MindTap™

M000305056

# Tap into **engagement**

MindTap empowers you to produce your best work—consistently.

MindTap is designed to help you master the material. Interactive videos, animations, and activities create a learning path designed by your instructor to guide you through the course and focus on what's important.

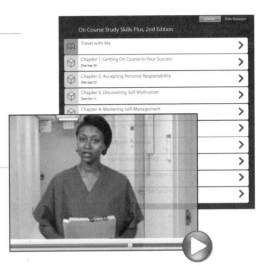

## MindTap delivers real-world activities and assignments

that will help you in your academic life as well as your career.

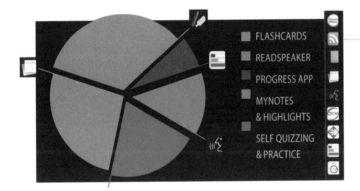

## MindTap helps you stay organized and efficient

by giving you the study tools to master the material.

## MindTap empowers and motivates

with information that shows where you stand at all times—both individually and compared to the highest performers in class.

*"MindTap was very useful – it was easy to follow and everything was right there."*
— Student, San Jose State University

*"I'm definitely more engaged because of MindTap."*
— Student, University of Central Florida

*"MindTap puts practice questions in a format that works well for me."*
— Student, Franciscan University of Steubenville

# Tap into more info at: **www.cengage.com/mindtap**

Engaged with you.
www.cengage.com

 CENGAGE Learning®

# Council for Exceptional Children CEC

## CEC Content Standards for All Beginning Special Education Teachers

The Council for Exceptional Children has established a comprehensive set of seven content standards for the preparation of all special education teachers. All newly prepared special educators are expected to develop a professional portfolio that includes evidence of their knowledge and skills across each of the seven domains.

## STANDARD 1:
### LEARNING DEVELOPMENT AND INDIVIDUAL LEARNING DIFFERENCES

Beginning special education professionals understand how exceptionalities may interact with development and learning and use this knowledge to provide meaningful and challenging learning experiences for individuals with exceptionalities.

1.1 Beginning special education professionals understand how language, culture, and family background influence the learning of individuals with exceptionalities.

1.2 Beginning special education professionals use understanding of development and individual differences to respond to the needs of individuals with exceptionalities.

## STANDARD 2:
### LEARNING ENVIRONMENTS

Beginning special education professionals create safe, inclusive, culturally responsive learning environments so that individuals with exceptionalities become active and effective learners and develop emotional well-being, positive social interactions, and self-determination.

2.1 Beginning special education professionals through collaboration with general educators and other colleagues create safe, inclusive, culturally responsive learning environments to engage individuals with exceptionalities in meaningful learning activities and social interactions.

2.2 Beginning special education professionals use motivational and instructional interventions to teach individuals with exceptionalities how to adapt to different environments.

2.3 Beginning special education professionals know how to intervene safely and appropriately with individuals with exceptionalities in crisis.

## STANDARD 3:
### CURRICULAR CONTENT KNOWLEDGE

Beginning special education professionals use knowledge of general and specialized curricula to individualize learning for individuals with exceptionalities.

3.1 Beginning special education professionals understand the central concepts, structures of the discipline, and tools of inquiry of the content areas they teach, and can organize this knowledge, integrate cross-disciplinary skills, and develop meaningful learning progressions for individuals with exceptionalities.

3.2 Beginning special education professionals understand and use general and specialized content knowledge for teaching across curricular content areas to individualize learning for individuals with exceptionalities.

3.3 Beginning special education professionals modify general and specialized curricula to make them accessible to individuals with exceptionalities.

## STANDARD 4:
### ASSESSMENT

Beginning special education professionals use multiple methods of assessment and data sources in making educational decisions.

4.1 Beginning special education professionals select and use technically sound formal and informal assessments that minimize bias.

4.2 Beginning special education professionals use knowledge of measurement principles and practices to interpret assessment results and guide educational decisions for individuals with exceptionalities.

4.3 Beginning special education professionals in collaboration with colleagues and families use multiple types of assessment information in making decisions about individuals with exceptionalities.

4.4 Beginning special education professionals engage individuals with exceptionalities to work toward quality learning and performance and provide feedback to guide them.

## STANDARD 5:
### INSTRUCTIONAL PLANNING AND STRATEGIES

Special educators actively create learning environments Beginning special education professionals select, adapt, and use a repertoire of evidence-based instructional strategies to advance learning of individuals with exceptionalities.

5.1 Beginning special education professionals consider an individual's abilities, interests, learning environments, and cultural and linguistic factors in the selection, development, and adaptation of learning experiences for individuals with exceptionalities.

5.2 Beginning special education professionals use technologies to support instructional assessment, planning, and delivery for individuals with exceptionalities.

5.3 Beginning special education professionals are familiar with augmentative and alternative communication systems and a variety of assistive technologies to support the communication and learning of individuals with exceptionalities.

5.4 Beginning special education professionals use strategies to enhance language development and communication skills of individuals with exceptionalities.

*(continued in the back)*

# Human Exceptionality

**TWELFTH EDITION**

## SCHOOL, COMMUNITY, AND FAMILY

**Michael L. Hardman**
*University of Utah*

**M. Winston Egan**
*Brigham Young University*

**Clifford J. Drew**
*University of Utah*

*with contributions from*

**Jayne McGuire**   *Humboldt State University*
**Tina Taylor Dyches**   *Brigham Young University*
**Gordon S. Gibb**   *Brigham Young University*
**Carol Hawkins Solomon**   *Brigham Young University*

CENGAGE
Learning®

Australia • Brazil • Mexico • Singapore • United Kingdom • United States

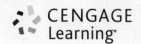

*Human Exceptionality: School, Community, and Family,* **Twelfth Edition**

Michael L. Hardman, M. Winston Egan, Clifford J. Drew

Product Director: Marta Lee-Perriard

Product Manager: Mark Kerr

Content Developer: Julia White

Product Assistant: Valerie Kraus

Marketing Manager: Christine Sosa

Content Project Manager: Samen Iqbal

Art Director: Andrei Pasternak

Manufacturing Planner: Doug Bertke

Intellectual Property Analyst: Jennifer Nonenmacher

Intellectual Property Project Manager: Brittani Morgan

Photo Researcher: Hemalatha Dhanapal

Text Researcher: Kavitha Balasundaram

Copy Editor: Heather McElwain

Production Service: Jill Traut, MPS Limited

Cover and Text Designer: Diane Beasley

Cover Image Credit: Anthony Gomez/ Creativity Explored

Compositor: MPS Limited

For product information and technology assistance, contact us at **Cengage Learning Customer & Sales Support, 1-800-354-9706.**

For permission to use material from this text or product, submit all requests online at **www.cengage.com/permissions**. Further permissions questions can be e-mailed to **permissionrequest@cengage.com**.

Library of Congress Control Number: 2015935646

Student Edition: ISBN: 978-1-305-50097-6

Loose-leaf Edition: ISBN: 978-1-305-63956-0

**Cengage Learning**
20 Channel Center Street
Boston, MA 02210
USA

Cengage Learning is a leading provider of customized learning solutions with employees residing in nearly 40 different countries and sales in more than 125 countries around the world. Find your local representative at **www.cengage.com**.

Cengage Learning products are represented in Canada by Nelson Education, Ltd.

To learn more about Cengage Learning Solutions, visit **www.cengage.com**.

Purchase any of our products at your local college store or at our preferred online store **www.cengagebrain.com**.

Printed in Canada
Print Number: 01   Print Year: 2015

# Dedication

*This book is dedicated to people with differing abilities everywhere, who have risen to the challenge of living in a world that is sometimes nurturing, but all too often ambivalent.*

*To our spouses, Monica, Linda, and Linda, our loving appreciation for being so patient and caring during the writing of this 12th edition and the more than 30 years of writing, rewriting, and revising this text. Their insightful contributions and constant support have been invaluable to the quality and success of this book.*

**M L H**
**M W E**
**C J D**

# Brief Contents

# Contents

# Guide to Selected Text Features

## ASSISTIVE TECHNOLOGY

## CASE STUDY ON EMBRACING DIVERSITY

## REFLECT ON THIS

# About the Authors

MICHAEL L. HARDMAN is Distinguished Professor of Special Education and Chief Global Officer at the University of Utah. He served as the University's Interim Senior Vice President for Academic Affairs (Chief Academic Officer) in 2012–2013 and was previously Dean of the College of Education (2007–2012). Dr. Hardman has numerous experiences within education and public policy, including appointment as Trustee of the Ensign College of Public Health, Ghana, West Africa; Matthew J. Guglielmo Endowed Chair at California State University, Los Angeles; Visiting Senior Scholar at Cambridge University; Senior Education Advisor and Kennedy Fellow, the Joseph P. Kennedy, Jr. Foundation; Legislative Staff to the United States Senate; the Governor's Representative to the California Advisory Commission on Special Education; University Coordinator for the Eunice Kennedy Shriver National Center for Community of Caring; President of the Higher Education Consortium for Special Education; and a member of the board of directors for several international organizations. He has directed or consulted on several international projects on school improvement for USAID (Bosnia-Herzegovina), the Organization for Economic Cooperation and Development (France and Italy), UNICEF (Zanzibar and Tanzania), and the government of Scotland.

Dr. Hardman has published widely in national and international journals in the field of education and has authored ten college textbooks of which two, *Human Exceptionality* and *Intellectual Disabilities Through the Lifespan*, are in their 12th and 9th editions, respectively. As a researcher, he has directed numerous national and international demonstration projects in the areas of educational policy and reform, teacher quality and professional development, inclusive education, and preparing tomorrow's leaders in education.

M. WINSTON EGAN is professor emeritus and served as the chair of the Teacher Education Department at the David O. McKay School of Education, Brigham Young University. Dr. Egan has taught children of all ages, preschool through high school. He began his special education career at Utah Boys Ranch. His writings appear in *Behavior Disorders, Journal of Teacher Education, Teacher Education and Special Education, American Journal of Distance Education, Journal of Special Education, Rural Special Education Quarterly,* and *Teaching and Teacher Education.* He has been honored with several university teaching awards including Professor of the Year, Blue Key National Honor Society, Brigham Young University; and Excellence in Teaching Award, College of Education, University of Utah. He has also been honored as an associate for the National Network for Education Renewal (NNER). His interests include youth development, teacher socialization, education for democracy, and emotional/behavioral disorders.

CLIFFORD J. DREW is professor emeritus of special education and educational psychology at the University of Utah since 1971, and was a faculty member at the University of Texas at Austin and Kent State University prior to coming to Utah. He has also served as associate dean for research and outreach in the College of Education, and as director of academic outreach and continuing education at the University of Utah. He received his master's degree from the University of Illinois and his PhD from the University of Oregon. He has published numerous articles in education and related areas including intellectual disabilities, research design, statistics, diagnostic assessment, cognition, evaluation related to the law, and information technology. His most recent book is *Adolescent Online Social Communication and Behavior* (IGI Global, 2010). His professional interests include research methods in education and psychology, human development and disabilities, applications of information technology, and outreach in higher education.

**JAYNE MCGUIRE** is an associate professor of Recreation Administration at Humboldt State University. She teaches courses in the Recreation Administration, Special Education, and College Faculty Preparation programs. Dr. McGuire is passionate about inclusion in the classroom and in the community. During her career, she has as served as a high school special education teacher, a therapeutic recreation specialist, an executive director of an accessible adventure organization, a Special Olympics coach and researcher, and an assistant professor of special education. Dr. McGuire has published articles, book chapters, and presented nationally and internationally on inclusion of people who experience disability, universal design for learning, and self-determination. She is actively involved with faculty development at Humboldt State University and regularly collaborates with the Office of Diversity and Inclusion, the College of eLearning and Extended Education, and the Student Disability Resource Center. Dr. McGuire was honored as the 2009 recipient for Outstanding Faculty Award through the Humboldt State University Student Disability Resource Center.

**TINA TAYLOR DYCHES** is a professor of special education at Brigham Young University and serves as an associate dean in the David O. McKay School of Education. Dr. Dyches earned her doctoral, master's, and undergraduate degrees at Illinois State University, Utah State University, and Brigham Young University, respectively. She has worked with individuals with disabilities and their families for 30 years as a special educator, consultant, professor, and administrator, and has received numerous awards including the Council for Exceptional Children's Burton Blatt Humanitarian Award and the Autism Society of America's Autism Professional of the Year Award. Her academic interests include adaptation of families raising children with disabilities, children's literature that includes characters with disabilities, multicultural issues affecting children with autism and their families, and provision of appropriate services to students with disabilities. She has published over 70 book chapters and refereed articles and has made over 190 professional presentations on topics related to individuals with disabilities. Dr. Dyches has co-authored several books, the most recent of which is *IEPs: Writing Quality Individualized Education Programs* (2015).

**GORDON S. GIBB** is associate professor of special education at Brigham Young University and serves as coordinator of undergraduate special education. Dr. Gibb taught students with mild/moderate disabilities for 16 years while earning his master's of education at Brigham Young University and doctoral degree at the University of Utah. As a teacher educator, Dr. Gibb focuses on effective reading and math instruction for students with learning disabilities and students for whom English is a second language. His research includes Tier 2 elementary reading instruction, first-generation immigrant parent and student knowledge and understanding learning disabilities, and the IEP process. He has authored and co-authored peer-reviewed publications, books, and book chapters that address effective classroom practice, parent understanding of special education, and the IEP process.

**CAROL HAWKINS SOLOMON** is the manager of TESOL K–12 teaching minor in the David O. McKay School of Education at Brigham Young University. She also coordinates a national professional development grant focused on the preparation of in-service and preservice teachers to support the academic language and content development of emergent bilingual learners in public schools. She earned her master's and undergraduate degrees at Western Oregon State College and Brigham Young University. She also earned a K–12 administrator/superintendent certification from Portland State University. Her professional experience includes 23 years in these roles: special education teacher and district coordinator, Title 1A teacher and district coordinator, ESL district coordinator, and elementary principal. For four years, she also served as an adjunct professor and grant coordinator in the Counseling Psychology and Special Education Department at Brigham Young University. Her professional life has been shaped profoundly by experiences with family members with disabilities and diverse cultural and linguistic backgrounds.

# Preface

The realization that we are all basically the same human beings, who seek happiness and try to avoid suffering, is very helpful in developing a sense of brotherhood and sisterhood; a warm feeling of love and compassion for others.

— Dalai Lama

Welcome to *Human Exceptionality: School, Community, and Family!* In this, our new 12th edition, we are very pleased to continue as a member of the Cengage Learning family. As authors in a partnership with Cengage Learning, we fully agree with our publisher's mantra that "engagement is the foundation of learning... engagement is at our core and our focus is on engaging with learners, both in the classroom and beyond, to ensure the most effective product design, learning solutions, and personalized services—all to help people learn."

In doing so, our goal in writing this new edition is to provide you, our readers, with a textbook that is current, informative, relevant, user-friendly, and meaningful in both your professional and personal life—a book that rises to the Cengage vision of fostering academic excellence and professional development, as well as providing *measurable and meaningful learning outcomes* to you, the readers.

For some of you, this book is the beginning of your journey into the lives of people who are exceptional, their families, and the schools and communities in which they live. This text is first and foremost about people—people with many different needs, desires, characteristics, challenges, and lifestyles—people who for one reason or another are described as *exceptional*. What does the word *exceptional* mean to you? For that matter, what do the words *disabled, challenged,* or *different* mean to you? Who or what influenced your knowledge and attitudes toward people with differing abilities and the labels we often use to describe them? You are most influenced by your life experiences. You may have a family member, friend, or casual acquaintance who is exceptional. It may be that you are a person who is exceptional in some way. Then again, you may be approaching a study of human exceptionality with little or no background. In reading and interacting with this book, we believe you will find that the study of human exceptionality is the study of being human. Perhaps you will come to understand yourself better in the process. As suggested by the novelist Louis Bromfield,

> *There is a rhythm in life, a certain beauty which operates by a variation of lights and shadows, happiness alternating with sorrow, content with discontent, distilling in this process of contrast a sense of satisfaction, of richness that can be captured and pinned down only by those who possess the gift of awareness.*

## About This Edition
### Organization
We have thoughtfully listened to the needs of our current adopters, the university instructors, and most importantly, you—the students who use our book. In doing so, we have organized our book into 15 chapters to easily coordinate with a 15-week semester, a common time frame for many university and college courses. Additionally, this book is organized into four parts that can be taught easily within a 10-week period, with each part addressed over a two-week period, which better accommodates universities or colleges that follow a quarter system.

The four parts reflect the major themes of the book. In Part 1, we begin with a focus on understanding exceptionality through the lifespan. Also, we examine exceptionality from the perspectives of many different disciplines. Part 2 looks into the meaning of diversity and the role of family and is followed by Part 3, a study of individuals who are identified as exceptional. Our new edition concludes with Part 4, an in-depth discussion on people with exceptional gifts and talents. In responding to the needs and desires of our audience of students and adopters who are currently using this text, as well as those who are considering adopting it for future use, we have completely rewritten and updated three chapters in Parts 2 and 3: "Cultural and Linguistic Diversity" (Chapter 5), "Learning Disabilities" (Chapter 7), and "Autism Spectrum Disorders" (Chapter 11).

### New and Updated Features

- In this edition, you will find that each chapter begins with the heading "A Changing Era in the Lives of People Who Are Exceptional" and concludes with "Looking Toward a Bright Future." The narratives within these headings begin and end each chapter on a positive note on the past, present, and future, while acknowledging the challenges that people with differences face and will continue to encounter in the years to come.

- The feature, *Learning through Social Media*, introduced in the 11th edition, is updated this edition to reflect the ever-increasing and changing use of social media in the 21st century. Social media on the Internet, which began more as a personal convenience, is moving rapidly into the realm of a necessity in every student's learning experience. In this new edition, many of the chapters highlight new and updated online blogs and social media sites by and for people who are exceptional, the purpose of which is to use this ever-changing technology to promote greater inclusion in schools, families, and communities.

- The features that have been so popular with our readers in past editions, including *Reflect on This, Case Study on Embracing Diversity,* and *Assistive Technology,* continue to appear in the 12th edition. Many of these have been updated and expanded to provide the most accurate and current information available in both the professional literature and the popular press.

- We continue to update and expand our unique topical coverage of multidisciplinary and collaborative approaches to education, health care, and social services with the *Community Support for Lifelong Inclusion* feature (formerly *Inclusion and Collaboration through the Lifespan*) that you'll find in Chapters 7 through 15. The change in this feature's title is reflective of the increasing emphasis on the important role the entire community plays in supporting social and academic inclusion throughout the life of a person who is exceptional.

- The content of this new 12th edition corresponds with the 2012 Council for Exceptional Children (CEC) Standards as highlighted in the margin icons within every chapter. The Standards Correlation Chart at the end of the book details where specific standards are addressed in the book.

- MindTap for Education is a first-of-its-kind digital solution with an integrated e-portfolio that prepares teachers by providing them with the knowledge, skills, and competencies they must demonstrate to earn an education degree and state licensure, and to begin a successful career. Through activities based on real-life teaching situations, MindTap elevates students' thinking by giving them experiences in applying concepts, practicing skills, and evaluating decisions, guiding them to become reflective educators.

- We are also very proud of the fact that the 12th edition contains nearly **1,200 citations** from sources that have been published within the last decade and many of which have been published within the last two years. As authors, we are very comfortable in saying to you, our readers, that the

12th edition of *Human Exceptionality* provides the most current sources available on the lives of people who are exceptional.

## Pedagogical Features and Student Learning System

In addition to providing you with current and informative content, we are committed to making your experience with this textbook, interesting, enjoyable, and productive. To this end, each chapter in this 12th edition contains new and continuing features that will significantly enhance your desire to learn more about human exceptionality.

## Learning Objectives and Chapter Review

At the beginning of each chapter, we have provided tools to assist you in locating and more effectively learning and retaining key content. A set of **learning objectives** opens each chapter and serves as an advanced organizer for your reading. Learning objectives are directly linked to **first-order headings** within the chapter narrative. For example, Learning Objective 4-3 at the beginning of Chapter 4 reads:

- Identify the purpose of person-centered transition planning and the basic steps in its formulation.

The first-order heading that corresponds with Learning Objective 4-3 can easily be found in chapter narrative since it has the same numbering (4-3) as its corresponding learning objective.

Each chapter concludes with a **Chapter Review** that reiterates the chapter's learning objectives, summarizing key concepts and content.

### Learning Objectives
*After you complete this chapter, you will be able to:*

**9-1** Describe how the lives of people with intellectual and developmental disabilities have changed since the advent of IDEA.

**9-2** Explain the various definitions and classifications of intellectual disabilities.

**9-3** Describe the characteristics and prevalence of children and youth with intellectual disabilities.

**9-4** List the causes and risk factors associated with intellectual disabilities.

**9-5** Describe the assessment procedures used to identify intellectual disabilities in children and youth.

**9-6** Describe the different interventions for children and youth with intellectual disabilities from early childhood through adulthood.

### Chapter Review

**9-1 Describe how the lives of people with intellectual disabilities have changed since the advent of IDEA.**

- As more children with intellectual disabilities enter school, developmental delays have become more apparent. Prior to the passage of IDEA, it was common for the cognitive and social differences of children with intellectual disabilities to be attributed to immaturity. Today, educators recognize the need for specialized services to support a child's development in the natural settings of school, neighborhood, and home.
- People with moderate to severe intellectual disabilities have challenges that often transcend the classroom. Today, we recognize that these children are able to learn and use adaptive skills that allow independence, with varying levels of support.

- Although dependent upon others for basic life needs, people with profound intellectual disabilities benefit from education and treatment beyond routine care and maintenance. The extent of profound disabilities is one reason why this group of children was excluded from the public schools prior to the passage of IDEA. Exclusion was often justified on the basis that schools did not have the resources, facilities, or trained professionals to deal with the needs of these students.

**9-2 Explain the various definitions and classifications of intellectual disabilities.**

- Definition
  - There are significant limitations in intellectual abilities.
  - There are significant limitations in adaptive behavior as expressed in conceptual, social, and practical adaptive skills.

## Snapshot

*Snapshot* features are personal insights into the lives of real people. These insights may come from teachers, family members, friends, peers, and professionals, as well as from people who are exceptional. Each chapter in the 12th edition opens with a narrative *Snapshot* of people who are exceptional, their family members, or teachers. We believe you will find *Snapshots* to be one of the most enriching aspects of your introduction to human exceptionality. For example, you'll learn about:

- Tara Hillegas's eight tips for new Special Education Teachers (Chapter 2)

- Jennifer and Linea and their unique mental health challenges (Chapter 8)

- Actress Lauren Potter from TV's *Glee* (Chapter 9)

- Trinity, a 7th grader with a fluency disorder (Chapter 10)

- Diagnosing "C", a mother's reflection on her son being diagnosed with autism (Chapter 11)

- Sarina's experiences in her neighborhood junior high school (Chapter 12)

## Community Support for Lifelong Inclusion

Another updated feature in this edition with a new title is *Community Support for Lifelong Inclusion.* This feature provides helpful information on ways to interact with, include, communicate with, or teach people who are exceptional across a variety of settings (home, school, and community) and age spans (early childhood through the adult years). We hope these ideas will provide motivation for further thinking about ways to fully include these individuals as family members, school peers, friends, or neighbors, as well as collaborate with other professionals concerned with improving the lives of people who are exceptional.

## Reflect on This

Every chapter includes one or more *Reflect on This* boxes. Each box highlights additional interesting and relevant information beyond the chapter narrative that will add to your learning and enjoyment of the topic, such as:

- "What's My Role on the Multidisciplinary School-Wide Assistance Team?" (Chapter 3)

- "Redefining Learning Disabilities Using a Response to Intervention Model" (Chapter 7)

 **SNAPSHOT**   Living with NO Boundaries: Meet Hector

*By the Disability.gov team*

Some people collect baseball cards. Others save coins or stamps. But Hector's collection is much more valuable. He is the proud owner of more than 24 library cards, which he actively uses around the state of California. It was simply by chance that the Disability.gov team chose a library as the setting for Hector's photo shoot. Little did we know that libraries are such an intricate part of his story.

Hector's insatiable thirst for knowledge started at a young age. After teaching himself to read, Hector spent hours on end at the local library, poring over books in every genre. One time, when he was living with his grandmother in Mexico, he learned that a new library was opening in town. Hector, who was only six years old, decided to skip school to visit it. Needless to say, his family wasn't too pleased with his little adventure.

Throughout the years, libraries became a safe haven from the overstimulation Hector sometimes experienced as a result of his autism and other invisible disabilities. Even though he wanted to socialize with his classmates, Hector said he couldn't always handle the stress after a long day at school. Library books offered access to the intimate thoughts of thousands of "friends" in a quiet environment. Hector still

reads every chance he gets, and the Internet has only enhanced his ability to learn, enabling him to quickly reach out to authors to ask them questions about their books.

Knowledge leads to not only awareness, but also understanding. Hector knows this fact all too well. As a Two Spirit member of the Chiricahua Apaches, Hector brings light to the presence of autism and mental health conditions (e.g., bipolar disorder, post-traumatic stress disorder) in the Native American community. Because his culture only recognizes disability as a limitation imposed by environmental factors, accessibility and accommodations for people with disabilities are scarce. Without increasing awareness, this situation is unlikely to change.

For this reason, Hector advocates for turning one's disability into what he calls a "purpose-ability," that is, finding a way to make a difference despite the challenges that may be presented by one's disabilities. A large part of his focus is on issues affecting people, families, and communities impacted by disabilities. He regularly volunteers for a number of organizations, including the National Alliance on Mental Illness, the Women Shelter of Long Beach, Organizing for Action (a grassroots movement to enroll U.S. citizens in

health care), the California Mental Health Services Oversight and Accountability Commission, and the Workforce Education and Training Consumer and Family Member Employment Advisory Committee.

In addition, Hector lends his expertise in mental health conditions to local government agencies and other organizations. As a self-employed public policy analyst, he provides consulting services, such as reviewing budgets for local mental health programs and evaluating whether they are research-based or successful after implementation. Hector says he enjoys owning his own business because it gives him more control of the end product, but sometimes it's hard waiting for a check to arrive. Even still, Hector appreciates the independence his job provides.

"I force myself to adapt and be independent," he says. "I traveled to Washington, D.C., for the first time by myself for this photo project. I was nervous, but I just said I was going to do it...and I did."

The Disability.gov team would like to thank the staff at the Arlington Public Library for graciously donating their time and space to the No Boundaries Photo Project.

SOURCE: Retrieved January 6, 2015, from https://usodep .blogs.govdelivery.com/2014/07/09/living-with-no -boundaries-meet-hector/#more-8542.

 **COMMUNITY SUPPORT FOR LIFELONG INCLUSION**

### People with Emotional/Behavioral Disorders (EBD)

**Early Childhood Years**

**Tips for Families**

- Become involved with parent training and other community support services.

- Work collaboratively with multidisciplinary personnel (educators, social workers, health care professionals, and parent–group volunteers) in developing effective child management strategies.

- Use the same evidence-based intervention strategies at home that are applied in the preschool settings.

- Establish family routines, schedules, and incentive systems that reward and build positive behaviors.

- Participate actively in advocacy or parent-support groups.

- Understand your rights regarding health care, education, and social services benefits.

**Tips for Preschool Teachers**

- Work collaboratively with the mul-

managing children with challenging behaviors.

- Make every effort to involve children with EBD in school-wide activities and special performances.

- Orient and teach preschool children without disabilities about how to appropriately respond to classmates with challenging behaviors such as teaching them to ignore, walk away, get help from the teacher, and so on.

- Collaborate with parents in using the same management systems and strategies in your preschool classroom as those used in the home.

**Tips for Neighbors and Friends**

- Become familiar with the things you can do as a neighbor or friend in responding to the challenging behaviors of a neighborhood child with EBD.

- Be patient with parents who are attempting to cope with their child's temper tantrums or other challenging behaviors in community settings (such

your spouse from community mental health agencies or other public or private sources.

- Help your other children and their friends understand the things they can do to support your child with EBD.

**Tips for General Education Classroom Teachers**

- Provide a positive, structured classroom/learning environment (i.e., with clearly stated rules, helpful positive and negative consequences, well-conceived classroom schedules, carefully taught classroom routines, and solid relationship-building activities).

- Teach social skills (how to deal with bullying, accept criticism, etc.) to all of the children with the help of members of the school's multidisciplinary teacher assistance team.

- Teach self-management skills (goal selection, self-monitoring, self-reinforcement, etc.) to all children with the aid of members of the school's multidisciplinary

**REFLECT ON THIS**

### What's My Role on the Multidisciplinary School-Wide Assistance Team?

A team is a group of professionals, parents, and students who join together to plan and implement an appropriate educational program for a student at risk or with a disability. Team members may be trained in different areas of study, including education, health services, speech and language, school administration, and so on. In the team approach, these individuals, regardless of where or how they were trained, sit down together and coordinate their efforts to help students. For this approach to work, all team members must clearly understand their roles and responsibilities as members of the team. Let's visit with some team members and explore their roles in working with students.

**Special Education Teacher**

It's my responsibility to coordinate the student's individualized education pro-

**Parents**

We work with each team member to ensure that our child is involved in an appropriate educational program. We give the team information about our child's life outside school and suggest experiences that might be relevant to the home and the community. We also work with our child at home to reinforce what is learned in school. As members of the team, we give our written consent for any evaluations of our child and any changes in our child's educational placement.

**School Psychologist**

I select, administer, and interpret appropriate psychological, educational, and behavioral assessment instruments. I consult directly with team members regarding the student's overall educational development. It is also my

experiences for the student during the time that he or she spends in my classroom. I ensure that the student's experiences outside my classroom are consistent with the instruction he or she receives from me. In carrying out my responsibilities, I keep an accurate and continuous record of the student's progress. I am also responsible for referring any other students in my classroom who are at risk and may need specialized services to the school district for an evaluation of their needs.

**Adapted Physical Education Teacher**

I am an adapted physical education specialist who works with the team to determine whether the student needs adapted physical education services as a component of his or her individual-

## Assistive Technology

The 12th edition offers new information on the expanding use of technology for people who are exceptional. *Assistive Technology* features highlight important innovations in computers, biomedical engineering, and instructional systems. The following are examples of *Assistive Technology* features:

- "Assistive Technology for People with Intellectual Disabilities" (Chapter 9)
- "Apps for Autism" (Chapter 11)
- "VGo: The Ultimate School-Based Robot" (Chapter 14)
- "From Science Fiction to Reality: Ekso Exoskeletons" (Chapter 14)
- "Renzulli Learning: Differentiation Engine" (Chapter 15)

## Case Study on Embracing Diversity

Each chapter includes a *Case Study on Embracing Diversity* feature, which is an in-depth look at a personal story of exceptionality. Each *Case Study on Embracing Diversity* also includes Application Questions to extend your knowledge and apply what you learned from each vignette. You'll find a variety of stories, such as:

- Ana, a first-grader from an impoverished and abusive home environment where English language usage is limited (Chapter 5)
- Ten-year-old Leon's challenging day as a boy with emotional/behavioral disorders (Chapter 8)
- Culturally and linguistically diverse children with ASD (Chapter 11)
- Xeeb, an 8-year-old Hmong boy with a hearing loss (Chapter 13)

## Learning through Social Media

The *Learning through Social Media* boxes provide interesting and informative online blogs and social media sites by and for people who are exceptional, and the use of this technology to promote inclusion in school, family, and society. Examples of *Learning through Social Media* boxes include:

- "10 Helpful and Compassionate Comments Heard at an IEP Meeting" (Chapter 2)
- "Edutopia on Culturally Responsive Teaching" (Chapter 5)
- "Bring Change 2 Mind" (Chapter 8)
- "Design Challenge: DIY Assistive Game Controllers" (Chapter 12)
- "Experiences of People with Sensory Impairments" (Chapter 13)
- "My Life With Cerebral Palsy: Removing the Fence around Social Barriers One Post at a Time" (Chapter 14)

## End-of-Chapter Features

In addition to the Chapter Review mentioned earlier, other end-of-chapter features include a list of Council for Exceptional Children standards (updated in 2012) addressed in the chapter and Mastery Activities and Assignments.

# Supplement Package

## MindTap™: The Personal Learning Experience

MindTap for Hardman/Egan/Drew, *Human Exceptionality: School, Community, and Family*, 12th edition, represents a new approach to teaching and learning. A highly personalized, fully customizable learning platform with an integrated e-portfolio, MindTap helps students elevate thinking by guiding them to:

- Know, remember, and understand concepts critical to becoming great teachers;
- Apply concepts, create curriculum and tools, and demonstrate performance and competency in key areas in the course, including national and state education standards;
- Prepare artifacts for the portfolio and eventual state licensure, to launch a successful teaching career; and
- Develop the habits to become reflective practitioners.

As students move through each chapter's Learning Path, they engage in a scaffolded learning experience, designed to move them up Bloom's taxonomy, from lower- to higher-order thinking skills. The Learning Path enables preservice students to develop these skills and gain confidence by:

- Engaging them with chapter topics and activating their prior knowledge by watching and answering questions about authentic videos of teachers teaching and children learning in real classrooms;
- Checking their comprehension and understanding through Did You Get It? assessments, with varied question types that are autograded for instant feedback;

- Applying concepts through mini-case scenarios—students analyze typical teaching and learning situations, and then create a reasoned response to the issue(s) presented in the scenario; and
- Reflecting about and justifying the choices they made within the teaching scenario problem.

MindTap helps instructors facilitate better outcomes by evaluating how future teachers plan and teach lessons in ways that make content clear and help diverse students learn, assessing the effectiveness of their teaching practice, and adjusting teaching as needed. MindTap enables instructors to facilitate better outcomes by:

- Making grades visible in real time through the Student Progress App so students and instructors always have access to current standings in the class.
- Using the Outcome Library to embed national education standards and align them to student learning activities, and also allowing instructors to add their state's standards or any other desired outcome.
- Allowing instructors to generate reports on students' performance with the click of a mouse against any standards or outcomes that are in their MindTap course.
- Giving instructors the ability to assess students on state standards or other local outcomes by editing existing or creating their own MindTap activities, and then by aligning those activities to any state or other outcomes that the instructor has added to the MindTap Outcome Library.

MindTap for Hardman/Egan/Drew, *Human Exceptionality: School, Community, and Family*, 12th edition, helps instructors easily set their course because it integrates into the existing Learning Management System and saves instructors time by allowing them to fully customize any aspect of the learning path. Instructors can change the order of the student learning activities, hide activities they don't want for the course, and—most importantly—create custom assessments and add any standards, outcomes, or content they do want (e.g., YouTube videos, Google docs). Learn more at www.cengage.com/mindtap.

## Online Instructor's Manual with Test Bank

An online Instructor's Manual accompanies this book. It contains information to assist instructors in designing the course, including sample syllabi, discussion questions, teaching and learning activities, field experiences, learning objectives, and additional online resources. For assessment support, the updated test bank includes true/false, multiple-choice, matching, short-answer, and essay questions for each chapter.

MindTap Moves Students Up Bloom's Revised Taxonomy

Create
Evaluate
Analyze
Apply
Understand
Remember & Know

Anderson, L. W., & Krathwohl, D. (Eds.). (2001). *A taxonomy for learning, teaching, and assessing: A revision of Bloom's taxonomy of educational objectives.* New York: Longman.

## PowerPoint Lecture Slides

These vibrant Microsoft PowerPoint lecture slides for each chapter assist you with your lecture by providing concept coverage using images, figures, and tables directly from the textbook.

## Cognero

Cengage Learning Testing Powered by Cognero is a flexible online system that allows you to author, edit, and manage test bank content from multiple Cengage Learning solutions; create multiple test versions in an instant; and deliver tests from your LMS, your classroom, or wherever you want.

## Acknowledgments

We begin with a very big thank you to our colleagues from across the country and around the world who provided such in-depth and constructive feedback on the 11th edition of *Human Exceptionality,* including the following:

> Glenda Baca, Montgomery College
> Deborah Anne Banker, Angelo State University
> Richard Carney, Community College of Allegheny County
> Katherine Ellis-Donner, Erie Community College
> Daniella Errett, Pennsylvania Highlands Community College
> Cheryl Every-Wurtz, Suffolk County Community College
> Peter Griswold, William Paterson University
> Laura Lane-Worley, Lee College
> Alfred Longo, Ocean County College
> Victoria Page-Voth, University of Maryland
> Stacey Pistorova, Terra State Community College
> Edward Schultz, Midwestern State University
> Joan Silver, St. Joseph's College
> Brenda-Jean Tyler, Radford University
> Barbara Wilson, Bloomsburg University of Pennsylvania

Special thanks to the people with disabilities and their families who participated in the *Snapshot, Case Study on Embracing Diversity,* and *Assistive Technology* features for this book. These are the people who make up the heart of what this book is all about. Throughout the writing and production of this book, they made us keenly aware that this book is first and foremost about people.

We are very proud that four outstanding author contributors are joining us for this new 12th edition. Our deep gratitude to chapter contributors Jayne McGuire from Humboldt State University in northern California, and Tina Taylor Dyches, Gordon S. Gibb, and Carol Hawkins Solomon from Brigham Young University in Provo, Utah, for their major contributions to this new edition.

As authors, we are certainly grateful for the commitment and expertise of the Cengage editorial and production team in bringing to fruition the highest-quality text possible. This team has sought to consistently improve the readability, utility, and appearance of this book. We want to thank Senior Product Manager Mark D. Kerr. This is our second opportunity to work with Mark and we appreciate his vision, insights, and patience with us while consistently supporting this text and its enhanced narrative and features.

A very special thank you to Julia White, associate content developer, who provided invaluable and substantive insight into both the content and writing style of the new edition. Julia kept us focused and on track, attending not only to the quality of the content but also ensuring that the book maintains its strong, user-friendly approach to instruction. Julia's attention to detail and in-depth editing of the manuscript has been critical in presenting a new edition of which we are all very proud. Thanks also to Joshua Taylor, associate content vendor services manager, for coordinating the supplements. Our thanks to Jill Traut, project manager for MPS, for her patience and expertise in leading the process for reviewing the copyedited pages, as well as the final page proofs for this text. The photo researcher for this book, Manojkiran Chander, did an outstanding job of locating photos that brought to life the text's printed word. Under Manojkiran's direction, we have included the most recent photographs from general education classes, including school systems throughout the country that work with the inclusion model, and current photos of families with children and adults with disabilities.

To those professors who have chosen this book for adoption, and to those students who will be using this book as their first information source on people with differences, we hope our 12th edition of *Human Exceptionality* meets your expectations.

A loving thank you to our families who have always been there during the past three decades of writing and rewriting this text. We have strived "oh so hard" to produce a book of which you can be proud.

*Michael L. Hardman*
*M. Winston Egan*
*Clifford J. Drew*

# Human
# Exceptionality

TWELFTH EDITION

## SCHOOL, COMMUNITY, AND FAMILY

## CHAPTER 1

# Understanding Exceptionalities in the 21st Century

Jim West/Alamy

## Learning Objectives

*After you complete this chapter, you will be able to:*

**1-1** Describe why we continue to label people even when we know it may have a negative effect on an individual.

**1-2** Identify three approaches to describe human differences.

**1-3** Explain how societal views on people with disabilities changed from widespread discrimination to an era of inclusion and support in the 21st century.

**1-4** Identify the catalyst, effects, and provisions of the Americans with Disabilities Act.

**1-5** Describe the role of health care, psychology, and social services professionals in meeting the needs of people with disabilities.

## A Blog by Joe Dolson

Many of those who could be considered disabled would not choose to self-identify as disabled. *Disability* is a label, and like any label, the members of the labeled group are diverse and may exhibit the label in unexpected ways. How many people with color blindness self-identify as disabled? How many people with children in strollers are unable to climb stairs with their child—would they self-identify as disabled? How many left-handed people struggle with right-handed scissors? Is this disability? An issue may appear trivial, but that makes the problem no less frustrating when encountered.

### What Is Disability?

Disability, at some level, affects every part of our day-to-day existence. Disability is nothing more than an inability to make use of a particular resource as it is presented to you. This is how disability is particularly differentiated from usability: With disability, you *cannot* use the resource on your own. If a resource has poor usability, you are *able* to use it, albeit with difficulty.

This is why disability is not an absolute. Disability only prevents you from using tools if alternatives are not made available to you in a manner that you *are* able to use. The blind can "see" if an object or action is described well enough.

The previous examples are situations that may only disable the person in certain circumstances. People with color blindness are disabled when a circumstance requires them to distinguish red from green with no other

Courtesy of Joseph Dolson

clarifying indicators. Some people may be able to carry their children and stroller up the stairs; others may not. An elevator, moving walkway, or escalator platform can resolve the problem. Some left-handed people can successfully switch to the right hand, or at least can manipulate right-handed scissors in such a manner as to successfully cut paper—but can many switch hands to write a letter?

Physical strength or handedness is not classically considered a disability, but there can be no question that they affect one's ability to accomplish certain tasks.

### But Some People Really Are "Normal"

Oh, yes, of course. I mean, *I'm* normal. But *you*? Well, I have some doubts.

I mean, there are tons of things that I can do that you can't. Doesn't that mean you're disabled? No? It just means that you have a different set of abilities than I do. Or, alternatively, a different set of *disabilities*. Neither of us is necessarily disabled; but we are "differently abled."

That's right…I forgot. Everybody has a different and independent

capability to perform tasks. Some people are impaired when it comes to math; others, art. Some people don't run very fast; others can't walk. These disabilities will always affect one's life. The degree to which disability affects one's life is highly variable. People who are classically considered disabled tend to have limitations that are severe enough to affect their life every day.

What is commonly called "normal" is truly just an abstract concept that we apply to our personal experience: Whether by attributing it to ourselves or to others, it is relative to our own perceptions and our environments.

The Web has a great power to reduce that effect. It's commonly remarked that people behave differently on the Web. This is because the Web divorces them from their mundane routine—and this is true for everybody. On the Web, with a well-designed and accessible website, people with disabilities such as cerebral palsy, sight impairment, or hearing impairment can have an experience fundamentally equal to the experience of the so-called "normal" user.

In any context, people with a disability are disabled not because of an inherent inability to compensate, but because they are in an environment that requires tasks they are unable to perform. If we change the environment, we can remove the disability.

# A Changing Era in the Lives of People with Disabilities

In our opening Snapshot, Joe Dolson, an Internet accessibility consultant, emphasizes the point that "disability is not an absolute." Yet, for good or bad, labeling is the fundamental way society chooses to describe human difference. The purpose of a label is to communicate specific differences in people who vary significantly from what is considered "typical or normal." Sociologists use labels to describe people who do not follow society's expectations (e.g., *sociopath*); educators and psychologists use labels to identify and provide services for students with learning, physical, and behavioral differences (e.g., *autistic*); and physicians use labels to distinguish the sick from the healthy (e.g., *diabetic*). Governments label people to identify who is eligible for, or entitled to, publicly funded services and supports (e.g., *disabled*).

## 1-1 Why Label People?

We use many labels, including *disorder, impairment, disability,* and *handicap,* to describe people who are different. These terms are not synonymous. Disorder, the broadest of the three terms, refers to a general abnormality in mental, physical, or psychological functioning. Impairment goes one step further to indicate that the disorder creates a barrier to typical functioning. A disability is more specific than an impairment and is associated with a loss of physical functioning (e.g., loss of sight, hearing, or mobility), or a challenge in learning and social adjustment that significantly interferes with typical growth and development. A handicap is a limitation imposed on an individual by demands in the environment and is related to the individual's ability to adapt or adjust to those demands. For example, Franklin Roosevelt, the 32nd president of the United States, used a wheelchair because of a physical disability—the inability to walk—that resulted from having polio as a child. He used a wheelchair to move from place to place. When the environment didn't accommodate his wheelchair (such as a building without ramps that was accessible only by stairs), his disability created a handicap. Historically, *handicap* has taken on a very negative connotation and is seldom used in today's society. The word *handicapped* literally means "cap in hand"; it originates from a time when people with disabilities were forced to beg in the streets merely to survive. For President Roosevelt, his advisers took great pains to disavow his "handicap" because many people in the 1930s and 1940s viewed it as a sign of weakness. However, there is hope that such negative attitudes are changing in the United States today. The national monument in Washington, D.C. that honors President Roosevelt includes a life-size bronze statue of him sitting in a wheelchair.

Exceptional is a comprehensive label. It describes an individual whose physical, intellectual, or behavioral performance differs substantially from what is typical (or normal), either higher or lower. People described as exceptional include those with extraordinary abilities (such as gifts and talents) and/or disabilities (such as learning disabilities or intellectual disabilities). People who are exceptional, whether gifted, disabled, or both, benefit from individualized assistance, support, or accommodations in school and community settings.

Labels are only rough approximations of characteristics. Some labels, such as deaf, might describe a permanent characteristic—loss of hearing; others, such as *overweight*, describe what is often a temporary condition. Some labels are positive, and others are negative. Labels communicate whether a person meets the expectations of the culture. A given culture establishes criteria that are easily exceeded by some but are unreachable for others. For example, one society may value creativity, innovation, and imagination, and will reward those who have such attributes with positive labels, such as *bright, intelligent,* or *gifted*. Another society, however, may brand anyone whose ideas significantly exceed the limits of conformity with negative labels, such as *radical, extremist,* or *rebel*.

---

**Disorder**
A disturbance in normal functioning (mental, physical, or psychological).

**Impairment**
A state of being diminished, weakened, or damaged, especially mentally or physically.

**Disability**
A condition resulting from a loss of physical functioning; or, difficulties in learning and social adjustment that significantly interfere with normal growth and development.

**Handicap**
A limitation imposed on a person by the environment and the person's capacity to cope with that limitation.

**Exceptional**
An individual whose physical, mental, or behavioral performance deviates so substantially from the average (higher or lower) that additional support is required to meet the individual's needs.

**Gifts and talents**
Extraordinary abilities in one or more areas.

**Learning disabilities**
A condition in which one or more of an individual's basic psychological processes in understanding or using language are deficient.

**Intellectual disabilities**
Substantial limitations in functioning, characterized by significantly subaverage intellectual functioning concurrent with related limitations in two or more adaptive skills. Intellectual disability is manifested prior to age 18.

**Deaf**
Individuals who have hearing losses greater than 75 to 80 dB, have vision as their primary input, and cannot understand speech through the ear.

Moreover, the same label may have different meanings within a culture. Let's take the example of Ellen who is labeled by her high school teachers as a *high achiever* because she always follows the rules and produces quality work. From the teachers' point of view, this is a positive characteristic, but to Ellen's peer group, it could be negative. She may be described by her high school classmates as an *overachiever* or *teacher's pet*.

As emphasized in our opening Snapshot, labels are not absolutes and are often based on perception and not fact. As such, what are the possible consequences of using labels to describe people? Although labels have always been the basis for developing and providing services to people, they have also promoted stereotyping, discrimination, and exclusion. Some researchers suggest that the practice of labeling people has perpetuated and reinforced both the label and the stereotypical behaviors associated with it (Hardman & McDonnell, 2008; Mooney, 2007; Shifrer, 2013).

**Standard 6**
Professional Learning and
Ethical Practice

If labels may have negative consequences, why is labeling used so extensively? One reason is that many social services and educational programs for people who are exceptional require the use of labels to distinguish who is eligible for services and who is not. Discussing the need to label students who have special educational needs, Woolfolk (2013) suggested that labeling may actually help protect a child with learning differences from a class bully who, knowing the child has an "intellectual disability," may be more willing to accept the learning differences. Others (Hardman & McDonnell, 2008; Rose, Swearer, & Espelage, 2012) argue that labeling a child often has just the opposite effect—the child becomes more vulnerable to discrimination and abuse.

As Woolfolk suggests, however, the fact remains that being "labeled" in today's society still opens doors to special programs, useful information, special technology and equipment, or financial assistance. To illustrate, Antonio, a child with a hearing loss, must be assessed and labeled as having a "hearing impairment" before specialized educational or social services can be made available to him in his school. Another reason for the continued use of labels is the "useful information" they provide to professionals in communicating effectively with one another; they also provide a common ground for evaluating research findings. Labeling helps people to identify the specific needs of a particular group of individuals. Labeling can also help people to determine degrees of needs or to set priorities for services when societal resources are limited.

## 1-2 Three Approaches to Understanding Human Differences

Differences are found in every society. Most people *conform* to what is expected of them. Conformity—acting as we are "supposed" to act, or looking the way we are "supposed" to look—is the rule for most of us, most of the time (Baron, Branscombe, & Byrne, 2008). Usually, we look the way we are expected to look, behave the way we are expected to behave, and learn the way we are expected to learn. When a person differs substantially from these expectations, three approaches may be used to describe the nature and extent of these differences (see Figure 1.1).

### 1-2a A Developmental Approach

To understand human differences, we must first establish the definition of typical development or what is often described as "normal." According to the developmental approach, typical development can be described by using statistics (and milestones)—that is, observing in large numbers of individuals those characteristics that occur most frequently at a specific age. For example, when stating that the average 3-month-old infant is able to follow a moving object visually, *average* is a statistical term based on observations of the behavior of 3-month-old infants. When comparing an individual child's growth to that group average, differences in development (either advanced or delayed) are labeled accordingly.

**Figure 1.1** *Three Approaches to Describing Human Differences*

Developmental Approach

Cultural View

Self-Labeling

© Cengage Learning: Image in U.S. Map Credit: KidStock/Blend Images/Getty Images

## 1-2b   A Cultural Approach

From a cultural view, "typical" is defined by what any given society values. Whereas a developmental approach considers only the frequency of behaviors to define differences, a cultural view suggests that differences can be explained to a large extent by examining the *values* inherent within a society. What constitutes a significant difference changes over time, from culture to culture, and among the various social groups within a culture. People are considered *different* when they do something that is not expected of or valued by other members within the dominant culture. For example, in some cultures, intelligence is described in terms of how well someone scores on a test measuring a broad range of cognitive abilities; in other cultures, intelligence relates much more to how skillful someone is at hunting or fishing. The idea that people are the products of their cultures has received its greatest thrust from anthropology, which emphasizes the diversity and arbitrary nature of cultural rules regarding dress, eating habits, sexual behaviors, politics, and religion.

## 1-2c   Self-Labeling

Everyone engages in a process of self-labeling that may not be recognized by others with whom they interact. Thus, self-imposed labels reflect how we perceive ourselves, not how others see us. Conversely, a person may be labeled by society as different, but the individual does not recognize or accept the label. Such was the case with Thomas Edison. In school, young Thomas Edison was described as "addled," unable to focus, terrible at mathematics, a behavior problem, dyslexic, and unable to express himself in a coherent manner (difficulty with speech). Although the schools imposed many negative labels on young Thomas Edison, he eventually recognized that he was an individualist, ignored the labels, and pursued his own interests as an inventor. (See the nearby Reflect on This feature, and take a quiz on other famous people with disabilities.)

## A Few Famous People Who Are Differently Abled (Yet Labeled As Having a Disability)

a. Albert Einstein

b. Frida Kahlo

c. Stephen Hawking

d. Whoopi Goldberg

e. R. J. Mitte

f. Tom Cruise

g. James Earl Jones

h. Jay Leno

i. Julia Roberts

### Match the Names to the Descriptions:

___ 1. He was diagnosed with amyotrophic lateral sclerosis (ALS–Lou Gehrig's disease) at the age of 21. He must use a wheelchair and have round-the-clock nursing care. His speech has been severely affected, and he communicates through a computer by selecting words from a screen that are expressed through a speech synthesizer. Acknowledged as one of the greatest physicists in history, he developed a theory on black holes that provided new insights into the origin of the universe. Currently, he is professor of mathematics at Cambridge University, a post once held by Sir Isaac Newton.

___ 2. She experienced severe pain and other health conditions as a result of a bus crash when she was a teenager. Her artwork is celebrated for its surreal style that was influenced by indigenous cultures of Mexico.

___ 3. A well-known, tireless humanitarian advocate for children, the homeless, and human rights, and also involved in the battles against substance abuse and AIDS, this Oscar-winning actress and Grammy winner is a high school dropout with an acknowledged reading disability.

___ 4. He is the voice of Darth Vader and the most in-demand narrator in Hollywood. Virtually mute as a child, he stuttered throughout most of his youth. With the help of his high school English teacher, he overcame stuttering by reading Shakespeare aloud to himself and then to audiences. He went on to debating and finally to stage and screen acting.

___ 5. He is an actor that strives to enlighten his audience about disability by selecting roles that have depth and reduce stereotypes. He lives with mild cerebral palsy caused from oxygen deprivation during his birth.

___ 6. He did not speak until the age of 3. Even as an adult he found that searching for words was laborious. Schoolwork, especially math, was difficult for him, and he was unable to express himself in written language. He was thought to be "simple-minded" (retarded) until he discovered that he could achieve through visualizing rather than the use of oral language. His theory of relativity, which revolutionized modern physics, was developed in his spare time. *Time* magazine named him the most important person of the 20th century.

___ 7. He didn't learn to read while in school due to severe dyslexia and was unable to finish high school. Today he is regarded as one of most accomplished actors of his time. Although unable to read early in his career, he could memorize his lines from a cassette tape or someone reading to him. He later learned to read as an adult.

___ 8. He is an American stand-up comedian and television host. From 1992 to 2009 and from 2010 to 2012, he was the host of NBC's *The Tonight Show*. He grew up in Andover, Massachusetts, and has confirmed that he is dyslexic. Although his high school guidance counselor recommended that he drop out of high school because of his grades, he not only graduated but also went on to receive a bachelor's degree in speech therapy from Emerson College in 1973. He also attended Bentley College in Waltham, Massachusetts.

___ 9. She is an Academy Award–winning American film actress and former fashion model. She became the highest paid actress in the world, topping the annual power list of top-earning female stars for four consecutive years (2002 to 2005). She acknowledged that she stuttered when she was child, but with therapy, she now speaks fluidly.

### Question for Reflection

Select two of these famous people, or another famous person with a disability that you know about, and write a short essay on how their disability has had a positive influence on their lives. Can you describe someone with a disability that you know and how he or she has met the challenges of being a person who is "differently abled"?

SOURCE: The original source of the information contained in this quiz is unknown.

Photo Credits: Einstein: Topham/The Image Works; Kahlo: Bettmann/Corbis; Hawking: AP Images/Banks; Goldberg: AP Images/Lisa Bul; Mitte: AP Images /Richard Shotwell; Cruise: Stephane Cardinale/Sygma/Corbis; Jones: AP Images/Bob Galbraith; Leno: © Featureflash/Shutterstock.com; Roberts: © Featureflash/Shutterstock.com

**Answers:** 1(c), 2(b), 3(d), 4(g), 5(e), 6(a), 7(f), 8(h), 9(i)

## 1-2d The Effects of Being Labeled

Reactions to a label differ greatly from one person to another but can often be negative (Hardman & McDonnell, 2008; Rose, Swearer, & Espelage, 2012; Woolfolk, 2013). In a study of the reactions of family members, professionals, and the general public to the commonly used label *mental retardation,* researchers found the label generated a more negative reaction than the more current terminology of "intellectual disabilities" (see Chapter 9) (Schroeder et al., 2002).

**Separating the Person and the Label** Once a label has been affixed to an individual, the two may become inseparable. For example, Becky has been labeled as having autism. The tendency is to refer to Becky and her condition as one in the same—Becky is autistic. She is described by a disability label, causing people to lose sight of the fact that she is first and foremost a person, and that her exceptional characteristics (intellectual and social differences) are only a small part of who she is as an individual. To treat Becky as a label rather than someone who is differently abled is discrimination, and an injustice, not only to Becky, but to everyone else as well.

The use of person-first language, putting the person before the disability, can offset the potentially hurtful effects of labels. As an example of person-first language, a teacher could say "this student has a learning disability," rather than "this is a learning disabled student." Snow (2005) emphasizes that inappropriate use of labels perpetuate negative stereotypes and potentially reinforce attitudinal barriers.

**? ⓘ LEARNING THROUGH SOCIAL MEDIA**

### "Spread the Word to End the Word!"

*A national campaign is under way to encourage everyone to pledge to stop using the words retard and retarded. Over 500,000 people have taken the pledge. Here are just a few of the comments made on the site:*

—From R-word.org (Retrieved October 1, 2014, from http://www.r-word.org/Stories/Stories/R-word_Stories.aspx)

#### By Fatou Jawara

I don't understand why people use the "R" word as a synonym for stupid or anything else flawed. It doesn't make them sound "cool." It just makes them ignorant. These people are completely apathetic. They don't think about the person who has an intellectual disability or knows someone that has an intellectual disability. And what grinds my gears is when people say that it's not "offensive" or "not that serious." It is! I'm so thankful that we have organizations like Spread the Word to End the Word that look at ending the "R" word. It makes me feel warm inside that other people have the same feelings that I have on

ending the derogatory use of the "R" word. Kudos to you guys for trying to make a difference.

#### By Selena Barrows

My little brother has autism. He is very low functioning and does not talk and cannot do basic things you and I can do. One day a boy called me retarded. It hurt me because I started thinking of what he would call my brother if he were to meet him with no knowledge of his disability. The boy continued to call me a retard. After I told the counselor, she called him in. It stopped. When I mention my brother in conversation, and forget to mention his autism, people sometimes hesitantly ask if he is dumb. I reply with a simple, "Nope. He has autism." While we can't make people stop using this word, we can at least make a difference. I also have Asperger's and fear I will be a victim of that cruel word if I tell people. I shouldn't have to live in fear of telling others about my differences. I shouldn't feel insecure. I hope for a change, something this site can hopefully bring.

#### By Sydney Neal

I have a friend named Sierra. She has Down syndrome. Ever since I met Sierra, I started realizing how many people throw around the R-word like it doesn't mean anything and like it won't hurt anyone. This seriously needs to stop. You have a million different words you could say and you choose the one that hurts tons of people who are amazing and don't deserve that. I know by being close to Sierra that those words hurt. She is not a label; she is a person. It doesn't matter whether you are just joking with a friend or actually calling someone with a mental disability the R-word. If everyone made this pledge, imagine what our world could be.

*Question for Reflection*

What can you do to get involved in "Spread the Word to End the Word"? Taking the pledge may be an important first step, but what else do you think is essential if the language of discrimination is to end? To take the pledge, go to www.r-word.org/.

**Contextual Bias** The context in which we view someone can clearly influence our perceptions of that person. In a classic study from 1973, psychologist David Rosenhan investigated this premise by having himself and seven other "sane" individuals admitted to a number of state-run hospitals that treat mental illness across the United States. Once admitted to the hospitals, these subjects behaved as they normally would. The question was whether the staff would perceive them as people who were mentally healthy instead of as patients who experienced mental illness. Rosenhan reported that the eight pseudopatients were never detected by the hospital staff but were recognized as imposters by several of the legitimate patients. Throughout their hospital stays, the pseudopatients were incorrectly labeled and treated as though they had schizophrenia. Rosenhan's investigation demonstrated that the context in which the observations are made could bias the perception of what is normal.

Another example of contextual bias can be seen in the peer-to-peer treatment of students with disabilities who are taught in self-contained special education classrooms compared to those who are taught in inclusive classrooms. Rose, Swearer, and Espelage (2012) found that children taught in segregated settings report being targets of bullying more frequently than peers in inclusive settings, suggesting that the context has an effect on the perceptions of classmates.

## 1-3 Changing Societal Views on People with Disabilities: From Discrimination to Inclusion

In the fourth century b.c., the Greek philosopher Aristotle openly declared, "As to the exposure and rearing of children, let there be a law that no deformed child shall live..." (Aristotle, 1941).

Aristotle's stark statement is inconceivable in a civilized 21st-century world, but from the beginning of recorded time, children with disabilities were vulnerable to practices such as infanticide, slavery, physical abuse, and abandonment. Many civilizations accepted infanticide as a necessary means of controlling population growth and ensuring that only the strongest would survive in societies highly dependent on "living off the land." Early Greek and Roman patriarchies practiced selected eugenics—the belief in the possibility of improving the human species by discouraging the reproduction of people having genetic defects or inheritable "undesirable" traits. Although there are notable exceptions to the barbarism that marked early history, such as the ancient Egyptians who viewed infanticide as a crime, many early civilizations viewed "deformed children" as a sign of weakness, shame, and an unnecessary burden on society. Such views continued well into the 20th century. In Nazi Germany, genocide had come full circle from early Greek and Roman history to reach its pinnacle in 1939, with the planned extermination of "the mentally and physically disabled" under Operation T4. In the Hitler era, people with disabilities were openly targeted for the "final solution." The German government actively terminated the lives of people with disabilities as a means to purify the human race and put these individuals whose "life wasn't worthy of life" out of their misery (United States Holocaust Memorial Museum, 2014).

The 20th century was an era of marked contradictions in societal and government support for people with disabilities and their families. On one hand, treatment and education that had been denied for centuries were becoming more accessible. Schools were offering special classes for slow learners, children with physical disabilities, and those who were deaf and blind. In contrast, the societal view became increasingly more negative and accusatory. Parents were blamed for both the genetic inferiority of their children and were held responsible for not being able to take care of their needs without additional government support. The fear grew that many disabilities were passed on from generation to generation, and that eventually these "defectives" would defile the human race (Braddock & Parish, 2002). The following quote from Spratting in 1912 (cited in Wolfensberger, 1975) describes this phenomenon:

*Photo 1.1* Early institutions were human warehouses intended to prevent the spread of genetic and social deviance, as well as protect society from a "defective" person.

Library of Congress Prints and Photographs Division [LC-D4-17317]

*We must come to recognize feeblemindedness, idiocy, imbecility and insanity as largely communicable conditions or diseases, just as the physician recognizes smallpox, diphtheria, etc. as communicable.*

In the United States, the response to this fear was the enforcement of 17th-century blue laws (such as the Connecticut Code of 1650) that prohibited "mental and moral defectives" from marrying. Eventually the legislation was expanded to include **sterilization**. For most countries throughout the world, this eugenics scare of the 20th century evolved from laws about marriage and sterilization to planned social isolation rather than extermination. The emphasis on keeping families together at all costs changed to a perspective that removing the child with disabilities from the family into a controlled, large congregate living facility would be in the best interests of society, the family, and the child. Such isolation would prevent the further spread of genetic and social deviance, as well as protect society from the defective person.

Large congregate living facilities for people with disabilities were subsumed under many different labels, such as institution, hospital, colony, prison, school, or asylum. The move away from treatment to isolation increased over a period of 50 years as these large institutions grew in size. Families faced the dilemma of either keeping the child at home, often with no medical, educational, or social supports, or giving children over to professionals to live in an institution where they could be with others of "their own kind." This situation remained virtually unchanged for nearly five decades and declined even further during the Depression of the 1930s and 1940s, when funds and human resources were in short supply. By the 1950s, more than a million people in the United States had been committed to mental hospitals and institutions.

## 1-3a Advocating for Change

Throughout the 20th century, people with disabilities and their families struggled with a society that, in the best of times, was apathetic to their needs and, in the worst of times, was downright discriminatory. In response to the apathy and discrimination that permeated their lives, new parent groups advocating for the rights of children with disabilities began to organize on a national level around 1950. The United Cerebral Palsy (UCP) was founded in 1949, and the National Association for Retarded Children[1] (NARC) began in 1950. These organizations had similar goals. Both were concerned with providing accurate information to the public regarding the people they represented; both wanted to ensure the rights of full citizenship for people with disabilities through access to medical treatment, social services, and education. Other parent groups followed the lead of these two landmark organizations, including the National Society for Autistic Children (1961) and the Association for Children with Learning Disabilities[2] (1964).

The advent of parent organizations as advocates for people with disabilities coincided with the civil rights movement in the 1950s. As courts throughout the country reaffirmed the civil rights of ethnic minorities, parent organizations seized the opportunity to lay a foundation for stronger federal and state roles in meeting the needs of individuals with disabilities. In 1956—only two years after the landmark U.S. Supreme Court decision in *Brown v. The Board of Education of Topeka, Kansas* declared that separate education for people of color was inherently unequal—the NARC presented a call to action for the federal government to expand teaching and research in the education of children with

**Sterilization**
The process of making an individual unable to reproduce, usually done surgically.

[1] The National Association for Retarded Children became the National Association for Retarded Citizens in 1974. It is now known as the ARC of the United States.
[2] The Association for Children with Learning Disabilities is now known as the Learning Disabilities Association (LDA).

intellectual disabilities. Other parent and professional organizations followed suit. By 1960, the Congress and state legislatures were actively engaged with both parents and professionals concerned with improving the lives of people with disabilities.

Parents and professionals received a major boost in 1961, with the election of President John F. Kennedy. Through the strong encouragement of his sister Eunice Kennedy Shriver, who passed away in August 2009, and out of a strong family commitment to his sister Rosemary (who had an intellectual disability), President Kennedy elevated the needs of people with disabilities to a major national concern. The first-ever President's Committee on Mental Retardation (now the President's Committee for People with Intellectual Disabilities) was formed, and legislation that eventually resulted in many federal initiatives on behalf of people with disabilities was passed. President Kennedy was also a strong advocate for institutional reform:

> We as a nation have long neglected the mentally ill and mentally retarded. This neglect must end... We must act...to stimulate improvements in the level of care given the mentally disabled in our state and private institutions, and to reorient those programs to a community centered approach. (Kennedy, 1963)

Spurred on by an emerging federal role in services for people with disabilities and the expanding civil rights movement in the United States, parents moved to the courts to fight discrimination. In 1972, parents of people who were institutionalized in Alabama filed a lawsuit claiming that people with intellectual disabilities were being deprived of the right to treatment that would provide the skills to live in a community and family setting. The court described the institution as a human warehouse steeped in an atmosphere of psychological and physical deprivation. The state was ordered to ensure that people residing in the institution had a therapeutic environment. The *Wyatt v. Stickney* case led to the development of federal standards for institutions across the country that mandated specific rights for people with disabilities, including privacy, management of their own affairs, freedom from physical restraint and isolation, and adequate medical programs. The *Wyatt v. Stickney* case was followed by several other landmark decisions on institutional reform, such as *Halderman v. Pennhurst State School and Hospital*, *Youngberg v. Romeo*, and *Homeward Bound v. Hissom Memorial Center*.

Parents were equally active in their efforts to reform education. In 1971, parents from the Pennsylvania Association for Retarded Citizens (PARC) filed a class-action suit

*Photo 1.2* Parents, family members, advocacy organizations, and people who have disabilities led the way in the effort to ensure full citizenship for people with disabilities.

Wally McNamee/Historical/Corbis

(*PARC v. Commonwealth of Pennsylvania*), claiming that their children were being denied the right to a free and appropriate public education on the basis of mental retardation. The court ordered Pennsylvania schools to provide a free public education to all children with mental retardation between the ages of 6 and 21. Later that same year, the Pennsylvania decision was expanded to include all children with disabilities in the case of *Mills v. Board of Education of the District of Columbia*. The Pennsylvania and Mills cases were catalysts for several court cases and legislation in the years that followed, culminating in the passage of federal legislation in 1975 mandating a free and appropriate public education for all students with disabilities. The passage of Public Law 94-142[3] brought together all of the various pieces of state and federal legislation into a national law requiring parent involvement in the education of their children, multidisciplinary and nondiscriminatory testing, education in the least restrictive environment, and the development of an individualized education plan for every student.

Paralleling the advocacy efforts of parents and family members, self-advocacy groups appeared in the early 1970s. People First is an example of a self-advocacy group that began as an offspring of a parent advocacy group. The purpose of the organization is to provide a platform for people who have developmental disabilities to speak for themselves, and share ideas, friendship, and information. The first conference for People First took place in Oregon in 1974, with 560 people in attendance. Today, People First and the self-advocacy movement have grown into an international movement in 43 countries, with an estimated 17,000 members.

Today, the rights of people with disabilities have come full circle from the early history of genocide, to an era of rights and family support. The humanitarian reforms of the past four decades have resulted in significant changes in the lives of people with disabilities and their families. The culmination of parent and professional advocacy on behalf of 57 million people with disabilities in the United States, coupled with an increased presence of people who have disabilities advocating for themselves, was the passage of the Americans with Disabilities Act (ADA) in 1990.

## 1-4 The Americans with Disabilities Act (ADA)

A precursor to the Americans with Disabilities Act and the national movement to end discrimination against people with disabilities came with the passage of **Section 504** of the Vocational Rehabilitation Act in 1973. Section 504 stated:

> *No otherwise qualified person with a disability…shall, solely on the basis of disability, be denied access to, or the benefits of, or be subjected to discrimination under any program or activity provided by any entity/institution that receives federal financial assistance.*

Section 504 of the Vocational Rehabilitation Act set the stage for passage of the **Americans with Disabilities Act (ADA)** of 1990, the most sweeping civil rights legislation in the United States since the **Civil Rights Act of 1964**. The purpose of ADA is to prevent discrimination on the basis of disability in employment, programs, and services provided by state and local governments, goods and services provided by private companies, and commercial facilities. (See the nearby Reflect on This feature, "One City's Response to ADA.")

In the past, people with disabilities had to contend with the reality that learning to live independently did not guarantee access to community services or jobs. Access to public restrooms, restaurants, and successful employment has often eluded people with disabilities, due to architectural and attitudinal barriers. The purpose of ADA was to change this discrimination and affirm the rights of more than 50 million

**Standard 1**
Learner Development and
Individual Learning Differences

---

[3] Public Law 94-142, the Education for All Handicapped Children Act, was renamed the Individuals with Disabilities Education Act (IDEA) in 1990.

## One City's Response to ADA

### Building a Barrier-Free Community for 10-Year-Old Brittany and Her Friends

Fernandina Beach, Florida, a resort community of 8,800 residents on Amelia Island between the Atlantic Ocean and the Amelia River, is Florida's second oldest city and the state's first resort area. With its 50-block downtown historic district, golf courses, parks and nature areas, beaches, and a resident shrimping fleet, the community welcomes visitors and vacationers from all corners of the country. And recently, Fernandina Beach became an even more welcoming place for people with disabilities.

The city of Fernandina Beach made a decision—and a commitment—to go above and beyond the minimum ADA requirements and to make the city as usable and accessible as possible for everyone. To do this, city officials and residents worked together to find new approaches to accessibility, an experience they found both gratifying and exciting.

The city is working to make all its playgrounds accessible. Each city playground will have new accessible equipment, accessible playground surfaces, and accessible paths to the playground equipment. Cheri Fisher is thrilled with the changes. She no longer has to lift her daughter onto the play equipment and can happily watch as Brittany and her buddy go down the slide together. "What's really good is that Brittany now can play longer because she's not as tired from trudging to the playground. She also can play on pretty much all the equipment and play together with her friends; she's not being excluded now." Ten-year-old Brittany, who uses crutches and sometimes a wheelchair to get around, agrees. "I like the rope things that go round and round and I like the slide with the bumps and I liked the three of us sliding together!" In addition to creating accessible playgrounds, the city installed an accessible route to the picnic pavilions in each of its city parks and accessible picnic tables in every pavilion. The city constructed a beach walkover at the Main Beach and constructed an accessible viewing area connected to the accessible beach path, allowing as many as eight people using wheelchairs to sit together on the beach and enjoy an unobstructed view of the surf. The city plans to construct two additional walkovers at opposite ends of the city at the North Park and Seaside Park Beaches to give wheelchair users access to the beach nearest them. The city also purchased two beach wheelchairs for those who wish to join family and friends near the water on the sandy beach. It has plans to buy more.

### Question for Reflection

Can you identify examples of how your city or town has removed physical

Jose Carrillo/PhotoEdit

James Shaffer/PhotoEdit

barriers for people with disabilities from parks, restaurants, schools, universities, or government buildings in order to facilitate every person's full participation in the life of the community?

SOURCE: United States Department of Justice. (2011). "A Resort Community Improves Access to City Programs and Services for Residents and Vacationers." Retrieved August 25, 2011, from http://www.ada.gov/fernstor.htm.

Americans with disabilities to participate in the life of their community. Much as the Civil Rights Act of 1964 removed barriers to the African American struggle for equality, the ADA promised to do the same for those with disabilities. Its success in eliminating fears and prejudices remains to be seen, but the need for this legislation was obvious. First, people with disabilities faced discrimination in employment, access to public and private accommodations (e.g., hotels, theaters, restaurants, grocery stores), and services offered through state and local governments (Kessler Foundation and the National Organization on Disability, 2010; NOD/Harris & Associates, 2004). Second, because the historic Civil Rights Act of 1964 did not even mention people with disabilities, they had

## The ADA: 20 Years Later

- Although there has been substantial improvement reported in education attainment and political participation since 1986, large gaps still exist between people with and without disabilities with regard to employment, household income, access to transportation, health care, socializing, going to restaurants, and satisfaction with life. In some instances, the gaps have actually worsened since the inception of the first NOD survey.

- Employment remains the largest gap between people with and without disabilities. Of all working-age people with disabilities, only 21 percent indicated that they are employed, compared to 59 percent of people without disabilities—a gap of 38 percentage points.

- As was true in 1990, people with disabilities living in the second decade of the 21st century remain more likely to be living in poverty and less likely than those without disabilities to socialize with friends, relatives, or neighbors. The survey suggests that significant barriers remain to participation in leisure activities for those with disabilities.

- The second-largest gap between people with and without disabilities is Internet access. Of those surveyed, 85 percent of adults without disabilities access the Internet, whereas only 54 percent of adults with disabilities report doing so—a gap of 31 percentage points.

- The 2010 survey continues to emphasize that there is no single indicator of the quality of lives of people with disabilities. They face a range of challenges, and have varied experiences and aspirations. This diversity is characterized not only by a broad spectrum of disability characteristics, specifically type and severity, but also by a range of personal characteristics and circumstances. Understanding this heterogeneity is crucial in our understanding of how to support people with disabilities with the tools, skills, and opportunities they need to succeed.

### Question for Reflection

Although ADA accomplished a great deal on behalf of people with disabilities in the past two decades, much remains to be done. Identify and discuss three key areas where you see more attention is needed from policy makers, businesses, and the community if we are truly to improve the quality of life for children and adults with disabilities.

SOURCE: Kessler Foundation and the National Organization on Disability. (2010). *Survey of Americans with Disabilities*. New York: Author.

---

no federal protection against discrimination. As stated by the United States Department of Justice (2014):

> *Barriers to employment, transportation, public accommodations, public services, and telecommunications have imposed staggering economic and social costs on American society and have undermined our well-intentioned efforts to educate, rehabilitate, and employ individuals with disabilities... The Americans with Disabilities Act gives civil rights protections to individuals with disabilities similar to those provided to individuals on the basis of race, color, sex, national origin, age, and religion. It guarantees equal opportunity for individuals with disabilities in public accommodations, employment, transportation, state and local government services, and telecommunications.*

**Standard 6**
Professional Learning and Ethical Practice

In 2010, the Kessler Foundation and National Organization on Disability (NOD) released the results of a survey on the quality of life of people with disabilities and the gaps in employment, services, and supports between people with and without disabilities. A summary of the survey results of more than 1,000 adults with disabilities and 788 adults without disabilities are found in the nearby Reflect on This feature, "The ADA: 20 Years Later."

## 1-4a   The ADA Definition of Disability

The original ADA was passed by the U.S. Congress in 1990. In 2008 Congress clarified the definition of disability and the provisions of the act with the American with Disabilities Act Amendments Act (ADAAA). According to the ADA, a person is considered to have a disability if he or she has (1) a physical or mental impairment that substantially limits him or her in one or more major life activity, (2) has a record of such an impairment, or (3) is regarded as having such an impairment (29 C.F.R. § 1630.2[g]). To clarify, the ADAAA states that a person will have to show only that he or she was discriminated against because of an actual or *perceived* impairment, even if the impairment doesn't limit or isn't perceived to limit a major life activity.

## 1-4b  Major Provisions of ADA

ADA mandates protections for people with disabilities in public and private-sector employment, all public services, and public accommodations, transportation, and telecommunications. The U.S. Department of Justice is charged with the responsibility of ensuring that these provisions are enforced on behalf of all people with disabilities. The intent of ADA is to create a "fair and level playing field" for eligible people with disabilities. To do so, the law specifies that reasonable accommodations need to be made that take into account each person's needs resulting from his or her disabilities. As defined in law, the principal test for a reasonable accommodation is its effectiveness: Does the accommodation provide an opportunity for a person with a disability to achieve the same level of performance and to enjoy benefits equal to those of an average, similarly situated person without a disability? The major provisions of the ADA include:

- *Employment*. ADA mandates that employers may not discriminate in any employment practices, including job application procedures, hiring, firing, advancement, compensation, training, and other terms, conditions, and privileges of employment. It applies to recruitment, advertising, tenure, layoff, leave, fringe benefits, and all other employment-related activities. The law applies to any business with 15 or more employees.

- *Transportation*. ADA requires that all new public transit buses, bus and train stations, and rail systems must be accessible to people with disabilities. Transit authorities must provide transportation services to individuals with disabilities who cannot use fixed-route bus services. All Amtrak stations are now accessible to people with disabilities. Discrimination by air carriers in areas other than employment is not covered by the ADA, but rather by the Air Carrier Access Act (49 U.S.C. §1374 [c]).

- *Public accommodations*. Restaurants, hotels, and retail stores may not discriminate against individuals with disabilities. Physical barriers in existing facilities must be removed, if removal is readily achievable. If not, alternative methods of providing the services must be offered. All new construction and alterations of facilities must be accessible.

- *Government*. State and local agencies may not discriminate against qualified individuals with disabilities. All government facilities, services, and communications must be accessible to people with disabilities.

- *Telecommunications*. ADA requires that all companies offering telephone service to the general public must offer telephone relay services to individuals with hearing loss who use telecommunication devices or similar equipment.

## 1-5  The Role of Health Care, Psychology, and Social Services Professionals in the Lives of People with Disabilities

This chapter continues with an initial discussion of three disciplines concerned with supporting people with disabilities and their families in community settings: health care, psychology, and social services. (Education is the focus of Chapter 2 in this text.) Each discipline is unique in its understanding of, and approach to, people with disabilities. Figure 1.2 provides the common terminology associated with each field.

### 1-5a  The Role of Health Care Professionals

The medical model has two dimensions: normalcy and pathology. *Normalcy* is defined as the absence of a biological problem. Pathology is defined as alterations in an organism caused by disease, resulting in a state of ill health that interferes with or destroys the integrity of the organism. The medical model, often referred to as the *disease model*, focuses

**Reasonable accommodations**
Requirements within ADA to ensure that a person with a disability has an equal chance of participation. The intent is to create a "fair and level playing field" for the person with a disability. A reasonable accommodation takes into account each person's needs resulting from their disability. Accommodations may be arranged in the areas of employment, transportation, or telecommunications.

**Medical model**
Model by which human development is viewed according to two dimensions: normal and pathological. Normal refers to the absence of biological problems; pathological refers to alterations in the organism caused by disease.

**Pathology**
Alterations in an organism that are caused by disease.

**Figure 1.2** *Common Terminology in Medicine, Psychology, and Sociology*

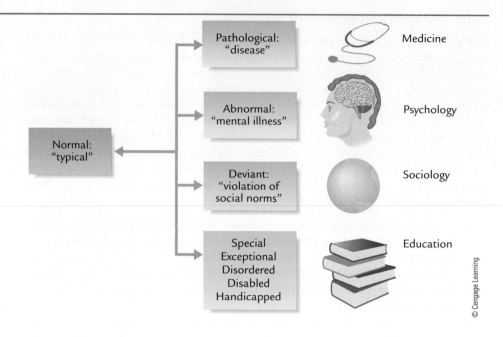

primarily on biological problems and on defining the nature of the disease and its pathological effects on the individual. The model is based on the premise that being healthy is better than being sick, regardless of the culture in which one lives. Although the model is essentially universal, there are some culturally relative values that guide understanding and treatment of illness.

When diagnosing a problem, a physician carefully follows a definite pattern of procedures that includes questioning the patient to obtain a history of the problem, conducting a physical examination and laboratory studies, and in some cases, performing surgical explorations. The person who has a biological problem is labeled the *patient*, and the deficits are then described as the *patient's disease*.

We must go back more than 200 years to find the first documented attempts to personalize health care to serve the needs of people with differences. In 1799, as a young physician and authority on diseases of the ear and education of those with hearing loss, Jean-Marc Itard (1775–1838) believed that the environment, in conjunction with physiological stimulation, could contribute to the learning potential of any human being. Itard was influenced by the earlier work of Philippe Pinel (1745–1826), a French physician concerned with mental illness, and John Locke (1632–1704), an English philosopher. Pinel advocated that people characterized as insane or idiots needed to be treated humanely, but his teachings emphasized that they were essentially incurable and that any treatment to remedy their disabilities would be fruitless. Locke, in contrast, described the mind as a "blank slate" that could be opened to all kinds of new stimuli. The positions of Pinel and Locke represent the classic controversy of nature versus nurture: What are the roles of heredity and environment in determining a person's capabilities?

Itard tested the theories of Pinel and Locke in his work with Victor, the so-called wild boy of Aveyron. Victor was 12 years old when hunters found him in the woods. He had not developed any language, and his behavior was virtually uncontrollable, described as savage or animal like. Ignoring Pinel's diagnosis that the child was an incurable idiot, Itard took responsibility for Victor and put him through a program of sensory stimulation that was intended to cure his condition. After five years, Victor developed some verbal language and became more socially aware as he grew accustomed to his new environment. Itard's work with Victor documented for the first time that learning is possible even for individuals that most professionals describe as totally helpless.

Health care services for people with disabilities have evolved considerably since Itard's groundbreaking work. The focus today is directly on the individual in family and community settings. In many cases, the physician is the first professional with whom parents have

**Nature versus nurture**
Controversy concerning how much of a person's ability is related to sociocultural influences (nurture) as opposed to genetic factors (nature).

contact concerning their child's disability, particularly when the child's challenges are identifiable immediately after birth or during the early childhood years. The physician is the family adviser and communicates with parents regarding the medical prognosis and recommendations for treatment. However, too often physicians assume that they are the family's only counseling resource (Drew & Hardman, 2007). Physicians should be aware of additional resources within the community, including other parents, social workers, mental health professionals, and educators.

Health care services are often taken for granted simply because they are readily available to most people. This is not true, however, for many people with disabilities. It is not uncommon for a pediatrician to suggest that parents seek treatment elsewhere for their child with a disability, even when the problem is a common illness such as a cold or a sore throat.

**Photo 1.3** Physicians in community practice must be willing to provide medical care to people with disabilities. What additional training do you think is needed for physicians to care for people with disabilities?

It would be unfair to stereotype health care professionals as unresponsive to the needs of people with disabilities. On the contrary, medical technology has prevented many disabilities from occurring and has enhanced the quality of life for many people. However, to ensure that people with disabilities receive comprehensive health care services in a community setting, several factors must be considered. The physician in community practice (e.g., the general practitioner, pediatrician) must receive more training in the medical, psychological, and educational aspects of disability conditions. This training could include instruction regarding developmental milestones; attitudes toward children with disabilities; disabling conditions; prevention; screening, diagnosis, and assessment; interdisciplinary collaboration; effective communication with parents; long-term health care and social programs; and community resources. Physicians need not become disability specialists, but they must have enough knowledge to refer patients to appropriate specialists when necessary and be willing to treat patients with disabilities for common illnesses. Some specialists that might be included as part of an individual's treatment plan include geneticists and genetic counselors, physical therapists and occupational therapists, public health nurses, and nutritional and dietary consultants.

**Geneticist**
A professional who specializes in the study of heredity.

**Genetic counselor**
A specially trained professional who counsels people about their chances of producing a seriously ill infant, in reference to their genetic history.

**Physical therapist**
A professional who provides services that help restore function, improve mobility, relieve pain, and prevent or limit permanent physical disabilities. They help restore, maintain, and promote overall fitness and health for people of all ages.

**Occupational therapist**
A professional who specializes in developing self-care, work, and play activities to increase independent function and quality of life, enhance development, and prevent disability.

## 1-5b The Role of Psychologists

Psychology is the science of human and animal behavior, the study of the acts and mental events that can be observed and evaluated. Broadly viewed, psychology is concerned with every behavior of an individual. Behavior is the focus of psychology, and when the behavior of an individual does not meet the criteria of normalcy, it is labeled *abnormal* and the person is labeled. Labels describing abnormal behavior include emotional disturbance, behavior disorders, psychosis, neurosis, and so on.

Psychology, as we know it today, is more than 125 years old. In 1879, Wilhelm Wundt (1832–1920) defined psychology as the science of conscious experience. His definition was based on the *principle of introspection*—looking into oneself to analyze experiences. William James (1842–1910) expanded Wundt's conception of conscious experience in his treatise, *The Principles of Psychology* (James, 1890), to include learning, motivation, and emotions. In 1913, John B. Watson (1878–1958) shifted the focus of psychology from conscious experience to observable behavior and mental events.

**Standard 7**
Collaboration

We cannot live in today's world without encountering behavior that is disturbing, socially unacceptable, distressing, or maladaptive. In psychology these are considered abnormal behaviors. The media are replete with stories ranging from burglary to mass murders, and embezzlement to child abuse. Each case represents a point on the continuum of *abnormal behavior* that exists in society. Levels of emotional and behavioral challenges range from actions that are slightly deviant or eccentric (but still within the confines of normal human experience) to **neurotic disorders** (partial disorganization characterized by combinations of anxieties, compulsions, obsessions, and phobias) to **psychotic disorders** (severe disorganization resulting in loss of contact with reality and characterized by delusions, hallucinations, and illusions).

The study of abnormal behavior historically has been based in philosophy and religion in Western culture. Until the Middle Ages, a person operating outside of the norm was thought to have made a "pact with the devil," and the psychological affliction was believed to be a result of divine punishment or the work of devils, witches, or demons residing within the person. The earliest known treatment for mental disorders, called *trephining,* involved drilling holes in a person's skull to permit evil spirits to leave (Carlson et al., 2009).

Today, psychologists play a critical role in the treatment of many individuals with disabilities. Depending upon their training and philosophy, psychologists provide treatments that include behavior therapy, rational-emotive therapy, group psychotherapy, family therapy, or client-centered therapy. According to Carlson et al. (2009), the majority of psychologists describe their therapeutic philosophy as eclectic. They choose from many different approaches in determining the best way to work with an individual in need of psychological help.

## 1-5c   The Role of Social Services Professionals

Whereas psychology focuses primarily on the behavior of the individual, social services professionals are concerned with modern cultures, group behaviors, societal institutions, and intergroup relationships. These professionals view individuals in relation to their physical and social environments. When individuals meet the social norms of the group, they are considered normal. When individuals are unable to adapt to social roles or to establish appropriate interpersonal relationships, their behaviors are considered **deviant**. Unlike medical pathology, social differences cannot be defined in universal terms. Instead, they are defined within the context of the culture, in any way the culture chooses to define them.

Even within the same society, different social groups often define human differences in myriad ways. Groups of people who share the same norms and values will develop their own rules about what is and what is not acceptable social behavior. Four principles serve as guidelines in determining who will be labeled socially different:

1.  Normal behavior must meet societal, cultural, or group expectations. Difference is defined as a violation of social norms.

2.  Social differences are not necessarily illnesses as defined by the medical model. Failure to conform to societal norms does not imply that the individual has pathological or biological deficits.

3.  Each culture determines the range of behaviors that are defined as normal or deviant and then enforces these norms. Those people with the greatest power within the culture can impose their criteria for normalcy on those who are less powerful.

4.  Social differences may be caused by the interaction of several factors, including genetic makeup and individual experiences within the social environment.

Today, many different kinds of social service professionals specialize across more than 50 subfields and specialties. Within each specialty area, these professionals undertake a systematic study of social groups, organizations, cultures, and societies on individual and group behavior. The social services professionals provide information about social behavior (including disability) in the context of the society as a whole. The following are just a few examples of specialties that may include an emphasis on disability: sociology, social work, gerontology (aging), criminology and criminal justice, and family and marriage. This chapter has examined many different perspectives on people with disabilities, including common terminology used to describe these individuals, bringing about social change and inclusion through the Americans with Disabilities Act, and understanding people with disabilities from the disciplines of medicine, psychology, and sociology.

## Looking Toward a Bright Future

The ADA seeks to ensure that comprehensive services (e.g., employment, housing, educational programs, public transportation, restaurant access, and religious activities) are available to all individuals with disabilities within or as close as possible to their families and communities. In 1999, the U.S. Supreme Court ruled in *Olmstead v. L.C. & E.W.* (now known as the *Olmstead decision*) that it is a violation of the ADA to discriminate against people with disabilities by providing services only in institutions when they could be served in a community-based setting. This historic decision encouraged policy makers to reevaluate how they deliver publicly funded services and supports to people with disabilities. Communities must have (1) a comprehensive, effective working plan for placing qualified people in less restrictive settings, and (2) a waiting list for community-based services that ensures people can receive services

Mika/Flame/Corbis

*Photo 1.4* As a result of ADA, people with disabilities and their families have opportunities to experience living in their neighborhood communities, paid employment, access to public transportation, and schooling that were not available even 20 years ago.

and be moved off the list at a reasonable pace. A recent report (U.S. Senate Committee on Health, Education, Labor and Pensions, 2014) concluded that the promise of community living assured through the Olmstead decision has yet to be realized. The report suggests that "Congress should amend the ADA to clarify and strengthen the law's integration mandate in a manner that accelerates *Olmstead* implementation and clarifies that every individual who is eligible for [long-term services and supports] LTSS under Medicaid has a federally protected right to a real choice in how they receive services and supports."

As a result of the ADA, federal and state support for community living is being redirected from isolated large congregate care settings to small, community-based residences located within local neighborhoods. Although the unemployment rate of people with disabilities is the highest of any group of people in the world, with antidiscrimination legislation, such as ADA, there is an increasing effort to help people who have disabilities obtain real jobs, earn wages, and work side by side with those who are not disabled. For families, there has been an expansion in services, such as respite care and in-home assistance, to provide help in balancing the everyday stress that can be associated with long-term care of individuals who have disabilities. People with disabilities and their families are also experiencing a stronger emphasis on person-centered supports. Through individualized program planning, adults with disabilities and their families are brought together with myriad agencies (such as social services, vocational rehabilitation, health care, Social Security) to plan, develop, and implement the supports necessary for individuals to participate in their communities.

To ensure a bright future, people with disabilities need access to their local community services, such as education, health care, transportation, recreation, and social networks. Access to these supports creates the opportunity to be included in community life. Successful inclusion requires a two-part approach: (1) Appropriate support needs to be provided to help individuals become more independent (education, job skill development, social skills), and (2) the community needs to strive for ways to reduce barriers and increase inclusion. Access to adequate housing and a barrier-free environment are essential for people with disabilities. **Barrier-free facilities** are created by requiring that buildings and public transportation incorporate barrier-free designs. People with disabilities need entrance ramps to and within public buildings; accessibility to public telephones, vending machines, and restrooms; and lifts for public transportation vehicles. Community living options should include apartments, small group homes, foster homes, and home ownership.

The availability of recreation and leisure experiences within the community vary substantially depending upon age and severity of disability. Many people with a disability may not have access to the arts and sports activities that are generally available to others within the community. Similar challenges exist for children, adolescents, and adults with disabilities, many of whom have limited opportunities for recreation and leisure experiences beyond solo or passive activities like playing video games and watching television.

Recreational programs must be developed in ways that assist individuals in accessing leisure activities of their choice and creating more satisfying lifestyles. Therapeutic recreation is a profession concerned specifically with the goal of increased independence and social connectedness through recreation.

Work is an essential component of quality of life for all adults, including those with disabilities. Yet many individuals with disabilities are unable to gain employment during their adult years. Brault (2012) states that although there are approximately 56.7 million people with disabilities who bring a unique set of skills to the workplace and thereby enhance, strengthen, and diversify the U.S. labor market, less than half of this group are employed. Additionally, median monthly earnings of working adults with disabilities are significantly less than those with no disability.

**Barrier-free facility**
A building or structure without architectural obstructions that allows people with mobility disabilities (such as those in wheelchairs) to move freely through all areas.

## Keani

Over the past several years, many changes have occurred in Keani's life. After spending the first half of her life in a large institution, Keani, now in her late 40s, lives in an apartment with two other women, both of whom have a disability. She receives assistance from a local supported-living program and is supported to make her own decisions as she becomes more independent in the community. Additionally, she is involved with the Polynesian Cultural Center in her community, which has provided her a wonderful support network.

Over the years, Keani has had many labels describing her disability, including intellectual disability, epilepsy, autism, physical disability, chronic health concerns, and serious emotional disturbance. She does have some significant challenges, both mentally and physically. Medical problems associated with epilepsy necessitate the use of medications that affect Keani's behavior (motivation, attitude, and so on) and her physical well-being. During her early 20s, while walking up a long flight of stairs, Keani had a seizure that resulted in a fall and broken neck. The long-term impact from the fall was a paralyzed right hand and limited use of her left leg.

Keani's life goal has been to work a real job, make money, and have choices about how she spends her money. For most of her life, the goal has been out of reach. Her only jobs have been in sheltered workshops, where she worked for next to nothing, doing piecemeal work such as sorting envelopes, putting together cardboard boxes, or folding laundry. Whereas most of the focus in the past has been on what Keani "can't do" (can't read, can't get along with supervisors, can't handle the physical requirements of a job), her family and the professionals on her support team are looking more at her very strong desire to succeed in a community job.

About three miles from Keani's apartment, a job has opened up for a stock clerk at a local video store. The store manager is looking to hire someone to work four to six hours a day stocking the shelves with videos and handling some basic tasks (such as cleaning floors, washing windows, and dusting furniture). Keani loves movies and is really interested in this job. With the support of family and her professional team, she has applied for the job.

### Application Questions

**1.** As Keani's potential employer, what are some of the issues you would raise about her capability to perform the essential functions of the job?

**2.** What would you see as the "reasonable accommodations" necessary to help Keani succeed at this job if she were hired?

A comparison of working and nonworking individuals with disabilities revealed that working individuals were more satisfied with life, had more money, and were less likely to blame their disability for preventing them from reaching their potential. For more insight into the employment of a person with disabilities, see the nearby Case Study on Embracing Diversity, "Keani."

Many of the changes in the last three decades have had a positive and dramatic impact on the lives of people with disabilities and their families. However, much remains to be done. As people with disabilities and their families engage in life in the 21st century, it will be critical to carefully listen to and support their individual needs and preferences. As suggested by the Center on Human Policy at Syracuse University (2011), support for people with disabilities should:

- be based on the principle "whatever it takes." Services should be flexible, individualized, and designed to meet the diverse needs of the individual and the family.
- build on existing social networks and natural sources.
- maximize each person's control over his or her services.
- be based on the assumption that the individual and the family, rather than governments and agencies, are in the best position to determine needs.
- encourage the inclusion of people with disabilities into the life of the family and community.

**1-1 Describe why we continue to label people even when we know it may have a negative effect on an individual.**

- Labels are an attempt to describe, identify, and distinguish one person from another.
- Many medical, psychological, social, and educational services require that an individual be labeled to determine who is eligible to receive special services.
- Labels help professionals communicate more effectively with one another and provide a common ground for evaluating research findings.
- Labels enable professionals to differentiate more clearly the needs of one group of people from those of another.

**1-2 Identify three approaches to describe human differences.**

- The developmental approach is based on differences in the course of human development from what is considered normal physical, social, and intellectual growth. Human differences are the result of interaction between biological and environmental factors. Observing large numbers of individuals and looking for characteristics that occur most frequently at any given age can explain normal growth.
- The cultural approach defines *normal* according to established cultural standards. Human differences can be explained by examining the values of any given society. What is considered normal will change over time and from culture to culture.
- Self-labeling reflects how we perceive ourselves, although those perceptions may not be consistent with how others see us.

**1-3 Explain how societal views on people with disabilities changed from widespread discrimination to an era of inclusion and support in the 21st century.**

- People with disabilities have historically been viewed as a burden to families and society. Discrimination has been prevalent since early civilizations.

- The 20th century brought about positive changes in societal and government support for people with disabilities and their families. Treatment and education that had been denied for centuries became more accessible. By 1960, the Congress and state legislatures were actively engaged with both parents and professionals concerned with improving the lives of people with disabilities.
- With the passage of the Americans with Disabilities Act in 1990, the rights of people with disabilities came full circle, from the early history of genocide to an era of rights and family support in the 21st century.

**1-4 Identify the catalyst, effects, and provisions of the Americans with Disabilities Act.**

- ADA is a U.S. federal civil rights law that provides a national mandate to end discrimination against individuals with disabilities in private-sector employment, in all public services, and in public accommodations, transportation, and telecommunications.

**1-5 Describe the role of health care, psychology, and social services professionals in meeting the needs of people with disabilities.**

- Health care professionals are focused directly on the individual in family and community settings. In many cases, the physician is the first professional with whom parents have contact concerning their child's disability, particularly when the child's challenges are identifiable immediately after birth or during early childhood. The physician is the family adviser and communicates with parents regarding the medical prognosis and recommendations for treatment.
- Psychologists use many different approaches in the treatment of mental health challenges, including behavior therapy, rational-emotive therapy, group psychotherapy, family therapy, or client-centered therapy.
- Whereas psychology focuses primarily on the behavior of the individual, social services professionals are concerned with modern cultures, group behaviors, societal institutions, and intergroup relationships. They view the individual in relation to the physical and social environment.

**Council for Exceptional Children (CEC) Standards to Accompany Chapter 1**

If you are thinking about a career in special education, you should know that many states use national standards developed by the Council for Exceptional Children (CEC) to assess a teacher candidate's knowledge and skills for working with students with disabilities. See a complete listing of the seven CEC Content Standards on the inside cover of this text.

1 Learner Development and Individual Learning Differences
2 Learning Environments
6 Professional Learning and Ethical Practice
7 Collaboration

## Mastery Activities and Assignments

To master the content within this chapter, complete the following activities and assignments:

1. Complete a written test of the chapter's content. If your instructor requires a written test of your content knowledge for this chapter, keep a copy for your portfolio.
2. Review the Case Study on Embracing Diversity, "Keani," and respond in writing to the Application Questions.

Keep a copy of the Case Study and your written response for your portfolio.

3. Participate in a community service learning activity. Community service is a valuable way to enhance your learning experience. Develop a reflective journal of the service learning experience for your portfolio.

## CHAPTER 2

# Education for All

Shaunl/E+/Getty Images

## Learning Objectives

*After you complete this chapter, you will be able to:*

**2-1** Describe the educational services that were available for students with disabilities during most of the 20th century.

**2-2** Identify the principal issues in the right-to-education cases that led to the eventual passage of the national mandate to educate students with disabilities.

**2-3** Describe special education and related services as they apply to each of the major provisions of the Individuals with Disabilities Education Act (IDEA).

**2-4** Discuss the special education referral, assessment, planning, and placement process.

**2-5** Describe what schools should do to assure accountability for student learning and access to the general curriculum.

**2-6** Distinguish between students with disabilities eligible for services under Section 504/ADA and those eligible under IDEA.

# Tara and Her 8 Tips for New Special Education Teachers

Tara Hillegas is a K–3 special education teacher in the Pine Richland School District in Pittsburgh, Pennsylvania. She graduated from Slippery Rock University with a bachelor's degree in elementary and special education and master's degree in special education. She has been teaching students with disabilities for seven years and was recently awarded the "Making a Daily Difference Award" from Fund It Forward, a nonprofit organization. She wrote these tips for the Special Education Guide blog.

Starting a new teaching job is an exciting time, but can be stressful. Here are a few tips to help ease the transition into the special education world.

Courtesy of Tara Hillegas

### Build a Reward System

A strong set of rules and consequences is important in a special education classroom, as is a reward system. My students really like to earn "behavior bucks" during learning sessions. They get paid for completing their work and are allowed to shop on Fridays if they demonstrate good behavior.

It is easy to set up a consequence system by using "fines" for inappropriate behaviors such as missed homework or calling out. I have used this type of system with high school students in a full-time emotional support classroom, as well as with K–2 learning support students in a pullout setting.

This type of system can be as involved or as basic as you would like to make it. It is also an excellent tool for behavioral data collection. I have individualized this system for all students in my classroom by using their specific IEP goals. Data are collected and counted at the end of the day to determine how much students have earned, and fines are subtracted.

### Establish a System to Collect and Analyze Data

Special education is all about collecting data. Data drive instruction and help teams make informed decisions about student learning. I collect daily behavioral data for students with behavior plans so that I have an accurate picture of all students and their day. This allows me to look at patterns of behavior and make modifications to programming.

I collect biweekly or weekly data on academic goals for students with learning disabilities. This data is then graphed on a chart so that parents or students are able to see progress whenever they would like. Kids like to know what their goals are and how they can beat them. Charts and graphs are visual representations that are easy for students and their parents to understand.

### Be Flexible

Just when you think you have everything figured out and things are working smoothly, something will change. It might be a new student added to your caseload, new behavioral problems with an existing student, a sudden reduction in staff, or a variety of other challenges. Although it can be frustrating to continually face change, it is necessary to be flexible.

### Keep Up with Your Paperwork

Special education teachers have a lot of paperwork to complete, and it can be easy to get behind. Between individual education plans (IEPs), progress monitoring, and planning individual lessons for multiple groups of students, it can be overwhelming for a new teacher. Ideally, it would be wonderful to have enough time to complete all of your paperwork during the school day, but that is not usually how it works out. One way to limit the amount of work that you take home is to get organized and make every minute of the day count.

### Get Organized

Organization is extremely important in a special education classroom. Being organized will help your classroom run more smoothly and will help alleviate some stress, but data collection can be overwhelming when you have a caseload of 20 students who have three or more IEP goals each. I use color-coded folders for each subject area for individual students based on their goals, and I rotate through them weekly.

My students also have individual work binders to work through during times when I am working with a student one on one. Valuable instructional time can be lost in a disorganized classroom, and since there is a limited amount of time to work with students in a pullout setting, organization is a crucial part of the successful special education classroom.

### Familiarize Yourself with Research-Based Programs and Interventions

One area in education that is continually changing is which programs and interventions are best for students with disabilities. Response to intervention (RTI) is an important process that allows teams to track and try research-based programs for students with and without disabilities. As a special education teacher, it is important to learn about programs that are research-based so that you can provide your students with the best possible interventions for their disabilities.

### Initiate Parent Contact

I suggest initiating contact with new families prior to the start of the school year. This will help ease your transition into the classroom, and parents will feel more comfortable if you have made the effort to contact them in advance. Email can be a great tool for quick messages to a parent, but for more in-depth conversations, I suggest using the telephone.

### Know When to Ask for Help

One piece of advice I like to give new teachers is to know when to ask for help. It really takes a team to work with students with disabilities. I could not implement behavior plans, collect data, or individualize student learning without the assistance of the regular education teachers and paraeducators in my building. Often, when you solve a problem together, you can come up with a better solution than if you were to tackle the issue on your own.

SOURCE: Hillegas, T. "8 Tips for New Special Education Teachers." Retrieved December 4, 2014, from http://www.specialeducationguide.com/blog/8-tips-for-new-special-education-teachers/.

## A Changing Era in the Lives of Students with Disabilities

Educating children with disabilities around the world has historically focused on caring for each student in a segregated setting away from nondisabled peers, or not providing any schooling at all. Today, many nations are acknowledging the importance of an education for these children as a critical factor in promoting independence in family and community settings. The view that children with disabilities should be excluded from school is being replaced with the call to provide an educational opportunity for every child. An example of this worldwide call for inclusive education is seen in the 1994 Salamanca Statement issued by the United Nations (UN) with the support of 92 different countries. The Salamanca Statement affirms that:

- Every child has unique characteristics, interests, abilities, and learning needs.
- Education systems should be designed, and educational programs should be implemented to take into account the wide diversity of characteristics and needs.
- Those with special educational needs must have access to regular [general education] schools that should accommodate them within a child-centered instructional program.
- Regular schools with this inclusive orientation are the most effective means of combating discriminatory attitudes, creating welcoming communities, building an inclusive society and achieving education for all. (United Nations Education, Scientific and Cultural Organization [UNESCO], 1994)

The UN further strengthened its strong view on *education for all* during the World Summit for Children (UNESCO, 2001), calling for schools to promote access to education for every child with a disability. To meet this call, schools are expected to provide students with the opportunity to learn and apply the necessary skills for a successful transition to adult life.

In the United States, access to education is a basic value, reflecting the expectation that all children should have an opportunity to learn and develop to the best of their ability. Schools are responsible for every student, from the most academically capable to those in need of specialized services and supports. All Tara Hillegas from the opening Snapshot wants for her students is the opportunity for them to learn the skills that would facilitate success in school, family, and community. As an experienced teacher, Tara provides some important and interesting insights into what it takes to be an effective special education teacher.

## 2-1 Educational Services for Students with Disabilities in the 20th Century

The goal of *education for all* is full participation for everyone—regardless of race, cultural background, socioeconomic status, physical disability, or intellectual challenges. It wasn't until 1975, however, that this value was translated into practice for all students with disabilities in the United States. The following section describes the beginnings of special education; a view from some professionals and national leaders that education is a privilege and not a right for students with disabilities; and the expanding role of the U.S. government in educating these students.

## 2-1a Early Special Education Programs

Throughout most of the last three centuries, many families who had a child with a disability were unable to get help for their most basic needs, such as medical and dental care, social services, or education. In the 18th and 19th centuries, educational services consisted of programs that were usually separate from the public schools, established mainly for children who were described as "slow learners" or who had hearing or sight loss. These students were usually placed in separate classrooms in a public school building or in separate schools. Special education meant segregated education. Moreover, students with very substantial learning and behavior differences were excluded from public education entirely.

## 2-1b Education as a Privilege but Not a Right

From 1920 to 1960, most states merely allowed for special education; they did not mandate it. Educational services to children with mild emotional disorders (e.g., discipline problems or inappropriate behavior) were initiated in the early 1930s, but mental hospitals continued to be the only alternative for most children with severe emotional problems. Special classes for children with physical disabilities expanded in the 1930s; separate schools for these children became increasingly popular during the late 1950s, with specially designed elevators, ramps, and modified doors, toilets, and desks.

During the 1940s, special school versus general education class placement emerged as an issue in the education of students with disabilities. Educators and parents began to advocate that these students be educated in a school setting that would promote social interaction with "typical" (nondisabled) peers.

By the 1950s, many countries around the world sought to expand educational programs for students with disabilities in special schools and classes. Additionally, many health care and social services professionals were advocating on behalf of individuals with disabilities, thus enriching our knowledge regarding effective programs and services. Researchers and families began calling into question the validity of segregated programs. Several studies in the 1950s and 1960s (e.g., Cassidy & Stanton, 1959; Johnson, 1961; Jordan & deCharms, 1959; Thurstone, 1959) examined the value of special classes. This research resulted in the development of a new model (*mainstreaming*) in which a child could remain in the general class program for the majority, if not all, of the school day, receiving special education when and where it was needed. Today, mainstreaming is often understood as the placement of a child into a general education setting without consideration of the supports needed for that child to succeed.

**Standard 6**
Professional Learning and
Ethical Practice

*Photos 2.1a–c* Special Education Schooling throughout History

## 2-1c John F. Kennedy and the Expanding Role of National Government

The 1960s brought significant changes in the education of students with disabilities. President John F. Kennedy expanded the role of the U.S. government, providing financial support to university programs for the preparation of special education teachers. The Bureau of Education for the Handicapped (BEH) in the Office of Education (now the Office of Special Education and Rehabilitative Services in the U.S. Department of Education) was created as a clearinghouse for information at the federal level. New projects were funded nationwide to meet the educational needs of students with disabilities in the public schools.

## 2-2 The Right to Education

The right to education for children with disabilities came about as a part of a larger social issue in the United States: the civil rights of people from differing ethnic and racial backgrounds. The civil rights movement of the 1950s and 1960s awakened the public to the issues of discrimination in employment, housing, access to public facilities (e.g., restaurants and transportation), and public education.

Education was reaffirmed as a right and not a privilege by the U.S. Supreme Court in the landmark case of *Brown v. Board of Education of Topeka, Kansas* (1954). In its decision, the Court ruled that education must be made available to everyone on an equal basis. A unanimous Supreme Court stated, "In these days, it is doubtful that any child may reasonably be expected to succeed in life if he is denied the opportunity of an education. Such an opportunity, where the state has undertaken to provide it, is a right which must be made available to all on equal terms" (*Brown v. Board of Education of Topeka, Kansas,* 1954). Although usually heralded for striking down racial segregation by acknowledging that separate is not equal, this decision also set a precedent for the right to inclusive education for students with disabilities. Yet, it was nearly 20 years later before federal courts confronted the issue of a free and appropriate education for these students.

The 1970s have often been described as a decade of revolution in the education of students with disabilities. Many of the landmark cases were brought before the courts to address the right to education for students with disabilities. Additionally, major pieces of state and federal legislation were enacted to reaffirm the right of students with disabilities to a free public education.

Table 2.1 summarizes court cases and legislation addressing the right to education for students with disabilities.

**Table 2.1** Major Court Cases and Federal Legislation Focusing on the Right to Education for Individuals with Disabilities

| Court Cases and Federal Legislation | Precedents Established |
|---|---|
| *Brown v. Board of Education of Topeka, Kansas* (1954) | Segregation of students by race is held unconstitutional. Education is a right that must be available to all on equal terms. |
| *Pennsylvania Association for Retarded Citizens v. Commonwealth of Pennsylvania* (1971) | Pennsylvania schools must provide a free public education to all school-age children with mental retardation. |
| *Mills v. Board of Education of the District of Columbia* (1972) | Exclusion of individuals with disabilities from free and appropriate public education is a violation of the due process and equal protection clauses of the 14th Amendment to the Constitution. Public schools in the District of Columbia must provide free education to all children with disabilities regardless of their functional level or ability to adapt to the present educational system. |

© Cengage Learning

**Table 2.1**　Major Court Cases and Federal Legislation Focusing on the Right to Education for Individuals with Disabilities (*continued*)

| Court Cases and Federal Legislation | Precedents Established |
|---|---|
| Public Law 93-112, Vocational Rehabilitation Act of 1973, Section 504 (1973) | Individuals with disabilities cannot be excluded from participation in, denied benefits of, or subjected to discrimination under any benefit or activity receiving federal financial assistance. |
| Public Law 94-142, Part B of the Education for All Handicapped Children Act (1975) | A free and appropriate public education must be provided for all children with disabilities in the United States. (Those up through age 5 may be excluded in some states.) |
| *Board of Education of the Hendrick Hudson School District v. Rowley* (1982) | The U.S. Supreme Court held that in order for special education and related services to be appropriate, they must be reasonably calculated to enable the student to receive education benefits. |
| Public Law 99-457, Education for All Handicapped Children Act Amendments (1986) | A new authority extends free and appropriate education to all children with disabilities aged 3 to 5, and provides a new early intervention program for infants and toddlers. |
| Public Law 101-336, Americans with Disabilities Act (1990) | Civil rights protections are provided for people with disabilities in private-sector employment, all public services, and public accommodations, transportation, and telecommunications. |
| Public Law 101-476, Individuals with Disabilities Education Act (1990) | The Education for All Handicapped Children Act Amendments are renamed the Individuals with Disabilities Education Act (IDEA). Two new categories of disability are added: autism and traumatic brain injury. IDEA requires that an individualized transition plan be developed no later than age 16 as a component of the IEP process. Rehabilitation and social work services are included as related services. |
| Public Law 105-17, Amendments to the Individuals with Disabilities Education Act (1997) (commonly referred to as IDEA 97) | IDEA 97 expands the emphasis for students with disabilities from public school access to improving individual outcomes (results). The 1997 amendments modify eligibility requirements, IEP requirements, public and private placements, disciplining of students, and procedural safeguards. |
| Public Law 108-446, Individuals with Disabilities Education Improvement Act of 2004 | IDEA 2004 eliminates IEP short-term objectives for most students; establishes new state programs for multiyear IEPs and paperwork reduction; and establishes qualifications to become a highly qualified special education teacher. |

© Cengage Learning

# 2-3　The Individuals with Disabilities Education Act (IDEA)

In 1975, the U.S. Congress brought together various pieces of state and federal legislation into one comprehensive national law. **The Education for All Handicapped Children Act (Public Law 94-142)** made available a free and appropriate public education to nearly four million U.S. school-age students with disabilities between the ages of 6 and 21. The law included provisions for an individualized education program, procedural safeguards to protect the rights of students and their parents, nondiscriminatory and multidisciplinary assessment, and education with nondisabled peers to the maximum extent appropriate (aka "the least restrictive environment"). Each of these provisions is discussed in depth later in this chapter.

In 1986, Congress amended the Education for All Handicapped Children Act to make available a free and appropriate public education for preschool-age students. **Public Law 99-457** extended all the rights and protections of school-age children (ages 6 through 21) to preschoolers ages 3 through 5. PL 99-457 also established a program for infants and toddlers up through 2 years old. Infants and toddlers with developmental delays became eligible for services that included a *multidisciplinary* assessment and an

**Education for All Handicapped Children Act (Public Law 94-142)**
This federal law, passed in 1975, made a free and appropriate public education available to all eligible students regardless of the extent or type of handicap (disability). Eligible students must receive special education and related services necessary to meet their individual needs. Renamed the Individuals with Disabilities Education Act in 1990.

**Public Law 99-457**
Passed in 1986, this law extended the rights and protections of Public Law 94-142 to children ages 3 through 5. The law also established an optional state program for infants and toddlers with disabilities.

**Individualized family service plan (IFSP)**
A plan of services for infants and toddlers and their families. It includes statements regarding the child's present development level, the family's strengths and needs, the major outcomes of the plan, specific interventions systems to accomplish outcomes, dates of initiation and duration of services, and a plan for transition into public schools.

**Individuals with Disabilities Education Act (IDEA; Public Law 101-476)**
The new name for the Education for All Handicapped Children Act (Public Law 94-142) as per the 1990 amendments to the law.

**Zero-exclusion principle**
Advocates that no person with a disability can be rejected for a service regardless of the nature or extent of the disabling condition.

**Special education**
Specially designed instruction provided at no cost to parents in all settings (such as the classroom, physical education facilities, the home, and hospitals or institutions).

**Related services**
Those services necessary to ensure that students with disabilities benefit from their educational experience. Related services may include special transportation, speech pathology, psychological services, physical and occupational therapy, recreation, rehabilitation counseling, social work, and medical services.

**Orthopedic impairments**
Bodily impairments that interfere with an individual's mobility, coordination, communication, learning, and/or personal adjustment.

**Autism spectrum disorders**
Autism spectrum disorders are characterized by persistent deficits in social communication and social interaction across multiple contexts, which impair an individual's ability to communicate and interact with others.

**Standard 1**
Learner Development and Individual Learning Differences

**Standard 6**
Professional Learning and Ethical Practice

individualized family service plan (IFSP). Although this provision did not mandate that states provide services to all infants and toddlers with developmental delays, it did establish financial incentives for state participation. (The IFSP and other provisions of PL 99-457 are discussed in depth in Chapter 3.)

In 1990, the same year that the Americans with Disabilities Act was signed into law, Congress renamed the Education for All Handicapped Children Act (Public Law 94-142) the **Individuals with Disabilities Education Act (IDEA; Public Law 101-476)**. The purpose of this name change was to reflect "person-first" language and promote the use of the term *disabilities* rather than handicapped.

## 2-3a   What Are Special Education and Related Services?

Referred to as the zero-exclusion principle, IDEA requires that public schools provide special education and related services to meet the individual needs of all eligible students, regardless of the extent or type of their disability. Special education means specially designed instruction provided at no cost to parents in all settings (such as the classroom, physical education facilities, the home, and hospitals or institutions). IDEA also stipulates that students with disabilities receive any related services necessary to ensure that they benefit from their educational experience. Related services include the following:

> *transportation, and such developmental, corrective, and other supportive services (including speech-language pathology and audiology services, interpreting services, psychological services, physical and occupational therapy, recreation, including therapeutic recreation, social work services, school nurse services designed to enable a child with a disability to receive a free appropriate public education as described in the individualized education program of the child, counseling services, including rehabilitation counseling, orientation and mobility services, and medical services, except that such medical services shall be for diagnostic and evaluation purposes only) as may be required to assist a child with a disability to benefit from special education, and includes the early identification and assessment of disabling conditions in children. (Exception: The term does not include a medical device that is surgically implanted, or the replacement of such device.) (IDEA, 2004, PL 108-446, Sec. 602[26])*

## 2-3b   Who Is Eligible for Special Education and Related Services?

For a student to receive the specialized services available under IDEA, two criteria must be met: First, the student must be identified as having one of the disability conditions identified in federal law, or a corresponding condition defined in a state's special education rules and regulations. These conditions include specific learning disabilities, intellectual disability, speech or language impairments, hearing impairments (including deafness), visual impairments (including blindness), serious emotional disturbances, orthopedic impairments, autism spectrum disorders, traumatic brain injury, multiple disabilities, or other health impairments (IDEA, 2004, PL 108-446, Sec. 602[3][A][i]). Each disability will be defined and described in depth in subsequent chapters of this text.

In the 1997 amendments to IDEA, states and school districts/agencies were given the option of eliminating categories of disability (such as serious emotional disturbance or specific learning disabilities) for children ages 3 through 9. For this age group, a state or school district may define a child with a disability as

> *experiencing developmental delays, as defined by the State and as measured by appropriate diagnostic instruments and procedures, in one or more of the following areas: physical development; cognitive development; communication development; social or emotional development; or adaptive development. (IDEA, 2004, PL 108-446, Sec. 602[3][B][i])*

The second criterion for special education eligibility is the student's demonstrated need for specialized instruction and related services in order to receive an appropriate education. This need is determined by a team of professionals and parents or caregivers. Both criteria for eligibility must be met. If this is not the case, it is possible for a student to be identified as disabled but not be eligible to receive special education and related services under IDEA. These students may still be entitled to accommodations or modifications in their educational program. (See heading "Section 504/ADA and Reasonable Accommodations" later in this chapter.)

## 2-3c Major Provisions of IDEA

The five major provisions of IDEA are:

1. All students with disabilities are entitled to a free and appropriate public education designed to meet their unique needs and prepare them for employment and independent living.

2. Schools must use nondiscriminatory and multidisciplinary assessments in determining a student's educational needs.

3. Parents have the right to be involved in decisions regarding their son's or daughter's special education program.

4. Every student must have an individualized education program (IEP).

5. Every student has the right to receive an education with nondisabled peers to the maximum extent appropriate.

**A Free and Appropriate Public Education (FAPE)** IDEA is based on the value that every student can learn. As such, all students with disabilities are entitled to a **free and appropriate public education (FAPE)** designed to meet their unique needs. Schools must provide special education and related services at no cost to parents. The IDEA provisions related to FAPE are based on the 14th Amendment to the U.S. Constitution guaranteeing equal protection of the law. No student with a disability can be excluded from a public education based on a disability (the zero-exclusion principle). A major interpretation of FAPE was handed down by the U.S. Supreme Court in *Board of Education of the Hendrick Hudson School District v. Rowley* (1982). The Supreme Court declared that an appropriate education consists of "specially designed instruction and related services" that are "individually designed" to provide "educational benefit." Often referred to as the "some educational benefit" standard, the ruling mandates that a state need not provide an ideal education, but must provide a beneficial one for students with disabilities.

**Nondiscriminatory and Multidisciplinary Assessment** IDEA incorporated several provisions related to the use of nondiscriminatory testing procedures in labeling and placing students for special education services. Among those provisions are the following:

- The testing of students in their native or primary language, whenever possible
- The use of evaluation procedures selected and administered to prevent cultural or racial discrimination
- Validation of assessment tools for the purpose for which they are being used
- Assessment by a team of school professionals, using several pieces of information to formulate a placement decision

Historically, students with disabilities were too often placed in special education programs on the basis of inadequate or invalid assessment information. This resulted in a disproportionate number of children from differing ethnic backgrounds, as well as those from disadvantaged backgrounds (e.g., living in poverty), being inappropriately placed in special education.

**Parental Safeguards and Involvement** IDEA granted parents the following rights in the education of their children:

- To give consent in writing before the child is initially assessed to determine eligibility for special education and related services
- To give consent in writing as to the educational setting in which the child will receive special education and related services

**Traumatic brain injury**
Direct injuries to the brain, such as tearing of nerve fibers, bruising of the brain tissue against the skull, brain stem trauma, and swelling.

**Free and appropriate public education (FAPE)**
Provision within IDEA that requires every eligible student with a disability be included in public education. The Supreme Court declared that an appropriate education consists of "specially designed instruction and related services" that are "individually designed" to provide "educational benefit."

**Standard 4**
Assessment

**Standard 1**
Learner Development and Individual Learning Differences

**Standard 5**
Instructional Planning and Strategies

**Standard 6**
Professional Learning and Ethical Practice

- To request an independent educational assessment if the parents believe the school's assessment is inappropriate

- To request an educational assessment at public expense if the parent disagrees with the school's assessment and recommendations

- To participate on the committee that considers the assessment of, placement of, and programming for the child

- To inspect and review educational records and challenge information believed to be inaccurate, misleading, or in violation of the privacy or other rights of the child

- To request a copy of information from the child's educational record

- To request a due process hearing concerning the school's proposal or refusal to initiate or change the identification, educational assessment, or placement of the child or the provision of a free and appropriate public education

The intent of these safeguards is twofold: first, to create an opportunity for parents to be more involved in decisions regarding their child's education program; and second, to protect the student and family from decisions that could adversely affect the child's education. Families thus can be secure in the knowledge that every reasonable attempt is being made to educate their child appropriately.

Some professionals and parents have argued that IDEA's promise for a parent and professional partnership has never been fully realized (Berry, 2009; Drew & Hardman, 2007). Several challenges may exist between the school and the home, including poor communication, a lack of trust, and inadequate service coordination (Friend & Bursuck, 2012; Wagner et al., 2012; Williams-Diehm et al., 2014). Byrnes (2011) suggested that schools must go beyond the procedural due process requirements in IDEA and assure that parents are actively involved in their child's education. As such, every attempt should be made to prevent adversarial relationships, such as those that often occur in due process hearings. Such hearings may lead to mistrust and long-term problems. IDEA responds to the need for a mediation process to resolve any conflict between parents and school personnel and to prevent long-term adversarial relationships. The law requires states to establish a mediation system in which parents and schools voluntarily participate. In such a system, an impartial individual would listen to parents and school personnel and attempt to work out a mutually agreeable arrangement in the best interest of the student with a disability. Although mediation is intended to facilitate the parent and professional partnership, it must not be used to deny or delay the parents' right to a due process hearing.

### The Individualized Education Program (IEP)

The individualized education program (IEP) is a written statement that is the framework for delivering a free and appropriate public education to every eligible student with a disability. The IEP provides an opportunity for parents and professionals to join together in developing and delivering specially designed instruction to meet student needs.

The team responsible for developing an IEP consists of the student's parents; at least one special education teacher; at least one general education teacher if the child is, or may be, participating in the general education environment; and a school district representative. The school district representative must be qualified to provide, or supervise the provision of, specially designed instruction to meet the unique needs of children with disabilities. This educator must also be knowledgeable about the general curriculum and the availability of resources within the school. The IEP team must also include a professional(s) who can interpret the eligibility and instructional implications of the various assessment results. When appropriate, other professionals who have knowledge or special expertise regarding the child (including related services personnel) as well as the student with a disability may be included on the team at the discretion of the parents or school district.

The purpose of the IEP process is to ensure continuity in the delivery of special education services and supports for each student on a daily and annual basis. The IEP is also

**Standard 1**
Learner Development and Individual Learning Differences

**Standard 5**
Instructional Planning and Strategies

**Individualized education program (IEP)**
A written framework for delivering appropriate and free education to every eligible disabled student.

**General curriculum**
Instructional content that all students are expected to learn in school. Specific content and performance standards for student achievement are set by individual states or local districts.

## 10 Helpful and Compassionate Comments Heard at an IEP Meeting

*Special Needs Resources (SNR) is a one-stop portal into the world of people with special needs and the people who love them. Sponsored by the Friendship Circle of Michigan, SNR is a nonprofit social media site with online learning and social media blogs to and from parents, siblings, volunteers, supporters, and even those with special needs themselves. (For more information, go to http://blog.friendshipcircle.org/.)*

The following is a blog post written by Karen Wang. Karen has been blogging about disabilities and caregiving for the Friendship Circle since 2011, and is the co-author of several e-books from the Friendship Circle. She is also a contributing author to the website SpecialEducationGuide.com and the 2009 anthology *My Baby Rides the Short Bus: The Unabashedly Human Experience of Raising Kids with Disabilities.*

### A Blog by Karen Wang

During most discussions about IEPs, we talk about the times that things went wrong and disgraceful things were said. But not all IEPs are like that! Recently a commenter on the Friendship Circle blog wrote, "Instead of ridiculous and offensive comments, why don't you write about helpful and compassionate things heard at an IEP meeting?"

After a few rough years and three different school districts, I have developed a good working relationship with my son's IEP team. My son does not receive 100 percent of the services that I request for him, but he is receiving an excellent education and is fully included in general education for most of the school day.

Over the years, many helpful and compassionate comments have stuck with me. Here is a sample of supportive comments that have been spoken to me as a parent, but I should note that I also make it a point to express my appreciation to the team as well. IEP support isn't just a two-way street: It's a busy construction site with administrators, educators, parents, and the student all interacting and choosing to build the future together:

**1. "Your child has so many strengths—what would you like to add to the list?"**

This question comes at the beginning of the IEP and really sets the tone for the whole meeting.

**2. "This IEP is designed to consider the needs of the whole child, and we value your input at every step."**

I heard this comment right after I moved out of a negative situation in another school district, and I was relieved to be treated with respect as a valued team member. This comment *should* be made at every IEP.

**3. "How can we make the transition between school and home as smooth as possible for your child?"**

This question is rare, and if you hear it, you will know that you have an excellent team!

**4. "Can you share one of the strategies that works well for you at home?"**

When presented in a respectful manner, this question demonstrates the team's confidence in the student's family.

**5. "Even though your child was found not to be eligible for this service, we know that you wanted additional information about it, so we prepared this packet for you."**

My son's team often sends home packets to help me research methods to help my son and to review academic material during school vacations.

**6. "Parent training is an important component of the IEP process, so we prepared this list of resources for you."**

Some parents are insulted at the suggestion of parent training and support groups, but I was happy to receive the information and chose what worked for me.

**7. "Can you suggest a better way to word this goal?"**

The IEP is a team effort and goals should not be prewritten. Goals should be written with input from all parties.

**8. "Your child comes to school ready to learn every morning."**

I smiled when my son's fifth grade teacher said this, because of my son's happy, eager-to-please personality. The teacher understood that preparing my son for school took effort on my end, and that preparation was an important part of our partnership.

**9. "The Behavior Support Plan has been working well because it's being reinforced at home."**

This comment helps to keep the tone positive and share responsibility for small successes.

**10. "We're so glad to work with you as part of a team. We appreciate having the home perspective."**

This is a great way to end any meeting, not just an IEP meeting!

SOURCE: Wang, K. (2014). The Art of Diplomacy. Retrieved November 25, 2014, from http://www.friendshipcircle .org/blog/2014/11/25/10-helpful-and-compassionate -comments-heard-at-an-iep-meeting/.

**Photo 2.2**

The development of an IEP is a collaborative process, involving parents, educators, and students. Why is it important for parents to participate in the development of the IEP?

intended to promote more effective communication between school personnel and the child's family. IDEA 2004 requires that each child's IEP must include:

- a statement of the child's present levels of academic achievement and functional performance, including how the child's disability affects the child's involvement and progress in the general education curriculum; for preschool children, as appropriate, also a statement of how the disability affects the child's participation in appropriate activities.

- a statement of measurable annual goals, including academic and functional goals, designed to meet the child's needs that result from the child's disability to enable the child to be involved in and make progress in the general education curriculum, and to meet each of the child's other educational needs that result from the child's disability; for children with disabilities who take *alternate assessments* aligned to alternate achievement standards, include a description of benchmarks or short-term objectives.

- a description of how the child's progress toward meeting the annual goals described will be measured and when periodic reports on the progress the child is making toward meeting the annual goals will be provided.

- a statement of the special education and related services and supplementary aids and services, based on peer-reviewed research to the extent practicable, to be provided to the child, or on behalf of the child, and a statement of the program modifications or supports for school personnel that will be provided for the child to (a) advance appropriately toward attaining the annual goals, (b) be involved in and make progress in the general education curriculum and to participate in extracurricular and other nonacademic activities, and (c) be educated and participate with other children with disabilities and nondisabled children.

- an explanation of the extent, if any, to which the child will *not* participate with nondisabled children in the regular [general education] class.

- a statement of any individual appropriate accommodations that are necessary to measure the academic achievement and functional performance of the child on state- and district-wide assessments, or if the IEP team determines that the child shall take an alternate assessment of student achievement, a statement of why the child cannot participate in the regular assessment; and the particular alternate assessment selected as appropriate for the child (IDEA, 2004, PL 108-446, Sec. 614[d]).

## Education in the Least Restrictive Environment
Building on the understanding that separate is not equal, students with disabilities have the right to learn in the least restrictive environment (LRE). IDEA mandated that:

> To the maximum extent appropriate, children with disabilities, including children in public or private institutions or other care facilities, are educated with children who are not disabled, and that special classes, separate schooling, or other removal of children with disabilities from the regular [general] education environment occurs only when the nature or severity of the disability is such that education in regular classes with the use of supplementary aids and services cannot be achieved satisfactorily. (IDEA, 2004, PL 108-446, Sec. 614[d])

To be certain that schools meet this mandate, federal regulations required districts to develop a continuum of educational placements based on the individual needs of students. The continuum may range from placement in a general classroom with support services to homebound and hospital programs. Placement in a setting along this continuum is based on the premise that this is the most appropriate environment to implement a student's individualized program as developed by the IEP team. An educational services model depicting seven levels on the continuum of placements is presented in Figure 2.1.

Some parents and professionals have criticized the concept of "a continuum of placements" in recent years. The concern is that, despite IDEA's strong preference for students with disabilities to be educated with their peers who are not disabled, the continuum has legitimized and supported the need for more restrictive, segregated settings.

**Least restrictive environment (LRE)**
Students with disabilities are to be educated with their peers without disabilities to the maximum extent appropriate.

**Standard 1**
Learner Development and Individual Learning Differences

**Figure 2.1** *Educational Service Options for Students with Disabilities*

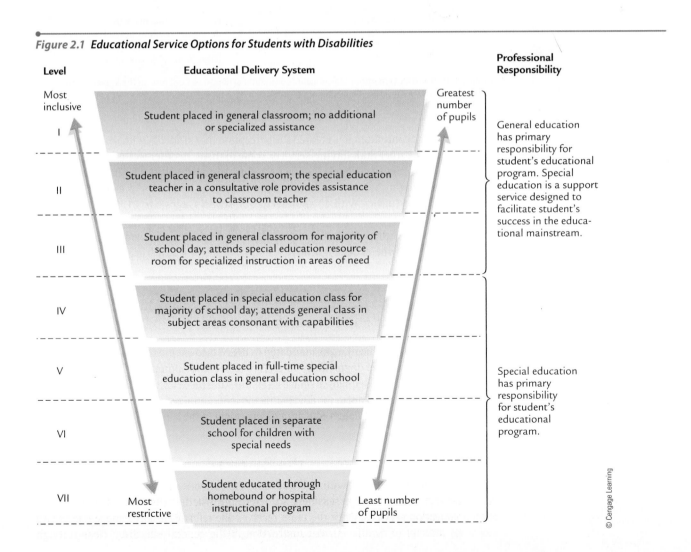

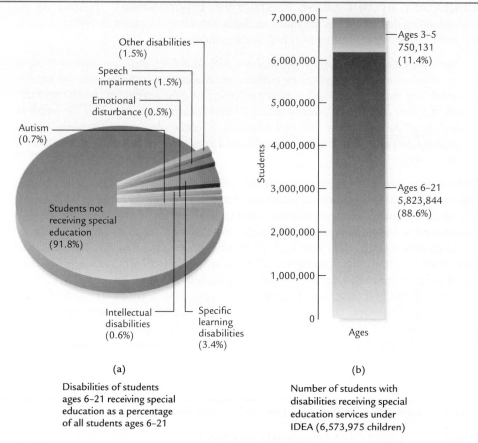

**Figure 2.2** *A Profile of Special Education in the United States*

Other disabilities (1.5%)

Speech impairments (1.5%)

Emotional disturbance (0.5%)

Autism (0.7%)

Students not receiving special education (91.8%)

Intellectual disabilities (0.6%)

Specific learning disabilities (3.4%)

Ages 3–5
750,131
(11.4%)

Ages 6–21
5,823,844
(88.6%)

Students

Ages

(a)

Disabilities of students ages 6–21 receiving special education as a percentage of all students ages 6–21

(b)

Number of students with disabilities receiving special education services under IDEA (6,573,975 children)

SOURCE: Data from U.S. Department of Education, 36th Annual Report to Congress on the Implementation of the *Individuals with Disabilities Education Act,* 2014.

Additionally, the continuum has created the perception that students with disabilities must "go to" services, rather than having services come to them. In other words, students could be placed in classrooms or schools that focus exclusively on students who have disabilities, because it is thought that they will have greater access to resources to meet their needs. Of the 5.8 million students with disabilities in U.S. schools, ages 6 to 21, 5 percent receive their education in separate schools, residential facilities, and homebound programs (U.S. Department of Education, 2013). For a closer look at who is being served in special education programs, and where, see Figure 2.2.

## 2-4 The Special Education Referral, Assessment, Planning, and Placement Process

The purpose of special education, as mandated in IDEA, is to ensure that all eligible students with disabilities have the opportunity to receive a free and appropriate public education. The process involves four sequential phases: (1) initiating the referral, (2) assessing student eligibility and educational need, (3) developing the individualized education program (IEP), and (4) determining the student's educational placement in the least restrictive environment (LRE). (See Table 2.2.)

### 2-4a Phase 1: Initiating the Referral

The referral process begins with a request to the school's *special services committee* or *child-study team* for an assessment to determine whether the student qualifies for special education services. Once the team receives the referral, it may choose one of two steps: (1) attempt to modify current instruction in the general education class through

## Table 2.2 The Special Education Referral, Assessment, Planning, and Placement Process

| Phase 1: Initiating the Referral | Phase 2: Assessing Student Eligibility and Educational Need | Phase 3: Developing the Individualized Education Program (IEP) | Phase 4: Determining the Least Restrictive Environment (LRE) |
|---|---|---|---|
| • School personnel or parents indicate concern about student's learning, behavior, or overall development.<br><br>• If referral is made by school personnel, parents are notified of concerns.<br><br>• Child-study team decides to provide additional support services and adapt student's instructional program prior to initiating formal assessment for eligibility. (This step may be bypassed, and team may choose to immediately seek parental permission to evaluate the student's eligibility for special education.)<br><br>• School seeks and receives parents' permission to evaluate student's eligibility for special education services. (This will occur if the additional support services and adaptive instruction are unsuccessful OR if the team has chosen to move directly to a formal evaluation to determine student eligibility.) | • Multidisciplinary and nondiscriminatory assessment tools and strategies are used to evaluate student's eligibility for special education services.<br><br>• Child-study team reviews assessment information to determine (1) whether student meets eligibility requirements for special education services under one of 12 disability classifications or meets the definition of developmentally delayed (for students between ages 3 and 9), and (2) whether student requires special education services.<br><br>• If team agrees that the student is eligible for and needs special education services, then the process moves to Phase 3: developing the IEP. | • Appropriate professionals to serve on an IEP team are identified. A team coordinator is appointed.<br><br>• Parents (and student when appropriate) participate as equal members of the team and are provided with written copies of all assessment information.<br><br>• Team meets and agrees upon the essential elements of the student's individualized education program plan:<br>  • Measurable annual goals<br>  • Skill areas needing special education and related services<br>  • People responsible for providing services and supports to meet student's identified needs<br>  • Criteria/evaluation procedures to assess progress<br>  • Student's access to the general education curriculum<br>  • Student's participation in statewide or school district assessments<br>  • Beginning and end dates for special education services<br>  • A process for reporting to parents on student's progress toward annual goals<br>  • Positive behavioral intervention plan if needed | • Identify potential educational placements based on student's annual goals and special education services to be provided.<br><br>• Adhering to the principle that students with disabilities are to be educated with their peers without disabilities to the maximum extent appropriate, justify any removal of the child from the general education classroom.<br><br>• With parents involved in the decision-making process, determine student's appropriate educational placement.<br><br>• Document, on the student's IEP, justification for any removal from the general education classroom.<br><br>• Team members agree in writing to the essential elements of the IEP and to the educational placement where special education and related services are to be provided.<br><br>• As members of the IEP team, parents must consent in writing to the agreed-upon educational placement for their child. |

© Cengage Learning

coordinated early intervening services, or (2) conduct a formal evaluation to determine the student's eligibility for special education services.

The first step, coordinated early intervening services, involves instructional adaptations, modifications, or accommodations designed to provide additional support to children who are at risk for educational failure prior to referring them for special education services. Adaptations may vary according to student need but most often involve modifying curriculum, changing a seating arrangement, changing the length and difficulty of homework or classroom assignments, using peer tutors or volunteer parents to assist with instructional programs, or implementing a behavior management program. It is the responsibility of the general education teacher to implement the modified instruction and to assess the student's progress over a predetermined period of time. If the modifications are successful, a referral for special education is not necessary.

Should the team determine that the student's educational progress is not satisfactory, even with the use of early intervening services, a formal referral for special education may

**Coordinated early intervening services**
The provision of services and supports for students who have not yet been identified as needing special education and related services but who need extra academic and behavior support to succeed in the general education classroom.

*Photo 2.3* Early intervening services involve adapting instruction to the need of the student before initiating a referral for special education services. What are some early intervening strategies that teachers can use in their classroom?

**CEC**

**Standard 1**
Learner Development and Individual Learning Differences

be initiated. The formal referral begins with the team's analysis of the information provided by education professionals and parents in order to further understand the child's educational needs. Documentation may include results from achievement tests, classroom performance tests, samples of student work, behavioral observations, or anecdotal notes (such as teacher journal entries). The team must also decide whether additional assessment information is needed to determine the child's eligibility for special education. At this time, a written notice must be provided to parents that includes all of the following:

- A full explanation of the safeguards available to the parents
- A description of the action proposed or refused by the school, why the school proposes or refuses to take the action, and a description of any options the school considered and the reasons why those options were rejected
- A description of each evaluation procedure, test, record, or report the school used as a basis for the proposal or refusal
- A description of any other factors relevant to the school's proposal or refusal to take action

Following a written notice, the school must seek written parental consent to move ahead with further evaluation. Informed consent means that parents

- have been fully informed of all information relevant to the activity for which consent is sought, in their native language or other mode of communication;
- understand and agree in writing to the carrying out of the activity for which his or her consent is sought; the consent describes that activity and lists the record (if any) that will be released and to whom; and
- understand that the granting of consent is voluntary on the part of the parent and may be revoked at any time.

**CEC**

**Standard 1**
Learner Development and Individual Learning Differences

**Standard 4**
Assessment

## 2-4b Phase 2: Assessing Student Eligibility and Educational Need

Once parents give written consent to evaluate, the school child-study team moves ahead to assess the student's eligibility for special education services under IDEA. The assessment should include the student's performance in both school and home environments. When the assessment process is complete, a decision is made regarding the student's eligibility for special education and his or her disability classification (such as specific learning disabilities, autism, and so on).

## 2-4c Phase 3: Developing the Individualized Education Program (IEP)

The IEP is a cornerstone of a free and appropriate public education (Huefner & Herr 2012; National Information Center for Children and Youth with Disabilities, 2011). Once it has been determined that the student is eligible for special education services under IDEA, the next step is to establish an IEP team. At a minimum, this team consists of the student's parents, the student (when appropriate), a special education teacher, a general education teacher (if the student is participating in the general education environment), and a representative of the local education agency (LEA) (aka school district). As stated in IDEA, the LEA representative must be qualified to provide, or supervise the provision of, specially designed instruction to meet the unique needs of children with disabilities; be knowledgeable about the general education curriculum; and be knowledgeable about the availability of resources of the local educational agency (IDEA, 2004, PL 108-446, Sec. 614[b][D][iv]). Additionally, IDEA requires that someone must be available (either a current team member or someone from outside of the team, such as a school psychologist) to interpret each student's assessment results. At the discretion of the parents or school district, other individuals with knowledge or special expertise, including related services specialists, may also be invited to participate on the IEP team.

Each IEP team should have a coordinator (most often the special education teacher or school psychologist) who serves as liaison between the school and the family. The coordinator has the responsibility to (1) inform parents and respond to any concerns they may have regarding the IEP process, (2) assist parents in developing specific goals they would like to see their child achieve, (3) schedule IEP meetings that are mutually convenient for both team members and parents, and (4) lead the IEP meetings. Prior to the initial IEP meeting, parents should be provided with written copies of all assessment information on their child. Individual conferences with members of the IEP team or a full team meeting may be necessary prior to developing the IEP. This will further assist parents in understanding and interpreting assessment information. Analysis of the assessment information should include a summary of the child's strengths as well as areas in which the child may require special education or related services.

Once there is mutual agreement between educators and parents on the interpretation of the assessment results, the team coordinator organizes and leads the IEP meeting(s). Such meetings are meant to achieve the following purposes:

- Document the student's present level of performance.
- Agree upon measurable annual goals (and objectives/benchmarks for children with disabilities who take alternate assessments aligned to alternate achievement standards).
- Identify skill areas needing special education (including physical education) and related services, the people responsible for delivering these services, and the criteria/evaluation procedures to assess progress.
- Document student access to the general curriculum.
- Document student participation in state- and district-wide assessment programs with individual modifications or adaptations made, as necessary, in how the tests are administered. For children who cannot participate in regular assessments, the team must document use of state-developed **alternate assessments**.
- Establish beginning and end dates for special education services.
- Determine a process for reporting to parents on student progress toward annual goals.

See Figure 2.3, a sample individualized education program for Haillee, an elementary-age student with disabilities.

## 2-4d Phase 4: Determining the Student's Educational Placement in the Least Restrictive Environment (LRE)

The decision regarding placement is based on the answers to two questions: First, what is the appropriate placement for the student, given his or her annual goals? Second, which of the placement alternatives under consideration is consistent with the least restrictive environment? As stated in the IDEA, the student is to be educated to the maximum extent appropriate with peers who are not disabled. To ensure that this principle is applied in making placement decisions, the IDEA begins with the premise that the general education classroom is where all children belong. As such, any movement away from the general education class must be justified and documented on the student's IEP. The IEP must be the result of a collaborative process that reflects the views of both the school and the family.

Once the school team has determined that a student is eligible for special education services, educators, related services personnel, parents, and students must consider many important issues in the development of IEP goals and objectives as well as determine the most appropriate educational placement. For a more in-depth look into these considerations, see the nearby Case Study on Embracing Diversity, "Yasmeen."

**Standard 1**
Learner Development and Individual Learning Differences

**Alternate assessments**
Assessments mandated in IDEA 1997 for students who are unable to participate in required state- or district-wide assessments. They ensure that all students, regardless of the severity of their disabilities, are included in the state's accountability system.

**Figure 2.3** A Sample Individualized Education Program (IEP) for Haillee: An Elementary-Age Student with Disabilities

Student Name __Haillee__

Date of Birth __5-3-2005__

Primary Language:

Home __English__   Student __English__

Date of IEP Meeting __April 27, 2016__

Entry Date to Program __April 27, 2016__

Projected Duration of Services __One school year__

Required __Specify amount of time in special education and/or related services per day or week__

General Education Class __4 to 5 hours/day__

Resource Room __1 to 2 hours/day__

Special Ed Consultation in General Ed Classroom __Co-teaching and consultation with general education teacher in the areas of academic and adaptive skills as indicated in annual goals__

Self-Contained __None__

Related Services __Group counseling sessions twice weekly with guidance counselor. Counseling to focus on adaptive skill development as described in annual goals and short-term objectives__

P.E. Program __45 minutes daily in general ed PE class with support from adapted PE teacher as necessary__

Assessment

Intellectual __WISC-V__

Educational __Key Math Woodcock Reading__

Behavioral/Adaptive __Burks__

Speech/Language _____

Other _____

Vision __Within normal limits__

Hearing __Within normal limits__

### STUDENT'S PRIMARY CLASSIFICATION: SERIOUS EMOTIONAL DISTURBANCE SECONDARY CLASSIFICATION: NONE

Classroom Observation __Done__

Dates __1/15–2/25/2016__

Personnel Conducting Observation __School Psychologist, Special Education Teacher, General Education Teacher__

Present Level of Performance Strengths

1. Polite to teachers and peers
2. Helpful and cooperative in the classroom
3. Good grooming skills
4. Good participation in physical education activities

Access to General Education Curriculum

Haillee will participate in all content areas within the general education curriculum. Special education services will be provided in the areas of math, reading, and social skills development. These services will be provided for no less than 1 to 2 hours per day, five days per week in the resource room, and on an as-needed basis in the general education classroom.

Effect of Disability on Access to General Education Curriculum

Emotional disabilities make it difficult for Haillee to achieve at expected grade-level performance in general education curriculum in the areas of reading and math. It is expected that this will further impact her access to the general education curriculum in other content areas (such as history, biology, English) as she enters middle school.

Participation in Statewide or District Assessments

Haillee will participate in all state- and district-wide assessments of achievement. No adaptations or modifications required for participation.

Justification for Removal from General Education Classroom

Haillee's objectives require that she be placed in a general education classroom with support from a special education teacher for the majority of the school day. Based on adaptive behavior assessment and observations, Haillee will receive instruction in a resource room for approximately 1 to 2 hours per day in the areas of social skills development.

Reports to Parents on Progress toward Annual Goals

Parents will be informed of Haillee's progress through weekly reports of progress on short-term goals, monthly phone calls from general ed teachers, special education teachers, and school psychologist, as well as regularly scheduled report cards at the end of each term.

*Figure 2.3 A Sample Individualized Education Program (IEP) for Haillee: An Elementary-Age Student with Disabilities (continued)*

**STUDENT'S PRIMARY CLASSIFICATION: SERIOUS EMOTIONAL DISTURBANCE**
**SECONDARY CLASSIFICATION: NONE**

Team Signatures _____    IEP Review Date _____

LEA Rep. _____

Parent _____

Sp Ed Teacher _____

Gen Ed Teacher _____

School Psych _____

Student (as appropriate) _____

Related Services Personnel (as appropriate) _____

Objective Criteria and Evaluation Procedures _____

Areas Needing Specialized Instruction and Support

**1.** Adaptive Skills

  • *Limited interaction skills with peers and adults* _____

  • *Excessive facial tics and grimaces* _____

  • *Difficulty staying on task in content subjects, especially reading and math* _____

  • *Difficulty expressing feelings, needs, and interests* _____

**2.** Academic Skills

  • *Significantly below grade level in math—3.9* _____

  • *Significantly below grade level in reading—4.3* _____

Annual Review: _____ Date: _____

Comments/Recommendations _____

_____

_____

_____

## Yasmeen

Yasmeen Al-Bayiti, a third-grade student and refugee from Iraq, arrived in the United States two years ago when her family was displaced due to conflict in their country. When she started first grade, she had very limited English. At this point she appears to be conversationally fluent in English, but has shown minimal academic progress this year. In addition to her low reading level, Yasmeen has difficulty paying attention in class and recalling information. Yasmeen's teacher, Mr. Ortiz, is concerned about her academic performance but is unsure if the delay is related to English language development or a learning disability. Yasmeen is no longer receiving support from the English language learning (ELL) program at her elementary school. Mr. Ortiz has tried to relate his concerns to Yasmeen's parents, but, unfortunately, there is a language barrier. Mr. Ortiz doesn't speak Arabic, and Yasmeen's parents aren't fluent in English.

Mr. Ortiz met with the child-study team at his school to learn how to best support Yasmeen. The meeting was very helpful. He learned that it is difficult to determine if a student's academic difficulty stems from limited English proficiency or from a learning disability. The team shared that the level of a student's proficiency in their second language can be compounded if they did not develop proficiency in their first language. Mr. Ortiz also discussed his concern about identifying Yasmeen as having a learning disability when she may actually be struggling for other reasons, such as limited English proficiency. They decided to contact Yasmeen's parents to learn more about her language

development, her literacy skills at home, and her family history. The team also suggested a few research-based strategies to modify instruction for Yasmeen. Specifically, they encouraged Mr. Ortiz to use a particular curriculum and increase the amount of time he worked with Yasmeen on language arts.

Two weeks later, the child-study team reconvened to share their findings. Mr. Ortiz reported that he implemented the strategies suggested and saw little improvement in Yasmeen's reading level. One member of the team was able to contact Yasmeen's parents and communicate through a translator. According to her parents, Yasmeen didn't begin talking until she was 3½ years old, and she is not fluent in Arabic at home. The team decided that a formal referral for special education assessment would give them more information. After Mrs. Al-Bayiti reluctantly gave written consent for the evaluation, Yasmeen was evaluated using formal assessments, along with information gathered from classroom observations and work samples.

When the testing was complete, Mrs. Al-Bayiti met with Yasmeen's teachers, the principal, and the school psychologist. The school psychologist read the evaluation results.

"Yasmeen's score on the Test of Nonverbal Intelligence was 105. This score is in the average range of intelligence. On the Woodcock–Johnson Test of Cognitive Abilities, she scored at least two standard deviations below the mean in the areas of auditory processing, short-term memory, comprehension knowledge, and fluid reasoning—tasks that typically

measure an individual's verbal abilities. She scored in the average range in sections that measure perceptual skills. On the Woodcock–Johnson Tests of Achievement, Yasmeen scored two standard deviations below the mean in reading, written language, and knowledge. She scored in the average range in math."

The school psychologist then turned to Mrs. Al-Bayiti and her translator to say: "This pattern of scores indicates that Yasmeen has a learning disability. There is also a wide gap between Yasmeen's verbal and nonverbal scores, which also can indicate a learning disability. Yasmeen would benefit from being in a special education classroom for most of her day at school." Everyone at the meeting nodded in agreement except Yasmeen's mother.

Mrs. Al-Bayiti, through her translator, said, "I don't think she has a disability; she is just quiet and thoughtful. Also, I don't want Yasmeen to go to a different class. She is happy in Mr. Ortiz's class. She has friends there." The school psychologist insisted that a separate class was best. The group then scheduled an IEP meeting to determine annual goals for Yasmeen.

### Application Questions

**1.** Were the referral, assessment, planning, and placement process followed correctly for Yasmeen?

**2.** Do you think Mrs. Al-Bayiti's concerns were taken seriously by the group?

**3.** In addition to academic achievement, what cultural/linguistic factors should have been considered when determining the most appropriate placement for Yasmeen?

## 2-5 Educating Students with Disabilities in the 21st Century: From Access to Accountability

The education of students with disabilities has gone through many changes during the past four decades. In this section, we take a closer look at 21st-century U.S. schools and the national policies that impact each student's opportunity for a free and appropriate public education. The rallying cry in today's schools is "higher expectations for all students."

National education policy under the Elementary and Secondary Education Act (authorized as the **No Child Left Behind Act [NCLB]** in 2001) uses a **standards-based approach** as the basis for improving the quality of U.S. schools. That is, schools must set high standards for what should be taught and how student performance should be measured based on these standards. Three principles that characterize a standards-based approach to school accountability are:

1. A focus on student achievement as the primary measure of school success
2. An emphasis on challenging academic standards that specify the knowledge and skills students should acquire and the levels at which they should demonstrate these skills in getting ready for college or beginning a career
3. A desire to extend the standards to all students, including those for whom expectations have been traditionally low (U.S. Department of Education, 2010)

Although improved academic achievement for all students was the focus of the 2001 Elementary and Secondary Education Act, the stringent requirements laid out in the reauthorization unintentionally created barriers to some states' efforts to improve outcomes (Duncan, 2011). In 2011, a formal process was implemented to allow individual states to request flexibility from the specific requirements of NCLB. As of 2014, 43 states have been approved for ESEA flexibility, and two additional states have requests under review (U.S. Department of Education, 2014).

Federal involvement has been, and continues to be, a strong influence on the reform of educational programs and services for students with disabilities. Prior to the congressional reauthorizations of IDEA in 1997 and 2004, federal policy concentrated on ensuring *access* to a free and appropriate public education (FAPE). In clarifying the definition of FAPE, the courts required schools to make available individualized, specially designed instruction and related services resulting in "some educational benefit." Eventually, the "some educational benefit standard" was further expanded to ensure meaningful progress that could be measured for each student.

Many advocates for educational reform have strongly emphasized the importance of including students with disabilities in a state and school district accountability system (Huefner & Herr, 2012). However, as much of the policy research suggests, the participation of students with disabilities in the general curriculum and statewide assessments of student performance varied considerably from state to state and district to district (Hardman & Dawson, 2008; Hardman & Mulder, 2004). Hehir (2002) suggests that "one of the reasons students with disabilities [were] not performing better is that they have not had sufficient access to the general curriculum" (p. 6). States and school districts were keeping students with disabilities out of their accountability systems because of fears that they would pull down scores.

In response to these concerns, the IDEA 2004 requires that a student's IEP must describe how the disability affects the child's involvement and progress *in the general curriculum*. The law requires an explanation of any individual modifications in the administration of state- or district-wide assessment of student achievement that are needed for the child to participate.

The promise of the IDEA 2004 is straightforward—all students can and will learn more than they are currently learning, and all students will succeed if schools expect the highest academic standards. If students don't succeed, then public schools must be held accountable for their failure. The definition of success is determined by student proficiency on content specified by the state and as measured by state performance standards. The promise of "all

**No Child Left Behind Act (NCLB) of 2001**
U.S. federal law that reauthorized the Elementary and Secondary Education Act originally passed in 1965. NCLB expanded the federal role in public education, mandated state assessments to measure student academic performance on an annual basis, increased state accountability for student learning by measuring schools' annual yearly progress (AYP), and prescribed teacher qualifications.

**Standards-based approach**
Instruction emphasizes challenging academic standards of knowledge and skills, and the levels at which students should demonstrate mastery of them.

**Standard 6**
Professional Learning and Ethical Practice

*Photo 2.4* Students with disabilities must have access to the general curriculum and be included in statewide testing programs when appropriate. Do you think participation in the general curriculum results in higher academic achievement for students with disabilities?

AP Images/Rusty Kennedy

means all" includes students with disabilities. Therefore, students with disabilities must be assured access to (1) "highly qualified and effective" teachers who are knowledgeable in the subject matter area(s) being taught; (2) a curriculum upon which the standards are based; (3) assessments that measure performance on the standards; and (4) inclusion in the reported results that determine how well a school is meeting the established performance criteria. During the past two decades, the promise that every student will learn and succeed has been translated into public policy. Although public policy provides the impetus for every student to learn and succeed, the critical issue is whether the promise becomes reality.

## 2-6 Section 504/ADA and Reasonable Accommodations

U.S. schools must provide supports and services to two groups of students with disabilities. One group qualifies for special education services under the IDEA because their disability limits their access to an appropriate education. Another group, not viewed as educationally limited by their disability and therefore ineligible for special education, is protected against discrimination under Section 504 of the Vocational Rehabilitation Act and the Americans with Disabilities Act (ADA). Together, Section 504 and ADA address issues of nondiscrimination and equal opportunity for students with disabilities.

**504/ADA plan**

Provides for reasonable accommodations or modifications in assessment and instruction to "create a fair and level playing field" for students who qualify as disabled under Section 504 of the Vocational Rehabilitation Act and the Americans with Disabilities Act.

Students with disabilities eligible under Section 504/ADA are entitled to have a *written plan* that ensures access to an education comparable to that of students who are not disabled. A 504/ADA plan is different from an IEP in its scope and intent. Whereas an IEP is concerned with ensuring access to a free and appropriate education designed to provide educational benefit, a 504/ADA plan provides for reasonable accommodations or modifications as a means to "create a fair and level playing field" for the student. For example, a student who uses as wheelchair, but does not require special education services, may still need a written 504/ADA plan to assure access to adapted transportation or physical therapy (Huefner & Herr, 2012). Table 2.3 provides a comparison of IDEA and 504/ADA provisions.

Numerous accommodations or modifications can be made for students, depending on identified need. Some examples include untimed tests, extra time to complete assignments, change in seating arrangement to accommodate vision or hearing loss or distractibility, opportunity to respond orally on assignments and tests, taped textbooks, access to peer tutoring, access to study carrel for independent work, use of supplementary materials such as visual or auditory aids, and so on.

**Table 2.3** A Comparison of the Purposes and Provisions of IDEA and Section 504/ADA

| | IDEA | Section 504/ADA |
|---|---|---|
| **General Purpose** | Provides financial aid to states in their efforts to ensure adequate and appropriate services for children and youth with disabilities. | Prevents discrimination on the basis of disability in employment, programs, and services provided by state and local governments, goods and services provided by private companies, and commercial facilities. |
| **Definition of Disability** | Identifies 12 categories of disability conditions. However, the law also allows states and school districts the option of eliminating categories for children ages 3 through 9 and defining them as developmentally delayed. | Identifies students as disabled if they meet the definition of a qualified handicapped (disabled) person (i.e., student has or has had a physical or mental impairment that substantially limits a major life activity, or student is regarded as disabled by others). |
| **Responsibility to Provide a Free and Appropriate Public Education (FAPE)** | Both statutes require the provision of a free and appropriate public education, including individually designed instruction, to students covered under specific eligibility criteria. | |
| | Requires a written IEP document. | Does not require a written IEP document but does require a written plan. |

**Table 2.3   A Comparison of the Purposes and Provisions of IDEA and Section 504/ADA** *(continued)*

| | IDEA | Section 504/ADA |
|---|---|---|
| | "Appropriate education" means a program designed to provide "educational benefit." | "Appropriate" means an education comparable to the education provided to students who are not disabled. |
| **Special Education or General Education** | Student is eligible to receive IDEA services only if the child-study team determines that the student is disabled under one of the 12 qualifying conditions and requires special education. Eligible students receive special education and related services. | Eligible student meets the definition of a qualified person with a disability: one who currently has or has had a physical or mental impairment that substantially limits a major life activity or who is regarded as disabled by others. The student is not required to need special education to be protected. |
| **Funding** | Provides additional funding if a student is eligible. | Does not provide additional funds. |
| **Accessibility** | Requires that modifications be made, if necessary, to provide access to a free and appropriate public education. | Includes regulations regarding building and program accessibility. |
| **Notice Safeguards** | Both statutes require notice to the parent or guardian with respect to identification, evaluation, and/or placement. | |
| | Requires written notice. | Does not require written notice, but a district would be wise to provide it. |
| | Delineates required components of written notice. | Particular components are not delineated. |
| | Requires written notices prior to *any* change in placement. | Requires notice only before a "significant change" in placement. |
| **Evaluations** | Requires consent before an initial evaluation is conducted. | Does not require consent but does require notice. |
| | Requires re-evaluations at least every three years. | Requires periodic re-evaluations. |
| | Requires an update and/or review before *any* change in placement. | Requires re-evaluation before a significant change in placement. |
| | Provides for independent educational evaluations. | Independent educational evaluations are not mentioned. |
| **Due Process** | Both statutes require districts to provide impartial hearings for parents or guardians who disagree with the identification, evaluation, or placement of a student with disabilities. | |
| | Specific requirements are detailed in IDEA. | Requires that the parent have an opportunity to participate and be represented by counsel. Other details are left to the discretion of the local school district. These should be covered in school district policy. |
| **Enforcement** | Enforced by the Office of Special Education Programs in the Department of Education. | Enforced by the Civil Rights Division of the Department of Justice. |

## Looking Toward a Bright Future

This chapter has briefly discussed a history of special education services within the overall context of educational reform in the United States. Over the last four decades, national policy in the United States has reaffirmed the rights of students with disabilities who are eligible for special education services to a free and appropriate public education (FAPE). In doing so, the Individuals with Disabilities Education Act established five basic tenets to assure every eligible student's access to FAPE. In looking to the future, it is certainly appropriate to say that "much has been accomplished and much remains to be done." As suggested by the President's Commission on Excellence in Special Education:

> Four decades ago, [the U.S.] Congress began to lend the resources of the federal government to the task of educating children with disabilities. Since then, special education has become one of the most important symbols of American compassion, inclusion, and educational opportunity. Over the years, what has become known as the Individuals with Disabilities Education Act has moved children with disabilities from institutions into classrooms, from the outskirts of society to the center of class instruction. Children who were once ignored are now protected by the law and given unprecedented access to a "free and appropriate public education." But America's special education system presents new and continuing challenges.... Hundreds of thousands of parents have seen the benefit of America's inclusive education system. But many more see room for improvement.... Although it is true that special education has created a base of civil rights and legal protections, children with disabilities remain those most at risk of being left behind. (2002)

Today, a number of important questions are yet to be answered. A formidable challenge lies ahead if educators and families are able to come together and ensure that every student has the opportunity to learn. The mantra of "education for all" remains more a promise than a reality in today's schools. Although there is considerable agreement with the intent of the IDEA 2004 to improve student learning, the means to achieve the goals are controversial. Clearly, research is needed to directly support or refute the assumption within national policy that a standards-based education system will improve results for all students, including those with disabilities. Without such evidence, educators will continue to operate in a vacuum of opinion. Finally, it will be critical that all general and special educators have the knowledge and skills to work collaboratively in partnership with families to provide an education experience that consistently reflects the stated value of an *education for all*.

## Chapter Review

**2-1  Describe the educational services that were available for students with disabilities during most of the 20th century.**

- Educational programs at the beginning of the 20th century were provided primarily in separate, special schools.
- For the first 75 years of the 20th century, the availability of educational programs for students with disabilities was sporadic and selective. Special education was allowed in many states but required in only a few.
- Research on the efficacy of special classes for students with mild disabilities suggested that there was little or no benefit in removing students from general education classrooms.

**2-2  Identify the principal issues in the right-to-education cases that led to the eventual passage of the national mandate to educate students with disabilities.**

- The U.S. Supreme Court reaffirmed education as a right and not a privilege.
- In Pennsylvania, the court ordered the schools to provide a free public education to all children with intellectual disabilities of ages 6 to 21.

- The *Mills* case extended the right to a free public education to all school-age children with disabilities.

**2-3  Describe special education and related services as they apply to each of the major provisions of the Individuals with Disabilities Education Act (IDEA).**

- The labeling and placement of students with disabilities in educational programs required the use of nondiscriminatory and multidisciplinary assessment.
- Parental safeguards and involvement in the educational process included consent for testing and placement, and participation as a team member in the development of an IEP.
- Procedural safeguards (e.g., due process) were included to protect the child and family from decisions that could adversely affect their lives.
- Every student with a disability is entitled to a free and appropriate public education.
- The delivery of an appropriate education occurs through an individualized education program (IEP).
- All children have the right to learn in an environment consistent with their academic, social, and physical needs. The law mandated

that children with disabilities receive their education with peers without disabilities to the maximum extent appropriate.

### 2-4 Discuss the special education referral, assessment, planning, and placement process.

- Initiating the referral: A student is referred for an assessment to determine whether he or she qualifies for special education services. Once the school's child-study team receives the referral, it may try to modify or adapt instruction in the general education classroom or conduct a formal assessment to determine whether the student is eligible for special education.
- Assessing student eligibility and educational need: A multidisciplinary team of professionals conducts a nondiscriminatory assessment of the student's needs, including performance in both school and home environments, to determine eligibility for special education.
- Developing the individualized education program (IEP): An IEP team is established that includes professionals and parents. This team is responsible for documenting the student's present level of performance; agreeing on measurable annual goals; identifying skill areas where special education and related services are needed; documenting access to the general curriculum and participation in state- and district-wide assessments; establishing beginning and ending dates for special education services; and determining a process for reporting to parents on student progress in meeting annual goals.
- Determining the least restrictive environment (LRE): Once the IEP team has agreed upon annual goals, a decision is made regarding the most appropriate educational placement to meet the student's individual needs.

### 2-5 Describe what schools should do to assure accountability for student learning and access to the general curriculum.

- Measuring student achievement is a primary measure of school success.
- Challenging academic standards should be emphasized that specify the knowledge and skills students should acquire and the levels at which they should demonstrate mastery of that knowledge.
- Standards should be extended to all students, including those for whom expectations have been traditionally low.
- IDEA 2004 requires that a student's IEP must describe how the disability affects the child's involvement and progress in the general curriculum. IEP goals must enable the child to access the general curriculum when appropriate.

### 2-6 Distinguish between students with disabilities eligible for services under Section 504/ADA and those eligible under IDEA.

- Students eligible under 504/ADA are entitled to accommodations and/or modifications to their educational program that will ensure that they receive an appropriate education comparable to that of their peers without disabilities.
- Students eligible under IDEA are entitled to special education and related services to ensure they receive a free and appropriate education.

 ## Council for Exceptional Children (CEC) Standards to Accompany Chapter 2

If you are thinking about a career in special education, you should know that many states use national standards developed by the Council for Exceptional Children (CEC) to assess a teacher candidate's knowledge and skills for working with students with disabilities. See a complete listing of the seven CEC Content Standards on the inside cover of this text.

1 Learner Development and Individual Learning Differences
4 Assessment
5 Instructional Planning and Strategies
6 Professional Learning and Ethical Practice

## Mastery Activities and Assignments

To master the content within this chapter, complete the following activities and assignments.

1. Complete a written test of the chapter's content. If your instructor requires a written test of your content knowledge for this chapter, keep a copy for your portfolio.
2. Review the Case Study on Embracing Diversity, "Yasmeen," and respond in writing to the Application

Questions. Keep a copy of the Case Study and your written response for your portfolio.
3. Participate in a community service learning activity. Service learning is a valuable way to enhance your learning experience. Develop a reflective journal of the service learning experience for your portfolio.

# Inclusion and Multidisciplinary Collaboration in the Early Childhood and Elementary School Years

E.D. Torial/Alamy

## Learning Objectives

*After you complete this chapter, you will be able to:*

**3-1** Define inclusive education.

**3-2** Describe the characteristics of evidence-based inclusive schools.

**3-3** Define multidisciplinary collaboration and identify its key characteristics.

**3-4** Describe (a) the importance of early intervention services for young children and families, (b) how Part C

of IDEA supports these services, and (c) evidence-based early childhood instructional approaches.

**3-5** Describe the special and general education teachers' roles in an inclusive classroom setting, and identify the characteristics of evidence-based instruction that enhance learning for all students.

**Matt**

One day, 4-year-old Matt was playing across the street from his house. As he crossed the street to return home, he was hit by a car. Matt sustained a traumatic brain injury as a result of the accident and was in a coma for more than two months. Now he's in school and is doing well.

Matt wears a helmet to protect his head, and he uses a walker in his general education kindergarten class in the morning and special education class in the afternoon. The general education kindergarten children sing songs together and work on handwriting, before they work at centers in the classroom. Matt's favorite center is the block area. He spends most of his time there. Recently, however, he

has become interested in the computer and math centers.

He is working on his fine motor skills and speech skills so he can learn to write and use a pencil again.

Jaren Wicklund/Age Fotostock

The focus of his academic learning is mastering the alphabet, learning how to count, and recognizing numbers. He also receives regular speech therapy. He speaks in sentences, but it is very difficult for others to understand what he is saying.

Matt is well liked by his classmates. His teacher enjoys seeing his progress: "Well, it's our plan for Matt to be fully included in first grade, and through the activities we do in the classroom here [in special education] and in the kindergarten class, we hope the kids will get to know him and interact with him and that this will help pull up his skills to the level where he can go back to the general education classroom for all his schoolwork."

## A Changing Era in the Lives of Students with Disabilities

This chapter explores inclusive education, collaboration, instructional programs, and services in the early childhood and elementary school years. For infants, toddlers, and preschool-age children, the world is defined primarily through family and a small group of same-age peers. As children progress in age and development, their world expands to include their neighborhood, school, and the larger community. For Matt in our opening Snapshot, learning takes place with "typical" peers in an inclusive classroom in the morning, followed by a more specialized classroom experience in the afternoon. Matt's inclusive classroom experiences give him the opportunity to develop friendships and learn the content typically covered in kindergarten. His afternoon class focuses more on his fine motor skill and speech development. These intensive and specialized afternoon sessions are intended to provide Matt with skills he will need when he is fully included next year.

**CEC**

**Standard 1**
Learner Development and Individual Learning Differences

**Standard 2**
Learning Environments

## 3-1  Inclusive Education

The history of education has seen continuous evolution in the terms used to describe the concept of educating students with disabilities in a general education setting, side by side with their peers without disabilities. The most common terms are *mainstreaming, least restrictive environment,* and *inclusive education.* We discussed the least restrictive environment in the context of IDEA in Chapter 2. The expression *mainstreaming* dates back to the very beginnings of the field of special education. It didn't come into widespread use until the 1960s, however, with the growth of public school classes for children with disabilities, most of which separated students with disabilities from their peers without disabilities.

At that time, some professionals called into question the validity of separate programs. Dunn (1968) charged that classes for children with mild retardation could not be justified:

**Mainstreaming**
Placement of students with disabilities into general education classrooms for some or all of the school day.

**Inclusive education**
Students with disabilities receive the services and supports appropriate to their individual needs within the general education setting.

**Full inclusion**
Students with disabilities receive all instruction in a general education classroom; support services come to the student.

**Partial inclusion**
Students with disabilities receive some of their instruction in a general education classroom with *"pull-out"* to another instructional setting when appropriate to their needs.

"Let us stop being pressured into continuing and expanding a special education program that we know now to be undesirable for many of the children we are dedicated to serve" (p. 225). Dunn, among others, called for a placement model whereby students with disabilities could remain in the general education class program for at least some portion of the school day and receive special education when and where needed. This model became widely known as **mainstreaming**. Although mainstreaming implied that students with disabilities would receive individual planning and support from both general and special educators, this did not always happen in actual practice. In fact, the term *mainstreaming* fell from favor when it became associated with placing students with disabilities in general education classes without providing additional support, as a means to save money and limit the number of students who could receive additional specialized services. However, the term *mainstreaming* remains in some use today as one way to describe educating students with disabilities in general education settings.

The terms *mainstreaming* and *inclusive education,* although often used interchangeably, are not synonymous. Whereas mainstreaming implies the physical placement of students with disabilities in the same school or classroom as students without disabilities, inclusive education suggests that placement alone is not enough. **Inclusive education** means students with disabilities receive the services and supports appropriate to their individual needs within the general education setting. This concept may be described as "push-in" services. Whereas the traditional model for special education "pulls the student out of the general education class to receive support," inclusive education focuses on "pushing services and supports into" the general education setting for both students and teachers.

Inclusive education may also be defined by the extent of the student's access to, and participation in, the general education classroom. **Full inclusion** is an approach whereby students with disabilities receive all instruction in a general education classroom; support services come to the student. **Partial inclusion** involves students with disabilities receiving some of their instruction in a general education classroom as well as relocation to another instructional setting when appropriate to their individual needs. The success of full and partial inclusion depends on several factors, including a strong belief in the value of inclusion on the part of professionals and parents. Equally important is the availability of a support network of general and special education teachers along with related services professionals (speech and language specialists, school psychologists, physical or occupational therapists, social workers, nurses, and so on), working together to assure each student's access to programs and services that meet individual needs.

*Photo 3.1* Inclusive classrooms promote diversity, acceptance, and belonging for all children. What are the responsibilities of professionals to ensure a successful inclusive program?

E.D. Torial/Alamy

A number of educators have argued that in spite of certain accomplishments, pull-out programs have caused negative effects or obstacles to the appropriate education of students with disabilities (Holzberg, 2012; Lipsky & Gartner, 2002; Shapiro-Barnard et al., 2002). The negative effects of pullout programs are sometimes discussed through the framework of social justice, which seeks to minimize marginalization or exclusion for all individuals including students who have disabilities (Theoharris, 2007). On the other hand, proponents of pullout programs have argued that the available research doesn't support the premise that full-time placement in a general education classroom is superior to special education classes for all students with disabilities (Dorn & Fuchs, 2004; Leafstedt et al., 2007; Worrell, 2008).

# 3-2 Characteristics of Evidence-Based Inclusive Schools

**Standard 1**
Learner Development and Individual Learning Differences

**Standard 6**
Professional Learning and Ethical Practice

The No Child Left Behind Act of 2001 and IDEA 2004 launched a great deal of discussion and controversy about which characteristics, taken together, constitute an evidence-based school and classroom for all students. There seems to be considerable agreement that schools are most effective in promoting student achievement and valued post-school outcomes when they:

- promote the values of diversity, acceptance, and belonging.
- ensure the availability of formal and natural supports within the general education setting.
- provide services and supports in age-appropriate classrooms in neighborhood schools.
- ensure access to the general curriculum while meeting the individualized needs of each student.
- provide a multidisciplinary school-wide support system to meet the needs of all students.

## 3-2a Diversity, Acceptance, and Belonging

An evidence-based inclusive school promotes acceptance and belonging within a diverse culture (Gollnick & Chinn, 2009; Hollins & Guzman, 2005; Sapon-Shevin, 2008). Wade and Zone (2000) described this value as "building community and affirming diversity. [S]truggling learners can be actively involved, socially accepted, and motivated to achieve the best of their individual and multiple abilities" (p. 22). These authors further suggested that the responsibility for ensuring a successful inclusive program lies with adults who create learning through individualized and appropriate educational instruction consistent with each student's abilities and interests.

## 3-2b Formal and Natural Supports

Within an effective inclusive school, students with disabilities must have access to both formal and natural support networks (Friend & Bursuck, 2012; Hogansen et al., 2008; McDonnell & Hardman, 2009). **Formal supports** are those available through the public school system. They include highly effective teachers, related services personnel, paraprofessionals, and access to instructional materials designed for, or adapted to, individual need. **Natural supports** consist of the student's family, classmates, and community members. These individuals constitute a support network of mutual caring that promotes greater inclusion within the classroom, school, and community, access to effective instruction, and the development of social relationships (friendships). Through these networks, students with disabilities achieve success within an inclusive environment. High-quality formal supports provide a foundation for each student as they learn valued instructional content. The natural support network builds on this foundation by connecting students with opportunities to bond with others who will listen, understand, and support them as they meet the challenges of the world around them.

## 3-2c Age-Appropriate Classrooms in a Neighborhood School

Evidence-based inclusive schools provide services and support to students with disabilities in age-appropriate classrooms in the same school they would attend if they were not disabled (National Association of School Psychologists, 2012). Inclusive programs are those in which students, regardless of the severity of their disability, receive appropriate specialized instruction and related services within an age-appropriate general education classroom in the school that they would attend if they did not have a disability.

**Access to the General Curriculum** Access to the general curriculum for students with disabilities is a critical provision of IDEA 2004. As suggested within the law,

**Formal supports**
Educational supports provided by, and funded through, the public school system. They include highly effective teachers, paraprofessionals, and access to instructional materials designed for, or adapted to, individual needs.

**Natural supports**
The student's family, classmates, and community; these individuals comprise a support network of mutual caring that promotes greater inclusion within the classroom, school, and community, access to effective instruction, and the development of social relationships (friendships).

"[more than] 30 years of research and experience has demonstrated that the education of children with disabilities can be made more effective by having high expectations for such children and ensuring their access in the general curriculum to the maximum extent possible" (IDEA, 2004, PL 108-446, Sec. 682[C][5]). A student's IEP must describe how the disability affects the child's involvement and progress in the general curriculum. An evidence-based inclusive school promotes meaningful participation for each student within the subject matter content areas identified in the general curriculum (e.g., reading, mathematics, science, etc.). As the movement toward a national set of standards, referred to as a Common Core, gains momentum, it is important to consider evidence-based strategies to support students who have disabilities. Meaningful participation in the general curriculum will necessitate the development and use of effective teaching strategies, such as universally designed curriculum, instructional adaptations, a **multitiered system of support** (aka **response to intervention [RtI]**), assistive technology, and cooperative learning. Each of these strategies is discussed in detail later in this chapter.

**School-Wide Support** Evidence-based inclusive schools are characterized by a school-wide support system that uses both general and special education resources in combination to benefit all students in the school (Humphrey, 2008; Mastropieri & Scruggs, 2013; Murawski, 2008; Peterson & Hittie, 2010; Scanlon & Barker, 2012). The leadership of the school principal is vital. The principal should openly support the inclusion of all students in the activities of the school, advocate for the necessary resources to meet student needs, and strongly encourage cooperative learning and peer support programs (Friend & Cook, 2010; Grenier, Rogers, & Iarusso, 2008; Tan & Cheung, 2008). In addition to instructional support, many schools have moved toward school-wide behavioral support or character building programs. These programs focus on the whole school context and aim to create a supportive and positive social climate for all children (Bal et al., 2014). Inclusive classrooms are characterized by a philosophy that celebrates diversity, rewards collaboration among professionals, and teaches students how to collaborate with and support one another. In the next section, we discuss the essential elements of school-wide collaboration, why it is an important concept within an inclusive school, and who must be involved for it to be effective.

## 3-3 Multidisciplinary Collaboration

**Multidisciplinary collaboration** is defined as professionals from across different disciplines, parents, and students *working together* to achieve the mutual goal of delivering an evidence-based educational program designed to meet individual need and access to the general curriculum. It should always be viewed as a cooperative, not a competitive, endeavor. As suggested by Friend and Bursuck (2012), collaboration is not *what* those involved do, but *how* they do it. This process can be described as a *collaborative ethic,* in which everyone works together as a multidisciplinary team to meet the needs of all students, including those with disabilities. The team focuses on mastering the process of collaboration as well as cultivating the professional values and skills necessary to work effectively as part of a team.

In an inclusive school, effective multidisciplinary collaboration has several key characteristics:

**Standard 7**
Collaboration

- Parents are viewed as active partners in the education of their children.
- Team members from various disciplines (such as education, health care, and psychological and social services) share responsibility; individual roles are clearly understood and valued.
- Team members promote peer support and cooperative learning.

### 3-3a Parents as Valued Partners

Inclusive schools are most effective when they value families and establish positive and frequent relationships with parents. A strong relationship between home and school is characterized by a clear understanding of the philosophical and practical approaches to meeting the needs of students with a disability within the general education setting. Collaboration among parents and professionals is most effective when everyone

- acknowledges and respects each other's differences in values and culture.
- listens openly and attentively to the others' concerns.
- values others' opinions and ideas.
- discusses issues openly and in an atmosphere of trust.
- shares in the responsibility and consequences for making decisions (Berry, 2009; Leader-Janssen et al., 2012; McDonnell & Hardman, 2009).

When parents feel valued as equal members of the team, they are more likely to develop a positive attitude toward school professionals. Consequently, educators are able to work more closely with parents to understand each student's needs and functioning level. Home–school collaboration will work only if communication is a two-way process where everyone feels respected.

## 3-3b   Sharing the Responsibility

An inclusive school is effective when professionals from across the disciplines work together to achieve a common goal: a free and appropriate education for students with disabilities. Unfortunately, professional isolation was the norm for teachers of students with disabilities for more than a century. Special education meant separate education. However, in the late 1980s, some parents and professionals questioned whether it was in the best interest of students with disabilities to be taught solely by special education teachers in separate classrooms or schools. A merger of general and special education, known as the **regular education initiative (REI)**, was proposed to ensure that these students would have access to qualified professionals from both disciplines. The goal of REI was for general and special education teachers to share responsibility in ensuring an appropriate educational experience for students with disabilities. Ultimately, the separate special education system would be eliminated. Although some viewed REI as an attempt on the part of the federal government to reduce the number of students with mild disabilities receiving special education, and thus ultimately to reduce the cost of special education, it did result in a reexamination of the roles of general and special educators within the inclusive school. "Shared responsibility" became the means by which students with disabilities could receive both the formal and the natural supports necessary for them to participate in the general curriculum and in the inclusive classroom.

## 3-3c   Multidisciplinary School-Wide Assistance Teams

To meet the needs of a diverse group of students, including those with disabilities, schools have developed support networks that facilitate collaboration among professionals. **Multidisciplinary school-wide assistance teams**, sometimes referred to as teacher assistance teams (TATs), involve groups of professionals from several different disciplines, students, and/or parents working together to solve problems, develop instructional strategies, and support classroom teachers. The team uses a variety of strategies to assist teachers in making appropriate referrals for students who may need specialized services, to adapt instruction or develop accommodations consistent with individual student needs, to involve parents in planning and instruction, and to coordinate services across the various team members.

## 3-3d   Working Together as a Professional and Parent Team

Students with disabilities have very diverse needs, ranging from academic and behavioral support to functional life skills, communication, and motor development. These needs require that students have access to many different education and related services professionals who work together in delivering instruction and providing appropriate resources.

**Regular education initiative (REI)**
A merger of general and special education proposed to ensure all educators would share responsibility in ensuring appropriate education for students with disabilities.

**Multidisciplinary school-wide assistance teams**
Groups of professionals, students, and/or parents working together to solve problems, develop instructional strategies, and support classroom teachers.

## What's My Role on the Multidisciplinary School-Wide Assistance Team?

A team is a group of professionals, parents, and students who join together to plan and implement an appropriate educational program for a student at risk or with a disability. Team members may be trained in different areas of study, including education, health services, speech and language, school administration, and so on. In the team approach, these individuals, regardless of where or how they were trained, sit down together and coordinate their efforts to help students. For this approach to work, all team members must clearly understand their roles and responsibilities as members of the team. Let's visit with some team members and explore their roles in working with students.

### Special Education Teacher

It's my responsibility to coordinate the student's individualized education program. I work with each member of the team to assist in selecting, administering, and interpreting appropriate assessment information. I maintain ongoing communication with each team member to ensure that we are all working together to help the student. It's my responsibility to compile, organize, and maintain good, accurate records on each student. I propose instructional alternatives for the student and work with others in the implementation of the recommended instruction. To carry this out, I locate or develop the necessary materials to meet each student's specific needs. I work directly with the student's parents to ensure that they are familiar with what is being taught at school and can reinforce school learning experiences at home.

### Parents

We work with each team member to ensure that our child is involved in an appropriate educational program. We give the team information about our child's life outside school and suggest experiences that might be relevant to the home and the community. We also work with our child at home to reinforce what is learned in school. As members of the team, we give our written consent for any evaluations of our child and any changes in our child's educational placement.

### School Psychologist

I select, administer, and interpret appropriate psychological, educational, and behavioral assessment instruments. I consult directly with team members regarding the student's overall educational development. It is also my responsibility to directly observe the student's performance in the classroom and assist in the design of appropriate behavioral management programs in the school and at home.

### School Administrator

As the school district's representative, I work with the team to ensure that the resources of my school and district are used appropriately in providing services to the student. I am ultimately responsible for ensuring that the team's decisions are implemented properly.

### General Education Classroom Teacher

I work with the team to develop and implement appropriate educational experiences for the student during the time that he or she spends in my classroom. I ensure that the student's experiences outside my classroom are consistent with the instruction he or she receives from me. In carrying out my responsibilities, I keep an accurate and continuous record of the student's progress. I am also responsible for referring any other students in my classroom who are at risk and may need specialized services to the school district for an evaluation of their needs.

### Adapted Physical Education Teacher

I am an adapted physical education specialist who works with the team to determine whether the student needs adapted physical education services as a component of his or her individualized education program.

### Related Services Specialist

I may be a speech and language specialist, social worker, school counselor, school nurse, occupational or physical therapist, juvenile court authority, physician, behavior specialist, or school technology coordinator. I provide any additional services necessary to ensure that the student receives an appropriate educational experience.

### *Question for Reflection*

What suggestions do you have for the members of the school's multidisciplinary team that would help them to collaborate more effectively in meeting the needs of children with disabilities?

Multidisciplinary collaborative teaming involves bringing key specialists together to develop an instructional program that views students from a holistic perspective. All members of the team work together to integrate instructional strategies and therapy concurrently within the classroom—and to evaluate the effectiveness of their individual roles in meeting the needs of each student.

Collaborative teaming is advantageous in an inclusive setting, but it may be difficult to implement because of differing philosophical orientations on the part of team members. If professionals believe that only they are qualified to provide instruction or support in a particular area of need (e.g., communication or motor development), then efforts to share successful strategies are inhibited (Klein & Hollingshead, 2015; McDonnell & Hardman, 2009; Vaughn, Bos, & Schumm, 2011). To overcome this barrier, several strategies could be used to facilitate successful multidisciplinary collaborative teaming:

- Always focus on the needs of the student first, rather than on the individual philosophy or expertise of each professional.

- View team members as collaborators rather than experts. Understand what each professional has to offer in planning, implementing, integrating, and evaluating instructional strategies in an inclusive setting.

- Openly communicate the value of each professional's role in meeting student needs. Maintain an open and positive attitude toward other professionals' philosophy and practices.

- Meet regularly and consult one another on how students are progressing. Identify what is working, what barriers to progress exist, and what steps will be taken next in furthering the students' learning and development (Spencer, 2005).

## 3-3e Peer Support and Cooperative Learning

Peers may serve as powerful natural supports for students with disabilities in both academic and social areas (Jimenez et al., 2012; Tannock, 2009). They often have more influence on their classmates' behavior than the teacher does. Peer support programs may range from simply creating opportunities for students with disabilities to interact socially with peers without disabilities to highly structured programs of peer-mediated instruction. **Peer-mediated instruction** involves a structured interaction between two or more students under the direct supervision of a classroom teacher. The instruction may use peer and cross-age tutoring and/or cooperative learning. **Peer and cross-age tutoring** emphasize the learning helper–helpee model, whereas **cooperative learning** emphasizes the simultaneous learning of students as they seek to achieve group goals. Although they are often an underrated and underused resource in general education, peers are very reliable and effective in implementing both academic and social programs with students who have disabilities (Jimenez et al., 2012; Mastropieri, Scruggs, & Berkeley, 2013). In addition, cooperative learning is beneficial to all students, from the highest achievers to those at risk of school failure. Cooperative learning builds self-esteem, strengthens peer relationships, and increases the acceptance of students with disabilities in inclusive classrooms. The effectiveness of peers, however, is dependent on carefully managing the program so that students both with and without disabilities benefit. It is important for teachers to carefully select, train, and monitor the performance of students working as peer tutors. Cooperative learning appears to be most effective when it includes goals for the group as a whole, as well as for individual members (Eggen & Kauchak, 2010; Guralnick et al., 2008; Vaughn, Bos, & Schumm, 2011).

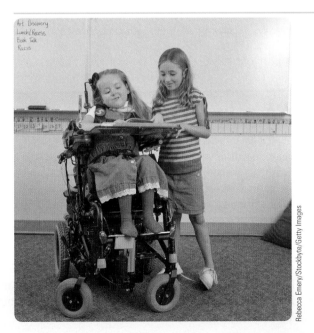

Rebecca Emery/Stockbyte/Getty Images

**Peer-mediated instruction**
Structured interaction between two or more students under direct supervision of a classroom teacher. Peers assist in teaching skills to other students.

**Peer tutoring**
An instructional method whereby one student provides instruction and/or support to another student or group of students.

**Cross-age tutoring**
An instructional method that pairs older students with younger students to facilitate learning.

**Cooperative learning**
Emphasizes the simultaneous learning of students as they work together to achieve group goals.

CEC

**Standard 5**
Instructional Planning and Strategies

*Photo 3.2* In addition to being effective teaching strategies, peer support and cooperative learning build self-esteem and increase the acceptance of students with disabilities in inclusive classrooms. Why do you think these strategies are often underutilized in general education classrooms?

## Is There a Role for Social Media in Special Education?

As technology continues to become an integral part of everyday life, the consideration of how to use technology in education and what technologies and formats to use in classrooms continues to be debated. Questions continue to be raised on the appropriate role of social media not only in higher education, but also in elementary, middle, and high schools as well. The debate also includes the role that using technology and social media should play in special education.

### Benefits of Social Media in Special Education

One area in which special education teachers use social media is for students with autism. Some experts believe that social media is an effective method for improving the socialization skills of students from all ranges of the autism spectrum. Sites such as Habbo.com and Club Penguin provide heavily monitored and filtered social interaction, and depending on development and age level, these could be appropriate to utilize in special education classrooms.

For high school students, social media sites such as Edmodo are helpful in learning to use appropriate language and communication skills while online. Because many everyday

activities take place online, it can be argued that this is an essential skill for special education students to have exposure to while supervised and in school. Examples include the ability to job search and post portfolios or resumes, and building skills with computers. One of the main goals of every educator in special education is to provide students with the same tools they will need to be successful in life, and appropriately using social media is one of these skills.

Social media also fosters the ability to collaborate, and instant feedback on ideas, pictures, and projects that are posted via social media can help all students, including those with special needs or developmental disabilities, to gain more confidence.

### Outside of the Classroom

Social media sites such as Twiducate, a social media site specifically designed for use in education, also allow educators to stay in touch with parents and students outside of school hours, providing better access for parents to track progress and stay in touch with what their children are doing in school.

One of the biggest challenges in any classroom is meeting the diverse needs of students, and this can be especially true in special education classes.

Facebook and other educational social media sites have additional resources, and applications can be added to supplement learning in school as well. Teachers can assess additional student needs and add the applications that will be most beneficial for each student to practice additional math, reading, or socialization skills.

### Teaching Resources

Social media can also provide benefits in the field of special education through teacher resources. Networking and sharing ideas are beneficial for all teachers at all levels of education: PCI Education and the We Are Teachers network developed a forum specifically for special educators to interact and use forums and blogs to learn new ideas for special education classrooms. Webinars and other tools are also available to special education teachers through the site.

Additional information on using technology and social media in special education classrooms can be found at www.emergingedtech.com/category /special-needs-students/.

SOURCE: Adapted from Master's in special education program guide. (2014). Retrieved January 5, 2015, from www.masters-in-special-education.com/faq/is-there-a -role-for-social-media-in-special-education/.

## 3-4　The Early Childhood Years

In the past two decades, we have seen a growing recognition of the educational, social, and health needs of young children with disabilities. This is certainly true for Yvonne from the nearby Snapshot. Yvonne was born with cerebral palsy, requiring immediate services and supports from many different professionals. Yvonne's early learning experiences provided a foundation for her future learning, growth, and development. Early intervention was also crucial to the family's understanding of Yvonne's needs and of the importance of a strong parent–professional partnership.

The first years of life are critical to the overall development of children, including those at risk for disabilities. Moreover, classic studies in the behavioral sciences from the 1960s and 1970s indicated that early stimulation is critical to the later development of language, intelligence, personality, and a sense of self-worth (Bloom, 1964; Hunt, 1961; Piaget, 1970; White, 1975).

Yvonne: The Early Childhood Years

Anita was elated. She had just learned during an ultrasound that she was going to have twin girls. As the delivery date neared, she thought about how much fun it would be to take them on long summer walks in the new double stroller. Two weeks after her estimated delivery date, she was in the hospital, giving birth to her twins. The first little girl arrived without a problem. Unfortunately, this was not the case for the second.

There was something different about her; it became obvious almost immediately after the birth. Yvonne just didn't seem to have the same body tone as her sister. Within a couple of days, Yvonne was diagnosed as having cerebral palsy. Her head and the left side of her body seemed to be affected most seriously. The pediatrician calmly told the family that Yvonne would undoubtedly have learning and physical problems throughout her life. She referred the parents to a division of the state health agency responsible for assisting families with children who have disabilities. Further testing was done, and Yvonne qualified for an early intervention program for infants with developmental disabilities. When Yvonne reached the age of 3, her parents enrolled her in a preschool program where she would have the opportunity to learn communication and social skills, while interacting with children of her own age with and without disabilities. Because neither of the parents had any direct experience with a child with disabilities, they were uncertain how to help Yvonne. Would this program really help her that much, or should they work with her only at home? It was hard for them to see this little girl go to school so very early in her life.

Advocates of **early intervention** for children at risk for disabilities believe that intervention should begin as early as possible in an environment free of traditional disability labels (such as "intellectual disabilities" and "emotionally disturbed"). Carefully selected services and supports can reduce the long-term impact of the disability and counteract any negative effects of waiting to intervene. The postponement of services may, in fact, undermine a child's overall development, as well as his or her acquisition of specific skills (Batshaw, Pellegrino, & Rozien, 2008; Berk, 2011; Hunt, McDonnell, & Crockett, 2014).

**Early intervention**
Comprehensive services for infants and toddlers who are disabled or at risk of acquiring a disability.

## 3-4a Importance of Early Intervention for Young Children and Families

For most of the 20th century, comprehensive educational and social services for young children with disabilities were nonexistent or were provided sporadically at best. For families of children with more severe disabilities, often the only option outside of the family home was institutionalization. As recently as the 1950s, many parents were advised to institutionalize a child immediately after birth if he or she had a recognizable physical condition associated with a disability (such as Down syndrome). By doing so, the family would not become attached to the child in the hospital or after returning home.

**Standard 6**
Professional Learning and Ethical Practice

The efforts of parents and professionals to gain national support to develop and implement community services for young children at risk began in 1968 with the passage of Public Law (PL) 90-538, the Handicapped Children's Early Education Program (HCEEP). The documented success of HCEEP eventually culminated in the passage of PL 99-457, in the form of amendments to the Education of the Handicapped Act, passed in 1986. The most important piece of legislation ever enacted on behalf of infants and preschool-age children with disabilities, PL 99-457 opened up a new era of services for young children with disabilities. It required that all states ensure a free and appropriate public education to every eligible child with a disability between 3 and 5 years of age. For infants and toddlers (birth to 2 years of age), a new program, Part H (changed to Part C in the 1997 amendments to IDEA), was established to help states develop and implement programs for early intervention services. Part C has the following purposes:

1. To enhance the development of infants and toddlers with disabilities, to minimize their potential for developmental delay, and to recognize the significant brain development that occurs during a child's first three years of life;

2. To reduce the educational costs to our society, including our nation's schools, by minimizing the need for special education and related services after infants and toddlers with disabilities reach school age;

3. To maximize the potential for individuals with disabilities to live independently in society;

4. To enhance the capacity of families to meet the special needs of their infants and toddlers with disabilities; and

5. To enhance the capacity of state and local agencies and service providers to identify, evaluate, and meet the needs of all children, particularly minority, low-income, inner-city, and rural children, and infants and toddlers in foster care (IDEA, 2004, PL 108-446, Part C Sec. 631[a]).

Although states are not *required* to participate, every state provides at least some services under Part C of IDEA.

**Early Intervention Programs and Services** Early intervention focuses on the identification and provision of education, health care, and social services as a means to enhance learning and development, reduce the effects of a disability, and prevent the occurrence of future difficulties for young children. IDEA 2004 defines eligible infants and toddlers as those under age 3 who need early intervention services for one of two reasons: (1) There is a developmental delay in one or more of the areas of cognitive development, physical development, communication development, social or emotional development, and adaptive development; or (2) there is a diagnosis of a physical or mental condition that has a high probability of resulting in a developmental delay.

Timing is critical in the delivery of early intervention services. The maxim, "the earlier, the better," says it all. Moreover, early intervention may be less costly and more effective than providing services later in an individual's life (Crane & Winser, 2008; Leppert & Rosier, 2008; Lipkin & Schertz, 2008). Effective early intervention services are directed not only to young children with a disability but also to family members (McDonnell, Hardman, & McDonnell, 2003; Neal, 2008; Shonkoff, 2010). All early intervention services must be designed and delivered within the framework of informing, supporting, and empowering family members. Comprehensive early intervention is broad in scope, as illustrated in the listing of IDEA, Part C services found in Figure 3.1.

The services under Part C of IDEA that are needed for a child and the family are identified through the development of an **individualized family service plan (IFSP)**. The IFSP is structured much like the individualized education program (IEP), but it broadens the focus to include all members of the family. Figure 3.2 lists the required components of the IFSP.

## 3-4b Evidence-Based Instructional Approaches for Preschool-Age Children

This section examines evidence-based models for delivering services and supports to infants and toddlers, including developmentally supportive care in hospitals, and center-based and family-centered programs. For these models to be effective, services and supports

**Individualized family service plan (IFSP)**
Service plan written to ensure that infants and toddlers receive appropriate services under Part C of IDEA; broadens the IEP's focus to include all family members.

*Figure 3.1 Services Provided to Infants and Toddlers under Part C of IDEA*

- Special instruction
- Speech and language instruction
- Occupational and physical therapy
- Psychological testing and counseling
- Service coordination
- Diagnostic and evaluative medical services
- Social work services
- Sign language and cued speech services

- Assistive technology devices and services
- Family training, counseling, and home visits
- Early identification, screening, and assessment
- Health services necessary to enable the infant or toddler to benefit from the other early intervention services
- Transportation and related costs as necessary to ensure that the infant or toddler and the family receive appropriate services

Figure 3.2 *Required Components of the IFSP*

1. Infant's or toddler's present levels of physical development, cognitive development, communication development, social or emotional development, and adaptive development, based on objective criteria;

2. Family's resources, priorities, and concerns related to enhancing the development of the family's infant or toddler with a disability;

3. Measurable results or outcomes expected to be achieved for the infant or toddler and the family, including preliteracy and language skills, as developmentally appropriate for the child, and the criteria, procedures, and timelines used to determine the degree to which progress toward achieving the results or outcomes is being made and whether modifications or revisions of the results or outcomes or services are necessary;

4. Specific early intervention services based on peer-reviewed research, to the extent practicable, necessary to meet the unique needs of the infant or toddler and the family, including the frequency, intensity, and method of delivering services;

5. Natural environments in which early intervention services will appropriately be provided, including a justification of the extent, if any, to which the services will not be provided in a natural environment;

6. Projected dates for initiation of services and the anticipated length, duration, and frequency of the services;

7. Identification of the service coordinator from the profession most immediately relevant to the infant's or toddler's or family's needs who will be responsible for the implementation of the plan and coordination with other agencies and people, including transition services; and

8. Steps to be taken to support the transition of the toddler with a disability to preschool or other appropriate services.

**SOURCE: IDEA, 2004, PL 108-446, Sec. 636(d).**

should focus on individualization, intense interventions, and a comprehensive approach to meeting the needs of each child and that child's family.

**Service Delivery** Advancements in health care have increased the number of at-risk infants who survive birth. **Intensive care specialists,** working with sophisticated medical technologies in newborn intensive care units and providing developmentally supportive care, are able to save the lives of infants who years ago would have died in the first days or weeks of life. **Developmentally supportive care** views the infant as "an active collaborator" in determining what services are necessary to enhance survival. With this approach, infant behavior is carefully observed to determine what strategies (such as responding to light, noise, or touch) the infant is using to try to survive. Specially trained developmental specialists then focus on understanding the infant's "developmental agenda" to provide appropriate supports and services to enhance the infant's further growth and development.

In addition to the critical services provided in hospital newborn intensive care units, early intervention may be delivered through center-based and family-based programs or a combination of the two (Case-Smith & Holland, 2009; Frankel & Gold, 2007). The center-based model requires families to take their child from their home to a setting where comprehensive services are provided. These sites may be hospitals, churches, schools, or other community facilities. The centers use various instructional approaches, including both developmental and therapeutic models, to meet the needs of infants and toddlers. Center-based programs tend to look like medical or health care facilities in which the primary orientation is individual or small-group therapy. In contrast to the center-based model, a family-centered program provides services to the child and family in their natural living environment. Using the natural resources of the home, professionals address the needs of the child in terms of individual family values and lifestyles.

Finally, early intervention may be provided through a combination of services at both a center and the home. Infants or toddlers may spend some time in a center-based program,

**Intensive care specialists**
Health care professionals trained specifically to treat newborns who are seriously ill, disabled, or at risk of serious medical problems; also referred to as *neonatal specialists*.

**Developmentally supportive care**
Approach to care that views the infant as "an active collaborator" in determining what services are necessary to enhance survival.

**Standard 2**
Learning Environments

receiving instruction and therapy in individual or group settings, and also receive in-home family-centered services to promote learning and generalization in their natural environment.

### Individualized, Intensive, and Comprehensive Services

Early intervention programs for infants and toddlers should be based on individual need, and they should be intensive over time and comprehensive. Intensity reflects the frequency and amount of time an infant or child is engaged in intervention activities. An intensive approach requires that a child participate in intervention activities that involve two to three hours of contact each day, at least four or five times a week. Until the 1980s, this child-centered model of service delivery placed parents in the role of trainers who provided direct instruction to the child and helped him or her transfer the learning activities from the therapeutic setting to the home environment. Many professionals and family members eventually questioned the model of parents as trainers. Families were dropping out of programs; many parents either did not use the intervention techniques effectively with their children or they simply preferred to be parents, not trainers (McDonnell, Hardman, & McGuire, 2007). With the passage of PL 99-457 in 1986 (now IDEA), early intervention evolved into a more family-centered approach in which individual family needs and strengths became the basis for determining program goals, supports needed, and services to be provided.

As our understanding of brain development and neuroscience increases, it has become clear that early intervention services should (1) begin as early as possible, (2) enhance the mental health, executive function skills, and self-regulation capacities of caregivers, and (3) include skill-building opportunities for a variety of service providers (Shonkoff, 2011). Providing the breadth of services necessary to meet the individual needs of an infant or toddler within the family constellation requires a *multidisciplinary intervention team*. It should include professionals with varied experiential backgrounds—such as speech and language therapy, physical therapy, health care, and education—and the parents or guardian. The multidisciplinary team should review the IFSP at least annually and issue progress updates to the parents every six months. Coordination of early intervention services across disciplines and with the family is crucial if the goals of the IFSP are to be realized.

The traditional academic-year programming (lasting approximately nine months) that is common to many public school programs is not in the best interests of infants and toddlers who are at risk or have disabilities. Year-round continuity is essential. Services and supports must be provided throughout the early years without lengthy interruptions.

### Preschool Services: Referral, Assessment, and IEP Development

Four-year-old Matt from the opening Snapshot began receiving preschool services as soon as he came out of a coma that resulted from being hit by a car. Although he sustained a severe head trauma and still wears a helmet and uses a walker, Matt is doing well in his kindergarten class. Preschool services for Matt began with a referral to his local school to assess the type and extent of his perceived delays relative to same-age peers without disabilities. Once Matt's needs were identified and the multidisciplinary team determined his eligibility for preschool special education services, appropriate developmental and age-appropriate instructional strategies were implemented in a school-based classroom.

*Referral Programs* Referral programs for preschool-age children with disabilities have several important components. First, a child-find system is set up in each state to locate preschool-age (ages 3 to 5) children at risk and to make referrals to the local education agency. Referrals may come from parents, the family physician, health care or social service agencies, or the child's day care or preschool teacher. Referrals for preschool services may be based on a child's perceived delays in physical development (such as not walking by age 2), speech and language delays (such as nonverbal by age 3), excessive inappropriate behavior (such as frequent temper tantrums, violent behavior, extreme shyness, or excessive crying), or sensory difficulties (unresponsive to sounds or unable to visually track objects in the environment).

**Standard 5**
Instructional Planning and Strategies

**Standard 5**
Instructional Planning and Strategies

**Child-find system**
A system within a state or local area that attempts to identify all children who are disabled or at risk in order to refer them for appropriate support services.

***Multidisciplinary Assessment*** Following a referral, a child-study team initiates assessments to determine whether the child is eligible for preschool special education services under IDEA 2004. Preschool-age children with disabilities are eligible if they meet both of the following requirements. First, developmental delays are evident as measured by appropriate diagnostic instruments and procedures, in one or more of the following areas: physical development, cognitive development, communication development, social or emotional development, or adaptive development. Second, as a result of these delays, the child needs special education and related services (IDEA, 2004, PL 108-446, Sec. 602[3]).

***Developing an IEP for Preschool-Age Children*** If a child is eligible, an individualized education program (IEP) is developed. Specialists from several disciplines—including physical therapy, occupational therapy, speech and language therapy, pediatrics, social work, and special education—participate in the development and implementation of IEPs for preschool-age children. The purpose of preschool programs for young children with disabilities is to assist them in living in and adapting to a variety of environmental settings, including home, neighborhood, and school. Depending on individual needs, preschool programs may focus on developing skills in communication, social and emotional learning, physical well-being, self-care, early academics, and coping (Raver, 2010). The decision regarding which skill areas are to be taught should be based on a **functional assessment** of the child and of the setting where he or she spends time. Functional assessments determine the child's skills, the characteristics of the setting, and the family's needs, resources, expectations, and aspirations (Harvey et al., 2008; Horner et al., 2006). Through a functional assessment, professionals and parents come together to plan a program that supports the preschool-age child in meeting the demands of the home, school, or community setting.

**Functional assessment**
Assessments to determine the child's skills, the characteristics of the setting, and the family's needs, resources, expectations, and aspirations.

## Developmentally Appropriate Practice

Early child educators share the conviction that programs for young children should be based on **developmentally appropriate practice (DAP)**. DAP is grounded in the belief that there has been too much emphasis on preparing preschool-age children for academic learning and not enough on activities that are initiated by the child, such as play, exploration, social interaction, and inquiry. As suggested by the National Association for the Education of Young Children (NAEYC, 2009), "high-quality early childhood programs do much more than help children learn numbers, shapes, and colors. Good programs help children learn how to learn: to question why and discover alternative answers; to get along with others; and to use their developing language, thinking, and motor skills."

DAP is viewed as culturally sensitive because it emphasizes interaction between children and adults. Adults become "guides" for student learning rather than controlling what, where, and how students acquire knowledge. DAP is strongly advocated by NAEYC, the largest national organization for professionals in early childhood education. NAEYC has developed several guiding principles for the use of DAP; these are illustrated in Figure 3.3.

## Age-Appropriate Placement

As we have noted, DAP is widely accepted throughout the early childhood community, but many special education teachers and related services personnel (such as speech and language pathologists and physical therapists) see DAP as a base or foundation to build on to meet the individual needs of young children with disabilities. These professionals indicate that early childhood programs for students with disabilities must also take into account age-appropriate placements and functional skill learning.

Age-appropriate placements emphasize the child's chronological age over developmental level. Thus, a 2-year-old with developmental delays is first and foremost a 2-year-old, regardless of whether he or she has disabilities. A young child with disabilities should be exposed to the same instructional opportunities and settings as a nondisabled peer of the same chronological age. Age-appropriate learning prepares children to live and learn in inclusive environments with same-age peers. Arguing that DAP and age-appropriate practice are compatible, McDonnell, Hardman, and McDonnell (2003) and Widerstrom (2005)

**Developmentally appropriate practices (DAP)**
Instructional approaches that use curriculum and learning environments consistent with the child's developmental level.

**Age-appropriate placement**
Educational placement based on instructional programs consistent with chronological age rather than developmental level.

- **Create a caring community of learners.** Developmentally appropriate practices occur within a context that supports the development of relationships between adults and children, among children, among teachers, and between teachers and families.

- **Teach to enhance development and learning.** Adults are responsible for ensuring children's healthy development and learning. From birth, relationships with adults are critical determinants of children's healthy social and emotional development, and they also serve as mediators of language and intellectual development.

- **Construct an appropriate curriculum.** The content of the early childhood curriculum is determined by many factors, including the subject matter of the disciplines, social or cultural values, and parental input. In developmentally appropriate programs, decisions about curriculum content also take into consideration the age and experience of the learners.

- **Assess children's learning and development.** Assessment of individual children's development and learning is essential for planning and implementing an appropriate curriculum. In developmentally appropriate programs, assessment and curriculum are integrated, with teachers continually engaging in observational assessment for the purpose of improving teaching and learning.

- **Establish reciprocal relationships with families.** Developmentally appropriate practices derive from deep knowledge of individual children and of the context within which they develop and learn. The younger the child, the more important it is for professionals to acquire this knowledge through relationships with the child's family.

SOURCE: Adapted from National Association for the Education of Young Children (2009). NAEYC position statement. Retrieved January 13, 2015, from www.naeyc.org/files/naeyc/file/positions/PSDAP.pdf.

suggested that there are many ways to create learning experiences for young children that are both developmentally appropriate and age-appropriate. The following is one example:

> *Mark is a 5-year-old with limited gross and fine motor movement and control. His cognitive development is similar to a typically developing 11-month-old. Mark is learning to use adaptive switches to activate toys and a radio or [CD] player. Mark enjoys listening to music and toys that make noise and move simultaneously. Mark would also enjoy the lullabies and battery-operated lamb and giraffe toys that might usually be purchased for an 11-month-old. However, he also enjoys Raffi songs and songs from Disney movies, as well as automated racetracks and battery-operated dinosaurs and robots. The latter selection of music and toys would also interest other children of his age...and could provide some familiar and pleasurable experiences for Mark to enjoy in classroom and play settings with typical peers. (McDonnell, Hardman, & McDonnell, 2003, p. 239)*

**Teaching Functional Life Skills** Consistent with the individualized needs of the child and the expectations of the family, teaching functional life skills facilitates the young child's learning in the natural setting (such as home and family). Functional skill development helps a child adapt to the demands of a given environment—that is, it creates an adaptive fit between the child and the setting in which he or she must learn to function. Functional skills focus on teaching and assisting a child to become more independent and to interact appropriately with family, friends, and professionals. In fact, it may be more important for some children to be able to dress themselves, brush their teeth, comb their hair, and take care of other personal hygiene needs than to be able to perform long division.

**Inclusive Preschool Classrooms** In the evidence-based inclusive classroom, young children with disabilities receive their educational program side by side with peers without disabilities in a regular preschool or day care program. Effective programs are staffed by child care providers, special education preschool teachers in a co-teaching or consultant role, paraprofessionals, and other related services personnel as needed by the children. One of the benefits of an inclusive classroom is the positive effect of typically developing peers on the

**Adaptive fit**
Compatibility between demands of a task or setting and a student's instructional needs and abilities.

language skills of a child who has a disability (Justice et al., 2014). Figure 3.4 describes the values that are at the foundation of an evidence-based inclusion preschool program, and the multidisciplinary resources that are essential to implement it.

In a study of child care providers, Devore and Hanley-Maxwell (2000) identified five critical factors that contributed to successfully serving young children with disabilities in inclusive, community-based child care settings: (1) a willingness on the part of the child care provider to make inclusion work; (2) a realistic balance

**Photo 3.3** Evidence-based inclusive preschool classrooms are staffed by highly trained professionals in both child care and special education. What other indicators of quality should we look for in an inclusive preschool classroom?

Fotosearch/Getty Images

- Inclusion, as a value, supports the right of all children, regardless of abilities, to participate actively in natural settings within their communities. Natural settings are those in which the child would spend time if he or she did not have a disability. These settings include (but are not limited to) home, preschool, nursery schools, Head Start programs, kindergartens, neighborhood school classrooms, child care, places of worship, recreational venues (such as community playgrounds and community events), and other settings that all children and families enjoy.

- Young children and their families have full and successful access to health, social, educational, and other support services that promote full participation in family and community life. The cultural, economic, and educational diversity of families is valued and supported as a process for identifying a program of services.

- As young children participate in group settings (such as preschool, play groups, child care, and kindergarten), their active participation should be guided by developmentally and individually appropriate curricula. Access to and participation in the age-appropriate general curriculum become central to the identification and provision of specialized support services.

- To implement inclusive practices, there must be
  - the continued development, implementation, evaluation, and dissemination of full inclusion supports, services, and systems that are of high quality for all children;
  - the development of preservice and in-service training programs that prepare families, services providers, and administrators to develop and work within inclusive settings;
  - collaboration among key stakeholders to implement flexible fiscal and administrative procedures in support of inclusion;
  - research that contributes to our knowledge of recommended practice; and
  - the restructuring and unification of social, educational, health, and intervention supports and services to make them more responsive to the needs of all children and families.

SOURCE: Adapted from Division for Early Childhood, Council for Exceptional Children and the National Association for the Education of Young Children. (2009). *Position statement on inclusion [online]*. Retrieved January 13, 2015, from http://dec.membershipsoftware.org/files/Position%20Statement%20and%20Papers/Inclusion%20Position%20statement.pdf.

*Figure 3.4* **Indicators of Quality in an Inclusive Preschool Program**

between the resources available in the program and the needs of the student; (3) continual problem solving with parents; (4) access to emotional support and technical assistance from special educators and early intervention therapists; and (5) access to other supports, such as other child care providers, respite care providers, and houses of worship.

There are many reasons for the increasing number of inclusive classrooms for preschool students with disabilities. Inclusive classrooms create opportunities for social interaction and for the development of friendships among children with disabilities and same-age peers without disabilities. The social development skills learned in inclusive settings are applied at home and community as well as in future educational and social settings. Preschool-age children without disabilities learn to value and accept diversity (Drew & Hardman, 2007).

**Head Start,** the nation's largest federally funded early childhood program, was enacted into law in 1965, and has served over 27 million children. The program was developed around a strong research base suggesting that early enrichment experiences for children with economic disadvantages would better prepare them for elementary school (Bierman et al., 2008; Phillips & Cabrera, 2006; U.S. Department of Health and Human Services, 2013). Although the original legislation did not include children with disabilities, the law was eventually expanded in 1982 to require that at least 10 percent of Head Start enrollment be reserved for these children. The U.S. Department of Health and Human Services (2013) reported that of the more than 1,130,000 children in Head Start programs, children with disabilities accounted for 11.5 percent of this population. Head Start has been hailed through the years as a major breakthrough in federal support for early childhood education.

Federal regulations under Head Start have been expanded to ensure that a disabilities service plan be developed to meet the needs of all children with disabilities and their families, that the programs designate a coordinator of services for children with disabilities, and that the necessary special education and related services be provided for children who are designated as disabled under IDEA.

### Transition from Preschool to Elementary School

Transitions, although a natural and ongoing part of everyone's life, are often difficult under the best of circumstances. For preschool-age children with disabilities and their families, the transition from early childhood programs to kindergarten can be very stressful. Early childhood programs for preschool-age children with disabilities commonly employ many adults (both professional and paraprofessional). In contrast, kindergarten programs are often not able to offer the same level of staff support, particularly in more inclusive educational settings. Therefore, it is important for preschool professionals responsible for transition planning to attend not only to the needs and skills of the individual students, but also to how they can match the performance demands of the elementary school and classroom setting. Guralnick et al. (2008) indicated that successful transition from preschool to elementary programs is a critical factor in inclusion. The *Handbook on Transition from Early Childhood Special Education Programs* (2005) makes several suggestions for professionals as they support parents throughout the transition process:

- Emphasize transition as a process and not as a single event.
- Begin discussions about transition early in the process.
- Plan steps to ensure the child's success and comfort in the new environment.
- Communicate with parents about the similarities and differences between programs and plans (IFSP and IEP).

To identify the skills needed in the elementary school environment, a preschool transition plan should begin at least one to two years before the child's actual move. This move is facilitated when the early intervention specialist, the child's future kindergarten teacher, and the parents engage in a careful planning process that recognizes the significant changes that the child and the family will go through as they enter a new and unknown situation (DeVore & Russell, 2007; Rosenkoetter et al., 2001).

**Head Start**
Federally funded preschool
program for economically disadvantaged children.

In summary, early childhood programs for children with disabilities focus on teaching skills that will improve a child's opportunities for living a rich life and on preparing the child to function successfully in family, school, and neighborhood environments. Young children with disabilities are prepared as early as possible to share meaningful experiences with same-age peers. Additionally, early childhood programs lessen the impact of conditions that may deteriorate or become more severe without timely and adequate intervention and that may prevent children from developing other, secondary disabling conditions. The intended outcomes of these programs will not, however, be accomplished without consistent family participation and professional collaboration.

## 3-5 The Elementary School Years

In the elementary school years, the focus is on supporting children's progress toward the expectations of the general education curriculum. The degree to which a child is able to meet these expectations depends on how effectively the school accommodates individual needs and provides evidence-based instructional programs. For Ricardo in the nearby Case Study, the school's expectations were a challenge, and he was struggling to connect with his classmates and was falling behind in most subjects. His first-grade teacher decided to initiate a referral to evaluate Ricardo's eligibility for special education services. Once it was determined that Ricardo qualified as a student with an autism spectrum disorder, a multidisciplinary team of special educators, general educators, related services personnel, and his mother worked together to develop his individualized education program (IEP) and meet his academic communication and social skills needs.

### 3-5a Meeting Student Needs in an Inclusive Classroom through a General Education/Special Education Partnership

Today's teachers are charged with preparing the next generation of students for a changing and diverse world. The growing student diversity includes increasing numbers from ethnically diverse backgrounds, those with disabilities, and children at risk of educational failure. Each of these factors contributes to the critical need for general education and special education teachers to work together in preparing all students for the many challenges of the next century, while at the same time not losing sight of individual learning needs, styles, and preferences.

The current wave of reform in U.S. schools, as mandated by federal law, is focused on finding new and more effective ways to increase student achievement by establishing high standards for *what* should be taught and *how* performance will be measured. Accountability for meeting high standards rests at several levels, but the ultimate test of success is what happens between teacher and student in the day-to-day classroom.

Increasing student diversity in the schools will require general educators to teach students whose needs exceed those of the traditionally defined "typical child." Correspondingly, special education teachers must have the specialized skills to meet the needs of students with disabilities, and will be called upon to apply this expertise to a much broader group of high-risk and disadvantaged students in a collaborative educational environment. The combination of these factors makes a very strong case for a partnership between general education and special education.

**The Many Roles of the Special Education Teacher** In an inclusive school, special educators are called upon to fill multiple roles sometimes referred to as the four C's: collaboration, consultation, coordination, and co-teaching. In the role of *collaborator,* special educators:

- work with school personnel (such as general educators, the school principal, and related services personnel) and parents to identify the educational needs of students with disabilities;

## Ricardo

Ricardo, a first-grader at Bloomington Hill Elementary School, has recently been referred by his teacher, Ms. Thompson, to the school's pre-referral team for an evaluation. During the first few months of school, Ricardo has continued to fall further behind in all content areas, and he has difficulty connecting with his peers. This is his first year at Bloomington Hill Elementary School, and he didn't have any school records when he enrolled. From the beginning of the year, Ms. Thompson noticed that Ricardo has very little language production, and some repetitive characteristics that caught her attention. Ricardo does not engage with the other students in the class and becomes frustrated when his peers attempt to use the tools that he is using. Ms. Thompson structures her curriculum around cooperative learning centers, which seem to work for most students, but not Ricardo. It was clear to Ms. Thompson that Ricardo's language development was delayed as well. He had a very limited expressive vocabulary and had some difficulty following directions if more than one or two steps were involved.

Ms. Thompson contacted Ricardo's mother, Maria Galleghos (a single parent), to inform her that she would like to refer Ricardo for an in-depth evaluation to determine is he is on the autism spectrum. A representative from the school would be calling her to explain what the evaluation meant and to get her approval for the necessary testing. The school psychologist, Jean Andreas, made the call to Ms. Galleghos. During the phone conversation, Ms. Galleghos reminded the school psychologist that the primary language spoken in the home was Spanish, even though she and his siblings spoke English, too. Ms. Andreas indicated that the assessment would be conducted in both Spanish and English to determine whether Ricardo's delays were related to a disability or perhaps to problems with English as a second language.

Having received written approval from Ricardo's mother, the school's pre-referral team conducted an evaluation of Ricardo's academic performance. The formal evaluation included achievement tests, classroom performance tests, samples of Ricardo's work, behavioral observations, and anecdotal notes from Ms. Thompson. Additionally, Ms. Thompson and Ms. Galleghos completed the Autism Behavioral Checklist (ABC).

An interview with Ms. Galleghos was conducted as part of the process to gain her perceptions of Ricardo's strengths and problem areas and to give her an opportunity to relate pertinent family history.

The evaluation confirmed his teacher's concerns. Ricardo was more than two years below what was expected for a child his age in both reading and language development and showed a deficit in social relation, language and communication skills, and social and adaptive skills on the ABC. Ricardo's difficulties in these areas did not seem to be related to his being bilingual, but the issue of English as a second language would need to be taken into careful consideration in developing an appropriate learning experience.

The team determined that Ricardo qualified for special education services as a student with autism spectrum disorder. Once again, Ms. Andreas contacted Ms. Galleghos with the results, indicating that Ricardo qualified for special education services. Ms. Andreas pointed out that, as a parent of a student with an identified disability, Ms. Galleghos had some specific legal rights that would be further explained to her both in writing and orally.

One of those rights is the right to participate as a partner in the development of Ricardo's individualized education program (IEP). Ms. Andreas further explained that a meeting would be set up at a mutually convenient time to develop a plan to assist Ricardo over the next year.

### Application Questions

**1.** Prior to the meeting, what could Ricardo's teachers do to help his mother feel valued as a member of the IEP team and to better understand her role in developing the IEP?

**2.** What additional information could Ricardo's mother provide that would help the team better understand his academic and social needs as a student who is an English language learner and whose primary language in the home is Spanish?

**3.** What do you see as important for Ricardo to learn in school?

---

**Standard 7**
Collaboration

- link student assessment information to the development of the IEP and access to the general curriculum;
- determine appropriate student accommodations and instructional adaptations; and
- deliver intensive instruction using specialized teaching methods.

Special educators provide instruction and support in academic, behavioral, and/or adaptive/functional areas, as well as fostering student self-determination and self-management skills. As collaborators, special education teachers use effective problem-solving strategies to facilitate student learning, co-teach with general educators, and apply effective accountability measures to evaluate individual students' progress and long-term results.

In the role of *consultant,* special education teachers must be able to serve as a resource to general educators and parents on effective instructional practices for students with disabilities. Expertise may be provided in content areas (such as effective approaches to teaching reading to students with special needs) and/or problem-solving skills (such as strategies to motivate students to participate in class activities).

In the role of *coordinator,* special education teachers take the lead responsibility for organizing the activities of the school team in developing, implementing, and evaluating student IEPs. They also may be responsible for organizing school resources to best meet the needs of students with disabilities; initiating professional development activities for school team members; supervising paraprofessionals, peer support, and volunteers; and facilitating positive communication with parents.

In the role of *co-teacher*, special education teachers enter a direct partnership with general education teachers. Together, they collaborate to meet the unique learning needs of students while teaching specific content. There are many models of co-teaching, but one common factor that connects them is that there are two teachers in the classroom with a shared responsibility for student success.

## The General Education Teacher: Meeting the Challenge to Educate All Students

General education teachers must continually meet the challenges of achieving increased academic excellence, as well as responding to students with many different backgrounds and instructional needs coming together in a common environment. The weight of these demands is felt even more profoundly while teachers are adapting to new standards, such as the Common Core State Standards. The inclusion of students with disabilities in general education classes need not be met with teacher frustration, anger, or refusal. These reactions are merely symptomatic of the confusion surrounding inclusive education. Huefner (2012) suggested that the IDEA 2004 requirement for general educators to be members of the IEP team gives them leverage to obtain the supports they need to be more effective with special education students and to work more collaboratively with special education teachers. As members of the IEP team, general educators are in a better position to share their knowledge and insight on individual students and to provide important information about the curriculum and strategies to support each student in the classroom.

Specific roles for general educators in working collaboratively with special education and related services personnel include:

- identifying and referring students who may be in need of additional support to succeed in an inclusive setting;
- understanding each student's individual strengths and limitations, and the effects on learning;
- implementing an appropriate individualized education program that is focused on supporting student success in the general education curriculum;
- communicating and collaborating with the special education teacher; and
- initiating and maintaining ongoing communication with parents.

Unfortunately, inclusive education is sometimes synonymous with placing a student with disabilities into a general education class without the necessary supports to the teacher or to the student, and at the expense of others in the class. Teachers may experience many different needs and challenges, such as disruptive students who must learn social and behavioral skills to succeed in a general education setting. General education teachers may need support from a special education teacher or other school personnel (such as a speech and language specialist, occupational therapist, social worker, or nurse), and access to appropriate instructional adaptations necessary to meet the needs of students with disabilities.

However, in a review of the literature on the attitudes and beliefs of general educators regarding students with disabilities, Pugach (2005) suggested that the discussion has shifted away from focusing on the barriers to inclusion to what it is that teachers need to know and what they can do to meet the needs of these students. To address these needs, Pugach further asserts,

> it will be crucial to take advantage of the natural progression [in universities] toward collaborative [teacher education] programs…conducted in a joint fashion, teams comprised of teacher educators from special and general teacher education, across content areas and multicultural education…. By joining forces in this manner we can begin to provide answers to a new generation of questions about how best to achieve the goal of delivering instruction of the highest quality to students with disabilities. (p. 578)

The role of a general education teacher extends not only to working with students with mild disabilities, but also to involvement with those with more severe disabilities. Success in a general education class for students with severe disabilities depends critically on the cooperative relationship among the general education teacher, the special education teacher, and the school support team. A general educator works with the team to create opportunities to include students with more severe disabilities. Inclusion may be achieved by having the general education class serve as a homeroom for the student; by developing opportunities for students with severe disabilities to be with their peers without disabilities as often as possible, both within the general education class and in school activities such as recess, lunch, and assemblies; by developing a peer support program; and by using effective practices, such as multitiered systems of support (RtI), universal design for learning, differentiated instruction, assistive technology, and curriculum-based measurement.

## 3-5b Evidence-Based Practices in Inclusive Elementary School Programs

Ensuring appropriate and effective educational learning experiences for all students, including those with disabilities, is dependent upon the provision of evidence-based educational services and supports. Characteristics of evidence-based instruction that enhance learning opportunities for students of all ages and across multiple settings include:

- *Individualization*, a student-centered approach to instructional decision making;
- *Intensive instruction*, frequent instructional experiences of significant duration; and
- An *"education for all" approach to teaching and learning,* developing and adapting instruction to meet the needs of every student. (Hardman & Dawson, 2008; Hardman & Mulder, 2004)

**CEC**

**Standard 1**
Learner Development and Individual Learning Differences

**Individualization**
A student-centered approach to instructional decision making.

**Individualization** The defining hallmark of special education has always been individualization—developing and implementing an appropriate educational experience based on the individual needs of each student. Research indicates that fundamental differences have characterized the ways in which special educators approach instruction, distinguishing them from their general education colleagues. Traditionally, instruction in general education has most often centered on the curriculum (content knowledge). Although general education has traditionally been guided by a utilitarian approach (the greatest good for the greatest number), special education practice is driven by individually referenced decision making. It is designed to meet the unique needs of every student, regardless of educational need or ability. Using an individually referenced approach to decision making, special education teachers continually plan and adjust curriculum and instruction in response to the students. However, the fact is that *all* teachers must have at their disposal multiple ways to adapt curriculum, modify their instructional approaches, and motivate every student to learn (Peterson & Hittie, 2010; Vaughn, Bos, & Schumm, 2011). Hardman and McDonnell (2008) suggested that the vast majority of teachers, whether in general or special education, unfortunately do not have this broad expertise in both the subject matter (content area) and in adapting curriculum and instruction (pedagogy) necessary to meet individual student needs. Thus, together, general and special educators must acquire a core of knowledge and skills, as well as the ability to work collaboratively to facilitate their effectiveness in providing evidence-based instruction to all students.

**Intensive Instruction** The instructional approach of intensive instruction involves (1) actively engaging students in their learning by requiring high rates of appropriate response to the material presented; (2) carefully matching instruction to student ability, interests, and skill level; (3) providing instructional cues and prompts to support learning and then fading them when appropriate; and (4) providing detailed feedback that is directly focused on the task the students are expected to complete. Intensive instruction may involve both group and one-to-one learning. Research suggests that intensive instruction can significantly improve both academic achievement and the student's life skills (Fuchs, Fuchs, & Vaughn, 2014; Vaughn, Bos, & Schumm, 2011). For all students, including those with disabilities, intensive instruction provided consistently over time and by qualified and effective teachers can result in significant gains in academic achievement and life skill learning.

## An "Educational for All" Approach to Teaching and Learning

Learning is a continual process of adaptation for all students as they attempt to meet the demands of school (Friend & Bursuck, 2012; Peterson & Hittie, 2010). Not every student learns in the same way or at the same rate. Some students do not learn as quickly or as efficiently as their classmates and are constantly fighting a battle against time and failure. Despite these challenges, however, all students, including those with disabilities, can learn the required skills that will orient them toward striving for success rather than fighting against failure. Success can be achieved only when educators remain flexible, constantly adjusting to meet the needs of their students. For example, an "education for all approach" to instruction in core academic areas (e.g., reading, math, and science) stresses that students must learn a specified set of sequenced skills, each a prerequisite to the next. This process can be illustrated by briefly analyzing the teaching of reading. When learning to read, students must acquire many individual skills and then be able to link them together as a whole. The students then have the ability to decode abstract information and turn it into meaningful content. When one of the separate skills required for reading is not learned, the entire process may break down. Teaching core academic skills, whether in reading or any other content area, lays the groundwork for further development and higher levels of functioning. Vaughn, Bos, and Schumm (2011) suggested that reading instruction is *appropriate* and *intensive* when:

- students have a clear understanding of teacher expectations and the goals of instruction;
- the reader's instructional reading level and needs match the instruction provided;
- instruction is *explicit* and direct in the skills and strategies the readers need to become more proficient and more independent;
- students are grouped appropriately, which includes ability-level grouping;
- instruction includes frequent opportunities for responding with feedback and ongoing progress monitoring; and
- teachers and peers support the students when necessary.

Not all children are able to learn core academic skills within the time frame dictated by schools. The degree to which students are able to meet the requirements of a school setting and the extent to which the school recognizes and accommodates individual diversity are known as adaptive fit. This fit is dynamic and constantly changes in the negotiations between the individuals and the environment.

For students with a disability, adaptive fit may involve learning and applying various strategies that will facilitate the ability to meet the expectations of a learning

**Intensive instruction**
An instructional approach that involves (1) actively engaging students in their learning by requiring high rates of appropriate response; (2) carefully matching instruction to student ability, interests, and skill level; (3) providing instructional cues and prompts to support learning and then fading them when appropriate; and (4) providing detailed feedback directly focused on the task the student is expected to complete.

environment. Such students may find that the requirements for success within a general education classroom are beyond their adaptive capabilities and that the system is unwilling to accommodate academic, behavioral, physical, sensory, or communicative differences. As a result, students develop negative attitudes toward school. Imagine yourself in a setting that constantly disapproves of how you act and what you do, a place in which activities are difficult and overwhelming, a setting in which your least desirable qualities are emphasized. What would you think about spending more than 1,000 hours a year in such a place?

Over the years, educators have responded in several ways to mismatches between the needs of students and the demands of the learning environment. Using the first alternative, the traditional approach, students remain in the negative situation and nothing is done until inevitable failure occurs. This changed with the second alternative—the advent of special education and the continuum of placements whereby students are pulled out of a setting and moved to a classroom or school more conducive to individual needs. In this approach, no attempt is made to modify the students' current environment.

For some time, the general classroom teacher has had to work with students who have disabilities without the assistance of any effective support. This is no longer the case in many of today's schools. The emergence of inclusive education programs in elementary schools throughout the United States has strengthened collaborative efforts between the general education classroom teacher and the network of supports available in the school.

In U.S. schools today, we see a greater emphasis on access to the general curriculum and on accountability for student learning. What does access to the general curriculum mean for students with disabilities? How can schools make the curriculum accessible to all students in an inclusive setting? What approaches are needed to measure student progress effectively? In the next section, we take a closer look at several evidence-based instructional approaches that have proved effective in creating access to the general education curriculum and facilitating student learning in an inclusive setting.

### Multitiered System of Support (aka Response to Intervention [RtI])
A multitiered system of support (MTSS), often used synonymously with "the three-tiered model of assessment and instruction" or "response to intervention" (RtI), has its origins in the research on school-wide positive behavioral supports (PBS) (Horner, Sugai, & Anderson, 2010; Sugai & Horner, 2010). See Chapter 8 for more discussion on PBS. MTSS is based on a system-wide approach to providing evidence-based instruction using a three-tiered model based on the instructional and behavioral needs of each child. It involves continuous monitoring of student progress in making decisions regarding the frequency and intensity of instruction. Data are used to guide instruction, appropriate intervention and practice, parent involvement, and other evidence-based practices (Vaughn, Bos, & Schumm, 2011). As described by Gargiulo and Metcalf (2013), "an RtI [MTSS] framework represents a conceptual shift in thinking from a 'wait to fail' approach to one that emphasizes early intervention and possibly prevention..." (p. 58).

The MTSS framework is most often described in terms of three assessment and instructional tiers. *Tier I* focuses on core classroom instruction that is provided to all students using evidence-based practices to teach the critical elements within a core curriculum. The general education teacher and special education teacher in conjunction with a school-wide support team provide instruction to students who are at various levels of development in critical academic and/or behavior skills. Most students will demonstrate proficiency with effective Tier I instruction. These students are able to acquire skills through the core instruction provided by the teacher, whereas others require more intensive instruction in specific skill areas. The use of universal design for learning, differentiated instruction (see the following section on differentiated instruction), and the targeting of specific skill development provide classroom teachers, in conjunction with the school-wide support team, with the tools to meet the needs of most students.

*Tier II* provides supplemental targeted instruction in addition to evidence-based practices taught at the Tier I level. For some students, core classroom instruction in the general classroom is not enough for them to demonstrate proficiency. These students require targeted supplemental instruction in addition to the skills taught through core instruction. Tier II meets the needs of these students by giving them additional time for intensive small-group instruction daily. The goal is to support and reinforce skills being taught by the general and special education teachers as well as the school-wide support team at the Tier I level. At this level of intervention, data-based monitoring is used to ensure adequate progress is being made on target skills. The frequency, intensity, and duration of this instruction vary for each student depending on the assessment and progress monitoring data.

A small number of students who receive targeted supplemental instruction (Tier II) continue to have difficulty becoming proficient in necessary content skills. *Tier III* provides intensive targeted instruction to the most at-risk learners who have not adequately responded to evidence-based practices. These students require instruction and/or behavioral intervention that is more explicit, more intensive, and specifically designed to meet their individual educational needs. Additional sessions of specialized one-to-one or small-group instruction are provided with progress monitoring of specific skills.

In summary, the key components of MTSS are (1) the use of evidence-based instruction designed to meet the needs of students at each level, and (2) assessment and progress-monitoring procedures that measure current skills and growth over time and that are used to provide new instruction to individual students.

## Universal Design for Learning and Adapted Instruction

Universal design as an applied concept began in the field of architecture where its initial focus was to create accessibility to a physical space (e.g., building and/or landscape) that would meet the needs of every individual without having to adapt or alter the critical elements of the space over time. As applied to architecture, the purpose of universal design is to accommodate everyone, including people who use wheelchairs, people with low vision, people with children, and people who are elderly. In schools, **universal design for learning (UDL)** shares with architecture the primary goal of assuring "accessibility." In education, however, the concept of "accessibility" is focused on developing common (universal) approaches to curriculum development that give all students equal opportunities to learn. UDL focuses on providing access to the content in multiple ways, giving students a variety of ways to interact with the content, and stimulating interest and motivation for learning.

Recording for the Blind and Dyslexic

**Photo 3.4** Universal design for learning helps make the curriculum accessible and applicable to all students, regardless of their abilities or learning styles. Here students are using a digital talking textbook. What are some other ways in which universal design for learning can help students with disabilities in an inclusive classroom?

Compared to universal design for learning, **adapted instruction** seeks to enhance individual student performance in a given content area (e.g., reading) by modifying the way in which instruction is delivered and by changing the environment where the learning takes place. This approach uses a variety of instructional procedures, materials, and alternative learning sequences in the classroom setting to help students master content consistent with their needs, abilities, and interests (Wood, 2006). For example, a student who is unable to memorize multiplication tables may be taught to use a calculator to complete the task. Learning to use the calculator would likely not take place in a large group setting but in a one-to-one or small-group situation. The degree of difficulty for the task is modified to fit with the capability of the student; the alteration within the learning environment allows the student to be taught the skill through intensive instruction.

**Universal design for learning (UDL)**
Instructional programs that work for all students to the greatest extent possible without the needs for adaption or specialized design.

**Adapted instruction**
Instruction that modified the learning environment to accommodate unique learner characteristics.

**In a UDL curriculum...**

- *Goals* provide an appropriate challenge for all students.

- *Materials* have a flexible format, supporting transformation between media and multiple representations of content to support all students' learning.

- *Methods* are flexible and diverse enough to provide appropriate learning experiences, challenges, and supports for all students.

- *Assessment* is sufficiently flexible to provide accurate, ongoing information that helps teachers adjust instruction and maximize learning.

**Teaching Math Using UDL**

Suppose a math teacher uses the UDL approach to convey the critical features of a right triangle. With software that supports graphics and hyperlinks, a document is prepared that shows:

- Multiple examples of right triangles in different orientations and sizes, with the right angle and the three points highlighted.

- An animation of the right triangle morphing into an isosceles triangle or into a rectangle, with voice and on-screen text to highlight the differences.

- Links to reviews on the characteristics of triangles and of right angles.

- Links to examples of right triangles in various real-world contexts.

- Links to pages that students can go to on their own for review or enrichment on the subject.

- The teacher could then project the documentation onto a large screen in front of the class. Thus, the teacher would present the concept not simply by explaining it verbally or by assigning a textbook chapter or workbook page, but by using many modalities and with options for extra support or extra enrichment.

SOURCE: From Hitchcock, C., Meyer, A., Rose, D., & Jackson, R. (2002, November/December). Providing new access to the general curriculum: Universal design for learning. *Teaching Exceptional Children 8, 13*.

Universal design for learning goes one step beyond adapted instruction, creating instructional programs and environments that work for all students, to the greatest extent possible, without the need for adaptation or specialized design.

As is true for adapted instruction, the basic premise of universal design for learning is to make the curriculum accessible and applicable to all students, regardless of their abilities or learning styles (Bender, 2008; Bolt & Roach, 2009; Ketterlin-Geller, 2008; Kotering, McClannon, & Braziel, 2008; Rose & Meyer, 2002). Rao, Ok, and Bryant (2014) reviewed the research that has been conducted on UDL and found that there are a variety of ways that universal design is being implemented. The evidence from the wide range of studies reinforces the idea that UDL supports student learning. Figure 3.5 describes the basic principles of the universal design curriculum and provides an example of its application in the teaching of mathematics.

**Standard 5**
Instructional Planning and Strategies

**Differentiated Instruction** Today's classrooms include children with many different needs and abilities. Haager and Klinger (2005) describe what it is like for teachers to face the challenges of a mixed-ability class:

*Mrs. Ryan [an elementary special education teacher] co-teaches in Mrs. Crawford's fourth-grade class during language arts time. Today Mrs. Crawford is explaining an assignment after reading aloud a chapter of a literature book. The students have their own copies of the literature book to use as a reference. The assignment is to write each vocabulary word written on the board, draw an illustration of the word, and write a sentence demonstrating its meaning. The students are using the class dictionaries and will complete any work they do not finish in class for homework. They will also write an entry in their reading journals for homework. Mrs. Ryan observes Marcel and Tomika, two students on her special education roster, during the reading time and makes some notes in her consultation log regarding Marcel's approved attention. He has refrained from talking aloud during reading, one of his goals. When the students begin their seat work, [Mrs. Ryan] implements adaptations for both students. They will both do only half of the words, and she and the teacher [Mrs. Crawford] have rearranged which words are most critical. Marcel and Tomika will do journal entries later with Mrs. Ryan's assistance. Mrs. Ryan quietly explains the modifications to Marcel and Tomika and directs them to begin with the assignment, reminding them that they should spell the vocabulary words correctly since they are copying them, but they need not worry about spelling all the words right in their sentences; the important thing is getting their ideas down. (pp. 54–55)*

In a mixed-ability class, students of the same age are clearly not alike in *how* they learn or in their *rate* of acquiring new knowledge. Therefore, teachers must use **differentiated instruction**, a teaching technique in which a variety of instructional approaches within the same curriculum are used to meet individual instructional need. At its most basic level, differentiated instruction provides students with many different ways to access and learn content within the general education curriculum. Peterson and Hittie (2010) describe differentiated instruction as "designing for diversity" and suggest several strategies for its implementation:

- Design lessons at multiple levels.
- Challenge students at their own level.
- Provide support to push children ahead to their next level of learning.
- Engage children in learning via activities related to the real world—to their lives at home and in the community.
- Engage the **multiple intelligences** and learning styles of children so that many pathways for learning and demonstrating achievement are available.
- Involve students in collaborative pair or group work in which children draw on each other's strengths. (p. 46)

To be effective, differentiated instruction requires that general and special education teachers work together to ensure access to the curriculum for all children in the class, while at the same time accepting individual goals for each child (Gartin et al., 2002; Haager & Klinger, 2005; Hammeken, 2007; Karen, 2007). Together with related services, these teachers use many different instructional strategies that are consistent with a student's level and rate of learning. Finally, students are able to demonstrate progress in many different ways (such as orally instead of in writing).

**Assistive Technology** Have you ever watched a program with closed-captioning or a foreign movie with subtitles? Do you turn on your television and open your garage door with a remote control device? Do you use speed dial or a digital address book on your cell phone? If so, you use assistive technology. **Assistive technology** is "any item, piece of equipment, or product system, whether acquired commercially off the shelf, modified, or customized, that is used to increase, maintain, or improve the functional capabilities of a child with disabilities" (Technology Related Assistance for Individuals with Disabilities Act, 20 U.S.C. 1401[1]).

Assistive technology can take many forms (high-tech or low-tech) and can be helpful to students with disabilities in several different ways. For students with reading problems, a high-tech digital textbook could assist with decoding and comprehending text. Students who have difficulty in verbally communicating with others might use a low-tech language board on which they point to pictures cut from magazines to indicate what they would like for lunch. Students with motor difficulties could learn to operate a joystick so they can move their power wheelchair in any direction.

**Curriculum-Based Assessment/Measurement** In this era of accountability, developing *assessments* that reliably *measure* student learning is an essential component of instruction (Arthur-Kelly et al., 2008; Hosp & Hosp, 2003; Lund & Veal, 2008). As Howell and Nolet (2000) put it, "Assessment is the process of collecting information by reviewing the products of student work, interviewing, observing, or testing" (p. 3). Educators assess students for the purpose of deciding whether they are making adequate progress and, if not, what additional or different services and supports are needed.

**Differentiated instruction**
Provides students with many different ways to access and learn content within the general education curriculum.

**Multiple intelligences**
A theory that human intelligence spans several domains: linguistic, logical-mathematical, spatial, musical, bodily-kinesthetic, interpersonal, intrapersonal, and naturalistic.

**Assistive technology**
An item or product used to increase, maintain, or improve the functional capabilities of a child with disabilities.

### The Strategy Tutor

The World Wide Web is an engaging, information-rich learning environment—but it also can present significant challenges for struggling learners. Unlike textbooks, which are laid out to help learn a specific curriculum, websites are created for a wide range of purposes and by a varied and often unknown group of authors. As a result, the Internet can be a challenging environment for students who struggle with reading.

Strategy Tutor, developed by the Center for Applied Special Technology and funded by the Carnegie Corporation of New York, is an instructional tool that supports students and their teachers in getting the most out of information-rich web pages. The program helps teachers implement reading strategy instruction while guiding students through specific online research projects. Teachers can add prompts and interactive features that will, through the Strategy Tutor interface, be displayed as part of websites they have preselected. On sites not customized by the teacher, Strategy Tutor gives generic tips intended to guide students through the process of web research, teaching strategies that will serve them well even without the Strategy Tutor interface. For more information on Strategy Tutor, visit http://cst.cast.org.

SOURCE: Center for Applied Special Technology. (2012). *Carnegie Strategy Tutor*. Retrieved January 15, 2012, from www.cast.org/research/projects/tutor.html (Coyne, P., & Dalton, B., Project Directors).

The hallmarks of any good assessment are its accuracy, fairness, and utility. Traditional standardized tests (such as intelligence quotient [IQ] or achievement tests) compare one student with another to determine how each individual compares with the overall average. For example, an average score on the Stanford-Binet Intelligence Test is 100. Any score (higher or lower) would be described as deviating from the average. Significantly higher scores may lead to the use of such descriptors as *gifted* or *talented*. Significantly lower scores may result in the label *intellectually disabled*.

Traditional assessments may be useful in determining a student's eligibility for special education (comparing the student with the average performance of peers), but many educators question their use in planning for instruction and measuring day-to-day student learning. An alternative approach to traditional assessment is the use of **curriculum-based assessments (CBAs)** and **curriculum-based measurements (CBMs)**. CBAs include "any procedure that evaluates student performance in relation to the school curriculum, such as weekly spelling tests," whereas CBMs are the "frequent, direct measurements of critical school behaviors, which could include timed (1- to 5-minute) tests of performance on reading, math, and writing skills" (Mastropieri & Scruggs, 2013, p. 297).

## Looking Toward a Bright Future

**Curriculum-based assessments (CBAs)**
Procedure that evaluates student performance in relation to the school curriculum.

**Curriculum-based measurements (CBMs)**
A direct measurement of a student's academic and behavioral performance in a specific subject area that takes place on a frequent basis (e.g., a timed three-minute math test).

In the nearly four decades since the passage of the Individuals with Disabilities Education Act, we have been witness to the most significant and positive improvements in educational services and supports for students with disabilities in our history. From isolation to inclusion and from research to practice, much has been accomplished to create access to appropriate schooling and improve the quality of education for these children. As we now move through the second decade of the 21st century, the future looks bright. The future will become even brighter if we continue to pay attention to what we know about best practices and use them in preparing our new and highly qualified teachers, focusing on quality professional development for practicing teachers, and providing the critical resources that schools must have to meet the individual needs of all students. It will be essential for general and special education teachers to find new and innovative ways to work together along with their related services colleagues to use evidence-based instruction that will create access to the general curriculum and increase student learning and achievement. We know what works, including differentiated instruction, universal design for learning, direct instruction, assistive technology, and curriculum-based assessment/measurement. A bright future will depend on our willingness and ability to use these practices with each child, all day, and in every school.

# Chapter Review

## 3-1 Define inclusive education.

- Inclusive education may be defined as placing students with disabilities in a general education setting within their home or neighborhood school while making available both formal and natural supports to ensure an appropriate educational experience.

- Full inclusion occurs when students with disabilities receive all instruction and support within the general education classroom. Partial inclusion occurs when students with disabilities receive most instruction within the general education classroom but are "pulled out" for specialized services part of the school day.

## 3-2 Describe the characteristics of evidence-based inclusive schools.

Evidence-based inclusive schools:

- promote the values of diversity, acceptance, and belonging.

- ensure the availability of formal and natural supports within the general education setting.

- provide services and supports in age-appropriate classrooms in neighborhood schools.

- ensure access to the general curriculum while meeting the individualized needs of each student.

- provide a school-wide support system to meet the needs of all students.

## 3-3 Define multidisciplinary collaboration and identify its key characteristics.

- Collaboration is defined as professionals, parents, and students *working together* to achieve the mutual goal of delivering an effective educational program designed to meet individual needs. Collaboration is not what those involved do; it is how they do it.

- In an inclusive school, effective collaboration has several key characteristics:

  - Parents are viewed as active partners in the education of their children.

  - Team members share responsibility; individual roles are clearly understood and valued.

  - Team members promote peer support and cooperative learning.

## 3-4 Describe (a) the importance of early intervention services for young children and families, (b) how Part C of IDEA supports these services, and (c) evidence-based early childhood instructional approaches.

- The first years of life are critical to the overall development of all children—normal, at-risk, and disabled.

- Early stimulation is crucial to the later development of language, intelligence, personality, and self-worth.

- Early intervention may prevent or reduce the overall impact of disabilities, as well as counteract the negative effects of delayed intervention.

- Early intervention may in the long run be less costly and more effective than providing services later in an individual's life.

- Part C of IDEA has several purposes, including:

  - enhancing the development of infants and toddlers with disabilities to minimize their potential for developmental delay, and recognizing the significant brain development that occurs during a child's first three years of life;

  - reducing the educational costs to our society by minimizing the need for special education and related services when infants and toddlers with reach school age;

  - maximizing the potential for individuals with disabilities to live independently in society;

  - enhancing the capacity of families to meet the special needs of their infants and toddlers with disabilities; and

  - enhancing the capacity of state and local agencies and service providers to identify, evaluate, and meet the needs of all children, particularly minority, low-income, inner-city, and rural children, and infants and toddlers in foster care.

Evidence-based instructional approaches for preschoolers with disabilities include:

- A child-find system in each state to locate young children at risk and make referrals to appropriate agencies for preschool services

- An individualized education program (IEP) that involves specialists across several disciplines

- Instruction that reflects developmentally appropriate practice, age-appropriate practice, and the teaching of functional skills

- Inclusive preschool classrooms where young children with disabilities are educated side by side with peers without disabilities

**3-5 Describe the special and general education teachers' roles in an inclusive classroom setting, and identify the characteristics of evidence-based instruction that enhance learning for all students.**

- Special education teachers have multiple roles that may be referred to as the "four C's": collaborator, consultant, coordinator, and co-teacher.

- In the role of *collaborator,* special educators work with a school to assess student needs, develop the IEP, determine appropriate accommodations and instructional adaptations, and deliver intensive instruction in academic, behavioral, and/or adaptive functional areas. Special education teachers use effective problem-solving strategies to facilitate student learning, co-teach with general educators, and apply effective accountability measures to evaluate individual student progress and long-term results.

- In the role of *consultant,* special education teachers serve as a resource to general educators and parents on effective instructional practices for students with disabilities.

- In the role of *coordinator,* special education teachers take the lead responsibility for organizing the activities of the school team in developing, implementing, and evaluating student IEPs. Special education teachers may also be responsible for organizing school resources; spearheading professional development activities; supervising paraprofessionals, peer support, and volunteers; and facilitating positive communication with parents.

- In the role of *co-teacher*, special education teachers enter a direct partnership with general education teachers. Together, the two teachers collaborate to meet the unique learning needs of students while teaching specific content. There are many models of co-teaching, but one common factor that connects them is that there are two teachers in the classroom with a shared responsibility for student success.

- General educators must be able to identify and refer students who may be in need of additional support; understand each student's individual strengths and limitations, and the effects on learning; implement an appropriate individualized instructional program that is focused on supporting student success in the general education curriculum; and initiate and maintain ongoing communication with special education teachers and parents.

- The characteristics of evidence-based instruction for all students are *individualization* (student-centered approach to instructional decision making); *intensive instruction* (frequent instructional experiences of significant duration); and *an "education for all" approach to teaching and learning* (developing and adapting instruction to meet the needs of every student).

- Multitiered systems of support (MTSS) (aka response to intervention [RtI]) are based on a system-wide approach to providing evidence-based instruction using a three-tiered model based on the instructional and behavioral needs of each child.

- Universal design for learning goes one step beyond adapted instruction, creating instructional programs and environments that work for all students, to the greatest extent possible, without the need for adaptation or specialized design.

- Students of the same age are clearly not alike in how they learn or in their rate of learning. For this reason, teachers must use *differentiated instruction* in which multiple teaching approaches within the same curriculum are *adapted* to individual need and functioning level.

- Assistive technology can take many forms and can be helpful to students with disabilities in several different ways (examples include a high-tech digital textbook, a low-tech language board, and a joystick to guide a power wheelchair).

- Although traditional assessments may be useful in determining a student's eligibility for special education, many educators question their use in planning for instruction and measuring day-to-day student learning. An alternative to traditional tests is the use of curriculum-based assessments (CBAs) and curriculum-based measurements (CBMs). CBAs include "any procedure that evaluates student performance in relation to the school curriculum." CBMs are "frequent, direct measurements of critical school behaviors, which could include timed (1- to 5-minute) tests of performance" (Mastropieri & Scruggs, 2013, p. 297).

## Council for Exceptional Children (CEC) Standards to Accompany Chapter 3

If you are thinking about a career in special education, you should know that many states use national standards developed by the Council for Exceptional Children (CEC) to assess a teacher candidate's knowledge and skills for working with students with disabilities. See a complete listing of the seven CEC Content Standards on the inside cover of this text.

1 Learner Development and Individual Learning Differences
2 Learning Environments
5 Instructional Planning and Strategies
6 Professional Learning and Ethical Practice
7 Collaboration

## Mastery Activities and Assignments

To master the content within this chapter, complete the following activities and assignments.

1. Complete a written test of the chapter's content. If your instructor requires a written test of your content knowledge for this chapter, keep a copy for your portfolio.
2. Review the Case Study on Embracing Diversity, "Ricardo," and respond in writing to the Application Questions. Keep a copy of the Case Study and of your written response for your portfolio.
3. Participate in a community service learning activity. Community service is a valuable way to enhance your learning experience. Develop a reflective journal of the service learning experience for your portfolio.

## CHAPTER 4

# Secondary Education and Transition Planning

fstop123/iStockphoto.com

## Learning Objectives

*After you complete this chapter, you will be able to:*

**4-1** Discuss the research on the lives of adults with disabilities.

**4-2** Describe the IDEA transition planning requirements.

**4-3** Identify the purpose of person-centered transition planning and the basic steps in its formulation.

**4-4** Describe the instructional focus used to prepare students for college and career readiness.

Living with NO Boundaries: Meet Hector

*By the Disability.gov team*

Some people collect baseball cards. Others save coins or stamps. But Hector's collection is much more valuable. He is the proud owner of more than 24 library cards, which he actively uses around the state of California. It was simply by chance that the Disability.gov team chose a library as the setting for Hector's photo shoot. Little did we know that libraries are such an intricate part of his story.

Hector's insatiable thirst for knowledge started at a young age. After teaching himself to read, Hector spent hours on end at the local library, poring over books in every genre. One time, when he was living with his grandmother in Mexico, he learned that a new library was opening in town. Hector, who was only six years old, decided to skip school to visit it. Needless to say, his family wasn't too pleased with his little adventure.

Throughout the years, libraries became a safe haven from the overstimulation Hector sometimes experienced as a result of his autism and other invisible disabilities. Even though he wanted to socialize with his classmates, Hector said he couldn't always handle the stress after a long day at school. Library books offered access to the intimate thoughts of thousands of "friends" in a quiet environment. Hector still

reads every chance he gets, and the Internet has only enhanced his ability to learn, enabling him to quickly reach out to authors to ask them questions about their books.

Knowledge leads to not only awareness, but also understanding. Hector knows this fact all too well. As a Two Spirit member of the Chiricahua Apaches, Hector brings light to the presence of autism and mental health conditions (e.g., bipolar disorder, post-traumatic stress disorder) in the Native American community. Because his culture only recognizes disability as a limitation imposed by environmental factors, accessibility and accommodations for people with disabilities are scarce. Without increasing awareness, this situation is unlikely to change.

For this reason, Hector advocates for turning one's disability into what he calls a "purpose-ability," that is, finding a way to make a difference despite the challenges that may be presented by one's disabilities. A large part of his focus is on issues affecting people, families, and communities impacted by disabilities. He regularly volunteers for a number of organizations, including the National Alliance on Mental Illness, the Women Shelter of Long Beach, Organizing for Action (a grassroots movement to enroll U.S. citizens in

health care), the California Mental Health Services Oversight and Accountability Commission, and the Workforce Education and Training Consumer and Family Member Employment Advisory Committee.

In addition, Hector lends his expertise in mental health conditions to local government agencies and other organizations. As a self-employed public policy analyst, he provides consulting services, such as reviewing budgets for local mental health programs and evaluating whether they are research-based or successful after implementation. Hector says he enjoys owning his own business because it gives him more control of the end product, but sometimes it's hard waiting for a check to arrive. Even still, Hector appreciates the independence his job provides.

"I force myself to adapt and be independent," he says. "I traveled to Washington, D.C., for the first time by myself for this photo project. I was nervous, but I just said I was going to do it...and I did."

The Disability.gov team would like to thank the staff at the Arlington Public Library for graciously donating their time and space to the No Boundaries Photo Project.

SOURCE: Retrieved January 6, 2015, from https://usodep.blogs.govdelivery.com/2014/07/09/living-with-no-boundaries-meet-hector/#more-8542.

# A Changing Era in the Lives of People with Disabilities

In the 21st century, our expectations for students leaving school and moving into adult life are college or career readiness. Early adulthood begins a new era in life. It is a time of change—a transition from dependence on the family to increasing responsibilities. Young adults are concerned with furthering their education, earning a living, establishing their pathways through life, and creating social networks. As an adolescent leaves high school, decisions need to be made. Each of us may reflect on several questions: What kind of career or job do I desire? Should I further my education to increase my career choices? Where shall

I live and with whom shall I live? How shall I spend my money? With whom do I choose to spend time? Who will be my friends?

Although most young people face these choices as a natural part of growing into adult life, the challenges confronting individuals with disabilities and their families may be different. For many, the choice may be to disappear into the fabric of society and try to make it on their own without the supports and services that were so much a part of their experience growing up. Others may choose to go to college, seeking the needed accommodations (such as more time to take tests, large-print books, or interpreters) that will give them a fighting chance to succeed in an academic world. Still others will need continuing supports to find and keep a job and to live successfully in the community.

Given the expectations for adult life, the school's responsibility is to teach the skills that will assist each individual with disabilities to achieve valued postschool outcomes. Much has been done to improve the quality of life for adults with disabilities, and much more remains to be done to ensure that every person with a disability is able to access the services or supports necessary for success following graduation from school.

**CEC**

**Standard 6**
Professional Learning and
Ethical Practice

## 4-1 Research on the Lives of Adults with Disabilities

One measure of the effectiveness of a school program is the success of its graduates. Nearly four decades have passed since the passage of the federal mandate to provide a free and appropriate public education to all students with disabilities. The educational opportunities afforded by this landmark legislation have not yet led to full participation of special education graduates in the social and economic mainstream of their local communities (Kessler Foundation and the National Organization on Disability [N.O.D.], 2010). However, there have been some very positive changes. Whereas follow-up studies of special education graduates in the 1990s suggested that these individuals had higher unemployment rates, lower rates of participation in postsecondary education, and less extensive support networks than their peers without disabilities (Hasazi, Furney, & Destefano, 1999; Wagner & Blackorby, 1996), the U.S. Department of Education's *National Longitudinal Transition Study-2* (NLTS-2) (Newman et al., 2011) reported that progress had been made in several areas. The study revealed that 60 percent of young adults with disabilities continued on to some level of postsecondary education within eight years of leaving high school, while 67 percent reported working full-time. Further, the study showed that within eight years of leaving high school, 59 percent of young adults with disabilities lived independently and 4 percent lived semi-independently.

**CEC**

**Standard 2**
Learning Environments

### 4-1a High School Completion and Access to Valued Postschool Outcomes

The increasing emphasis on the transition from school to adult life has altered many earlier perceptions about people with disabilities. Without question, the potential of adults with disabilities has been significantly underestimated. In recent years, professionals and parents have begun to address some of the crucial issues facing students with disabilities as the students prepare to leave school and face life as adults in their local communities. More than 400,000 students with disabilities exit school each year, but the dropout rate for these students is nearly twice that of their typical nondisabled peers (Thurlow, Sinclair, & Johnson, 2009). Of the students with disabilities exiting school (ages 14 to 21), only 56.5 percent leave with a high school diploma, compared with 90 percent of their peers without disabilities (U.S. Department of Education, 2011). Although there has been improvement, as evidenced by the results of the NLTS-2 (Newman et al., 2011), too many of the current graduates from special education programs are not adequately prepared for employment and have difficulty accessing further education. They are also unable to locate the critical programs and services necessary for success as adults in their local communities (Kessler and N.O.D., 2010; Wehman, 2011). For people with more severe disabilities, long waiting

## Meet Ellie and Kari and Their "Education for All" Approach to Teaching Math in a High School Classroom

Ellie Goldberg is a general education high school math teacher. Kari Abdal-Khallaq is a special education teacher who specializes in math-related learning problems for high school students with disabilities. Each day Ellie and Kari come together in an inclusive high school classroom to provide math instruction for students who have varying ranges of abilities, learning styles, behavioral challenges, and instructional needs. Together, these teachers use many different strategies to assure every student is focused and on task during instructional time, including classroom rules and expectations, large- and small-group instruction, individual tutoring, tactile activities, written and oral feedback, and extended instructional time. Ellie and Kari have been co-teaching together for three years and have developed a system that truly brings the best of what each teacher has to offer to the students. When asked about the secret to their success, they both agree that communication is the most important factor, followed closely by having enough time for planning together. Their co-teaching arrangement is being used as a model throughout the district.

*Question for Reflection*

What barriers do you think might exist for Ellie and Kari as they plan their curriculum together?

---

lists for employment and housing services prove frustrating (Crockett & Hardman, 2009). Furthermore, individuals with disabilities who enroll in postsecondary education often find that the supports and services they need to achieve success in college are also not available (Babbitt & White, 2002; McDonnell, Kiuhara, & Collier, 2009; Schindler & Kientz, 2013).

## 4-1b   Employment

The U.S. Department of Education's NLTS-2 (Newman et al., 2011) reported that the *probability* of young adults with disabilities working for pay at some time during the first few years out of high school had increased significantly (from 55 percent to 89 percent) between 1987 and 2011. However, the rate of employment for young adults with disabilities lagged significantly behind that of same-age peers without disabilities in 2003 (41 percent versus 63 percent). Worse yet, the unemployment rate Newman et al. reported in 2011 was significantly higher than the findings of the 2010 Kessler and N.O.D. poll, in which only 21 percent of the people with disabilities indicated that they were employed.

## 4-1c   Closing the Gap: Transition Planning and Services

The transition from school to adult life is a complex and dynamic process. Transition planning should culminate with the transfer of support from the school to an adult service agency, access to postsecondary education, or life as an independent adult. The planning process involves a series of choices about which experiences in their remaining school years will best prepare students with disabilities for what lies ahead in the adult world. A successful transition from school to the adult years requires both formal (government-funded) and natural supports (Muller, Schuler, & Yates, 2008; Steere, Rose, & Cavaiuolo, 2007; Wehman, 2011). Historically, providing *formal supports*, such as health care, employment preparation, and supported living, has been emphasized. Only recently has society begun to understand the importance of the family and other *natural support* networks in preparing adolescents with a disability for adult life. Research suggests that the family unit may be the single most powerful force in preparing an adolescent with a disability for the adult years (Drew & Hardman, 2007).

The principal components of an effective transition system include:

- Effective middle (junior high) and high school programs that link instruction to further education (such as college or trade schools) and to valued postschool outcomes (such as employment, independent living, and recreation/leisure activities);

**Standard 5**
Instructional Planning and Strategies

**Transition services**
Coordinated activities designed to help students with disabilities move from school to employment, further education, vocational training, independent living, and community participation.

- A cooperative system of transition planning that involves public education, adult services, and an array of natural supports (family and friends) to ensure access to valued postschool outcomes; and

- The availability of formal government-funded programs following school that meet the unique educational, employment, residential, and leisure needs of people with disabilities in a community setting.

## 4-2  IDEA Transition Planning Requirements

IDEA requires that every student with a disability receives transition services. **Transition services** are a coordinated set of activities for students with disabilities that are designed to facilitate the move from school to employment, further education, vocational training, independent living, and community participation. To be more specific, transition services should possess the following attributes:

- They are designed to be within a results-oriented process—that is, focused on improving the academic and functional achievement of the child with a disability to facilitate the child's movement from school to postschool activities, including postsecondary education, vocational education, integrated employment (including supported employment), continuing and adult education, adult services, independent living, and community participation.

- They are based on the individual child's needs, taking into account the child's strengths, preferences, and interests.

- They are designed to include instruction, related services, community experiences, the development of employment and other postschool adult living objectives, and, when appropriate, acquisition of daily living skills and functional vocational evaluation (IDEA, 2004, PL 108-446, Sec. 602[34]).

IDEA requires that, beginning at age 16 and updated annually, a student's individualized education program (IEP) should include measurable postsecondary goals based on age-appropriate transition assessments related to training, education, employment, and, where appropriate, independent living skills. The IEP must include a statement of transition services related to various courses of study (such as participation in advanced placement courses or a vocational education program) that will assist the student in reaching her or his goals (IDEA, 2004, PL 108-446, Sec. 614[d]).

**Standard 6**
Professional Learning and Ethical Practice

### 4-2a  Other Federal Laws Linked to IDEA and Transition Planning

Five other pieces of federal legislation are linked directly to the IDEA transition requirements to facilitate an effective transition planning process. They are the Vocational Rehabilitation Act, the Carl D. Perkins Vocational and Applied Technology Education Act, the Americans with Disabilities Act (ADA), the School-to-Work Opportunities Act, and the Ticket to Work and Work Incentives Improvement Act. The Vocational Rehabilitation Act provides services through rehabilitation counselors in several areas (such as guidance counseling, vocational evaluation, vocational training and job placement, transportation, family services, interpreter services, and telecommunication aids and devices). Amendments to the act have encouraged stronger collaboration and outreach between the schools and the rehabilitation counselors in transition planning.

Greater connections between education and vocational rehabilitation are expected to help students with disabilities to move on to postsecondary education or obtain employment. The Carl D. Perkins Vocational and Applied Technology Education Act provides students with disabilities greater access to vocational education services. ADA addresses equal access to public accommodations, employment, transportation, and telecommunication services following the school transition years (see Chapter 1). Such services are often directly targeted as a part of the student's transition plan.

The School-to-Work Opportunities Act provides all students in public schools with education and training to prepare them for first jobs in high-skill, high-wage careers, and for further education following high school. Students with disabilities are specifically identified as a target population of the act. The Ticket to Work and Work Incentives Improvement Act provides people with disabilities greater opportunities for employment by allowing them to work and still keep critical health care coverage. Prior to the passage of this act, many people with disabilities were not able to work because federal Social Security laws put them at risk of losing Medicaid and Medicare coverage if they accrued any significant earnings. Thus, there was little incentive for people with disabilities to work because they could not access health insurance. The Work Incentives Improvement Act made health insurance available and affordable when a person with a disability went to work or developed a significant disability while working.

**Person-centered transition planning**
Planning process based on an understanding of and a commitment to each student's needs and preferences, and developed and implemented within each student's IEP.

## 4-3 Person-Centered Transition Planning

Transition involves more than the mere transfer of administrative responsibility from the school to an adult service agency. **Person-centered transition planning** is based on an understanding of and commitment to each student's needs and preferences, and must be developed and implemented within each student's IEP. The process includes access to the general education curriculum and a focus on the adaptive and functional skills that will facilitate life in the community following school (Bakken & Obiakor, 2008; Hagner et al., 2014; Steere, Rose, & Cavaiuolo, 2007; Wehman, 2011).

See Figure 4.1 for an illustration of person-centered transition planning in the area of employment preparation. The purpose of the transition statement is to (1) identify the type and range of transitional services and supports, and (2) establish timelines and personnel responsible for completing the plan. Wehman (2011) identifies six basic steps in the person-centered transition planning process. These are listed in Figure 4.2.

**CEC**

**Standard 5**
Instructional Planning and Strategies

### 4-3a Facilitating Student and Parent Involvement

In the transition from school to adult life, many students and parents receive quite a shock. Once they leave school, students may not receive any further assistance from government programs or, at least, they may be placed on long waiting lists for employment training,

**CEC**

**Standard 6**
Professional Learning and Ethical Practice

---

**👥 CASE STUDY ON EMBRACING DIVERSITY**

### LoQuisha

LoQuisha is a 17-year-old junior in high school who has a learning disability and uses a wheelchair due to spina bifida. She and her three siblings are being raised by their grandmother, Evi Stevens. Evi works two jobs to provide for the children and is rarely available to participate in meetings. In many ways LoQuisha is a typical teenager in this high-poverty school. She is popular, outgoing, and loves to create art. She and her teacher, Mr. Milner, have been discussing her transition plan, and she has indicated that she would like to go to college to study art. LoQuisha is

afraid to share her plans with her grandmother because she doesn't think she will be supported. Her grandmother is concerned about funding LoQuisha's college because her resources are already stretched so thin to provide for LoQuisha and her siblings.

LoQuisha lives near a community college and has access to public transportation. Mr. Milner is supportive of LoQuisha's goal and has offered to schedule a visit to the community college. He has assured her that she can be successful in college and that the

school offers support for students who have disabilities. LoQuisha is worried that her grandmother will not approve her transition plan if it includes college.

*Application Questions*

**1.** When is LoQuisha's transition plan required to be in place?

**2.** What strategies could Mr. Milner use to help LoQuisha prepare for college?

**3.** How would you help LoQuisha address her grandmother's concerns about college tuition?

Student: *Robert Brown*

Meeting Date: *January 20, 2015*

Graduation Date: *June, 2016*

IEP/Transition Planning Team Members: *Robert Brown (student), Mrs. Brown (parent), Jill Green (teacher), Mike Weatherby (Vocational Education), Dick Rose (Rehabilitation), Susan Marr (SPED)*

TRANSITION PLANNING AREA: *Employment*

Student Preferences and
Desired Postschool Goals: *Robert would like to work in a grocery store as a produce stocker.*

Present Levels of Performance: *Robert has held several work experience placements in local grocery stores (see attached work placement summaries). He requires a self-management checklist using symbols to complete assigned work tasks. His rate of task completion is below the expected employer levels.*

Needed Transition Services: *Robert will require job placement, training, and follow-along services from an employment specialist. In addition, he needs bus training to get to his job.*

ANNUAL GOAL: *Robert will work Monday through Friday from 1:00 to 4:00 p.m. at Safeway's Food Center as a produce stocker, completing all assigned tasks without assistance from the employment specialist on ten consecutive weekly performance probes.*

**Benchmarks Aligned with Alternate Achievement Standards:**

1. When given his bus pass, Robert will independently take the number 5 outbound bus to Safeway's Food Center on five consecutive daily performance probes.
2. When given his bus pass, Robert will independently take the number 11 inbound bus to the Mill Hollow bus stop on five consecutive daily performance probes.
3. When given a self-management checklist using symbols, Robert will initiate all assigned tasks without prompts from the employment specialist on five consecutive daily performance probes.
4. During break, Robert will purchase a drink and snack from the deli without prompts from the employment specialist on five consecutive daily performance probes.

| Activities | Person | Completion Date |
|---|---|---|
| 1. Place Robert on the state-supported employment waiting list. | Susan Marr | May 1, 2015 |
| 2. Obtain a monthly bus pass. | Mrs. Brown | February 1, 2016 |
| 3. Schedule Robert for employee orientation training. | | February 16, 2016 |

SOURCE: Adapted from Polychronis, S., & McDonnell, J. (2009). "Developing IEPs/transition plans." In J. McDonnell & M.L. Hardman (Eds.), *Successful transition programs* (pp. 81–100). Los Angeles: Sage Publishing Co.

housing, or education assistance. Thus, a person with a disability may experience a significant loss in services at a crucial time. Many students and their parents know little, if anything, about what life may bring during the adult years.

To fully prepare for the transition from school, students and parents must be educated about critical components of adult service systems, including the characteristics of service agencies and what constitutes a good program, as well as current and potential opportunities for employment, independent living, or further education (Margolis & Prichard, 2008; Payne-Christiansen & Sitlington, 2008; Winn & Hay, 2009). Wehmeyer (2014) describes the important role a family plays in helping their young adult with a disability develop self-determination skills, which will be discussed in the following section. Families and schools should work together in the transition process to ensure that the student's hopes, plans, and needs are central in the planning process. One way

1. Convene IEP teams, individualized to reflect the wants and needs of each transition-age student.
   - Identify all transition-age students.
   - Identify appropriate school service personnel.
   - Identify appropriate adult service agencies.
   - Identify appropriate members of the student's networks.

2. Review assessment data and conduct additional assessment activities.
   - Meet with transition-age student and a small circle of friends, family members, co-workers, neighbors, church members, and/or staff to establish the individual's needs and preferences for adult life.

3. Teams develop IEPs/Transition IEPs.
   - Schedule the IEP meeting.
   - Conduct the IEP meeting.
   - Open the IEP/transition IEP meeting.

4. Implement the IEP or transition IEP.
   - Operate according to guidelines defined in interagency agreements.
   - Use the Circle of friends/Circle of support: a group of individuals who meet regularly to work on behalf of and support a person with disabilities. These circles work to "open doors" to new opportunities for the person with disabilities, including establishing new friendships.

5. Update the IEP/transition IEP annually and implement follow-up procedures.
   - Phase out involvement of school personnel, while increasing involvement of adult service agencies.
   - Contact people responsible for completion of IEP/transition IEP goals to monitor progress.

6. Hold an exit meeting.
   - Ensure most appropriate employment outcome or access to further education.
   - Ensure most appropriate community living and recreation outcome.
   - Ensure referrals to all appropriate adult agencies and support services.

SOURCE: Wehman, P. (2006). Individualized transition planning. In P. Wehman (Ed.), *Life beyond the classroom: Transition strategies for young people with disabilities,* 4th ed. (pp. 78–95). Baltimore: Paul H. Brookes.

to do this is using a person-centered approach to transition planning, where the student is at the core of the planning process and the school works with parents to identify the student's preferences and expectations.

## 4-3b Working with Adult Services

In addition to the student, parents, and school personnel, professionals from adult service agencies (such as vocational rehabilitation counselors, representatives from university or college centers for students with disabilities, and the state developmental disability agency) may also be involved in transition planning. **Adult service agencies** assist individuals with disabilities in accessing postsecondary education, employment, supported living, and/or leisure activities.

**Photo 4.1** Schools have many roles in the transition planning process. What do you think are a school's most important responsibilities in facilitating a successful transition from school to adult life?

altrendo images/Getty Images

**Adult service agencies** Agencies that provide services and supports to assist people with disabilities to become more independent as adults.

## Reflections on Inclusive Education and Parent Involvement at the Secondary Level

### A Blog by Lisa Dieker and Selma Powell

*Dr. Lisa Dieker is a parent of a student with a disability as well as a professor and Lockheed Martin Eminent Scholar at the University of Central Florida. Selma Powell is a doctoral candidate at the University of Central Florida.*

To include or not to include? That is the question every parent has to struggle with as his or her child progresses through the school; issues related to placement options for students with disabilities are challenging. This question is a complex one for parents, teachers, administrators, and even students to answer, as grade point averages become more and more important for college admissions or future career options. Therefore, what *is* the least restrictive environment for all students? That is a question that becomes even more complex as students enter middle and high school.

As an educator and a parent of a student with a disability, I (Lisa Dieker) can share that our family has had these same struggles. Compound the parent role with what both of us (Lisa and Selma) know about secondary schools and we will share some of the reasons the struggle at the secondary level exists. Many parents struggle with the right balance between their child participating in inclusive settings and closing gaps that might still exist for students as they progress in grade level. In addition, parents must consider a range of service delivery options when GPAs count, and there are few instances of general and special educators teaching together. Not only are students transforming intellectually, emotionally, sexually, and socially, but also teachers' identities seem to change from foregrounding children to foregrounding discipline knowledge. In this blog, we share what we have seen that works for secondary schools that develop successful inclusive education contexts.

We both have worked with students, families, teachers, and administrators in the roles of special educator, general educator, administrator, and researcher in secondary schools. We want to celebrate the great secondary schools we have seen that have successfully included students with disabilities to the maximum extent possible and appropriate, a decision we believe can only be made by students with disabilities and their parents/guardians. So what do these successful secondary schools look like? From visiting hundreds of schools at this level, we have seen common themes to what works…

- **Technology use and adoption:** Schools provided students with disabilities with tools that they were taught to use to meet their unique needs to become successful independent learners.

- **Self-advocacy preparation:** Students were aware of their disability and how to advocate for their own needs.

- **Grading:** Grading was discussed across schools and teams as a way to report to parents student progress (e.g., standard-based report cards, portfolios).

- **Homework:** Teachers coordinated efforts across the school and teams to provide a logical structure to when homework was assigned and was due.

- **Teams:** Teachers (both general and special education) were aligned by content teams, grade-level teams, or professional learning communities to work together toward the success of all students.

- **Collaborative teaching:** Teachers were in classrooms working together with special educators, general educators, English as a second language teachers, reading specialists, and speech therapists.

- **Behavior:** Schools had discussed the need for similar rules and consequences, with many using positive behavioral intervention support models.

- **Active learning:** Students were not in rows, but actively engaged in cooperative learning or peer support groups.

SOURCE: Adapted from Dieker, L., & Powell, S. (2012). "reflection on inclusive practices at the secondary level." Retrieved February 19, 2012, from www.niusileadscape.org/bl/?p=762# more-762.

Agencies may provide support in vocational rehabilitation, social services, and mental health. Examples of supports include career, education, or mental health counseling, job training and support (such as a job coach), further education (college or trade school), attendant services, and interpreter services. Adult service agencies should become involved early in transition planning to begin targeting the services that will be necessary once the student leaves school. Adult service professionals should collaborate with the school in establishing transition goals and identifying appropriate activities for the student during the final school years. Additionally, adult service professionals must be involved in developing information systems that can effectively track students as they leave school, and should monitor the availability and appropriateness of services to be provided during adulthood (Wehman, 2011).

# 4-4 Preparing Students for Adult Life: Instructional Focus for College and Career Readiness

Successful transition begins with a solid foundation, and the school is an essential component of that foundation. Secondary schools have many roles in the transition process: teaching students the skills they need for college and career; assessing individual needs; helping each student develop an IEP/transition plan; coordinating transition planning with adult service agencies; participating with parents and students in the planning process; and providing experiences to facilitate access to community services and employment. For one student, these experiences may include learning to shop in a neighborhood grocery store and training for a job in the community. For another student with a disability who has different needs and abilities, the activities may be more academically oriented to prepare the student for college.

Several outcomes are expected for students with disabilities as they enter adulthood. First, they should be able to function as independently as possible in their daily lives; their reliance on others to meet their needs should be minimized. As students with disabilities leave school, they should be able to make choices about where they will live, how they will spend their free time, and whether they will be employed in the community or go on to college. Secondary schools are in the unique position of being able to coordinate activities that enhance student participation in the community and link students with needed programs and services. College and career readiness require that students take ownership of learning (e.g., self-determination), which includes goal setting, persistence, self-awareness, motivation, progress monitoring, and self-efficacy (Conley, 2012). Several instructional practices are at the core of evidence-based secondary programs for students with disabilities. These include teaching self-determination, academic skills, adaptive and functional life skills, college preparation, and employment preparation (McDonnell, Hardman, & McGuire, 2007; Rowe, Mazzotti, & Sinclair, 2015).

## 4-4a Teaching Self-Determination

Self-determination plays a critical role in the successful transition from school to adult life (Bremer, Kachgal, & Schoeller, 2003; Getzel & Thoma, 2008; Pierson et al., 2008; Shogren et al., 2014; Wehmeyer, Gragoudas, & Shogren, 2006). Definitions of self-determination focus on a person's ability to consider options and make appropriate decisions and to exercise free will, independence, and individual responsibility (University of Illinois at Chicago National Research and Training Center, 2009). The need for secondary schools to teach self-determination skills is evident from research on positive transition outcomes. Wehmeyer, Gragoudas, and Shogren (2006) indicate that "teaching effective decision-making and problem-solving skills has been shown to enhance positive transition outcomes for youth and young adults" (p. 45). These include the reduction of problem behaviors, improved outcomes in community-based instruction, and the promotion of choice-making opportunities in vocational tasks. Teaching self-determination skills to students with disabilities helps them become more efficient in acquiring knowledge and solving problems (Agran et al., 2008; Bambara, Browder, & Kroger, 2006; Finn, Getzel, & McManus, 2008; Smith et al., 2008; Wehmeyer, 2014). Students become better able to achieve goals that will facilitate their transition out of school and become aware of the specific challenges they will face in the adult years. Ultimately, students leave school with a more highly developed sense of personal worth and social responsibility and with better problem-solving skills.

Creating opportunities for individual choice and decision making is an important element in the transition from school to adult life. Each individual must be able to consider options and make appropriate choices. This means less problem solving and decision making on the part of service providers and family members and a greater focus on teaching and promoting choice. The planning process associated with the development of a student's IEP is an excellent opportunity to promote self-determination. Unfortunately, very few adolescents with disabilities attend their IEP meetings, and even fewer actively participate (Wehman, 2011).

**CEC**

**Standard 1**
Learner Development and Individual Learning Differences

**Standard 5**
Instructional Planning and Strategies

## 4-4b   Teaching Academic Skills and Access to the General Curriculum

Research suggests that students with disabilities are not faring as well as they could be in the academic content of high school programs or in postsecondary education (U.S. Department of Education, 2011). As mentioned earlier, these students have higher school dropout rates and lower academic achievement than their peers without disabilities. However, the research also suggests that students with disabilities can achieve in academic content beyond their current performance (Friend & Bursuck, 2006; Lock & Layton, 2008). The Partnership for 21st Century Skills (2014) developed a vision for student success that integrates the essential skills necessary for the workplace with the support systems schools can offer. The model can be seen in Figure 4.3. High school programs can support student success using the following strategies:

**Standard 1**
Learner Development and Individual Learning Differences

**Standard 5**
Instructional Planning and Strategies

- Develop teaching strategies based on the unique learning characteristics of each student.
- Take into account the cultural background of each student and its effect on learning.
- Determine each student's strongest learning modes (visual, auditory, and/or tactile) and adapt instruction accordingly.
- Use technology to support learning (e.g., tablets, laptops, and smartphones) to help students capitalize on their strengths.
- Create positive learning environments to enable students to feel motivated and build their self-esteem.
- Teach students to advocate for themselves with a clear understanding of accommodations that support their learning.

For students with moderate to severe disabilities, the purpose of academic learning may be more functional and compensatory—to teach skills that have immediate and frequent use in the students' environment (McDonnell & Copeland, 2011). Instruction concentrates on skills needed in the students' daily living routine. For example, safety skills may include reading street signs, railroad crossings, entrance/exit signs, or product labels. Information skills may include completing a job application, reading recipes, using transit maps, and accessing smart technology and computers.

With an increasing emphasis on academics and increasing access to the general curriculum, there is a growing concern about students with disabilities and the opportunity to earn a high school diploma. Because employers view the high school diploma as a

*Figure 4.3  Key Elements for 21st-Century Learning*

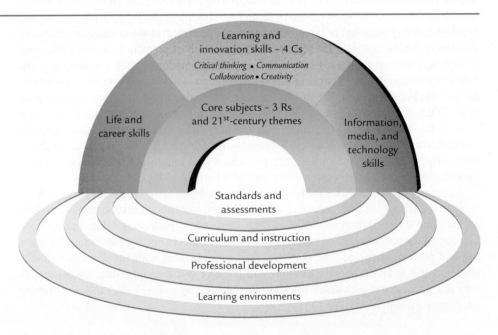

minimum requirement signaling competence, what does this mean for students with disabilities who are unable to meet academic criteria? Many students with disabilities do not receive the same high school diploma as their peers without disabilities. Some states and local school districts have adopted graduation requirements that specify successful completion of a number of credits to receive a diploma. Students with disabilities must meet the same requirements as their peers to receive a "regular" high school

*Photo 4.2* In many school districts, students with disabilities must meet the same requirements as their peers without disabilities to receive a high school diploma. Do you think students with disabilities should be held to the same academic standard as those who are not disabled?

diploma. Many states have instituted exit exams as part of the high school graduation requirements. If a student with a disability fails to meet graduation requirements, he or she may be awarded an "IEP diploma," marking progress toward annual goals, or a certificate of high school completion (or attendance). IEP diplomas and certificates of completion communicate that a student was unable to meet the requirements to obtain a standard diploma.

Other states award students with disabilities the standard high school diploma based on modified criteria that are individually referenced, reflecting the successful completion of IEP goals and objectives as determined by a multidisciplinary team of professionals and the student's parents.

## 4-4c Teaching Adaptive and Functional Life Skills

Students with disabilities in the secondary school years need access to social activities. Adaptive and functional life skills training may include accessing socialization activities in and outside school and learning to manage one's personal affairs. It may be important to provide basic instruction on how to develop positive interpersonal relationships and the behaviors that are conducive to successfully participating in community settings (Allen, Ciancio, & Rutkowski, 2008; Hansen & Morgan, 2008; Harchik & Ladew, 2008; Joseph & Konrad, 2009; Manley et al., 2008; McDonnell, 2009; Wehman, 2011). Instruction may include co-teaching among general and special education teachers, as well as the use of peer tutors to both model and teach appropriate social skills in community settings such as restaurants, theaters, or shopping malls. See the nearby Reflect on This, "Tips and Strategies for Co-Teaching at the Secondary Level."

## 4-4d College Preparation

Going to college is often a lifelong dream for people with and without disabilities. Today, students who received special education services in high school are attending career and vocational schools, two- and four-year colleges, and universities at higher rates than in the past (Newman et al., 2011). High school teachers play a pivotal role in preparing students to transition to higher education. Hamblet (2014) suggests these steps to improve college transition planning:

- Educate the IEP team members and the special education faculty about legal and systematic changes in colleges.
- Reach out to families to help them understand what support services are in place in colleges.
- Encourage students' future independence by developing skills that will be necessary in college (e.g., developing study guides and organizing schedules).
- Teach students to use assistive technology.

## Tips and Strategies for Co-Teaching at the Secondary Level

Co-teaching can be a powerful tool in meeting the needs of all students, including those with disabilities in middle and high school settings. However, the success of a co-teaching experience is dependent upon many factors, including but certainly not limited to:

- Clearly defined roles for both the general and special education teacher in regard to teaching instructional content and pedagogical approaches to learning;
- Taking advantage of the unique teaching styles of both the general and special education teacher;
- Instruction in subject matter areas that is focused on access to the general education curriculum while at the same time meeting the individualized needs of students with disabilities;

- Continuous progress monitoring of student learning within and across subject matter areas;
- Creating time to plan a curriculum, teaching, and evaluation strategies together; and
- Strong administrative support for instructional planning time, scheduling, and ongoing professional development.

Nierengarten (2013) suggests strategies for secondary-level general and special education teachers and administrators to consider in developing a co-teaching model:

- Involve an administrator and be sure that she/he has training to understand co-teaching.
- Allow teachers to choose to participate in co-teaching. Choice will give a

sense of ownership and increase the likelihood of success.

- Train teachers prior to implementing co-teaching.
- Select appropriate ratios of students with and without IEPs. It is best to keep in mind natural proportions.
- Nurture an inclusive attitude in school.
- Create a common planning time before the implementation begins.

### Question for Reflection

Several strategies for enhancing the success of co-teaching at the secondary level are presented in this feature. What additional tips would you offer to general and special education teachers who are just beginning to work together in a co-teaching situation?

---

- Give students the documentation they need. Most colleges will not accept an evaluation that is more than three years old.
- Educate students about their disabilities and their strengths.
- Explicitly teach learning and organizational strategies.
- Ensure that students are prepared to apply for accommodations at college.
- Support students in understanding the differences between the systems of service provision in high schools and in higher education.

**CEC**

**Standard 5**
Instructional Planning
and Strategies

**Work experience program**
Programs that allow students to spend a portion of the school day in a classroom setting (focusing on academic and/or vocational skills) and a portion of the day at an off-campus site receiving on-the-job training.

## 4-4e Employment Preparation

People with disabilities are sometimes characterized as consumers of society's resources rather than as contributors, but employment goes a long way toward dispelling this idea. Paid employment means earning wages, through which individuals can buy material goods and enhance their quality of life; it also contributes to personal identity and status (Crockett & Hardman, 2009; Drew & Hardman, 2007).

In the past, high schools have been somewhat passive in their approach to employment training, focusing primarily on teaching vocational readiness through simulations in a classroom setting. More recently, high schools have begun to emphasize employment preparation for students with disabilities through work experience, career education, and community-based instruction. In a **work experience program**, students spend a portion of the school day in classroom settings (which may emphasize academic and/or vocational skills) and the rest of the day at an off-campus site receiving on-the-job training. Responsibility for the training may be shared among the high school special education teacher, vocational rehabilitation counselor, and vocational education teacher.

**Career education** includes training in social skills as well as general occupational skills. Career education programs usually concentrate on developing an awareness of various career choices, exploring occupational opportunities, and developing appropriate attitudes, social skills, and work habits.

Whereas career education is oriented to developing an awareness of various occupations, **community-referenced instruction** involves direct training and ongoing support, as necessary, in a community employment site. The demands of the work setting and the functioning level, interests, and wishes of each individual determine the goals and objectives of the training. The most notable difference between community-referenced instruction and work experience programs is that the former focuses on the activities to be accomplished at the work site rather than on the development of isolated skills in the classroom. An employment training program based on a community-referenced approach includes the following elements:

- Primary focus on student and family needs and preferences
- A balance between time spent in inclusive general education classrooms and in placement and employment preparation at least until age 18
- A curriculum that reflects the job opportunities available in the local community
- An employment training program that takes place at actual job sites
- Training designed to sample the student's performance across a variety of economically viable alternatives
- Ongoing opportunities for students to interact with peers without disabilities in a work setting
- Training that culminates in employment placement
- Job placement linked to comprehensive transition planning, which focuses on establishing interagency agreements that support the student's full participation in the community (Drew & Hardman, 2007)

For more insight into transition preparation during the high school years, see the Case Study on Embracing Diversity, "LoQuisha," earlier in this chapter.

## Looking Toward a Bright Future

During the middle and high school years, the challenges associated with receiving quality services and supports for students with disabilities are ever-changing, varied, and complex. For middle and high school-age students, there are clear expectations that they must achieve the same high academic standards as their peers without disabilities in general education classrooms. This expectation will become reality only when there is positive and ongoing communication between educators and families, as well as new and innovative approaches to address diverse learning needs across the curriculum (Stenhoff, Davey, & Lignugaris/Kraft, 2008; Wehmeyer, 2014; Worrell, 2008).

As students with disabilities transition from school to adult life, these young adults must be able to participate in a coordinated system of services and supports that will help them find work, housing, or recreational and leisure activities (McGuire & McDonnell, 2008). Many will find jobs or go on to postsecondary education if they have been taught the academic, technical, and social skills necessary to find and/or maintain employment. The transition requirements of the IDEA are designed to help students successfully leave school to live and work within the community or go on to further education. Today, more students with disabilities are participating in postsecondary education than ever before. Nearly 60 percent of these students go on to attend some courses at a college, university, or applied technical school (Newton & Dell, 2010).

**Career education**
Education that focuses on developing an awareness of various career choices, exploring occupational opportunities, and developing the skills and attitudes that lead to greater success in the workplace.

**Community-referenced instruction**
Involves direct training and ongoing support, as necessary, in a community employment site. The demands of the work setting and the functioning level, interests, and wishes of each individual determine the goals and objectives of the training.

## 4-1 Discuss the research on the lives of adults with disabilities.

- The educational opportunities afforded under IDEA have not yet led to full participation of special education graduates in the social and economic mainstream of their local communities.
- However, there has been considerable improvement. The National Longitudinal Transition Study-2 reports that progress has been made in several areas (high school completion, living arrangements, social involvement, further education, and employment rates).
- Adult service systems have inadequate resources to meet the needs of students with disabilities following the school years.
- The capabilities of adults with disabilities are often underestimated.

## 4-2 Describe the IDEA transition planning requirements.

- IDEA requires that every student with a disability receive transition services.
- Transition planning is designed to be a results-oriented process focused on improving the academic and functional achievement of a child with a disability to facilitate the child's movement from school to postschool activities.
- Transition services must be based on the individual student's needs, taking into account the student's preferences and interests.
- Transition services must include a focus on postsecondary education, vocational education, integrated employment (including supported employment), continuing and adult education, adult services, independent living, and/or community participation.
- IDEA requires that, beginning at age 16 and updated annually, a student's individualized education program (IEP) should include measurable postsecondary goals based on age-appropriate transition assessments related to training, education, employment, and, where appropriate, independent living skills.
- The IEP must include a statement of transition services related to various courses of study (such as participation in advanced placement courses or a vocational education program) that will assist the student in reaching her or his goals.

## 4-3 Identify the purpose of person-centered transition planning and the basic steps in its formulation.

- Person-centered transition planning is based on an understanding of and commitment to each student's needs and preferences; it must be developed and implemented within each student's IEP.
- It is a process that ensures each student's access to the general education curriculum and/or a focus on the adaptive and functional skills that will facilitate life in the community following school. The basic steps in person-centered transition planning include
  - Convening the IEP team organized in terms of the preferences and needs of each student
  - Reviewing assessment data and conducting additional assessment activities
  - Developing IEPs/transition IEPs
  - Implementing the IEP/transition IEP
  - Updating the IEP/transition IEP annually and implementing follow-up procedures
  - Holding an exit meeting

## 4-4 Describe the instructional focus used to prepare students for college and career readiness.

- Self-determination skills help students to solve problems, consider options, and make appropriate choices as they transition into adult life.
- Academic skills are essential in meeting high school graduation requirements and preparing students with disabilities for college. A functional academic program helps students learn applied skills in daily living, leisure activities, and employment preparation.
- Adaptive and functional life skills help students learn how to socialize with others, maintain personal appearance, and make choices about how to spend free time.
- College preparation should start early and include a deep understanding of the differences and similarities between high school and higher education. Employment preparation during high school increases the probability of success on the job during the adult years and places the person with a disability in the role of a contributor to society.

## Council for Exceptional Children (CEC) Standards to Accompany Chapter 4

If you are thinking about a career in special education, you should know that many states use national standards developed by the Council for Exceptional Children (CEC) to assess a teacher candidate's knowledge and skills for working with students with disabilities. See a complete listing of the seven CEC Content Standards on the inside cover of this text.

1 Learner Development and Individual Learning Differences
2 Learning Environments
5 Instructional Planning and Strategies
6 Professional Learning and Ethical Practice

## Mastery Activities and Assignments

To master the content within this chapter, complete the following activities and assignments.

1. Complete a written test of the chapter's content. If your instructor requires a written test of your content knowledge for this chapter, keep a copy for your portfolio.
2. Review the Case Study on Embracing Diversity, "LoQuisha," and respond in writing to the Application Questions. Keep a copy of the Case Study and of your written response for your portfolio.
3. Participate in a community service learning activity. Community service is a valuable way to enhance your learning experience. Develop a reflective journal of the service learning experience for your portfolio.

## CHAPTER 5

# Cultural and Linguistic Diversity

CEFutcher /istockphoto.com

## Learning Objectives

*After you complete this chapter, you will be able to:*

**5-1** Describe how the lives of students with disabilities from culturally and/or linguistically diverse backgrounds have changed since the advent of IDEA.

**5-2** Describe the purposes and approaches of bilingual/ESL education and culturally and linguistically responsive education.

**5-3** Describe population trends among culturally and linguistically diverse learners, especially prevalence by race and ethnicity, speakers of other languages, poverty, and migrancy.

**5-4** Describe how these population trends affect public education.

**5-5** Identify ways that public schools can decrease the disproportionality of culturally and linguistically diverse learners (CLDLs) in special education and significantly improve their education.

**5-6** Describe culturally and linguistically responsive special education that supports student learning for CLDLs.

**5-7** Identify promising changes in public education that support culturally and linguistically diverse learners with disabilities.

José came to the United States from Mexico last year with his mother, father, and younger brother. José's father is a mechanic by trade but could not find employment in Mexico. The family moved to the United States hoping to find work with the help of relatives already living there.

José attended school in Mexico for only two years but struggled to perform academically in his rural Mexican school. He was unable to master the alphabet or learn to read in his native language of Spanish. However, José enjoyed the social aspects of school and found friends with whom he played soccer, basketball, and baseball.

Upon arriving in the United States, José entered a fourth-grade mainstream classroom. He was shy and quiet but always had a smile. José tried to assimilate to his new school by learning English phrases such as "Where is the bathroom?", "Can I go and play?", and "What?" He found new friends who could translate for him and who helped him understand the barrage of English he heard each day. He mastered the U.S. school system and understood his responsibilities—to bring back homework, to get

AP Images/Damian Dovarganes

notes to his mother, to be quiet in class, and to draw as little attention to himself as possible.

José continued to have difficulty learning to read in English and in Spanish. He could not recognize the letters in his name or write his last name. He was able to read only four words in English and ten words in Spanish. He diligently took his homework to his parents, and together they tried to complete the tasks he had to do, but no one in the home had enough education or understanding of English to help José. In an attempt to help her son, José's mother insisted he bring books home from the school library, which she had him look at for 45 minutes each afternoon. Though

she only had a third-grade education, José's mother knew that education was vital for her son's future.

Throughout the school year, José made friends and continued to play soccer and other sports. He worked hard but became increasingly frustrated with his lack of academic skill. Because he was unable to do his classroom assignments, he developed coping strategies to pass the time—looking at books, talking to other students, searching for lost papers, and running errands for the teacher. Much of his literacy instruction throughout the year took place outside his classroom. He spent hours in ESL classes and in the remedial reading program.

José, his younger brother, and his mother returned to Mexico. José's father remains in the United States and hopes to be able to support his family through his work as a mechanic. It is the first time the family has ever been separated, and José's mother is hopeful that they will soon be reunited.

SOURCE: Teemant, A., Smith, M. E., Pinnegar, S. (2003). *Bilingual/ESL Endorsement through Distance Education Program: Assessment for Linguistically Diverse Students Instruction Guide*, 2nd ed. Provo, UT: Brigham Young University.

## 5-1 A Changing Era in the Lives of Students with Disabilities from Culturally and/or Linguistically Diverse Backgrounds

Families with culturally and linguistically diverse backgrounds live in an exciting time of change in our U.S. communities. No place represents this better than the public schools. Significant numbers of **culturally and linguistically diverse learners (CLDLs)** are entering public school systems. A vitally important subset of this group of learners includes **emergent bilingual learners (EBLs)**. EBLs are children and youth whose heritage or first language is not English. As such, these learners (CLDLs and EBLs), especially ones with disabilities or presumed disabilities, are important catalysts for change for all educators and service providers. These children, youth, and their parents bring with them a variety of strengths and challenges that create tensions as well as opportunities for educators and others to expand their horizons and fine-tune their practices.

**Culturally and linguistically diverse learners (CLDL)**
Individuals whose culture and/or language is different from the majority of the population. Examples include a person whose first language is Russian living in the United States, or Navajo American Indians who follow the culture of their forefathers.

**Emergent bilingual learner (EBL)**
A person who is in the process of becoming a fluent speaker of two or more languages, including the academic language of the languages.

**Standard 2**
Learning Environments

**English as a second language (ESL)/bilingual education** and **culturally and linguistically responsive education** evolved from a belief that the academic needs of children whose linguistic or cultural backgrounds differed from those of the majority are best supported when we understand who they are, what they and their families bring to the education enterprise, and how this knowledge influences our instructional decision making (González, Moll, & Amanti, 2005).

For children whose heritage language is one other than English, there is clear research that developing academic language in both the L1, their heritage language, and the L2, their emerging English language, support overall academic growth. As you might guess, providing instruction in many L1 languages like Somali, Hmong, and Arabic is exceedingly challenging.

To understand linguistic and cultural diversity, we will first explore educational responses to diversity, ESL/bilingual education, and culturally responsive education, as well as their underlying purposes and approaches. Then, we will examine population trends, disproportionality in special education, and means for addressing disproportionality through culturally responsive special education.

Some of the terms and descriptions used in this chapter to describe culturally and linguistically diverse populations and effective educational practices may be unfamiliar to you because they are emerging terminologies with the goal of more positively describing these individuals. They are the positive terms and descriptions related to serving CLDLs, the "can do's" (WIDA, 2014).

Terms used for students who are English language learners have included **limited English proficient (LEP)** and **English learners (ELs)** or **English language learners (ELLs)**. All of these terms place children or youths in a position of having a deficit. The term *emergent bilingual learners* (EBLs), coined by Ofelia García, is used in this chapter. This term better describes students who are becoming bilingual as they learn English and retain their home language, a much sought-after ability in our present multilingual world of work (Freeman & Freeman, 2014). **Culturally and linguistically responsive teaching (CRT)** is another term used to describe instruction and interactions that respond in positive and effective ways to support decisions about unbiased and accurate assessments and the instructional needs of CLDLs by using culturally and linguistically responsive education models (National Center for Culturally Responsive Educational Systems, 2008).

## 5-2 The Purposes and Approaches of Bilingual/ESL Education and Culturally and Linguistically Responsive Education

Important differences exist between the fundamental purposes of general education, bilingual/ESL education, culturally and linguistically responsive education, and special education. The differences among the goals and approaches of general, special, and culturally and linguistically responsive education often create challenges for school systems and among educators as they struggle to implement state and federally mandated policies, respond to accountability demands and standards, and strive to provide effective instruction to make a difference in the lives of all students.

### 5-2a Dual-Language Immersion/ESL Education and Its Role

The number of states experiencing dramatic increases in populations of EBLs have soared, amplifying the need for public schools to provide educational responses that support the academic and language development of these learners (Freeman & Freeman, 2011). It is important to remember that among this group, we also find all of the same learning challenges and opportunities found in our English-speaking student populations: disabilities, giftedness, lack of academic language for school success, and varying family circumstances that either enhance or impede a child's development.

A lively debate of the "right way" to provide effective teaching and education for EBLs has existed for some time. Two major models for teaching English language proficiency with an emphasis on academic language include different forms of **dual-language or dual-immersion education** and ESL approaches. Dual-language immersion education includes a variety of language instruction programs provided in two languages; for example, one involves EBLs learning English as the target language, and the other involves English speakers learning a target language such as Spanish or Chinese. EBLs benefit from strengthening the heritage language because it supports their learning of academic English. In the first instance, the focus is on the development of academic language skills in the mother tongue or first language (e.g., Spanish, Portuguese) as well as the second language (English). English as a second language (ESL) programs focus on English only. These programs are often pullout programs that include isolated newcomer programs to support students as they learn basic English skills before moving into a regular classroom. The amount of pullout service and the type of scaffolding of these services are determined by the **language development level (LDL)** of the individual learner as determined by state-required language assessments. Currently, this assessment is used in over 37 states in the United States by using the ACCESS test developed by WIDA (WIDA, 2014).

Although we have solid research that bilingual or multilingual educational programs work very well for our EBLs, there are two major reasons why U.S. school systems in general have resisted this approach. First, there are strongly held beliefs that people coming to the United States speaking languages other than English should learn English and that this should be a relatively quick process. Because of this, schools that have bilingual programs (also known as dual immersion) are closely monitored and assessed. The second reason is that these types of programs are generally feasible only with large linguistically similar groups of students such as Spanish speakers. In addition, finding teachers who are dual-immersion trained can also be an issue. Because of this, ESL classes (pullout models) are the typical approaches used in most schools (Freeman & Freeman, 2007; Ovando, Combs, & Collier, 2006). There is usually no support for the first language (L1) in these programs. An important note here is that ESL teachers, because of their professional preparation, are immersed in culturally responsive practices, thus allowing them to be very adept in responding to children, their backgrounds, and cultures. The importance of understanding cultural sameness and difference in strengthening academic learning outcomes is imperative to the academic success of EBLs (Ovando, Combs, & Collier, 2006).

## 5-2b Culturally and Linguistically Responsive Education and Its Role

Culturally and linguistically responsive education seeks positive changes in how schools think about children from diverse backgrounds and how to develop instruction and practices that supports their learning (Banks, 2008; Moule, 2012). Understanding this and the impact of collective culture on each individual is an ongoing challenge for professionals in schools (Carpenter, Zarate, & Garza, 2007; Deaux, Reid, & Martin, 2006). The National Center for Culturally Responsive Educational Systems (NCCRESt) defines **cultural responsiveness** as "the ability to learn from and relate respectfully with people of your own culture as well as those from another culture" (National Center for Culturally Responsive Educational Systems, 2008, p. 12). To better understand what culturally and linguistically responsive education is, we briefly examine two theories that support and help define it: modified cultural pluralism and social capital.

The theory of **modified cultural pluralism** encourages the idea of cultural groups retaining their unique characteristics but also building relationships across cultures (Grant, Sleeter, & Grant, 2009). This theory describes the U.S. society as a "patchwork quilt," rather than a "melting pot." Modified cultural pluralism incorporates the ideas associated with **social capital**, which is made up of two kinds of social interactions: (1) bonding capital that strengthens the cultural characteristics within a group, such as a family, a particular religion, or a specific ethnic group; and (2) bridging capital that promotes more formal social ties across cultures to create mutual interests that strengthen the shared society, be it local, state, or national (Flora, 2011).

Standard 2
Learning Environments

Communities high in social capital are characterized by individuals and families that trust one another, join together in achieving common and worthwhile causes, and spend celebratory times together. Cultural pluralism, the teaching about cultural diversity, and how it functions in a culturally pluralistic society is not exclusively aimed at students from linguistically or culturally diverse backgrounds, but all students (Ornstein & Moses, 2005; Riad, 2007). Asserting that **multicultural education** is a concept that addresses cultural diversity, Gollnick and Chinn (2009) cited six beliefs and assumptions on which it is based:

1. Cultural differences have strength and value.

2. Schools should be models for the expression of human rights and respect for cultural differences.

3. Social justice [fairness] and equal access [based on individual rather than the same needs] for all people should be of paramount importance in the design and delivery of curricula.

4. Attitudes and values necessary for the continuation of a democratic society can be promoted in schools.

5. Schooling can provide the knowledge, skills, and dispositions—and the values, attitudes, and commitments—to help students from diverse groups learn.

6. Educators working with families and communities can create an environment that is supportive of multiculturalism [cultural responsiveness]. (p. 4)

This theory and its related practices counter the once-prevalent view that schools should minimize cultural differences (Baldwin, Faulkner, & Hecht, 2006). Further, this notion of cultural pluralism promotes the philosophy that collaboration among multiple cultures creates a stronger, more unified citizenry that can contribute both socially and economically to the well-being of a community and country.

Culturally linguistically responsive education is intended to reduce discrimination, but also to provide the tools necessary to navigate among diverse cultures and within the "majority" culture (Banks, 2008; Sleeter & Grant, 2009). Young people develop many of their enduring attitudes and related knowledge bases, including their thoughts and feelings about diverse cultures, in their classrooms and homes. Incomplete information and clichéd presentations about different cultures detract from deepening students' understanding of the variety of peoples and cultures that characterize our country and world (Arrendondo & Perez, 2006; Vásquez, Lott, & Garcia-Vazquez, 2006). One effective application of cultural pluralism that is being implemented in many schools today is CRT, which will be discussed later in this chapter.

## 5-3 Population Trends Among Culturally and Linguistically Diverse Learners in the United States

It is important to understand the meaning of two terms when discussing the effects of population trends in schools: prevalence and disproportionality. First, **prevalence** refers to the number of people in a given population who exhibit a condition or are placed in a particular category, such as those individuals with a hearing loss, those who speak Spanish, or those of a specific gender. Prevalence is determined by counting how often something occurs in a given population. In this section, we will examine prevalence by certain factors relevant to the relationship between human exceptionalities and CLDL issues.

**Disproportionality** is the overrepresentation or underrepresentation of a specific cultural or ethnic group within a specified setting when compared to the percentage of their representation or prevalence in the general population. For instance, African American male children are overrepresented as students with emotional and behavior disorders. Asian and Pacific Islander students are underrepresented in special education. The opposite is true in gifted and talented programs where Asian students are overrepresented and black American children are underrepresented (Artiles, Kozleski, Trent, Osher, & Ortiz, 2010; Gollnick & Chinn, 2009; National Education Association [NEA], 2008a; Sullivan, 2011). As you might surmise, there is a disproportionate number of CLDLs labeled as disabled and who are served in special education programs.

**Prevalence**
The number of people in a given population who exhibit a condition or particular state; it is determined by counting how often it occurs (e.g., the number of people who speak Spanish or who are identified for special education).

**Disproportionality**
The over- or underrepresentation of a specific cultural or linguistic group represented within a specified setting when compared to the percentage of their representation in the general population.

Although the United States is home to immigrants from around the world, at least one commentator has dubbed the changing population as the "browning of America." This change is primarily a function of significant increases in the number of Hispanic individuals and families that have come to the United States since 1990 (Funkhouser, 2013; Johnson & Kasarda, 2011; Stavans, 2002). Current population estimates suggest that all people of color will make up 41.5 percent of the U.S. population by 2060 (Colby & Ortman, 2015). This change includes both linguistic and cultural diversity affecting both education and the workforce.

In this section, we will examine the prevalence figures for several groups that are proving to be catalysts for change in schools. In this regard, we will examine statistics on prevalence for ethnic and cultural diversity, language diversity, poverty, as well as migrancy. We will also highlight a new phenomenon of unaccompanied minors (children and youth) entering the United States.

**Standard 1**
Learner Development and
Individual Learning
Differences

## 5-3a Cultural and Ethnic Diversity

Several culturally or ethnically diverse groups of people are growing rapidly. In some cases, this rate of growth is twice that of the white population, much in part because of high birthrates and increased entry of individuals entering the southern borders of the United States. The general population for July 1, 2013 was up by an estimated 2.4 percent. Also, an estimated 23.3 percent of the population were 18 and younger (U.S. Census Bureau, 2015). The July 2014 population estimates indicate that Hispanics represented 17.2 percent of the total population, slightly down from 19.2 percent in 2010, but up significantly from 15.1 percent in 2000 (U.S. Census Bureau, 2014b). Hispanics are having children at a much higher rate than their white peers (Perlich, 2011; U.S. Census Bureau, 2012). Figure 5.1 graphically portrays predicted population growth rates in the United States for several key groups between the years of 1990 and 2060. As of 2014 in the United States, the percentage of children of color under 18 had approached majority status (Colby & Ortman, 2015). This increase of culturally and linguistically diverse children does and will have profound impacts on education, challenging school systems and other support services to deliver instruction and assistance that is genuinely helpful to these diverse children, youth, and their families.

## 5-3b Language Diversity

People with diverse language backgrounds constitute a rapidly growing sector of the U.S. population. Between 1990 and 2000, the number of children between 5 and 17 who were EBLs increased by 54.6 percent, and, of those, emergent bilinguals who reported speaking English "not well" or "not at all" grew by 45.7 percent. This represented about 1.33 million children in 2000. By 2007, that number had increased by 5 percent according to recent surveys (Glimpse, 2012; Skinner, Wight, Aratani, Cooper, & Thampi, 2010).

Obviously, the academic language of schooling in the United States is English. Students who do not speak, write, read, or understand English well are at a pronounced disadvantage in benefitting from public education. Thus, it is common for EBLs to struggle with the content

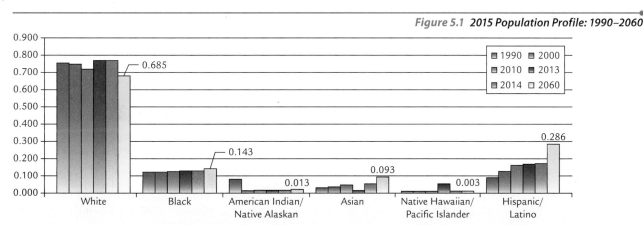

*Figure 5.1 2015 Population Profile: 1990–2060*

SOURCE: From Colby & Ortman, 2015; Grieco & Cassidy, 2001; U.S. Census Brief, 2011; U.S. Department of Commerce, 1995.

learning they must accomplish and eventually master if they are to go on and benefit from any kind of postsecondary education. However, not just the EBL population struggles with academic language issues, as you will learn in the following discussions about poverty and migrancy.

## 5-3c Poverty

From 2007 to 2011, of all children 18 and younger, very close to 20 percent were living in poverty as defined by established federal standards (Macartney, Bishaw, & Fontenot, 2013). This was a significant increase from 2000. For children by race or ethnicity, poverty among African Americans remains the highest at 36.9 percent, an increase of 5.7 percent since 2000. The prevalence rate for Hispanic children in poverty went from 28.4 percent in 2000 to 30.4 percent in 2014. When these two groups of children are compared to the white, non-Hispanic groups, there is almost a 20 percent difference, which is highly significant statistically. White children had a poverty rate of 9.1 percent in 2000 and 10.7 percent between 2007 and 2011. It is interesting to note here that the highest level of child poverty exists in families where the mother (any race or ethnicity) is the head of household with no spouse present, a rate of 45.8 percent (ASPE Issue Brief, 2014; Macartney, Bishaw, & Fontenot, 2013; U.S. Census Bureau, 2014a).

Poverty is found more often in CLDL populations than in mainstream populations and is also associated with higher risk of academic problems. Examples that graphically describe the difference in ethnic or cultural groups include the 2013 comparison of white and Asian children in poverty, 15.9 and 9.8 percent, respectively, to black and Hispanic children in poverty, 36.7 and 30 percent, respectively (U.S. Census Bureau, 2014b). Figure 5.2 summarizes

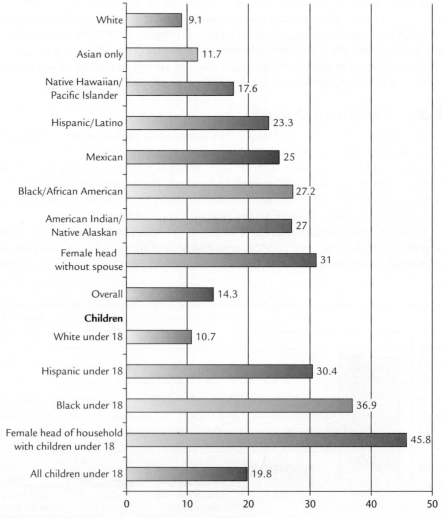

*Figure 5.2  U.S. Poverty Rates: 2007–2011 by Selected Characteristics*

SOURCE: Adapted from Macartney, Bishaw, & Fontenot (2013).

poverty rates across several demographic characteristics (Bratter & Eschbach, 2005; Evans & Kim, 2007; Feldman, 2005; Skiba, Poloni-Staudinger, & Simmons, 2005; U.S. Census Bureau, 2014a).

Environmental factors such as lack of pre- and postnatal nutrition, potential exposure to high-risk environments, and limited health care for children from impoverished settings may also play strong roles in the lives of these children and their challenges in benefitting from education. These factors also contribute to the likelihood of these children developing disabilities (Emerson & Hatton, 2007; McDonough, Sacker, & Wiggins, 2005). In addition, recent research suggests increased risk is related to diminished brain development in areas affecting school success such as attention, problem-solving skills, as well as vocabulary and language development (Kishiyama, Boyce, Jimenez, Perry, & Knight, 2008). The effects of impoverished environments continue to cast shadows of health risk beyond childhood and often over a lifetime, which may give rise to shortened life expectancies, more chronic health problems, and neurological problems (Hallerod & Larsson, 2008; Kishiyama et al., 2008; McDonough, Sacker, & Wiggins, 2005; Skiba, Poloni-Staudinger, & Simmons, 2005).

## 5-3d Migrancy

The United States is the top migrant destination in the world. The largest surge in **immigration** happened between 1900 and 1910; the next biggest surge was in 1990, spiking at about 1.8 million. Immigration decreased until the most recent surge in 2010, but it was still significantly below the 1990 influx. As of 2013, immigration is down to below one million (Banks, 2008; Monger & Yankay, 2013; Perlich, 2010).

According to 2013 statistics on immigration, 990,553 individuals obtained green cards for permanent residency. Of this group, 400,000 were from Asia, and 301,479, or 30 percent, were from North and Central America, not including Canada. Mexico leads all other countries in the number of individual immigrants receiving permanent residency. About half of these new permanent residents were sponsored by families already living in the United States (Peoplemovin, 2010; Monger & Yankay, 2014). Of this group of legal immigrants, 165,713 came for professional jobs, 160,301 are working in farm, fishery, forestry, production, transportation, or moving industries, while 181,041 of the work-eligible people remained unemployed (Department of Homeland Security, 2014).

Another group to consider are refugees seeking asylum. Of the 69,909 refugees, 19,793 were school-aged children (Department of Homeland Security, 2014). These children come to school often with very limited education and often having been traumatized by life-threatening situations. Many have known nothing but the poverty and the challenges of growing up in refugee camps where they resided before coming to the United States.

A new term, **in-migration**, has immerged to explain the increasing movement between states (Perlich, 2010). This moving is usually for the purpose of securing employment with the hope of finding a permanent residence (Gollnick & Chinn, 2009).

**Children from Migrant Families** During 2013, the number of permanent residents between the ages of 5 and 24 was 269,084 (Department of Homeland Security, 2014). Although the largest percentage of these children and families being served in public schools speaks some form of Spanish, other languages included Mandarin Chinese, Korean, Arabic, Tagalog, Somali, Russian, and Hmong, to name just a few. Many school districts in the United States have scores of different languages spoken by their immigrant students and families.

In many cases, the circumstances of **migrancy** are associated with economic disadvantage as well as linguistic and cultural differences, creating social and physical isolation from much of the larger communities in which they reside. In other cases, migrancy or in-migration becomes a way of life for many families seeking means to sustain themselves. Large numbers of these individuals are employed in farming, fishery, forestry, and food processing–related industries.

**Unaccompanied Minors** Children or youth under the age of 18 who come across the American border without an adult are known as **unaccompanied minors**. Although the

*Photo 5.1* Huge numbers of unaccompanied minors make long and treacherous journeys to cross the southern border of the United States from Central America.

TERESITA CHAVARRIA/Getty Images

**CEC**

**Standard 1**
Learner Development and Individual Learning Differences

**Standard 2**
Learning Environments

entrance of unaccompanied minors is not new, the challenges schools and communities face are profound, creating enormous demands for many affected schools and their communities. These children, some as young as 9, take perilous and exceedingly long journeys to escape the violence in their places of origin, often reuniting with family members already here in the United States. During the fiscal year 2009, there were 19,418 unaccompanied minor children with the largest group coming from Mexico. In the fiscal year of 2014, 67,339 unaccompanied minor children came to the United States, with the majority, 51,705, from El Salvador, Guatemala, and Honduras (Kandel et al., 2014; O'Neil, 2015).

## 5-4  Effect of Population Trends on Schools

Regular education programs and specialized services are impacted greatly by the number of children who enter their doors with English language learning needs, with poverty-related issues, or with the challenges associated with migrancy. Classroom teachers find it a daunting task to develop and provide the variety of effective materials and instruction needed to support the academic growth of these learners (Crawford-Brooke, 2013). How do school systems respond to these needs? How do these systems provide the needed supports and services, including culturally and linguistically responsive education, interpreters, professional development for teachers, and additional funds to underwrite these programs and related services?

### 5-4a  Language Learning and Schools

Significant growth in the number of EBLs compared to other groups of students is impacting many school systems (Barnum-Martin et al., 2006; Barrera, 2006; Nippold, 2006; Solarsh & Alant, 2006; Wiese, 2006; (see Table 5.1). Some schools have as many as 70 different heritage languages spoken by their students and families (see Figure 5.3). There is an ever-increasing need to provide linguistically appropriate assessments and instruction in classrooms. It is vitally important to note here that not all of these students will need special supports or programs, though many will require a substantial amount of supplementary assistance and support for language development, especially academic language development.

**Table 5.1  Types of Emergent Bilingual Learners**

| | |
|---|---|
| Newly arrived with adequate schooling | • Recent arrivals (less than 5 years in the United States)<br>• Typically in grades 2–12<br>• Adequate schooling in native country<br>• Soon catch up academically<br>• May still score low on standardized tests given in English<br>• Social and economic factors can influence positively or negatively |
| Newly arrived with limited formal schooling | • Recent arrivals (less than 5 years in the United States)<br>• Typically in grades 2–12<br>• Interrupted or limited schooling in native country<br>• Limited native language literacy<br>• Below grade level in math<br>• Poor academic achievement<br>• Social and economic factors can influence positively or negatively |

**Table 5.1** Types of Emergent Bilingual Learners *(continued)*

| Long-term English learner | • 7 or more years in the United States |
|---|---|
| | • Typically in grades 6–12 |
| | • Limited literacy in both native language and English |
| | • Some may get adequate grades but score low on tests |
| | • Struggle with content classes |
| | • Often have been retained and are at risk of dropping out |
| | • Are students with inconsistent/subtractive schooling |
| | • Have had ESL or bilingual instruction, but no consistent program |
| Potential long-term English learner | • Recent arrivals in grades K–1 |
| | • Students in grades K–5 who have lived in the United States most of their lives and begin their schooling speaking a language other than English |
| | • Parents with low levels of education |
| | • Parents struggling financially and/or socially |

Many EBLs come from academically and experience-rich backgrounds in their mother tongue (L1) that enable them to develop the English academic language so vital for success in their current classrooms and for postsecondary education. Many students with diminished academic language development in their first language or mother tongue come from backgrounds of poverty. As you might hypothesize, first language expertise, especially that tied to academic learning, is extraordinarily helpful in learning a new language. If students already know how to read and write in their heritage language, these skills and competencies can be very helpful in learning a new language (in this case, English). The range of academic language includes (1) not having any understanding of the language

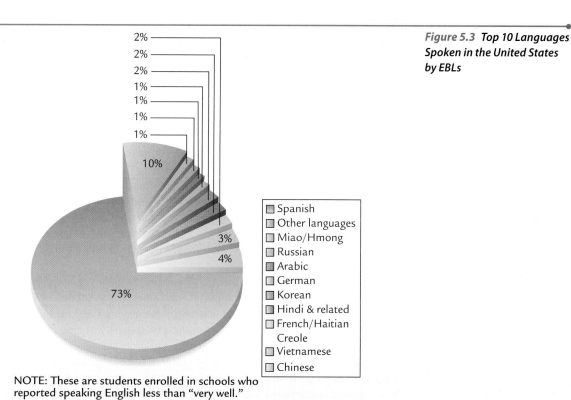

*Figure 5.3* **Top 10 Languages Spoken in the United States by EBLs**

2%
2%
2%
1%
1%
1%
1%
10%
3%
4%
73%

- Spanish
- Other languages
- Miao/Hmong
- Russian
- Arabic
- German
- Korean
- Hindi & related
- French/Haitian Creole
- Vietnamese
- Chinese

NOTE: These are students enrolled in schools who reported speaking English less than "very well."

SOURCE: Batalova & McHugh (2010). MPI analysis of the 2009 American Community Survey.

at all; (2) being able to communicate in informal social settings with friends due to **basic interpersonal communication skills (BICS)**; and (3) being able to succeed academically due to their **cognitive/academic language proficiency (CALP)**.

It is necessary to make instructional adaptations for EBLs, especially those who may need a more intense focus due to their identified disabilities. Moreover, the overall school environment for these children is altered significantly as they spend time away from regular classrooms, receive specialized instruction, and experience diminished classroom interaction with peers. The broad range of educational curricula requires school systems to reevaluate how they provide optimal learning opportunities for these students (Edelsky, 2006; Vaughn et al., 2006) and then regularly assess the effects of these opportunities on student learning and development with precision and care.

## 5-4b   Poverty and Schools

Poverty does not exert a simple, singular influence as mentioned earlier; rather, it is accompanied by a complex set of other influential factors, including challenging physical surroundings, psychological influences that diminish children's assessments of their own abilities and talents, often inaccurate judgments about children's performances by educators, and economic challenges that cause their own negative consequences—diminished nutrition, inadequate health care, and so on (Evans & Kim, 2007; Hallerod & Larsson, 2008). Research evidence indicates that thoughtfully developed, culturally responsive early intervention programs provided by well-trained professionals have beneficial effects on academic performance, cognitive development, and the general health on children in poverty (Coll-Black, Bhushan, & Fritsch, 2007; Emerson & Hatton, 2007; Kline & Huff, 2008; MacFarlane, 2007; Reschly, 2009). Family assistance such as home visitation programs, nutrition assistance, and health care along with guidance in accessing these programs generally contributes to very positive outcomes.

**Poverty and Academic Language**   Poverty and academic language are directly linked to how successful a child will be in academic settings. Because all learning is language-based, vocabulary knowledge is a critical element of the language development and school readiness of young children. Subsequently, another major risk factor for school success in children from poverty, no matter their race, gender, or ethnic group, is their reduced number of language interactions with parents and others. Also, the level of language complexity evidenced in their conversations with parents and caregivers is less than optimal or often lacking or absent. Language interactions with parents and others set the stage for the development of school-related, academic language. If young children's interactions with parents and others have been limited, they begin their formal schooling behind other children who have experienced rich language interaction with parents and other family members (Blachowicz, Fisher, & Watts-Taffe, 2005; Center on Teaching and Learning, 2015).

In 1995, a seminal longitudinal study examined the language interactions or talking between parents and their young children (Hart & Risley, 1995). Findings from this and other subsequent studies indicate that the amount and type of language interactions are strong predictors of children's cognitive ability and school success (Lucchese & Tamis-LeMonda, 2007). The amount and type of vocabulary used with young children is critical. Children by age 3 differ greatly in their vocabulary development (500 versus 1,100 words) depending on the stimulation provided by their families and other child care givers (Hart & Risley, 1995).

Vocabulary-rich homes and other child care settings increase children's exposure to a wide variety of words (quantity, quality, and complexity) that set the stage for academic language development and related learning (Lucchese & Tamis-LeMonda, 2007). By the time children are 6 years of age, the vocabulary disparity among and between them can be enormous—5,000-word vocabularies for children deprived of rich language experiences and 20,000-word vocabularies for children from language-rich environments (Hart & Risley, 1995; Lucchese & Tamis-LeMonda, 2007). As you might surmise, children from impoverished environments do not experience the language richness that is provided in more advantaged environments, including less exposure to books, less complex language interactions, and less conversations in general. This language gap persists and, by the time these children are in sixth grade, many children from impoverished environments are far behind because they lack the skills needed to comprehend more complex reading content and engage in more demanding writing tasks (Dahlgren, 2008). Language gaps can put children at risk throughout their educational careers and increase the chances that they will be identified for special education services whether or not they have an identifiable disability (Blachowicz, Fisher, & Watts-Taffe, 2005; Marulis & Neuman, 2010).

## 5-4c Migrancy and Schools

Migrancy poses significant challenges for children, families, and school systems, and their learning. Imagine the potential trauma associated with constantly making and developing new friendships with peers and others, adjusting to varied academic materials and practices, and adjusting to various teachers and school cultures. It is no wonder that migrant children experience major challenges in achieving solid school success and developing enduring relationships with peers, teachers, and other adults (Clare & Garcia, 2007; Levin, 2006).

For example, children who move three or four times each year may begin the school year in one reading program and finish only a lesson or two before moving to another school that uses a totally different program and approach to literacy development. They may also have little access to essential services because of their short-term enrollment. Children with potential disabilities may never be referred or identified as needing specialized instructional assistance or support. Migrant education programs are available to support districts and schools and provide extended learning opportunities for migrant children, but determining the programs' success is difficult because of the mobility of these children (U.S. Department of Education, 2014).

Schools are required to enroll all students—even undocumented, unaccompanied migrant students. As these children await the decisions of immigration judges, schools are scrambling to find suitable resources, including appropriate books and instructional materials, adequately prepared teachers and counselors, and appropriate space and facilities for additional students. Needed services may include ESL/bilingual instruction, physical and mental health services and supports, and specialized instruction such as Title IA or special education. Often these students come with limited educational experience and most do not speak English. Many have been traumatized by their circumstances before and as they traveled to the United States. Often, these children are moved to a different setting before decisions about educational needs can even be established. Even enrolling these children can be an arduous task. Although they are guaranteed immediate access to education, they usually are not able to meet the entry requirements regarding vaccinations, proper documentation, and residency, which creates another barrier that education services must work around (Kandel et al., 2014; Maxwell, 2014; O'Neil, 2015). Another issue facing educators is the relatively short time teachers and others might have to work with these students.

## 5-5 Decreasing Disproportionality of Culturally and Linguistically Diverse Children in Special Education

As addressed earlier in this chapter, there are certain risk factors for CLDLs in school settings. However, it is important to emphasize that, although these factors pose significant challenges for schools, they do not necessarily set the fate and futures of these children—school failure or placement in special education programs. Yet a continuing concern is the disproportionate number (both overrepresentation and underrepresentation) of special education students who come from linguistic and culturally diverse backgrounds (Artiles et al., 2010; Harry & Klingner, 2006; NEA, 2008a; Skiba, Poloni-Staudinger, & Simmons, 2005). Concerns related to disproportionality have been around for almost 40 years, since the inception of special education. The complexity of these concerns should not be underestimated.

The good news is that, over the past 20 years, progress has been made in reducing disproportionality (Artiles et al., 2010; Reschly, 2009; Waitoller, Artiles, & Cheney, 2010).

Often we hear the phrase "good teaching is good teaching"; however, this is a very simplistic view of what is needed to assure that appropriate educational decisions are made for CLDLs in regular and special education settings. Forming appropriate teams for decision making, understanding rules and regulations around identification, involving parents, using unbiased assessments, and designing specialized instruction for students with disabilities who come from culturally and linguistically diverse backgrounds—all of these activities and processes are challenging. Decisions must be centered on information gathered from culturally and linguistically responsive evaluations and aligned to their individual learning strengths and needs. IEPs must include specific linguistic and cultural considerations that are relevant for a particular child. Often, regular teachers and special education teachers are not aware of the types of instruction they should implement for CLDLs because they have not had adequate training that would provide them with the knowledge and tools they need to make these crucial professional judgments. In addition, schools must carefully examine their educational goals and the methods used to achieve them (Barrera, 2006; Rodriguez, 2005; Rueda & Yaden, 2006). Unfortunately, some aspects of providing services to these children become politicized as legislators enact laws that dictate matters of language that may not be informed by current research. So, what can be done? To address this question, we will discuss culturally and linguistically responsive teaching, building relationships with parents, collaborating across disciplines, using appropriate assessments and related procedures, and providing focused training for professionals.

**? LEARNING THROUGH SOCIAL MEDIA**

## *Edutopia on Culturally Responsive Teaching*

Edutopia is a nonprofit social media site sponsored through the What Works in Education, George Lucas Educational Foundation. Here you will find a variety of resources and interactive networking for teachers working in K–12 classrooms that support general, special education, working with EBLs, authentic formative assessment, and culturally responsive teaching to name a few. Along with resources are examples of innovative school programs. For more information, visit Edutopia's website.

The following is part of a question and answer session that Elena Aguilar had with Zaretta Hammond, author of the book *Culturally Responsive Teaching and the Brain: Promoting Authentic Engagement and Rigor among Culturally and Linguistically Diverse Students.*

**What are three things that you hope readers will take away from your book?**

First I want teachers to get that you don't have to learn 19 different cultures to be effective. Teachers need to simply begin with understanding the cultural dimensions of communalism—most communities of color have this cultural trait in common, namely a focus on the interdependence of the group. It can be summed up in the African proverb, "I am because we are." This way of being is contrasted with our dominant culture's more individualist, pull-yourself-up-by-your-bootstraps worldview.

The second thing is how important it is to build trusting relationships with students who feel marginalized or misunderstood. The neuroscience is clear on the connection between emotions, trust, and learning. Stress hormones from mistrust block cognition. Students respond to a teacher's focus on care by giving her permission to be tough and push them toward higher achievement.

And last, I hope they take from the book new processes and strategies for operationalizing culturally responsive teaching. I see a lot of school districts using the term, but there isn't much guidance to help teachers build the routines, processes, and structures in their classrooms so that it becomes more than a gimmick.

**I'm most intrigued by the title of Chapter 3, "This Is Your Brain on Culture." Can you give a quick synopsis of that chapter?**

This is where the neuroscience is so cool in helping us understand the role of culture in learning. It is like software that programs our "hardware" (the brain). Cultural values and learning practices transmitted from our parents and community guide how the brain wires itself to process information and handle relationships. Neural pathways are overdeveloped around one's cultural ways of learning.

Culturally responsive teachers know this and piggyback on these well-developed neural pathways with similar types of instruction. Tapping into these neural pathways can help students accelerate their own learning.

SOURCE: Aguilar, E. (2015). "Making Connections: Culturally Responsive Teaching and the Brain." Retrieved from www.edutopia.org/blog/making-connections-culturally-responsive-teaching-and-brain-elena-aguilar.

## 5-5a Culturally and Linguistically Responsive Teaching

The importance of CRT models versus **deficit education models** is magnified considerably when we take into account other cultural and economic factors, such as poverty, migrancy, time in country, and language levels in L1 (the home or heritage language) and L2 (English). All children bring their language and culture into classroom. Culturally and linguistically responsive teaching makes vital connections among and between children's classrooms, their schools, families, and the broader community to support students' learning and development. This includes incorporating students' culturally and linguistically relevant information, forming collaborative interactions, and identifying the funds of knowledge that students and their families bring with them based on their life experiences and backgrounds. Funds of knowledge represent the skills, experiences, and competencies children, youth, and adults bring with them from their experiences in their homes, communities, and countries of origin. These funds can be used by teachers and others to link school activities and to previous learning and life experiences. For example, a teacher of a child discovered that he and his family were extremely knowledgeable about horses, their care, and training. The teacher used this information in selecting reading materials, providing writing assignments, and selecting art projects. The child also became known to others in his classroom as the horse specialist.

One of the most important qualities of culturally and linguistically responsive teaching is safety—creating environments that are safe and supportive for teachers, learners, and their families. For CLDLs who are eligible for special education, significant attention is directed at providing appropriate services in least restrictive environments—environments that are very responsive to the child's and family's needs and desires.

U.S. public education predominantly reflects the philosophy of the cultural majority; the social customs of the diverse subcultures may continue to flourish in private and often emerge in individual interactions and behaviors (Collier, 2004; Gollnick & Chinn, 2009; Skinner & Weisner, 2007). Differences often surface in discussions about disabilities, particularly when they involve children and youth who are culturally and linguistically diverse. When educators are aware of their cultural and attitudinal biases, they are empowered to make better decisions about providing appropriate educational services for their CLDLs. **Cultural bias** can be defined as beliefs that dominant or mainstream cultural ways of being, learning, and knowing are superior to others' cultures and ways of viewing the world (Tyler, Stevens, & Uqdah, 2009). Moreover, **attitudinal bias** represented in negative attitudes about language, accents, poverty, and migrancy often cloud **professional judgments**

**Standard 5**
Instructional Planning and Strategies

**Standard 6**
Professional Learning and Ethical Practice

**Deficit education models**
Models of educational practice that first look at what a child is deficient in (specific academic skills such as reading, spelling, math, or language deficits in English) to plan educational interventions.

**Cultural bias**
Negative attitudes about cultures different than our own, usually based on myths or stereotyping, that often cloud professional judgment.

**Attitudinal bias**
Negative attitudes about language, accents, poverty, and migrancy that often cloud professional judgment.

**Professional judgment**
An informed opinion based on specialized training in the area being evaluated that bridges the gap between quantitative data and qualitative information when making decisions.

*Photo 5.2* Culturally responsive teaching provides a safe environment in which parents and teachers together support the learning of children.

Kali Nine LLC/Getty Images

related to assessment practices and outcomes, as well as determining what placement and instruction are optimally needed (Ovando, Combs, & Collier, 2006).

Sensitivity in interpersonal communication is very important when professionals deliver services to culturally and linguistically diverse children and their families (Arias & Morillo-Campbell, 2008; De Von Figueroa-Moseley, Ramey, & Keltner, 2006). This includes being aware of the meaning and interpretation of certain facial expressions, because the expression of emotions, manners, and behaviors denoting respect and interpersonal matters vary greatly among cultures. Caring and competent professionals become familiar with these nuances of effectively communicating and forming successful partnerships with diverse parents and families.

Keep in mind that CRT is the key to addressing these challenges by forming positive and affirming relationships with the families and their children (Banks, 2008; Deaux, Reid, & Martin, 2006; Díaz-Rico & Weed, 2010; Sleeter & Grant, 2009). Effective teachers and other support personnel come to understand the questions they need to ask themselves for each of their students and families (Teemant et al., 1998). These questions include:

1. Who is this child?
2. What are this child's strengths and needs?
3. What are the policies in place to support this child?
4. What programs and practices are available to support this child in the school setting?
5. How can I collaborate with others to support this child's learning and development?
6. How can I position this child for success in my classroom?
7. What does the student already know—what valuable experiences and knowledge does he or she bring to the classroom? What do their families bring in the way of learning, experiences, and knowledge?

When we address these aforementioned questions accurately and completely, we dramatically increase the chances for success and optimal development and learning for these students who are diverse and also students with disabilities. For example, an IEP might necessarily address the type of language intervention needed (e.g., enrichment, either in a native language or in English). Instruction may be targeted at language enhancement using existing core curriculum materials, such as children's literature or activities that include the funds of knowledge children bring with them from home environment and life experiences.

It is also important to note that most children from culturally diverse backgrounds do not require special education. This is an exceedingly important point. Sometimes, in an attempt to provide specialized services for these children, they are placed in special education programs with the intent to provide them individualized instruction—instruction beyond that provided in their regular education settings. When this is done, it is a mistake to label such students as having disabilities. Table 5.2 outlines factors that educators should consider as they address various elements of the referral process for children from diverse linguistic and cultural backgrounds.

These are only examples of the considerations that may need attention when teachers provide educational interventions for children who may have disabilities. Environmental conditions, such as extreme poverty and developmental deprivation, may dictate that services and supports focus on environmental stimulation lacking in the child's early learning experiences (Blachowicz, Fisher, & Watts-Taffe, 2005; Emerson & Hatton, 2007; Hendrick & Weissman, 2007). Keep in mind that children of poverty have had a variety of experiences and that these experiences may be useful for supporting instruction and language development. Thus, individual strategies for promoting learning and language development are as varied as the factors that make up a child's background.

The CRT model is vitally important to understanding children in the context of their families (De Von Figueroa-Moseley, Ramey, & Keltner, 2006; González, Moll, & Amanti, 2005; Rodriguez, 2005). Because CRT focuses on the strengths, prior knowledge, and experiences of learners and their families to create rich learning environments, one of the most

**Table 5.2**  Process Checklist for Serving Children from Culturally and Linguistically Diverse Backgrounds

This checklist provides professionals with points to consider in the process of educating children from culturally and linguistically diverse backgrounds. These matters should be considered during each of the following: referral, testing, or diagnostic assessment; classification, labeling, or class assignment change; and teacher conferences or home communication.

| Process | Issues | Questions to Be Asked |
|---|---|---|
| Referral, Testing, or Diagnostic | Language issues | Is the native language different from the language in which the child is being taught, and should this be considered in the assessment process? What is the home language? What is the normal conversational language? In what language can the student be successfully taught or assessed (academic language)? |
|  | Cultural issues | What are the views toward schooling in the culture from which the child comes? Do differences exist in expectations between the school and family for the child's schooling goals? What are the cultural views toward illness or disability? |
|  | Home issues | What is the family constellation, and who are the family members? What is the family's economic status? What is the level of education of the parents? What funds of knowledge exist in the family? |
| Classification, Labeling, or Class Assignment Change | Language issues | Does the proposed placement change account for any language differences that are relevant, particularly academic language? |
|  | Cultural issues | Does the proposed placement change consider any unique cultural views regarding schooling? Is the change viewed as safe by the student and the family? |
|  | Home issues | Does the proposed placement change consider pertinent family matters? |
| Teacher Conferences or Home Communication | Language issues | Is the communication to parents or other family members in a language they understand? |
|  | Cultural issues | Has a relationship been developed between the teachers and the family? Do cultural views influence communication between family members and the school as a formal governmental organization? Is there a cultural reluctance of family members to come to the school? Are home visits a desirable alternative? Is communication from teachers positive? |
|  | Home issues | Is the family constellation such that communication with the schools is possible and positive? Are family members positioned economically and otherwise to respond to communication from the schools in a productive manner? If the family is of low socioeconomic status, is transportation a problem for conferences? What can the school do to support family communication and access to school in a culturally and linguistically responsive way? |

important elements in providing successful interventions is gathering information in a culturally responsive way by learning who the family and child are without prejudice. Gay (2002) describes this process as:

- Recognizing and understanding personal attitudes and behaviors toward differing cultural groups;
- Understanding and using students' strengths, background knowledge, and previous experience to enhance instruction in a way that will strengthen new learning experiences;
- Creating an inviting and caring classroom community that supports the development of interdependence and collaboration;
- Building strong relationships with and among students and their families; and
- Holding students highly accountable for their own learning.

Examples of excellent culturally and linguistically responsive teaching models and methods can be found at the University of Hawaii's Center for Research on Education, Diversity & Excellence (CREDE), and Arizona State University's National Center for Culturally Responsive Educational Systems.

Think again about José presented in the opening Snapshot. What are José's funds of knowledge, his strengths, and interests? Have his teachers considered his funds of knowledge and those of his family, and how might these funds be used to support and motivate his learning and development? Should José be considered to have a disability because of his academic performance or because of his CLD background? As you receive more professional preparation and develop more skills, you will position yourself to be a part of a collaborative team that will be capable of skillfully answering these questions and making informed and defensible decisions that benefit CLDLs and their families.

**Standard 7**
Collaboration

### 5-5b Increasing Parent Involvement

Many factors interfere with parent involvement in the education of their children. These factors may include a lack of understanding about culture and processes of public education in the United States, past negative experiences with education personnel, a perception that their involvement might place them at risk for legal action, a reluctance to attend events that do not attend to their needs for interpretation, and potentially unwelcoming school environments.

The manner in which parents are involved is important to achieving maximum benefits (Arias & Morillo-Campbell, 2008; De Von Figueroa-Moseley, Ramey, & Keltner, 2006; Epstein, 2011; NEA, 2008b). Building relationships with families, knowing who they are, and learning what their funds of knowledge are and what they believe can be critical to collaborative teams that wish to be genuinely helpful to CLDLs and their families.

Parents of children with disabilities who are economically limited, ethnically diverse, and speak a primary language other than English face enormous disadvantages in interacting with school personnel and related systems (Arias & Morillo-Campbell, 2008). The language barrier and lack of knowledge about American public schooling make it extremely difficult for these parents to fully benefit from public education, thus impacting their right to fully participate in and support their children's learning and development. Many helpful

*Photo 5.3* Parents as partners with teachers in the education of children provide the greatest potential for their achieving maximum benefits academically in school.

Ariel Skelley/Blend Images/Getty Images

websites are now available that help parents inform themselves about issues, responsibilities, and helpful supports available in their local communities. These resources may help bridge gaps in building productive and satisfactory relationships, and provide appropriate supports for parents to participate knowledgably in regular and special education–related processes. Sensitivity in interpersonal communication is very important when professionals deliver services to children of families who are CLDLs (Arias & Morillo-Campbell, 2008; De Von Figueroa-Moseley, Ramey, & Keltner, 2006). Professionals need to be aware of the meaning and interpretation of certain facial expressions: the expression of emotions, manners, and behaviors denoting respect.

**Funds of knowledge**
The belief that all families are competent and have knowledge based on their life experiences, and that they use this knowledge to develop social relationships and connections necessary for the survival of their family and to make sense of their everyday experiences.

## Funds of Knowledge

As you have learned, what parents and children bring from their own experiences and knowledge can be very useful to school personnel. Parents' **funds of knowledge** as contributors to school success encompass the belief that all families are competent and have important and valuable knowledge based on their life experiences. They use these funds of knowledge to develop social relationships and connections necessary for the survival of their families and to make sense of their everyday experiences (González, Moll, & Amanti, 2005). Understanding how these funds of knowledge contribute to school success can best be described by a story about Miguel (names changed throughout).

*Photo 5.4* Home visits can be a useful way of learning about the funds of knowledge within a family that can support student learning.

When Miguel came to school in the United States for the first time, he entered the second-grade classroom of Mrs. Crane. Right away she realized she would need to understand some things about Miguel to open learning opportunities for him. Even as an EBL, he seemed to be coming along nicely in all his subjects but math. Mrs. Crane tried everything she could think of but nothing seemed to make a difference. She decided it was time to talk with the parents about the situation, maybe even consider special education services. Instead of having them come to the school, she made an appointment to visit them at their home. The parents were delighted that a teacher would have such interest in their son and graciously opened their home, giving her a tour as they talked. When they got to the garage, she found herself gazing at a group of wonderful birdhouses carefully measured and precisely built. Miguel's father explained that he and his son spent many hours together building them. Immediately, Mrs. Crane knew what she needed to do to support Miguel's math development. As you might surmise, with Mrs. Crane's careful attention to the funds of knowledge Miguel already had about math concepts, she was able to start from what he knew and helped him move forward. Careful evaluation of families' and students' funds of knowledge can make the difference in a child's educational progress as this example clearly demonstrates.

**Standard 7**
Collaboration

## 5-5c Nondiscriminatory and Multidisciplinary Collaboration

**Multidisciplinary collaboration** is a very important tool in education, particularly in providing culturally and linguistically responsive special education. Effective collaboration requires that all of the professionals have a student- and family-centered focus, which includes knowing their funds of knowledge and building a productive and supportive relationship with them. Achieving these ends, teams can effectively bridge the needs and experiences of the child and family with an appropriate education and related services. Multidisciplinary collaboration that is culturally responsive improves outcomes related to

**Multidisciplinary collaboration**
Collaboration between parents and professionals with different expertise such as the classroom teacher, assessment specialist, disability specialist, ESL specialist, and school administrator in planning for the individual learning needs of a child.

assessment, language development, family satisfaction, and the achievement of IEP goals (Dettmer, Thurston, & Dyck, 2005; Friend & Cook, 2007).

## 5-5d Culturally and Linguistically Responsive Assessment

Assessment has two main purposes in schools. First, it provides teachers with accurate information to develop instruction that is understandable and meaningful to a child and promotes demonstrable learning (Teemant, Smith, & Pinnegar, 2003). Second, it provides useful information to the public about how schools are performing. The history of assessment for children from CLDL backgrounds raises serious issues about its accuracy, fairness, and the ability to shed light on identifying appropriate services and placements for children.

Perhaps nowhere is the interface between special, bilingual/ESL, and culturally responsive educational practices more prominent than in issues of **nondiscriminatory assessment**.

*Photo 5.5* Special care must be taken when assessing CLDLs to avoid assessment bias by considering who the child is, what the child can do, and what can be done to support the child's continued academic learning.

As noted earlier, disproportionate numbers of students from CLDL backgrounds are found in special education classes (Artiles et al., 2010; Sullivan, 2011). Decisions regarding referral and placement in these classes are based on assessments that are typically based on standardized evaluations of intellectual, academic, and social functioning. Using assessments constructed with a specific language or content that favors the majority culture often leads to bias, especially for CLDLs. Whenever possible, EBLs should be assessed in their native language. However, this is not always possible given the sheer number of different languages that might be represented in a given school system. Additionally, bias assessments may lead to results and placements that are detrimental to a child (Moule, 2012; Wright, 2007). Professionals who are not properly trained to interpret results for CLDLs may lead to misdiagnoses as well as inappropriate interventions and placements (Rodriguez, 2006).

When trying to decide whether a child has a language disability, professionals often mistakenly identify a child as needing special education services when, in fact, the issue is a language learning issue. This can happen because of a lack of knowledge about the difference between language learning and language deficits (Fujiki & Brinton, 2010). In several early cases, courts determined that reliance on academic and psychological assessments discriminated against Latino students (*Diana v. State Board of Education*, 1970, 1973) and African American students (*Larry P. v. Riles*, 1972, 1979). Assessment and instruction for Asian American children were addressed in the case of *Lau v. Nichols* (1974). These California cases had a national impact and greatly influenced the reauthorization of Individuals with Disabilities Education Act (IDEA).

Two prominent precedents based in IDEA were established in the case of *Diana v. State Board of Education*: (1) Children tested for potential placement in special education must be assessed in their native or primary language, and (2) children cannot be placed in special classes on the basis of culturally biased tests. Interestingly, IDEA mandates that evaluation involve a multidisciplinary team using several sources of information in making placement decisions. To put these safeguards in context, it is necessary to examine the assessment process and how linguistic and cultural bias occurs.

**Test Bias, Assessment Errors, and Measurement** Test bias, assessment errors, and measurement in psychological assessment have been recognized as problems for many years and continue to concern professionals (Artiles et al., 2010; Gregory, 2007; Moule, 2012; Sullivan, 2011). Some assessment procedures simply fail to reveal comparable levels of performance in CLDLs and "majority" culture learners, even if they have very

**Nondiscriminatory assessment**

Testing conducted in a child's preferred language without cultural or racial discrimination through the use of validated assessment tools.

similar abilities. This phenomenon is referred to as **assessment bias**. These biases threaten the validity of the assessment results. There are a variety of assessment biases to be aware of, including cultural bias, attitudinal bias, assessment bias, and norming bias (Ovando, Combs, & Collier, 2006). **Measurement bias** produces errors during the testing, leading to unfair or inaccurate test results that do not reflect a student's actual abilities or skills (Gregory, 2007; Harry & Klingner, 2006; Hays, 2008; Reynolds, Livingston, & Willson, 2006). Test bias gives rise to results that do not accurately reflect the true skills, capacities, or achievements of CLDLs, including EBLs (Erevelles, Kanga, & Middleton, 2006; McMillan, 2007; Spinelli, 2006).

**Avoiding Measurement Bias** So what can be done to avoid measurement bias? Measurement bias is in part addressed by carefully considering not only the selection of potential assessment instruments and processes, but also by carefully interpreting the results in light of such things as a student's language development, cultural nuances related to test vocabulary and usage, and other natural, real-life observations of the student in school and home settings. Understanding the linguistic and cultural differences of students contributes significantly to determining learners' needs and capacities as well as weighing information related to qualifying learners for special education services. For example, a second-grader being assessed for learning disabilities using a commonly used intelligence test as part of the evaluation was asked to name the four seasons of the year. After thinking about it for a few minutes, he responded, "fishing season, deer season, duck season and," pausing to think, "rabbit season?" Although the answer did not fit the pattern required by the standardization of the test, it was a reasonable answer given this child's cultural background and provides important insight into the language and everyday life experiences of this child. Another example is a Navajo child who may not respond to questions about snakes in a testing situation because the cultural custom is not to speak of such matters. If a test administrator assumes this lack of response means the child does not know the answer, it may be classified as an error on the test without providing the context for the nonresponse. However, if the administrator has a cultural understanding of the issue, a different conclusion is reached that benefits the child.

Examiners must be trained to recognize the biases present in standardized assessments so that they can better evaluate the data they gather. They are now required by law to use more than one instrument in making decisions. This is especially important when assessing CLDLs and EBLs for special education.

There are several effective tools that can be used in making decisions for EBLs. All identified EBLs in schools are required to take an annual language proficiency test. Information from this test helps determine the student's English language development (ELP) and language development plans (LDP). This information is vital when determining if a child has a disability, because it can show the pattern of language growth over time. Two other tools for CLDLs are professional judgment and authentic assessment.

**Professional Judgment** Professional judgment is an informed opinion based on training that bridges the gap between quantitative and qualitative data gathered about a child. Quantitative data is derived from various formal and standardized assessments about a given child's performance. Qualitative data may come from other processes such as classroom observations, teacher appraisals, home observations, and more naturalistic information provided by parents based on experiences outside school settings. For all children being evaluated for high-incidence disabilities, such as learning disabilities, intellectual delays, and emotional and behavior disorders, professional judgment in evaluating the data collected is absolutely essential. However, too often, bias on the part of assessors or members of the multidisciplinary team plays a prejudicial role in interpreting both types of data (Artiles et al., 2010). To decrease the chance of bias, evaluators and multidisciplinary team members must be adequately trained to consider all relevant assessment information with sensitivity to culturally and linguistically relevant information and findings.

**Authentic Assessment** An important element of teacher candidate preparation programs is the use of **authentic assessments** in regular, special, and ESL/bilingual education. Wiggins (1998) defined authentic assessment as performance-based assessments

**Assessment bias**
A test or testing procedure that creates a disadvantage for one group as a consequence of factors unrelated to ability, such as culture, linguistic or racial background, or gender.

**Measurement bias**
An unfairness or inaccuracy of test results or their interpretation that is related to cultural or linguistic background, gender, or race.

**Authentic assessments**
Performance-based assessments based on real tasks carried out by the student as part of the regular classroom assignments and usually evaluated with a rubric.

**Table 5.3** Key Elements and Challenges in Using Authentic Assessments

| Criteria (Key Elements) | Challenges |
|---|---|
| • Use of higher-level thinking skills | • Setting clear criteria that is fair to learners |
| • Use of meaningful and cognitively challenging tasks | • Designing tasks that are meaningful and cognitively challenging |
| • Integration of academic language skills | • Making professional judgments about student work |
| • Deepening student knowledge rather than widening the variety of skills | • Creating time for professional development to collaborate on the design of the assessments/assignments |
| • Involving students in monitoring and self-assessing their work | |

SOURCE: Ovando, C. J., Combs, M. C., & Collier, V. P. (2006). *Bilingual and ESL classrooms: teaching in multicultural contexts.* New York: McGraw-Hill.

generated from classroom assignments that relate to the real classroom performance and functioning (Ovando, Combs, & Collier, 2006). There are specific criteria and challenges that teachers should be aware of in conducting and interpreting authentic assessments (see Table 5.3).

A good example of authentic assessments is the use of portfolio information gathered from students' classroom assignments. For example, keeping a portfolio of writing assignments that students do over time reveals their pattern of progress or lack thereof. These writing samples may also help teachers plan the next steps in the skill development process. Also, when working with parents, it can be a very visual way for them to see the progress their child has made on IEP writing goals and to help with determining what goals need to be pursued next.

## 5-5e   Language Acquisition

Attending to language acquisition for children who are culturally and linguistically diverse in special education programs is especially important. Because all language acquisition is based on developmental stages and experience, it is important for teachers to have training in language acquisition (Krashen, 2002). To assume that all English language learners lack language acquisition can be a costly mistake. A child who enters the classroom speaking only Spanish may have highly developed levels of academic language, previous education in the native language, and extensive background knowledge developed through life experiences. On the other hand, a child speaking only English but who comes from a language-impoverished environment with little access to experiences that enhance academic language development will not have the same academic language foundation for learning new concepts. Making sure that appropriate related services for language acquisition as well as language-rich instructional interventions are central to the ongoing success of CLDLs.

**Standard 6**
Professional Learning and Ethical Practice

## 5-5f   Proper Training of Professionals

Selection of culturally and linguistically responsive practices requires a knowledge base that is beyond that of many education professionals. Researchers found major gaps in teachers' understanding of language structure and reading instruction as well as the meaning of student assessments and work samples (Moats, 2015). Fortunately, many professional education programs are including coursework and related field experiences that prepare professionals and paraprofessionals for working successfully with CLDLs (Kauffman, Conroy, Gardner, & Oswald, 2008). Effective training in culturally and linguistically responsive practices is one of the best ways to assure appropriate use of professional judgment in the interpretation of test results and implementation of interventions when working with children from diverse backgrounds. This is particularly important in achieving effective collaboration for students with disabilities (Alvarez, 2007; Dettmer, Thurston, & Dyck, 2005; Friend & Cook, 2007; Gimbert, Cristol, & Sene, 2007; Ralabate, 2007; Rodriguez, 2005).

Culturally and linguistically responsive professional education prepares teachers and other professionals to be constantly aware of potential bias due to language and cultural differences, as well as other factors that may mask students' true abilities (Merrell, 2007; O'Hara & Pritchard, 2008; Reynolds, Livingston, & Willson, 2006). Learning how to gather information about what children know from their home life and other environments, their funds of knowledge, matters greatly. This information can provide valuable insights to evaluators and instructors in administering assessments, interpreting results, and considering appropriate interventions, services, and placements. That gathering of information includes what languages are spoken in the household and by whom, who a child's caregivers are (parents and others), how much time the child spends with caregivers, and what types of activities (e.g., cooking, gardening, religion, carpentry, bowling, baseball) the family and child know about and participate in. Highly skilled assessment personnel need to be adept in determining what information derived from formal and informal testing, communications, and observations are important in making decisions (Mueller, 2011; Sleeter & Grant, 2009; Teemant, Smith, & Pinnegar, 2003). Such preparation is essential for professionals to obtain accurate data for the development of effective instructional strategies and to minimize misinterpretations that may lead to disproportionality in identifying CLDLs as individuals with disabilities (Artiles et al., 2010; Gregory, 2007; Merrell, 2007).

**CEC**

**Standard 5**
Instructional Planning and Strategies

## 5-6 Culturally Responsive Special Education

For all children identified for special education, the first things to consider in developing an individual education program (IEP) are the educational strengths and needs of children as established by a collaborative team of professionals in concert with parents. IEP development includes instructional interventions and related services provided in a linguistically and/or culturally responsive manner. Education professionals should avoid making conventional assumptions about children's cultural background, which means getting to know the children and their families well. When specific cultural content is included in instruction, content must be relevant to the required general curriculum and each student's identified learning needs, and interventions must be informed by relevant cultural and linguistic knowledge specifically related to each student.

IEPs written for children from culturally and linguistically diverse backgrounds as well as the systematic monitoring of language and academic progress must accurately be attended to in an individualized fashion, perhaps even more so than for children with disabilities who come from the cultural majority. Teachers who are mindful about a child's cultural and linguistic experiences will use these observations and related information to strengthen and motivate individual academic performance and achievement, and to develop highly functional social and adaptive skills.

In addition to developing an IEP, IDEA requires the specification of a subsequent placement in the least restrictive environment for each student with a disability. Most school districts have considerable experience in moving through this process. However, special care must be exerted in determining placements for CLDLs/EBLs who are also identified as children or youth with disabilities (Hendrick & Weissman, 2007). As you might conclude, culture and language play significant roles in determining not only the IEP components but also the placement of a given child or youth. Better decisions and placements are made by professionals who have the necessary skills and knowledge related to CLDLs/EBLs and their families. Therefore, personnel with training in culturally responsive techniques become crucial (Baca & Cervantes, 2004; Gollnick & Chinn, 2009).

The guiding principle is that instruction for students with disabilities should take place in an environment as similar to that of the educational mainstream as possible, alongside peers without disabilities to the greatest extent appropriate. However, supplemental language or cultural instruction may be needed in addition to general and special education instruction, making inclusion in the educational mainstream more difficult. In all cases, settings must be culturally and linguistically responsive, sensitive to family language and cultural differences, and their funds of knowledge.

Although children with exceptionalities who have language differences may also receive assistance from ESL or dual-language education staff, this language instruction should be incorporated across learning environments (August & Shanahan, 2006; Harrington & Brisk, 2006; Hellerman & Vergun, 2007). In situations where the disability is more severe or the language difference is extreme, the student may be placed in a separate setting for a portion of the instructional time, with the staff carefully monitoring the acquisition of skills so that the child can be moved into more inclusive settings as soon as possible for optimum learning and social opportunities.

As you know, placement options for LRE vary along the continuum of needs and levels of fluency with the goal of embracing inclusive pedagogy (see Figure 5.4)—decisions and instructional practices that center on the needs of the children and are supported through active collaboration with all essential parties: parents, regular educators, and so on. This

**Figure 5.4** *Inclusive Pedagogy Framework*

## Inclusive Pedagogy Framework:
## Collaboration for Common Understanding and United Advocacy:
### Who is this Child?

| | | |
|---|---|---|
| What are this child's needs and strengths? *CRITICAL LEARNING DOMAINS* | **\*Cognitive:** How can I support my students' learning by building on their previous knowledge and encouraging use of appropriate strategies and skills? <br> **\*Social/affective:** How can I help students recognize, participate in and master playing the school game? <br> **\*Linguistic:** How do I teach in ways that support this student's language and literacy development? | *How can my teaching embody my understanding of diverse learners commonalities and uniqueness?* |
| What programs and practices are available to support this child in the school setting? *ESSENTIAL POLICY* | **\*Standards:** How do I attend to the standards for teaching and learning for all learners? <br> **\*Classifications:** How do classifications both expand and limit my ability to advocate for all learners? <br> **\*Legalities:** How do policies, programs, and legislation impact the students' school environment? | *What are my moral obligations to all students?* |
| How can I collaborate to support this child's learning? *GUIDING PRINCIPLES* | **\*Multiple Perspectives:** How could I think about this differently? <br> **\*High Expectations:** How can I hold high expectations for all students? <br> **\*Knowledge-based Practice:** What do I already know and what do I need to learn to support the learning of all students? <br> **\*Accountability:** How can I hold myself and my students accountable? | *How can I apply my guiding principles in my teaching?* |
| How can I position this child for success in my classroom? *CLASSROOM STRATEGIES* | **\*Planning:** How can I respond to all children's needs and strengths in my planning? <br> **\*Teaching:** How can I accommodate all students in my teaching? <br> **\*Assessing:** How can I make sure that my assessment practice allows all students to demonstrate what they know? | *What specific changes will I make in my own teaching to accommodate all students?* |

**Reflection for Change:** *How can I engage with other people in different disciplines and classrooms within my educational setting to support students' development as knowers and learners?*

SOURCE: Teaching English Language Learners Program, Brigham Young University (1998).

## Ana

Five-year-old Ana traveled with her mother, father, and two sisters to a small town in the United States from their home in a rural community in Mexico because of her special needs. She had been living with her grandmother in a town that had a special preschool for children like Ana. When Ana's grandmother could no longer care for her because of her behaviors, an uncle living in the United States suggested Ana's family come to his town where he would provide a job at a salvage yard for her father and the family could get help for Ana.

The local school district was made aware of Ana when her mother registered her and her sisters at the local elementary school. The district special education coordinator contacted Ana's mother through an interpreter to gather some information and to set an appointment to meet and learn more about Ana and her family. Based on the conversation with Ana's mother, it was clear that Ana needed more services than the district alone could provide. Through the school health nurse, local medical and special needs funding resources were contacted to be a part of the multidisciplinary team (MDT) meeting that would include the district and local school representatives, the school nurse, the Education Services District (a state-funded organization that supported low-incidence special needs services), a community medical resource group, the Spanish-speaking interpreter, and Ana's mother (her father was working and unable to come). Ana's mother was asked if she had any of Ana's paperwork from the school in

KidStock/Blend Images/Getty Images

Mexico and, if so, to please bring it to the meeting.

At the beginning of the meeting, Ana's mother expressed through the interpreter how grateful she and her husband were for this opportunity. As the MDT communicated with her, they learned how much the family loved Ana but how worried they were about her learning and her behavior. She had brought with her in a blue plastic file folder all of the paperwork from Ana's previous school. She had been identified in Mexico as a child with severe developmental delays and behavioral issues. Her mother explained that they had a very hard time keeping her safely in a car seat. She was able to get out of everything they had tried. The MDT received information about her physical health and the concerns of her family. The MDT learned that Ana did not speak. She did scream, poke, push, pull hair, pinch, shred and tear, scratch, and run as means of communicating with her family. The family could not afford a telephone and were concerned about how to communicate with the school.

As the MDT heard the concerns presented, it was apparent that a lot of services would be needed for Ana and her family. Two very special and expensive car seats were purchased by a community agency, one for the bus and one for the family car. A phone was installed that allowed the family to call and receive calls from the school. Health services were set up for the family. It was determined that, educationally, Ana would be best served in a self-contained setting and, within that setting, she would need to be physically isolated from her peers but still have access to all of the conversation and other appropriate supervised activities. The Spanish interpreter was also hired as a personal assistant for Ana. She also served as the family trainer and visited their home to train Ana's parents in using the same language, behavioral, and social interventions being used at school.

By the end of the first year, Ana was speaking in both English and Spanish. She was able to join her peers using appropriate skills for group settings. She was no longer screaming, pinching, poking, or running. Her parents were ecstatic—now they could all sit down together for a meal, all of their daughters could play together, and they began to dream about what Ana might be able to do when she grew up.

*Application Questions*

**1.** What were Ana's mother's funds of knowledge?

**2.** What culturally responsive educational practices did the school and community use?

approach for EBLs represents an important framework for factoring in potential disability needs as well as language diversity status. Although this concept is logical, Collier (2004) noted "there is still considerable debate concerning how and where the bilingually exceptional child should be served" (p. 305). It is important to keep in mind that, even at the beginning stages of second-language acquisition, many children can progress quite nicely in inclusive environments such as regular classrooms with proper instructional strategies and support. Collaboration is absolutely essential in creating supports and effective interventions for CLDLs with disabilities. For example, if a student needs total assistance to interact and is in the very early stages of language development, this child may be provided inclusive instruction with targeted pullout programs to provide highly focused assistance.

## Looking Toward a Bright Future

Linguistic and cultural diversity is more visible than it has been in the past and continues to be an integral part of our daily lives in the United States. We are in the midst of a revolution of school change as it relates to cultural and language diversity, including services for **culturally and linguistically diverse learners with disabilities**.

We are much more aware of culturally and linguistically responsive educational practices in the schools and classrooms and that these practices matter significantly to the well-being of these learners. We are more aware of assessment bias and how to negate it. Additionally, we are coming to see the immense value of authentic assessments—assessments that include student work, classroom observations, self-evaluations, peer reviews, and parent perceptions. We are also more adept in knowing how to gather appropriate information about diverse learners' capacities as well using this information in an ongoing fashion to adjust instruction to meet the needs of individual students.

Increasingly, data regarding student performance are playing important roles in shaping and motivating educational reforms. Although many question this current emphasis, findings from these data have provided important catalysts for significant and important changes in education practices. Language and culture matter on many levels. Children who master and speak multiple languages well can and do contribute in significant ways to their families, the economies of which they are a part, and their communities.

*Photo 5.6* Increasing the number of graduating CLDLs with and without disabilities is important, as they have much to offer our communities and our society.

©Volt Collection/Shutterstock.com

Unfortunately, too many CLDL with disabilities are exiting their schooling prematurely without the necessary skills and knowledge to be full participants in our democratic society. However, we are coming to recognize the immense value of these students and their families as partners in the successful education of children. Significant progress has been made in preparing CLDLs for active roles in our society—learners with and without disabilities. Moreover, educators and other professionals are now receiving training that heightens their capacities to connect with CLDLs and their families. Increasingly, professionals are recognizing the value of funds of knowledge that children and parents bring to education, and their importance in advancing learning and development.

Educators, in particular, are coming to understand the vital role of developing academic language in CLDLs. Advanced postsecondary schooling requires high levels of academic language proficiency in reading and writing. With solid language development, young people are able to access and profit from higher education and other advanced training.

Finally, there has been an explosion in the clinical and theoretical research about CLDLs, especially those with disabilities. Now more than ever, we are learning what we need to do to benefit these children and their families.

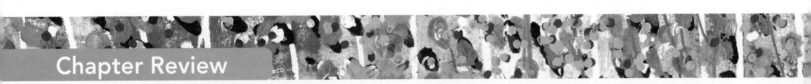

## Chapter Review

**5-1 Describe how the lives of students with disabilities from culturally and/or linguistically diverse backgrounds have changed since the advent of IDEA.**

- Significant numbers of culturally and linguistically diverse learners (CLDLs) are entering public school systems.
- CLDLs and emergent bilingual learners (EBLs), especially ones with disabilities or presumed disabilities, are important catalysts for change for all educators and service providers.
- Two approaches schools are taking up for CLDLs are ESL/bilingual education and culturally and linguistically responsive education.

**5-2 Describe the purposes and approaches of bilingual/ESL education and culturally and linguistically responsive education.**

- Bilingual/ESL education focuses on English academic language development for emergent bilingual learners and supports their success in accessing school learning and development as a citizen.
- Culturally and linguistically responsive education uses the strengths children bring with them (their funds of knowledge) into the learning environment to support the bonding and bridging capitals students need to appreciate and work with the differences and similarities they find in their classroom community and the larger community in which they live.

**5-3 Describe population trends among culturally and linguistically diverse learners, especially** prevalence by race and ethnicity, speakers of other languages, poverty, and migrancy.

- Culturally and linguistically diverse groups represent a substantial portion of the U.S. population. Next to English, the most often spoken language in the United States is Spanish.
- It is expected that people of color will represent 41.5 percent of the population by 2060.
- The number of children of color in 2014 was almost half of all children under 18.
- Several of these groups are growing rapidly—in some cases, at twice the rate of growth of the white population because of increasing birthrates and immigration levels.
- Poverty levels among the black and Hispanic populations are significantly higher than white populations.
- Migration continues at a high rate, with a surge in unaccompanied minors from Central America.

**5-4 Describe how these population trends affect public education.**

- School funding is stretched.
- EBLs require well-trained teachers who know how to support the academic English language development.
- For many children in poverty, limited vocabulary affects their academic growth in the school system.
- Migrancy interrupts the continuity of schooling and has an impact on learning, teacher and peer relationships, and general academic progress.

**5-5** Identify ways that public schools can decrease the disproportionality of culturally and linguistically diverse learners (CLDL) in special education and significantly improve their education.

- Build strong and trusting relationships with students and their families.

- Understanding children's real academic language development in their native tongue and in English allows more accurate information for making decisions about which assessments to use, interpretations to be made, and the development of appropriate instruction.

- Gathering information from children and the families about their funds of knowledge in culturally responsive ways supports making successful decisions for assessment and intervention.

- Providing instruction that leads to language and academic growth is critical and based on constant assessment.

- Proper training of educators increases culturally responsive practices, collaborative relationships with parents and school teams, and creates safe environments for these students and their parents.

- Understanding that some parents from different linguistic or cultural backgrounds may view school involvement or special programs differently allows educators and other key personnel to communicate more successfully with parents and design culturally responsive programs for the children.

- Developing a safe environment in which parents can comfortably participate supports learning for CLDLs.

- Parents' funds of knowledge are important contributors in supporting family/school connections, and student learning and growth.

**5-6** Describe culturally and linguistically responsive special education that supports student learning for CLDLs.

- Focusing on the strengths of students and then their needs provides a basis for positive and supportive instruction.

- Students' cultural and linguistic experiences are useful in strengthening their individual academic performance in the core curriculum.

- Real-life, ongoing classroom assignments can be effectively used to measure academic growth.

- Strong collaborative working relationships with parents and school teams contribute exponentially to the success of CLDLs.

- Using the principle of least restrictive environments in culturally responsive ways creates safe and optimal learning settings for CLDLs and their families.

**5-7** Identify promising changes in public education that support culturally and linguistically diverse learners with disabilities.

- Linguistic and cultural diversity is more visible than it has been in the past and continues to be an integral part of our daily lives in the United States.

- Educators recognize that language learning and culturally responsive practices matter significantly.

- We are also more adept in knowing how to gather appropriate information about diverse learners' capacities as well as in using this information in an ongoing fashion to adjust instruction to meet the needs of individual students.

- We are coming to recognize the immense value of these students and their families as partners in the successful education of children.

- Data from a variety of formal and informal sources, including authentic classroom assessments, if carefully considered, give rise to effective practice and educational outcomes.

- We hope that these practices will reduce the significant number of CLDL students with and without disabilities leaving the education system early.

- We look forward to these students advancing to higher education and other advanced training opportunities, and that these students will have active roles as contributors in our society.

**Council for Exceptional Children (CEC) Standards to Accompany Chapter 5**

If you are thinking about a career in special education, you should know that many states use national standards developed by the Council for Exceptional Children (CEC) to assess a teacher candidate's knowledge about and skills for working with students with disabilities. See a complete listing of the seven CEC Content Standards on the inside cover of this text.

1 Learner Development and Individual Learning Differences
2 Learning Environments

4 Assessment
5 Instructional Planning and Strategies
6 Professional Learning and Ethical Practice
7 Collaboration

Additional training in ESL teaching and culturally responsive teaching can better prepare you for working with children who are linguistically or culturally diverse and who may also be children with disabilities.

## Mastery Activities and Assignments

To master the content within this chapter, complete the following activities and assignments:

1. Complete a written test of the chapter's content. If your instructor requires a written test of your content knowledge for this chapter, keep a copy for your portfolio.
2. Review the Case Study on Embracing Diversity, "Ana," and respond in writing to the Application Questions.

Keep a copy of the Case Study and your written response for your portfolio.

3. Participate in a community service learning activity. Community service is a valuable way to enhance your learning experience. Develop a reflective journal of the service learning experience for your portfolio.

## CHAPTER 6

# Exceptionalities and Families

©Monkey Business Images/Shutterstock.com

## Learning Objectives

*After you complete this chapter, you will be able to:*

**6-1** Describe how the lives of families with children with disabilities have changed since the advent of IDEA.

**6-2** Describe the family systems approach and how it applies to families with members with disabilities, and describe the strengths and challenges of families raising children with disabilities.

**6-3** Describe common reactions of parents when obtaining a diagnosis for their children with disabilities.

**6-4** Describe factors that influence the relationship between children with disabilities and their mothers, fathers, siblings, grandparents, and other extended family members.

**6-5** Describe essential behaviors that nurturing and competent professionals exhibit when interacting with families with children with disabilities.

Courtesy of Ellen Burkett

Teela is a beautiful, fun, 16-year-old young lady who happens to be severely disabled. When she was born, doctors didn't realize that there was anything wrong. By the time she was a year old, it was very apparent that Teela was not the perfect baby I had planned on. This realization was so devastating to me that I honestly believed I could never be happy again for the rest of my life. While the ensuing years have certainly had disappointments and heartache, I have also had a lot of joy from Teela, and my family and I have learned that happiness is indeed still possible.

Teela has two younger siblings—Marissa is 14 and Travis is 9. When asked what kind of an effect Teela has had on our family, both replied that it isn't really a good or bad effect, it's just what our family is and they can't imagine anything else. They don't feel like they've missed out on anything by having Teela as a sibling. Marissa even suggested that other families miss out on our experiences by not having a special needs member. As their mother, I put a lot of effort into making sure we have "normal" family activities. This means researching and planning carefully and making adaptations, but we have great times together and our efforts to include Teela help to unify us. We love to participate in outdoor activities such as camping and walking. We always make sure to go places where Teela can also go in her "Teela-mobile"—this is what we call her stroller because teenagers don't ride in strollers.

Caring for Teela and keeping her safe from the multiple seizures she suffers every day is also a family effort. Everyone helps with opening doors, physical therapy, and other small tasks. I do have to be careful to not ask too much of her siblings in order to avoid feelings of resentment. I worry that the extra time I spend with Teela could cause the rest of my family to feel neglected. I am always conscious of this and try to make sure that they are also getting enough of my time and attention. This puts a lot of pressure on me. I feel responsible for holding my family together and making sure their needs are all met while also meeting the special needs of Teela. It's an overwhelming task that I have to just take one day at a time. I have noticed that the way I treat Teela has a huge influence on how my other kids perceive her. When I'm feeling frustrated with her, they tend to also have negative feelings about her. I have had to work very hard to develop coping skills so that we can be a happy family. As I have learned to appreciate Teela and focus more on the positive, my family has followed suit.

Being the mother of a child with disabilities is by far the biggest challenge of my life but by no means has it ruined my life. This isn't exactly the family life I had envisioned, but we have all learned from Teela and have grown closer together because of her.

SOURCE: Ellen Burkett, personal communication, September 19, 2011.

## 6-1  A Changing Era in the Lives of People with Disabilities

Times have changed for families raising children with disabilities. Prior to the Education for All Handicapped Children Act of 1975 (renamed the Individuals with Disabilities Education Act), families did not have access to appropriate services for their children with disabilities, including free and appropriate public education. For example, in the 1930s, Don Kirkendall was denied access to public schooling because he had a physical disability due to having polio. He recalls this distinctly, indicating that before his mother had the chance to register him for elementary school, three school board members visited Don's parents and told them, "It has been brought to [our] attention that you folks have a son in a wheelchair. It is our duty to inform you he will be unable to attend school" (Warren & Kirkendall, 1973, p. 91).

The Individuals with Disabilities Education Act was landmark legislation that assured important rights to families with members with disabilities, unavailable to youngsters with disabilities prior to 1975. No longer were children with disabilities overwhelmingly excluded from school, placed in institutions, and excluded from society. With this and other subsequent legislation along with changing attitudes, families gained more rights and became stronger advocates for their children.

Along with families becoming more empowered over the years, education professionals have gained greater knowledge, skills, and nurturing attitudes toward students with disabilities and their families. They are becoming more inclusive in the ways they partner with, care for, and build helpful relationships with families. Increasingly, those who work with families and children with disabilities seek to understand their needs and aspirations, realizing that family members are the primary caregivers, the most constant sources of ongoing support, and powerful repositories of knowledge about their children and youth with disabilities. Moreover, professionals are now more adept in providing assistance and interventions that are home- and family-based, helping parents and siblings address important issues such as challenging behaviors, accessing respite care, and finding appropriate resources.

This chapter focuses on various types of families who live with children with disabilities. Many children with disabilities are raised by foster parents, single parents, parents of blended families, and grandparents, as well as by LGBTQ (lesbian, gay, bisexual, transgender, questioning) couples (Lee & Gardner, 2010). Furthermore, about a half million children are cared for through various state social services organizations and agencies (Fish, 2000; Kresak, Gallagher, & Kelley, 2014). It is clear that child care professionals need to work effectively and respectfully with all families, learning about their unique needs, and responding with family-sensitive programs and effective interventions (Dunst & Dempsey, 2007; McKie, 2006; Tellegen & Sanders, 2013; Ulrich, 2003).

The nature of families may vary, but one common factor is the presence of a child with a disability. All children deserve the attention and support of school personnel and other professionals—regardless of the type of family unit to which they belong. The people who serve as primary caregivers or legal guardians of these children should be invited to participate fully in all programs and support services (Fish, 2000).

## 6-2 Family Systems Approach

As revealed in the opening Snapshot, families play essential roles in caring for and nurturing children, particularly families who have children with disabilities. A family member with a disability impacts the family, just as family members impact the individual with a disability. This **family systems approach** recognizes the bidirectional influence of each family member on each other and on the family as a whole (Cridland, Jones, Magee, & Caputi, 2014; Seligman & Benjamin, 1989). Early research on families raising children with disabilities often studied the family in parts rather than as a whole, viewing individuals with disabilities as the cause or source of challenges in families. However, more recent research affirms the family as a system of interconnected parts that affect one another and the family as whole (Bavelas & Segal, 1982; Falik, 1995; Smith, Greenberg, & Seltzer, 2011). See Figure 6.1 for a graphic representation of this model.

Think about your own family and how each member influenced or impacted others in your family over time. Think about the role your parents played in attending to special events, challenges, or crises. How did their behaviors affect you and other members of your family? How did your family and its individual members respond to periodic problems and challenges? What kinds of support were available within your family when things went awry? How did your family members communicate and interact with each other? How helpful were you to each other in times of crises? Use your answers to these questions to think about families with children with disabilities.

One family systems approach is the Olson Circumplex Model. This model, supported by over 1,200 studies, defines family interactions with three central variables: flexibility, cohesion, and communication skills (Olson, 2011). When family members have good communication skills and manifest flexibility and cohesion, they are more likely to function in healthy and helpful ways with one another. Although too much flexibility leads to chaos in the family (e.g., lack of leadership, erratic discipline, too much change), too much rigidity leads to authoritarian leadership, strict discipline, and little change. Too much cohesion or the emotional bonding between family members leads to enmeshed families (e.g., little

**Family systems approach**
An approach in which all of the constituent parts, attributes, functions, and roles of a family are examined and considered in selecting and providing interventions, training, support, and care.

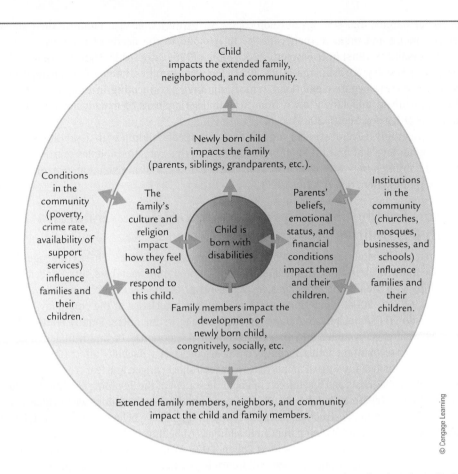

*Figure 6.1 Social/Ecological Model: Spheres of Influence*

Child impacts the extended family, neighborhood, and community.

Newly born child impacts the family (parents, siblings, grandparents, etc.).

Conditions in the community (poverty, crime rate, availability of support services) influence families and their children.

The family's culture and religion impact how they feel and respond to this child.

Child is born with disabilities

Parents' beliefs, emotional status, and financial conditions impact them and their children.

Institutions in the community (churches, mosques, businesses, and schools) influence families and their children.

Family members impact the development of newly born child, congnitively, socially, etc.

Extended family members, neighbors, and community impact the child and family members.

© Cengage Learning

tolerance for private space, rejection of non–family members). On the other hand, too little cohesion leads to disengaged families where there is little closeness, a lack of loyalty, and a high degree of independence (Olson, 2011).

The presence of a child with a disability impacts families in positive and challenging ways. Again, think about your own family's communication, flexibility, and cohesion. Consider the positive as well as the negative ways in which others in your family, particularly siblings, influenced your well-being and the quality of your family life. Thinking about your own experiences in your family will help you relate to families with children with disabilities.

## 6-2a Positive Impacts of Children with Disabilities on Their Families

The presence of a child with a disability in the family creates conditions for growth in siblings and parents (Connors & Stalker, 2003; Hastings, Beck, & Hill, 2005; Moyson & Roeyers, 2011). This growth may be evidenced in improved levels of empathy and patience, heightened communication skills, positive family relations, and greater emotional and psychological strength (Burbidge & Minnes, 2014; Flaherty & Glidden, 2000; Glidden & Schoolcraft, 2003). Mothers may grow in their capacity for compassion, selflessness, and resilience (Bayat, 2007; Cridland et al., 2014). The child with a disability may be a source of unity that bonds family members together and strengthens their relationships (Ferguson, 2002).

A recent study of thousands of households with children with Down syndrome affirms the positive views of parents regarding their sons or daughters with Down syndrome (Skotko, Levine, & Goldstein, 2011). Nearly 80 percent believed their outlook on life was more positive because of these children. These same families reported good relationships between and among their children with and without disabilities.

Interestingly, another study addressing the psychological well-being of fathers with and without children with disabilities provides some interesting findings (Boyraz & Sayger, 2010). Fathers with children with disabilities reported higher levels of self-acceptance and better adjustment in some domains than fathers of children without disabilities.

Some parents and siblings develop coping skills over time that enhance their sense of well-being and improve their capacity to respond to the needs of a family member with a disability (Baskin & Fawcett, 2006; Falik, 1995; Gray, 2002; Hauser-Cram, 2006; Pipp-Siegel, Sedey, & Yoshinaga-Itano, 2002). For some families, humor plays an important role in releasing negative emotions, remedying stress, connecting in unique ways with family members, and moving away from "terminal seriousness," a malady no family wants or needs (Rieger & Scotti, 2004).

Interestingly, several studies suggest that parents of children with disabilities experience higher levels of marital happiness, suggesting that for some couples rearing a child with disabilities may strengthen marital bonds, unity, and satisfaction (Kazak, 1987; Taanila, Kokkonen, & Jaervelin, 1996).

## 6-2b Family Challenges Related to Raising Children with Disabilities

Children with disabilities may present unique challenges for families. These challenges may include financial pressures, strained relationships with family members, altered social relationships with friends and associates, as well as physical and health problems (Newacheck, Inkelas, & Kim, 2004). Sometimes the disabling characteristics of the child may put the family into crisis, precipitating major conflicts among its members. Family relationships may be weakened by added and unexpected physical, emotional, or financial demands.

The birth of an infant with a disability or discovery of a disability affects the family as a social system in many ways. Parents may react with shock, anger, and fear. They may refuse to accept the diagnosis and feel uncertain about the extent of the disabling condition on their child (Huang, Kellett, & St. John, 2010). Moreover, youth with disabilities who evidence pronounced demanding, destructive, disruptive, and/or aggressive behaviors pose special challenges to the well-being of their parents and siblings (Abbeduto et al., 2004; Lach et al., 2009; McCarthy, Cuskelly, van Kraayenoord, & Cohen, 2006; Woodman & Hauser-Cram, 2013).

In general, families that include children with disabilities experience greater stress and more intense concerns about quality of life issues than families without children with disabilities (Baker-Ericzén, Brookman-Frazee, & Stahmer, 2005; Griffith et al., 2011; McCarthy et al., 2006; Theule, Wiener, Tannock, & Jenkins, 2012; Werner et al., 2009). These concerns relate to such factors as financial well-being, emotional health, social well-being, family interaction, parenting skills, and the challenges of other co-occurring disabilities in their children, particularly behavior problems (Lach et al., 2009; Neece, Blacher, & Baker, 2010; Poston et al., 2003; Segal, 2010; Stoneman, 2007; Wang et al., 2004).

Families caring for children with disabilities report difficulties with accessing services, finding high-quality care, qualifying for and receiving adequate insurance coverage, and shared decision making (Vohra, Madhavan, Sambamoorthi, & St. Peter, 2014). Parents often experience stress due to the intense caregiving responsibilities associated with raising their child with a disability, the personal emotional and physical challenges they experience, their efforts to maintain a healthy marital relationship, their desires to attend to the needs of their other children, and their need to seek for and obtain effective services (Freedman, Kalb, Zablotsky, & Stuart, 2012; McStay et al., 2014).

In extreme cases, families experience housing instability, greatly diminished access to health care, and a host of other problems (Parish et al., 2008). One research study indicated that more than one-fifth of children who have suffered maltreatment have disabilities, most commonly emotional/behavior disorders. These children are twice as likely to be in out-of-home placements than children without disabilities who have suffered maltreatment (Lightfoot, Hill, & Laliberte, 2011).

## 6-3 Parental Reactions

Parents' discovery that their infant or child has a disability can be heart wrenching and may have a profound impact on the family (MacInnes, 2008). The expected or fantasized child that the parents and other family members had anticipated does not arrive; generally parents are thrown into a state of emotional shock or disequilibrium. Carefully think about

Teela's mother and how she felt when she realized her one-year-old girl was not the "perfect baby" she had expected. Also, consider the perspectives and feelings shared by the mother of Andrew and Mariah (see later Snapshot).

## 6-3a Determining a Diagnosis

Some conditions, such as **spina bifida** and **Down syndrome**, are often apparent at or before birth, whereas others are not immediately detectable. Even if attending physicians and other professionals suspect the presence of a disabling condition, they may be unable to give a firm diagnosis without the passage of some time and further testing. When parents suspect a child is not developing normally, waiting for a diagnosis can be agonizing (Fox & Dunlap, 2002; Frost, 2002; Siklos & Kerns, 2007).

A variety of responses are present in parents of infants and toddlers when they obtain a diagnosis of disability (Bingham, Correa, & Huber, 2012; Feinger-Schaal & Oppenheim, 2013). Sometimes the concern that something is "wrong" with their child lasts only a few hours, while other parents' negative feelings last weeks or months (Bingham, Correa, & Huber, 2012). However, obtaining a diagnosis after the child has begun school is also difficult for family members. Many children with attention deficit/hyperactivity disorder (ADHD), specific learning disabilities, and other mild conditions are not diagnosed until they begin struggling in school.

**CEC**

Standard 4
Assessment

**Spina bifida**
A developmental defect of the spinal column.

**Down syndrome**
A condition caused by a chromosomal abnormality that results in unique physical characteristics and varying degrees of intellectual disabilities.

---

**? LEARNING THROUGH SOCIAL MEDIA**

### Shasta Kearns Moore

*This writer, author, self-publisher, and stay-at-home mama has twins, JJ and Malachi, one of whom has cerebral palsy.*

*Check out this one of many social media postings produced by Shasta, the mother of an identical twin with cerebral palsy. Increasingly, mothers and fathers are using social media to share their experiences, ideas, and concerns. They are also sharing their feelings about what they are learning about themselves and their children.*

#### Floor Time Frustration

Something I've really incorporated during the past year is how important it is to stay positive. As in, it actually improves outcomes to focus on what is going right and ignore what isn't.

That said, it's time for a rant.

A year after we first discovered the Anat Baniel Method, we went pretty hardcore into it. During the past two years, we've spent tens of thousands of dollars on lessons with senior practitioners, including Anat Baniel herself.

Jessie Kirk

A key point of ABM is to leave the child on his back on the floor as much as possible. Anat Baniel believes that special needs children, when given the proper information and treatments, will progress on more or less the same path as a neurotypical baby, just slower. For the same reasons physical therapists across the nation discourage the use of Johnny Jump-Ups and other standing devices for neurotypical babies, Anat argues that most equipment, such as walkers, standers, and the like, only serve to ingrain bad habits and teach the child ways of moving that won't lead toward independent and pain-free movement.

This has never quite felt right to me, but Anat is right about so much else that we decided to give it a try. For at least a year—during Malachi's most critical period of brain development—we gave

him as much floor time as he would tolerate and had him in supported sitting the rest of the time. A year ago, we relaxed this policy to try out a gait trainer, but rarely used it until Malachi suddenly learned how in September.

Throughout the past two years, we've had the exact same pattern with floor time repeated over and over again. Malachi will roll over one day, and I think joyfully: "This is it! He is finally putting it together! Pretty soon, he'll be rolling all over the house!" But he doesn't really do it again for months. Then Malachi will learn how to crawl, and I think joyfully: "This is it! He is finally putting it together! Pretty soon he'll be crawling all over the house!" But then he doesn't really do it again for months.

I keep waiting for him to feel internally motivated to use these skills, to get that object, to explore the house on his own, but no matter how much I wish and wait and leave him alone to surprise me, IT NEVER HAPPENS.

SOURCE: Adapted from *Floor Time Frustration*. Retrieved February 24, 2015, from www.outrageousfortune.net /2014/04/floor-time-frustration.html

Parents and professionals need to be patient with each other, especially when the manifestations of potential disabilities are vague, inconsistent, or complicated. Keeping the lines of communication open, positive, and appropriately factual generally produces good outcomes for all—physicians, parents, psychologists, and other care providers.

Although parents of children with disabilities may experience similar feelings and reactions to receiving a diagnosis, their responses to specific challenges and related time periods as well as their eventual adjustments vary immensely (Poston et al., 2003; Turnbull & Turnbull, 2002). There is no consistent path or sequence of specific stages of adjustment through which all parents move (Hauser-Cram, 2006). The stage approach simply helps us think about the ways in which parents and others might respond to an infant or child with a disability over time. Emotions associated with one stage or phase may overlap and resurface during another period. Some parents may go through distinct periods of adjustment, whereas others may adjust without passing through any identifiable stages. The process of adjustment for parents is continuous and uniquely individual (Baxter, Cummins, & Yiolitis, 2000; Fine & Nissenbaum, 2000; Ulrich, 2003).

## 6-3b Experiencing Shock

The initial response to the birth of an infant with a disability is generally shock, distinguished by feelings of anxiety, guilt, numbness, confusion, helplessness, anger, disbelief, denial, and despair. Parents sometimes have feelings of grief, detachment, bewilderment, or bereavement. At this time, when many parents are most in need of support, the least amount of help may be available.

Here are the responses of several parents as they learned they were mothers of children with disabilities. "The day my child was diagnosed as having a disability, I was devastated—and so confused that I recall little else about those first days other than the heartbreak." Another parent described this event as a "black sack" being pulled down over her head, blocking her ability to hear, see, and think in normal ways. Another parent described the trauma as "having a knife stuck in her heart" (Smith, 2015).

During the initial period of shock, parents may be unable to process or comprehend information provided by medical and other health care personnel. For this reason, information may need to be communicated later to parents—even several times in loving and understandable ways. Moreover, parents may experience major assaults to their self-worth and belief systems during this period. They may blame themselves for their child's disability and may seriously question their once positive views of themselves. Likewise, they may be forced to reassess the meaning of their lives, the reasons for their present challenges, and how they will adjust to their current circumstances and powerful feelings.

The ways in which parents react during this period depend on the nature of their psychological makeup, the types of support available, their cultural and religious beliefs, the type and severity of the disability, and other factors. Over time, many parents migrate from being victims to becoming survivors of what they experienced initially as trauma (Gray, 2002; Ravindran & Myers, 2012).

Another common reaction is depression, often exhibited in the form of grief or mourning (Brown, 2014; Parentlink, 2011). Some parents describe such emotions as very much like those suffered after the death of a loved one (Bingham, Correa, & Huber, 2012). Recurrent sorrow and frequent feelings of inadequacy are emotions that parents may experience as they gradually adjust to having an infant or child with a disability (Lee et al., 2001). These ongoing feelings may be triggered by health or behavior challenges presented by the child, perplexing care demands, the child's inability to meet developmental milestones such as walking and talking, and the insensitivity of extended family and/or community members (Gray, 2002; Lee et al., 2001).

The process of adjustment, as indicated earlier, is continuous and uniquely individual (Baxter, Cummins, & Yiolitis, 2000; Fine & Nissenbaum, 2000; Ulrich, 2003).

Consider this revealing reflection of a mother of a child with autism:

> *But I could not stay in denial long. I reread every single book and highlighted paragraphs that supported Rocky's autism diagnosis, this time in neon yellow. By the end of my research, my books were suffering from severe jaundice.*

*I showed the diseased pages to my doubting spouse. Together we conceded defeat in the battle against the dreaded label.*

*After sobering up from the intoxication of denial, grief and despair overwhelmed me. I sank into a deep depression. Friends urged me to get help, so I reluctantly went to a support group.... (Mara, 2010, p. 17)*

Some parents, siblings, and even relatives of children with disabilities employ a kind of cognitive coping that enables them to think about the child, sibling, or grandchild with a disability in ways that enhance their sense of well-being and increase their capacity for responding positively to the child (Baskin & Fawcett, 2006; Chapadjiev, 2009). For example, consider the following account of one mother concerning her response to the birth of a child with a disability:

*Brian, my husband, was so completely calm and supportive, he comforted me (and still does) many a many a many a time! We believed that God would show us miracles— maybe not in the way of miraculously having a "normal" baby, but that all would be well and His will, and that we would be HAPPY. Things changed. I started looking at life differently and noticing what was really important. Earlier challenges seemed so trivial now. I had my faith in God, my family, and an active baby boy growing inside of me.*

*I was grateful for each kick and bump I felt the baby make, as well as the bond that mama and baby were creating. I wrote a special song and sang it to him often. Pregnancy is so amazing. (Bree, 2011)*

This mother was able to interpret the birth and subsequent events in a positive manner. Her thinking or cognitive coping helped her reduce or successfully manage potential feelings of shock, distress, and depression. Additionally, her positive interpretation of this event aided her adjustment and contributed to her capacity to respond effectively to her child's needs. In this regard, parents and others can be taught effective cognitive coping strategies that can greatly enhance their emotional well-being and improve their overall functioning, thus heightening their effectiveness as parents (Woodman & Hauser-Cram, 2013).

## 6-3c  Coming to a Realization

When parents come to realize that their child has a disability, they may engage in several types of behavior. They may be anxious or fearful about their ability to cope with the demands of caring for a child with unique needs. They may be easily irritated or upset and spend considerable time in self-accusation, self-pity, or self-hatred. They may continue to reject or deny information provided by care providers and medical personnel. During this stage, however, parents begin to understand the actual demands and constraints of raising a child or youth with a disability (Lee et al., 2001). For example, one parent wrote:

*"It's probably cerebral palsy," said the early intervention therapist. Rachel was only four months old during this initial evaluation. She couldn't hold her head up, roll over, sit up, or crawl. She couldn't even lift her arms or legs. She had no eye contact, cried constantly, and never slept. I knew something was wrong and feared she would never bond with me.*

*I remember starting to cry. The grandmothers looked on, tried to hold back their tears, but they couldn't. My perfect child was officially not perfect. After collecting my thoughts and trying to shed the feeling of devastation, I tried to think of the positives. As long as it's CP, I thought, this diagnosis meant that she would be physically disabled, but her mental faculties would be intact. We called to make an appointment with a neurologist within 10 minutes of the initial CP diagnosis. (Epstein & Bessell, 2002, p. 56)*

## 6-3d  Moving Away from Retreat

During the defensive retreat stage, parents attempt to avoid dealing with the anxiety-producing realities of their child's condition. Gradually, with appropriate support, parents begin to embrace coping strategies that center on problem solving, pursuing professional support, actively seeking information relevant to their child, and obtaining support from family, friends, and advocacy groups. Additionally, with help often provided by other parents who have children with disabilities, parents begin to reframe their challenges by looking for the positive aspects of their and their children's lives.

## 6-3e   Coming to Acknowledgment

Acknowledgment is the stage in which parents mobilize their strengths and skills to confront the conditions created by having a child with a disability. At this time, parents begin to involve themselves more fully in interventions and treatments. They are also better able to comprehend information or directions provided by care providers. Some parents join advocacy groups that contribute to their adjustment. Parents begin to accept the child with the disability (Capitani, 2007; Friend & Cook, 2003). During this stage, parents begin to direct their energies and abilities at their children's challenges and capitalize on their strengths.

 **SNAPSHOT**   # Autism in the Family

### Christie Allred

My qualifications to write to you on families of children with disabilities do not stem from a formal education, but rather, from two of my six children being diagnosed on different quadrants of the autism spectrum. Our story begins over 26 years ago, with the birth of my oldest son, Andrew, who has Asperger's syndrome, and continues through the birth of my youngest daughter, Mariah, who was diagnosed with high-functioning autism 10 years later. This story also reaches across two generations, with my grandson being diagnosed with autism five years ago and with one other grandchild, still too young to be diagnosed, showing those all-too-familiar symptoms of the disorder.

When I started my parenting years, *autism* was not a familiar term. Teachers interacting with Andrew referred to him as "unteachable" and an "odd duck." In fact, one middle school principal stated that Andrew brought the bullying on himself by playing the constant victim.

However, for us, Andrew stood out with his gentle disposition and extremely focused individual play. Most of the time, he created his own world. When given numbers to add, he never used his fingers or counted

Courtesy of Christie Allred

individual items. Even as early as 3 years old, he could add large numbers in his head, immediately knowing the answer. His brilliance was just beginning to show through his blank, and often emotionless, face.

With greater understanding in later years, our family became closer and stronger, building up a defensive wall against the outside world. Siblings, who were once resentful, now stuck together to protect their autistic brother from those who would try to tease or single him out.

The diagnosis finally came for Andrew when he was 17, way too late to stop the painful years of suffering from bullies, overmedication, misdiagnosis, and hospitalization. He continues to need assistance with the basic needs in his life. His intellect, however, is as bright as ever. He is currently a senior at a university, majoring in mathematics and physics.

In stark contrast to Andrew's early school years, Mariah now has the benefit of increased educational focus on the social and behavioral challenges of autistic children. Mariah was diagnosed at age 11, and was allowed special accommodations that helped her succeed in school. With education on how to teach students with autism, teachers provided Mariah a positive and creative learning experience, specially developed to meet her needs.

My grandson was diagnosed with severe autism. At the age of 2, he would not communicate or acknowledge anyone when called. He wears a tracking device on his ankle to provide security in case he wanders away. Today, he is thriving, with positive experiences of early intervention at home and school. The school district was providing speech therapy and developmental classes to help him succeed by the time he was 3 years old. Now he is included in a classroom two grade levels above his age group.

As time passes, we have grown to understand that autism is not just a disability of children, but is a lifelong family commitment, as autistic children become autistic adults. Even so, we continue to feel blessed to have these special individuals as part of our family.

## 6-4 Family Relationships

The birth of a child with a disability and its continued presence strongly influence how family members respond to one another, particularly if the child has severe disabilities and presents behavior problems. Providing ongoing care for multiple children with disabilities can be especially challenging, potentially reducing family cohesion and adaptability (Orsmond, Lin, & Seltzer, 2007).

When mothers are drawn away from the tasks they once performed, other family members—usually daughters—often must assume more responsibility and new roles (Laman & Shaughnessy, 2007). Adjusting to new roles and routines may be difficult for some family members.

Many relationships may be affected when caring for a family member with a disability: spousal, mother–child, father–child, and sibling relationships, as well as relationships between the child and his or her grandparents and extended family members.

### 6-4a Spousal or Partner Relationships

Research related to spousal or partner relationships is often contradictory (Lach et al., 2009; McCarthy et al., 2006; Stoneman & Gavidia-Payne, 2006). Also, there is a paucity of research on diverse couples (LGBTQ, parents of blended families, unmarried couples, etc.) raising children with disabilities (Baumle & Compton, 2014; Leung, Erich, & Kanenberg, 2005). With the passage of time and increased numbers of diverse couples adopting and caring for children with disabilities, more research will inevitably surface.

Some families with children with disabilities experience extreme spousal turmoil, often culminating in separation and eventually divorce, yet others experience the usual joys and challenges of being married and serving as parents (McCarthy et al., 2006). Recent research suggests that there "is a detectable overall negative impact on marital adjustment, but this impact is small and much lower than would be expected given earlier assumptions about the supposed inevitability of damaging impacts of children with disabilities on family well-being" (Risdal & Singer, 2004, p. 101).

There are significant benefits for children with disabilities who are reared in families with high parent self-efficacy—this has been defined as parents who believe they can positively impact the behavior and development of their children. Research affirms that parent self-efficacy is strongly related to children's development, effective parenting, and parental competence (Boyraz & Sayger, 2011; Dyches et al., 2012). Parental efficacy also contributes to overall family well-being and family cohesiveness.

What follows is a discussion of relevant factors that contribute to spousal happiness and success. These factors include coming to understand the adjustments that need to be embraced, the kinds of spousal support and nurturing that are so useful, how to respond to newly discovered demands, and the benefits of respite care.

A child with a significant disability may require immediate and prolonged attention from the mother for feeding, treatment, and general care (Smith et al., 2010). Thus, her attention may become riveted on the life of the child with a disability. The balance that once existed between being a mother and being a spouse no longer exists. The mother may become so involved with caring for the child that other relationships lose some of their quality and intensity. Feelings of loss, neglect, and dissatisfaction are typical for some fathers (Boström & Broberg, 2014).

**Husband Support and Involvement** As indicated, mothers deeply involved in caregiving often feel overworked, overwhelmed, and in need of a break. They may wonder why their spouses are not more helpful and understanding. Husbands who assist with the burdens of caring for a child with a disability serve as a buffer, contributing to their partner's well-being and resilience. Day-to-day physical and psychological support provided by husbands is invaluable to mothers of children with disabilities (Rummel-Hudson, 2008; Simmerman, Blacher, & Baker, 2001). This support is also predictive of couple-centered satisfaction and contentment. Moreover, husbands who effectively employ

**Photo 6.1** Parents of children with disabilities need time to be together. This is often made possible through respite care.

©Tyler Olson/Shutterstock.com

**Respite care**
Assistance provided by individuals outside of the immediate family to give parents and other children time away from the child with a disability.

problem-focused coping, actively confronting stressful problems associated with rearing a child with disabilities, contribute to higher marital adjustment and greater life satisfaction in their spouses (Stoneman & Gavidia-Payne, 2006). Also, stable and supportive marriages protect fathers of children with disabilities from depression and related conditions (Boyraz & Sayger, 2011).

**Marital Distress** Fear, anger, guilt, and resentment often interfere with a couple's capacity to communicate and seek realistic solutions. Fatigue itself profoundly affects how couples function and communicate. As a result, some parents of children with disabilities join together to create **respite care** programs, which give them opportunities to get away from the demands and stress of child rearing. These programs give couples opportunities to relax, renew, and sustain their relationships (Baskin & Fawcett, 2006). Just one hour of respite care per week has been shown to help couples in distressed marriages have more satisfactory relationships (Harper et al., 2013).

Other factors also contribute to stress: unusually heavy financial burdens for medical treatment or therapy; frequent visits to treatment facilities; foregone time in couple-related activities; lost sleep and fatigue, particularly in the early years of the child's life; and potential social isolation from relatives and friends.

---

 **REFLECT ON THIS**

## Friday's Kids Respite

Friday's Kids Respite (www.fridayskids .org) is a unique service for families. Simply expressed, it delivers high-quality respite care—allowing parents and family members a reprieve from the demands of caring for an infant or child with a disability. As mirrored in its name, Friday is the night on which parents and others can be free for several hours to be with each other, knowing their child with simple or profound needs will be fully cared for while having a fun and even stimulating evening with caring volunteers and well-trained professionals.

One of Friday's Kids Respite's most unique features is its capacity to care for children with unique medical or other needs. Children with all kinds of conditions and disabilities are gladly accepted. Feeding, medical regimens, and

medications—all factors are attended to in providing the respite care.

The program strengthens families and communities by giving parents and other caregivers opportunities to catch their breath, to enjoy an evening out, or to give some concentrated attention to their other children in family-centered activities. Children with disabilities receive one-on-one attention in a safe and yet stimulating environment with caring youth, adults, and medical professionals who attend to their unique needs and capacities.

Concerned individuals can play wonderful roles in their communities by volunteering regularly to give respite care.

Locating a youth or adult who is willing and able to provide quality care for an evening or weekend is extremely

difficult. In some areas of the country, however, enterprising teenagers have developed babysitting businesses that specialize in tending children with disabilities. Frequently, local disability associations and parent-to-parent programs help families find qualified babysitters or other respite care providers.

### Questions for Reflection

1. Now that you are familiar with the concept of respite care, what are the skills and dispositions you would need to participate fully and effectively in a program such as Friday's Kids Respite?

2. What would motivate you to give one night each month to this kind of enterprise?

SOURCE: Adapted from Friday's Kids, retrieved September 29, 2011, from www.fridayskids.org.

Time away from a child with a disability or serious illness gives parents and siblings a chance to meet some of their own needs (Chan & Sigafoos, 2000). (See the related Reflect on This, "Friday's Kids Respite.") Parents can recharge themselves for demanding regimens, and siblings can use the exclusive attention of their parents to reaffirm their importance and their value as family members. When parents cannot take a break, the added stress of caring for a child with a disability continues to grow.

## 6-4b Mother–Child Relationships

Mothers play significant roles in the lives of their children, especially children with disabilities. In most cases, if a child's impairment is readily apparent at birth, the mother often becomes responsible for relating to the child and attending to his or her needs. If an infant is born prematurely or needs extensive, early medical assistance, the mother may be prevented from engaging in the typical feeding and caregiving routines that bring about attachment and provide the foundation for vitally important bonding. Moreover, mothers responsible for caring for multiple children with disabilities are likely to experience "greater challenges to their personal well-being and family functioning" (Orsmond, Lin, & Seltzer, 2007, p. 264).

In many families, the mother experiences the greatest amount of trauma and strain. In caring for such a child, she may no longer be able to do many of the tasks she once did, and her attention to other family members may be greatly altered. Thus, powerful relationships often develop between mothers and their children with disabilities.

**Dyadic and Bidirectional Relationships** As alluded to earlier, mothers frequently develop strong **dyadic relationships** with their children with disabilities (Hauser-Cram, 2006). Dyadic relationships are characterized by very close ties between these children and their mothers. Bidirectional relationships are those in which both individuals are impacted by the relationship. The child impacts the mother, and the mother impacts the child. This is also true in sibling relationships. Influences, both positive and negative, flow in both directions.

Rather than communicating with all members of the family, a child with a disability may use his or her mother as the exclusive channel for communicating needs and making requests. Dyadic relationships may also develop between other members of the family. Certain siblings may turn to each other for support and nurturing. Older siblings, particularly daughters, may take on the role of parent substitutes as a result of their new caregiving responsibilities, and their younger siblings may develop strong relationships with them (Burbidge & Minnes, 2014).

**Overprotectiveness** Mothers who develop very close relationships with their children who have disabilities often walk a variety of tightropes (Larson, 2000). In their

**Dyadic relationships**
Relationships involving two individuals who develop and maintain a significant affiliation over time.

---

### CASE STUDY ON EMBRACING DIVERSITY

#### Halgan

Halgan is a recent refugee from Somalia. She is a single mother with three children—two daughters, 8 and 10, and one son—Abuukar. He is a six-year-old with severe disabilities. Halgan knows little about public schooling in the United States and knows even less about services available for children and youth with disabilities. Moreover, she is learning English as a second language.

You are Abuukar's special education teacher. He has just become a member

of your class. You sense Halgan's concern and confusion about what to do for her son and how to relate to you and the school system. Because of your commitment to your students and their families, you genuinely want to be helpful to Abuukar, his mother, and their family.

*Application Questions*

**1.** What do you do immediately to communicate more effectively with Halgan?

**2.** How do you gain her trust?

**3.** What do you need to learn potentially about her culture and experiences?

**4.** What skills and knowledge will help you more fully serve Abuukar and his family?

**5.** Whom should you seek out to help you become informed in relating well to Halgan and her family?

desire to protect their children, they may be overprotective and, thus, deny their children of opportunities to practice the skills and participate in the activities that ultimately lead to independence. Mothers may also underestimate their children's capacities and may be reluctant to allow them to engage in challenging activities. In contrast, other mothers may neglect their children with disabilities and not provide the stimulation so critical to their optimal development.

The mother's long-term vision for her child with a disability dramatically influences her behavior in preparing her son or daughter for adulthood and appropriate independence. For many mothers, conquering the tendency to be overprotective is extremely difficult, but it can be accomplished with help from other parents who have already experienced and overcome this particular challenge. If the mother or other care providers continue to be overprotective, the results can be counterproductive, especially when the child reaches late adolescence and is unprepared for entry into adulthood or semi-independent living.

## 6-4c Father–Child Relationships

Research about fathers of children with disabilities is growing in scope and depth (Boström & Broberg, 2014; MacDonald & Hastings, 2010a, 2010b; Parette, Meadan, & Doubet, 2010; Pleck, 2010; Saloviita, Itälinna, & Leinonen, 2003). New research sheds light on the relationships fathers have with their sons or daughters with disabilities.

**Responses of Fathers** Some research suggests that the involvement of fathers with children who have disabilities is not significantly different from that of fathers of children without disabilities (Turbiville, 1997; Young & Roopnarine, 1994). Moreover, fathers are generally more reserved and guarded in expressing their feelings in contrast to other family members (Boström & Broberg, 2014). Fathers are also more likely to internalize their feelings. Research suggests that fathers respond differently than mothers to the challenges and stressors associated with caring for and rearing a child with a disability, particularly sons who display behavior problems (McCarthy et al., 2006).

However, the aforementioned research outcomes are changing with more fathers engaging in the primary and routine roles of caring for and nurturing children with disabilities in their families (Boström & Broberg, 2014). Historically, fathers spent less time with their children with disabilities; thus, their psychological wellness was not impacted as much as that of their spouses. However, with increasingly greater gender equity and involvement of fathers in caring for children with disabilities, they may experience similar emotional outcomes as their spouses in terms of stress, depression, and fatigue.

Generally, fathers of children with intellectual disabilities are typically more concerned than mothers about their children's social development and eventual educational status, particularly if they are boys (Turbiville, 1997). Likewise, fathers are more affected than mothers by the visibility and severity of their children's conditions (Lamb & Meyer, 1991; Turbiville, 1997; Wang et al., 2004). Often fathers of children with severe disabilities spend less time interacting with them, playing with them, and engaging in school-related tasks. Fathers are more likely to be involved with their children with disabilities if the children are able to speak or interact with words and phrases.

The relationships that emerge between fathers and their children with disabilities are influenced by the same factors as mother–child relationships. As indicated earlier, one important factor may be the gender of the child (Turbiville, 1997). If the child is male and if the father has idealized the

*Photo 6.2* Supportive fathers contribute to the happiness of their children and their spouses by being available for child care and other home-centered support.

©Jaren Jai Wicklund/Shutterstock.com

role he would eventually assume in interacting with a son, the adjustment for the father can be very hard. The father may have had hopes of playing football with the child, of the son eventually becoming a business partner, or of participating with his son in a variety of recreational activities. Many of these hopes may not be realized with a son who has a severe disability.

**CEC**

**Standard 7**
Collaboration

**Training Preferences of Fathers** Fathers of children with disabilities prefer events and learning activities that are directed at the whole family, not just themselves (Turbiville & Marquis, 2001). They want to learn with other family members about encouraging learning, fostering language development, and promoting other skills (Johnson, 2000). Also, support for fathers centers on helping them develop closer relationships with their children with disabilities, which contributes significantly to their development and positive feeling about themselves (Boström & Broberg, 2014).

Service providers sometimes neglect fathers, not realizing the important contributions they are capable of making. Also, fathers prefer programs that clearly address their preferences and priorities—programs that focus on their needs (Turbiville & Marquis, 2001). Children whose fathers are involved in their education perform better in school, evidence better social skills, are more highly motivated to succeed in school, and are less likely to exhibit violent or delinquent behavior later on in their lives (Johnson, 2000; Turbiville, 1997).

## 6-4d Sibling Relationships

Sibling relationships are often the longest lasting relationships individuals with disabilities have. Siblings are present at birth, through childhood, and frequently throughout adulthood, long after their parents have passed away. Because of these lifelong relationships, siblings play important roles in the lives of people with disabilities (Burbidge & Minnes, 2014).

About 6.5 million children in the United States have a sibling with a disability (Laman & Shaughnessy, 2007). The vast majority of siblings of children with a disability are essentially identical to siblings in families without disabilities (Neece, Blacher, & Baker, 2010). Having a sister or a brother with a disability does not cause or promote psychological problems per se (Hastings, 2006). Across a spectrum of behaviors and attributes (self-concept, perceived ability, and so on), siblings of children with a disability are remarkably similar to siblings of families without disabilities (Stoneman, 2005; Verté, Hebbrecht, & Roeyers, 2006). However, as indicated earlier, recent research affirms a strong relationship between the presence of behavior problems in children and negative impacts on their siblings as well as their parents, especially if behavior problems co-occur with other disabilities in a child or youth (Lach et al., 2009; Neece, Blacher, & Baker, 2010; Orsmond & Seltzer, 2009; Pinkham, 2010).

**Common Questions of Siblings** Responses of siblings to a sister or brother with a disability vary (Brown, 2004; Laman & Shaughnessy, 2007; McHugh, 2003; Meyer, 2005; Skotko & Levine, 2009; Strohm, 2005). Upon learning that a brother or sister has a disability, siblings may be burdened with different kinds of concerns about their quality of life and other factors (Davys, Mitchell, & Haigh, 2011).

A number of questions are commonly asked: "Why did this happen?" "Is my brother contagious?" "Can I tell others about my brother?" "What am I going to say to my friends?" "Am I going to have to take care of him all of my life?" "Will I have children who are disabled too?" "How will I later meet my responsibilities to my brother with a disability and also meet the needs of my future wife and children?"

Like their parents, siblings generally want to know and understand as

*Photo 6.3* Siblings may play many roles in nurturing a brother or sister with a disability.

much as they can about the disability of their siblings. They want to know how they should respond and how their lives may be different as a result of having a brother or sister with a disability. If these concerns can be adequately addressed, the prospects for positive involvement with the brother or sister with a disability are much better (Brown, 2004; Darley, Porter, Werner, & Eberly, 2002).

What follows are comments made by siblings of children with disabilities. These comments give you a sense for the perceptions and feelings of youth regarding their siblings (Meyer, 2005, p. 72–73): "You get more clothes because she doesn't care about them" (Lydia Q., 13, Massachusetts). "If my sister wasn't a part of my life, I would be so ignorant about people who have disabilities" (Margaret C., 14, Illinois). "It gives you a different outlook on life. You don't take anything in life for granted. Jeremy helps me to slow down and just take a moment to relax and love life" (Lindsay D., 17, North Carolina). "One thing is that we have a handicap sticker for parking. She also brings happiness to our family" (Katelyn C., 16, Virginia). "You become sensitive to other people's needs and more understanding and accepting of people's differences. You also get to be part of special groups like Sibshops" (Erin G., 14, Alberta). "I think David's made me a better person. Definitely a less judgmental one" (Katie J., 19, Illinois).

### Effects of Parents' Attitudes and Behaviors on Siblings

Parents' attitudes and behaviors significantly impact their children's views of a sibling with a disability (Grissom & Borkowski, 2002; Stoneman, 2005). Don Meyer, a specialist in sibling relationships, expressed it this way:

> If parents perceive their child's disability as this life-searing tragedy from which there's no escape, they shouldn't be a bit surprised to find that their typically developing kids perceive it that way as well. On the other hand, if they perceive it as being a series of challenges that they have little choice but to meet with as much grace and humor as they can muster, then they have every reason to believe that their typically developing kids will face it that way as well. (Laman & Shaughnessy, 2007, p. 46)

If parents are optimistic and realistic in their views toward the child with a disability, then siblings are likely to mirror these attitudes and related behaviors.

### Sibling Concerns

With increased inclusion of students with disabilities in neighborhood schools and other general education settings, siblings are often "called into action." They may be asked to explain their brother's or sister's behavior, to give ongoing support or modeling, and to respond to questions teachers and others might ask. Furthermore, they may be subject to teasing and related behaviors. Because of these and other factors, some siblings are at greater risk for developing behavior problems.

Some siblings resent the time and attention parents devote to their sister or brother with a disability. This resentment may also take the form of jealousy. Some siblings feel emotionally neglected, convinced that their parents are unaware of their need for attention and emotional support (McHugh, 2003). For some siblings, the predominant feeling is one of bitter resentment or even rage. For others, the predominant attitude is deprivation, believing that their social, educational, and recreational pursuits have been seriously limited.

The following statements are examples of such feelings: "We never went on a family vacation because of my brother, Steven." "How could I invite a friend over? I never knew how my autistic brother would behave." "How do you explain to a date that you have a sister who is retarded?" "Many of my friends stopped coming to my house because they didn't know how to handle my brother, Mike, who is deaf. They simply could not understand him." "I was always shackled with the responsibilities of tending my little sister. I didn't have time to have fun with my friends." "I want a real brother, not a retarded one."

Siblings of children with disabilities may also believe they must compensate for their parents' disappointment about having a child with a disability (McHugh, 2003). They may feel an undue amount of pressure to excel or to be successful in a particular academic or artistic pursuit.

**Positive Perspectives and Influences of Siblings** Generally, siblings have positive feelings about having a sister or brother with a disability and believe that their experiences with this sibling with a disability made them better individuals (Chambers, 2007; Nielson et al., 2012; Plat et al., 2014; Roper et al., 2014; Stoneman, 2005; Taunt & Hastings, 2002). Siblings who are kindly disposed toward assisting the child with a disability can be a real source of support (Brown, 2004; Harland & Cuskelly, 2000). One mother of an 11-year-old son put it this way:

> In the past he has said, "I wish I had a regular brother, I wish I had someone to play with." And there are really some hard, sad things like that. But over the years, he has been such a support, and he will help in any way that we ask. I'm pleased with the qualities that I see in him. (Darley et al., 2002, pp. 34–35)

Many siblings play crucial roles in fostering the intellectual, social, and cognitive development of a brother or sister with a disability. Some even become special educators and care providers in part because of their experiences in growing up with a sibling with a disability (Chambers, 2007; Marks, Matson, & Barraza, 2005).

**Sibling Support Groups** Support groups for siblings of children with disabilities can be particularly helpful to adolescents (Laman & Shaughnessy, 2007). These groups introduce youth to the important aspects of having a sibling with a disability. They assist in setting appropriate expectations and discussing questions siblings may be hesitant to ask in family settings. These groups and related support services also provide helpful means for analyzing problems and identifying practical solutions (McHugh, 2003; Williams, Piamjariyakul, Graff, & Stanton, 2010).

### 6-4e Extended Family Relationships

The term *extended family* is frequently used to describe a household in which an immediate (nuclear) family lives with relatives. In this section, this term is used to refer to close relatives or friends with whom the immediate family has regular and frequent contact, even though they do not necessarily live in the same household. These individuals may include grandparents, uncles, aunts, cousins, close neighbors, or friends.

**Grandparents** Research indicates that grandparents, particularly during the disability identification process, are influential in how their children—the new parents—respond to the child with a disability. If grandparents and others show understanding, offer emotional support, and provide good role models of effectively coping, they may positively impact a struggling mother and father. If grandparents are critical and nonresponsive, they may add to the parents' burdens and worsen an already challenging situation (Lee & Gardner, 2010; Seligman & Darling, 1989).

When a grandchild with a disability is born, the joy of the birth event may dissipate. Like parents, grandparents may be hurled into a crisis that necessitates reevaluation and reorientation (Lee & Gardner, 2010). They must decide not only how they will respond to their child, who is now a parent, but also how they will relate to the new grandchild. Many grandparents, having grown up in a time when deviation from the norm was barely tolerated, much less understood, enter the adjustment process without much prior understanding.

However, things are changing with the inclusion of children with disabilities in general education classrooms and schools. Many yet-to-be parents and grandparents will have had many experiences with children and youth with disabilities because of their elementary and secondary school experiences.

*Photo 6.4* Grandparents or other close relatives may be very helpful in providing respite care.

©Monkey Business Images/Shutterstock.com

**CEC**

**Standard 7**
Collaboration

**Support for Grandparents and the Extended Family** Grandparents and other extended family members may contribute a great deal to the primary family unit and increase its overall happiness (Baskin & Fawcett, 2006; Darley et al., 2002; Fox et al., 2002; Luckner & Velaski, 2004). The correlation between grandparent support and positive paternal adjustment is significant (Sandler, Warren, & Raver, 1995). One mother of a child with a disability described a grandmother's actions in this way: "She would play with my son and make a big game out of things that the therapist wanted him to practice. I believe because of her...[my son] is able to walk today" (Baranowski & Schilmoeller, 1999, p. 441). If grandparents or other relatives live near the family, they may become integral parts of the support network and, as such, may be able to provide assistance before the energies and resources of their children are so severely depleted that they require additional costly help. To be of assistance, grandparents must be prepared and informed, which can be achieved in a variety of ways. They must have an opportunity to voice their questions, feelings, and concerns about the disability and its complications (Lee & Gardner, 2010). Parents can aid in this process by sharing with their own parents and siblings the pamphlets, materials, and books suggested by health, advocacy, medical, and educational support groups.

Grandparents may be helpful in providing much-needed respite care and sometimes financial assistance in the form of a "special needs" trust for long-term support of a grandchild (Bertelli, Silverman, & Talbot, 2009; Carpenter, 2000). Furthermore, they may be able to give parents a weekend reprieve from the pressures of maintaining the household and assisting with transportation or babysitting. Grandparents may often serve as third-party evaluators, providing solutions to seemingly irresolvable problems. The child with a disability profits from the unique attention that only grandparents can provide. This attention can be a natural part of special occasions such as birthdays, outings, and other traditional family activities.

Interestingly, millions of children with disabilities now live with their grandparents who are their primary caregivers. These grandparents struggle with many of the same issues and challenges as other parents, including depression, stress, and anxiety—often related to finances and housing. They, like other parents, need access to respite care and support services (Kresak, Gallagher, & Kelley, 2014). Additionally, some of their needs are greater because of their own heightened physical and emotional circumstances. The needs of grandparents may be more pronounced if they are less culturally assimilated; if they have limited English skills; or if they have no legal custody of their grandchildren (Cox, 2008), thus limiting the role they can play in formal deliberations related to IEPs and placements.

**Standard 6**
Professional Learning and Ethical Practice

**Standard 7**
Collaboration

# 6-5 Providing Nurturing and Competent Family Support

The relationships between parents and children with disabilities are a function of many factors. Some of the most crucial factors include the child's age and gender; the family's socioeconomic status; the family's culture, their relative coping strength, and the type of the family (one-parent family, two-parent family, or blended family); and the nature and seriousness of the disability. Families go through developmental phases in responding to the needs and nuances of caring for children with disabilities:

1. The time at which parents learn about or suspect a disability in their child

2. The period in which the parents make plans regarding the child's education

3. The point at which the individual with a disability has completed his or her education

4. The period when the parents are older and may be unable to care for their adult offspring (Knox & Bigby, 2007; Turner, 2000)

The nature and severity of the disability and the willingness of the parents to adapt and educate themselves regarding their roles in helping their children move through these phases have an appreciable influence on the parent–child relationships that eventually emerge.

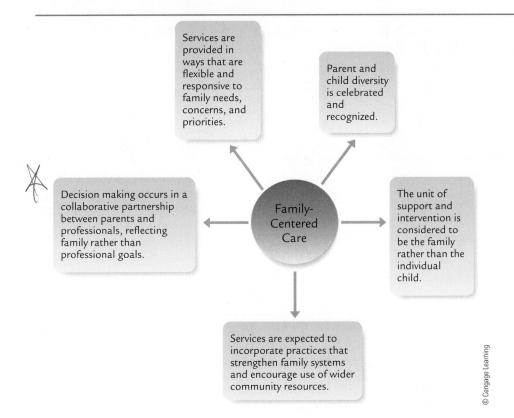

**Figure 6.2** *Attributes of Family-Centered Care*

Services are provided in ways that are flexible and responsive to family needs, concerns, and priorities.

Parent and child diversity is celebrated and recognized.

Decision making occurs in a collaborative partnership between parents and professionals, reflecting family rather than professional goals.

Family-Centered Care

The unit of support and intervention is considered to be the family rather than the individual child.

Services are expected to incorporate practices that strengthen family systems and encourage use of wider community resources.

© Cengage Learning

## 6-5a  Family-Centered Support, Services, and Programs

Family-centered support, services, and programs encourage families to take the lead in establishing and pursuing their priorities (Dempsey & Keen, 2008; Epley et al., 2010; Migerode, Maes, Buysse, & Brondeel, 2012; see Figure 6.2). Professionals who embrace a family-centered philosophy focus on the strengths and capabilities of families, not their deficits (Muscott, 2002; Raver, 2005; Ulrich, 2003). These professionals move away from a "fix and serve" framework to seeing individuals with disabilities as children, youth, and adults with unique kinds of practical knowledge that can be strengthened and actualized through participation in family-centered support services. Furthermore, family-centered services and social support are directed at the entire family, not just the mother and the child or youth with a disability (Keen, 2007; Lach et al., 2009).

## 6-5b  Early Childhood Years

Patterns of family-centered support vary as a function of the life cycle of the family, the severity of the disabling condition(s), and the changing needs of parents, children with disabilities, and their siblings (Dunst, 2002; Turnbull & Turnbull, 2002; Kyzar, Turnbull, Summers, & Gómez, 2012; Vacca & Feinberg, 2000). Family support during the early childhood years focuses on delivering appropriate services in natural settings and on helping family members develop an understanding of the child's disability. Support may also center on addressing child behavior problems, becoming knowledgeable about legal rights, learning how to deal with ongoing challenges, and learning how to communicate and work effectively with caregivers and school personnel (Bruder, 2000; Gallagher, Rhodes, & Darling, 2004; Raver, 2005; Shelden & Rush, 2001).

Family support may focus on helping parents create effective home rules; develop functional family routines for dinner, bedtime, and study/homework times; use daily report cards; build behavior monitoring devices; establish effective incentive systems; and create simple contracts. See Figure 6.3 for an example of a behavioral incentive contract designed to help the child and the family.

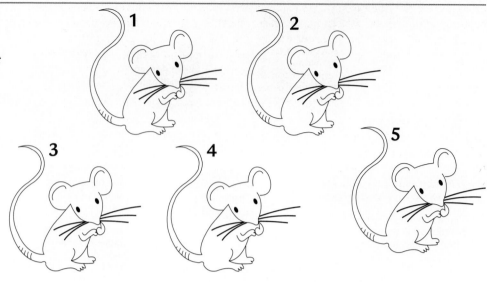

I, _____*Jamal*_____ agree to _____*follow instructions immediately and complete two chores each week day*_____ .
If I am successful, then I may color in a mouse for the day. When all five mice are colored in nice, I will get:

_____*a Saturday afternoon with Dad doing something of my choice (movie, shooting baskets, trip to favorite fast-food, etc.)*_____ .

Date: _____*March 12*_____

Child: _____*Jamal*_____

Parent: _____*Dad*_____

Family-centered, home-based services delivered by educational and social services professionals are directed at fostering appropriate motor development, promoting speech and language development, assisting with toilet training, and encouraging cognitive development. Other assistance may be targeted at helping parents address specific physical or health conditions that may require special diets, medications, or therapy regimens. The thrust of these services is to enhance capacity and build competence (Raver, 2005).

## 6-5c Elementary School Years

During the elementary school years, parents become increasingly concerned about their children's academic achievement and social relationships. With the movement in many school systems to more inclusionary programs, parents may be particularly anxious about their children's social acceptance by peers without disabilities and about the intensity and appropriateness of instructional programs delivered in general education settings. Overall, parents seem to be pleased with inclusion, particularly its social aspects. Intervention efforts during this period are based on the individualized education program (IEP).

Consistent collaboration between parents and various multidisciplinary team members is crucial to the actual achievement of IEP goals and objectives. Unfortunately, many parents find the IEP process intimidating, confusing, and discouraging (Gallagher & Konjoian, 2010). Many parents would like to be more fully involved in the IEP-related decision-making processes, but feel unskilled in representing their views or conclude they will not be taken seriously if they speak out. Others have been taught by their cultures to respect authority and to defer to those above them; thus they rely on others, particularly the more educated, in determining the specifics of their child's IEP. These individuals are merely passive participants in the creation of their child's IEP (Ong-Dean, 2009).

## 6-5d Secondary School Years

The secondary school years frequently pose significant challenges for adolescents with disabilities, their parents, and their families. Like their peers, adolescents with disabilities confront significant physical and psychological issues, including learning how to deal with their

**CEC**

**Standard 7**
Collaboration

emerging sexuality, how to develop satisfactory relationships with individuals outside of the home environment, and how to become appropriately independent. Parents of adolescents with disabilities agree that academic achievement is vitally important; nevertheless, they want their sons and daughters to develop essential social skills and other behaviors associated with empathy, perseverance, and character (Geisthardt, Brotherson, & Cook, 2002; Kolb & Hanley-Maxwell, 2003). Other issues must also be addressed during these years, including preparation for employment, development of appropriate self-regulation, provision of instruction in how to access adult services, and development of community living skills.

During their children's adolescence, parents often experience less compliance with their requests and greater resistance to their authority. Parents who are attuned to the unique challenges and opportunities work closely with educators and other support personnel to develop IEPs and related interventions that address these issues and prepare the adolescents for entry into adulthood. As appropriate, youth with disabilities are now actively prepared for and often participate in IEP meetings with parents and professionals (Martin et al., 2006).

## 6-5e Transition to the Adult Years

The transition from high school to community and adult life can be achieved successfully by adolescents with disabilities if parents and professionals carefully plan for this transition (Levinson, McKee, & DeMatteo, 2000). Transition planning is mandated by IDEA and is achieved primarily through the IEP planning process. IEP goals during this period are directed at providing instruction that is specifically related to succeeding in the community, using public transportation, and functioning as an adult. These adult skills include behaviors related to self-regulation, self-realization, and autonomy. The challenge for parents and care providers is to help adolescents with disabilities achieve as much independence as possible, given their unique strengths and challenges. Some research suggests that parents are often the greatest impediments to adults with disabilities in achieving their own independence and autonomy (Steeves, 2006).

**Standard 7**
Collaboration

## 6-5f Parents, Families, and Partnerships

The interaction among professionals, parents, and families is often marked by confusion, dissatisfaction, disappointment, and anger (Blue-Banning et al., 2004; Keen, 2007). Available research and other new developments have led many observers to believe that partnerships and relationships among parents, families, and professionals can be significantly improved (Dunst & Dempsey, 2007; Keen, 2007). One parent described the emotional support she received in this way:

> *Every time I talk to him he'll give me words of encouragement. He'll say something like, "You know you are Devante's primary caretaker and the best thing you can do for him is to love him." I mean, this is regardless of if I bring him in for a scraped knee or ear infection, it's always something about just loving him and being there for him and understanding. (Fox et al., 2002, p. 444)*

## 6-5g Strengthening Family Supports

The primacy of the family in contributing to the well-being of all children is obvious. Research indicates that family members provide one another with the most lasting, and often the most meaningful, support (Dunlap & Fox, 2007; Raver, 2005; Turnbull & Turnbull, 2002). Much of what has been done to assist children with disabilities, however, has supplanted rather than supported families in their efforts to care and provide for their children. Historically, monies and resources have been directed at services and supports outside the family or even beyond the neighborhood or community in which the family lives.

**Standard 6**
Professional Learning and Ethical Practice

**Standard 7**
Collaboration

## 6-5h Positive Behavior Support

Indeed, progress has been made in helping professionals partner and relate more effectively and compassionately to parents, families, and others responsible for children and youth with disabilities (Dunst & Dempsey, 2007; Keen, 2007). This is particularly true in the preparation of special educators and others who serve as direct and indirect service providers in family-, school-, and community-based programs (Correa, Hudson, & Hayes, 2004; Rupiper & Marvin, 2004).

One such partnering approach is positive behavior support (PBS) (Bambara & Knoster, 2009; Fox & Dunlap, 2002; Frankland, Edmonson, & Turnbull, 2001; Lee, Poston, & Poston, 2007; Young, Calderella, Richardson, & Young, 2011). This approach focuses on changing disruptive behaviors and supporting behaviors that are valued and naturally supported by parents, neighbors, teachers, and other community members. In effect, all important players in the child's or youth's life become interveners, working together to achieve highly functional positive behaviors—behaviors that are valued and supported in family, school, and community settings (Dunlap & Fox, 2007). These may include skills related to making and keeping friends, replacing loud vocalizations with more appropriately toned speech and language, making requests, expressing appreciation, and developing new ways of responding to events that normally produce aggression or property destruction. Again, the primary focus of PBS is to develop behaviors that are useful and highly valued at home, at school, and in the community—behaviors that "facilitate and promote comprehensive lifestyle changes for enhancing [the] quality of life of both the individual and his or her family" (Lee, Poston, & Poston, 2007, p. 418).

## 6-5i Elements of Successful Partnerships

Effective professional partners and care providers strive to establish trust and respect, empower families, create supportive environments, demonstrate sensitivity to family issues, affirm the positive features of the child with a disability, share valuable information, contribute to the parent's confidence, clarify expectations, and listen well (Blue-Banning et al., 2004; Dunst & Dempsey, 2007; Keen, 2007; Luckner & Velaski, 2004). Care providers seek to understand the family, its ecology, and its culture, taking the time to listen and to build trusting and nurturing relationships, as indicated earlier (Dunlap & Fox, 2007; Frankland, Turnbull, Wehmeyer, & Blackmountain, 2004; Zhang & Bennett, 2001).

Healthy, well-functioning families of children with disabilities contribute greatly to the well-being of all family members. The same is true of marriages that are cohesive and strong. Supportive marriages also protect fathers from depression and other related conditions (Boyraz & Sayger, 2011).

On the other hand, family tension and disorganization may negatively affect siblings of children with disabilities, heightening their chances for developing behavior problems, lessening their social competence, and diminishing their capacity for developing important problem-solving skills (Lobato, Kao, & Plante, 2005; Stoneman, 2005). Parent-to-parent programs, communities of practice—groups of people who share common concerns and frequently interact with one another and other family support programs—are directed at helping families function more optimally, thus contributing positively to the development of the child with a disability and other children within the family (Gotto, Beauchamp, & Simpson, 2007; Lucyshyn, Dunlap, & Albin, 2002; Santelli, Ginsberg, Sullivan, & Niederhauser, 2002).

Superb family support programs keep families together, enhancing their capacity to meet the needs of an individual with a disability, reducing the need for out-of-home placement, and giving families access to typical social and recreational activities (Heiman & Berger, 2008). The following statement expresses a parent's wonderment at the effectiveness of family-centered support:

> *They never give up. I am just astounded by the many creative ways they keep coming up with to help him. Oftentimes they do not understand him, but they never give up. At one point I had to ask myself: Are these people for real?... I cannot believe how genuine and real they really are. (Worthington, Hernandez, Friedman, & Uzzell, 2001, p. 77)*

Increasingly, policy makers and program providers are realizing the importance of the family, emphasizing its crucial role in the development and ongoing care of a child with a

**CEC**

**Standard 7**
Collaboration

**CEC**

**Standard 2**
Learning Environments

disability. Services are now being directed at the family as a whole, rather than just at the child with the disability (Raver, 2005). This support is particularly evident in the individualized family service plan (IFSP). Such an orientation honors the distinctive and essential roles of parents, siblings, and other extended family members as primary caregivers, nurturers, and teachers (Heiman & Berger, 2008). Additionally, these services provide parents and siblings with opportunities to engage in other respite-related activities that are important to their physical, emotional, and social well-being.

Because of family support services and parent-to-parent programs, many children and youth with disabilities enjoy relationships and activities that are a natural part of living in their own homes, neighborhoods, and communities. These services allow children and youth with disabilities to truly be a part of their neighborhoods and communities.

**CEC**

**Standard 6**
Professional Learning and Ethical Practice

## 6-5j Training for Families

Parent training is an essential part of most early intervention programs for children with disabilities. As part of IDEA, parent training is directed at helping parents acquire the essential skills that assist them in implementing their child's IEP or IFSP (Tynan & Wornian, 2002; Whitbread, Bruder, Fleming, & Park, 2007). No longer is the child viewed as the primary recipient of services; instead, services and training are directed at the complex and varied needs of each family and its members. Much of the training is conducted by experienced and skilled parents of children with disabilities, who volunteer their time as part of their affiliation with an advocacy or support group. These support groups are invaluable in helping parents, other family members, neighbors, and friends respond effectively to children or youth with a disability (Gallagher & Konjoian, 2010). In describing her experiences with parent training, one mother made the following observations:

> Oh yes, she [the parent trainer] was excellent. Our third child was a 29 weeker. We didn't know any of that stuff…. I enjoyed finding out what was going on and knowing the signals, because if he's going to throw up a red flag to me, I want to know how to react…. I couldn't believe all the stuff that she told me that I didn't know…. [S]he related to all members of the family…. I appreciated what she did. (Ward, Cronin, Renfro, Lowman, & Cooper, 2000)

Training may be focused on general parenting skills: feeding techniques, language development, toilet training programs, managing challenging behaviors, motor development, employment, or other related issues important to parents (Buschbacher, Fox, & Clarke, 2004; Francis, Gross, Turnbull, & Parent-Johnson, 2013).

For parents of youth or adults with disabilities, the training may be directed at accessing adult services, using functional assessment and positive behavior support, accessing recreational programs, finding postsecondary vocational programs, locating appropriate housing, qualifying for Social Security benefits, or legal planning for guardianship (Brooke & McDonough, 2008; Chambers, Hughes, & Carter, 2004; Russell & Grant, 2005). In some instances, the training and preparation center on giving parents meaningful information about their legal rights, preparing them to participate effectively in IEP meetings, helping them understand the nature of their child's disability, making them aware of recreational programs in their communities, or alerting them to specific funding opportunities. On the forefront of parent training are efforts targeted at dramatically increasing parental efficacy, building and strengthening beliefs of parents regarding their capacity to effectively promote positive behaviors and development in their children (Boyraz & Sayger, 2011; Dyches et al., 2012; Jones & Prinz, 2005).

Through these training programs, parents learn how to promote the growth and development of their children, engage effectively in problem solving and conflict resolution and, thus, are empowered and prepared to advocate for their children and themselves. Parent involvement in the education of their children with disabilities significantly benefits their children's learning and overall school performance. Training also contributes to the overall physical, social, psychological, and emotional well-being of parents.

### 6-5k  Training for Siblings, Grandparents, and Extended Family Members

Training may also be directed at siblings, grandparents, and other relatives. It may even involve close neighbors or caring friends who wish to contribute to the well-being of the family. Often these are individuals who are tied to the family through religious affiliations or long-standing friendships (Poston & Turnbull, 2004).

Siblings of children with disabilities need information about the nature and possible course of disabilities affecting their brother or sister (Chambers, Hughes, & Carter, 2004). Furthermore, they need social and emotional support, including acknowledgment of their own needs for nurturing, attention, and affirmation. Some research suggests that many siblings know very little about their brother or sister's disability, its manifestations, and its consequences. Siblings need to understand that they are not responsible for a particular condition or disability. Other questions also need addressing. These questions deal with the heritability of the disability, the siblings' future role in providing care, the ways in which siblings might explain the disability to their friends, and the ways the presence of the brother or sister with a disability will affect their family and themselves.

In most instances, the training of siblings occurs through support groups or workshops sometimes referred to as "Sibshops," as indicated earlier (Laman & Shaughnessy, 2007). These groups are age-specific so that siblings can express feelings, vent frustrations, and learn from others. They may also get advice on how to deal with predictable situations—that is, what to say or how to respond. Some learn how to use sign language, how to complete simple medical procedures, how to manage misbehavior, or how to use certain incentive systems. In some cases, siblings may become prepared for the eventual death of a brother or sister who has a life-threatening condition.

Training of grandparents, other relatives, neighbors, and friends is also crucial. They, like the siblings of children with disabilities, must be informed, must have opportunities to express feelings, must be able to ask pertinent questions, and must receive training that is tailored to their needs. If they are informed and well trained, they often provide the only consistent respite care that is available to families. Also, they may contribute invaluable transportation, recreational activities, babysitting, critical emotional support, and/or short-term and long-term financial assistance (French, 2008; Gorman, 2004).

**Standard 6**
Professional Learning and Ethical Practice

### 6-5l  Training for Professionals

Collaborative training involves professionals, such as educators, social workers, psychologists, and health care professionals. This training focuses primarily on building positive relationships, collaborating effectively, understanding cross-cultural matters, and providing meaningful instruction and support—all centered on improving the quality of life for families and their children (Robey et al., 2013; Romer & Walker, 2013; Shogren et al., 2013). Training is also aimed at helping professionals understand the complex nature of family cultures, structures, functions, and interactions, as well as at encouraging them to take a close look at their own attitudes, feelings, values, and perceptions about families that include children, youth, and adults with disabilities (Gorman, 2004; Iezzoni & Long-Bellil, 2012; Stone, 2005; Turnbull & Turnbull, 2002).

**Standard 6**
Professional Learning and Ethical Practice

### 6-5m  Cultures and Disability Perspectives for Professionals

Responses of siblings, other family members, and neighbors vary according to their cultural backgrounds and related beliefs about children with disabilities (Banks, 2003; Bui & Turnbull, 2003; Frankland et al., 2004; Hu, Wang, & Fei 2012). We are just beginning to understand the influence of various cultures on the ways in which children with disabilities are viewed, treated, and reared by their parents and families (Banks, 2003; Blacher, Begum, Marcoulides, & Baker, 2013; Boscardin, Brown-Chidsey, & Gonzalez-Martinez, 2001; McHatton & Correa, 2005; Ortiz, 2006; Rivers, 2000).

Teachers and other care providers need to learn about the cultures of families and the children they serve. They need to become aware of and sensitive to issues related to child-rearing practices, family religious beliefs, cultural perspectives, and family views about the role of education (Chapadjiev, 2009; McHatton & Correa, 2005; Poston & Turnbull, 2004; Shogren, 2012; Zhang & Bennett, 2001). Professionals also need to be aware of the different meanings that parents assign to disabilities (Banks, 2003). Furthermore, greater efforts must be directed at finding well-trained interpreters who play essential roles in helping parents and educators understand one another as they develop individualized family service plans (IFSPs) and individualized education plans (IEPs) for children and youth with disabilities. Moreover, teachers and other care providers need to become skilled in cross-cultural communication: learning how to do home visits and becoming proficient in connecting with diverse families and communities (Matuszny, Banda, & Coleman, 2007; McHatton, 2007). Parents and families sense and know when they are being treated with respect and trust by professionals. This trust and respect gives rise to better outcomes for families and their children with disabilities.

**Standard 6**
Professional Learning and Ethical Practice

## Looking Toward a Bright Future

As we know, families play vitally important roles in the development and well-being of all children—this is particularly true of children and youth with disabilities. Now more than ever, educational, medical, social, and other health care professionals seek to understand the needs, concerns, and aspirations of families of children with disabilities. Increasingly, the preparation of physicians, nurses, school administrators, and other care providers includes experiences about and with these families. Professionals are becoming more inclusive and innovative in the ways they connect with, care for, and build rewarding partnerships and relationships with families.

Professionals now understand more completely that family members are the primary nurturers, the first and most consistent teachers, the crucial providers of care, and powerful sources of knowledge about children and youth with disabilities. Increasingly, professionals are listening more, giving more of themselves and their expertise, and providing services and interventions that were often reserved for children and youth without disabilities. Moreover, professionals are much more skilled in providing assistance that is home- and family-based, helping parents and siblings deal with real and often challenging behaviors their children present, providing increased access to respite care, and giving material and emotional assistance when needed.

Families, siblings, grandparents, and other family members, particularly fathers, now have vastly improved access to support groups, social networks, and systems of care, each of which is designed to benefit not only the child with disabilities, but also the family and its constituent members.

We are also beginning to understand the role of culture in working with families with children who have a disability, becoming sensitive to the unique perspectives of parents and other family members about disabilities. More and more, talented clinicians and other professionals are involving interpreters and other community members in meaningful ways, genuinely seeking to understand and respond to diverse families in respectful, sensitive, and supportive ways.

We can all contribute to this bright future for families with children who have a disability as we seek to inform ourselves, to alter our attitudes, and to commit to new levels of involvement and service. Our contributions might include providing respite care for a family in our neighborhood, actively recruiting and preparing individuals with a disability for employment, being more inclusive in our social and recreational activities, and expressing care and regard in our communications.

**6-1   Describe how the lives of families with children with disabilities have changed since the advent of IDEA.**

- Families now have access to free and appropriate education for their child with disabilities.

- Families have been empowered to play important roles in approving the kinds of special education and related services their children with disabilities receive.

- There is much greater public awareness about the needs and challenges of children with disabilities.

- Professionals are more adept in providing services in more inclusive and natural environments, delivering needed support to parents and siblings of children with disabilities.

**6-2   Describe the family systems approach and how it applies to families with members with disabilities, and describe the strengths and challenges of families raising children with disabilities.**

- The family systems or social/ecological approach recognizes the bidirectional influence of each family member on each other and on the family as whole.

- The family is viewed as a system of interconnected parts that influence each other in a variety of ways.

- Families vary in behaviors and actions associated with being communicative, flexible, and cohesive—healthy families use good communications skills, are appropriately unified and cohesive, and are suitably flexible in responding to challenges and opportunities.

- Parents and siblings may grow in behaviors related to empathy, patience, emotional and psychological strength, family unity, as well as positive relationships.

- Mothers and fathers may become more compassionate, resilient, and selfless.

- The presence of a child with a disability may enhance stronger family bonds.

- Fathers may experience growth in self-acceptance and achieve better adjustment in various psychological domains.

- Parents and siblings of children with disabilities often develop highly functional coping skills that improve their capacity to support the child with a disability.

- Humor can and does play a role in releasing negative emotions, responding to stress, and connecting with family members.

- For some couples, their marriages are improved and enhanced.

- Common challenges include financial pressures, strained relationships, altered social relationships, and physical and health problems.

- Powerful emotions accompany the discovering and formalization of diagnosis.

- Generally, the stress parents experience is greater in families with children with disabilities.

- Other challenges include finding appropriate support services—everything from babysitting and respite care to appropriate and sensitive medical treatment.

**6-3   Describe common reactions of parents when obtaining a diagnosis for their children with disabilities.**

- Reactions of parents vary widely in response to obtaining a diagnosis, including shock, realization, moving away from retreat, and coming to acknowledgment.

- Because of these reactions, professionals need to be sensitive to these strong emotions and the ways in which they might impact parents learning about and responding to a child with a newly discovered disability.

**6-4   Describe factors that influence the relationship between children with disabilities and their mothers, fathers, siblings, grandparents, and other extended family members.**

- There is a negative detectable influence on marital relationships, but research reveals that this impact is much lower than would be expected as reported in earlier studies.

- The responses of parents to a child with a disability profoundly influence the ways in which siblings, grandparents, and others respond.

- Older daughters in families may assume an increasingly large role in caring for siblings without disabilities.

- Couples who evidence high parent self-efficacy (strong beliefs in their capacity to positively impact their children's development) contribute greatly to their children's development—both children with and without disabilities.

- Generally, the primary caregiver, the mother, develops a very strong relationship with the child.

- Mothers who have a long-term vision for her child with a disability can conquer the tendency to be overprotective.

- Supportive husbands play an immensely important role in sustaining the well-being of their spouses—this support is predictive of couple-centered satisfaction and contentment.

- Respite care for parents and families contributes much to their emotional well-being.

- Increasingly, fathers are becoming the primary caregivers for children with disabilities given the shifts in employment patterns and the changes in societal expectations.

- Fathers who receive appropriate training and support provide invaluable assistance to their families and children with disabilities.

- Progressively, training is available to fathers that is particularly suited to their needs and preferences for help.

- Siblings have common questions and concerns related to their sibling with disabilities, and parents' attitudes can influence siblings' reactions.
- Siblings profit significantly from information and support tailored to their needs.
- Grandparents can be very helpful to families and their children, but they need to be informed and knowledgeable about the support they can provide.
- Grandparent input and support is particularly critical during the formalization of the diagnosis.
- Grandparents who are rearing grandchildren with disabilities need and want support that is sensitive to their needs.

### 6-5 Describe essential behaviors that nuturing and competent professionals exhibit when interacting with families with children with disabilities.

- Caring and competent professionals encourage families to take the lead in directing the services for their children from early childhood throughout adulthood.

- Professionals focus on strengths and capacities of families, not just their deficits.
- Professionals consider all the factors that may impact the child and family, including the severity of the disability, the ever-changing needs of the family, the culture of the family, the present social supports or lack thereof, and the developmental needs of the child with a disability.
- Professionals are sensitive to the factors that contribute to positive collaborations: listening, trust building, cultural sensitivity, openness to ideas, positive and affirming conversations, and a focus on positive behavior support.
- Increasingly, professionals are focusing on the family quality of life, the degree to which the family is satisfied with its growth, success, and happiness.

 ## Council for Exceptional Children (CEC) Standards to Accompany Chapter 6

If you are thinking about a career in special education, you should know that many states use national standards developed by the Council for Exceptional Children (CEC) to assess a teacher candidate's knowledge and skills for working with students with disabilities. See a complete listing of the seven CEC Content Standards on the inside cover of this text.

1 Learner Development and Individual Learning Differences
2 Learning Environments
4 Assessment
6 Professional Learning and Ethical Practice
7 Collaboration

## Mastery Activities and Assignments

To master the content within this chapter, complete the following activities and assignments:

1. Complete a written test of the chapter's content. If your instructor requires a written test of your content knowledge for this chapter, keep a copy for your portfolio.
2. Review the Case Study on Embracing Diversity, "Halgan," and respond in writing to the Application

Questions. Keep a copy of the Case Study and your written response for your portfolio.
3. Participate in a community service learning activity. Community service is a valuable way to enhance your learning experience. Develop a reflective journal of the service learning experience for your portfolio.

# Learning Disabilities

© Cengage Learning

## Learning Objectives

*After you complete this chapter, you will be able to:*

**7-1** Describe how the lives of people with learning disabilities (LD) have changed since the advent of IDEA.

**7-2** Explain the various definitions and classifications of LD.

**7-3** Describe the characteristics and prevalence of children and youth with LD.

**7-4** List the causes and risk factors associated with LD.

**7-5** Describe the assessment procedures used to identify LD in children and youth.

**7-6** Describe the different interventions for children and youth with LD from early childhood through adulthood.

# Mathew

*Note: The following is an excerpt from a statement prepared by an upper-division psychology undergraduate student who has learning disabilities. Mathew tells his story in his own words, recounting some of his school experiences, his diagnosis, and how his learning disabilities affect his academic efforts.*

Imagine having the inability to memorize times tables, not being able to "tell time" until the ninth grade, and taking several days to read a simple chapter from a school textbook.

In elementary and high school, I was terrified of math classes for several reasons. First, it did not matter how many times I practiced my times tables or other numerical combinations relating to division, subtraction, and addition. I could not remember them. Second, I dreaded the class time itself, for inevitably the teacher would call on me for an answer to a "simple" problem. Multiplication was the worst! Since I had to count on my fingers to do multiplication, it would take a lot of time and effort. Do you know how long it takes to calculate 9 3 7 or 9 3 9 on your fingers? Suffice it to say, too long, especially if the teacher and the rest of the class are waiting.

When I was a sophomore at a junior college, I discovered important information about myself. After two days of clinical cognitive testing, I learned that my brain is wired differently than most individuals. That is, I think, perceive, and process information differently. They discovered several "wiring jobs" that are called learning disabilities. First, I have a problem with processing speed. The ability to bring information from long-term memory to consciousness (into short-term memory) takes me a long time. Second, I have a deficit with my short-term memory. This means that I cannot hold information there very long. When new information is learned, it must be put into long-term memory. This is an arduous process requiring the information to be rehearsed several times. Third, I have a significant problem with fluid reasoning. Fluid reasoning is the ability to go from A to G without having to go through B, C, D, E, and F. It also includes drawing inferences, coming up with creative solutions to problems, solving unique problems, and the ability to transfer information and generalize. Hence, my math and numerical difficulties....

With all of this knowledge, I was able to use specific strategies that will help me in compensating for these neurological wiring patterns. Now I tape all lectures rather than trying to keep up taking notes. I take tests in a room by myself and they are not timed. Anytime I need to do mathematical calculations I use a calculator...

SOURCE: Adapted from Gelfand, D. M., & Drew, C. J. (2003). *Understanding child behavior disorders*, 4th ed. (p. 238). Belmont, CA: Wadsworth. Used with permission.

## 7-1 A Changing Era in the Lives of People with Learning Disabilities

Learning disabilities have likely always been a part of the human condition, but it is only since the latter half of the 20th century that we have focused on this particular area of disorder. Often called one of the invisible disabilities, learning disabilities affect people of all ages and walks of life but cannot be detected simply by appearance, dress, or behavior. In the opening Snapshot, Mathew did not learn the reasons for his struggles until he was in college, yet learning disabilities affected his entire school experience.

Mathew's case is not altogether unusual. Although parents, educators, and other professionals in the field have learned much about recognizing the condition, some people do not learn the reasons for their academic or social struggles until high school or college or beyond. Still, it is most common to see indicators of possible learning disabilities in the early years of school. The cognitively complex activities of learning to read, write, and do math usually bring concerns to the fore when knowledgeable teachers and parents notice a student's lack of progress compared to other children.

We are fortunate to live at a time of great progress in assessing, affirming, planning for, and instructing individuals with learning disabilities. However, this is not to say that we have all the answers; the field continues to evolve. This chapter discusses the continuing debate over the definition of learning disabilities and estimates of the prevalence of the

**Learning disability**
A condition in which one or more of the basic psychological processes involved in understanding or using language are deficient.

disorder. It then presents the characteristics and possible causes of learning disabilities, and explores the current understanding of appropriate learning disabilities practice and effective interventions.

## 7-2 Definitions and Classifications of Learning Disabilities

The field of learning disabilities was virtually unrecognized prior to the 1960s. These disabilities are often considered mild because people with learning disabilities usually have average or near-average intelligence, although learning disabilities can occur at all intelligence levels. People with learning disabilities achieve at unexpectedly low levels, particularly in reading and mathematics. The term *learning disabilities* has become a generic label representing a very heterogeneous group of conditions that range from mild to severe in intensity (Bender, 2008a; Buttner & Hasselhorn, 2011). Individuals with learning disabilities exhibit a highly variable and complex set of characteristics and needs. Consequently, they present a substantial challenge to family members and professionals. This set of challenges, however, is repeatedly met with significant success, as evidenced by many stories of outstanding achievement by adults who have histories of learning disabilities in childhood.

Confusion, controversy, and polarization have been associated with learning disabilities as long as they have been recognized as a family of disabilities. In the past, many children now identified as having specific learning disabilities would have been labeled remedial readers, remedial learners, emotionally disturbed, or even children with intellectual disabilities. Delayed academic performance is a major element in most current definitions of learning disabilities (Fletcher, Stuebing, Morris, & Lyon, 2013; Scanlon, 2013). Today, services related to learning disabilities represent the largest single program for exceptional children in the United States. Those with learning disabilities represented about 25 percent of all students with disabilities in 1975, rose to a high of 46 percent in 1999, and decreased to 36 percent in 2014 (U.S. Department of Education, 2014a).

**CEC**

**Standard 1**
Learner Development and Individual Learning Differences

### 7-2a Definitions

The definitions of learning disabilities vary considerably. This inconsistency may be due to the field's unique evolution, rapid growth, and strong interdisciplinary nature. The involvement of multiple disciplines (such as medicine, psychology, speech and language, and education) has also contributed to confusing terminology (Buttner & Hasselhorn, 2011; Scanlon, 2013). A child with a brain injury is described as having an organic impairment resulting in perceptual problems, thinking disorders, and emotional instability. A child with minimal brain dysfunction manifests similar challenges but often shows evidence of difficulties in language, memory, motor skills, and impulse control.

The Individuals with Disabilities Education Act (IDEA) of 2004 stated that:

> *"Specific learning disability" means a disorder in one or more of the basic psychological processes involved in understanding or in using language, spoken or written, which may manifest itself in an imperfect ability to listen, think, speak, read, write, spell, or to do mathematical calculations. The term includes such conditions as perceptual disabilities, brain injury, minimal brain dysfunction, dyslexia, and developmental aphasia. The term does not include children who have learning challenges which are primarily the result of visual, hearing, or motor disabilities, of [intellectual disabilities], of emotional disturbance, or of environmental, cultural, or economic disadvantage. (IDEA, 2004, PL 108-446, Sec. 602[30])*

This definition codified into federal law many of the concepts found in earlier descriptions. It also furnished a legal focus for the provision of services in the public schools. Service guidelines through the IDEA definition matured over the years with criteria from the companion "Rules and Regulations." Figure 7.1 summarizes the criteria, published in the *Federal Register* in 2006, used for identifying a specific learning disability. These criteria are consistent with the IDEA definition presented earlier.

Figure 7.1 *Criteria for Identifying a Specific Learning Disability*

1. A team may determine that a child has a specific learning disability if the child does not achieve adequately for the child's age or meet state-approved grade-level standards in one or more of the following seven areas, when provided with learning experiences and instruction appropriate for the child's age or state-approved grade-level standards. Criteria adopted by a state must permit the use of a process based on the child's response to research-based intervention and cannot prohibit the use of a severe discrepancy between intellectual ability and achievement:

    i. Oral expression
    ii. Listening comprehension
    iii. Written expression
    iv. Basic reading skill
    v. Reading comprehension
    vi. Mathematical calculation
    vii. Mathematical reasoning

2. The team may not identify a child as having a specific learning disability if the lack of achievement is primarily the result of:

    i. A visual, hearing, or motor impairment,
    ii. [Intellectual disabilities],
    iii. Limited English proficiency,
    iv. Emotional disturbance,
    v. Environmental, cultural, or economic disadvantage, or
    vi. Lack of instruction

SOURCE: Adapted from Rules and regulations. (2006, August 14). Federal Register, section [300.309, p. 46,786].

The IDEA definition and the guidelines in Figure 7.1 primarily describe conditions that are *not* learning disabilities and give little substantive explanation of what *does* constitute a learning disability (i.e., a discrepancy between achievement and ability in areas of oral expression, listening, written expression, and so on). This use of exclusionary criteria still surfaces in a variety of circumstances (e.g., Hoover, 2010; Kavale, Spaulding, & Beam, 2009). The IDEA definition is also somewhat ambiguous because it prescribes no clear way to measure a learning disability.

This definition is important to our discussion for several reasons. First, it describes *learning disabilities* as a generic term that refers to a heterogeneous group of disorders. Second, a person with learning disabilities must manifest significant difficulties. The word *significant* is used in an effort to remove the connotation that a learning disability constitutes a mild problem. Finally, this definition makes it clear that learning disabilities are lifelong challenges and places them in a context of other disabilities and cultural differences.

Varying definitions and terminology related to learning disabilities emerged partly because of different theoretical views of the condition. For example, perceptual-motor theories emphasize an interaction between various channels of perception and motor activity. Children with learning disabilities are seen as having unreliable and unstable perceptual-motor abilities, which present challenges when such children encounter activities that require an understanding of time and space. Language disability theories, on the other hand, concentrate on a child's reception or production of language (Berninger & May, 2011; Troia, 2011). Because language is so important in learning, these theories emphasize the relationship between learning disabilities and language deficiencies.

Still another view of learning disabilities has emerged in the past several years. Some researchers have suggested that many different, specific disorders have been grouped under one term. They see *learning disabilities* as a general umbrella term that includes both academic and behavioral problems; they have developed terminology to describe particular conditions falling within the broad category of learning disabilities. Some of these terms refer to particular areas of functional academic difficulty (such as math, spelling, and reading), whereas others reflect difficulties that are behavioral in nature. This perspective was adopted by the American Psychiatric Association in the fifth edition of its *Diagnostic and Statistical Manual of Mental Disorders* (American Psychiatric Association, 2013). This manual uses *specifiers* to refer specifically to disorders in reading, mathematics, and written expression (e.g., specific learning disorder [SLD] with impairment in reading).

Research on learning disabilities also reflects the difficulties inherent when attempting to define a specific disability. The wide range of characteristics associated with children who have learning disabilities, along with various methodological challenges (such as heterogeneous populations and measurement error), has caused many difficulties in conducting research on learning disabilities (Gall, Gall, & Borg, 2007; Jitendra, Burgess, & Gajria, 2011).

The notion of severity has largely been ignored in earlier definitions and concepts related to learning disabilities. Although this has changed somewhat, severity still receives only limited attention (see Pierangelo & Giuliani, 2006; Porter, 2005). Learning disabilities have probably been defined in more ways by more disciplines and professional groups than any other type of disability (Buttner & Hasselhorn, 2011; Kavale, Spaulding, & Beam, 2009). See the nearby Reflect on This, "Redefining Learning Disabilities Using a Response to Intervention Model," for one perspective.

## 7-2b   Classification

*Learning disabilities* is a term applied to a complex constellation of behaviors and symptoms. Many of these symptoms or characteristics have been used for classification purposes at one time or another. Three major elements have a substantial history of being employed in classifying learning disabilities: discrepancy, heterogeneity, and exclusion—all points that we noted earlier. Discrepancy approaches to classification are based on the notion that there is an identifiable gap between intelligence and achievement in particular areas, such as reading, math, and language. Heterogeneity classification addresses the differing array of academic domains where these children often demonstrate performance problems (as in the seven areas noted in Figure 7.1). The exclusion approach reflects the idea that the learning disabilities cannot be due to selected other conditions. The evidence supporting the use of discrepancy and exclusion as classification parameters is not strong, whereas heterogeneity seems to be supported (Hoover, 2010; National Joint Committee on Learning Disabilities, 2011b).

Reference to severity appears in the literature on learning disabilities fairly often, even though it is not accounted for in most definitions (Swanson, 2011; Waesche, Shatschneider, Maner, Ahmed, & Wagner, 2011). Prior to 2004, IDEA mandated that any criterion for classifying a child as having learning disabilities must be based on a preexisting severe discrepancy between intellectual capacity and achievement. A child's learning disability must be determined on an individual basis, and there must be a severe discrepancy between achievement and intellectual ability in one or more of the following areas: oral expression, listening comprehension, written expression, basic reading skill, reading comprehension, mathematical calculation, or mathematical reasoning. The determination of referral for special services and type of educational placement was related to the following criteria:

1. Whether a child achieves commensurate with his or her age and ability when provided with appropriate educational experiences

2. Whether the child has a severe discrepancy between achievement and intellectual ability in one or more of seven areas related to communication skills and mathematical abilities

The meaning of the term *severe discrepancy* is debated among professionals (e.g., Buttner & Hasselhorn, 2011; Maehler & Schuchardt, 2011). Although it is often stipulated as a classification parameter, there is no broadly accepted way to measure it. What is an "acceptable" discrepancy between a child's achievement and what is expected at his or her grade level? 25 percent? 35 percent? 50 percent? Research on discrepancy classifications, particularly

## Redefining Learning Disabilities Using a Response to Intervention Model

**Response to intervention**, or RtI, is a strategy for addressing the individual learning and behavior needs of all students within a school. Rather than waiting for students to fail before finding a way to help them, RtI employs assessment and data-based decisions to identify students that need extra help and then provides individualized and intensive interventions to help those who are not progressing adequately.

Referred to as a multitiered system, RtI begins with primary prevention, or general classroom instruction for all students. This must be effective, evidence-based practice that provides the primary prevention of failure for most students. Those who do not respond adequately to good primary instruction may be served in secondary prevention with moderately intensive interventions to remediate learning difficulties. A very small percentage of

students who do not respond to secondary prevention may then be served at the tertiary level, with very intensive individual or small-group interventions to address specific needs. RtI success depends on effective instruction at each level and progress monitoring to determine each student's progress.

RtI is developing as a way to identify learning disabilities in lieu of the traditional discrepancy approach. As noted earlier in the chapter, educators and psychologists are challenging the use of discrepancy between aptitude and achievement to identify learning disabilities. Within an RtI approach, progress-monitoring data can be combined with other valid assessments to ensure that students are not being identified with learning disabilities when the real cause of difficulty is inappropriate learning opportunities. For those who do have learning disabilities, RtI data

can be used to help make the determination of eligibility for special education services. Though not yet universal, several states either require or allow the use of RtI to determine whether students have specific learning disabilities. As yet, there is no one accepted method for doing so, but the steady increase in the knowledge base about RtI and its usefulness for determining learning disabilities will no doubt inform the future of this approach.

### Questions for Reflection

How does RtI provide a proactive approach to addressing student needs? How does RtI promote inclusion for instruction?

SOURCE: Adapted from National Center on Response to Intervention. (2010). *Essential Components of RtI—A Closer Look at Response to Intervention*. Retrieved from www.rti4success.org/resource/essential-components-rti -closer-look-response-intervention.

---

in reading, reveals that the discrepancy concept has mixed empirical support, particularly in field applications (Callinan, Cunningham, & Theiler, 2013; O'Donnell & Miller, 2011).

In recognizing the controversy surrounding the use of a "discrepancy formula" as the only criterion for determining eligibility for special education services, current IDEA regulations no longer *require* that school districts determine whether a child has a severe discrepancy between intellectual ability and achievement. Schools now have the option of using a process that determines a child's response to intervention (RtI), which is aimed at evidence-based decisions and is research-based (National Center on Response to Intervention, 2010). The basic concept of RtI is empirically based decision making—that is, determining intervention success on the basis of data reflecting the student's performance. This approach has considerable appeal for several reasons. In particular, RtI is focused on the child's academic response to specific instruction, and it is also another perspective for assessing children with learning disabilities. This latter rationale is very useful for some children who are struggling with early academic work but may not evidence a severe discrepancy. RtI is attracting increased interest generally—and particularly regarding children with learning disabilities (Bender & Waller, 2011; Johnson, Semmelroth, Mellard, & Hopper, 2012; Lindstrom & Sayeski, 2013). The Reflect on This box summarizes key elements of the RtI model.

Lack of agreement about concepts basic to the field has caused difficulties in both research and treatment for those with learning disabilities. Nonetheless, many people who display the challenging characteristics of learning disabilities are successful in life and have become leaders in their fields (an example is Charles "Pete" Conrad, Jr., who became an astronaut in the 1960s).

**Response to intervention (RtI)**
A student's response to instructional interventions that have been determined to be effective through scientifically based research.

# 7-3 Characteristics and Prevalence of Learning Disabilities

Although specific learning disabilities are often characterized as representing mild disorders, few attempts have been made to validate this premise empirically. Identification of subgroups, subtypes, or severity levels in this heterogeneous population was largely neglected in the past. However, some attempts have been made in recent years to address these issues (Buttner & Hasselhorn, 2011; Davis & Broitman, 2011). Subtype and **comorbidity** research are appearing in the current literature at increasing rates (Buttner & Hasselhorn, 2011; O'Brien, Wolf, & Lovett, 2012). Subtype research investigates the characteristics of children and youth to identify distinctive groups within the broad umbrella of learning disabilities. Comorbidity research investigates the degree to which youngsters exhibit evidence of multiple disabilities or conditions (such as learning disabilities and communication disorders, or personality disorders) (Fasmer et al., 2011; McGillivray & Baker, 2009).

*Photo 7.1* Many students with learning disabilities have difficulties with word recognition, word knowledge, and the use of context in learning to read.

© Cengage Learning

**CEC**

**Standard 1**
Learner Development and Individual Learning Differences

Researchers have investigated a broad array of subgroups ranging from people with reading problems to those with hyperactivity (e.g., Egeland, Ueland, & Johansen, 2012; Mangina & Beuzeron-Mangina, 2009). Attention deficit/hyperactivity disorder (ADHD) is a condition often associated with learning disabilities, with some estimates as high as 45 percent (DuPaul, Gormley, & Laracy, 2013).

Challenges in determining the numbers of people with learning disabilities are amplified by differing definitions, theoretical views, and assessment procedures. The number of students with learning disabilities identified and served under IDEA has fallen sharply between 2002 and 2011, as noted in Table 7.1, declining 18 percent, while total enrollment in special education declined about 3 percent. Reasons for this decline may be related to earlier and more effective intervention, especially in reading, and shifts in the ways the condition is identified (National Center for Learning Disabilities, 2014). Currently, about 3.4 percent of students in U.S. schools are identified with learning disabilities using the IDEA definition (U.S. Department of Education, 2014b).

Because learning disabilities emerged as a category, their prevalence has been high compared with other exceptionalities. In 2013, over 6,429,000 children with disabilities were served under IDEA in the United States. Of that number, over 2,277,000 were classified as having learning disabilities, a figure that represents about 35 percent of the population with disabilities being served (U.S. Department of Education, 2014b). (See Figure 7.2.)

Although discrepancies in prevalence estimates occur in all fields of exceptionality, the area of learning disabilities seems more variable than most. Prevalence figures gathered through various studies are unlikely to match when different definitions determine what is counted.

## 7-3a Academic Achievement

Problems and inconsistencies in academic achievement largely prompted the recognition of learning disabilities as an area of exceptionality. Individuals with learning disabilities, though generally of average or near-average intelligence, seem to have many academic challenges. These challenges usually persist from the primary grades through the end of formal schooling, including college (Gerber, 2012; Goldstein, 2011). Researchers are suggesting that educational planning for students with learning disabilities

**Table 7.1** Changes in Number of Students Ages 6 through 21 Served under IDEA by Disability Category, 2002 and 2013

| Disability | 2002 | 2013 | Change in Number |
|---|---|---|---|
| Specific learning disabilities | 2,848,000 | 2,277,000 | –571,000 |
| Speech or language impairments | 1,412,000 | 1,356,000 | –56,000 |
| Intellectual disability | 602,000 | 430,000 | –172,000 |
| Emotional disturbance | 485,000 | 362,000 | –123,000 |
| Hearing impairments | 78,000 | 77,000 | –1,000 |
| Orthopedic impairments | 83,000 | 59,000 | –24,000 |
| Other health impairments | 403,000 | 779,000 | 376,000 |
| Visual impairments | 29,000 | 28,000 | –1,000 |
| Multiple disabilities | 138,000 | 133,000 | –5,000 |
| Deafness/blindness | 2,000 | 1,000 | –1,000 |
| Autism | 137,000 | 498,000 | 361,000 |
| Traumatic brain injury | 22,000 | 26,000 | 4,000 |
| Developmental delay | 283,000 | 402,000 | 119,000 |
| All disabilities | 6,523,000 | 6,429,000 | –94,000 |

SOURCE: U.S. Department of Education, National Center for Education Statistics. (2014). *Digest of Education Statistics*, 2013, Table 204.30.

should offer a variety of long-range alternatives, including options and academic preparation for postsecondary education (Barron & Hassiotis, 2008; Grigal, Hart, & Migliore, 2011).

**Reading**   Reading problems are found among students with learning disabilities more often than in any other area of academic performance. Historically, as the learning disabilities category began to take shape, it was applied to youngsters who had earlier been identified as remedial reading students. Estimates have suggested that as many as 60 to

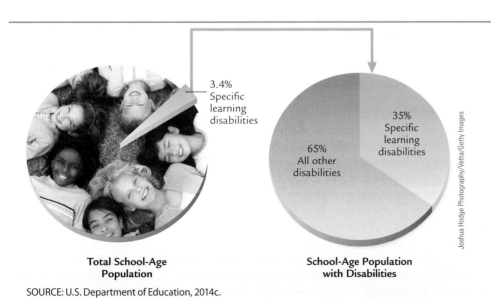

3.4%
Specific learning disabilities

65%
All other disabilities

35%
Specific learning disabilities

**Total School-Age Population**

**School-Age Population with Disabilities**

SOURCE: U.S. Department of Education, 2014c.

Joshua Hodge Photography/Vetta/Getty Images

*Figure 7.2  The Prevalence of Learning Disabilities for Students 6–21 Years of Age*

## Dyslexia: Searching for Causes

Throughout history, people have always speculated about the cause of learning disabilities, particularly the most severe forms, such as **dyslexia** (a rare condition). Dyslexia is a rare type of learning disability that impairs the ability to read. The search for the most prominent cause is jokingly called looking for the "bullet theory" by professionals in the field, most of whom believe that matters are more complicated than singular causation.

*Time* magazine followed a bullet theory on August 29, 1994, with "Brain Bane: Researchers May Have Found a Cause for Dyslexia." Beginning with background information on dyslexia, this article then moved to the final paragraph (where barely one-third of the article was devoted to the main topic, causation). Here it was noted that Dr. Albert Galaburda of Harvard and Beth Israel Hospital in Boston had been conducting research on the brains of people with dyslexia who have died. Essentially, the research team sampled brain tissue from people with dyslexia (postmortem) and compared it with brain tissue collected from people who did not have dyslexia. These researchers found a difference in the size of nerve cells between the left and right hemispheres in tissue from people with dyslexia, but they found no such difference in the tissue from individuals without dyslexia. The researchers noted that the size differential was only between 10 percent and 15 percent, but that was enough to capture the attention of *Time*. The public thirst for bullet theories was alive and well.

### Question for Reflection

How does searching for causes of dyslexia provide clues for instructional effectiveness?

SOURCE: Adapted from Alexander, C. P. (1994). "Brain Bane: Researchers May Have Found a Cause for Dyslexia." *Time, 144*(9), 61.

**Dyslexia**
Dyslexia is a severe type of learning disability that impairs the ability to read.

90 percent of students with learning disabilities have reading difficulties (Bender, 2008a). Clearly, difficulties with the reading process are prevalent among students identified as having learning disabilities (Judge & Bell, 2011; National Center for Learning Disabilities, 2014). However, the specific challenges that they have in reading vary as much as the many components of the reading process. (See the nearby Reflect on This, "Dyslexia: Searching for Causes.")

Both word knowledge and word recognition are vitally important parts of reading skill, and they both cause a challenge for people with learning disabilities (Janse, de Bree, & Brouwer, 2010; Sheehy, 2009; Taub, 2011). When most of us encounter a word that we know, we recall its meaning from our "mental dictionary," but for unfamiliar words, we must "sound out" the letters and pronounce the words by drawing on our knowledge of typical spelling patterns and pronunciation rules. This ability is important, both because we cannot memorize all words and because we constantly encounter new ones.

Students must also be able to generalize letter patterns and draw analogies with considerable flexibility. Good readers usually accomplish this task rather easily, quite quickly, and almost automatically after a little practice (Deacon, Leblanc, & Sabourin, 2011). Students with reading disabilities, however, experience substantial difficulty with this process, and when they can, they do it, only slowly and laboriously. Such students need training and practice in strategies that help them succeed at recognizing words (Morris & Gaffney, 2011; Shaul, Arzouan, & Goldstein, 2012).

Some students with learning disabilities focus on minor details within a text, without distinguishing the important ideas from those of less significance. A specific focus on learning strategies can help these students. Teaching them skills like organizing and summarizing, using mnemonics, problem solving, and relational thinking can help them avoid these difficulties and enhance academic performance (Berkeley, Mastropieri, & Scruggs, 2011; Harris, Schumaker, & Deshler, 2011; Rosenzweig, Krawec, & Montague, 2011).

Reading involves many skills (e.g., an ability to remember and an ability to focus on important, rather than irrelevant, aspects of a task) that also affect performance in other subjects (Cerdan, Gilabert, & Vidal-Arbaca, 2011; Mason, 2013). Some difficulties experienced by people with learning disabilities emerge in more than one area. For example, does a child with reading disabilities have attention difficulties or working memory deficits? The problem could be caused by either disability or by a combination of the two. Specific instruction may improve performance, but if the focus of the training is too narrow, the student may not generalize it to other relevant areas. Instruction that combines different methods (e.g., using both phonological awareness and instruction in specific skills) may serve students with reading disabilities better than applying a single method (Berkeley, Mastropieri, & Scruggs, 2011; Mason, 2013; Stothers & Klein, 2010).

**Writing and Spelling** Children with learning disabilities often exhibit quite different writing performance than their peers without disabilities. This problem affects their academic achievement and frequently persists into adulthood. Difficulties may occur in handwriting (slow writing, spacing problems, poor formation of letters), spelling, and composition or general written expression (Datchuk & Kubina, 2013; Gardner, 2011; Overvelde & Hulstijn, 2011). Some children are poor at handwriting because they have not mastered basic developmental skills required for the process, such as grasping a pen or pencil. Handwriting also involves understanding spatial concepts, such as up, down, top, bottom, and letter alignment. These abilities frequently are less developed in youngsters with learning disabilities than their peers without disabilities (Kushki, Schwellnus, & Ilyas, 2011; Overvelde & Hulstijn, 2011). Some children with rather mild handwriting problems exhibit slowness in development that will improve as they grow older, receive instruction, and practice. However, in more severe cases, age and practice may not result in mastery of handwriting skills. Several such difficulties are found in Figure 7.3.

Some researchers view the handwriting, writing, and composition skills of students with learning disabilities as closely related to their reading ability. A number of processes, ranging from basic skills to strategies employed, seem to contribute significantly to writing problems among students with learning disabilities (Gardner, 2011; Mason, Harris, & Graham, 2011). Letter reversals and, in severe cases, **mirror writing** have been used as illustrations of poor handwriting. However, it is questionable whether children with learning disabilities make these types of errors more often than their peers without disabilities at the same reading level.

Poor spelling (evident in Figure 7.3) is often a problem among students with learning disabilities. Research indicates that spelling problems are associated with other linguistic shortcomings. Limitations in overall language abilities often give rise to difficulties with spelling for students with learning disabilities. These children frequently omit letters or add incorrect ones. Their spelling may also show evidence of letter-order confusion and developmentally immature pronunciation (Friend & Olson, 2008; Kohnen, Nickels, &

**Mirror writing**
Writing backward from right to left, making letters that look like ordinary writing seen in a mirror.

*Figure 7.3* *Writing Samples of a College Freshman with a Learning Disability*

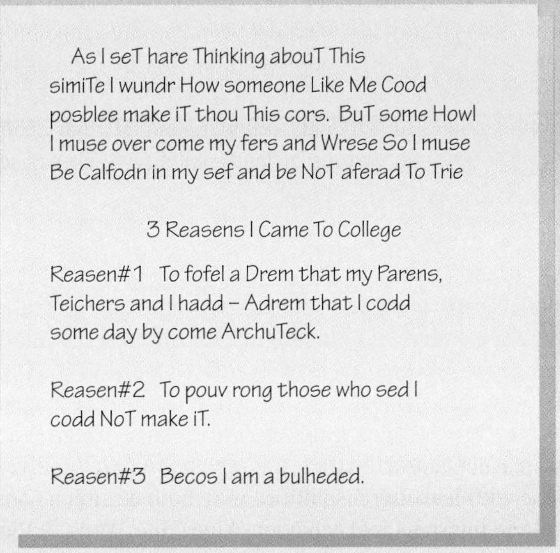

As I seT hare Thinking abouT This simiTe I wundr How someone Like Me Cood posblee make iT thou This cors. BuT some Howl I muse over come my fers and Wrese So I muse Be Calfodn in my sef and be NoT aferad To Trie

3 Reasens I Came To College

Reasen#1 To fofel a Drem that my Parens, Teichers and I hadd – Adrem that I codd some day by come ArchuTeck.

Reasen#2 To pouv rong those who sed I codd NoT make iT.

Reasen#3 Becos I am a bulheded.

**The text of these samples reads as follows:**

As I sit here thinking about this semester, I wonder how someone like me could possibly make it through this course. But somehow I must overcome my fears and worries. So I must be confident in myself and be not afraid to try.

Three Reasons I Came To College

Reason #1. To fulfill a dream that my parents, teachers, and I had—a dream that I could some day become architect.

Reason #2. To prove wrong those who said I could not make it.

Reason #3. Because I am bullheaded.

© Cengage Learning

Coltheart, 2010; Moats, 2009). Some studies have shown promise in the remediation of spelling difficulties. Encoding instruction (Weiser & Mathis, 2011), error self-correction (Viel-Ruma, Houchins, & Fredrick, 2007), mapping sounds (Murray & Steinen, 2011), and explicit instruction with feedback provided by the teacher or a peer accompanied by immediate practice (Sayeski, 2011) all resulted in significant gains for spellers with learning disabilities. Research literature suggests that the spelling skills of students with learning disabilities follow developmental patterns similar to those of their peers without disabilities but that they are delayed (Bender, 2008a; Sayeski, 2011).

**Mathematics** Arithmetic is another academic area that causes individuals with learning disabilities considerable difficulty. Such individuals often have trouble with counting, writing numbers, and mastering other simple math concepts (Mammarella, Lucangeli, & Cornoldi, 2010; Stock, Desoete, & Roeyers, 2010; Wei, Lenz, & Blackorby, 2013). Counting objects is perhaps the most fundamental mathematics skill and is a foundation for development of the more advanced, yet still basic, skills of addition and subtraction. Some youngsters omit numbers when counting sequences aloud (e.g., 1, 2, 3, 5, 7, 9), and others can count correctly but do not understand the relative values of numbers. Students with arithmetic learning disabilities have difficulties when asked to count beyond 9, which requires the use of more than one digit. This skill is somewhat more advanced than single-digit counting and involves knowledge about place value.

Place value, a function of base-10 understanding, is a more complex concept than the counting of objects and is fundamental to understanding addition and subtraction. Many students with learning disabilities in math have problems understanding the base-10 principle of place value, particularly that the same digit (such as 6) represents different values according to its position in a written number (as in 16, 61, and 632). Research has shown that early place value misunderstanding can predict later difficulties with math understanding and procedures (Moeller, Pixner, & Zuber, 2011). Such complexities require strategic problem solving, which presents particular difficulties for students with learning disabilities (Krawec, 2014; Powell, 2011). Research on the provision of math problem-solving instruction indicates significant success at both elementary and middle school levels (Jitendra & Star, 2011; Swanson, Moran, Bocian, Lussier, & Zheng, 2013). Some of these math difficulties are often major obstacles in the academic paths of students with learning disabilities; they frequently continue to cause challenges through high school and into the college years (Morris, Schraufnagel, Chudnow, & Weinberg, 2009).

**Achievement Discrepancy** Students with learning disabilities perform below expectations based on their measured potential, in addition to scoring below their peers in overall achievement. Attempts to quantify the discrepancy between academic achievement and academic potential for students with learning disabilities have appeared in the literature, but the field still lacks a broadly accepted explanation of the phenomenon (Cahan, Fono, & Nirel, 2012; Maehler & Schuchardt, 2011). Early in the school years, youngsters with learning disabilities may find themselves two to four or more years behind their peers in academic achievement; many fall even further behind as they continue in the educational system. This discouraging pattern often results in students dropping out of high school or graduating without proficiency in basic reading, writing, or math skills (U.S. Department of Education, 2013a).

## 7-3b Intelligence

Certain assumptions about intelligence are being reexamined in research on learning disabilities. Populations with behavior disorders and learning disabilities are thought to include people generally considered above average, average, or near average in intelligence (Swanson, 2011; Kebir, Grizenko, Sengupta, & Joober, 2009). Differences between students with behavior disorders and those with specific learning disabilities have been defined on the basis of social skill levels and learner characteristics. It is well known that individuals with intellectual deficits and those with learning disabilities may both exhibit a considerable amount of maladaptive social and interpersonal behavior (Algozzine, Wang, & Violette, 2011; Semrud-Clikeman, Walkowiak, Wilkinson, & Minne, 2010).

These insights have affected ideas about the distinctions between learning disabilities and intellectual disabilities. Marked discrepancy between measured intelligence and academic performance has long been viewed as a defining characteristic of people with learning disabilities (Dunn, 2010; Machek & Nelson, 2010). Also, descriptions of learning disabilities have often emphasized great intraindividual differences between skill areas. For example, a youngster may exhibit very low performance in reading but not in arithmetic. However, intraindividual variability is sometimes evident in students with intellectual disabilities and those with behavior disorders. Further, intraindividual variability in students with learning disabilities does not always appear; here again, the research evidence is mixed (Branum-Martin, Fletcher, & Stuebing, 2013; Wilcutt et al., 2013).

**Cognition and Information Processing** People with learning disabilities have certain characteristics related to **cognition**, or **information processing**, the way a person acquires, retains, and manipulates information (e.g., Geary, Hoard, Nugent, & Bailey, 2011; Maehler & Shurchardt, 2009). These processes often emerge as challenges for individuals with learning disabilities. For example, teachers have long complained that such children have poor memory function. In many cases, these students seem to learn material one day but cannot recall it the next. Memory function is also centrally involved in language skill and development, a challenging area for many children with learning disabilities (Baird, Dworzynski, Slonims, & Simonoff, 2010; Passolunghi, 2011).

Attention problems have also been associated with learning disabilities. Such problems have often been characterized as short attention span. Parents and teachers note that their children with learning disabilities cannot sustain attention for more than a very short time and that some of them exhibit considerable daydreaming and high distractibility. Some researchers have observed **short attention spans** in these children while others indicate that they have difficulty in certain types of attention problems and, in some cases, attend selectively (Bender, 2008a; Obrzut & Mahoney, 2011). **Selective attention** problems make it difficult to focus on centrally important tasks or information rather than on peripheral or less relevant stimuli. Attention problems remain in the spotlight as the information-processing problems of children with learning disabilities are investigated (e.g., Iseman & Naglieri, 2011; Shiran & Breznitz, 2011).

## 7-3c Learning Characteristics

The study of perceptual problems had a significant role early in the history of learning disabilities although interest in this topic has declined. Some researchers, however, continue to view perception difficulties as important. Perception difficulties in people with learning disabilities represent a constellation of behavior anomalies, rather than a single characteristic. Descriptions of these problems have referred to the visual, auditory, and **haptic** sensory systems. Difficulty in visual perception has been closely associated with learning disabilities. This type of abnormality can cause a child to see a visual stimulus as unrelated parts rather than as an integrated pattern; for example, a child may not be able to identify a letter in the alphabet because he or she perceives only unrelated lines, rather than the letter as a meaningful whole (Bender, 2008a). Visual perception problems may emerge in **figure–ground discrimination**, the process of distinguishing an object from the background. Most of us have little difficulty with figure–ground discrimination, but children with learning disabilities may have trouble focusing on a word or sentence in a textbook because they cannot distinguish it from the rest of the page.

Other discrimination difficulties have also surfaced in descriptions of people with learning disabilities. Individuals with difficulties in **visual discrimination** may be unable to distinguish one visual stimulus from another (they cannot tell the difference between words such as *sit* and *sat*, for example, or between letters such as V and W, and they commonly reverse letters such as b and d). This type of error is common among young children, causing great concern for parents. Yet most youngsters overcome this problem in the course of normal development, and by about 7 or 8 years of age, show few reversal or rotation errors with visual image. Children who make frequent errors beyond that age might be viewed as potential problem learners and may need additional instruction specifically aimed at improving such skills.

**Cognition**
The act of thinking, knowing, or processing information.

**Information processing**
A model used to study the way people acquire, remember, and manipulate information.

**Short attention span**
An inability to focus one's attention on a task for more than a few seconds or minutes.

**Selective attention**
Attention that often does not focus on centrally important tasks or information.

**Haptic**
Related to the sensation of touch and to information transmitted through body movement or position.

**Figure–ground discrimination**
The process of distinguishing an object from its background.

**Visual discrimination**
Distinguishing one visual stimulus from another.

**Auditory processing disorder**
A condition resulting in difficulties distinguishing the sounds of language, but not with general understanding or use of language.

**Kinesthetic**
Related to the sensation of body position, presence, or movement, resulting chiefly from stimulation of sensory nerve endings in the muscles, tendons, and joints.

Auditory perception problems have historically been associated with learning disabilities. The current discussion in the field addresses **auditory processing disorder** as a condition resulting in difficulties understanding receptive language. As described by the American Speech-Language-Hearing Association, this condition can result in difficulties isolating one sound in a blend, discriminating similar sounds, and recognizing sound patterns—all of which are important for processing spoken language (American Speech-Language-Hearing Association, 2005; Kamhia, 2011). Affected children may be unable to distinguish /ch/ from /sh/, hear the difference between /b/ and /d/, or recognize the identical sound endings in *stone* and *own*. In addition, the condition makes it difficult for listeners to understand and remember what others say, even though there are no problems with hearing acuity. At this time there is no generally agreed-upon definition of auditory processing disorder, and debate continues about appropriate and effective interventions (Moore, 2011; National Coalition of Auditory Processing Disorders, 2015).

Another area of perceptual difficulty long associated with learning disabilities involves haptic perception (touch, body movement, and position sensation). For example, handwriting requires haptic perception, because tactile information about the grasp of a pen or pencil must be transmitted to the brain. In addition, **kinesthetic** information regarding hand and arm movements is transmitted as one writes. Children with learning disabilities have often been described by teachers as having poor handwriting and difficulties in spacing letters and staying on the lines of the paper (Cahill, 2009; Overvelde & Hulstijn, 2011). Figure 7.3 shows examples of writing by a college freshman with learning disabilities. The two samples in this figure were from consecutive days, each in a 40-minute period. The note beside the samples translates what was written.

## 7-3d Social and Emotional Characteristics

Children and adolescents with learning disabilities often have emotional and interpersonal difficulties that are quite serious and highly resistant to treatment (Cowden, 2010b). Because of their learning challenges, they frequently have low self-esteem and a negative emotional status (Alesi, Rappo, & Pepi, 2012; Semrud-Clikeman et al., 2010). They may not be able to interact effectively with others because they misunderstand social cues or cannot discriminate among, or interpret the subtleties of, typical interpersonal associations. For some with learning disabilities, social life poses greater challenges than their academic deficits.

## 7-3e Hyperactivity

Hyperactivity has commonly been linked to children labeled as having learning disabilities (Harrison, Vannest, & Reynolds, 2011; Knowles, 2010). Also termed **hyperkinetic behavior**, **hyperactivity** is typically defined as a general excess of activity. Not all children with learning disabilities are hyperactive, and not all hyperactive children have learning disabilities.

## 7-4 Causes of Learning Disabilities

Researchers have theorized about a number of possible causes for learning disabilities. There are probably many different causes of learning disabilities, and in some cases, a specific type of learning disability may have multiple causes (Buttner & Hasselhorn, 2011; Kaufman, 2008; Miller & McCardle, 2011). Also, a single cause may underlie multiple disorders, such as learning disabilities and hyperactivity, in the same child (Mangina & Beuzeron-Mangina, 2009; Stothers, & Cardy, 2012). Because it is imperative to help affected students even though we do not yet fully understand the cause of learning disabilities, the practical issues of assessment and intervention have frequently taken priority in research so that specialized instruction can be offered to such students (Bender, 2008b; National Joint Committee on Learning Disabilities, 2011b).

**Hyperkinetic behavior**
A general excess of behavior in an inappropriate setting.

**Hyperactivity**
A general excess of behavior in an inappropriate setting.

## 7-4a Neurological Factors

For many years, some have viewed the cause of learning disabilities as structural neurological damage, abnormal neurological development, or some type of abnormality in neurological function (e.g., Bender, 2008a; Miller & McCardle, 2011). Neurological damage associated with learning disabilities can occur in many ways. Damage may occur in the neurological system at birth by conditions such as anoxia (a lack of oxygen), low birth weight, or abnormal fetal positioning during delivery (Taylor, Espy, & Anderson, 2009). Infections may also cause neurological damage and learning disabilities, as can certain types of physical injury. However, magnetic resonance imaging (MRI) is generating research that supports some unusual neurological functioning in these children (Cleary & Scott, 2011; Norton, Beach, & Gabrieli, 2015).

## 7-4b Maturational Delay

In many ways, the behavior and performance of children with learning disabilities resemble those of much younger individuals (Pieters, Desoete, Roeyers, Vanderswalmen, & Van Waelvelde, 2012). They often exhibit delays in skills maturation, such as slower development of language skills and problems in the visual-motor area and several academic areas, as already noted. Although maturational delay is probably not a causative factor in all types of learning disabilities, there is evidence that it contributes to some (Houston et al., 2014).

## 7-4c Genetic Factors

Genetic abnormalities, which are inherited, are thought to cause or contribute to one or more of the challenges categorized as learning disabilities (Miller & McCardle, 2011; Rubenstein, Raskind, Berninger, Matsushita, & Wijsman, 2014). Some research, including studies of **identical twins** and **fraternal twins**, has suggested that such disorders may be inherited (Davis & Plomin, 2010; Haworth et al., 2009). These findings must be viewed cautiously because of difficulty in separating the influences of heredity and environment, but selected evidence supports the idea that some learning disabilities are inherited (Sampango-Sprouse et al., 2014; Scerri & Schulte-Korne, 2010).

## 7-4d Environmental Factors

The search for the causes of learning disabilities has also implicated certain environmental influences: Dietary inadequacies, food additives, radiation stress, fluorescent lighting, unshielded television tubes, alcohol consumption, drug consumption, and inappropriate school instruction have all been investigated at one time or another (Loomis, 2006; Walker & Plomin, 2005). Some environmental factors, such as irradiation, lead ingestion, maternal smoking, illicit drugs, and family stress, are also known to have negative effects on development (Anderko, Braun, & Auinger, 2010; Dufault et al., 2009; U.S. Department of Education, 2011).

# 7-5 Identification and Assessment of Learning Disabilities

Assessment, or the evaluation of individuals with learning disabilities, has several purposes. The ultimate goal is to provide an appropriate intervention, if warranted, for the child or adult being evaluated. Assessment and intervention involve a series of related steps, which include screening, identification, placement, and delivery of specialized assistance. Deciding how to meet an individual student's needs requires data obtained through specialized assessment procedures (Decker, 2012; Rosenblum, Larochette, Harrison, & Armstrong, 2010).

## 7-5a Formal and Informal Assessment

Formal versus informal assessment has come to mean standardized tests versus teacher-made tests or techniques. Standardized instruments, such as intelligence tests and

**Identical twins**
Twins from a single fertilized egg and a single placental sac. Such twins are of the same sex and usually resemble one another closely.

**Fraternal twins**
Twins from two fertilized eggs and two placental sacs. Such twins do not resemble each other closely.

**Standard 4**
Assessment

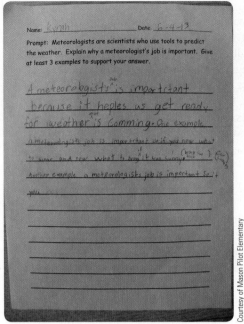

**Photo 7.2** By comparing a student's skill level with a criterion-based assessment, a teacher is able to make a specific instruction plan for the student.

*Courtesy of Mason Pilot Elementary*

achievement tests, are published and distributed commercially. Teacher-made techniques or instruments (or those devised by any professional) are ones that are not commercially available. These may be constructed for specific assessment purposes and are often quite formal, in that great care is taken in the evaluation process (Beirne-Smith & Riley, 2009; Miller, 2009).

**Norm-referenced assessment** compares an individual's skills or performance with that of others, such as peers, usually on the basis of national average scores. Thus, a student's counting performance might be compared with that of his or her classmates, with that of others in the school district of the same age, or with state or national average scores. In contrast, **criterion-referenced assessment** does not compare an individual's skills with a norm but with a desired performance level (criterion) or a specific goal. For example, the goal may involve counting to 100 with no errors by the end of the school year. One application of criterion-referenced assessment, **curriculum-based assessment**, has received attention recently. It uses a student's curriculum objectives as the criteria by which progress is evaluated (McMaster, Du, & Yeo, 2011; Seethaler & Fuchs, 2011). Curriculum-based assessment, used to screen students for individual strengths and needs, is sometimes contrasted with ongoing curriculum-based *measurement* as used for progress monitoring (monitoring a student's progress), or repetitive measures given over time to monitor students' progress toward learning goals (Jenkins & Terjeson, 2011; Luckner & Bowen, 2010). The relationship between evaluation and instructional objectives makes instruction planning and assessment more efficient. The purpose of measuring from the students' curriculum is to determine the effectiveness of instruction and make changes as needed to ensure student success.

Both norm- and criterion-referenced assessments are useful for working with students with learning disabilities. Norm-referenced assessment is used for administrative purposes, such as compiling census data on how many students achieve at or above the state or national average. Criterion-referenced assessment is helpful for specific instructional purposes and planning. These two assessments do not require separate types of assessment instruments or procedures. Depending on how a technique, instrument, or procedure is employed, it may be used in a norm-referenced or a criterion-referenced manner. Some areas, such as intelligence, are more typically evaluated using norm-referenced procedures. However, even a standardized intelligence test can be scored and used in a criterion-referenced fashion. Assessment should always be undertaken with careful attention to the purpose and future use of the evaluation (Dombrowski & Gischlar, 2014; Keeley, 2011).

## 7-5b Screening

**Screening** of students who have learning disabilities has always been an important facet of assessment. Screening occurs prior to determining eligibility or treatment of a student, although clinicians or others (e.g., parents) often suspect that a problem exists. Assessment for potential learning disabilities most often takes place during the school years. This is partly because the types of performance that are most problematic for these children are not usually required until a child goes to school and partly because one of the important markers for learning disabilities (a discrepancy between ability and achievement) does not seem to show as well very early.

The role of screening is to "raise a red flag," or suggest that investigation is needed. Four questions are relevant at this point: (1) Is there a reason to investigate the abilities

**Norm-referenced assessment**
Assessment wherein a person's performance is compared with the average of a larger group.

**Criterion-referenced assessment**
Assessment that compares a person's performance with a specific established level (the criterion). This performance is not compared with that of other people.

**Curriculum-based assessment**
Assessment in which the objectives of a student's curriculum are used as the criteria against which progress is evaluated.

**Screening**
A preliminary assessment to decide if further study of a child's functioning level is necessary. Screening raises "a red flag" if a problem is indicated.

of the child more fully? (2) Is there a reason to suspect that the child in any way has disabilities? (3) If the child appears to have disabilities, what are their characteristics, and what sort of intervention is appropriate? (4) How should we plan for the future of the individual? Answers to these questions might point to a variety of needs such as further classification of the disability, planning of intervention services such as psychological treatment or individualized instruction, or ongoing evaluation of progress. For students with learning disabilities, assessment is not a simple, isolated event resulting in a single diagnosis. Rather, it is a complex process with many different steps (Gilbert, Compton, Fuchs, & Fuchs, 2012; National Joint Committee on Learning Disabilities, 2011b).

## 7-5c Intelligence

For the most part, individuals with learning disabilities are described as having average or near-average intelligence, although they experience many challenges in school that are typical of students with lower intelligence levels. In many cases, measures of intelligence may be inaccurate because of specific visual, auditory, or other limitations that may affect the student's performance (Lund, Miller, & Ganz, 2014; Roivainen, 2014). However, intelligence remains an important matter for individuals with learning disabilities; assessment of intelligence is often done with a standardized instrument such as an intelligence test. Where measured intelligence fits into the definition of learning disabilities is somewhat controversial (Dunn, 2010; Maehler & Schuchardt, 2011).

## 7-5d Adaptive Skills

People with learning disabilities are frequently described as exhibiting poor adaptive skills—that is, they lack a sense of what constitutes appropriate behavior in a particular environment. Such descriptions have appeared primarily in clinical reports, though evaluation of adaptive skills has not historically been a routine part of assessment of learning disabilities to the same degree as in other areas of exceptionality. However, some work has been undertaken to address adaptive and social skills and their assessment for individuals with learning disabilities (e.g., Cowden, 2010a; Galway & Metsala, 2011).

## 7-5e Academic Achievement

Academic achievement has always been a major problem for students with learning disabilities. Assessment of academic achievement helps evaluate a student's level of functioning in one or more specific academic areas. Instruments have been developed and used to diagnose specific academic challenges. For example, a number of reading tests, including the Woodcock Reading Mastery Tests, the Diagnostic Reading Scales, and the Stanford Diagnostic Reading Test, determine the nature of reading problems. Likewise, mathematics assessment employs instruments such as the KeyMath Diagnostic Arithmetic Test and the Stanford Diagnostic Mathematics Test (Gronlund & Waugh, 2009).

Academic assessment for students with learning disabilities is very important. Assessment techniques resemble those used in other areas of exceptionality, because deficits in academic achievement are a common problem among students with a variety of disabilities. Diagnosis of deficits in specific skills, however, has a more prominent history in learning disabilities and has prompted the development of focused, skills-oriented assessment of academic achievement in other disability areas as well.

## 7-6 Interventions and Treatments for People with Learning Disabilities

Interventions for people with learning disabilities focus on evidence-based practices for addressing individual academic and behavioral needs throughout the life span. Researchers and practitioners refine practice by collecting and analyzing student outcome data, and making instructional changes as needed for elementary students, adolescent students, and those transitioning to adulthood.

Alice found herself very frustrated with school. She was in the fourth grade, and her grades were very bad. She had worked hard, but many of the things that were required just didn't seem to make sense.

History was a perfect example. Alice had looked forward to learning more about history; it was so interesting when her grandfather told his stories. Alice thought it would have been fun to live back then, when all the kids got to ride horses. But history in school was not fun, and it didn't make any sense at all. Alice had been reading last night, supposedly about a girl who was her age and was moving west with a wagon train. As Alice looked at the book, she read strange things. One passage said, "Mary pelieveb that things would detter. What they hab left Missouri they hab enough foob dut now there was darely enough for one meal a bay. Surely the wagon-master woulb finb a wet to solve the brodlem." Alice knew that she would fail the test, and she cried quietly in her room as she dressed for school.

## 7-6a Elementary Education Programs

Services and supports for children with learning disabilities have changed over time as professionals have come to view learning disabilities as a constellation of specific individualized needs. Specific disabilities, such as cognitive learning problems, attention deficit and hyperactivity, social and emotional difficulties, and problems with spoken language, reading, writing, spelling, and mathematics, are all receiving research attention (e.g., Ashkenazi, Black, Abrams, Hoeft, & Menon, 2013; Connor, Alberto, Compton, & O'Connor, 2014; Orosco & O'Connor, 2014). This approach has resulted in services and supports focused on individual need. Greater attention is being paid to social skills instruction for children with learning disabilities and to the effective use of tutors and peer tutors (Roberts, Solis, Ciullo, McKenna, & Vaughn, 2015; Scheeler, Macluckie, & Albright, 2010).

An overarching concept for this approach to intervention is the RtI model for making decisions about instructional focus. RtI tends to be associated with assessment because of its prominent and ongoing measurement components (Beach & O'Connor, 2015; Lindstrom & Sayeski, 2013). Although the assessment element is important, the comprehensive RtI concept also includes other important components related to evidence-based decisions about interventions (Lembke, Hampton, & Byers, 2012; Lieberman-Betz, Vail, & Chai, 2013). As indicated in Figure 7.4, the three-tiered service triangle involves a carefully designed comprehensive academic core to which a very large proportion of students with learning disabilities will respond—perhaps as high as 80 to 85 percent. In tier two, more intensive or supplemental instruction is undertaken to help the next 10 to 15 percent make progress. Tier three involves even more specialized and intense instruction needed by about 5 percent of students with the most serious academic challenges. Of course, these proportions are rough estimates and will vary (Mellard, McKnight, & Jordan, 2010). A balanced RtI concept focuses on both the assessment and intervention elements of the evidence-based decision making that is crucial for both general and special education.

Services and supports for adolescents or adults with learning disabilities may differ from those for children. Some changes in approach are due to shifting goals as individuals grow older (e.g., the acquisition of basic counting skills versus instruction in preparation for college). Individuals from varied professions must function as a team and also as unique

**CEC**

**Standard 2**
Learning Environments

**Standard 5**
Instructional Planning and Strategies

*Figure 7.4 RtI Model for Instruction and Service Delivery*

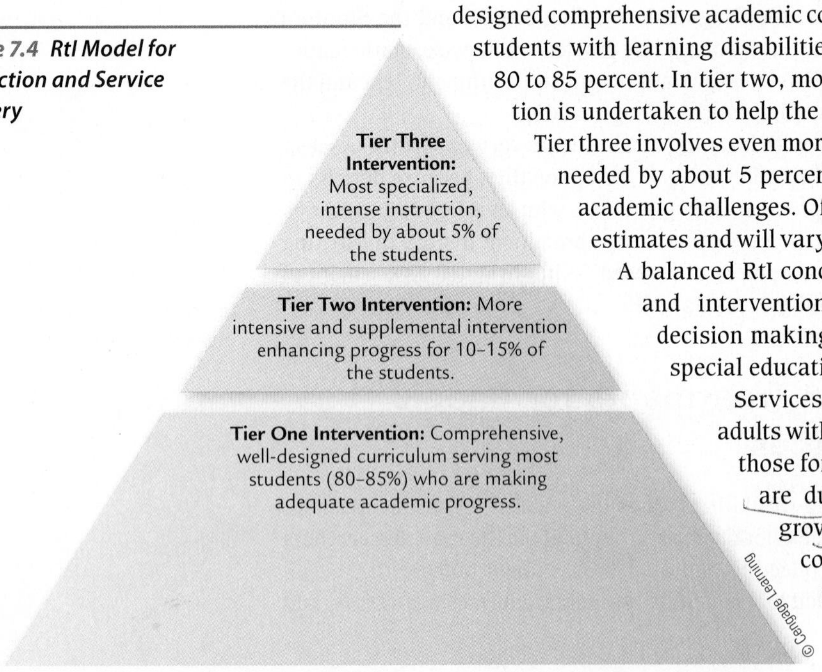

**Tier Three Intervention:** Most specialized, intense instruction, needed by about 5% of the students.

**Tier Two Intervention:** More intensive and supplemental intervention enhancing progress for 10–15% of the students.

**Tier One Intervention:** Comprehensive, well-designed curriculum serving most students (80–85%) who are making adequate academic progress.

© Cengage Learning

contributors to create well-balanced programs for students with learning disabilities (Shapiro et al., 2012; Unruh & McKellar, 2013).

**Academic Instruction and Support** A wide variety of instructional approaches has been used over the years for children with learning disabilities. These include strategies to develop cognition, attention, spoken language, and skill in reading, writing, and mathematics (Connor et al., 2014; Orosco & O'Connor, 2014). Even within each area, a whole array of instructional procedures has been used to address specific problems. For example, cognitive training has incorporated problem solving, strategies for attacking problems, and instruction in social competence (Hord & Xin, 2013; Montague, Enders, & Dietz, 2011).

Various approaches to cognitive instruction are needed to teach the heterogeneous population of children with learning disabilities. Such strategies or tactics are often customized or reconfigured to individualize the program and target a student's specific needs. For example, if a youngster exhibits adaptive skills deficits that interfere with inclusion in general education, such skills may form an instructional focus. Flexible and multiple services or supports may make inclusion possible, providing a well-defined instructional environment, teaching the child important skills, and addressing interpersonal or social-emotional needs (Abbott, McConkey, & Dobbins, 2011; McLeskey & Waldron, 2011).

**Mathematics** Students with learning disabilities often have difficulties with four foundational math skills: counting, memorizing and retrieving math facts, base-10 understanding, and problem solving (Becker, McLaughlin, Weber, & Gower, 2009; Martin et al., 2013; Montague, Enders, & Dietz, 2011; Swanson et al., 2013). Counting may be most effectively taught with manipulative objects. Repetitive experience with counting buttons, marbles, or any such objects provides practice in counting, as well as exposure to the concepts of magnitude associated with numbers. Counting and grouping sets of 10 objects can help children begin to grasp rudimentary place-value concepts. These activities must often be quite structured for students with learning disabilities (Doabler & Fien, 2013; Manci, Miller, & Kennedy, 2012). Effective strategies for memorizing and retrieving math facts depend on consistent oral and written rehearsal with immediate corrective feedback and practice to mastery, as used in the cover, copy, and compare approach (Becker et al., 2009). Teaching base-10 understanding involves helping students understand that multidigit numbers are made up of groups of ones, tens, and hundreds rather than numerals in a certain place or position. This can be taught by having students manipulate units, tens, and hundreds using counting sticks or base-10 blocks (Cooper & Tomayko, 2011; Lopez Fernandez & Velazquez Estrella, 2011). Recent research on teaching problem solving indicates that cognitive strategy instruction increases achievement for students with learning disabilities (Hord & Xin, 2013; Montague, Enders, & Dietz, 2011).

Information and communication technology have replaced much traditional seat and board work for teaching students with learning disabilities. Laptop computers, tablet computers, and interactive whiteboards are commonly used for a variety of teaching and learning activities in general and special education classrooms. These devices allow teachers and students to engage in interactive teaching and learning just as they would with pencils, paper, books, or math manipulatives. Downloadable web applications provide almost unlimited strategies for teaching and learning with tablet computers. Math applications ranging from basic counting, sorting, and classifying activities to algebra and geometry make it possible for teachers to customize practice for students with learning disabilities (Kalloo & Mohan, 2012; Kiger, Herro, & Prunty, 2012; Olsen, LeMire, & Baker, 2011). The only drawback to using new technologies for these purposes seems to be inadequate teacher preparation for keeping up with quickly evolving possibilities (Blue & Tirotta, 2011; Handal, Campbell, Cavanaugh, Petocz, & Kelly, 2013).

**Reading** It has long been recognized that students with learning disabilities have great difficulty with reading. Because of this, many different strategies have been developed to address the problem (Dexter & Hughes, 2011; Narkon & Wells, 2013; Wilson, 2012). Each procedure has succeeded with certain children, but none with all. Research on particular types of skill instruction has produced significant improvements for students with learning disabilities (see Connor et al., 2014; Watson, Gable, Gear, & Hughes, 2012).

## Teen Use of Social Media on the Rise

Teen use of social media is nearly ubiquitous. Quickly replacing blogging as the preferred way to update status and communicate with others, the use of social networking increased from 55 percent of teens in 2006 to 81 percent in 2012. Facebook and Twitter are the current preferred group forums for communicating with friends, building relationships, and sharing social comment, but text messaging is still the most used form of digital communication other than voice. Current data indicate that older kids are more likely to use Twitter than younger ones, and high school girls are more likely to use Twitter than any other

school-aged group (Lenhart, Purcell, Smith, & Zickuhr, 2010).

Are there useful applications for social media in the classroom? Many writers answer in the affirmative. Teachers are exploring student use of Twitter for taking and sharing notes, and encouraging students to use Facebook to work together on shared assignments. Others are helping students prepare and produce podcasts that are then used to mentor younger students using iPads or smartphones (Koenig, 2011). For some, answering class questions using Twitter proves to be less threatening than traditional oral responses. Out-of-class

sharing and peer-to-peer homework help are now accomplished largely through social media (Jackson, 2011).

There is little research on the use of social media to specifically address the needs of students with learning disabilities, but technology-savvy teachers are finding ways to use the latest devices and applications to empower this population. The challenges that those with learning disabilities have with reading textbooks or literature, expressing themselves in writing, or using math in appropriate and functional ways present opportunities for creative teachers to explore applications of social media in and out of the classroom.

The largest-ever analysis of reading research, conducted by the National Reading Panel (2000), found that all readers must master five fundamental skills to read fluently and with comprehension: phonemic awareness, phonics, fluency, vocabulary, and text comprehension. Phonemic awareness is the ability to hear, discriminate, and manipulate the sounds of language. Phonics refers to the alphabetic principle, or the system of representing sounds with letters. Fluent reading is the ability to read with speed, accuracy, and correct intonation. Vocabulary refers to the number and variety of words that children can read and speak. Text comprehension is the ability to understand and enjoy what one reads without relying on illustrations or other images (Armbruster, Lehr, & Osborn, 2006).

Students can be classified as having learning disabilities in either basic reading skills or in reading comprehension, or both (Ritchey, 2011). Helping children with learning disabilities master the skills of reading is best accomplished by teaching practices with strong research support, or evidence-based practice (practice that is based on evidence or data). Explicit, intensive, and systematic instruction is integral to one evidence-based class of instructional practices, whether for teaching basic skills or helping students master strategies for specific types of comprehension (Connor et al., 2014; Nelson-Walker et al., 2013; Ritchey, 2011; Stockard, 2010). Explicit instruction is exemplified by specific learning objectives, teacher modeling, high rates of students responding with affirmative and corrective feedback, praise for success, and practice to mastery (Archer & Hughes, 2011, Kim & Axelrod, 2005). Effective strategies for improving reading beyond the basic level include self-monitoring for comprehension, cognitive strategy instruction, attribution retraining, and computer-assisted instruction (Berkeley, Mastropieri, & Scruggs, 2011; Boudah, 2014; Joseph & Eveleigh, 2011; Ponce, Lopez, & Mayer, 2012). It is important to note that focusing on isolated skills is not effective for overall reading improvement. Instead, teachers must engage students in consistent application of the complete reading process through reading, discussing, and making meaning from what is read (Berkeley, Mastropieri, & Scruggs, 2011; Hollenbeck, 2011).

Computer-assisted instruction has successfully enhanced the reading skills of students with learning disabilities. Researchers have studied computer instruction for phonemic awareness, phonics, fluency, vocabulary acquisition, and text comprehension, all of which have shown promise (Macaruso & Rodman, 2011; Ponce, Lopez, & Mayer, 2012; Torgesen,

### Software for Writing

Writing has long been recognized as an academic area that presents considerable difficulty for children with learning disabilities. Advances in educational applications of technology, especially the development of new computer software, have the potential to assist children with writing problems (Moorman, Boon, & Keller-Bell, 2010; Stetter & Hughes, 2011). An example of such software is Starter Paragraph Punch©, used in elementary schools to help students master basic paragraph writing by guiding them through the topic sentence, body, and conclusion. It includes a teaching monitoring system and comes in both CD software and web versions (Merit, 2011). Grammar Fitness© is a companion program that includes a speak-aloud text talker to guide students while learning to identify and correct errors in punctuation, usage, and tenses.

WriteOnline© is another program for guiding student writing in upper elementary and secondary schools (Crick, 2011). The program includes a word processor, a word-prediction feature that uses word bars to present word choices to writers, a speech function, and a system to help teachers analyze student writing. Teachers can choose either the CD software or online versions for use in their classrooms.

The proliferation of tablet computers such as the Apple iPad makes interactive teaching and learning readily available to individual students. Downloadable web applications ("apps") are available for just about any educational purpose with more coming available at a dizzying rate. Several current apps apply specifically to a variety of language arts skills, including writing. One such is StoryBuilder© for beginning writers (Northwest Kinematics, 2010). The program uses audio recording to capture a student's spoken story and then replays the audio clips to form a complete narrative. The idea is that students can learn to form and present their ideas as spoken stories before committing them to text.

Another is My Writing Spot©, developed for students with special needs. The program lets students write in portrait or landscape, tracks word count, has a dictionary/thesaurus, and emails documents (PT Software, 2010). The autosave function ensures that students do not lose their work between sessions.

Many state offices of education and school district websites are adding lists of approved or recommended downloadable apps. These and other resources can help teachers as they address specific needs for students with learning disabilities (Kendall, Nino, & Stewart, 2010).

Wagner, & Rashotte, 2010). Whether on a desktop computer, a smartphone, or a tablet computer, students can learn and practice skills ranging from letter names and sounds to text comprehension using a wide variety of software and apps (Castek & Beach, 2013; King-Sears, Swanson, & Mainzer, 2011). Teachers should be careful to evaluate the actual instructional effectiveness of any program before adopting it for the classroom. Studies of software design show that many lack helpful features, such as tracking student performance and providing timely feedback to users (Zipke, 2014).

Progress monitoring for reading is an important strategy to help teachers make decisions regarding the effectiveness of particular instruction for student achievement. As mentioned previously, frequent systematic measurement of student progress toward learning goals and objectives provides the data needed to either continue a particular strategy or change to something more effective (Fuchs & Fuchs, 2011; Jenkins & Terjeson, 2011). Good teachers also monitor other important factors of the classroom learning environment, including student grouping, behavior management, access to materials, the emotional climate, and physical appearance. Such attention to the whole child and common human needs can greatly enhance motivation, emotional health, and achievement (Gettinger, Schieneback, Seigel, & Vollmer, 2011).

**Behavioral Interventions** Distinctions between behavioral and academic interventions are not always sharp and definitive. Both involve students in learning skills and changing behavior. Behavioral interventions, however, generally use practical applications of learning principles such as reinforcement. Behavioral interventions, such as the structured presentation of stimuli (e.g., letters or words), reinforcement for correct responses, and self-monitoring of behavior and performance, are used in many instructional approaches (Joseph & Eveleigh, 2011; Stockard, 2010).

**Behavioral contract**
An agreement, written or oral, stating that if one party behaves in a certain manner, the other will provide a specific reward.

**Token reinforcement system**
A system in which students, by exhibiting positive behavior changes, may earn plastic chips, marbles, or other tangible items that they can exchange for rewards.

Some students with learning disabilities who experience repeated academic failure, despite their great effort, become frustrated and depressed (e.g., Nelson & Harwood, 2011b; Toland & Boyle, 2008). They may not understand why their classmates without disabilities seem to do little more than they do and yet achieve more success. These students with learning disabilities may withdraw or express frustration and anxiety by acting out or becoming aggressive. When this type of behavior emerges, it may be difficult to distinguish individuals with learning difficulties from those with behavior disorders as a primary disability (e.g., Evans, Clinkinbeard, & Simi, 2015; Langberg, Vaughn, Brinkman, Froehlich, & Epstein, 2010). Social and behavioral difficulties of students with learning disabilities are receiving increasing attention (Cowden, 2010a; Roberts et al., 2015).

**Behavioral contracts** are one type of intervention that is often used to change undesirable behavior. Using this approach, a teacher, behavior therapist, or parent establishes a contract with the child that provides him or her with reinforcement for appropriate behavior. Such contracts are either written or spoken, usually focus on a specific behavior, and reward the child with something that she or he really likes and considers worth striving for (such as going to the library or using the class computer). It is important that the pupil understand clearly what is expected and that the event or consequence be appealing to the child. Behavioral contracts have considerable appeal because they give students some responsibility for their own behavior (Bowman-Perrott, Burke, de Marin, Zhang, & Davis, 2015; Lane, Menzies, & Bruhn, 2010).

Token reinforcement systems represent another behavioral intervention often used with youngsters experiencing learning difficulties. **Token reinforcement systems** allow students to earn tokens for appropriate behavior and to exchange them eventually for a reward of value to them (Bullock & Hackenberg, 2015; Gilley & Ringdahl, 2014). Token systems resemble the work-for-pay lives of most adults, and therefore, can be generalized to later life experiences.

Behavioral interventions are based on fundamental principles of learning largely developed from early research in experimental psychology. These principles have been widely applied in many settings for students with learning disabilities as well as other exceptionalities. One of their main strengths is that once the basic theory is understood, behavioral interventions can be modified to suit a wide variety of needs and circumstances.

## 7-6b Adolescent Education and Transition to Adulthood

Services and supports for adolescents and young adults with learning disabilities differ from those used for children. New issues emerge during the teen years; assistance appropriate for a young child will not typically work for a preteen or teenager. Adolescents and young adults with learning disabilities may, like their peers without such disabilities, become involved in alcohol use, drug use, gambling, and sexual activity (McNamara & Willoughby, 2010; Shandra, 2012). Although teens have peer pressures and temptations to behave like their friends, they are also influenced by their parents' expectations of them. Effective services and supports for adolescents with learning disabilities must be individually designed to be age-appropriate.

**Academic Instruction and Support** Research suggests that the educational system often fails adolescents with learning disabilities. These students have lower school completion rates than their peers without learning disabilities, as well as higher unemployment rates (U.S. Department of Education, 2011). Often these adolescents still need to develop basic academic survival skills; they may also lack social skills and comfortable interpersonal relationships (Cowden, 2010a; Roberts et al., 2015). Adolescents with learning disabilities are attending college in greater numbers than ever, but they also tend to drop out at higher rates than their peers without disabilities (U.S. Department of Education, 2011). A comprehensive model needs to be developed to address a broad spectrum of needs for adolescents and young adults with learning disabilities (Elias & Leverett, 2011; Rojewski, Lee, Gregg, & Gemici, 2012).

Relatively speaking, adolescents with learning disabilities have received considerably less attention than their younger counterparts. Adolescents tend to overestimate their academic abilities (Heath, Roberts, & Toste, 2013; Job & Klassen, 2012), but academic deficits that first appeared during the younger years tend to grow more marked as students face progressively more challenging schoolwork; by the time many students with learning disabilities reach secondary school or adolescence, they may be further behind academically than they were in the early grades (McDonald, Keys, & Balcazar, 2009; Morris et al., 2009). Problems with motivation, self-reliance, learning strategies, social competence, and skill generalization all emerge related to adolescents and young adults (e.g., Farmer, Hall, & Weiss, 2011; Greenbank & Sharon, 2013).

Time constraints represent one difficulty that confronts teachers of adolescents with learning disabilities. Learning disabilities and attendant academic deficits persist (Geary, 2011), and adolescents are reaching an age at which life grows more complex. A broad array of issues must be addressed, including possible college plans (an increasingly frequent goal for students with learning disabilities), employment goals, and preparation for social and interpersonal life during the adult years. In many areas, instead of building and expanding on a firm foundation of knowledge, many adolescents with learning disabilities are operating only at a beginning to intermediate level.

The challenge of time constraints has led researchers to seek alternatives to traditional teaching of academic content to students with learning disabilities. Even with the press of time, each individual requires specific instructional planning. For example, evidence suggests that direct instruction may also be effective when focused on key areas such as writing skills (Sundeen, 2012; Viel-Ruma, Houchins, Jolivette, Fredrick, & Gama, 2010). However, in other cases, learning strategies may be the focus of instruction (Orosco, 2014; Swanson et al., 2013). Teaching learning strategies to students is one widely used approach that focuses on the learning process. Learning strategies instruction often employs mnemonic acronyms that help students remember steps for the strategy process.

Secondary school instruction for adolescents with learning disabilities may also involve teaching compensatory skills to make up for those not acquired earlier. For example, audio recording may be used in class to offset difficulties in note taking during lectures, and thus, compensate for a listening (auditory-input) problem. For some individuals, personal problems related to disabilities require counseling or other mental health assistance. And to complicate matters further, hormonal changes with strong effects on interpersonal behavior come into play during adolescence. Research results are beginning to emerge on such issues for adolescents with learning disabilities (Evans, Clinkinbeard, & Simi, 2015; Rojewski, Lee, & Gregg, 2014).

Many of the difficulties that adolescents with learning disabilities experience do not disappear as they grow older; specialized services are often needed throughout adolescence and perhaps into adulthood (Devine, Taggart, & McLornian, 2010). The National Center for Learning Disabilities (2014) emphasized this developmental need, noting that "reports of LD across the life span provide irrefutable evidence that the condition is lifelong and does not disappear upon leaving school" (p. 26). We may find that this period of life is characterized by some unique challenges, just as it is for young people with other disabilities (Ferguson, Jarrett, & Terras, 2011; Yew & O'Kearny, 2014).

**Transition Services** The transition from school to adult life is a central concern for planning and instruction in secondary settings for students with learning disabilities. Preparing students for post–school life usually involves a combination of high school classes directed toward adult skills and/or preparation for postsecondary education, and supervised opportunities to experience work, service, and other aspects of adult living through collaboration with community agencies (Carter, Trainor, & Ditchman, 2011; Hughes, Banks, & Terras, 2013). IDEA 2004 requires IEP teams to begin transition planning no later than a student's 16th birthday, but effective practices have been slow to evolve. Programs that show promise have turned their focus to providing as much mainstream academic course work as possible and to enhancing students' self-determination skills as they consider their interests and goals for the future (Daviso, Denney, & Baer, 2011; Shogren, 2011). Students who actively participate in their own transition planning report higher levels of satisfaction with the process and the outcomes (Johnson, Serrano, & Veit, 2013; Woods, Sylvester, & Martin, 2010).

## Alice Revisited

Remember Alice, who we met in the last Snapshot? When we last saw her, Alice was in the fourth grade and was extremely frustrated with school. Unfortunately, she failed the history test for which she was preparing. She could not obtain enough information from the narrative and consequently could not answer the questions on the test. The exam was a paper-and-pencil test, which to Alice, looked like the book that she was supposed to read about the family who was moving west with the wagon train. When she received her graded test, Alice broke into tears. This was not the first time she had wept about her schoolwork, but it was the first time her teacher had observed it.

Alice's teacher, Mr. Dunlap, was worried about her. She was not a troublesome child in class, and she seemed attentive. But she could not do the work. On this occasion, Mr. Dunlap consoled Alice and asked her to stay after school briefly to chat with him about the test. He was astonished when they sat together and he determined that Alice could not even read the questions. If she could not read

the questions, he thought, then she undoubtedly cannot read the book. But he was fairly certain that she was not lacking in basic intelligence. Her conversations simply didn't indicate such a problem.

Mr. Dunlap sent her home and then contacted her parents. He knew a little about exceptional children and the referral process. He set that process in motion, meeting with the parents, the school psychologist, and the principal, who also sat in on all the team meetings at this school. After a diagnostic evaluation, the team met again to examine the psychologist's report. Miss Burns, the psychologist, had tested Alice and found that her scores fell in the average range in intelligence (with a full-scale WISC-V score of 114). Miss Burns had also assessed Alice's abilities with a comprehensive structural analysis of reading skills; she concluded that Alice had a rather severe form of dyslexia, which interfered substantially with her ability to read.

Alice's parents expressed a strong desire for her to remain in Mr. Dunlap's

class. This was viewed as a desirable choice by each member of the team, and the next step was to determine how an intervention could be undertaken to work with Alice while she remained in her regular class as much as possible. All team members, including Alice's parents, understood that effectively meeting Alice's educational and social needs would be challenging for everyone. However, they all agreed that they were working toward the same objectives—a very positive first step.

*Application Questions*

Placing yourself in the role of Mr. Dunlap, and given the information that you now have about Alice, respond to the following questions:

**1.** How could you facilitate Alice's social needs, particularly her relationships with classmates?

**2.** Who should be a part of this broad educational planning?

**3.** Should you talk with Alice about it?

Those who are planning transition programs for adolescents with learning disabilities must consider that these adolescents' life goals may approximate those of adolescents without disabilities. Some students look forward to employment that will not require education beyond high school. Some plan to continue their schooling in vocational and trade schools (Daviso, Denney, & Baer, 2011; Grigal, Hart, & Migliore, 2011). Employment preparation activities—occupational awareness programs, work experience, career and vocational assessment, development of job-related academic skills, and interpersonal skills—should all be part of transition plans and should benefit these students. In addition, professionals may need to negotiate with employers to secure some accommodations at work for young adults with learning disabilities.

**College Bound** As we have noted, growing numbers of young people with learning disabilities plan to attend a college or university (National Center for Learning Disabilities, 2014). There is little question that they will encounter difficulties and that careful transition planning is essential to their success. It is also clear that with some additional academic assistance, they not only will survive but also can be competitive college students (Cowden, 2010b; Shifter, Callahan, & Muller, 2013). But there is considerable difference between the relatively controlled setting of high school and the more unstructured environment of college. In their preparation for this transition, students profit from focused assistance, planning, and goal setting (e.g., Dunn, Rabren, Taylor, & Dotson, 2012; Johnson, Serrano, & Veit, 2013).

College-bound students with learning disabilities may find that many of their specific needs are related to basic survival skills in higher education. It is assumed that students can already take notes and digest lecture information auditorily and that they have adequate writing skills, reading ability, and study habits. Transition programs must strengthen these abilities as much as possible (Daviso, Denney, & Baer, 2011). Students with reading disabilities can obtain the help of readers who audio record the content of textbooks so that they can listen to the material, rather than making painfully slow progress if reading is difficult and time-consuming. College students with learning disabilities must seek out educational support services and social support networks to offset emotional immaturity and personality traits that may impede college achievement (Lewandowski, Cohen, & Lovett, 2013; Reed, Kennett, & Lewis, 2011).

Perhaps the most helpful survival technique that can be taught to an adolescent with learning disabilities is actually more than a specific skill; it is a way of thinking about survival—an overall attitude of resourcefulness and a confident approach to solving problems. Recall Mathew, the psychology student in one of this chapter's first Snapshots. Mathew has an amazing array of techniques that he uses to acquire knowledge while compensating for the specific areas where he has deficits.

Another key transition element involves establishing a support network. Students with learning disabilities should be taught how to establish an interpersonal network of helpers and advocates. An advocate on the faculty can often be more successful than the student in requesting special testing arrangements or other accommodations (at least to begin with). However, faculty are bombarded with student complaints and requests, and many assertions are not based on extreme needs. Consequently, many faculty are wary of granting special considerations. However, an appeal from a faculty colleague may carry more weight and enhance the credibility of a student's request.

Concern about the accommodations requested by students who claim to have learning disabilities is genuine and growing. Because learning disabilities are invisible, they are hard to understand; there is much room for abuse in students' requests for accommodations due to a disability. Such requests have increased dramatically, and many faculty are skeptical about their legitimacy. Although the Americans with Disabilities Act clearly mandates accommodation, college students with learning disabilities should be aware that many higher-education faculty are skeptical about the merits of this mandate (Quinlan, Bates, & Angell, 2012). The process of getting special arrangements approved is not simple; accessing support services requires adequate documentation, and there is no requirement for high schools to prepare and provide it (National Center for Learning Disabilities, 2014). In addition, colleges and universities do not have uniform requirements for disability determination (Harrison, Lovett, & Gordon, 2013). Providing clear diagnostic evidence of a learning disability will enhance the credibility of a request for accommodation.

Students with learning disabilities can lead productive, even distinguished, adult lives. But some literature suggests that even after they complete a college education, adults with learning disabilities have limited career choices (Bender, 2008a). We know that notable individuals have been identified as having learning disabilities. They include scientist and inventor Thomas Edison, former U.S. president Woodrow Wilson, scientist Albert Einstein, and former vice president of the United States and former governor of New York Nelson Rockefeller. We also know that the young man whose writing we saw in Figure 7.3 became a successful architect. Such achievements are not accomplished without considerable effort, but they show that the outlook for people with learning disabilities is very promising.

## 7-6c Multidisciplinary Collaboration: Education and Other Services

**Standard 7**
Collaboration

Multidisciplinary collaboration is particularly crucial for those with learning disabilities because of the wide range of characteristics that may emerge in these individuals. Providing effective inclusive education and the full range of other services requires a wide variety of professionals (Pugach, Blanton, & Correa, 2011). There is an enormous heterogeneity of ability and disability configurations that emerge and evolve at various ages in those with learning disabilities (Fuchs, Fuchs, & Compton, 2013; Nelson & Harwood, 2011a).

**Collaboration on Inclusive Education** Definitions and descriptions of various approaches to inclusive education were introduced in earlier chapters. A very large proportion of students with learning disabilities receive educational services in settings that are either fully or partially inclusive (McLeskey & Waldron, 2011). In 2011, less than 7 percent of students with learning disabilities from 6 to 21 years of age were served mostly outside the regular classroom. The U.S. Department of Education defines this service pattern as being more than 60 percent of the time outside the regular class (U.S. Department of Education, 2013b).

Inclusive approaches have received increasing attention in the learning disability literature, which has prompted thought-provoking debate about appropriate formats and the advantages and limitations of placing students with learning disabilities in fully inclusive educational environments (McLeskey & Waldron, 2011; Nowicki & Brown, 2013). To be successful, inclusive education requires commitment to collaboration among general and special educators and other team members. Individualized educational programs (IEPs) at this stage evolve with a student's chronological age and as his or her skills develop. The academic focus may be on a reading problem or on difficulties in some content area. Social and behavioral issues may emerge in the inclusive environment; related interventions may form part of the spectrum of services and supports (Maxam & Henderson, 2013; Watson & Gable, 2013).

Teacher attitudes about inclusive education are very influential. Some evidence suggests that general education teachers feel unprepared to teach students with disabilities, to collaborate with special educators, and to make academic adaptations or accommodations. Adequate teacher preparation requires a significant collaborative partnership between general education and special education teacher education programs. In addition to teachers' curriculum and instructional skills, their personal attitudes toward inclusive education are vitally important. General education teachers often have less positive attitudes toward and perceptions of inclusive education than special education teachers do (Hills, 2011; Maxam & Henderson, 2013).

Successful inclusion requires much more than just placing students with learning disabilities in the same classroom with their peers without disabilities. Some researchers have noted that successful inclusion might better be described as *supported* inclusion. Inclusive education must be undertaken only after careful planning of the instructional approach, services, and supports (Ciullo, Falcomata, Pfannenstiel, & Billingsley, 2015; Prater, Redman, Anderson, & Gibb, 2014).

**Collaboration on Health and Other Services** A variety of other services may be marshaled for students and adults with learning disabilities, and here again, collaboration and communication are essential. Collaboration between educators, speech and language specialists, physical therapists, and occupational therapists is essential for a smoothly functioning personal plan (Bock, Michalak, & Brownlee, 2011; Darsaklis, Snier, Majnemer, & Mazer, 2013). One area that often receives attention for those with learning disabilities involves health care professionals. Medical personnel are sometimes involved in the diagnosis of learning disabilities and in prescribing medications used in treating conditions that may coexist with learning disabilities.

*Childhood* Physicians often diagnose a child's abnormal or delayed development in the areas of language, behavior, and motor functions. Physicians may have early involvement with a child with learning disabilities because of the nature of the problem, such as serious developmental delay or hyperactivity. More often, a medical professional sees the young child first because he or she has not yet entered school; the family physician becomes a primary adviser for parents (Glascoe & Trimm, 2014; Langkamp, McManus, & Blakemore, 2015).

One example of medical service appropriate for some children with disabilities involves controlling hyperactivity and other challenging behaviors. Many children with learning disabilities receive medication such as Ritalin to control hyperactivity (generic name, methylphenidate). Although their action is not completely understood, such psychostimulants appear to result in general improvement for a large proportion of children with hyperactivity (Dalsgaard, Nielsen, & Simonsen, 2014; Holmes et al., 2010; Paton et al., 2014). Some researchers have expressed caution about such treatment, however, focusing on matters of effectiveness, overprescription, and side effects (e.g., Clemow, & Walker, 2014; Hoekstra, 2011). Uncertainty regarding medications and dosage levels, and the fact that high doses may have toxic effects, add to the confusion. Although there are benefits to medication, it may be overprescribed (Graf, Miller, & Nagel, 2014; Kalikow, 2011).

**Adolescence** As in other treatment areas, medical services for adolescents and young adults with learning disabilities differ somewhat from those for children. In some cases, psychiatric treatment may be involved either through interactive therapy or antidepressant medication. Additionally, efforts are under way to improve the assessment of medical, developmental, functional, and growth variables for those with learning difficulties (e.g., Lobo & Galloway, 2013; Schieve et al., 2012; Wilkinson-Smith & Semrud-Clikeman, 2014).

Some adolescents receiving medication to control hyperactivity may have been taking it for a number of years. Many physician assessments are made during the childhood years of patients with learning disabilities; as a result, medications are prescribed when these patients are still children. On the other hand, some treatments are of rather short duration and may terminate within two years (Dalsgaard, Nielsen, & Simonsen, 2014; Powell, Thomsen, & Frydenberg, 2011).

## Looking Toward a Bright Future

Nearly 50 years ago, "learning disabilities" became a formally recognized category within the disability field. Over the years, there have been many different perspectives on what constitutes a learning disability, and the idea that students with learning disabilities can be effectively taught in general education settings with children who were not disabled is still evolving (Prater et al., 2014; Watson & Gable, 2013). Today, learning disabilities are central to our understanding of effective instructional approaches for all children, as reflected through emerging approaches such as with response to intervention (RtI) (Bender & Waller, 2011; Johnson et al., 2012; Lindstrom & Sayeski, 2013). As a concept, RtI focuses on the individual needs of each child within an inclusive educational setting. This means that educational assessments must focus on each child's strengths and challenges for educators to prescribe effective academic instruction (Swanson, 2011). In doing so, research suggests that we will find that children with learning disabilities have a great deal more variability in their skill levels across academic subject areas than their nondisabled peers. These students may have difficulty focusing on specific academic tasks and appear to be overly active in certain circumstances (DuPaul, Gormley, & Laracy, 2013).

In teaching students with learning disabilities, it will be important for educators to collaborate with other disciplines, such as behavior and language specialists, health care providers, and school psychologists. With the individual as the focal point, and the support of family members, we may find that medical intervention in conjunction with new and innovative approaches to learning will be effective in meeting the needs of students with learning disabilities. This can only be determined in a consultative manner with other professions, including health care (for assessment and prescriptions), educational professionals (for assessment and instructional planning), school psychologists and counseling professionals, and family members (for information, assessment, and planning for the future) (National Joint Committee on Learning Disabilities, 2011a; Nguyen, 2012; Schieve et al., 2012). Through the use of evidence-based instruction, students with learning disabilities can and will learn to survive and thrive in our complex world. This represents a promising future for those with learning disabilities.

**7-1** Describe how the lives of people with learning disabilities (LD) have changed since the advent of IDEA.

- We live at a time of great progress in assessing, affirming, planning for, and instructing individuals with learning disabilities, and the field continues to evolve.

**7-2** Explain the various definitions and classifications of LD.

- The term *learning disabilities* has become a generic label representing a very heterogeneous group of conditions that range from mild to severe in intensity.
- Varying definitions and terminology related to learning disabilities emerged partly because of different theoretical views of the condition.
- Definitions of LD vary between medicine, psychology, and education, but the IDEA definition is used in special education.
- Classifications of LD are based on discrepancy between aptitude and expected performance, on heterogeneous distinctions between academic deficits such as reading or mathematics, and on exclusionary criteria, which name LD as the probable condition when all other possibilities have been excluded.

**7-3** Describe the characteristics and prevalence of children and youth with LD.

- Learning disabilities can include specific academic deficits in reading, math, or written expression, difficulties with memory and other cognitive functions, and difficulties with emotional and interpersonal issues.
- LD subtypes refer to distinctive groups within the broad umbrella of learning disabilities. Comorbidity refers to the degree to which youngsters exhibit evidence of multiple disabilities or conditions (such as learning disabilities and communication disorders, or personality disorders).
- The prevalence of LD has fallen sharply since 2002, now including about 35 percent of individuals with disabilities or 3.4 percent of the total school population.

**7-4** List the causes and risk factors associated with LD.

- Possible causes of LD include abnormal neurological development, maturational delay in skill development, inherited genetic abnormalities, and environmental factors ranging from dietary inadequacies to illicit drugs, family stress, and inappropriate school instruction.

**7-5** Describe the assessment procedures used to identify LD in children and youth.

- Assessment for LD begins with measures of IQ, or capacity to learn, and formal or informal measures of academic achievement in specific areas of concern. These data are used by a multidisciplinary team to determine if a student fits the LD profile as described in the IDEA definition.
- Additional assessment can identify deficits in adaptive skills, meaning appropriate behaviors in particular environments.
- LD assessment has evolved to focus on identifying specific deficits as a means for targeting interventions efficiently and effectively.

**7-6** Describe the different interventions for children and youth with LD from early childhood through adulthood.

- A wide variety of instructional approaches are used for children with learning disabilities, including strategies to develop cognition, attention, spoken language, and skill in reading, writing, and mathematics.
- Elementary school interventions usually address basic academic and social skills, often using small-group explicit instruction formats with the goal of bringing students' skills to grade level.
- Intervention at all levels may include strategy instruction, in which students learn ways to think, plan, and execute effective behaviors for completing assignments.
- Computer-assisted instruction is increasingly common as students access programs and apps to address skill deficits and to learn and use strategies.
- Behavioral interventions that teach self-monitoring and focused effort can help students with LD learn and use productive social and learning behaviors.
- Adolescents with LD benefit from compensatory skills to bridge the gap between learning demands and deficits in reading, writing, and math skills. This age group also benefits from strategy instruction and activities that prepare them for future employment, postsecondary education, and independent living goals.
- Transition planning and preparation should include school course work, work experiences, and collaboration with community agencies that individuals will work with upon leaving school.

**Council for Exceptional Children (CEC) Standards to Accompany Chapter 7**

If you are thinking about a career in special education, you should know that many states use national standards developed by the Council for Exceptional Children (CEC) to assess a teacher candidate's knowledge about and skills for working with students with disabilities. See a complete listing of the seven CEC Content Standards on the inside cover of this text.

1 Learner Development and Individual Learning Differences
2 Learning Environments
4 Assessment
5 Instructional Planning and Strategies
7 Collaboration

## Mastery Activities and Assignments

To master the content within this chapter, complete the following activities and assignments:

1. Complete a written test of the chapter's content. If your instructor requires a written test of your content knowledge for this chapter, keep a copy for your portfolio.
2. Review the Case Study on Embracing Diversity, "Alice Revisited," and respond in writing to the Application Questions. Keep a copy of the Case Study and your written response for your portfolio.
3. Participate in a community service learning activity. Community service is a valuable way to enhance your learning experience. Develop a reflective journal of the service learning experience for your portfolio.

## CHAPTER 8

# Emotional/Behavioral Disorders

©Suzanne Tucker/Shutterstock.com

## Learning Objectives

*After you complete this chapter, you will be able to:*

**8-1** Describe how the lives of people with emotional and behavioral disorders (EBD) have changed since the advent of IDEA.

**8-2** Explain the various definitions and classifications of EBD.

**8-3** Describe the characteristics and prevalence of children and youth with EBD.

**8-4** List the causes and risk factors associated with EBD.

**8-5** Describe the assessment procedures used to identify EBD in children and youth.

**8-6** Describe the different interventions for children and youth with EBD from early childhood through adulthood.

"[My] mother always said, 'There must be nothing worse than losing a child.'" Patty never understood what her mother meant until she had a child of her own, and thought she might lose her, though in a different way.

*What are we doing here?* Patty wondered to herself. *This can't be happening! She had, after all, led a happy, normal childhood.... Now she was leaving her 11-year-old daughter, Jennifer, in a real hospital. A mental hospital.*

At that moment, Patty wasn't sure if she had lost her daughter forever. But the truth was, she had been losing Jennifer for a few years.

She actually knew something was terribly wrong when Jennifer was just 8. Patty and her family were on a dream family vacation in Disney World—"the Happiest Place on Earth."

The evening parade had just ended. Mickey, Minnie, and the gang had floated away into the sunset, leaving Patty's family and her favorite characters . . . behind. Patty couldn't help but smile as she looked up and down the colorful streets at all the families grinning from mouse ear to mouse ear.

That is, until she was interrupted by an all-too-familiar and painful screech.

"Why do they have to leave? Why!" shouted 8-year-old Jennifer, who was sitting on the curb, hugging the Minnie Mouse on her sweatshirt and flailing her legs.

"Oh that's just great! It's even happening here!" muttered Patty, helplessly realizing that the Magic Kingdom, the place where "dreams come true," was about to turn into her personal nightmare.

It really shouldn't have surprised her. Over the past few months, Jennifer's moods had become increasingly unpredictable. She would cry for hours and become violent about the smallest things.

Courtesy of Jenn & Patricia Konjoian

"Why? Why can't I wear my jelly shoes?"

"Because, Jenns, it's 30 degrees outside and snowing."

"WAAAAAHHHH! I hate you!"

She was also becoming alarmingly destructive.

"Jennifer Marie! What are you doing with my scissors and the family picture?"

"I'm cutting myself out. I don't want to be part of this family anymore."

And during that dream vacation to Disney—the one Jennifer had been excited about for months ("How many days till we go, Mom? Tell me! Tell me!")—her moods were just as unpredictable. Somehow Patty had actually thought Jenn's problems would disappear, but instead of seeing Snow White, Patty saw her daughter magically transform into Grumpy, Saddy, and Angry (Gallagher & Konjoian, 2010, p. 15–17).

## Linea (excerpted from her high school journal)

I was numb, a smile plastered on my face like the one I wore every day. I couldn't feel anything. The pills prescribed to me after witnessing my best friend slash open her arms kept me from the pain of sadness. They also robbed me of the euphoria of joy. I was at an even keel all the time. My life was bland while all my outside interaction and activities suggested excitement, adventure, and pride.

As I developed new and increasingly dangerous coping methods such as self-mutilation, and drug and alcohol use, I began to question myself as a perfectionist. I began seeing myself as a perfectionist. I began seeing myself in a dualist view, the stable productive side as the "good" me and the unstable often incontrollable side as the "bad" me.... What I truly needed was a comforting voice outside my loving family, to tell me that it was okay if I failed, or even broke a few rules.

My training as a perfectionist in high school taught me to hide my feelings. I found ways to act like nothing had changed and found ways to make myself appear happy to the average population. And though I did a good job of feigning composure to the general population, the people I saw daily, friends, boyfriend, and teachers, should have been aware of my changing interaction with the world.

I believe had I even one teacher who knew me well enough to see the stress and pain that came from my endless search for perfection, I would have felt more comfortable confronting my feelings earlier. It is so important for teachers and educational professionals to be aware of their students' patterns and personalities in order to help the students trust themselves and others when it comes to emotional crises. By fearing that my emotions would ruin my reputation as a good student and mature young adult, I let myself get to increasingly dangerous levels of depression.

SOURCE: Adapted from Johnson, C., Eva, A. L., Johnson, L., & Walker, B. (2011). "Don't Turn Away: Empowering Teachers to Support Students' Mental Health." *The Clearing House: A Journal of Educational Strategies, Issues and Ideas*, 84(1), 9–11.

# 8-1 A Changing Era in the Lives of People with Emotional/Behavioral Disorders

Since the passage of the Individuals with Disabilities Education Act (IDEA) in 1975, much has changed about the ways that children and youth with emotional and behavioral disorders (EBD) are served. There is now a much greater focus on supporting children and youth who appear to be at risk for developing EBD. Newly developed school-wide programs seek to support all children in their social and academic development and growth. There are also more efforts targeted at helping children and youth with EBD before their behaviors become potentially more serious or chronic in nature. Contemporary interventions may include pre-referral interventions (practices designed to prevent the onset of serious behavior problems), school-wide efforts to promote positive and functional behaviors in all children and youth, evidence-based approaches provided by collaborative teams of skilled professionals, increased access to inclusive settings (regular education classrooms and related experiences), a focus on preventing serious, violent, or destructive behaviors, and the provision of community-based and family-sensitive care systems. Each of these interventions is addressed in greater depth later in this chapter.

Individuals with **emotional and behavioral disorders** (EBD)—such as Jennifer and Linea in the opening Snapshot—may experience great difficulties in relating appropriately to peers, siblings, parents, teachers, and other adults. However, recent advances in intervention approaches are making a difference for many children and youth with EBD, allowing them to be served in integrated settings, such as regular classrooms and neighborhood schools, and in other community-based programs.

As you might guess, many children and youth with EBD have difficulty responding to academic and social tasks that are essential parts of their schooling (Lane et al., 2008). Generally, they are deficient in vitally important academic and social behaviors. This chapter explores issues and opportunities related to EBD in greater detail, giving you a framework for understanding these children and youth.

# 8-2 Definitions and Classifications of Emotional/Behavioral Disorders

As you will see, several terms have been developed to describe individuals with EBD. Think about Jennifer and Linea as you move through this section. These terms include *emotionally disturbed*, *conduct disordered*, *behavior disordered*, and *socially maladjusted*. In reading this chapter, think about the labels you have used over time to describe peers, relatives, classmates, or other acquaintances who frequently exhibited atypical behaviors. Use these experiences with others as reference points for thinking about and coming to understand children and youth with EBD. How are your experiences similar to those revealed by Jennifer's mother and Linea?

Emotional disturbance is defined in the Individuals with Disabilities Education Act (IDEA) as:

**Standard 1**
Learner Development and Individual Learner Differences

*(I). A condition exhibiting one or more of the following characteristics over a long period of time and to a marked degree that adversely affects educational performance:*

    *A. An inability to learn that cannot be explained by intellectual, sensory, or health factors;*

    *B. An inability to build or maintain satisfactory interpersonal relationships with peers and teachers;*

    *C. Inappropriate types of behavior or feelings under normal circumstances;*

    *D. A general pervasive mood of unhappiness or depression; or*

    *E. A tendency to develop physical symptoms or fears associated with personal or school problems.*

*(II). The term does not include children who are socially maladjusted, unless it is determined that they are seriously emotionally disturbed.* (U.S. Department of Education, 2006)

This definition of severe emotional disturbance, or EBD, was adapted from an earlier definition created by Bower (1959). The IDEA definition for EBD has been criticized for its lack of clarity, incompleteness, and exclusion of individuals described as *socially maladjusted*—sometimes referred to as juvenile delinquents (Dikel & Stewart, 2011; Merrell & Walker, 2004; U.S. Department of Education, 2006). Furthermore, this definition mandates that assessment personnel—teachers, special educators, and school psychologists—demonstrate that EBD adversely impacts students' school performance and achievement. In some cases, students with serious EBD—such as eating disorders, mood disorders (depression and bipolar disorder), suicidal tendencies, and social withdrawal—do not receive appropriate care and treatment, merely because their academic achievement in school appears to be normal or above average (Crundwell & Killu, 2007; Johnson, Johnson, & Walker, 2011). This is also true for young preschool children who do not manifest "substantial deficits in academic achievement," but evidence high levels of aggressive and antisocial behavior (Maag & Katsiyannis, 2010, p. 472).

The National Mental Health and Special Education Coalition in 1990 attempted to address many of the problems associated with the IDEA definition. This definition attempts to provide greater clarity and precision in describing EBD:

(I). *The term emotional or behavioral disorder means a disability characterized by behavioral or emotional responses in school so different from appropriate age, cultural, or ethnic norms that they adversely affect educational performance. Educational performance includes academic, social, vocational, and personal skills. Such a disability*
   A. *is more than a temporary, expected response to stressful events in the environment;*
   B. *is consistently exhibited in two different settings, at least one of which is school-related; and*
   C. *is unresponsive to direct intervention in general education or the child's condition is such that general education interventions would be insufficient.*
(II). *Emotional and behavioral disorders can co-exist with other disabilities.* (Forness & Kavale, 2000, p. 266)

This definition provides a more precise basis for identifying children and youth with EBD. Its advantages include a consideration of cultural and ethnic norms, the inclusion of challenging emotional and behavioral responses of children and youth, the durability of the problematic behaviors, a specification of multiple settings in which the behaviors occur, a documented lack of responsiveness to general education interventions, and the fact that EBD can co-occur with other disabilities.

*Photo 8.1* Youth with EBD often engage in destructive behaviors directed at themselves or others.

©Axente Vlad/Shutterstock.com

## 8-2a Classification Systems

Professionals use a variety of classification systems to describe various groups and kinds of challenging behaviors. These systems provide descriptions, uniform terminology, and characteristics for diagnosis. First, they provide professionals with a shared means for describing various types of behavior problems in children and youth. Second, they provide professionals with common terminology for communicating with one another (Cullinan, 2004). Third, physicians and other mental health specialists use these characteristics and other information as a basis for diagnosing and treating individuals. Unfortunately, "[c]lassifications as yet have limited validity for the most important purpose of classification: specifying interventions [and treatments] that are best suited to improve any particular form of EBD" (Cullinan, 2004, p. 41).

The field of EBD is broad and includes many different types of problems, so it is not surprising that many approaches have been used to classify these individuals. Some classification systems describe individuals according to statistically derived categories—patterns of strongly related behaviors are identified through sophisticated statistical techniques. Other classification systems are clinically derived; they are derived from the experiences of physicians and other mental health specialists who work directly with children, youth, and adults with EBD.

## 8-2b A Statistically Derived Classification System

For a number of years, researchers have collected information about children with EBD using parent and teacher questionnaires, interviews, and behavior rating scales. Applying sophisticated statistical techniques, two broad categories of behavior have been identified from these sources: externalizing behaviors and internalizing behaviors. Children or youth who exhibit externalizing behaviors may be described as engaging in behaviors that are directed more at others than at themselves. These behaviors could be characterized as aggressive, noncompliant, defiant, resistive, disruptive, and dangerous. These behaviors significantly affect parents, families, siblings, classmates, teachers, and neighbors. The average ratio of males to females referred for externalizing behaviors is 5:1 (Young et al., 2010). Children's internalizing behaviors are directed more at the self than at others (Johnson, Johnson, & Walker, 2011). Withdrawal, depression, shyness, and phobias are examples of internalized behaviors; some clinicians would describe individuals with these conditions as *emotionally disturbed*. The average ratio of males to females referred for internalized behaviors is 2:1 (Young et al., 2010).

## 8-2c Clinically Derived Classification Systems

Although several clinically derived classification systems have been developed, the system primarily used by medical and psychological professionals is that contained in the *Diagnostic and Statistical Manual of Mental Disorders: DSM-5* (American Psychiatric Association [APA], 2013). This and previous editions were developed by groups of psychiatric, psychological, and health care clinicians—hence, the term clinically derived classifications. Professionals in each of these groups included people who worked closely with children, adolescents, and adults with mental disorders or, using our terminology, EBD.

The categories and subcategories of *DSM-5* were developed after years of investigation and field testing and were most recently revised in 2013. These psychiatric categories are not used by school personnel in identifying children or adolescents for special education services. However, school personnel and other care providers should be familiar with these categories as they often work with medical specialists and clinicians in hospitals, clinics, and residential settings with young people with EBD.

The *DSM-5* identifies seven major groups of childhood disorders under the general heading of neurodevelopmental disorders that may be exhibited by infants, children, or adolescents. Again, not all of these disorders are included within the IDEA definition of EBD. Some of the *DSM-5* disorders are related to other special education designations such as intellectual disabilities and learning disabilities. The *DSM-5* disorders include (1) intellectual disabilities; (2) communication disorders; (3) autism spectrum disorder; (4) attention deficit/hyperactivity disorder; (5) specific learning disorder; (6) motor disorders; and (7) other neurodevelopmental disorders. In addition, *DSM-5* describes disruptive, impulse control, and conduct disorders that can be manifest by children with EBD. As indicated earlier, this classification system is not used in schools or by school psychologists for identifying and classifying children and youth with EBD. What follows are brief descriptions of emotional and behavioral disorders drawn from this clinical classification system.

**Attention Deficit/Hyperactivity Disorder (ADHD)** This disorder is characterized by "a persistent pattern of inattention and/or hyperactivity-impulsivity that interferes with functioning or development" (APA, 2013, p. 59). Attention deficit/hyperactivity disorder (ADHD) can manifest throughout the lifespan and negatively impacts individuals' academic achievement, social behavior, and occupational activities. Children with ADHD can be primarily inattentive, or they can manifest hyperactivity and impulsivity. Those who are inattentive have difficulty attending to tasks, maintaining effort, or staying focused on learning or play activities. They may show a pattern of careless mistakes, fail to follow through with instructions, or leave assigned tasks unfinished. Children who are hyperactive demonstrate excessive and inappropriate motor activity, such as moving about the classroom, fidgeting, or tapping. As they grow older, these individuals may seem overly active and restless. Children who are impulsive act in haste and show little or no forethought. These individuals may blurt out in class, interrupt others in conversation, or make decisions or act without proper consideration for consequences.

### Disruptive, Impulse Control, and Conduct Disorders

These disorders are manifested in individuals who have difficulty regulating their emotions and behaviors, resulting in conflict with other people in the learning or social environment, or with those in authority.

**Oppositional defiant disorder** is a condition in which an individual shows an established pattern of anger, argumentativeness, and/or defiance of authority. Individuals may be easily irritated, argue with teachers, refuse to follow directions or requests, or lash out at others with no apparent reason.

**Intermittent explosive disorder** affects individuals who engage in volatile verbal or physical aggression at least twice per week. Outbursts come on suddenly, often with little provocation, and usually end in less than half an hour.

**Conduct disorder** describes individuals who regularly violate the rights of others by threatening, bullying, fighting, destroying property, stealing, or defying school or parental rules. People with conduct disorder often lack remorse and are unconcerned with the effects of their behavior on others.

In addition to outwardly aggressive disorders, students with EBD may manifest a variety of other conditions, including eating disorders, tic disorders, and reactive attachment disorder. These may be less outwardly impactful but can affect individuals' learning and progress.

### Feeding and Eating Disorders

Feeding and eating disorders are behaviors that interfere with normal eating and digestion, resulting in health or psychosocial functioning. The disorder known as pica consists of the persistent eating of nonnutritive materials for at least one month. Materials consumed may be cloth, string, hair, plaster, or even paint. Often children with pervasive developmental disorders manifest pica.

Anorexia nervosa and bulimia nervosa are common eating disorders evidenced by gross disturbances in eating behavior (Levitt, Sansone, & Cohn, 2004). In the case of **anorexia nervosa**, the most distinguishing feature is body weight that is less than minimally normal (APA, 2013). These individuals are intensely afraid of weight gain and exhibit grossly distorted perceptions of their bodies. **Bulimia nervosa** is characterized by repeated episodes of bingeing, followed by self-induced vomiting or other extreme measures to prevent weight gain. Both anorexia nervosa and bulimia nervosa may result in depressed mood, social withdrawal, irritability, and other serious medical conditions. The National Institute of Mental Health estimates that about 10 percent of individuals with anorexia nervosa and bulimia nervosa die each year, but it is unknown what percentage die from metabolism collapse and what percentage die from suicide (Insel, 2012). **Rumination disorder** is characterized by repeated regurgitation and rechewing of food.

### Tic Disorders

Tic disorders involve movements or vocalizations that are involuntary, rapid, and recurrent over time. Tics may take the form of excessive eye blinking, facial gestures, sniffing, snorting, repeating certain words or phrases, or grunting. Stress often exacerbates the nature and frequency of tics. **Tic disorders** include Tourette's syndrome, persistent (chronic) motor or vocal tic disorder, and provisional tic disorder.

**Oppositional defiant disorder**
A disorder characterized by a pattern of anger, argumentativeness, and/or defiance of authority.

**Intermittent explosive disorder**
A disorder characterized by volatile verbal or physical aggression at least twice per week.

**Conduct disorder**
A disorder in which an individual regularly violates the rights of others and may lack remorse about or concern for their behavior.

**Pica**
A disorder characterized by consumption of nonnutritive materials (cloth, hair, plaster, etc.) for at least one month.

**Anorexia nervosa**
A disorder characterized by a fear of weight gain, distorted body perception, and body weight less than minimally normal.

**Bulimia nervosa**
A disorder characterized by episodes of bingeing followed by self-induced vomiting or other measures.

**Rumination disorder**
A disorder characterized by repeated regurgitation and rechewing of food.

**Tic disorders**
A disorder characterized by involuntary, rapid, and current movements or vocalizations.

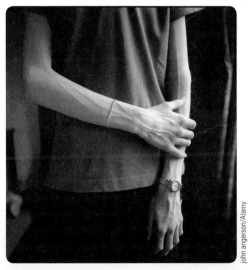

john angerson/Alamy

*Photo 8.2* Anorexia and bulimia may lead to very serious medical problems.

**Elimination disorders**
Disorders characterized by soiling (encopresis) and wetting (enuresis) in older children.

**Anxiety disorders**
Disorders characterized by difficulty dealing with fear-provoking situations and with separation from attachment figures.

**Selective mutism**
A disorder characterized by refusal to speak in specific social situations.

**Reactive attachment disorder**
A disorder characterized by noticeably abnormal or developmentally inept social relatedness.

**Childhood schizophrenia**
A disorder characterized by severe behaviors such as hallucinations, delusions, irrational behavior, and strange thinking.

**Elimination Disorders and Childhood Anxiety Disorders** Elimination disorders entail soiling (encopresis) and wetting (enuresis) in older children. Children who continue to have consistent problems with bowel and bladder control past their fourth or fifth birthday may be diagnosed as having an **elimination disorder**, particularly if the condition is not a function of any physical problem.

Children and youth with **anxiety disorders** have difficulty dealing with fear-provoking situations and with separating themselves from parents or other attachment figures (e.g., close friends, teachers, coaches). Unrealistic worries about future events, concern about achievement, excessive need for reassurance, and somatic complaints are characteristics of young people who exhibit anxiety disorders. Behaviors indicative of this disorder include persistent refusal to go to school, excessive worry about personal harm or injury to themselves or other family members, reluctance to go to sleep, and repeated complaints about headaches, stomachaches, nausea, and other related conditions.

The last condition included within this subset of disorders is **selective mutism**. Young children with this condition are able to speak but do not speak in specific social situations. Most commonly, this disorder appears in the first days or weeks of attending school or participating in a new social environment. These children are able to talk and do speak at home with their parents or other care providers, but they are verbally silent in school and other social settings.

**Reactive Attachment Disorder** In infancy or early childhood, **reactive attachment disorder** is represented by noticeably abnormal and developmentally inept social relatedness. This disorder appears as a result of grossly inadequate care, such as physical or emotional neglect, frequent changes in major caregivers, and other abuse. Behaviors common to this disorder include extreme inhibitions, inability to form appropriate attachments, complete lack of ability to respond to or instigate social interaction with others, and hypervigilance or complete absence of attention to surrounding social opportunities.

**Childhood Schizophrenia** A chronic condition called **childhood schizophrenia** is characterized by hallucinations, delusions, irrational behavior, strange thinking, and other severe behaviors. Less than 1 in 10,000 preadolescents develop this serious illness. Often referred to as childhood-onset schizophrenia, its impacts are profound. Causes of the condition seem to be combinatorial: genetic, environmental, and biochemical. Early medical and educational treatments and interventions are essential to the well-being of children with schizophrenia.

Again, these clinically derived classifications of behavior disorders are primarily used by psychiatric and other related personnel who work in hospital and clinical settings.

---

**?i LEARNING THROUGH SOCIAL MEDIA**

### Bring Change 2 Mind

Bring Change 2 Mind, a nonprofit organization, seeks to counter the prevailing myths, misconceptions, and misinformation about mental illness. It was launched by Glenn Close and other organizations interested in changing public opinion about children, youth, and adults with emotional and behavioral disorders. Glenn's interests were spawned by her own interactions with her sister and nephew who are individuals with mental illnesses.

What follows are some recent story entries on the Bring Change 2 Mind website.

Donna Svennevik/Disney ABC Television Group/Getty Images

**Community Story: Bri**

I was first diagnosed with bipolar disorder in 7th grade. I really didn't

understand what was happening, I used to be such a happy person; suddenly I was trapped inside my mind. Of course not knowing what to do, I went to my friends for help, not realizing middle schoolers have no concept about mental illness. I ended up pushing them all away; what I was going through was too hard for them to understand. It was like I was a different person to them.

I started cutting, using anything sharp I could find. I also planned out a suicide and would have gone through with it, but then, God I didn't know how to get the child's lock off the pill bottle! I was hospitalized September of my eighth grade year. I almost then felt guilty because some people there had been raped or abused by their parents. I had a good loving family and a "good life," so what was wrong with me? Why was I doing all of this?

I isolated myself from everyone, spent a lot of time in my head, which wasn't good. Even when I received correct medication, I still wasn't quite right. Not until I went to high school and met my friends with other mental illness did I become determined to be there and be the friend I didn't have in my time of need. Now, still in high school, I hear the jokes about mental illness go around all the time. They don't realize it's such a real thing; to them it's just a punch line. I feel like I have to hide the fact that I'm bipolar, not wanting to be just another joke. Kids now are so uneducated about mental illness, making kids like me hide it like it's something to be ashamed of. We need to end the stigma of mental illness.

## Community Story: K.D.

I've been living with mental illness since I was a young girl, and although I've been in therapy since I was 13, it has taken years to correctly diagnose me with bipolar and schizoaffective disorder. I've struggled a long time in this fight, but refuse to give up. I have a wonderful, supportive husband, and two beautiful children that keep me going. I've also been through the stigma that surrounds what I have, including people who had said that it's all in my head or tried to tell me that I need to have self-worth. In truth, they have only made me feel worse about myself then. I've been in the hospital twice, and battled self-injury as well. It's been a long, hard struggle, but I have sworn to myself that I will make it, so I keep up with taking care of my family and have taken up writing novels as a coping method.

For now, I have been sharing articles in wonderful places like BC2M to let people know and understand how mental illness is just that, an illness. No one should judge someone who's struggling with it or to overcome it. In fact, they should support them just as much as they'd support someone with any other illness. Those of us who suffer from this will never give up, and never stop hoping for a day when it can be defeated for good.

### Question for Reflection

What have you learned from these brief personal reflections from individuals with mental illnesses that is useful for you?

SOURCE: Bring Change 2 Mind. (2012). "Bri" and "K.D." Retrieved April 3, 2015, from http://bringchange2mind.org /bris-story/ and http://bringchange2mind.org/k-d/

# 8-3 Characteristics and Prevalence of Emotional/Behavioral Disorders

**Standard 1**
Learner Development and Individual Learner Differences

If you had to describe children or youth with EBD, what would you say about their intellectual capacity, their behavior, their academic performance, and their long-term prospects for employment and success? How many males are identified? How many females? This section provides answers to some of these questions. However, note that these figures represent averages. We must view each child or youth with EBD individually, focusing on his or her strengths and potential for growth and achievement.

## 8-3a Intelligence

Researchers from a variety of disciplines have studied the intellectual capacity of individuals with EBD. Research suggests that children and youth with EBD tend to have average to below-average IQs compared with their peers (Algozzine, Serna, & Patton, 2001; Coleman & Webber, 2002).

What impact does intelligence have on the educational and social–adaptive performance of children with EBD? Is the intellectual capacity of a child with EBD a good predictor of other types of achievement and social behavior? The answer is yes. The IQs of students with EBD are the best predictors of future academic and social achievement (Kauffman, 2005). The below-average IQs of many of these children contribute to the challenges they experience in mastering academic content and developing other important school-related social and adaptive skills.

## 8-3b Social–Adaptive Behavior

Children and youth with EBD exhibit a variety of problems in adapting to their home, school, and community environments (Burke, Davis, Hagan-Burke, Lee, & Fogarty, 2012;

Wicks-Nelson & Israel, 2006). Furthermore, they usually exhibit difficulties in relating socially and responsibly to peers, parents, teachers, and other authority figures. In short, students with EBD are generally difficult to teach and to parent. In contrast to their peers who generally follow rules and respond well to their teachers and parents, children and youth with EBD often defy their parents and teachers, disturb others, are aggressive toward others, and behave in ways that invite rejection by those around them. Children and youth with EBD experience the highest rate of suspensions from school. Moreover, they have the highest rate of "interim alternative placements" for drug or weapon offenses that occur in school settings (U.S. Department of Education, 2014).

Socially, children and youth with EBD have difficulties sharing, playing typical age-appropriate games, and apologizing for actions that hurt others. They may be unable to deal appropriately with situations that produce strong feelings, such as anger and frustration. Problem solving, self-control, accepting consequences for misbehavior, negotiating, expressing affection, and reacting appropriately to failure are social skills that are generally underdeveloped or absent in these children and youth. Because these children and youth have deficits in these social–adaptive behaviors, they frequently experience difficulties in meeting the demands of classrooms and other social environments (Hansen & Lignugaris-Kraft, 2005; Polsgrove & Smith, 2004; Vazsonyi & Huang, 2010).

Several studies shed considerable light on the social difficulties these children experience. Researchers have found that about three out of four children with EBD show clinically significant language deficits (Hollo & Wehby, 2014; Mattison, Hooper, & Carlson, 2006; Nungesser & Watkins, 2005). These include problems related to processing and understanding verbal communication and using language to communicate (Benner, Nelson, & Epstein, 2002; Mackie & Law, 2010). Benner et al. also found that one out of two children with language deficits is identified as having EBD. These language deficits contribute to the social problems these children experience.

Children and adolescents who are anxious and withdrawn frequently exhibit behaviors such as seclusiveness and shyness. They may find it extremely difficult to interact with others in typical social settings. They tend to avoid contact with others and may often be found daydreaming. In the extreme, some of these youth begin to avoid school or refuse to attend (Graczyk, Connolly, & Corapci, 2005). Their school avoidance or refusal is marked by persistent fear of social situations that might arise in school or related settings. These youth fear being humiliated or embarrassed. Their anxiety may be expressed in tantrums, crying, and other bodily complaints (stomachaches, sickness, etc.).

Other children and youth with EBD may struggle with mood disorders (Doerfler, Conner, & Toscano, 2011; Roberts & Bishop, 2005). These may include depression and bipolar disorder (National Institute of Mental Health, 2008). Left untreated, these individuals are at risk for suicide, poor school performance, and relationship problems with peers, siblings, parents, teachers, and spouses. Manifestations of depression in children and youth include sleep disturbance (nightmares, night terrors, and so on), fatigue or loss of energy, excessive feelings of guilt or worthlessness, inability to concentrate, and suicidal thoughts.

**Bipolar disorders** are characterized by episodes of manic behavior and depression. Manic behaviors may include defiance of authority, agitation, distractibility, sleeping very little, strong frequent cravings, inappropriate sexual behavior, unrealistic beliefs about abilities, impaired judgment, racing thoughts, and destructive rages.

Depressive behaviors may include sleeping too much, extreme sadness, lack of interest in play or highly preferred activities, crying spells, persistent thoughts of death or suicide, irritability, and inability to concentrate (Child and Adolescent Bipolar Foundation, 2009). Jennifer, identified in the opening Snapshot, is challenged with this disorder.

Bullying perpetration and victimization are persistent problems among students with disabilities, occurring about twice as often as in the general student population. **Bullying** can be described as behavior that involves using physical, emotional, verbal, or sexual aggression to gain a position of strength or authority over others (Maag & Katsiyannis, 2012). **Cyberbullying** involves using any social media outlet to accomplish the same purposes (Kowalski & Fedina, 2011). Students with EBD engage in higher rates of fighting and bullying behavior than students with other disabilities (Rose & Espelage, 2012), but they

**Bipolar disorders**
Disorders characterized by episodes of manic and depressive behaviors.

**Bullying**
Behavior that uses physical, emotional, verbal, or sexual aggression to gain strength or authority over others.

**Cyberbullying**
Use of social media for bullying.

are also victimized at higher rates than other students (Cummings et al., 2006). Among adolescent girls, those with oppositional defiant disorder tend to bully, while those with ADHD are more often victims (Scibarras, Ohan, & Anderson, 2012).

Once thought to be spontaneous confrontations between aggressor and victim, bullying is now characterized as a more complex phenomenon influenced by family, peer group, and community environments (Espelage & Swearer, 2011). Students who feel accepted report fewer incidents of bullying (Birchmeier, 2009). Researchers posit that deficits in age-appropriate social skills such as assertiveness, anger control, and interpreting social cues may underlie propensities to bully or to be bullied (Rose & Espelage, 2012).

Youth gang activities, drug abuse, truancy, violence toward others, and other delinquent acts characterize children and adolescents who are often identified as being "socially maladjusted" or having a conduct disorder (see Figure 8.1). Serious conduct

**Figure 8.1** *Diagnostic Criteria for Conduct Disorder*

A. A repetitive and persistent pattern of behavior in which the basic rights of others or major age-appropriate societal norms or rules are violated, as manifested by the presence of three (or more) of the following criteria in the past 12 months, with at least one criterion present in the past 6 months:

**Aggression to People and Animals**

1. Often bullies, threatens, or intimidates others
2. Often initiates physical fights
3. Has used a weapon that can cause serious physical harm to others (e.g., a bat, brick, broken bottle, knife, gun)
4. Has been physically cruel to people
5. Has been physically cruel to animals
6. Has stolen while confronting a victim (e.g., mugging, purse snatching, extortion, armed robbery)
7. Has forced someone into sexual activity

**Destruction of Property**

8. Has deliberately engaged in fire setting with the intention of causing serious damage
9. Has deliberately destroyed others' property (other than by setting fire)

**Deceitfulness or Theft**

10. Has broken into someone else's house, building, or car
11. Often lies to obtain goods or favors or to avoid obligation (i.e., "cons" others)
12. Has stolen items of nontrivial value without confronting a victim (e.g., shoplifting, but without breaking and entering; forgery)

**Serious Violations of Rules**

13. Often stays out at night despite parental prohibitions, beginning before age 13 years
14. Has run away from home overnight at least twice while living in parental or parental surrogate home (or once without returning for a lengthy period)
15. Is often truant from school, beginning before age 13 years

B. The disturbance in behavior causes clinically significant impairment in social, academic, or occupational functioning.

C. If the individual is age 18 years or older, criteria are not met for antisocial personality disorder.

SOURCE: Adapted from the *Diagnostic and statistical manual of mental disorders,* 5th ed., pp. 469–470), Copyright 2013 American Psychiatric Association.

problems in children and youth often foreshadow poor adult adjustment—substance abuse, spousal and friendship violence, and serious criminal activity (Lopez-Romero, Romero, & Luengo, 2012).

Adolescents with conduct problems are often seen as impulsive, hyperactive, irritable, and excessively stubborn. Teen girls with conduct disorders are more likely to become pregnant, give birth, or have abortions (Pedersen & Mastekaasa, 2011). Furthermore, many students with EBD engage in behaviors that draw attention to themselves. Other behaviors associated with this condition include cruelty to others, drug trafficking, and participation in other illegal activities (Capaldi & Eddy, 2005). It is easy to see how the behaviors associated with these categories are maladaptive and interfere with youths' opportunities for success in schools, families, communities, and employment settings.

## 8-3c Academic Achievement

As we have noted, students with EBD experience significant difficulties and deficits in academic subject areas, and rarely catch up academically (Allen-DeBoer, Malmgren, & Glass, 2006; Griffith et al., 2009; Johnson, McGue, & Iacono, 2009; Kostewicz & Kubina, 2008; Lane et al., 2008). In contrast to other students with high-incidence disabilities such as learning disabilities, students with EBD exhibit the "poorest academic outcomes" (Shriner & Wehby, 2004, p. 216). Some attribute these poor outcomes to the preparation of the teachers who work with these students and to the poor quality of the academic instruction these students often receive (Gable, 2004; Lane, 2004; Shriner & Wehby, 2004). Additionally, interventions for students with EBD have often been directed primarily at controlling behavior and developing social competence rather than building academic skills and promoting achievement (Ryan, Reid, & Epstein, 2004). Thus, many, if not most, students with EBD are not prepared to perform well on state- or federally mandated tests or on other measures of academic achievement (Carter et al., 2005).

The dropout and graduation rates for students with EBD are staggering. In 2012, 38 percent of these students dropped out of school, a greater percentage than for any other disability group. In addition, only 51 percent earned regular diplomas (U.S. Department of Education, 2014). Only one in five youth with EBD participate in postsecondary schooling (Wagner et al., 2005).

Studies dealing with employment rates of students with EBD after high school are frankly disheartening. In 2009, when last reported by the government, only 41 percent of students with EBD who exited high school were employed two years later, compared with 63 percent of typical adolescents who have left or completed high school (U.S. Department of Education, 2013b). Significant challenges persist in preparing young people with EBD for meaningful employment and involvement in our communities (Nochajski & Schweitzer, 2014).

The postsecondary school years for youth with EBD are often tragic. Many are incarcerated, some are involved in domestic abuse, and many or most are unemployed or underemployed (Kauffman & Landrum, 2009; Menzies & Lane, 2011). Later in this chapter, we highlight collaborative approaches to intervention that are designed to address the social, educational, transition, and employment challenges of youth and adults with EBD.

Estimates of the prevalence of EBD vary greatly from one study to the next, ranging from 2 percent to 20 percent (Harry et al., 2009; Kauffman, Simpson, & Mock, 2009; Young et al., 2010). A sensible estimate is 3 to 6 percent (Kauffman & Landrum, 2009). Sadly, during the past thirty years in the United States, 1 percent or less of children and youth 3 to 21 years of age have been identified and served as exhibiting EBD (National Center for Education Statistics, 2013).

Unfortunately, significant numbers of children and youth with EBD remain unidentified and do not receive the care or special education they need to succeed (Forness, Kim, & Walker, 2012; Johnson, Johnson, & Walker, 2011). Equally distressing is the disproportionate number of young African American males who are identified as having EBD, vastly exceeding the percentage that would be expected in the general population of school-age students (U.S. Department of Education, 2013a). Reasons for this are unclear, but recent research indicates that disproportionality is more strongly correlated with poverty than with race or ethnicity (Wiley, Brigham, Kauffman, & Bogan, 2013).

**Standard 1**
Learner Development and Individual Learner Differences

## 8-4  Causes of Emotional/Behavioral Disorders

What causes children and youth to develop EBD? As you read this section, think about your own patterns of behavior. How would you explain these patterns? What gives rise to your own behaviors?

Throughout history, philosophers, psychologists, and others have attempted to explain why people behave as they do. Historically, people who were mentally ill were viewed as being possessed by evil spirits. The treatment of choice was religious in nature. Later, Sigmund Freud (1856–1939) and others advanced the notion that behavior could be explained in terms of subconscious phenomena and/or early traumatic experiences. More recently, researchers have attributed disordered behaviors to inappropriate learning and complex interactions among factors such as native temperament, family environment, poverty, health care, and so on (Ensor, Marks, Jacobs, & Hughes, 2010; Rutter, 2006). Others, approaching the issue from a biological perspective, suggest that aberrant behaviors are caused by certain biochemical substances (Haltigan et al., 2011), brain abnormalities or injuries, chromosomal irregularities, and other inherited genetic factors (Forsman et al., 2010; Johnson, McGue, & Iacono, 2009; Vazsonyi & Huang, 2010).

With such a wealth of explanations, it is easy to see why practitioners might select different approaches in identifying, treating, and preventing EBD. As you will see, the causes of behavioral disorders are multifaceted and often complex (Burt, 2009; Burt & Neiderhiser, 2009; Heilbrun, 2004; Rutter, 2006).

Clearly, many factors contribute to the emergence of EBD (Crews et al., 2007). Family and home environments play critical roles (Barber, Stolz, & Olsen, 2005; Murray et al., 2010; Whitted, 2011). Economic stress, involvement of primary caregivers with drugs and alcohol, child abuse and neglect, malnutrition, dysfunctional family environments, family discord, and inept parenting have a profound impact on the behaviors that emerge in children and adolescents (Burt, 2009; Conroy & Brown, 2004; Murray et al., 2010; Wicks-Nelson & Israel, 2006). For example, "minimal rules in the home, poor monitoring of children, and inconsistent rewards and punishments create an environment in which behavior problems flourish" (Sampers et al., 2001, p. 94).

Photo 8.3 Children who have been abused are at risk for the development of emotional/behavioral disorders.

Children reared in low-income families and communities bear increased risks for wide-ranging challenges, including low cognitive stimulation, deficient school achievement, and high rates of EBD. Antisocial behaviors often emerge in children whose family poverty is accompanied by other stressors, such as homelessness, the death of a parent, maternal depression, placement in foster care, or persistent child abuse or neglect (Murray et al., 2010).

Family discord also plays a role in the development of EBD in some children. Extended marital conflict and distress are associated with several serious child outcomes, including aggressive behavior, difficulty with schoolwork, depression, health problems, and lower social competence (Wicks-Nelson & Israel, 2006).

Procedures used in child management and discipline also play important roles in the development of EBD (Nelson et al., 2007). However, the way in which child management may trigger EBD is highly complex. Parents who are extremely permissive, who are overly restrictive, or who use highly aggressive discipline approaches often produce children with conduct disorders (Vieno et al., 2009). Again, home environments that are devoid of consistent rules and consequences for negative behaviors, that lack parental supervision, that reinforce aggressive behavior, and that use aggressive child-management practices produce children who are very much at risk for developing conduct disorders (see Figure 8.1; Barker et al., 2011; Wicks-Nelson & Israel, 2006).

Child abuse plays a major role in the development of aggression and other problematic behaviors in children and adolescents. Effects of child abuse on young children include withdrawal, noncompliance, aggression, enuresis (bed-wetting), and physical complaints. Physically abused children exhibit high rates of adjustment problems of all kinds (Wicks-Nelson & Israel, 2006). Neglected children often experience difficulty in academic subjects and receive below-average grades. Children who have been sexually abused manifest an array of problems, including inappropriate, premature sexual behavior; poor peer relationships; and serious mental health problems. Similar difficulties are evident in adolescents who have been abused. These include low self-esteem, depression, poor peer relationships and school problems, and self-injurious and suicidal behaviors.

The pathways to EBD are multidimensional. However, the more we learn about these pathways, the greater our opportunities are to prevent EBD or to lessen its overall impact (Eivers, Brendgen, & Borge, 2010). Much can be done for children, at-risk youth, and their families if appropriate preventive measures, protective factors, and interventions are actively pursued and put in place, especially during the early childhood years (Adelman & Taylor, 2006; Crews et al., 2007; Quinn & Poirier, 2004; Whitted, 2011).

## 8-5 Identification and Assessment of Emotional/Behavioral Disorders

**Standard 1**
Learner Development and Individual Learner Differences

Many factors influence the ways in which we perceive the behaviors of others. Our perceptions of behavior are significantly influenced by our personal beliefs, standards, and values about what constitutes normal behavior. Our range of tolerance varies greatly, depending on the behavior and the related context. What some may view as normal, others may view as abnormal.

As was indicated earlier, the contexts in which behaviors occur dramatically influence our views of their appropriateness. For example, teachers and parents expect children to behave reasonably well in settings where they have interesting things to do or where children are doing things they seem to enjoy. Often, children with EBD misbehave in these settings. At times, they seem to be oblivious to the settings in which they find themselves.

Many factors influence the types of behaviors that children and youth exhibit or suppress: (1) the parents' and teachers' management/discipline approaches, (2) the school or home environments, (3) the social and cultural values of the family, (4) the social and economic conditions of the community, (5) the expectations and responses of peers and siblings, and (6) the biological, intellectual, and social–emotional temperaments of the individuals.

### 8-5a Screening, Pre-Referral Interventions, and Referral for Assessment

Screening is the first step in the assessment process. It is designed to identify children and youth who may or may not present EBD. Once these children and youth are identified, teachers and other support personnel may provide targeted pre-referral interventions. These interventions are designed to address the presenting problems, often using **positive behavior support (PBS)** strategies without formally labeling the child or youth as having EBD (Vincent & Tobin, 2011). If the child or youth is unresponsive to these carefully conceived and applied interventions over time, a referral would be made for further observations and testing, thus potentially qualifying the child or youth for more intensive services and potential placements. We will speak more about PBS in the next section.

**Standard 4**
Assessment

Screening is based on the belief that early identification leads to early treatment, which may reduce the overall impact of the EBD on the individual, family, and community (Davis et al., 2011; Eivers, Brendgen, & Borge, 2010). As suggested earlier in this chapter, significant numbers of children and youth with EBD are not identified, and thus do not receive appropriate services and interventions.

Screening approaches are multiagent and multigated; that is, they do not rely on one professional, one method, or one observation for assessing a child or youth when EBDs are suspected (Conroy, Hendrickson, & Hester, 2004). Screeners move through successive "gates" to identify children or youth for more intensive assessment and pre-referral interventions.

**Positive behavior support (PBS)**

A school-wide approach to supporting all children in developing highly functional social and academic skills supported by all teachers and school personnel through clearly stated expectations and powerful incentives.

One such approach is **systematic screening for behavior disorders** (SSBD; see Walker, Severson, & Feil, 2014). This approach has been very effective in identifying young children who need interventions and other services before being seriously considered for formal referrals for special education services. SSBD is a three-stage process, beginning with nominations by a general education teacher. Teachers think about the children in their classes and then group them according to various behavior patterns, some of which mirror the characteristics of children with EBD. Once the children have been grouped, each child is ranked within the group according to the severity and frequency of his or her behaviors. The last step is a series of systematic observations conducted in classrooms and in other school environments to see how the children who were ranked most severely behave in these environments. As children are progressively and systematically identified through this multiple-gating process, assessment team members determine which children ought to be considered for pre-referral interventions or other more intensive assessments.

**Collaborative Teams** Pre-referral interventions are designed to address students' identified behavioral and academic problems and to reduce the likelihood of further, more restrictive placements. These interventions are applied generally when the academic and behavior challenges of children are more amenable to change and amelioration (Lane, 2007). Often, these interventions are developed, planned, and implemented under the direction of multidisciplinary collaborative teams. Many states now require the application of scientifically based interventions specifically tailored to the needs of all students experiencing learning or behavior problems based on informal and formal assessments. Commonly referred to as the **response to intervention (RtI)**, regular and special educators join together with other professionals in conducting ongoing assessments and applying carefully selected, evidence-based interventions in working with *all* children (Hughes & Dexter, 2011; Ryan, Pierce, & Mooney, 2008). These interventions and practices, often referred to as positive behavior support (PBS), hold great promise for helping students from diverse backgrounds and those with challenging behaviors remain and succeed in general education classrooms and in other less restrictive settings (Arter, 2007; Reinke, Herman, & Tucker, 2006). PBS "is a systems approach for establishing a continuum of proactive, positive discipline procedures for all students and staff members in all types of school settings" (Eber et al., 2002, p. 171).

Instead of treating the symptom(s) and ignoring the underlying problems, the thrust of PBS is to address all features and factors that may be related to a child's or youth's negative behaviors or academic challenges. The primary goals of PBS systems are improved behaviors for all children and youth at home, at school, and in the community; enhanced academic performance; and the prevention of serious violent, aggressive, or destructive behaviors (Lane, Kalberg, & Menzies, 2009).

Schools in which PBS systems are evident define school-wide expectations and rules; actively and regularly build social competence through active and intense teaching of social skills; provide rewards for targeted, prosocial behaviors; and make decisions on the basis of frequently collected, pertinent data (Gresham, Van, & Cook, 2006; Lewis et al., 2010; Miller, Lane, & Wehby, 2005; Reinke, Herman, & Tucker, 2006). Additionally, collaborative teams of professionals develop and put into action individually tailored plans for students who present chronic, challenging behaviors. These plans evolve from carefully completed functional behavior assessments conducted by key individuals in the students' school, home, and community settings (Young et al., 2011).

Several response to intervention cycles using PBS would be applied before school administrators seriously considered any student for referral for special education services. In effect, RtI and PBS efforts are both proactive and preventive; that is, they are focused on helping any child or youth who is not succeeding in school as soon as possible and lessening the emergence of more serious learning or behavior problems.

The actual submission of a referral for a student is generally preceded by several parent–teacher conferences. These conferences help teachers and parents determine what actions should to be taken. For example, the student's difficulties may be symptomatic of family problems such as a parent's extended illness, marital difficulties, or severe financial challenges. If the parents and concerned teachers continue to be perplexed by a child's or youth's behavior, a referral may be initiated. Referrals are generally processed by school principals who review them, consult with parents, and then forward the referred families to a licensed psychologist or other qualified professionals.

Once a referral has been appropriately processed and a parent's or guardian's permission for testing and evaluation has been obtained, assessment team members carefully observe and assess the child's present levels of performance: intellectually, socially, academically, and emotionally. Their task is to determine whether the child has EBD and whether he or she qualifies for special education services.

**Assessment Factors** As we noted earlier in this chapter, emotional and behavioral disorders have many causes. Likewise, the behaviors of children and youth being assessed for EBD serve many functions. In other words, behaviors are purposeful. For example, a young child may throw a tantrum to avoid schoolwork that is too difficult. Or a youth may engage in destructive behavior to gain attention that he or she does not otherwise derive from peers or parents.

Behavior is also a function of interactions with environmental factors. Some conditions set off negative behaviors, and other conditions reward or reinforce these same behaviors. Interpersonal factors—such as depression, anxiety, or erroneous interpretations of environment events—may contribute to a child's or youth's problems. If a child or youth is showing behaviors that are highly problematic, teachers and other professionals have an obligation to look at them from a functional point of view—to see what purposes these behaviors serve and what conditions give rise to them.

Current IDEA regulations require assessment team members to conduct **functional behavioral assessments** and to document the impact of the EBD on the child's or youth's academic achievement (U.S. Department of Education, 2006; Witt, VanDerHeyden, & Gilbertson, 2004). Simply defined, "Functional assessment is a collection of methods for obtaining information about antecedents [things a child experiences before the behavior of concern], behaviors [what the child does], and consequences [what the child experiences after the behavior of concern]. The purpose is to identify potential reasons for the behavior and to use the information to develop strategies that will support positive student performance while reducing the behaviors that interfere with the child's successful functioning" (Witt, Daly, & Noell, 2000, p. 3). The purpose of completing a functional behavioral assessment is to identify the roles and purposes of a student's behavior in relationship to various school, home, or community settings (Crone, Hawken, & Horner, 2015).

Assessment team members collect information through interviews, make careful observations, and examine the effects of probes or experimental manipulations over a period of several days. Through these procedures, team members, general education teachers, and parents discover reliable relationships among specific problem behaviors, the settings or events that give rise to these behaviors, and their consequences for the child or youth.

If the functional behavioral assessment is done well, it provides grounding for the development of **behavior intervention plans (BIPs)** that may be used to assist the child or youth in developing new, more useful behaviors for school and home (Arter, 2007; Etscheidt, 2006; Lane et al., 2007). Additionally, the BIP may include new curricular or instructional approaches tailored to the student's learning needs and preferences. The BIP may also identify changes to be implemented in the school setting or home. These might include peer and paraprofessional support, use of conflict resolution specialists, home-based specialists and programs, and other carefully selected interventions. In the end, BIPs seek to prevent problem behaviors, and in their place, build useful, functional behaviors that advance the youth's social, emotional, and academic development using evidence-based practices (Mueller, Bassett, & Brewer, 2012).

**Assessment Approaches and Procedures** Several approaches and procedures are used to identify children with EBD. As we have seen, the identification and classification of a child or youth with EBD is preceded by screening procedures accompanied by a functional behavior assessment, motivational assessments, teacher and parent interviews, diagnostic academic assessments, behavior checklists, a variety of sociometric devices (e.g., peer ratings), and the use of teacher and parent rating scales (Conroy & Brown, 2004; Cunningham & O'Neill, 2007; Rosenberg et al., 2004).

**CEC**
**Standard 4**
Assessment

Figure 8.2 *Representative Items from the Child Behavior Checklist for Ages 4 to 18*

0 = Not True (as far as you know)
1 = Somewhat or Sometimes True
2 = Very True or Often True

| 0 | 1 | 2 | 1. Acts too young for his/her age |
|---|---|---|---|
| 0 | 1 | 2 | 5. There is very little he/she enjoys |
| 0 | 1 | 2 | 10. Can't sit still, restless, or hyperactive |
| 0 | 1 | 2 | 15. Cruel to animals |
| 0 | 1 | 2 | 20. Destroys his/her own things |
| 0 | 1 | 2 | 25. Doesn't get along with other kids |
| 0 | 1 | 2 | 30. Fears going to school |
| 0 | 1 | 2 | 35. Feels worthless or inferior |
| 0 | 1 | 2 | 40. Hears sounds or voices that aren't there (describe): |
| 0 | 1 | 2 | 45. Nervous, high strung, or tense |
| 0 | 1 | 2 | 50. Too fearful or anxious |

SOURCE: From Achenbach, 1. M., & Rescorla, L. A. *Manual for the ASEBA school-age forms and profiles.* Burlington, VT: University of Vermont, Research Center for Children, Youth, and Families. Copyright 2001 by L. M. Achenbach. Reproduced by permission.

Typically, parents and teachers are asked to respond to a variety of rating-scale items that describe behaviors related to various classifications of EBD. The number of items marked and the rating given to each item contribute to the behavior profiles generated from the ratings (see Figure 8.2). In making their assessments, parents and professionals are asked to consider the child's behavior during the past several months.

A positive development in assessing children and youth for EBD is **strength-based assessment** (Donovan & Nickerson, 2007; Epstein, 1998). In contrast to deficit-oriented instruments, this approach focuses on the child's or youth's strengths. One such instrument is the *Behavioral and Emotional Rating Scale—Second Edition* (BERS-2) (Epstein & Sharma, 1997). Using this instrument, parents, teachers, and other caregivers rate the child's or youth's strengths in several important areas, including interpersonal strength, involvement with family, intrapersonal assets, school functioning, and affective or emotional strengths. Clinicians use the BERS and other similar approaches to develop strength-centered, rather than deficit-centered, IEPs for children and youth with EBD (see Figure 8.3).

Once the screening process has been concluded, specialists or consultants—including psychologists, special educators, and social workers—complete in-depth assessments of the child's academic and social–emotional strengths and weaknesses in various settings. The assessment team may analyze the child with EBD in classroom and playground interactions with peers, using functional behavioral assessment techniques; may administer various tests to evaluate personality, achievement, and intellectual factors; and may interview the parents and the child. Additionally, the assessment team may observe the child at home, again making use of functional behavioral assessment procedures.

Photo 8.4 When completing behavioral assessments, parents are asked to assess their child's behavior at home, such as how well the child interacts with siblings.

©2015 Cengage Learning®

**Strength-based assessment**
Assessment that rates a child's strengths and uses this information to develop a strength-centered individualized education program.

**Standard 2**
Learning Environments

**Standard 5**
Instructional Planning and Strategies

**Standard 7**
Collaboration

A particularly complex problem for clinicians is the assessment of children and youth who have limited English proficiency and/or are culturally diverse (Artiles et al., 2012). Unfortunately, many of these children and youth are disproportionately represented in special education settings for students with EBD (Moreno, Wong-Lo, & Bullock, 2014). Some hope for improvement is merited, especially as practitioners collaborate and use functional behavioral assessment and related procedures, pre-referral interventions, and positive behavioral support (PBS) for all students (Lane, Kalberg, & Menzies, 2009).

## CASE STUDY ON EMBRACING DIVERSITY

### Leon

I have had an IEP since first grade. I don't read very well and don't write very well either. I had to go to resource room for extra help in reading and writing. It was embarrassing to go there because kids would make fun of me.

When I started school I had a lot of problems. I couldn't sit still, pay attention, and basically I was jumping all over the room. I had trouble getting my work done in class because I couldn't concentrate. This would make my teachers mad at me. What was worse, the kids in my class would laugh at me.

As I got older I got more and more different diagnoses and more and more different medicines.

I started getting angry in school. I was also having problems at home. I didn't like listening to any adults.

I [was] tired of all the crap in school and at home. One of my best friends committed suicide so I decided to commit suicide too. I cut my wrists, but I didn't die; instead I had to go to a hospital. They told me that if I didn't straighten up, I would never be able to go back home and be with my family. I didn't like therapists saying they understood what I was going through. I asked them if they were bipolar or ADHD, and they said no. They can't possibly understand it, unless they live with it.

Sometimes I feel like a lab rat. I have been on lots of different meds. Some of them have had horrible side effects. Everyone needs to understand about the side effects. It's not just about gaining weight, or being sleepy. Some of meds have done the opposite. Some have made me do crazy stuff and act differently.

But I have strengths, too: I am a third degree black belt in tae kwon do, I can write rap and perform rap music, I have a good sense of humor, I'm helpful to others, a good listener, friendly, and a loyal friend.

*Application Questions*

**1.** What would you do as a teacher for and with Leon, if he were in your classroom?

**2.** How could the wraparound approach be used in Leon's case?

**3.** Given what you have learned in this chapter, what are some recommendations that you would make to Leon's parents?

SOURCE: Adapted from Midwest Symposium for Leadership in Behavior Disorders. *Kid's Stories*. Retrieved from http://www.mslbd.org/kids_stories.htm.

# 8-6 Interventions and Treatments for Emotional/Behavioral Disorders

Historically, most children and youth with EBD received treatments and interventions in isolation from their families, homes, neighborhoods, and communities. These treatments and interventions were based on the assumption that students' problems were primarily of their own making. Services, if they were delivered at all, were rarely coordinated. Fragmentation was the rule (Eber & Keenan, 2004).

## 8-6a Multidisciplinary Collaboration: Systems of Care

Increasingly, care providers for children and youth with EBD are establishing systems of care (Adelman & Taylor, 2006; National Mental Health Information Center, 2006). One very promising practice is the **wraparound approach (WRAP)** (Eber et al., 2008). "Wraparound is not a service or set of services; it is a [collaborative] planning process. This process is used to build consensus within a team of professionals, family members, and natural support providers to improve the effectiveness, efficiency, and relevance of supports and services developed for children and their families" (Eber et al., 2002, p. 173). We will have more to say about the wraparound process in subsequent sections of this chapter.

Community-based and family-centered systems for delivering services to children and youth with EBD are also emerging. In these systems, educational, medical, and community care providers are beginning to pay greater attention to youth with EBD and their families, as well as to the communities in which they live (see Figure 8.4). This new approach is based on several core values and guiding principles (see Figure 8.5). One of the basic features of the systems of care concept is that it does not represent a prescribed structure for assembling a network of services and agencies. Rather, it reflects a philosophy about the way in which services should be delivered to children, youth, and their families. The child and family become the focus of the delivery system, with vital services surrounding them. These services might include home-based interventions, special class placement, therapeutic foster care, financial assistance, primary health care, outpatient treatment, career education, after-school programs, and carefully tailored family support.

An integral part of the systems of care is school-wide primary prevention (Adelman & Taylor, 2006; Eber et al., 2008). Interventions associated with this kind of prevention include systems for positive behavior support (PBS), response to intervention (RtI) practices as identified earlier, multidisciplinary collaboration, teaching conflict resolution, emotional literacy, **cognitive–behavioral therapy**, and anger management for all students in the school—not just to those identified with EBD (Guerra, Boxer, & Kim, 2005; Mayer,

**CEC**

**Standard 1**
Learner Development and Individual Learner Differences

**Standard 2**
Learning Environments

**Standard 5**
Instructional Planning and Strategies

**Standard 7**
Collaboration

**Wraparound approach (WRAP)**
An intensive, complete, team/community approach of involving children and youth and their families so that they can thrive in their homes, local schools, and communities and develop the skills and behaviors needed for successful living and learning.

**Cognitive–behavioral therapy**
Therapy that focuses on the role of thinking and language and how they influence behavior(s) and related feelings.

*Figure 8.4* **The System of Care Framework**

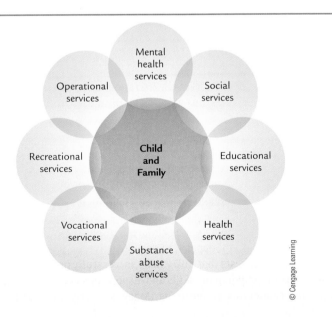

© Cengage Learning

**Figure 8.5** *Core Values and Guiding Principles of Systems of Care*

**Core Values**

1. The system of care should be child-centered and family-focused, with the needs of the child and family dictating the types and mix of services provided.

2. The system of care should be community-based, with the locus of services as well as management and decision-making responsibility resting at the community level.

3. The system of care should be culturally competent, with agencies, programs, and services that are responsive to the cultural, racial, and ethnic differences of the population they serve.

**Guiding Principles**

1. Children with emotional disturbances should have access to a comprehensive array of services that address physical, emotional, social, and educational needs.

2. Children with emotional disturbances should receive individualized services in accordance with the unique needs and potentials of each child and guided by an individualized service plan.

3. Children with emotional disturbances should receive services within the least restrictive, most normative environment that is clinically appropriate.

4. The families and surrogate families of children with emotional disturbances should be full participants in all aspects of the planning and delivery of services.

5. Children with emotional disturbances should receive services that are integrated, with linkages between child-serving agencies and programs and mechanisms for planning, developing, and coordinating services.

6. Children with emotional disturbances should be provided with case management or similar mechanisms to ensure that multiple services are delivered in a coordinated and therapeutic manner and that they can move through the system of services in accordance with their changing needs.

7. Early identification and intervention for children with emotional disturbances should be promoted by the system of care to enhance the likelihood of positive outcomes.

8. Children with emotional disturbances should be ensured smooth transitions to the adult service system as they reach maturity.

9. The rights of children with emotional disturbances should be protected, and effective advocacy efforts for children and youth with emotional disturbances should be promoted.

10. Children with emotional disturbances should receive services without regard to race, religion, national origin, sex, physical disability, or other characteristics, and services should be sensitive and responsive to cultural differences and special needs.

SOURCE: From Stroul, B., & Friedman, R. M. (1986). *A system of care for children and adolescents with severe emotional disturbances.* rev. ed. (p. xxiv). Washington, D.C.: Georgetown University Child Development Center, National Technical Assistance Center for Children's Mental Health. Copyright 1986 by B. Stroul and R. M. Friedman.

Lochman, & Van Acker, 2005; Powell et al., 2011; Robinson, 2007; Ryan, Pierce, & Mooney, 2008). These kinds of interventions can prevent 75 to 85 percent of student adjustment and behavior problems.

## 8-6b  Early Childhood Education

"Increasingly, it is understood that serious and persistent challenging behaviors in early childhood are associated with subsequent problems in socialization, school adjustment, school success, and educational and vocational adaptation in adolescence and adulthood" (Dunlap et al., 2006, p. 29). The early childhood years are vitally important for all children, but they are particularly crucial for young children with EBD—young children who are consistently noncompliant, defiant, oppositional, destructive, aggressive, and so on (Whitted, 2011). Recent research suggests that EBD can be successfully prevented and ameliorated by developing within young children the skills and dispositions needed for successful schooling, relationships, and community connections (Maag & Katsiyannis, 2010). Many children

**Standard 4**
Assessment

**Standard 5**
Instructional Planning and Strategies

**Standard 7**
Collaboration

would not develop serious EBD if they and their families received early, child-centered, intensive, community-based, and family-focused services and interventions. Moreover, the cost of delivering these prevention services would be far less than that of providing services to these same individuals as teens, young adults, and adults. Society seems unwilling to make investments that would yield remarkable financial, social, and emotional dividends for us, our children, and our communities (Lopes, 2005). Key elements of the prevention process include early identification, family-driven needs assessment, home-based and community-based interventions, parent training, and collaboration with an array of educational and community agencies (Brotman et al., 2011; Dunlap et al., 2006; Kendziora, 2004).

Interventions for young children with EBD are child-, family-, and home-centered. Often, they are directed at reducing the impacts of EBD, replacing challenging behaviors with more functional ones, and preventing more serious emotional and behavioral problems from developing (Brotman et al., 2011; Dunlap et al., 2006; Kendziora, 2004). Thus, the goals associated with individualized family service plans (IFSPs) go well beyond the typical educational goals found in individualized education programs (IEPs) for older children. Interventions for young children with EBD include teaching them to manage their feelings; developing empathy skills (how to read and interpret others' behaviors); problem solving (how to take turns and ask for help, and to develop self-control); and learning how to manage impulses, how to delay gratification, and how to deal with anger (Whitted, 2011). Additionally, interventions are directed at building positive replacement behaviors for challenging behaviors, promoting appropriate social interactions with peers and others, and creating positive behavioral supports across a child's natural environments (Essa, 2003; Powell et al., 2011).

Family-centered interventions focus on respite care; parent training directed at managing a young child with EBD at home and in other community settings; the delivery of family, marital, or drug therapy; treatment for maternal depression; and the provision of specialized day care or day treatment. The nature, intensity, and duration of these multiagency services and interventions are determined by the needs of the families and the speed with which they develop new skills and coping strategies. The interventions are delivered in multiple contexts—the places where children, family members, and others play, work, learn, and associate.

Catherine Ledner/Stone/Getty Images

*Photo 8.5* Children with emotional/behavioral disorders can pose challenges for general education teachers.

Often the interventions for young children with EBD are directed at functional communication skills—learning how to get attention, learning how to make a request, or recruiting praise; developing appropriate social interaction with siblings, parents, and peers; learning targeted and useful social skills; and mastering developmentally appropriate tasks. Also, in keeping with the movement toward inclusion, family intervention and transition specialists are focused on preparing young children for successful participation in less restrictive environments (Chang et al., 2011).

## 8-6c Elementary Education

Elementary children with EBD often present overlapping behavioral problems. These problems center on accepting appropriate consequences, building appropriate academic skills, interacting successfully with others, using self-control, following directions, and expressing strong feelings appropriately. Such behaviors become the focus of intervention efforts. With the assistance of parents, IEP team members strive to construct a complete picture of each child, determining his or her present levels of intellectual, social, emotional, and academic performance and the contexts that give rise to and support these behaviors (Beard & Sugai, 2004). These levels of performance and the outcomes derived from the functional behavioral assessment become the basis for identifying important goals for the child's IEP and for developing behavior intervention plans (Lewis et al., 2004).

**CEC**

**Standard 2**
Learning Environments

**Standard 4**
Assessment

**Standard 5**
Instructional Planning and Strategies

**Standard 7**
Collaboration

## People with Emotional/Behavioral Disorders (EBD)

### Early Childhood Years

#### Tips for Families

- Become involved with parent training and other community support services.

- Work collaboratively with multidisciplinary personnel (educators, social workers, health care professionals, and parent–group volunteers) in developing effective child management strategies.

- Use the same evidence-based intervention strategies at home that are applied in the preschool settings.

- Establish family routines, schedules, and incentive systems that reward and build positive behaviors.

- Participate actively in advocacy or parent–support groups.

- Understand your rights regarding health care, education, and social services benefits.

#### Tips for Preschool Teachers

- Work collaboratively with the multidisciplinary professionals in your preschool (the director, psychologist, social worker, parent trainers, special educators, and health care professionals) to identify evidence-based instructional strategies.

- Establish clear schedules, class routines, rules, and positive consequences for all children in your classroom.

- Create a learning and social environment that is nurturing for everyone.

- Explicitly teach social behaviors (e.g., following directions, greeting other children, sharing toys, using words to express anger, etc.) to all children.

- Ask for help from the multidisciplinary teacher support team—remember collaboration is the key to success.

#### Tips for Preschool Personnel

- Engage older socially competent peers to assist with academic readiness and social skills training.

- Help others (teaching assistants, aides, volunteers, etc.) know what to do in managing children with challenging behaviors.

- Make every effort to involve children with EBD in school-wide activities and special performances.

- Orient and teach preschool children without disabilities about how to appropriately respond to classmates with challenging behaviors such as teaching them to ignore, walk away, get help from the teacher, and so on.

- Collaborate with parents in using the same management systems and strategies in your preschool classroom as those used in the home.

#### Tips for Neighbors and Friends

- Become familiar with the things you can do as a neighbor or friend in responding to the challenging behaviors of a neighborhood child with EBD.

- Be patient with parents who are attempting to cope with their child's temper tantrums or other challenging behaviors in community settings (such as at a grocery store, in the mall, etc.).

- Assist parents who would benefit from some time away from their preschooler by offering respite care for short periods of time.

- Involve the neighborhood child with EBD in your family activities.

- Encourage parents to involve their child in neighborhood and community events (e.g., parades, holiday celebrations, and birthday parties).

### Elementary Years

#### Tips for Families

- Use the effective management techniques that are being applied in your child's classroom in your home environment.

- Establish clear rules, set routines, and consequences that are consistent with your child's developmental age and interests.

- Obtain counseling when appropriate for yourself, your other children, and your spouse from community mental health agencies or other public or private sources.

- Help your other children and their friends understand the things they can do to support your child with EBD.

#### Tips for General Education Classroom Teachers

- Provide a positive, structured classroom/learning environment (i.e., with clearly stated rules, helpful positive and negative consequences, well-conceived classroom schedules, carefully taught classroom routines, and solid relationship-building activities).

- Teach social skills (how to deal with bullying, accept criticism, etc.) to all of the children with the help of members of the school's multidisciplinary teacher assistance team.

- Teach self-management skills (goal selection, self-monitoring, self-reinforcement, etc.) to all children with the aid of members of the school's multidisciplinary teacher assistance team.

- Promote the positive peer interaction that develops positive relationships among students.

- Ask for targeted help from members of your school's multidisciplinary teacher assistance team or the youth's parents.

#### Tips for School Personnel

- Use same-age or cross-age peers to provide tutoring, coaching, and other kinds of assistance in developing the academic and social skills of children with EBD.

- Establish school-wide management programs and positive behavioral supports that reinforce individual and group accomplishments.

- Work closely and collaboratively with members of the multidisciplinary teacher assistance team to create a school environment that is positive and caring.

- Use collaborative problem-solving techniques in dealing with difficult or persistent behavior problems—work with your school multidisciplinary teacher assistance team.

- Help all children in the school develop an understanding of how to appropriately respond to students with challenging behaviors.

### Tips for Neighbors and Friends

- Involve the child with EBD in appropriate after-school activities (recreational events, informal sports, etc.).

- Invite the child to spend time with your family in appropriate excursions and recreational activities (swimming, hiking, boating, etc.).

- Teach your children how to support appropriate behaviors and how to ignore inappropriate behaviors when they occur.

- As a youth leader, coach, or recreational specialist, get to know each child with behavior disorders well so that you can respond with confidence when providing support and potential corrections/consequences.

## Secondary and Transition Years

### Tips for Families

- Continue your efforts to focus on the positive behaviors of your child with EBD.

- Assist your child in understanding and selecting appropriate postsecondary training, education, and/or employment.

- Give yourself a regular break from the task of being a parent and engage in activities that are totally enjoyable for you.

- Seek help from community mental health services, clergy, or a close friend when you are feeling overwhelmed or stressed.

- Consult regularly with support personnel to monitor progress and develop ideas for maintaining the behavioral and academic gains made by your child.

- Maintain involvement in advocacy and parent–support groups.

### Tips for General Education Classroom Teachers

- Create positive relationships within your classroom with cooperative learning teams and group-oriented assignments.

- Engage all students in creating standards for conduct as well as consequences for positive and negative behaviors.

- Provide relevant/engaging instruction.

- Incorporate your students' interests and strengths.

- Focus your efforts on developing a positive relationship with students with EBD by greeting them regularly in your class, informally talking with them at appropriate times, attending to improvements in their performance, and becoming aware of their interests and concerns.

- Promote the positive peer interactions that develop positive relationships among students.

- Work closely with members of the school multidisciplinary teacher assistance team to be aware of teacher behaviors that may positively or adversely affect the student's performance.

- Understand that changes in behavior often occur very gradually with periods of regression and sometimes tumult.

### Tips for School Personnel

- Create a school climate that is positive and supportive.

- Provide students with an understanding of their roles and responsibilities in responding to peers with disabilities.

- Engage peers in providing social skills training, job coaching, and academic tutoring.

- Engage members of the school multidisciplinary teacher assistance team to help you deal with crisis situations and to provide other supportive therapies and interventions.

- Establish school-wide procedures for dealing quickly and efficiently with particularly difficult behaviors.

### Tips for Neighbors, Friends, and Potential Employers

- If you have some expertise in a content area (such as math, English, history, etc.), offer to provide assistance with homework or other related school assignments for students with EBD.

- Provide opportunities for students with EBD to be employed in your business.

- Give parents an occasional respite by inviting the adolescent with EBD to join your family for a cookout, movie night, or other family-oriented activities.

- Encourage other children and adolescents to volunteer as peer partners, job coaches, and social skills trainers.

- Do not allow others to tease, harass, or ridicule an adolescent with behavior disorders in your presence.

## Adult Years

### Tips for Families

- Build on efforts to develop appropriate independence and interdependence.

- Maintain contact with appropriate multidisciplinary personnel (health care professionals and social services personnel), particularly if the adult with EBD is on medication or receiving counseling.

- Work collaboratively with appropriate adult service agencies that are required by law to assist with your adult child's employment, housing, and recreation.

- Prepare your other children or other caregivers as appropriate to assume the responsibilities that you may be unable to assume over time.

### Tips for Neighbors, Friends, and Employers

- As an employer, be willing to make sensible and reasonable adjustments in the work environments.

- Understand adjustments that may need to take place with new medications or treatment regimens.

- Get to know the individual as a person —his/her likes or dislikes, who they admire, and preferred leisure activities.

- Be willing to involve the individual in appropriate holiday and special occasion events such as birthdays, athletic activities, and other social gatherings.

- Understand what might be irritating or uncomfortable to the individual.

- Be available to communicate with others who may be responsible for the individual's well-being—a job coach, an independent living specialist, and others.

**Curriculum of control**
Classroom routines, structures, and instructional strategies focused on controlling children rather than teaching them success-related behaviors.

**Standard 2**
Learning Environments

**Standard 7**
Collaboration

**Standard 4**
Assessment

**Standard 2**
Learning Environments

**Standard 5**
Instructional Planning and Strategies

Typically, programs for children with EBD focus on replacing maladaptive with adaptive behaviors, increasing self-regulation, building appropriate academic skills and dispositions, increasing self-awareness, increasing cooperative behavior, and acquiring age-appropriate self-control (Lane, Kalberg, & Menzies, 2009). Children need these skills and behaviors to succeed in their classrooms, homes, and communities.

In the past, many programs for children with EBD were restrictive, controlling, and punitive in nature. Rather than teaching new behaviors, these programs focused on controlling the behaviors of children and youth. These programs employed the **curriculum of control** (Knitzer, Steinberg, & Fleisch, 1990) or the *curriculum of noninstruction* (Shores & Wehby, 1999, p. 196). Rather than developing replacement behaviors or new behaviors, children and youth in many of these programs languished or regressed. Even today, many children and youth with behavior disorders are served in settings that remove them from natural interactions with students without disabilities. Some of these programs are boot camp–like in nature (Jeter, 2010). Most young people with EBD have friends that are neighborhood-based rather than school-centered—just the opposite of young people without disabilities.

**Collaboration: Wraparound Services** New systems of care for children and adolescents with EBD have emerged (Eber & Keenan, 2004; Eber, Hyde, & Suter, 2011). As mentioned earlier, these systems deliver wraparound services to children and youth with EBD and their families (Eber et al., 2008) (see Reflect on This, "Henry: Wraparound"). As is implied by the word *wraparound*, children, youth, and their families receive the support they need to address the problems uncovered through carefully conducted assessments. Preliminary research regarding the provision of these services is very positive for youth with complex and challenging EBD. Results include successfully living at home, positive emotional and behavioral growth, reduced recidivism rates for delinquent-related behaviors, and better performance at school as evidenced in improved attendance and grades (Eber, Hyde, & Suter, 2011).

Services may include in-home child management training, employment assistance, and family therapy—whatever is needed to help families become successful. Figure 8.6 reveals essential phases of wraparound systems and related programs.

Again, at the heart of many new programs is positive behavioral support (PBS). Instead of trying to exclusively control behaviors, teachers, parents, and clinicians collaborate, working together to build new replacement behaviors—behaviors that are highly regarded and especially functional in school, home, and community settings.

As highlighted in the assessment section of this chapter, professionals use functional behavioral assessment to determine the patterns and functions of certain behaviors. Once these patterns and functions are well understood, teachers, parents, and others help children and youth with EBD develop new behaviors, grow academically, achieve worthwhile goals, and learn how to deal with their thoughts and feelings in positive ways (Beard & Sugai, 2004).

Children who exhibit moderate to severe EBD may be served in special classes (see Reflect on This, "Henry: Wraparound"). In some school systems, special classes are found in elementary, middle, and high schools. They may be grouped in small clusters of two to three classes in selected buildings. Other special classes may be found within hospital units, special schools, residential programs, juvenile units, and other specialized treatment facilities.

Most special classes for children with moderate to severe disorders share certain characteristics. The first is a high degree of structure and specialized instruction. In other words, rules are clear and consistently enforced; helpful routines are in place; high-quality academic and social instruction are provided; and both adult–child relationships and child–child relationships are fostered and developed (Kauffman, Bantz, & McCullough, 2002; Rorie et al., 2011). Other features include close teacher monitoring of student performance, frequent feedback, and reinforcement based on students' academic and social behaviors. Students learn how to express themselves, how to address individual and group problems, and how to deal effectively with very strong feelings and emotions. Often, point systems or token economies are used, although some concerns have been raised about these systems. These systems provide students with a specific number of points or tokens when they maintain certain behaviors or achieve certain goals. The points can be exchanged for various rewards, such as treats, school supplies, or activities that students enjoy. Furthermore, all members of special classes are well informed about behavioral and academic expectations

Figure 8.6 Phases of the Wraparound Process

**Phase I: Engagement and Team Preparation**
**Facilitator . . .**

- Meets with family and key team members to gather their perspectives.
- Guides family to generate a strengths list (multiple settings and perspectives) and a list of needs.
- Generates a team member list, which includes natural supports, with the family.
- Documents and shares baseline data about student's strengths/needs.

**Phase II: Initial Plan Development**
**Team . . .**

- Begins regular meeting schedule.
- Documents and reviews strengths and needs data (home/school/community).
- Chooses a few needs for team to focus action planning, with special priority assigned to family concerns.
- Develops an intervention plan (including function-based behavior supports as needed) to respond to home, school, and community strengths/needs.
- Assesses community supports/resources available to meet needs identified by family.

**Phase III: Plan Implementation and Refinement**
**Team . . .**

- Documents accomplishments of student and team at each meeting.
- Meets frequently, checking follow-through and assessing progress of different interventions.
- Receives regular documentation including data and plan updates.
- Facilitates ongoing communication among those providing interventions in home, school, and community.

**Phase IV: Transition Team . . .**

- Discusses transitioning out of wraparound.
- Considers the concerns of all team members in transition planning.
- Communicates methods for future access to services to all team members.
- Negotiates methods of introducing student and family to future teachers or providers.

SOURCE: Adapted from Eber, L., Breen, K., Rose, J., Unizycki, R. M., & London, T. H. (2008, July/August). "Wraparound as a Tertiary Level Intervention for Students with Emotional/Behavioral Needs." *Teaching Exceptional Children*, 40(6), p. 19. Copyright © 2008 Council for Exceptional Children (CEC).

(see Figure 8.7). One of the greatest challenges in teaching and treating students with EBD is treatment intensity and generalization—having them use their newly learned knowledge and social skills outside their "treatment" environments or special class settings—at home, in the community, and in the workplace (Gresham, Van, & Cook, 2006; Maag, 2006).

In addition to behaviorally oriented interventions, students may also receive individual counseling or group and family therapy (Wicks-Nelson & Israel, 2006). Also, many children with EBD profit from carefully prescribed and monitored drug therapies and regimens—about 50 percent of the youth identified with behavior disorders take medications for their

Figure 8.7 Point Card for IEP Goals

Name: _____ Date: <u>September 25</u>

1. My IEP goal today is: Raising my hand to get teacher help, to answer questions, or to participate in class discussions:

| Goal "Positives" | Goal " Negative" | | Percent "Positives" |
|---|---|---|---|
| /// | // | | 8/10 = 80% |

2. Returned Daily Home Note:    Yes <u>X</u>    No ___    Points Earned on Daily Home Note <u>10</u>

3. Bus Report: Poor <u>X</u>    Good _____    Excellent _____    Points Earned on Bus Report <u>3</u>

© Cengage Learning

⌄ Professional Resource Download

8-6 INTERVENTIONS AND TREATMENTS FOR EMOTIONAL/BEHAVIORAL DISORDERS **199**

## Henry: Wraparound

"Henry," a student at Sunnyside Elementary School, had extremely poor attendance, failing grades, and poor homework completion. He had experienced trouble with the law in the community, which resulted in a court-assigned probation officer and a mandated Department of Children and Family Services (DCFS) counselor.

### First Phase

During the first phase of wraparound, engagement and team preparation, Henry's family was introduced to the wraparound program. When Henry's mother shared a pamphlet she had been given for a short-term residential treatment center, the school social worker started the conversation by offering Henry's mother the opportunity to develop a comprehensive support plan so Henry could experience success in his own home, school, and community settings.

### Second Phase

In the second phase of wraparound, initial plan development, the team identified and documented Henry's strengths and needs. Henry's strengths included a good relationship with his teacher, responsiveness to positive attention from adults he liked, leadership among his peers, and effective self-advocacy. The school social worker helped the team identify two big needs for Henry: (1) "Henry needs to feel as if he fits in with the other kids at school," and (2) "Henry needs to feel successful at school." By focusing on needs rather than problems, Henry's team changed the tone of both meetings and interventions from reactive to proactive. Rather than using preexisting interventions or services that are more deficit-oriented, the team designed interventions to respond to Henry's unique strengths and needs.

Because Henry had a positive relationship with his teacher, he was included in the check-and-connect intervention being delivered to other students in the school, some of whom were not on wraparound plans. Henry's teacher would greet him each morning by saying, "Thank you for coming; I am so glad you are here today." Henry and his teacher would talk about the individual behavior goals listed on his daily point card. This intervention was selected because Henry's expected behavior could be "corrected" in advance and positive behavior encouraged in other settings, with extra support or reminders as needed.

Henry's plan included strategies that he selected along with his family and teachers and that were based on his expressed strengths and needs. For example, he joined the school safety patrol, with the goal of acting as a positive role model; this helped him monitor and improve his own behavior in the hallways.

### Third Phase

In the third phase of wraparound, plan implementation and refinement, the team focused on (1) regularly using data for decision making; (2) checking with the family, student, and teacher(s) to ensure that the plan was working; (3) adjusting the wraparound plan based on feedback from team members; and (4) addressing additional needs that may have been identified but were not priorities at the onset of the wraparound process....

Classroom interventions included homework adjustments, fewer spelling words, checking that Henry understood directions and extra reading support in class from the Title I teacher. In addition, the team designed unique progress criteria for Henry so he could be eligible for the school-wide Student of the Month recognition. His classroom duties included putting stickers on the homework chart for everyone in class. The school also referred Henry and his family to a local interagency network so they could receive financial support to participate in community recreation activities.

### Fourth Phase

During the fourth phase, transition, Henry's accomplishments will continue to be reviewed and celebrated. The team will develop a transition plan to ensure success as it adjusts to less frequent team meetings and/or moves to natural supports without the ongoing wraparound team. As Henry's school performance improved, the team had to plan for increasing the use of natural supports and for ensuring successes during and after summer breaks.

*Questions for Reflection*

1. What are the advantages of helping Henry succeed in his own home setting and neighborhood rather than treating him in a residential treatment center?

2. How do we help students like Henry feel successful at school when they may not naturally have some of the necessary social skills for making and sustaining friendships?

3. Given what you know about the wraparound process, what are the natural supports in a child's life? How can they be strengthened?

SOURCE: Adapted From Eber, L., Breen, K., Rose, J., Unizycki, R. M., & London, T. H. (2008). "Wraparound: A Tertiary Level Intervention for Students with Emotional/Behavioral Needs. *Teaching Exceptional Children*, 40(6), 18–21.

conditions (Konopasek & Forness, 2004; Shoenfeld & Konopasek, 2007). These medications help students who struggle with depression, hyperactivity, impaired attention, and mood variations. These medications may be prescribed by a psychiatrist, pediatrician, or primary care physician.

## 8-6d Adolescent Education and Transition to Adulthood

Individually and collectively, adolescents with EBD pose significant challenges for parents, teachers, and other care providers. These problems include violent exchanges with parents and others, delinquency, school refusal, bullying, fighting, withdrawal, substance abuse, and other difficult behaviors. In the past, interventions and programs for adolescents with EBD, like those created for elementary children, were often punitive, controlling, and negative.

**Systems of Care** Fortunately, perspectives and practices are changing. Professionals in education, medicine, social work, and mental health are developing systems of care. Again, these systems of care are characterized by family-friendly, multidisciplinary collaborations (Kendziora et al., 2001; Woodruff et al., 1999). Ideally, the care is community-based, family-driven, individualized, based on strengths rather than weaknesses, sensitive to diversity, and team-based. In these systems, the knowledge and views of parents and family members are taken very seriously. Parents and key providers help design, shape, and assess interventions and transition programs (Sitlington & Neubert, 2004). If a family needs parent training, family therapy, and employment assistance, the agencies and school work together to provide these services. If the youth needs services beyond those typically delivered in a school, they are secured.

Another approach that is beginning to gather momentum is individualized care (IC). IC is also linked to the wraparound approach (WRAP). As you recall, WRAP focuses on improving the outcomes for children and adolescents with EBD through coordinated, flexible approaches to integrated, family-centered care. Rather than being provided to students in school settings or at a mental health agency exclusively, these services are delivered to children and adolescents, their parents, and families where they are needed—frequently in their homes. Henry's case provides powerful examples of IC and WRAP in action (see Reflect on This, "Henry: Wraparound").

Increasingly, mental health professionals are readying young people with EBD for additional education, employment, and fuller participation in our neighborhoods and communities (Benitez, Lattimore, & Wehmeyer, 2005). With recent advances in psychotropic medications and other innovative interventions, entry into meaningful schooling and employment for youth with behavior disorders is now a greater reality. Features associated with successful programs include program locations that are unique and separate from adult program sites, a focus on strengths and assets of each respective youth, access to a range of transitional housing options, and individually tailored, youth-friendly interventions (Woolsey & Katz-Leavey, 2008).

**Standard 2**
Learning Environments

**Standard 4**
Assessment

**Standard 5**
Instructional Planning and Strategies

**Standard 7**
Collaboration

**Standard 7**
Collaboration

**Individualized care (IC)**
Improving the outcomes for children and adolescents with EBD through coordinated, flexible approaches to integrated, family-centered care.

*(Muscombe, B 2014)*

---

**ASSISTIVE TECHNOLOGY**

### SymTrend ADL Activities for Daily Living

SymTrend ADL is a mobile app that tracks behavior data for activities of daily living, such as eating, dressing, toileting, and more. The program also lets parents and caregivers track health, medication, and therapy data. The mobile data syncs to a website that provides suggested strategies based on the child's progress and produces charts and reports that let the user determine the success of strategies and other interventions. The

EasyChild Software, 2009. Encourage Software

website is an affordable subscription program that allows users to share reports with teachers, therapists, and other interveners. Users also have access to a blog to stay current with information and suggestions (SymTrend ADL, 2012).

## Looking Toward a Bright Future

As we anticipate the future for children and youth with EBD and their families, there is room for optimism. This optimism is centered in having professionals and others actively apply evidence-based practices—practices that are supported by rigorous research. Also, the movement to family-sensitive and family-responsive interventions is a step in the right direction. Listening to families, focusing on their assets and strengths, and giving families the support they need to nurture and connect with their children in healthy and productive ways are causes for hope and positive anticipation.

Systems of care—often delivered in the form of wraparound programs—are being embraced by communities, schools, and other mental health agencies. These systems give rise to new ways of thinking about and responding to children and youth with EBD. Rather than a deficit orientation, these programs focus on the strengths, possibilities, and assets of children and youth, their families, and their communities. Also, these systems present possibilities for being appropriately sensitive to cultural and ethnic concerns of families and communities.

Progressively, we are seeing the development of early intervention programs for young children who are at risk for EBD. Although relatively few in number, these programs focus on providing nurturing and supportive environments for young children, giving parents the skills and dispositions needed for developing feelings of competence, self-determination, and connectedness in their children, and fostering a sense of community and increased personal capacity in all participants.

More and more schools are embracing and applying school-wide, positive behavioral support systems for all children. These systems give rise to thriving school communities where the primary goals are solid learning and growth for every child. Such schools generate the protective buffers children need to sustain themselves and grow into healthy citizens and adults. These schools spawn safe and caring environments, positive relationships with peers, and strong bonds with caring teachers and adults.

Finally, well-respected leaders on every level are challenging and expecting all parents to play more significant roles in nurturing and caring for their children—turning off their televisions, listening to their children read, helping children with homework, and engaging in relationship-forming activities. There are many challenges in serving children and youth with emotional and behavioral disorders, but there is cause for hope and optimism on many fronts.

## Chapter Review

### 8-1 Describe how the lives of people with emotional and behavioral disorders (EBD) have changed since the advent of IDEA.

- Increasingly, children and youth at risk for EBD are receiving preventative treatment and support for developing appropriate social and academic behaviors.

- Greater efforts are directed at children and youth who have been diagnosed with EBD so their behaviors and related conditions do not worsen or become more chronic over time.

- Contemporary interventions improve outcomes for children and youth through pre-referral interventions, school-wide efforts to promote positive behaviors in all children and youth, evidence-based approaches provided by collaborative teams of skilled professionals, increased access to inclusive settings

(regular education classrooms and related experiences), a focus on preventing serious, violent, or destructive behaviors, and provision of community-based and family-sensitive systems.

### 8-2 Explain the various definitions and classifications of EBD.

- The IDEA definition of EBD describes a chronic condition that causes an inability to learn and/or to build or maintain normal relationships. It may also include inappropriate types of behavior, depression, or tendencies to develop physical symptoms or fears.

- An alternate definition proposed but not adopted by IDEA provides more precision in identification, considers cultural and ethnic norms, and admits co-occurrence with other disabilities.

- Classification systems provide common descriptions and terminology among professionals, parents, and affected individuals. The two common classification systems are derived from statistics about externalizing and internalizing behaviors and from clinical practice.

### 8-3  Describe the characteristics and prevalence of children and youth with EBD.

- Children and youth with EBD tend to have average or below-average intellectual capacity, reflected in challenges mastering academic, social, and adaptive skills.

- Social and adaptive skill challenges are manifested in poor relationships, inappropriate classroom behaviors, bullying perpetration and victimization, social fears, depression and other mood disorders, conduct disorders, and/or delinquency.

- Students with EBD often experience significant academic deficits and finish high school at much lower rates than the general population and students with other disabilities. Adults with EBD have low rates of employment and higher rates of incarceration.

- A reasonable estimate of 3 to 6 percent of children and youth have EBD, but most remain unidentified.

### 8-4  List the causes and risk factors associated with EBD.

- Behavior disorders are likely caused by complex interactions among a variety of personal, familial, socioeconomic, and biological factors. Researchers have identified connections to parenting styles; family dysfunction including discord, abuse, and neglect; the stresses of poverty; and inherited tendencies.

### 8-5  Describe the assessment procedures used to identify EBD in children and youth.

- Assessment procedures are conducted by multiple professionals using multiple methods.

- Systematic screening for behavior disorders (SSBD) proceeds through three stages: (1) nomination of potential cases by classroom teachers, (2) ranking nominated students by severity and frequency of behaviors, and (3) systematic observations across school environments.

- Identified children are then assessed with more specific and intensive measures.

### 8-6  Describe the different interventions for children and youth with EBD from early childhood through adulthood.

- Collaborative teams design and implement pre-referral interventions to address behavior needs in the least restrictive environment, as with response to intervention (RtI) and positive behavior support (PBS) systems.

- If students are served in special education, then the multidisciplinary team conducts functional behavior assessments to learn the antecedents and consequences of the behavior. Planned interventions then manipulate these aspects to shape more appropriate behaviors.

- Systems of care strive to involve all important individuals and sources of support in an individual's life to address behavior concerns.

- As in all disability intervention, the earlier, the better. Prevention is better and easier than addressing ingrained behaviors in later years. Early childhood identification and intervention with children and their families is both timely and effective. ●

- Programs for children and youth focus on replacing maladaptive behavior with appropriate and productive skills and dispositions. This may be accomplished through individual counseling, group therapy, and family therapy. Some individuals respond well to medications for controlling their conditions.

## Council for Exceptional Children (CEC) Standards to Accompany Chapter 8

If you are thinking about a career in special education, you should know that many states use national standards developed by the Council for Exceptional Children (CEC) to assess a teacher candidate's knowledge and skills for working with students with disabilities. See a complete listing of the seven CEC Content Standards on the inside cover of this text.

1 Learner Development and Individual Learner Differences
2 Learning Environments
4 Assessment
5 Instructional Planning and Strategies
7 Collaboration

## Mastery Activities and Assignments

To master the content within this chapter, complete the following activities and assignments:

1. Complete a written test of the chapter's content. If your instructor requires a written test of your content knowledge for this chapter, keep a copy for your portfolio.
2. Review the Case Study on Embracing Diversity, "Leon," and respond in writing to the Application Questions.

Keep a copy of the Case Study and your written response for your portfolio.

3. Participate in a community service learning activity. Community service is a valuable way to enhance your learning experience. Develop a reflective journal of the service learning experience for your portfolio.

## CHAPTER 9

# Intellectual and Developmental Disabilities

©karelnoppe/Shutterstock.com

## Learning Objectives

*After you complete this chapter, you will be able to:*

**9-1** Describe how the lives of people with intellectual and developmental disabilities have changed since the advent of IDEA.

**9-2** Explain the various definitions and classifications of intellectual disabilities.

**9-3** Describe the characteristics and prevalence of children and youth with intellectual disabilities.

**9-4** List the causes and risk factors associated with intellectual disabilities.

**9-5** Describe the assessment procedures used to identify intellectual disabilities in children and youth.

**9-6** Describe the different interventions for children and youth with intellectual disabilities from early childhood through adulthood.

I'm Lauren Potter. I'm just a 24-year-old girl who is working hard to live my dreams and make my difference in the world.

In order to do that, I've had to face challenges. Sometimes even seemingly simple things, like walking and talking, have been a challenge. But I never let that stop me. I have *always* continued to dream big and to fight hard to pursue those dreams.

When I was young, my dream was to be an actress. Sure people told me I'd never be able to do it, but I replied, "Just watch me!" Now they are watching me, but this time on the big screen. I filmed my first movie when I was 16 years old, and I am currently an actress on Fox's hit TV show *Glee* that just celebrated its 100th episode.

As a girl who has accomplished things that many didn't think were possible, I know that people can be wrong when they judge someone else just because they are different. We are *all* different. And that isn't bad, it's just, well, different!

Because of *Glee* I have been given a chance to pursue another dream of mine—to make the world a more

©Helga Esteb/Shutterstock.com

welcoming place for people who are different—especially for people like me who have always been told "you can't" instead of "you can." I want to live in a world where everyone can live, go to school and go to work without having to be afraid. Afraid of being judged, afraid of being bullied or cyberbullied. Afraid of new things. Afraid of failure. Afraid of dreaming. In fact, I want to live in a world where people are actually celebrated for their differences, just as I celebrate mine!

Do you want to live in that world? Do you want to join me in "being the change"?

I believe we can be the generation that makes it happen! That's why I'm taking a stand for acceptance and inclusion. And I'm hoping that everyone will join me.

Special Olympics is an organization that celebrates differences and gives people of all abilities the chance to be a champion and a star. At the Special Olympics World Games Los Angeles 2015, the whole world will have a chance to show that they too stand up for acceptance and inclusion of all people by celebrating the joy, courage, and determination of the 7,000 athletes who will participate. I am so proud and honored to be a part of this wonderful mission as a World Games Goodwill Ambassador. I will continue to cheer on the athletes and stand with them as we tell those who still may say or think we can't do it, "Just watch me!"

SOURCE: Potter, Lauren. (2104, June 2). "I'm Talking a Stand to Make My Difference in the World." Huffington Post. *The Blog*. Retrieved February 7, 2015, from http://www.huffingtonpost.com/lauren-potter/im-taking-a-stand-to-make_b_5431373.html

## 9-1   A Changing Era in the Lives of People with Intellectual Disabilities

This chapter is about people whose ability to understand the world and develop meaning from social networks may differ significantly from what is considered "typical." Their growth and development depend on the educational, social, and medical supports made available throughout life. Lauren from our opening Snapshot is a young woman with an intellectual disability who has drive, talent, and a wonderful support network of family, friends, and teachers. As she moves through her adult years, she is achieving the dream of being an actress, but still longs for being viewed first and foremost as "Lauren," a typical person who just happens to have Down syndrome.

Lauren is also a person with an intellectual disability, but she is not necessarily representative of the wide range of ability that characterizes people who have this condition. For example, this wide range of ability may include 6-year-old Juliana, described as having a mild intellectual disability who may be no more than one or two years behind the normal development of academic and social skills. Prior to the passage of IDEA, many children with intellectual disabilities were not identified until they entered elementary

**Intellectual disability**
Limited ability to reason, plan, solve problems, think abstractly, comprehend complex ideas, learn quickly, and learn from experience.

school at age 5 or 6, because they may not have exhibited physical or learning delays that are readily identifiable during the early childhood years. As these children enter school, developmental delays become more apparent. During early primary grades, it is common for the cognitive and social differences of children with intellectual disabilities to be attributed to immaturity. However, with the passage of IDEA, educators now recognize the need for specialized services to support a child's development in the natural settings of school, neighborhood, and home.

People with moderate to severe intellectual disabilities have challenges that often transcend the classroom. Some have significant, multiple disabling conditions, including sensory, physical, and emotional problems. People with moderate intellectual disabilities are able to learn and use adaptive skills that allow independence, with varying levels of support. These skills include the abilities to dress and feed themselves, to meet their own personal care and health needs, and to develop safety skills that enable them to be more independent in the community. These individuals often have the ability to communicate their needs and desires. Most people develop spoken language skills; others may rely on manual forms of communication like sign language or communication boards. Their social interaction skills may be limited, which makes it a challenge for them to interact spontaneously with others.

People with profound intellectual disabilities often depend on others to maintain even their most basic life functions, including eating, hygiene, communicating, and dressing. This certainly does not mean that education and treatment beyond routine care and maintenance are not beneficial. The extent of profound disabilities is one reason why this group of children was excluded from public schools prior to passage of IDEA. Exclusion was often justified on the basis that schools did not have the resources, facilities, or trained professionals to deal with the needs of these students.

## 9-2 Definitions and Classification of Intellectual Disabilities

People with intellectual disabilities have been labeled with pejorative terms for centuries, including "feebleminded," "idiot," "imbecile," and "moron." More recently, they have been stereotyped with one of the most derogatory terms in the English language—*retard*. As Lauren Potter stated in an interview with Buxton (2015):

> The R-word is a hateful word. We need to stop, to end the R-word in every place. I don't know why people are so mean. All I want from you is to stop saying the R-word.... That's what I am trying to let my fans know, that's a really bad word. You can't say anything bad about other people—it will hurt other people.

The terms *mental retardation* and *mentally retarded* were officially stripped from United States federal health, education, and labor policy in 2010, when Rosa's Law (PL 111-256) was passed. "Intellectual disability" or "individuals with an intellectual disability" are now used to replace those outdated terms. Although the policy has changed, the pejorative use of the r-word is too frequently used today.

### 9-2a Definition

The American Association on Intellectual and Developmental Disabilities (AAIDD) states that intellectual disability is characterized by significant limitations in both intellectual functioning and in adaptive behavior, and must originate before the age of 18 (AAIDD, 2013).

The AAIDD definition has evolved through years of effort to more clearly reflect the ever-changing understanding of intellectual disabilities. In recent years, the concept of adaptive behavior has played an increasingly important role in defining and classifying people with intellectual disabilities.

**Intellectual Functioning** Intellectual functioning, often referred to as intelligence, includes an individual's ability to reason, plan, solve problems, think abstractly, comprehend complex ideas, and learn from experience (AAIDD, 2013). These abilities are assessed

**CEC**

**Standard 6**
Professional Learning and Ethical Practice

**American Association on Intellectual and Developmental Disabilities (AAIDD)**
Professionals across multiple disciplines engaged in the advocacy for, study, treatment, and education of intellectual disabilities.

by a standardized intelligence test in which a person's score is compared with the average of other people who have taken the same test (referred to as a *normative sample*). The statistical average for an intelligence test is generally set at 100. We state this by saying that the person has an intelligence quotient (IQ) of 100. Psychologists use a mathematical concept called the **standard deviation** to determine the extent to which any given individual's score deviates from this average of 100. An individual who scores more than two standard deviations below 100 on an intelligence test meets AAIDD's definition of significant limitations in intellectual functioning. This means that people with IQs of approximately 70 to 75 and lower would be considered as having intellectual disabilities.

**Adaptive Behavior** AAIDD defines **adaptive behavior** as a collection of conceptual, social, and practical skills that have been learned by people to function in their everyday lives. (Figure 9.1 provides several examples of adaptive behavior.) If a person has limitations in these adaptive skills, he or she may need some additional assistance or supports to participate more fully in both family and community life.

As is true with intelligence, adaptive skills also may be measured by standardized tests. These tests, most often referred to as *adaptive behavior scales*, generally use structured interviews or direct observations to obtain information. Adaptive behavior scales measure the individual's ability to take care of personal needs (such as hygiene) and to relate appropriately to others in social situations. Adaptive skills may also be assessed through informal appraisal, such as observations by family members or professionals who are familiar with the individual, or through anecdotal records.

**Age of Onset** The AAIDD definition specifies that the intellectual disabilities must originate before a person is 18 years old. The reason for choosing age 18 as a cutoff point is that intellectual disabilities belong to a family of conditions referred to as developmental disabilities. **Developmental disabilities** are mental and/or physical impairments that are diagnosed at birth or during the childhood and adolescent years. A developmental disability results in substantial functional limitations in at least three areas of major life activity, such as self-care, language, learning, mobility, self-direction, capacity for independent living, and economic self-sufficiency.

AAIDD emphasizes the importance of a positive environment for fostering growth, development, and individual well-being. Thus, a person's participation and interaction within the environment are indicators of adaptive functioning. The more an individual engages in activities in their communities, such as work, leisure, and community living, the more likely that an "adaptive fit" will develop between the person and his or her environment.

**Standard deviation**
A statistical measure of the amount that an individual score deviates from the average.

**Adaptive behavior**
Conceptual, social, and practical skills that people have learned to function in their everyday lives.

**Developmental disabilities**
Mental and/or physical impairments that limit substantial functioning in at least three areas of major life activity.

**Standard 1**
Learner Development and Individual Learning Differences

---

**Conceptual**

Language (receptive and expressive)

Reading and writing

Money concepts

Self-direction

**Social**

Interpersonal skills

Responsibility

Self-esteem

Gullibility

Naiveté

Follows rules

Obeys laws

Avoids victimization

**Practical**

Activities of daily living
- Eating
- Transfer/mobility
- Toileting
- Dressing
Occupational skills
Maintains safe environments

Instrumental activities of daily living
- Meal preparation
- Housekeeping
- Transportation
- Taking medication
- Money management
- Telephone use

*Figure 9.1 Examples of Conceptual, Social, and Practical Adaptive Skills*

The physical and mental health of an individual influences his or her overall intellectual and adaptive functioning. AAIDD indicates that the functioning level for people with intellectual disabilities is significantly affected (facilitated or inhibited) by the effects of physical and mental health. Some individuals [with intellectual disabilities] enjoy good health with no significant activity limitations; others, however, have a variety of health limitations, such as seizure disorder or cerebral palsy, that could create compounding conditions that lead to restricted activities and social participation. Additionally, people with intellectual disabilities have a 50 percent higher rate of psychiatric disorders than the general population (Werner & Stawski, 2012). When a person has a dual diagnosis, a co-occurrence of intellectual disability and a psychiatric disorder, the compounded effects of the two conditions can create a greater need for support.

The level of independence a person with an intellectual disability has will be affected by the environmental context of their lives. *Environmental context* is the term for the inter-related conditions in which people live their lives. Context is based on an environmental perspective with three different levels: (1) the immediate social setting that includes the person and her or his family, (2) the broader neighborhood, community, or organizations that provide services and supports (such as public education), and (3) the overarching patterns of culture and society. The various levels are important to people with intellectual disabilities because they provide differing opportunities and can foster well-being.

**Putting the Definition into Practice**   There are five criteria that professionals should apply as they put the definition into practice:

1. Limitations in a person's present functioning must be considered within the context of community environments typical of the individual's age, peers, and culture.

2. Valid assessment considers cultural and linguistic diversity as well as differences in communication, sensory, motor, and behavioral factors.

3. Within an individual, limitations often coexist with strengths.

4. An important purpose of describing limitations is to develop a profile of needed supports.

5. With appropriate personalized supports over a sustained period, the life functioning of the person with [intellectual disabilities] generally will improve. (AAIDD, 2013)

## 9-2b   Classification

To more clearly understand the diversity of people with intellectual disabilities, several classification systems have been developed. Each classification method reflects an attempt by a particular discipline (such as medicine or education) to better understand and respond to the needs of individuals with intellectual disabilities. We will discuss four of these methods.

**Severity of the Condition**   The extent to which a person's intellectual capabilities and adaptive skills differ from what is considered "normal" can be described by using terms such as *mild*, *moderate*, *severe*, or *profound*. *Mild* describes the highest level of performance; *profound* describes the lowest level. Distinctions between severity levels associated with intellectual disabilities are determined by a clinician's impression of the severity of adaptive functioning. Severity is assessed across three domains. These are conceptual, social, and practical life skills (American Psychiatric Association, 2013).

**Medical Descriptors**   Intellectual disabilities may be classified on the basis of the biological origin of the condition. A classification system that uses the cause of the condition to differentiate people with intellectual disabilities is often referred to as a *medical classification* system because it emerged primarily from the field of medicine. Common medical descriptors include fetal alcohol syndrome, chromosomal abnormalities (e.g., Down syndrome), metabolic disorders (e.g., phenylketonuria, thyroid dysfunction), and infections (e.g., syphilis, rubella). These medical conditions will be discussed more thoroughly in the section on causation.

## Classification Based on Needed Support

Today, AAIDD uses a classification system based on the type and extent of the support that the individual requires to function in the natural settings of home and community. Four levels of support are recommended:

- *Intermittent*. Supports are provided on an "as-needed basis." These supports may be (1) episodic—that is, the person does not always need assistance; or (2) short-term, occurring during lifespan transitions (e.g., job loss or acute medical crisis). Intermittent supports may be of high or low intensity.

*Photo 9.1* School and community programs are moving away from pejorative classification categories (such as "trainable") to descriptions of the individual based on type and extent of support needed to function in natural settings.

- *Limited*. Supports are characterized by consistency; the time required may be limited, but the need is not intermittent. Fewer staff may be required, and costs may be lower than those associated with more intensive levels of support (examples include time-limited employment training and supports during transition from school to adulthood).

- *Extensive*. Supports are characterized by regular involvement (e.g., daily) in at least some environments, such as work or home; supports are not time-limited (e.g., long-term job and home-living support will be necessary).

- *Pervasive*. Supports must be constant and of high intensity. They have to be provided across multiple environments and may be life-sustaining in nature. Pervasive supports typically involve more staff and are more intrusive than extensive or time-limited supports.

The AAIDD's emphasis on classifying people with intellectual disabilities on the basis of needed support is an important departure from the more restrictive perspectives of the traditional approaches. Supports may be described not only in terms of the level of assistance needed, but also by type—that is, as formal or natural support systems. Formal supports may be funded through government programs, such as income maintenance, health care, education, housing, or employment. Another type of formal support is the advocacy organization (e.g., **The ARC of the United States**) that lobbies on behalf of people with intellectual disabilities for improved and expanded services, as well as for providing family members a place to interact and support one another. **Natural supports** differ from formal supports in that they are provided not by agencies or organizations, but by the nuclear and extended family members, friends, or neighbors. Natural supports are often more effective than formal supports in helping people with intellectual disabilities access and participate in a community setting. Research suggests that adults with intellectual disabilities who are successfully employed following school find more jobs through their natural support network of friends and family than through formal support systems (Crockett & Hardman, 2009).

# 9-3 Characteristics and Prevalence of Intellectual Disabilities

We now examine the myriad characteristics commonly found in people with intellectual disabilities that can affect their academic learning, as well as their ability to adapt to home, school, and community environments.

## 9-3a Characteristics Common to Children and Youth with Intellectual Disabilities

People who have an intellectual disability are each unique. They have strengths and challenges just like their typically developing peers. The following is a list of characteristics commonly occurring with intellectual disability, but will vary in severity with each person.

**The ARC of the United States**
A national organization that works to enhance the quality of life for people with intellectual disabilities.

**Natural supports**
Supports for people with disabilities that are provided by family, friends, and peers.

**Learning and Memory** Intelligence is the ability to acquire, remember, and use knowledge. A primary characteristic of intellectual disabilities is diminished intellectual ability that translates into a difference in the rate and efficiency with which the person acquires, remembers, and uses new knowledge, compared to the general population.

The learning and memory capabilities of people with intellectual disabilities are significantly below average in comparison to peers without disabilities. Children with intellectual disabilities, as a group, are less able to grasp abstract, as opposed to concrete, concepts. Accordingly, they benefit from instruction that is meaningful and useful, and they learn more from contact with real objects than they do from representations or symbols.

Intelligence is also associated with learning how to learn, often referred to as metacognition, and with the ability to apply what is learned to new experiences, known as generalization. Children and adults with intellectual disabilities learn at a slower pace than peers without disabilities, and they have difficulty relating information to new situations (Beirne-Smith, Patton, & Hill, 2010; Hua, Morgan, Kaldenbers, & Goo, 2012). Generalization happens "when a child applies previously learned content or skills to a situation in which the information has not been taught" (Drew & Hardman, 2007; Falcomata, Wacker, Ringdahl, Vinquist, & Dutt, 2013). The greater the severity of intellectual deficit, the greater the difficulties with memory. Memory problems in children with intellectual disabilities have been attributed to several factors. People with intellectual disabilities have trouble focusing on relevant stimuli in learning and in real-life situations, sometimes attending to the wrong things (Kittler, Krinsky-McHale, & Devenny, 2004; Westling & Fox, 2009).

**Self-Regulation** People with intellectual disabilities do not appear to develop efficient learning strategies, such as the ability to rehearse a task (to practice a new concept, either out loud or to themselves, over and over). The ability to rehearse a task is related to a broad concept known as **self-regulation** (Beirne-Smith, Patton, & Hill, 2009). Whereas most people will rehearse to try to remember, individuals with intellectual disabilities do not appear to be able to apply this skill.

Some researchers have begun to focus on **information-processing theories** to better understand learning differences in people with intellectual disabilities. Information-processing theorists study how a person processes information from sensory stimuli to motoric output (Sternberg, 2008). In information-processing theory, the learning differences in people with intellectual disabilities are seen as the underdevelopment of metacognitive processes. Metacognitive processes help the person plan how to solve a problem. First, the person decides which strategy he or she thinks will solve a problem. Then the strategy is implemented. During implementation, the person monitors whether the strategy is working and makes any adaptations necessary. Finally, the results of the strategy are evaluated in terms of whether the problem has been solved and how the strategy could be used in other situations (Sternberg, 2008). Even though children with intellectual disabilities may have difficulty applying the best strategy when confronted with new learning situations, they can learn ways to do so.

**Generalization**
The process of applying previously learned information to new settings or situations.

**Self-regulation**
The ability to regulate one's own behavior.

**Information-processing theories**
Theories on how a person processes information from sensory stimuli to motoric output.

## E-Buddies

Best Buddies International, founded by Anthony K. Shriver (son of Sargent and Eunice Kennedy Shriver), offers a social media program called e-Buddies, which provides opportunities for Internet friendships among people with intellectual and developmental disabilities and people who do not have a disability. The e-Buddies program has proven to be a fun and safe way for people with intellectual disabilities to make new friends. E-mail matches are made on the basis of similar age, gender, geography, and shared interests. The e-Buddies program provides individuals with an intellectual disability an opportunity to develop new friendships through social media while also acquiring computer skills. For people without disabilities, e-Buddies is a unique opportunity to change a life and make a friend. (For more information, visit the e-Buddies website.)

Social stories are one method that is used to teach self-regulation to individuals who have intellectual disabilities. A social story is a personalized narrative that embeds social cues and actions that are appropriate in particular social situations (Flores et al., 2014).

**Adaptive Skills** The abilities to adapt to the demands of the environment, relate to others, and take care of personal needs are all important aspects of an independent lifestyle. In the school setting, adaptive behavior is defined as the ability to apply skills learned in a classroom to daily activities in natural settings.

The adaptive skills of people with intellectual disabilities often lag behind those of their peers without disabilities. A child with intellectual disabilities may have difficulty in both learning and applying skills for a number of reasons, including a higher level of distractibility, inattentiveness, failure to read social cues, and impulsive behavior. Thus, these children will need to be taught appropriate reasoning, judgment, and social skills that lead to more positive social relationships and personal competence. Adaptive skill differences for people with intellectual disabilities may also be associated with a lower self-image and a greater expectancy for failure in both academic and social situations.

**Academic Achievement** Research on the academic achievement of children with mild to moderate intellectual disabilities has suggested that they will experience significant delays in the areas of literacy and mathematics. Reading comprehension is usually considered the weakest area of learning. In general, students with mild intellectual disabilities are better at decoding words than comprehending their meaning (Drew & Hardman, 2007), and they tend to read below their own developmental level (Katims, 2000; Thurlow et al., 2012).

*Photo 9.2* The academic performance of children with intellectual disabilities varies greatly, depending on the level of intellectual ability and adaptive skills. Many children with mild intellectual disabilities may learn to read, though at a slower rate, whereas those with moderate intellectual disabilities benefit from a functional academic program.

Children with intellectual disabilities also perform poorly on mathematical computations, although their performance may be closer to what is typical for their developmental level. These children may be able to learn basic computations but may be unable to apply concepts appropriately in a problem-solving situation (Beirne-Smith, Patton, & Hill, 2010; Thurlow et al., 2012).

A growing body of research has indicated that children with moderate or severe intellectual disabilities can be taught academics as a means to gain information, participate in social settings, increase their orientation and mobility, and make choices (Browder, Ahlgrim-Delzell, Courtade-Little, & Snell, 2011; Browder, Jimenez, & Trela, 2012; Browder & Spooner, 2011). Reading helps students develop a useful vocabulary that will facilitate their inclusion in school and community settings (Browder et al., 2011). People with moderate to severe intellectual disabilities who struggle with phonetic reading can often learn to memorize whole words. Sight word reading often begins with learning their names and those of significant others in their lives, as well as common survival words, including *help*, *exit*, *danger*, and *stop*. Math assists students in learning such skills as how to tell time, how to add and subtract small sums to manage finances (such as balancing a checkbook), and how to appropriately exchange money or use debit cards for products in community settings (e.g., grocery stores, movie theaters, and vending machines).

**Speech and Language** One of the most serious and obvious characteristics of individuals with intellectual disabilities is delayed speech and language development. The most common speech difficulties involve articulation problems, voice problems, and stuttering. Language problems are generally associated with delays in language development rather than with a bizarre use of language (Beirne-Smith, Patton, & Hill, 2010; Moore & Montgomery, 2008). Kaiser (2000) emphasized that "the overriding goal of language intervention is to increase the functional communication of students" (p. 457).

**Articulation problems**
Speech problems such as omissions, substitutions, additions, and distortions of words.

**Voice problems**
Abnormal acoustical qualities in a person's speech.

**Stuttering**
A speech problem involving abnormal repetitions, prolongations, and hesitations as one speaks.

There is considerable variation in the language skills of people with intellectual disabilities. In general, the severity of the speech and language problems is positively correlated with the cause and severity of the intellectual disabilities: The milder the intellectual disabilities, the less pervasive the language difficulty (Moore & Montgomery, 2008). Speech and language difficulties may range from minor speech defects, such as articulation problems, to the complete absence of expressive language. Speech and language pathologists are able to minimize speech differences for most students with intellectual disabilities.

**Physical Development** The physical appearance of most children with intellectual disabilities does not differ from that of same-age children who are not disabled. However, a relationship exists between the severity of the intellectual disabilities and the extent of physical differences for the individual (Beirne-Smith, Patton, & Hill, 2010; Drew & Hardman, 2007). For people with severe intellectual disabilities, there is a significant probability of related physical challenges; genetic factors are likely to underlie both disabilities. Individuals

REFLECT ON THIS

## Eunice Kennedy Shriver: A Celebration of an Extraordinary Life Dedicated to People with Intellectual Disabilities

As founder and honorary chairperson of Special Olympics and executive vice president of the Joseph P. Kennedy, Jr. Foundation, Eunice Kennedy Shriver was a leader in the worldwide struggle to improve and enhance the lives of individuals with intellectual disabilities for more than five decades. Born in Brookline, Massachusetts, the fifth of nine children of Joseph P. and Rose Fitzgerald Kennedy and sister to President John F. Kennedy, she received a bachelor of arts degree in sociology from Stanford University....

In 1957, Eunice Shriver took over the direction of the Joseph P. Kennedy, Jr. Foundation. The foundation, established in 1946 as a memorial to Joseph P. Kennedy, Jr.—the family's eldest son, who was killed in World War II—has two major objectives: to seek the prevention of intellectual disabilities by identifying its causes, and to improve the means by which society deals with citizens who have intellectual disabilities. Under Eunice Shriver's leadership, the foundation has helped achieve many significant advances, including the establishment by President Kennedy of the President's Committee on Mental Retardation in 1961 (now called the President's Committee for People with Intellectual Disabilities); development

of the National Institute of Child Health and Human Development (NICHD) in 1962 (now the Eunice Kennedy Shriver NICHD); the establishment of a network of university-affiliated facilities and mental retardation [intellectual disabilities] research centers at major medical schools across the United States in 1967; the establishment of Special Olympics in 1968; the creation of major centers for the study of medical ethics at Harvard and Georgetown Universities in 1971; the founding of the "Community of Caring" for the reduction of intellectual disabilities among babies of teenagers in 1981...and the establishment of "Community of Caring" programs in 1,200 public and private schools (now the Eunice Kennedy Shriver National Center for Community of Caring at the University of Utah).

Recognized throughout the world for her efforts on behalf of people with intellectual disabilities, Shriver received many honors and awards, including the Presidential Medal of Freedom, the Legion of Honor Award, the Prix de la Couronne Francaise, the Mary Lasker Award, the Philip Murray-William Green Award (presented to Eunice and Sargent Shriver by the AFL-CIO), the American Association on Mental Deficiency (AAMD) Humanitarian Award, the Laetare Medal of

the University of Notre Dame, the Order of the Smile of Polish Children, the Franklin D. Roosevelt Four Freedoms Freedom from Want Award, the National Women's Hall of Fame, the Laureus Sports Award, the National Collegiate Athletics Association (NCAA) Theodore Roosevelt Award, and the International Olympic Committee Award....

In 1984, U.S. President Reagan awarded Eunice Shriver the Presidential Medal of Freedom, the nation's highest civilian award, for her work on behalf of people with intellectual disabilities, and in 2005, she was honored for her work with Special Olympics as one of the first recipients of a sidewalk medallion on The Extra Mile Points of Light Pathway in Washington, D.C. Eunice passed away on August 11, 2009 at the age of 88. To learn more about Eunice Kennedy Shriver, visit the Eunice Kennedy Shriver or the Special Olympics websites.

*Question for Reflection*

Eunice Kennedy Shriver is an example of how one very special person can make a profound difference. How have you made a difference in the lives of people with intellectual disabilities? Volunteering for Special Olympics, Best Buddies, or the Community of Caring schools where you live?

with mild intellectual disabilities, in contrast, may exhibit no physical differences because the intellectual disabilities may be associated with environmental, not genetic, factors.

The majority of children with severe and profound intellectual disabilities have multiple disabilities that often affect nearly every aspect of their intellectual and physical development (Westling & Fox, 2009). Increasing health problems for children with intellectual disabilities may be associated with genetic or environmental factors. For example, people with Down syndrome have a higher incidence of congenital heart defects and respiratory problems directly linked to their genetic condition. On the other hand, some children with intellectual disabilities experience health problems because of their living conditions. A significantly higher percentage of children with intellectual disabilities come from low socioeconomic backgrounds in comparison to peers without disabilities. Children who do not receive proper nutrition and who are exposed to inadequate sanitation have a greater susceptibility to infections (Drew & Hardman, 2007). Health services for families in these situations may be minimal or nonexistent, depending on whether they are able to access government medical support, so children with intellectual disabilities may become ill more often than those who do not have disabilities. Consequently, children with intellectual disabilities may miss more school or not get involved in healthy activities, such as sports and recreation.

In the area of health and physical fitness, one individual truly stands alone as recognizing the importance of engaging people with intellectual disabilities in fitness activities, particularly sports. This person was Eunice Kennedy Shriver, founder of the Special Olympics, and sister of President John F. Kennedy. More than any other notable figure in history, Eunice Shriver changed society's perceptions of what is possible for people with intellectual disabilities. For more information on the unparalleled accomplishments of Eunice Shriver, see the nearby Reflect on This feature, "Eunice Kennedy Shriver: A Celebration of an Extraordinary Life Dedicated to People with Intellectual Disabilities."

## 9-3b   Prevalence of Intellectual Disabilities

The prevalence of intellectual disabilities worldwide and across all ages is estimated at 1 percent of the total population (Maulik et al., 2011). For school-age children between ages 6 and 21, the most recent annual report from the U.S. Department of Education (2014) reported that approximately 414,000 students were labeled as having intellectual disabilities and were receiving services under IDEA. Approximately 7 percent of all students with disabilities between the ages of 6 and 21 are identified as having intellectual disabilities (see Figure 9.2).

The President's Committee for People with Intellectual Disabilities (2014) estimates that approximately 7 to 8 million Americans of all ages have intellectual disabilities. Intellectual disabilities affect about one in ten families in the United States. Note that we are able only to estimate prevalence, because no one has actually counted the number of people with intellectual disabilities.

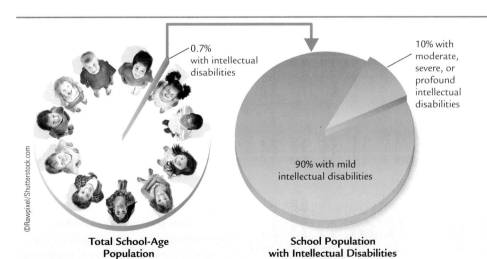

**Total School-Age Population**

0.7% with intellectual disabilities

**School Population with Intellectual Disabilities**

10% with moderate, severe, or profound intellectual disabilities

90% with mild intellectual disabilities

©Rawpixel/Shutterstock.com

**Figure 9.2** *Prevalence of Intellectual Disabilities*

SOURCE: U.S. Department of Education. (2011). To Assure the Free Appropriate Public Education of All Children with Disabilities. *Thirtieth Annual Report to Congress on the Implementation of the Individuals with Disabilities Education Act.* Washington, DC: U.S. Government Printing Office.

## 9-4 Causes of Intellectual Disabilities

Intellectual disabilities result from multiple causes, some known, many unknown (The ARC, 2011a). Possible known causes of intellectual disabilities include genetic conditions, problems during pregnancy, problems at birth, problems after birth, and poverty-related deprivation.

### 9-4a Genetic Conditions

Many genetic conditions are associated with intellectual disability. These conditions may result from genes inherited from parents, errors when genes combine, or from external factors, such as infections during pregnancy or overexposure to X-rays. Genetic disorders can be classified into three types: chromosomal, single gene, and multifactorial disorders. Chromosomal disorders are caused by a person having too many or two few chromosomes or by a change in the structure of the chromosome that disrupts its function.

One of the most widely recognized types of intellectual disabilities, Down syndrome, results from chromosomal abnormality. There are more than 400,000 people living in the United States with Down syndrome. About one in every 700 babies in the United States is born with Down syndrome (National Down Syndrome Society [NDSS], 2015). Physical characteristics of a person with Down syndrome include slanting eyes with folds of skin at the inner corners (epicanthal folds); excessive ability to extend the joints; short, broad hands with a single crease across the palm on one or both hands; broad feet with short toes; a flat bridge of the nose; short, low-set ears; a short neck; a small head; a small oral cavity; and/or short, high-pitched cries in infancy.

Down syndrome has received widespread attention from medical, education, and social services professionals for many years. Part of this attention is due to the ability to identify a cause with some degree of certainty. The cause of such genetic errors has become increasingly associated with the age of both the mother and the father. The most common type of Down syndrome is **trisomy 21**. In about 25 percent of the cases associated with trisomy 21, the age of the father (particularly when he is over 55 years old) is also a factor.

Other chromosomal disorders associated with intellectual disabilities include **Williams syndrome** and **fragile X syndrome**. Williams syndrome, a rare genetic disease that occurs in about 1 in every 20,000 births, is characterized by an absence of genetic materials on the seventh pair of chromosomes. Most people with Williams syndrome have some degree of intellectual disabilities and associated medical problems (such as heart and blood vessel abnormalities, low weight gain, dental abnormalities, kidney abnormalities, hypersensitive hearing, musculoskeletal problems, and elevated blood calcium levels). While exhibiting deficits in academic learning and spatial ability typical of people with intellectual disabilities, they are often described as highly personable and verbal, exhibiting unique abilities in spoken language.

Fragile X syndrome is a common hereditary cause of intellectual disabilities associated with genetic anomalies in the 23rd pair of chromosomes. Males are usually more severely affected than females because they have only one X chromosome. Females have more protection because they have two X chromosomes; one X contains the normal functioning version of the gene and the other is nonfunctioning. The normal gene partially compensates for the nonfunctioning gene. The term *fragile X* refers to the fact that this gene is pinched off in some blood cells. For those affected by fragile X syndrome, intellectual differences can range from mild learning disabilities and a normal IQ to severe intellectual disabilities

*Photo 9.3* **The most common cause of Down syndrome is a chromosomal abnormality known as trisomy 21, in which the 21st chromosomal pair carries one extra chromosome.**

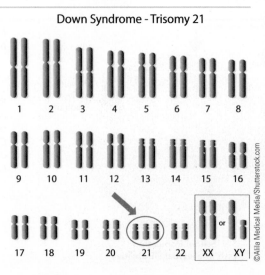

**Down Syndrome - Trisomy 21**

©Alila Medical Media/Shutterstock.com

and autism. Physical features may include a large head and flat ears; a long, narrow face with a broad nose; a large forehead; a squared-off chin; prominent testicles; and large hands. People with fragile X are also characterized by speech and language delays or deficiencies and by behavioral problems. Some people with fragile X are socially engaging and friendly, but others have autistic-like characteristics (poor eye contact, hand flapping, hand biting, and a fascination with spinning objects) and may be aggressive. Males may also exhibit hyperactivity.

**Single-gene disorders** occur when cells cannot produce proteins or enzymes needed to process (metabolize) certain substances that can then become poisonous and damage tissue in the central nervous system. With **phenylketonuria (PKU)**, one such inherited metabolic disorder, the baby is not able to process phenylalanine, a substance found in many foods, including milk ingested by infants. The inability to process phenylalanine results in an accumulation of poisonous substances in the body. If it goes untreated or is not treated promptly (mostly through dietary restrictions), PKU causes varying degrees of intellectual disabilities, ranging from moderate to severe deficits. If treatment is promptly instituted, however, damage may be largely prevented or at least reduced. For this reason, most states now require mandatory screening for all infants to treat the condition as early as possible and prevent lifelong problems.

**Multifactorial disorders** occur when one or several genes on different chromosomes in combination with environmental factors result in abnormal inheritance patterns. Many researchers are investigating the complex effects of specific genetic combinations and environmental factors. One example of a multifactorial disability is spina bifida, which is discussed in Chapter 14.

## 9-4b  Problems during Pregnancy

Prenatal environmental factors such as exposure to drugs and alcohol, toxins, maternal illnesses, and malnutrition can result in intellectual disability. *Intoxication* is cerebral damage that results from an excessive level of some toxic agent in the mother–fetus system. Excessive maternal use of alcohol or drugs or exposure to certain environmental hazards, such as X-rays or insecticides, can damage the child. Damage to the fetus from maternal alcohol consumption is characterized by facial abnormalities, heart problems, low birth weight, small brain size, and intellectual disabilities. The terms **fetal alcohol syndrome (FAS)** and *fetal alcohol effects* (*FAE*) (a lesser number of the same symptoms associated with FAS) refer to a group of physical and mental birth defects resulting from a woman's drinking alcohol during pregnancy. FAS is recognized as a leading preventable cause of intellectual disabilities. The National Organization on Fetal Alcohol Syndrome (2015) estimated that one in every 100 live births involves FAS and that more than 40,000 babies with alcohol-related problems are born in the United States each year. Similarly, pregnant women who smoke are at greater risk of having a premature baby with complicating developmental problems such as intellectual disabilities (Centers for Disease Control and Prevention, 2015). The use of drugs during pregnancy has varying effects on an infant, depending on frequency of use and drug type. Drugs known to produce serious fetal damage include LSD, heroin, morphine, and cocaine.

Maternal substance abuse is also associated with gestation disorders involving prematurity and low birth weight. **Prematurity** refers to infants delivered before 37 weeks from the first day of the last menstrual period. **Low birth weight** characterizes babies that weigh 2,500 grams (5½ pounds) or less at birth. Prematurity and low birth weight significantly increase the risk of serious problems at birth, including intellectual disabilities.

Bill Roth/MCT /Landov

*Photo 9.4* Fetal alcohol syndrome is a leading cause of preventable intellectual disabilities.

**Single-gene disorders**
Disorders that occur when cells cannot produce proteins or enzymes needed to process (metabolize) certain substances that can then become poisonous and damage tissue in the central nervous system.

**Phenylketonuria (PKU)**
A disorder in which an infant cannot digest a substance found in many foods, including milk; may cause intellectual disabilities if left untreated.

**Multifactorial disorders**
Disorders that occur when one or several genes on different chromosomes in combination with environmental factors result in abnormal inheritance patterns.

**Fetal alcohol syndrome (FAS)**
Damage caused to the fetus by the mother's consumption of alcohol.

**Prematurity**
Infants delivered before 37 weeks from the first day of the mother's last menstrual period.

**Low birth weight**
A weight of 2,500 grams (5½ pounds) or less at birth.

Several types of maternal infections may result in difficulties for an unborn child. The probability of damage is particularly high if the infection occurs during the first three months of pregnancy. Congenital rubella (German measles) causes a variety of conditions, including intellectual disabilities, deafness, blindness, cerebral palsy, cardiac problems, seizures, and a variety of other neurological problems. The widespread administration of a rubella vaccine is one major reason why the incidence of intellectual disabilities as an outcome of rubella has declined significantly in recent years.

Another infection associated with intellectual disabilities is the human immunodeficiency virus (HIV). When transmitted from the mother to an unborn child, HIV can result in significant intellectual deficits. The virus actually crosses the placenta and infects the fetus, damaging the infant's immune system. HIV is a major cause of preventable infectious intellectual disabilities (Gargiulo, 2011).

Several conditions associated with unknown prenatal influences can result in severe disorders. One such condition involves malformations of cerebral tissue. The most dramatic of these malformations is anencephaly, a condition in which the individual has a partial or even complete absence of cerebral tissue. In some cases, portions of the brain appear to develop and then degenerate. In hydrocephalus, which also has unknown origins, an excess of cerebrospinal fluid accumulates in the skull and results in potentially damaging pressure on cerebral tissue. Hydrocephalus may involve an enlarged head and cause decreased intellectual functioning. If surgical intervention occurs early, the damage may be slight because the pressure will not have been serious or prolonged.

## 9-4c Problems during Birth

Difficulties during the birth process can result in injuries that cause intellectual disabilities. The continuing supply of oxygen and nutrients to a baby is a critical factor during delivery. Certain fetal positions may result in damage to the fetus as delivery proceeds. A baby's oxygen supply may be reduced for a period of time until the head is expelled and the lungs begin to function; this lack of oxygen may result in damage to the brain. Such a condition is known as anoxia (oxygen deprivation). Temporary oxygen deprivation, abnormal labor and delivery, neonatal seizures, and head trauma at birth are examples of the types of injuries that can occur. Additionally, low birth weight and premature delivery correlate with other serious problems that can lead to intellectual disabilities.

## 9-4d Problems after Birth

Childhood diseases such as whooping cough, chicken pox, measles, and Hib disease that may lead to meningitis and encephalitis can cause brain damage. In recent years there has been an increase in American parents electing to not vaccinate their children. Some states are reporting rates as low as 83 percent immunization for incoming kindergarten children. As a result, there have been reported outbreaks of mumps, whooping cough, and measles (CDC, 2015).

Injuries such as a blow to the head or near drowning can also lead to intellectual disability. Additionally, lead, mercury, and other environmental toxins can cause irreparable damage to the brain and nervous system.

## 9-4e Poverty-Related Deprivation

Children living in poverty are at higher risk for malnutrition, childhood diseases, and exposure to environmental health hazards, and often receive inadequate health care. Each of these factors increases the risk of intellectual disability. For individuals with mild intellectual disabilities, the cause is often not apparent. A significant number of these individuals come from families living in poverty; their home situations often offer few opportunities for learning, which only further contributes to their challenges at school. Additionally, because these high-risk children live in such adverse economic conditions, they generally do not receive proper nutritional care. In addition to poor nutrition, high-risk groups are in greater jeopardy of receiving poor medical care and living in unstable families (Children's Defense Fund, 2011).

An important question to be addressed concerning people who have grown up in adverse sociocultural situations is this: How much of the person's ability is related to sociocultural influences, and how much to genetic factors? This issue is referred to as the **nature versus nurture** controversy. Numerous studies over the years have focused on the degree to which heredity and environment contribute to intelligence. These studies show that although we are reaching a better understanding of the interactive effects of both heredity and environment, the exact contribution of each to intellectual growth remains unknown.

The term used to describe intellectual disabilities that may be attributable to both sociocultural and genetic factors is **cultural–familial intellectual disabilities**. People with this condition are often described as (1) having mild intellectual disabilities, (2) having no known biological cause for the condition, (3) having at least one parent or sibling who has mild intellectual disabilities, and (4) growing up in a low socioeconomic status (low SES) home environment.

Although we have presented a number of possible causal factors associated with intellectual disabilities, the cause is unknown and undeterminable in many cases. Additionally, many conditions associated with intellectual disabilities are due to the interaction of hereditary and environmental factors. Although we cannot always identify the causes of intellectual disabilities, measures can be taken to prevent their occurrence.

## 9-5 Identification and Assessment of Intellectual Disabilties

As discussed in the definition section, intellectual disability has three distinct eligibility criteria: IQ, adaptive behavior, and age of onset. To determine if a person has an intellectual disability, assessments of intelligence and adaptive behavior must be completed and it must be determined that the deficits began prior to the age of 18. Intelligence is typically assessed using an IQ test, which assesses the mental capacity for learning, reasoning, and problem solving. IQ tests are **norm-referenced standardized assessments** that set the average score at 100. If an individual scores at 70 to 75 or lower (two standard deviations below the norm), they meet the intelligence criteria for intellectual disability. Many different assessments can be used to determine eligibility. Some of the most commonly used IQ tests include the Wechsler Intelligence Scale for Children (WISC-V), Stanford-Binet Intelligence Scales (SB5), Woodcock Johnson Tests of Cognitive Abilities, and the Test of Nonverbal Intelligence (TONI).

In addition to intelligence assessments, a comprehensive evaluation of adaptive behaviors must be completed. Adaptive behavior includes the collection of conceptual, social, and practical skills that people have learned and perform in their everyday lives. Like the IQ tests, many different tools are available to measure adaptive behaviors, including the Vineland Adaptive Behavior Scales, Adaptive Behavior Scale-School, Scales of Independent Behavior, and the Adaptive Behavior Assessment System. The final criterion for eligibility is the age onset. An intellectual disability must manifest or become present by the age of 18.

## 9-6 Interventions and Treatments for Intellectual Disability

We now turn our attention to educating students with intellectual disabilities from early childhood through the transition from school to adult life. The provision of appropriate services and supports for individuals with intellectual disabilities is a lifelong process. For children with mild intellectual disabilities, educational services may not begin until they are in elementary school. However, for those with more severe intellectual disabilities, services and supports will begin at birth and may continue into the adult years.

**Nature versus nurture**
Controversy concerning how much of a person's ability is related to sociocultural influences (nurture) as opposed to genetic factors (nature).

**Cultural–familial intellectual disabilities**
Intellectual disabilities that may be attributable to both sociocultural and genetic factors.

**Standard 1**
Learner Development and Individual Learning Differences

**Standard 4**
Assessment

**Norm–referenced standardized assessments**
Assessments that are designed to compare and rank test takers in relation to one another. Norm-referenced tests report whether test takers performed better or worse than a hypothetical average student, which is determined by comparing scores against the performance results of a statistically selected group of test takers, typically of the same age or grade level, who have already taken the exam.

## 9-6a  Early Childhood Education

Children with mild intellectual disabilities may exhibit subtle developmental delays in comparison to age-mates, but parents may not view these discrepancies as significant enough to seek intervention during the preschool years. Even if parents are concerned and seek help for their child prior to elementary school, they are often confronted with professionals who are apathetic toward early childhood education. Some professionals believe that early childhood services may actually create problems, rather than remedy them, because the child may not be mature enough to cope with the pressures of structured learning in an educational environment. Simply stated, the maturation philosophy means that before entering school, children should reach a level of growth at which they are ready to learn certain skills. Unfortunately, this philosophy has kept many children out of the public schools for years.

The antithesis of the maturation philosophy is the prevention of further problems in learning and behavior through intervention. **Head Start**, funded as a federal preschool program for students from low-income families, is a prevention program that attempts to identify and instruct at-risk children before they enter public school. Although Head Start did not have the results that were initially anticipated (the virtual elimination of school adjustment problems for students from low-income families), it has represented a significant move forward and continues to receive widespread support from parents and professionals alike. The rationale for early education is widely accepted in the field of special education and is an important part of the IDEA mandate.

Intervention based on normal patterns of growth is referred to as *developmental milestones* because it seeks to develop, remedy, or adapt learner skills based on a child's variation from what is considered normal. This progression of skills continues as children age chronologically; rate of progress depends on the severity of the condition. Some children with profound intellectual disabilities may never exceed a developmental age of 6 months. Those with moderate intellectual disabilities may develop to a level that will enable them to lead fulfilling lives as adults, with varying levels of support.

The importance of early intervention cannot be overstated. Significant advances have been made in the area of early intervention, including improved assessment, curricula, and instructional technologies; increasing numbers of children receiving services; and appreciation of the need to individualize services for families as well as children (Batshaw, Pellegrino, & Rozien, 2007; Berk, 2011; McDonnell et al., 2014). Early intervention techniques, such as **infant stimulation** programs, focus on the acquisition of sensorimotor skills and intellectual development. Infant stimulation involves learning simple reflex activities and equilibrium reactions. Subsequent intervention then expands into all areas of human growth and development.

## 9-6b  Elementary Education

Public education is a relatively new concept as it relates to students with intellectual disabilities, particularly those with more severe characteristics. Historically, many of these students were defined as *noneducable* by public schools because they did not fit the programs offered by general education. Because such programs were built on a foundation of academic learning that emphasized reading, writing, and arithmetic, students with intellectual disabilities could not meet the academic standards set by the schools and, thus, were excluded. Public schools were not expected to adapt to the needs of students with intellectual disabilities; rather, the students were expected to adapt to the schools.

With the passage of Public Law 94-142 (now IDEA), schools that excluded these children for so long now face the challenge of providing an appropriate education for all children with intellectual disabilities. Education has been redefined on the basis of a new set of values. Instruction and support for children of elementary school age with intellectual disabilities focus on decreasing dependence on others, while concurrently teaching adaptation to the environment. Therefore, instruction must concentrate on those skills that facilitate the child's interaction with others and emphasize independence in the community. Instruction for children with intellectual disabilities generally includes development of academic skills, self-help skills, social skills, communication skills, and motor skills.

**Academic Skills** Students with intellectual disabilities can benefit from instruction in traditional or functional academic programs. In the area of literacy, students with intellectual disabilities benefit from a systematic instructional program that allows for differences in the rate of learning, but they can learn to read when given rich, intensive, and extensive literary experiences. In fact, some students may achieve as high as a fourth- or fifth-grade level in reading. Students with intellectual disabilities can make significant progress in literacy programs that emphasize **direct instruction** (the direct teaching of letters, words, and syntactic, phonetic, and semantic analysis) in conjunction with written literature that is meaningful to the student or that draws on the student's own writings.

A significant relationship exists between measured IQ and reading achievement: Students with intellectual disabilities read well below the level of students of the same age without disabilities. Although this relationship seems to suggest that reading instruction should be limited to higher-functioning students, a growing body of research indicates that students with more severe intellectual disabilities can learn academic skills. According to Browder and colleagues (2011), "The emerging research shows that students with severe disabilities can master academic skills. However, educators continue to have substantial work ahead to demonstrate effective practices for teaching them the wide range of academic skills typical of the general curriculum" (p. 493).

A functional reading program uses materials that are a part of a person's normal routines in work, everyday living, and leisure activities. For example, functional reading involves words that are frequently encountered in the environment, such as those used on labels or signs in public places; words that warn of possible risks; and symbols such as the skull and crossbones to denote poisonous substances.

Students with intellectual disabilities also have challenges in developing math skills, but the majority of those with mild intellectual disabilities can learn basic addition and subtraction. However, these children will have significant difficulty in the areas of mathematical reasoning and problem-solving tasks (Beirne-Smith, Patton, & Hill, 2010). Math skills are taught most efficiently through the use of money concepts. For example, functional math involves activities such as learning to use a bank account, shopping in a grocery store, or using a vending machine. The immediate practical application motivates the students. Regardless of the approach used, arithmetic instruction must be concrete and practical to compensate for a child's deficiencies in reasoning ability.

**Self-Help Skills** The development of self-help skills is critical to a child's progression toward independence from caregivers. Self-help skills include eating, dressing, and maintaining personal hygiene. Eating skills range from finger feeding and drinking from a cup to using proper table behaviors (such as employing utensils and napkins), serving food, and following rules of etiquette. Dressing skills include buttoning, zipping, buckling, lacing, and tying. Personal hygiene skills are developed in an age-appropriate context. Basic hygiene skills include toileting, face and hand washing, bathing, tooth brushing, hair combing, and shampooing. Skills associated with adolescent and adult years include skin care, shaving, hair care, and the use of deodorants and cosmetics.

**Social Skills** Social skills training emphasizes the importance of learning problem-solving and decision-making skills and of using appropriate communication in a social context. Difficulty with problem solving and decision making have been barriers to the success of people with intellectual disabilities in community and school settings. Students with intellectual disabilities will not learn these skills through observation but must be specifically taught how to solve problems.

Westling and Fox (2009) suggested several learning outcomes for students in the use of appropriate communication in a social context. They must be able to initiate and maintain a conversation (verbal, signed, or pictorial) while using appropriate social conventions and courtesies (e.g., staying on topic, not interrupting a speaker, and using appropriate body posture). These authors suggested a list of social skills that are important instructional targets for students with intellectual disabilities (see Figure 9.3).

**Direct instruction**
Teaching academic subjects through precisely sequenced lessons involving drill, practice, and immediate feedback.

**Standard 2**
Learning Environments

Figure 9.3 *Instructional Targets in Social Skills Training*

| | |
|---|---|
| Establish eye contact. | Make requests. |
| Establish appropriate proximity. | Respond to requests. |
| Maintain appropriate body posture during conversation. | Ask for information. |
| Speak with appropriate volume, rate, and expression. | Provide information. |
| Maintain attention during exchange. | Ask for clarification. |
| Initiate greetings. | Respond to requests for clarification. |
| Respond to greetings. | Extend social invitation. |
| Initiate partings. | Deliver refusals. |
| Respond to partings. | Respond to refusals. |
| Discriminate appropriate times to greet or part. | Use social courtesies (please, thank you, apology). |
| Answer questions. | Maintain topic. |
| Ask questions. | Initiate a new topic. |

SOURCE: From Westling, D., & Fox, L. (2009). *Teaching students with severe disabilities*. Upper Saddle River, NJ: Merrill.

**Communication Skills** The ability to communicate with others is an essential component of growth and development. Without communication, there can be no interaction. Communication systems for children with intellectual disabilities take three general forms: verbal language, augmentative communication (including sign language and language boards), and a combination of the verbal and augmentative approaches. The approach used depends on the child's capability. A child who can develop the requisite skills for spoken language will have greatly enhanced everyday interactive skills. For a child unable to develop verbal skills as an effective means of communication, manual communication must be considered. Such children must develop some form of communication that will facilitate inclusion with peers and family members throughout their lives. The use of computer-based, tablet-style devices appears to be making communication more accessible to students with limited speech (Kagohara et al., 2013). For some specific tips on effective ways to include people with intellectual disabilities from early childhood through the adult years, see the nearby Community Support for Lifelong Inclusion feature, "People with Intellectual Disabilities."

Some students with intellectual disabilities benefit from the use of **assistive technology** and communication aids. Assistive technology may involve a variety of communication approaches that aid people with intellectual disabilities who have limited speech ability. These approaches may be low-tech (a language board with pictures) or high-tech (a tablet with voice output). Regardless of the approach, a communication aid can be a valuable tool in helping people with intellectual disabilities communicate with others. For more information, see the nearby feature, "Assistive Technology for People with Intellectual Disabilities."

**Assistive technology**
Devices such as computers, hearing aids, wheelchairs, and other equipment that help individuals adapt to the natural settings of home, school, and family.

**Motor Skills** The acquisition of motor skills is fundamental to the developmental process and a prerequisite to successful learning in other content areas, including self-help and social skills. Gross motor development involves general mobility, including the interaction of the body with the environment. Gross motor skills are developed in a sequence, ranging from movements that make balance possible to higher-order locomotor patterns. Locomotor

## People with Intellectual Disabilities

### Early Childhood Years

#### Tips for Families

- Promote family learning about the diversity of all people in the context of understanding a child with intellectual differences.

- Create opportunities for friendships to develop between your child and children without disabilities, in preschool and in family and neighborhood settings.

- Help facilitate your child's opportunities and access to neighborhood preschools by actively participating in the education planning process and collaborating with professionals with multidisciplinary backgrounds (health care, social services, education, etc.).

- Become familiar with the individualized family service plan (IFSP) and how it can serve as a planning tool to support the inclusion of your child in preschool programs that involve students without disabilities.

#### Tips for General Education Preschool Teachers

- Focus on the child's individual abilities first. Whatever labels have been placed on the child will have little to do with instructional needs.

- When teaching a child, focus on presenting each component of a task clearly while reducing outside stimuli that may distract the child from learning.

- Begin with simple tasks, and move to more complex ones as the child masters each skill.

- Verbally label stimuli, such as objects or people, as often as possible to provide the child with both auditory and visual input.

- Provide a lot of practice in initial learning phases, using short but frequent sessions to ensure that the child has mastered the skill before moving on to more complex tasks.

- Create successful experiences by rewarding correct responses to tasks as well as appropriate behavior with peers who are not disabled.

- Help young children with intellectual disabilities be able to transfer learning from school to the home and neighborhood. Facilitate such transfer by providing information that is meaningful to the child and noting how the initial and transfer tasks are similar.

#### Tips for Preschool Personnel

- Support the inclusion of young children with intellectual disabilities in classrooms and programs.

- Collaborate with the team of multidisciplinary professionals, including teachers, staff, related services professionals (such as speech and language pathologists), and volunteers as they attempt to create success experiences for the child in the preschool setting.

- Integrate families as well as children into the preschool programs. Offer parents as many opportunities as possible to be part of the program (e.g., advisory boards, volunteer experiences).

#### Tips for Neighbors and Friends

- Look for opportunities for young neighborhood children who are not disabled to interact during playtimes with a child who has an intellectual disability.

- Provide a supportive community environment for the family of a young child who has an intellectual disability. Encourage the family, including the child, to participate in neighborhood activities (e.g., outings, barbecues, outdoor yard and street cleanups, crime watches).

- Try to understand how a young child with intellectual disabilities is similar rather than different to other children in the neighborhood. Focus on those similarities in your interactions with other neighbors and children in your community.

### Elementary Years

#### Tips for Families

- Actively participate with the multidisciplinary team in the development of your son's or daughter's individualized education program (IEP). Through active participation, advocate for those goals that you would like to see on the IEP that will focus on your child's developing social interaction and communication skills in natural settings (e.g., the general education classroom).

- To help facilitate your son's or daughter's inclusion in the neighborhood elementary school, help the multidisciplinary team of professionals better understand the importance of inclusion with peers who are not disabled (e.g., riding on the same school bus, going to recess and lunch at the same time, participating in school-wide assemblies).

- Participate in as many school functions for parents (e.g., PTA, parent advisory groups, volunteering) as is reasonable, to connect your family to the mainstream of the school.

- Create opportunities for your child to make friends with same-age children without disabilities.

#### Tips for General Education Classroom Teachers

- View children with intellectual disabilities as children, first and foremost. Focus on their similarities to other children rather than on their differences.

- Recognize children with intellectual disabilities for their own accomplishments within the classroom, rather than comparing them to those of peers without disabilities.

- Employ cooperative learning strategies wherever possible to promote effective learning by all students. Use peers without disabilities as support for students with intellectual disabilities. This may include establishing peer–buddy programs or peer and cross-age tutoring.

- Consider all members of the classroom when you organize the physical environment. Find ways to meet the individual needs of each child (e.g., establishing aisles that will accommodate a wheelchair and organizing desks to facilitate tutoring on assigned tasks).

### Tips for School Personnel

- Integrate the multidisciplinary resources within the school to meet the needs of all children.

- Wherever possible, help general classroom teachers access the collaborative and multidisciplinary resources necessary to meet the needs of students with intellectual disabilities. Make available instructional materials and programs to whomever needs them, not just to those identified as being in special education.

- Help general and special education teachers develop peer–partner and support networks for students with intellectual disabilities.

- Promote the heterogeneous grouping of students. Avoid clustering large numbers of students with intellectual disabilities in a single general education classroom. Integrate no more than two in each elementary classroom.

- Maintain the same schedules for students with intellectual disabilities as for all other students in the building. Recess, lunch, school assemblies, and bus arrival and departure schedules should be identical for all students.

- Create opportunities for the multidisciplinary personnel in the school to collaborate in the development and implementation of instructional programs for individual children.

### Tips for Neighbors and Friends

- Support families who are seeking to have their child with intellectual disabilities educated with children who are not disabled. This will give children with intellectual disabilities more opportunities for interacting with children who are not disabled, both in school and in the local community.

## Secondary and Transition Years

### Tips for Families

- Create opportunities for your son or daughter to participate in activities that are of interest to him or her, beyond the school day, with same-age peers who are not disabled, including high school clubs, sports, or just hanging out in the local mall.

- Promote opportunities for students from your son's or daughter's high school to visit your home. Help arrange get-togethers or parties involving students from the neighborhood and/or school.

- Become actively involved in the development of the individualized education and transition program. Explore with the high school's team of advisers what should be done to assist your son or daughter in the transition from school to adult life.

### Tips for General Education Classroom Teachers

- Collaborate with the school's multidisciplinary team (special educators, related services personnel, administrators, paraeducators) to adapt subject matter in your classroom (e.g., science, math, or physical education) to the individual needs of students with intellectual disabilities.

- Let students without disabilities know that students with intellectual disabilities belong in their classroom. The goals and activities of these students may be different from those of other students, but with support, students with intellectual disabilities will benefit from working with you and the other students in the class.

- Support students with intellectual disabilities in becoming involved in extracurricular activities. If you are the faculty sponsor of a club or organization, explore whether these students are interested and how they could get involved.

### Tips for School Personnel

- Advocate for parents of high school–age students with intellectual disabilities to participate in the activities of the school (e.g., committees and PTA).

- Help facilitate parental collaboration in the IEP process during the high school years by helping the school's multidisciplinary team value parental input that focuses on a desire to include their child in the mainstream of the school. Parents will be more active when school personnel have general and positive contact with the family.

- Provide human and material support to high school special education or vocational teachers seeking to develop community-based instruction programs that focus on students learning and applying skills in actual community settings (e.g., grocery stores, malls, theaters, parks, and work sites).

### Tips for Neighbors, Friends, and Potential Employers

- Work with the family and school personnel to create opportunities for students with intellectual disabilities to participate in community activities (such as going to the movies, "hanging out" with peers without disabilities in the neighborhood mall, and going to high school sports events).

- As a potential employer, work with the high school to locate and establish community-based employment-training sites for students with intellectual disabilities.

## Adult Years

### Tips for Families

- Become aware of what life will be like for your son or daughter in the local community during the adult years. What formal supports (government-funded advocacy organizations) from various disciplines (such as health care and social services) and informal supports are available in your community? What are the characteristics of adult service programs? Explore adult support systems in the local community in the areas of supported living, employment, and recreation and leisure.

patterns are intended to move a person freely through the environment. Gross motor movements include controlling the head and neck, rolling, body righting, sitting, crawling, standing, walking, running, jumping, and skipping.

Fine motor development requires more precision and steadiness than the skills developed in the gross motor area. The development of fine motor skills, including reaching, grasping, and manipulating objects, is initially dependent on the ability of the child to visually fix on an object and visually track a moving target. Coordination of the eye and hand is an integral factor in many skill areas, as well as in fine motor development. Eye–hand coordination is the basis of social and leisure activities and is essential to the development of the object-control skills required in employment.

**Inclusion in School**  Historically, special education for students with intellectual disabilities meant segregated education. Today, however, the focus is on including these students in general education schools and classrooms. Some students with intellectual disabilities are included for only a part of the school day and attend only those general education classes that their individualized education program (IEP) teams consider consistent with their needs and functioning levels (such as physical education, industrial arts, or home economics). Other students with intellectual disabilities attend general education classes for all or the majority of the school day. For these students, special education consists primarily of services and supports intended to facilitate their opportunities and success in the general education classroom. Placement information from the U.S. Department of Education (2014) indicates that approximately 94 percent of students with intellectual disabilities between the ages of 6 and 21 were placed in general education schools for the entire day. Of these students, about 18 percent were served in a general education class for at least 80 percent of the time, and 45 percent spent more than half of their time outside the general education class. Inclusion in our schools opens doors for inclusion in the community.

Another placement option for students with disabilities is the special school. Special schools are defined as facilities exclusively for students with intellectual disabilities or other disabilities. Approximately 6 percent of students with intellectual disabilities attend public special schools, and less than one percent attend private special schools (U.S. Department of Education, 2014). In this era of inclusion, considerable controversy exists as to whether there is *any* justification for placing students with intellectual disabilities in special schools.

## 9-6c  Adolescent Education and Transition to Adulthood

The goals of an educational program for adolescents with intellectual disabilities are to increase personal independence, enhance opportunities for participation in the local community, prepare for employment, and facilitate a successful transition to the adult years.

**Personal Independence and Participation in the Community**  The term *independence* refers to the development and application of skills that lead to greater self-sufficiency in daily personal life, including personal care, self-help, and appropriate

## Assistive Technology for People with Intellectual Disabilities

### How Do People with Intellectual Disabilities Use Technology?

**Communication.** For individuals who cannot communicate vocally, technology can help them communicate. Augmentative and alternative communication (ACC) may involve technology ranging from low-tech message boards to computerized voice output communication aids and synthesized speech.

**Mobility.** Simple to sophisticated computer-controlled wheelchairs and mobility aids are available. Technology may be used to aid in finding directions, guiding users to destinations. Computerized cueing systems and robots have also been used to guide users with intellectual disabilities.

**Environmental control.** Assistive technology can help people with severe or multiple disabilities to control electrical appliances, operate audio/video equipment such as home entertainment systems, or perform basic tasks such as locking and unlocking doors.

**Activities of daily living.** Technology is assisting people with disabilities to successfully complete everyday tasks of self-care:

- Automated and computerized dining devices allow individuals who need assistance at mealtime to eat more independently.

- Audio prompting devices can assist people with memory difficulties to complete a task or to follow a sequence of steps from start to finish in such activities as making a bed or taking medication.

- Video-based instructional materials can help people learn functional life skills such as grocery shopping, writing a check, paying the bills, or using the ATM.

**Education.** Technology is used in education to aid communication, support activities of daily living, and to enhance learning. Computer-assisted instruction can help in many areas, including word recognition, math, spelling, and even social skills. Computers have also been found to promote interaction with non-disabled peers.

**Employment.** Technology, such as video-assisted training, is being used for job training and job skill development and to teach complex skills for appropriate job behavior and social interaction. Prompting systems using digital recorders and computer-based prompting devices have been used to help workers stay on task. Computerized prompting systems can help people manage their time in scheduling job activities.

**Sports and recreation.** Toys can be adapted with switches and other technologies to facilitate play for children. Computer or video games provide age-appropriate social opportunities and help children learn cognitive and eye–hand coordination skills. Specially designed Internet access software can help people with intellectual disabilities access the World Wide Web. Exercise and physical fitness can be supported by video-based technology.

### What Barriers to Technology Use will People with Intellectual Disabilities Encounter?

Even though it is the goal of most technology development efforts to incorporate the principles of universal design, cognitive access is not carefully considered. Universal design ensures that all people may use technology without adaptation. An example of cognitive access can be found in computer use—if someone with a disability is using a computer, the onscreen messages should last long enough or provide enough wait time to allow a disabled person to consider whether to press a computer key. Or the time should be sufficient between making a phone call and pressing the numbers to complete the call using a rechargeable phone card as payment. Because individuals with intellectual disabilities have a range of learning and processing abilities, it is difficult to develop assistive technology solutions that are appropriate for all skill levels.

### Do Schools have to Provide Assistive Technology to Students Who Need It?

IDEA requires that the need for assistive technology be considered for all students when developing individualized education programs. The intention of the special education law is this: If a student with disabilities needs technology to be able to learn, the school district will (1) evaluate the student's technology needs; (2) acquire the necessary technology; (3) coordinate technology use with other therapies and interventions; and (4) provide training for the individual, the individual's family, and the school staff in the effective use of technology. If a student's individualized education program specifies that assistive technology is needed for home use to ensure appropriate education, the school must provide it. If the school purchases an assistive technology device for use by a student, the school owns it. The student cannot take it when moving to another school or when leaving school.

SOURCE: Adapted from "Technology for People with Intellectual Disabilities," 2009, www.thearc.org.

Figure 9.4 *Categories of Supports Needed During the Adult Years*

**Family Supports**

Family crisis            Family counseling

Family education         Respite care
and training

**Community Supports**

Information      Protective
and referral     services

Early identification   Public
and treatment        awareness

Health care         Advocacy

**Leisure Supports**

Therapeutic     Fitness
recreation
                Outdoor
Sports and      recreation
games
                Entertainment
Access to
community events

**Community Support Needs**

**Supported Living**

Group          Individual
homes          house

Foster          Apartment
homes          living

**Employment Supports**

Vocational          Training
counseling referral,
job placement,      Supported
follow-up           employment

leisure activities. Participation in the community includes access to programs, facilities (grocery stores, shopping malls, restaurants, theaters, and parks), and services that people without disabilities often take for granted. Adolescents with intellectual disabilities need opportunities for interaction with peers without disabilities (other than caregivers), access to community events, sustained social relationships, and involvement in choices that affect their lives. An illustration of the range of community services and supports that can facilitate the transition of an adolescent with intellectual disabilities into the adult years is shown in Figure 9.4.

The ARC (2015) released a position statement that describes the types of supports that are needed to ensure that people who have intellectual disabilities have full and meaningful lives in the community. The statement addresses the rights for individuals with intellectual disabilities to have access to early intervention, and education and behavioral supports that offer opportunities for choice and social integration. The statement continues to describe the rights for this groups of people to have the same opportunities as other citizens to enjoy full lives in their community, including access to employment, health care, housing, transportation, and services provided for seniors. The right to personal choices around sexuality and spirituality are also listed as essential for full, independent community lives.

**Standard 6**
Professional Learning
and Ethical Practice

**Employment Preparation** Work is a crucial measure of any person's success during adulthood, providing the primary opportunity for social interaction, a basis for personal identity and status, and a chance to contribute to the community. These needs are basic to adults who have intellectual disabilities, just as they are for their peers without disabilities.

Fortunately, employment training for students with intellectual disabilities is shifting from the isolation and "getting ready" orientation of a **sheltered workshop** to authentic community employment. Goals and objectives are developed according to the demands

**Sheltered workshop**
A segregated vocational training and employment setting for people with disabilities.

**Photo 9.5** For adolescents with moderate and severe intellectual disabilities, employment preparation during high school is shifting away from segregated sheltered workshops to supported employment in inclusive community settings.

Robin Nelson/PhotoEdit

of the community work setting and the functioning level of the individual. The focus is on helping each person learn and apply skills in a job setting while receiving the support necessary to succeed. Providing ongoing assistance to the individual on the job is the basis of an approach known as supported employment. **Supported employment** is work in an inclusive setting for individuals with disabilities (including those with intellectual disabilities) who are expected to need continuous support services and for whom competitive employment has traditionally not been possible.

Research indicates that people with intellectual disabilities can work in community employment if adequate training and support are provided (Crockett & Hardman, 2009; Siperstein, Heyman, & Stokes, 2014; Wehman, 2011). Following are some suggested guidelines in developing a comprehensive employment-training program for students with intellectual disabilities:

**Supported employment**
Jobs for individuals with severely disabilities who will need continuous support, and for whom competitive jobs have traditionally not been possible.

- Students should have the opportunity to make informed choices about what jobs they want to do and where they want to work.

- Students should receive employment training in community settings prior to graduation from high school.

---

### CASE STUDY ON EMBRACING DIVERSITY

#### Lucy

When Lucy was 4 years old, she had a meningitis incident that resulted in a mild intellectual disability. Now, Lucy is an 18-year-old student at Central Valley High School. School has never been easy for Lucy, but high school has been particularly hard. For the last three years, she bounced between her dad's home on a rancheria 60 miles away and her mom's apartment. She attended different schools depending on which parent she was living with. Earlier this year, following her mother's death, Lucy told the school psychologist that she didn't feel safe living with her father. She announced that she would be living with friends as she finishes high school at CVHS.

Lucy's schedule includes remedial math and English classes, culinary class, jewelry making, theater, and a career development course. She has expressed an interest in working with animals and is currently exploring jobs as

a veterinarian assistant. Ms. Alvarez, the special education teacher at CVHS who manages Lucy's progress, is concerned about several things. Following a discussion with the school social worker, Ms. Alvarez asked Lucy about her living arrangements. Lucy shared that she is living in a homeless shelter for a short time, while she figures out what to do next. Lucy told Ms. Alvarez that she was considering dropping out of school because it is too hard to get to school. She has attempted to pass the high school exit exam twice, failing the math section both times by a very narrow margin. She is also concerned that she does not have a parent or advocate to attend her upcoming transition IEP meeting.

Ms. Alvarez is committed to helping Lucy find sustainable living arrangements, pass the exit exam, and complete high school with a diploma. She assures Lucy that as an 18-year-old, she

can attend and sign off on her own IEP. Next, she gathers together the transition IEP team, including Lucy, her theater teacher, the assistant principal, the school social worker, and a local representative for the homeless youth project. Together, they develop a plan including a coordinated set of activities and support services that will lead Lucy to achieving the post-school goals she envisioned for herself!

##### Application Questions

**1.** Why is Lucy able to represent herself at her transition IEP meeting?

**2.** Why is it so important to include a broad range of people (teachers, administrators, social works, community advocates) on Lucy's transition planning meeting?

**3.** What are some coordinated activities that would support Lucy in moving toward her adult goals?

- Employment training should focus on work opportunities present in the local area where individuals currently live.

- The focus of the employment training should be on specific job training as students approach graduation.

- Collaboration between the school and adult service agencies must be part of an employment-training program (Drew & Hardman, 2007).

**CEC**

**Standard 2**
Learning Environments

## Looking Toward a Bright Future

Historically, services for people with intellectual disabilities have been primarily focused on isolating and caring for individuals rather than facilitating their access and participation in school, family, and community life. With the passage of civil rights and federal education legislation in the late 20th century, the promise of autonomy, choice, and independence for people with intellectual disabilities has become a reality for some but remains a dream for others. Even today, more than 100,000 people with intellectual and developmental disabilities remain institutionalized in the United States. Others, although not institutionalized, have little control over where, with whom, and how they live in their communities (Lakin, 2005). And then there are the Troy Daniels of this world. Troy, a young man with Down syndrome who uses a wheelchair, was selected to stand and deliver the senior speech before his graduating class at Northfield High School in Vermont. Here is what Troy had to say to friends, family, and neighbors on that special day:

> *Not long ago people with disabilities could not go to school with other kids; they had to go to special schools. They could not have real friends; they call people like me "retard." That breaks my heart.... The law says that I can come to school but no law can make me have friends. But then some kids started to think that I was okay, first just one or two kids were nice to me.... Others started to hang out with me and they found out we could be friends. I cared about them and they cared about me.... I want all people to know and see that these students I call my friends are the real teachers of life.*

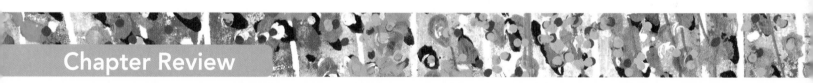

## Chapter Review

**9-1 Describe how the lives of people with intellectual disabilities have changed since the advent of IDEA.**

- As more children with intellectual disabilities enter school, developmental delays have become more apparent. Prior to the passage of IDEA, it was common for the cognitive and social differences of children with intellectual disabilities to be attributed to immaturity. Today, educators recognize the need for specialized services to support a child's development in the natural settings of school, neighborhood, and home.

- People with moderate to severe intellectual disabilities have challenges that often transcend the classroom. Today, we recognize that these children are able to learn and use adaptive skills that allow independence, with varying levels of support.

- Although dependent upon others for basic life needs, people with profound intellectual disabilities benefit from education and treatment beyond routine care and maintenance. The extent of profound disabilities is one reason why this group of children was excluded from the public schools prior to the passage of IDEA. Exclusion was often justified on the basis that schools did not have the resources, facilities, or trained professionals to deal with the needs of these students.

**9-2 Explain the various definitions and classifications of intellectual disabilities.**

- Definition
  - There are significant limitations in intellectual abilities.
  - There are significant limitations in adaptive behavior as expressed in conceptual, social, and practical adaptive skills.

- Disability originates before the age of 18.
- The severity of the condition is tempered by the individual's participation, interactions, and social roles within the community; by her or his overall physical and mental health; and by the environmental context.

- Classifications systems
  - Severity of the condition may be described in terms of mild, moderate, severe, or profound intellectual disabilities.
  - Medical descriptors classify intellectual disabilities on the basis of the origin of the condition (e.g., infection, intoxication, trauma, chromosomal abnormality).
  - Type and extent of support needed categorizes people with intellectual disabilities as having intermittent, limited, extensive, or pervasive needs for support to function in natural settings.

### 9-3 Describe the characteristics and prevalence of children and youth with intellectual disabilities.

- Intellectual characteristics may include learning and memory deficiencies, difficulties with metacognition, and generalization skills.
- Self-regulation characteristics include difficulty in mediating or regulating behavior.
- Adaptive skill characteristics may include difficulties in coping with the demands of the environment, developing interpersonal relationships, developing language skills, and taking care of personal needs.
- The prevalence of intellectual disabilities worldwide and across all ages is estimated at one percent of the total population.
- There are approximately 447,000 students between the ages of 6 and 21 labeled as having intellectual disabilities and receiving service under IDEA. Approximately 7 percent of all students with disabilities between the ages of 6 and 21 have intellectual disabilities.
- Overall, students with intellectual disabilities constitute about 0.88 percent of the total school population.

### 9-4 List the causes and risk factors associated with intellectual disabilities.

- Intellectual disabilities are the result of multiple causes, some known, and many unknown. Genetic conditions, problems during pregnancy, problems at birth, problems after birth, and poverty-related deprivation can lead to intellectual disabilities.

### 9-5 Describe the assessment procedures used to identify intellectual disabilities in children and youth.

- Three separate factors need to be considered to determine if an individual has an intellectual disability. A test of intellectual functioning (IQ test) must reveal a score of 70 to 75 or lower. A formal assessment of adaptive behavior must be completed and indicate a significant delay. Finally, the onset of the disability must occur prior to the age of 18.

### 9-6 Describe the different interventions for children and youth with intellectual disabilities from early childhood through adulthood.

- Inclusive education should be a primary focus across the full range of the education system. Regardless of the severity of their condition, students with intellectual disabilities benefit from placement in general education environments where opportunities for inclusion with nondisabled peers are systematically planned and implemented.
- Early intervention programs focus on the development of communication skills, social interaction, and readiness for formal instruction.
- Programs for elementary-age children with intellectual disabilities balance the curriculum between academics and functional skills. Focus in often on:
  - Academic skills
  - Self-help skills
  - Social skills
  - Communication skills
  - Motor development skills
- Programs for adolescents with intellectual disabilities focus on transition to adulthood by placing emphasis on:
  - Increasing the individual's personal independence
  - Enhancing opportunities for participation in the local community
  - Preparing for employment
  - Facilitating a successful transition to the adult years

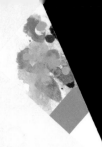

If you are thinking about a career in special education, you should know that many states use national standards developed by the Council for Exceptional Children (CEC) to assess a teacher candidate's knowledge and skills for working with students with disabilities. See a complete listing of the seven CEC Content Standards on the inside cover of this text.

1 Learner Development and Individual Learning Differences
2 Learning Environments
4 Assessment
5 Instructional Planning and Strategies
6 Professional Learning and Ethical Practice

## Mastery Activities and Assignments

To master the content within this chapter, complete the following activities and assignments:

1. Complete a written test of the chapter's content. If your instructor requires a written test of your content knowledge for this chapter, keep a copy for your portfolio.
2. Review the Case Study on Embracing Diversity, "Lucy," and respond in writing to the Application Questions.

Keep a copy of the Case Study and your written response for your portfolio.

3. Participate in a community service learning activity. Community service is a valuable way to enhance your learning experience. Develop a reflective journal of the service learning experience for your portfolio.

## CHAPTER 10

# Communication Disorders

BSIP/Getty Images

## Learning Objectives

*After you complete this chapter, you will be able to:*

**10-1** Describe how the lives of people with communication disorders have changed since the advent of IDEA.

**10-2** Describe the primary components of typical communication development.

**10-3** Describe language disorders, their prevalence, causation, identification, and related interventions.

**10-4** Describe speech sound disorder, its prevalence, causation, identification, and related interventions.

**10-5** Describe child onset fluency disorder, its prevalence, causation, identification, and related interventions.

**10-6** Describe social (pragmatic) communication disorder, its prevalence, causation, identification, and related interventions.

**10-7** Describe voice and resonance disorders, their prevalence, causation, identification, and related interventions.

## SNAPSHOT Trinity

### Stuttering Is Like a Car Going Too Fast

Trinity, 7th grade, Henrico, Virginia

My stuttering is like a car going too fast. When the car goes too fast it can crash. The car is my speech. When I speak fast I stutter. My stutter is like the car crashing. My brain is like the driver of the car. The driver goes to driving school to learn how to drive. I go to therapy to help my brain learn how to use speech rules. When people tell me to go slow it is like the police giving a ticket to the driver to slow down. The speed limit and traffic signals remind the driver to slow down like my therapist gives me signs and signals to slow down.

SOURCE: www.stutteringhelp.org/drawings-and-letters-kids.

## 10-1 A Changing Era in the Lives of People with Communication Disorders

**Standard 6**
Professional Learning and Ethical Practice

Evidence of communication disorders has existed for thousands of years. One of the first recognized individuals in written history who appears to have had a communication disorder as well as therapy to correct the condition was Demosthenes (384–322 BCE), a popular Greek orator, politician, and speechwriter. It is believed Demosthenes was challenged with a fluency disorder (stuttering), which he "overcame and rendered more distinct by speaking with pebbles in his mouth; his voice he disciplined by declaiming and reciting speeches or verses when he was out of breath, while running or going up steep places; and that in his house he had a large looking-glass, before which he would stand and go through his exercises" (Plutarch, 75).

Much has changed in the field of communication disorders since the time of the ancient Greeks, both in how we view such disorders and how we assess and treat them. With the advent of the Individuals with Disabilities Education Act (IDEA) in 1975, students with communication disorders now have rights to be assessed by a multidisciplinary team of trained professionals and, for those eligible, to receive free and appropriate services individualized to meet their needs. IDEA's primary purpose is to improve early intervention and to improve educational attainment and functional outcomes for children with disabilities, including those with communication disorders (U.S. Department of Education, 2014).

Communication is one of the most frequent activities we undertake. Think about how often you communicate using various modalities each day. You may order food in a restaurant, thank a stranger for helping you, send a text message to a friend, ask a question in class, email your instructor, smile at a person across the room, and give directions to someone who is lost, all within a short period of time. Our lives revolve around communication in many crucial ways, but communication rarely gets much attention unless we have a problem with it. Because our society places such an emphasis on interpersonal communication, the challenges people with communication disorders face are sometimes daunting and have a significant impact on their behavior. This chapter will focus on the broad and complex field of communication development, communication disorders, and their impact on children and youth.

## 10-2 Communication Development

**Standard 1**
Learner Development and Individual Learning Differences

Communication is a relational, nonlinear, transactional process between a sender and a receiver of a message (Dyches, Carter, & Prater, 2012). See Figure 10.1 for a conceptual model of this communication process. The message may be an exchange of ideas, opinions, facts, or simply social etiquette conventions (e.g., please, thank you, excuse me). The medium is

**Figure 10.1** *A Conceptual Model of the Communication Process*

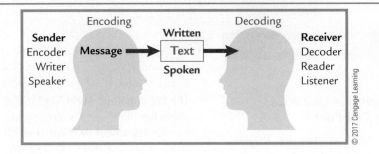

often oral (e.g., speech, song, sounds), written (e.g., text messages, emails, books, handwritten notes), manual (e.g., gestures, sign language), or visual (e.g., photographs, drawings). This chapter will focus primarily on oral communication.

Effective communication is very complex. Think about what must happen to have clear understanding in any communicative action. First, a "message is intended, composed, sent, received, detected, and recognized as a message, opened, processed, understood, and interpreted, with an externally observable response" (Steinfatt, 2009, p. 299). Many elements are critical for effective communication: deliberate behavioral cues, private and public cues, message content and form, coding, and decoding among the communication partners. At any point in the communicative exchange, a communication breakdown may occur. For example, during an exchange between a teacher and a parent of one of her students, "The message may be received but not opened (e.g., the parent heard you but was not really listening); the message may be received, recognized as a message, but not processed (e.g., the parent acknowledges you said something by saying, "Uh-huh," but does not understand what you have said); and so forth" (Dyches et al., 2012, p. 19).

Consider the childhood game of "Telephone," where all participants sit in a circle and the leader whispers a message to the person to her left, who receives this message and relays it to the person on his left, and so forth, until they reach the end of the circle. Oftentimes, the original message is distorted, either because a sender did not clearly communicate the message, or because a receiver did not clearly understand the message. In either case, the message was not communicated accurately. What may have started out as "Harry Potter wears very cool glasses" can turn out to be "Every hothead tears shoes and smashes!" Although this game is fun to play, in reality, when one's message is not communicated clearly, frustration, confusion, and despair may abound. Therefore, it is important that school professionals learn the characteristics of communication disorders so children at risk of having these difficulties can be identified early, assessed, and served appropriately.

## 10-2a Expressive and Receptive Language

Because communication involves at least two partners, both need skills to send as well as to receive messages. These two primary components of communication are called expressive and receptive language.

**Expressive language** involves many skills that help an individual communicate a message to another. In oral expression, the communicator needs to be able to formulate a thought, have the motor skills to produce the sounds of the words, phrases, and sentences related to that thought, speak the message using correct form, and use appropriate intonation, gestures, and other communicative acts to help the receiver comprehend the message. Other forms of expressive communication include orthography (written words), Braille, sign language, and pictures, among others.

**Receptive language** involves many skills that help the receiver of a message to both receive and understand the message that is sent. With oral communication, the receiver must attend to the speaker, hear what the speaker is saying, and comprehend the words, phrases, and sentences of the speaker. The receiver must also understand the intonation, gestures, and other communicative acts of the speaker to more accurately receive the message that was intended by the communicative partner. Similar to expressive language, for the receiver to understand other forms of communication such as Braille, sign language, and traditional

**Expressive language**
Skills that help an individual communicate a message to another.

**Receptive language**
Skills that help the receiver of a message to both receive and understand the message that is sent.

Figure 10.2 *A Conceptual Model of Communication, Language, and Speech*

**Language**

Language expressed through speech and through other means (e.g., manual sign language, written communication)

**Spoken Language**

**Speech**

Speech without language (e.g., a parrot's sounds)

© 2017 Cengage Learning

Language can exist without speech (left), and not all speech constitutes language (right), but spoken language (center) is one outcome of typical human development. Communication is the broad umbrella concept that includes speech and language. Although communication can be achieved without these components, it is greatly enhanced by them.

orthography, he must know the language in which the message is sent. For example, if a person writes a message to you in Arabic, but you do not have the language skills or resources to interpret the message, there is a communication breakdown between you and the speaker.

## 10-2b Speech and Language

Two highly interrelated components of communication are speech and language; however, although they are related, they are not the same thing (see Figure 10.2). **Speech** is the physical production of sounds that take the form of words and is one means of expressing language. **Language** represents a symbolic, rule-based system that gives meaning to the things we speak, write, read, and understand. It is possible to have language without speech, such as sign language used by people with hearing impairments, and speech without language, such as some patients with certain types of aphasia who produce speech without meaning.

Language focuses on three primary aspects: form, content, and use (when and why we say something, or pragmatics). Each of these will be described.

**Language Form** Language form, or how we say something, is comprised of phonology, morphology, and syntax. **Phonology** is the system of speech sounds that an individual utters—that is, rules regarding how sounds can be used and combined (Pfeiffer & Adkins, 2012). For example, the word cat has three phonemes, C-A-T. **Morphology** is concerned with the form and internal structure of words—that is, the transformations of words in terms of areas such as tense (e.g., present to past tense), number (singular to plural), and so on. When we add an s to cat, we

*Photo 10.1* Language can exist without speech and not all speech includes language. Spoken language is one outcome of typical human development.

©Lucky Business/Shutterstock.com

have produced the plural form, cats, with two morphemes, or units of meaning: the concept of cat and the concept of plural. Such transformations involve prefixes, suffixes, and inflections (Owens, 2008; Plante & Beeson, 2013). **Syntax** involves the rules governing sentence structure, the ways in which words are combined into phrases and sentences. For example, the sentence "Will you help Sheyenne?" changes in meaning when the order of only two words is changed to "You will help Sheyenne."

A combination of syntax and morphology constitutes **grammar**. For example, instead of saying, "We were at the mall," Colton says, "Me and him was to the mall," which is grammatically incorrect because of the pronoun, prepositional, and subject-verb agreement

**Speech**
The physical production of sounds that take the form of words and is one means of expressing language.

**Language**
A symbolic, rule-based system that gives meaning to the things we speak, write, read, and understand.

**Phonology**
The system of speech sounds that an individual utters.

**Morphology**
The form and internal structure of words.

**Syntax**
The rules governing sentence structure, the way sequences of words are combined into phrases and sentences.

**Grammar**
A combination of syntax and morphology.

*Photo 10.2* Language is made up of several components, such as phonology, syntax, morphology, semantics, and pragmatics. These will vary as the children mature and grow in their ability to communicate, and as they learn from interacting with others.

errors. However, young children learning their native language often do not follow standard grammatical rules. It is important to note that dialects based upon regional speech patterns, social class, and ethnic groups may have different grammatical conventions, and are not considered language disorders.

**Language Content** Language content includes the "what" of the communication message, its **semantics**, or understanding the meaning of language. Semantics addresses whether the speaker's intended message is conveyed by the words in an age-appropriate manner. For example, the sentence "The tree ate the color four" is syntactically correct, but it has no meaning because trees do not eat and, even if they could, they cannot eat something that does not exist (the color four).

**Language Use** Language use, or **pragmatics**, represents how language is used in social situations. Pragmatics can be illustrated by the fact that teachers talk differently depending on whether they are instructing students, making a point in a faculty meeting, or chatting at a party. Pragmatics includes processes such as turn taking, and initiating, maintaining, and ending conversations.

In the vast percentage of cases, children develop speech and language normally, without significant delays or disruptions to the process. Understanding the typical developmental process helps school professionals and others identify and serve students whose speech and language characteristics differ from the norm and therefore interfere with effective communication.

### 10-2c Speech and Language Development

Young children normally advance through several stages in acquiring language, from babbling, using words, stringing words together, to expressing their own thoughts in relatively complex sentences. An infant's initial verbal output is primarily limited to crying and, hence, is usually associated with discomfort (from hunger, pain, or being soiled or wet). Before long (around 2 months), babies begin to cry and to coo vocally, expressing reactions to pleasure as well as discomfort. At about 4 to 6 months of age, they begin to babble, which involves making some consonant and vowel sounds. At this point, babies often make sounds repeatedly when they are alone, seemingly experimenting with their sound-making abilities and not necessarily trying to communicate with anyone (Fogle, 2013; Owens, 2008). They may also babble when their parents or others are playing with or otherwise caring for them.

A baby's first word is a momentous, long-anticipated event. In fact, eager parents often interpret as "words" sounds that probably have no meaning to the child. What usually happens is that the baby begins to string together sounds that occasionally resemble words. To the parents' delight, these sounds frequently include utterances such as "Da-Da" and "Ma-Ma," which, of course, are echoed, repeated, and reinforced greatly by the parents. As the baby actually begins to listen to the speech of adults, exchanges or "conversations" seem to occur, where the baby responds by saying "Da-Da" when a parent says that sound. Although this type of interchange sounds like a conversation, the child's vocal productions may be understood only by those close to him or her (such as parents or siblings); people other than immediate family members may not be able to interpret their meaning. The baby also begins to use different tones and vocal intensity, which makes his or her vocalizations vaguely resemble adult speech. The interactions between babies and their parents are critical for enhancing babies' developing speech and language. Parents often provide a great deal of reinforcement, such as praise in excited tones, or hugs, for word approximations. They also provide stimulus sounds and words for the baby to mimic, giving the baby considerable practice.

**CEC**

**Standard 1**
Learner Development and Individual Learning Differences

**Semantics**
The understanding of language, the component most directly concerned with meaning.

**Pragmatics**
A component of language that represents the rules that govern the reason(s) for communicating.

The timing of a baby's actual first word is open to interpretation, although it usually happens between 12 and 18 months (Tager-Flusberg et al., 2009). These words often involve echoing (repeating what has been heard) or mimicking responses based on verbalizations of those nearby. At first the words may have little or no meaning, although they soon become attached to people or objects in the child's immediate environment, such as daddy, mommy, or milk. Before long, these words begin to have more perceptible intent, as the child uses them for requests and as a means of pleasing parents. Strings of two and three words that resemble sentences typically begin between 18 and 30 months of age (Tager-Flusberg et al., 2009). At this stage, meaning is usually unmistakable because the child can clearly indicate that he or she wants something. The child uses fairly accurate syntax, with word order generally consisting of subject-verb-object.

Most children with normally developing language are able to use all the basic syntactical structures by 30 to 48 months (Tager-Flusberg et al., 2009). By 5 years, they have progressed to using six-word sentences, on the average. Children who are developing language at a normal pace articulate nearly all speech sounds correctly, and in context, somewhere between 4 and 8 years of age. These illustrations are couched in terms of when children produce language—that is, in terms of expressive language development. However, research indicates that children's receptive skills precede their abilities to express language (Mayor & Plunkett, 2014). Thus, children are able to understand a great deal more than they can express. Most children show some understanding of language as early as 6 to 9 months, often responding first to commands such as "no-no" and their names (Vinson, 2012; Williams, 2011).

Variable age ranges are used for each milestone in outlining normal language development, some with rather broad approximations. Several factors contribute to this variability. For one thing, even children who are developing normally exhibit substantial differences in their rates of development. Some variations are due to a child's general health and vitality, others to inheritance, and still others to environmental influences, such as the amount and type of interaction with parents and siblings (Phillips & Lowenstein, 2012; Vinson, 2012). Also, age ranges become wider in more advanced stages of development. Therefore, observation of when receptive and expressive language first occurs is perhaps less accurate. Considerable variability also occurs with abnormal language and speaking ability. In some cases, the same factors that contribute to variability in normal language are considered disorders if they result in extreme performance deviations. In other cases, the definitions differ and characteristics vary among people—the same variability we have encountered with other disorders.

When a child speaks like a much younger person, she may have a speech delay. For youngsters with a speech delay, the development follows a normal pattern, but is substantially slower than in most children of the same age. From a developmental point of view, this problem involves both delayed speech and language development.

Young children can typically communicate, at least to some degree, before they learn verbal behaviors. They use gestures, gazing or eye contact, facial expressions, other physical movements, and nonspeech vocalizations, such as grunts or squeals. This early development illustrates the relationship among communication, language, and speech.

Very young children with **delayed speech** often have few or no verbalizations that can be interpreted as conventional speech at a period of time when speech is expected. Some communicate solely through physical gestures. Others may use a combination of gestures and vocal sounds that are not approximations of words. Although some may speak, but in a very limited manner, perhaps using single words (typically nouns without auxiliary words, such as "ball" instead of "my ball"), they often have fewer syllables per word, or primitive sentences like "Want ball" rather than "I want the ball" (Kaderavek, 2011). Such communication is normal for infants and toddlers, but it is abnormal for children beyond the age when most have at least a partially fluent speech (Weber-Fox & Hampton, 2008).

Because there are several forms of delayed speech, the causes of these problems also vary greatly. For example, partial or complete hearing loss may seriously limit an individual's sensory experience and, hence, cause serious delays in speech development (e.g., Owens, 2011; Radziewicz & Antonellis, 2009). For those with normal hearing, the broader environment may also contribute to delayed speech (e.g., Bernstein & Levy, 2009). For

**Delayed speech**
A deficit in speaking proficiency whereby the individual speaks like someone much younger.

example, in some children's homes, there is minimal conversation, little chance for the child to speak, and, thus, little opportunity to learn and engage in speech. Also, related language experiences such as reading to young children may be limited or totally absent. Parental negativism, or conflicts between parents' expectations and a child's ability to perform, may also contribute to speech delays (Bernstein & Levy, 2009; Owens, 2010). Other developmental conditions, such as cerebral palsy, autism, intellectual disabilities, emotional disturbance, or brain injuries may also contribute to delayed speech (e.g., Drew & Hardman, 2007; Froemling, Grice, & Skinner, 2011).

Treatment approaches for delayed speech teach the child appropriate speaking proficiency for his or her age level. When physiological conditions are the cause of the delayed speech (e.g., hearing impairments), then specific treatments such as surgery or hearing aids must be considered (Owens, 2010; Radziewicz & Antonellis, 2009). However, for many cases, treatment is likely to focus on the basic principles of learned behavior where the stimulus and reinforcement patterns that are contributing to delayed speech are changed so that appropriate speaking behaviors can be learned, actively practiced, and reinforced (Froemling, Grice, & Skinner, 2011). Some success has been achieved through direct instruction aimed at increasing spontaneous speech. Such instruction emphasizes positive reinforcement of speaking to shape the child's behavior in the direction of more normal speech. All interventions should involve the collaborative efforts of speech-language pathologists (SLPs), teachers, and parents to focus on modifying and enhancing the child's speech and the communication environments (Tiegerman-Farber, 2009; Weiss, 2009).

Although speech delays are concerns for parents and professionals, they are not considered to be disorders. In the field of speech-language pathology, communication disorders are categorized into nine areas, referred to as the "Big Nine" (American Speech-Language-Hearing Association [ASHA], 2015a) and include: articulation, fluency, voice and resonance, receptive and expressive language, hearing, swallowing, cognitive assessments of communication (e.g., attention, memory), social aspects of communication (e.g., challenging behavior, ineffective social skills), and communication modalities (e.g., oral, manual, assistive technology).

For the purposes of this chapter, communication disorders are categorized according to the *Diagnostic and Statistical Manual of Mental Disorders* (*DSM-5*; American Psychiatric Association, 2013) and generally comprise the "Big Nine." These categories include five distinct disorders. Voice and resonance disorders are also included in this chapter, although they are not considered to be mental or developmental disorders; rather, they result from physiological problems. The disorders discussed in this chapter include the following:

1. Language disorder,
2. Speech sound disorder (articulation),
3. Child onset fluency disorder (stuttering),
4. Social (pragmatic) communication disorder, and
5. Voice and resonance disorders.

This chapter will discuss these five communication disorders, including their definitions; characteristics and prevalence; causes and risk factors; identification and assessment processes; and interventions and treatments. Disorders that require highly specialized training to assess and treat (e.g., swallowing disorders, cognitive assessments of communication) are not covered, and communication disorders related to hearing impairments are addressed in Chapter 13 of this text. Furthermore, this chapter does not cover selective mutism, as it is considered to be emotionally based rather than developmentally based.

## 10-3 Language Disorders

This section presents information related to language disorders, including their definitions and classifications, characteristics and prevalence, causes and risk factors, identification and assessment, and finally, interventions and treatments.

## 10-3a Definitions and Classifications of Language Disorders

The diagnostic criteria for individuals with a language disorder include persistent challenges in acquiring and using language with various modalities (e.g., spoken, written, sign language) because of deficits in comprehension or production. These difficulties with language are substantially and measurably below age expectations (American Psychological Association, 2013). Stated simply, language disorders represent significant difficulties in one's ability to understand or express ideas in his or her native communication system.

In public schools, however, professionals use the classification system provided by the federal government, according to the Individuals with Disabilities Education Act (IDEA). The classification for students with communication disorders under IDEA is "Speech or Language Impairment" (SLI) and generally means a communication disorder such as impaired articulation, language impairment, stuttering, or a voice impairment that adversely affects a student's educational performance. Students with the communication disorders discussed in this chapter are likely to be considered eligible for speech-language therapy and/or other services under the classification of "Speech Language Impairment," if the multidisciplinary team determines this is appropriate.

*Photo 10.3* Interactions between individuals are complex and may reflect language maturation challenges in the child.

©Serhiy Kobyakov/Shutterstock.com

## 10-3b Characteristics and Prevalence of Language Disorders

The terminology applied to the processes involved in language, and to disorders in those processes, varies widely. In this chapter, we will discuss three language disorders: expressive language disorders, receptive language disorders, and aphasia.

Individuals who experience difficulty in language production, or formulating and using spoken or written language, may have an **expressive language disorder**. Some have limited vocabularies and use the same array of words regardless of the situation. Expressive language disorders may appear as immature speech, often resulting in interaction difficulties (Freed, 2012).

People with **receptive language disorders** have difficulty comprehending what others say. In many cases, receptive language problems in very young children are noticed when they do not follow an adult's instructions. These children may seem inattentive, may be very slow to respond, and process only part of what is being said to them (Pfeiffer & Adkins, 2012).

It is not uncommon for receptive language problems to appear in students with specific learning disabilities (Fogle, 2013). Such language deficits contribute significantly to their problems with academic performance as well as their social skills. Receptive language disorders appear as high-risk indicators of other disabilities, especially emotional and behavioral disorders.

Individuals with **mixed receptive and expressive language disorders** experience delays in comprehending and using the rules related to combining elements of words. For example, a child might not use *the* or *a* correctly, use verb tenses incorrectly (e.g., "he runned"), or use third-person singular verbs incorrectly (e.g., "He want"). They also have difficulty in formulating their own questions and in inferring meaning from what someone says to them (Boyle, McCartney, O'Hare, & Law, 2010).

**Aphasia** involves a loss of the ability to speak or comprehend language. It can affect all language modalities (e.g., speech, comprehension, writing, reading). Aphasia may be found both during childhood and in the adult years. The term **developmental aphasia** has been used widely for children; however, these children are also referred to as having an expressive language disorder. Regardless of the label, children with developmental aphasia struggle to acquire and use words to express their needs and wants to others.

Because communication disorders are comprised of many types of impairments, estimating prevalence is difficult. However, national data indicates that 18.2 percent of all children (ages 6 to 21) served in programs for those with disabilities are categorized as having speech or language impairments. It must be remembered, however, that only approximately 12 percent of all U.S. children K through 12 are served in programs for students with disabilities (U.S. Department of Education, 2014).

Also, of children between ages 3 to 5 being treated under IDEA, almost half (44.7 percent) are served for speech and language impairments (U.S. Department of Education, 2014). These figures do not deviate greatly from other estimates, although some data have suggested substantial geographical differences (e.g., significantly higher percentages in some areas of California than in parts of the Midwest). Speech and language impairments are the second most frequently occurring disability (next to specific learning disabilities) to receive special services (U.S. Department of Education, 2014). Speech and language disorders are identified in more children in kindergarten through the middle grades, but decline as age increases.

Obviously, students with speech and language disorders that do not significantly impact their progress in the general curriculum are not eligible for specialized educational services. It may be possible for some of these students to receive accommodations with a 504 plan, or they may receive privately funded services, such as speech therapy paid for by the students' parents. Yet other students may receive no services at all, with the hope that the speech disorder will correct itself with time. The prevalence of language delays in children ages 2 to 7 ranges from 2.3 to 19 percent, and these children often have difficulty with attention, reading, writing, and socialization (McLaughlin, 2011).

## 10-3c Causes and Risk Factors of Language Disorders

Many physiological problems may cause language difficulties. Neurological damage that may affect language functioning may occur prenatally, during birth, or any time throughout life (Williams, 2011). For example, language problems may result from oxygen deprivation before or during birth. Serious emotional disorders may accompany language disturbances if an individual's perception of the world is substantially distorted (Freed, 2012).

Language disorders may also occur if learning opportunities are seriously deficient or are otherwise disrupted. As with speech, children may not learn their native language if the environment is not conducive to such learning (Froemling, Grice, & Skinner, 2011). Modeling in the home may be so infrequent or disordered that a child may not learn language in a normal fashion.

Aphasia is typically the result of an acquired brain injury or sometimes a developmental abnormality in the brain. Adult aphasia typically is linked to accidents or injuries such as gunshot wounds, motorcycle and auto accidents, and strokes. Current research suggests that different symptoms result from damage to different parts of the brain (Bastiaanse & Thompson, 2012; Manasco, 2014). Injury to one area of the brain may result in impaired expression, poor articulation, slow and labored speech, and grammatical omissions (e.g., *of, the, an*). However, if a neighboring area of the brain is injured, the resulting speech and language complications differ greatly. Individuals with this neurological damage may show more fluent, but nonsensical, speech known as jargon. Their comprehension is often impaired, resulting in a lack of awareness about their own jumbled speech and deficits. Individuals with aphasia resulting from injury to the back part of the brain seem to have more fluent speech, but the speech lacks important content. The speech of these individuals appears to reflect impaired comprehension (Martin, 2009; Sampson & Faroqi-Shah, 2011).

Pinpointing the causes of different language disorders can be difficult. We do not know precisely how normal language acquisition occurs or how malfunctions influence language disorders. We do know that certain sensory and other physiological systems must be intact for language processes to develop normally. For example, impaired vision or hearing may result in a language deficit (Freed, 2012; Reed, 2012). Likewise, serious brain damage may inhibit normal language functioning. Learning must also progress in a systematic, sequential fashion for speech and language to develop appropriately (Bernstein & Levy, 2009).

## 10-3d Identification and Assessment of Language Disorders

**CEC**

**Standard 4**
Assessment

As we have seen with other disabilities, referrals may come from several stakeholders, notably parents and teachers or other educational personnel (Miller & Wagstaff, 2011). Parents play the most critical role in initial identification of potential problems, because their child's communication skills develop during the early years. Such initial assessments are likely to emerge when the child's communication performance attracts someone's attention, such as when a child does not meet major communication milestones. Parents working with speech-language pathologists become key figures in coordinating multidisciplinary team collaboration (Pfeiffer & Adkins, 2012). Referrals, screening procedures, diagnoses, and interventions will follow trajectories that are mapped specifically on the features of a child's communication disability and other contextual matters, such as family circumstances (Moore & Montgomery, 2008).

Because language disorders are varied, effective assessment components must reflect that variation to adequately serve the needs of the individual (Schwartz, 2012). Such cooperation is crucial for students with communication disorders because of the broad array of challenges that fall into the purview of different disciplines ranging from medical and health-related specialties to those involving teaching and positive behavior development.

**CEC**

**Standard 7**
Collaboration

Assessments for classification of language disorder include natural language samples through direct observation in different communicative contexts, formal and informal interaction with the child, and observing interactions between the child and her parents, usually with the observation lasting at least 30 minutes so the speech-language pathologist has sufficient time to observe the quantity and quality of utterances (Tager-Flusberg et al., 2009). Assessments also include parent-report measures to provide observations that are not readily observed in clinic settings. Finally, multidisciplinary teams may conduct direct assessments of a child's language skills using standardized measures. Although few instruments are valid for children younger than 24 months of age (Tager-Flusberg et al., 2009), the *Bayley Scales of Infant and Toddler Development* (Bayley, 2005) is one test that has been used to help diagnose infants and toddlers with language disorders. Having an early diagnosis helps and guides multidisciplinary teams in providing early and effective interventions for these children (Torras-Mañá, Guillamón-Valenzuela, Ramírez-Mallafré, Brun-Gasca, & Fornieles-Deu, 2014). Comprehensive evaluations are critical, particularly for children who are not meeting expected developmental milestones, because disordered language development may be a red flag for the possibility of other physical or developmental problems that manifest themselves first as a language problems (McLaughlin, 2011).

Assessment typically involves the development of an individual's profile of strengths, limitations, age, developmental level, monolingual or bilingual background, and literacy, as well as considerations regarding temperament that may affect therapy. From such a profile, an individualized treatment plan is designed and put in place (Bastiaanse & Thompson, 2012).

Speech-language pathologists assessing bilingual clients must be able to differentiate between a speech-language disorder and difficulties resulting from speech-language differences. Thus, SLPs must be familiar with a wide variety of cultural and linguistic differences and, when assessing, must consider many factors such as family dynamics, socioeconomic status, cultural traditions, gender, and class that make up an individual's cultural identity. Without considering these factors, clinicians may perform a skewed and biased assessment, failing to accurately represent a child's speech and language abilities. These misdiagnoses result in time and effort being wasted treating those who need no speech or language intervention, but who may possibly need culturally and linguistically relevant instruction.

So, how can assessment be carried out in such a way as to prevent misdiagnoses of culturally and linguistically diverse students? Simply translating standardized assessments into the native language fails to be the answer. Because various cultures do not put the same emphasis on labeling items or the acquiring knowledge of prepositions, for example, a translated assessment will fail to accurately depict the native language abilities of an emergent bilingual child. Thus, a more nuanced, sociocultural approach, involving dynamic assessment (test–teach–retest format), ethnographic interviewing, and direct observation, should be taken when assessing culturally and linguistically diverse students.

**Standard 5**
Instructional Planning and Strategies

## 10-3e Interventions and Treatments for Language Disorders

Treatments for language disorders must account for many elements as the multidisciplinary team develops a treatment plan (Pfeiffer & Adkins, 2012). Interventions are individualized, and significant planning is required, especially by speech-language pathologists (Meinzen-Derr, Wiley, Grether, & Choo, 2011; Schwartz, 2012). Furthermore, early interventions are critical for the success of infants and toddlers at risk for and diagnosed with communication disorders. Research indicates that the earlier a child is diagnosed and receives services individualized to the changing needs, preferences, and priorities of the family, the more positive the outcomes (Paul & Roth, 2011).

Interventions for all communication disorders must consider multiple elements: the nature of the problem, the impact on the individual, and the individualized delivery of services (Fogle, 2013; Pfeiffer & Adkins, 2012). Two areas of primary importance while serving students with language impairments are to create an individualized language plan, and to consider augmentative and alternative communication strategies or devices.

When a student is identified as having a language disorder, the multidisciplinary team, including parents, should develop an **individualized language plan (ILP)**, similar in concept to the individualized education programs (IEPs) mandated by IDEA (Tiegerman-Farber, 2009). These intervention plans often include several components:

- Long-range goals (annual)
- Short-range and specific behavioral objectives
- A statement of the resources to be used in achieving the objectives
- A description of evaluation methods
- Program beginning and ending dates
- Evaluation of the individual's generalization of skills
- A statement regarding service delivery location(s)

**Standard 2**
Learning Environments

After the team decides upon these items, services are then delivered. In some cases, speech-language services are provided in a therapy room; however, in other situations, the team determines the services are most appropriately delivered in the general or special education classroom. Some students receive services in multiple locations, under the direction of the speech-language pathologist, who works to assure skills learned in isolated or small group settings are generalized to more natural environments.

Several questions immediately arise, including what to teach or remediate first and whether teaching should focus on an individual's strong or weak areas. These questions have been raised with respect to many disabilities. Teaching exclusively to children's weaknesses may result in more failure than is either necessary or helpful to their progress. That is, children may experience so little success and receive so little reinforcement that they become discouraged. Good clinical judgment needs to be exercised in deciding how to divide one's attention between the students' strengths and their weaknesses. One program, Systematic Engaging Early Literacy (SEEL), has been developed to balance instruction to meet the unique needs of young children with speech and language impairments, while attending to their strengths as curious, active, and playful children. See the accompanying Learning through Social Media box for a description of this free and effective resource.

For adults with aphasia, an individualized treatment plan also involves evaluation, profile development, and teaching/therapy in specific areas within each of the broad domains (Chabon & Cohn, 2011). Such training should begin as soon as possible, depending on the person's condition. The most noticeable recovery of speech and language abilities happens within the first couple months following a stroke. After about six months, however, the rate of recovery slows significantly (Vukovic, Vuksanovic, & Vukovic, 2008). Advances in technology are often used in diagnosis and treatment (Fogle, 2013); for example, brain stimulation and medication are relatively new treatments for individuals with aphasia (Fama & Turkeltaub, 2014).

## Treating Language Delays

Preschool children with language delays benefit from literacy activities that are systematic and engaging. A free curriculum, SEEL (Systematic Engaging Early Literacy), is available for those who teach children in preschool through first grade who have language delays or reading difficulties, as well as typically developing children. The lessons are engaging, motivating children to participate playfully in meaningful activities. They explore learning through informal and spontaneous conversations, receive frequent and varied practice opportunities, make meaningful connections, and learn explicitly "what, why, and how." For example, in the lesson plan to teach students the short *Aa* sound, students engage in word play about Andy, who loves ants, and says "Aachoo!" when he hears a word that begins with the *Aa* sound. Resources are also available in Spanish. To access these free resources, visit http://education.byu.edu/seel.

Some people with communication disorders require intervention through communication other than oral language. In some cases, the person may be incapable of speaking because of a severe physical or cognitive disability, so a nonspeech means of communication must be selected, designed, and implemented. Known as **augmentative and alternative communication (AAC)**, this area of practice is intended to either augment an individual's existing speech and language or to serve an alternative to speech, and requires collaboration among professionals from many disciplines, such as speech-language pathology, special education, vocational rehabilitation, and engineering.

**CEC**

**Standard 7**
Collaboration

Some AAC strategies may be "no tech" or "low tech," such as the use of sign language, picture communication books, or communication boards. Other strategies might be more "moderate" or "high tech," such as the use of communication applications on an iPad, highly specific software and hardware on a computer, or a special device dedicated for the sole purpose of providing communication access to users. Research results suggest that carefully chosen techniques and devices can be quite effective (Fogle, 2013; Johnston, Reichle, Feeley, & Jones, 2012). See the nearby Assistive Technology feature about one of the world's greatest astrophysicists, Stephen Hawking, who lost the ability to speak after tracheotomy surgery. Dr. Hawking uses a dedicated device to communicate expressively and has delivered many speeches and written many best-selling books using his alternative means of speech.

*Photo 10.4* Technology devices such as iPads or similar may be used effectively for children as they learn to name items, to speak to others when the tablets are programmed in this fashion, or flexibly as both with different applications installed.

© Racorn/Shutterstock.com

Individuals use AAC to not only to provide them with a "voice" with which they can communicate in their social environments, but to increase their participation in their home and community environments, elevate their quality of life, enhance their relationships, and overcome barriers (Beukelman & Mirenda, 2012). Augmentative and alternative communication devices and strategies have received increasing attention in the past few years, partly because of the availability of affordable technology and partly because of prominent coverage provided in the popular press.

Users of AAC include those with a variety of conditions that affect communication including intellectual disabilities, autism, physical disabilities, and multiple disabilities (Johnston et al., 2012). These strategies must also be individualized to meet the specific needs of those being treated and to take into account their strengths and limitations in operating the technology.

**Augmentative and alternative communication (AAC)**
An area of practice intended to either augment an individual's existing speech and language or to serve an alternative to speech.

## World-Renowned Astrophysicist Stephen Hawking's Use of Assistive Technology

Since 1997, my computer-based communication system has been sponsored and provided by Intel® Corporation. A tablet computer mounted on the arm of my wheelchair is powered by my wheelchair batteries, although the tablet's internal battery will keep the computer running if necessary.

My main interface to the computer is through a program called EZ Keys, written by Words Plus Inc. This provides a software keyboard on the screen. A cursor automatically scans across this keyboard by row or by column. I can select a character by moving my cheek to stop the cursor. My cheek movement is detected by an infrared switch that is mounted on my spectacles. This switch is my only interface with the computer. EZ Keys includes a word prediction algorithm, so I usually only have to type the first couple of characters before I can select the whole word.

When I have built up a sentence, I can send it to my speech synthesizer. I use a separate hardware synthesizer, made by Speech+. It is the best I have heard, although it gives me an accent that has been described variously as Scandinavian, American, or Scottish.

Through EZ Keys I can also control the mouse in Windows. This allows me to operate my whole computer. I can check my email using the Eudora email client, surf the Internet using Firefox, or write lectures using Notepad. My latest computer from Intel, based on an Intel® Core™ i7 Processor and Intel® Solid-State Drive 520 Series, also contains a webcam which I use with Skype to keep in touch with my friends. I can express a lot through my facial expressions to those who know me well.

I can also give lectures. I write the lecture beforehand and save it on disk.

I can then send it to the speech synthesizer a sentence at a time using the Equalizer software written by Words Plus. It works quite well and I can try out the lecture and polish it before I give it.

I keep looking into new assistive technologies, and recently Intel [has] sponsored a team of its engineers to design a new facial recognition system aimed at improving my communication speed. They also have some new ideas regarding my software interface and it will be interesting to see the results of this. It looks quite promising. I have also experimented with Brain Controlled Interfaces to communicate with my computer; however, as yet these don't work as consistently as my cheek-operated switch.

SOURCE: Hawking, S. "The Computer." Retrieved on April 13, 2015, from www.hawking.org.uk/the-computer.html.

**Standard 1**
Learner Development and Individual Learning Differences

# 10-4 Speech Sound Disorders

This section presents information related to speech sound disorders, including their definitions and classifications, characteristics and prevalence, causes and risk factors, identification and assessment, and finally, interventions and treatments.

## 10-4a Definitions and Classifications of Speech Sound Disorders

To be diagnosed with a speech sound disorder, individuals must experience persistent challenges with speech sound production, and those difficulties must interfere with intelligibility of speech (American Psychological Association, 2013). Speech sound disorder (or articulation disorder) represents the largest category of all speech problems. Additionally, much of the past and current speech and language research attends to this disorder (American Psychiatric Association, 2013; Plante & Beeson, 2013).

## 10-4b Characteristics and Prevalence of Speech Sound Disorders

Speech is very important in contemporary society. Speaking ability can influence a person's success or failure in personal, social, and professional arenas. Most people are average in their speaking ability, and they may envy those who are unusually articulate and pity those who have a difficult time with speech. What is it like to have a serious deficit in speaking ability? It is different for each individual, depending on the circumstances in which he or she operates and the severity of the disorder.

People with articulation problems often carry strong emotional reactions to their speech that may significantly influence their behavior, such as restricting their speech or not speaking at all. Speech is so critical to functioning in society that speech disorders often have a significant impact on affected individuals. It is not difficult to imagine the impact poor articulation may have in classroom settings or social environments. Children may be ridiculed by peers, feel inadequate, suffer emotional stress, and even struggle academically. That stress may continue into adolescence (Brinton, Fujiki, & Baldridge, 2010) and even adulthood, limiting their social lives and influencing their vocational choices.

Speech sound disorders are characterized by problems with articulation (making sounds) and sound patterns (phonological processing), resulting in the inaccurate or otherwise inappropriate execution of speaking (Hartmann, 2008). Individuals may make certain types of errors or distribute errors incorrectly (e.g., the position of the sound in the word) (ASHA, 2015b).

The error types can be remembered by the acronym SODA: substitutions, omissions, distortions, and additions (Daymut, 2009). Substitutions happen when a speaker substitutes one phoneme for another, such as saying /w/ for /r/ (e.g., wight for right), /w/ for /l/ (e.g., fowo for follow), and /th/ for /s/ (e.g., thtop for stop, and thoup for soup). Omissions (or deletions) most frequently involve dropping consonants from the ends of words (e.g., los for lost), although omissions may occur in any position in a word. Distortions happen when a speaker produces an unfamiliar sound (e.g., nasalized, where /p/ may sound more like /m/). Additions involve adding an extra sound (e.g., dog-uh for dog). Articulation errors may also involve transitional lisps, where a /th/ sound precedes or follows an /s/ (e.g., sthoup for soup or yeths for yes) (Plante & Beeson, 2013).

Speech sound disorders are a rather prevalent type of speech problem. Research suggests that most problems encountered by speech clinicians involve articulation disorders (American Psychiatric Association, 2013), with a prevalence rate of 1.06 percent of elementary school children having a speech sound disorder (McKinnon, McLeod, & Reilly, 2007).

## 10-4c Causes and Risk Factors of Speech Sound Disorders

Speech sound disorders are believed to develop for three primary reasons: structural, neurological, and functional. Structural reasons include physiological problems such as abnormal mouth, jaw, or teeth structures, or cleft palate. Neurological problems include those resulting from nerve injury or brain damage (Plante & Beeson, 2013; Raposa & Perlman, 2012).

**Functional articulation disorders** refer to articulation problems that are not due to structural physiological defects, but rather are likely to have resulted from environmental or psychological influences. The vast majority of articulation disorders are functional. However, such categories of causation overlap in practice, and even the line between functional and structural articulation disorders is indistinct. Function and structure, though often related, are not perfectly correlated: Some people with physical malformations that "should" result in articulation problems do not have such problems, and vice versa.

Despite this qualifying note, we will examine the causes of speech sound disorders due to either structural or functional reasons. These distinctions remain useful for instructional purposes because it is unusual for individuals to overcome a physical abnormality and articulate satisfactorily.

Many different physical structures influence speech formulation, and all must be synchronized with learned muscle and tissue movements, auditory feedback, and a multitude of other factors. These coordinated functions are almost never perfect, but for most people they develop in a remarkably successful manner. Oral structure malformations alter the manner in which coordinated movements must take place, and sometimes they make normal or accurate production of sounds extremely difficult, if not impossible.

One faulty oral formation recognized by most people is the **cleft palate**, which speech-language pathologists often refer to as clefts of the lip, palate, or both. The cleft palate is a gap in the soft palate and roof of the mouth, sometimes extending through the hard palate and upper lip. The roof of the mouth serves an important function in accurate sound production. A cleft palate reduces the division between the nasal and mouth cavities, influencing

**Functional articulation disorders**
Articulation problems that are likely the result of environmental or psychological influences.

**Cleft palate**
A gap in the soft palate and roof of the mouth, sometimes extending through the upper lip.

*Figure 10.3  Normal and Cleft Palate Configuration*

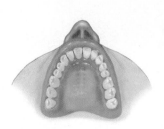
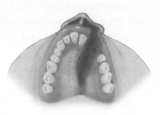

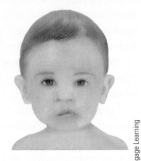

(a) Normal palate configuration    (b) Unilateral cleft palate    (c) Bilateral cleft palate    (d) Repaired cleft palate

the movement of air that is so important to articulation performance (Klinto, Salameh, Svensson, & Lohmander, 2011). Clefts are congenital defects that occur in about one of every 700 births and may take any of several forms (e.g., Owens, Metz, & Farinella, 2011; Raposa & Perlman, 2012). Figure 10.3 shows a normal palate in part (a) and unilateral and bilateral cleft palates in parts (b) and (c), respectively; it is easy to see how articulation would be impaired. These problems are caused by prenatal developmental difficulties and are often corrected with surgery.

Articulation performance is also significantly influenced by a person's dental structure. Because the tongue and lips work together with the teeth to form many sounds, dental abnormalities may result in serious articulation disorders. Some dental malformations are side effects of cleft palates, as shown in parts (b) and (c) of Figure 10.3, but other dental deformities not associated with clefts also cause articulation difficulties.

The natural meshing of the teeth in the upper and lower jaws is important to speech production. The general term used for the closure and fitting together of dental structures is **occlusion**. When the fit is abnormal, the condition is known as **malocclusion**. Occlusion involves several factors, including the biting height of the teeth when the jaws are closed, the alignment of teeth in the upper and lower jaws, the nature of curves in upper and lower jaws, and teeth positioning. A normal adult occlusion is illustrated in part (a) of nearby Figure 10.4. The upper teeth normally extend slightly beyond those of the lower jaw, and the bite overlap of those on the bottom is about one-third for the top front teeth when the jaw is closed.

Occlusion abnormalities take many forms, although we will discuss only two. When the overbite of the top teeth is unusually large, normal difference between the lower and upper dental structures is exaggerated. Such conditions may be due to the positioning of the upper and lower jaws, as illustrated in part (b) of Figure 10.4. In other cases, nearly the

**Occlusion**
The closing and fitting together of dental structures.

**Malocclusion**
An abnormal fit between the upper and lower dental structures.

*Figure 10.4  Normal and Abnormal Dental Occlusion*

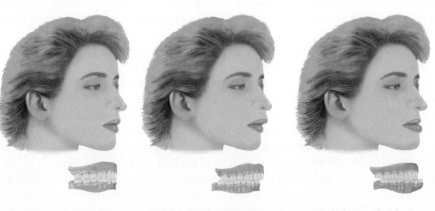

(a) Normal dental occlusion    (b) Overbite malocclusion    (c) Underbite malocclusion opposite occurs, as illustrated in part (c) of Figure 10.4, forming another kind of jaw misalignment. Exaggerated overbites and underbites may result from atypical teeth positions or angles as well as from atypical jaw alignment. All can cause articulation difficulties.

Many disorders are thought to be due to faulty language learning or functional articulation disorders. The sources of defective speech learning are often unknown or difficult to identify precisely (Robinson & Robb, 2009; Snowling & Hulme, 2012). Like other articulation problems, those of a functional nature have numerous specific causes. For example, interactions between children and their adult caretakers (parents and others) make a major contribution to language acquisition (Bernstein & Levy, 2009; Williams, 2011). In some cases, existing stimulus and reinforcement patterns may not support accurate articulation. For example, parents may be inconsistent in encouraging and prompting accurate articulation. Urging their children to speak properly may not be high on their priority list. However, such encouragement is important, particularly if misarticulation begins to emerge as a problem.

Many parents speak differently to infants and toddlers than they do to older children, youth, or adults. This has been called "parentese" or "motherese" and has been found to promote vocal productions and language development in infants and toddlers. However, when still used as the child grows older, this can be detrimental to speech, language, and social development.

Also, adults may encourage baby talk in children and youth by reinforcing and modeling such speech. For example, such speech may be powerfully reinforced by parents asking the child to say a particular word in the presence of grandparents or other guests and rewarding him or her with laughter, hugs, and kisses. Such potent rewards can result in misarticulations that linger long beyond the time when normal maturation would diminish or eliminate them. Related defective learning may come from modeling. Modeling is a potent tool in shaping speech and language behavior. Although the negative influence of baby talk between parents and children has been questioned, modeling and imitation are used in interventions and are thought to influence natural verbal development (Aarts, Demir, & Vallen, 2011; Syrja, 2011).

## 10-4d Identification and Assessment of Speech Sound Disorders

**Standard 4**
Assessment

Identification and assessment of speech sound disorders occur in similar ways as for language disorders. Typically, the family members are concerned about the young child's speech, either because of poor intelligibility, minor articulation problems, or other related speech problems. However, a predictable developmental progression occurs in a substantial number of functional articulation disorders. In such cases, articulation problems diminish and may even cease to exist as the child matures. For instance, the /r/, /s/, and /th/ problems disappear for many children after the age of 5. Therefore, many articulation problems that occur early in a child's life will not become problematic. However, when they do remain, parents are encouraged to have their child evaluated by a speech-language pathologist.

If the child is determined to have a speech sound disorder, speech therapy is often prescribed. If in a school setting, the child may receive a classification by the multidisciplinary team as having a developmental delay in the area of speech (in children younger than 9), or as having a speech-language impairment (for children 9 or older, although teams may give the SLI label to children under 9 if they so choose). Such children can then receive free and appropriate services tailored to meet their individual needs.

## 10-4e Interventions and Treatments for Speech Sound Disorders

**Standard 5**
Instructional Planning
and Strategies

Many types of treatment exist for speech sound disorders. Clearly, the treatment for disorders due to physical abnormalities differs from that for functional disorders. In many cases, however, treatment may include a combination of procedures. The treatment of articulation disorders has also been somewhat controversial, partly because of the prevalence in young children whose articulation skills are most likely to diminish and even disappear over time.

**CEC**

**Standard 5**
Instructional Planning
and Strategies

Thus, many school administrators are reluctant to provide services to treat functional articulation disorders in younger students. In other words, if a significant proportion of articulation disorders is likely to be corrected as the child continues to develop, why expend precious resources on early treatment? This logic has a certain appeal, particularly in times when there is a shortage of educational resources and their use is constantly questioned. However, this argument must be applied with considerable caution. In general, improvement of articulation performance continues until a child is about 9 or 10 years old (see the nearby Reflect on This feature to hear from 7½-year-old Timothy). If articulation problems persist beyond this age, they are unlikely to improve without intense intervention. Furthermore, the longer such problems are allowed to continue, the more difficult treatment becomes and the less likely it is to be successful. Although some researchers suggest that the impact of articulation difficulties is ultimately minimal, others believe that affected individuals may still evidence residuals of the disorder many years later (Owens, Metz, & Farinella, 2011; Plante & Beeson, 2013).

One treatment option is to combine articulation training provided by speech-language pathologists with other instruction for all very young children. This approach may serve as an interim measure for those who have continuing problems, by facilitating the development of articulation for others and not overly taxing school resources. It does, however, require some training for teachers of young children. Other treatment options include medical professionals, particularly if there are surgical needs.

Considerable progress has been made over the years in various types of surgical repair for cleft palates. Current research addresses a number of related matters, such as complex patient assessment before and after intervention (Chabon & Cohn, 2011; Reed, 2012). The surgical procedures may be intricate because of the dramatic nature of the structural defect. Some such interventions include Teflon implants in the hard portion of the palate, as well as stretching and stitching together the fleshy tissue. As nearby Figure 10.3 suggests, surgery is often required for the upper lip and nose structures, and corrective dental work may be undertaken as well. It may also be necessary to train or retrain an individual in articulation and to assess his or her emotional status insofar as it is related to appearance or speech skills, depending on the child's age at the time of surgery (Snowling & Hulme, 2012). A child's continued development may introduce new problems later; for example, the physical growth of the jaw or mouth may create difficulties for someone who underwent surgery at a very young age. Although early correction results in successful healing and speech for a very high percentage of treated cases, the permanence of such results is uncertain in light of later growth spurts.

Treatment of cleft palate may involve the use of prosthetic appliances as well. For example, a prosthesis that basically serves as the upper palate may be used. Such an appliance may be attached to the teeth to hold it in position; it resembles the palate portion of artificial dentures.

Dental malformations other than those associated with clefts can also be corrected. Surgery can alter jaw structure and alignment. In some cases, orthodontic treatment may involve the repositioning of teeth through extractions and the use of braces. Prosthetic appliances, such as full or partial artificial dentures, may also be used. As in other challenges, the articulation patient who has orthodontic treatment often requires speech therapy to learn proper speech performance.

Treatment of functional articulation disorders often focuses on relearning certain speaking acts; in some cases, muscle control and usage are the focus. Specific causes of improper learning are difficult to identify precisely, but the basic assumption is that an inappropriate stimulus and reinforcement situation was present in the environment during speech development (Owens, Metz, & Farinella, 2011; Plante & Beeson, 2013). Accordingly, treatment includes attempts to correct that set of circumstances so that accurate articulation can be learned. Several behavior modification procedures have been employed successfully in treating functional articulation disorders. In most cases, treatment techniques are difficult to implement because interventions must teach proper articulation, must be tailored to the individual, and must promote generalization of the new learning to a variety of word configurations and diverse environments beyond the treatment setting (Owens, Metz, & Farinella, 2011).

## Timothy: "I Think I Talk Okay, Don' You?"

My name is Timothy. I am almost 7½ years old. Mondays after school, I go to the university where I meet "wif a lady who help me talk betto. It was my teacha's idea 'cause she said I don' say 'l' and 'r' good an some othos too. I kinda like it [coming here] but I think I talk okay, don' you? I can say 'l' good now all the time and 'r' when I reeeally think about it. I have lots of friends, fow, no—five. I don' talk to them about comin' hea, guess I'm jus not in the mood. Hey, you witing this down, is that good? You know the caw got hit by a semi this mowning and the doow hanle came off. I'm a little dizzy 'cause we wecked."

Timothy, age 7½

### Question for Reflection

Timothy thinks he talks okay. What do you think? Although Timothy is already receiving some assistance, given his age, do you think additional intervention is needed?

It should also be noted that differences in language and accent can create some interesting issues regarding treatment. When a child's first language is other than English or involves an accent different from the mainstream, that youngster may demonstrate a distinctiveness of articulation that makes his or her speech different and perhaps hard to understand (Aarts, Demir, & Vallen, 2011; Battle, 2009; Snowling & Hulme, 2012). Does this circumstance require an intervention similar to that applied for articulation disorders? Such a question involves cultural, social, and political implications beyond those typically considered by communication professionals. See the Case Study on Embracing Diversity for more information related to differentiating between dialects and articulation disorders.

Speech-language pathologists are often concerned about the level of intensity and frequency of their services. What does the child need in order to correct her speech sound disorder? Some research indicates that for preschool children, three sessions per week yield greater success than only once per week after 24 sessions. It is important to have at least 80 to 100 responses made by the child per session (Allen, 2013).

### Emilio

It may be difficult for speech-language pathologists to conduct culturally relevant and appropriate assessments for English language learners. For example, 7-year-old Emilio is a student whose parents speak only Spanish, and he is the oldest of three children. He has been in a dual-immersion program for two and a half years and is experiencing difficulties producing particular sounds in English. It seems to the SLP that Emilio is slower to articulate some sounds than his other native Spanish-speaking peers. How can the SLP determine whether this is an articulation problem or an influence from Emilio's native language? For example, he says the word "espaghetti" rather than "spaghetti" (a phoneme distortion). This is typical for native Spanish speakers, where there is no initial /s/ cluster in their language, but the SLP does not have significant experience working with Spanish-speaking students, so she is not aware of these differences. Therefore, she seeks assistance from her multidisciplinary team, which includes native Spanish-speaking professionals.

When school personnel distinguish speech and language differences from disorders, they can develop treatment plans that are individualized and appropriate for each student. Bilinguistics has developed free downloadable files that show the common deletions, distortions, and replacements in second-language learners.

### Application Questions

As a member of the multidisciplinary team, what advice would you give to Emilio's speech-language pathologist regarding differentiating between speech-language disabilities and speech-language differences?

## 10-5  Child Onset Fluency Disorder

This section presents information related to child onset fluency disorder, including its definitions and classifications, characteristics and prevalence, causes and risk factors, identification and assessment, and finally, interventions and treatments.

### 10-5a  Definitions and Classifications of Child Onset Fluency Disorder

Child onset fluency disorder, or stuttering, occurs when the individual's normal fluency and time patterning of speech is disturbed, and this causes anxiety about speaking. The onset is in the child's early developmental period, but deficits may occur as social communication demands increase (American Psychological Association, 2013).

### 10-5b  Characteristics and Prevalence of Child Onset Fluency Disorder

In typical speech, we are accustomed to a reasonably smooth flow of words and sentences. For the most part, speech has a rhythm that is steady, regular, and rapid. Most of us also have times when we pause to think about what we are saying, either because we have made a mistake or because we want to mentally edit what we are about to say. However, these interruptions are considered typical, occur infrequently, and do not disturb the ongoing flow of our speaking. Our speech is generally fluent in speed and continuity.

However, when an individual has childhood onset fluency disorder (stuttering), typical flow of speech is abnormally interrupted by repetitions, blocks, or prolongations of sounds, syllables, words, or phrases (Chang & Zhu, 2013; Fogle, 2013). When conversing, it becomes apparent when an individual stutters. Interruptions in speech flow are very evident to both speaker and listener, and are disruptive to communication. Listeners may grow uncomfortable and try to assist the stuttering speaker by providing missing or incomplete words (Flynn & St. Louis, 2011; Przepiorka, Blachnio, St. Louis, & Wozniak, 2013).

Some people have a fluency disorder known as cluttered speech, or **cluttering**, which is characterized by overly rapid speech that is disorganized, and occasionally filled with unnecessary words (Bretherton-Furness & Ward, 2012). However, the most recognized fluency disorder is stuttering.

Stuttering generally presents itself in childhood and, in some circumstances, lasts into adulthood. The majority of children who stutter start to do so around two and a half years of age (ASHA, 2015c). Common symptoms of child onset fluency disorder are the frequent repetition of sounds and syllables. They may frequently use broken words, where long pauses interrupt the completion of a single word. Because some words may be so difficult to say, children with fluency disorders may avoid the use of certain words altogether. This is known as circumlocutions. In order to produce words, some children may demonstrate excessive physical tension, like increased eye blinking, twitching, tremors, and clenching of fists (American Psychiatric Association, 2013). See the Snapshot, "Trinity: Stuttering Is Like a Car Going Too Fast" by a seventh-grade student who stutters.

Although not an initial symptom of child onset fluency disorder, many children experience increased stress and anxiety as a result of stuttering, especially in social situations. They may be embarrassed to speak because of their stuttering, which may decrease the amount of social interactions they have. It may also negatively affect their academic and occupational performance (American Psychiatric Association, 2013). Oftentimes, the severity of stuttering increases under social pressure. For example, a person's stuttering may worsen when it is necessary to give a presentation in front of a group of people. However, in other situations such as when the speaker is reading out loud, singing, or communicating with a pet or an inanimate object, the stuttering may be completely absent (American Psychiatric Association, 2013).

Although stuttering is a familiar concept to most people, it occurs rather infrequently. Prevalence differs in the literature, but some research shows that 5 to 8 percent of the general population has experienced stuttering at some point in their lives (Chang & Zhu, 2013). According to research conducted by the Centers for Disease Control and Prevention,

**Child onset fluency disorder (stuttering)**
A symptom of child-onset fluency disorder that occurs when the flow of speech is abnormally interrupted by repetitions, blocking, or prolongations of sounds, syllables, words, or phrases.

**Cluttering**
A speech disorder characterized by excessively rapid, disorganized speaking, often including words or phrases unrelated to the topic.

approximately 1 to 2 percent of children between ages 3 and 17 have child onset fluency disorder (ASHA, 2015c), with boys being 3 to 4 times as likely to develop stuttering as girls (National Institute on Deafness and Other Communication Disorders, 2014). Child onset fluency disorder has one of the lowest prevalence rates among all speech disorders (Chang & Zhu, 2013).

## 10-5c   Causes and Risk Factors of Child Onset Fluency Disorder

For many years, it was believed that stuttering was caused by overly strict parenting, such as young children experiencing traumatic toilet training. However, this psychogenic theory has not been generally supported by empirical research. Most research supports two primary causes of child onset fluency disorder: developmental stuttering and neurogenic stuttering.

Developmental stuttering occurs when a child's speech and language abilities do not meet verbal demands. This type of stuttering has a genetic basis, with a breakthrough discovery in 2010 of three genes that cause stuttering. Children of parents who stutter are three times more likely to develop a stutter than the general population (American Psychiatric Association, 2013). Neurogenic stuttering occurs after brain injury such as a stroke or head trauma (National Institute on Deafness and Other Communication Disorders, 2010).

*Photo 10.5* The way in which parents speak greatly affects their child's speech patterns.

Although parenting styles may not cause child onset fluency disorder, environmental factors may worsen the symptoms (ASHA, 2015c). Stuttering may also be a by-product of another sensory deficit, like a hearing impairment. In some cases, stuttering may be a side effect of some medications.

**CEC**

**Standard 4**
Assessment

## 10-5d   Identification and Assessment of Child Onset Fluency Disorder

Parents often become concerned about stuttering as their children learn to talk. Most children exhibit some normal dysfluencies that diminish and cease with maturation. Approximately 80 to 90 percent of children who are diagnosed with child onset fluency disorder present symptoms by age 6. However, the age when children are usually diagnosed ranges between 2 and 7 years old (American Psychiatric Association, 2013). Children who present symptoms of child onset fluency disorder are referred to a speech-language pathologist. The child is then assessed over a period of time and in various social situations to determine the severity of the stuttering and to assess the settings in which the stuttering is absent, diminished, or elevated (ASHA, 2015c). Speech-language pathologists also pay special attention to how parents, peers, and others react to the stuttering.

When making a diagnosis, SLPs pay particular attention to how severe the child's stuttering is and how inhibiting it is in the child's family, social, emotional, and academic life. They also consider how the child is impacted emotionally by the stuttering (ASHA, 2015c). However, stuttering alone does not necessarily prevent success in school, extracurricular, or other life areas. The Snapshot "Windows to the World" describes the early influence of a teacher on Tom Holdman, a second-grade boy with a fluency disorder. With the encouragement and guidance from his parents and teachers, Tom found an additional way to communicate with the world—through art. He is now a world-renowned artist and owns his own studio, specializing in an ancient art form of using crushed glass in his stained glass windows, some over 5,000 square feet and consisting of over 40,000 individual pieces. His artwork has been showcased in many national and international venues.

*by Brad Wilcox*

Tom was a bright boy. His mind was quick. His hands were quicker. He loved learning at school, but he faced one problem. His parents didn't like to call it a problem. They called it a challenge. Tom stuttered. It took him forever to get out the simplest sentence. Each...word...came...with...great... effort. When he spoke he would squint his eyes, tighten the muscles in his neck, and ball his little hands into fists. He made it through first grade... with...great...effort.

Mrs. Wilcox was Tom's second-grade teacher. Her mind was creative. Her hands were nurturing. She had been told about Tom's problem, but she didn't like to call it a problem. She called it an opportunity.

Tom's favorite time of the day was story time when Mrs. Wilcox gathered her students on the shag rug at the back of the classroom. Then she would sit in her wooden rocking chair and read story after story. Tom would close his eyes and listen to the rhythm of her words. In his mind he would see images and his hands would move across the carpet bringing the images to life. He ran his fingers through the long carpet yarn standing it up into walls, shaping it into patterns.

When Mrs. Wilcox excused the students to return to their desks she would linger where Tom had been sitting. She would smile down at his creations and sense the talent inside this boy, just waiting to come out.

One day the class stood to say the Pledge of Allegiance as they always did. Tom usually remained quiet, but this day he tried to repeat the words along with the class: "I... p...p...pledge..." He had only said a few words and the children began to giggle. "You sound like Porky Pig," said a boy standing near. Then the boy yelled loudly, "Th...Th...That's all folks." Everyone laughed.

*Courtesy of Tom Holdman*

Mrs. Wilcox quickly quieted the children and moved ahead with the lesson, but she could see Tom with his head down on his desk. She could see his little shoulders quivering.

Later that morning, Mrs. Wilcox pulled Tom aside and looked at him lovingly over her reading glasses. "Tom," she said. "You have so much to say, but words are only one way to express all the wonders inside you. There are other ways." And she handed him a sketch pad and a brand new pencil.

"But... I...can't...draw..." Tom protested.

"Yes, you can. I've seen you do it on the carpet."

"But...what can I...draw?" He asked.

Mrs. Wilcox looked around the room until her eyes settled on the corner. "Draw the flag," she said with a smile.

Later that day, some of the other second-graders saw Tom busy at his desk and wondered what he was doing. They circled around and were surprised at the wonderful picture he was finishing.

"Wow!" said one of the girls. "Tom drew the flag. He's an artist." All the other students hurried to see.

"Will you draw a picture for me?" asked one of the boys.

Tom smiled at Mrs. Wilcox who was smiling back from across the room.

Later in the year a student teacher visited Tom's class and was doing the reading lesson. Before anyone could explain, she called on Tom to read aloud. He swallowed hard, looked at the words on the page and began: "The...boy...ran..."

When some of the children started to snicker, Tom threw his book down and ran out of the room. Mrs. Wilcox followed him into the hall. "Tom," she said placing her hands on his shoulders. "You have so much to say, but words are only one way of talking. There are other ways too." She went back into the classroom and returned with a set of watercolor paints.

"But...what...can...I...paint?" asked Tom.

"Use your imagination!" Mrs. Wilcox responded. Soon Tom was painting pictures that were so imaginative that they were displayed in the hall.

Later in the year, Tom was playing at recess when a boy said, "Let's play Red Rover, Red Rover." Everyone formed into teams and began to chant. Tom couldn't keep up with the others and was holding up his team. Some of the second-graders from another class began to mimic him. When it was his turn to run, he ran as hard as he could and didn't stop when he broke through the line. He just kept going.

Mrs. Wilcox watched him round the corner of the building and calmly followed after him. "Tom," she called out. "Tom, wait!" When she finally caught up, she knelt down next to him. "You have so much to say, but words are only one way to communicate. There are other ways too. Have you ever heard of clay?"

Soon Tom was making snakes and pots and masks for all the other children to enjoy. With his clay he even made their school with all its doors and windows.

When he showed Mrs. Wilcox, she admired the detail. "You've done a wonderful job," she said happily. Then she pointed to one of the windows and said, "That's what art is, Tom. It is a window to the world. Always keep developing your talents and you will be able to speak what's in your heart."

And Tom did just that. When he left second grade, he kept drawing and painting and shaping clay. Then one day in high school his art teacher demonstrated how to make a stained glass window. He was fascinated by the process and colors and how the light behind the window changed it—as if one piece of art were actually a hundred. He closed his eyes and saw images in his mind. His hands began to move creating shapes and patterns.

Many years have passed. Tom still talks...with...great...effort, but he now knows that words are only one way of speaking. There are other ways, and he has found them. He creates incredible stained glass windows that are displayed all over the world. The art window Mrs. Wilcox helped open for Tom, he now opens for many others as he speaks loudly, smoothly, beautifully, and confidently through his windows.

## 10-5e  Interventions and Treatments for Child Onset Fluency Disorder

**Standard 5**
Instructional Planning and Strategies

Fortunately, treatments are much more sophisticated today than those Demosthenes used by putting pebbles in his mouth while speaking. For several years, treatment models have increasingly focused on direct behavioral therapy—that is, attempting to teach children who stutter to use fluent speech patterns (e.g., Carey et al., 2010). In some cases, individuals are taught to monitor and manage their stuttering by speaking more slowly or rhythmically. Using this model, they are also taught to reward themselves for increasing periods of fluency. Some behavioral therapies include information regarding physical factors (such as regulating breathing) and direct instruction about correct speaking behaviors. The overall therapy combines several dimensions, such as an interview regarding the inconvenience of stuttering, behavior modification training, and follow-up. Because stuttering is a complex problem, effective interventions are likely to be complicated.

Additionally, interventions such as modeling, self-monitoring, counseling, and the involvement of support group assistance have all been studied and shown to be somewhat useful for children who stutter (e.g., Ramig & Dodge, 2010; Reed, 2012). Some research on medication treatment has shown improvements, although pharmacological intervention is not widely selected as a treatment option (Yairi & Seery, 2011). Speech rhythm has been the focus of some therapy, as well as developing the naturalness of speaking patterns. Relaxation therapy and biofeedback have also been used, because tension and anxiety are often observed in people who stutter (Fogle, 2012; Owens, Metz, & Farinella, 2011). In all the techniques noted, outcomes are mixed, and people who stutter are likely to try several approaches (Fogle, 2012; Weber-Fox & Hampton, 2008). However, even with the uncertainties in available interventions, some research has shown that 65 to 85 percent of children diagnosed with child onset fluency disorder overcome their dysfluency (American Psychiatric Association, 2013). The inability of any one treatment or cluster of treatments to consistently help people who stutter demonstrates the complexity of this disorder and ongoing need for research in this area.

## 10-6  Social (Pragmatic) Communication Disorder

This section presents information related to social (pragmatic) communication disorder, including its definitions and classifications, characteristics and prevalence, causes and risk factors, identification and assessment, and finally, interventions and treatments.

## 10-6a   Definitions and Classifications of Social (Pragmatic) Communication Disorder

Social (pragmatic) communication disorder (SCD) is characterized by sustained difficulties in using verbal and nonverbal communication, as related to the social purposes of communicating with others. These deficits significantly limit an individual's ability to communicate effectively, participate socially, develop and maintain social relationships, and may even affect academic and occupational performance. The symptoms have an early developmental onset; however, these deficits may not be observable until social communication demands exceed the individual's limited capabilities (American Psychiatric Association, 2013). This disorder is new to the *DSM-5*, although the concept and other clinically similar disorders have been identified and treated for a number of years with terms such as social communication disorder and pragmatic language impairment (Rapin & Allen, 1983).

To be diagnosed with SCD, the individual's communication barriers cannot be better explained by low structural language performance or cognitive ability (American Psychiatric Association, 2013). Furthermore, a diagnosis of SCD should be considered only if "the developmental history fails to reveal any evidence of restricted/repetitive patterns of behavior, interests, or activities" (Norbury, 2014, p. 204) that would rule out other diagnoses such as autism spectrum disorder. Also, intellectual disability and global developmental delay must be ruled out for an individual to be diagnosed with SCD.

## 10-6b   Characteristics and Prevalence of Social (Pragmatic) Communication Disorder

Social pragmatic communication requires several different constructs for effective communication. They include using skills such as making joint attention, greeting others, sharing information, and being flexible in communicating effectively with a range of communication partners. It also includes conversational turn-taking and nonverbal communication such as using gestures and making eye contact. Other skills include the ability to connect to others' emotional states and take another's perspective (Tierney, Kurtz, Panchik, & Pitterle, 2014). These skills are difficult for those with SCD.

Social (pragmatic) communication disorder has four primary characteristics. First, individuals with SCD have deficits in the use of communication for social reasons. Persistent difficulty in using verbal and nonverbal communication impairs their ability to engage appropriately in social contexts. For example, although they may have normal or even advanced use of language form and content, their use of language may be impaired. They compose well-structured sentences, deliver them according to conventional grammatical and linguistic rules, have accurate articulation, but how, when, and with whom they communicate is significantly impaired.

Next, they experience significant challenges in changing their communication to match various contexts. Using the earlier example related to pragmatics in this chapter, teachers talk differently depending on whether they are teaching students, making a point in a faculty meeting, or chatting at a party. Individuals with SCD cannot make the necessary adjustments for appropriate communication in different settings. For example, they may use overly formal language where informal language is appropriate. This may make it more difficult for them to make, maintain, and enjoy friendships (Tierney et al., 2014), as they may be more comfortable communicating with adults who understand them and can relate to them better. Adults also are more able to repair communicative breakdowns than children. The most prevalent characteristic of SCD is "persistent difficulties in the social use of verbal and nonverbal communication" (*DSM-5*, 2013). This includes difficulty communicating "for social purposes, such as greeting and sharing information, in a manner that is appropriate for the social context" (*DSM-5*, 2013).

Another characteristic of SCD is difficulty following conversational and storytelling rules. They may not take turns appropriately in conversations, realize they are misunderstood and work to repair the communication breakdown, and ineffectively use verbal or nonverbal signals to regulate their communication interactions (American Psychiatric Association, 2013). For example, they may not understand nonverbal cues such as when a conversational partner looks at his watch to indicate he is ready to exit the conversation.

Finally, those with SCD lack the ability, or experience extreme difficulty, understanding messages that are not explicitly stated. This means that they struggle to make inferences and have difficulty understanding language that depend on context for understanding such as idioms, metaphors, and some types of humor such as sarcasm (American Psychiatric Association, 2013). For example, when Andy heard his grandmother exclaim "Good grief!" he asked her, "How can grief be good, Grandma?" Andy took his grandmother's words literally, not realizing that she was using a figure of speech.

At the current time there are no reliable records that show the prevalence of SCD, which may be because so many symptoms of SCD overlap with other disorders (ASHA, 2015d).

## 10-6c Causes and Risk Factors of Social (Pragmatic) Communication Disorder

Because the communication symptoms of SCD are similar to those with other disorders such as high-functioning autism spectrum disorders (ASD), it is difficult to pinpoint a specific cause or cluster of causes of SCD. However, a family history of communication disorders, ASD, and specific learning disabilities appear to increase the risk for SCD (American Psychiatric Association, 2013).

Individuals with attention deficit/hyperactivity disorder may experience social communication limitations and social participation difficulties similar to those with SCD. Similarly, those with social anxiety disorders have similar characteristics; however, for those with social anxiety, their symptoms occur after appropriate development and due to anxiety or fear of social interactions. Finally, those with intellectual disability or global developmental delay may have concomitant impaired social communication skills, but SCD is not the appropriate diagnosis unless the social communication impairments are significantly exaggerated in light of the intellectual limitations (American Psychiatric Association, 2013).

## 10-6d Identification and Assessment of Social (Pragmatic) Communication Disorder

Symptoms of SCD normally present themselves in early childhood (American Psychiatric Association, 2013). However, it is uncommon that SCD would be diagnosed in a child younger than 4 or 5 years old. After this age most children have sufficient language and speech abilities, and any abnormalities or deficits in social communication may be more easily identified. Milder forms of SCD are not generally apparent until early adolescence (American Psychiatric Association, 2013; Norbury, 2014).

**Standard 4**
Assessment

Parents, teachers, and speech-language pathologists are key players in the process of making a diagnosis for SCD (ASHA, 2015d), particularly because some standardized measures do not detect functional difficulties that are evident to teachers and parents (Adams et al., 2012).

When initially screening a child for SCD, parents and teachers are carefully interviewed regarding the child's normal behaviors. The child is usually observed for a period of time, and typically a hearing test is administered to make sure that hearing loss is not contributing to poor social communicative interaction (ASHA, 2015d). When children are suspected of having a communication disorder after the initial screening, they are referred to a speech-language pathologist, where the SLP and the multidisciplinary team conduct further assessments. As the speech-language pathologists assess children, they look for individual and cultural aspects of how the children orient to their own names, the amount of eye contact they engage in, how much interest they show in objects around them, their ability to engage in pretend play and imitation, their nonverbal communication, and their language development (ASHA, 2015d).

A comprehensive assessment of children with SCD includes gathering information from standardized assessments, parent/teacher child report measures, ethnographic interviewing, analog tasks (e.g., observing the child in simulated social situations), and naturalistic observations. Upon completion of these assessments, the child may be diagnosed with a social pragmatic communication disorder, another disorder, or no diagnosis at all (if he does not meet eligibility requirements). The report should include a description of the symptoms and severity of the disorder, recommendations for intervention, and referral to other professionals as needed (ASHA, 2015d).

Because so many similarities can be seen between SCD and other disorders, it can be difficult to make a clear diagnosis (Norbury, 2014). For example, stereotyped phrases, intonation, and some nonverbal interactions may seem similar between those with SCD and those with ASD (Adams et al., 2012). It is important for multidisciplinary assessment teams to collaborate in their assessments to make accurate diagnosis or educational classification.

## 10-6e   Interventions and Treatments for Social (Pragmatic) Communication Disorder

Because there is great heterogeneity in the social communication skills of students with SCD, there are a number of intervention options available to help promote and develop positive social interaction (Adams et al., 2012). Treatment packages should follow a social communication approach, recognizing the "social, cognitive, and linguistic influences on pragmatics" (Adams, 2008, p. 191). Three primary components should be included with any intervention: social interaction and social understanding, pragmatics, and language processing (Adams, 2008).

Treatments related to developing positive social interactions and understanding others often include instruction and activities to help students understand social context, emotions, social cues, and nonstated social information. These treatments also focus on developing and maintaining friendships, and developing flexibility (Adams, 2008). Many software programs and tablet applications have been developed for students to learn to read facial expressions and understand the emotions of others.

Treatments related to pragmatics frequently focus on conversational turn-taking, learning mechanics of conversations, matching style to context, and managing topics (Adams, 2008). For example, some students need to be taught to not ask too many questions or to not talk too much during a communicative exchange. Manuel, a junior high school student, was taught to avoid sexual topics with his female teachers and classmates.

Interventions related to language processing help students to find the right words for the situation, construct narratives, monitor comprehension, and appropriately use idiomatic language and complex sentences (Adams et al., 2012). Students may need to learn how to make inferences—that is, how to fill in the unstated information in conversations, in ways that are developmentally appropriate (Adams, 2008). Some therapy has included direct instruction in teaching idioms and other figurative language to these students, using online resources, activity books, as well as children's books.

These social communication skills are taught in a number of ways. Some instruction happens during one-on-one therapy with a speech-language pathologist, but that alone is not likely to help students to generalize their skills to other situations or with other people. Small-group instruction, such as social skills groups, helps students to learn and practice social communication skills and to develop friendships in more functional contexts. Research supports the use of social skills groups for improving behavioral outcomes and self-esteem, increasing social competence, and generalizing social skills (Tierney et al., 2014).

These groups can be comprised of students with similar communication difficulties, or integrated with typically developing peers who can model appropriate social communication (Tierney et al., 2014). Sometimes instruction is provided within general education classrooms, with the SLP serving as a consultant to the classroom teacher or special educator (Adams, 2008). Furthermore, training can occur in the home or other settings, with siblings, co-workers, and others serving as role models.

Effective treatments do not need to be conducted solely by the SLP. Evidence exists for the effectiveness of training typically developing peers and siblings to model and reinforce appropriate social skills to increase social communication of preschoolers, helping them to generalize and maintain skills across other settings (Tierney et al., 2014). Furthermore, parents and sometimes even extended family members are critical members of the treatment team, particularly when they are the primary caregivers and frequent communication partners.

Various treatment approaches are used to provide therapy. Behavioral approaches are used to model and reinforce appropriate communication responses, and can be used individually or in groups. Also, cognitive-behavioral approaches have some levels of evidence for effectiveness (Tierney et al., 2014). Most strategies use a variety of philosophical approaches.

One specific strategy that includes multiple approaches is the use of Social Stories™. This strategy explicitly teaches social skills using visual supports written as a story to teach students what to do and say in different situations. They can be written by the student or someone who knows the student well, or a number of stories are available online. They can be illustrated, or use written words combined with graphic symbols, photographs, or even videotaped and watched repeatedly to match each student's unique learning needs (Gray, 1995).

Social scripts are another strategy that focus on the student's strengths in following rigid structures. Usually, the student or someone who knows the student well writes the script, which relates to social encounters that may be difficult for that student. For example, Merilee does not know how to ask her peers to join in a game of kickball during recess. Her teacher, under the consultation of the SLP, works with her to write a typical script of what she can say and what her peers might say in order to enter this social situation. Merilee practices this script with her teacher or other school personnel, her peers, and typically developing students. She then receives prompting, guidance, and feedback before using this script on the playground.

Another strategy to help students with SCD is video modeling. This is an observational learning technique where a student watches a video of himself or someone else engaging in appropriate social communicative interactions, then practices this skill in natural contexts. More information on video modeling is described in Chapter 11, "Autism Spectrum Disorders."

In addition to helping in the diagnostic or classification process, speech-language pathologists are critical in creating and carrying out treatment plans for children and adolescents with SCD. However, it requires the collaborative efforts of the whole multidisciplinary team, including the parents, to provide services across a range of circumstances, for the student to learn, maintain, and generalize the important skills learned for social communicative competence.

**Standard 5**
Instructional Planning
and Strategies

## 10-7   Voice and Resonance Disorders

This section presents information related to voice and resonance disorders, including their definitions and classifications, characteristics and prevalence, causes and risk factors, identification and assessment, and finally, interventions and treatments.

### 10-7a   Definitions and Classifications of Voice and Resonance Disorders

**Standard 1**
Learner Development
and Individual Learning
Differences

Voice and resonance disorders are not included in the *DSM-5*, as they are physiological rather than developmental or mental disorders. Voice disorders involve unusual or abnormal acoustical qualities in the sounds made when a person speaks. All voices differ significantly in pitch, loudness, and other features from the voices of others of the same gender, cultural group, and age. However, voice disorders involve acoustical qualities that are so different that they are noticeable and divert attention away from the content.

Resonance disorders occur when there is abnormal sound vibration in the oral, nasal, or pharyngeal cavities while speaking. This often leads to too little or too much nasality in one's speech (Kummer, 2006).

### 10-7b   Characteristics and Prevalence of Voice and Resonance Disorders

Most people have experienced problems with their voices. Think of the last time you screamed so loudly at a sporting event, and then had a hoarse voice for a period of time thereafter. This is an example of having a temporary problem with one's voice, but it is not

**Voice and resonance disorders**
A condition in which an individual habitually speaks with a voice that differs in pitch, loudness, or quality from the voices of his or her peer group.

**Photo 10.6** Factors in voice disorders that interfere with communication are pitch, quality, and volume. A voice disorder exists when these factors, singly or in combination, cause the listener to focus on the sounds being made rather than the message to be communicated.

a voice disorder. Those with voice and resonance disorders often speak with an unusual hoarseness, breathiness, or nasality.

Like so many speech problems, the nature of voice and resonance disorders varies greatly. Our description provides considerable latitude, but also outlines general parameters of voice disorders often dismissed in the literature: pitch, quality, and volume. An individual with a voice disorder may exhibit problems with one or more of these factors, and they may interfere with communication (Boone, McFarlane, Von Berg, & Zraick, 2010; Ferrand, 2012).

Appropriate pitch is efficient and is suited to the situation and the speech content as well as to the speaker's laryngeal structure. Normal pitch permits inflection without voice breaks or excessive strain, varies as emotion and meaning change, and does not distract attention from the message. Pitch disorders take several forms. The person's voice may have an abnormally high or low pitch, may be characterized by pitch breaks or a restricted pitch range, or may be monotonal or monopitched. Many individuals experience pitch breaks as they progress through adolescence. Although more commonly associated with young males, pitch breaks also occur in females. Such pitch breaks are a normal part of development, but if they persist much beyond adolescence, they may signal laryngeal difficulties. They may be learned from certain circumstances, as when a person in a position of authority believes a lower voice pitch evokes the image of power. Organic conditions, such as a hormone imbalance, may result in abnormally high- or low-pitched voices.

The acoustical characteristics of voice and resonance quality include such factors as nasality, breathy speech, and hoarse-sounding speech. **Hypernasality** occurs when there is too much nasality due to the failure of the soft palate to actively close off the nasal cavity during speech, resulting in air and energy being lost through the nasal passage and the speaker becoming less intelligible, usually with vowels and voice oral consonants. **Hyponasality** or **denasality** is the type of voice quality experienced that has too little nasality, usually on nasal consonants (e.g., /m/, /n/, and /ng/; Kummer, 2006), and sounds as though the child has a continual cold or a stuffy nose. People with voice disorders of hoarseness have a constant husky sound to their speech, as though they had strained their voices by yelling.

As for the final element of voice, volume is subjective. A normal voice is not habitually characterized by undue loudness or unusual softness. The typical level of loudness depends greatly on circumstances. Breathiness is a voice disorder with very low volume, like a whisper; it sounds as though not enough air is flowing past the vocal cords. Some research indicates 0.12 percent of elementary school-aged students have voice disorders (McKinnon, McLeod, & Reilly, 2007).

## 10-7c Causes and Risk Factors of Voice and Resonance Disorders

There are three main reasons that cause voice and resonance disorders: structural anomalies, neurological issues, and functional problems (e.g., environmental or psychological). Sometimes a combination of these factors results in voice and resonance disorders. Any one of these reasons can influence the pitch, loudness, or quality of a person's voice, resulting in a disorder.

Hypernasality can be due to improper tissue movement in the speech mechanism, or it may result from physical flaws such as an imperfectly repaired cleft palate (Nyberg,

**Hypernasality**
A resonance disorder that occurs when excessive air passes through the nasal cavity.

**Hyponasality**
A resonance disorder whereby too little air passes through the nasal cavity; also known as denasality.

**Denasality**
A voice resonance problem that occurs when too little air passes through the nasal cavity; also known as hyponasality.

Peterson, & Lohmander, 2014). Excessive hypernasality may also be learned, as in the case of certain rural dialects. Hyponasility, or the type of voice quality experienced during a head cold or hay fever, may also be a result of learning or of abnormal physical structures (Ferrand, 2012), including the presence of large tonsils (Kummer, 2006).

Voice disorders involving volume have varied causes. Voices that are excessively loud or soft may be learned through imitation, perceptions and characteristics of the environment, and even aging (Ferrand, 2012; Portone, Johns, & Hapner, 2008). An example is mimicking the soft speaking of a female movie star. Other cases of abnormal vocal intensity occur because an individual has not learned to monitor loudness. Some structural reasons that may cause issues with volume include paralysis of vocal cords, laryngeal trauma (e.g., laryngeal surgery for cancer, damage through accident or disease), and pulmonary diseases like asthma or emphysema (e.g., Chavira, Garland, Daley, & Hough, 2008; Richardson, Russo, Lozano, McCauley, & Katon, 2008). Loud speech may also be the consequence of hearing impairments or brain damage.

## 10-7d   Identification and Assessment of Voice and Resonance Disorders

**Standard 4**
Assessment

Determining the extent and nature of voice and resonance disorders is difficult for various reasons. First, the determination of voice and resonance normalcy involves a great deal of subjective judgment and varies considerably with the circumstances (e.g., football games, informal conversations, or seminar discussions) and with geographical location (e.g., the West, a rural area, New England, or the Deep South). Another factor that complicates analysis of voice disorders is related to the acceptable ranges of the normal voice. Most individuals' voices fall within acceptable ranges. Children with voice disorders are often not referred for help, and untreated problems may be persistent (Ferrand, 2012; Portone, Johns, & Hapner, 2008).

Disorders of resonance can be determined using a simple test where the speech-language pathologist places one end of a bending straw at the entrance to the child's nose and the other end at the examiner's ear. If while the child produces specific speech samples, the examiner can hear sound through the straw on vowel sounds, this is an indicator of hypernasality, whereas if little sound comes through the straw on nasal consonants, this is an indication of hyponasality (Kummer, 2006).

The typical process for evaluation and treatment is followed as in other disability determination. First there is a referral, followed by evaluation, diagnosis, and if eligible, treatment and evaluation.

## 10-7e   Interventions and Treatments for Voice and Resonance Disorders

**Standard 5**
Instructional Planning
and Strategies

The approach to treatment for a voice and resonance disorder depends on its cause, which can be structurally, neurologically, or functionally based. In cases where abnormal tissue development and/or dental structures result in unusual voice production, surgical intervention may be necessary. Surgery may also be part of the intervention plan if removal of the larynx is required. Such an intervention will also involve relearning communication through alternative mechanisms, including prostheses, and learning communication techniques to replace laryngeal verbalizations (Kosowski, Weathers, Wolfswinkel, & Ridgway, 2012). In some situations, treatment may include direct instruction to enhance the affected individual's learning or relearning of acceptable voice production. These efforts are more difficult if the behavior has been long-standing and is well ingrained.

As is typical of interventions with other language disorders, active participation at treatment sessions and related home implementation is crucial to the success of voice therapy (Starmer, Liu, Akst, & Gourin, 2014). One important element in planning interventions for voice and resonance disorders is clear and open communication with the person seeking treatment (Ferrand, 2012). It is important to avoid setting unrealistic expectations about outcomes and to remember that those being treated are the ultimate arbiters of that treatment's success.

# People with Communication Disorders

## Early Childhood Years

### Tips for Families

- Respond to babbling and other noises the young child makes with age-appropriate verbal and vocal social engagement, reinforcing early verbal output.

- Do not overreact if your child is not developing speech at the same rate as someone else's infant; great variation is found between children.

- If you are concerned about your child's speech development, have his or her hearing tested to determine whether that source of stimulation is normal.

- Observe other areas of development to assure yourself that your child is progressing within the broad boundaries of normal variation.

- If you are seeking day care or a preschool program, search carefully for one that will provide a rich, systematic communication environment.

- Be proactive in collaborating with professionals who serve your child, such as preschool teachers, speech-language pathologists, and other relevant service providers.

### Tips for Preschool Teachers

- Encourage parents to be involved in all dimensions of their child's program, including systematic speech and language stimulation at home.

- Consider all situations and events as opportunities to teach speech and language.

- Use all occasions possible to increase the child's vocabulary.

- Ask "wh" questions, such as what, who, when, and where, giving the child many opportunities to practice speaking as well as thinking.

### Tips for Preschool Personnel

- Communicate with the young child and all of those who are interacting with him or her.

- Collaborate with others in providing communication instruction, under the guidance of the licensed speech-language pathologist.

### Tips for Neighbors and Friends

- Interact with young children with communication disorders as you would with any others, speaking to them normally and directly modeling appropriate communication.

- Intervene if you encounter other children ridiculing the speech and language of these youngsters; encourage sensitivity to individual differences among your own children and other neighborhood children.

## Elementary Years

### Tips for Families

- Stay proactively involved in your child's educational program through active participation with the school.

- Work in collaboration with the child's teacher on speaking practice, blending it naturally into family and individual activities.

- Communicate naturally with the child; avoid "talking down" and thereby modeling the use of "simpler language."

### Tips for General Education Classroom Teachers

- Continue collaborating with and promoting parents' involvement in their child's intervention program in whatever manner they can participate.

- Encourage the child with communication disorders to talk about events and things in his or her environment and to describe experiences in as much detail as possible.

- Use all situations possible to provide practice for the child's development of speech and language skills.

- Promote vocabulary enhancement for the child in different topic areas.

### Tips for School Personnel

- Promote an environment where all who are available and in contact with the child are involved in communication instruction, if not directly then indirectly through interaction and modeling.

- Encourage student involvement in a wide array of activities that can also be used to promote speech and language development.

### Tips for Neighbors and Friends

- Interact with children with communication disorders normally; do not focus on the speaking difficulties that may be evident.

- Support the child's parents as appropriate, particularly if they are struggling with difficult feelings about their child's communication skills.

## Secondary and Transition Years

### Tips for Families

- Recognize that some teenagers and young adults who still exhibit communication problems may perform on a lower cognitive level due to other disabilities such as autism spectrum disorders, intellectual disabilities, or multiple disabilities.

- Encourage frequent and appropriate functional communication training, including AAC strategies and devices, particularly if students engage in maladaptive behavior due to the inability to adequately express themselves.

- Encourage your child to make and keep genuine friendships, particularly for those who are teased and bullied due to their communication disabilities.

### Tips for General Education Classroom Teachers

- Embed communication instruction in the context of functional areas (e.g., social interactions, requests for assistance, choice making).

- If AAC strategies and devices are part of the student's IEP or individualized language plan, specifically target their use in the classroom (e.g., let the student ask and answer questions using her AAC device).

### Tips for School Personnel

- Encourage students with communication disorders to participate in school activities that will require a broad variety of skill levels in speaking (e.g., debate club, drama club).

- Collaborate with others in the school to find the best way you can contribute to the student's communication development.

### Tips for Neighbors and Friends

- To the degree that you are comfortable doing so, interact with children using alternative communication approaches (e.g., sign language, gestures, pictures).

## Adult Years

### Tips for Families

- Interact with the adult who has a communication disorder on a level that is functionally appropriate for his or her developmental level while respecting her chronological age.

### Tips for Therapists or Other Professionals

- Recognize the maturity level of the person with whom you are working.

Do not assume you know the interests or inclinations of a younger client simply because the individual has a communication difficulty.

- Encourage adults with communication disorders to develop strengths and talents in their areas of choice.

### Tips for Neighbors and Friends

- Communicate in as normal a fashion as possible, given the severity and type of disorder. If the person uses AAC strategies or device, consider learning about them to the degree that you feel comfortable.

## Looking Toward a Bright Future

Communicating effectively with others is very important to us in nearly every aspect of our lives. Because our society places a great emphasis on interpersonal interaction, the challenges people with communication disorders face are paramount and have a significant impact. And yet the future of science, understanding, and intervention is very promising.

Research standards have been developed to guide researchers and practitioners in determining diagnosis, as well as the level of evidence for a given intervention or set of treatments. Evidence-based practices are those that have converging evidence such as meta-analytic research, include designs with experimental control, avoid subjectivity and bias, include effect sizes that are deemed clinically important, and relate to interventions that are relevant and feasible for practitioners to apply (American Speech-Language-Hearing Association, 2004). As more research is conducted that adheres to these practices, greater understanding, improved practice, and positive outcomes for individuals with communication disorders are likely to occur.

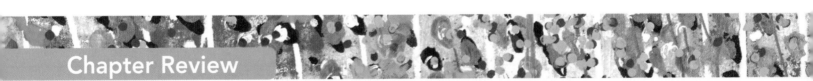

## Chapter Review

**10-1  Describe how the lives of people with communication disorders have changed since the advent of IDEA.**

- Students with communication disorders now enjoy the right to be assessed by a multidisciplinary team of trained professionals to determine their eligibility for services specifically targeted at their strengths and challenges.

- For students who are eligible, free and appropriate individualized services are provided.

- The intent of these services is to promote optimal speech and language development of each student with identifiable communication disorders.

**10-2  Describe the primary components of typical communication development.**

- Incrementally, children learn to compose, send, receive, detect, recognize, process, understand, and interpret communicative messages.

- Gradually infants begin to coo, then babble, using some consonant and vowel sounds, which gradually become simple utterances resembling real words.

- Attention, modeling, and reinforcement play important roles in shaping infants' and young children's speech and language development.

- Most children 18 to 30 months of age begin to use strings of two- and three-word expressions to communicate wants and needs.
- Most children between 30 and 48 months of age have developed to the point that they can apply most of the syntactical structures of their language to communicate using six-word sentences, and they can string together six-word sentences by age 5.
- With appropriate opportunities and encouragement for speech and language development, children and youth continue to develop their prowess and capacities for many kinds of communication (e.g., written, verbal, nonverbal).

## 10-3 Describe language disorders, their prevalence, causation, identification, and related interventions.

- Language disorders represent significant and persistent difficulties in students' abilities to understand or express ideas using their natural communication system.
- Language disorders are often characterized by challenges in receptive and expressive language.
- Some individuals have aphasia—they have lost their capacity to speak and comprehend language.
- The prevalence of language delays and related disorders in children ages 2 to 7 ranges from 2.3 to 19 percent.
- Almost half of all preschoolers receiving special education services have speech or language impairments.
- Almost 20 percent of all children (ages 6 to 21) served in programs for students with disabilities are categorized as having speech or language impairments.
- Causes of language disorders are associated with neurological damage, significantly deficient or disrupted opportunities for learning speech and language, sensory and physiological impairments, and, in cases of aphasia, brain injury.
- Identification of language disorders begins with referral provided by parents and others, including preschool personnel, teachers, and others.
- A variety of observations and assessment tools are used to gather typical language samples in formal and informal settings (e.g., home, school).
- Interventions begin with an individualized language plan for addressing both strengths and challenges.
- This plan may include carefully selected technologies, the use of augmentative and alternative communication strategies or devices, and specific treatments provided by licensed clinicians and specialists.

## 10-4 Describe speech sound disorder, its prevalence, causation, identification, and related interventions.

- Speech sound disorders are characterized by persistent challenges with speech sound production—these challenges interfere with the intelligibility of speech produced by children and adults.
- Speech sound disorders include problems with articulation (making sounds) and phonological processes (sound patterns).

- Approximately 1 percent of elementary-aged students have speech sound disorders.
- Speech sound disorders are believed to develop for three primary reasons: structural, neurological, and functional.
- Identification and assessment of speech sound disorders occur in similar ways as for language disorders: formal and informal observations in a variety of settings, formal assessments, and so on.
- Interventions include treatments for physical abnormalities, no treatments (i.e., waiting for normal development to take its corrective course), integrating articulation training with relevant instruction, teaching and relearning certain speaking acts, and regular and focused speech therapy.

## 10-5 Describe child onset fluency disorder, its prevalence, causation, identification, and related interventions.

- Child onset fluency disorder (stuttering) is characterized by disruptions of the production of speech sounds.
- This disorder often causes children, youth, and adults to have anxiety about speaking to and with others.
- Prevalence rates indicate that approximately 6 percent of the general population experience stuttering at some point in their lives.
- About 1 percent of children between ages 3 and 17 evidence child onset fluency disorder.
- Boys are three to four times more likely to develop stuttering than girls.
- Causes of stuttering include: genetic inheritance, brain injury, other sensory deficits such as hearing impairments, and some medications.
- Certain environmental factors may worsen the stuttering.
- Care is taken to determine the severity of the stuttering; to assess the settings in which the stuttering is absent, diminished, or elevated; the emotional and social impact on affected individuals; and to assess the response of others (e.g., peers, teachers, parents) to the stuttering.
- Most individuals with child onset fluency disorder receive more than one type of treatment, including approaches such as direct behavior therapy, regulation of breathing, modeling, self-monitoring, counseling, medication, speech-rhythm therapy, and participation in support groups.

## 10-6 Describe social (pragmatic) communication disorder, its prevalence, causation, identification, and related interventions.

- Individuals with social (pragmatic) communication disorder (SCD) experience significant difficulties in the social use of language.
- Behaviors associated with this disorder include difficulties in applying and using the social rules and appropriate behaviors associated with communicative interchanges with others.
- There are no reliable prevalence rates for SCD, mainly because symptoms of this disorder overlap with other conditions.

- Causes associated with SCD are varied, including genetic inheritance, associations with other identifiable disabilities or disorders, and the causes that give rise to them.
- Identification begins with interviews with key care providers (e.g., parents, teachers) to obtain their observations about the child's social interactions.
- Often hearing tests are completed to rule out any hearing impairments.
- Observations are made by a speech-language pathologist, observing the child's responsiveness in these and other areas: eye contact, interest in objects in the immediate environment, and patterns of play and imitation.
- Interventions center on teaching positive social interactions, pragmatics, and language processing. These interventions are taught in various ways.

**10-7 Describe voice and resonance disorders, their prevalence, causation, identification, and related interventions.**
- Voice disorders involve unusual or abnormal acoustical qualities in the sounds made when children, youth, or adults speak.
- Resonance disorders relate to abnormal sound vibration in the oral, nasal, or pharyngeal cavities while speaking.
- Voice disorders affect only 0.12 percent of elementary-aged students.
- Main causes for voice and resonance disorders include structural anomalies, neurological issues, and functional problems—any of these may influence the pitch, quality, and volume of a person's voice.
- Identification of voice and resonance disorders is challenging given the subjective nature of some of the required judgments.
- Like identification processes associated with communication assessments, formal and informal observations are made, appropriate assessments are provided, and determinations are made about potential interventions and services.
- Interventions are focused on the causes of the disorder, including surgical interventions, prostheses, direct instruction targeted at acceptable voice production, and frequent collaboration among and between parents, therapists, and therapy recipients.

**CEC** **Council for Exceptional Children (CEC) Standards to Accompany Chapter 10**

If you are thinking about a career in special education, you should know that many states use national standards developed by the Council for Exceptional Children (CEC) to assess a teacher candidate's knowledge and skills for working with students with disabilities. See a complete listing of the seven CEC Content Standards on the inside cover of this text.

1 Learner Development and Individual Learning Differences
2 Learning Environments
4 Assessment
5 Instructional Planning and Strategies
6 Professional Learning and Ethical Practice
7 Collaboration

## Mastery Activities and Assignments

To master the content within this chapter, complete the following activities and assignments:
1. Complete a written test of the chapter's content. If your instructor requires a written test of your content knowledge for this chapter, keep a copy for your portfolio.
2. Review the Case Study on Embracing Diversity, "Emilio," and respond in writing to the Application Questions.

Keep a copy of the Case Study and your written response for your portfolio.
3. Participate in a community service learning activity. Community service is a valuable way to enhance your learning experience. Develop a reflective journal of the service learning experience for your portfolio.

## CHAPTER 11

# Autism Spectrum Disorders

© 2015 Cengage Learning®

## Learning Objectives

*After you complete this chapter, you will be able to:*

**11-1** Describe how the lives of people with autism spectrum disorders (ASD) have changed since the advent of IDEA.

**11-2** Explain the various definitions and classification of ASD.

**11-3** Describe the characteristics and prevalence of children and youth with ASD.

**11-4** List the causes and risk factors associated with ASD.

**11-5** Describe the assessment procedures used to identify ASD in children and youth.

**11-6** Describe the different interventions for children and youth with ASD from early childhood through adulthood.

### A Blog by Abbey Marshall

When C was 13 months old I started to notice something was a little off about him. Was he a little behind? Was he just different from the rest of my other children? I remember looking up signs of autism on the Internet and he seemed to fit some of the criteria but I still wasn't sure. I confronted my husband and asked him what he thought and he just disregarded it and told me not to worry about it. Three months later things had started to progress and people were starting to make comments and ask questions about little C. I was seriously starting to look up the signs of autism at this point. This time I printed the list off and handed it to my husband after the kids had gone to bed and we had a serious conversation about what was going on with C. I still remember the look on my husband's face; it was almost blank as if he knew something was going on. Neither one of us wanted to really talk about it because if we did we were admitting that something was wrong. So many questions popped into my head: the how's, why's, and so on and so on. Then my heart sank, not that my kid might have autism but I knew that things were going to change for us. Our life was going to take a huge turn.

A couple of weeks after digesting the conversation with my husband, I realized that C had a doctor's appointment coming up. I decided I would talk to him about C and what he thought.

"C" Today

When we showed up to the doctor, he asked me if I had any concerns so far and then I slowly brought up the idea that C is showing signs of autism. My doctor said, "Ok, let's have you take a test for him." He handed me what they called an M-CHAT test. It's a bunch of questions about your child to see where they are developmentally, and several questions that would go along with autism: Does your child flap his hands? Will he look when you point at something? Does your child point at things? Will your child make eye contact for X amount of time? And so on. As I was answering all of these questions, I wanted so badly to just lie and mark that everything was ok, but I just couldn't do it. I handed the test back to the doctor, and he looked over it for quite some time. He then said, "C is showing several signs of AUTISM." There it was: the word that I knew I didn't want to hear. Suddenly I lost it. I didn't want to cry in front of the doctor nor my son. I wanted to be this strong mom that could take on anything, but in that moment I broke and realized that I wasn't the only one saying that word, AUTISM. Then my doctor quickly grabbed his nurse (probably worried that I was going to go all psycho in the office) and asked her to grab the packet of papers that went along with autism. There was that word again, AUTISM. He slowly sat beside me and said, "Everything is going to be okay." He handed me the packet and told me to please call him if I had any questions and if he could do anything to just call him.... He told me to take my time in the room and to come out when I was ready. I felt like I sat there for an hour, trying to compose myself and trying really hard to not look like I just went two rounds with Mike Tyson in there. I somehow made it out to my car with little C, and we called dad with the news.

A couple of hours later I received a phone call from C's doctor asking if I was okay and saying he was worried about me. I was so grateful for that phone call. I knew that we had one more person in our corner and another person to love C as much as we do.

SOURCE: Marshall, Abbey. (2014). "Is there a chance C has autism?" C is for Autism (blog). www.cisforautism .blogspot.com/2014_10_01_archive.html.

## 11-1 A Changing Era in the Lives of People with Autism Spectrum Disorders

Although most people nowadays know or have interacted with someone with an autism spectrum disorder (ASD), this widespread awareness is a relatively recent phenomenon. Autism was first described in the early 1800s (Volkmar & Wiesner, 2009), but the term *autism* was not used until the early 1900s, when Johns Hopkins University psychiatrist Leo Kanner wrote his seminal paper describing children with "autistic disturbances of affective contact"

*Courtesy of Abbey Marshall*

(Kanner, 1943, p. 217). Research conducted during subsequent decades focused on etiology, and in some cases blamed "cold, refrigerator mothers" for causing their child's autism, encouraging treatment that separated children from their mothers (Bettelheim, 1967).

It wasn't until the passage of the Education for All Handicapped Children Act of 1975 that children with autism were permitted a free and appropriate public education. However, autism was not yet a distinct educational category, so these students were served under disability labels that were then called mental retardation and serious emotional disturbance, often being taught by teachers who were not trained to meet their unique needs. When federal law recognized autism as a disability category in the Individuals with Disabilities Education Act of 1990 (IDEA), services became more widely available to students with autism and their families.

In the 1980s and early 1990s, autism was no longer considered to be only a condition that severely limited individuals' behavior, communication, and intellectual functioning; it began to be viewed as a disorder with a broad range of functioning, including those with extraordinary talents such as those with **savant syndrome** (Treffert, 2009). The 1981 English translation of Hans Asperger's 1944 paper describing a condition later to be named **Asperger's syndrome** brought greater awareness of the unique strengths of some individuals with ASD (Asperger, 1944). But popular media, most notably the 1988 movie *Rain Man*, starring Dustin Hoffman as an institutionalized adult with autism, raised awareness beyond the research and educational communities. *Autism* became a household word.

Today, autism and Asperger's syndrome are considered to be **autism spectrum disorders (ASD)** and have received significant attention from both the academic world and popular media. More than ever, popular media includes individuals with ASD, with actors playing characters with the condition as well as entertainers diagnosed with ASD or self-identifying their autistic symptoms, such as Jerry Seinfeld in a 2014 interview on *NBC Nightly News*. Because ASD is not always portrayed realistically, users are cautioned to not rely solely on popular media as reliable sources of knowledge regarding ASD (Draaisma, 2009; Dyches, Prater, & Leininger, 2009). The Council for Exceptional Children's Division on Autism and Developmental Disabilities has developed guidelines for evaluating the quality of depictions of characters with ASD and other developmental disabilities and biennially presents the Dolly Gray Children's Literature Award to the best picture books and adolescent/young adult books that realistically portray characters with developmental disabilities, including ASD. A list of award winners as well as all books considered for this award is found on the Dolly Gray Award website. See Table 11.1 for examples of recent popular media depictions of individuals with ASD or who have autistic characteristics.

**Standard 1**
Learner Development and Individual Learning Differences

**Savant syndrome**
A rare and extraordinary condition in which unusual skills are performed, usually in one of five areas: music, art, calculating, mathematics, and mechanical or spatial skills, characterized by obsessive preoccupation with specific items or memorization of facts, trivia, sequences, or patterns that are in stark contrast to the developmental level of the individual, including splinter skills, extraordinary talents, and prodigious savant skills.

**Asperger's syndrome**
A condition that shares unusual social interactions and behaviors with autism, but historically has included no general language delay. It is no longer given as an initial diagnosis, but may be incorporated into the diagnosis of ASD.

**Autism spectrum disorders (ASD)**
A range of functioning among many dimensions related to social communicative and social interactive functioning, with restricted and repetitive repertoire of behavior, interests, or activities.

| Table 11.1 | Examples of Individuals with ASD or Autistic-Like Symptoms in Popular Media |
|---|---|
| Picture Books | *My Brother Charlie* by Holly Robinson Peete and Ryan Elizabeth Peete |
| | *Understanding Sam and Asperger Syndrome* by Clarabelle van Niekerk & Liezl Venter, MA CCC-SLP |
| Adolescent Books | *Al Capone Does My Shirts* by Gennifer Choldenko |
| | *The Curious Incident of the Dog in the Night-Time* by Mark Haddon |
| | *Memoirs of an Imaginary Friend* by Matthew Dicks |
| | *Mockingbird* by Kathryn Erskine |
| | *Remember Dippy* by Shirley Reva Vernick |
| Comics | Black Manta in *DC Comics* |
| Manga | Hikaru Azuma in *With the Light: Raising an Autistic Child* |
| Movies | *Autism: The Musical* |
| | *Dear John* |
| | *Extremely Loud and Incredibly Close* |
| | *The Horse Boy* |
| | *Temple Grandin* |

| Table 11.1 | Examples of Individuals with ASD or Autistic-Like Symptoms in Popular Media (*continued*) |
|---|---|
| TV Shows | Sheldon Cooper in *The Big Bang Theory* |
| | Temperance Brennan in *Bones* |
| | Gil Grissom in *CSI: Crime Scene Investigation* |
| | Abed Nadir in *Community* |
| | Max Braverman and Hank Rizzoli in *Parenthood* |
| Video Games | Patricia Tannis in *Borderlands 2* |
| | David Archer in *Mass Effect 2* |

# 11-2  Definitions and Classification of Autism Spectrum Disorders

Several definitions have been used to describe autism spectrum disorders, and when these individuals are students, they may receive an educational classification of *autism* in order to receive special education services. The following sections will describe these definitions and educational classifications.

## 11-2a  Definitions of Autism Spectrum Disorders

Historically, many terms have been used to describe the condition we now call autism spectrum disorders: *autism, infantile autism, atypical autism, high-functioning autism, Asperger's syndrome, pervasive developmental disorder*, among others. Some are diagnostic terms while others are used for convenience.

**Standard 1**
Learner Development and Individual Learning Differences

Individuals are diagnosed by a medical professional such as a psychologist or psychiatrist based upon the criteria designated in the *Diagnostic and Statistical Manual of Mental Disorders* (*DSM*; American Psychiatric Association, 2013). This diagnostic manual has undergone several revisions since its first edition in 1952. Initially, autism was incorrectly associated with childhood schizophrenia; it was not mentioned as a separate diagnosis until 1980. The fourth edition of the *DSM* used the umbrella term *pervasive developmental disorders* (PDD) to characterize those with five specific conditions (American Psychiatric Association, 2000). The most recent edition (the *DSM-5*) changed the terminology to *autism spectrum disorder* (ASD) to reflect the variability within the diagnosis and because distinctions have been inconsistent over time. It also removed the diagnostic label of Asperger's syndrome. Table 11.2 includes the various names used by the *DSM* over time to describe autism.

Currently, ASD is defined as the early presence of a dyad of persistent deficits that are present early in a child's life and that cause clinically significant impairment in everyday functioning in multiple contexts. The dyad of deficits includes (1) social communication and social interaction; and (2) restrictive, repetitive patterns of behavior, interests, or activities.

Many individuals with ASD have disabilities as well as strengths along a spectrum of other characteristics such as gross and fine motor skills, measured IQ, and sensory sensitivities. For example, while one child with ASD might be highly verbal, socially quirky, awkward in physical movements, hypersensitive, intellectually gifted, and engages in repetitive self-calming behavior, another child with ASD might be nonverbal, socially self-absorbed, physically agile, hyposensitive, destructive to self and others, with a low IQ. Many different combinations of characteristics within the spectrum are possible. Figure 11.1 illustrates this concept of the autism spectrum. Examples of symptoms across the spectrum in very young children can be viewed on the Autism Speaks website. These videos give parents and practitioners examples of the "red flags" they may see in children suspected of having ASD. Table 11.3 profiles several school-aged children and youth, showing the diverse range of ability within the autism spectrum.

**Table 11.2** Terms Used in the *Diagnostic and Statistical Manual of Mental Disorders (DSM)* to Describe Autism Spectrum Disorders

| Edition | Year | Diagnostic Labels |
|---|---|---|
| I | 1952 | Schizophrenic reaction, childhood type |
| II | 1968 | Schizophrenia, childhood type |
| III | 1980 | Infantile autism |
| III-R | 1987 | Autistic disorder |
| IV | 1994 | Pervasive developmental disorders |
|  |  | Autistic disorder |
|  |  | Rett's disorder |
|  |  | Childhood disintegrative disorder |
|  |  | Asperger's disorder |
|  |  | Pervasive developmental disorder—Not otherwise specified |
| 5 | 2013 | Autism spectrum disorder |

Some argue that Asperger's syndrome is a distinct disorder; others contend it is a higher-functioning version of autism. A review of the literature implies several overlaps between the two disorders, with the existence of some finer differences in motor skills, speech patterns, and the nature of social interactions (Sharma, Woolfson, & Hunter, 2011). The *DSM-5* attempted to resolve this issue by making it clear that those who have well-established diagnoses under *DSM-IV* should qualify under the current edition, and those

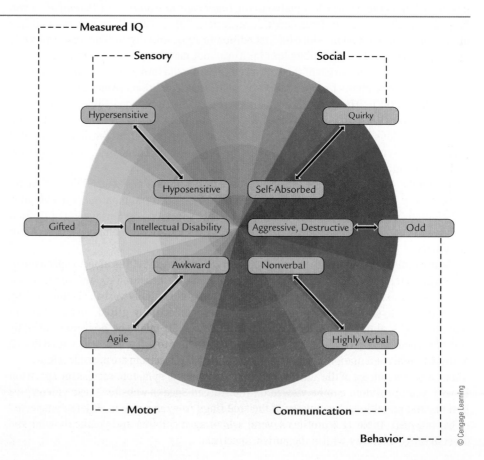

*Figure 11.1 The Autism Spectrum*

**Table 11.3** Social and Communication Skills Associated with Behaviors, Interests, and Activities

| Social Communication and Social Interaction Skills | Restricted, Repetitive Patterns of Behavior, Interests, or Activities |
| --- | --- |
| Three-year-old Nobuo uses both immediate and delayed echolalia. When asked, "What do you want?" he replies, "What do you want?" He often sings jingles from TV commercials. | Three-year-old Nobuo bites his wrist to the point of bleeding when he is prevented from getting what he wants. He appears to not feel any pain. |
| Seven-year-old Martina can say *please*, *cookie*, and *want*, and uses rudimentary sign language to communicate other wants and needs. | Seven-year-old Martina rocks back and forth for long periods of time if she is not redirected. She also toe walks and flaps her hands when she is excited. |
| Ten-year-old Jonell uses the paraeducator's hand as a tool to get a desired object rather than reaching for the object himself. | Ten-year-old Jonell appears to not notice when his peer tutor approaches his desk. Jonell continues to watch the spinning Frisbee he brought in from recess. |
| Eleven-year-old Brantley does not speak, but uses an iPad with special software to communicate his wants and needs, share his ideas, tell jokes, interact with friends, and complete his grade-level homework. | Eleven-year-old Brantley becomes anxious when his classmates touch him on the shoulder and ask him to play. He averts his eyes from their gaze and responds to them by typing on his iPad. |
| Fifteen-year-old Rory tries to engage his friends in conversations by telling them facts about his special interests, such as "Did you know that Saturn is known as the 'jewel of the solar system' and that it is nothing like our very own planet Earth?" | Fifteen-year-old Rory insists that his friends watch him play video games during their lunch break. When they refuse, he squeezes himself into his locker to "get away from those ignorant fools." |
| Eighteen-year-old Esther refers to herself in the third person, using phrases such as, "Esther wants to watch TV now." | Eighteen-year-old Esther becomes highly anxious when she has a substitute bus driver, teacher, or paraeducator. Agitated, she paces the room for long periods of time and repeats, "Esther wants the regular people." |

who do not meet criteria for ASD are to be evaluated for social (pragmatic) communication disorder, a separate disorder that is manifested by functional limitations due to ongoing difficulties in using verbal and nonverbal communication. See Chapter 10, "Communication Disorders," for more information on social (pragmatic) communication disorders.

## 11-2b Educational Classification of Autism Spectrum Disorders

Although medical diagnoses are important for families to obtain appropriate services and available insurance coverage, school personnel are not required to rely on *DSM* diagnoses to serve students with ASD. If a child is suspected of having ASD, the multidisciplinary team must evaluate that child to determine if he or she has a disability that adversely impacts the student's progress in the general curriculum and by reason thereof requires special education. It is important to note that, depending on the state in which the family lives, the child may not need to have a medical diagnosis to qualify for an educational classification of autism (MacFarlane & Kanaya, 2009). Conversely, when students diagnosed with ASD are experiencing success in school so that their educational progress is not significantly impacted, they may not qualify for special education services. Such students may be served with an accommodation plan, also called a 504 plan, with services provided by the general classroom teacher, rather than the special education teacher.

The law governing educational classification of students with ASD, the Individuals with Disabilities Education Improvement Act (IDEA), employs the following definition of autism:

> *Autism means a developmental disability significantly affecting verbal and nonverbal communication and social interaction, generally evident before age three, that adversely affects educational performance. Other characteristics often associated with autism are engagement in repetitive activities and stereotyped movements, resistance to environmental change or change in daily routines, and unusual responses to sensory experiences. (34 C.F.R. 300.8(c)(1))*

**Standard 1**
Learner Development and Individual Learning Differences

The IDEA definition is based largely upon the *DSM-IV* criteria; however, because it is stated generally, there is great variability from state to state and district to district in how students along the autism spectrum are classified (MacFarlane & Kanaya, 2009). It is the responsibility of the multidisciplinary team to determine if students qualify for services under the educational classification of autism, under another category, or if they qualify for accommodations under Section 504 of the Rehabilitation Act.

## 11-3 Characteristics and Prevalence of Autism Spectrum Disorders

This section will discuss the characteristics, associated conditions, unique strengths, and prevalence of autism spectrum disorders.

### 11-3a Characteristics of Autism Spectrum Disorders

The two primary distinguishing features of individuals with ASD are their deficits in social communication/social interaction and their restricted, repetitive patterns of behavior, interests, or activities. Some people with ASD also have other conditions that will be discussed in the following sections.

**Social Communication and Social Interaction Skills** Individuals with ASD have persistent deficits in social skills involving communication and interactions with others. These social skills are interrelated and are hallmark features of people with ASD.

Typical social communication impairments for those with ASD include difficulties with social–emotional reciprocity. For example, while some with ASD do not respond to their name being called, others struggle to engage in back-and-forth conversations.

Those with Asperger's syndrome and high-functioning autism have difficulties primarily with the social components of using language, specifically related to social-emotional reciprocity. They may engage in inappropriate turn taking, make poor judgments about how much or how little to say, struggle with taking another person's perspective, and ask inappropriate questions during conversations (Paul, Orlovski, Marcinko, & Volkmar, 2009). Often considered to be "little professors," students with Asperger's syndrome are often exceptionally bright, but use high-level or awkward vocabulary rather than the slang or common language their peers use (e.g., a teenage boy saying to a peer, "I am very pleased to meet you," rather than "Hey").

Although some people with ASD avoid social contact, many still yearn for friends and social interactions but are challenged by developing and keeping rewarding relationships. They may have a significantly abnormal social approach with limited or no initiation of social interactions or sharing of interests with others.

Impaired nonverbal elements include difficulty using and understanding gestures, body language, and facial expressions. For example, while other students respond readily to the "teacher look" when they are misbehaving, children with ASD may have difficulty understanding the interpretation of this emotional means of communication, because they find it hard to process and understand facial and vocal emotion in others (Stewart, McAdam, Ota, Peppé, & Cleland, 2013).

Speech is an element of verbal communication that may be impaired in children with ASD. The variation of speech abilities in those with ASD ranges from being completely absent to having overly formal speech with difficulties managing topics, reciprocity, and intonation (Paul et al., 2009). Approximately 30 percent of those with autism do not develop functional speech (Wodka, Mathy, & Kalb, 2013). Many who do speak often engage in unusual stereotypical speech, such as echolalia, where they repeat or "echo back" what has been said to them or what they have heard previously, such as lines from a favorite movie. Additionally, the tonal quality of their speech is often unusual or flat with little variation in pitch or volume; in some cases, their speech appears to serve the purpose of self-stimulation rather than communication.

Language skills are another aspect of verbal ability that is often impaired in children with ASD. They may exhibit an uneven level of development between their cognitive

**Standard 1**
Learner Development and Individual Learning Differences

**Echolalia**
Imitation or repetition of words that have been spoken, either immediate or delayed.

# Krista: A Girl with Asperger's Syndrome

Everything is literal to my daughter, Krista. When she was 5, I said that she had "rats" in her hair. She began screaming, "Get them out!" I explained that people say that when you have knots in your hair. A few days later she asked me to get the knots out of her hair, but one knot was really bad. When I told her I couldn't get the knot out, she informed me that the knot must be "double-knotted."

When she was 8, my husband said, "I have a backache." She began to argue with him, informing him that he didn't have a backache. The argument was getting pretty heated, so I asked my husband to stop and see what she

Courtesy of Jennifer Fletcher

meant. I asked her why she thought Dad didn't have a backache. She grabbed his hands and said, "Look,

there is nothing in his hands!" To her, "to have" meant that your hands had to be holding an object. She didn't understand a more abstract meaning of "have," where your body could possess something such as a backache.

Moments like these continue, even though she is now 15. She was visiting a friend and was told to come home at 6:30. The rest of the family got home at 7:00 and she wasn't there. When we asked her about it she said, "But I did come home at 6:30! Then I went back."

SOURCE: Copyright © Jennifer M. Fletcher. Reprinted with permission.

abilities and their receptive and expressive language skills, and fail to use pronouns in speech directed at other people (Tiegerman-Farber, 2009; Weismer, Lord, & Esler, 2010), preferring to call people by their names, and sometimes their full names, even when they know them quite well. They may fail to grasp grammatical complexity and make little use of semantics in sentence structure (Perkins, Dobbinson, Boucher, Bol, & Bloom, 2006). Although not inherent to the diagnosis, many with ASD engage in aggressive behaviors, often due to their inability to communicate verbally (Kanne & Mazurek, 2011).

Many with ASD tend to use and understand language that is concrete and literal. Words that depend upon contextual factors for understanding meaning such as homonyms (e.g., *which* for *witch*), pronouns, jokes, sarcasm, and figurative language are often difficult to interpret. The Snapshot on Krista illustrates how an individual with Asperger's syndrome interprets language literally.

## Restricted, Repetitive Patterns of Behavior, Interests, or Activities
In addition to social impairments, individuals with ASD exhibit stereotyped or repetitive patterns of behavior, interests, or activities. This is another hallmark feature and can include four types of patterns: repetitive use of objects, speech, or movements; inflexibility; fixated interests; and sensory sensitivities (American Psychiatric Association, 2013).

### Repetitive Motor Movements, Use of Objects, or Speech
Individuals with ASD engage in patterns of movement, use of objects, and speech that are stereotypical or repetitive. Typical motor repetitions include flicking hands in front of their faces, flapping hands, rocking, and spinning (Bruns & Thompson, 2012). These repetitive behaviors are sometimes termed **stereotypic behavior** or **self-stimulation** and may continue for a few seconds or, if unattended, for hours. Some behaviors that seem to start as stereotypy or self-stimulation may worsen or take different forms, creating the potential for injury. Examples include hair pulling, face slapping, biting, and head banging (Cannon, Kenworthy, Alexander, Werner, & Anthony, 2011). Behavior that becomes self-injurious is more often found in low-functioning children and can understandably cause concern and stress for parents and others around them (Butrimaviciute & Grieve, 2014).

**Stereotypic behavior**
Behavior or stereotypy involving repetitive movements such as rocking, hand flicking, or object manipulation.

**Self-stimulation**
Repetitive body movements used to stimulate one's senses. Often colloquially referred to as "stimming."

Individuals with ASD may use objects in a stereotypic way, such as spinning objects and playing with objects in an unusual and repetitive manner. For example, when given a toy truck to play with, instead of pushing the truck along the ground, a child with ASD may turn the truck upside down and spin the wheels for long periods of time. Often, items must be arranged in a symmetrical or orderly fashion to seem proper to those with ASD. They may line up their toys in a particular way or keep items in their desk in an organized fashion, becoming distraught or panicked if their items are moved or disrupted.

Stereotypical or ritualized language includes echolalia where the person says the same words, phrases, or scripts repetitively. Other children may use idiosyncratic language, which may not be known to others except for knowledgeable communicative partners such as their family members or teachers. For example, a child may say, "Wanna push?" to indicate "I want to go on the swing." Still others may be preoccupied with certain sounds, words, phrases, or ideas, and may say them repeatedly, having difficulty switching their attention to other topics.

Although the purposes and origins of stereotypic behavior are not well understood, for some, such activity may provide sensory input whereas for others it may provide a sense of organization. Stereotypic behavior is one area, among others, where autobiographic material by high-functioning individuals with ASD may significantly enhance our understanding (Koegel & Koegel, 2012). Classic autobiographies and memoirs that describe these behaviors include *Emergence: Labeled Autistic* by Temple Grandin and Margaret M. Scariano, *Nobody Nowhere* by Donna Williams, and *There's a Boy in Here* by Judy Barron and Sean Barron. Many more books and other personal accounts, including through social media and podcasts, have been produced since these accounts were first published, giving people insights regarding the personal experiences of those with autism.

**Inflexibility** Intense and rigid insistence on sameness, inflexible adherence to routines, or ritualized patterns of verbal/nonverbal behavior are characteristic of those with ASD. Occurring among a spectrum of severity, a mild case might include repetitive questioning (e.g., "Is the fire drill today?"), distress at small changes (e.g., substitute teacher, change in the arrangement of desks, unannounced school assembly), or insistence on a particular food for a given meal (e.g., pizza for school lunch only on Fridays). Extreme adherence to rituals and routines may lead to "meltdowns" or uncontrollable tantrums if a familiar routine is disrupted.

**Fixated Interests** Unusually intense and focused interests that are highly restricted are common for individuals with ASD. They may be fixated on certain topics, objects, or activities. These interests are abnormally intense and can be all-consuming. Some have an unusually strong attachment to or preoccupation with certain objects such as trains, string, or maps. They may have a preoccupation with parts of objects such as the wheels on a toy car or the blades of a toy helicopter.

Others may have excessively narrow interests that they continue to explore or discuss. Such extreme focus on these circumscribed interests is often called perseveration. For example, verbal children with ASD may investigate with great intensity and perseverance specialized topics such as the list of all passengers on the *Titanic,* and attempt to share their knowledge with anyone who will listen.

Some people with ASD wash themselves, collect certain items, and demand sameness in a manner reminiscent of those with obsessive-compulsive disorder (Zandt, 2007). However, ASD and obsessive-compulsive disorder are two distinct conditions and require different treatment protocols (Leininger, Dyches, Prater, & Heath, 2010).

**Sensory Sensitivities** People with ASD may have hyper- or hypo-responsivity to particular elements in the environment, or they may have unusual interests in sensory aspects of the environment. These sensory-processing responses can be manifest in any sensory area: sight, hearing, smell and taste, touch, balance, body position/awareness, and pain. Those who are hypo-responsive appear to be unresponsive to stimuli such as pain, heat, or cold. Hyper-responsive (hypersensitive) children have an exaggerated reaction to a stimulus, such as covering one's ears when the school bell rings, when a vacuum is turned on, or

**Standard 2**
Learning Environments

**Perseveration**
An extreme focus on circumscribed interests, topics, or activities.

**Hypo-responsive**
A low degree of reaction to a stimulus, such as a physical or emotional stimulus.

**Hyper-responsive**
A high degree of reaction to a stimulus, such as a physical or emotional stimulus.

when a toilet is flushed. Some textures may bother them, leading them to wear only certain articles of clothing, or demanding that the tags from their shirts be removed. They may also be bothered by physical touch. These sensitivities are likely to last into adulthood and should be considered when designing sensory-friendly work, home, and other environments (Tavassoli, Miller, Schoen, Nielsen, & Baron-Cohen, 2014).

Such restricted patterns of behaviors create numerous problems for people with ASD as well as their families. For example, most people pay little attention to the exact route they take when driving to the grocery store, or to the precise pattern of moving through the store once they arrive. For parents who take their child with ASD along, minor deviations may cause a serious crisis for the child as well as the parent. One mother indicated that while being out in the community with her child, she "grew immune to the stares and thoughtless comments from casual observers, such as, 'That girl is evil' or 'Your child is so rude'" (Smith, 2007, p. 324).

It is important to remember that we all engage in repetitive behavior that may be self-soothing or that provides other types of sensory feedback to the nervous system. Do you frequently chew on your pencil? Bite your fingernails? Wrap your hair around your finger? Wiggle your foot when sitting cross-legged? These are all self-stimulatory behaviors, but most people do not engage in these behaviors with the intensity and duration as do those with ASD, nor is it as limiting and all-encompassing. The poem by Mayer Shevin highlights the way language can be used inappropriately when describing behaviors that are common between people with and without disabilities. See Figure 11.2.

## 11-3b   Other Conditions Associated with Autism Spectrum Disorders

Many children with ASD have other conditions that impact their daily functioning, commonly described as "comorbid" conditions. This term implies a condition separate from the primary diagnosis, but in the case of ASD, it may be difficult to differentiate between conditions, as many symptoms of a secondary diagnosis can be typical features of ASD. These co-occurring conditions include developmental, mental health, and medical conditions. Approximately four out of five young children with ASD have at least one other condition, making accurate diagnosis difficult (Levy et al., 2010).

**Developmental Conditions** Developmental disorders are the most frequently co-occurring condition with ASD. Most commonly, these include language disorders, ADHD, and intellectual disabilities (American Psychiatric Association, 2013), but can also include motor coordination difficulties, hyperactivity, and other maladaptive behaviors (Bolton, Golding, Emond, & Steer, 2012; Stacy et al., 2014). Intellectual ability varies among those with ASD, and high-functioning individuals may test at a normal level or gifted range

| Us | Them |
|---|---|
| We like things. | They fixate on objects. |
| We try to make friends. | They display attention-seeking behavior. |
| We take breaks. | They display off-task behavior. |
| We stand up for ourselves. | They are noncompliant. |
| We have hobbies. | They self-stim. |
| We choose our friends wisely. | They display poor peer socialization. |
| We persevere. | They perseverate. |
| We like people. | They have dependencies on people. |
| We go for a walk. | They run away. |
| We insist. | They tantrum. |
| We change our minds. | They are disoriented and have short attention spans. |
| We have talents. | They have splinter skills. |
| We are human. | They are…? |

Figure 11.2  *The Language of Us and Them by Mayer Shevin*

(Koegel & Koegel, 2012). Approximately half have average or above-average intellectual ability, compared to approximately one-third of children surveyed a decade ago (Bolton et al., 2012; Centers for Disease Control and Prevention [CDC], 2014). However, IQ testing may not be valid for these children, because most intelligence tests rely on verbal and reasoning skills that may mask their intellectual capabilities.

**Mental Health Conditions** Mental health or psychiatric disorders are found among many children with ASD. Young children may be diagnosed with conditions such as oppositional defiant disorder, anxiety disorder, emotional disturbance, obsessive-compulsive disorder, among other conditions (Levy et al., 2010; Stacy et al., 2014). Children and adolescents with ASD are at an increased risk for depression and anxiety symptoms (Strang et al., 2012).

**Medical Conditions** Neurological and other medical conditions also occur in children with ASD. Most common is epilepsy, affecting up to 46 percent (Viscidi et al., 2014). Although relatively rare, conditions such as fragile X syndrome, tuberous sclerosis, and 15q duplication syndrome have also been found in children with ASD (Abrahams & Geschwind, 2008; Levy et al., 2010).

## 11-3c Unique Strengths

Some individuals with ASD have savant syndrome, or "spectacular 'islands of genius' in jarring juxtaposition to overall limitations" (Treffert, 2014, p. 564). Most common are the "splinter skill savants" who are preoccupied with information such as historical facts, sports trivia, or train schedules. The "talented savants" are those who have musical, art, or other talents such as **hyperlexia** that are not only remarkable in light of their disabilities, but also compared to their peers. The third type includes the rare "prodigious savants" who are prodigies or geniuses (Treffert, 2014). Approximately half of those with savant syndrome have autism, and 10 percent of those with ASD have savant syndrome. Their savant skills usually occur in one of five areas: music, art, calculating, mathematics, and mechanical or spatial skills (Treffert, 2014). For example, Stephen Wiltshire, who has ASD, creates architectural drawings accurately from memory with minute detail and perfect scale and perspective after a brief flight over a city such as New York; he now has his own gallery in London and a website that highlights his work, including videos showing his incredible skills. Profiles and videos of others with savant syndrome can be found at the Wisconsin Medical Society's Savant Syndrome website.

Parents and teachers are strongly recommended to "train the talent" rather than to suppress or eliminate these unusual skills (Treffert, 2009, p. 1,335). Instead of viewing the student's intense fascination as perseveration that is annoying or bothersome, create learning activities in which the student can demonstrate "perseverance" in meeting the learning objectives. Strategies to capitalize on strengths, interests, and talents associated with these focused fascinations do not demand much time, but do require creative thinking and student input (Lanou, Hough, & Powell, 2012). For example, if a student is fascinated with bus schedules, teachers can use this special interest to teach geography, math, reading, and other subjects. These highly focused skills can become a means toward achieving normalization, socialization, and independence.

Also, the use of memory for daily purposes appears to be impaired in some individuals with ASD (Jones et al., 2011); others seem to have relatively strong, specific long-term memory skills, particularly for factual information like names, numbers, and dates (Koegel & Koegel, 2012). Once these students have learned a piece of information, they may not forget it. Their long-term memory skills may equal or exceed those of their typically developing peers. The juxtaposition of unique skills with difficulty in social interactions is highlighted in the description of Donald T. in the nearby Reflect on This box.

**CEC**

**Standard 5**
Instructional Planning and Strategies

## 11-3d Prevalence of Autism Spectrum Disorders

Challenges in determining the prevalence of people with ASD have existed ever since researchers began collecting such data. Due to numerous uncontrollable factors, it is difficult to report an accurate prevalence rate. Nevertheless, there appears to be a real increase in

## Donald T.: First Child Diagnosed with Autism

Young Donald's behavior was perplexing to his parents. While he seemed slow and backward in some areas, he also displayed sparks of brilliance. At age 1, Donald could hum and sing tunes accurately; at age 2, he could name the U.S. presidents, along with many of his ancestors and relatives. Later he could recite short poems, the 23rd Psalm, and 25 questions and answers from the Presbyterian catechism. However, at age 3, Donald did not feed himself and exhibited problematic behaviors, and his mother believed that he was "hopelessly insane."

Following the recommendations of the family physician, Donald's parents had him institutionalized in a Mississippi town aptly named Sanatorium. Yet after one year of institutionalization, minimal progress, and a diagnosis of "some glandular disease," his parents took him home. Two months later, in October 1938, 5-year old Donald was examined by Austrian American psychiatrist Leo Kanner, who observed him not to be feebleminded, insane, or affected with schizophrenia. Donald, along with 10 other children, was described in the now-famous 1943 report as having a condition that "differs so markedly and uniquely from anything reported so far," something Kanner called "autistic disturbance of affective contact" (Kanner, 1943, p. 217).

Donald T., as he was known in the report, was the first child reported to have autism. His parents and Dr. Kanner noted Donald's triad of impairments

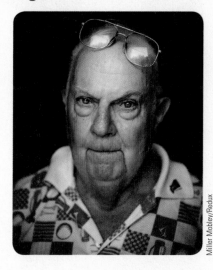

Miller Mobley/Redux

that have typically characterized a diagnosis of autism—qualitative impairments in both social interaction and communication, and patterns of behavior, activities, and interests that are restricted, repetitive, and stereotyped. When examined at age 5, Donald was described as being happiest when left alone, oblivious to his social environment, and having no apparent affection to others. Although he could enunciate words clearly, he asked questions only in single words, parroted words and phrases from others, and repetitively made irrelevant utterances such as "chrysanthemum," "dahlia, dahlia, dahlia," and "Through the dark clouds shining." He jumped up and down jubilantly while watching blocks, pans, and other round objects spin, had temper tantrums when interrupted, and had unusual body movements with his fingers and head.

Seventy-two years after being examined by Leo Kanner, the identity of "Case 1: Donald T." was discovered in Forest, Mississippi. Donald Gray Triplett, then 77 years old, grew up in a community of approximately 3,000 where he was educated, included, and accepted decades before the term *autism* became a household word. Today, Donald is an avid golfer and world traveler. He lives alone in the home he grew up in and enjoys his morning ritual of drinking coffee with his friends, going for a walk, watching *Bonanza* reruns, then driving to the golf course for a round of golf, preferring to play by himself. He has dinner with his brother and sister-in-law every Sunday night. Still showing signs of autism, Donald's life is tranquil, familiar, stable, and secure, particularly for a man with autism, and most notably for the first person diagnosed with autism.

### Questions for Reflection

**1.** What are some of the characteristics of autism that Donald exhibited when he was a young child and as a grown man?

**2.** How can misdiagnosis affect individuals with autism?

**3.** What types of adult outcomes are possible for those diagnosed with a utism today?

SOURCES: Donovan, J. & Zucker, C. (2010, October). Autism's First Child. *The Atlantic*. Retrieved February 25, 2012, www.theatlantic.com/magazine/archive/2010/10/autism-8217-s-first-child/8227/; Kanner, L. (1943). "Autistic Disturbances of Affective Contact." *Nervous Child*, 2, 217–250.

prevalence across the United States and in other countries. Although prevalence rates vary from study to study, a thorough analysis of recent epidemiological surveys estimates the prevalence of autism to be 22 to 70 per 10,000 for those along the spectrum (Saracino, Noseworthy, Steiman, Reisinger, & Fombonne, 2010), translating to approximately 1 child of 143 diagnosed with ASD.

However, the most recent report from the Centers for Disease Control and Prevention (2014) has gained much media attention, citing the prevalence of ASD in 14 U.S. sites as one out of every 68 children and one out of every 42 boys. Because studies like this do not comprise nationally representative samples, the CDC cautions that this prevalence

## Identifying Culturally and Linguistically Diverse Children with ASD

Recently, much attention has been paid to the differences in acquiring an ASD diagnosis and receiving appropriate services for various races and ethnicities. For example, a recent comprehensive study in Los Angeles County has found that in their sample of 7,540 children with autism, there were increased risks of being diagnosed with autism if the mothers were foreign-born and black, Central/South American, Filipino, or Vietnamese. Also, children born to U.S.-born mothers who were Hispanic or African American had a greater likelihood of being diagnosed with autism than those born of U.S.-born white mothers (Becerra et al., 2015). However, other research with slightly over 100 participants indicates children of Latina mothers are diagnosed approximately one year later, have greater unmet service needs, and receive fewer specialty services than children of non-Latina mothers (Magaña, Lopez, Aguinaga, & Morton, 2013). Contributing factors to these differences were the level of education of the mothers and number of sources of information about autism.

### Application Questions

**1.** How should professionals interpret research that may seem contradictory?

**2.** How might immigration status and decreased ability in speaking and understanding English contribute to racial/ethnic discrepancies in diagnosis and treatment?

**3.** How can school personnel provide unbiased assessments to appropriately identify and serve students with ASD?

**CEC**

**Standard 1**
Learner Development and Individual Learning Differences

rate cannot be generalized to the United States as a whole; however, the media presents these rates as if they are applicable to the nation at large, sounding out a warning cry of an autism "epidemic." When citizens hear these statistics, they may picture individuals with the most significant of autistic symptoms. Yet, due to the broadening definition of ASD, many individuals with ASD are not profoundly affected. Furthermore, researchers question the methods used by the CDC to obtain their prevalence rates and consider it a mistake to use these data for determining "meaningful estimates of prevalence" (Mandell & Lecavalier, 2014, p. 483).

The variation in prevalence rates is likely due to a number of factors. Current knowledge points to changes in diagnostic criteria, case identification, and reporting over time; variations in measurement; earlier identification; heightened awareness among parents and professionals; additional policies and services; and a true increase in the population (CDC, 2014; Hansen, Schendel, & Parner, 2015; Mandell & Lecavalier, 2014; Saracino et al., 2010). The wide range in prevalence may diminish over time as greater consensus about what constitutes ASD is achieved.

Gender differences are evident in autism; males outnumber females substantially. Estimates of these prevalence differences are typically reported to be around 5 to 1 (CDC, 2014). Some researchers attribute this gender difference to girls with autism being less socially aberrant than males, "camouflaging" their symptoms and making diagnoses more difficult, although girls with autism often have less intellectual ability (CDC, 2014; Lai et al., 2011; Nicholas et al., 2008).

Identification of ASD has been shown to vary by race and ethnicity. Some reports indicate greater prevalence among non-Hispanic white children than among non-Hispanic black children and Hispanic children, with Hispanic children being diagnosed later than their white, non-Latino counterparts (CDC, 2014). Evidence exists supporting the cross-cultural validity of ASD according to the *DSM-5* definitions, with some variability in those with milder autistic characteristics (Mandy, Charman, Puura, & Skuse, 2014). See the "Case Study on Embracing Diversity" for more information.

It is clear that the debate over accurately determining prevalence of ASD is not ending in the near future. What is most important to teachers, however, is that more children with ASD are being served in public schools than ever before. These increases necessitate better preparation of both preservice and in-service teachers to serve students with ASD using evidence-based strategies in appropriate environments.

## 11-4 Causes and Risk Factors of Autism Spectrum Disorders

**Etiology**
The cause or reason a condition occurs.

The cause or **etiology** of autism has been a topic that has been a concern since Leo Kanner first described it in 1943. Although Kanner noted that a biological component might be involved, later theories implicated parenting practices, in particular, the interactions of mothers, who were described as being cold and indifferent to their children. The hypothesis was that the child would withdraw from the mother's rejection and erect defenses against psychological pain, retreating to an inner world without contact with the outside environment (Bettelheim, 1967). This psychodynamic theory has largely been refuted, although some "failure to bond" theories occasionally gain attention.

**Standard 1**
Learner Development and Individual Learning Differences

Current research points to an integrated etiology. It is well accepted that neither is there one cause nor one cure for ASD. Rather, ASD appears to be an assortment of symptoms that require varied treatments. Possible contributors to the cause of ASD include genetic, infectious, neurologic, metabolic, and immunologic factors.

Widespread media attention has led many to believe that vaccinations cause autism, theorizing that stimulation of the immune system with vaccinations results in damage to the developing brain, thereby causing abnormal neural pathway development that leads to autism. However, meta-analytic research with over one million children with ASD indicates there is no relationship between vaccinations and ASD (Taylor, Swerdfeger, & Eslick, 2014). Nevertheless, the autism–vaccination link continues to be explored by researchers.

Clearly, various causes of ASD remain unsolved puzzles in the face of ongoing research and widespread interest in the condition. Accumulated evidence has strongly implicated biological factors. Although the environment may play a role in the development of ASD, strong evidence supports a genetic link, not as a single gene that causes ASD, but as gene expression that may be stimulated by certain environmental conditions (Hall & Kelley, 2014), with common gene variants and other mutations accounting for 59 percent of the causes of ASD (Gaugler et al., 2014). Breakthrough international research has implicated 60 contributing genes, with a 90 percent risk factor of a child developing autism (DeRubeis et al., 2014). This genetic link is supported by studies citing the occurrence of autism in identical twins as 36 to 95 percent of the time and in nonidentical twins 0 to 31 percent of the time. Also, parents with one child with ASD have a 2 to 18 percent chance of having another child who also has ASD (CDC, 2014).

As with many areas of disability, an understanding of causation is important as we attempt to improve treatment. Research continues to unravel the sources of this perplexing disability, and improved research methodology is vital for further progress in the investigation of ASD.

## 11-5 Identification and Assessment of Autism Spectrum Disorders

**Standard 4**
Assessment

Throughout this book, we have discussed collaboration between multiple disciplines as we have examined other disabilities. Because of the wide variation of characteristics presented in this spectrum of disorders, the diversity of the assessment team is quite broad and may include professionals from the fields of medicine, psychology, education, speech–language pathology, occupational pathology, physical therapy, social work, counseling, and other fields, depending on the student's presenting behaviors and needs (Cannon et al., 2011).

Often, parents are concerned about symptoms of ASD in their toddlers. Typical parental concerns during the child's first year of life are related to vision and hearing, along with social, communication, and fine motor skills. During the second year of life, parents notice red flags regarding the child's play, imitation skills, feeding habits, and temperament (Bolton et al., 2012). However, sometimes autistic characteristics do not concern parents for many years, particularly for children with high-functioning autism, because

**Standard 7**
Collaboration

their behaviors may appear to be just "odd" or "quirky," and their high intelligence often compensates for some of their autistic symptoms.

When parents observe their children persistently engaging in unusual and atypical behaviors, they may visit their pediatrician for evaluation. However, a thorough evaluation must be completed since time constraints during office visits generally prevent physicians from reaching informed conclusions about potential ASD. It is important for physicians to use formal screening tools and developmental tests to provide sufficient information for accurate referrals (Gabrielsen et al., 2015).

The diagnosis of ASD is often delayed and ranges from an average of approximately 3 to 10 years. The age of diagnosis has been decreasing over time (Daniels & Mandell, 2014). Children who have more severe autistic symptoms and whose parents show great concern and have high socioeconomic status are more likely than others to be diagnosed at younger ages. When children are diagnosed early, parents often have an ongoing relationship with their pediatrician, which puts medical professionals on the multidisciplinary team very early, preferably by 18 months for a child's universal screening or at the 24- or 33-month screening (Kogan et al., 2008). These screenings should be covered through the Affordable Care Act, as most health insurance plans are no longer allowed to deny, limit, or exclude insurance coverage to any person based on a preexisting condition, including ASD (Johnson, Danis, & Hafner-Eaton, 2014). As of 2014, at least 38 states have passed laws that mandate coverage of services for individuals with ASD (Autism Speaks, 2014). The Snapshot of "C" illustrates the process from parental concern to diagnosis.

**Standard 4**
Assessment

As a child's evaluation begins, assessment is typically undertaken in multiple skill areas, including communication and language, intelligence, and social interaction (Anckarsater, 2006). Following the assessment process, a multidisciplinary team plans, delivers, and evaluates the interventions. From the parents' perspective, the important outcome of this collaboration is to allow their child to receive effective and individualized service in appropriate environments (White, Scahill, Klin, Koenig, & Volkmar, 2007). Although the nature of the multidisciplinary collaboration evolves over time as circumstances change, the need for collaboration on assessments and interventions will continue as the child grows older, reaches adolescence, and transitions into adulthood (Henault, 2006). A primary goal of these multidisciplinary teams is to facilitate post-school outcomes that the person with ASD and his family value. These might include appropriate social outlets, recreation, employment, education, housing, finances, and respite care for the family (Billstedt, Gillberg, & Gillberg, 2011; Eaves & Ho, 2008).

## 11-6 Interventions and Treatments for Autism Spectrum Disorders

**Standard 5**
Instructional Planning and Strategies

For decades, there have been a wide variety of treatments, some of which have little to no empirical evidence, yet are still popular with families and in schools. Different approaches have been based on theories of causation, while others have focused on specific observable behaviors (National Autism Center, 2009). Significant progress has been made in providing successful interventions for people with ASD, although investigators continually emphasize the importance of further systematic research on the effectiveness of various intervention and treatment strategies. Research affirms the use of a variety of evidenced-based strategies—strategies that are tailored to the strengths as well as the challenges individuals with ASD experience (National Research Council, 2001; Stahmer, Schriebman, & Cunningham, 2011).

### 11-6a Early Childhood Education

When children with ASD are identified before age 3, they can receive early intervention through a provider of services to children with disabilities or delays. Some parents choose to supplement these services, or even replace them, with in-home therapy. At age 3, children with ASD may qualify for early childhood special education, which can range from typical preschool programs with specialized support, to programs designed specifically for students with ASD. Along with specialized instruction, most preschoolers with ASD receive speech therapy, occupational therapy, behavior management programs, learning strategies, and study skills assistance (Bitterman, Daley, Misra, Carlson, & Markowitz, 2008).

Early intervention is critical in treatment for young children with ASD. Research is replete with evidence that early, intense treatments (minimum of five hours per day) have long-lasting positive effects, particularly in the areas of measured IQ, expressive and receptive language, and adaptive behavior (Maglione, Gans, Das, Timbie, & Kasari, 2012; National Research Council, 2001; Peters-Scheffer, Didden, Korzilius, & Sturmey, 2011). To help parents and practitioners understand various treatment options, Autism Speaks has developed a Video Glossary of more than 100 video clips from actual therapy sessions with young children with ASD. The therapy sessions illustrate more than 20 treatments that focus on building skills, connecting with peers and family, and reducing challenging behaviors.

**Standard 2**
Learning Environments

## 11-6b Elementary Education

By age 5, children with ASD who qualify for special education will receive services as determined on their IEP. Each IEP should include statements of short- and long-term goals that relate to the two core deficits of the disorder (social communication/interaction and restrictive, repetitive behavior). IEPs and instructional plans should focus on individual strengths, interests, and talents required for maximum independence (Lanou, Hough, & Powell, 2012).

The type and amount of services, as well as location of these services, are determined by the child's IEP team. The type of services provided often includes special education and related services such as speech, physical, and occupational therapy. Location of service delivery can range along a continuum of placements. Although some students with ASD are educated in general education classes for all or part of the day, others are self-contained in a neighborhood school or in a school designed for students with ASD. Some students receive instruction at the home, hospital, or institution, depending upon the decision the IEP team makes (Gibb & Dyches, 2015). The IEP team has the right to determine which placement allows students to be educated to the maximum extent appropriate with their nondisabled peers, with educational placement and instructional programming dependent on the student's age and functioning level (White et al., 2007). The ultimate goal is to prepare all students, and not just those who have high-functioning ASD, to live high-quality lives in their home communities.

**Standard 7**
Collaboration

Students with high-functioning ASD may not qualify for special education in some circumstances because their disability does not significantly impact their progress in the general curriculum. These students may be served in general education settings with adaptations and accommodations provided according to a 504 plan. Other students may not be served with any special services or may be in gifted and talented education programs.

## 11-6c Adolescent Education and Transition to Adulthood

Adolescence can be a difficult time for many students because it is a time of several life changes, increased independence, and a time to make important life decisions such as college, employment, vocational training, and housing. When a student has ASD, these aspects can be increasingly difficult, particularly if they are anxious about change. Multidisciplinary teams must not leave these transitions to chance; a detailed plan must be in place, and students with ASD should be primary contributors to the plan. If a student cannot participate in a meaningful way, the student's desires, interests, and abilities should be considered (Gibb & Dyches, 2015).

Transition planning for youth and young adults with ASD is critical because, after age 22, they no longer qualify for a free and appropriate public education. If they have not secured a job or educational opportunities, there may be no state or local services available to assist them in meeting their postsecondary goals. However, those who do have effective transition plans can be successful in their lives. The example of Taylor Crowe as depicted in the Snapshot is just one example of a successful adult with ASD.

Five steps for transition planning have been developed to help adolescents with ASD move from secondary school to post-school activities:

1. Identify transition goals—postsecondary education, employment, independent living.

2. Link postsecondary goals with IEP goals—at least one IEP goal should support and align with each of the goals.

3. Troubleshoot and adjust transition and IEP goals—make goals that are measurable and encourage active participation.

4. Provide opportunities to teach skill—balance academic skills with social–emotional skill development.

5. Evaluate progress—measure student progress and make instructional decisions using these data. (Szidon, Ruppar, & Smith, 2015)

Instructional strategies for adolescents with ASD are often qualitatively similar to strategies for youth with ASD. For example, a recent meta-analysis indicates that behavioral treatments for concerns such as academics, problem behavior, phobic avoidance, and social, adaptive, and vocational skills demonstrate positive benefits for adolescents and adults with ASD (Roth, Gillis, & DiGennaro Reed, 2014).

**CEC**

**Standard 5**
Instructional Planning and Strategies

## 11-6d Evidence-Based Practices

To facilitate the success of students with ASD, multidisciplinary teams have the professional responsibility to use evidence-based practices (Alexander, Ayers, & Smith, 2015). Unfortunately, the field is filled with so many interventions claiming to be effective for students with ASD that parents and professionals may be confused and frustrated in selecting the most appropriate treatments. They may rely upon what is currently available or, alternatively, invest in treatments that claim to cure the condition, but have little or no empirical support. It is the professionals' responsibility to know the current research regarding effective treatments and to verify the evidence base by analyzing student progress data. Although it is nearly impossible for practicing teachers to review the thousands of research articles on treatments for students with ASD, recent comprehensive reviews and meta-analyses of research are good resources for staying well informed on current research.

One recent meta-analytic report investigated more than 400 studies related to interventions for children, youth, and young adults with ASD related to outcomes such as social skills, communication, behavior, school readiness, and adaptive skills (Wong et al., 2015). Previous reviews and meta-analyses have been conducted, but some focus on only young children, yet the 2015 report includes interventions from ages 0 to 22. However, very few practices have been deemed evidence-based for those ages 15 to 22, specifically related to increasing skills in joint attention, cognitive performance, academics, motor skills, vocational skills, and mental health. Results indicated 27 intervention practices that met the scientific criteria for being evidence-based practices. See Table 11.4 for a list of these interventions.

Another meta-analytic research report evaluated types of behavioral treatments, rather than specific focused interventions, and found varying levels of evidence for treatments for children with ASD ages 0 to 12. The interventions with the highest positive effects were those that addressed commonly associated conditions using cognitive behavior therapy (for children with at least average IQ). The interventions with moderate positive effects included early intensive behavioral and developmental interventions based upon applied behavior analysis (ABA), and play/interaction-based interventions for joint attention (Weitlauf et al., 2014).

Most educational interventions for students with ASD include communication services, behavioral strategies, visual structure and support, social skills development,

## Table 11.4 Evidence-Based Practices for Children, Youth, and Young Adults with ASD

- Antecedent-based intervention
- Cognitive behavioral intervention
- Differential reinforcement of alternative, incompatible, or other behavior
- Discrete trial teaching
- Exercise
- Extinction
- Functional behavior assessment
- Functional communication training
- Modeling
- Naturalistic intervention
- Parent-implemented intervention
- Peer-mediated instruction and intervention
- Picture Exchange Communication System (PECS)
- Pivotal learning variables
- Pivotal response training
- Prompting
- Reinforcement
- Response interruption/redirection
- Scripting
- Self-management
- Social narratives
- Social skills training
- Structured play groups
- Task analysis
- Technology-aided instruction and intervention
- Time delay
- Video modeling
- Visual supports

Adapted from Wong, C., Odom, S. L., Hume, K. A., Cox, A. W., Fettig, A., Kucharczyk, S....Schultz, T. R. (2015). "Evidence-Based Practices for Children, Youth, and Young Adults with Autism Spectrum Disorder: A Comprehensive Review." *Journal of Autism and Developmental Disorders*. Advance online publication. doi:10.1007/s10803-014-2351-z

and functional skills development. Some students also receive psychological and medical interventions.

**Communication Services** The most critical and frequently used approach for students with ASD is the collaborative provision of social communication services. It is not solely the work of the speech-language therapist to provide students with access to appropriate communication devices, aids, and strategies. The classroom teacher, special educator, and others who serve the student will see fewer communicative breakdowns, tantrums, and other maladaptive behavior when they work together to use evidence-based, naturalistic interventions (Kane, Connell, & Pellecchia, 2010).

Because many students with ASD are nonverbal or minimally verbal, the use of **augmentative and alternative communication (AAC)** strategies and devices are common. Examples of high-tech devices are devices dedicated for the purpose of facilitating communication, software programs for computers, and specialized applications for phones, handheld devices, or tablet computers. Low-tech devices include

**Augmentative and alternative communication (AAC)**
The use of aided and unaided strategies (such as communication devices, sign language, gestures, and written language) to communicate wants/needs, transfer information, engage in social closeness, and use social etiquette.

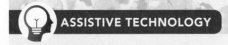

### Apps for Autism

The phenomenal success of tablets with the general public has spawned thousands of applications for individuals with ASD, many of which are free or low in cost. Having strong visual skills, students with autism are motivated to participate in learning activities presented on electronic devices. Some apps are designed for individuals without disabilities (e.g., academic programs such as names of the U.S. presidents, math flash cards, spelling, graphic organizers), while other apps are designed specifically for individuals with disabilities such as ASD (e.g.,

social skills, eye contact, visual timers, sign language). Apps that have the greatest impact on nonverbal students are those that can be used for augmentative and alternative communication (AAC). Typical electronic AAC devices are expensive, but apps for tablets provide similar functionality at a lower price and with greater portability.

Because thousands of apps are available online and many of them are appropriate for individuals with ASD, it can be overwhelming to parents and

professionals to choose the most appropriate app for the right purpose for each person. Some apps and websites have been designed to address this issue. On the AppyAutism site, users select their operating system, type of device, category of app (e.g., communication, social, learning), and keyword, and the site lists the apps matching the user's search criteria. Prices, screenshots, videos, and scholarly articles accompany some of the app listings. The site is available updated monthly and presented in English and Spanish.

**CEC**

**Standard 5**
Instructional Planning and Strategies

communication boards and books with pictures, words, or more complex and abstract forms of communication. Some worry that the use of AAC will suppress speech; however, research indicates AAC increases communication skills and speech production (Schlosser & Wendt, 2008). See the nearby Assistive Technology feature, "Apps for Autism," for more information.

One frequently used intervention for students with ASD who are nonverbal or who have little to no communicative initiation skills is the Picture Exchange Communication System (PECS). This system teaches children to initiate a communicative exchange with a partner by using pictures. Meta-analytic research indicates that the use of PECS enhances the functional communication skills of children with ASD, especially preschool children, and that the students who continued in the PECS protocol phases had the most positive outcomes (Ganz, Davis, Lund, Goodwyn, & Simpson, 2012).

**Behavioral Strategies** Many educational and therapeutic approaches for students with ASD are based upon applied behavior analysis (ABA) principles. This model of intervention has been used in a wide array of circumstances within education, psychology, medicine, and family therapy.

ABA is used in educational contexts by breaking large tasks into small, manageable parts and reinforcing successive approximations to the goal. For example, instead of expecting a student with ASD to sit quietly in his chair for a 30-minute language arts lesson, the child may be allowed to hold a favorite "comfort toy" while sitting and is praised every 10 minutes for sitting and participating. Another student may be reinforced with praise and a favorite item for her attempts to speak. Instead of waiting for the child to say, "I want a cookie," the teacher reinforces the child for saying "cook," an approximation of the word *cookie*. Common strategies and programs such as discrete trial training, PECS, pivotal response treatment, positive behavior intervention and support, among many others, are based upon ABA principles (National Autism Center, 2009). Decades of research support the efficacy of ABA strategies.

**Positive behavior intervention and support (PBIS)**

A proactive framework used to establish a positive social environment and provide behavioral supports for all students to succeed socially, emotionally, and academically.

One outgrowth of ABA is the field of **positive behavior intervention and support (PBIS)**, which aims to analyze the function of a challenging behavior and create structures and supports that reduce the barriers for engaging in more appropriate behaviors. PBIS interventions are used in natural settings, are family-centered, avoid using punishment strategies, use a collaborative, assessment-based approach, and result in multifaceted support plans (Carr et al., 2002).

In the PBIS model, an individual receiving support is the most important decision maker in the behavior-change process. The individual's preferences are used to make data-based decisions, and those people who this person values give their perspectives regarding developing interventions and support plans (Dunlap, Carr, Horner, Zarcone, & Schwartz, 2008).

Behavioral interventions may focus on challenging behavior such as self-stimulation, tantrums, or self-inflicted injury, and have substantially reduced or eliminated these problem behaviors in many cases (Northey, 2009). Behavioral interventions have also been effective in remediating deficiencies in fundamental social skills and language development, as well as in facilitating community integration for children with ASD (Bauminger et al., 2008). Furthermore, parental involvement in behavioral interventions has shown promising results. Research has demonstrated that certain students with ASD can be effectively taught to employ self-management skills, which further enhance efficiency (Blacher & McIntyre, 2006; Rogers & Ozonoff, 2006). Some evidence indicates adapted group therapy is effective in reducing anxiety symptoms for children with ASD (McConachie et al., 2014; Sung et al., 2011).

**Visual Structure and Support** Providing visual structure and support is another strategy to set up the environment in such a way that capitalizes on the student's visual strengths. Teachers who establish visually structured classrooms post their class rules/expectations in a prominent place along with consequences for maintaining or not maintaining those expectations (see Figure 11.3). They teach the expectations to the students, reteach as necessary, and reinforce frequently. Also, these teachers have the daily schedule posted and refer to it often. Some students may need individualized schedules, either in writing or accompanied with pictures (see Figure 11.4 and Figure 11.5). Schedules help students know what to predict for their school day, which decreases their anxiety. Effective teachers also prevent problems during transition times by providing structured verbal and visual cues to smooth these transitions (Bondy & Frost, 2008). To facilitate a predictable environment, teachers establish logical routines that are taught and reinforced throughout the year (e.g., what to do upon entering the classroom, where to put completed work, what to do if students finish work early, when students are allowed to leave their seats). They also establish areas in the class designated for certain activities or items (e.g., a quiet zone, a one-on-one instructional area with teacher or paraeducator, specific locations to keep various instructional items). Labeling the areas in the room with written words, photographs, or pictures and referring to these labels is one strategy to reinforce the concepts and to increase literacy skills. For some students, color-coding facilitates understanding. For example, Noah, who is currently unable to understand the meaning of pictures and written words, has his items labeled in his favorite color—yellow. His desk is labeled with his name on a yellow card, as is his coat hook and his storage bin with his personal calming and reinforcement items.

**Standard 2**
Learning Environments

**Standard 5**
Instructional Planning and Strategies

Visual supports can also be provided via technological means. One common strategy is to use video modeling, where a student with ASD watches himself or another person perform a target behavior that has previously been videotaped. Any prompts or errors that were made during the video shoot are edited out, so the student can view an errorless execution of the skill. After viewing the video, the student then practices the skill. Video modeling is often used to teach language, self-help, and daily living skills (Bellini & Akullian, 2007; LeBlanc, 2010), but has also been used to teach academic skills (Burton, Anderson, Prater, & Dyches, 2013) and vocational skills (Kellems & Morningstar, 2012).

**Social Skill Development** Interventions that focus on enhancing positive social relationships are based upon developmental theory and can be delivered in a variety of settings. Examples include programs such as the Early Start Denver Model, Floortime therapy, Relationship Developmental Intervention, and responsive teaching. These treatments are considered to have "emerging" levels of evidence (National Autism Center, 2009), and continued meta-analytic research may find greater evidence for the effectiveness of these treatments.

Programs that focus on the development of social skills target a primary core deficit of children with ASD. Social skills can be taught in a variety of ways in various settings:

*Figure 11.3* ***Classroom Rules with Natural Consequences Depicted in Writing and Pictures for Greater Comprehension***

| Class Rules | What If We Do? | What If We Don't? |
|---|---|---|
| 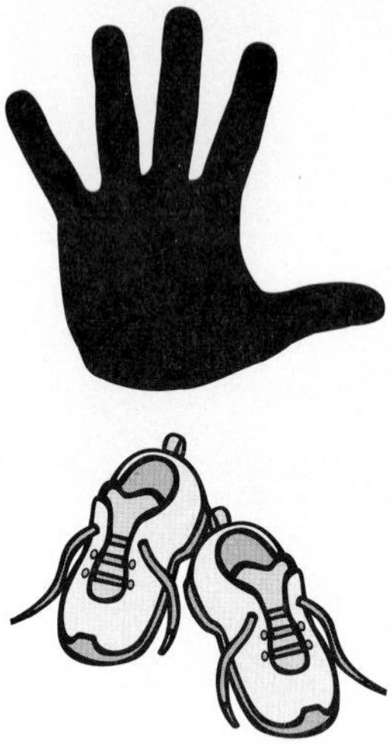<br>We keep **hands** and **feet** to self.<br>© Dr.G/Shutterstock.com<br>©Miguel Angel Salinas Salinas/Shutterstock.com | 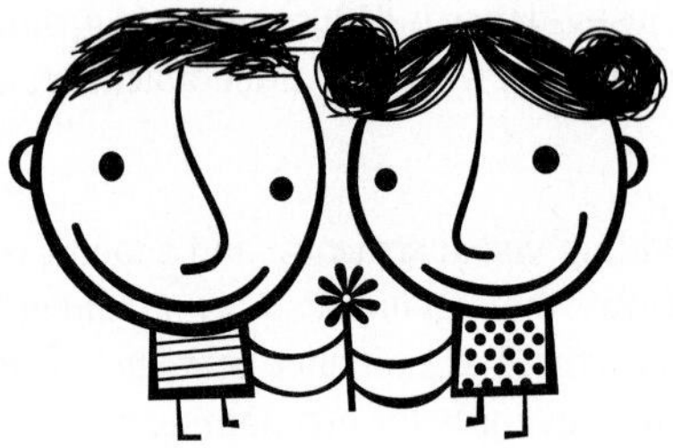<br>We make friends.<br>©Complot/Shutterstock.com | 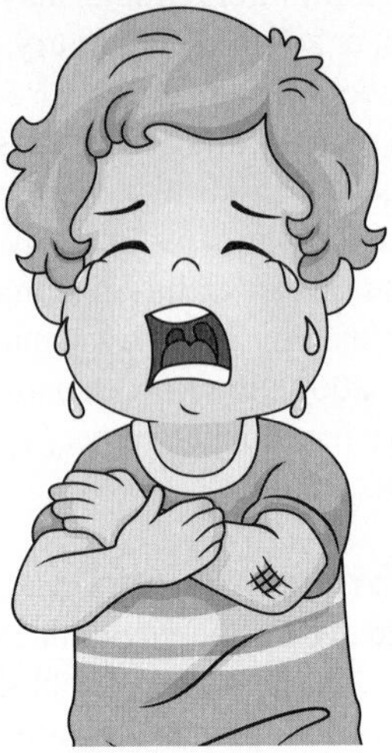<br>People can get hurt.<br>©Lorelyn Medina/Shutterstock.com |
| 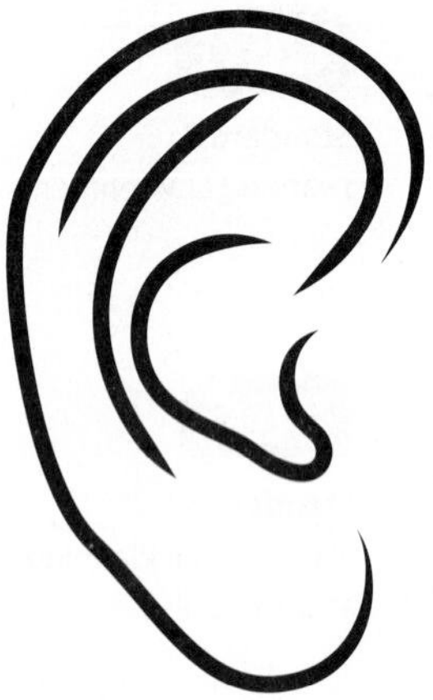<br>We **listen**.<br>©nikolae/Shutterstock.com | 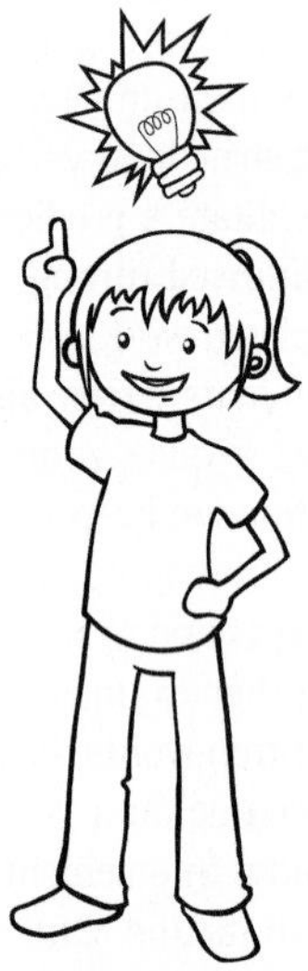<br>We understand.<br>virtute/Getty Images | 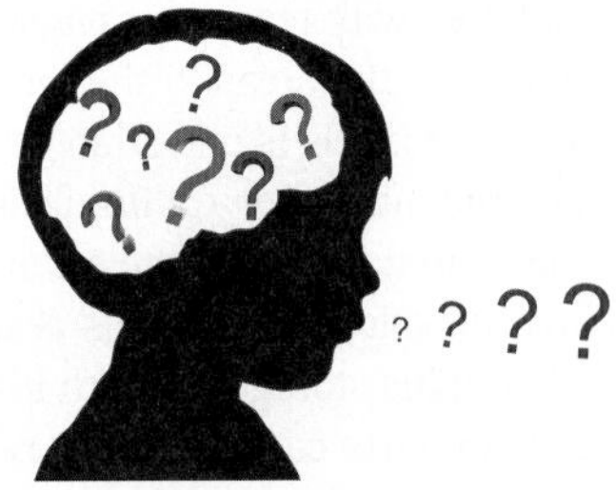<br>We don't understand.<br>©Trifonenko Ivan. Orsk/Shutterstock.com |
| 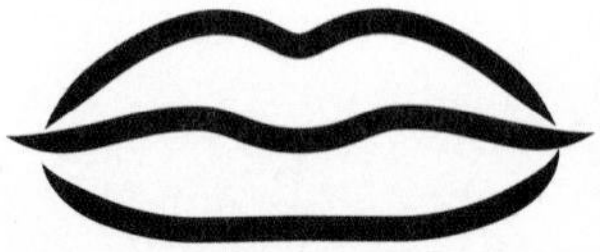<br>We have **quiet mouths**.<br>©nikolae/Shutterstock.com | 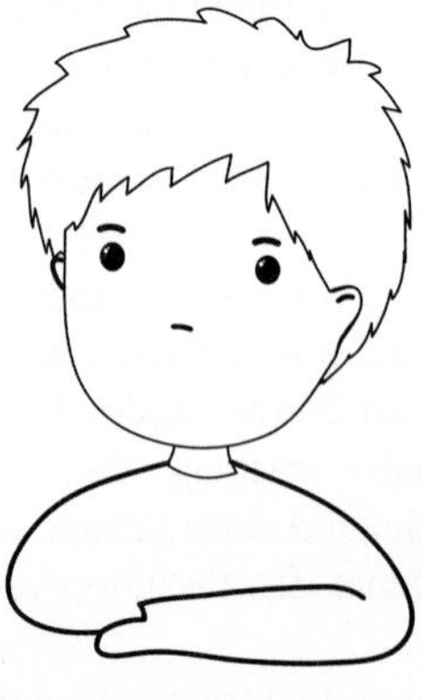<br>We can hear and learn.<br>©kvitka/Shutterstock.com | 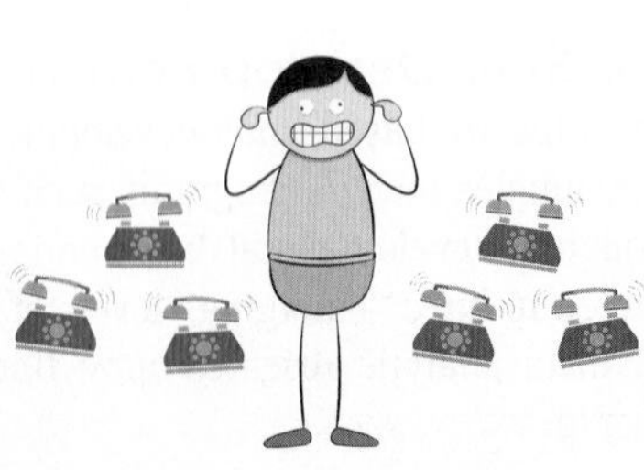<br>It's too noisy to learn.<br>©zetwe/Shutterstock.com |

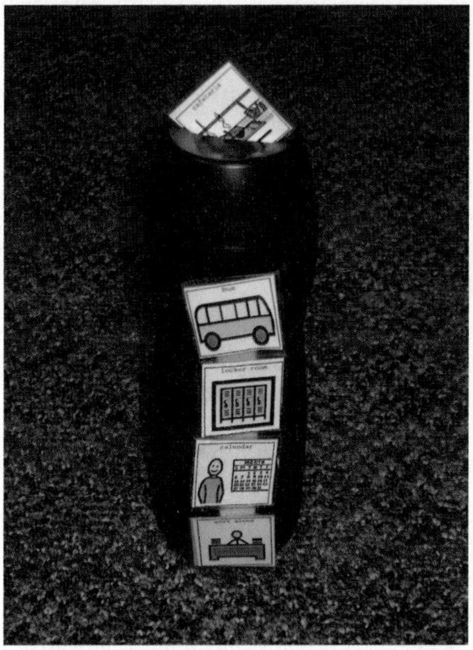

**Figure 11.4** *Portable Picture Schedule Made from Potato Chip Container*

**Figure 11.5** *Daily Picture Schedule with "To Do" and "Done" Velcro Strips*

special or general education classrooms, friendship groups, buddy or mentoring programs, and social skill groups. Examples of strategies with an established level of scientific support include joint attention intervention, peer training, pivotal response treatment, and story-based interventions (National Autism Center, 2009). Other common strategies to teach social skills are direct instruction, role playing, modeling, constructive feedback (Toth & King, 2008), peer networks (Kamps et al., 2014), social script training (Hundert, Rowe, & Harrison, 2014), and more recently, multimedia social skills programs (Radley, Ford, Battaglia, & McHugh, 2014).

Technology to teach social skills, emotion and face recognition, and language, academic, and other skills are gaining empirical support (Grynszpan, Weiss, Perez-Diaz, & Gal, 2014;

Wass & Porayska-Pomsta, 2014). Additional research on the effectiveness of such technology presents intriguing possibilities as hardware, software, and applications continue to mature.

Teaching social skills to students with ASD is critical because they are likely targets for bullying (Cappadocia, Weiss, & Pepler, 2012) and are teased more often their than nondisabled peers, particularly when they have higher cognitive functioning, less severe symptoms, and spend more time in inclusive educational settings (Nowell, Brewton, & Goin-Kochel, 2014; Zablotsky, Bradshaw, Anderson, & Law, 2014). When students with ASD have serious concerns about their school achievement, self-esteem, stress and coping, difficulties learning, and being bullied, then their quality of life is decreased (Lee, Harrington, Louie, & Newschaffer, 2008).

**Functional Skills Instruction** Because functional skills vary among individuals with ASD, instruction must be individualized. Some will receive instruction in communication, social, self-help, and self-protection skills (Koegel & Koegel, 2006; Legoff & Sherman, 2006). For others, functional skills instruction will focus on academic subjects with skills that can be used in everyday life, as well as subjects not always included in general education curricula, such as sex education; other topics may be those of special concern to the children's parents (Dale, Jahoda, & Knott, 2006; Harrington, Patrick, & Edwards, 2006; U.S. Department of Education, 2011).

**Providing Positive and Creative Educational Services** Creative, innovative, and positive teachers are particularly important in providing effective education for students with ASD (e.g., Willis, 2009). As noted earlier, these children present some unique challenges for instruction. Some seemingly insignificant actions by teachers can create great difficulties for students who have ASD—difficulties that can easily be avoided if teachers receive training and support for implementation. For example, many interpret speech literally, so it is important to teach them the meanings of slang, idioms, and sarcasm. An individual with ASD might take such phrases literally and learn something very different from what was intended. The Snapshot by Taylor Crowe illustrates how teachers can be more effective with students with ASD.

To capitalize on the unique characteristics of students with ASD, teachers need to plan in advance. These four steps offer structure to follow: (1) List the student's strengths, interests, and talents; (2) identify whether the student's specific area of need is behavioral, academic, social, or emotional; (3) consider and select evidence-based strategies to teach the student; and (4) pair the strategy with a strength, interest, or talent (Lanou, Hough, & Powell, 2012). For example, Kaleb has a fascination with Captain America. He has a collection of Captain America comics and has memorized facts from the movies. However, he does not initiate conversation with his classmates, so his teacher decided to use direct instruction and role playing to teach Kaleb how to initiate a conversation. She then chose the power card strategy (Gagnon, 2001) to help Kaleb perform the skill more frequently with peers. Using his special interest in Captain America, she created a story and a power

**LEARNING THROUGH SOCIAL MEDIA**

### Assessing and Treating ASD

Many different interventions are aimed at teaching those on the autism spectrum. After reviewing evidence-based practices, one has to experiment with individual interventions to determine particular treatment(s) that will facilitate the most growth for the person. Autism Internet Modules are available and may be reviewed to learn how to accurately assess students with ASD, and how to teach children with ASD at home, school, the workplace, and in the community. Many instructional strategies are described in text and video, shown in photographs, and demonstrated with case studies (see the Autism Internet Modules website). This set of modules includes a large number of particular applications that may be modified to fit a child's or adult's needs for social interaction with others, academic instruction, or skill acquisition to build or offset problems or promote growth.

# My Thoughts about the Education of High-Functioning Individuals with Autism

### By Taylor Crowe

My name is Taylor Crowe, and I have autism. As I write this, I am 30 years old. I am a graduate of the California Institute of the Arts, where I studied character animation. Like many students with special needs in the United States, I attended public school until just before my 21st birthday.

After undergoing extreme behavioral changes and losing almost all of my language skills at age 3, I was diagnosed with severe autism one year later. From those earliest days, my parents worked to surround me with other children who knew me, and who, as we grew older, accepted me and understood that my autism shouldn't be a barrier to our friendships. In a very real sense, those neurotypical kids taught me how to be a kid, and were some of the best "teachers" I ever had. I've come to learn that a wonderful side effect of these relationships was that teasing and bullying were never a serious problem for me because my friends protected me from those things. Unlike many kids with special needs, my memories of school and childhood are very pleasant.

My parents arranged for a speech therapist to give me language therapy beginning at age 4½. I worked with her for 15 years, slowly building language skills and learning to use language. My mom and dad say that as my ability to communicate started to develop, my "meltdowns" decreased, probably because I was able to communicate what I was thinking and wasn't as frustrated as I was when I couldn't speak.

After two years of kindergarten to build my social skills, I was "mainstreamed" in first grade, but that didn't work very well because I

AP Images/ADAM VOGLER

couldn't keep up with my classmates. I couldn't communicate very well and I was easily overwhelmed, both verbally and socially. I was placed in a special needs classroom in the second grade, attending the "regular ed" classroom only for art and music class. During these years, my teachers worked to facilitate my friendships with the other kids in school, so I never felt isolated.

I've learned that early on in school, a lot of focus was placed on survival language skills and community-based education. This created lots of opportunities to meet other people and created a lot of "real-world" social challenges for me. It also helped a lot of people in our community get to know me and understand more about autism.

Something I think all teachers should know is that most people with autism are visual learners: In my case, *seeing* something and learning from it visually meant a lot more to me than hearing something and trying to learn. Language was very confusing to me. It often still is.

Idioms and figures of speech were very hard for me to figure out. I spent years in language therapy slowly learning about these very difficult parts of language. If you believe exactly what you hear, what does "It's raining cats and dogs" mean? What

about "Keep your eye on the ball," "Ants in your pants," or "Bite the hand that feeds you"? If you interpret everything literally, things like this can be very confusing or upsetting.

All teachers should be very careful not to tease or exaggerate when working with individuals who have autism. I once had a teacher who told me I couldn't go home until I finished a worksheet and that if I didn't finish it, I'd just have to spend the night in school. I believed her and thought she wanted to kidnap me, so I was absolutely terrified! I remained scared of her for years.

My best teachers were the ones who treated me as if I was their own child and went out of their way to help me. My seventh-grade mainstream English teacher discovered that I was really good at spelling. Every week, when it was time to work on spelling in her class, she'd have me come down from the special needs classroom to take part in a spelling exercise. She said I was as good or better than anyone else in the class in spelling, and she wanted all the other kids to see what I was capable of. She did this on her own, because she wanted to; no one told her to do it.

Early in my school years, teachers discovered my interests in art. They encouraged those interests, not just to help me become a better artist, but also to create social situations for me in an environment in which I was comfortable. Those opportunities enhanced my social skills and helped me get to where I am today.

Having good teachers and friends who cared about me has had a huge impact on my life. Those relationships gave me levels of freedom that no one believed I was capable of when I was a preschooler.

**Figure 11.6** *Captain America Talks to Friends*

Captain America is good at talking to friends. When Captain America wants to be friendly, he finds a person to talk to, says "Hey," and the person's name, and then asks them a question. He waits for them to answer the question before saying something else. When Captain America does this, he makes a new friend, and they have fun together. Captain America likes talking to his friends!

Captain America wants you to talk to your friends! He knows that when you talk to your friends, you will have a lot of fun. It will make you happy and it will make others happy when you talk to your friends.

Captain America wants you to remember these four steps when you are making friends:

1. Find a person to talk to.
2. Say "Hey" and the person's name.
3. Ask the person a question.
4. Wait for the person to answer before asking another question.

card with Captain America, encouraging Kaleb to talk to his friends. See Figure 11.6 for an example of the story and a power card.

Parental participation in preparing children with ASD for school and other aspects of life is critical (Ashbaker, Dyches, Prater, & Sileo, 2012; Dyches, Carter, & Prater, 2011). Such preparation can include objectives like instilling a positive attitude in the child, helping him or her with scheduling, and teaching him or her how to find the way around in school. Also helpful is identifying a "safe" place and a "safe" person to seek out should the child become confused or encounter a particularly upsetting event. Other issues and strategies related to families are found in Chapter 6.

**CEC**

**Standard 7**
Collaboration

## 11-6e Psychological and Medical Interventions

As mentioned earlier, multidisciplinary collaboration for individuals with ASD may include psychological and medical professionals, often from the very early stages of the child's life. Their support will most often continue in various forms throughout the individual's lifespan, depending on needs and specific contextual circumstances.

Psychological interventions in schools often consist of services from a school psychologist, behavior support team, or other psychological service providers. Students may receive one-on-one instruction and support, engage in small therapeutic groups, or receive services by special or general education teachers in consultation with the school psychologist.

Various medical treatments have been used for individuals with ASD, primarily to alleviate or eliminate symptoms rather than to "cure" the autism. Research indicates at least 50 percent of individuals with ASD receive psychotropic medications during their lives (Mohiuddin & Ghaziuddin, 2013). Parents should make informed decisions when they are investigating the possible pros and cons of medications. Some concerns include financial burden, side effects, and the possibility that the medicine will not work. Parents should also be informed that medication is not likely to solve problems related to the child not following directions, learning slowly, not talking, and having poor social skills. Some benefits include the possibility of the child having reduced symptoms, functioning better, sleeping better, and fitting in better with peers (Autism Speaks, 2011).

Specific medications have been used in the past with individuals with ASD to treat certain symptoms. For example, stimulant medications such as Ritalin and Adderall have been used to treat hyperactivity, short attention span, and impulsive behavior. Antianxiety medications such as Prozac, Luvox, and Zoloft have been used to treat depression, anxiety, and repetitive thoughts and behaviors. Second-generation/atypical antipsychotics such as Risperdal and Zyprexa have been used to treat irritability, aggression, and sleep problems. Certain medications such as Tegretol and Depakote have been used to treat seizures and mood problems (Mohiuddin & Ghaziuddin, 2013). Autism Speaks offers a simple toolkit to aid parents in making informed decisions about medications (Autism Speaks, 2011).

Generally, medications have shown some promise in the treatment of ASD. There appears to be potential for improvement, but such treatment should be used thoughtfully in conjunction with a multicomponent, comprehensive treatment plan. Parents can receive research-based medical care from the Autism Treatment Network, where hospitals, physicians, researchers, and families work together to provide the most effective medical approach to individuals with ASD.

The tips found in this chapter's Community Support for Lifelong Inclusion illustrate the need for individualizing the varied and complicated treatment packages for enhancing the quality of life for those with ASD.

**Standard 7**
Collaboration

## People with Autism Spectrum Disorders (ASD)

### Early Childhood Years

#### Tips for Families

- Learn the signs of ASD. The Centers for Disease Control and Prevention's "Learn the Signs. Act Early" campaign helps parents to spot red flags in their children and to get early treatment.

- Look for and celebrate your child's milestones, and identify delays as early as possible. The CDC's *Birth to 5: Watch Me Thrive!* campaign helps parents with developmental and behavioral screening.

- Watch videos available on the Autism Speaks website to help detect red flags or diagnostic features children may exhibit.

- Contact your local Early Intervention Agency (for children younger than 3) or your Early Childhood Special Education program (for children ages 3 to 5) for an evaluation.

- Complete a developmental checklist, such as the *Communication and Symbolic Behavior Scales Developmental Profile Infant/Toddler Checklist* available free from the Florida State University's *FIRST WORDS Project*, and discuss it with your child's pediatrician.

- Complete the Modified Checklist for Autism in Toddlers (M-CHAT) on the Autism Speaks website if your child is between 16 and 30 months old,

and go over the results with your pediatrician.

- Obtain a 100 Day Kit from Autism Speaks. The kit includes basic information about autism and dealing with the news of a diagnosis and can be accessed free on the Autism Speaks website.

- Create a filing system for compiling important information and documents (e.g., personal documentation, developmental milestones, diagnostic history, education history, social skill development).

- Be an active partner in the treatment of your child. Collaborate proactively on the multidisciplinary team for your child, facilitating communication and coordinating interventions.

- Involve all family members in learning about your child's strengths, interests, and talents as well as her weaknesses.

- Protect your own health by obtaining respite care when you need a rest or a break. You may need to devise a family schedule that allows adequate time for ongoing sleep and respite. Plan ahead for respite; otherwise, when you need it most, you may be too exhausted to find it.

- Help prepare your child for school by instilling a positive attitude about

it; help him or her with the idea of a school schedule and how to find a "safe" place and a "safe" person at school.

#### Tips for Preschool Personnel

- Depending on a child's level of functioning, you may have to use physical cues or clear visual modeling to encourage her to do something; children with autism may not respond naturally to social cues.

- Establish, teach, and reinforce class expectations/consequences and natural routines throughout the school day. Use pictures or photographs to facilitate understanding.

- Pair physical cues with verbal cues and systematically fade cues as the child becomes more independent.

- Limit instruction to one item at a time; focus on what is concrete rather than abstract.

- Avoid verbal overload by using short, direct sentences.

- Encourage the development of programs where other children model good behavior and interact positively with children with ASD.

- Initiate and maintain communication with the child's parents to enhance the information flow and to promote consistent collaboration across environments.

- Promote ongoing collaborative relationships between the preschool and related service providers who can provide advice and assistance to children with ASD.
- Promote the appropriate collaborative involvement of support staff through workshops that provide information and awareness.

### Tips for Neighbors and Friends

- Be supportive of the parents and siblings of a child with ASD. They may be under high levels of stress and may need moral support.
- Be positive with the parents. They may receive information that places blame on them, which should not be magnified by their friends.
- Offer parents respite care to give them a short but important time away to do things that other families take for granted, such as going to the store or going on a date.

## Elementary Years
### Tips for Families

- If your child has recently been diagnosed, contact your local district to obtain an educational evaluation, classification, and service through an IEP or a 504 (accommodation) plan.
- Consistently follow through with the basic principles of your child's treatment program at home. This may mean taking more workshops or training on various topics to effectively collaborate as part of the intervention team.
- Learn to use applications of positive behavior support in your home, perhaps by enrolling in a parent training class.
- When working with your child, concentrate on one behavior at a time as the target for change; emphasize increasing positive, appropriate behaviors rather than focusing solely on decreasing or eliminating inappropriate behavior.
- Be active in community efforts for children with ASD; join local or national parent groups to provide support for and gain support from others.

- Provide siblings with information and opportunities to discuss the issues they are concerned about. Provide them with appropriate levels of support and attention, particularly if they feel neglected, embarrassed, or jealous of the sibling with ASD. See Chapter 6 for resources for siblings.
- Take an online introductory course such as the Autism 101 course sponsored by the Autism Society of America or similar online courses provided by the Geneva Centre for Autism or Yale.
- Learn about the law and your rights in your child's education. If your child is being served by a publicly funded organization, they will give you a document detailing your "Parents' Rights." This may be a lengthy document accompanied by a brief summary. You may also access information about education law at sites such as Wrightslaw.
- It may be necessary to take safety precautions in the home (e.g., installing locks on all doors and windows).

### Tips for General Education Classroom Teachers

- Help with collaborative organizational strategies, assisting students regarding matters that are difficult for them (e.g., remembering where to turn in homework).
- Use concrete examples to help students with ASD understand abstract concepts.
- Communicate with specific directions or questions, not vague or open-ended statements.
- If a student becomes agitated or upset, help him identify his emotions by using a visual scale, similar to a pain scale found in doctor's offices. Depending on the student's emotional level, he may need to change activities or go to a place in the room that is "safe" for a period of time.
- Together with the student, create a self-monitoring chart to track appropriate behavior. This can serve as a "home note" to celebrate the child's daily successes.

- Collaborate with parents and other school personnel to determine classroom expectations, consequences, and schedules. Explicitly teach students so they understand what is expected of them. Accompany the written expectations and schedules with pictures to enhance comprehension.
- Begin preparing students with ASD for a more variable environment by teaching adaption to changes in routine. Involve the children in planning for changes, mapping out what they might be.

### Tips for School Personnel

- Promote an environment throughout the school where children model appropriate behavior and receive reinforcement for it. Proactively collaborate with all members of the team, including parents.
- Develop peer assistance programs, where older students can help tutor and model appropriate behavior for children with ASD.
- Encourage the development of strong, ongoing collaborative school–parent relationships and support groups working together to meet children's needs.
- Find a reliable way to communicate with parents. Some students with ASD may not be able to take messages home with them, as the notes may get lost.

### Tips for Neighbors and Friends

- When possible, ignore trivial disruptions or misbehaviors; focus on positive behaviors.
- Don't take misbehaviors personally; the child is not trying to make your life difficult or to manipulate you.
- Avoid sarcasm and idiomatic expressions, such as "beating around the bush." Children with ASD may not understand and may interpret what you say literally.

## Secondary and Transition Years
### Tips for Families

- Be alert to developmental and behavioral changes as the individual grows older, such as the onset of a seizure disorder or difficulties dealing with puberty.

- Continue as a proactive collaborative partner in your child's educational and treatment program, planning for the transition to adulthood.
- Begin acquainting yourself with the adult services that will be available when your child leaves school. Together with your child, plan for adult living in environments and with activities that he or she prefers.

### Tips for General Education Classroom Teachers

- Gradually increase the level of abstraction in teaching, remaining aware of the individual challenges that young adults with ASD face.
- Continue preparing students for an increasingly variable environment through specific instruction and peer modeling.
- Focus increasingly on matters of vital importance to students as they mature (e.g., social awareness and interpersonal issues between the sexes).
- Teach students with an eye toward post-school community participation, including matters such as navigating the community, recreational and social activities, and employment. Teach students about interacting with police in the community, because they require responses different from those appropriate for other strangers.

### Tips for School Personnel

- Prepare in advance for students' transition plan. Check state guidelines for when these plans must be in place.
- See the National Secondary Transition Technical Assistance Center (NSTTAC)

website for information regarding transition assessments, best practices, toolkits, products, and other resources.

- Promote involvement in social activities and clubs that enhance interpersonal interaction.
- Encourage the development of functional academic programs that are combined with transition planning.
- Consider and encourage participation in gifted or other programs that facilitate unique interests and skills.
- Promote a continuing collaborative relationship with parents, other school staff, and agency personnel who might be involved in students' overall treatment program (e.g., health care providers, social service agencies, vocational rehabilitation).
- Work with other agencies that may encounter children in the community (e.g., law enforcement, medical services). Provide workshops, if possible, to inform officers regarding behavioral characteristics of people with autism.

### Tips for Neighbors and Friends

- Encourage a positive understanding of people with ASD among other neighbors and friends who may be in contact with young adults; help them to provide environmentally appropriate interactions.
- Assist families in providing opportunities for socialization with nondisabled peers in leisure, school, and work settings.
- Support the parents as they consider the issues of adulthood for their child with ASD. Topics such as guardianship

and community living may be difficult for parents to discuss.

## The Adult Years

### Tips for Families

- Continue to be alert for behavioral or developmental changes that may occur as an individual matures. Continued biological maturation may require medication adjustments as well as adjustments in behavioral intervention programming.
- Seek opportunities for continuing education that are appropriate and preferred.
- Continue to seek out adult services that are available to individuals with disabilities.
- Seek legal advice regarding plans for the future when you are no longer able to care for a family member with an ASD. Plan for financial arrangements and other needs that are appropriate, such as naming an advocate. Backup plans should be made; do not always count on the person's siblings. Consider guardianship by other people or agencies.

### Tips for Therapists or Other Professionals

- Remain cognizant of the maturity level of individuals with whom you are working. Despite the presence of an ASD, some individuals have mature interests and inclinations. Do not treat them as children.
- Proactively promote collaboration between appropriate adult service agencies to provide the most comprehensive services.

# Looking Toward a Bright Future

Autism spectrum disorders (ASD) have received substantial attention in the popular press during the past decade. A brighter picture is emerging due to this media attention. As recent as 40 years ago, the picture of autism was bleak—most people with autism were denied a free and appropriate public education, those with severe behavioral challenges were institutionalized, most had intellectual disabilities, and few lived enviable lives. However, today, the diagnosis of an autism spectrum disorder can bring unexpected joys and success in many life pursuits. As we move forward, we can take several points from this chapter that both guide us and present a bright future for those with autism spectrum disorders.

**11-1    Describe how the lives of people with autism spectrum disorders (ASD) have changed since the advent of IDEA.**

- Since 1975, individuals on the autism spectrum have the right to a free and appropriate public education.
- Increased media attention has encouraged greater awareness, acceptance, and inclusion.

**11-2    Explain the various definitions and classification of ASD.**

- The definition of autism has changed many times over the years and is currently viewed as a spectrum disorder with varying levels of functioning.
- Individuals with ASD have two primary impairments that are pervasive and significantly affect their functioning:
  - Social communication and social interaction
  - Restricted, repetitive patterns of behavior, interests, or activities
- Medical professionals diagnose an individual with ASD, but a diagnosis is not necessary to receive an educational classification of autism.

**11-3    Describe the characteristics and prevalence of children and youth with ASD.**

- Social communication and interactions skills are impaired along a broad continuum.
- Restricted, repetitive patterns of behaviors, interests, or activities limit functional living, and have great variation.
- Other comorbid conditions often exist, such as developmental, mental health, and medical conditions.
- Prevalence rates of ASD range from approximately 22 to 70 cases per 10,000, or 1 out of every 143 children.
- The most recent report from the Centers for Disease Control and Prevention (2014) has gained much media attention, citing the prevalence of ASD as 1 of every 68 children.
- Variation in prevalence rates is due to numerous factors such as changes in diagnostic criteria and earlier identification. However, there may be a true increase.

**11-4    List the causes and risk factors associated with ASD.**

- It is well accepted that there is no one specific cause of ASD.
- ASD is likely caused by genetic, infectious, neurologic, metabolic, and immunologic factors, with the bulk of research supporting genetic etiologies.

**11-5    Describe the assessment procedures used to identify ASD in children and youth.**

- Multidisciplinary teams of professionals from the fields of medicine, psychology, education, speech–language pathology, occupational therapy, physical therapy, social work, and counseling collaborate to identify, diagnose, and classify students with ASD.
- Parents are often the first to notice autistic characteristics in their children.

**11-6    Describe the different interventions for children and youth with ASD from early childhood through adulthood.**

- Early intervention and early childhood special education are critical for achieving positive outcomes in young children with ASD and are provided in many developmentally appropriate settings.
- Elementary students with ASD may qualify for special education services or accommodations through a 504 plan, and some may qualify for gifted and talented programs.
- Evidence-based services are provided to young adults with ASD as they prepare to transition to post-high school environments, such as college, vocational training, work, and other appropriate settings.
- Evidence-based practices should include instruction in communication skills, behavioral strategies, visual structure and support, social skills development, functional skills instruction, positive and creative educational services, and for some, psychological or medical services.

**Council for Exceptional Children (CEC) Standards to Accompany Chapter 11**

If you are thinking about a career in special education, you should know that many states use national standards developed by the Council for Exceptional Children (CEC) to assess a teacher candidate's knowledge and skills for working with students with disabilities. See a complete listing of the seven CEC Content Standards on the inside cover of this text.

1 Learner Development and Individual Learning Differences
2 Learning Environments
4 Assessment
5 Instructional Planning and Strategies
7 Collaboration

## Mastery Activities and Assignments

To master the content within this chapter, complete the following activities and assignments:

1. Complete a written test of the chapter's content. If your instructor requires a written test of your content knowledge for this chapter, keep a copy for your portfolio.
2. Review the Case Study on Embracing Diversity, "Identifying Culturally and Linguistically Diverse Children with ASD," and respond in writing to the Application Questions. Keep a copy of the Case Study and your written response for your portfolio.
3. Participate in a community service learning activity. Community service is a valuable way to enhance your learning experience. Develop a reflective journal of the service learning experience for your portfolio.

## CHAPTER 12

# Severe and Multiple Disabilities

Courtesy of Tribune News Service

## Learning Objectives

*After you complete this chapter, you will be able to:*

**12-1** Describe how the lives of people with severe and multiple disabilities have changed since the advent of IDEA.

**12-2** Explain the various definitions and classifications of severe and multiple disabilities.

**12-3** Describe the characteristics and prevalence of children and youth with severe and multiple disabilities.

**12-4** List the causes and risk factors associated with severe and multiple disabilities.

**12-5** Describe the assessment procedures used to identify severe and multiple disabilities in children and youth.

**12-6** Describe the different interventions for children and youth with severe and multiple disabilities from early childhood through adulthood.

Sarina never had the opportunity to go to preschool and didn't begin her formal education in the public schools until the age of 6. She is now 15 years old and goes to Eastmont Junior High, her neighborhood school. Sarina does not verbally speak, walk, or hear, and she has limited sight. Professionals have used several labels to describe her, including *severely disabled, severely multiply disabled, deaf–blind,* and *profoundly intellectually disabled.* Her teenage classmates at Eastmont call her Sarina.

Throughout the day, Sarina has a support team of administrators, teachers, paraprofessionals, and peers who work together to meet her instructional, physical, and medical needs. And she has many, many needs. Sarina requires some level of support in nearly everything she does, ranging from eating and taking care of personal hygiene to communicating with others. In the last few years, she has learned to express herself through the use of assistive technology. Sarina has a personal communication board with picture symbols that keeps her in constant contact with teachers, friends, and family. Through the use of a power wheelchair and her ability to use various switches, Sarina is able to maneuver her way through just about any obstacle in her environment. She is also learning to feed herself independently.

Sarina lives at home with her family, including three older brothers. Her parents, siblings, and grandparents are very supportive, always looking for ways to help facilitate Sarina's participation in school, family, and community activities. What she loves to do most is go shopping with her mom at the local mall, eat with friends at a fast-food restaurant, relax on the lawn in the neighborhood park, and play miniature golf at Mulligan's Pitch and Putt.

## 12-1  A Changing Era in the Lives of People with Multiple Disabilities

Sarina, in the opening Snapshot, is a person with **severe and multiple disabilities**. In one way or another, she will require services and support in nearly every facet of her life. Some people with multiple disabilities have significant intellectual, learning, and behavioral differences; others have physical disabilities with vision and hearing loss. The layered effect of disabilities is often referred to as multiple disabilities. People who have multiple disabilities are often said to have a severe disability. Sarina has multiple needs, one of which is communication. Yet, although she is unable to communicate verbally, she is able to express herself through the use of an assistive communication device, a language board. Thus, in many circumstances, a disability may be described as severe, but through today's technology and our understanding of how to adapt the environment, individuals with severe disabilities are able to lead constructive, happy, and productive lives in school, family, and community. Prior to 1975, when IDEA went into effect, children with multiple disabilities were often excluded from school due to the severity of their disabilities. However, educators now recognize that each individual has potential and will benefit from specialized services offered by a team of professionals.

This chapter is about *people* with severe and multiple disabilities. These individuals are often described and labeled by the severity of their disability. Yet, they bring unique personalities, characteristics, and life experiences to this world. We begin our discussion of the various definitions and characteristics associated with multiple disabilities. Sarina from our opening Snapshot is a 15-year-old teenager. Instead of initially describing Sarina as a teenager with green eyes and a beautiful smile who loves to listen to Kings of Leon with her brothers and attends Eastmont High School, she is too often described solely by her deficits: multiply disabled with a profound intellectual disability, blindness, or physical impairments. In this chapter, regardless of whether we are talking about definitions, characteristics, or causation, the language will be "people first." As such, Sarina is a teenager who also happens to have multiple disabilities.

**Severe and multiple disabilities**
Disabilities that involve significant physical, sensory, intellectual, and/or social-interpersonal performance deficits.

## 12-2 Definitions of People with Severe and Multiple Disabilities

**CEC**

**Standard 6**
Professional Learning and Ethical Practice

The needs of people with severe and multiple disabilities cannot be met by one professional. The nature of their disabilities extends equally into the fields of education, medicine, psychology, and social services. Because these individuals present such diverse characteristics and require the attention of several professionals, it is not surprising that numerous definitions have been used to describe them.

Throughout history, terminology associated with severe disabilities has communicated a sense of hopelessness and despair. The condition was described as "extremely debilitating," "inflexibly incapacitating," or "uncompromisingly crippling." In the 1970s, Abt Associates (1974) described individuals with severe disabilities as unable "to attend to even the most pronounced social stimuli, including failure to respond to invitations from peers or adults, or loss of contact with reality" (p. v). The definition went on to use terms such as *self-mutilation* (e.g., head banging, body scratching, and hair pulling), *ritualistic behaviors* (e.g., rocking and pacing), and *self-stimulation* (e.g., masturbation, stroking, and patting). The Abt definition focused almost exclusively on the individual's deficits and negative behavioral characteristics.

Justen (1976) proposed a definition that moved away from negative terminology to descriptions of an individual's developmental characteristics. "The 'severely disabled' refers to those individuals...who are functioning at a general development level of half or less than the level which would be expected on the basis of chronological age and who manifest learning and/or behavior problems of such magnitude and significance that they require extensive structure in learning situations" (p. 5).

Whereas Justen emphasized a discrepancy between normal and atypical development, Sailor and Haring (1977) proposed a definition that was oriented to the educational needs of each individual:

> A child should be assigned to a program for the severely/multiply disabled according to whether the primary service needs of the child are basic or academic.... If the diagnosis and assessment process determines that a child with multiple disabilities needs academic instruction, the child should not be referred to the severely disabled program. If the child's service need is basic skill development, the referral to the severely/multiply disabled program is appropriate. (p. 68)

In the 1990s, Snell (1991) further elaborated on the importance of defining severe disabilities on the basis of educational need, suggesting that the emphasis be on supporting individuals in inclusive classroom settings. TASH (a human rights and advocacy organization), agreeing in principle with Snell, proposed a definition that focused on inclusion in *all* natural settings: family, community, and school (Meyer, Peck, & Brown, 1991).

TASH describes the individuals it serves as follows:

> People with significant disabilities and support needs who are most at risk for being excluded from society; perceived by traditional service systems as most challenging; most likely to have their rights abridged; most likely to be at risk for living, working, playing, and learning in segregated environments; least likely to have the tools and opportunities necessary to advocate on their behalf; and are most likely to need ongoing, individualized supports to participate in inclusive communities and enjoy a quality of life similar to that available to all people. (TASH, 2014a)

TASH focuses on the relationship of the individual within the environment (adaptive fit), the need to include people of all ages, and "ongoing support" in life activities. The adaptive fit between the person and the environment is a two-way proposition. First, it is important to determine the capability of the individual to cope with the requirements of family, school, and community environments. Second, the extent to which these various environments recognize and accommodate the need of the person with severe disabilities is vital. The adaptive fit of the individual within the environment is a dynamic process requiring continuous adjustment that fosters a mutually supportive coexistence. The TASH definition suggests that an adaptive fit can be created only when there is ongoing support (formal and/or natural) for each person as he or she moves through various life activities, including social interactions, taking care of personal needs, and making choices about lifestyle, working, and moving from place to place.

## 12-2a The IDEA Definitions of Multiple Disabilities

As defined in IDEA federal regulations, *multiple disabilities* means:

> *concomitant impairments (such as intellectual disabilities–blindness, intellectual disabilities–orthopedic impairment, etc.), the combination of which causes such severe educational needs that they cannot be accommodated in special education programs solely for one of the impairments. The term does not include deaf–blindness. (34 C.F.R. 300.8[c][7], August 14, 2006)*

This definition includes multiple conditions that can occur in any of several combinations. One such combination is described by the term **dual diagnosis** and involves people who have serious emotional disturbance or who present challenging behaviors in conjunction with severe intellectual disabilities. Estimates of the percentage of people with intellectual disabilities who also have serious challenging behaviors vary, ranging from 5 percent to 15 percent of those living in the community to a much higher percentage for people living in institutions (Beirne-Smith, Patton, & Hill, 2011). Why do people with intellectual disabilities and other developmental disabilities often have higher rates of challenging behaviors? These individuals are more likely to live in situations that are restrictive, are prejudicial, limit their independence, and result in victimization. Additionally, when a person has limited means of communication, challenging behaviors can develop as a primary way to express wants and frustrations (Oliver, Petty, Ruddick, & Bacarese-Hamilton, 2012). For more insight into the life of a person with multiple disabilities, see the nearby Reflect on This, "Mat's Story."

## 12-2b Deaf–Blindness

For some with multiple disabilities, intellectual disabilities may not be a primary symptom. One such condition is deaf–blindness. The concomitant vision and hearing difficulties (sometimes referred to as **dual sensory impairments**) exhibited by people with **deaf–blindness** result in severe communication deficits as well as in developmental and educational difficulties that require extensive support across several professional disciplines. IDEA defines deaf–blindness in federal regulation as:

> *concomitant hearing and visual impairments, the combination of which causes such severe communication and other developmental and educational needs that they cannot be accommodated in special education programs solely for children with deafness or children with blindness. (34 C.F.R. 300.8[c][2], August 14, 2006)*

Although deaf–blindness sounds like a very specific set of characteristics, people who have this combination of sensory limitations span a continuum of ability. The impact of both vision and hearing loss on the educational needs of a student will vary depending on the individual student. One person with deaf–blindness may have such severe intellectual disabilities that both vision and hearing are also affected while another may have average intelligence and lost their hearing and sight after they acquired language. Intellectual functioning for people with deaf–blindness may range from normal or gifted to severe intellectual disabilities. All people with deaf–blindness experience challenges in learning to communicate, access information, and comfortably move through their environment. These individuals may also have physical and behavioral disabilities. However, the specific needs of each person will vary enormously, depending on age, age at onset, and type of deaf–blindness.

**Dual diagnosis**
Identification of both serious emotional problems and intellectual disabilities in the same individual.

**Standard 1**
Learner Development and Individual Learning Differences

**Standard 6**
Professional Learning and Ethical Practice

**Dual sensory impairments**
A condition, characterized by both vision and hearing sensory impairments (deaf–blindness), which can result in severe communication problems.

**Deaf–blindness**
A disorder involving simultaneous vision and hearing impairments.

## Mat's Story: Joining the Community

Mat is a 23-year-old man with severe and multiple disabilities (including autism and intellectual disabilities). He lives in a home with one roommate and holds two jobs. One job involves cleaning at a local bar and restaurant for an hour each morning. The second job is delivering a weekly advertiser to 170 homes in his neighborhood. In addition to working in the community, Mat goes shopping, takes walks around a nearby lake, goes to the movies, attends concerts and special events, and eats at a fast-food restaurant where he uses a wallet-sized communication picture board to order his meal, independently.

Mat hasn't always been so integrated into his local community. In the past he engaged in a number of challenging behaviors, including removing pictures from the wall, taking down drapes and ripping them, dismantling his bed, ripping his clothing, breaking windows, smearing his bowel movements on objects, urinating on his clothing, hurting others, stripping naked, and similar behaviors. For almost one entire year, Mat refused to wear clothing and spent most of his time wrapped in a blanket. He would often cover his head with the blanket and lie on the couch for hours. He frequently stripped in community settings, on those few occasions when staff were able to coax him to go out. After this had continued for months, the assistance of a behavioral analyst was sought. An analysis of the function that the behaviors served revealed that Mat's stripping and subsequent refusal to wear clothing were the result

of his attempt to exert control over his environment, primarily to escape or avoid undesirable events. For this reason, the behavior analyst suggested not focusing directly on the issue of wearing clothing but, rather, addressing the development of a communication system for Mat.

Mat was reported to know over 200 signs, but he was rarely observed to use the signs spontaneously. When he did sign, others in his environment were unable to interpret his signing. Consequently, the behavior analyst and a consultant in augmentative and alternative communication suggested that a communication system using pictures or symbols be implemented to supplement his existing system.

The support program that was developed for Mat had two main components. The first was to enhance his communication and choice-making skills; the second was to provide opportunities for him to participate in activities that were motivating and required him to wear clothing. To address communication and choice-making skills, several photographs were taken of people Mat knew and had worked with, activities he liked or was required to engage in (e.g., watching YouTube videos, going to McDonald's, shaving, taking a shower), and a variety of objects (e.g., lotion, pop, cookies). Then, a minimum of four times each hour, Mat was presented with a choice. Mat would then pick one of the pictures, and staff would help him complete whatever activity he had chosen. Soon he had over 130 photographs in

his communication system. The photographs were mounted on hooks in the hallway of the house where he lived, ensuring that he had easy access to them. Staff reported that over time, Mat began spontaneously using some of the pictures to request items. He would, for example, bring staff the photo of a Diet Pepsi to request a Diet Pepsi. Thus, the communication served to enhance his ability to make his wants and needs known, as well as to help him understand choices presented to him.

While Mat's communication system was being developed, staff was also trying to address indirectly his refusal to wear clothes by capitalizing on the fact that he seemed to genuinely like to go out into the community. Staff would periodically encourage Mat to dress. On those occasions when he would dress, he was able to participate in a community activity that was reinforcing for him. The length of these outings was gradually increased.

### Questions for Reflection

**1.** Why do you believe the two components of Mat's community support program were so effective in helping him to participate more in community activities?

**2.** What ideas do you have for supporting Mat's opportunities to "join the community"?

SOURCE: Hewitt, A., & O'Nell, S. (2009). *I Am Who I Am. A Little Help from My Friends.* Washington, DC: President's Committee on Intellectual Disabilities. Adapted from Piche, L., Krage, P., & Wiczek, C. (1991). Joining the community. IMPACT, 4(1), 3, 18. Retrieved May 5, 2009, from www.acf. hhs.gov/programs/pcpid/pcpid_help.html.

## 12-3 Characteristics and Prevalence

Although there are many possible combinations of disabilities and characteristics that can occur together, few people are identified as having severe and multiple disabilities.

## 12-3a Characteristics of Individuals with Severe and Multiple Disabilities

The multitude of characteristics exhibited by people with multiple disabilities is mirrored by the numerous definitions associated with these conditions. A close analysis of these definitions reveals a consistent focus on people whose life needs cannot be met without substantial support from others, including family, friends, and society. With this support, however, people with multiple disabilities have a much greater probability of escaping the stereotype that depicts them as totally dependent consumers of societal resources. People with multiple disabilities can become contributing members of families and communities.

Giangreco (2011) suggests that "inclusion-oriented people seek to establish an ethic that welcomes all children into their local schools and simultaneously pursues a range of individually meaningful learning outcomes through effective education practices" (p. 4). For Sarina in the opening Snapshot, this would mean concentrating on educational outcomes that will decrease her dependence on others in her environment and create opportunities to enhance her participation at home, at school, and in the community. Instruction would be developed with these outcomes in mind, rather than on the basis of a set of general characteristics associated with the label *severely disabled*.

**Standard 1**
Learner Development and Individual Learning Differences

### Intelligence and Academic Achievement
Most people with multiple disabilities have intellectual disabilities as a primary condition. Thus, their learning and memory capabilities are reduced. The greater the intellectual disabilities, the more difficulty the individual will have in learning, retaining, and applying information. People with multiple disabilities will likely require specialized and intensive instruction to acquire and use new skills across a number of settings.

Given the reduced intellectual capability of many people with multiple disabilities, academic learning is often a low instructional priority. The vast majority of students with multiple disabilities struggle to access content from basic academic programs in reading, writing, and mathematics. Instruction in functional academic skills that facilitate access to the general curriculum is the most effective approach to academic learning. Basic academic subjects are taught in the context of daily living. For example, functional reading focuses on those words that facilitate a child's access to the environment (*restroom, danger, exit,* and the like). Functional math skill development involves developing strategies for telling time or the consumer's use of money. A more in-depth discussion of teaching functional skills to students with severe disabilities appears later in this chapter.

### Adaptive Skills
The learning of **adaptive skills** is critical to success in natural settings. These skills involve both personal independence and social interaction. Personal independence skills range from the ability to take care of one's basic needs—eating, dressing, and hygiene—to living on one's own in the community (including getting and keeping a job, managing money, and finding ways to get around in the environment). Social interaction skills involve being able to communicate one's needs and preferences, as well as listening and appropriately responding to others. People with multiple disabilities often do not have age-appropriate adaptive skills; they need ongoing services and supports to facilitate learning and application in this area. We do know that when given the opportunity to learn adaptive skills through participation in inclusive settings with peers without disabilities, children with multiple disabilities have a higher probability of maintaining and meaningfully applying this learning over time (Snell & Brown, 2011; Westling & Fox, 2009).

### Speech and Language
People with severe and multiple disabilities generally have significant deficits and delays in speech and language skills, ranging from articulation and fluency disorders to an absence of any expressive oral language (Westling & Fox, 2009). Speech and language deficits and delays are positively correlated with the severity of intellectual disabilities (Moore & Montgomery, 2008). As is true for adaptive skill learning,

**Adaptive skills**
Conceptual, social, and practical skills that facilitate an individual's ability to function in community, family, and school settings.

**Epilepsy**
A condition that produces brief disturbances in brain function, resulting in seizures of varying intensity.

**Spasticity**
A condition that involves involuntary contractions of various muscle groups.

**Athetosis**
A condition characterized by constant, contorted twisting motions in the wrists and fingers.

**Standard 1**
Learner Development and Individual Learning Differences

people with multiple disabilities will acquire and use appropriate speech and language if these skills are taught and applied in natural settings. Functional communication systems (such as signing, picture cards, communication boards, and gesturing) are also an integral part of instruction. Regardless of the communication system(s) used to teach speech and language skills, they must be applied across multiple settings. For example, if picture cards are used in the classroom, they must also be a part of the communication system used at home and in other environments.

**Physical and Health** People with multiple disabilities typically have significant physical and health care needs. For instance, these individuals have a higher incidence of congenital heart disease, epilepsy, respiratory problems, diabetes, and metabolic disorders. They also exhibit poor muscle tone and often have conditions such as spasticity, athetosis, and hypotonia. Such conditions require that professionals in the schools and other service agencies know how to administer medications, catheterization, gastronomy tube feeding, and respiratory ventilation (Rues, Graff, Ault, & Holvoet, 2006).

**Vision and Hearing** Although the prevalence of vision and hearing loss is not well documented among people with severe disabilities, sensory impairments do occur more frequently in people with severe disabilities than in the general population (Drew & Hardman, 2007). Some individuals, particularly those described as deaf–blind, have significant vision and hearing disorders that require services and supports beyond those for a person with blindness *or* deafness.

### 12-3b Prevalence of Multiple Disability

People with multiple disabilities constitute a very small percentage of the general population. Even if we consider the multitude of conditions, prevalence is no more than 0.1 percent to 1.0 percent. The U.S. Department of Education (2013) reported that more than 130,000 students between the ages of 6 and 21 were served in the public schools under the label *multiple disabilities*. These students account for about 2 percent of the over 7 million students considered eligible for services under IDEA. The Department of Education also reported that more than 1,600 students between the ages of 6 and 21 were labeled as deaf–blind. These students account for 0.0002 percent of students with disabilities served under IDEA. Overall, about 14,000 individuals in the United States are identified as deaf–blind.

*Photo 12.1* Students with deaf–blindness require extensive support to meet their educational needs, particularly in the area of communication.

Courtesy of Tribune News Service

**Hypotonia**
Poor muscle tone.

**Catheterization**
The process of introducing a hollow tube (catheter) into body cavities to drain fluid, such as introducing a tube into an individual's bladder to drain urine.

**Gastronomy tube feeding**
The process of feeding a person through a rubber tube that is inserted into the stomach.

**Respiratory ventilation**
Use of a mechanical aid (ventilator) to supply oxygen to an individual with respiratory problems.

## 12-4 Causes and Risk Factors Associated with Multiple Disabilities

Multiple disabilities result from multiple causes. For the vast majority of people with multiple disabilities, the differences are evident at birth. Multiple disabilities may be the result of genetic or metabolic disorders, including chromosomal abnormalities, and phenylketonuria (See Chapter 9 for more in-depth information on these disorders.) Most identifiable causes of multiple disabilities that include severe intellectual disabilities are genetic in origin (The ARC, 2014). Other causes include prenatal conditions: poor maternal health during pregnancy, drug abuse, infectious diseases (e.g., HIV), radiation exposure, venereal disease, and advanced maternal age. Multiple disabilities can also result from incidents or conditions that occur later in life, such as accidents, poisoning, malnutrition, physical and emotional abuse or neglect, and disease.

## 12-5 Assessment Procedures Used to Identify Severe and Multiple Disabilities

Children who have severe and multiple disabilities are often identified at a very young age due to the overarching nature of the disability. It is not unusual for a pediatrician to make a diagnosis soon after birth or within the first year as the infant misses developmental milestones. Once a concern has been identified, further information is typically gathered through formal assessments given by pediatricians, speech and language pathologists, physical therapists, and early intervention specialists. These assessments often include evaluation of fine and gross motor skills, reflexes, vision, hearing, and a complete health screening. Infants and toddlers who have severe and multiple disabilities start early intervention services as soon as a deficit or concern is identified.

## 12-6 Interventions for Children and Youth with Multiple Disabilities

**CEC**

Standard 4
Assessment

The axiom "the earlier, the better" is certainly applicable to educational assessments and supports for children with severe and multiple disabilities. Such services must begin at birth and continue throughout the lifespan. Traditionally, there has been a heavy reliance on standardized assessments, particularly IQ tests, in identifying people with severe and multiple disabilities, particularly when the primary condition is intellectual disabilities (see Chapter 9). Some professionals (Bishop, 2005; Brown & Snell, 2011) have suggested that standardized tests, particularly the IQ test, do not provide information useful in either diagnosing the disability or providing instruction to individuals with severe disabilities. Others (McDonnell, Hardman, & McDonnell, 2003) believe that standardized tests may be appropriate as one tool in a battery of multidisciplinary assessments to determine eligibility for special education services, but that they provide no meaningful information for making curriculum decisions such as what and how to teach.

Assessments that focus on valued skills to promote independence and quality of life in natural settings are referred to as functional, ecological, or **authentic assessment** (Horner, Albin, Todd, & Sprague, 2006; McDonnell, Hardman, & McDonnell, 2003). Authentic assessment refers to the systematic recording of developmental observations over time, focused on behaviors and competencies of the person being assessed (Bagnato, Goins, Pretti-Frontczak, & Neisworth, 2014). These assessments focus on the match between the needs of the individual and the demands of the environment (adaptive fit). The purpose of the assessment is to determine what supports are necessary to achieve the intended outcomes of access and participation in natural settings. Skills are never taught in isolation from actual performance demands. Additionally, the individual does not "get ready" to participate in the community through a sequence of readiness stages as in the developmental model but, rather, learns and uses skills in the setting where the behavior is expected to occur. Bagnato et al. (2014) found authentic assessments to be superior to conventional assessments for the purpose of diagnosing early childhood disorders.

During the past decade, there has been increasing emphasis on holding schools more accountable for student learning and progress. States are setting educational standards and then assessing how students progress toward the intended goals. A major challenge for education is to demonstrate accountability for all students, including those with the most significant disabilities:

> *Regardless of one's perspective on the wisdom and implications of this [accountability] movement, it promises to have a significant effect on curricular guidance and foci for students with [severe] disabilities.... A major question facing educators and parents is how can those concerned with the education of students with significant disabilities ensure a continued and focused emphasis on full membership and meaningful outcomes during this era? (Ford, Davern, & Schnorr, 2001, p. 215)*

**Authentic assessment**
An alternative basis used to measure student progress. Assessment is based on student progress in meaningful learning activities.

**Alternate assessments**
Assessments mandated in IDEA for students who are unable to participate in required state- or district-wide assessments. It ensures that all students, regardless of the severity of their disabilities, are included in the state's accountability system.

IDEA requires that schools must include students with disabilities in district-wide or statewide assessments of achievement or provide a statement of why that assessment is not appropriate for the child. The law also requires that individual modifications in the administration of statewide or district-wide assessments be provided as appropriate for children to participate. Examples of student accommodations include large-print text, testing in a separate setting, and extended time. Ysseldyke, Olsen, and Thurlow (2012) estimate that about 85 percent of students with disabilities have mild or moderate disabilities and can take state or district assessments, either with or without accommodations. For many students with severe disabilities, these assessments are inappropriate; such students are excluded from taking them. Schools are still accountable, however, for the progress of these students. IDEA mandated that states conduct **alternate assessments** to ensure that all students are included in the state's accountability system. Quenemoen and Thurlow (2012) identified five characteristics of good alternate assessments:

- There have been careful stakeholder and policy-maker development and definition of desired student outcomes for the population, reflecting the best understanding of research and practice.
- Assessment methods have been carefully developed, tested, and refined.
- Professionally accepted standards are used to score evidence (e.g., adequate training, dual-scoring third-party tiebreakers, reliability tests, and rechecks of scorer competence).
- An accepted standards-setting process has been used so that results can be included in reporting and accountability.
- The assessment process is continuously reviewed and improved.

Alternate assessment systems should include as key criteria the extent to which the system provides the supports and adaptations needed and trains students to use them.

Alternate assessments may involve either normative or absolute performance standards (Ysseldyke & Olsen, 2012). If a normative assessment is used, then a student's performance is compared to that of peers (other students of comparable age or ability participating in the alternate assessment). If an absolute standard is used, then a student's performance is compared against a set criterion, such as being able to cross the street when the "walk" sign is flashing 100 percent of the time without assistance.

## 12-6a The Early Childhood Years

Effective early intervention services that start when a child is born are critical to the prevention and amelioration of social, medical, and educational problems that can occur throughout the life of an individual (Batshaw, Pellegrino, & Rozien, 2008; Berk, 2005). During the early childhood years, services and supports are concentrated on two age groups: infants and toddlers, and preschool-age children.

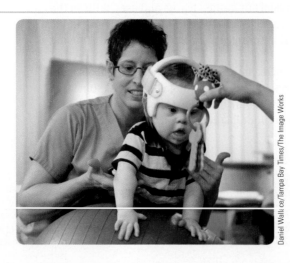

*Photo 12.2* Effective programs for infants and toddlers with severe and multiple disabilities are both child- and family-centered. Therapists work closely with the infant and the family to promote early learning and development.

Daniel Wallace/Tampa Bay Times/The Image Works

**Services and Supports for Infants and Toddlers** Effective programs for infants and toddlers with severe and multiple disabilities are both child- and family-centered. A child-centered approach focuses on identifying and meeting individual needs. Services begin with infant stimulation programs intended to elicit in newborns the sensory, cognitive, and physical responses that will connect them with their environment. As the child develops, health care, physical therapy, occupational therapy, and speech and language services may become integral components of a child-centered program.

Family-centered early intervention focuses on a holistic approach that involves the child as a member of the family unit. The needs, structure, and preferences of the family drive the delivery of services and supports. The overall purpose of family-centered intervention is to enable family members first to cope with the birth of a child with a severe disability and eventually to grow together and support one another. Family-centered approaches build on and increase family strengths, address the needs of every family member, and support mutually enjoyable family relationships. Supports for families may include parent-training programs, counseling, and **respite care**.

**CEC**

**Standard 1**
Learner Development and Individual Learning Differences

**Standard 5**
Instructional Planning and Strategies

### Services and Supports for Preschool-Age Children

Preschool programs for young children with severe and multiple disabilities continue the emphasis on family involvement while extending the life space of the child to a school setting. McDonnell, Hardman, and McDonnell (2003) suggest four goals for preschool programs serving children with severe disabilities:

1. Maximize the child's development in a variety of important developmental areas. These include social communication, motor skills, cognitive skills, pre-academic skills, self-care, play, and personal management.

2. Develop the child's social interaction and classroom participation skills. Focus should be on teaching the child to follow adult directions while developing peer relationships, responding to classroom routines, and becoming self-directed (that is, completing classroom activities without constant adult supervision).

3. Increase community participation through support to family members and other caregivers. Work to identify alternative caregivers so that the family has a broader base of support and more flexibility to pursue other interests. Help the family to identify activities within the neighborhood that their preschooler would enjoy to provide the child with opportunities to interact with same-age peers. Activities may involve swimming or dancing lessons, joining a soccer team, attending a house of worship, and so on.

4. Prepare the child for inclusive school placements, and provide support for the transition to elementary school. The transition out of preschool will be facilitated if educators from the receiving elementary school work collaboratively with the family and preschool personnel.

To meet these goals, preschool programs for children with severe disabilities blend the principles and elements of developmentally appropriate practices (DAP), multicultural education, and special education. DAP was developed by the National Association for the Education of Young Children as an alternative to an academic curriculum for preschoolers. It emphasizes age-appropriate child exploration and play activities that are consistent with individual needs. Multicultural education emphasizes acceptance of people from different cultural and ethnic backgrounds within and across the preschool curriculum. Successful culturally inclusive programs blend principles and practices that guide special education, inclusive education, and multicultural education (Gollnick & Chinn, 2012). Special education focuses on assessing individual needs, providing intensive instruction, and teaching explicit skills within the context of an individualized education program (IEP). Families, educators, and other professionals committed to DAP, multicultural education, and special education work together to provide a quality experience for preschool-age children with severe disabilities.

**Respite care**
Assistance provided by individuals that allows parents and other children within the family time away from the child with a disability.

*Photo 12.3* Culturally inclusive preschool programs blend the principles and practices that guide special education, inclusive education, and multicultural education.

Amelie Benoist/BSIP/Photoshot

## 12-6b  The Elementary School Years

Historically, services and supports for students with severe and multiple disabilities have been oriented to protection and care. The objective was to protect the individual from society, and society from the individual. This philosophy resulted in programs that isolated the individual and provided physical care rather than preparation for life in a heterogeneous world. Today, educators working together with parents are concentrating their efforts on preparing students with severe and multiple disabilities to participate actively in the life of the family, school, and community. Given the emphasis on lifelong learning and living as independently as possible in natural settings, educators have identified several features that characterize quality programs for elementary-age students with severe and multiple disabilities:

**Standard 5**
Instructional Planning
and Strategies

- Self-determination is important—student preferences and needs are taken into account in developing educational objectives.
- The school values and supports parental involvement.
- Instruction focuses on frequently used functional skills related to everyday life activities and the provision of plenty of opportunities to practice the skills.
- Assistive technology and augmentative communication are available to maintain or increase the functional capabilities of the student with severe and multiple disabilities.

**Self-Determination** People with severe and multiple disabilities, like everyone else, must be in a position to make their own life choices as much as possible. School programs that promote self-determination enhance each student's opportunity to become more independent in the life of the family and in the larger community. Providing students with severe disabilities the opportunity to communicate their needs and preferences enhances autonomy, problem-solving skills, adaptability, and self-efficacy expectations (Gaumer Erickson, Noonan, Zheng, & Brussow, 2015; Wehmeyer, Gragoudas, & Shogren, 2006). Self-determination skills have been shown to be positively correlated with achievement in math and reading, as well as overall adult outcomes (Gaumer et al., 2015; Wehmeyer et al., 2011).

**Parental Involvement** Schools are more successful in meeting the needs of students when they establish positive relationships with the family. The important role parents play during the early childhood years must continue and be supported during elementary school. Parents who actively participate in their child's educational program promote the development and implementation of instruction that is consistent with individual needs and preferences. Parental involvement can be a powerful predictor of post-school adjustment for students with severe and multiple disabilities. A strong home–school partnership requires that parents and educators acknowledge and respect each other's differences in values and culture, listen openly and attentively to one another's concerns, value varying opinions and ideas, discuss issues openly and in an atmosphere of trust, and share in the responsibility and consequences of making a decision.

**Teaching Functional Skills** Effective educational programs focus on the functional skills that students with severe and multiple disabilities need to live successfully in the natural settings of family, school, and community. A functional skill is one that will have frequent and meaningful use across multiple environments. Instruction should involve the following elements:

- Many different people
- A variety of settings within the community
- Varied materials that will interest the learner and match performance demands

If the student with severe disabilities is to learn how to cross a street safely, shop in a grocery store, play a video game, or eat in a local restaurant, the necessary skills should

## Design Challenge: DIY Assistive Game Controllers

Video gaming is a social activity that can empower participants. According to the Entertainment Software Association (ESA, 2014), "59% of Americans play video games"—many of whom are children. Those with physical disabilities, however, may find it nearly impossible to participate alongside their peers. Controllers—like those included with Xbox, PlayStation, and Wii consoles—can have over a dozen buttons, often requiring two hands to operate.

The AbleGamers Foundation is a non-profit organization that "aims to improve the overall quality of life for those with disabilities through the power of video games." To that end, it published Includification, a game accessibility guideline to help developers extend accessibility for all.

### Simple Switch Interfaces

A switch simply turns an electrical signal on or off (e.g., a light switch, the right-click button on a mouse, the space bar on a keyboard). Makey Makey is an easy-to-use kit that can serve as a switch interface. Costing about $50, Makey Makey is built on an Arduino circuit board and includes a USB cable, alligator clips, and additional wires. Almost anything that carries an electrical current—pencil graphite, bananas, modeling clay—can become part of the circuit. When the USB is plugged in, the computer's keyboard interface becomes shared with Makey Makey. There are assistive guides posted on its web page, in which a computer's keys are remapped (rerouted) to best work with a person's needs.

### Design Challenges

More often than not, a teacher or paraprofessional is responsible for adapting a device to fit a person's need. The following are sample challenges that can be met using Makey Makey as a do-it-yourself (DIY) assistive game controller:

*1. Mini-Keyboard Challenge*
Able gamers with muscular dystrophy can find movement across a keyboard to be difficult. However, there are ways to move with greater precision. For example, a trackball interface is often used instead of a mouse—the ball can be rolled without moving or stretching one's arms. The challenge is to use Makey Makey to move game keys very close together. A solution might be creating a dedicated mini-keyboard for the WASD keys (common in PC games: W = up, A = left, S = down, D = right), along with the arrow keys, space bar (in some games this is jump or shoot), and enter button. Users must be able to operate the controller with one idle hand.

*2. Macro-Keyboard Challenge*
Able gamers with cerebral palsy can find fine motor activity to be nearly impossible. The challenge is to use Makey Makey to spread out the WASD keys, along with the arrow keys, space bar, and enter buttons. Modeling clay on a desk can be used to spread out the input keys.

*3. Head Mobility Challenge*
Some able gamers can move only their heads. The challenge is to design a game controller using head movement to take the place of arrow keys. It can work well with dancing games created on Scratch (an online community for building interactive games and animations, sponsored by MIT).

*4. Simple Switch Challenge*
Some able gamers have very restricted mobility. A hand chop, shoulder shrug, or even a tongue move can be used to interact with one-button games. Try Flabby Physics, playable with just the space bar.

I attempted to create a directional head movement interface using Makey Makey. Moving my head could, theoretically, take the place of arrow keys on my laptop. I could touch my left shoulder with my head to turn left in a game world. First I had a brainstorming session—paper towel rolls, hats, shirt collars, and other apparatus were considered as materials. I discovered that the most flexible tool for the head movement interface was a small necklace made from pipe cleaners. Wearing the contraption proved uncomfortable and awkward. Upon observing this, my wife suggested that I use a travel neck pillow. This accomplished two things: an object to prop up the pipe cleaner ring and something to provide added comfort. Of course, I was testing my own design. To be most effective, try your prototype with a person of need.

### Teaching Students to Be Designers

Design thinking is considered to be a desirable 21st-century or "soft" skill. Bringing in students as designers can make the process even more inclusive. Working in teams can create a learning environment in which solutions emerge. A jigsaw cooperative structure would work effectively in the testing phases. Students would then have the opportunity to watch their prototypes used through someone else's eyes. (Herein lies another challenge—something obvious to a designer may not be obvious to users.) Testers can move from group to group. No one should test the same design twice. If you only have one kit, then groups can work in a station, out of view from the rest of the class. The goal is for other students to not see the prototyped design.

Makey Makey is a tool that can make video games accessible for able gamers. Take the systemic rather than technocentric approach to integrating this tool. The technology that you're introducing should not be the sole focus of the activity. Keep in mind that you're using Makey Makey to remap a keyboard that will enable students of all abilities to play.

SOURCE: From Farber, M. (2014). Design Challenge: DIY Assistive Game Controllers. *Edutopia*. Retrieved March 1, 2015, from www.edutopia.org/blog/design-diy-assistive-game-controllers-matthew-farber.

**Photo 12.4** An assistive device, such as this computerized touch screen language board, helps students who are nonverbal to communicate with parents, teachers, and friends.

be taught in the actual setting where the behavior is to be performed. It should not be assumed that a skill learned in a classroom will simply transfer to a setting outside of the school. Instruction in a more natural environment can ensure that the skill will be useful and will be maintained over time.

As suggested by Drew and Hardman (2007), a functional approach teaches academic skills in the context of environmental cues. The learning of new skills is always paired directly with environmental stimuli. Snell and Brown (2011) stressed that the teacher must use instructional materials that are real and meaningful to students. Traditional materials, such as workbooks, basal readers, and flash cards, do not work for students with severe disabilities. Students must be taught using *real objects in real situations* in the home or community setting. For example, when teaching the word *exit*, pair it with an actual exit sign in a movie theater. Or when teaching the word *stop*, pair it with a stop sign on a street corner.

### Assistive Technology and Augmentative Communication

Assistive technology is any item, piece of equipment, or product system that can be used to increase, maintain, or improve the functional capabilities of students with disabilities (The Technology-Related Assistance for Individuals with Disabilities Act, PL 100-407 [20 U.S.C. Sec. 140(25)]). An assistive technology service "directly assists an individual with a disability in the selection, acquisition, or use of an assistive technology device" (20 U.S.C. Sec 140[26]). Johnston (2003) identified several types of assistive technology:

- Aids for daily living (such as nonslip placement to hold a bowl, utensils with built-up handles to provide a better gripping surface, and two-handed mugs to allow for two-handed grasping)
- Communication aids (computers with voice output, hearing aids)
- Aids for working, learning, and playing (braces, artificial limbs, prosthetic hands)
- Mobility aids (wheelchairs, lifts, walkers)
- Positioning aids (cushions, pelvic strips or hip guides, head supports on a wheelchair)

Students with severe and multiple disabilities benefit from any one or more of these assistive devices or activities. For students with severe disabilities who are unable to use speech and need an additional communication mode, **augmentative communication** will nearly always be an integral component of their individualized education program. Augmentative communication involves adapting existing vocal or gestural abilities into meaningful communication; teaching manual signing (such as American Sign Language), static symbols, or icons (such as **PECS**), and using manual or electronic communication devices (such as electric communication boards, picture cues, or synthetic speech; Westling & Fox, 2009). For more insight into the use of PECS in an instructional setting for students with severe disabilities, see the nearby Case Study on Embracing Diversity, "Ernesto."

### 12-6c  The Adolescent Years

Societal perceptions about the capabilities of people with severe and multiple disabilities have changed a great deal over the past several years. Until very recently, the potential of these individuals to learn, live, and work in community settings was significantly underestimated. People with severe and multiple disabilities can become active participants in the lives of their community and family. This realization has prompted professionals

**Augmentative communication**
Communication systems that involve adapting existing vocal or gestural abilities into meaningful communication, or using manual or electronic devices.

**PECS**
A symbol-based communication system developed in 1985 as a unique augmentative alternative communication method for people with developmental disabilities.

**CEC**

**Standard 6**
Professional Learning and Ethical Practice

## Meet Ashley

In the vignette that follows, Kimberly Voss describes how she taught her daughter Ashley, a child born with Down syndrome and severe disabilities, to learn reading through the use of assistive technology. Kimberly describes Ashley's odyssey through life as one of "getting Ashley out":

Trapped inside a body that does not always do what she asks it to do, we have had to invent and create from scratch numerous methods that allow her to emerge. Her medical diagnosis and developmental label have not been an accurate measure of her human potential. Unwilling to accept "can't" as an option, we have focused on "what if?" Ashley's determination, as well as mine, has been our key to unlocking door after door, every day revealing more of Ashley's abilities and character. While she lives with many challenging and complex disabilities, Ashley has emerged as an assertive, independent, loving, and spirited young woman with a zest for life and wonderfully keen sense of humor. She will face adversity throughout her life, but we will face it, as we have all the changes that came before, one day and one creative solution at a time (from Voss, 2005, pp. 9–10).

### Teaching Ashley to Read Using Assistive Technology

When Ashley was quite young, I had the good fortune to attend a workshop Patricia Oelwein gave before her 1995 book, *Teaching Reading to Children with Down Syndrome*, was published. Her technique began by following a three-step progression (matching, selecting, and naming) and was very visual, initially teaching sight words rather than phonics or text decoding. Pat suggested starting off by playing simplified matching-type games, matching text to text—for example, putting the word "Daddy" on "Daddy." After that was mastered, Pat suggested matching text to an image and then selecting the correct word from a set of different word choices. We would ask, "Give me the card that says 'Daddy.'" This approach worked very well for Ashley.

For Ashley, teaching sight words held real potential. Because of her complex speech problems, Ashley could not verbally describe what letters she was seeing or what words she was reading, making it even more of a challenge to teach her to read. But Pat's approach of matching words and selecting words required no speech at all. Using these methods, Ashley was quickly able to learn to read a number of meaningful sight words, matching text to text, matching text to image, and then selecting a requested word from a set. Over time, she significantly increased her sight word vocabulary and eventually completed the final step of naming: expressively communicating her identification of many words using sign language. As she began to read and sign, lo and behold, along came speech.

Sight word cards really show the advantages of designing the materials by computer, including the opportunity to customize the word choices and to keep it constantly fresh and new. And the computer enables uniformity. If the words are to be matched, it is best if they are an exact copy of one another (so that they are truly visually the same), which they cannot be if handwritten. It is quick and easy to accomplish this using a computer.

SOURCE: Voss, K. S. (2005). *Teaching by Design*. Bethesda, MD: Woodbine House (pp. 9, 215).

and parents to seek significant changes in the ways that schools prepare students for the transition to adult life.

In a review of the research on successful community living for people with severe disabilities, Crockett and Hardman (2009) address four tasks that are important in planning for the transition to adult life:

- Establish a network of friends and acquaintances.
- Develop the ability to use community resources on a regular basis.
- Secure a paid job that supports the use of community resources and interaction with peers.
- Establish independence and autonomy in making lifestyle choices.

## 12-6d   Inclusive Education

The provision of services and supports in an inclusive educational setting is widely viewed as a critical factor in delivering a quality program for students with severe and multiple

**Standard 2**
Learning Environments

**Standard 3**
Curricular Content
Knowledge

## Ernesto

Ernesto is a 6-year-old kindergarten student at Armstrong Elementary School. Like most of his friends in his inclusive class, he likes Pokémon and Transformers. Unlike his peers, Ernesto has spina bifida and uses a wheelchair. When he was 2 years old, following a series of seizures, he had a shunt surgically implanted in his head to drain fluids and relieve pressure. Additionally, Ernesto has an intellectual disability and is nonverbal. Ernesto has lived in the United States all of his life, but his parents immigrated from Peru 15 year ago. The family is bilingual and uses both Spanish and English at home.

The kindergarten teacher, Mr. Carmichael, was excited when he learned Ernesto would be joining his class, but he also had some concerns about how to best meet the needs of all the students in his class. Ms. Rice, the speech and language pathologist, and Ms. Lopez, the inclusion specialist, met with Mr. Carmichael to introduce him to the communication board and the PECS (Picture Exchange Communication System) program that Ernesto was going to learn this year. Together, with Ernesto's parents, they considered strategies to support Ernesto's bilingualism. They decided to introduce Ernesto to PECS with a dozen picture cards that include both languages on each card. This strategy was selected to ensure that the communication system would be effective across multiple environments.

Ernesto's teacher and friends have been communicating with him using the PECS program, and they have learned some Spanish along the way. Mr. Carmichael is excited about Ernesto's progress and plans to add even more symbols to his communication board, including Pokémon!

### Application Questions

**1.** Why is it important for Ernesto to use bilingual PECS when he is nonverbal?

**2.** What are the benefits for Ernesto to be included in his neighborhood kindergarten class? What are the benefits for his peers?

**3.** Why is it important to include Pokémon on Ernesto's communication board?

disabilities (The ARC, 2012). Effective educational programs include continual opportunities for interaction between students with severe disabilities and peers without disabilities. Frequent and age-appropriate interactions between students with disabilities and their peers without disabilities can enhance opportunities for successful participation in the community during the adult years. Social interaction can be enhanced by creating opportunities for these students to associate both during and after the school day. Successful inclusion efforts are characterized by the following features:

- Physical placement of students with severe and multiple disabilities in the general education schools and classes they would attend if they didn't have disabilities
- High-level expectations and supports to allow students to access the grade-level standards
- Participation in alternative assessments to monitor growth and achievement
- Systematic organization of opportunities for interaction between students with severe and multiple disabilities and students without disabilities
- Specific instruction in valued post-school outcomes that will increase the competence of students with severe and multiple disabilities in the natural settings of family, school, and community (Ryndak, Alper, Hughes, & McDonnell, 2012)

One of the most important characteristics of the natural settings in which students ultimately must function is frequent interaction with people without disabilities. Consequently, it is logical to plan educational programs that duplicate this feature of the environment and that actively build skills required for successful inclusion. As students with severe and multiple disabilities are included in general education schools and classrooms, it is important to find ways to encourage social interactions between these students and students who are not disabled. Planned opportunities for interaction may include the use of in-class peer supports (tutors, circles of friends) as well as access to everyday school activities such as assemblies, recess, lunch, and field trips. For more tips on supporting people with severe and multiple disabilities in natural settings, see this chapter's Community Support for Lifelong Inclusion.

## People with Severe and Multiple Disabilities

### Early Childhood Years

**Tips for Families**

- During the infant and toddler years, seek out family-centered programs that focus on communication and the building of positive relationships among all individual members.

- Seek supports and services for your preschool-age child that promote communication and play activities with same-age peers without disabilities.

- Seek opportunities for friendships to develop between your child and children without disabilities in family and neighborhood settings.

- Use the individualized family service plan and the individualized education plan as a means for the multidisciplinary team to establish goals that develop your child's social interaction and classroom participation skills.

**Tips for Preschool Teachers**

- Establish a classroom environment that promotes and supports diversity.

- Use a child-centered approach to instruction that acknowledges and values every child's strengths, preferences, and individual needs.

- Ignore whatever labels have been used to describe the child with severe and multiple disabilities. There is no relationship between the label and the instruction needed by the child to succeed in natural settings.

- Set high expectations for academic and social success and support the student in meeting them.

- Create opportunities for ongoing communication and play activities among children with severe disabilities and their same-age peers without disabilities. Nurture interactive peer relationships across a variety of instructional areas and settings.

**Tips for Preschool Personnel**

- Support the inclusion of young children with severe and multiple disabilities in all preschool classrooms and programs.

- Always refer to children by name, not label. If you must employ a label, use "child-first language." For example say, "children with severe disabilities," not "severely disabled children."

- Communicate genuine respect and support for all teachers, staff, and volunteers who look for ways to include children with severe disabilities in preschool classrooms and collaborative school-wide activities.

- Welcome families into the preschool programs. Listen to what parents have to say about the importance of, or concerns about, including their child in school programs and activities.

- Create opportunities for parents to become involved in their child's program through collaborative projects with school personnel, including volunteering, school governance, and the like.

**Tips for Neighbors and Friends**

- Most importantly, see the child with severe disabilities as an individual who has needs, preferences, strengths, and weaknesses. Avoid the pitfalls of stereotyping and "self-fulfilling prophecies."

- Support opportunities for your children and those of friends and neighbors to interact and play with a child who has severe and multiple disabilities.

- Help children without disabilities build friendships with children who have severe and multiple disabilities, rather than merely playing caregiving roles.

- Provide a supportive and collaborative community environment for the family of a young child with severe and multiple disabilities. Encourage the family, including the child, to participate in neighborhood activities.

### Elementary Years

**Tips for Families**

- Actively collaborate with the multidisciplinary team in the development of your son's or daughter's IEP. Write down the priorities and educational goals that you see as important for your child in the natural settings of home, school, and community.

- Follow up at home on activities that the school suggests are important for helping your child generalize skills learned at school to other natural settings.

- Actively collaborate with school personnel, whether in your child's classroom or in extracurricular activities. Demonstrate your appreciation and support for administrators, teachers, and staff who openly value and support the inclusion of your child in the school and classroom.

- Continually collaborate with administrators and teachers on the importance of children with severe disabilities being included with peers without disabilities during classroom and school-wide activities (such as riding on the same school bus, going to recess and lunch at the same time, and participating in school-wide assemblies).

**Tips for General Education Classroom Teachers**

- See children with severe and multiple disabilities as individuals, not labels. Focus on their similarities with other children rather than on their differences.

- Openly value and support diversity and collaboration in your classroom. Set individualized goals and objectives for all children.

- Develop a classroom environment and instructional program that recognize multiple needs and abilities.

- Become part of a team that continually collaborates to meet the needs of all children in your classroom. View the special education teacher as a resource who can assist you in developing an effective instructional program for the child with severe and multiple disabilities.

### Tips for School Personnel

- Communicate that diversity is strength in your school. Openly value diversity by providing the resources necessary for teachers to work with students who have a range of needs and come from differing backgrounds.

- Integrate school resources as well as children. Develop school-wide teacher-assistance or teacher-support teams that work collaboratively to meet the needs of every student.

- Collaborate with general and special education teachers in the development of peer-partner and support networks for students with severe and multiple disabilities.

- Include all students in the programs and activities of the school.

### Tips for Neighbors and Friends

- Openly communicate to school personnel, friends, and neighbors your support of families who are seeking to have their child with severe and multiple disabilities be a part of an inclusive school setting.

- Communicate to your children and those of friends and neighbors the value of collaboration and inclusion. Demonstrate this value by creating opportunities for children with severe disabilities and their families to play an active role in the life of the community.

## Secondary and Transition Years

### Tips for Families

- Seek opportunities for students from your son's or daughter's high school to visit your home. Help arrange get-togethers or parties involving students from the neighborhood and/or school.

- Communicate to the school what you see as priorities for your son or daughter as they transition from school into adult life. Suggest goals and objectives that promote and support social

interaction and community-based activities with peers who are not disabled. Collaborate with the school to translate your goals into an individualized education plan that includes transition activities from school to adult life.

### Tips for General Education Classroom Teachers

- Become part of a school-wide team that collaborates to meet the needs of all students in high school. Value the role of the special educator as teacher, collaborator, and consultant who can serve as a valuable resource in planning for the instructional needs of students with severe disabilities. Collaborate with special education teachers and other specialists to adapt subject matter in your classroom (e.g., science, math, or physical education) to the individual needs of students with severe and multiple disabilities.

- Communicate the importance of students with severe disabilities being included in school programs and activities. Although the goals and activities of this student may be different from those of other students, with support, she or he will benefit from working with you and other students in the class.

- Encourage the student with severe disabilities to become involved in extracurricular high school activities. If you are the faculty sponsor of a club or organization, explore whether this student is interested and how he or she could get involved.

### Tips for School Personnel

- Advocate for parents of high school–age students with severe and multiple disabilities to participate in the activities and governance of the school.

- Collaborate with parents in the transition-planning process during the high school years by listening to parent input that focuses on a desire for their son or daughter to be included as a valued member of the high school community.

- Support high school special education or vocational teachers seeking to develop community-based instruction programs that focus on students

learning and applying skills in actual community settings (e.g., grocery stores, malls, theaters, parks, work sites).

### Tips for Neighbors, Friends, and Potential Employers

- Collaborate with the family and school personnel to create opportunities for students with severe and multiple disabilities to participate in community activities (such as going to the movies, "hanging out" with peers who are not disabled in the neighborhood mall, and going to high school sporting events) as often as possible.

- As a potential employer, collaborate with the high school to locate and establish community-based employment training sites for students with severe and multiple disabilities.

## Adult Years

### Tips for Families

- Develop an understanding of life after school during your son's or daughter's adult years. What are the formal (government-funded or parent organizations) and informal supports (family and friends) available in your community? What are the characteristics of adult service programs? Explore adult support systems in the local community in the areas of supported living, employment, and recreation/leisure.

### Tips for Neighbors, Friends, and Potential Employers

- Become part of the community support network for the individual with severe and multiple disabilities. Be alert to ways in which this individual can become and remain actively involved in community employment, neighborhood recreational activities, and local church functions.

- As a potential employer in the community, seek information on employment of people with severe and multiple disabilities. Find out about programs (such as supported employment) that focus on establishing work for people with mental retardation while meeting your needs as an employer.

## Looking Toward a Bright Future

Throughout history, individuals with severe and multiple disabilities have been forgotten and neglected people, often being denied opportunities for education, social services, and health care. Today, these individuals are receiving more services and supports than ever before, although there is much left to do to assure their full access to and participation in school, family, and community life. As such suggested by TASH (2014b):

> *Children and adults with disabilities should have opportunities to develop relationships with neighbors, classmates, co-workers, and community members. Adults, whether married or single, should make decisions about where and with whom they live. The preferences of each individual should be honored in regards to their decisions on community life and participation. Individuals with disabilities and families must be entitled to quality educational supports, decent and affordable housing, financial security, recreation, and employment.*

The attitudes and progressive policies of the 21st century bring considerable hope to the lives of people with severe and multiple disabilities. Inclusive education is increasing in our schools; opportunities to live and work in the community are no longer just a dream; and every day the critical support that is needed from family, friends, neighbors, and professionals becomes more and more a natural part of the lives of people with severe disabilities.

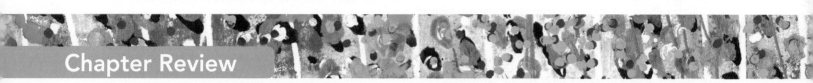

## Chapter Review

**12-1  Describe how the lives of people with severe and multiple disabilities have changed since the advent of IDEA.**

- Prior to 1975, when IDEA went into effect, children with multiple disabilities were often excluded from school due to the severity of their disabilities. However, educators now recognize that each individual has potential and will benefit from specialized services offered by a team of professionals.

- People with severe and multiple disabilities have challenges that transcend the classroom. Although often dependent upon support from others, people with severe and multiple disabilities can accomplish much in academics and independent life skills.

**12-2  Explain the various definitions and classifications of severe and multiple disabilities.**

- *Severe disabilities* as defined by TASH includes three elements:
  - The relationship of the individual within the environment (adaptive fit)
  - The value of inclusion of people of all ages
  - The necessity of extensive ongoing support in life activities
- *Multiple disabilities* refers to the layering or concomitance of disabilities (such as intellectual disabilities and orthopedic impairments).

- *Deaf–blindness* involves concomitant hearing and visual impairments. The combination causes communication and other developmental and educational problems so severe that they cannot be accommodated in special education programs designed solely for children who are deaf or blind.

**12-3  Describe the characteristics and prevalence of children and youth with severe and multiple disabilities.**

- Having intellectual disabilities is often a primary condition.

- Most children will not benefit from basic academic instruction in literacy and mathematics. Instruction in functional academics is the most effective approach to learning academic skills.

- People with severe and multiple disabilities often may not have age-appropriate adaptive skills and need ongoing services and supports to facilitate learning in this area.

- Significant speech and language deficits and delays are a primary characteristic.

- Physical and health needs are common, involving conditions such as congenital heart disease, epilepsy, respiratory problems, spasticity, athetosis, and hypotonia. Vision and hearing loss are also common.

- Prevalence estimates generally range from 0.1 percent to 1 percent of the general population.

- Students with multiple disabilities recently accounted for about 2 percent of the 7 million students with disabilities served in the public schools. Approximately 0.0002 percent of students with disabilities were labeled deaf–blind.

### 12-4 List the causes and risk factors associated with severe and multiple disabilities.

- Many possible causes of severe and multiple disabilities exist. Most severe and multiple disabilities are evident at birth. Birth defects may be the result of genetic or metabolic problems. Most identifiable causes of severe intellectual disabilities and related developmental disabilities are genetic in origin. Factors associated with accidents, poisoning, malnutrition, physical and emotional abuse and neglect, and disease are also known causes.

### 12-5 Describe the assessment procedures used to identify severe and multiple disability in children and youth.

- Children who have severe and multiple disabilities are often identified at a very young age due to the overarching nature of the disability. Once a concern has been identified, further information in typically gathered through formal assessments. These assessments often include evaluation of fine and gross motor skills, reflexes, vision, hearing, and a complete health screening.
- Traditionally, there has been a heavy reliance on standardized assessments, particularly the IQ test, in identifying people with severe and multiple disabilities.
- Assessments that focus on valued skills to promote independence and quality of life in natural settings are referred to as *functional*, *ecological*, or *authentic assessment*.

### 12-6 Describe the different interventions for children and youth with severe and multiple disabilities from early childhood through adulthood.

- Services and supports must begin at birth.
- Programs for infants and toddlers are both child- and family-centered.
- The goals for preschool programs are to maximize development across several developmental areas, to develop social interaction and classroom participation skills, to increase community participation through support to family and caregivers, and to prepare the child for inclusive school placement.

- Effective and inclusive preschool programs have a holistic view of the child, see the classroom as a community of learners, base the program on a collaborative ethic, use authentic assessment, create a heterogeneous environment, make available a range of individualized supports and services, engage educators in reflective teaching, and emphasize multiple ways of teaching and learning.
- Self-determination is important—student preferences and needs are taken into account in developing educational objectives.
- Students with disabilities must participate in statewide and district-wide assessments of achievement, or the school must explain why that assessment is not appropriate for the child. For many students with severe disabilities, these assessments are inappropriate, and the students with disabilities are excluded from taking them. Alternate assessments are conducted instead.
- Instruction focuses on grade-level standards and frequently used functional skills related to everyday life activities.
- Assistive technology and augmentative communication are available to maintain or increase the functional capabilities of the student with severe and multiple disabilities.
- Programs for adolescents and young adults who have severe and multiple disabilities should focus on the following:
  - Establishing a network of friends and acquaintances
  - Supporting students' access to grade-level standards
  - Developing the ability to use community resources on a regular basis
  - Securing a paid job that supports the use of community resources and interaction with peers
  - Establishing independence and autonomy in making lifestyle choices
- Physical placement of students with severe and multiple disabilities in the general education schools and classes they would attend if they didn't have disabilities
- Systematic organization of opportunities for interaction between students with severe and multiple disabilities and students without disabilities
- Specific instruction in valued post-school outcomes that will increase the competence of students with severe and multiple disabilities in the natural settings of family, school, and community

**Council for Exceptional Children (CEC) Standards to Accompany Chapter 12**

If you are thinking about a career in special education, you should know that many states use national standards developed by the Council for Exceptional Children (CEC) to assess a teacher candidate's knowledge and skills for working with students with disabilities. See a complete listing of the seven CEC Content Standards on the inside cover of this text.

1 Learner Development and Individual Learning Differences
2 Learning Environments
3 Curricular Content Knowledge
4 Assessment
5 Instructional Planning and Strategies
6 Professional Learning and Ethical Practice

## Mastery Activities and Assignments

To master the content within this chapter, complete the following activities and assignments:

1. Complete a written test of the chapter's content. If your instructor requires a written test of your content knowledge for this chapter, keep a copy for your portfolio.
2. Review the Case Study on Embracing Diversity, "Ernesto," and respond in writing to the Application Questions.

Keep a copy of the Case Study and your written response for your portfolio.

3. Participate in a community service learning activity. Community service is a valuable way to enhance your learning experience. Develop a reflective journal of the service learning experience for your portfolio.

## CHAPTER 13

# Sensory Disabilities:
## Hearing and Vision Loss

Chris Jackson/Getty Images News/Getty Images

## Learning Objectives

*After you complete this chapter, you will be able to:*

**13-1**  Describe how the lives of people with sensory disabilities have changed since the advent of IDEA.

**13-2**  Explain the various definitions and classifications of sensory disabilities.

**13-3**  Describe the characteristics and prevalence of children and youth with sensory disabilities.

**13-4**  List the causes and risk factors associated with sensory disabilities.

**13-5**  Describe the assessment procedures used to identify sensory disabilities in children and youth.

**13-6**  Describe the different interventions for children and youth with sensory disabilities from early childhood through adulthood.

Throughout childhood, we all pondered the question "What do you want to be when you grow up?" The average grade-schooler had a handful of rotating answers that changed on a daily basis: firefighter, veterinarian, teacher, singer, astronaut, sports star—the list goes on. For most of us, those fanciful dreams were soon replaced with more practical career paths. Tamika Catchings, however, is an exception.

Raised in a family known for their love of sports, Tamika decided in the seventh grade that she was going to play in the NBA. It's worth noting that professional women's basketball didn't even exist when she first scribbled that goal on her bathroom mirror. Tamika had a vision for her life, and she pursued it ruthlessly from a very young age.

In college, Tamika played for arguably the best basketball coach of all time, Pat Summitt, who eventually became a friend and mentor. It was Pat who encouraged Tamika to accept and acknowledge the hearing disability she'd been dealing with since birth—a life-changing decision that would make Tamika a role model for more than just her athletic abilities. Going on to win a national championship title in the WNBA, Tamika can honestly say that her childhood dreams have come true. However, it doesn't surprise us that she's still hungry for more. Today, Tamika shares her unique story about how faith, hard work, passion, and sacrifice got her to the top of her game.

**Prior to joining the WNBA with the Indiana Fever, you played college basketball for the legendary University of Tennessee Lady Vols, and before that you played high school basketball. When did your love of sports, specifically basketball, begin?**

I was raised in a sports family. My father, Harvey Catchings, played in

Darrell Walker/UTHM/Icon SMI/Photoshot

the NBA. With us moving around when I was young as he went to different teams, sports was introduced very early. I was also born with a hearing and speech problem, which created a need for hearing aids. As a child, I was always the one that got teased for the way I looked, the way I talked, or the hearing aids in my ears. That's how sports became so important to me. On the playing field, I knew that if I practiced and got really good, that no one could make fun of me for any of my disabilities. I used sports and faith as the two outlets that could keep me "safe." That has shaped me into the person that I am today because my faith, basketball, and my family are my top three priorities. I love giving back to the community, and I love what I do as far as basketball goes, but God and my family have been there for me when nothing else has been.

The best advice our dad gave us was regarding pursuing our passions. He always said, "Play the game as long as you enjoy playing it. Once you don't enjoy it, it's time to move on and find out what your next passion is." I still live by that and love what I'm doing on and off the court.

**In college, you began to speak publicly about your hearing disability. We can only imagine that this must have been difficult for you growing up. Tell us what that was like. What was it that prompted you to start talking about it?**

I was born with a hearing deficiency, and I grew up with hearing aids, glasses, braces—the whole nine yards. I remember going to school when I was younger, and I was made fun of every day—whether it was about the way I looked because I wore big, clunky hearing aids or the way I talked. I just wanted to be normal. I just wanted to fit in. I didn't want people to notice me. I wasn't comfortable talking because people made fun of me. I just wanted to be invisible.

One day, I'd just finally had enough. I was walking home from school with my sister, crying. Walking past a field of grass near my home, I tore off my hearing aids and threw them as far as I could.

Over time, I accepted myself for being different. Eventually, Pat Summitt broke it down for me the best when she said, "When people can't see, they wear glasses; when their teeth need correction, they wear braces; and when people can't hear, they wear hearing aids." Having the support of Pat and our trainer Jenny Moshak meant a lot. They sat down with me and showed me how much I could impact the world and change lives just by being able to hear, continuing to be the best that I could be and being able to share my differences with other people. So, ever since then, I've embraced that deficiency and I try to help kids who maybe felt the same as I did.

**What would you say to someone reading this who is struggling with feeling "different"?**

I know it's easier said than done, but find something that you can become passionate about. While my differences brought struggles, being able to play different sports allowed me to not dwell on the negativity.

**In 2004, you started your own foundation, Catch the Stars, which "empowers youth to achieve their dreams" by focusing on literacy, fitness, and mentoring. Tell us about why you started your foundation. What have been the greatest challenges in running a charity? Greatest rewards?**

I love being able to make a difference in the community. We started the Catch the Stars Foundation (CTSF) to be able to provide opportunities for the youth in our community to achieve their dreams. I knew that I wanted to have my own basketball camp, and that was the first thing we started. Then, from there, we just kept adding programs until we put everything under the Catch the Stars Foundation umbrella in 2004. Growing up, I had a lot of people that stepped in and helped me get to where I am today, and I aim to provide that same guidance for these kids.

**What advice would you give to your 23-year-old self?**

Continue to strive to be the best you can be, but don't forget to enjoy the process while you're going through it. And, let the past be the past.

SOURCE: Cook, B. (2013). *The Everygirl Career Profile: Tamika Catchings of the WNBA*. Retrieved March 21, 2015, from http://theeverygirl.com/feature/tamika-catchings-of-the -wnba.

## 13-1 A Changing Era in the Lives of People with Sensory Disabilities

In a world controlled by sight and sound, the ability to see and hear is a critical link to our overall development and perspectives on the world. Children who can hear learn to talk by listening to those around them. Everyday communication systems depend on sound. What, then, would it be like to live in a world that is silent? People talk, but you hear nothing. The television and movie screens are lit up with moving pictures, but you cannot hear and understand what is going on. Your friends talk about their favorite music and hum tunes that have no meaning to you. A fire engine's siren wails as it moves through traffic, but you are oblivious to its warning. To people with hearing, the thought of such a world can be very frightening. To those without hearing, it is quite simply their world—a place that can be lonely, frustrating, and downright discriminatory. People with a hearing loss may live in isolation from everyday interactions that make life enjoyable. They may feel alienated from friends, family, and the community, and this alienation can evolve into a strong sense of fear and a need to avoid the hearing world.

The frustration of a hearing loss may be felt not only by the person experiencing the loss, but also by those who are close to the individual. This is exemplified by siblings who often feel they are being ignored because their brother or sister with a hearing loss does not respond when called from another room or when their back is turned. Because hearing loss is an "invisible disability," people who are able to hear often forget to make needed accommodations. It is all too common for a person who can hear accuse a person with a hearing loss of "selectively listening"—that is, choosing what they do or don't want to hear.

Yet, the most common emotion for people with a hearing loss is the embarrassment that comes from not hearing oral instructions, missing key points in a conversation, or not laughing at someone else's joke. Unfortunately, isolation, fear, frustration, and embarrassment may also characterize the everyday life experiences for individuals with a vision loss. Through the visual process, we observe the world around us, and develop an appreciation for the physical environment and a greater understanding of it. Vision is one of our most important avenues for the acquisition and assimilation of knowledge, but we often take it for granted. From the moment we wake up in the morning, our dependence on sight is obvious. We rely on our eyes to guide us around our surroundings, inform us through the written word, and give us pleasure and relaxation.

What if this stream of visual information were lost or impaired? How would our perceptions of the world change? Losing sight is one of our greatest fears, partly because of the misconception that people with vision loss are helpless and unable to lead satisfying or productive lives. It is not uncommon for people with sight to have little understanding of those with vision loss. People who are sighted may believe that most adults who are blind are likely to be marginalized socially, economically, and culturally. Children who have sight may believe that their peers who are blind are incapable of learning many basic skills, such as telling time and using a computer, or of enjoying leisure and recreational activities such as swimming, watching movies, or playing video games. Throughout history, some religions have even promoted the belief that blindness is a punishment for sins. As you will see in this chapter, the negative perceptions about people with a hearing or vision loss are often inaccurate and misleading. The vast majority of people with a sensory impairment lead active and productive lives and do not allow their hearing or vision loss to deprive them of the life activities they love and value. They experience joy, fulfillment, and a life of endless possibilities no different from that experienced by people who can hear or see. The quality of life for a person with a sensory impairment has been dramatically enhanced since the passage of IDEA, which promises each individual a free and appropriate public education in the most inclusive setting possible. Advances in technology often supported by IDEA research funding have also led to greater independence and opportunities for people who experience vision or hearing loss.

In this chapter, we take a closer look into the lives of people with sensory disabilities—those with vision or hearing loss. We begin our journey with the nearby Snapshot of Tamika Catchings, professional basketball player, all-star, and community leader who also happens to be a person with a hearing loss.

## 13-2 Definitions and Classifications of Sensory Disabilities

Sensory disabilities can include hearing loss, vision loss, or both. Regardless of the nature of the sensory disability, a diagnosis can range from a mild loss to a complete loss of input from vision or hearing.

### 13-2a Hearing Loss

Although Tamika from our opening Snapshot is unable to hear many sounds, her life is one of independence, success, and fulfillment. For Tamika, just as for many people who are deaf or hard of hearing, the obstacles presented by the loss of hearing are not insurmountable. People with a hearing loss are able to learn about the world around them in any number of ways, such as lip-reading, gestures, pictures, and writing. Some people are able to use their residual hearing with the assistance of a hearing aid. For others, a hearing aid doesn't help because it only makes distorted sounds louder. To express themselves, some people prefer to use their voices; others prefer to use a visual sign language. Most people with a hearing loss use a combination of speech and signing. People with a hearing loss, such as Tamika, may seek and find success in a fully inclusive community. Others seek to be part of a deaf community or deaf culture to share a common language (American Sign Language) and customs. In a deaf culture, those within the community share a common heritage and traditions. People often select life partners from within the community. They also have a shared literature and participate in the deaf community's political, business, arts, and sports programs. People in the deaf community do not see the loss of hearing as a disability. From their perspective, being deaf is not an impairment and should not be looked upon as a pathology or disease that requires treatment. It is simply another way of being that focuses on a communication system that is unique to people who have hearing loss.

**The Hearing Process** To understand hearing loss, we must first understand how normal hearing works. Audition is the act or sense of hearing. The auditory process involves the transmission of sound through the vibration of an object to a receiver. The process originates with a vibrator—such as a string, reed, membrane, or column of air—that causes displacement of air particles. To become sound, a vibration must have a medium to carry it. Air is the most common carrier, but vibrations can also be carried by metal, water, and other substances. The displacement of air particles by the vibrator produces a pattern of circular waves that move away from the source.

**Audition**
The act or sense of hearing.

**Figure 13.1** *Structure of the Ear*

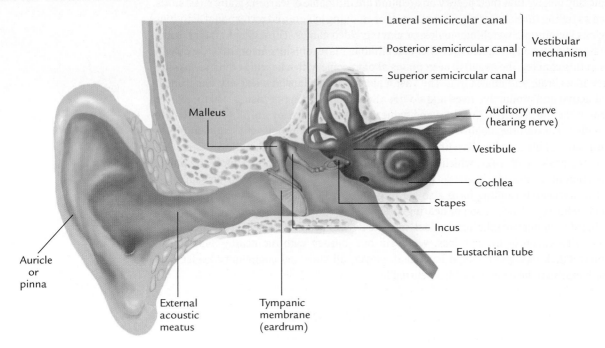

This movement, which is referred to as a sound wave, can be illustrated by imagining the ripples resulting from a pebble dropped in a pool of water. Sound waves are patterns of pressure that alternately push together and pull apart in a spherical expansion. Sound waves are carried through a medium (e.g., air) to a receiver. The human ear is one of the most sensitive receivers there is; it is capable of being activated by incredibly small amounts of pressure and being able to distinguish more than a half million different sounds. The ear is the mechanism through which sound is collected, processed, and transmitted to an area in the brain that decodes the sensations into meaningful language. The anatomy of the hearing mechanism is discussed in terms of the outer, middle, and inner ears. These structures are illustrated in Figure 13.1.

**Definitions of Hearing Loss** Two terms, *deaf* and *hard of hearing* (or *partial hearing*), are commonly used to indicate the severity of a person's hearing loss. *Deaf* is often overused and misunderstood and is commonly applied to describe a wide spectrum of hearing loss. However, as discussed in this chapter, the term should be used in a more precise fashion.

Hearing loss may be defined according to the degree of hearing impairment, which is determined by assessing a person's sensitivity to loudness (sound intensity) and pitch (sound frequency). The unit used to measure sound intensity is the decibel (dB); the range of human hearing is approximately 0 dB to 130 dB. Sounds louder than 130 dB (such as those made by jet aircraft at 140 dB) are extremely painful to the ear. Conversational speech registers at 40 dB to 60 dB, loud thunder at about 120 dB, and a rock concert at about 110 dB.

The frequency of sound is determined by measuring the number of cycles that vibrating molecules complete per second. The unit used to measure cycles per second is the **hertz (Hz)**. The higher the frequency, the greater the measure in hertz. The human ear can hear sounds ranging from 20 to approximately 13,000 Hz. Speech sounds range in pitch from 300 Hz to 4,000 Hz, whereas the pitches made by a piano keyboard range from 27.5 Hz to 4,186 Hz. Although the human ear can hear sounds at the 13,000 Hz level, the vast majority of sounds in our environment range from 300 Hz to 4,000 Hz.

**Deafness** Deafness describes people whose hearing loss is in the extreme: meaning they can only hear at 90 dB or greater. Even with the use of hearing aids or other forms of amplification, the primary means for developing language and communication for people who are

**Hertz (Hz)**
A unit used to measure the frequency of sound in terms of the number of cycles that vibrating molecules complete per second.

deaf is through the visual channel. **Deafness** as defined by the Individuals with Disabilities Education Act (IDEA) means "a hearing impairment that is so severe that the child is impaired in processing linguistic information through hearing, with or without amplification, which adversely affects educational performance" (IDEA, 34 C.F.R. 300.7).

People who are deaf are most often described as those who cannot hear sound. Consequently, individuals are unable to understand human speech. Many people who are deaf have enough residual hearing to recognize sound at certain frequencies, but they still may be unable to determine the meaning of the sound pressure waves.

### Hard of Hearing (Partial Hearing)
For people defined as **hard of hearing**, audition is deficient but remains somewhat functional. Individuals who are hard of hearing have enough residual hearing that, with the use of a hearing aid, they are able to process human speech auditorily.

The distinction between deaf and hard of hearing, based on the functional use of residual hearing, is not as clear as many traditional definitions imply. New breakthroughs in the development of hearing aids, as well as improved diagnostic procedures and medical procedures, have enabled many children labeled deaf to use their hearing functionally under limited circumstances.

In addition to the individual's sensitivity to loudness and pitch, two other factors are involved in defining deafness and hard of hearing: the age of onset and the anatomical site of the loss.

### Age of Onset
Hearing loss may be present at birth (congenital) or acquired at any time during life. **Prelingual loss** occurs prior to the age of 2, or before speech development. **Postlingual loss** occurs at any age following speech acquisition. In nine out of ten children, deafness occurs at birth or prior to the child's learning to speak. The distinction between a congenital and an acquired hearing loss is important. The age of onset will be a critical variable in determining the type and extent of interventions necessary to minimize the effect of the individual's disability. This is particularly true in relation to speech and language development. A person who is born with hearing loss has significantly more challenges, particularly in the areas of communication and social adaptation (Centers for Disease Control, 2015a; Correa-Torres, 2008).

### Anatomical Site of the Hearing Loss
In terms of anatomical location, the two primary types of hearing loss are peripheral problems and central auditory problems. There are three types of peripheral hearing loss: conductive, sensorineural, and mixed. A **conductive hearing loss** is caused by something that blocks the sounds from getting through the outer or inner ear. The loss may result from a blockage in the external canal, as well as from an obstruction interfering with the movement of the eardrum or ossicle. The overall effect is a reduction or loss of loudness. A conductive loss can be offset by amplification (hearing aids) and medical intervention. Surgery has been effective in reducing a conductive loss or even in restoring hearing.

A **sensorineural hearing loss** occurs when there is a problem in the way the inner ear or hearing nerve works. A sensorineural loss may distort sound, affecting the clarity of human speech; it cannot presently be treated adequately through medical intervention. A sensorineural loss is generally more severe than a conductive loss and is permanent. Losses of greater than 70 dB are usually sensorineural and involve severe damage to the inner ear. One common way to determine whether a loss is conductive or sensorineural is to administer an air and bone conduction test. An individual with a conductive loss would be unable to hear a vibrating tuning fork held close to the ear, because of blocked air passages to the inner ear, but may be able to hear the same fork applied to the skull just as well as someone with normal hearing would. An individual with a sensorineural loss would not be able to hear the vibrating fork, regardless of its placement. This test is not always accurate, however, and must therefore be used with caution in distinguishing between conductive and sensorineural losses. **Mixed hearing loss**, a combination of conductive and sensorineural problems, can also be assessed through the use of an air and bone conduction test. In the case of a mixed loss, abnormalities are evident in both tests.

**Deafness**
A hearing loss greater than 90 dB. Individuals who are deaf have vision as their primary input and cannot understand speech through the ear.

**Hard of hearing**
A sense of hearing that is deficient but somewhat functional.

**Prelingual loss**
Pertaining to hearing impairments occurring prior to the age of 2, or the time of speech development.

**Postlingual loss**
Pertaining to hearing impairments occurring at any age following speech development.

**Conductive hearing loss**
A hearing loss resulting from poor conduction of sound along the passages leading to the sense organ.

**Sensorineural hearing loss**
A hearing loss resulting from an abnormal sense organ (inner ear) and a damaged auditory nerve.

**Mixed hearing loss**
A hearing loss resulting from a combination of conductive and sensorineural problems.

| Table 13.1 Classification of Hearing Loss | | |
|---|---|---|
| **Hearing Loss in Decibels (dB)** | **Classification** | **Effect on Ability to Understand Speech** |
| 0 to 13 | Normal hearing | None |
| 16 to 25 | Slight hearing loss | Minimal difficulty with soft speech |
| 26 to 40 | Mild hearing loss | Difficulty with soft speech |
| 41 to 55 | Moderate hearing loss | Frequent difficulty with normal speech |
| 56 to 70 | Moderate to severe hearing loss | Occasional difficulty with loud speech |
| 71 to 90 | Severe hearing loss | Frequent difficulty with loud speech |
| >91 | Profound hearing loss | Near total or total loss of hearing |

Although most hearing losses are peripheral, as are conductive and sensorineural problems, some occur where there is no measurable peripheral loss. This type of loss, which is referred to as a central auditory disorder, occurs when there is a dysfunction in the cerebral cortex. The cerebral cortex, the outer layer of gray matter of the brain, governs thought, reasoning, memory, sensation, and voluntary movement. Consequently, a central auditory problem is not a loss in the ability to hear sound, but a disorder of symbolic processes, including auditory perception, discrimination, comprehension of sound, and language development (expressive and receptive).

**Classification of Hearing Loss** Hearing loss may be classified according to the severity of the condition. The symptom severity classification system shown in Table 13.1 presents information relative to a child's ability to understand speech patterns at the various severity levels.

Classification systems based solely on a person's degree of hearing loss should be used with a great deal of caution when determining appropriate services and supports. These systems do not reflect the person's capabilities, background, or experience; they merely suggest parameters for measuring a physical defect in auditory function. As a young child, for example, Tamika from the opening Snapshot was diagnosed as having a hearing loss in both ears, yet throughout her life she successfully adjusted to both school and community experiences. Clearly, many factors beyond the severity of the hearing loss must be assessed when determining an individual's potential. In addition to severity of loss, factors such as general intelligence, emotional stability, scope and quality of early education and training, the family environment, and the occurrence of other disabilities must also be considered.

## 13-2b Vision Loss

To more fully understand the nature of vision loss within the context of normal sight, we begin with a Snapshot, a personal story about Darran who is a college student with a vision impairment. We then review the physical components of the visual system and define the terms *blind* and *partially sighted*.

The physical components of the visual system include the eye, the visual cortex in the brain, and the optic nerve, which connects the eye to the visual cortex. The basic anatomy of the human eye is illustrated in Figure 13.2. The cornea is the external covering of the eye, and in the presence of light, it bends or refracts visual stimuli. These light rays pass through the pupil, which is an opening in the iris. The pupil dilates or constricts to control the amount of light entering the eye. The iris, the colored portion of the eye, consists of membranous tissue and muscles whose function is to adjust the size of the pupil. The lens, like the cornea, bends light rays so that they strike the retina directly. As in a camera lens, the lens of the eye reverses the images. The retina consists of light-sensitive cells that transmit the image to the brain via the optic nerve. Images from the retina remain upside down until they are neurally flipped over in the visual cortex occipital lobe of the brain.

**Standard 1**
Learner Development and Individual Learning Differences

**Visual cortex**
The visual center of the brain, located in the occipital lobe.

**Optic nerve**
The nerve that connects the eye to the visual center of the brain.

**Cornea**
The external covering of the eye.

**Pupil**
The expandable opening in the iris of the eye.

**Iris**
The colored portion of the eye.

**Lens**
The clear structure of the eye that bends light rays so they strike the retina directly.

**Retina**
Light-sensitive cells in the interior of the eye that transmit images to the brain via the optic nerve.

*Figure 13.2 The Parts of the Human Eye*

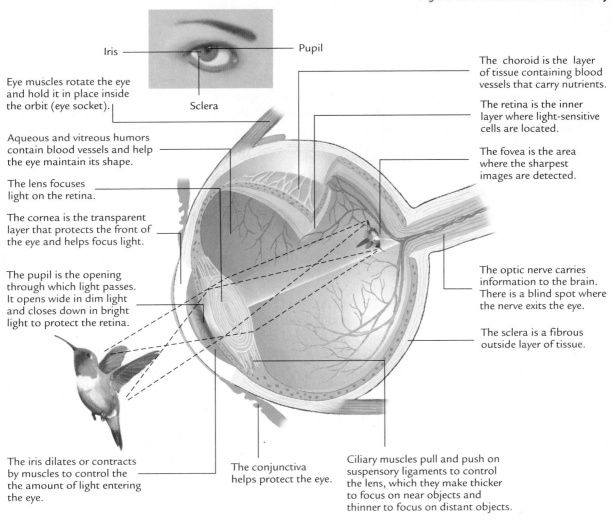

Iris — Pupil

Eye muscles rotate the eye and hold it in place inside the orbit (eye socket).

Sclera

Aqueous and vitreous humors contain blood vessels and help the eye maintain its shape.

The lens focuses light on the retina.

The cornea is the transparent layer that protects the front of the eye and helps focus light.

The pupil is the opening through which light passes. It opens wide in dim light and closes down in bright light to protect the retina.

The iris dilates or contracts by muscles to control the the amount of light entering the eye.

The conjunctiva helps protect the eye.

Ciliary muscles pull and push on suspensory ligaments to control the lens, which they make thicker to focus on near objects and thinner to focus on distant objects.

The choroid is the layer of tissue containing blood vessels that carry nutrients.

The retina is the inner layer where light-sensitive cells are located.

The fovea is the area where the sharpest images are detected.

The optic nerve carries information to the brain. There is a blind spot where the nerve exits the eye.

The sclera is a fibrous outside layer of tissue.

The visual process is much more complex than suggested by a description of the physical components involved. The process is an important link to the physical world, helping us to gain information beyond the range of other senses, while also helping us to integrate the information acquired primarily through hearing, touch, smell, and taste. For example, our sense of touch can tell us that what we are feeling is furry, soft, and warm, but only our eyes must tell that it is a brown rabbit with a white tail and pink eyes. Our nose may perceive something with yeast and spices cooking, but our eyes must confirm that it is a large pepperoni pizza with bubbling mozzarella and green peppers. Our hearing can tell us that a friend sounds angry and upset, but only our vision can register the scowl, clenched jaw, and stiff posture. The way we perceive visual stimuli shapes our interactions with and reactions to the environment, while providing a foundation for the development of a more complex learning structure.

The term *vision loss* encompasses people with a wide range of conditions, including those who have never experienced sight, those who had normal vision prior to becoming partially or totally blind, those who experienced a gradual or sudden loss of acuity across their field of vision, and those with a restricted field of vision. A variety of terms are used to define vision loss; this has created some confusion among professionals in various fields of study. The rationale for the development of multiple definitions is directly related to their intended use. For example, eligibility for income tax exemptions or special assistance from the American Printing House for the Blind requires that individuals with vision loss qualify under one of two general subcategories: **blind** or partially sighted (low vision).

**Blind**
Condition in which central visual acuity does not exceed 20/200 in the better eye with correcting lenses, or in which visual acuity, if better than 20/200, is limited in the central field of vision.

Meeting the challenges of graduate school, no matter which program, can be daunting. Among the second-year students at the University of Utah is Darran Zenger. His dream is to become a social worker, which involves a demanding list of classes and practicums and training in different areas—learning people skills and understanding government aid.

Darran and his guide dog, Archer, maneuver campus and the social work program with determination. Darran has Usher syndrome: Born deaf, he wears cochlear implants. And his sight continues to deteriorate with retinitis pigmentosa. He believes he knows exactly how to help others with disabilities.

"My experience growing up, it was normalized," he said. "You lose vision, you lose hearing, so what? It's just a challenge, that's all it is."

Holding his arms outstretched, he slowly brings them in to demonstrate his sight range.

In Darran's presentation to fellow students earlier this semester, titled "Seeing through Blindness," he described one of his pet peeves: people who say, "You don't look blind."

"I mean, not to be rude or anything, but you don't look stupid," Darran said.

His classmates laugh. He understands who needs him.

Twenty million people suffer from total blindness in the United States, the narrator in Darran's presentation video says. "Losing vision is a very traumatic experience for many people," Darran explained. When people become legally blind, he says, it affects their family relationships, their social life and their employment. "For blind or visually impaired individuals, the unemployment rate, just in that population, is 70 to 75 percent," Darran said.

Darran's fellow classmates see him as not only a regular member of the group, but also, because of his disabilities, a little more caring than most. Callie Tatum took notes for Darran their first year in grad school. She says he was always more concerned about her. "He's looking out for his individual peers," Tatum said. "That's kind of a humbling, eye-opening moment to experience."

Mary Beth Fitzpatrick says Darran never defines himself by his disabilities. "He talks it and he walks it so that 98 percent of the time I'm really not aware that there's anything crazier about him than the rest of us who are doing social work, you know?" Fitzpatrick said.

His professors say he speaks volumes just being who he is. "Just the fact that there is a Darran, that will speak to the people he works with whether they're children or teens or grown-ups," professor David Derezotes said.

Darran will receive his degree this spring and then hopes to deliver a message of possibilities. "We can't change the world overnight but we can change the world one person at a time," he said. He carries that message of hope to families and individuals who need to hear from him.

SOURCE: Mikita, C. (2014). "Despite Disabilities, U. Student Spreads Message of Hope." Retrieved November 20, 2014, from www.ksl.com/?nid=148&sid=32239160#Asmv0R7VX9OZwthx.03.

**Blindness** The term blindness has many meanings. In fact, there are over 150 citations for blind in an unabridged dictionary. **Legal blindness**, as defined by the Social Security Administration (2015), means either that vision cannot be corrected to better than 20/200 in the better eye or that the visual field is 20 degrees or less, even with a corrective lens. Many people who meet the legal definition of blindness still have some sight and may be able to read large print and get around without support (i.e., without a guide dog or a cane).

As we have noted, the definition of legal blindness includes both acuity and field of vision. **Visual acuity** is most often determined by reading letters or numbers on a chart using the **Snellen test** or by using an index that refers to the distance from which an object can be recognized. People with normal eyesight are defined as having 20/20 vision. However, if an individual is able to read at 20 feet what a person with normal vision can read at 200 feet, then his or her visual acuity would be described as 20/200. Most people consider those who are legally blind to have some light perception; only about 20 percent are totally without sight. A person is also considered blind if his or her field of vision is limited at its widest angle to 20 degrees or less (see Figure 13.3). A restricted field is also referred to as **tunnel vision** (or pinhole vision or tubular vision). A restricted field of vision severely limits a person's ability to participate in athletics, read, or drive a car.

Blindness can also be characterized as an educational disability. Educational definitions of blindness focus primarily on students' ability to use vision as an avenue for learning. Children who are unable to use their sight and rely on other senses, such as hearing

**Legal blindness**
Visual acuity of 20/200 or worse in the best eye with best correction as measured on the Snellen test, or a visual field of 20 percent or less.

**Visual acuity**
Sharpness or clearness of vision.

**Snellen test**
A test of visual acuity.

**Tunnel vision**
A restricted field of vision that is 20 degrees or less at its widest angle.

Figure 13.3 The Field of Vision

(a) 180°
Normal field of vision is about 180°.

(b) 20°
A person with a field of vision of 20° or less is considered blind.

and touch, are described as functionally blind. Functional blindness, in its simplest form, may be defined in terms of whether vision is used as a primary channel of learning. Regardless of the definition used, the purpose of labeling a child as functionally blind is to ensure that he or she receives an appropriate instructional program. This program must assist a student who is blind in utilizing other senses as a means to succeed in a classroom setting and, in the future, as an independent and productive adult.

### Partial Sight (Low Vision)
People with partial sight or low vision have a visual acuity greater than 20/200 but not greater than 20/70 in the best eye after correction. The field of education also distinguishes between being blind and being partially sighted when determining what level and extent of additional support services a student requires. The term **partially sighted** describes students who are able to use vision as a primary source of learning.

A vision specialist often works with students with vision loss to make the best possible use of remaining sight. This includes the elimination of unnecessary glare in the work area, removal of obstacles that could impede mobility, use of large-print books, and use of special lighting to enhance visual opportunities. Although children with low vision often use printed materials and special lighting in learning activities, some use **braille** because they can see only shadows and limited movement. These children benefit from the use of tactile or other sensory channels to gain maximum benefit from learning opportunities (Anghel, 2012; Lund & Troha, 2008; Poon & Ovadia, 2008; Supalo, Malouk, & Rankel, 2008). Children with low vision should be given opportunities to use their residual sight in conjunction with visual stimulation training to improve their ability to use sight as an avenue for learning. Additionally, Anghel (2012) found that engaging children with low vision in rich pretend play and dialogue about toys that have surprises, tricks, or secrets can aid in their development of theory of mind, which forms the foundation for early social skills.

### Classifying Vision Loss
Vision loss may be classified according to the anatomical site of the problem. Anatomical disorders include impairment of the refractive structures of the eye, muscle anomalies in the visual system, and problems of the receptive structures of the eye.

### Refractive Eye Problems
The most common types of vision loss occur when the refractive structures of the eye (cornea or lens) fail to focus light rays properly on the retina. The four types of **refractive problems** are hyperopia, or farsightedness; myopia, or nearsightedness; astigmatism, or blurred vision; and cataracts.

**Hyperopia** occurs when the eyeball is excessively short from front to back (has a flat corneal structure), forcing light rays to focus behind the retina. People with hyperopia can clearly visualize objects at a distance but cannot see them at close range. These individuals may require convex lenses so that a clear focus will occur on the retina.

**Myopia** occurs when the eyeball is excessively long (has increased curvature of the corneal surface), forcing light rays to focus in front of the retina. People with myopia can view objects at close range clearly but cannot see them from a distance (such as 100 feet). Eyeglasses may be necessary to assist in focusing on distant objects. Figure 13.4 illustrates the myopic and hyperopic eyeballs, and compares them to the normal human eye.

**CEC**

**Standard 1**
Learner Development and Individual Learning Differences

**Standard 6**
Professional Learning and Ethical Practice

**CEC**

**Standard 6**
Professional Learning and Ethical Practice

**Partially sighted**
Visual acuity greater than 20/200 but not greater than 20/70 in the better eye after correction.

**Braille**
A writing system for the blind that involves combinations of six raised dots punched into paper, which can be read with the fingertips.

**Refractive problems**
Visual disorders that occur when the refractive structures of the eye fail to properly focus light rays on the retina.

**Hyperopia**
Farsightedness; a refractive problem wherein the eyeball is excessively short, focusing light rays behind the retina.

**Myopia**
Nearsightedness; a refractive problem wherein the eyeball is excessively long, focusing light in front of the retina.

Figure 13.4 *Normal, Myopic, and Hyperopic Eyeballs*

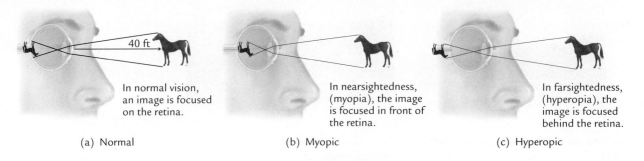

In normal vision, an image is focused on the retina.

(a) Normal

In nearsightedness, (myopia), the image is focused in front of the retina.

(b) Myopic

In farsightedness, (hyperopia), the image is focused behind the retina.

(c) Hyperopic

**Astigmatism**
A refractive problem that occurs when the cornea surface is uneven or structurally defective, preventing light rays from converging at one point.

**Cataract**
A clouding of the eye lens, which becomes opaque, resulting in visual problems.

**Nystagmus**
Uncontrolled rapid eye movements.

**Strabismus**
Crossed eyes (internal) or eyes that look outward (external).

**Amblyopia**
Loss of vision due to an imbalance of eye muscles.

**Esotropia**
A form of strabismus causing the eyes to be pulled inward toward the nose.

**Exotropia**
A form of strabismus in which the eyes are pulled outward toward the ears.

**Optic atrophy**
A degenerative disease caused by deteriorating nerve fibers connecting the retina to the brain.

**Retinitis pigmentosa**
A hereditary condition resulting from a break in the choroid.

**Retinal detachment**
A condition that occurs when the retina is separated from the choroid and sclera.

**Retinopathy of prematurity (ROP)**
A term now used in place of retrolental fibroplasia.

Astigmatism occurs when the curvature or surface of the cornea is uneven, preventing light rays from converging at one point. The rays of light are refracted in different directions, producing unclear, distorted visual images. Astigmatism may occur independently of or in conjunction with myopia or hyperopia.

Cataracts occur when the lens becomes opaque, resulting in severely distorted vision or total blindness. Surgical treatment for cataracts (such as lens implants) has advanced rapidly in recent years, returning most of the vision that was lost.

**Muscle Disorders** Muscular defects of the visual system occur when one or more of the major muscles within the eye are weakened in function, resulting in a loss of control and an inability to maintain tension. People with muscle disorders cannot maintain their focus on a given object for even short periods of time. The three types of muscle disorders are nystagmus (uncontrolled rapid eye movement), strabismus (crossed eyes), and amblyopia (an eye that appears normal but does not function properly). Nystagmus is a continuous, involuntary, rapid movement of the eyeballs in either a circular or a side-to-side pattern. Strabismus occurs when the muscles of the eyes are unable to pull equally, thus preventing the eyes from focusing together on the same object. Internal strabismus (esotropia) occurs when the eyes are pulled inward toward the nose; external strabismus (exotropia) occurs when the eyes are pulled out toward the ears. The eyes may also shift on a vertical plane (up or down), but this condition is rare. Strabismus can be corrected through surgical intervention. People with strabismus often experience a phenomenon known as double vision, because the deviating eye causes two very different pictures to reach the brain. To correct the double vision and reduce visual confusion, the brain attempts to suppress the image in one eye. As a result, the unused eye loses its ability to see. This condition, known as amblyopia, can also be corrected by surgery or by forcing the affected eye into focus by covering the unaffected eye with a patch.

**Receptive Eye Problems** Disorders associated with the receptive structures of the eye occur when there is a degeneration of or damage to the retina and the optic nerve. These disorders include optic atrophy, retinitis pigmentosa, retinal detachment, retinopathy of prematurity, and glaucoma. Optic atrophy is a degenerative disease that results from the deterioration of nerve fibers connecting the retina to the brain. Retinitis pigmentosa, the most common hereditary condition associated with loss of vision, appears initially as night blindness and gradually causes degeneration of the retina. Eventually, it results in total blindness.

Retinal detachment occurs when the retina separates from the choroid and the sclera. This detachment may result from disorders such as glaucoma, retinal degeneration, or extreme myopia. It can also be caused by trauma to the eye, such as a boxer receiving a hard right hook to the face.

Retinopathy of prematurity (ROP) is one of the most devastating eye disorders in young children. It occurs when too much oxygen is administered to premature infants, resulting in the formation of scar tissue behind the lens of the eye, which prevents light rays from reaching the retina. ROP gained attention in the early 1940s, with the advent of better incubators for infants born premature. These incubators substantially improved the concentration of oxygen available to infants, but resulted in a drastic increase in the number of children with vision loss. The disorder has also been associated with neurological, speech, and behavior problems in children and adolescents. Now that a relationship has been established between increased oxygen levels and blindness, premature infants can be protected by careful control of the amount of oxygen received in the early months of life.

# 13-3 Characteristics and Prevalence of Sensory Disabilities

Hearing loss and vision loss can result in a range of characteristics discussed in the following sections. Both classifications are considered low incidence because relatively few people are diagnosed with these disabilities.

## 13-3a Characteristics of Hearing Loss

The effects of hearing loss on the learning or social adjustment of individuals are extremely varied, ranging from far-reaching (as in prelingual sensorineural deafness) to quite minimal (as in a mild postlingual conductive loss). Fortunately, prevention, early detection, and intervention have recently been emphasized, resulting in a much-improved prognosis for individuals who are deaf or hard of hearing.

**Intelligence** Research on the intellectual characteristics of children with hearing loss has suggested that the distribution of IQ scores for these individuals is similar to that of hearing children (Moores, 2008; Phillips, Wiley, Barnard, & Meinzer-Derr, 2014). Findings suggest that intellectual development for people with hearing loss is more a function of language development than of cognitive ability. Any difficulties in performance appear to be closely associated with speaking, reading, and writing the English language, but are not related to level of intelligence. For example, children using sign language have to divide their attention between the signs and the instructional materials. Although the child may seem slower in learning, it may be that the child simply needs more time to process the information.

**Speech and English Language Skills** Speech and English language skills are the areas of development most severely affected for those with a hearing loss, particularly for children who are born deaf. These children develop speech at a slower pace than their peers with normal hearing; thus, they are at greater risk for emotional difficulties and isolation from their peers and family (Ching & Dillon, 2013; Hintermair, 2008; Kaland & Salvatore, 2012). The effects of a hearing loss on English language development vary considerably. For children with mild and moderate hearing losses, the effects may be minimal. Even for individuals born with moderate losses, effective communication skills are possible because the voiced sounds of conversational speech remain audible. Although individuals with moderate losses cannot hear unvoiced sounds (such as a sigh or cough) and distant speech, English language delays can be prevented if the hearing loss is diagnosed and treated early (Hintermair, 2008; Jackson & Schatschneider, 2014). The majority of people with hearing loss are able to use speech as the primary mode of English language acquisition.

**Standard 1**
Learner Development
and Individual Learning
Differences

For the person who is congenitally deaf, most loud speech is inaudible, even with the use of the most sophisticated hearing aids. These people are unable to receive information through speech unless they have learned to lip-read. Spoken language produced by people who are deaf may be difficult to understand. Children who are deaf exhibit significant problems in articulation, voice quality, and tone discrimination. Even as early as 8 months of age, babies who are deaf appear to babble less than babies who can hear. One way to assist these babies in developing language is to provide early and specialized training in English language production and comprehension. Another approach is to teach them sign language long before they learn to speak. Because hand–eye coordination develops earlier in infants than verbal skills, signs, such as "yes," "no," "please," "more," "stop," or "milk," can be learned before any speech develops. For an infant or toddler with a hearing loss, the ability to communicate with parents, teachers, and caregivers is critical. Sign language can be a very functional form of communication as exemplified in the following situation.

*"Languishing in front of the TV, watching a gripping episode of* Teletubbies, *a baby of 10 months waves down Mom and signals for a bottle of the good stuff. No crying, no fuss. He just moves his hands in a pantomime of milking a cow—the international sign for milk. Mom smiles, signs back her agreement, and fetches Junior's bottle." (McKeen, 2012)*

*Photo 13.1* Sign language can enhance the communication and language skills of young children with a hearing loss.

Courtesy of Tribune News Service

Parents of infants with a hearing loss often ask the question, "At what age can I begin to teach sign language?" It is important to remember that a hearing loss is most often not related to cognitive ability. Therefore, infants with a hearing loss can learn cognitive tasks, such as signing, at the same age as their hearing peers (about 8 months). Gestures, such as throwing kisses or waving "bye-bye," are forms of sign language.

**Educational Achievement** The educational achievements of students with a hearing loss may be significantly delayed compared with achievements of students who can hear. Students who are deaf or have a partial hearing loss have considerable difficulty succeeding in an educational system that depends primarily on the spoken word and written language to transmit knowledge. Low achievement is characteristic of students who are deaf (Heine & Slone, 2008; Marschark, Shaver, Nagle, & Newman, 2015); they average three to four years below their age-appropriate grade levels. Reading is the academic area most negatively affected for students with a hearing loss. Any hearing loss, whether mild or profound, appears to have detrimental effects on reading performance (Cupples et al., 2014; Narr, 2008). To counteract the difficulty with conventional reading materials, specialized instructional programs have been developed for students with a hearing loss (Marschark & Spencer, 2011; McAnally, Rose, & Quigley, 2005; Poobrasert & Cercone, 2009).

**Social Development** A hearing loss affects a person's capacity to receive and process auditory stimuli. People who are deaf or have a partial hearing loss receive a reduced amount of auditory information. That information is also distorted, compared with the auditory input received by those with normal hearing. Thus, the perceptions of auditory information by people with a hearing loss, particularly those who are deaf, will differ from those who can hear. Ultimately, this difference in perception has a direct effect on each individual's social adjustment to the hearing world.

Reviews of the literature on children's social and psychological development suggest that there are developmental differences between children who are deaf and children who can hear (Kaland & Salvatore, 2012; Scheetz, 2004; Stanzione & Schick, 2014). Different or delayed language acquisition may lead to more limited opportunities for social interaction. Children who are deaf may have more adjustment challenges when attempting to communicate with children who can hear. However, they appear to be more secure when conversing with peers who have a hearing loss.

For some people who are deaf, social isolation from the hearing world is not considered an adjustment problem. On the contrary, it is a natural state of being where people are bonded together by a common language, customs, and heritage. People in the **deaf culture** seek out one another for social interaction and emotional support. The language of the culture is sign language, where communication occurs through hand signs, body language, and facial expressions. Sign language is not one universal language. American Sign Language (ASL) is different from Russian Sign Language (RSL), which is different from French Sign Language (FSL), and so on. ASL is not a form of English or of any other language. It has its own grammatical structure, which must be mastered in the same way as the grammar of any other language. (American Sign Language is discussed in greater detail later in this chapter.)

**Deaf culture**
A culture where people who are deaf become bonded together by a common language (sign language), customs, and heritage, and rely on each other for social interaction and emotional support.

In addition to a common language, the deaf culture also has its own unique set of interactive customs. For example, people who are deaf value physical contact with one another even more than people in a hearing community. It is common to see visual and animated expressions of affection, such as hugs and handshakes in both greetings and departures. Regardless of the topic, discussions are frank, and there is no hesitation in getting to the point. Gatherings within the deaf culture may last longer because people like to linger. This may be particularly true at a dinner, where it is perfectly okay to sign (talk) with your mouth full. It will obviously take longer to eat because it is difficult to sign and hold a knife and fork at the same time.

Within the deaf community, the social identity of being a person who is deaf is highly valued, and there is a fierce internal loyalty. Everyone is expected to support activities within the deaf culture, whether in sports, arts and literature, or political networks. The internal cohesion among the community's members includes a strong expectation that people will marry within the group. In fact, nine out of ten people in the deaf culture marry others within the same community. This loyalty is so strong that parents who are deaf may hope for a child who is deaf to pass on the heritage and tradition of the deaf culture to their offspring. Although hearing people may be welcomed within the deaf community, they are seldom accepted as full members.

CEC

**Standard 6**
Professional Learning
and Ethical Practice

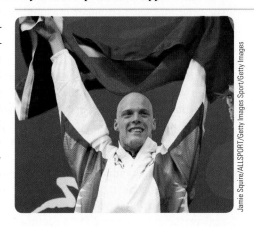

*Photo 13.2* When 20-year-old Terence Parkin arrived at the Sydney 2000 Olympic Games, his goal was to make his mark for South Africa and show the world what people who are deaf can accomplish. Terence, who was born with a severe hearing disability and uses sign language to communicate with his coach, achieved his goal by swimming to a silver medal in the 200-meter breaststroke. "I think it will confirm that deaf people can do things," he said afterward. "Other people will hopefully think now that we're just like other people. The only thing deaf people can't do is hear."

## 13-3b Prevalence of Hearing Loss

Hearing loss usually gets worse over time and increases dramatically with age. Estimates of hearing loss in the United States go as high as 30 million people. Of these 30 million, approximately 11 million people have significant irreversible hearing loss, and one million are deaf. Only 5 percent of people with hearing loss are under the age of 17; nearly 43 percent are over the age of 65. Contrast this to the fact that only 12 percent of the general population is over the age of 65 years (Centers for Disease Control, 2015a; National Institute on Deafness and Other Communication Disorders, 2015a). Men are more likely than women to have a hearing loss; Caucasians are proportionately overrepresented among people with a hearing loss. The prevalence of hearing loss decreases as family income and education increase.

The U.S. Department of Education (2014) indicated that more than 69,000 students defined as having a hearing impairment and between the ages of 6 and 21 are receiving special education services. These students account for approximately 0.1 percent of school-age students identified in the United States as having a disability. It is important to note that these figures represent only those students who receive special education services; a number of students with hearing loss who could benefit from additional services do not receive them. Of the students with a hearing loss receiving special education, approximately 58 percent were being served in general education classrooms for at least 80 percent of the school day. Another 29 percent spent at least a part of their day in a general education classroom, and 13 percent in separate public/private day schools or residential living facilities for students with a hearing loss (ibid.).

## 13-3c Characteristics of Vision Loss

A vision loss present at birth will have a more significant effect on individual development than one that occurs later in life. Useful visual imagery may disappear if sight is lost prior to the age of 5. If sight is lost after the age of 5, it is possible for the person to retain some visual memories. These memories may be maintained for years to come, assisting the person to better understand newly learned concepts. Total blindness that occurs prior to age 5 has the greatest negative influence on overall functioning. However, many people who are blind from birth or early childhood are able to function at about the same level as sighted people of equal ability.

**Intelligence** Children with vision loss sometimes base their perceptions of the world on input from senses other than vision. This is particularly true of children who are congenitally blind, whose learning experiences are significantly restricted by the lack of vision. Consequently, everyday learning opportunities that people with sight take for granted, such as reading the morning newspaper or watching television news coverage, may be substantially altered.

Reviews of the literature on intellectual development suggest that children with vision loss differ from children with sight in some areas of intelligence, ranging from understanding spatial concepts to a general knowledge of the world (Batshaw, Roizen, & Lotrecchiano, 2012; McLinden & McCall, 2006). However, comparing the performances of individuals with and without sight may not be appropriate because those with sight have an advantage. The only valid way to compare the intellectual capabilities of these children must be based on tasks in which vision loss does not interfere with performance.

**Speech and Language Skills** For children with sight, speech and language development occur primarily through the integration of visual experiences and the symbols of the spoken word. Depending on the degree of loss, children with vision loss are at a distinct disadvantage in developing speech and language skills because they are unable to visually associate words with objects. As a result, such children must rely on hearing or touch for input, and their speech may develop at a slower rate. Once these children have learned speech, however, it is typically fluent.

Preschool-age and school-age children with vision loss may develop a phenomenon known as verbalisms, or the excessive use of speech (wordiness), in which individuals may use words that have little meaning to them (e.g., "Crusaders are people of a religious sex" or "Lead us not into Penn Station"). Some research suggests that children with visual impairments may have a restricted oral vocabulary, compared with that of sighted peers, because they lack the visual input necessary to piece together all of the information available in a given experience (Papadopoulos, Argyropoulos, & Kouroupetroglou, 2008; Sacks & Silberman, 2000).

**Academic Achievement** The academic achievement of students with vision loss may be significantly delayed, compared with that of students with sight. Numerous factors may influence academic achievement for students with vision loss. In the area of written language, these students have more difficulty organizing their thoughts to write a composition because they lack the same opportunities as children with sight to read newspapers and magazines. Decoding in the area of reading may be delayed because students with visual impairments often use braille or large-print books as the media to decode. Decoding is a much slower process when a reader is using these two media. Reading comprehension is also affected because it depends so much on the experiences of the reader. Once again, the experience of students with visual impairments may be much more limited than that of students with sight; therefore these children don't bring as much information to the reading task (Papadopoulos, Argyropoulos, & Kouroupetroglou, 2008).

Other possible reasons for delays in academic achievement range from excessive school absences due to the need for eye surgery or treatment to years of failure in programs that did not meet each student's specialized needs. On the average, children with vision loss lag two years behind sighted children in grade level. Thus, any direct comparisons between students with vision loss and those with sight would indicate significantly delayed academic growth for the visually impaired. However, this might have resulted from children with vision loss entering school at a later age, from frequent absence due to medical problems, or from lack of appropriate school resources and facilities.

**Social Development** The ability of children with vision loss to adapt to the social environment depends on a number of factors, both hereditary and experiential. It is true that each of us experiences the world in his or her own way, but common bonds provide a foundation on which to build perceptions of the world around us. One such bond is vision. Without vision, perceptions about ourselves and those around us can be drastically distorted.

For people with vision loss, these differences in perception may produce some social-emotional challenges. Children with vision loss are less likely to initiate a social interaction and have fewer opportunities to socialize with other children (Anghel, 2012; Leigh & Barclay, 2000; Steinweg, Griffin, Griffin, & Gingras, 2005). They are often unable to imitate the physical mannerisms of others and, therefore, do not develop one very important component of social communication: body language. Because the subtleties of nonverbal communication can significantly alter the intended meaning of spoken words, people's inability to learn and use visual cues (such as facial expressions and hand gestures) has profound consequences for interpersonal interactions. People with vision loss can neither see the visual cues that accompany the messages received from others nor sense the messages that they may be conveying through body language.

Differences between people with a vision loss and those who are sighted may also result from exclusion of the person with a vision loss from social activities that are integrally related to the use of sight (such as sports and movies). People with vision loss are often excluded from such activities without a second thought, simply because they cannot see. This reinforces the mistaken notion that they do not want to participate and would not enjoy these activities. Social skills can be learned and effectively used by people with vision loss. Excluding them from social experiences more often stems from negative public attitudes than from the individuals' lack of social adjustment skills.

**Orientation and Mobility** A unique limitation facing people with vision loss is the challenge of moving about from place to place. These individuals may be unable to orient themselves to other people or objects in the environment simply because they cannot see them and therefore do not understand their own relative position in space. Consequently, they may be unable to move in the right direction and may fear getting injured, so they may try to restrict their movements to protect themselves. Parents and professionals may contribute to such fears by overprotecting an individual who has vision loss from the everyday risks of life. Shielding in this way will hinder the person's acquisition of independent mobility skills and create an atmosphere that promotes lifelong overdependence on caregivers.

Photo 13.3 Author and mountain climber Erik Weihenmayer didn't let blindness interfere with his life's passion: to scale some of the world's highest mountains.

AAron Ontiveroz/The Denver Post/Getty Images

Vision loss can affect fine motor coordination and interfere with the ability to manipulate objects. Poor eye–hand coordination interferes with learning how to use tools related to job skills and daily living skills (such as using eating utensils, a toothbrush, or a screwdriver). Prevention or remediation of fine motor problems may require training in the use of visual aid magnifiers and improvement of basic fine motor skills. This training must begin early and focus directly on experiences that will enhance opportunities for independent living.

**Perceptual-Motor Development** Perceptual-motor development is essential in the development of locomotion skills, but it is also important in the development of cognition, language, socialization, and personality. Most children with vision loss appear to have perceptual discrimination abilities (such as discriminating texture, weight, and sound) comparable to those of children with sight (Hallemans, Ortibus, Truijen, & Meire, 2011). Children with vision loss do not perform as well on more complex tasks of perception, including form identification, spatial relations, and perceptual-motor integration (Bouchard & Tetreault, 2000).

## 13-3d Prevalence of Vision Loss

The prevalence of vision loss is often difficult to determine. For example, although about 20 percent of children and adults in the United States have some vision loss, most of these conditions can be corrected to a level where they do not interfere with everyday tasks (such

**Standard 1**
Learner Development
and Individual Learning
Differences

**Standard 2**
Learning Environments

as reading, playing, or driving a car). Approximately 1 in 3,000 U.S. children is considered legally blind (American Printing House for the Blind, Inc., 2014), while 3 percent of the total population (9 million people) have a significant vision loss that will require some type of specialized services and supports. About 5 percent of U.S. children (approximately 1.2 million) have a serious eye disorder (KidSource, 2012). This figure increases to 20 percent for people over the age of 65. If cataracts are included, nearly 50 percent of people over the age of 65 have a significant vision loss. The U.S. Department of Education (2014) reports that approximately 23,000 students with a visual impairment between the ages of 6 and 21 received specialized services under IDEA in U.S. public schools. This accounts for 0.4 percent of all students with disabilities receiving special education services.

## 13-4   Causes Associated with Sensory Disabilities

There are many causes and risk factors that can lead to sensory disabilities, including conditions present at birth, those resulting from illnesses, and as a result of an injury.

### 13-4a   Hearing Loss: Causes and Risk Factors

A number of congenital (existing at birth) or acquired factors may result in a hearing loss. Approximately one child in a thousand is born deaf because of factors associated with heredity, maternal rubella or German measles, or drugs taken during pregnancy. Substance abuse, disease, and constant exposure to loud noises are all causes of hearing loss. Loss of hearing is also a normal part of the aging process, beginning as early as the teen years when the high-frequency hearing of childhood starts to diminish.

**Heredity** Although more than 200 types of deafness have been related to hereditary factors, the cause of 18 percent of prelingual hearing loss remains unknown. Because genetic defects that cause hearing loss are usually rare, they are not included in routine prenatal genetic screenings. One of the most common diseases affecting the sense of hearing is otosclerosis. The cause of this condition is unknown, but it is generally believed to be hereditary and is manifested most often in early adulthood. The condition is characterized by abnormal bone remodeling in the middle ear. About 10 percent of adults have otosclerosis; it can be passed from one generation to the next but not manifest itself for several generations. Hearing loss results in about 13 percent of all cases of otosclerosis and at a rate for females that is twice the rate for males. People with otosclerosis experience high-pitched throbbing or ringing sounds known as tinnitus. There is no specific treatment or any medication that will improve the hearing in people with otosclerosis. Surgery (stapedectomy) may be recommended when the stapes (stirrup) bone is involved.

**Prenatal Disease** Several conditions, although not inherited, can result in sensorineural loss. The major cause of congenital deafness is infection, of which rubella, cytomegalovirus (CMV), and toxoplasmosis are the most common. The rubella epidemic of 1963 to 1965 dramatically increased the incidence of deafness in the United States. During the 1960s, approximately 10 percent of all congenital deafness was associated with women contracting rubella during pregnancy. For about 40 percent of the individuals who are deaf, the cause is rubella. About 50 percent of all children with rubella incur a severe hearing loss. Most hearing losses caused by rubella are sensorineural, although a small percentage may be mixed. In addition to hearing loss, children who have had rubella sometimes acquire heart disease (50 percent), cataracts or glaucoma (40 percent), and intellectual disabilities (40 percent). Since the advent of the measles, mumps, rubella (MMR) vaccine, the elimination of this disease has become a nationwide campaign, and the incidence of rubella has dramatically decreased. However, the Center for Disease Control (2015) data indicate a 300 percent increase in rubella rates from 2009 to 2014. This increase could be due to selective nonparticipation in MMR vaccination.

Congenital cytomegalovirus (CMV) is viral infection that is spread through body fluids. CMV is the most frequently occurring virus among newborns and is characterized

**Otosclerosis**
A disease of the ear characterized by destruction of the capsular bone in the middle ear and the growth of a weblike bone that attaches to the stapes. The stapes is restricted and unable to function properly.

**Tinnitus**
High-pitched throbbing or ringing sounds in the ear, associated with disease of the inner ear.

**Congenital cytomegalovirus (CMV)**
Viral infection that spreads by close contact with another person who is shedding the virus in body secretions.

by jaundice, microcephaly, hemolytic anemia, mental disabilities, hepatosplenomegaly (enlargement of the liver and spleen), and hearing loss. Although no vaccine is currently available to treat CMV, some preventive measures can be taken—such as ensuring safe blood transfusions, practicing good hygiene, and avoiding contact with people who have the virus. CMV is detectable in utero through amniocentesis.

Congenital toxoplasmosis infection is characterized by jaundice and anemia, but frequently the disease also results in central nervous system disorders (such as seizures, hydrocephalus, and microcephaly). Approximately 13 percent of infants born with this disease are deaf.

Other factors associated with congenital sensorineural hearing loss include maternal Rh-factor incompatibility and the use of ototoxic drugs. Maternal Rh-factor incompatibility does not generally affect a firstborn child, but as antibodies are produced during subsequent pregnancies, multiple problems can result, including deafness. Fortunately, deafness as a result of Rh-factor problems is no longer common. Since the advent of an anti-Rh gamma globulin (RhoGAM) in 1968, the incidence of Rh-factor incompatibility has significantly decreased. If RhoGAM is injected into the mother within the first 72 hours after the birth of the first child, she does not produce antibodies that harm future unborn infants.

A condition known as atresia is a major cause of congenital conductive hearing loss. Congenital aural atresia results when the external auditory canal is either malformed or completely absent at birth. A congenital malformation may lead to a blockage of the ear canal through an accumulation of cerumen, which is a wax that hardens and blocks incoming sound waves from being transmitted to the middle ear.

**Postnatal Disease** One of the most common causes of hearing loss in the postnatal period is infection. Postnatal infections—such as measles, mumps, influenza, typhoid fever, and scarlet fever—are all associated with hearing loss. Meningitis is an inflammation of the membranes that cover the brain and spinal cord and is a cause of severe hearing loss in school-age children. Sight loss, paralysis, and brain damage are further complications of this disease. The incidence of meningitis has significantly declined over the three decades, however, thanks to the development of antibiotics and chemotherapy.

Another common problem that may result from postnatal infection is otitis media, an inflammation of the middle ear. This condition, which can result from severe colds that spread from the eustachian tube to the middle ear, is the most common cause of conductive hearing loss in younger children. Otitis media (also called "ear infection") ranks second to the common cold as the most common health problem in preschool children. Three out of every four children have had at least one episode by the age of 3. The disease is difficult to diagnose, especially in infancy, at which time symptoms are often absent. Otitis media has been found to be highly correlated with hearing problems (Moore, 2007; National Institute on Deafness and Other Communication Disorders, 2015b).

*Photo 13.4* Loud noise is a leading cause of hearing problems. Adolescents are subjected to damaging noise levels when headphones and earbuds on smartphones or MP3 or DVD players are turned up too high.

© Antoniodiaz/Shutterstock.com

**Environmental Factors** Environmental factors—including extreme changes in air pressure caused by explosions, physical abuse of the cranial area, impact from foreign objects during accidents, and loud music—also contribute to acquired hearing loss. Loud noise is rapidly becoming a major cause of hearing problems; about 30 million people are subjected to dangerous noise levels in everyday life (National Institute on Deafness and Other Communication Disorders, 2015b; Owen, 2007). Most of us are subjected to hazardous noise, such as noise from jet engines and loud music, more often than ever before. With the popularity of headphones and earbuds, such as those used with iPods or MP3 players, many

**Congenital toxoplasmosis infection**
Characterized by jaundice and anemia, this disease frequently results in central nervous system disorders.

**Hydrocephalus**
Condition resulting in excess cerebrospinal fluid in the brain.

**Atresia**
The absence of a normal opening or cavity.

**Otitis media**
An inflammation of the middle ear.

**Albinism**
Lack of pigmentation in eyes, skin, and hair.

**Photophobia**
An intolerance to light.

**Retinoblastoma**
A malignant tumor in the retina.

**Microphthalmia**
An abnormally small eyeball.

**Anophthalmia**
Absence of the eyeball.

**Glaucoma**
A disorder of the eye, which is characterized by high pressure inside the eyeball.

**Buphthalmos**
An abnormal distention and enlargement of the eyeball.

**Standard 1**
Learner Development and Individual Learning Differences

**Xerophthalmia**
Vitamin A deficiency that can lead to a lack of mucous-producing cells (known as dry eye) or blindness.

**Cortical visual impairment (CVI)**
A leading cause of acquired blindness, which involves damage to the occipital lobes and/or the visual pathways to the brain, resulting from severe trauma, infections, or drug abuse.

**Trachoma**
Infectious bacterial disease associated with poor living standards and inadequate hygiene. Leads to blindness due to repeated infections causing irritation and scars on the eyelids.

people (particularly adolescents) are subjected to damaging noise levels. Occupational noises (such as those from jackhammers, tractors, and sirens) are now the leading cause of sensorineural hearing loss. Other factors associated with acquired hearing loss include degenerative processes in the ear that may come with aging, cerebral hemorrhages, allergies, and intercranial tumors.

## 13-4b   Vision Loss: Causes and Risk Factors

Vision loss may be associated with both genetic and acquired disorders. A number of genetic conditions can result in vision loss, including:

- **albinism** (resulting in **photophobia** because of lack of pigmentation in eyes, skin, and hair),
- retinitis pigmentosa (degeneration of the retina),
- **retinoblastoma** (malignant tumor in the retina),
- optic atrophy (loss of function of optic nerve fibers),
- cataracts (opaque lens resulting in severely distorted vision),
- severe myopia associated with retinal detachment,
- lesions of the cornea,
- abnormalities of the iris (coloboma or aniridia),
- **microphthalmia** (abnormally small eyeball),
- hydrocephalus (excess cerebrospinal fluid in the brain) leading to optic atrophy,
- **anophthalmia** (absence of the eyeball), and
- **glaucoma** or **buphthalmos** (abnormal distention and enlargement of the eyeball).

Glaucoma results from increased pressure within the eye that damages the optic nerve if left untreated. It is responsible for about 4 percent of all blindness in children (Batshaw, Roizen, & Lotrecchiano, 2012). The incidence of glaucoma is highest in people over the age of 40 who have a family history of the disease. Glaucoma is treatable, either through surgery to drain fluids from the eye or through the use of medicated eye drops to reduce pressure.

Acquired disorders associated with vision loss may occur prior to, during, or after birth. Several factors present prior to birth, such as radiation or the introduction of drugs into the fetal system, may result in vision loss. A major cause of blindness in the fetus is infection, which may be due to diseases such as rubella and syphilis. Other diseases that can result in blindness include influenza, mumps, and measles.

One of the leading causes of acquired blindness in children worldwide is vitamin A deficiency (**xerophthalmia**). Xerophthalmia is ranked among the World Health Organization's top ten leading causes of death through disease in developing countries (United Nations World Food Programme, 2012).

Another cause of acquired blindness is retinopathy of prematurity (ROP). As noted earlier, ROP results from administering oxygen over prolonged periods of time to infants with low birth weight. Almost 80 percent of preschool-age blind children lost their sight as a result of ROP during the peak years of the disease (1940s through 1960s).

Vision loss after birth may be due to several factors. Trauma, infections, inflammations, and tumors are all related to loss of sight. **Cortical visual impairment (CVI)** is a leading cause of acquired blindness. CVI, which involves damage to the occipital lobes and/or the visual pathways to the brain, can result from severe trauma, asphyxia, seizures, infections of the central nervous system, drugs, poisons, or other neurological conditions. Most children with CVI have residual vision.

The most common cause of preventable blindness is **trachoma**. This infectious disease affects more than 150 million people worldwide. Trachoma is associated with compromised living standards and hygiene (such as lack of water and unsanitary conditions) within a community. Although the incidence of trachoma has been reduced worldwide, it remains a serious health risk to millions of people in rural areas with significant levels of poverty (Lewallen et al., 2008).

The most common vision problems in adults, particularly those over the age of 60, are caused by macular degeneration. This condition is the result of a breakdown of the tissues in the macula (a small area in the middle of the retina). Macular degeneration affects more than 165,000 people each year, and 16,000 of them go blind as a result of the disease. Nearly two million Americans have impaired vision due to macular degeneration. With macular degeneration, central vision becomes distorted and blurry. The individual also has considerable difficulty differentiating colors (Riddering, 2008). New advances in the treatment of macular degeneration include laser surgery and drug therapy.

## 13-5  Identification and Assessment of Sensory Disabilities in Children and Youth

Sensory disabilities are often noticed first by parents or caregivers and then formally diagnosed by a medical specialist.

### 13-5a  Assessment of Hearing Loss

Early detection of a hearing loss can prevent or at least minimize the impact of the disability on the overall development of individuals. Generally, it is the responsibility of the pediatrician or family practitioner to be aware of a problem and to refer the family to an appropriate hearing specialist. This requires that the physician be familiar with family history and conduct a thorough physical examination of the child. The physician must be alert to any symptoms (such as delayed language development) that indicate potential sensory loss.

An otologist is a medical specialist who is most concerned with the hearing organ and its diseases. Otology is a component of the larger specialty of diseases of the ear, nose, and throat. Otologists, like pediatricians, screen for potential hearing problems, but the process is much more specialized and exhaustive. Otologists also conduct an extensive physical examination of the ear to identify syndromes that are associated with conductive or sensorineural loss. This information, in conjunction with family history, provides data used to recommend appropriate medical treatment that may involve medical therapy or surgical intervention.

Common therapeutic procedures include monitoring aural hygiene (e.g., keeping the external ear free from wax), blowing out the ear (e.g., a process to remove mucus blocking the eustachian tube), and administering antibiotics to treat infections. Surgical techniques may involve the cosmetic and functional restructuring of congenital malformations such as a deformed external ear or closed external canal (atresia). Fenestration is the surgical creation of a new opening in the labyrinth of the ear to restore hearing. A stapedectomy is a surgical process conducted under a microscope whereby a fixed stapes is replaced with a prosthetic device capable of vibrating, thus permitting the transmission of sound waves. A myringoplasty is the surgical reconstruction of a perforated tympanic membrane (eardrum).

Another widely used surgical procedure is the cochlear implant. This electronic device is surgically placed under the skin behind the ear. It consists of four parts: (1) a microphone for picking up sound, (2) a speech processor to select and arrange sounds picked up by the microphone, (3) a transmitter and receiver/stimulator to receive signals from the speech processor and convert them into electric impulses, and (4) electrodes to collect the impulses from the stimulator and send them to the brain. The implant does not restore or amplify hearing. Instead, it provides people who are deaf or profoundly hard of hearing with a useful "sense" of sound in the world around them. The implant overcomes "nerve deafness" (sounds blocked from reaching the auditory nerve) by getting around damage to the tiny hair cells in the inner ear and directly stimulating the auditory nerve. An implant electronically finds useful or meaningful sounds, such as speech, and then sends these sounds to the auditory nerve.

Cochlear implants are becoming more widely used with both adults and children. More than 219,000 children and adults worldwide have had the surgery (National Institute on Deafness and Other Communication Disorders, 2015c). Some adults who were deafened in their later years reported useful hearing following the implant; others still needed

**Macular degeneration**
An age-related condition in which the macula (tissues within the retina) break down, resulting in distorted and blurred central vision.

**Otologist**
Specialist involved in the study of the ear and its diseases.

**Cochlear implant**
Procedure that implants an electronic device under the skin behind the ear to directly stimulate the auditory nerve.

speech-reading to understand the spoken word. Most children receive the implants between the ages of 2 and 6 years. Debate continues about which age is optimal for the surgery, but it appears that the earlier, the better. The American Speech-Language-Hearing Association (2012) suggests that the younger a child who was born deaf receives an implant, the greater the benefit achieved in the areas of speech perception and speech and language development. The existing research suggests that cochlear implants assist in the learning of speech, language, and social skills, particularly for young children. However, there are still issues to be addressed, such as understanding the risk of possible damage to an ear that has some residual hearing, as well as the risk of infection from the implant (Berg, Ip, Hurst, & Herb, 2007).

Whereas an otologist offers a biological perspective on hearing loss, an audiologist emphasizes the functional impact of losing one's hearing. Audiologists first screen individuals for a hearing loss and then determine both the nature and the severity of the condition. Social, educational, and vocational implications of the hearing loss are then discussed and explored. Although audiologists are not specifically trained in the field of medicine, these professionals interact constantly with otologists to provide a comprehensive assessment of hearing.

Working together, audiologists and otologists provide assistance in the selection and use of hearing aids. At one time or another, most people with a hearing loss will probably wear hearing aids. Hearing aids amplify sound, but they do not correct hearing. Hearing aids have been used for centuries. Early acoustic aids included cupping one's hand behind the ear as well as the ear trumpet. Modern electroacoustic aids do not depend on the loudness of the human voice to amplify sound, but utilize batteries to increase volume. Electroacoustic aids come in three main types: body-worn aids, behind-the-ear aids, and in-the-ear aids. Which hearing aid is best for a particular person depends on the degree of hearing loss, the age of the individual, and his or her physical condition.

The behind-the-ear aid (also referred to as an ear-level aid) is a common electroacoustic device for children with a hearing loss. All components of the behind-the-ear aid are fitted in one case behind the outer ear. The case then connects to an earmold that delivers the signal directly to the ear. In addition to their portability, behind-the-ear aids have the advantage of producing the greatest amount of electroacoustic flexibility (amount of amplification across all frequencies). The primary disadvantage is a problem with acoustic feedback. As discussed earlier in this chapter, the behind-the-ear aid may be used with an FM-RF system. These aids may be fitted monaurally (on one ear) or binaurally (on both ears).

The in-the-ear aid fits within the ear canal. All major components (microphone, amplifier, transducer, and battery) are housed in a single case that has been custom-made for an individual user. The advantage of the in-the-ear aid is the close positioning of the microphone to the natural reception of auditory signals in the ear canal. In-the-ear aids are recommended for people with mild hearing losses who do not need frequent changes in earmolds. Accordingly, these aids are not usually recommended for young children.

Although the quality of commercially available hearing aids has improved dramatically in recent years, they have distinct limitations. Commercial hearing aids make sounds louder, but do not necessarily make them more clear and distinct. The criteria for determining the effectiveness of a hearing aid must be based on how well it fits, as well as each individual's communication ability. The stimulation of residual hearing through a hearing aid enables most people with a hearing loss to function as hard of hearing. However, the use of a hearing aid must be implemented as early as possible, before sensory deprivation takes its toll on a child. It is the audiologist's responsibility to weigh all the factors involved (such as convenience, size, and weight) in the selection and use of an aid for an individual. The individual should then be directed to a reputable hearing aid dealer.

## 13-5b Assessment of Vision Loss

Much like the assessment of hearing loss, early detection of vision loss is critical to maximize vision and minimize the effects often associated with low vision. Pediatricians or family practitioners are often the first professionals to complete a formal vision assessment. The assessment process typically includes a variety of activities and tools to measure the level of vision and function a child has. It is considered best practice to use a variety of methods to assess vision. Once a vision loss has been detected, interventions generally involve the following steps:

- Correction of the vision to the greatest extent possible
- Prevention or reduction of developmental problems that typically occur in children with limited vision
- Support and education for the family (New York State Department of Health [NYSDOH], 2015)

Initial screenings for vision loss are usually based on an individual's visual acuity. Visual acuity may be measured through the use of the Snellen test, developed in 1862 by Dutch ophthalmologist Herman Snellen. This visual screening test is used primarily to measure central distance vision. The subject stands 20 feet from a letter chart, or E chart (the standard eye chart for testing vision), and reads each symbol, beginning with the top row. The different sizes of each row or symbol represent what a person with normal vision would see at the various distances indicated on the chart. As indicated earlier in this chapter, a person's visual acuity is then determined via an index that refers to the distance at which an object can be recognized. People with normal eyesight are defined as having 20/20 vision.

Because the Snellen test measures only visual acuity, it must be used primarily as an initial screening device that is supplemented by more in-depth assessments, such as a thorough ophthalmological examination. Parents, physicians, school nurses, and educators must also carefully observe a child's behavior, and document a complete history of possible symptoms of a vision loss. These observable symptoms fall into three categories: appearance, behavior, and complaints. Table 13.2 describes some warning signs of vision loss. The existence of symptoms does not necessarily mean a person has a significant vision loss, but it does indicate that an appropriate specialist should be consulted for further examination.

**Prevention** Prevention of vision loss is one of the major goals of the field of medicine. Because some causes of blindness are hereditary, it is important for the family to be aware of genetic services. One purpose of genetic screening is to identify those who are planning to have a family and who may possess certain detrimental genotypes (such as albinism or retinoblastoma) that can be passed on to their descendants. Screening may also be conducted after conception to determine whether an unborn fetus possesses any genetic abnormalities.

**Table 13.2** Warning Signs of Visual Problems

| Physical Symptoms | Observable Behavior | Complaints |
|---|---|---|
| Eyes are crossed. | Blinks constantly | Frequent dizziness |
| Eyes are not functioning in unison. | Trips or stumbles frequently | Frequent headaches |
| Eyelids are swollen and crusted, with red rims. | Covers one eye when reading | Pain in the eyes |
| Eyes are overly sensitive to light. | Holds reading material either very close or very far away | Itching or burning of the eyes or eyelids |
| Sties occur frequently. | Distorts the face or frowns when concentrating on something in the distance | Double vision |
| Eyes are frequently bloodshot. | Walks cautiously | |
| Pupils are of different sizes. | Fails to see objects that are to one side or the other | |
| Eyes are constantly in motion. | | |

**Epiphora**
An overflow of tears from obstruction of the lachrymal ducts of the eye.

Following screening, a genetic counselor informs the parents of the test results so that the family can make an informed decision about conceiving a child or carrying a fetus to term.

Adequate prenatal care is another means of preventing problems. Parents must be made aware of the potential hazards associated with poor nutritional habits, the use of drugs, and exposure to radiation (such as X-rays) during pregnancy. One example of preventive care during this period is the use of antibiotics to treat various infections (influenza, measles, and syphilis, for example), thus reducing the risk of infection to an unborn fetus.

Developmental screening is also a widely recognized means of prevention. Early screening of developmental problems enables the family physician to analyze several treatment alternatives and, when necessary, refer the child to an appropriate specialist for a more thorough evaluation of developmental delays.

This screening—which includes examination of hearing, speech, motor, and psychological development—includes attention to vision as well. Early screening involves a medical examination at birth, assessing the physical condition of the newborn, and also obtaining a complete family medical history. The eyes should be carefully examined for any abnormalities, such as infection or trauma.

At 6 weeks of age, visual screening forms part of another general developmental assessment. This examination should include input from the parents about how their child is responding (e.g., smiling and looking at objects or faces). The physician should check eye movement and search for infection, crusting on the eyes, or epiphora, an overflow of tears resulting from obstruction of the lachrymal ducts.

The next examination should occur at about 6 months of age. A defensive blink should be present at this age, and eye movement should be full and coordinated. If any imbalance in eye movements is noted, a more thorough examination should be conducted. Family history is extremely important, because in many cases there is a familial pattern of vision problems.

Between the ages of 1 and 5 years, visual evaluation should be conducted at regular intervals. An important period occurs just prior to the child entering school. Visual problems must not go undetected as children attempt to cope with the new and complex demands of the educational environment.

## 13-6 Interventions and Treatments for Sensory Disabilities from Early Childhood Through Adulthood

Regardless of the age of a person when diagnosed with a sensory disability, interventions and treatment are essential to assist in academic or occupational skills, independence, and confidence.

### 13-6a Intervention Strategies for Youth Who Are Deaf or Hard of Hearing

In the United States, educational programs for children who are deaf or hard of hearing emerged in the early 19th century. The residential school for the deaf was the primary model for delivery of educational services; it was a live-in facility where students were segregated from the family environment. In the latter half of the 19th century, day schools were established in which students lived with their families while attending special schools exclusively for deaf students. As the century drew to a close, some public schools established special classes for children with a hearing loss within general education schools.

The residential school continued to be a model for educational services well into the 20th century. However, with the introduction of electrical amplification, advances in medical treatment, and improved educational technology, more options became available within the public schools. Today, educational programs for students who are deaf or hard of hearing range from the residential school to inclusive education in a general education classroom with support services.

**Standard 2**
Learning Environments

**Standard 5**
Instructional Planning and Strategies

Research strongly indicates that children with a hearing loss must receive early intervention as soon as possible if they are to learn the language skills necessary for reading and other academic subjects (Gilbertson & Ferre, 2008; Lederberg, Miller, Easterbrooks, & McDonald, 2014; McGowan, Nittrouer, & Chenausky, 2008). There is little disagreement that the education of children with a hearing loss must begin at the time of the diagnosis. Educational goals for students with a hearing loss are comparable to those for students who can hear. Students with a hearing loss bring many of the same strengths and weaknesses to the classroom as hearing students. Adjustment to learning experiences is often comparable for both groups, as well. Students with a hearing loss, however, face the formidable problems associated with being unable to communicate effectively with teachers and students who can hear. For more information on interacting with people who have a hearing loss, see this chapter's Community Support for Lifelong Inclusion.

**Teaching Communication Skills** The approaches commonly used to teach communication skills to students with a hearing loss include auditory, oral, manual, and total communication. There is a long history of controversy regarding which approach is the most appropriate. However, no single method or combination of methods can meet the individual needs of all children with a hearing loss. Our purpose is not to enter into the controversy regarding these approaches but to present a brief description of each approach.

***The Auditory Approach*** The auditory approach emphasizes the use of amplified sound and residual hearing to develop oral communication skills. The auditory channel is considered the primary avenue for language development, regardless of the severity or type of hearing loss. The basic principles of the auditory-verbal approach are to:

1. Promote early diagnosis of hearing loss in newborns, infants, toddlers, and young children, followed by immediate audiologic management and auditory-verbal therapy;

2. Recommend immediate assessment and use of appropriate, state-of-the-art hearing technology to obtain maximum benefits of auditory stimulation;

3. Guide and coach parents to help their child use hearing as the primary sensory modality in developing spoken language without the use of sign language or emphasis on lip-reading;

4. Guide and coach parents to become the primary facilitators of their child's listening and spoken language development through active, consistent participation in individualized auditory-verbal therapy;

5. Guide and coach parents to create environments that support listening for the acquisition of spoken language throughout the child's daily activities;

6. Guide and coach parents to help their child integrate listening and spoken language into all aspects of the child's life;

7. Guide and coach parents to use natural developmental patterns of audition, speech, language, cognition, and communication;

8. Guide and coach parents to help their child self-monitor spoken language through listening;

9. Administer ongoing formal and informal diagnostic assessments to develop individualized auditory-verbal treatment plans, to monitor progress, and to evaluate the effectiveness of the plans for the child and family; and

10. Promote education in regular schools with peers who have typical hearing and with appropriate services from early childhood onward. (Alexander Graham Bell Academy, 2012)

The auditory approach uses a variety of electroacoustic devices to enhance residual hearing, such as binaural hearing aids, acoustically tuned earmolds, and FM units. FM units employ a behind-the-ear hearing aid connected to a high-powered frequency-modulated radio-frequency (FM-RF) system. These units use a one-way wireless system on radio frequency bands. The student wears the receiver unit (about the size of a deck of cards), and the teacher wears a wireless microphone-transmitter-antenna unit. One advantage of using an FM-RF system is that the teacher can be connected to several students at a time.

**CEC**

**Standard 5**
Instructional Planning
and Strategies

## Xeeb

Xeeb Chang is an 8-year-old boy at Jefferson Elementary School who uses hearing aids to amplify sound due to a moderate hearing loss. He is from a Hmong family that emigrated from Laos to the United States 25 years ago. Both of his parents are hearing.

Xeeb's teacher, Mr. Homem, wanted to develop a close working relationship with each of the families of his students. He was particularly eager to learn more about Xeeb and his family so that he could create a successful inclusive environment for Xeeb. Mr. Homem invited Xeeb's parents to meet him at a local ice cream parlor to get to know each other and to discuss strategies to support Xeeb's success. Xeeb's parents shared some interesting details with Mr. Homem about their understanding of Xeeb's hearing loss and their rights as partners in the education process. He learned that Xeeb's parents noticed that Xeeb was not responding to sounds in the same way his siblings did, but they were reluctant to seek medical assessment. They both confirmed that the elders in their community were not supportive of medical interventions, but they eventually did bring Xeeb to the doctor for a hearing screening. Upon learning about their son's hearing loss, they felt despair and great apprehension. They shared that they accepted Xeeb unconditionally,

Chris Bernard Photography Inc/iStockphoto.com

yet they felt his hearing loss would create a barrier to learning and therefore they had lower expectations for him than his peers. They added that they have a strong value of education and its role in improving the lives of their children.

The Changs stated that they believe that parents must play a role in their children's learning, but they did not have a clear understanding of the general education system and had an even weaker understanding of the special education process. Mr. Homem invited the Changs to take an active role in all school and class activities and shared that their involvement would be beneficial for everyone.

Mr. Homem asked the Changs about what Xeeb enjoyed doing at home and what his study habits were. They reported that he loves to play video games, basketball, and is particularly fond of all things *Star Wars*. He is not an avid reader, but enjoys doing math and

spelling work. They shared that their children, Xeeb and two older siblings, do homework at the kitchen table after dinner.

Noticing that Xeeb often leaves his hearing aids at home, Mr. Homem asked the Changs how they felt about their son's use of an amplification system. The Changs assured Mr. Homem that they had no reservations about Xeeb using hearing aids but noted that Xeeb strongly dislikes wearing them. They said that they do not require him to wear the aids at home.

Mr. Homem thanked the Changs for their time and for sharing their son's and their history with him. He left the meeting feeling like he had a better understanding of Xeeb and his family.

### Application Questions

**1.** What are some strategies Mr. Homem could use to help the Changs better understand the general and special education system at Jefferson Elementary School?

**2.** How can Mr. Homem capitalize on Xeeb's interests in the classroom?

**3.** It is important to Mr. Homem that the Changs support his high expectations of Xeeb's success. What are some strategies he could use to help build a stronger understanding of their son's ability?

**The Oral Approach** The oral approach to teaching communication skills also relies on the use of amplified sound and residual hearing to develop oral language. This approach emphasizes the need for people with a hearing loss to function in the hearing world. Individuals are encouraged to speak and be spoken to. In addition to electroacoustic amplification, teachers may employ speech-reading, reading and writing, and moto-kinesthetic speech training (feeling an individual's face and reproducing breath and voice patterns). **Speech-reading** is the process of understanding another person's speech by watching lip movement and facial and body gestures. This skill is difficult to master, especially for people who have been deaf since an early age and, thus, never acquired speech. Problems with speech-reading include the fact that many sounds are not distinguishable on the lips; readers must attend carefully to every word spoken, a difficult task for preschool and primary-age children. Additionally, speech-readers must be able to see the speaker's mouth at all times.

**Speech-reading**
The process of understanding another person's speech by watching lip movement and facial and body gestures.

If a severe or profound hearing loss automatically made an individual neurologically and functionally "different" from people with normal hearing, then the oral approach may not be tenable. However, outcome studies show that individuals who have been taught through the active use of amplified residual hearing since early childhood are indeed independent, speaking, and contributing members of mainstream society.

**The Manual Approach** The manual approach to teaching communication skills stresses the use of signs in teaching children who are deaf to communicate. The use of signs is based on the premise that many such children are unable to develop oral language; consequently, they must have some other means of communication. Manual communication systems are divided into two main categories: sign languages and sign systems.

Sign languages are systematic and complex combinations of hand movements that communicate whole words and complete thoughts rather than the individual letters of the alphabet. One of the most common sign languages is the American Sign Language (ASL) with a vocabulary of more than 6,000 signs. Examples of ASL signs are shown in Figure 13.5.

ASL is currently the most widely used sign language among many adults who are deaf, because it is easy to master and has historically been the preferred mode of communication. It is a language, but it is not English. Its signs represent concepts rather than single words. The use of ASL in a school setting has been strongly recommended by some advocates for people who are deaf because it is considered their natural language (National Institute on Deafness and Other Communication Disorders, 2015d).

Sign systems differ from sign languages in that they attempt to create visual equivalents of oral language through manual gestures. With finger spelling, a form of manual communication that incorporates all 26 letters of the English alphabet, each letter is signed independently on one hand to form words. It is common to see a person who is deaf using finger spelling when there is no ASL sign for a word. The four sign systems used in the United States are Seeing Essential English, Signing Exact English, Linguistics of Visual English, and Signed English.

There is a continuing debate regarding the use of ASL and signing English systems in providing academic instruction to students who are deaf. Should ASL or English be the primary language for instruction? Those advocating a bicultural–bilingual approach

**Sign languages**
Complex combinations of hand movements that communicate whole words and complete thoughts rather than the individual letters of the alphabet.

**American Sign Language (ASL)**
A type of sign language commonly used by people with hearing impairments. ASL signs represent concepts rather than single words.

**Sign systems**
Differing from sign languages, sign systems create visual equivalents of oral language through manual gestures. For example, finger spelling uses a separate sign for each letter of the English alphabet.

**Bicultural–bilingual approach**
Instructional approach advocating ASL as the primary language and English as the second language for students who are deaf.

**Figure 13.5** *Examples of "Faint" Expressed in American Sign Language*
*Example Usage of Faint: My mother fainted from the ammonia fumes.*

Alabama, Hawaii

Arkansas, Florida, Maine, Kentucky, Louisiana, Virginia, North Carolina, South Carolina

California, Illinois, Utah

Colorado, Texas (1 of 2)

Massachusetts

Michigan, Ohio

**Total communication**
A communication approach that uses elements from manual, oral, and any other techniques available to facilitate understanding.

**Cued speech**
Cued speech facilitates the development of oral communication by combining eight hand signals in four different locations near the person's chin.

**Closed-caption television**
TV broadcasts that provide translated dialogue in the form of subtitles. Also called the "line-21" system because the caption is inserted into blank line 21 of the picture.

believe that ASL should be the primary language and English the second language. As the primary language, ASL would then serve as the foundation for the learning of English. The rationale for ASL as the primary language emerges from the values held dear by the deaf community: Children who are deaf must learn academic content in the language of their culture, their natural language. The primary language for children who are deaf is visual, not verbal. Children who are deaf should be considered bilingual students, not students with disabilities. As is true in bilingual education programs for students with differing language backgrounds, there is also the debate about whether ASL should be taught first and then English, or whether both should be taught simultaneously. One side emphasizes the importance of the child's first acquiring the natural language (ASL). The other stresses the need to expose the child to both ASL and English simultaneously and as early as possible. There is little research to support either position.

*Total Communication* Total communication has roots traceable to the 16th century. Over the past four centuries, many professionals advocated for an instructional system that employed every method possible to teach communication skills: oral, auditory, manual, and written. This approach was known as the combined system or simultaneous method. The methodology of the early combined system was imprecise; essentially, any recognized approach to teaching communication was used as long as it included a manual component. The concept of total communication differs from the older combined system in that it is used not only when the oral method fails or when critical learning periods have long since passed, but also in a much broader sense—as a total communication philosophy, not a system.

The philosophy of total communication holds that the simultaneous presentation of signs and speech will enhance each person's opportunity to understand and use both systems more effectively.

Total communication programs use residual hearing, amplification, speech-reading, speech training, reading, and writing in combination with manual systems. A method that may be used as an aid to total communication but is not a necessary component of the approach is cued speech. Cued speech facilitates the development of oral communication by combining eight different hand signals in four different locations near the person's chin. These hand signals provide additional information about sounds not identifiable by speech-reading. The result is that an individual has access to all sounds in the English language through either the lips or the hands.

## Assistive Technology
Educational and leisure opportunities for people with a hearing loss have been greatly expanded through technological advances such as closed-caption television, computers, and the Internet. In this section, we examine 21st-century technology for people with a hearing loss.

*Closed-Captioning* Closed-caption television translates dialogue from a television program into printed words (captions or subtitles). These captions are then converted into electronic codes that can be inserted into the television picture on sets specially adapted with decoding devices. The process is called the line-21 system because the caption is inserted into blank line 21 of the picture.

In its first year of operation in 1958, national closed-caption programming was available about 30 hours a week. By 1987, more than 200 hours a week of national programming were captioned in a wide range of topics, from news and information to entertainment and commercials. By 1993, all major broadcast networks were captioning 100 percent of their prime-time broadcasts, national news, and children's programming. With the passage of the Television Decoder Circuitry Act of 1993, the numbers of viewers watching closed-caption television expanded even more dramatically. This act required that all television sets sold in the United States that measure 13 inches or larger be equipped with a decoder that allows captions to be placed anywhere on the television screen. (This prevents captions from interfering with on-screen titles or other information displayed on the TV broadcast.) In 1997, the U.S. Congress passed the Telecommunications Act, which required virtually all new television programming to be captioned by January 2006. The clear intent of the law was to expand access to television for millions of people who are deaf.

**Standard 5**
Instructional Planning and Strategies

**Computers, Smartphones, Tablets, and the Internet** Personal computers, electronic tablets, and smartphones add an exciting dimension to information access for people with a hearing loss. These widely used devices place people with a hearing impairment in an interactive setting using Internet applications ("apps") and computer software. Learning can be individualized so that students can gain independence by working at their own pace and level.

Various apps are now available for instructional support across academic subject areas from reading and writing to learning basic sign language. Software is available that will display a person's speech in visual form on the screen to assist in the development of articulation skills. Another innovative computer system is called C-Print, developed by the National Technical Institute for the Deaf. Using a laptop computer equipped with a computer shorthand system and commercially available software packages, C-Print provides real-time translations of the spoken word. C-Print provides a major service to students with a hearing loss as they attend college classes or oral lectures; they typically find note taking an extremely difficult activity, even when an oral interpreter is available (National Technical Institute for the Deaf, 2006).

Through e-mail, texting, interactive chat rooms, smartphones, and the infinite number of websites, the Internet offers people with a hearing loss access to all kinds of visual information through the quickest and most convenient means possible. Harris Communications and the American Sign Language Browser at Michigan State University are just two examples of sites designed specifically for people who are deaf.

**Telecommunication Devices** A major advance in communication technology for people with a hearing loss is the telecommunication device (TDD). In 1990, the Americans with Disabilities Act renamed these devices **text telephones (TTs)**. TTs send, receive, and print messages through thousands of stations across the United States. People with a hearing loss can now dial an 800 number to set up conference calls, make appointments, or order merchandise or fast food. Anyone who wants to speak with a person using a TT can do so through the use of a standard telephone.

The teletypewriter (TTY) and printer system is another effective use of technology for people who are deaf. It allows them to communicate by phone via a typewriter that converts typed letters into electric signals through a modem. These signals are sent through the

**Text telephones (TTs)**
Telephones that send, receive, and print messages through thousands of stations across the United States.

## LEARNING THROUGH SOCIAL MEDIA

## *Experiences of People with Sensory Impairments*

In 2010, four Norwegian researchers (Tollefsen, Dale, Berg, & Nordby, 2011) conducted a survey of Norwegian citizens with disabilities, including those with sensory impairments, to better understand their use of social media. The researchers asked specifically about the use of Facebook, Twitter, and Skype, but respondents were free to talk about other forms of social media in their lives. A few highlights of responses from people with hearing and vision loss follow:

> I am severely hard of hearing (hearing aid user) and visually impaired. Facebook has become an extremely important arena for me to keep updated. The social aspects of visual or

hearing impairments do not matter here. I use what I have learned on Facebook when I later meet people face to face, and this has made it much easier for me to follow and understand the context of conversations. It has also become much easier to keep in touch with people I otherwise would not have had the resources to keep in contact with. For me, Facebook provides the opportunity for a more active social life out in "real life."

The previous quote ... suggests that social media actually provide a significant added value in relation to social participation in "real life." A woman who is blind says:

I use whatever I have found on Facebook when I meet people. For example, others can see that someone is pregnant and ask how it's going. I can't see this, but I have often found out about it on Facebook. Then I can ask!

### Questions for Reflection

Why do you think many people with sensory impairments in this survey view social media as a "valued-added" part of their lives? What are the challenges for people with sensory impairments in accessing social media sites?

SOURCE: Tollefsen, M., Dale, Ø, Berg, M, & Nordby, R. (2011). *Connected!: Disabled and use of social media.* Retrieved March 12, 2012, from http://medialt.no/news/en-US /connected-disabled-and-use-of-social-media/737.aspx.

## Motor Skill Development for Young Children with Vision Loss

Children with sight develop motor skills by watching how other people move and by engaging in physical play. Children who are blind or have limited sight do not share the same experiences as their sighted peers. As a result, they have significant delays in their motor skill development and physical fitness levels. These delays can be minimized by creating opportunities for physical play, especially play that involves exploring the environment around them. Adapted physical education programs can improve fitness levels, strengthen motor skills, bolster self-confidence with regard to independent mobility, and establish social connections that lead to friendships. The following is a list of strategies for students with visual impairments in physical education programs:

• Allow students to position themselves to maximize their residual vision.

• Make sure play areas are well lit.

• Encourage students with visual impairment to explore the entire physical education area to become familiar with it.

• Keep instructional areas free from clutter and keep students with visual

Marmaduke St. John / Alamy

impairment up-to-date on changes in the environment.

• Modify activities and equipment when necessary. Use audible bells, guide ropes for running, larger equipment when available, and employ the buddy system.

• Provide arm support if needed for jumping activities.

• Use touch to demonstrate body movements.

• Use good verbal descriptions when sharing a new activity or movement pattern.

• Resist the urge to overprotect students who have visual impairments.

• Teach skills from least difficult to most difficult (catching a ball from a short

distance first, then extend to a greater distance).

• Use the student's name before they are expected to engage.

• Use bells on the "it" person during tag games.

• Consider limiting the playing space when appropriate.

Adapting games and activities increases the opportunity for fun, skill development, and self-confidence. Learning a new sport or recreational activity can improve a person's general sense of well-being and competence as well as lead to improved fitness levels.

### Questions for Reflection

**1.** What are some of ways in which children with a vision loss are able to participate in physical education?

**2.** How can educators, parents, and caregivers assure that children with a vision loss have the opportunity to develop motor skills?

SOURCE: Letcher, K. (2015). *Adapted Physical Education for the Blind and Visually Impaired.* Overbrook School for the Blind. Retrieved March 21, 2015, from www.s118134197 .onlinehome.us/page.php?ITEM=39.

**Standard 1**
Learner Development and Individual Learning Differences

**Standard 4**
Assessment

**Standard 6**
Professional Learning and Ethical Practice

phone lines and are then translated into typed messages and printed on a typewriter connected to a phone on the other end. Computer software is now available that can turn a personal computer into a TTY.

## 13-6b Intervention Strategies for Youth Who Are Blind or Have Low Vision

A popular misconception regarding the perceptual abilities of people with vision loss is that because of their diminished sight, they develop greater capacity in other sensory areas. For example, people who are blind are supposedly able to hear or smell some things that people with normal vision cannot perceive. This notion has never been empirically validated.

**Education Strategies** When determining the appropriate educational strategies for a student with a vision loss, an IEP team must also focus on how a student utilizes any remaining vision (visual efficiency) in conjunction with other senses. The Visual Efficiency Scale (see Barraga & Erin, 2002) assesses the overall visual functioning of individuals to determine how they use sight to acquire information. As suggested by Bishop (2005), if an individual has remaining vision, it is important that professionals and parents promote its use.

A functional approach to determining appropriate educational strategies for individuals with a vision loss focuses on visual capacity, attention, and processing. Visual capacity includes both acuity and field of vision; it also encompasses the response of the individual to visual information. The assessment of visual attention involves observing the individual's sensitivity to visual stimuli (alertness), ability to use vision to select information from a variety of sources, attention to a visual stimulus, and ability to process visual information. Visual-processing assessment determines which, if any, of the components of normal visual functioning are impaired.

The educational needs of students with vision loss are comparable to those of their sighted counterparts. In addition, many instructional methods currently used with students who are sighted are appropriate for students with vision loss. However, educators must be aware that certain content areas that are generally unnecessary for sighted students are essential to the success, in a classroom, of students with vision loss. These areas include mobility and orientation training as well as acquisition of daily living skills.

**Standard 1**
Learner Development and Individual Learning Differences

**Standard 5**
Instructional Planning and Strategies

The ability to move safely, efficiently, and independently through the environment enhances an individual's opportunities to learn more about the world and, thus, be less dependent on others for survival. Lack of mobility restricts individuals with vision loss in nearly every aspect of educational life. Such students may be unable to orient themselves to physical structures in the classroom (desks, chairs, and aisles), hallways, rest rooms, library, and cafeteria. Whereas people with sight can automatically establish a relative position in space, individuals with vision loss must be taught some means of compensating for a lack of visual input. This may be accomplished in a number of ways. It is important that students with vision loss not only learn the physical structure of their school, but also develop specific techniques to orient themselves to unfamiliar surroundings.

*Photo 13.5* Guide dogs and electronic mobility devices (such as this global positioning device) assist people who are blind in moving safely, efficiently, and independently through their environment.

These orientation techniques involve using the other senses. For example, the senses of touch and hearing can help students identify cues that designate where the bathroom is in the school. Although it is not true that people who are blind have superior hearing abilities, they may learn to use their hearing more effectively by focusing on subtle auditory cues that often go unnoticed. The efficient use of hearing, in conjunction with the other senses (including any remaining vision), is the key to independent travel for people with vision loss.

Independent travel with a sighted companion, but without the use of a cane, guide dog, or electronic device, is the most common form of travel for young school-age children. The major challenges for children with low vision in moving independently and safely through their environment include:

- Knowing where landmarks are throughout the school setting;

- Being familiar with the layout of classrooms and common areas, such as the library, gym, and cafeteria;

- Knowing where exits, rest rooms, the main office, and other relevant school and classroom areas are located; and

- Understanding the school's emergency procedures, such as fire, tornado, or earthquake drills. (Cox & Dykes, 2001)

Other challenges for students with low vision include adapting to changes in lighting, negotiating stairs and curbs, and walking in bad weather.

With the increasing emphasis on instructing young children in orientation at an earlier age, use of the long cane (Kiddie Cane) for young children has become more common. As these children grow older, they may be instructed in the use of a Mowat sensor. The Mowat sensor, approximately the size of a flashlight, is a handheld ultrasound travel aid that uses high-frequency sound to detect objects. Vibration frequency increases as objects become closer; the sensor vibrates at different rates to warn of obstacles in front of the individual. The device ignores everything but the closest object within the beam.

Guide dogs or electronic mobility devices may be appropriate for adolescents or adults, because the need to travel independently increases significantly with age. A variety of electronic mobility devices are currently being used for everything from enhancing hearing efficiency to detecting obstacles.

The Laser Cane converts infrared light into sound as light beams strike objects in the path of the person who is blind. It uses a range-finding technique with a semiconductor laser and a position-sensitive device (PSD). Proximity to an obstacle is warned by vibration at different levels of frequency.

The SonicGuide or Sonic Pathfinder, worn on the head, emits ultrasound and converts reflections from objects into audible noise in such a way that individuals can learn about the structure of objects. For example, loudness indicates size: The louder the noise, the larger the object. To use the SonicGuide effectively, people with low vision should have mobility skills. It is designed for outdoor use in conjunction with a cane, a guide dog, or residual vision.

The acquisition of daily living skills is another content area important to success in the classroom and to overall independence. Most people take for granted many routine events of the day, such as eating, dressing, bathing, and toileting. People with sight learn very early in life the tasks associated with perceptual-motor development, including grasping, lifting, balancing, pouring, and manipulating objects. These daily living tasks become more complex during the school years as children learn personal hygiene, grooming, and social etiquette. Eventually, people with sight acquire many complex daily living skills that later contribute to their independence as adults. Money management, grocery shopping, doing laundry, cooking, cleaning, making minor household repairs, sewing, mowing the lawn, and gardening are all daily tasks associated with adult life and are learned from experiences that are not usually a part of an individual's formal educational program.

For children with vision loss, however, routine daily living skills are not easily learned through everyday experiences. These children must be encouraged and supported as they develop life skills; they must not be overprotected from everyday challenges and risks by family and friends.

**Academic Content** Mobility training and daily living skills are components of an educational program that must also include an academic curriculum.

Particular emphasis must be placed on developing receptive and expressive language skills. Students with vision loss must learn to listen in order to understand the auditory world more clearly. Finely tuned receptive skills contribute to the development of expressive language, which allows these students to describe their perceptions of the world orally. Some research suggests the use of a language experience approach (LEA) as a means to develop language skills and prepare students for reading (Dorr, 2006; Koenig & Holbrook, 2005). The LEA involves several steps, as described in Figure 13.6.

Oral expression can be expanded to include handwriting as a means of communication. The acquisition of social and instructional language skills opens the door to many areas, including reading and mathematics. Reading can greatly expand the knowledge base for children with vision loss. For people who are partially sighted, various optical aids are available: video systems that magnify print, handheld magnifiers, magnifiers attached to eyeglasses, and other telescopic aids. Another means to facilitate reading for partially sighted students is the use of large-print books, which are generally available

*Figure 13.6  General Steps in the Language Experience Approach*

1. Arrange for and carry out a special event or activity for the child (or a group of children), such as a visit to the town's post office or a nearby farm. A naturally occurring experience such as a classmate's birthday or a school assembly may also be used, but it is important to continue to expand the child's experiences through unique and special activities (such as attending a circus or riding in a rowboat). Use a multisensory approach and active learning to immerse the child fully in the experience.

2. After the activity, have the child tell a story about what happened. If he or she has trouble getting started, use some brief prompts ("What happened first?"). As the child tells the story, write it down word for word with a braillewriter. Generally, the stories are relatively short at this stage in the student's literacy development. Three important points need to be emphasized:

   • Use a braillewriter (rather than a computer) to write the story so that the child knows that what he or she is saying is being recorded through writing. Have the child follow along with his or her finger just behind the embossing head, if appropriate.

   • Write the story in braille as the child is speaking. It is not instructionally effective to write it in print and later transcribe it into braille. Writing immediately in braille makes the child aware of the natural relationship between spoken and written words.

   • Write down the child's words exactly as he or she says them. Do not fix grammatical errors or attempt to control the vocabulary in any way. One of the goals of using this approach is to build the child's trust. If the child thinks that his or her story needs to be "fixed," then this feeling of trust is interrupted, and the child may be less willing to share his or her experiences and stories in the future.

3. Reread the story immediately with the child, using the shared reading strategy just discussed. The child will remember much of the story and will be able to read along, saying many of the words. Do not stop or pause during this step to have the child sound out or analyze words. The immediate rereading should be a holistic experience recounting the child's story.

4. Continue rereading the story through shared reading on subsequent days. Soon, the child will independently know more of the words and may even begin to recognize some of the words out of context.

5. Arrange contextually appropriate reading-strategy lessons based on the story, especially as the child approaches kindergarten. For example, if the story has several *p* words in it, talk about the initial /p/ sound. The child can scan to find the *p* words in the story and make a list, perhaps in a shared writing experience, of other *p* words. A comprehension activity may involve writing a new ending of the story by changing one feature (e.g., "How would your story have ended if … ?"). Related art activities or binding the story into a book may also be fun and motivating for the child.

SOURCE: Koenig, A. J., & Holbrook, M. C. (Eds.). (2005). Literacy skills. In *Foundations of education: Volume II, Instructional strategies for teaching children and youths with visual impairments,* 2nd ed. (pp. 276–277). New York: AFB Press.

in several print sizes through the American Printing House for the Blind and the Library of Congress. Other factors that must be considered in teaching reading to students who are partially sighted include adequate illumination and the reduction of glare. Advance organizers prepare students by previewing the instructional approach and materials to be used in a lesson. These organizers essentially identify the topics or tasks to be learned, give the student an organizational framework, indicate the concepts to be introduced, list new vocabulary, and state the intended outcomes for students.

Abstract mathematical concepts may be difficult for students who are blind. These students will probably require additional practice in learning to master symbols, number facts, and higher-level calculations. As concepts become more complex, additional aids may be necessary to facilitate learning. Specially designed talking microcomputers, calculators, rulers, and compasses have been developed to assist students in this area.

**Communication Media** For students who are partially sighted, their limited vision remains a means of obtaining information. The use of optical aids in conjunction with auditory and tactile stimuli provides these individuals with an integrated sensory approach to learning. However, this approach is not possible for students who are blind. Because they do not have access to visual stimuli, they may have to compensate through the use of tactile and auditory media. Through these media, children who are blind develop an understanding of themselves and of the world around them. One facet of this development process is the acquisition of language, and one facet of language acquisition is learning to read.

For students who are blind, the tactile sense represents entry into the symbolic world of reading. The most widely used tactile medium for teaching reading is the braille system.

This system, which originated with the work of Louis Braille in 1829, is a code that utilizes a six-dot cell to form 63 different alphabetical, numerical, and grammatical characters. To become proficient braille readers, people must learn 263 different configurations, including alphabet letters, punctuation marks, short-form words, and contractions. Braille is not a tactile reproduction of the standard English alphabet, but a separate code for reading and writing.

Braille is composed of from 1 to 6 raised dots depicted in a cell or space that contains room for two vertical rows of three dots each. On the left, the dots are numbered 1, 2, and 3 from top to bottom; on the right the dots are numbered 4, 5, and 6. This makes it easy to describe braille characters. For example, "a" is dot 1, "p" is dots 1, 2, 3, and 4, and "h" is dots 1, 2, and 5.

In braille any letter becomes a capital by putting dot 6 in front of it. For example, if "a" is dot 1, then "A" is dot 6 followed by dot 1, and if "p" is dots 1, 2, 3, and 4, then "P" is dot 6 followed by dots 1, 2, 3, and 4. This sure is easier than print, which requires different configurations for more than half of the capital letters. If "h" is dots 1, 2, and 5, what is "H"? Research has shown that the fastest braille readers use two hands. Using two hands also seems to make it easier for beginning braille readers to stay on the line. Do you think this might have something to do with two points constituting a line as my geometry teacher used to tell us (Pester, 2012)?

Braille is used by about one of every ten students who are blind and is considered by many to be an efficient means for teaching reading and writing. The American Printing House for the Blind produces about 28 million pages in English braille each year (Pester, 2012). Critics of the system argue that most readers who use braille are much slower than those who read from print and that braille materials are bulky and tedious. It can be argued, however, that without braille, people who are blind would be much less independent. Some people who are unable to read braille (such as people with diabetes who have decreased tactile sensitivity) are more dependent on sight readers and recordings. Simple tasks—such as labeling cans, boxes, or cartons in a bathroom or kitchen—become nearly impossible to complete.

Braille writing is accomplished through the use of a slate and stylus. Using this procedure, a student writes a mirror image of the reading code, moving from right to left. The writing process may be facilitated by using a braillewriter, a hand-operated machine with six keys that correspond to each dot in the braille cell.

Innovations for braille readers that reduce some of the problems associated with the medium include the Mountbatten Brailler and the Braille 'n Speak. The Mountbatten Brailler is electronic and, hence, easier to operate than a manual unit. The Mountbatten Brailler weighs about 15 pounds and can be hooked up to a computer keyboard attachment to input information.

The Braille 'n Speak is a pocket-size battery-powered braille note taker with a keyboard for data entry with voice output. The device can translate braille into synthesized speech or print. Files may be printed in formatted text to a printer designed to enable users to input information through a braille keyboard. The Braille 'n Speak has accessories for entering or reading text for a host computer, for reading computer disks, and for sending or receiving a fax.

In regard to educational programs for students who are blind, the U.S. Congress responded to concerns that services for these students were not addressing their unique educational and learning needs, particularly their needs for instruction in reading, writing, and composition. In IDEA, Congress mandated that schools make provision for instruction in braille and the use of braille unless the IEP team determines that such instruction and use are not appropriate to the needs of the student (U.S. Department of Education, 2014).

One tactile device that does not use the braille system is the Optacon scanner. This machine exposes printed material to a camera and then reproduces it on a fingerpad, using a series of vibrating pins that are tactile reproductions of the printed material. Developed by J. C. Bliss, Optacons have been available commercially since 1971, and thousands are currently in use worldwide. Although the Optacon greatly expands access to the printed word, it has drawbacks as well. It requires tactile sensitivity, so reading remains a slow, laborious process. Additionally, considerable training is required for individuals to become skilled users. These drawbacks, along with the development of reading machines, have resulted in the declining use and production of the Optacon scanner.

Photo 13.6 The Braille 'n Speak translates braille into synthesized speech and is so portable that it can be carried anywhere.

Many of the newer communication systems do not make use of the tactile sense because it is not functional for all people who are blind (many, including some elderly people, do not have tactile sensitivity). Such individuals must rely solely on the auditory sense to acquire information. Specialized auditory media for people who are blind are becoming increasingly available. One example is the reading machine, hailed as a major breakthrough in technology for people with a vision loss. Reading machines convert printed matter into synthetic speech at a rate of 1 to 2.5 pages per minute. They can also convert print to braille. The costs associated with reading machines have decreased substantially in the past few years; most can be purchased with computer accessories for about $1,000. Several advocacy organizations for those with blindness and many banks throughout the United States currently provide low-interest loans for people with vision loss so that they can purchase the device. The first commercial reading machines were invented by Ray Kurzweil in the 1970s, culminating in today's L&H Kurzweil 1000 and 3000 Reading Systems. The Kurzweil 1000 makes any printed or electronic text easily accessible to people with low vision or blindness. The Kurzweil 3000 provides struggling readers the opportunity to learn from the same content and curriculum materials as their peers by facilitating assigned readings, assisting in the learning of critical study skills, and independently completing writing projects and tests (Kurzweil Technologies, 2012).

Reading machines are now readily available and affordable for people with low vision through a number of companies worldwide. The most recent reading machine software and newly developed "apps" can be found in pocket-size devices, including smartphones and tablets (i.e., iPad.), in addition to desktop personal computers and laptops. E-readers, such as the Amazon Kindle and Nook, have the capability of increasing text size with one touch, thus significantly enhancing availability for people with low vision to all types and forms of text. Although printed text is not likely to go away anytime in the foreseeable future, the affordable e-readers and new tablet technologies are clearly changing the face of publishing. Such technologies can only mean good news for people with low vision or blindness. Other auditory aids that assist people who are blind include personal computers, smartphones, electronic tablets, calculators, watches, calendars and e-readers with voice output; digital recorders; and numerous other personal digital assistants (PDAs). For example, the Note Teller is a small, compact machine that can identify denominations of U.S. currency using a voice synthesizer that communicates in either English or Spanish.

**Standard 2**
Learning Environments

Communication media that facilitate participation of people with vision loss in the community include specialized library and newspaper services that offer books in large print, on cassette, and in braille. The *New York Times*, for example, publishes a weekly special edition with type three times the size of its regular type. The sale of large-print books has increased during the past ten years; many have also become available through the Internet or on computer disc (electronic books).

Responding to a human voice, devices known as **personal digital assistants (PDAs)** can look up a telephone number and make a phone call. Using a synthesized voice, some PDAs can read a newspaper delivered over telephone lines, balance a checkbook, turn home appliances on and off, and maintain a daily appointment book.

***Closed-Circuit Television*** Closed-circuit television (CCTV) systems are another means to enlarge the print from books and other written documents. Initially explored in the 1950s, CCTV systems became more practical in the 1970s, and they are now in wider use than ever before. The components of the CCTV systems include a small television camera with variable zoom lens and focusing capacity, a TV monitor, and a sliding platform table for printed materials. An individual sits in front of the television monitor to view printed material that can be enhanced up to 60 times its original size through the use of the TV camera and zoom lens. Some CCTVs are also available with split-screen capability to allow near and distant objects to be viewed together. These machines can also accept input directly from a computer as well as printed material.

More recently, some residential schools have advocated an open system of intervention. These programs are based on the philosophy that children who are blind should have every opportunity to gain the same experiences that would be available if they were growing up in their own communities. Both open and closed residential facilities exist today as alternative intervention modes; they are no longer the primary social or educational systems available to people who are blind. Just like Darran in one of the chapter Snapshots, the vast majority of people who are blind or partially sighted now live at home, attend local public schools, and interact within the community. For more information about including people with vision loss in family, school, and community, see this chapter's Community Support for Lifelong Inclusion on p. 348.

Educational programs for students with vision loss are based on the principle of flexible placement. Thus, a wide variety of services are available to these students, ranging from general education class placement, with little or no assistance from specialists, to separate residential schools. Between these two placements, the public schools generally offer several alternative classroom structures, including the use of consulting teachers, resource rooms, part-time special classes, or full-time special classes. Placement of students in one of these programs depends on the extent to which the loss of vision affects their overall educational achievement. Many students with vision loss are able to function successfully within inclusive educational programs if the learning environment is adapted to meet their needs.

Some organizations advocating for students who are blind strongly support the concept of flexible placements within a continuum ranging from general education classroom to residential school (American Foundation for the Blind, 2015). The American Foundation for the Blind recommends a full continuum of alternative placements, emphasizing that students who are visually impaired are most likely to succeed in educational systems where appropriate instruction and services are provided in a full array of program options by qualified staff to address each student's unique educational needs. Whether the student is to be included in the general education classroom or taught in a special class, a vision specialist must be available, either to support the general education classroom teacher or to provide direct instruction to the student. A vision specialist has received concentrated training in the education of students with vision loss. This specialist and the rest of the educational support team have knowledge of appropriate educational assessment techniques, specialized curriculum materials and teaching approaches, and the use of various communication media. Specialized instruction for students who have vision loss may include a major modification in curricula, including teaching concepts that children who are sighted learn incidentally (such as walking down the street, getting from one room to the next in the school building, getting meals in the cafeteria, and using public transportation).

**Access to Health Care and Other Community Services** The nature of health care services depends on the type and severity of the loss. For people who are partially sighted, use of an optical aid can vastly improve access to the visual world. Most of these aids take the form of corrective glasses or contact lenses, which are designed to magnify the image on the retina. Some aids magnify the retinal image within the eye, and others clarify the retinal image. Appropriate use of optical aids, in conjunction with regular medical examinations, not only helps correct existing visual problems but may also prevent further deterioration of existing vision.

Surgery, muscle exercises, and drug therapy have also played important roles in treating people with vision loss. Interventions may range from complex laser surgical procedures and corneal transplants to the process known as atropinization, in which the dominant eye use is strategically reduced to allow muscle control to develop in the less dominant eye.

Social services can begin with infant stimulation programs and counseling for the family. As children grow older, group counseling can help the family cope with their feelings about blindness and provide guidance in the area of human sexuality (limited vision may distort perception of the physical body). Counseling eventually extends into matters focusing on marriage, family, and adult relationships. For adults with vision loss, special guidance may be necessary in preparation for employment and independent living.

Mobility of people with vision loss can be enhanced in large cities by the use of auditory pedestrian signals known as audible traffic signals (ATS) at crosswalks. The *walk* and *don't walk* signals are indicated by auditory cues, such as actual verbal messages (e.g., "Please do not cross yet"), different bird chirps for each signal, or a Sonalert buzzer. ATS is somewhat controversial among people who are blind and professionals in the field. Those who do not support the use of ATS have two basic concerns: First, the devices promote negative public attitudes, indicating a presumption that such assistance is necessary for people who are blind to be mobile. Second, the devices may actually contribute to unsafe conditions because they mask traffic noise for people who are blind.

Restaurant menus, elevator floor buttons, and signs in buildings (such as rest rooms) can be produced in braille. Telephones, credit cards, personal checks, ATM cards, special mailing tubes, and panels for household appliances are also available in braille. Access to community services is greatly enhanced by devices that use synthesized speech for purchasing subway and rail tickets and for obtaining money from automatic teller machines.

**Atropinization**
Treatment for cataracts that involves washing the eye with atropine, permanently dilating the pupil.

**Standard 4**
Assessment

## Looking Toward a Bright Future

In the United States, nearly 11 million people have an irreversible hearing loss, and 9 million people have vision loss that will require some type of specialized services and supports. For these individuals, life in the 21st century is very different than for the generations that came before them. New research on effective education, health care, and social services, as well as advances in new technologies, is enhancing life in school, family, and community every day. Major advances in computer programs are now readily available to assist school-age students with a hearing loss across a variety of academic subject areas, from reading and writing to learning basic sign language. The Internet has created a whole new world for those with a hearing loss as well as their hearing peers through social networking, interactive chat rooms, and an infinite number of websites.

For people with vision loss, print-to-speech reading machines, such as the Kurzweil 3000, have become very small, inexpensive, palm-sized devices that can read books, printed documents, and other real-world texts such as signs and displays. GPS technology has made available user-friendly navigation devices that assist people in getting around; these devices are particularly helpful for those with a vision loss who need to avoid physical obstacles in their path and move easily through their environment (Kurzweil Technologies, 2012). Braille readers can now read their books on the Internet thanks to a historic technological breakthrough by the Library of Congress called Web-Braille. Readers now have access to more than 3,000 electronic braille books recently placed on the Internet. Many hundreds of new titles are added each year. As a result of new computer technology, braille readers may now access Web-Braille digital braille book files with a computer and a refreshable braille display (electronic device that raises or lowers an array of pins to create a line of braille characters) or a braille embosser (Library of Congress, 2012). It is indeed a changing world for those with sensory disability—a world that holds the promise of a bright future.

## COMMUNITY SUPPORT FOR LIFELONG INCLUSION

## People with Hearing and/or Vision Loss

### Early Childhood Years

#### Tips for Families

- Orient your family members (children, cousins, and other extended family members) so they have a good understanding about their supportive roles and how they can be understanding, helpful, and encouraging.

- Keep informed about organizations that can provide support to your child with a vision or hearing loss.

- Get in touch with your local health, social services, and education agencies about infant, toddler, and preschool programs for your child.

- Become familiar with the individualized family service plan (IFSP) and how it can serve as a planning tool to support the inclusion of your child in early intervention programs.

- Collaborate with professionals to determine what modes of communication (oral, manual, and/or total communication) will be most effective in developing early language skills in your child with a hearing loss.

- Provide appropriate and multiple sources of input for your child with a vision or hearing loss.

- Help your child with a vision loss to become oriented to the environment

by removing all unnecessary obstacles around the home (e.g., shoes left on the floor, partially opened doors, a vacuum cleaner left out).

#### Tips for Preschool Teachers

- Focus on developing expressive and receptive communication in the classroom as early as possible in your child with a hearing loss.

- Help classmates interact with children with a hearing or vision loss in appropriate ways. Parents and other specialists can give you helpful suggestions.

- If a child with a hearing loss doesn't respond to sound, have the hearing children learn to stand in the line of sight.

- Work closely with parents so that early communication and skill development for a young child with a hearing loss are consistent across school and home environments.

- Become very familiar with acoustical devices (e.g., hearing aids) that a young child with a hearing loss may use. Make sure that these devices are worn properly and that they work in the classroom environment.

- Instruction in special mobility techniques should begin as early as possible with a young child who has vision loss.

#### Tips for Preschool Personnel

- Support the inclusion of young children with a hearing or vision loss in your classrooms and programs.

- Support teachers, staff, and volunteers as they attempt to create successful experiences for young children with a hearing or vision loss in the preschool setting.

- Collaborate with families to keep them informed and active members of the school community.

#### Tips for Neighbors and Friends

- Collaborate with the family of a young child with a hearing or vision loss to seek opportunities for interactions with peers in neighborhood play settings.

- Focus on the capabilities of young children with a hearing or vision loss, rather than on the disabilities. Understand how children with a hearing loss communicate: Orally? Manually? Or both? If a child uses sign language, take the time to learn fundamental signs that will enhance your communication with him or her.

- Help children with a vision loss to develop a sense of touch and to use hearing to acquire information. Young children may also need assistance in learning to smile and make eye contact with others.

- Help children in the classroom who have sight interact with a child with vision loss by teaching them to speak directly in a normal tone of voice.

- Become very familiar with both tactile (e.g., braille) and auditory aids (e.g., personal readers) that young children may use to acquire information.

## Elementary Years

### Tips for Families

- Learn about your rights as parents of a child with a hearing or vision loss. Actively collaborate with professionals in the development of your child's individualized education program (IEP). Through active participation, establish goals on the IEP that will focus on your child's unique and particular needs.

- Participate in as many school functions for parents as possible (e.g., PTA, parent advisory groups, volunteering) to connect your family to the school.

- Seek information on in-school and extracurricular activities available that will enhance opportunities for your child to interact with school peers.

- Keep the school informed about the medical needs of your child with a hearing loss. If he or she needs or uses acoustical devices to enhance hearing capability, help school personnel understand how these devices work.

- If your child with a vision loss needs or uses specialized mobility devices to enhance access to the environment, help school personnel understand how these devices work.

### Tips for General Education Classroom Teachers

- Outline schoolwork (e.g., the schedule for the day) on paper or the blackboard so a student with a hearing loss can see it.

- Remember that students with hearing loss don't always know how words fit together to make understandable sentences. Help students develop skills by always writing in complete sentences.

- Have students with a hearing loss sit where they can see the rest of the class as easily as possible. Choose a buddy to sit nearby to help a student with a hearing loss stay aware of what is happening within the classroom.

- Don't be surprised to see gaps in learning. Demonstrations of disappointment or shock will make students feel at fault.

- Be sure to help students with a hearing or vision loss know what is going on at all times (e.g., pass on announcements made over the intercom).

- Have scripts (or outlines of scripts) for movies and videotapes used in class. Let a student with a hearing loss read the script for the movie.

- When working with an interpreter, remember to:

  - Introduce the interpreter to the class at the beginning of the year, and explain his or her role.

  - Always speak directly to the student, not to the interpreter.

  - Pause when necessary to allow the interpreter to catch up, because he or she may often be a few words behind.

- Face the class when speaking. (When using a blackboard, write on the board first, then face the class to speak.)

- Include students who are deaf in class activities, and encourage these students to participate in answering questions.

- Introduce the vision specialist to the class. A professional trained in the education of students with vision loss can serve as an effective consultant in several areas (e.g., mobility training, use of special equipment, communication media, and instructional strategies).

- Encourage peer support, an effective tool for learning, in the classroom setting. Peer buddy systems can be established in the school to help children with initial mobility needs and/or to provide any tutoring that would help them succeed in the general education classroom.

### Tips for School Personnel

- Integrate school resources as well as children. Wherever possible, help general education classroom teachers access the human and material resources necessary to meet the needs of students with a hearing or vision loss. For example:

  - Keep in close contact with the *audiologist*, and seek advice on the student's hearing and the acoustic devices being used.

  - The *special education teacher* trained in hearing loss is necessary both as a teacher of students with a hearing loss and as a consultant to general educators. Activities can range from working on the development of effective communication skills to dealing with behavioral difficulties. General education teachers may even decide to work with the special education teacher on learning sign language, if appropriate.

  - Work with *speech and language specialists*. Many students with a hearing loss will need help with speech acquisition and application in the school setting.

  - A *vision specialist* trained in the education of students with vision loss can serve as an effective consultant to you and the children in several areas (e.g., mobility training, use of special equipment, communication media, and instructional strategies).

  - Students with a vision loss often have associated medical problems. An *ophthalmologist* is helpful for helping teachers understand any related medical needs that can affect a child's educational experience.

  - Students with sensory disabilities often lag in motor development. Create opportunities with an *adapted physical educator* for physical play that can build motor skills, balance, social connections, and self-confidence.

### Tips for Neighbors and Friends

- Help families with a child with a hearing or vision loss to be an integral part of neighborhood and friendship networks. Seek ways to include the family and the child in neighborhood activities (e.g., outings, barbecues, outdoor yard and street cleanups, crime watches).

## Secondary and Transition Years

### Tips for Families

- Become familiar with adult services systems (e.g., rehabilitation, Social Security, health care) while your son or daughter is still in high school. Understand the type of vocational or employment training needed prior to graduation.
- Create opportunities outside of school for your son or daughter to participate in activities with same-age hearing peers.
- Allow teens and young adults opportunities for independence that balance risk and risk management.

### Tips for General Education Classroom Teachers

- Collaborate with specialists in hearing or vision loss and other school personnel to help students adapt to subject matter in your classroom (e.g., science, math, physical education).
- Become aware of the needs of students with a hearing or vision loss in your classroom and with the resources available for them. Facilitate student learning by establishing peer support systems (e.g., note takers) to help students with a hearing loss be successful.
- Use diagrams, graphs, and visual representations whenever possible when presenting new concepts to a student with a hearing loss.
- Help students with a hearing or vision loss become involved in extracurricular high school activities. If you are the faculty sponsor of a club or organization, explore whether students are interested and how they could get involved.
- Maintain positive and ongoing contact with the family.

### Tips for School Personnel

- Encourage parents of high school–age students with a hearing or vision loss to participate in school activities (such as committees and PTA).
- Parents will be more active when school personnel have general and positive contact with the family.

### Tips for Neighbors, Friends, and Potential Employers

- Collaborate with family and school personnel to create opportunities for students with a hearing or vision loss to participate in community activities as much as possible with peers.
- As a potential employer for people with a hearing or vision loss, work with the high school and vocational rehabilitation counselors to locate and establish employment training sites.

## Adult Years

### Tips for Families

- Become aware of the supports and services available for your son or daughter in the local community in which they will live as adults. What formal supports are available in the community through government-funded programs or advocacy organizations for people with a hearing loss?
- Explore adult services in the local community in the areas of postsecondary education, employment, and recreation.

### Tips for Neighbors, Friends, and Potential Employers

- Seek ways to become part of a community support network for individuals with a hearing or vision loss. Be alert to ways in which these individuals can become and remain actively involved in community employment, neighborhood recreational activities, and local church functions.
- As potential employers in the community, seek out information on employment of people with a hearing or vision loss. Locate programs that focus on establishing employment opportunities for people with a hearing or vision loss, while meeting your needs as an employer.

## Chapter Review

**13-1 Describe how the lives of people with sensory disabilities have changed since the advent of IDEA.**

- IDEA's commitment to education in the least restrictive environment has resulted in classroom inclusion of many children and youth who have sensory disabilities.
- Technological advances over the last three decades have led to improved outcomes in academics, social opportunities, and independence for people who have sensory disabilities.

**13-2 Explain the various definitions and classifications of hearing and vision loss.**

*Hearing Loss*

- People who are deaf typically have profound or total loss of auditory sensitivity and very little, if any, auditory perception.
- For people who are deaf, the primary means of information input is through vision; speech received through the ears is not understood.

- People who are hard of hearing (partially hearing) generally have residual hearing through the use of a hearing aid, which is sufficient to process language through the ear successfully.

*Vision Loss*

- Legal blindness is determined by visual acuity of 20/200 or worse in the best eye after correction or by a field of vision of 20 percent or less.

- Educational definitions of blindness focus primarily on students' inability to use vision as an avenue for learning.

- People who are partially sighted have a visual acuity greater than 20/200 but not greater than 20/70 in the best eye after correction.

- People who are partially sighted can still use vision as a primary means of learning.

## 13-3  Describe the characteristics and prevalence of children and youth with sensory disabilities.

*Hearing Loss*

- Estimates of hearing loss in the United States are as high as 28 million people; approximately 11 million people have significant irreversible hearing loss, and one million are deaf.

- More than 69,000 students between the ages of 6 and 21 have a hearing impairment and are receiving special education services in U.S. schools. These students account for approximately 1.2 percent of school-age students identified as having a disability.

*Vision Loss*

- Approximately 20 percent of all children and adults have some vision loss; 3 percent (9 million people) have a significant vision loss that will require some type of specialized services and supports.

- Fifty percent of people over the age of 65 experience a significant loss of vision (including cataracts).

- Over 23,000 students have visual impairments and receive specialized services in U.S. public schools.

## 13-4  List the causes and risk factors associated with sensory disabilities.

*Hearing Loss*

- Although more than 200 types of deafness have been related to hereditary factors, the cause of 50 percent of all hearing loss remains unknown.

- A common hereditary disorder is otosclerosis (bone destruction in the middle ear).

- Nonhereditary hearing problems evident at birth may be associated with maternal health problems: infections (e.g., rubella), anemia, jaundice, central nervous system disorders, the use of drugs, sexually transmitted disease, chicken pox, anoxia, and birth trauma.

- Acquired hearing losses are associated with postnatal infections, such as measles, mumps, influenza, typhoid fever, and scarlet fever.

- Environmental factors associated with hearing loss include extreme changes in air pressure caused by explosions, head trauma, foreign objects in the ear, and loud noise. Loud noise is rapidly becoming one of the major causes of hearing problems.

- Intellectual development for people with hearing loss is more a function of language development than of cognitive ability. Any difficulties in performance appear to be closely associated with speaking, reading, and writing the English language but are not related to level of intelligence.

- Speech and English language skills are the areas of development most severely affected for those with a hearing loss. The effects of a hearing loss on English language development vary considerably.

- Most people with a hearing loss are able to use speech as the primary mode for language acquisition. People who are congenitally deaf are unable to receive information through the speech process unless they have learned to speech-read.

- Reading is the academic area most negatively affected for students with a hearing loss.

- Social and psychological development in children with a hearing loss may be delayed due to barriers in language acquisition, which may lead to limited opportunities for social interaction. Children who are deaf may have more adjustment challenges when attempting to communicate with children who can hear, but they appear to be more secure when conversing with children who are also deaf.

*Vision Loss*

- A number of genetic conditions can result in vision loss, including albinism, retinitis pigmentosa, retinoblastoma, optic atrophy, cataracts, severe myopia associated with retinal detachment, lesions of the cornea, abnormalities of the iris, microphthalmia, hydrocephalus, anophthalmia, and glaucoma.

- Acquired disorders that can lead to vision loss prior to birth include radiation, maternal drug use, and infections. Vision loss after birth may be due to several factors, including trauma, infections, inflammations, and tumors.

- The leading cause of acquired blindness in children worldwide is vitamin A deficiency (xerophthalmia). Cortical visual impairment (CVI) is also a leading cause of acquired blindness.

- Refractive eye problems occur when the cornea or lens fail to focus light rays properly on the retina. Refractive problems include hyperopia (farsightedness), myopia (nearsightedness), astigmatism (blurred vision), and cataracts.

- Muscle disorders occur when the major muscles within the eye are inadequately developed or atrophic, resulting in a loss of control and an inability to maintain tension. Muscle disorders include nystagmus (uncontrolled rapid eye movement), strabismus (crossed eyes), and amblyopia (loss of vision due to muscle imbalance).

- Receptive eye problems occur when the retina and/or optic nerve degenerate or become damaged. Receptive eye problems include optic atrophy, retinitis pigmentosa, retinal detachment, retinopathy of prematurity, and glaucoma.

## 13-5  Describe the assessment procedures used to identify sensory disabilities in children and youth.

- Early detection of hearing and vision loss can prevent or minimize the impact of the disability on the overall development of an individual.

*Hearing Loss*
- A multidisciplinary approach is often used in the assessment of hearing loss. Specialists may include pediatricians or family practitioners, geneticists, otologists, and audiologists.
- Following assessment of hearing loss, treatment may include medical therapy, sound amplification techniques, or surgical procedures.

*Vision Loss*
- Much vision loss can be prevented through genetic screening and counseling, appropriate prenatal care, and early developmental assessment.

## 13-6 Describe the different interventions for children and youth with sensory disabilities from early childhood through adulthood.

*Hearing Loss*
- Most children and youth who have hearing loss (77 percent) are taught in inclusive classrooms for at least part of the school day.
- There are four approaches to education for students who have hearing loss:
  - The auditory approach to communication emphasizes the use of amplified sound and residual hearing to develop oral communication skills.
  - The oral approach to communication emphasizes the use of amplified sound and residual hearing but may also employ speech-reading, reading and writing, and speech training.
  - The manual approach stresses the use of signs in teaching children who are deaf to communicate.
  - Total communication employs the use of residual hearing, amplification, speech-reading, speech training, reading, and writing in combination with manual systems to teach communication skills to children with a hearing loss.

*Vision Loss*
- Children with vision loss are at a distinct disadvantage in developing speech and language skills because they are unable to visually associate words with objects. Preschool-age and school-age children with vision loss may develop a phenomenon known as verbalisms, or the excessive use of speech (wordiness), which may lead to using words that have little meaning to them.
- In the area of written language, students with vision loss have more difficulty organizing thoughts to write a composition. Decoding for reading may be delayed because such students often use braille or large-print books as the media to decode.

Reading comprehension is also affected because it depends so much on the experiences of the reader.
- Other factors that may influence academic achievement include (1) late entry into school; (2) failure in inappropriate school programs; (3) loss of time in school due to illness, treatment, or surgery; (4) lack of opportunity; and (5) slow rate of acquiring information.
- People with vision loss are unable to imitate the physical mannerisms of sighted peers and thus do not develop body language, an important form of social communication.
- People with vision loss are often excluded from social activities that are integrally related to the use of vision, thus reinforcing the mistaken idea that they do not want to participate.
- Lack of sight may prevent people from understanding their own relative position in space, and may affect fine motor coordination and interfere with their ability to manipulate objects.
- People who are blind do not perform as well as people with sight on complex tasks of perception, including form identification, spatial relations, and perceptual-motor integration.
- Education programs for students who are blind or have partial sight should include the following:
  - *Mobility and orientation training* focuses on the ability to move safely, efficiently, and independently through the environment, enhancing individuals' opportunities to learn more about the world and thus be less dependent on others. Lack of mobility restricts individuals with vision loss in nearly every aspect of educational life.
  - *Daily living skills* acquisition for children with vision loss should include routine daily living skills that are not easily learned through everyday experiences. These children must be encouraged and supported as they develop life skills, and not be overprotected from everyday challenges and risks by family and friends.
- The development of optical aids, including corrective glasses and contact lenses, has greatly improved access to the sighted world for people with vision loss.
- Medical treatment may range from complex laser surgical procedures and corneal transplants to drug therapy (such as atropinization).
- Mobility of people with vision loss can be enhanced by the use of auditory pedestrian signals. Restaurant menus, elevator floor buttons, and signs in buildings (such as rest rooms) can be produced in braille. Access to community services is greatly enhanced by devices that use synthesized speech.

## Council for Exceptional Children (CEC) Standards to Accompany Chapter 13

If you are thinking about a career in special education, you should know that many states use national standards developed by the Council for Exceptional Children (CEC) to assess a teacher candidate's knowledge and skills for working with students with disabilities. See a complete listing of the seven CEC Content Standards on the inside cover of this text.

1 Learner Development and Individual Learning Difference
2 Learning Environments
4 Assessment
5 Instructional Planning and Strategies
6 Professional Learning and Ethical Practice

## Mastery Activities and Assignments

To master the content within this chapter, complete the following activities and assignments:

1. Complete a written test of the chapter's content. If your instructor requires a written test of your content knowledge for this chapter, keep a copy for your portfolio.
2. Review the Case Study for Embracing Diversity, "Xeeb," and respond in writing to the Application Questions.

Keep a copy of the Case Studies and your written responses for your portfolio.

3. Participate in a community service learning activity. Community service is a valuable way to enhance your learning experience. Develop a reflective journal of the service learning experience for your portfolio.

## CHAPTER 14

# Physical Disabilities and Other Health Disorders

© Lisa F. Young/Shutterstock.com

## Learning Objectives

*After you complete this chapter, you will be able to:*

**14-1** Describe how the lives of people with physical disabilities and other health disorders have changed since the advent of IDEA.

**14-2** Describe cerebral palsy, its prevalence, causation, and related interventions.

**14-3** Describe spina bifida, its prevalence, causation, and related interventions.

**14-4** Describe spinal cord injury, its prevalence, causation, and related interventions.

**14-5** Describe muscular dystrophy, its prevalence, causation, and related interventions.

**14-6** Describe AIDS, its prevalence, causation, and related interventions.

**14-7** Describe asthma, its prevalence, causation, and related interventions.

**14-8** Describe epilepsy, its prevalence, causation, and related interventions.

**14-9** Describe diabetes, its prevalence, causation, and related interventions.

**14-10** Describe cystic fibrosis, its prevalence, causation, and related interventions.

**14-11** Describe sickle-cell disease, its prevalence, causation, and related interventions.

**14-12** Describe traumatic brain injury, its prevalence, causation, and related interventions.

**14-13** Describe attention deficit/hyperactivity disorder (ADHD), its prevalence, causation, and related interventions.

# I Have Cerebral Palsy ... It Doesn't Have Me!

Hi! My name is Michael Anwar, and I am a fifth-grade general education student at Evergreen Elementary in the Mead School District in Mead, Washington. I was born with cerebral palsy. The doctors told my mom that I would never be able to do things like most kids. For instance, I would never be able to walk.

There are many different types of cerebral palsy. I have ataxic cerebral palsy, which is characterized by fluctuating muscle tone and uncoordinated movement patterns. My cerebral palsy affects my gross motor skills (balance, posture, functional mobility), fine motor skills (hand skills), and communication skills (articulation and breathing).

When I first started school, I had difficulty walking, talking, singing, maintaining balance to sit at a table, getting on and off the school bus, eating, keeping up with my assignments, managing my clothing and backpack, using the bathroom, and all of the other typical things that preschoolers do (e.g., cutting, coloring, gluing, holding a crayon).

At school, I have an individualized education plan (IEP). This is a legally binding document that defines my education program. My team is comprised of me, my mom and dad, a paraeducator, teacher, education

Courtesy of Michael Anwar

specialist, school psychologist, as well as occupational, physical, and speech therapists. Through the years, they have taught me to be my own self-advocate.

Thanks to a lot of hard work on my part and with my therapist's help, I am now independent in almost everything I do at school. I can independently walk, talk, and sing. I can sit at a regular desk and get on and off the school bus with my neighborhood friends. During lunch, I can carry my own lunch tray, eat with my friends, and play safely on the playground. I am able to keep up with all of my classroom assignments because my teacher and paraeducator support me in using assistive technology. I use a laptop with technology that allows me to scan in worksheets so

I can type on them instead of write. Throughout the school day, I am able to take my coat on and off all by myself. I can also put on my backpack at the end of the day. I am able to use the bathroom all by myself. I can hold a crayon, color, and glue, beautifully. I am also able to be independent in PE, music, and library because my teachers adapt or modify assignments as necessary.

My ability to be independent in school has inspired me to participate in outside activities. My outside interests include wheelchair basketball, football, adapted snowboarding, four-wheeling, weight lifting, playing with my two dogs, and swimming.

In the past, people with cerebral palsy did not have many options. Today, I know that I can accomplish any goal that I set for myself. The reasons that I have been able to overcome many obstacles in my life are because of my great sense of humor, my flexibility, my self-acceptance, and, besides, I am irresistibly cute! I look forward to driving, holding a job, dating, getting married, and raising a family. My disability does not disable ME ... I disable it!!!!

SOURCE: Adapted from Anwar, M., Boyd, B., & Romesburg, A. M. (2007). "I Have Cerebral Palsy ... It Doesn't Have Me!" *Exceptional Parent*, 37(6), 100.

## 14-1 A Changing Era in the Lives of People with Physical Disabilities and Other Health Disorders

Advancements and inventions in many fields are bringing hope to many children, youth, and adults with physical disabilities as well as their families. Physical disabilities may influence a person's ability to move about, to use arms and legs effectively, to swallow food, and/or to breathe independently. Physical disabilities may also affect other primary functions, such as vision, cognition, speech, language, hearing, and bowel and bladder control. However, as indicated earlier, technologies, inventions, and developments in many fields are improving the lives of young people and adults with physical disabilities.

The degree to which individuals with physical disabilities participate in their neighborhoods and communities is directly related to the quality and timeliness of treatments

**CEC**

**Standard 1**
Learner Development
and Individual Learning
Differences

**Standard 1**
Learner Development and Individual Learning Differences

**Standard 1**
Learner Development and Individual Learning Differences

received from various professionals; the nurturing and encouragement provided by parents, siblings, and teachers; the support and acceptance offered by peers, neighbors, relatives, and other community members; and the careful application of assistive and related technologies.

Developments in assistive technologies, stem cell research, person-specific medications, advanced surgical techniques, transplants, gene therapies, and other preventative and early therapies have and will continue to have lasting and positive impacts on infants, children, youth, and adults with physical disorders.

The Individuals with Disabilities Education Act (IDEA) uses the term orthopedic impairment to describe students with physical disabilities and the term other health impaired to describe students with health disorders.

The discussion of physical disabilities will be limited to a representative sample of physically disabling conditions: cerebral palsy, spina bifida, spinal cord injuries, and muscular dystrophy. We will present important information about definitions, prevalence, causation, and interventions.

As described in IDEA, health disorders cause individuals to have "limited strength, vitality, or alertness, due to chronic or acute health problems such as a heart condition, tuberculosis, rheumatic fever, nephritis, asthma, sickle-cell anemia, hemophilia, epilepsy, lead poisoning, leukemia, or diabetes which adversely affect... educational performance" (23 Code of Federal Regulations, Section 300.5 [7]). In recent years, new subgroups have emerged within the health disorders area. They are often referred to as medically fragile and/or technologically dependent (American Federation of Teachers, 2009). These individuals are at risk for medical emergencies and often require specialized support in the form of ventilators or nutritional supplements. Often children or youth who are medically fragile have progressive diseases such as cancer or AIDS. Other children have episodic conditions that lessen their attentiveness, stamina, or energy.

Health disorders affect children, youth, and adults in a variety of ways. For example, a child with juvenile diabetes who has engaged in a vigorous game of volleyball with classmates may need to drink a little fruit juice or soda pop just before or after an activity to regulate blood sugar levels. An adult with diabetes may need to follow a special diet and regularly receive appropriate doses of insulin. The following health disorders will be reviewed in this section: acquired immune deficiency syndrome (AIDS), asthma, seizure disorders (epilepsy), diabetes, cystic fibrosis (CF), sickle-cell disease (SCD), traumatic brain injury (TBI), and attention deficit/hyperactivity disorder (ADHD).

Again, there is cause for optimism for children, youth, and adults with health disorders. This optimism centers on research and development efforts in many fields that are producing new person-specific medications, gene therapies, assistive devices, new surgical procedures, and a host of other inventions that heighten an individual's capacity to function more fully and to mitigate some of the effects of the health disorders.

## 14-2 Cerebral Palsy

Cerebral palsy (CP) represents a group of chronic conditions that affect muscle coordination and body movement. It is a neuromuscular disorder caused by damage to one or more specific areas of the brain, most often occurring during fetal development usually before birth, but may follow during or shortly after birth. *Cerebral* refers to the brain, and *palsy* speaks to muscle weakness and poor motor control. Secondary conditions may develop with CP, which may improve, worsen, or remain the same (American Academy for Cerebral Palsy and Developmental Medicine, 2011; Parkes & Hill, 2010).

Movement characteristics of individuals with CP include spastic—stiff and difficult movement; athetoid—involuntary and uncontrolled movement; and ataxic—disturbed depth perception and very poor sense of balance. Individuals with spastic CP may experience ongoing challenges with pain (Gorodzinsky, Hainsworth, & Weisman, 2011). There are several categories for cerebral palsy, which depend on the part of parts of the body affected (see Table 14.1).

Individuals with CP are likely to have mild to severe problems in nonmotor areas of functioning, including hearing impairments, speech and language disorders, intellectual

| Table 14.1 | Topographical Descriptions of Paralytic Conditions |
| --- | --- |
| **Description** | **Affected Area** |
| Monoplegia | One limb |
| Paraplegia | Lower body and both legs |
| Hemiplegia | One side of the body |
| Triplegia | Three appendages or limbs, usually both legs and one arm |
| Quadriplegia | All four extremities and usually the trunk |
| Diplegia | Legs more affected than arms |
| Double hemiplegia | Both halves of the body, with one side more affected than the other |

© 2014 Cengage Learning

deficits, visual impairments, and general perceptual problems. Because of the multifaceted nature of this condition, many individuals with CP are considered people with multiple disabilities. Thus, CP cannot be characterized by any one set of common symptoms or attributes; it is a condition in which a variety of problems may be present in differing degrees of severity.

## 14-2a Prevalence and Causation

About 764,000 individuals in the United States display clinical features of CP. Nearly 10,000 infants are born each year with CP or develop it shortly after birth. The prevalence rate for CP is 3.3 per 1,000, with many more boys affected than girls (4:1) (United Cerebral Palsy, 2012). The fundamental causes of CP are insults to the brain (Cerebral Palsy Alliance, 2015). Seventy percent of these insults take place during the intrauterine period of development (Yamamoto, 2007). Thirty percent of these insults occur during the birthing process. Any condition that can adversely affect the brain can cause CP. Environmental toxins, malnutrition, radiation damage, maternal disease, infections (measles, HIV, syphilis, etc.), prematurity, trauma, multiple births, insufficient oxygen to the brain—all of these and many more are risk factors for the development of CP (United Cerebral Palsy, 2012). Early symptoms of CP include delayed motor development, abnormal muscle tone, and atypical motor functioning.

## 14-2b Interventions

There is no cure for CP; rather, professionals and parents must work to manage the condition and its various manifestations, beginning as soon as the CP is diagnosed. Early and ongoing interventions and therapies center on the child's movement, social and emotional development, learning, language, speech, and hearing.

Effective interventions for the various forms of CP are based on accurate and continuous assessments. Motor deficits and other challenges associated with CP are not unchanging but evolve over time. Continuous assessment allows care providers to adjust treatment programs and select placement options in accordance with the emerging needs of the child, youth, or adult (Parkes & Hill, 2010).

Management of CP is a multifaceted process that involves many medical and human service specialties working in teams (United Cerebral Palsy, 2012). These teams, composed of medical experts, physical and occupational therapists, teachers, social workers, volunteers, and family members, join together to help children, youth, and adults with CP realize their potential and self-selected goals. Vital goals of management/therapy may include developing or improving existing skills, decreasing complications of CP, lessening skeletal deformity, improving mobility, and developing communication skills.

**Standard 2**
Learning Environments

The thrust of the management efforts depends on the nature of the problems and strengths presented by the individual child, youth, or adult. More specifically, interventions are directed at

- preventing additional physical deformities;
- decreasing adverse symptoms;
- developing useful posture and movements;
- providing appropriate surgeries when needed;
- dealing with feeding and swallowing problems;
- developing appropriate motor skills;
- securing suitable augmentative communication and other assistive devices;
- prescribing appropriate medications to reduce spasticity, drooling, muscle spasms, seizures, and to aid body control; and
- developing mobility and appropriate independence skills. (Kahn, 2009; United Cerebral Palsy, 2012)

Because of the multifaceted nature of CP, other specialists may also be involved, including ophthalmologists, audiologists, massage therapists, speech and language clinicians, and vocational and rehabilitation specialists.

Physical and occupational therapists play significant roles in the lives of children and youth with CP (Palisano et al., 2012). These individuals provide essentially three types of crucial services: (1) assessments to detect deformities and deficits in movement quality; (2) program planning, such as assisting with the writing of IEPs and other treatment plans, selecting adaptive equipment and assistive devices, and developing home and school programs for parents and other family members; and (3) delivery of therapy services.

---

**LEARNING THROUGH SOCIAL MEDIA**

## My Life with Cerebral Palsy: Removing the Fence Around Social Barriers One Post at a Time

*Laura Forde is a young adult. She has been blogging for several years. As a child, she felt quite lonely and secluded because others her age did not know how to communicate with her. However, as she moved through her schooling, she developed greater independence, becoming a "spunky and determined adult." She now communicates regularly from her blog. What follows is one of her recent postings:*

### Why I Am Glad I Grew Up in the Time I Did

In coming up with today's post, I found myself in a reflective space.... [O]ut my window, the snow is softly falling and the forecast later today looks bleak so I am told. It is this weather that leaves the thought of going out to be an undesired one, and yet I have a strong need: the need for community.

### The Digital Age Helps the Disabled

I often wonder what my life would be like if I grew up in a different time. The Internet helps to maintain or build a community that I otherwise wouldn't have. The digital age has helped me be less lonely, less aware of my physical limitation. That isn't just because of this blog; it's Facebook, Twitter, AbilityOnline, and the other places online that I frequent.

### Why I Love Blogging and Think We All Should Have a Blog

We all have a story worth telling, and I love how the blog for me does not require any adaptation to participate; it simply requires learning and a learning curve and some dedication. But I don't "look" different nor do I do things differently from the next guy that runs a blog. Blogs are about shared experience and I hope you will do me the honor of sharing my blog with your friends and family and your community online. I feel like this blog is helping to reduce social stigma, and without the Internet, this blog wouldn't be here.

SOURCE: Copyright © 2012 by Laura Forde. Laura Forde is a blogger and public speaker from Ontario Canada you can learn more about her at http://lifeofthedifferently abled.com

School-centered services may include indirect treatment provided in the form of consultation, training, and informal monitoring of student performance; direct service through regular treatment sessions in out-of-class settings; and in-class or multisite service delivery to students in general education classrooms, in their homes, or at other community sites (Laverdure & Rose, 2012).

Recent developments in augmentative communication and computer-centered technologies have had a tremendous impact on children, youth, and adults with CP and other conditions that impair speech and language production (Light & McNaughton, 2012). Smartphone and tablet applications have revolutionized communication for these individuals. Mobile devices are more affordable and easier to manipulate than older technologies, and allow users full access to the Internet, social networks, and the ever-increasing range of specialized communication applications (McNaughton & Light, 2013). These applications allow users or caregivers to build sentences for text-to-speech production or to simply touch an icon to speak a word, phrase, or sentence. Speech recognition software allows individuals with limited movement to type by speaking into a computer or other device.

Selecting augmentative communication devices and applications for a child or youth is a team effort. Teachers, parents, speech and language specialists, physical and occupational therapists, and rehabilitation engineers play important roles in assisting with the selection process. Major benefits of augmentative and alternative communication in general education classrooms include increased interaction of students with disabilities with classroom peers, increased acceptance of students with disabilities, and greater connections with teachers—thus, resulting in improved relationships, greater learning, and better understanding of children with disabilities. As people with CP move into adulthood, they may require various kinds of support, including continuing therapy, personal assistance services, independent living services, vocational training, and counseling.

## ASSISTIVE TECHNOLOGY

### VGo: The Ultimate School-Based Robot

#### For Some Students, Attending School Isn't Possible

Injuries, extended illnesses, immune deficiencies, and other physical challenges prevent students from physically being able to attend school. School districts try to accommodate these children with special needs by providing online courses, in-home tutors, special busing, videoconferencing, and more. But these are expensive and very limiting because students miss out on the classroom experience and social life that come with attending school. Now, they can participate in classroom discussions and share in the social aspects of locker-side chats, lunch period, and moving from class to class.

#### VGo Enables Students to Attend School from a Distance

At VGo, we love putting the spotlight on Lyndon Baty, a high school student

in Knox City, Texas, who has an illness that requires him to remain at home because of the risk of physically being in class. He's a perfect example of the type of student who benefits greatly by being able to "attend" school via his VGo—or "BatyBot" as it's affectionately known at Lyndon's school.

From the safety of his home, in the morning, Lyndon gets on his computer

instead of the bus. He uses VGo to move around school, interact with teachers, chat with his friends between classes, and spend the lunch period with them without endangering his health.

Lyndon operates his VGo simply with an Internet-connected computer equipped with audio capabilities and a webcam. VGo runs for a full school day before needing to be recharged.

VGo for Remote Students has opened up academic and social environments to other students who are disabled or have immune deficiencies as well. There are no longer boundaries between them and the world that was previously inaccessible.

SOURCE: Adapted from VGo. (2012). VGo Communications, Inc. Retrieved February 22, 2012, from www.vgocom .com/remote-student.

## 14-3  Spina Bifida

"*Spina Bifida* [SB] or *myelodysplasia* is a collective term for malformations of the spinal chord and is the most common NTD [neural tube deficit]. This defect can occur at any level of the spinal cord, although it more commonly affects the lumbar and sacral spine" (Lazzaretti & Pearson, 2010, p. 671). Spina bifida (SB) is characterized by an abnormal opening in the spinal column. It originates in the first days of pregnancy, often before a mother even knows that she is expecting. Through the process of cell division and differentiation, a neural tube forms in the developing fetus. At about 26 to 27 days, this neural tube fails to completely close. This failure results in various forms of spina bifida, frequently causing paralysis of various portions of the body, depending on the location of the opening. It may or may not influence the individual's intellectual functioning. Spina bifida is usually classified as either spina bifida occulta or spina bifida cystica.

Spina bifida occulta is a very mild condition in which a small slit is present in one or more of the vertebral structures. Most people with spina bifida occulta are unaware of its presence unless they have had a spinal X-ray for diagnosis of some other condition. Spina bifida occulta has little, if any, impact on a developing infant.

Spina bifida cystica is a malformation of the spinal column in which a tumorlike sac herniates through an opening or cleft on the infant's back (see Figure 14.1). Spina bifida cystica exists in many forms; however, two prominent forms will receive attention in our discussion: spina bifida meningocele and spina bifida myelomeningocele. In spina bifida meningocele, the sac contains spinal fluid but no nerve tissue. In the myelomeningocele type, the sac contains nerve tissue.

Spina bifida myelomeningocele is the most serious form of neural tube defect (NTD). It generally results in weakness or paralysis in the legs and lower body, an inability to control the bladder or bowel voluntarily, and the presence of other orthopedic problems (club feet, dislocated hip, and so on). There are two types of myelomeningocele. In one, the tumorlike sac is open, revealing the neural tissue; in the other, the sac is closed or covered with a combination of skin and membrane.

*Figure 14.1*  ***Side Views of the Spine***

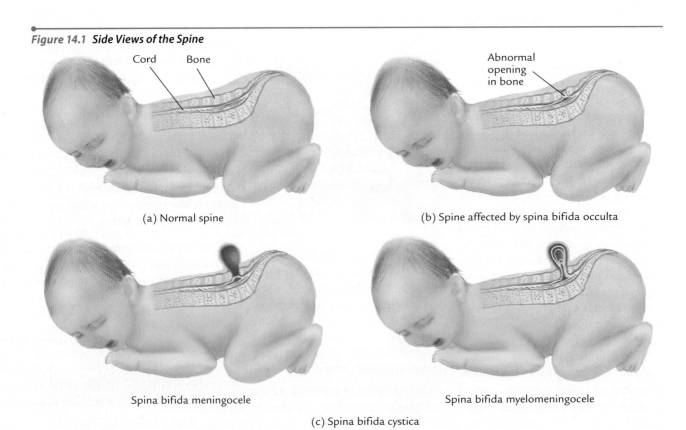

(a) Normal spine

(b) Spine affected by spina bifida occulta

Spina bifida meningocele

Spina bifida myelomeningocele

(c) Spina bifida cystica

## 14-3a  Prevalence and Causation

Prevalence figures for SB is one in 1,500 births. The highest rates for these defects occur with Hispanic women and the lowest rates appear in Asian and African American women. The prevalence of spina bifida (SB) has decreased over time in part because of prenatal screening, increased consumption of folic acid by pregnant mothers, and elective terminations of pregnancies (Centers for Disease Control and Prevention, 2014a).

The exact cause of SB is unknown, although there is a slight tendency for the condition to run in families. In fact, myelomeningocele appears to be transmitted genetically, probably as a function of certain prenatal and environmental factors interacting with genetic predispositions (Nehring, 2010). It is also possible that certain antiseizure medications taken by the mother prior to or at the time of conception, or during the first few days of pregnancy, may be responsible for the defect. Environmental factors such as nutrition and diet also play a role.

Folic acid deficiencies have been implicated strongly in the causation of SB. Pregnant mothers should take particular care to augment their diets with 0.4 mg of folic acid each day. Folic acid is a common water-soluble B vitamin. Intake of this vitamin reduces the probability of neural tube defects in developing infants (Spina Bifida Association of America, 2012). The regular use of vitamin B12 may also reduce the incidence of SB and NTDs (Nehring, 2010).

Infant exposure to various **teratogens** may also induce defects in the spine. These include valproic acid, carbamazepine (a seizure control medication), and other agents/drugs. Other causative factors include radiation, maternal hyperthermia (high fever), and excess glucose. Also, congenital rubella has been implicated in causing SB and NTDs (Nehring, 2010).

## 14-3b  Interventions

Several tests are now available to identify babies with myelomeningocele before they are born. One such test involves analysis of the mother's blood for the presence of a specific fetal protein (alpha-fetoprotein, AFT). AFT leaks from the developing child's spine into the amniotic fluid of the uterus and subsequently enters the mother's bloodstream. If blood tests prove positive for this AFT, ultrasonic scanning of the fetus may be performed to confirm the diagnosis. SB may also be detected through an ultrasound of an emerging fetus, potentially revealing a malformation of the spine.

Confirmation of the myelomeningocele creates intense feelings in parents. If the diagnosis is early in the child's intrauterine development, parents are faced with the decision of continuing or discontinuing the pregnancy or subjecting the emerging fetus to intrauterine surgery. There are, however, increased risks associated with this surgery for mothers and infants. These include early labor and delivery, fetal demise, and potential problems with bladder and bowel functioning in affected infants (Nehring, 2010). If parents decide to continue the pregnancy, they have time to process their intense feelings and to prepare for the child's surgery, birth, and care. If the decision is to discontinue the pregnancy, they must deal with the feelings produced by this action as well. If the condition is discovered at the time of the child's birth, it also produces powerful and penetrating feelings, the first of which is generally shock. All members of the health team (physicians, nurses, social workers, and so on), as well as other people (clergy, siblings, parents, and close friends), can help parents cope with the feelings they experience and the decisions that must be made.

Immediate action is often called for when the child with myelomeningocele is born, depending on the nature of the lesion, its position on the spine, and the presence of other related conditions. Decisions regarding medical interventions are extremely difficult to make, for they often entail problems and issues that are not easily or quickly resolved. For example, in 80 percent of children with myelomeningocele, a portion of the spinal cord is exposed, placing them at great risk for developing bacterial meningitis, which has a mortality rate of over 50 percent.

The decision to undertake surgery is often made quickly if the tissue sac is located very low on the infant's back. The purpose of the surgery is to close the spinal opening and lessen the potential for infection.

**Teratogens**
Substances or conditions that cause malformations.

*Figure 14.2  Ventriculoperitoneal Shunt*

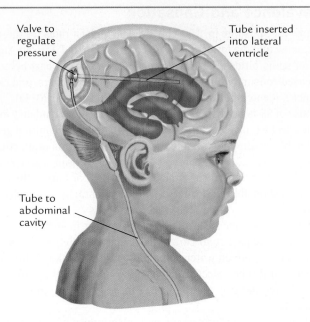

Valve to
regulate
pressure

Tube inserted
into lateral
ventricle

Tube to
abdominal
cavity

**Standard 2**
Learning Environments

**Standard 2**
Learning Environments

**Standard 7**
Collaboration

Another condition that often accompanies myelomeningocele is hydrocephalus, a condition characterized by excessive accumulation of cerebral fluid within the brain. More than 25 percent of children with myelomeningocele exhibit this condition at birth. Moreover, 70 to 90 percent of all children with myelomeningocele develop it after they are born. Surgery may also be performed for this condition in the first days of life. The operation includes inserting a small, soft plastic tube between the ventricles of the brain and connecting this tube with an absorption site in the abdomen. The excessive spinal fluid is diverted from the ventricles of the brain to a thin layer of tissue, the peritoneum, which lines the abdominal cavity (see Figure 14.2).

Children with spina bifida myelomeningocele may have little if any voluntary bowel or bladder control. This condition is directly attributable to the paralysis caused by malformation of the spinal cord and removal of the herniated sac containing nerve tissues. However, children as young as 4 years old can be taught effective procedures to manage bladder problems. As they mature, they can develop effective regimens and procedures for bowel management (Velde, Biervliet, Bruyne, & Winckel, 2013).

Physical therapists play a critical role in helping children as they learn to cope with the paralysis caused by myelomeningocele (Stark et al., 2014). Paralysis obviously limits the children's exploratory activities, so critical to later learning and perceptual–motor performance. With this in mind, many such children are fitted with modified skateboards or other wheeled devices that allow them to explore their surroundings. Utilizing the strength in their arms and hands, they become quite adept in exploring their home and neighborhood environments. Gradually, they move to leg braces, crutches, a wheelchair, or a combination of the three. Some children are ambulatory and do not require the use of a wheelchair.

Education programs for students with serious forms of spina bifida vary according to the needs of each student (Jahns, 2008). The vast majority of students with myelomeningocele are served in general education classrooms. School personnel can contribute to the well-being of these students in several ways: making sure that physical layouts permit students to move effectively with their crutches or wheelchairs through classrooms and other settings; supporting students' efforts in using various bladder and bowel management procedures and ensuring appropriate privacy in using them; requiring these students to be as responsible as anyone else in the class for customary assignments; involving them fully in field trips, physical education, and other school-related activities; and communicating regularly with parents. Additionally, if a student has a shunt, teachers should be alert to signs of its malfunctioning, including fever, irritability, neck pain, headache, vomiting, reduced alertness, and decline in school performance. These symptoms may appear very quickly and may be mistaken for flu-like symptoms. Teachers should take any of these aforementioned symptoms very seriously. As with all physical disabilities, collaboration and cooperation among all caregivers are vitally important to the well-being of each child or youth.

## 14-4  Spinal Cord Injury

**Standard 1**
Learner Development and Individual Learning Differences

Spinal cord injuries happen without any advanced notice. They are generally a result of some normal activity—driving a car, hiking, skiing, sledding, or diving. About 12,500 spinal cord injuries take place each year in the United States (National Spinal Cord Injury Statistical Center, 2014). "Spinal cord injury (SCI) is damage to the spinal cord that results in a loss of function such as mobility or feeling. Frequent causes of damage are trauma (car accident, gunshot, falls, etc.) or disease (polio, spina bifida, Friedreich's ataxia, etc.). The spinal cord does not have to be severed for a loss of functioning to occur. In fact, in most people with an SCI, the spinal cord is intact, but the damage to it results in loss of functioning" (Spinal Cord Injury Resource Center, 2012).

When the spinal cord is traumatized or severed, **spinal cord injury (SCI)** occurs. Trauma can result through extreme extension or flexing from a fall, an automobile accident, or a sports injury. The cord can also be severed through the same types of accidents, although such occurrences are extremely rare. Usually in such cases, the cord is bruised or otherwise injured, after which swelling and (within hours) bleeding often occurs. Gradually, a self-destructive process ensues, in which the affected area slowly deteriorates and the damage becomes irreversible (Spinal Cord Injury Resource Center, 2012).

The overall impact of injury on an individual depends on the site and nature of the insult. If the injury occurs in the neck or upper back, the resulting paralysis and effects are usually quite extensive. If the injury occurs in the lower back, paralysis is confined to the lower extremities. Similar to individuals with spina bifida, those who sustain spinal cord injuries may experience loss of voluntary bowel and bladder function.

Spinal cord injuries rarely occur without individuals sustaining other serious damage to their bodies. Accompanying injuries may include head trauma, fractures of some portion of the trunk, and significant chest injuries.

The physical characteristics of spinal cord injuries are similar to those of spina bifida myelomeningocele except there is no tendency for the development of hydrocephalus. The terms used to describe the impact of spinal cord injuries are *paraplegia*, *quadriplegia*, and *hemiplegia*. Note, however, that these terms are global descriptions of functioning and are not precise enough to convey accurately an individual's actual level of motor functioning.

### 14-4a  Prevalence and Causation

About 450,000 individuals live with SCIs in the United States. Causes include motor vehicle accidents (42 percent); violence—primarily gunshot wounds (15.3 percent); sports-related injuries (7.4 percent); falls (27.1 percent); and other causes (8.1 percent). Significant numbers, nearly 25 percent, of the SCIs are alcohol-related (Mayo Clinic, 2012). The average age for SCI injuries is now 38 years (Spinal Cord Injury Resource Center, 2012). About 5 percent of the SCIs occur in children, primarily from automobile-related accidents and falls (Liverman, Altevogt, Joy, & Johnson, 2005).

### 14-4b  Interventions

The immediate care rendered to a person with SCI is crucial. The impact of the injury can be magnified if proper procedures are not employed soon after the accident or onset of the condition. Only properly trained personnel should move and transport a child, youth, or adult with a suspected SCI (Stiens, Fawber, & Yuhas, 2013).

The first phase of treatment provided by a hospital is the management of shock. Quickly thereafter, the individual is immobilized to prevent movement and possible further damage. As a rule, surgical procedures are not undertaken immediately. The major goal of medical treatment at this point is to stabilize the spine, manage swelling, and prevent further

**Spinal cord injury (SCI)**
An injury derived from the bruising, traumatizing, or severing of the spinal cord, producing bleeding and swelling that often produce irreversible damage resulting in a loss of motor and/or sensory functioning.

## What Do You Know About Stem Cells?

Many of us hear news and talk show commentaries about stem cells, related research, and anticipated applications of the research. What follows is a series of questions and linked answers that will help you speak more knowledgeably about this exciting field of study that has profound implications for children, youth, and adults with all kinds of disabilities, diseases, and injuries.

### What is A Stem Cell?

*Stem cell* is an umbrella term used to categorize a group of cells. Stem cells come in different varieties and might be specific to a particular tissue type.

Usually, when people use the term *stem cell*, they are referring to embryonic stem cells. A stem cell is a cell that is capable of dividing asymmetrically into two daughter cells that are not exactly alike. The overwhelming majority of cells in your body cannot do this.

This may not sound too compelling, but consider that you originated from one cell. The clear cells lining the cornea of your eye and the skin cells gripping this paper originally came from the same cell. A stem cell line can grow and mature into different cell types and tissues.

### Medically, What Are the Potential Uses for Stem Cells?

Stem cells can give rise to any tissue. There are types of tissues in adults that do not regrow, or that have the potential to do so very slowly.

Neural (brain and spinal cord) tissue is an example. If scientists can figure out how to trigger neural stem cells to regrow, it may be possible to help paralyzed patients walk again or to treat diseases such as Parkinson's, Alzheimer's, or dementia.

There also exists the possibility of growing tissues for implantation, such as skin for a burn victim or an organ transplant for a cancer patient. The potential uses are numerous and it is likely that more possibilities will come forth once more is known about stem cells.

### How Are Human Embryonic Stem Cells Obtained?

Human embryonic stem cells are obtained from the inner cell mass of a blastocyst, an extremely small spherical cluster of cells present about five days after fertilization.

### Do Scientists have to Create New Embryos Specifically to Destroy Them?

Yes and no. There are already over 400,000 extra embryos that have been created via in-vitro fertilization that will never be implanted into surrogate mothers. Essentially, there are a lot of potential resources.

#### Questions for Reflection

**1.** What still puzzles you about the talk and debate about stem cells and stem cell research?

**2.** Should stem cell research be advanced to help treat individuals who have serious debilitating conditions such as Parkinson's, Alzheimer's, or dementia?

SOURCE: Adapted from Graf, R. (2009). Stem cells for dummies: A few questions answered. New University. Retrieved April 17, 2009, from www.newuniversity .org/2007/10/features/stem_cells_for_dummies42/.

complications. Pharmacological interventions are also critical during this phase of treatment. Recent studies support the use of high and frequent doses of methylprednisolone. This medication often reduces damage to nerves cells, decreases swelling near the injury site, and improves the functional outcome for the affected individual, thus reducing secondary damage. Catheterization may be employed to control urine flow, and steps may be taken to reduce swelling and bleeding at the injury site. Traction may be used to stabilize certain portions of the spinal column and cord.

Medical treatment of SCIs is lengthy and often tedious. See the nearby Reflect on This, "What Do You Know about Stem Cells?" for answers to questions about new stem cell–related treatments. Once physicians and other medical personnel have successfully stabilized the spine and treated other medical conditions, the rehabilitation process promptly begins. Individuals with SCI are taught to use new muscle combinations and to take advantage of any and all residual muscle strength. They are also taught to use orthopedic equipment, such as hand splints, braces, reachers, headsticks (for typing), and plate guards.

Traumatic SCI is accompanied by various pain syndromes—sometimes phantom pain. Relieving pain is a significant challenge over the lifespan of individuals with an SCI.

Psychiatric and other support personnel are also engaged in rehabilitation activities. Psychological adjustment to SCI and its impact on an individual's functioning can take a great deal of time and effort. The goal of all treatment is to help an injured person become as independent as possible.

## From Science Fiction to Reality: Ekso Exoskeletons

We've all seen exoskeletons in some of the most popular science fiction, even if we didn't know that's what they were called. Sigourney Weaver used an exoskeleton designed for cargo lifting in outer space to kill the alien queen in *Aliens*. Tony Stark used a more personalized and high-tech one to save the world as *Iron Man*. Believe it or not, paraplegics could be using one sooner rather than later to walk again.

Introducing the personal exoskeleton—the mechanical bodysuit that could get people with spinal cord injuries back on their feet. The military already has them, rehab clinics are using them, and with costs coming down and technology improving, it looks like they're going to be available for personal use in the near future.

courtesy of Ekso Bionics

When a skiing accident left Amanda Boxtel a T11-12 paraplegic 18 years ago, doctors told her what they have told hundreds of thousands of people with spinal cord injuries: You'll never walk again. Undeterred, she carved out a new life for herself. She started a nonprofit, helped create adaptive skiing programs, and spoke often as a motivational speaker. Still, Boxtel missed the natural feeling of simply standing

up and moving around. The closest she felt to natural body movements was when she was on horseback.

That was before she was invited to try the Ekso exoskeleton (earlier called eLegs) in 2010. The Ekso is the signature product of Ekso Bionics, one of the pioneering companies manufacturing exoskeletons. Walking with the aid of the Ekso proved even more natural than horseback riding, according to Boxtel. "I had forgotten how tall I was. How it is to look someone eye to eye," says Boxtel, adding, "[Using Ekso] was the most powerful psychological and emotional experience for me."

SOURCE: From Ramachandran, Priya. (2012). "From Science Fiction to Reality: Exoskeletons." Copyright © 2012 National Spinal Cord Injury Association a program of United Spinal Association. Reprinted with permission.

As individuals master necessary self-care skills, other educational and career objectives can be pursued with the assistance of the rehabilitation team. The members of this collaborative team change constantly in accordance with the needs of each individual.

Education for individuals with spinal cord injuries is similar to that for uninjured children or adults. Teachers must be aware, however, that some individuals with spinal cord injuries will be unable to feel pressure and pain in the lower extremities, so pressure sores and skin breakdown may occur in response to prolonged sitting. Opportunities for repositioning and movement will help prevent these problems. Parents and teachers should be aware of signs of depression that may accompany reentry into school.

## 14-5   Muscular Dystrophy

"The muscular dystrophies (MD) are a group of more than 30 genetic diseases characterized by progressive weakness and degeneration of the skeletal muscles that control movement. Some forms of MD are seen in infancy or childhood, while others may not appear until middle age or later. The disorders differ in terms of the distribution and extent of muscle weakness (some forms of MD also affect cardiac muscle), age of onset, rate of progression, and pattern of inheritance" (National Institute of Neurological Disorders and Stroke, 2012b). The muscles of the heart and some other involuntary muscles are also affected in some forms of muscular dystrophy, and a few forms involve other organs as well. Muscular dystrophy is a progressive disorder that may affect the muscles of the hips, legs, shoulders, and arms, progressively causing these individuals to lose their ability to walk and to use their arms and hands effectively and functionally. The loss of ability is attributable to fatty tissue that gradually replaces healthy muscle tissue. Heart muscle may also be affected, resulting in symptoms of heart failure. The seriousness of the various dystrophies is influenced by heredity, age of onset, the physical location and nature of onset, and the rate at which the condition progresses (National Institute of Neurological Disorders and Stroke, 2012b).

**Standard 1**
Learner Development and Individual Learning Differences

Duchenne-type muscular dystrophy (DMD) is the most common form of childhood muscular dystrophy. DMD generally manifests when children are between the ages of 2 and 6. Early in the second decade of life, individuals with DMD use wheelchairs to move from place to place. By the end of the second decade of life, or early in the third, young adults with DMD die from respiratory insufficiency or cardiac failure (Muscular Dystrophy Association, 2012).

DMD is first seen in the pelvic girdle, although it sometimes begins in the shoulder girdle muscles. With the passage of time, individuals begin to experience a loss of respiratory function and are unable to cough up secretions that may result in pneumonia. Also, severe spinal curvature develops over time with wheelchair use, although this curvature may be prevented with spinal fusion.

## 14-5a Prevalence and Causation

About 200,000 people are affected by muscular dystrophies and related disorders. About one in every 4,700 males is affected by DMD (Dooley, Gordon, Dodds, & MacSween, 2010). Mothers who are carriers transmit this condition to 50 percent of their male offspring. One-third of the cases of DMD arise by mutation in families with no history of the disease.

Abnormalities in muscle protein genes cause muscular dystrophies. Each human cell contains tens of thousands of genes. Each gene is a string of DNA and is the code or recipe for a given protein. If the recipe for a muscle-related protein is lacking or is missing a key ingredient, the results can be tragic. The missing or diminished ingredient is dystrophin, an essential and critical component of healthy muscle fibers (Muscular Dystrophy Association, 2011). Without dystrophin, muscle cells explode and eventually die.

## 14-5b Interventions

There is no known cure for muscular dystrophy. Treatments focus on maintaining or improving the individual's functioning and preserving his or her ambulatory independence for as long as possible. The first phases of maintenance and prevention are handled by physical therapists, who work to prevent or correct contractures (a permanent shortening and thickening of muscle fibers).

Drugs identified as *catabolic steroids* may have significant benefits for children and youth with DMD. The most often prescribed of these drugs is prednisone. It lessens the loss of muscle function or increases muscle strength in individuals with DMD. These drugs may lengthen the period of time in which individuals with DMD may be able to walk and to use their arms—several months to a couple of years (Parent Project Muscular Dystrophy, 2012). However, prednisone also has many potentially damaging side effects, which can be severe over a prolonged period, including loss of bone and muscle tissue, significant weight gain, loss of bone and (ironically) muscle tissue, thinning of the skin, elevated blood pressure and blood sugar, and serious psychological side effects, including depression and sleeping problems.

As DMD becomes more serious, treatment generally includes prescribing supportive devices, such as walkers, braces, night splints, surgical corsets, and hospital beds. Eventually, a person with muscular dystrophy will need to use a wheelchair.

Major symptoms that may be experienced include pain, nausea, vomiting, seizures, convulsions, decreased appetite, mouth sores, fatigue, cough, difficulty swallowing foods, and skin problems.

The terminal nature of DMD and other health conditions pose challenging problems to affected individuals, their families, and caregivers. Fortunately, significant progress has been made in helping individuals with terminal illnesses deal with death. Programs developed for families who have a terminally ill child, youth, or adult serve several purposes. They give children with terminal illnesses opportunities to ask questions about death; to express their concerns through writing, play, or other means; and to work through their feelings.

Programs for parents are designed to help them understand their children's conceptions about death, to suggest ways in which the parents might respond to certain questions or concerns, and to outline the steps they might take in successfully preparing for and responding to the child's death and related events. One such program is Compassionate Friends (Compassionate Friends, 2012). This organization, which is composed of parents who have lost children to death, provides sensitive support and resources to other parents who have lost a child to injury or disease.

At this juncture, you may want to examine the Community Support for Lifelong Inclusion feature toward the end of this chapter. It offers valuable suggestions for interacting with young children, school-age children, youth, and adults with physical disabilities.

## 14-6 Human Immunodeficiency Virus (HIV) and Acquired Immunodeficiency Syndrome (AIDS)

Acquired immunodeficiency syndrome (AIDS) is a set of symptoms and infections in individuals resulting from the specific injury to the **immune system** caused by infection with the human immunodeficiency virus (HIV). AIDS in children and youth is defined by two characteristics: (1) the presence of the **human immunodeficiency virus (HIV)**, a virus that attacks certain white blood cells within the body, and/or the presence of antibodies to HIV in the blood or tissues as well as (2) recurrent bacterial diseases (National Center for HIV/AIDS, Viral Hepatitis, STD, and TB Prevention, 2012).

Individuals with AIDS move through a series of disease stages. The first stage is the exposure stage, or the period during which the transmission of the HIV occurs. Young people may be infected with HIV but may not yet exhibit the life-threatening conditions associated with AIDS. The second stage is characterized by the production of antibodies in infected individuals. These antibodies appear about 2 to 12 weeks after the initial transmission of the virus. About 30 percent of individuals experience flu-like symptoms for a few days to several weeks. During stage three, the immune system declines, and the virus begins to destroy cells of the immune system. However, many individuals with HIV are asymptomatic during this stage. This asymptomatic phase may continue for 3 to 10 years. About half of all individuals with HIV develop AIDS within 10 years.

Most children with HIV infection are diagnosed before the illness manifests itself (Fahrner & Romano, 2010). For children, the onset of AIDS ranges from one to three years. Generally, AIDS manifests itself within two years of the initial infection (Ball & Bindler, 2008). At stage four, individuals begin to manifest symptoms of a damaged immune system, including weight loss, fatigue, skin rashes, diarrhea, and night sweats. In more severe cases, opportunistic diseases appear in individuals with AIDS. At stage five, recurrent and chronic diseases begin to take their toll on individuals. Gradually, the immune system fails and death occurs.

Researchers have identified several patterns of disease development in HIV-infected children. The mean age of onset in exposed children is about 4.1 years. About 33 percent of exposed children remain AIDS-free until up to 13 years of age. Often the most serious symptoms do not appear until these children enter school or begin their adolescent years.

### 14-6a Prevalence and Causation

The Centers for Disease Control and Prevention "estimates that 1,201,000 persons aged 13 years and older are living with HIV infection, including 168,300 (14%) who are unaware of their infection. Over the past decade, the annual number of people living with HIV has increased, while the annual number of new HIV infections has remained relatively stable. Still, the pace of new infections continues at far too high a level" (Centers for Disease Control and Prevention, 2014b). In 2012, approximately 47,989 Americans were diagnosed with HIV infection (Centers for Disease Control and Prevention, 2014b).

Increasingly, heterosexual adolescents are at greater risk than infants to contract HIV—this is because of unprotected sexual activities. Statistics indicate that nearly 2,300 adolescents aged 13 to 19 are infected annually, or about six per day (Centers for Disease Control and Prevention, 2015a). Left untreated or undiagnosed, youth may not evidence any symptoms of AIDS until 10 years later as adults.

The cause of AIDS is the human immunodeficiency virus (HIV). This virus is passed from one person to another through various means, including the exchange of bodily fluids, usually semen or vaginal secretions; blood exchange through injection drug use (IDU); and

**Immune system**
A system of organs, tissues, cells, and cell products that attack potentially disease-causing organisms or substances.

**Standard 1**
Learner Development and Individual Learning Differences

**Human immunodeficiency virus (HIV)**
A class of viruses that infect and destroy helper T cells of the immune system, making the body unable to combat and counter opportunistic infections.

**Opportunistic infection**
An infection caused by germs that are not usually capable of causing infection in healthy people but can do so given certain changes in the immune system (opportunity).

exchange through blood transfusions, perinatal contact, and breast milk. Mothers who are infected with HIV can dramatically reduce the transmission of the virus to their yet-to-be born children by taking zidovudine during pregnancy.

Many children with AIDS do not grow normally, do not make appropriate weight gains, are slow to achieve important motor milestones (crawling, walking, and so on), and evidence neurological damage (Fahrner & Romano, 2010). As HIV turns into AIDS, these children are attacked by life-threatening **opportunistic infections**. Also, many of the children, as indicated earlier, develop more serious neurological problems associated with mental retardation, cerebral palsy, and seizure disorders.

## 14-6b   Interventions

To date, there is no known cure for AIDS. The best cure for AIDS in children and youth is prevention. Treatment is generally provided by an interdisciplinary team composed of medical, educational, and health care professionals.

Much progress has been made in testing and applying new antiretroviral therapies to combat AIDS and in developing agents to treat opportunistic infections. Early diagnosis of infants with HIV is crucial. Early antiviral therapy and prophylactic treatment of opportunistic diseases can contribute significantly to the infected child's well-being and prognosis over time. Some infants benefit significantly from highly active antiretroviral therapy (HAART) (Fahrner & Romano, 2010). The frequency and nature of various treatments depend on the age of onset and the age at which the child develops the first opportunistic infection.

Providing appropriate interventions for infants with AIDS can be challenging. These infants, like infants without AIDS, are totally dependent on others for their care. Many mothers who pass the AIDS virus on to their children are not adequately prepared to care effectively for their infants. Typically, these mothers come from impoverished environments with little access to health care and other appropriate support services. Additionally, these mothers may be intravenous drug users and, therefore, are not reliable or trustworthy caregivers.

Treating adolescents with HIV and AIDS can be challenging. For example, compliance with medical regimens for all age groups is difficult. However, for those who are HIV-positive and have no obvious symptoms, keeping regular medical appointments and taking antiviral medications are not only highly problematic, but also constant reminders of a chronic, if not fatal, disease. Current treatment advances and carefully maintained drug regimes "have turned a disease that used to be a death sentence into a chronic, manageable one for individuals who live in countries where antiretroviral therapy is available" (Ricci & Kyle, 2009b, p. 164). These regimens need to be adhered to with almost perfect precision—otherwise the drug resistance sets in and the outcomes are tragic.

Youth with HIV and AIDS need to learn how to make medical regimens a regular part of their lives to maintain good health and longevity. They also require assistance in dealing with the psychological reactions of anxiety and depression that often accompany the discovery of HIV infection. Finally, they and others benefit significantly from instruction directed at helping them to understand AIDS, to make wise decisions about their sexual and other high-risk behaviors, to use assertiveness skills, and to communicate effectively with others.

**Standard 2**
Learning Environments

Laws regarding the disclosure of AIDS to others vary across states. Many states and some cities have *partner-notification* laws—meaning that, if you test positive for HIV, you (or your health care provider) may be legally obligated to tell your sex or needle-sharing partner(s). In some states, if you are HIV-positive and don't tell your partner(s), you can be charged with a crime. Some health departments require health care providers to report the name of your sex and needle-sharing partner(s) if they know that information—even if you refuse to report that information yourself.

"Some states also have laws that require clinic staff to notify a 'third party' if they know that person has a significant risk for exposure to HIV from a patient the staff member knows is infected with HIV. This is called 'duty to warn'" (AIDS.gov, 2012).

In many states, neither students with AIDS nor their parents are compelled by law to disclose their HIV medical status to school personnel or child care providers (Child Care Law Center, 2005; Fahrner & Romano, 2010). Nevertheless, the parents or students may share this information with a limited number of school-based personnel if they determine

---

**Universal Precautions**

- Thorough hand washing, before and after contacting individuals, objects, or secretions.

- Use of personal protective equipment (barrier protection) (gloves, masks, etc.).

- Application of safe methods of disposing waste, cleaning up spills, and handling laundry.

- Procedures for dealing with accidental exposure to potentially infectious materials.

**Benefits of Adhering to Universal Precautions**

- They protect infected individuals from further infection.

- They protect the privacy of infected individuals.

- They protect the health of service providers.

- They protect the health of other students.

SOURCE: Adapted from Best, S. J., Heller, K. W., & Bigge, J. L. (2005). *Preventing infectious disease transmission and implementing universal precautions in Chapter 3: Health impairments and infectious diseases in teaching individuals with physical or multiple disabilities* (p. 79).

---

this would benefit their child, including the school nurse, the principal, and the child's or youth's teacher(s). This information should be treated with the utmost confidentiality.

"Unfortunately, there is widespread but unwarranted anxiety among parents whose children attend school with a youngster with AIDS, fearing that their own child may contract the disease. The AIDS virus (human immunodeficiency virus, or HIV) is transmitted only through blood, blood products, and sexual contact. Casual physical contact—including touching or holding hands with someone with AIDS, or sharing a drinking glass—will not transfer the AIDS virus" (American Academy of Pediatrics, 2011).

Students with HIV who are on strict medical regimens will need time to take their medications. Missing dosages could seriously jeopardize a student's health. Fatigue is a common occurrence in these students. Ample opportunities should be available for rejuvenation and respite from demanding physical activities.

Essential teacher-related behaviors in working with children and youth with AIDS include working collaboratively with care providers, providing sensitive and nonjudgmental services, heeding the guidelines to prevent blood-borne infections (see Figure 14.3, "Universal Precautions and Their Benefits in School Settings"), helping young people adhere to their medication regimens, modeling appropriate respectful behaviors, and maintaining privacy and confidentiality. Also, teachers, parents, and other community organizations play key roles providing instruction related to preventing AIDS and its transmission.

**Standard 1**
Learner Development and Individual Learning Differences

## 14-7 Asthma

Asthma is evidenced by swelling and inflammation of the air passages that transport air from the mouth and nose to the lungs. This swelling within the affected passages causes them to narrow, thus limiting the air entering and exiting the individual. Symptoms can be activated by allergens, drugs, foods, inhalants, or other irritants that are drawn into the lungs, resulting in swollen, constricted, or blocked airways. Symptoms include diminished breathing capacity, coughing, wheezing, tightness in the chest, and excessive sputum (Ratcliffe & Kiechhefer, 2010). In severe cases, asthma can be life-threatening (Asthma and Allergy Foundation of America, 2012d).

### 14-7a Prevalence and Causation

Nearly one in ten children in the United States is affected by asthma. Most recent studies suggest that 8 percent of adults and 9.3 percent of children have asthma (Centers for Disease Control and Prevention, 2015b).

Asthma is genetic in its origin—it is inherited. However, for asthma to display itself, to be awakened, it must be triggered. Triggers vary greatly across children, youth, and adults (Asthma and Allergy Foundation of America, 2012c). In response to these triggers, the large airways (bronchi) contract into spasm. Swelling soon follows, leading to a further narrowing of the airways and excessive mucus production, which leads to coughing and other breathing difficulties.

Triggers include waste from common household insects (house dust mites, cockroaches, and so on), grass pollens, mold spores, and pet dander. Other triggers involve medications, air pollution (ozone, nitrogen dioxide, sulfur dioxide, and so on), cleaning agents, tobacco smoke, and various chemicals and industrial compounds. Also, some early childhood infections, particularly respiratory infections, set the stage for the potential development of asthma. Emotional stress has also been implicated as a potential trigger or aggravator (Asthma and Allergy Foundation of America, 2012c).

## 14-7b Interventions

Several interventions are useful to children, youth, and adults with asthma. It is important for all age groups with asthma to eliminate or moderate exposure to potential triggers—appropriate actions may prevent or moderate asthma symptoms (Asthma and Allergy Foundation of America, 2012a). Interventions include increasing the anti-inflammatory medication in advance of anticipated exposure to certain triggers, using appropriate bronchodilators for much the same purpose, and limiting the time of exposure to potential or known triggers.

As indicated earlier, medications play a key role in treating and managing asthma. Bronchodilators, appropriately administered, reduce the swelling and inflammation in the affected airways and generally provide short-term reprieves from common symptoms. Other physician-prescribed, anti-inflammatory medications regularly administered contribute significantly to the management of the disease and its symptoms. For moderate to severe cases of asthma, anti-IgE therapy is recommended. This is a relatively new and very expensive therapy (Asthma and Allergy Foundation of America, 2012b).

Generally, the side effects of the asthma-prescribed medications are minimal. However, frequent use of bronchodilators may indicate a need for further medical consultation. Also, some forms of asthma are cold- or exercise-induced. In these cases, parents and other care providers will want to determine the benefits and related risks in having their children engage in activities that may activate asthma and its symptoms.

Like so many other health conditions, teachers and others who have regular and frequent access to children and youth with asthma need to understand the disease and its consequences. Many families will have created an "asthma management plan" with two primary purposes: effectively managing the disease on a daily basis and creating a rescue plan in the event of a severe asthmatic attack. The plan outlines warning signs, identifies rescue medicines, provides steps to take with an attack, and describes conditions that would warrant calling a doctor. The asthma management or action plan is an incredibly helpful tool for school personnel to have on hand (see Table 14.2).

**Standard 2**
Learning Environments

**Standard 7**
Collaboration

| **Table 14.2**  Contents of an Asthma Management Plan |
| --- |
| **Brief history of the student's asthma:** |
| • Asthma symptoms |
| • Information on how to contact the student's health care provider, parent/guardian |
| • Physician and parent/guardian signature |
| • List of factors that make the student's asthma worse |
| • The student's personal best peak flow reading if the student uses peak flow monitoring |
| • List of the student's asthma medications |
| • A description of the student's treatment plan, based on symptoms or peak flow readings, including recommended actions for school personnel to help handle asthma episodes |

SOURCE: Adapted from "Asthma and Physical Activity in the School: Asthma Management Plan," www.kidneeds.com/diagnostic_categories/articles/asthmaphysicalactiv.htm.

Frequently, the symptoms associated with asthma are more evident during the day when children or youth participate in various school-related activities (recess, physical education, or other physically demanding activities). If there is some likelihood of severe asthmatic attacks, medications should be available within the school, teachers should know how to administer them, and the medications should be adequately stored in a secure cabinet, generally located in the school nurse's office. Communication and collaboration among and between teachers, parents, and other school personnel are vital to the successful treatment of asthma in children and youth.

## 14-8 Seizure Disorders (Epilepsy)

"Epilepsy is a brain disorder in which clusters of nerve cells, or neurons, in the brain sometimes signal abnormally. In epilepsy, the normal pattern of neuronal activity becomes disturbed, causing strange sensations, emotions, and behavior or sometimes convulsions, muscle spasms, and loss of consciousness. … Having a seizure does not necessarily mean that a person has epilepsy. Only when a person has had two or more seizures is he or she considered to have epilepsy. EEGs and brain scans are common diagnostic tests for epilepsy" (National Institute of Neurological Disorders and Stroke, 2012a). Several classification schemes have been employed to describe the various types of seizure disorders. We will briefly discuss two types of seizures: tonic/clonic and absence.

**Standard 1**
Learner Development and Individual Learning Differences

Generalized tonic/clonic seizures, formerly called *grand mal seizures*, affect the entire brain. The tonic phase of these seizures is characterized by a stiffening of the body; the clonic phase is distinguished by repeated muscle contractions and relaxations. Tonic/clonic seizures are often preceded by a warning signal known as an aura, in which the individual senses a unique sound, odor, or physical sensation just prior to the onset of the seizure. In some instances, the seizure is also signaled by a cry or similar sound. The tonic phase of the seizure begins with a loss of consciousness, after which the individual falls to the ground. Initially, the trunk and head become rigid during the tonic phase. The clonic phase follows and consists of involuntary muscle contractions (violent shaking) of the extremities. Irregular breathing, blueness in the lips and face, increased salivation, loss of bladder and bowel control, and perspiration may occur (Epilepsy Foundation, 2009b).

The nature, scope, frequency, and duration of tonic/clonic seizures vary greatly from person to person. Such seizures may last as long as 20 minutes or less than one minute (see Figure 14.4). One of the most dangerous aspects of tonic/clonic seizures is potential injury from falling and striking objects in the environment.

A period of sleepiness and confusion usually follows a tonic/clonic seizure. The individual may exhibit drowsiness, nausea, headache, or a combination of these symptoms. Such symptoms should be treated with appropriate rest, medication, or other therapeutic

*Figure 14.4  First Aid for Seizures*

1. Cushion the head.

2. Loosen tight necktie or collar.

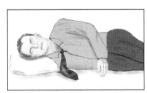
3. Turn on side.

4. Put nothing in the mouth.

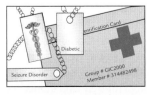
5. Look for identification.

6. Don't hold the person down.

7. Seizure ends.

8. Offer help

remedies. The characteristics and aftereffects of seizures vary in many ways and should be treated with this in mind.

"Absence seizure—also known as petit mal—involves a brief, sudden lapses of consciousness. Absence seizures are more common in children than adults. Someone having an absence seizure may look like he or she is staring into space for a few seconds" (Mayo Clinic, 2012a). During these seizures, the brain ceases to function as it normally would. The individual's consciousness is altered in an almost imperceptible manner. Young people with this type of seizure disorder may experience these seizures as often as 100 times a day. Such inattentive behavior may be viewed as daydreaming by teachers or work supervisors, but the episode is really due to momentary bursts of abnormal brain activity that individuals cannot control. The lapses in attention caused by this form of epilepsy can greatly hamper an individual's ability to respond properly to or profit from a teacher's presentations or a supervisor's instructions. Treatment and control of absence seizures are generally achieved through prescribed medications.

## 14-8a Prevalence and Causation

Prevalence figures for seizure disorders vary, in part because of the social stigma associated with them. Epilepsy affects approximately 468,000 children age 17 and younger in the United States (Centers for Disease Control and Prevention, 2013). About 150,000 new cases of epilepsy are diagnosed in children and adults each year (Epilepsy Foundation, 2014). Half of all of the cases of seizure disorders in children appear before 10 years of age. Unfortunately, large numbers of adults and children have seizure disorders that remain undiagnosed and untreated.

The causes of seizure disorders are many, including perinatal factors, tumors of the brain, complications of head trauma, infections of the central nervous system, vascular diseases, alcoholism, infection, maternal injury or infection, and genetic factors (Blosser & Reider-Demer, 2009; Epilepsy Foundation, 2009a). Also, some seizures are caused by ingestion of street drugs, toxic chemicals, and poisons. Nevertheless, no explicit cause can be found in six out of ten individuals with seizure disorders (Epilepsy Foundation, 2014).

Researchers are endeavoring to determine what specific biophysical features give rise to seizures. If they can discover the underlying parameters, they may be able to prevent seizures from occurring.

## 14-8b Interventions

The treatment of seizure disorders begins with a careful medical investigation in which the physician develops a thorough health history of the individual and completes an in-depth physical examination. Moreover, it is essential that the physician receive thorough descriptions of the seizure(s). These preliminary diagnostic steps may be followed by other assessment procedures, including blood tests, video capturing of seizure episodes, CT scans or MRIs, cranial ultrasounds, and spinal fluid taps to determine whether or not the individual has meningitis (Ricci & Kyle, 2009a). EEGs (electroencephalograms) may also be performed to confirm the physician's clinical impressions. The electroencephalogram is a test to detect abnormalities in the electrical activity of the brain. However, it should be noted that many seizure disorders are not detectable through electroencephalographic measures. As indicated earlier, accurate diagnoses are essential to providing effective treatments (National Institute of Neurological Disorders and Stroke, 2012a).

Many types of seizures can be treated successfully with precise drug management. Significant headway has been made with the discovery of effective drugs, particularly for children with tonic/clonic and absence seizures. Maintaining regular medication regimens can be very challenging for children or youth and their parents. Anticonvulsant drugs must be chosen very carefully, however. The potential risk and benefit of each medication must be balanced and weighed. Once a drug has been prescribed, families should be educated in its use, in the importance of noting any side effects, and in the need for consistent administration. In some instances, medication may be discontinued after several years of seizure-free behavior. This is particularly true for those young children who do not have some form of underlying brain pathology.

Other treatments for seizure disorders include surgery, stress management, a vagus nerve stimulator (an electronic device designed to prevent seizures by sending small bursts of electrical energy to the brain), brain infusion of the chemical muscimol into affected areas of the brain, and diet modifications. The goal of surgery is to remove the precise part of the brain that is damaged and is causing the seizures. Surgery is considered primarily for those individuals with uncontrollable seizures, essentially those who have not responded to anticonvulsant medications. Using a variety of sophisticated scanning procedures, physicians attempt to isolate the damaged area of the brain that corresponds with the seizure activity. The outcomes of surgery for children and youth with well-defined foci of seizure activity are excellent. Of individuals who undergo surgery, 55 to 90 percent experience positive outcomes (National Institute of Neurological Disorders and Stroke, 2012c, 2012d). Obviously, the surgery must be done with great care. Brain tissue, once removed, is gone forever, and the function that the tissue performed is eliminated or only marginally restored.

Stress management is designed to increase a child's or youth's general functioning. Because seizures are often associated with illnesses, inadequate rest, and other stressors, parents and other care providers work at helping children, youth, and adults understand the importance of attending consistently to their medication routines, developing emotional resilience, and maintaining healthful patterns of behavior.

Diet modifications are designed to alter the way the body uses energy from food. Typically, our bodies convert the carbohydrates we consume into glucose (sugar). Several types of seizures can be controlled by instituting a ketogenic diet (National Institute of Neurological Disorders and Stroke, 2012a; 2012c). This diet focuses on consuming fats rather than carbohydrates. Instead of producing glucose, individuals on this diet produce ketones, a special kind of molecule. This change in food consumption causes alterations in the metabolism of the brain that normally uses sugars to "fire" its functions. For reasons that are not completely understood, the brain is less receptive to certain kinds of seizures under this diet. However, the diet is extraordinarily difficult to maintain on a long-term basis and is now rarely used or recommended.

**Standard 2**
Learning Environments

Individuals with seizure disorders need calm and supportive responses from others— teachers, parents, and peers. The treatment efforts of various professionals and family members must be carefully orchestrated to provide these individuals with opportunities to use their abilities and talents. Educators should be aware of the basic fundamentals of seizure disorders and their management. They should also be aware of their critical role in observing seizures that may occur at school. The astute observations of a teacher may be invaluable to a health care team that is developing appropriate medical and other interventions for a child or youth with seizure disorders. Additionally, teachers should have the necessary skills to attend to seizures before, during, and following their occurrence. It is vitally important that teachers and parents be able to accurately and sensitively describe to other children and youth what has happened when a student experiences a seizure in their classroom and what they might do in a similar situation, thus lessening the chances for misunderstanding and the development of stigmas associated with seizure disorders.

## 14-9 Diabetes

**Standard 1**
Learner Development and Individual Learning Differences

The term *diabetes mellitus* refers to a developmental or hereditary disorder characterized by inadequate secretion or use of insulin, a substance that is produced by the pancreas and used to process carbohydrates. There are two types of diabetes mellitus: insulin-dependent diabetes mellitus (IDDM), commonly known as type 1 or juvenile-onset diabetes, and noninsulin-dependent diabetes mellitus (NIDDM), referred to as type 2 or adult-onset diabetes (American Diabetes Association, 2014; Doyle & Grey, 2010).

Glucose—a sugar, one of the end products of digesting carbohydrates—is used by the body for energy. Some glucose is used quickly, whereas some is stored in the liver and muscles for later use. However, muscle and liver cells cannot absorb and store the energy released by glucose without insulin, a hormone produced by the pancreas that converts glucose into energy that body cells use to perform their various functions.

Without insulin, glucose accumulates in the blood, causing a condition known as hyperglycemia. Left untreated, this condition can cause serious, immediate problems for people with IDDM, leading to loss of consciousness or to a diabetic coma (American Diabetes Association, 2014).

Typical symptoms associated with glucose buildup in the blood are extreme hunger, thirst, and frequent urination. Although progress has been made in regulating insulin levels, the prevention and treatment of the complications that accompany diabetes—blindness, cardiovascular disease, and kidney disease—still pose tremendous challenges for health care specialists and affected individuals.

Consider this revealing description of a 9-year-old who had been diagnosed with type 1 diabetes at age 6: "She had pricked her finger for a blood test 9,000 times and received more than 2,000 insulin shots in the past three years. She typically has four blood checks a day, eats on a relentlessly regular schedule, and may wake up out-of-kilter at night when her blood-sugar level drops. The 'adjustments' necessitated by diabetes—which as far as she knows will be lifelong—are wrenching" (Clark, 2003, p. 6). This brief description helps us sense the challenges that children and youth with diabetes and their families experience.

IDDM, or juvenile-onset diabetes, is particularly troublesome. Compared with the adult form, juvenile-onset diabetes tends to be more severe and progresses more quickly, thus increasing the likelihood of the onset of conditions associated with type 2 diabetes. Generally, the symptoms of type 1 diabetes are easily recognized. The child develops

*Photo 14.1* Consistent insulin delivery is essential to the well-being of young people with diabetes.

an unusual thirst for water and other liquids. His or her appetite also increases substantially, but listlessness and fatigue occur despite increased food and liquid intake. Young people with type 1 diabetes need insulin to convert starches, sugars, and other foods for vitally important energy. Thus, insulin injections are imperative in managing the disease.

In contrast to type 1 diabetes, with type 2 diabetes, insulin injections are not always necessary because the pancreas is still able to produce insulin, but often it does not make sufficient amounts for cell usage. Type 2 diabetes (NIDDM) is the most common form of diabetes and is often associated with obesity in individuals over age 40. Individuals with this form of diabetes are at less risk for diabetic comas; most individuals with NIDDM can manage the disorder through exercise and dietary restrictions. If these actions fail, insulin therapy may be necessary.

## 14-9a    Prevalence and Causation

Almost 9 percent of the U.S. population has diabetes—29.1 million individuals. Of this number, 21 million have been diagnosed with the condition. Eight million are undiagnosed, and 86 million are prediabetic. Each year, 1.7 million new cases of diabetes are identified in adults 20 and older (American Diabetes Association, 2014). Type 2 diabetes has become increasingly common in children—primarily as a result of staggering growth rates in childhood obesity (Science Codex, 2009). According to the Centers for Disease Control and Prevention (2012a), "Childhood obesity has more than tripled in the past 30 years."

The causes of diabetes remain obscure, although considerable research has been conducted on the biochemical mechanisms responsible for it. Diabetes develops gradually in individuals. A combination of genetic dispositions and environmental triggers and conditions give rise to type 1 diabetes. The exact variables that underlie this form of diabetes are still unclear.

Individuals who develop type 2 diabetes incrementally create conditions in their body in which their cells become unresponsive to the effects of insulin. Additionally, the pancreas is unable to make sufficient insulin to overcome this unresponsiveness. Thus, sugars accumulate in the bloodstream with very negative outcomes for affected individuals. Like in type 1 diabetes, genetic and environmental variables play a role in the onset of

## Sarah and the "Pump"

Sarah, who has juvenile-onset diabetes and is now in sixth grade, migrated from her regular, self-administered shots for her diabetes to an insulin infusion pump several years ago. Sarah, however, believes that the pump makes her look different among her peers and wants to return to the shots. Recently, she "disinstalled" her pump. Her mom is worried about her and her health, knowing that she has played an important role in monitoring Sarah's pump regimens and related insulin doses.

*Application Questions*

**1.** How could you help Sarah with the transition she is making?

**2.** How could you help Sarah's mother with her concerns about Sarah's social and medical well-being?

type 2 diabetes. Interestingly, becoming overweight is strongly linked to the development of type 2 diabetes, although not every individual with type 2 diabetes is overweight (Mayo Clinic, 2012b).

## 14-9b   Interventions

Medical treatment centers on the regular administration of insulin, which is essential for children and youth with juvenile diabetes. Several exciting advances have been made in recent years in the monitoring of blood sugar levels and the delivery of insulin to people with diabetes. Also, recent success with pancreas transplants has virtually eliminated the disease for some individuals. Significant progress is also being made in the development of the bioartificial pancreas and gene therapies (Gebel, 2012).

Solid progress has been made in transplanting insulin-producing islet cells to individuals with type 1 diabetes. However, this approach is complicated by shortages in the availability of whole pancreases and by the rejection of these new cells in recipients. Other sources of pancreatic tissue are present in fetal tissue. This controversial approach makes use of tissues—stem cells derived from aborted or unused fetuses. Also, animal islet cells are currently being investigated, particularly islet cells derived from pigs, whose insulin differs by only one molecule from that of humans. However, transplantation of these cells poses similar rejection problems for recipients.

Hybrid technologies are also being pursued. Perhaps the most promising is the production of artificial beta cells that could be used in an artificial pancreas. This approach entails inserting new genes into naturally occurring cells that would produce insulin and be sensitive to the rise and fall of blood glucose.

Maintaining normal levels of glucose is now achieved in many instances with insulin infusion pumps, which are worn by people with diabetes and are powered by small batteries. The infusion pump operates continuously and delivers the dose of insulin that the physician and patient determine. This form of treatment is effective only when used in combination with carefully followed diet and exercise programs. These pumps, if carefully monitored and operated, contribute greatly to "controlling" diabetes, thus reducing or slowing the onset and risks for eye disease, nerve damage, and kidney disease.

Juvenile-onset diabetes is a lifelong condition that can have a pronounced effect on children or youth in a number of areas. Complications for children with long-standing diabetes include blindness, heart attacks, skin disorders, neuropathy (weakness and numbness) in the feet, and kidney problems. Many of these problems can be delayed or prevented by maintaining adequate blood sugar levels with appropriate food intake, exercise, and insulin injections.

Teachers and other care providers need to work carefully with parents and other medical personnel in monitoring treatment and medication regimens, supporting blood sugar monitoring efforts, and being alert to changes in student behavior or performance that may merit immediate action or consultation with medical or other therapeutic personnel. Also, teachers play key roles in helping children and youth embrace and engage in activities and events that enhance their physical well-being, lessening the likelihood of problems with

childhood obesity and related conditions. Communication between teachers and parents is essential in caring for and educating children and youth with diabetes.

## 14-10   Cystic Fibrosis

"Cystic fibrosis is an inherited chronic disease that affects the lungs and digestive system of about 30,000 children and adults in the United States (70,000 worldwide). A defective gene and its protein product cause the body to produce unusually thick, sticky mucus that clogs the lungs and leads to life-threatening lung infections; and obstructs the pancreas and stops natural enzymes from helping the body break down and absorb food" (Cystic Fibrosis Foundation, 2012a). Cystic fibrosis (CF) "is the most common life-shortening genetic illness among white children, adolescents, and young adults" (Hazle, 2010, p. 405). Fortunately, great progress has been made in significantly lengthening the life expectancies of individuals with CF to more than 37 years—some into their 40s (Cystic Fibrosis Foundation, 2012a).

### 14-10a   Prevalence and Causation

In the United States, about 30,000 children and adults have cystic fibrosis. More than 10 million individuals—one in every 31 are carriers of the defective CF gene but do not have the disease (Cystic Fibrosis Foundation, 2012b).

CF is a genetically transmitted disease. A child must inherit a defective copy of the CF gene from each parent to develop the disease. The gene for the CF transfer regulator (CFTR) is very large; some 2,000 mutations have already been identified with the disease. CFTR, a protein, produces improper transportation of sodium and salt (chloride) within cells that line organs such as the lungs and pancreas. CFTR prevents chloride from exiting these cells. This blockage affects a broad range of organs and systems in the body, including reproductive organs in men and women, the lungs, sweat glands, and the digestive system.

The prognosis for individuals with CF depends on a number of factors. The two most critical are early diagnosis of the condition and the quality of care provided after the diagnosis. If the diagnosis occurs late, irreversible damage may be present. With early diagnosis and appropriate medical care, most individuals with CF can achieve weight and growth gains similar to those of their normal peers. Early diagnosis and improved treatment strategies have lengthened the average lifespan of individuals with CF; more than half now live into their 30s and 40s.

### 14-10b   Interventions

The best and most comprehensive treatment is provided through CF centers located throughout the United States. These centers provide talented medical and support staff (respiratory care personnel, social workers, dieticians, genetic counselors, and psychologists). Moreover, they maintain diagnostic laboratories especially equipped to perform pulmonary function testing and sweat testing. Sweat of children with CF has abnormal concentrations of sodium or chloride; in fact, sweat tests provide the definitive data for a diagnosis of CF in infants and young children.

Interventions for CF are varied and complex, and treatment continues throughout the person's lifetime. Consistent and appropriate application of the medical, social, educational, and psychological components of treatment enables these individuals to live longer and with less discomfort and fewer complications than in years past. Treatment of CF is designed to achieve a number of goals. The first is to diagnose the condition before any severe symptoms are exhibited. Other goals include control of chest infection, maintenance of adequate nutrition, education of the child and family regarding the condition, and provision of a suitable education for the child.

Management of respiratory disease caused by CF is critical. If respiratory insufficiency can be prevented or minimized, the individual's life will be greatly enhanced and prolonged. Antibiotic drugs, postural drainage (chest physical therapy), airway clearance systems, and medicated vapors play important roles in the medical management of CF (Alba & Chan, 2007).

Diet management is also essential for children with CF. Generally, children with this condition require more caloric intake than their normal peers. The diet should be high in protein and should be adjusted if a child fails to grow and/or make appropriate weight gains. Individuals with CF benefit significantly from the use of replacement enzymes that assist with food absorption. Also, the intake of vitamins is very important to individuals with digestive system problems.

The major social and psychological problems of children with CF are directly related to chronic coughing, small stature, offensive stools, gas, delayed onset of puberty and secondary sex characteristics, and potentially unsatisfying social relationships. Also, these children and youth may spend significant amounts of time away from school settings for aggressive pulmonary and antibiotic therapies (Brady, 2009). Thus teachers, counselors, and other support personnel play essential roles in helping these students feel at home in school, assisting them in making up past-due work, forming friendships, taking medications including enzyme treatments, providing appropriate privacy for rest and coughing episodes, helping other children and youth understand the condition, and receiving other appropriate school-based care (Hazle, 2010). Collaboration between school personnel, parents, and health care providers is essential to the well-being of children and youth with CF. Moreover, support groups play important roles in helping students with CF understand themselves and their disease and develop personal resilience and ongoing friendships.

**Standard 1**
Learner Development and Individual Learning Differences

**Standard 7**
Collaboration

## 14-11   Sickle-Cell Disease

**Standard 1**
Learner Development and Individual Learning Differences

"Sickle-cell disease (SCD) is a group of inherited red blood cell disorders" (Centers for Disease Control and Prevention, 2015c). Sickle-cell disease profoundly affects the structure and functioning of red blood cells. The hemoglobin molecule in the red blood cells of individuals with SCD is abnormal in that it is vulnerable to structural collapse when the blood–oxygen level is significantly diminished. As the blood–oxygen level declines, these blood cells become distorted and form bizarre shapes. This process, which is known as sickling, distorts the normal doughnutlike shapes of cells into shapes like microscopic sickle blades. Obstructions in the vessels of affected individuals can lead to stroke and to damage of other organs in the body (see Figure 14.5).

People affected by sickle-cell disease (SCD) may experience unrelenting anemia. In some cases, it is tolerated well; in others, the condition is quite debilitating. Another aspect of SCD involves frequent infections and periodic vascular blockages, which occur as sickled cells block microvascular channels. These blockages can often cause severe and chronic pain in the extremities, abdomen, or back. In addition, the disease may affect any organ system of the body. SCD also has a significant negative effect on the physical growth and development of infants and children.

### 14-11a   Prevalence and Causation

About 1 in 12 African Americans is a carrier of the sickle-cell gene. A thousand infants are born with SCD each year. In the United States, 90,000 to 100,000 individuals are impacted by this disease. One in every 36,000 Hispanics is born with SCD (Centers for Disease Control and Prevention, 2015d).

Sickle-cell disease is caused by various combinations of genes. A child who receives a mutant S-hemoglobin gene from each parent exhibits SCA to one degree or another. The disease usually announces itself at 6 months of age and persists throughout the individual's lifetime.

### 14-11b   Interventions

A number of treatments may be employed to deal with the problems caused by sickle-cell disease, but the first step is early diagnosis. Babies—particularly infants who are at risk for this disease—should be screened at birth. Early diagnosis lays the groundwork for the prophylactic use of antibiotics to prevent infections in the first five years of life. This treatment, coupled with appropriate immunizations and nutrition, prevents further complications of

**Anemia**
A condition in the body where the blood is abnormally low in red blood cells or the red cells do not have enough hemoglobin to carry oxygen from the lungs to the other cells of the body.

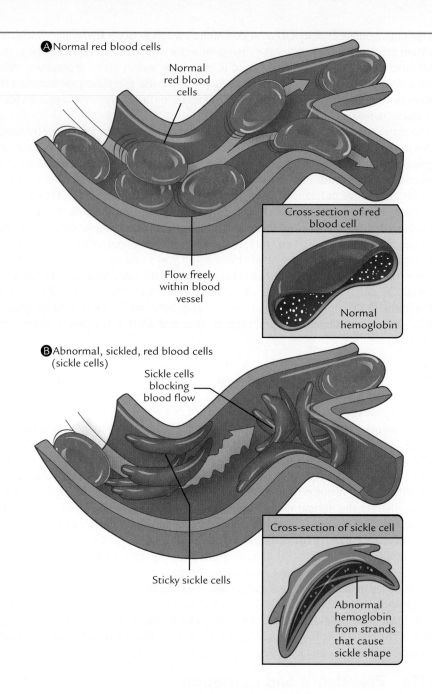

**Figure 14.5** *Normal and Sickled Red Blood Cells*

(A) Normal red blood cells

Normal red blood cells

Flow freely within blood vessel

Cross-section of red blood cell

Normal hemoglobin

(B) Abnormal, sickled, red blood cells (sickle cells)

Sickle cells blocking blood flow

Sticky sickle cells

Cross-section of sickle cell

Abnormal hemoglobin from strands that cause sickle shape

the disease. Moreover, these treatments significantly reduce death rates associated with SCD. One of the primary goals of treatment is the prevention of crises and related sickling episodes.

Children, youth, and adults usually learn to adapt to their disease and lead relatively normal lives. When their lives are interrupted by crises, a variety of treatment approaches can be used. For children, comprehensive and timely care is crucial. For example, children with SCD who develop fevers should be treated aggressively. In fact, parents of these children may be taught how to examine the spleen and recognize early signs of potentially serious problems. Hydration is also an important component of treatment. Lastly, pain management may be addressed with narcotic and nonnarcotic drugs.

Several factors predispose individuals to SCD crisis: dehydration from fever, reduced liquid intake, and hypoxia (a result of breathing air that is poor in oxygen content). Those who have a history of SCD crises should avoid stress, fatigue, and exposure to cold temperatures.

Treatment of crises is generally directed at keeping the individual warm, increasing liquid intake, ensuring good blood oxygenation, and administering medication for infection.

**CEC**

**Standard 7**
Collaboration

Assistance can also be provided during crisis periods by partial-exchange blood transfusions with fresh, normal red cells. Transfusions may also be necessary for individuals with SCA who are preparing for surgery or who are pregnant.

Teachers and other care providers may assist with the following: dispensing medications in keeping with school regulations and policies; honoring recommendations for activity restrictions; making referrals to appropriate medical personnel if pain and fever become evident; encouraging affected students to dress warmly during cold weather; and responding immediately in the event of SCA crises. As with all physical and health disorders, collaboration and communication among caregivers are key elements of serving children and youth so affected.

**Standard 1**
Learner Development and Individual Learning Differences

**Standard 7**
Collaboration

## 14-12   Traumatic Brain Injuries

"Traumatic brain injury (TBI), a form of acquired brain injury, occurs when a sudden trauma causes damage to the brain. TBI can result when the head suddenly and violently hits an object, or when an object pierces the skull and enters brain tissue. Symptoms of a TBI can be mild, moderate, or severe, depending on the extent of the damage to the brain" (National Institute of Neurological Disorders and Stroke, 2012e). TBI injuries happen, for example, in car accidents when the head hits the windshield and in bicycle accidents when the head hits the ground. The trauma caused by the rapid acceleration or deceleration of the brain may cause the tearing of important nerve fibers in the brain, bruising of the brain itself as it undergoes impact with the skull, brain stem injuries, and swelling of the brain.

Medical professionals describe two types of brain damage, primary and secondary. *Primary damage* is a direct outcome of the initial impact to the brain. *Secondary damage* develops over time as the brain responds to the initial trauma. For instance, an adolescent who is hit accidentally with a baseball bat may develop a hematoma, an area of internal bleeding within the brain. This may be the primary damage. However, with the passage of time, the brain's response to the initial injury may be pervasive swelling, which may cause additional insult and injury to the brain.

**Standard 1**
Learner Development and Individual Learning Differences

In the school context, the Individuals with Disabilities Act (IDEA) defines traumatic brain injury as "an acquired injury to the brain caused by an external physical force, resulting in total or partial functional disability or psychosocial impairment, or both, that adversely affects a child's educational performance. Traumatic brain injury applies to open or closed head injuries resulting in impairments in one or more areas, such as cognition; language; memory; attention; reasoning; abstract thinking; judgment; problem-solving; sensory, perceptual, and motor abilities; psychosocial behavior; physical functions; information processing; and speech. Traumatic brain injury does not apply to brain injuries that are congenital or degenerative, or to brain injuries induced by birth trauma" (U.S. Department of Education, 2006).

Head injures may result in disabilities that adversely and severely affect individuals' information processing, social behaviors, memory capacities, reasoning and thinking, speech and language skills, and sensory and motor abilities.

### 14-12a   Prevalence and Causation

The statistics associated with traumatic brain injury are sobering. About 2.5 million people sustain TBIs each year. Of this number, about 50,000 individuals die and 280,000 are hospitalized (Centers for Disease Control and Prevention, 2015c). About 475,000 TBIs take place with children (0 to 14 years of age). About 80,000 to 90,000 are permanently disabled from their accidents or injuries. About 180 per 100,000 children under age 15 experience a TBI. Of that number, about 5 to 8 percent experience a severe TBI. The rate of TBI caused by sports and recreation-related injuries rose 57 percent in just eight years for children ages 19 or younger (Centers for Disease Control and Prevention, 2015c). Also, significant numbers of military personnel, more than 229,000, were diagnosed with a TBI between 2000 and 2011. Tragically, TBI is the signature injury of veterans of the Iraq and Afghanistan wars (Defense and Veterans Brain Injury Center, 2014).

It is now estimated that 5.3 million children and adults in the United States are living with the consequences of sustaining a traumatic brain injury. Of all the head injuries that occur, 40 percent involve children. About 2 to 5 percent of the children and youth who experience a TBI develop severe neurologic complications; others develop lasting behavior problems, and over one-third experience lifelong disabilities.

"The single most preventative risk factor is alcohol usage" (Cifu, Kreutzer, Slater, & Taylor, 2007, p. 1,134). If youth and young adults controlled their alcohol consumption, many TBIs would not occur. Additionally, many TBIs could be prevented with proper use of seat belts, air bags, child restraints, and helmets, and securing guns from accidental discharge and misuse by children.

**Standard 2**
Learning Environments

For small children, the most common cause of TBIs is a fall from a short distance. Such children may fall from a tree, playground equipment, their parents' arms, or furniture. Another major cause of injury in young children is physical abuse. These injuries generally come from shaking or striking infants, which may cause sheering of brain matter or severe bleeding. Common causes of head injuries in older children include falls from playground swings or climbers, bicycles, or trees; blows to the head from baseball bats, balls, or other sports equipment; gunshot wounds; and pedestrian accidents (Centers for Disease Control and Prevention, 2015c).

The number of children and others who experience serious head trauma would be significantly reduced if seat belts and other child restraint devices were consistently used. Further reductions in such injuries would be achieved by significantly decreasing accidents due to driving under the influence of alcohol and other mind-altering substances.

Programs directed at reducing the number of individuals who drive while under the influence of alcohol or other substances should be vigorously supported. Likewise, children (and everyone else) should wear helmets when bicycling, skateboarding, skiing, snowboarding, horseback riding, and similar activities; and should obey safety rules that reduce the probability of serious accidents.

## 14-12b Interventions

Individuals with a TBI present a variety of challenges to families and professionals. The injuries may affect every aspect of an individual's life (see Figure 14.6 for effects on children) (Bullough, 2011). The resulting disabilities also have a profound effect on an individual's family. Often the injuries radically change the individual's capacities for learning and making sense of different kinds of incoming information (verbal, written, nonverbal, visual, and so on).

Generally, individuals with a TBI will need services and supports in several areas: cognition, speech and language, social and behavioral skills, as well as physical functioning. Cognitive problems have an impact on thinking and perception. For example, people who have sustained a brain injury may be unable to remember or retrieve newly learned or processed information. They may be unable to attend or concentrate for appropriate periods of time. Another serious problem is their inability to adjust or respond flexibly to changes in home, school, community, or work environments.

**Standard 1**
Learner Development
and Individual Learning
Differences

A person with TBI may also struggle with speech, producing unintelligible sounds or indistinguishable words. Speech may be slurred and labored. Individuals with a TBI may know what they want to say, but are unable to express it. Professionals use the term aphasia to describe this condition. Expressive aphasia is an inability to express one's own thoughts and desires.

Language problems may also be evident. For example, a school-age student may be unable to retrieve a desired word or expression, particularly during a "high-demand" instructional session or during an anxiety-producing social situation. Given their difficulties with word retrieval, individuals with a TBI may reduce their overall speech output or use repetitive expressions or word substitutions. Many children with a brain injury express great frustration at knowing an answer to a question, but being unable to retrieve it when called on by teachers.

Social and behavioral problems may present the most challenging aspects of TBI. For many individuals, the injury produces significant changes in their personality, their temperament, their disposition toward certain activities, and their behaviors. These social

*Figure 14.6* **Characteristics of Children with Traumatic Brain Injury**

**Medical/Neurological Symptoms**

- Sensory deficits affecting vision, hearing, taste, smell, or touch
- Decreased motor coordination
- Difficulty breathing
- Dizziness
- Headache
- Impaired balance
- Loss of intellectual capabilities
- Partial to full paralysis
- Poor eye–hand coordination
- Reduced body strength
- Seizure activity (possibly frequent)
- Sleep disorders
- Speech problems (e.g., stuttering, slurring)

**Cognitive Symptoms**

- Decreased attention
- Decreased organizational skills
- Decreased problem-solving ability
- Difficulties keeping up at school
- Difficulty with abstract reasoning
- Integration problems (e.g., sensory, thought)
- Poor organizational skills
- Memory deficits
- Perceptual problems
- Poor concentration
- Poor judgment
- Rigidity of thought

- Slowed information processing
- Poor short- and long-term memory
- Word-finding difficulty

**Behavioral/Emotional Symptoms**

- Aggressive behavior
- Denial of deficits
- Depression
- Difficulty accepting and responding to change
- Loss of reduction of inhibitions
- Distractibility
- Feelings of worthlessness
- Flat affect (expressionless, lacking emotion)
- Low frustration level
- Unnecessary or disproportionate guilt
- Helplessness
- Impulsivity
- Inappropriate crying or laughing
- Irritability

**Social Skills Development**

- Difficulties maintaining relationships with family members and others
- Inability to restrict socially inappropriate behaviors (e.g., disrobing in public)
- Inappropriate responses to the environment (e.g., over-reactions to light or sound)
- Insensitivity to others' feelings
- Limited initiation of social interactions
- Social isolation

SOURCE: Adapted from Pierangelo, R., and G. A. Giuliani. (2001). *What every teacher should know about students with special needs: Promoting success in the classroom*, pp. 98–100. Champaign, IL: Research Press. Copyright © 2001 by R. Pierangelo and G. G. Giuliani. Reprinted by permission.

and behavioral problems may worsen over time, depending on the nature of the injury, the preinjury status of the brain, the postinjury adjustment of the individual and family, the person's age at the time of the injury, and the treatment provided immediately after the injury. Behaviors emanating from a TBI include increased irritability and emotionality, compromised motivation and judgment, an inability to restrict socially inappropriate behaviors, insensitivity to others, and low thresholds for frustration and inconvenience.

Neuromotor and physical disabilities are also characteristic of individuals with a TBI. Neuromotor problems may be exhibited through poor eye–hand coordination. For example, an adolescent may be able to pick up a ball, but be unable to throw it to someone else. In addition, a person with a TBI may have impaired balance, an inability to walk unassisted, significantly reduced stamina, or paralysis. Impaired vision and hearing may also be present. The array and extent of the challenges individuals with brain injuries and their families face can be overwhelming and disheartening. However, with appropriate support and coordinated, interdisciplinary treatment, individuals and their families can move forward with their lives and develop effective coping skills.

**Standard 4**
Assessment

**Computerized tomography (CT)**

A method of examining body organs by scanning them with X-rays and using a computer to construct a series of cross-sectional scans of the organs.

**Magnetic resonance imaging (MRI)**

A medical imaging technique used in radiology to visualize internal structures of the body in detail.

**Voxel-based morphometry (VBM)**

A neuroimaging analysis technique that allows investigation of specific areas of brain anatomy.

Like other people with disabilities, individuals with a TBI significantly benefit from systems of care—collaborative/multidisciplinary approaches and interventions that address unique family and individual needs. Because of the nature and number of the deficits that might ensue as a result of a head injury, many specialists must be involved in a coordinated and carefully orchestrated fashion. Early comprehensive care is vital to the long-term, functional recovery of individuals with a TBI.

Furthermore, new medical technologies have revolutionized diagnostic and treatment procedures for TBIs. In previous decades, the vast majority of these individuals died within a short time of their accidents. With the development of **computerized tomography (CT)** scans, intracranial pressure monitors, **magnetic resonance imaging (MRI)**, **voxel-based morphometry (VBM)**, and the capacity to control bleeding and brain swelling, many individuals with traumatic brain injury survive. Also, CT scans and voxel-based morphometry of individuals without brain injuries now provide physicians and other health care providers with essential, normative information about the extent of the injury to the brain to compare with the uninjured brains of other individuals of the same age and gender. Voxel-based morphometry is a computational method for measuring differences in local concentrations of brain tissue, through comparisons of multiple brain images from individuals with and without injuries.

Head injuries may be described in terms of the nature of the injury. Injuries include concussions, contusions, skull fractures, and epidural and subdural hemorrhages:

- *Concussions.* The most common effects of closed-head injuries, concussions occur most frequently in children and adolescents through contact sports such as football, hockey, and martial arts. They are characterized by a temporary loss of consciousness with amnesia. Children who display weakness on one side of the body, exhibit a dilated pupil, or experience vomiting may have a concussion and should be examined immediately by a physician.

- *Contusions.* This kind of injury is characterized by extensive damage to the brain, including laceration of the brain, bleeding, swelling, and bruising. The resulting effect of a brain contusion is intense stupor or coma. Individuals with a contusion should be hospitalized immediately.

- *Skull fractures.* The consequences of **skull fractures** depend on the location, nature, and seriousness of the fracture. Unfortunately, some fractures are not easily detectable through radiologic examination. Injuries to the lower back part of the head are particularly troublesome and difficult to detect. These basilar skull fractures may set the stage for serious infections of the central nervous system. Immediate medical care is essential for skull fractures to determine the extent of the damage and to develop appropriate interventions.

- *Epidural and subdural hemorrhages.* Hemorrhaging, or bleeding, is the central feature of epidural and subdural hematomas. Hematomas are collections of blood, usually clotted. An epidural hematoma is caused by damage to an artery (a thick-walled blood vessel carrying blood from the heart) between the brain and the skull (see Figure 14.7). If this injury is not treated promptly and appropriately, an affected individual will die. A subdural hematoma is caused by damage to tiny veins that draw blood from the outer layer of the brain (cerebral cortex) to the heart. The aggregation of blood between the brain and its outer covering (dura) produces pressure that adversely affects the brain and its functioning (see Figure 14.8). If the subdural bleeding is left untreated, the result can be death.

Medical treatment of TBI proceeds generally in three stages: acute care, rehabilitation, and community integration. During the acute stage, medical personnel focus on maintaining the child's or youth's life, treating the swelling and bleeding, minimizing complications, reducing the level of coma, and completing the initial neurologic examination. This stage of treatment is often characterized by strained interactions between physicians and parents. Some physicians are challenged in responding to the overwhelming psychological needs of parents and family members because of the complex medical demands presented by the

**Skull fractures**

A break in one or more of the bones in the skull, usually occurring as a result of blunt force trauma.

## Reflections from Soldiers

Many soldiers who return from the Iraq and Afghanistan wars experience mild to severe traumatic brain injuries. At least 15 to 25 percent of returning soldiers experience mild traumatic brain injuries (TBIs), often characterized by chronic and severe headaches, emotional irritability, sleep problems, impaired cognition, and other challenging health issues. What follows are personal reflections of soldiers about the impact of their brain injuries:

> You tell yourself that physical injuries always happen to someone else, that it'll never happen to you. It took a long time for me to come to terms with my injury. (Source: "Physical Injury." Make the Connection. Retrieved July 20, 2012 from http://maketheconnection.net/events/injury.)

> I was having trouble seeing. Everything was blurry, the headaches were nonstop, ... I was confused all the time. All of these were symptoms of a brain injury—we just didn't know it yet. (Source: "Effects of Traumatic Brain Injury." Make the Connection. Retrieved July 20, 2012 from http://maketheconnection.net/conditions/traumatic-brain-injury.)

> At times, I wish that my spouse would just "get it" and understand all the things that I am dealing with. What I figured out is that the more honest and up front I am, the more that happens and better things get. We take it one day at a time. (Source: "Family and Relationship." Make the Connection. Retrieved July 20, 2012 from http://maketheconnection.net/events/family-relationships#1.)

> I had a short fuse. If you looked at me the wrong way I'd basically walk up to you and say, "You got an issue?" (Source: "Anger and Irritability." Make the Connection. Retrieved July 20, 2012 from http://maketheconnection.net/symptoms/anger-irritability/.)

> I'd say that the biggest thing that I had to deal with was frustration. I didn't know why I was forgetful all the time or always in a bad mood. I didn't know that I had a traumatic brain injury. (Source: Make the Connection: What are the mental health-related effects of TBI that I need to be aware of? Retrieved May 6, 2015 from http://maketheconnection.net/conditions/traumatic-brain-injury)

> It's entirely too easy to get too down, and not want to work on the things to get you back to where you need to be.... (Source: "Matthew James." Traumatic Brain Injury: The Journey Home. Retrieved July 20, 2012 from www.traumaticbraininjuryatoz.org/Personal-Journeys/Personal-Journeys/Matthew-James.)

> You gotta do your part and it's hard. You gotta just reach inside and be the soldier or marine that you are, and go forward. (Source: "Michael Welch." Traumatic Brain Injury: The Journey Home. Retrieved July 20, 2012 from www.traumaticbraininjuryatoz.org/Personal-Journeys/Personal-Journeys/Michael-Welsh.)

> ... [I]t's very important early on to be realistic about what you're facing. But also, find some hope in that reality.... [D]on't give up hope.... (Source: "Ted Wade." Traumatic Brain Injury: The Journey Home. Retrieved July 20, 2012 from www.traumaticbraininjuryatoz.org/Personal-Journeys/Personal-Journeys/Ted-Wade.)

> I've learned a lot about my own brain over the past years, probably more than the average person would ever want to know, but sadly knowing what's wrong doesn't help fix it. The only thing that does help is repetition and retraining. I know there are still many things that I have to work on, but thankfully I believe there is still hope. (Source: crlynch.com/: Update January 2008. Retrieved May 6, 2015 from www.crlynch.com/2012page13.html)

> Some days I can't distinguish the PTSD (post-traumatic stress disorder) from the head injury.... The PTSD can be cured, but the head injury, I don't know. It's just going to take time. (Source: "Charlie." NM Brain Injury Advisory Council. Retrieved July 20, 2012 from http://nmbiac.com/stories.html.)

### Questions for Reflection

**1.** If you were a spouse, parent, or sibling of a returning soldier with a TBI, what steps would you take to prepare yourself for assisting with the care and treatment of your loved one?

**2.** What services would you access?

**3.** How would you inform yourself?

**4.** Who would be your most reliable information providers?

injured child or youth. Other trained personnel—including social workers, psychologists, and clergy—play vital roles in supporting parents and other family members. Again, we see the importance of systems of care where talented professionals work together to achieve optimal outcomes for all concerned.

**Figure 14.7** *An Epidural Hematoma*

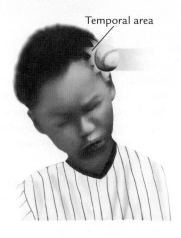

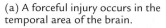

Temporal area

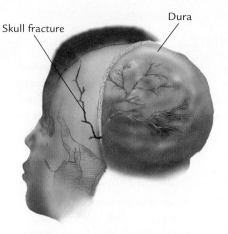

Skull fracture

Dura

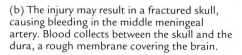

Dura

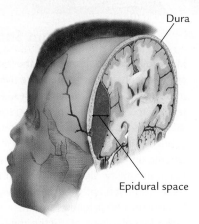

Dura

Epidural space

(a) A forceful injury occurs in the temporal area of the brain.

(b) The injury may result in a fractured skull, causing bleeding in the middle meningeal artery. Blood collects between the skull and the dura, a rough membrane covering the brain.

(c) As the blood collects, pressure builds on vital structures within the brain.

If a child, youth, or adult remains in a coma, medical personnel may use special stimulation techniques to reduce the depth of the coma. If the patient with a TBI becomes agitated by stimuli in the hospital unit, such as visitors' conversations, noises produced by housecleaning staff, obtrusive light, or touching, steps may be taken to control or reduce these problems. As an injured individual comes out of the coma, orienting him or her to the environment becomes a priority. This may include explaining where the patient is located, introducing care providers, indicating where loved ones are, sharing what has happened since the injury, and responding to the individual's other questions. Many people who have been injured do not remember the accident or the medical interventions administered.

The next stage of treatment is rehabilitation. During this phase, individuals seek to relearn and adequately perform preinjury skills and behaviors. This treatment may take time—often months—and considerable effort. Children and youth are prepared gradually for return to their homes and appropriate school environments. Their families prepare as well, receiving ongoing support and counseling. Additionally, arrangements are also

**Figure 14.8** *A Subdural Hematoma*

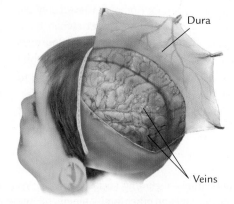

Dura

Veins

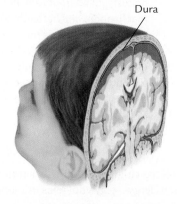

Dura

(a) Violently shaking or hitting a child may cause damage to the cerebral cortex.

(b) Trauma to the brain results in the rupturing of small veins.

(c) Blood gathers between the dura and the brain, resulting in pressure on vital brain structures.

made for appropriate speech/language, physical, and occupational therapies and for any specialized teaching necessary.

Many individuals return to their homes, schools, or employment settings as vastly different people. These differences often take the shape of unpredictable or extreme expressions of emotion. Furthermore, these individuals may have trouble recognizing and accepting their postinjury challenges and deficits.

The last stage of intervention is community reintegration, focusing on providing counseling and therapy to help individuals cope with their injuries and their residual effects; helping families maintain the gains that have been achieved; terminating specific head injury services; further developing language facility and skills; seeking disability determination; and referring individuals to community agencies, educational programs, and vocational rehabilitation for additional services as needed.

**Standard 5**
Instructional Planning
and Strategies

**Standard 7**
Collaboration

Educational supports focus on environmental changes that facilitate daily living and address critical transition issues that arise in preparing a child's or youth's return to appropriate school settings. Communication and collaboration are absolutely essential to the transition from the hospital/care facility to the school environment. Several groups are involved in ensuring that the care and support are optimal: parents and teachers, professionals within the school, and school professionals working with clinical/medical personnel outside the school. It is essential that educators and health providers work together to blend clinical, educational, and family interventions effectively.

Unfortunately, many children and youth with a TBI leave hospitals or rehabilitation settings without adequate preparation for the demands inherent in returning to home and school environments. Also, many teachers who receive these students are not adequately prepared to respond to their cognitive, academic, and behavioral needs.

Students with traumatic brain injury may return to one of several school placements, depending on their needs. Appropriate teaching activities include establishing high expectations, reducing stimuli and conditions that elicit challenging behaviors, using appropriate reductive techniques for stopping or significantly reducing aggressive or noncompliant behaviors, eliminating rewards for negative or problematic behaviors, providing precise feedback, giving students strategies for organizing information, and providing many opportunities for practice.

Educational services are tailored to a student's specific needs. Efforts are directed at improving students' general behaviors, such as problem solving, planning, and developing insight. Teaching strategies focus on developing appropriate social behaviors (performing in stressful situations, improving initiative taking, working with others, etc.), building expressive and receptive language skills (word retrieval, event description, understanding instructions, reading nonverbal cues, etc.), and writing skills (sentence development, legibility, etc.; see Figure 14.9). Also, some individuals with a TBI may benefit greatly from assistive technology devices that aid in communication, information processing, learning, and recreation. These technologies help individuals with a TBI and other disabilities communicate with others, display what they know, access information, and participate in various learning and recreational activities.

**Standard 2**
Learning Environments

The initial individualized education programs (IEPs) for students with a brain injury should be written for short periods of time, perhaps six to eight weeks. Moreover, these IEPs should be reviewed often to make adjustments based on the progress and growth of students. Often, students improve dramatically in the first year following their injuries. Children and youth with a TBI generally experience the most gains in the first year following the injury, with little progress made thereafter. Flexibility and responsiveness on the part of teachers and other support staff are essential to the well-being of students with a traumatic brain injury.

**Standard 7**
Collaboration

For students who want to move on to postsecondary education, interdisciplinary team members may contribute significantly to the transition process. Critical factors include the physical accessibility of the campus, living arrangements, support for academic achievement, social and personal support systems, and career/vocational training and placement.

For students who might find it difficult to continue their schooling after high school, transition planning for employment is essential. Prior to leaving high school, students

*Figure 14.9 Classroom Strategies for Children and Youth with TBI*

- **Study guide or content outline.** Students may need an outline to follow so they can anticipate content.
- **Pictures or visual cues.** Signals are a good way to alert students that they need to do something differently.
- **Systematic verbal rehearsal.** Students may have to "practice" a verbal cue and what is expected of them.
- **Homework assignment book.** All assignments will need to be written down because of poor short-term memory.
- **Teach memory strategies.** Students may need to learn memory tricks such as mnemonics, pictures, or limericks.
- **Scribe or note taker.** Classmates may want to take turns taking good notes and having them photocopied at the end of class to give to the student. TBI victims often can listen but cannot take notes and listen at the same time.
- **Recognition versus recall.** Do not assume, when students recognize information, that they recall how it fits into the big picture. Check for understanding.
- **Modify work amounts.** Because focusing may be a serious problem, shorten assignments to the minimum necessary. Increase assignments gradually if the students are successful.
- **Alternative forms of expression.** General statements and satire may go right over their heads. Be very specific and to the point.
- **Provide feedback on responses.** Always state that an answer is correct or needs more input. The students may not pick up on a smile or nod that would be affirming.
- **Classroom aides.** It is often necessary to hire a classroom aide to help a student stay on task, organize, and plan homework.
- **Assist with confusion.** Watch for the confused look. These students are not likely to raise their hands and ask questions.
- **Avoid overreactions.** These students may ask the same question over and over because of poor short-term memory. Be patient. Repeat as needed.
- **Accept inconsistencies in performance.** These students may do very well on, say, Tuesday. This raises the bar for expectations. Remember that they may not be able to do this well the rest of the week.
- **Routine and schedule.** Be prepared for problems if there is a late start, a substitute teacher, early dismissal, or shortened classes. Changes do not come easy to students with a TBI.
- **Behavior management strategy.** Have a plan in mind for misbehavior. The regular plan may not work well. Preferably, talk with students ahead of time and let them know how you plan to discipline them.
- **Simple, concrete language.** Use short sentences that are to the point. Try to keep directions down to as few steps as possible.
- **Alert to transitions.** State that the bell is going to ring in five minutes and that they should begin putting things away in an orderly fashion. It may help to state which class is next.
- **Communication book.** While students are given time to do homework at the end of class, it would be good to communicate with parents how things are going in class, to note positives, and to discuss areas that need work.

with a TBI should have skills associated with filling out job applications, interviewing for jobs, and participating in supervised work experiences. State vocational agencies also play key roles in assisting young people with a TBI following high school. They provide services related to aptitude assessment, training opportunities after high school, and trial job placements.

Collaboration and cooperation are the key factors in achieving success with individuals who have a traumatic brain injury. A great deal can be accomplished when families, students, and care providers come together, engage in appropriate planning, and work collaboratively.

# People with Physical Disabilities and Other Health Disorders

## Early Childhood Years

### Tips for Families

- Work closely with medical and other health-related personnel to lessen the overall impact of the disorder or injury over time.

- Become familiar with special services available in your community and region for the disability or disorder.

- Learn about simple applications of behavior modification for use in your home environment by completing a parent training class.

- Seek out appropriate assistance through advocacy and support groups.

- Pursue family or individual counseling for persistent relationship-centered problems.

- Develop sensible routines and schedules for the child or youth.

- Communicate with siblings, friends, and relatives; help them become informed about the disability and disorder and their role in the treatment process.

- Join advocacy and support groups that provide the information and assistance you need.

- Do not overprotect your child or youth. Provide boundaries, discipline, responsibility, and encouragement.

### Tips for Preschool Teachers

- Communicate and collaborate with parents, special education personnel, and health care providers to develop appropriate expectations, management, and instruction.

- Watch for abrupt changes in the child's behavior. If they occur, notify parents and other professionals immediately.

- Involve socially sophisticated and sensitive peers and other older children in working with a preschooler.

- Become familiar with events that "set off" a child or pose special problems for the child's involvement.

- Be sure that the physical environment in the classroom lends itself to the needs of children who may have physical or health disorders (e.g., that aisles in the classroom are sufficiently large for the free movement of a wheelchair).

- Use management procedures that promote appropriate independence, give rise to following instructions, and foster appropriate learning.

### Tips for Preschool Personnel

- Participate in team meetings with the preschool teacher.

- Communicate frequently with the student's parents about concerns and promising developments.

- Employ appropriate management strategies used by the parents and the preschool teacher.

- Help other children understand and accept the child with a disability or disorder.

- Become aware of specific needs and potential talents of the child by consulting with parents.

- Be sure that other key personnel in the school who interact directly with the child are informed of his or her needs; collaborate in offering the best services and supports possible.

- Orient all children in your setting to the needs of the child with a disability or disorder. This could be done by you, the parents or siblings, or other educational personnel in the school. Remember, your behavior toward the child will say more than words will ever convey.

- Be sure to make arrangements for emergency situations. For example, some peers may know exactly what to do if a fellow class member begins to have a seizure or an asthmatic attack. Additionally, classmates should know how they might be helpful in directing and assisting a child during a fire drill or other emergency procedures.

### Tips for Neighbors and Friends

- Involve a child with a physical disability or health disorder and his or her family in holiday gatherings.

- Be sensitive to dietary regimens, opportunities for repositioning, and alternative means for communicating if needed.

- Become aware of the things that you may need to do. For example, you may need to learn what to do if a child with insulin-dependent diabetes shows signs of glucose buildup.

- Offer to become educated about the condition and its impact on the child.

- Become familiar with recommended management procedures for directing a child.

- Teach your own children about the dynamics of the condition; help them understand how to react and respond to variations in behavior.

## Elementary Years

### Tips for Families

- Maintain a healthy and ongoing relationship with the care providers who are part of your child's life.

- Acknowledge their efforts and express appreciation for actions that are particularly helpful to you and your child.

- Continue to be involved with advocacy and support groups.

- Stay informed by subscribing to newsletters and magazines disseminated by advocacy organizations.

- Develop and maintain positive relationships with the people who teach and serve your child within the school setting.

- Remember that the transition back to school and family environments requires very explicit planning and preparation.

- Learn about and use management procedures that promote the child's well-being, growth, and learning.

- Establish functional routines and schedules for family activities.

### Tips for General Education Classroom Teachers

- Be informed and willing to learn about the unique needs of a child or youth with a disability or disorder in your classroom. For example, schedule a conference with the child's parents before the year begins to talk about medications, prosthetic devices, levels of desired physical activities, and so on.

- Remember that teamwork and coordination among caring professionals and parents are essential to a child's success.

- Use socially competent and mature peers to assist you (e.g., providing tutoring, physical assistance, social support in recess activities).

- Be sure that plans have been made and practiced for dealing with emergency situations (e.g., some children may need to be carried out of a building or room).

- If the child's condition is progressive and life-threatening, consult with parents and other professionals to prepare peers and others for the potential death of the child or youth.

### Tips for School Personnel

- Become informed; seek to understand the unique characteristics of a disability or disorder.

- Seek to understand and use instructional and management approaches that are well suited to a child's emerging strengths and challenges.

- Use the expertise that is available in the school and school system; collaborate with other specialists.

- Take advantage of opportunities to profit from parent training.

- Be sure that all key personnel in the school setting who interact with the child on a regular basis are informed about treatment regimens, dietary requirements, and signs of potentially problematic conditions such as fevers and irritability.

- Meet periodically as professionals to deal with emergent problems, brainstorm for solutions, and identify suitable actions.

- Institute cross-age tutoring and support. When possible, have a child with a physical or health condition become a tutor.

### Tips for Neighbors and Friends

- Adopt an inclusive attitude about family and neighborhood events; invite the child or youth to join in family-centered activities, picnics, and holiday events.

- Learn how to respond effectively and confidently to the common problems that the child or youth may present.

- Communicate concerns and problems immediately to parents in a compassionate and caring fashion.

- Provide parents with respite care.

## Secondary and Transition Years

### Tips for Families

- Work closely with school and adult services personnel in developing transition plans.

- Develop a thoughtful and comprehensive transition plan that includes education, employment, housing, and use of leisure time.

- Become aware of all the services and resources that are available through state and national adult services programs.

- Remember that for some individuals with physical or health disabilities, the secondary or young adult years may be the most trying, particularly if the student's condition is progressive in nature.

- Begin planning early in the secondary school years for the youth's transition from the public school to the adult world (schooling, work, transportation, independent living, etc.).

- Be sure that you are well informed about the adult services offered in your community and state.

### Tips for General Education Classroom Teachers

- Be sure that appropriate steps have been taken to prepare the youth to return to school, work, and related activities.

- Work closely with members of the multidisciplinary team in developing appropriate schooling and employment experiences.

- Report any subtle changes in behavior immediately to parents and other specialists within the school.

- Continue to be aware of the potential needs for accommodation and adjustment.

- Treat the individual as an adult.

- Realize that the youth's studies or work experiences may be interrupted from time to time for specialized or regular medical treatments or other important health care services.

### Tips for School Personnel

- Determine what environmental changes need to be made.

- Employ teaching procedures that best fit the youth's current cognitive status, attention deficits, physical functioning, and academic achievement.

- Be prepared for anger, depression, and rebellion in some youth with a TBI.

- Focus on the youth's current and emerging strengths.

- Acknowledge individuals by name, become familiar with their interests and hobbies, joke with them occasionally, and involve them in meaningful activities such as fund-raisers, community service projects, and decorating for various school events.

- Provide opportunities for all students to receive recognition and be involved in school-related activities.

- Realize that peer assistance and tutoring may be particularly helpful to certain students. Social involvement outside the school setting should be encouraged (e.g., going to movies, attending concerts, etc.).

- Use members of the multidisciplinary team to help with unique problems that surface from time to time. For example, you may want to talk with special educators about management or instructional ideas that may improve a given child's behavior and academic performance in your classroom.

### Tips for Neighbors, Friends, and Potential Employers

- Involve the youth in appropriate family, neighborhood, and community activities, particularly youth activities.
- Become informed about the youth's capacities and interests.
- Provide employment explorations and part-time employment.
- Be aware of assistance that you might provide in the event of a youth's gradual deterioration or death.
- Encourage your own teens to volunteer as peer tutors or job coaches.

### Adult Years

#### Tips for Families

- Begin developing appropriate independence skills throughout the school years.

- Determine early what steps can be taken to prepare the youth for meaningful part-time or full-time employment, or postsecondary training.
- Become thoroughly familiar with postsecondary educational opportunities and adult services for individuals with disabilities.
- Explore various living and housing options early in the youth's secondary school years.
- Work with adult service personnel and advocacy organizations in lining up appropriate housing and related support services.
- Know your rights and how you can qualify your son or daughter for educational or other support services.

### Tips for Neighbors, Friends, and Employers

- Create opportunities for the adult to be involved in age-relevant activities, including movies, sports events, going out to dinner, and so on.
- Be sure to regularly provide people with a physical disability or health disorder specific information, recognition, and feedback about their work performance. Feedback may include candid comments about their punctuality, rate of work completion, and social interaction with others. Withholding information, not making reasonable adjustments, and not expecting these individuals to be responsible for their behaviors are great disservices to them.

## 14-13   Attention Deficit/Hyperactivity Disorder

**Standard 1**
Learner Development and Individual Learning Differences

Attention deficit/hyperactivity disorder (ADHD) is one of the most common mental disorders in children and adolescents. Symptoms include difficulty staying focused and paying attention, difficulty controlling behavior, and very high levels of activity (Goldstein, 2011). "Studies show that the number of children being diagnosed with ADHD is increasing, but it is unclear why" (National Institute of Mental Health, 2012b). ADHD often persists into adulthood, requiring treatment and attention throughout the adult years (Barkley, 2006a; National Institute of Mental Health, 2008; Willcutt, 2012). Examine the attendant definition of ADHD found in Figure 14.10.

Children with ADHD—especially boys—often evidence problems in developing school-related academic skills and in achieving satisfactory behavior/emotional adjustment (Daley & Birchwood, 2010). They frequently experience significant challenges with grade retention, expulsions, and suspensions. Left untreated as children and youth, adults with ADHD may encounter serious problems, many related to drug abuse, criminality, and unsatisfactory relationships with others (Barkley, 2006b; Frodl, 2010; Froehlich, Lanphear, Epstein, Barbaresi, Katusic, & Kahn, 2010; Glass, Flory, Martin, & Hankin, 2011; Wilens, et al., 2011).

Three different types of ADHD have been proposed:

- **Predominantly inattentive type:** It is hard for these individuals to organize or finish a task, to pay attention to details, or to follow instructions or conversations. These people are easily distracted or forget details of daily routines.

- **Predominantly hyperactive-impulsive type:** These people fidget and talk a lot. It is hard to sit still for long (e.g., for a meal or while doing homework). Smaller children may run, jump, or climb constantly. Individuals feel restless and have trouble with impulsivity. Someone who is impulsive may interrupt others a lot, grab things from people, or speak at inappropriate times. It is hard for these people to wait their turn or listen to directions. People with impulsiveness may have more accidents and injuries than others.

- **Combined type:** Symptoms of the previous two types are equally present in these people. (Centers for Disease Control and Prevention, 2012b)

**Standard 4**
Assessment

There is not a single test for ADHD. Licensed professionals collect information about the child, youth, or adult using a variety of approaches, each tailored to the respective age

A. Either (1) or (2):

1. Six (or more) of the following symptoms of *inattention* have persisted for at least six months to a degree that is maladaptive and inconsistent with developmental level:

*Inattention*

a. Often fails to give close attention to details or makes careless mistakes in schoolwork, work, or other activities

b. Often has difficulty sustaining attention in tasks or play activities

c. Often does not seem to listen when spoken to directly

d. Often does not follow through on instructions and fails to finish schoolwork, chores, or duties in the workplace (not due to oppositional behavior or failure to understand instructions)

e. Often has difficulty organizing tasks and activities

f. Often avoids, dislikes, or is reluctant to engage in tasks that require sustained mental effort (such as schoolwork or homework)

g. Often loses things necessary for tasks or activities (e.g., toys, school assignments, pencils, books, or tools)

h. Is often easily distracted by extraneous stimuli

i. Is often forgetful in daily activities

2. Six (or more) of the following symptoms of *hyperactivity-impulsivity* have persisted for at least six months to a degree that is maladaptive and inconsistent with developmental level:

*Hyperactivity*

a. Often fidgets with hands or feet or squirms in seat

b. Often leaves seat in classroom or in other situations in which remaining seated is expected

c. Often runs about or climbs excessively in situations in which it is inappropriate (in adolescents or adults, may be limited to subjective feelings or restlessness)

d. Often has difficulty playing or engaging in leisure activities quietly

e. Is often "on the go" or often acts as if "driven by a motor"

f. Often talks excessively

*Impulsivity*

g. Often blurts out answers before questions have been completed

h. Often has difficulty awaiting turn

i. Often interrupts or intrudes on others (e.g., butts into conversations or games)

B. Some hyperactive-impulsive or inattentive symptoms that caused impairment were present before age 7 years.

C. Several inattentive or hyperactive-impulsive symptoms are present in two or more settings (e.g., at school [or work] and at home).

D. There must be clear evidence of clinically significant impairment in social, academic, or occupational functioning.

E. The symptoms do not occur exclusively during the course of a pervasive developmental disorder, schizophrenia, or other psychotic disorder and are not better accounted for by another mental disorder (e.g., mood disorder, anxiety disorder, dissociative disorder, or a personality disorder).

Code based on type:
*Attention deficit/hyperactivity disorder, combined presentation:* if both Criteria A1 and A2 are met for the past six months
*Attention deficit/hyperactivity disorder, predominantly inattentive presentation:* if Criterion A1 is met but Criterion A2 is not met for the past six months
*Attention deficit/hyperactivity disorder, predominantly hyperactive-impulsive presentation:* if Criterion A2 is met but Criterion A1 is not met for the past six months
*Coding note*: For individuals (especially adolescents and adults) who currently have symptoms that no longer meet full criteria, "In Partial Remission" should be specified.

SOURCE: Reprinted with permission from American Psychiatric Association. (2013). *Diagnostic and statistical manual of mental disorders, 5th ed.* Copyright 2013 American Psychiatric Association.

groups and settings in which the behaviors may occur, carefully determining their frequency, function, and impact on the affected individual. These might include behavior rating scales, ongoing structured observations, and diagnostic interviews with individuals who know the child or youth well—parents, coaches, babysitters, and others (Batstra, Nieweg, Pijl, Van Tol, & Dadders-Algra, 2014; DuPaul & Kern, 2011a; Efron & Sciberras, 2010).

## 14-13a Prevalence and Causation

The prevalence of ADHD has increased dramatically in the United States. Whereas an estimated 7.8 percent of children were diagnosed in 2003, numbers from 2011 indicate 11 percent of school-age children have the condition, although there is significant variance between states (Centers for Disease Control and Prevention, 2014a). Obviously, many "normal" children evidence mild features of the disorder, but are not diagnosed as such. About two and one half times as many boys as girls have ever been diagnosed with ADHD (Centers for Disease Control and Prevention, 2014c). However, the presenting symptoms in both boys and girls are very similar (Barkley, 2006c).

ADHD is presumed to be a function of a central nervous system disorder. Also, ADHD can co-occur with other disorders, including intellectual disabilities, sensory impairments, and serious emotional and behavior disorders (Harty, Miller, Newcorn, & Halperin, 2009; Selekman, 2010; Thorell & Rydell, 2008; Youngstrom, Arnold, & Frazier, 2010).

The exact causes and precise factors that give rise to ADHD remain unclear. However, there is a clear relationship between ADHD and genetic/environmental factors (Nikolas & Burt, 2011). "Genetic research strongly supports the role of genetic risk factors in ADHD" (Schachar, 2014, p. 46).

In this regard, magnetic resonance imaging (MRI) is helping researchers uncover some of the neurological factors associated with ADHD. Some children with ADHD appear to be wired differently than their same-age peers without the condition. In some children with ADHD, their brain development follows a normal path of development but progresses in a delayed fashion. This delay in development on average is generally three years behind children without the disorder (National Institute of Mental Health, 2012a).

**Standard 2**
Learning Environments

## 14-13b Interventions

Treatments and interventions for individuals with ADHD are centered on reducing symptoms and improving everyday functioning in home, classroom, social, and work settings. ADHD requires multiple interventions that fall into two broad categories: behavioral and medical. As is true in many disability areas, effective treatment involves a multidisciplinary team approach and includes combinations of techniques as determined by individual needs (Pugach & Winn, 2011; Reid & Johnson, 2011; Williamson & McLeskey, 2011).

Controlling hyperactive and impulsive behavior in children appears to be most effectively accomplished with medication (often methylphenidate or Ritalin) (Barbaresi, 2014; Ryan, Katsiyannis, & Hughes, 2011). Evidence is emerging that pharmacological control of behavioral challenges is more effective than nonmedical interventions, such as behavioral treatment (Powell, Thomsen, & Frydenberg, 2011; Ryan, Katsiyannis, & Hughes, 2011; Stroh, Frankenberger, Cornell-Swanson, Wood, & Pahl, 2008; Vaughan, Roberts, & Needelman, 2009). Research supporting the effectiveness of medication is accumulating, but such medical intervention shows no effect, or very limited influence, on academic performance (DuPaul & Kern, 2011b; Graziano, Geffken, & Lall, 2011; Hale et al., 2011). Current thinking suggests that even though there are clear benefits to the use of medication, it may be overprescribed; side effects and issues of potential abuse need further research (Frodl, 2010; Kalikow, 2011; Lee, Humphreys, Flory, Liu, & Glass, 2011).

Some researchers advise caution in the use of psychostimulants for both theoretical and practical reasons. First, there are concerns regarding side effects, as one would expect. In some cases, it is difficult to distinguish psychological characteristics that may appear to be side effects (such as increased anxiety) from the symptoms of ADHD itself. Additionally, some researchers express uneasiness about appropriate dosage, overprescription, and unhealthy side effects such as increased tobacco and alcohol use. There are also matters of potential for abuse and issues related to management planning and implementation for children being treated with medication (Comstock, 2011; Rabiner, Anastopoulos, & Costello, 2010).

Children who are young when they begin to receive medication may take it over a very long period; however, it is unclear what the cumulative effects may be on physical or intellectual development (van de Loo-Neus, Rommelse, & Buitelaar, 2011). For preschoolers, there is some evidence that susceptibility to side effects might be greater (DuPaul & Kern, 2011b; Posey, Bassin, & Lewis, 2009). Further investigation in both these areas is certainly warranted. Concerns about medication interventions have been raised in the popular press and continue to arise periodically as the field grapples with the challenges these children and youth present (Higgens, 2009; Shute, 2009).

The hyperactive and impulsive behaviors of many children with ADHD clearly present a significant challenge to parents, teachers, and other school personnel during the elementary school years. Elementary teachers describe these children as fidgety, impulsive, often off-task, and constantly disruptive (DuPaul, Weyandt, & Janusis, 2011; National Institute of Mental Health, 2008). These behaviors are often accompanied by deficits in academic performance (Bussing, Porter, Zima, Mason, Garvan, & Reid, 2012; McConaughy, Volpe, & Antshel, 2011).

Nonmedical, school-based interventions can also be effective in improving the classroom behaviors of elementary-age school children with ADHD. In general, targeted behavior modification strategies appear to be more effective for controlling behavioral problems than those that involve cognitive-behavioral or cognitive interventions. Cognitive-behavioral therapies are based on combining behavioral techniques with efforts to change the way a person thinks about his or her behaviors. Research evidence suggests limited beneficial results from cognitive-behavioral interventions for children with ADHD (Levine & Anshel, 2011).

Educators should arrange the classroom setting to enhance the child's ability to respond, attend, and behave in a manner that is conducive to learning. Teachers may have to monitor the directions they give students with ADHD, often cuing them to the fact that a direction or message is about to be delivered. This might be done with a prompt such as "Listen, John" or some other signal that the teacher is comfortable making and is well understood by the student as meaning a directive is to follow (Fowler, 2010; Geng, 2011).

Student learning is enhanced by strategies that involve considerable structure (Reid & Johnson, 2011). Instruction, such as writing lessons, may be more effective if reinforcement is combined with modeling and increased practice (Browder & Spooner, 2011; Hedin, Mason, & Gaffney, 2011). These children often require individualized instruction from a teacher or aide, focused on the specific content area needing attention, such as reading, math, or spelling (Riley, McKevitt, Shriver, & Allen, 2011; van Kraayenoord, Miller, & Moni, 2009).

Multiple treatment approaches (often termed *multimodal treatments*), such as drug and behavior therapies, are more effective than just one kind of treatment for children with ADHD (Beljan, Bree, Reuter, Reuter, & Wingers, 2014; Owens & Fabiano, 2011; Springer & Reddy, 2010). This is important in the case of children with ADHD, because a high proportion receive both medical treatment and school-based instruction. All collaborating parties must pay special attention to facilitating communication among physicians and others providing treatment.

## 14-13c   Adolescence and Adulthood

Once viewed as a childhood condition, ADHD is now known to have a significant presence beyond those early years and is accompanied by an array of other behaviors and conditions in adolescence and adulthood (Bussing, Mason, & Bell, 2010; Elkins, Malone, Keyes, Iacono, & McGue, 2011; Mao, Babcock, & Brams, 2011; Taylor, Deb, & Unwin, 2011). These include social impairments, greater number of driving-related problems (license suspensions, accidents, and traffic citations), continuing academic challenges, underachievement in work settings, presence of other psychiatric conditions, and inhibition/self-control issues (Barkley, 2006b; Kent et al., 2011). Current research suggests that ADHD is far more persistent into adulthood than once was thought; it often requires continuing treatment (Cahill, Coolidge, Segal, Klebe, Marle, & Overmann, 2012; Sprich, Knouse, & Cooper-Vince, 2010). Interventions appropriate for adolescents and adults with ADHD must be reassessed, and where appropriate, modified in an age-appropriate manner (Kraft, 2010; Mao, Babcock, and Brams, 2011; Mitchell, Robertson, Kimbrel, & Nelson-Gray, 2011). However, cognitive challenges such as the impulse control and memory problems found in children with ADHD occur in many adults with ADHD as well (Mitchell et al., 2011; Storm & White, 2010). Further, medication remains an effective treatment for the impulsivity and difficulty in focusing on tasks that continue into the adolescent and adult years for many people with ADHD.

Adolescents and adults with ADHD may not exhibit hyperactivity but may still have considerable difficulty in focusing on tasks, controlling impulses, and using appropriate social skills. Again, medication may be an effective treatment for some of these behaviors as many of the adult/adolescent-prescribed medications enhance the individuals' executive function of the brain—the brain's capacity to help adolescents or adults manage and control their behavior and impulses (National Resource Center on ADHD, 2012). There is still much to be learned about the treatment of adults with ADHD. Future research will help us understand the salient aspects of treatment and how they play out in managing the symptoms of ADHD and achieving worthwhile long-term outcomes for adolescents and adults with this disorder.

## Looking Toward a Bright Future

This is so much to be positive about in considering the future for children, youth, and individuals with physical disabilities and health disorders. Consider for a moment the comments made by young Michael Anwar, cited at the outset of the chapter, when he wrote "I have cerebral palsy…it doesn't have me!" Michael is proof positive that caring professionals can help children and youth respond with more resilience and optimism in coping with their conditions and grow in uniquely positive ways throughout their lives.

Some of our greatest causes for hope center on medical advances in gene therapies, stem cell research, uniquely person-specific medications, early treatment procedures, and highly innovative surgical techniques—too many to describe in great detail. Also, we are benefiting from the talents and skills of highly creative engineers and inventors who are developing new orthotics, highly functional assistive and augmentative devices, artificial limbs, exoskeletons, home and office control systems, and robotics.

Finally, we are becoming more inclusive, spontaneous, and caring in our responses to individuals with physical disabilities, disorders, and injuries—much in part because they are now so much a natural part of all of our daily experiences in our neighborhoods, schools, and communities. We know them. They have been in our classrooms. We feel more comfortable around them because of our own face-to-face interactions with them, their families, and their unique talents and capacities.

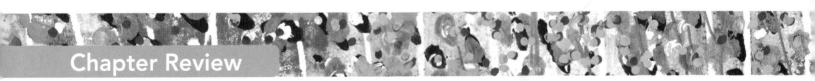

## Chapter Review

**14-1  Describe how the lives of people with physical disabilities and other health disorders have changed since the advent of IDEA.**

- Technologies, inventions, and developments in many fields are improving the lives of young people and adults with physical disabilities and other health disorders.

- Developments in assistive technologies, stem cell research, person-specific medications, advanced surgical techniques, transplants, gene therapies, and other preventative and early therapies have and will continue to have lasting and positive impacts on infants, children, youth, and adults with physical disorders.

- Health disorders cause individuals to have limited strength, vitality, or alertness, due to chronic or acute health problems.

- Optimism for people with health disorders centers on producing new person-specific medications, gene therapies, assistive devices, new surgical procedures, and a host of other inventions.

**14-2  Describe cerebral palsy, its prevalence, causation, and related interventions.**

- Cerebral palsy (CP) is a neuromuscular disorder caused by damage to one or more specific areas of the brain that affects muscle coordination and body movement.

- About 764,000 individuals in the United States display clinical features of CP.

- The fundamental causes of CP are insults to the brain.

- Early and ongoing interventions and therapies center on the child's movement, social and emotional development, learning, language, speech, and hearing.

**14-3  Describe spina bifida, its prevalence, causation, and related interventions.**

- *Spina bifida* (SB) is a collective term for malformations of the spinal cord. SB is the most common neural tube defect.

- SB occurs in about 1 in 1,500 births.

- The exact cause of SB is unknown. There is a slight tendency for it to run in families, and it is possible that certain medications or toxic substances ingested by the mother may be responsible. Folic acid deficiency is implicated.

- Physical therapy plays a critical role in intervention. Education programs and school care requirements vary according to the needs of each student.

**14-4  Describe spinal cord injury, its prevalence, causation, and related interventions.**

- "Spinal cord injury (SCI) is damage to the spinal cord that results in a loss of function such as mobility or feeling. Frequent causes of damage are trauma (car accident, gunshot, falls, etc.) or disease (polio, spina bifida, Friedreich's ataxia, etc.).

- About 450,000 individuals live with an SCI in the United States. SCIs result from any number of types of falls or other causes of trauma to the spinal cord.

- SCI patients are first treated for shock and then immobilized to prevent movement and possible further damage.

- Medical treatment is often lengthy and tedious. Relieving pain is a significant challenge over the lifespan of individuals with an SCI.

**14-5  Describe muscular dystrophy, its prevalence, causation, and related interventions.**

- The muscular dystrophies (MD) are a group of more than 30 genetic diseases. MDs are characterized by weakness and degeneration of the skeletal muscles that control movement. MDs are progressive disorders.

- About 200,000 Americans have MD. Some forms of MD are seen in infancy or childhood, whereas others may not appear until middle age or later.

- MD is caused by abnormalities wherein muscle protein genes are missing or lacking sufficient dystrophin.

- There is no known cure for muscular dystrophy. Treatments focus on maintaining or improving individuals' functioning and preserving their ambulatory independence for as long as possible.

**14-6  Describe AIDS, its prevalence, causation, and related interventions.**

- Acquired immunodeficiency syndrome (AIDS) is a set of symptoms and infections in individuals resulting from the specific injury to the immune system caused by infection with the human immunodeficiency virus (HIV).

- About 1.2 million people in the United States have HIV. About 50,000 become infected each year, including nearly 2,300 adolescents.

- HIV is passed from one person to another through various means, including the exchange of bodily fluids, usually semen or vaginal secretions; blood exchange through injection drug use (IDU); and exchange through blood transfusions, perinatal contact, and breast milk.

- To date, there is no known cure for AIDS. The best cure for AIDS in children and youth is prevention. Treatment is generally provided by an interdisciplinary team composed of medical, educational, and health care professionals.

**14-7  Describe asthma, its prevalence, causation, and related interventions.**

- Asthma is evidenced by swelling and inflammation of the air passages that transport air from the mouth and nose to the lungs. This swelling within the affected passages causes them to narrow, thus limiting the air entering and exiting the individual.

- Nearly one in ten children in the United States is affected by asthma.

- Asthma is an inherited condition that must be triggered to display. Triggers vary greatly across children, youth, and adults.

- Interventions include increasing the anti-inflammatory medication in advance of anticipated exposure to certain triggers, using appropriate bronchodilators for much the same purpose, and limiting the time of exposure to potential or known triggers.

**14-8  Describe epilepsy, its prevalence, causation, and related interventions.**

- Epilepsy is a seizure disorder in which the normal pattern of neuronal activity becomes disturbed. Epilepsy may cause abnormal sensations, emotions, and behavior, convulsions, muscle spasms, and loss of consciousness.

- Epilepsy affects approximately 468,000 children age 17 and younger in the United States.

- Epilepsy and other seizure disorders can be caused by perinatal factors, tumors of the brain, complications of head trauma, infections of the central nervous system, vascular diseases, alcoholism, infection, maternal injury or infection, and genetic factors.

- The treatment of seizure disorders involves careful medical investigation and then prescription and management of drugs. Other treatments for seizure disorders include surgery, stress management, a vagus nerve stimulator (an electronic device designed to prevent seizures by sending small bursts of electrical energy to the brain), brain infusion of the chemical muscimol into affected areas of the brain, and diet modifications.

**14-9  Describe diabetes, its prevalence, causation, and related interventions.**

- Diabetes mellitus is a developmental or hereditary disorder characterized by inadequate secretion or use of insulin, a substance that is produced by the pancreas and used to process carbohydrates. The two types of diabetes are type 1, insulin-dependent or juvenile-onset, and type 2, noninsulin-dependent or adult-onset.

- Approximately 21 million Americans have been diagnosed with diabetes and up to eight million are undiagnosed.

- A combination of genetic dispositions and environmental triggers and conditions cause type 1 diabetes, but the exact variables are unclear. Individuals who develop type 2 diabetes incrementally create conditions in their body in which their cells become unresponsive to the effects of insulin.

- Medical treatment centers on the regular administration of insulin for children and youth with juvenile diabetes.

**14-10 Describe cystic fibrosis, its prevalence, causation, and related interventions.**

- Cystic fibrosis (CF) is an inherited chronic disease in which a defective gene and its protein product cause the body to produce unusually thick, sticky mucus that clogs the lungs and leads to life-threatening lung infections, and obstructs the pancreas and stops natural enzymes from helping the body break down and absorb food.
- In the United States, about 30,000 children and adults have CF.
- CF is genetically transmitted and manifests in children who have the defective gene from both parents.
- Interventions for CF include consistent and appropriate application of the medical, social, educational, and psychological components of treatment to enable individuals to live longer and with less discomfort and fewer complications than in years past.

**14-11 Describe sickle-cell disease, its prevalence, causation, and related interventions.**

- Sickle-cell disease (SCD) is a group of inherited red blood cell disorders that profoundly affects the structure and functioning of red blood cells.
- SCD affects from 90,000 to 100,000 people in the United States.
- Sickle-cell disease is caused by various combinations of genes. A child who receives a mutant S-hemoglobin gene from each parent exhibits SCD to one degree or another. The disease usually announces itself at 6 months of age and persists throughout the individual's lifetime.
- SCD in the first five years of life is treated with antibiotics. The disease is then managed through immunizations, nutrition, hydration, and pain relief.

**14-12 Describe traumatic brain injury, its prevalence, causation, and related interventions.**

- Traumatic brain injury (TBI) results in open- or closed-head injuries resulting in impairments in one or more areas, such as cognition; language; memory; attention; reasoning; abstract thinking; judgment; problem solving; sensory, perceptual, and motor abilities; psychosocial behavior; physical functions; information processing; and speech.
- About 2.5 million people sustain a TBI each year; about 475,000 TBIs happen to children from birth to age 14 and account for 40 percent of all head injuries.
- TBI occurs when a sudden trauma causes damage to the brain. TBI can result when the head suddenly and violently hits an object, or when an object pierces the skull and enters brain tissue.
- Individuals with a TBI can receive services and supports in cognition, speech and language, social and behavioral skills, as well as physical functioning, according to individual need.

**14-13 Describe attention deficit/hyperactivity disorder (ADHD), its prevalence, causation, and related interventions.**

- Symptoms of ADHD include difficulty staying focused and paying attention, difficulty controlling behavior, and very high levels of activity. Children with ADHD—especially boys—often evidence problems in developing school-related academic skills and in achieving satisfactory behavior/emotional adjustment.
- About 11 percent of school-aged children are diagnosed with ADHD; about two and one half times as many boys as girls.
- The causes of ADHD remain unclear. However, there is a clear relationship between ADHD and genetic/environmental factors.
- ADHD requires multiple interventions that fall into two broad categories: behavioral and medical. Effective treatment involves a multidisciplinary team approach and includes combinations of techniques as determined by individual needs. Hyperactive behavior can sometimes be controlled with medication; nonmedical interventions center on behavioral therapies. Combinations of medication and behavioral therapies can also be effective.

 **Council for Exceptional Children (CEC) Standards to Accompany Chapter 14**

If you are thinking about a career in special education, you should know that many states use national standards developed by the Council for Exceptional Children (CEC) to assess a teacher candidate's knowledge and skills for working with students with disabilities. See a complete listing of the seven CEC Content Standards on the inside cover of this text.

1 Learner Development and Individual Learning Differences
2 Learning Environments
4 Assessment
5 Instructional Planning and Strategies
7 Collaboration

## Mastery Activities and Assignments

To master the content within this chapter, complete the following activities and assignments:

1. Complete a written test of the chapter's content. If your instructor requires a written test of your content knowledge for this chapter, keep a copy for your portfolio.
2. Review the Case Study on Embracing Diversity, "Sarah and the 'Pump'," and respond in writing to the Application Questions. Keep a copy of the Case Study and your written response for your portfolio.
3. Participate in a community service learning activity. Community service is a valuable way to enhance your learning experience. Develop a reflective journal of the service learning experience for your portfolio.

## CHAPTER 15

# Gifted, Creative, and Talented

© 2015 Cengage Learning®

## Learning Objectives

*After you complete this chapter, you will be able to:*

**15-1** Describe how the lives of people who are gifted, creative, and talented have changed since the advent of IDEA.

**15-2** Explain the various definitions and classifications of gifted, creative, and talented.

**15-3** Describe the characteristics and prevalence of children and youth who are gifted, creative, and talented.

**15-4** List the causes associated with gifts and talents.

**15-5** Describe the assessment procedures used to identify gifts and talents in children and youth.

**15-6** Describe the different interventions for children and youth with gifts and talents from early childhood through adulthood.

# Natalie: Reflections of a Very Talented Communicator and Community Builder

Natalie grew up in a large family and struggled to find her own identity. She already had a sibling who was a gifted artist, another who was a talented musician, another who was a beauty queen, and still another who was a scholar. She possessed native abilities and motivation to succeed, but finding a strong sense of identity proved difficult in a crowded field.

One thing Natalie clearly excelled at was athletics. Her natural-born eye–hand coordination coupled with a household filled with seven brothers provided ample opportunities for her to play basketball in the family gym (really an enclosed garage with 6-foot-high basketball hoops at each end) and touch football in the backyard. Unfortunately, Natalie grew up before women realized the benefit of equal opportunity in public school athletics (Title IX of the Education Amendments of 1972). All of her sports' heroes were men, which was not helpful and discouraged her from pursuing athletics. Even worse, being a tomboy was not a compliment in many settings. Natalie declined to play school-sanctioned sports in high school and often hid her athletic talents, even letting her older brother win when they played one-on-one basketball (she still doesn't confess this to him!).

Natalie still remembers the moment when, while attending the 1999 Women's FIFA World Cup soccer match final (China versus USA) at the Rose Bowl, she saw a young boy wearing a Mia Hamm jersey. It was a profound reminder of how far society has progressed in appreciating women's natural abilities and how everything works out in the end.

With athletics proving to be a dead end and a family setting that did not lend itself easily to finding her way, Natalie turned inward. Over many years she watched and learned. She learned she had a strong preference for cooperation instead of competition, harmony instead of discord. She learned that human kindness is a foundational virtue that should guide all human interactions. She learned not to feel a sense of entitlement, but rather to value a simpler life—the peace that comes from nature, a modest living environment, and deeply fulfilling personal relationships. She learned to place a high value on authenticity, civility, humility, patience, gratitude, and balance—attributes that would guide her later in life. She developed a strong sense of inner worth and personal identity…not from how others viewed her, but from how she viewed herself and what she knew to be true and right.

During her college years, Natalie's intellect, knack for team sports, and hard-earned emotional intelligence began to pay off. She thrived in her economics coursework. She played soccer for her college team and won multi-state competitions. More importantly, she continued to develop the personality attributes that she had developed in her youth and that are rewarded in the professional work environment. She finished undergraduate and graduate degrees in economics and began working in a governor's office as an economist.

It is in the professional work setting where the lessons learned growing up in a challenging, competitive, and even discriminatory environment began to blossom. Natalie's innate giftedness in language, computation, and relationship building joined with her emotional maturity to form a powerful combination, particularly in positions close to power where poise, confidence, and humility are at a premium. Natalie served under three different governors, rising to become the governor's director of policy and communications spokesperson. Most people do either public policy or communications; Natalie thrived at both and became a trusted senior adviser to a governor.

Later she was asked to serve as a political appointee in President George W. Bush's administration. Once again putting her technical versatility, gift for language, and ability to use emotional information to guide her thinking and behavior, Natalie oversaw the media operations for an entire federal agency and then served as a counselor to the secretary of the largest federal department. Today she serves as an associate dean of a nationally ranked business school and writes monthly columns for her city's daily newspaper and business magazine. Natalie continues to live modestly and spends her time building community and promoting civil society.

The terms *gifted*, *creative*, and *talented* are associated with children, youth, and adults who have extraordinary abilities in one or more areas of performance. Some believe that gifts and talents are overrated—that outstanding performance in most endeavors comes from consistent and deliberate practice (Colvin, 2008). What do you think? What really gives rise to individuals like Natalie—the talented musician and academic?

The gifted, creative, and talented are a diverse array of individuals. Intellectual prowess exhibited by Confucius, Plato, al-Biruni, Isaac Newton, and Maryam Mirzakhani; timeless creative works by Jochi, Michelangelo, Dostoyevsky, Rabindranath Tagore, and Maya Angelou; and the remarkable talents of Johann Bach, George Eliot, Dai Ailian, Margaret Court, and Gustavo Dudamel are testaments to achievements beyond the norm. Because of their unusual abilities and skills, educators and policy makers frequently assume that gifted individuals will reach their full potential without any specialized programs or targeted encouragement.

## 15-1  A Changing Era in the Lives of People Who Are Gifted, Creative, and Talented

For years, behavioral scientists described children and youth with exceptionally high intelligence as being **gifted**. Only recently have researchers and practitioners included the adjectives **creative** and **talented**, to suggest domains of performance other than those measured by traditional intelligence tests. Now more than ever, children, youth, and adults with remarkable talents or creative capacities are being identified for participation in programs designed to encourage and nourish their gifts and capacities. No longer are gifted programs solely targeted at those with high IQs. Obviously, not all individuals who achieve high scores on intelligence tests are creative or talented. Capacities associated with creativity include *elaboration* (the ability to embellish or enrich an idea), *transformation* (the ability to construct new meanings or change an idea into something new and novel), and *visualization* (the capacity to manipulate ideas or see images mentally) (Sternberg, Jarvin, & Grigorenko, 2011). Individuals who are talented may display extraordinary skills in mathematics, sports, music, or other performance areas (Sternberg, 2006; Treffinger, 2004). "A child [or individual] may demonstrate gifted behavior at one point in development, but not necessarily at another point in development or may exhibit gifted behavior in one domain, but not necessarily across all domains …" (Horowitz, 2009, p. 9). Some individuals soar to exceptional heights in a talent domain, others achieve in intellectual areas, and still others excel in creative endeavors. A select few exhibit remarkable achievement across several domains like Natalie featured in our opening Snapshot.

### 15-1a  Historical Developments

Definitions that describe the unusually able in terms of intelligence quotients and creativity measures are recent phenomena. Not until the beginning of the 20th century was there a suitable method for potentially quantifying or measuring the human attribute of intelligence. The breakthrough occurred in Europe when Alfred Binet, a French psychologist, constructed the first developmental assessment scale for children in the early 1900s. This scale was created by observing children at various ages to identify specific tasks that ordinary children were able to perform at each age. These tasks were then sequenced according to age-appropriate levels. Children who could perform tasks well above that which was normal for their chronological age were identified as being developmentally advanced.

Binet and Simon (1905; 1908) developed the notion of **mental age**. The mental age of a child was derived by matching the tasks (memory, vocabulary, mathematical, and comprehension, etc.) that a child was able to perform according to the age scale (which gave the typical performance of children at various stages). Although this scale was initially developed and used to identify children with mental retardation in the Parisian schools, it eventually became an important means for identifying those who had higher-than-average mental ages as well.

Lewis M. Terman, an American educator and psychologist, expanded the concepts and procedures Binet developed. He was convinced that Binet and Simon had discovered an approach that would be useful for measuring intellectual abilities in all children. This belief prompted him to revise the Binet instrument, adding greater breadth to the scale. In 1916, Terman published the **Stanford-Binet Intelligence Scale** in conjunction with Stanford University. During this period, Terman introduced the term **intelligence quotient**, or **IQ**. The IQ score was obtained by dividing a child's mental age (MA) by his or her chronological age (CA) and multiplying that figure by 100 (MA/CA $\times$ 100 = IQ). For example, a child with a mental age of 12 and a chronological age of 8 would have an IQ of 150 (12/8 $\times$ 100 = 150). See the nearby Reflect on This, "An IQ of 228: Is That Possible?" for an example of a person with an extraordinary IQ.

---

**Gifted, creative, and talented**
Terms applied to individuals with extraordinary abilities or the capacity for developing them.

**Mental age (MA)**
A score that represents the individual's mental age according to various tasks he or she is able to perform on a given IQ test. Children who are able to complete tasks well beyond their chronological age (CA) will have a higher mental age (MA) and thus a higher-than-average IQ score (MA, 12 years/CA, 8 years $\times$ 100 = IQ 150).

**Stanford-Binet Intelligence Scale**
A standardized individual intelligence test, originally known as the Binet-Simon scales, which was revised and standardized by Lewis Terman at Stanford University.

**Intelligence quotient (IQ)**
A score obtained from an intelligence test that reflects the relationship between one's chronological age and one's mental age (MA, 12 years/CA, 8 years $\times$ 100 = IQ, 150).

## An IQ of 228: Is that Possible?

At the age of 10, Marilyn vos Savant answered every question on the Stanford-Binet correctly. At the time, her mental age was "22 years and 11 months," and her calculated IQ was 228. Since that time, she has been listed in the *Guinness Book of World Records* for five years under "Highest IQ" for her childhood and adult scores (Savant, 2012, p. 1). Marilyn currently lives in New York with her husband. She is an executive at Jarvik Heart, Inc., and she writes a regular column for *Parade* magazine, which is a supplement to Sunday newspapers (Knight, 2009).

### Question for Reflection

What experiences as a child (in addition to her native endowment) do you think contributed to this test performance at 10 years of age?

SOURCES: Knight, S. (2009). *Is High IQ a Burden as Much as a Blessing?* Retrieved May 15, 2009, from www.ft.com /cms/s/0/4add9230-23d5-11de-996a-00144feabdc0.html; Savant, M. (2012). *About Marilyn.* Retrieved April 10, 2012, from http://marilynvossavant.com/about-marilyn/.

Gradually, other researchers became interested in studying the nature and assessment of intelligence. They tended to view intelligence as an underlying ability or capacity that expressed itself in a variety of ways. The unitary IQ scores that were derived from the Stanford-Binet tests were representative of and contributed to this notion.

Over time, however, other researchers came to believe that intellect was represented by a variety of distinct capacities and abilities (Cattell, 1971; Guilford, 1959). This line of thinking suggested that each distinct intellectual capacity could be identified and assessed. Several mental abilities were investigated, including memory capacity, divergent thinking, vocabulary usage, and reasoning ability (see Figure 15.1). Gradually, use of the multiple-ability approach outgrew that of the unitary-intelligence notion. Proponents of the multiple-ability approach were convinced that the universe of intellectual functions was extensive and that the intelligence assessment instruments utilized at that time measured

Each little cube represents a unique combination of one kind of operation, one kind of content, and one kind of product—and hence a distinctly different intellectual ability or function.

**Figure 15.1** *Guilford's Structure of the Intellect Model*

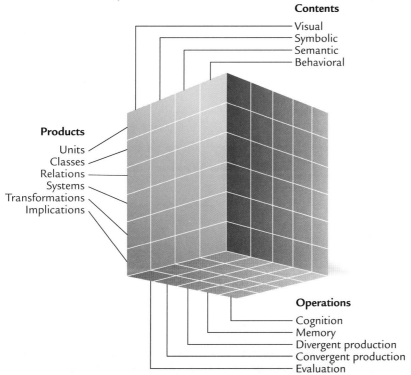

**Contents**
- Visual
- Symbolic
- Semantic
- Behavioral

**Products**
- Units
- Classes
- Relations
- Systems
- Transformations
- Implications

**Operations**
- Cognition
- Memory
- Divergent production
- Convergent production
- Evaluation

a very small portion of an individual's true intellectual capacities (Sternberg, Jarvin, & Grigorenko, 2011).

One of the key contributors to the multidimensional theory of intelligence was J. P. Guilford (1950, 1959). He saw intelligence as a diverse range of intellectual and creative abilities. Guilford's work led many researchers to view intelligence more broadly, focusing their scientific efforts on the emerging field of creativity and its various subcomponents, such as divergent thinking, problem solving, and decision making. Gradually, tests or measures of creativity were developed, using the constructs drawn from models Guilford and others created (Treffinger, 2004).

In summary, conceptions of giftedness during the early 1920s were closely tied to the score that an individual obtained on an intelligence test. Thus, a single score—one's IQ—was the index by which one was identified as being gifted. Beginning with the work of Guilford (1950, 1959) and Torrance (1961, 1965, 1968), notions regarding giftedness were greatly expanded. *Giftedness* began to be used to refer not only to those with high IQs, but also to those who demonstrated high aptitude on creativity measures. More recently, the term *talented* has been added to the descriptors associated with giftedness. As a result, individuals who demonstrate remarkable skills in the visual or performing arts or who excel in other areas of performance may be designated as gifted. Figure 15.2 reveals how

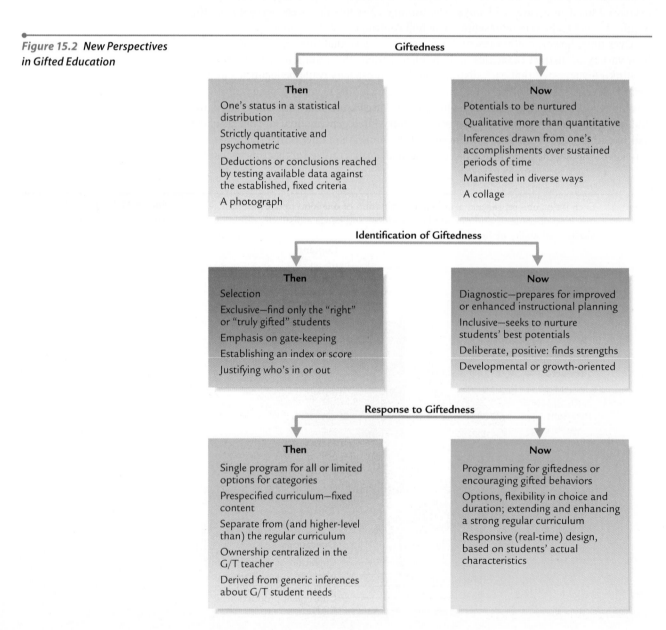

*Figure 15.2 New Perspectives in Gifted Education*

**Giftedness**

| Then | Now |
| --- | --- |
| One's status in a statistical distribution | Potentials to be nurtured |
| Strictly quantitative and psychometric | Qualitative more than quantitative |
| Deductions or conclusions reached by testing available data against the established, fixed criteria | Inferences drawn from one's accomplishments over sustained periods of time |
| A photograph | Manifested in diverse ways |
| | A collage |

**Identification of Giftedness**

| Then | Now |
| --- | --- |
| Selection | Diagnostic—prepares for improved or enhanced instructional planning |
| Exclusive—find only the "right" or "truly gifted" students | Inclusive—seeks to nurture students' best potentials |
| Emphasis on gate-keeping | Deliberate, positive: finds strengths |
| Establishing an index or score | Developmental or growth-oriented |
| Justifying who's in or out | |

**Response to Giftedness**

| Then | Now |
| --- | --- |
| Single program for all or limited options for categories | Programming for giftedness or encouraging gifted behaviors |
| Prespecified curriculum—fixed content | Options, flexibility in choice and duration; extending and enhancing a strong regular curriculum |
| Separate from (and higher-level than) the regular curriculum | Responsive (real-time) design, based on students' actual characteristics |
| Ownership centralized in the G/T teacher | |
| Derived from generic inferences about G/T student needs | |

our perspectives on giftedness have changed over time with the acceptance of new, multifaceted definitions of giftedness.

Currently, there is no federal mandate in the United States requiring educational services for students identified as gifted, as is the case with other exceptionalities. Only 32 states have mandated services for gifted students (National Association for Gifted Children, 2014). The actual funding of services for individuals who are gifted is a state-by-state, local challenge, so there is tremendous variability in the quality and types of programs offered to students in various states (Clark, 2013).

In coming years, we will probably see *talent development* replace gifted education as the guiding concept (Claxton & Meadows, 2009; Treffinger, Nassab, & Selby, 2009). Clark (2013) describes talent as specific areas of academic or artistic aptitude, and talent development as efforts directed toward identifying and developing those aptitudes. This description suggests a kind of programming that is directed at all students, not just those identified as gifted, talented, or creative (Clark, 2008; Davis, Rimm, & Siegle, 2011). A "benefit [of this kind of programming] is that the talent development orientation eliminates the awkwardness of the words *gifted* and, by exclusion, *not gifted*" (Davis & Rimm, 2004, p. 28). Currently, talent identification and development is most common in out-of-school university and community programs (Thomsen & Olszewski-Kubilius, 2014). Writers are calling for schools to adopt a developmental concept of gifts and talents, recognizing that intellectual and nonintellectual factors change over time, and that schools should do more to enrich learning environments to promote individual talent development (Subotnik, Olszewski-Kubilius, & Worrell, 2011).

## 15-2 Definitions and Classifications of People Who Are Gifted, Creative, and Talented

Capturing the essence of any human condition in a definition can be very perplexing. This is certainly true in defining the human attributes, abilities, and potentialities that constitute giftedness, creativity, and talent (Davis, Rimm, & Siegle, 2011; Worrell & Erwin, 2011). Throughout this chapter, we will use the terms *gifted* and *giftedness* to represent all forms of talents, capacities, and creativity.

Definitions of giftedness serve several important purposes (Horowitz, 2009; Worrell & Erwin, 2011). For example, definitions may have a profound influence on the number and kinds of students ultimately selected in a school system, on the types of instruments and selection procedures used, on the scores students must obtain to qualify for specialized instruction and/or programs, on the amount of funding required to provide services, and on the types of preparation educators need to teach students who are gifted. Thus, definitions are important from both practical and theoretical perspectives (Moon, 2006).

Definitions of giftedness have been influenced by a variety of knowledgeable individuals (Cattell, 1971; Gardner, 1983; Guilford, 1959; Piirto, 1999; Ramos-Ford & Gardner, 1997; Renzulli & Reis, 2003; Sternberg, 1997; Torrance, 1966). As you will soon discover, there is no universally accepted definition of giftedness (Clark, 2013).

The current definition, a derivative of an earlier government report—the *Marland Report to Congress*, is as follows:

> *Students, children, or youth who give evidence of high achievement capability in areas such as intellectual, creative, artistic, or leadership capacity, or in specific academic fields, and who need services and activities not ordinarily provided by the school in order to fully develop those capabilities. (National Association for Gifted Children, 2012)*

Definitions like these guide school personnel and others in pursuing several important objectives. These include identifying students across disciplines with diverse talents, using many different kinds of assessment measures to identify gifted students, identifying "achievement capabilities" and not necessarily demonstrated performance in students, searching actively for giftedness in all student populations (cultural, ethnic, economic, etc.), and considering students' drives and passions for achievement in various areas.

**Standard 1**
Learner Development and Individual Learning Differences

Also, new conceptions of giftedness and intelligence have emerged from theoretical and research literature (Esping & Plucker, 2008; Passow, 2004; Ramos-Ford & Gardner, 1997; Sternberg, 1997). One of these approaches is Sternberg's triarchic theory of human intelligence (Sternberg, 1997; Sternberg, Jarvin, & Grigorenko, 2011). In this approach, intellectual performance is divided into three parts: analytic, synthetic, and practical. Analytic intelligence is exhibited by people who perform well on aptitude and intelligence tests. Individuals with synthetic giftedness are unconventional thinkers who are creative, intuitive, and insightful. People with practical intelligence are extraordinarily adept in dealing with problems of everyday life and those that arise in their work environments. Recently, Sternberg (2009) coined the term *WICS*: wisdom, intelligence, creativity, synthesized—a form of giftedness. His premise is that wisdom, intelligence, and creativity are developed and formed—they are not entirely innate, but must be cultivated and nurtured (Sternberg, Jarvin, & Grigorenko, 2011). Gagné (1999) has also identified catalysts that give rise to gifts and talents in young people (see Figure 15.3).

Another view of giftedness has been developed by Ramos-Ford and Gardner (1997). They have defined intelligence or giftedness as "an ability or set of abilities that permit an individual to solve problems or fashion products that are of consequence in a particular cultural setting" (Ramos-Ford & Gardner, 1991, p. 56). This perspective on giftedness is referred to as the theory of multiple intelligences. Intelligence is assumed to manifest itself in linguistic, logical–mathematical, spatial, bodily–kinesthetic, musical, interpersonal, and intrapersonal behaviors (Esping & Plucker, 2008). Table 15.1 provides brief definitions of each of these behaviors, as well as the child and adult roles associated with each type of intelligence.

These and other definitions of giftedness have moved us from unitary measures of IQ to multiple measures of creativity, problem-solving ability, talent, and intelligence. However,

**Figure 15.3 *Catalysts for the Development of Gifts and Talents***

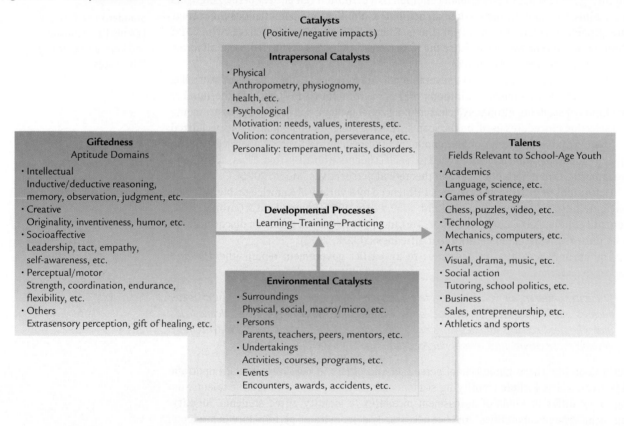

**Table 15.1**  **The Seven Intelligences**

| Intelligence | Brief Description | Related Child and Adult Roles |
|---|---|---|
| Linguistic | The capacity to express oneself in spoken or written language with great facility | Superb storyteller, creative writer, or inventive speaker: Novelist, lyricist, lawyer |
| Logical–mathematical | The ability to reason inductively and deductively and to complete complex computations | Thorough counter, calculator, notation maker, or symbol user: Mathematician, physicist, computer scientist |
| Spatial | The capacity to create, manipulate, and represent spatial configurations | Creative builder, sculptor, artist, or skilled assembler of models: Architect, talented chess player, mechanic, navigator |
| Bodily–kinesthetic | The ability to perform various complex tasks or activities with one's body or part of the body | Skilled playground game player, emerging athlete or dancer: Surgeon, dancer, professional athlete |
| Musical | The capacity to discriminate musical pitches, to hear musical themes, and to sense rhythm, timbre, and texture | Good singer, creator of original songs or musical pieces: Musician, composer, director |
| Interpersonal | The ability to understand others' actions, emotions, and intents and to act effectively in response to verbal and nonverbal behaviors of others | Child organizer or orchestrator, child leader, or a very social child: Teacher, therapist, political social leader |
| Intrapersonal | The capacity to understand well and respond to one's own thoughts, desires, feelings, and emotions | A sensitive child, a resilient child, or an optimistic child: Social worker, therapist, counselor, hospice worker |

despite the movement away from IQ scores and other changes in definitions of giftedness, critics argue that many if not most local, district, and state definitions are elitist in nature and favor the "affluent" and "privileged" (Borland, 2003; Ford, 2003).

The definitions of giftedness are diverse (Clark, 2013; Moon, 2006; Stephens & Karnes, 2000). Each of the definitions we have examined reveals the challenges associated with defining the nature of giftedness (Worrell & Erwin, 2011). In a multicultural, pluralistic society, such as that of the United States, different abilities and capacities are encouraged and valued by different parents, teachers, and communities. Also, definitions of giftedness are often a function of educational, societal, and political priorities at a particular time and place (Phillipson & McCann, 2007; Sternberg, Jarvin, & Grigorenko, 2011).

# 15-3   Characteristics and Prevalence of People Who Are Gifted, Creative, and Talented

Determining the number of children who are gifted is a challenge. The complexity of the task is directly related to problems inherent in determining who is gifted and what constitutes giftedness (Gallagher, 2004). The numerous definitions of giftedness range from quite restrictive (in terms of the number of children to whom they apply) to very inclusive and broad descriptions. Consequently, the prevalence estimates are highly variable.

Prevalence figures compiled before the 1950s were primarily limited to the intellectually gifted: those identified primarily through intelligence tests. At that time, 2 to 3 percent of the general population was considered gifted. During the 1950s, when professionals in the field advocated an expanded view of giftedness (Conant, 1959; DeHann & Havighurst, 1957), the prevalence figures suggested for program planning were substantially affected. Terms such as *academically talented* were used to refer to the upper 15 to 20 percent of the general school population.

Thus, prevalence estimates have fluctuated, depending on the views of politicians, policy makers, researchers, and professionals during past decades. Currently, 2 to 5 percent may be identified as gifted, increasing to 10 to 25 percent if individuals identified through talent development programs are included (Clark, 2013).

Accurately identifying the characteristics of gifted people is an enormous task. Different types of studies have generated many characteristics attributed to those who are gifted (see Table 15.2; MacKinnon, 1962; Terman, 1925). Gradually, what emerged from these studies were oversimplified, incomplete views of giftedness.

Unfortunately, much of the initial research related to the characteristics of giftedness was conducted with limited population samples. Generally, the studies did not include adequate samples of females or individuals from various ethnic and cultural groups, nor did early researchers carefully control for factors directly related to socioeconomic status. Therefore, the characteristics generated from these studies were not representative of gifted individuals as a whole but, rather, reflected the characteristics of gifted individuals from advantaged environments.

Given the present multifaceted definitions of giftedness and emerging views of intelligence, we must conclude that gifted individuals come from all population sectors. Consequently, research findings of the past must be interpreted with great caution as practitioners weigh and assess a particular youth's behaviors, attributes, talents, motivations, and dispositions.

Davis and Rimm (2004) have identified a number of positive and negative characteristics of student who are gifted (see Table 15.2).

Gifted students, who are intellectually able, demonstrate one resounding trait—"they are developmentally advanced in language and thought" (Davis & Rimm, 2004, p. 35). Many learn to speak and read very early. Their mental ages, as revealed in intelligence tests, far exceed their chronological ages. Moreover, their innate curiosity and capacity for asking questions can drive some parents and even teachers to the brink of exhaustion and desperation (Morawska & Sanders, 2009). These students can be unusually tenacious in pursuing ideas, discussing concerns, and raising questions. They may also have interests that would be characteristic of older children and/or adults.

Generally, gifted students are well adjusted and socially adept. There are, of course, exceptions (Reis & Renzulli, 2004). One of the more interesting attributes of gifted children and youth is their penchant for "emotional excitability" and "high sensitivity" (Davis & Rimm, 2004, p. 37). In this regard, their reactions can be more intense—that is, they may feel more joy and also experience greater sadness than age-mates. Table 15.2 lists characteristics often evident in gifted students.

Students who are described as creative share a number of personality attributes and dispositions. They often exhibit high energy and high motivation to succeed or perform. They have a real zest for pursuing tasks and seeking solutions to problems they encounter. Furthermore, they also have a proclivity for risk taking. They love to try new activities, to experiment with new behaviors, and to consider novel ways of processing problems or

**Standard 1**
Learner Development and Individual Learning Differences

*Photo 15.1* People with gifts and talents come from every ethnic, cultural, and socioeconomic background. While some individuals achieve in intellectual endeavors, others excel through athletics.

Gary bogdon/Epa/Newscom

**Table 15.2** Characteristics of Students Who Are Gifted

| Positive Characteristics | General Characteristics | Negative Characteristics |
|---|---|---|
| Unusual alertness in infancy and later | Wide interests, interested in new topics | Uneven mental development |
| Early and rapid learning | High curiosity, explores how and why | Interpersonal difficulties, often due to intellectual differences |
| Rapid language development as a child | Multiple capabilities (multipotentiality) | Underachievement, especially in uninteresting areas |
| Superior language ability—verbally fluent, large vocabulary, complex grammar | High care ambitions (desire to be helpful to others) | Nonconformity, sometimes in disturbing directions |
| Enjoyment of learning | Overexcitability | Perfectionism, which can be extreme |
| Academic superiority, large knowledge base, sought out as a resource | Emotional intensity and sensitivity | Excessive self-criticism |
| Superior analytic ability | High alertness and attention | Self-doubt, poor self-image |
| Keen observation | High intellectual and physical activity level | Variable frustration and anger |
| Efficient, high-capacity memory | High motivation, concentrates, perseveres, persists, task-oriented | Depression |
| Superior reasoning, problem solving | Active—shares information, directs, leads, offers help, eager to be involved | |
| Thinking that is abstract, complex, logical, insightful | Strong empathy, moral thinking, sense of justice, honesty, intellectual honesty | |
| Insightful, sees "big picture," recognizes patterns, connects topics | Aware of social issues | |
| Manipulates symbol systems | High concentration, long attention span | |
| Uses high-level thinking skills, efficient strategies | Strong internal control | |
| Extrapolates knowledge to new situations, goes beyond what is taught | Independent, self-directed, works alone | |
| Expanded awareness, greater self-awareness | Inquisitive, asks questions | |
| Greater metacognition (understanding own thinking) | Excellent sense of humor | |
| Advanced interests | Imaginative, creative, solves problems | |
| Needs for logic and accuracy | Preference for novelty | |
| | Reflectiveness | |
| | Good self-concept | |

SOURCE: Adapted from Davis, G. A., & Rimm, S. B. (2004). *Education of the Gifted and Talented*, 5th ed. (p. 33). San Francisco: Allyn and Bacon.

creating things (artistic, mechanical, etc.). Table 15.3 lists characteristics often evident in students described as creative.

No student who is identified as gifted will exhibit all of the characteristics described in this section. However, parents, teachers, coaches, and mentors have an opportunity, as well as an obligation, to encourage these traits, behaviors, proclivities, and dispositions. Studies of the lives of prominent gifted and talented individuals reveal that mentoring, special activities, and the efforts of parents have had more impact on success than have school activities (Olszewski-Kubilius & Lee, 2004).

**Standard 1**
Learner Development and Individual Learning Differences

**Table 15.3** Characteristics of Students Who Are Creative

| Positive Traits | Approximate Synonyms |
| --- | --- |
| Original | Imaginative, resourceful, flexible, unconventional, thinks metaphorically, challenges assumptions, irritated and bored by the obvious, avoids perceptual set, asks "what if?" |
| Aware of creativeness | Creativity-conscious, values originality, values own creativity |
| Independent | Self-confident, individualistic, nonconforming, sets own rules, unconcerned with impressing others, resists societal demands |
| Risk taking | Not afraid to be different or to try something new, willing to cope with hostility, willing to cope with failure |
| Motivated | Energetic, adventurous, sensation seeking, enthusiastic, excitable, spontaneous, impulsive, intrinsically motivated, persevering, works beyond assigned tasks |
| Curious | Questions norms and assumptions, experiments, inquisitive, wide interests, is a problem finder, asks "why?" |
| Sense of humor | Playful, plays with ideas, childlike freshness in thinking |
| Attracted to complexity | Attracted to novelty, asymmetry, the mysterious, theoretical and abstract problems; is a complex person; tolerant of ambiguity, disorder, incongruity |
| Artistic | Artistic and aesthetic interests, attracted to beauty and order |
| Open-minded | Receptive to new ideas, other viewpoints, new experiences, and growth; liberal; altruistic |
| Needs alone time | Reflective, introspective, internally preoccupied, sensitive, may be withdrawn, likes to work alone |
| Intuitive | Perceptive, sees relationships, finds order in chaos, uses all senses in observing |
| Intelligent | Verbally fluent, articulate, logical, good decision maker, detects gaps in knowledge, visualizes |

SOURCE: Adapted from Davis, G. A., & Rimm, S. B. (2004). *Education of the Gifted and Talented*, 5th ed. (p. 42). San Francisco: Allyn and Bacon.

## 15-4 Causes Associated with People Who Are Gifted, Creative, and Talented

**Standard 1**
Learner Development and Individual Learning Differences

**Nature versus nurture**
Controversy concerning how much of a person's ability is related to sociocultural influences (nurture) and how much is due to genetic factors (nature).

Scientists have long been interested in identifying the origins of intelligence. Conclusions have varied greatly. For years, many scientists adhered to a hereditary explanation of intelligence: that people inherit their intellectual capacity at conception. Thus, intelligence was viewed as an innate capacity that remained relatively fixed during an individual's lifetime. The prevailing belief then was that little could be done to enhance or improve intellectual ability.

During the 1920s and 1930s, scientists such as John Watson began to explore the new notion of behavioral psychology, or behaviorism. Like other behaviorists who followed him, Watson believed that the environment played a vitally important role in the development of intelligence as well as personality traits. Initially, Watson largely discounted the role of heredity and its importance in intellectual development. Later, however, he moderated his views, moving toward a theoretical perspective in which both heredity and environment contributed to an individual's intellectual ability.

During the 1930s, many investigators sought to determine the relative influence of heredity and environment on intellectual development. Some proponents of genetics asserted that as much as 70 to 80 percent of an individual's capacity was determined by heredity and the remainder by environmental influences. Environmentalists believed otherwise. The controversy over the relative contributions of heredity and environment to intelligence (known as the **nature versus nurture** controversy) is likely to continue for some time, in part because of the complexity and breadth of the issues involved. For example, studies of identical twins raised in different environments suggest that 44 to 72 percent of their intelligence (general cognitive ability) is inherited. With regard to environmental factors, we are just beginning to understand the dynamic relationships between nature and nurture and how giftedness manifests itself developmentally over time (Horowitz, 2009). Again, "bright children select and are selected by peers and educational programs that foster their abilities. They read and think more. This is the profound meaning of finding genetic influences on measures of the environment. Genes contribute to the experience itself" (Plomin & Price, 2003, p. 120). Plomin and Price (2003) captured it best when they said "it may well be more appropriate to think about [general cognitive ability] as an appetite rather than an aptitude" (p. 121). This appetite allows gifted children and youth to profit more fully from environmental influences over their lifetimes.

Thus far, we have focused on the origins of intelligence rather than on giftedness per se. Many of the theories about the emergence of giftedness have been derived from the study of general intelligence. Few authors have focused directly on the origins of giftedness. Moreover, the ongoing changes in the definitions of giftedness have further complicated the precise investigation of its origins.

The "Star Model" for explaining the causes and antecedents of giftedness is composed of five elements, each of which contributes to gifted behavior (see Figure 15.4). These elements are superior general intellect, distinctive special aptitudes, nonintellective factors, environmental supports, and chance. Associated with each are the descriptors *dynamic* and *static*. The static dimension includes factors that remain relatively constant or unchanged, such as the child's or youth's race and economic status. The dynamic dimension includes factors that are fluid and responsive to contextual or environmental changes or interventions. Elaborating on this notion, Hughes (2009) wrote: "Giftedness evolves and factors are developmental: It cannot be definitively fixed or measured. It is grown, not diagnosed" (p. 168). Increasingly, we will move from finding and labeling giftedness to developing it, that is, putting in place the conditions that give rise to talents, creativity, and giftedness.

The abilities associated with superior intelligence are generally factors assessed through intelligence tests (verbal, spatial, and memory capacity). Special abilities are those found, for example, in child prodigies who demonstrate extraordinary musical, mathematical, or other emerging talents. Nonintellective factors are a wide-ranging set of attributes, including, believe it or not, psychopathology and perfectionism. Many gifted artists and writers show clear signs of pathological deviance or emotional distress (Callard-Szulgit, 2003; Reis & Renzulli, 2004). Other, more positive factors associated with this element include motivation, self-concept, and resilience. The influence of environmental support

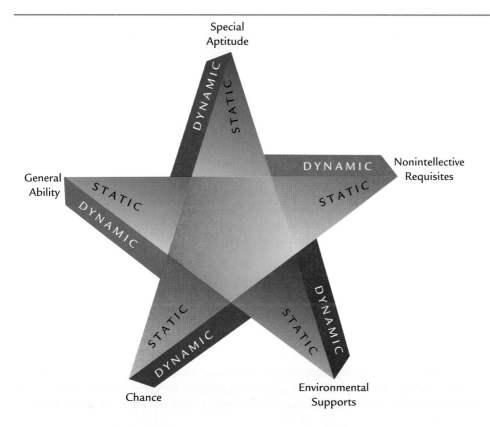

*Figure 15.4* **The Star Model: Psychosocial Factors Associated with Gifted Achievements**

### Steve Jobs: "I Will Never Forget that Moment."

Like most kids, [Jobs] became infused with the passions of the grown-ups around him. "Most of the dads in the neighborhood did really neat stuff.... I grew up in awe of that stuff and asking people about it." The most important of these neighbors, Larry Lang "...was my model of what an HP engineer was supposed to be: a big ham radio operator, hard-core electronics guy," Jobs recalled. "He would bring me stuff to play with." As we walked up to Lang's old house, Jobs pointed to the driveway: "He took a carbon microphone and a battery and a speaker, and he put it on this driveway. He had me talk into the carbon mike and it amplified out of the speaker." Jobs had been taught by his father that microphones always required an electronic amplifier. "So I raced home, and I told my dad that he was wrong."

"No, it needs an amplifier," his father assured him. When Steve protested otherwise, his father said he was crazy. "It can't work without an amplifier. There's some trick."

"I kept saying no to my dad, telling him he had to see it, and finally he actually walked down with me and saw it. And he said, 'Well I'll be a bat out of hell.'"

Jobs recalled the incident vividly because it was his first realization that his father did not know everything. Then a more disconcerting discovery began to dawn on him: He was smarter than his parents. He had always admired his father's competence and savvy. "He was not an educated man, but I had always thought he was pretty damn smart. He didn't read much, but he could do a lot. Almost everything mechanical, he could figure it out." Yet the carbon microphone incident, Jobs said, began a jarring process of realizing that he was in fact more clever and quick than his parents. "It was a very big moment that's burned into my mind. When I realized that I was smarter than my parents, I felt tremendous shame for having thought that. I will never forget that moment...."

Another layer of awareness occurred soon after. Not only did he discover that he was brighter than his parents, but he discovered that they knew this. Paul and Clara Jobs were loving parents, and they were willing to adapt their lives to suit a son who was very smart—and also willful. They would go to great lengths to accommodate him. And soon Steve discovered this fact as well. "Both my parents got me. They felt a lot of responsibility once they sensed that I was special. They found ways to keep feeding me stuff and putting me in better schools. They were willing to defer to my needs" (Isaacson, 2011, p. 10–12).

#### Questions for Reflection

What role did Steve's parents play in nurturing his talents and capacities? How do parents come to know that a child is "special"?

is obvious. "Giftedness requires [a] social context that enables it to mature. ... Human potential needs nurturance, urgings, encouragement, and even pressures from a world that cares" (Tannenbaum, 2003, p. 54). Last is the element of chance. Often, external factors that coincide with one's preparation and talent development contribute to one's eventual imminence or greatness (Worrell, 2009). All of these factors come together in a unique fashion to produce various kinds of giftedness.

Finally, Colvin (2008), in his book *Talent Is Overrated: What Really Separates World-Class Performers from Everybody Else*, suggests that many innate or naturally occurring gifts and talents are overvalued—that outstanding performance in most fields of expertise comes from consistent and deliberate practice—even hard work. In the absence of pronounced and persistent practice, giftedness in its various forms is not achieved. Additionally, the significant contributions these individuals could have made never come to light—the artwork, the medical advances, the musical works, the inventions, the artistic performance—all remain dormant and unexpressed.

## 15-5 Identification and Assessment of People Who Are Gifted, Creative, and Talented

The focus of assessment procedures for identifying giftedness is beginning to change (Sternberg, Jarvin, & Grigorenko, 2011). Elitist definitions and exclusive approaches are being replaced with more defensible, inclusive methods of assessment (Davis, Rimm, & Siegle, 2011; Richert, 2003). Tests for identifying people with potential for gifted performance are being more carefully selected; that is, tests are being used with the children for whom they were designed. Children who were once excluded from programs for the gifted because of formal or standard cutoff scores that favored particular groups of students are now being included (Richert, 2003; Tomlinson & Jarvis, 2014). Multiple sources of information are now collected and reviewed in determining who is potentially gifted (Johnsen, 2008; Worrell & Erwin, 2011). Ideally, the identification process is now directed at identifying needs and potentials rather than merely labeling individuals as gifted. Again, the new thrust is talent development as well as talent identification (Sosniak & Gabelko, 2008; Subotnik & Calderon, 2008).

Standard 4
Assessment

Several approaches have also been developed to identify children who are disadvantaged and also gifted. Some theorists and practitioners have argued for the adoption of a contextual paradigm or approach. Rather than using information derived solely from typical intelligence tests or other talent assessments, this approach relies on divergent views of giftedness as valued and determined by community members, parents, grandparents, and competent informants. Similar approaches focus on nontraditional measures of giftedness. These approaches use multiple criteria, broader ranges of scores for inclusion in special programs, peer nomination, assessments by people other than educational personnel, and information provided by adaptive behavior assessments. Furthermore, these approaches seek to understand students' motivations, interests, capacities for communication, reasoning abilities, imagination, and humor (Briggs et al., 2006; Davis, Rimm, & Siegle, 2011; Richert, 2003). For example, if 60 percent of students in a given school population come from a certain cultural minority group and only 2 percent are identified as gifted via traditional measures, the screening committee may want to reexamine and adjust its identification procedures.

Elementary and secondary students who are gifted are identified in a variety of ways. The first step is generally screening (Worrell & Erwin, 2011). During this phase, teachers, psychologists, and other school personnel attempt to select all students who are potentially gifted. A number of procedures are employed in the screening process. Historically, information obtained from group intelligence tests and teacher nominations has been used to select the initial pool of students. However, many other measures and data-collection techniques have been instituted since the approach to assessment of giftedness changed from one-dimensional to multidimensional. These techniques may include developmental inventories, classroom observations, parent and peer nominations, achievement tests, creativity tests, motivation assessments, teacher nominations, and evaluations of student projects (Worrell & Erwin, 2011).

## 15-5a   Teacher Nomination

Teacher nomination has been an integral part of many screening approaches. This approach is fraught with problems, however. Teachers often favor children who are cooperative, well mannered, and task-oriented. Bright underachievers who are confrontive and/or disruptive may be overlooked. Students from low socioeconomic and ethnic minority groups are much less likely to be recognized as potentially gifted or talented (Tomlinson & Jarvis, 2014). Also, many teachers are unfamiliar with the general traits, behaviors, and dispositions that underlie various forms of giftedness.

Fortunately, some of these problems have been addressed. Several scales, approaches, and guidelines are now available to aid teachers and others who are responsible for making nominations (Davis, Rimm, & Siegle, 2011; Renzulli & Reis, 2003). Teachers who have a thorough understanding of the various kinds of giftedness are in a much better position to provide good information in the nomination, screening, and selection processes (Johnsen, 2008; Johnsen, VanTassel-Baska, & Robinson, 2008).

## 15-5b   Intelligence and Achievement Tests

Intelligence testing continues to be a major source of information for screening and identifying general ability or intellectual giftedness in children and adolescents. These tests must be carefully selected. For example, some intelligence tests have low ceilings; that is, they do not allow participating children or youth to demonstrate their remarkable potential. The same is true of some group-administered intelligence tests. They are not designed to identify students who may have exceptionally high intellectual abilities.

One advantage of intelligence testing is that it often identifies underachievers. Intelligence test scores often reveal students who have wonderful intellectual capacity that may have gone unrecognized because of their pattern of poor school performance.

**Ceiling effects**
A restricted range of test questions
or problems that does not permit
academically gifted students to
demonstrate their true capacity or
achievement.

**Off-level**
Assessments or materials designed
for higher-grade students.

A serious limitation associated with intelligence tests emerges when they are administered to individuals for whom the tests were not designed. Very few intelligence tests adequately assess the abilities of children and adolescents who are substantially different from the core culture for whom the tests were created. However, some progress is being made in helping educators identify gifted children who are members of minority groups, underachievers, or at risk (Renzulli, 2004).

Similar problems are inherent in achievement tests, which, like intelligence tests, are not generally designed to measure the true achievement of children who are academically gifted. Such individuals are often prevented from demonstrating their unusual prowess because of the restricted range of the test items. These **ceiling effects** prevent youth who are gifted from demonstrating their achievement at higher levels. Professionals now recommend that schools address ceiling effects by using **off-level** (sometimes called above-level) achievement testing to more accurately gauge the potential of notably advanced students (Olszewski-Kubilius & Lee, 2011; Thomsen & Olszewski-Kubilius, 2014). This means that schools use higher grade-level assessments for promising students to avoid the ceiling effect and determine where they are actually functioning.

## 15-5c   Creativity Tests

Tests for creativity serve several purposes. Often they help teachers or practitioners discover capacity that may not be evident in normal classroom interactions and performances. However, the degree to which these tests actually measure creativity is often called into question. Because of the nature of creativity and the many forms in which it can be expressed, developing tests to assess its presence and magnitude is a formidable task (Piffer, 2012; Renzulli, 2004; Treffinger, 2004). In spite of these challenges, a number of creativity tests have been formulated (Rimm, 1982; Rimm & Davis, 1983; Torrance, 1966; Williams, 1980). A typical question on a test of divergent thinking might read, "What would happen if your eyes could be adjusted to see things as small as germs?"

Once the screening steps have been completed, the actual identification and selection of students begins. During this phase, each of the previously screened students is carefully evaluated again, using more individualized procedures and assessment tools. Ideally, these techniques should be closely related to the definition of giftedness used by the district and to the program offered to students (Eckert, 2006; Gubbins, 2006; Rogers, 2006). It is important to note that tests measure creative potential, not creative achievement (Piffer, 2012). Once identified, students are most likely to turn potential to achievement when provided sufficient time and opportunities to explore and develop their unique abilities (Moran, 2010).

A series of recommendations and statements that summarize this section on assessment and identification have been identified in Table 15.4. If these recommendations are carefully followed, more appropriate and equitable decisions will be made in identifying and serving children and youth who are gifted or potentially gifted.

---

**Table 15.4   Current Thinking and Recommendations for Identifying Gifted Students**

- Adopt a clearly defined but broadened conception of giftedness.
- Avoid using a single cutoff score.
- Use multiple alternative criteria—not multiple required hurdles—from several different sources.
- Use separate instruments or procedures for different areas of giftedness; be sure that tests (including ratings and nominations) are reliable and valid.
- Include authentic assessment (e.g., portfolios, examples of work) and performance-based procedures (e.g., evaluation tasks that elicit problem solving and creativity).
- Be aware that giftedness may appear in different forms in different cultural or socioeconomic groups.
- Repeat assessments over time to identify additional gifted students.
- Use identification data to enhance your understanding of students.

SOURCE: Adapted from Davis, G. A., & Rimm, S. B. (2004). "Identifying Gifted and Talented Students." In *Education of the Gifted and Talented*, 5th ed. (p. 81). San Francisco: Allyn and Bacon.

# 15-6 Interventions and Treatment for People Who Are Gifted, Creative, and Talented

Strategies for meeting the needs of gifted, creative, and talented individuals vary according to age and access to formal and informal opportunities for growth. Beginning in the home and extending through the school years and into adulthood, a variety of interventions have been used successfully.

## 15-6a Early Childhood Education

Current research suggests that many young children with high cognitive ability (HCA) can be identified in the middle of the second year of life (Colombo, Shaddy, Blaga, Anderson, & Kannass, 2009). Parents may contribute to HCA and other attributes of their children through a number of pathways (Gottfried, Gottfried, & Guerin, 2009; Horowitz, 2009; Rimm, 2008). During the first 15 months of life, 90 percent of all social interactions with children take place during such activities as feeding, bathing, changing diapers, and dressing. Parents who are interested in advancing social and cognitive development use these occasions for stimulating and talking to their children; providing varied sensory experiences such as bare-skin cuddling, tickling, and smiling; and conveying a sense of trust. Early, concentrated, language-centered involvement with young children gives rise to substantial cognitive, social, and linguistic skills (Horowitz, 2009).

As children progress through the infancy, toddler, and preschool periods, the experiences provided become more varied and uniquely suited to the child's emerging interests and capacities (Subotnik & Calderon, 2008). Language and cognitive development are encouraged by means of stories that are read and told. Children are also urged to make up their own stories. Brief periods are reserved for discussions or spontaneous conversations that arise from events that have momentarily captured their attention. Requests for help in saying or printing a word are promptly fulfilled. Thus, many children who are gifted learn to read before they enter kindergarten or first grade.

A variety of preschool programs have been developed for young children who are gifted.

**Standard 2**
Learning Environments

**Standard 5**
Instructional Planning and Strategies

Comstock Images/Stockbyte/Getty Images

**Photo 15.2** Parents play essential roles in nurturing and stimulating children with potential gifts and talents.

Some children are involved in traditional programs that focus on activities and curricula devoted primarily to the development of academic skills. Many of the traditional programs emphasize affective and social development as well (Mooij, 2013). The entry criteria for these programs are varied, but the primary considerations are usually the child's IQ and social maturity.

Creativity programs are designed to help children develop their natural endowments in a number of artistic and creative domains (Lubbard, Georgsdottir, & Besançon, 2009; Treffinger, 2004). Another purpose of such programs is to help children discover their own areas of promise. Children in these programs are also prepared for eventual involvement in traditional academic areas of schooling.

## 15-6b Elementary Education

Giftedness in elementary students may be nurtured in a variety of ways. A number of service delivery systems and approaches are used in responding to the needs of students who are gifted (Purcell & Eckert, 2006; Robinson, Shore, & Enersen, 2007; VanTassel-Baska,

2012). The nurturing process has often been referred to as **differentiated education**—that is, an education uniquely and predominantly suited to the natural abilities and interests of individuals who are gifted (Firmender, Reis, & Sweeny, 2013; Scott, 2014). Programs for children are targeted at delivering content more rapidly, using a variety of engaging instructional strategies, delivering more challenging content, examining content in greater depth, pursuing highly specialized content, and/or dealing with more complex and higher levels of subject matter (Caraisco, 2007; Cross & Coleman, 2014).

## Instructional Approaches

Instructional approaches for gifted students are selected on the basis of a variety of factors (Tomlinson & Hockett, 2008). First, the school system must determine what types of giftedness it is capable of serving and supporting. It must also establish identification criteria and related measures that enable it to select qualified students fairly. For example, if the system is primarily interested in enhancing creativity, measures and indices of creativity should be utilized. If the focus of the program is

---

### CASE STUDY ON EMBRACING DIVERSITY

#### Don-Wook Shin

Don-Wook Shin was doing long division in his head before the age of 5. He began learning calculus in fifth grade, took his first Advanced Placement (AP) test in seventh grade, and then proceeded to teach himself the curriculum to seven other AP math and science courses over the next three years. By the end of 10th grade, he'd done so well on all those AP tests that he was named a Siemens Award winner as the highest-scoring male student in California.

Catherine Cloughesy, his kindergarten teacher, noticed Shin's unusual facility with math and started throwing out long division with three-digit numbers. She stated, "I would sit next to him and I could see that he did it in his head and then wrote it down. It was quite shocking." She added, "You wouldn't know if you just met him. I've met a lot of gifted children and it's a rare trait to be able to joke and laugh about yourself like he can."

Catherine Harrington, a part-time inclusion specialist, worked with Shin before or after school, "giving up her own time to tutor me one-on-one," said Shin, to make sure he could continue progressing at his own rate in math. Harrington eventually enlisted another teacher to help Shin with calculus.

The story of this gifted child is also the story of a community of family and

Courtesy of davisenterprise

teachers who decided when Shin was still very young that this exceptional student, who could have gone to college as early as seventh grade, should be given a true childhood—a chance to grow up among his peers and become a well-rounded individual. The whole idea of Shin taking AP tests at such a young age was really more about measuring what he was learning. By the time he was in the ninth grade, Shin had taken and received top scores of 5 on calculus BC, statistics, both physics tests, and biology.

When his parents asked Harrington what Shin should work on over the summer, "I told them he needed to work on

riding his bike, swimming, and playing," Harrington said. That insistence that this child should remain a child is why, Harrington and Cloughesy said, Shin has become such a well-rounded teenager. Keeping him with his peers—who academically were all over the place—not only taught him humility, Harrington said, but how to be socially appropriate.

"My parents wanted to give me time to enjoy high school and develop on my own," Shin said of his journey. "It was my own decision to skip one year ahead. I'm really looking forward to college and being able to study what I want to study."

##### Application Questions

**1.** What difficulties would you anticipate if Shin was a student in your first-grade class? Be sure to consider and address academic, social, emotional, and behavioral concerns.

**2.** How did Shin's school address the disparity between his cognitive functioning and his chronological age?

**3.** In what other ways could his school have addressed Shin's needs if teachers were unwilling or unable to provide out-of-contract service?

Source: Ternus-Bellamy, A. (2013, March 7). "The Story of a Gifted Child." *The Davis Enterprise*, p. A1. Retrieved from www.davisenterprise.com/local-news/the-story-of-a -gifted-child/.

accelerating math achievement and understanding, instruments that measure mathematical aptitude and achievement should be employed. Second, the school system must select the organizational structures through which children who are gifted are to receive their differentiated education. Third, school personnel must select the instructional approaches to be utilized within each program setting. Fourth, school personnel must select continuous evaluation procedures and techniques that help them assess the overall effectiveness of the program. Data generated from such evaluations can serve as catalysts for making appropriate and meaningful changes (Callahan, 2008; Johnsen, 2013). Take a moment to think about Don-Wook Shin featured in the accompanying Case Study. What kinds of instructional approaches might be helpful to him in capitalizing on his intellectual gifts?

**Service Delivery Systems** Once the types of giftedness to be emphasized have been selected and appropriate identification procedures have been established, planning must be directed at selecting suitable service delivery systems. Organizational structures for students who are gifted are similar to those found in other areas of special education. Several options have been developed to provide services for students who are gifted (see Figure 15.5). Each of the learning environments in the model has advantages and disadvantages. For example, students who are enrolled in regular education classrooms and are given opportunities to spend time in seminars, resource rooms, special classes, and other novel learning environments profit from these experiences because they are responsive to their interests, talents, and capacities. Furthermore, such pullout activities provide a means for students to interact with one another and to pursue interests for which the usual school curriculum offers little access. However, the disadvantages of such a program are numerous. Major parts of the school week may be spent doing things that may not be appropriate or engaging for students who are gifted. Also, when gifted students return to general education classes, they are frequently required to make up missed assignments.

**CEC**

**Standard 5**
Instructional Planning and Strategies

**CEC**

**Standard 2**
Learning Environments

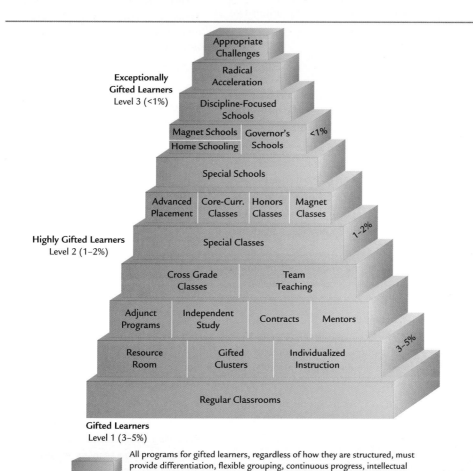

*Figure 15.5  Clark's Structuring Gifted Program*

All programs for gifted learners, regardless of how they are structured, must provide differentiation, flexible grouping, continuous progress, intellectual peer interaction, continuity, and teachers with specialized education.

## People Who Are Gifted, Creative, and Talented

### Early Childhood Years

#### Tips for Families

- Realize that giftedness is evidenced in many ways (e.g., concentration, memory, pleasure in learning, sense of humor, social skills, task orientation, ability to follow and lead, capacity and desire to compete, information capacity).

- Provide toys that may be used for a variety of activities and purposes.

- Take trips to museums, exhibits, fairs, and other places of interest to your child.

- Talk to the child in ways that foster give-and-take conversation.

- Begin to expose the child to picture books and ask him or her to find certain objects or animals or to respond to age-appropriate questions.

- Avoid unnecessary restrictions.

- Provide play materials that are developmentally appropriate and may be a little challenging.

#### Tips for Preschool Teachers

- Look for ways in which various talents and skills may be expressed or developed (e.g., cognitive, artistic, leadership, socialization, motor ability, memory, imagination).

- Capitalize on the child's curiosity. Develop learning activities related to his or her passions and emerging interests.

- Allow the child to experiment with all the elements of language—even written language—as he or she is ready.

- Give the child highly engaging learning experiences.

#### Tips for Preschool Personnel

- Remember that conversation is critical to the child's development. Do not be reluctant to spend a great deal of time asking the child questions as he or she engages in various activities.

- Become a specialist in looking for and developing gifts and talents across a variety of domains (e.g., artistic, social, cognitive).

- Allow for rapid mastery of concepts, and then allow the child to move on to other, more challenging activities rather than holding him or her back.

#### Tips for Neighbors and Friends

- Provide preschool opportunities for all children who are potentially gifted to have the necessary environmental ingredients to use their talents or gifts fully—that is, support and encourage talent development.

- Enjoy and sometimes endure the neighborhood child who has chosen your home as his or her lab for various experiments in cooking, painting, and building.

- Collaborate with friends and family in talking about potentially gifted children, considering ways to nurture their development.

### Elementary Years

#### Tips for Families

- Maintain the search for individual gifts and talents; some qualities may not be evident until a child is older.

- Collaborate with other professionals in providing appropriate experiences and options for gifted learners.

- Provide out-of-school experiences that foster talent or skill development (e.g., artistic, physical, academic, social).

- Enroll a child who is gifted in summer programs offered by universities or colleges.

- Monitor the child's school environment to be sure that adequate steps are being taken to respond to your child's unique skills, interests, and abilities.

- Join an advocacy group for parents in your community and consider taking a parenting class.

- Subscribe to child publications related to your child's current interests.

- Encourage your child's friendships and associations with other children who have like interests and aptitudes.

#### Tips for General Education Classroom Teachers

- Provide opportunities for enrichment as well as acceleration.

- Allow students who are gifted to pursue individual or group projects that require sophisticated forms of thinking, production, or problem solving.

- Become involved in professional associations that provide assistance to teachers of students who are gifted.

- Take a course that specifically addresses the instructional strategies that might be helpful children who are gifted.

- Encourage children to become active participants in various events that emphasize particular skills or knowledge areas (e.g., science fairs, music competitions).

#### Tips for School Personnel

- Develop clubs and programs that enable children who are gifted to pursue their talents.

- Create award programs that encourage talent development across a variety of domains.

- Involve and collaborate with community members (e.g., artists, engineers, writers) in offering enrichment and acceleration activities.

- Foster the use of inclusive procedures for identifying students who are potentially gifted from groups that are culturally diverse, are disadvantaged, or have disabilities.

#### Tips for Neighbors and Friends

- Contribute to organizations that foster talent development.

- Volunteer to serve as judges for competitive events.

- Be willing to share your talents with young, emergent scholars, musicians, athletes, and artists.

- Become a mentor for someone in your community.

## Secondary and Transition Years

### Tips for Families

- Continue to provide sources of support for talent development outside of the home.
- Regularly counsel with your child about courses he or she may take—collaborate with counselors and other school personnel.
- Provide access to tools (e.g., computers, video cameras, instruments, brushes and paints) and resources (e.g., magazines, websites, specialists, coaches, mentors) that contribute to your child's development.
- Expect variations in performance from time to time—give your child appropriate breathing room.
- Provide opportunities for relaxation and rest from demanding schedules.
- Continue to encourage involvement with peers who have similar interests and aptitudes.

### Tips for General Education Classroom Teachers

- Provide a range of activities for students with varying abilities.
- Provide opportunities for students who are gifted to deal with real problems or develop actual products.
- Give opportunities for genuine enrichment activities, not just more work—collaborate with professional peers within your discipline and others in making challenging and engaging activities available.

- Remember that giftedness manifests itself in many ways. Determine how various types of giftedness may be expressed in your content domain.
- Help to eliminate the conflicting and confusing signals about career choices and fields of study that are often given to young women who are gifted.

### Tips for School Personnel

- To the degree possible, provide a variety of curriculum options, activities, clubs, and creative outlets for gifted students.
- Acknowledge and celebrate excellence in a variety of performance areas (e.g., leadership, visual and performing arts, academics).
- Continue to use inclusive procedures in identifying individuals who are potentially gifted and talented.
- Encourage participation in competitive activities in which students are able to use and hone their gifts and talents (e.g., science fairs, debate tournaments, music competitions).

### Tips for Neighbors, Friends, and Potential Employers

- Provide opportunities for students to "shadow" talented professionals, artists, and clinicians in your network of employees or friends.
- Volunteer as a professional to work directly with students who are gifted in pursuing a real problem or producing an actual product.
- Become a mentor for a student who is interested in what you do professionally.

- Support the funding of programs for students who are gifted and talented and who come from disadvantaged environments.
- Provide summer internships for students who have a particular interest in your profession, talent domain, or specialty.
- Serve as an adviser for a high school club or other organization that gives students additional opportunities to pursue talent areas.

## Adult Years

### Tips for Families

- Continue to nurture appropriate independence.
- Celebrate the individual's accomplishments and provide support for challenges.
- Let go.

### Tips for Educational Personnel

- Exhibit behaviors associated with effective mentoring.
- Provide meaningful ways to deal with pressure.
- Allow individuals to be themselves.
- Provide adequate time for discussion and interaction—unhurried listening.
- Be aware of other demands in the individuals' lives.

### Tips for Potential Employers

- Establish appropriately high expectations.
- Be sensitive to changing interests and needs.
- Encourage and support employees who wish to mentor young gifted students on a volunteer basis.

As you may recall from Figure 15.5, Clark identified various structures through which gifted children and youth could be served. One of these is assignment to a special class, supplemented with opportunities for course work integrated with regular classes. This may occur at any level of schooling, elementary through high school. This approach has many advantages. Students have the best of both worlds, academically and socially. Directed independent studies, seminars, mentorships, and cooperative studies are possible through this arrangement. Students who are gifted are able to interact in an intensive fashion with other gifted students, as well as with regular students in their integrated classes. This program also has disadvantages, however. A special class requires a well-prepared, competent teacher; many school systems simply do not have sufficient funds to hire specialists in gifted education. Without skilled teachers, special-class instruction or other specialized learning activities may just be more of the general education curriculum.

Implementing service delivery and designing curricula for gifted students are significant but rewarding challenges (Burns, Purcell, & Hertberg, 2006; VanTassel-Baska, 2013). They demand the availability of sufficient financial and human resources, flexibility in determining student placement and progress, a focus on high-quality achievement and growth, and a climate of excellence characterized by high standards and significant student engagement (Cooper, 2006). Optimally, delivery systems should facilitate the achievement of specific curricular goals, mesh with state standards, correspond with the types of giftedness being nurtured, and prepare students for other experiences yet to come in elementary, secondary, and postsecondary settings (Adams, 2006; Tomlinson, Doubet, & Capper, 2006).

Conditions and strategies associated with successful classrooms and programs for gifted students include teachers who have advanced preparation and knowledge specifically related to gifted education, who relish change, and who enjoy working collaboratively with other professionals. Furthermore, effective teachers believe in differentiated instruction and actively implement it, have access to a variety of strategies for delivering this kind of instruction, and have a disposition for leadership and some autonomy in fulfilling their teaching responsibilities (Firmender, Reis, & Sweeney, 2013; Leppien & Westberg, 2006).

**Standard 5**
Instructional Planning
and Strategies

## Acceleration

**Acceleration** "Acceleration is an intervention that moves students through an education program at rates faster, or at younger ages, than typical. It means matching the level, complexity, and pace of the curriculum to the readiness and motivation of the student" (Colangelo, Assouline, & Gross, 2004a, p. xi). Many forms of acceleration can be pursued and adopted (Colangelo & Assouline, 2009). Acceleration enables gifted students to progress more rapidly and learn at a rate commensurate with their abilities. Early entrance to kindergarten or college, part-time grade acceleration, self-paced instruction, curriculum compacting, subject-matter acceleration, and grade skipping are all examples of acceleration (Tomlinson & Hockett, 2008).

Another practice related to grade skipping is telescoped or condensed schooling, which enables students to progress through the content of several grades in a significantly reduced time. An allied practice is allowing students to progress rapidly through a particular course or content offering. Acceleration of this nature provides students with the sequential, basic learning at a pace commensurate with their abilities. School programs that are ungraded are particularly suitable for telescoping. Regardless of their chronological ages, students may progress through a learning or curriculum sequence that is not constricted by artificial grade boundaries.

Some years ago, eminent researchers published a two-volume series entitled *A Nation Deceived: How Schools Hold Back America's Brightest Students* (Colangelo, Assouline, & Gross, 2004a, 2004b). Findings from studies presented in this two-volume series affirmed the value of various forms of acceleration (Colangelo, Assouline, & Gross, 2004b). Consider these prominent findings: Students who experience acceleration are more likely to pursue advanced degrees than those who do not (Kulik, 2004). Virtually all forms of acceleration advance growth in academic achievement (Rogers, 2004). Programs that embrace radical acceleration often produce "extraordinary levels of academic success" (Gross, 2004, p. 94). Social-emotional effects of acceleration are not harmful—as a rule, gifted children and youth tend to be more mature socially and emotionally than their same-age peers (Hoogeveen, van Hell, & Verhoeven, 2014). Whole-grade acceleration is a "low-risk/high-success intervention for qualified students" (Colangelo, Assouline, & Lupkowski-Shoplik, 2004, p. 85).

## Enrichment

**Enrichment** Experiences tied to enrichment extend, deepen, broaden, or enrich a person's knowledge (Tomlinson & Hockett, 2008). Music appreciation, foreign languages, and mythology are enrichment courses that are added to a student's curriculum and are usually not any more difficult than other classes in which the student is involved. Other examples of enrichment involve experiences in which the student develops sophisticated thinking skills (i.e., synthesis, analysis, interpretation, and evaluation), or has opportunities to master advanced concepts in a particular subject area. Some forms of enrichment are actually types of acceleration. A student whose enrichment involves fully pursuing mathematical concepts that are well beyond his or her present grade level is experiencing a form of acceleration. Obviously, the two approaches are interrelated.

**Acceleration**
A process whereby students are allowed to achieve at a rate that is consistent with their capacity, achievement, and interests.

**Enrichment**
Educational experiences for gifted students that enhance their thinking skills and extend their knowledge in various areas.

## How Grade Skipping Changed Everything

I've only been knee-deep in the world of gifted and talented education for three-plus years. Prior to that, my exposure was somewhat minor. I read scores of parenting books (some on gifted children), and we had both girls tested for programming at the Center for Talent Development at Northwestern University. We also considered sending them to Quest Academy in Palatine, Illinois, prior to our move to Colorado. However, it wasn't until this summer that we heard the words about our DD10 (dearest daughter who is 10), "She's an excellent candidate for a grade skip, and she wants to. ..."

Then, a week or so later, the same scenario repeated itself with my younger daughter at the Gifted Development Center in Denver, Colorado. "She, too, would be a prime candidate for acceleration."

My first reaction was, "Really? Are you serious?" For one, I thought acceleration was primarily geared toward early entrance to kindergarten and profoundly gifted kids entering college. Our two daughters, ages 9 and 10, were smack dab in the middle of elementary school. Did people really grade skip at this juncture? I had loads of questions:

- How will we know if it's the right decision?

- What happens if one skips and the other one doesn't want to?

- What about the fact that one daughter doesn't seem to be particularly fond of school? She's not even getting top marks.

- What about my perfectionist daughter? Will it be too challenging for her?

- What about socially? Are they mature enough to handle a skip?

- Will the school be amenable? How do I even initiate the process of discussing acceleration?

- Should we be concerned that there are equally bright students (perhaps even more advanced) in their current classes? They do have peers. Shouldn't they simply stay where they are?

- Will they feel too much pressure? Is this just a novel idea that will wear off when the work seems harder?

- What about learning gaps? What happens if they don't know what they're supposed to learn about Colorado history and/or certain science requirements?

- What if they start and then hate it?

Thankfully, we got all of these questions answered and then some. Between Dr. Linda Silverman, Barbara ("Bobbie") Jackson Gilman, and Kim Boham at the Gifted Development Center, we not only discussed each question thoroughly, but we also learned an extraordinary amount about research on acceleration, how vital it is for the students (not parents) to initiate the idea, and how to advocate with the school to ensure the best possible outcomes.

We're now several months into the school year, and I must say, the grade skips have had such an extraordinarily positive impact on both girls. We're fortunate that the receiving teachers welcomed the girls with open arms and understanding. The principal, GT [gifted and talented] teacher, GT coordinator, and counselor proved so supportive and insightful. The adjustment has been much smoother than I anticipated. DD10 has confidence navigating the halls of middle school and has made good friends. She even went to her first dance right before Halloween! DD09 has finally gotten comfortable with not immediately knowing the answers in class and is developing much more of a growth mind-set. She says this is her favorite year of school by far.

SOURCE: Adapted from Mersino, Deborah. (2012). "How Grade Skipping Changed Everything." *Ingenious: Strategic Communication, Gifted Perspective* (blog). Copyright © Deborah Mersino. Reprinted with permission. www.ingeniosus.net/archives/category/acceleration.

Enrichment is the most common administrative approach to serving gifted students. It is also the most abused approach because it is often applied in name only and in a sporadic fashion, without well-delineated objectives or rationale. There are also other problems with the enrichment approach. It is often implemented superficially, as a token response to the demands of parents. Some professionals view enrichment activities as periods devoted to educational trivia or to instruction heavy in student assignments but light in content. Quality enrichment programs are characterized by carefully selected activities, modules, or units; challenging but not overwhelming assignments; and evaluations that are rigorous yet fair. Additionally, good enrichment programs focus on thoughtful and careful plans for student learning and on engaging activities that stress higher-order thinking and application skills. Current enrichment practices make full use of the capacities of the Internet, using wikis, blogs, podcasts, and aggregators for collecting information and completing real-world products and research (Eckstein, 2009). The nearby Assistive Technology feature, "Renzulli Learning: Differentiation Engine," shows how a specialized database can provide personalized learning options for gifted students.

## Renzulli Learning: Differentiation Engine

Because children learn more when instruction is tailored to their abilities and interests, one of the most effective—and most challenging—pedagogic practices is differentiating instruction. For teachers, Renzulli Learning makes differentiating as easy as choosing options from three series of drop-down menus concerning subject, topic, assessment preferences, and due date. This unique engine allows educators to differentiate automatically in three easy steps—for all grades, abilities, and subjects.

Based on student information from the Renzulli Profiler as well as the teacher's input, the Differentiation Engine selects from *more than 25,000* activities, building Web-based lessons. When students log into Renzulli Learning, they see a unique, personalized lesson library filled with the following:

- Unique, differentiated activities
- Engaging, interest-based resources
- Assessment questions
- Teacher-created questions

SOURCE: Adapted from Renzulli Learning. (2012). "Differentiation Engine." Retrieved March 17, 2012, from www.renzullilearning.com/ToolsAndServices/differentiation engine.aspx.

Enrichment may include such activities as exploring exciting topics not normally pursued in the general curriculum, group-centered activities that focus on cognitive or affective skills and/or processes, and small-group investigations of actual, real-life problems. The keys to these endeavors are high student interest, excellent teaching, and superb mentoring.

There is a paucity of systematic experimental research on enrichment programs. Despite many of the limitations of current and past research, evidence supports the effectiveness of enrichment, particularly when it is delivered to specific ability groups and when the content and rigor of the curriculum coincide with the abilities of the targeted students.

Enrichment activities do not appear to detract from the success students experience on regularly administered achievement tests. Sociometric data on students who are pulled out of general education classrooms for enrichment activities are also positive. Students do not appear to suffer socially from involvement in enrichment programs that take place outside their general education classrooms. Acceleration and enrichment are complementary parts of curricular and service delivery systems for gifted children and youth.

**Special Programs and Schools** Programs designed to nurture the talents of individuals in nonacademic and academic areas, such as the visual and performing arts and mathematics, have grown rapidly in recent years (Olszewski-Kubilius & Lee, 2008). Students involved in these programs frequently spend half their school day working in academic subjects and the other half in arts studies. Often an independent institution provides the arts instruction, but some school systems maintain their own separate schools. Most programs provide training in the visual and performing arts, but a few emphasize instruction in creative writing, motion picture and television production, and photography. There are also residential schools for gifted students who specialize in developing stellar academic achievement and growth (Coleman, 2005). Also, distance education is beginning to play a major role in providing challenging, advanced, and stimulating learning experiences to gifted children and youth (Olszewski-Kubilius & Lee, 2008).

So-called governor's schools (distinctive summer programs generally held at university sites), talent identification programs, and specialized residential schools or high schools in various states also provide valuable opportunities for students who are talented and academically gifted (Olszewski-Kubilius & Lee, 2008). Competitively selected students are provided with curricular experiences that are closely tailored to their individual aptitudes and interests. These schools provide unique opportunities for young people to develop strong friendships and support networks that contribute to their social and emotional well-being as well as their talent development (McHugh, 2006). Faculties for these schools are meticulously selected for their competence in various areas and for their ability to stimulate, motivate, and engage students. However, these schools and special programs are few and serve only a small number of the students who would profit from them.

During the school years, parents can continue to encourage their children's development by providing opportunities that correspond to their strengths and interests. The simple identification games played during the preschool period become more complex and demanding. Discussions frequently take place with peers and other interesting adults in addition to parents. Parents help their children move to higher levels of learning by asking questions that involve analysis (comparing and contrasting ideas), synthesis (integrating and combining ideas into new and novel forms), and evaluation (judging and disputing books, newspaper articles, etc.). Parents can also help by

- furnishing books and reading materials on a broad range of topics;
- providing appropriate equipment as various interests surface (e.g., microscopes, musical instruments, art materials);
- providing access to various technologies (computers, sensors, GPS devices, etc.);
- encouraging regular trips to public libraries and other resource centers;
- providing opportunities for participation in cultural events, lectures, and exhibits;
- encouraging participation in extracurricular and community activities outside the home; and
- fostering relationships with potential mentors and other resource people in the community. (Rimm, 2008; Robinson, Shore, & Enersen, 2007)

## 15-6c Adolescent Education and Transition to Adulthood

Programs for gifted adolescents include those previously described, in addition to providing career education, career guidance, and counseling as essential components of a comprehensive program (Liu, Shepherd, & Nicpon, 2008; North, 2007; Rimm, 2008; Robinson, Shore, & Enersen, 2007). Ultimately, career education activities and counseling are designed to help students make educational, occupational, and personal decisions. Because of their multipotentiality (their capacity for doing so many things well), it is difficult for some gifted students to make educational and career choices.

Differentiated learning experiences give elementary and middle school students opportunities to investigate and explore (Benjamin, 2013). When gifted middle school and high school students were asked to comment about teachers who encouraged them to learn at high levels, they responded with the following: "They personally 'zoom in' on you and your work and help you learn at a different level. They expect a high level of performance from you. They give me stimulating questions to answer and something new to learn. If the teacher is excited and passionate about his or her subject, it makes it much easier for me to put in a lot of effort into whatever I'm doing" (Roberts, 2008, p. 249). Many opportunities are career-related and designed to help students understand what it might be like to be a zoologist, neurosurgeon, or filmmaker. What are the time demands? How stressful is the profession or occupation? Students also become familiar with the preparation and effort necessary for work in these fields. For gifted students in the elementary grades, these explorations often take place on Saturdays or weekends. They help such students understand themselves, their talents, and the essential experiences needed for entry into specific fields of advanced study or practice.

As students mature both cognitively and physically, the scope of their career education activities becomes more sophisticated and varied. In group meetings, gifted students and talented professionals may discuss the factors that influenced a scientist or group of researchers to pursue a given problem or conduct experiments that led to important discoveries or products. Condensed programming found at the high school level includes earning credit through examination, enrolling in extra courses for early graduation, reducing or eliminating certain course work, enrolling in intensive summer programs, and taking advanced placement courses while completing high school requirements. Many of these options enable students to enter college early or begin bachelor programs with other advanced students. Many students who are gifted are ready for college-level course work at age 14, 15, or 16—and some even at younger ages. Some students of unusually high abilities are prepared for college-level experiences prior to age 14.

**Mentoring**  Some students are provided opportunities to work directly with research scientists, artists, musicians, or other professionals. Students may spend as many as three or four hours a day, two days a week, in laboratory facilities, mentored by scientists and professionals. Other students rely on intensive workshops or summer programs in which they are exposed to specialized careers through internships and individually tailored instruction.

The benefits of mentoring for gifted students are numerous. Students have sophisticated learning experiences that are highly motivating and stimulating. They gain invaluable opportunities to explore careers and to confirm their commitment to certain areas of study or reexamine their interests. Mentoring experiences may affirm potential in underachieving students or students with disabilities—potential that was not being tapped through conventional means. Mentoring may also promote the development of self-reliance, specific interpersonal skills, and lifelong, productive friendships.

**Career Choices and Challenges**  Career interests, values, and dispositions appear to crystallize early in gifted students. In fact, their interests are neither broader nor more restricted than those of their classmates. Some gifted students know quite early what paths they will follow in postsecondary schooling. These paths often lead to careers in engineering, health professions, and physical sciences.

Counseling programs are particularly helpful to adolescents who are gifted. Often they know more about their academic content than they know about themselves. As gifted students come to understand themselves, their capacities, and their interests more fully, they will make better choices in selecting courses of study and professional careers.

Family counseling may also be helpful to parents and other family members. Problems caused by excessive or inappropriate parental expectations may need to be addressed in a family context. Counselors and therapists may help parents develop realistic expectations consistent with their child's abilities, aspirations, and true interests. As with other exceptionalities, counseling services are best provided through interdisciplinary/collaborative efforts.

## 15-6d  Problems and Challenges of Giftedness

Students who are gifted must cope with a number of problems. One problem is expectations—the expectations they have of themselves and those expectations that parents, teachers, and others have explicitly and implicitly imposed upon them (Berlin, 2009). Students who are gifted frequently feel an inordinate amount of pressure to achieve high grades or to select particular professions. They often feel obligated or duty-bound to achieve excellence in every area, a syndrome called perfectionism. Sadly, such pressure can foster a kind of conformity and prevent students from selecting avenues of endeavor that truly fit them and reflect their personal interests.

Several social-emotional needs that differentiate students who are gifted from their same-age peers have been identified:

- Understanding how they are different from and how they are similar to their peers
- Appreciating and valuing their own uniqueness as well as that of others
- Understanding and developing relationship skills
- Developing and valuing their high-level sensitivity
- Gaining a realistic understanding of their own abilities and talents
- Identifying ways of nurturing and developing their own abilities and talents
- Adequately distinguishing between the pursuit of excellence and the pursuit of perfection
- Developing behaviors associated with negotiation and compromise (VanTassel-Baska, 1989)

Students who are gifted need ongoing and continual access to adult role models who have interests and abilities that parallel theirs; the importance of these role models cannot

**CEC**

**Standard 1**
Learner Development
and Individual Learning
Differences

## What a Colossal Loss!

He started reading as a toddler, played piano at age 3, and delivered a high school commencement speech in cap and gown when he was just 10—his eyes barely visible over the podium.

Brandenn Bremmer was a child prodigy: He composed and recorded music, won piano competitions, breezed through college courses with an off-the-charts IQ, and mastered everything from archery to photography, hurtling through life precociously.

Then Brandenn was found dead in his Nebraska home from an apparent self-inflicted gunshot wound to his head.

He was just 14. He left no note.

"Sometimes we wonder if maybe the physical, earthly world didn't offer him enough challenges and he felt it was time to move on and do something great," his mother, Patricia, said

from the family home in Venango, Nebraska, a few miles from the Colorado border.

Brandenn showed no signs of depression, she said. He had just shown his family the art for the cover of his new CD that was about to be released.

He was, according to his family and teachers, an extraordinary blend of fun-loving child and serious adult. He loved Harry Potter and Mozart. He watched cartoons and enjoyed video games, but gave classical piano concerts for hundreds of people—without a hint of stage fright.

"He wasn't just talented, he was just a really nice young man," said David Wohl, an assistant professor at Colorado State University, where Brandenn studied music after high school. "He had an easy smile. He really was unpretentious."

Patricia Bremmer—who writes mysteries and has long raised dogs with her husband, Martin—said they both knew their son was special from the moment he was born. The brown-haired, blue-eyed boy was reading when he was 15 months old and entering classical piano competitions by age 4.

"He was born an adult," his mother said. "We just watched his body grow bigger."

He scored 178 on one IQ test—a test his mother said he was too bored to finish.

### Question for Reflection

What potential steps, if any, could have been taken to prevent this colossal tragedy?

SOURCE: Adapted from Cohen, S. (2005). *Child Prodigy's Apparent Suicide: "He Knew He Had To Leave," Mother Says.* New York: Associated Press, March 19. Copyright © 2005 Associated Press. Reprinted with permission.

---

be overstated. Role models are particularly important for gifted students who grow up and receive their schooling in rural and remote areas. Such students often complete their public schooling without the benefit of having a mentor or professional person with whom they can talk or discuss various educational and career-related issues. By using the Internet and telementoring, some students who live in rural or remote communities now have access to mentoring at a distance.

## 15-6e  Historically Neglected Groups

Girls and individuals with disabilities are less likely to be recognized as gifted and talented for a variety of reasons. Some girls wish to hide their giftedness, believing that their social prospects with girls as well as boys will be diminished. Thus, they hide or do not fully use their remarkable capacities or talents. With regard to children and youth with disabilities who are also gifted, who are twice exceptional, we are still uncovering means for assessing and calibrating their giftedness.

**Standard 1**
Learner Development and Individual Learning Differences

**Females** Girls usually tend to deny their giftedness and value their academic abilities lower than boys (Robinson, Shore, & Enersen, 2007). Also, the number of girls identified as gifted appears to decline with age. This phenomenon is surprising when we realize that girls tend to walk and talk earlier than their male counterparts; that girls, as a group, read earlier; that girls score higher than boys on IQ tests during the preschool years; and that the grade-point averages of girls during the elementary years are higher than those of boys.

Just exactly what happens to girls? Is the decline in the number of girls identified as gifted related to their socialization? Does some innate physiological or biological mechanism account for this decline? Why do some gifted females fail to realize their potential? To what extent do value conflicts about women's roles contribute to mixed achievement in gifted women? The answers to these and other important questions are gradually emerging.

One of the explanations given for this decline is the gender-specific socialization that girls receive. Behaviors associated with self-efficacy, competitiveness, risk taking, and independence are not generally encouraged in girls. Behaviors that are generally fostered in girls include dependence, cooperation, conformity, and nurturing. One researcher views the elimination of independent behaviors in girls as being the most damaging aspect of their socialization (Silverman, 1986). Rather than delighting in their emerging skills, talents, and capacities, girls tend to mask or hide them from others (Manning & Bestnoy, 2008).

More recent research suggests that girls who develop social self-esteem, "the belief that one has the ability to act effectively and to make decisions independently," are more likely to realize their potential (Davis & Rimm, 2004). Without independence, girls' ability to develop high levels of creativity, achievement, and leadership is severely limited. Overcoming the impact of sociocultural influences requires carefully applied interventions, counseling, and heightened levels of awareness on the part of parents, teachers, and counselors.

Females who are gifted and talented experience additional problems, including fear of appearing "unfeminine" or unattractive when competing with males; competition between marital and career aspirations; stress induced by traditional, cultural, and societal expectations; and self-imposed and/or culturally imposed restrictions related to educational and occupational choices (Davis, Rimm, & Siegle, 2011). Although many of these problems are far from being resolved at this point, some progress is being made. Women in vastly greater numbers are successfully entering professions men traditionally pursued.

Fortunately, multiple role assignments are emerging in many families, wherein the tasks mothers traditionally performed are shared by all members of the family or are completed by someone outside the family. Cultural expectations are changing; as a result, options for women who are gifted are rapidly expanding.

### People with Disabilities: Twice Exceptional

For some time, intellectual giftedness has been largely associated with high IQs and high scores on aptitude tests. These tests, by their very nature and structure, measure a limited range of mental abilities. Because of such limitations, they have not been particularly helpful in identifying people with disabilities who are intellectually or otherwise gifted. However, people with disabilities such as cerebral palsy, learning disabilities, emotional and behavior disorders, and other disabling conditions can be gifted (Montgomery, 2009; Robinson, Shore, & Enersen, 2007; Sternberg, Jarvin, & Grigorenko, 2011). Helen Keller, Vincent van Gogh, and Ludwig van Beethoven are prime examples of individuals with disabilities who were also gifted. Some theorists and practitioners suggest that as many as 2 percent of individuals with disabilities are gifted.

In this context, the twice exceptional are individuals with outstanding ability or potential who achieve high performance despite a physical, emotional, learning, or chronic health disability. Although many challenges are still associated with identifying individuals with disabilities who are gifted, much progress has been made.

Unfortunately, the giftedness of children with disabilities is often invisible to parents and teachers. Factors critical to the recognition of giftedness include environments that

*Photo 15.3* Stevie Wonder is a twice exceptional individual with remarkable musical talents.

elicit signs of talent and capacity, and availability of information about the individual's performance gathered from many sources. With regard to these eliciting environments, it is important that children be given opportunities to perform tasks on which their disabling condition is no impediment (Baum, Schader, & Hebert, 2014). Also, if and when tests of mental ability are used, they must be appropriately adapted, both in administration and scoring. Furthermore, the identification screening should occur at regular intervals. Some children with disabilities change dramatically with appropriate instruction and related assistive technologies. The developmental delays present in children with disabilities and the disabilities themselves pose the greatest challenges to identification efforts (Baum, 2004; Davis & Rimm, 2004).

Differential education for children with disabilities who are gifted is still in its infancy. A great deal of progress has been made, particularly in the adaptive uses of computers and related technologies, but much remains to be done. Additionally, a great deal is still unknown about the service delivery systems and materials that are best suited for these individuals. One of the best approaches parents and teachers can take with gifted children and youth with disabilities is fostering self-confidence, independence, and a sense of personal efficacy—I have what it takes to learn, to succeed, to manage my life, and to realize success (Manning & Bestnoy, 2008).

## Children and Youth from Diverse Cultural, Linguistic, Ethnic, and Economic Backgrounds

Rarely are culturally diverse and economically disadvantaged youth identified as gifted (Ford, Coleman, & Davis, 2014; Graham, 2009). These youth are dramatically underrepresented in programs for the gifted and talented (Gibbons, Pelchar, & Cochran, 2012; King, Kozleski, & Lansdowne, 2009; Matthews & Shaunessy, 2008). This underrepresentation is a function of several factors: racism; social and economic inequities; excessive reliance on testing and test scores that may not accurately capture potential and talent in these youth; IQ-based definitions of giftedness; identification practices based on achievement test scores; and a lack of teacher referrals of children for gifted education programs (Bireda, 2011; Center for Comprehensive School Reform and Improvement, 2008; Warwick & Matthews, 2009). Social and motivational variables also contribute to these diminished numbers, particularly with African American students who are pressured to "act black"—giving a false appearance of not being smart, acting dumb, exhibiting high levels of aggressiveness, being antiauthority, and other related behaviors (Graham 2009). Some districts are now using a checklist and other appropriate identification measures to help teachers and others look more inclusively and broadly for potentially gifted students (see Figure 15.6).

**Figure 15.6** *Javits Gifted Characteristics Checklist for Underrepresented Populations*

**VERBAL ABILITIES**
1. Has an expanded vocabulary
2. Asks unusual questions to find out more information
3. Expresses ideas well
4. Elaborates on questions for information

**LEARNING CHARACTERISTICS**
5. Exhibits quick mastery of skills
6. Has long-term recall of information
7. Has interest in how things work
8. Has the ability to see relationships and make connections
9. Is able to retain more information with less repetition
10. Displays creativeness, originality, putting things and ideas together in novel ways
11. Has a lot of information about one topic
12. Has a questioning attitude
13. Signals perfectionist tendencies
14. Likes to solve puzzles and trick questions
15. Has a wide range of interests
16. Performs well mathematically
17. Stays with a project until it is completed

**MOTIVATIONAL CHARACTERISTICS**
18. Sets high standards for self
19. Is inquisitive
20. Has a tendency to lose awareness of time/intense concentration
21. Becomes easily impatient with drill-and-routine procedures
22. Is persistent

23. Has keen powers of observation
24. Requires little direction

**SOCIAL ABILITIES**
25. Tends to dominate peers or situation
26. Has unusual, often highly developed sense of humor
27. Is independent
28. Often finds and corrects own or others' mistakes
29. Is anxious to complete tasks
30. Is often overly sensitive

**LEADERSHIP**
31. Adapts readily to new situations
32. Is well liked by classmates and demonstrates leadership
33. Carries responsibility well
34. Is self-confident with own age group
35. Is cooperative with teacher and classmates

**CREATIVITY**
36. Makes up games and activities displaying imagination
37. Expresses original ideas in other ways
38. Demonstrates ability to express feelings and emotions
39. Is articulate in role playing and storytelling
40. Displays a richness in imagery and informal language
41. Demonstrates ability in fine or practical arts

SOURCE: Adapted from Project Bright Horizon, Washington Elementary School District, Glendale, Arizona. Retrieved May 8, 2009, from www.ade.az.gov/asd/gifted/downloads/Project%20 BrightHorizon-GiftedCharacteristicsChecklist.pdf.

Behaviors that are receiving increased attention in identifying giftedness in diverse children and youth are resilience, acculturation, code switching, and bilingualism. Children who are diverse in some fashion, who maintain positive views of themselves despite challenging problems and environments, may be candidates for gifted programs. The same could be said of children who adjust more quickly, that is, acculturate more rapidly than same-age peers to their surrounding environments. With regard to code switching and bilingualism, children who are adept in their heritage language and who develop another language, and who use both with skill, may be candidates for gifted programs and related activities (Matthews & Shaunessy, 2008). As suggested at the beginning of this chapter, we are now focusing more on inclusive practices in identifying giftedness and are paying more attention to talent development in children and youth who are diverse in some fashion (Harris, Plucker, Rapp, & Marinez, 2009; Horowitz, 2009; Matthews & Shaunessy, 2008; VanTassel-Baska, 2009).

Effective instructional programs for children and adolescents who are disadvantaged and gifted have several key components. First, the teachers in these programs are well trained in adapting and differentiating instruction for these students, providing culturally responsive teaching and content (Center for Comprehensive School Reform and Improvement, 2008; Robinson, Shore, & Enersen, 2007). These teachers understand learning preferences, how to build and capitalize on students' interests, and how to maximize students' affective, cognitive, and ethical capacities. In addition to providing the typical curricular options for enrichment, acceleration, and talent development, the best programs for these children and youth embrace and celebrate ethnic diversity, provide extracurricular cultural enrichment, attend to differences in learning styles, provide counseling, supply mentoring, create culturally responsive classrooms, foster parent support groups and community connections, provide supportive and stimulating tutoring, and give these children and youth access to significant role models (Bireda, 2011; Sosniak & Gabelko, 2008).

There is general agreement that programs for these children and youth should begin early and should be tailored to the needs and interests of each identified child. They should focus on individual potentialities rather than deficits and should help parents and others understand their roles in fostering giftedness and talent development (Baum, 2004; Sosniak & Gabelko, 2008). Often, the emphasis in the early years is on reading instruction, language development, and foundation skills. Other key components include experiential education that provides children with many opportunities for hands-on learning, activities that foster self-expression, plentiful use of mentors and role models who represent the child's cultural or ethnic group, involvement of the community, and counseling throughout the school years that gives serious consideration to the cultural values of the family and the child who is gifted.

## Looking Toward a Bright Future

In spite of challenging problems in providing all gifted children and youth with appropriate opportunities for talent development, acceleration, and enrichment, there is cause for optimism on several fronts. We are beginning to see concerted efforts in identifying all potentially gifted children and youth. We are broadening the ways in which we seek to identify these children and youth. These efforts are particularly pronounced in recognizing and developing talent and capacity in historically neglected groups: girls, children and youth with disabilities (the twice exceptional), and young people from diverse cultural, linguistic, ethnic, and economic backgrounds.

Recent research is also helping teachers and other professionals understand the underserved and underrepresented gifted populations more thoroughly—recognizing hindrances to talent and capacity development, the vital role of motivation or lack thereof, and cultural factors that contribute to or interfere with talent development. Lastly, we are beginning to understand the trajectory of giftedness over a lifespan, giving us a reasonably complete picture of what it takes to nurture and sustain gifted children, youth, and adults who have the potential to contribute significantly on so many important fronts.

## 15-1 Describe how the lives of people who are gifted, creative, and talented have changed since the advent of IDEA.

- Formerly referred to as gifted individuals, researchers and practitioners now include creative and talented as descriptors not identified by traditional tests of intelligence. Programs now target creativity and exceptional talents along with high IQ.

- IDEA does not require services for children and youth who are gifted, creative, or talented; however, identifying and serving these individuals has increased greatly since the original passage of IDEA in 1975.

- Twenty-six states mandate services for gifted students, but funding affects the quality and types of programs offered.

- Talent development will likely replace gifted education in the coming years, with efforts directed toward identifying and developing intellectual gifts, creative abilities, and talents.

## 15-2 Explain the various definitions and classifications of gifted, creative, and talented.

- Definitions are essential for identifying those who will be served, for calculating funding, and for discussion among researchers and practitioners.

- The current definition comes from the National Association for Gifted Children (2012):

  Students, children, or youth who give evidence of high achievement capability in areas such as intellectual, creative, artistic, or leadership capacity, or in specific academic fields, and who need services and activities not ordinarily provided by the school in order to fully develop those capabilities.

## 15-3 Describe the characteristics and prevalence of children and youth who are gifted, creative, and talented.

- Children and youth with outstanding talent perform or show the potential for performing at remarkably high levels of accomplishment when compared with others of their age, experience, or environment.

- Gifted children and youth exhibit high performance capability in intellectual, creative, and/or artistic areas, possess an unusual leadership capacity, or excel in specific academic fields.

- Gifted children and youth require services or activities that schools do not ordinarily provide.

- Outstanding talents are present in children and youth from all cultural groups, across all economic strata, and in all areas of human endeavor.

## 15-4 List the causes associated with gifts and talents.

- Genetic endowment certainly contributes to giftedness.

- Environmental stimulation provided by parents, teachers, coaches, tutors, and others contributes significantly to the emergence of giftedness.

- The interaction of innate abilities with environmental influences and encouragement fosters the development and expression of giftedness.

## 15-5 Describe the assessment procedures used to identify gifts and talents in children and youth.

- Developmental checklists and scales
- Parent and teacher inventories
- Intelligence and achievement tests
- Creativity tests
- Other diverse observational information provided by parents, grandparents, and other knowledgeable adults involved in the gifted child's life

## 15-6 Describe the different interventions for children and youth with gifts and talents from early childhood through adulthood.

- Naturally interacting with and stimulating young children during bathing, feeding, and dressing young children

- Providing appropriate sensory experiences: cuddling, tickling, and touching

- Developing trust: establishing appropriate regimens, providing predictability in schedules and routines, and giving positive support for new experiences and learning

- Lots of language—lots of talking

- Providing experiences with appropriate picture books and other related materials—the reading of stories, talking about stories, having young children make predictions about what will happen next

- Having children tell their own stories and capturing them in print—establishing the rudiments of written language

- Providing many kinds of experiences—visits to different places, making things, engaging in dress-up activities—giving children opportunities for spontaneous and rich play

- Differentiated instruction: an approach to gifted education that attends to the natural abilities and interests of children and adolescents

- Enrichment: activities designed to extend, deepen, broaden, or enrich a person's knowledge

- Acceleration: allowing students to move through content and related experiences at a rate that is commensurate with their abilities and capacities

- Governor's schools: highly specialized programs, generally offered at or through universities, to encourage talent development, to give able students opportunities to connect with other talented students, and to work with skilled content specialists and mentors

- Mentoring: allowing gifted students to work with carefully selected specialists or experts who provide ongoing direction and experiences in a given talent or academic domain

Council for Exceptional Children (CEC) Standards to Accompany Chapter 15

If you are thinking about a career in special education, you should know that many states use national standards developed by the Council for Exceptional Children (CEC) to assess a teacher candidate's knowledge and skills for working with students with disabilities. See a complete listing of the seven CEC Content Standards on the inside cover of this text.

1 Learner Development and Individual Learning Differences
2 Learning Environments
4 Assessment
5 Instructional Planning and Strategies

## Mastery Activities and Assignments

To master the content within this chapter, complete the following activities and assignments:

1. Complete a written test of the chapter's content. If your instructor requires a written test of your content knowledge for this chapter, keep a copy for your portfolio.
2. Review the Case Study on Embracing Diversity, "Don-Wook Shin," and respond in writing to the Application Questions. Keep a copy of the Case Study and your written response for your portfolio.
3. Participate in a community service learning activity. Community service is a valuable way to enhance your learning experience. Develop a reflective journal of the service learning experience for your portfolio.

# References

## Chapter 1

Americans with Disabilities Act of 1990, PL 101-336.

Aristotle. (1941). Politics. In R. McKeon (Ed.), *The basic works of Aristotle (Book 7)* (p. 1,302). New York: Random House.

Baron, R. A., Branscombe, N. R., & Byrne, D. (2008). *Social psychology: Understanding human interaction*, 12th ed. Boston: Allyn & Bacon.

Braddock, D., & Parish, S. L. (2002). An institutional history of disability. In D. Braddock (Ed.), *Disability at the dawn of the 21st century and the state of the states* (pp. 1–61). Washington, D.C.: American Association on Mental Retardation.

Brault, Matthew W. (2012). Americans with Disabilities: 2010. *Current population reports*, P70-131. Washington, D.C.: U.S. Census Bureau.

Carlson, N. R., Miller, H., Heth, C. D., Donahoe, J. W., & Martin, N. (2009). *Psychology: The science of behavior*, 7th ed. Boston: Allyn & Bacon.

Center on Human Policy at Syracuse University. (2011). A statement in support of families and their children. Retrieved August 14, 2011, from http://thechp.syr.edu/resources/position-statements/families-and-their-children/.

Connecticut Code of 1650

Dolson, J. (2011). Leveling the playing field: We're all differently abled. Retrieved August 2, 2011, from http://accessites.org/site/2009/03/leveling-the-playing-field-were-all-differently-abled/.

Drew, C. J., & Hardman, M. L. (2007). *Intellectual disabilities across the lifespan*, 9th ed. Columbus, OH: Merrill.

Hardman, M., & McDonnell, J. (2008). Teachers, pedagogy, and curriculum. In M. McLaughlin & L. Florian, *Perspectives and purposes of disability classification systems in research and clinical practice* (pp. 153–169). London: Sage Publishing Co.

James, W. (1890). *Principles of psychology*. New York: Henry Holt.

Kennedy, J. F. (1963, October 31). *Remarks upon signing Bill for the Construction of the Mental Retardation Facilities and Community Mental Health Centers*. Washington, D.C.: The White House.

Kessler Foundation and the National Organization on Disability. (2010). *Survey of the employment of Americans with disabilities.* New York: Author.

Mooney, J. (2007). *The short bus: A journey beyond normal*. New York: H. Holt.

NOD/Harris, L., & Associates (2004). *National Organization on Disability/Harris Survey of Americans with Disability*. New York: Author.

Rose, C., Swearer, S. & Espelage, D. (2012). Bullying and students with disabilities: The untold narrative. *Focus on Exceptional Children, 45*(2), 1–10.

Rosenhan, D. I. (1973). On being sane in insane places. *Science, 179*, 250–258.

Schroeder, S. R., Gerry, M., Gertz, G., & Velazquez, F. (2002). *Usage of the term "mental retardation": Language, image and public education (Final Project Report)*. Lawrence, Kansas: University of Kansas Center on Developmental Disabilities and the Center for the Study of Family, Neighborhood and Community Policy.

Shifrer, D. (2013). Stigma of a label: Education expectations for high school students labeled with learning disabilities. *Journal of Health and Social Behavior, 54*(4), 462–480.

Snow, K. (2005). To ensure inclusion, freedom, and respect for all, it's time to embrace people first language. Retrieved September 26, 2014, from https://www.disabilityisnatural.com/images/PDF/pfl09.pdf.

United States Department of Justice. (2014). A resort community improves access to city programs and services for residents and vacationers. Retrieved October 17, 2014, from www.ada.gov/fernstor.htm.

United States Department of Justice, Equal Employment Opportunity Commission (2014). Americans with Disabilities Act: Questions and Answers. Retrieved October 17, 2014, from www.ada.gov/q&aeng02.htm.

United States Holocaust Memorial Museum. (2014). *People with disabilities*. Retrieved October 18, 2014, from http://www.ushmm.org/research/research-in-collections/search-the-collections/bibliography/people-with-disabilities.

United States Senate Committee on Health, Education, Labor and Pensions. (2014). Separate and unequal: States fail to fulfill the community living promise of the Americans with Disabilities Act. Retrieved September 2, 2014, from http://www.help.senate.gov/imo/media/doc/Olmstead Report July 20131.pdf.

Wolfensberger, W. (1975). *The origin and nature of our institutional models*. Syracuse, NY: Human Policy Press.

Woolfolk, A. (2013). *Educational psychology*, 12th ed. Boston: Allyn & Bacon.

## Chapter 2

Berry, J. (2009). *Lifespan perspectives on the family and disability*. Austin, TX: Pro-Ed.

*Brown v. Board of Education of Topeka, Kansas*, 347 U.S. 483 (1954).

Byrnes, M. A. (2011). *Taking sides: Clashing views on controversial issues in special education*, 2nd ed. Guilford, CT: McGraw-Hill Dushkin.

Cassidy, V. M., & Stanton, J. E. (1959). *An investigation*

of factors involved in the educational placement of mentally retarded children: A study of differences between children in special and regular classes in Ohio. U.S. Office of Education Cooperative Research Program, Project No. 043. Columbus, OH: Ohio State University.

Drew, C. J., & Hardman, M. L. (2007). *Intellectual disabilities across the lifespan*, 9th ed. Columbus, OH: Merrill.

Duncan, A. (2011). Letters from the education secretary or deputy secretary, September 23, 2011. Retrieved March 6, 2015, from http://www2.ed.gov /policy/gen/guid/secletter /110923.html.

Friend, M. P., & Bursuck, W. D. (2012). *Including students with special needs: A practical guide for classroom teachers*, 6th ed. Boston: Pearson.

Hardman, M. L., & Dawson, S. (2008, winter). The impact of federal public policy on curriculum and instruction for students with disabilities in the general classroom. *Preventing School Failure 52*(2), 5–11.

Hardman, M., & Mulder, M. (2004). Critical issues in public education: Federal reform and the impact on students with disabilities. In L. M. Bullock, & R. A. Gable (Eds.), *Quality personnel preparation in emotional/behavior disorders* (pp. 12–36). Dallas, TX: Institute for Behavioral and Learning Differences.

Hehir, T. (2002). IDEA 2002 Reauthorization: An opportunity to improve educational results for students with disabilities. *A timely IDEA: Rethinking federal education programs for children with disabilities.* Washington, D.C.: Center on Educational Policy.

*Board of Education of the Hendrick Hudson Central School District v. Rowley*, 458 U.S. 176 (1982).

Hillegas, T. (2014). 8 tips for new special education teachers. Retrieved December 4, 2014, from www.specialeducation guide.com/blog/8-tips -for-new-special -education-teachers/.

Huefner, D. S., & Herr, C. M. (2012). *Navigating special education law and policy.* Verona, WI: Attainment Company.

Johnson, G. O. (1961). *A comparative study of the personal and social adjustment of mentally handicapped children placed in special classes with mentally handicapped children who remain in regular classes.* Syracuse, NY: Syracuse University Research Institute, Office of Research in Special Education and Rehabilitation.

Jordan, A. M., & deCharms, R. (1959). Personal-social traits of mentally handicapped children. In T. G. Thurstone (Ed.), *An evaluation of educating mentally handicapped children in special classes and regular classes.* Chapel Hill, NC: School of Education, University of North Carolina.

*Mills v. Board of Education of District of Columbia*, 348 F. Supp. 866 (D.D.C. 1972).

National Information Center for Children and Youth with Disabilities. (2011).

*Questions often asked by parents about special education services.* Washington, D.C.: Author. Retrieved December 23, 2011, from http:// www.parentcenterhub .org/wp-content/uploads /repo_items/lg1.pdf.

*Pennsylvania Association for Retarded Citizens v. Commonwealth of Pennsylvania*, 334 F. Supp. (1971).

President's Commission on Excellence in Special Education. (2002). *A new era: Revitalizing special education for children and their families.* Washington, D.C.: Education Publications Center, U.S. Department of Education.

Thurstone, T. G. (1959). *An evaluation of educating mentally handicapped children in special classes and regular classes.* U.S. Office of Education, Cooperative Research Project No. OE-SAE 6452. Chapel Hill, NC: University of North Carolina.

United Nations Educational, Scientific and Cultural Organization (UNESCO). (1994). *World Conference on Special Needs Education: Access and quality.* Salamanca, Spain: Author.

United Nations Educational, Scientific, and Cultural Organization (UNESCO). (2001). *We the children: Meeting the promises of the World Summit for Children.* New York: Author.

U.S. Department of Education, (2010). *A blueprint for reform: The reauthorization of the Elementary and Secondary Education Act.* Washington, D.C.: U.S. Retrieved January 16, 2015, from www2 .ed.gov/policy/elsec/leg /blueprint/blueprint.pdf

U.S. Department of Education. (2013). *Thirty-fifth annual report to congress on the implementation of the* Individuals with Disabilities Education Act, *2013.* Washington, D.C.: U.S. Government Printing Office.

U.S. Department of Education (2014). ESEA Flexibility Page. Retrieved November 16, 2014, from http://www2.ed.gov /policy/elsec/guid/esea -flexibility/index.html.

Wagner, M., Newman, L., Cameto, R., Javitz, H., & Valdes, K. (2012). A national picture of parent and youth participation in IEP and transition planning meetings. *Journal of Disability Policy Studies, 23*(3), 140–155.

Wang, K. (2014). The art of diplomacy. Retrieved November 16, 2014, from http://www.friendship circle.org/blog/2014 /06/18/the-art-of-iep -diplomacy/.

Williams-Diehm, K., Brandes, J., Chesnut, P., & Haring, K. (2014). Student and parent IEP collaboration: A comparison across school settings. *Rural Special Education Quarterly, 33*(1), 3–11.

## Chapter 3

Arthur-Kelly, M., Foreman, P., Bennette, D., & Pascoe, S. (2008). Interaction, inclusion and students with profound and multiple disabilities: Toward an agenda for research and practice. *Journal of Research in Special Educational Needs, 8*(3), 161–166.

Bal, A., Kozleski, E. B., Schrader, E. M., Rodriguez, E. M., & Pelton, S. (2014). Systemic transformation from the ground up: Using learning lab to design culturally responsive schoolwide positive behavioral supports. *Remedial & Special Education, 35*(6), 327–339.

Batshaw, M., Pellegrino, L., & Rozien, N. J. (2008). *Children with disabilities*, 6th ed. Baltimore: Paul H. Brookes.

Bender, W. N. (2008). *Differentiating instruction for students with learning disabilities: Best teaching practices for general and special educators*, 2nd ed. Thousand Oaks, CA: Corwin Press.

Berk, L. E. (2011). *Development through the lifespan*, 2nd ed. Upper Saddle River, NJ: Prentice-Hall.

Berry, J. (2009). *Lifespan perspectives on the family and disability.* Austin, TX: Pro-Ed.

Bierman, K. L., Nix, R. L., Greenberg, M. T., Blair, C., & Domitrovich, C. E. (2008). Executive functions and school readiness intervention: Impact, moderation, and mediation in the Head Start REDI program. *Development and Psychopathology, 20*(3), 821–843.

Bloom, B. S. (1964). *Stability and change in human characteristics*. New York: Wiley & Sons.

Bolt, S. E., & Roach, A. T. (2009). *Inclusive assessment and accountability: A guide to accommodations for students with diverse needs.* New York: Guilford Press.

Case-Smith, J., & Holland, T. (2009). Making decisions about service delivery in early childhood programs. *Language, Speech & Hearing Services in Schools, 40*(4), 416–423.

Center for Applied Special Technology. (2012). *Carnegie Strategy Tutor.* Retrieved January 15, 2012, from www.cast.org/research/projects/tutor.html (Coyne, P., & Dalton, B., Project Directors).

Crane, J. L., & Winser, A. (2008). Early autism detection: Implications for pediatric practice and public policy. *Journal of Disability Policy Studies, 18*(4), 245–253.

Devore, S., & Hanley-Maxwell, C. (2000). "I wanted to see if we could make it work": Perspectives on inclusive childcare. *Exceptional Children, 66*(2), 241–255.

Devore, S., & Russell, S. (2007). Early childhood education and care for children with disabilities: Facilitating inclusive practice. *Early Childhood Education Journal, 35*(2), 189–198.

Division for Early Childhood, Council for Exceptional Children and the National Association for the Education of Young Children. (2009). *Position statement on inclusion.* Retrieved January 13, 2015, from http://dec.membershipsoftware.org/files/Position%20Statement%20and%20Papers/Inclusion%20Position%20statement.pdf.

Dorn, S., & Fuchs, D. (2004). Trends in placement issues. In A. M. Sorrells, H. J. Rieth, & P. T. Sindelar (Eds.), *Critical issues in special education: Access, diversity, and accountability* (pp. 57–72). Boston: Allyn & Bacon.

Drew, C. J., & Hardman, M. L. (2007). *Mental retardation*, 9th ed. Upper Saddle River, NJ: Prentice-Hall.

Dunn, L. M. (1968). Special education for the mildly retarded. Is much of it justifiable? *Exceptional Children, 35*, 229–237.

Eggen, P., & Kauchak, D. (2010). *Educational psychology: Windows on classrooms*, 8th ed. Upper Saddle River, NJ: Merrill Prentice-Hall.

Frankel, E. B., & Gold, S. (2007). Principles and practices of early intervention. In I. Brown & M. Percy (Eds.), *A comprehensive guide to intellectual and developmental disabilities* (pp. 451–466). Baltimore: Paul H. Brookes.

Friend, M. P., & Bursuck, W. D. (2012). *Including students with special needs: A practical guide for classroom teachers*, 5th ed. Boston: Allyn & Bacon.

Friend, M. P., & Cook, L. (2010). *Interactions: Collaboration skills for school professionals*, 6th ed. Upper Saddle River, NJ: Prentice-Hall.

Fuchs, D., Fuchs, L. S., & Vaughn, S. (2014). What is intensive instruction and why is it important? *Teaching Exceptional Children, 46*(4), 13–18.

Gargiulo, R., & Metcalf, D. (2013). *Teaching in today's inclusive classrooms: A universal design for learning approach.* Belmont, CA: Wadsworth Cengage Learning.

Gartin, B. C., Murdick, N. L., Imbeau, M., & Perner, D. E. (2002). *How to use differentiated instruction with students with developmental disabilities in the general education classroom.* Alexandria, VA: Council for Exceptional Children.

Gollnick, D., & Chinn, P. C. (2009). *Multicultural education in a diverse society*, 8th ed. Boston: Allyn & Bacon.

Grenier, M., Rogers, R., & Iarusso, K. (2008). Including students with Down syndrome in adventure programming. *Journal of Physical Education, 79*(1), 30–35.

Guralnick, M. J., Neville, B., Hammond, M. A., & Connor, R. T. (2008). Continuity and change from full inclusion early childhood programs through the early elementary period. *Journal of Early Intervention, 30*(3), 237–250.

Haager, D., & Klinger, J. K. (2005). *Differentiating instruction in inclusive classrooms: The special educator's guide.* Boston: Allyn & Bacon.

Hammeken, P. A. (2007). *Inclusion: An essential guide for the paraprofessional*, 2nd ed. Thousand Oaks, CA: Corwin Press.

California Department of Education. (2005). Handbook on Transition from Early Childhood Special Education Programs. California Department of Education. Sacramento, CA.

Hardman, M. L., & Dawson, S. (2008, winter). The impact of federal public policy on curriculum and instruction for students with disabilities in the general classroom. *Preventing School Failure, 52*(2), 5–11.

Hardman, M., & McDonnell, J. (2008). Teachers, pedagogy, and curriculum. In M. McLaughlin & L. Florian (Eds.), *Perspectives and purposes of disability classification systems in research and clinical practice* (pp. 153–169). London: Sage Publishing Co.

Hardman, M., & Mulder, M. (2004). Critical issues in public education: Federal reform and the impact on students with disabilities. In L. M. Bullock & R. A. Gable (Eds.), *Quality personnel preparation in emotional/behavior disorders* (pp. 12–36). Dallas, TX: Institute for Behavioral and Learning Differences.

Harvey, A., Robin, J., Morris, M. E., Graham, H. K., & Baker, R. (2008). A systematic review of measures of activity limitation for children with cerebral palsy. *Developmental Medicine and Child Neurology, 50*(3), 190–198.

Hogansen, J. M., Powers, K., Geenen, S., Gil-Kashiwabara, E., & Powers, L. (2008). Transition goals and experiences of females with disabilities: Youth, parents, and professionals. *Exceptional Children, 74*(2), 225–234.

Hollins, E. R., & Guzman, M. T. (2005). Research on preparing teachers for diverse populations. In M. Cochran-Smith & K. M. Zeichner (Eds.), *Studying teacher education: The report of the AERA panel on research and teacher education*

(pp. 477–548). Mahwah, NJ: Lawrence Erlbaum Associates.

Holzberg, C. (2012). *Helping all learners succeed: Special education success stories.* Retrieved January 7, 2012, from www.washington.edu /doit/Press/learning .html. (Originally published in *Technology and Learning,* January 1998.)

Horner, R. H., Albin, R. W., Sprague, J. R., & Todd, A. W. (2006). Positive behavior support. In M. E. Snell & F. Brown (Eds.), *Instruction of students with severe disabilities* (pp. 206–250). Baltimore: Paul H. Brookes.

Horner, R. H., Sugai, G., & Anderson, C. M. (2010). Examining the evidence base for school-wide positive behavior support. *Focus on Exceptional Children, 42*(8).

Hosp, M. K., & Hosp, J. L. (2003). Curriculum-based measurement for reading, spelling, and math: How to do it and why. *Preventing School Failure, 48*(1), 10–17.

Howell, K. W., & Nolet, V. (2000). *Curriculum-based evaluation.* Stamford, CT: Wadsworth.

Huefner, D.S. (2012). *Navigating special education law and policy.* Verona, Wisconsin: Attainment Company.

Humphrey, N. (2008). Autistic spectrum and inclusion: Including pupils with autistic spectrum disorders in mainstream schools. *Support Learning, 23*(1), 41–47.

Hunt, J. M. (1961). *Intelligence and experience.* New York: Ronald Press.

Hunt, P. h., McDonnell, J., & Crockett, M. A. (2012).

Reconciling an ecological curricular framework focusing on quality of life outcomes with the development and instruction of standards-based academic goals. *Research & Practice For Persons with Severe Disabilities, 37*(3), 139–152.

Jimenez, B., Browder, D, Spooner, F., & Dibiase, W. (2012). Inclusive inquiry science using peer-mediated embedded instruction for students with moderate intellectual disability. *Exceptional Children, 78*(3), 301–317.

Justice, L. M., Logan, J. R., Tzu-Jung, L., & Kaderavek, J. N. (2014). Peer effects in early childhood education: Testing the assumptions of special-education inclusion. *Psychological Science, 25*(9), 1722–1729.

Karen, T. J. (2007). *More inclusion strategies that work: Aligning student strengths with standards.* Thousand Oaks, CA: Corwin Press.

Ketterlin-Geller, L. R. (2008). Testing students with special needs: A model for understanding the interaction between assessment and student characteristics in a universally designed environment. *Educational Measurement: Issues and Practices, 27*(3), 3–16.

Klein, E., & Hollingshead, A. (2015). Collaboration between special and physical education: the benefits of a healthy lifestyle for all students. *Teaching Exceptional Children, 47*(3), 163–171.

Kotering, L., McClannon, T. W., & Braziel, P. M. (2008). Universal design

for learning: A look at what algebra and biology students with and without high incidence conditions are saying. *Remedial and Special Education, 29*(6), 352–363.

Leader-Janssen, E., Swain, K. D., Delkamiller, J., & Ritzman, M. J. (2012). Collaborative relationships for general education teachers working with students with disabilities. *Journal of Instructional Psychology, 39*(2), 112–118.

Leafstedt, J. M., Richards, C., Lamonte, M., & Cassidy, D. (2007). Perspectives on co-teaching: Views from high school students with learning disabilities. *Learning Disabilities: A Multidisciplinary Journal, 14*(3), 177–184.

Leppert, M. L., & Rosier, E. M. (2008). In P. J. Accardo (Ed.), *Capute and Accardo's neurodevelopmental disabilities in infancy and childhood: Vol 1: Neurodevelopmental diagnosis and treatment,* 3rd ed. (pp. 395–404). Baltimore: Paul H. Brookes.

Lipkin, P. H., & Schertz, M. (2008). Early intervention and efficacy. In P. J. Accardo (Ed.) *Capute and Accardo's neurodevelopmental disabilities in infancy and childhood: Vol 1: Neurodevelopmental diagnosis and treatment,* 3rd ed. (pp. 519–552). Baltimore: Paul H. Brookes.

Lipsky, D. K., & Gartner, A. (2002). Taking inclusion into the future. In M. Byrnes (Ed.), *Taking sides: Clashing views on controversial issues in special education* (pp. 198–203). Guilford, CT: McGraw-Hill Dushkin.

Lund, J. L., & Veal, M. L. (2008). Chapter 4: Measuring pupil learning—How do student teachers assess within instructional models? *Journal of Teaching in Physical Education, 27*(4), 487–511.

Mastropieri, M. A., & Scruggs, T. E. (2013). *The inclusive classroom: Strategies for effective instruction.* Upper Saddle River, NJ: Merrill.

McDonnell, A. P., Hawken, L. S., Johnston, S. S., Kidder, J. E., Lynes, M. J., & McDonnell, J. J. (2014). Emergent literacy practices and support for children with disabilities: a national survey. *Education & Treatment of Children, 37*(3), 495–529.

McDonnell, J. M., & Hardman, M. L. (2009). *Secondary and transition programs for students with intellectual and developmental disabilities.* London: Sage Publishing.

McDonnell, J., Hardman, M., & McDonnell, A. P. (2003). *Introduction to persons with moderate and severe disabilities* (p. 299). Boston: Allyn & Bacon.

McDonnell, J., Hardman, M. L., & McGuire, J. (2007). Teaching and learning in secondary education. In L. Florian (Ed.), *The handbook of special education* (pp. 378–389). London: Sage Publishing.

Murawski, W. W. (2008). Five keys to co-teaching in inclusive classrooms. *School Administrator, 65*(8), 29.

National Association for the Education of Young Children. (2009). *NAEYC position statement.* Retrieved January 13, 2015, from www.naeyc.org /files/naeyc/file/positions /PSDAP.pdf.

National Association of School Psychologists. (2012). *Position statement on inclusive programs for students with disabilities.* Retrieved January 15, 2012, from www.nasponline.org /about_nasp/pospaper _ipsd.aspx.

Neal, P. (2008). Are we making a difference? Measurement of family outcomes in early intervention. Chapel Hill, NC: *Dissertation Abstracts International Section A: Humanities and Social Sciences, 68*(7), 2802.

Peterson, J. M., & Hittie, M. M. (2010). *The journey toward effective schools for all learners.* Upper Saddle River, NJ: Prentice-Hall.

Phillips, D. A., & Cabrera, N. J. (2006). *Beyond the blueprint: Directions for research on Head Start families.* Washington, D.C.: National Academies Press.

Piaget, J. (1970). Piaget's theory. In P. H. Mussen (Ed.), *Carmichael's manual of child psychology,* 3rd ed., Vol. 1. New York: Wiley.

Pugach, M. C. (2005). Research on preparing general education teachers to work with students with disabilities. In M. Cochran-Smith & K. M. Zeichner (Eds.), *Studying teacher education: The report of the AERA panel on research and teacher education* (pp. 549–590). Mahwah, NJ: Lawrence Erlbaum Associates.

Rao, K., Ok, M. W., & Bryant, B. R. (2014). A review of research on universal design educational models. *Remedial & Special Education, 35*(3), 153–166.

Raver, S. (2010). *Early childhood special education—0 to 8 years: Strategies for positive outcomes.* Upper Saddle River, NJ: Prentice-Hall.

Rose, D. H., & Meyer, A. (2002). *Teaching every student in the digital age: Universal design for learning.* Alexandria, VA: Association for Supervision and Development.

Rosenkoetter, S. E., Whaley, K. T., Hains, A. H., & Pierce, L. (2001). The evolution of transition policy for young children with special needs and their families: Past, present, and future. *Topics in Early Childhood Education, 21*, 3–15.

Sapon-Shevin, M. (2008). Learning in an inclusive community. *Educational Leadership, 66*(1), 49–53.

Scanlon, D., & Baker, D. (2012). An accommodations model for the secondary inclusive classroom. *Learning Disability Quarterly, 35*(4), 212–224.

Shapiro-Barnard, S., Tashie, C., Martin, J., Malloy, J., Schuh, M., Piet, J., Lichtenstein, S., & Nisbet, J. (2002). Petroglyphs: The writing on the wall. In M. Byrnes (Ed.), *Taking sides: Clashing views on controversial issues in special education* (pp. 210–214). Guilford, CT: McGraw-Hill Dushkin.

Shonkoff, J. P. (2011). Protecting brains, not simply stimulating minds. *Science, 333*(6045), 982–983.

Spencer, S. (2005). Lynne Cook and June Downing: The practicalities of collaboration in special education service delivery (Interview). *Intervention in School and Clinic, 40,* 296–300.

Sugai, G., & Horner, R. (2010). School-wide positive behavior support: Establishing a continuum of evidence-based practices. *Journal of Evidence-Based Practices in Schools, 11*(1), 62–83.

Tan, T. S., & Cheung, W. S. (2008). Effects of computer collaborative group work on peer acceptance of a junior pupil with attention deficit hyperactive disorder. *Computers and Education, 50*(3), 725–741.

Tannock, M. T. (2009). Tangible and intangible elements of collaborative teaching. *Intervention in School and Clinic, 44(3),* 173–178.

Theoharris, G. (2007). Social justice educational leaders and resistance: Toward a theory of social justice leadership. *Educational Administration Quarterly, 43,* 221–258.

U.S. Department of Health and Human Services. (2013). *Head Start Program fact sheet.* Washington, D.C.: Administration on Families and Children. Retrieved April 4, 2015, from http:// eclkc.ohs.acf.hhs.gov /hslc/data/factsheets /docs/hs-program-fact -sheet-2013.pdf.

Vaughn, S., Bos, C. S., & Schumm, J. S. (2011). *Teaching students who are exceptional, diverse, and at-risk students in the general education classroom,* 5th ed. Boston: Prentice-Hall.

Wade, S. E., & Zone, J. (2000). Creating inclusive classrooms: An overview. In S. E. Wade (Ed.), *Inclusive education: A casebook and readings for prospective and practicing teachers* (pp. 1–27). Mahwah, NJ: Lawrence Erlbaum Associates.

White, B. L. (1975). The first three years of life. Englewood Cliffs, NJ: Prentice Hall. *Journal of the Division for Early Childhood Education, 9*, 11–26.

Widerstrom, A. H. (2005). *Achieving learning goals through play: Teaching young children with special needs*, 2nd ed. Baltimore: Paul H. Brookes.

Wood, J. W. (2006). *Teaching students in inclusive settings; Adapting and accommodating instruction*, 5th ed. Boston: Prentice-Hall.

Worrell, J. L. (2008). How secondary schools can avoid the seven deadly sins of inclusion. *American Secondary Education, 36*(2), 43–45.

## Chapter 4

Agran, M., Wehmeyer, M. L., Cavin, M., & Palmer, S. (2008). Promoting student active classroom participation skills through instruction to promote self-regulated learning and self-determination. *Career Development for Exceptional Individuals, 31*(2), 106–114.

Allen, P., Ciancio, J., & Rutkowski, S. (2008). Transitioning students with disabilities into work. *Techniques: Connecting Education and Careers, 83*(2), 22–25.

Babbitt, B. C., & White, C. M. (2002). RU ready? Helping students assess their readiness for postsecondary education. *Teaching Exceptional Children, 35*(2), 62–66.

Bakken, J. P., & Obiakor, F. E. (2008). *Transition planning for students with disabilities: What educators and service providers can do.* Springfield, IL: Charles C. Thomas, Publisher, Ltd.

Bambara, L., Browder, D., & Kroger, X. (2006). Home and community. In M. Snell & F. Brown (Eds.), *Instruction of students with severe disabilities*, 6th ed. (pp. 526–568). Upper Saddle River, NJ: Merrill Publishing/Prentice Hall.

Bremer, C. D., Kachgal, M., & Schoeller, K. (2003, April). Self-determination: Supporting successful transition. *Research to Practice Brief of the National Center on Secondary Education and Transition, 2*(1), 1–5.

Conley, D. T. (2012). *A complete definition of college and career readiness.* Portland, OR: Educational Policy Improvement Center. Retrieved from www.epiconline.org.

Crockett, M., & Hardman, M. L. (2009). Expected outcomes and emerging values. In J. McDonnell & M. L. Hardman, *Successful transition programs*, 2nd ed. (pp. 25–42). Los Angeles: Sage Publishing.

Drew, C. J., & Hardman, M. L. (2007). *Intellectual disabilities across the lifespan*, 9th ed. Upper Saddle River, NJ: Merrill.

Finn, D., Getzel, E. E., & McManus, S. (2008).

Adapting the self-determined learning model for instruction for college students with disabilities. *Career Development for Exceptional Individuals, 31*(2), 85–93.

Friend, M. P., & Bursuck, W. D. (2006). *Including students with special needs: A practical guide for classroom teachers*, 4th ed. Boston: Allyn & Bacon.

Getzel, E. E., & Thoma, C. A. (2008). Experiences of college students with disabilities and the importance of self-determination in higher education settings. *Career Development for Exceptional Individuals, 31*(2), 77–84.

Hagner, D., Kurtz, A., May, J., & Cloutier, H. (2014). Person-centered planning for transition-aged youth with autism spectrum disorders. *Journal of Rehabilitation, 80*(1), 4–10.

Hamblet, E. C. (2014). Nine strategies to improve college transition planning for students with disabilities. *Teaching Exceptional Children, 46*(3), 53–59.

Hansen, D. L., & Morgan, R. L. (2008). Teaching grocery store purchasing skills to students with intellectual disabilities using computer-based instruction program. *Education and Training in Developmental Disabilities, 43*(4), 431–442.

Harchik, A., & Ladew, P. (2008). Strategies to help children with special needs enjoy successful community outings. *Exceptional Parent, 38*(12), 75–77.

Hasazi, S. B., Furney, K. S., & Destefano, L. (1999).

Implementing the IDEA transition initiatives. *Exceptional Children, 65*(4), 555–566.

Joseph, L. M., & Konrad, M. (2009). Have students self-manage their academic performance. *Intervention in School and Clinic, 44*(4), 246–249.

Kessler Foundation and the National Organization on Disability. (2010). *Survey of the employment of Americans with disabilities.* New York: Author.

Lock, R. H., & Layton, C. A. (2008). The impact of tutoring attendance on the GPAs of postsecondary students with learning disabilities. *Learning Disabilities: A Multidisciplinary Journal, 15*(2), 55–60.

Manley, K., Collins, B. C., Stenhoff, D. M., & Kleinert, H. (2008). Using a system of least prompts procedure to teach telephone skills to elementary students with cognitive disabilities. *Journal of Behavioral Education, 17*(3), 221–236.

Margolis, H. S., & Prichard, E. (2008). What to do when your child turns 18. *Exceptional Parent, 38*(11), 24–26.

McDonnell, J. (2009). Curriculum. In J. McDonnell & M. L. Hardman, *Successful transition programs* (pp. 63–80). Los Angeles: Sage Publishing.

McDonnell, J., & Copeland, S. (2011). Teaching academic skills. In M. Snell & F. Brown (Eds.), *Instruction of students with severe disabilities*, 7th ed. (pp. 492–528). Boston: Pearson Group.

McDonnell, J., Hardman, M. L., & McGuire, J. (2007). Teaching and learning in secondary education. In L. Florian (Ed.), *The handbook of special education* (pp. 378–389). London: Sage Publishing Co.

McDonnell, J. Kiuhara, S., & Collier, P. (2009). Transition to post-secondary education. In J. McDonnell & M. L. Hardman, *Successful transition programs*, 2nd ed. (pp. 320–340). Los Angeles: Sage Publishing.

McGuire, J., & McDonnell, J. (2008). Relationships between recreation and levels of self-determination for adolescents and young adults with disabilities. *Career Development for Exceptional Individuals, 31*(3), 154–163.

Muller, E., Schuler, A., & Yates, G. B. (2008). Social challenges and supports from the perspective of individuals with Asperger syndrome and other autism spectrum disabilities. *Autism: The International Journal of Research and Practice, 12*(2), 173–190.

Newman, L. Wagner, M., Knokey, A., Marder, C., Nagle, K., Shaver, D. & Wei, X. (2011). *The post-high school outcomes for young adults with disabilities up to 8 years after high school: A report from the National Longitudinal Transition Study-2 (NLTS2).* Washington, D.C.: National Center for Special Education Research.

Newton, D. A., & Dell, A. G. (2010). Supporting transitions of assistive technology users. *Journal of Special Education Technology, 25*(1), 57–62.

Nierengarten, G. (2013). Supporting co-teaching teams in high schools: Twenty research-based practices. *American Secondary Education, 42*(1), 73–83.

Partnership for 21st Century Skills. (2014). Framework for 21st century learning. Retrieved January 6, 2015, from www.p21.org/about-us /p21-framework.

Payne-Christiansen, E. M., & Sitlington, P. L. (2008). Guardianship: Its role in the transition process for students with developmental disabilities. *Education and Training in Developmental Disabilities, 43*(1), 3–19.

Pierson, M. R., Carter, E. W., Lane, K. L., & Glaeser, B. C. (2008). Factors influencing the self-determination of transition-age youth with high incidence disabilities. *Career Development for Exceptional Individuals, 31*(2), 115–125.

Polychronis, S., & McDonnell, J. (2009). Developing IEPs/transition plans. In J. McDonnell & M.L. Hardman, *Successful transition programs* (81–100). Los Angeles: Sage Publishing.

Rowe, D. A., Mazzotti, V. L., & Sinclair, J. (2015). Strategies for teaching self-determination skills in conjunction with the Common Core. *Intervention in School & Clinic, 50*(3), 131–141.

Schindler, V. P., & Kientz, M. (2013). Supports and barriers to higher education and employment for individuals diagnosed with mental illness. *Journal of Vocational Rehabilitation, 39*(1), 29–41.

Shogren, K. A., Kennedy, W., Dowsett, C., & Little, T. D. (2014). Autonomy, psychological empowerment, and self-realization: Exploring data on self-determination from NLTS2. *Exceptional Children, 80*(2), 221–235.

Smith, T. L., Beyer, J. F., Polloway, E. A., Smith, D. J., & Patton, J. R. (2008). Ethical considerations in teaching self-determination: Challenges in rural special education. *Rural Special Education Quarterly, 27*(1/2), 30–35.

Steere, D. E., Rose, E., & Cavaiuolo, D. (2007). *Growing up: Transition to adult life for students with disabilities.* Boston: Allyn & Bacon.

Stenhoff, D. M., Davey, B. J., & Lignugaris/Kraft, B. (2008). The effects of choice on assignment completion and percent correct by a high school student with a learning disability. *Education and Treatment of Children, 31*(2), 203–211.

Thurlow, M. L., Sinclair, M. F., & Johnson, D. (2009). Students with disabilities who drop out of school: Implications for policy and practice. *Issues Brief: Examining Current Issues in Secondary Education and Transition.* Retrieved April 11, 2009, from www.ncset.org /publications/viewdesc .asp?id=425.

University of Illinois at Chicago National Research and Training Center. (2009). *Self-determination framework for people with psychiatric disabilities.* Chicago, IL: Author. Retrieved April 2, 2009, from www.cmhsrp.uic .edu/download/uicnrtc -sdbib.pdf.

U.S. Department of Education. (2011). *To assure the free appropriate public education of all children with disabilities: Thirtieth annual report to congress on the implementation of the Individuals with Disabilities Education Act.* Washington, D.C.: U.S. Government Printing Office.

Wagner, M., & Blackorby, J. (1996). Transition from high school to work or college: How special education students fare. In the Center for the Future of Children, *Special education for students with disabilities, 6*(1), 103–120. Los Angeles: The Center for the Future of Children.

Wehman, P. (2011). *Essentials of transition planning.* Baltimore: Paul H. Brookes.

Wehmeyer, M. L. (2014). Self-determination: A family affair. *Family Relations, 63*(1), 178–184.

Wehmeyer, M. L., Gragoudas, S., & Shogren, K. A. (2006). Self-determination, student involvement, and leadership development. In P. Wehman, *Life beyond the classroom: Transition strategies for young people with disabilities*, 4th ed. (pp. 41–69). Baltimore: Paul H. Brookes.

Winn, S., & Hay, I. (2009). Transition from school for youths with a disability: Issues and challenges. *Disability & Society, 24*(1), 103–115.

Worrell, J. L. (2008). How secondary schools can avoid the seven deadly school "sins" of inclusion. *American Secondary Education, 36*(2), 43–56.

# Chapter 5

Aguilar, E. (2015). Making connections: Culturally responsive teaching and the brain. Retrieved from www.edutopia.org/blog /making-connections -culturally-responsive -teaching-and-brain -elena-aguilar.

Alvarez, H. K. (2007). The impact of teacher preparation on responses to student aggression in the classroom. *Teaching and Teacher Education, 23,* 1113–1126.

Arias, M. B., & Morillo-Campbell, M. (2008). Promoting ELL parental involvement: Challenges in contested times. Tempe: Arizona State University. Retrieved from http://epsl.asu.edu /epru/documents/EPSL -0801-250-EPRU.pdf.

Arrendondo, P., & Perez, P. (2006). Historical perspectives on the multicultural guidelines and contemporary applications. *Professional Psychology: Research and Practice, 37,* 1–5.

Artiles, A. J., Kozleski, E. B., Trent, S. C., Osher, D., & Ortiz, A. (2010). Justifying and explaining disproportionality, 1968–2008: A critique of underlying views of culture. *Exceptional Children, 76*(3), 279–299.

ASPE Issue Brief. (2014). *Information on poverty and income statistics: A summary of 2014 current population survey data.* Washington, D.C.: Department of Health and Human Services. Retrieved from http:// aspe.hhs.gov/hsp/14 /PovertyAndIncomeEst /ib_poverty2014.pdf.

August, D., & Shanahan, T. (2006). Introduction and methodology. In D. August & T. Shanahan (Eds.), *Developing literacy in second-language learners: Report of the national literacy panel on language-minority children and youth* (pp. 1–42). Mahwah, NJ: Lawrence Erlbaum Associates Publishers.

Baca, L. M., & Cervantes, H. T. (2004). *The bilingual special education interface,* 4th ed. Columbus, OH: Merrill/Macmillan.

Baldwin, J. R., Faulkner, S. L., & Hecht, M. I. (2006). *Redefining cultures: Perspective across the disciplines.* Mahwah, NJ: Lawrence Erlbaum Associates.

Banks, J. A. (2008). *An introduction to multicultural education,* 4th ed. Boston: Pearson.

Barnum-Martin, L., Mehta, P. D., Fletcher, J. M., Carlson, C. D., Ortiz, A., Carlo, M., & Francis, D. J. (2006). Bilingual phonological awareness: Multilevel construct validation among Spanish-speaking kindergartners in transitional bilingual education classrooms. *Journal of Educational Psychology, 98,* 170–181.

Barrera, M. (2006). Roles of definitional and assessment models in the identification of new or second language learners of English for special education. *Journal of Learning Disabilities, 39,* 142–156.

Batalova, J. & McHugh, M. (2010). *Top Languages Spoken by English Language Learners Nationally and by State.* Washington, DC: Migration Policy Institute.

Blachowicz, C. L. Z., Fisher, P. J., & Watts-Taffe, S. (2005). *Integrated vocabulary instruction: Meeting the needs of diverse learners in grades K–5.* Learning Point Associates, North Central Regional Educational Laboratory. Retrieved from www.learningpt .org/pdfs/literacy /vocabulary.pdf.

Bratter, J. L., & Eschbach, K. (2005). Race/ethnic differences in nonspecific psychological distress: Evidence from the National Health Interview Survey. *Social Science Quarterly, 86,* 620–644.

Carpenter, S., Zarate, M. A., & Garza, A. A. (2007). Cultural pluralism and prejudice reduction. *Cultural Diversity and Ethnic Minority Psychology, 13,* 83–93.

Center on Teaching and Learning. (2015). Big ideas in beginning reading—Vocabulary. Eugene: University of Oregon. Retrieved from http://reading.uoregon .edu/big_ideas/voc/voc _what.php.

Clare, M. M., & Garcia, G. (2007). Working with migrant children and their families. In G. B. Esquivel, E. C. Lopez, & S. Nahari (Eds.), *Handbook of multicultural school psychology: An interdisciplinary perspective* (pp. 549–572). Mahwah, NJ: Lawrence Erlbaum Associates Publishers.

Colby, S. L. & Ortman, J. M. (2015). *Projections of the size and composition of the U.S. population: 2014 to 2060. Table 2. Population by race and Hispanic origin: 2014 and 2060.* Issued March 2015. Washington, D.C.: U.S. Bureau of Census. Retrieved from www .census.gov/content/dam /Census/library/publications/2015/demo/p25 -1143.pdf.

Coll-Black, S., Bhushan, A., & Fritsch, K. (2007). Integrating poverty and gender into health programs: A sourcebook for health professionals. *Nursing and Health Sciences, 9,* 246–253.

Collier, C. (2004). Including bilingual exceptional children in the general education classroom. In L. M. Baca & H. T. Cervantes (Eds.), *The bilingual special education interface,* 4th ed. (pp. 298–335). Columbus, OH: Merrill/Macmillan.

Crawford-Brooke, E. (2013). The critical role of oral language in reading for Title I students and English language learners. *Lexia, a Rosetta Stone Company.* Retrieved from http://lexialearning.com /lexiaresearch/white papers/oral-language -whitepaper.

Dahlgren, M. E. (2008). Oral language and vocabulary development kindergarten & first grade. Reading First National Conference, 2008. Retrieved from www2.ed.gov /programs/readingfirst /2008conferences /language.pdf.

Deaux, K., Reid, A., & Martin, D. (2006). Ideologies of diversity and inequality: Predicting collective action in groups varying in ethnicity and immigrant status. *Political Psychology, 27,* 123–146.

Department of Homeland Security. (2014). *Yearbook*

of *Immigration Statistics 2013,* Washington, D.C.: Department of Homeland Security.

Dettmer, P., Thurston, L. P., & Dyck, N. J. (2005). *Consultation, collaboration, and teamwork for students with special needs,* 5th ed. Boston: Allyn & Bacon.

De Von Figueroa-Moseley, C., Ramey, C. T., & Keltner, B. (2006). Variations in Latino parenting practices and their effects on child cognitive developmental outcomes. *Hispanic Journal of Behavioral Sciences, 28,* 102–114.

*Diana v. State Board of Education* (1970, 1973). C-70, 37 REP (N. D. Cal., 1970, 1973).

Díaz-Rico, L. T., & Weed, K. Z. (2010). *The cross-cultural, language, and academic development handbook: A complete K–12 reference guide,* 4th ed. Boston: Allyn & Bacon.

Edelsky, C. (2006). *With literacy and justice for all: Rethinking the social in language and education,* 3rd ed. Mahwah, NJ: Lawrence Erlbaum Associates.

Emerson, E., & Hatton, C. (2007). Poverty, socioeconomic position, social capital and the health of children and adolescents with intellectual disabilities in Britain: A replication. *Journal of Intellectual Disability Research, 51,* 866–874.

Epstein, J. L. (2011). *School, family and community partnerships: Preparing educators and improving schools,* 2nd ed. Washington, D.C.: Westview Press.

Erevelles, N., Kanga, A., & Middleton, R. (2006). How does it feel to be a problem? Race, disability, and exclusion in education al policy. In E. A. Brantlinger (Ed.), *Who benefits from special education? Remediating (fixing other people's children* (pp. 77–99). Mahwah, NJ: Lawrence Erlbaum Associates.

Evans, G. W., & Kim, P. (2007). Childhood poverty and health: Cumulative risk exposure and stress dysregulation. *Psychological Science, 18,* 953–957.

Feldman, S. (2005). The war for children. *Professional Psychology: Research and Practice, 36,* 615–617.

Flora, C. B. (2011). *The community capitals framework: A transparent tool for participatory development.* A presentation given at Brigham Young University, English Language Learners Symposium. Retrieved from http://education.byu.edu/ellsymposium/2011/resources.html.

Freeman, D. E., & Freeman, Y. S. (2007). *English language learners: The essential guide.* New York: Scholastic Teaching Resources.

Freeman, D. E., & Freeman, Y. S. (2011). *Beyond worlds: access to second language acquisition,* 3rd ed. Portsmouth, NH: Heinemann.

Freeman, Y. S., & Freeman, D. E. (2014). Introduction. In Y. S. Freeman & D. E. Freeman (Eds.), *Research on preparing preservice teachers to work effectively with emergent bilinguals* (pp. xi–xvii). Bingley, UK: Emerald Group Publishing Limited.

Friend, M., & Cook. L. (2007). *Interventions: Collaboration skills for school professionals,* 5th ed. Boston: Allyn & Bacon.

Fujiki, M. & Brinton, B. (2010). Distinguishing between language difference and language deficit for ELLs. Presentation at Brigham Young University English Language Learners Annual Symposium, 2010. McKay School of Education vimeo production. Retrieved from http://vimeo.com/13835949.

Funkhouser, M. (2013). The political future of the browning of America. *Governing: States and Localities.* Retrieved from www.governing.com/gov-institute/col-political-future-browning-america-population-growth.html.

Gay, G. (2002). Culturally responsive teaching in special education for ethnically diverse students: Setting the stage. *Qualitative Studies in Education, 15,* 613–629.

Gimbert, B. G., Cristol, D., & Sene, A. M. (2007). The impact of teacher preparation on student achievement in algebra in a "hard-to-staff" urban preK–12-university partnership. *School Effectiveness and School Improvement, 18,* 245–272.

Glimpse, W. (2012). Assessing English language proficiency. Retrieved from http://proximityone.com/elp.htm.

Gollnick, D. M., & Chinn, P. C. (2009). *Multicultural education in a pluralistic society,* 8th ed. Upper Saddle River, NJ: Merrill.

González, N., Moll, L. C., & Amanti, C., Eds. (2005). *Funds of knowledge, theorizing practices in households, communities and classrooms.* Mahwah, NJ: Lawrence Erlbaum Associates, Publishers.

Grant C. A., Sleeter, C. E., & Grant, C. A. (2009). *Making choices for multicultural education: Five approaches to race, class, and gender,* 6th ed. Danvers, MA: John Wiley & Sons, Inc.

Gregory, R. J. (2007). *Psychological testing: History, principles, and applications,* 5th ed. Boston: Allyn & Bacon.

Grieco, E. M. & Cassidy, R. C. (2001). *Overview of race and Hispanic origin: Census 2000 Brief.* Washington, D.C.: U.S. Bureau of Census.

Hallerod, B., & Larsson, D. (2008). Poverty, welfare problems and social exclusion. *International Journal of Social Welfare, 17,* 15–25.

Harrington, M. M., & Brisk, M. E. (2006). *Bilingual education: From compensatory to quality schooling,* 2nd ed. Mahwah, NJ: Lawrence Erlbaum Associates.

Harry, B. & Klingner, J. (2006). *Why are so many minority students in special education?: Understanding race & disability in schools.* New York: Teachers College Columbia University.

Hart, B. & Risley, T. R. (1995). Meaningful Differences in the everyday experiences of young American children (3rd printing, January 2003).

Baltimore: Brookes Publishing.

Hays, P. A. (2008). Putting culture to the test: Considerations with standardized testing. In P. A. Hays (Ed.), *Addressing cultural complexities in practice: Assessment, diagnosis, and Therapy*, 2nd ed. (pp. 129–151). Washington, D.C.: American Psychological Association.

Hellerman, J., & Vergun, A. (2007). Language which is not taught: The discourse marker use of beginning adult learners of English. *Journal of Pragmatics, 39*, 157–179.

Hendrick, J., & Weissman, P. (2007). *The whole child: Developmental curriculum for the young child,* 7th ed. Upper Saddle River, NJ: Pearson, Prentice Hall.

Johnson, J. H. Jr., & Kasarda, J. D. (January 2011). Six disruptive demographic trends: What census 2010 will reveal. Chapel Hill: University of North Carolina. Retrieved from www.kenaninstitute.unc .edu/Census2010Trends/.

Kandel, W. A., Bruno, A., Meyer, P. J., Seelke, C. R., Taft-Morales, M., & Wasem, R. E. (2014). Unaccompanied alien children: Potential factors contributing to recent immigration. Washington, D.C.: Congressional Research Service. Retrieved from http://fas.org/sgp /crs/homesec/R43628.pdf.

Kauffman, J. M., Conroy, M., Gardner, R., & Oswald, D. (2008). Cultural sensitivity in the application of behavior principles to education. *Education and Treatment of Children, 31*, 239–262.

Kishiyama, M. M., Boyce, W. T., Jimenez, A. M., Perry, L. M., & Knight, R. T. (2008). Socioeconomic disparities affect prefrontal function in children. *Massachusetts Institute of Technology, Journal of Cognitive Neuroscience, 21*(6), 1106–1115.

Kline, M. V., & Huff, R. M. (2008). *Health promotion in multicultural populations: A handbook for practitioners and students.* Thousand Oaks, CA: Sage Publications.

Krashen, S. D. (2002, Dec.). *Second language acquisition and second language learning.* Internet Edition. First printed edition 1981 by Pergamon Press Inc. Retrieved from www .sdkrashen.com/content /books/sl_acquisition _and_learning.pdf.

*Larry P. v. Riles.* (1972). C-71-2270 U.S. C, 343 F. Supp. 1306 (N. D. Cal. 1972).

*Larry P. v. Riles.* (1979). 343 F. Supp. 1306, 502 F. 2d 963 (N. D. Cal. 1979).

*Lau v Nichols.* (1974). 414, U.S., 562–572 (1974, January 21).

Levin, B. (2006). Schools in challenging circumstances: A reflection on what we know and what we need to know. *School Effectiveness and School Improvement, 17*, 399–407.

Lucchese, F., & Tamis-LeMonda, C. S. (2008). Fostering language development in children from disadvantaged backgrounds. *Encyclopedia of Language and Literacy Development* (pp. 1–11). London, ON: Canadian Language and Literacy Research Network. Retrieved from www

.literacyencyclopedia.ca /pdfs/topic.php?topId=229.

Monger, R., & Yankay, J. (2014). U.S. lawful permanent residents: 2013. Homeland Security, Office of Immigration Statistics, Policy Directorate.

Macartney, S., Bishaw, A., & Fontenot, K. (2013). *Poverty rates for selected detailed race and Hispanic groups by state and place: 2007–2011: American Community Survey Briefs.* Issued February 2013. U.S. Census Bureau. Retrieved from www.census .gov/prod/2013pubs /acsbr11-17.pdf.

MacFarlane, S. B. (2007). Researching health, poverty, and human development. *Critical Public Health, 17*, 191–193.

Marulis, L. M., & Neuman, S. B. (2010). The effects of vocabulary intervention on young children's word learning: A meta-analysis. *Review of Educational Research, 80*, 300–335.

Maxwell, L. A. (2014). After journey from Honduras, boy starts school in U.S. *Education Week,* August 27, 2014, Vol. 34, Issue 03, pg. 6. Retrieved from www.edweek.org/ew/arti cles/2014/08/27/02unacc ompanied.h34.html.

McDonough, P., Sacker, A., & Wiggins, R. D. (2005). Time on my side? Life course trajectories of poverty and health. *Social Science and Medicine, 61*, 1795–1808.

McMillan, J. H. (2007). *Classroom assessment: Principles and practices for effective standards-based instruction,* 4th ed. Boston: Allyn & Bacon.

Merrell, K. W. (2007). *Behavioral, social, and

emotional assessment of children and adolescents.* Abingdon, UK: Routledge.

Moats, L. C. (unknown). Implementing research-based reading instruction in high poverty schools: Lessons learned from a five-year research program. University of Michigan Conference. Retrieved from www .umich.edu/~rdytolrn /pathwaysconference /presentations/moats.pdf.

Monger, R. & Yankay, J. (2014). U.S. lawful permanent residents: 2013, Annual flow report. Washington, D.C.: Office of Immigration Statistics. Retrieved from www.dhs .gov/sites/default/files /publications/ois_lpr _fr_2013.pdf.

Moule, J. (2012). *Cultural competence; a primer for educators,* 2nd ed. Belmont, CA: Cengage Learning.

Mueller, J. (2011). Authentic assessment toolbox. Retrieved from http:// jfmueller.faculty.noctrl .edu/toolbox/whatisit.htm.

Nippold, M. A. (2006). *Later language development: School age children and young adults,* 3rd ed. Austin, TX: Pro-Ed.

National Center for Culturally Responsive Educational Systems. (2008). *Academy 1 Module 2: Culturally responsive pedagogy and practice, Academy 1: Understanding cultural responsiveness.* Participant's handout (pg. 12). Tempe: Arizona State University. Retrieved from www .nccrest.org/publications /NCCREST-PL-Modules /CRPP/A1/CR%20 Pedagogy%20and%20

Practice%20Academy%201%20Participant%20Handouts%20ver%201.0%20FINAL%20kak.pdf.

National Education Association (2008a). Disproportionality: Inappropriate identification of culturally and linguistically diverse children. An NEA policy brief. Washington, D.C. Retrieved from www.nea.org/assets/docs/HE/mf_PB02_Disproportionality.pdf.

National Education Association (2008b). Parent, family, community involvement in education. NEA Policy Brief. Washington, D.C. Retrieved from www.nea.org/assets/docs/PB11_ParentInvolvement08.pdf.

O'Hara, S., & Pritchard, R. H. (2008). Meeting the challenge of diversity: professional development for teacher educators. *Teacher Education Quarterly, 35*, 43–61.

O'Neil, S. (March 6, 2015). Central America's unaccompanied minors. *Latin America's Moment*. Retrieved from http://blogs.cfr.org/oneil/2015/03/06/central-americas-unaccompanied-minors/.

Ornstein, E., & Moses, H. (2005). One nation many voices. *School Social Work Journal, 30*, 87–89.

Ovando, C. J., Combs, M. C., & Collier, V. P. (2006). *Bilingual and ESL classrooms: teaching in multicultural contexts.* New York: McGraw-Hill.

Peoplemovin. (2010). A visualization of migration flows. Retrieved from http://peoplemov.in/.

Perlich, P. (2011). *Coming to our census*. Retrieved from http://education.byu.edu/ellsymposium/2010/.

Ralabate, P. (2007). Truth in labeling: Disproportionality in special education. Washington, D.C.: National Education Association. Retrieved from www.nea.org/assets/docs/HE/EW-TruthInLabeling.pdf.

Reschly, D. J. (2009). Overview document: Prevention of disproportionate special education representation using response to intervention. *National Comprehensive Center for Teacher Quality.* Washington, D.C.: ETS, Learning Point Associates, and Vanderbilt University.

Reynolds, C. R., Livingston, R., & Willson, V. (2006). *Measurement and assessment in education.* Boston: Allyn & Bacon.

Riad, S. (2007). Of mergers and cultures: "What happened to shared values and joint assumptions?" *Journal of Organizational Change Management, 2*, 26–43.

Rodriguez, D. (2005). *A conceptual framework for bilingual special education teacher programs.* Proceedings of the 4th International Symposium on Bilingualism. Sommerville, MA: Cascadilla Press.

Rueda, R., & Yaden, D. B., Jr. (2006). The literacy education of linguistically and culturally diverse young children: An overview of outcomes, assessment, and large-scale interventions. In B. Spodek & O. N. Saracho (Eds.), *Handbook of research on the education of young children,* 2nd ed., (pp. 167–186). Mahwah, NJ: Lawrence Erlbaum Associates.

Skiba, R. J., Poloni-Staudinger, L., & Simmons, A. B. (2005). Unproven links: Can poverty explain ethnic disproportionality in special education: *Journal of Special Education, 39*, 130–144.

Skinner, D., & Weisner T. S. (2007). Sociocultural studies of families of children with intellectual disabilities. *Mental Retardation and Developmental Disabilities Research Reviews, 13*, 302–312.

Skinner, C., Wight, V. R., Aratani, Y, Cooper, J. L., & Thampi, K. (2010). English language proficiency, family economic security, and child development. *National Center for Children in Poverty.* Retrieved from http://nccp.org/publications/pub_948.html.

Sleeter, C. E., Grant, C. A. (2009). *Turning on learning: Five approaches for multicultural teaching plans for race class, gender, and disability,* 5th ed. Danvers, MA: John Wiley & Sons, Inc.

Solarsh, B., Alant, E. (2006). The challenge of cross-cultural assessment: The test of ability to explain for Zulu speaking children. *Journal of Communication Disorders, 39, 109–138.*

Spinelli, C. (2006). *Classroom assessment for students in special and general education,* 2nd ed. Upper Saddle River, NJ: Pearson.

Stavans, I. (2002, May 30). The browning of America. *The Nation*. Retrieved from www.thenation.com/article/browning-america.

Sullivan, A. (2011). Disproportionality in special education and placement of English language learners. *Exceptional Children V 77(3),* pp. 317–334. Arlington, VA: Council for Exceptional Children.

Teemant, A., Cutri, R., Squires, & Gibb, G. (1998). *Inclusive Pedagogy Framework: Developing Common Understanding and United Advocacy.* Provo, UT: Brigham Young University.

Teemant, A., Smith, M. E., Pinnegar, S. (2003*). Bilingual/ESL endorsement through distance education program: Assessment for linguistically diverse students instruction guide,* 2nd ed. Provo, UT: Brigham Young University.

Tyler, K., Stevens, R., & Uqdah, A. (updated 2009). Cultural bias in teaching. Retrieved from www.education.com/reference/article/cultural-bias-in-teaching/.

U.S. Census Bureau. (2012). The 2012 Statistical Abstract, Table 79. Retrieved from www.census.gov/compendia/statab/cats/births_deaths_marriages_divorces.html.

U.S. Census Bureau. (2014a). QuickFacts. Retrieved from www.census.gov/quickfacts/table/PST045214/00.

U.S. Census Bureau. (2014b). Table 15. Projected components of change by race and Hispanic origin for the United States: 2015 to 2016 (NP2014-T15) Source: U.S. Census Bureau, Population Division Release Date: December 2014. Retrieved from www.census.gov

/.../projections/files/summary/NP2014-T15.xls.

U.S. Census Bureau (2015). Quick Facts: USA. Retrieved from http://quickfacts.census.gov/qfd/states/00000.html.

U.S. Department of Commerce (1995). *Population Profile of the United States 1995.* Washington, D.C.: U.S. Department of Commerce.

U.S. Department of Education. (2014). Migrant education—Purpose. Washington, D.C.: Office of Migrant Education. Retrieved from www2.ed.gov/programs/mep/index.html.

Vásquez, M J. R., Lott, V., & Garcia-Vázquez, E. (2006). Personal reflections: Barriers and strategies in increasing diversity in psychology. *American Psychologist, 61,* 157–172.

Vaughn, S., Linan-Thompson, S., Mathes, P. G., Cirino, P. T., Carlson, C. D., Pollard-Durodola, S. D., Gardenas-Hagan, E., & Francis, D. J. (2006). Effectiveness of Spanish intervention for first-grade English language learners at risk for reading difficulties. *Journal of Learning Disabilities, 39,* 56–73.

Waitoller, F. R., Artiles, A. J., Cheney, D. A. (2010). The Miner's Canary: A review of overrepresentation research and explanations. *The Journal of Special Education, 44*(1), 29–49. Austin, TX: Hamill Institute on Disabilities.

WIDA (2014). "The WIDA can do philosophy." Madison: University of Wisconsin. Retrieved from www.wida.us/aboutUs/AcademicLanguage/index.aspx.

Wiese, A. M. (2006). Educational policy in the United States regarding bilinguals in early childhood education. In B. Spodek (Ed.), *Handbook of research on the education of young children,* 2nd ed. Mahwah, NJ: Lawrence Erlbaum Associates.

Wiggins, G. P. (1998). *Educative assessment: Designing assessments to inform and improve student performance.* San Francisco: Jossey-Bass Publishers.

Wright, R. J. (2007). *Educational assessment: Tests and measurements in the age of accountability.* Thousand Oaks, CA: Sage Publications.

**Chapter 6**

Abbeduto, L., Seltzer, M. M., Shatuck, P., Krauss, M. W., Orsmond, G., & Murphy, M. M. (2004). Psychological well-being and coping in mothers of youths with autism, Down syndrome, and fragile X syndrome. *American Journal of Mental Retardation, 109*(3), 237–254.

Baker-Ericzén, M. J., Brookman-Frazee, L., & Stahmer, A. (2005). Stress levels and adaptability in parents of toddlers with and without autism spectrum disorders. *Research and Practice for Persons with Severe Disabilities, 30*(4), 194.

Bambara, L. M., & Knoster, T. P. (2009). *Designing positive behavior support plans,* 2nd ed. Washington, D.C.:

American Association on Intellectual and Developmental Disabilities.

Baumle, A. K., & Compton, D. R. (2014). Identity versus identification: How LGBTQ parents identify their children on census surveys. *Journal of Marriage and Family, 76*(1), 94–104.

Banks, M. E. (2003). Disability in the family: A life span perspective. *Cultural Diversity and Ethnic Minority Psychology, 9*(4), 367–384.

Baranowski, M. D., & Schilmoeller, G. L. (1999). Grandparents in the lives of grandchildren with disabilities: Mothers' perceptions. *Education and Treatment of Children, 22,* 427–446.

Baskin, A., & Fawcett, H. (2006). *More than a mom: Living a full and balanced life when your child has special needs.* Bethesda, MD: Woodbine House.

Bavelas, J.B., & Segal, L. (1982). Family systems theory: Background and implications. *Journal of Communication, 32*(3), 99–107.

Baxter, C., Cummins, R. A., & Yiolitis, L. (2000). Parental stress attributed to family members with and without disability: A longitudinal study. *Journal of Intellectual & Developmental Disability, 25,* 105–118.

Bayat, M. (2007). Evidence of resilience in families of children with autism. *Journal of Intellectual Disability Research, 51*(9), 702–714.

Bertelli, Y., Silverman, J., & Talbot, S. (2009). *My baby rides the short bus.* Oakland, CA: PM Press.

Bingham, A., Correa, V. I., & Huber, J. J. (2012). Mothers voices: Coping with their children's initial disability diagnosis. *Infant Mental Health Journal, 33*(4), 372–385.

Blacher, J., Begum, G. F., Marcoulides, G. A., & Baker, B. L. (2013). Longitudinal perspectives of child positive impact on families: Relationship to disability and culture. *American Journal on Intellectual and Developmental Disabilities, 118*(2), 141–155.

Blue-Banning, M., Summers, J. A., Frankland, H. C., Nelson, L. L., & Beegle, G. (2004). Dimensions of family and professional partnerships: Constructive guidelines for collaboration. *Council for Exceptional Children, 70*(2), 167–184.

Boscardin, M. L., Brown-Chidsey, R., & Gonzalez-Martinez, J. C. (2001). The essential link for students with disabilities from diverse backgrounds. *Journal of Special Education Leadership, 14*(2), 89–95.

Boström, P. K., & Broberg, M. (2014). Openness and avoidance—a longitudinal study of fathers of children with intellectual disability. *Journal of Intellectual Disability Research, 58*(9), 810–821.

Boyraz, G. & Sayger, T. V. (2011). Psychological well-being among fathers of children with and without disabilities: Family cohesion, adaptability, and paternal self-efficacy. *American Journal of Men's Health, 5*(4), 286–296.

Bree (2011). *Mama tells the whole story.* Retrieved

February 9, 2015, from http://thebuggslife .blogspot.com/2011/02 /buggs-story.html.

Brooke, V., & McDonough, J. T. (2008). The facts ma'am, just the facts: Social security disability benefit programs and work incentives. *Teaching Exceptional Children, 41*(1), 58–65.

Brown, G. (2004). Family-centered care, mothers occupations of caregiving and home therapy programs. In S. A. Esdaile & J. A. Olson (Eds.), *Mothering occupations: Challenge, agency, and participations* (pp. 346–371). Philadelphia: F. A. Davis.

Brown, M. W. (2014). *Caregiver depression and social support in families with children with autism* (Doctoral dissertation). Eugene: University of Oregon.

Bruder, M. B. (2000). Family-centered early intervention: Clarifying our values for the new millennium. *Topics in Early Childhood Special Education, 20,* 105–115, 122.

Bui, Y. N., & Turnbull, A. (2003). East meets West: Analysis of person-centered planning in the context of Asian American values. *Education and Training and Mental Retardation and Developmental Disabilities, 38*(1), 18–31.

Burbidge, J., & Minnes, P. (2014). Relationship quality in adult siblings with and without developmental disabilities. *Family Relations, 63,* 148–162.

Buschbacher, P., Fox, L., & Clarke, S. (2004). Recapturing desired family routines: A parent-professional behavioral collaboration. *Research and Practice for Persons with Severe Disabilities, 2*(1), 25–39.

Capitani, J. (2007). What to do with a boy. In K. L. Soper & M. Sears (Eds.), *Gifts: Mothers reflect on how children with Down syndrome enrich their lives* (pp. 10–15). Bethesda, MD: Woodhouse, Inc.

Carpenter, B. (2000). Sustaining the family: Meeting the needs of families of children with disabilities. *British Journal of Special Education, 27,* 135–144.

Chambers, C. R. (2007). Siblings of individuals with disabilities who enter careers in the disability field. *Teacher Education and Special Education, 30*(3), 115–127.

Chambers, C. R., Hughes, C., & Carter, E. W. (2004). Parent and sibling perspectives on the transition to adulthood. *Education and Training in Developmental Disabilities, 39*(2), 79–94.

Chan, J. B., & Sigafoos, J. (2000). A review of child and family characteristics related to the use of respite care in developmental disability services. *Child and Youth Care Forum, 29,* 27–37.

Chapadjiev, S. (2009). My mama drove the short bus. In Y. Bertelli, J. Silverman, & S. Talbot (Eds.), *My baby rides the short bus: The unabashedly experience of raising kids with disabilities* (pp. 201–211). Oakland, CA: PM Press.

Connors, C., & Stalker, K. (2003). *The views and experiences of disabled children and their siblings: A positive outlook.* London: Jessica Kingsley Publishers.

Correa, I., Hudson, R. F., & Hayes, M. T. (2004). Preparing early childhood special educators to serve culturally and linguistically diverse children and families: Can a multicultural education course make a difference? *Teacher Education and Special Education, 27*(4), 323–341.

Cox, C. (2008), Supporting grandparent-headed families. *The Prevention Researcher, 15,* 14–16.

Cridland, E. K., Jones, S. C., Magee, C. A., and Caputi, P. (2014, October). Family-focused autism spectrum disorder research: A review of the utility of family systems, *Autism, 3.* Retrieved February 12, 2015, from http://aut .sagepub.com/content /early/2013/10/02 /1362361312472261.

Darley, S., Porter, J., Werner, J., & Eberly, S. (2002). Families tell us what makes families strong. *Exceptional Parent, 32,* 34–36.

Davys, D., Mitchell, D., & Haigh, C. (2011). Adult sibling experience, roles, relationships and future concerns—a review of the literature in learning disabilities. *Journal of Clinical Nursing, 20,* 2837–2853.

Dempsey, I., & Keen, D. (2008). A review of processes and outcomes in family-centered services for children with a disability. *Topics in Early Childhood Special Education, 28*(1), 42–52.

Dunlap, G., & Fox, L. (2007). Parent-professional partnerships: A valuable context for addressing challenging behaviors. *International Journal of Development, Disability and Education, 54*(3), 273–285.

Dunst, C. J. (2002). Family-centered practices: Birth through high school. *Journal of Special Education, 36,* 139–147.

Dunst, C. J., & Dempsey, I. (2007). Family–professional partnerships and parenting competence, confidence, and enjoyment. *International Journal of Disability, Development and Education, 54*(3), 305–318.

Dyches, T. T., Smith, T. B., Korth, B. B., Roper, S. O., & Mandleco, B. (2012). Positive parenting of children with developmental disabilities: A meta-analysis. *Research in Developmental Disabilities, 33*(6), 2213–2220.

Epley, P., Gotto, G. S., Summer, J. A., Brotherson, M. J., Turnbull, A. P., & Friend, A. (2010). Supporting families of young children with disabilities: Examining the role of administrative structures. *Topics in Early Childhood Special Education, 30*(1), 20–31.

Epstein, S. H., & Bessel, A. G. (2002). A parent's determination and a pre-K dream realized. *Exceptional Parent, 32,* 56–60.

Falik, L. H. (1995). Family patterns of reaction to a child with a learning disability: A mediational perspective. *Journal of Learning Disabilities, 28,* 335–341.

Falik, L. H. (1995). Family patterns of reaction to a child with a learning disability: A mediational perspective. *Journal of Learning Disabilities, 28,* 335–341.

Feinger-Schaal, R., & Oppenheim, D. (2013). Resolution of the diagnosis and maternal sensitivity among mothers of children with intellectual disability. *Research in Developmental Disabilities, 34*(1), 306–313.

Ferguson, P. M. (2002). A place in the family: An historical interpretation of research on parental reactions to having a child with a disability. *Journal of Special Education, 36,* 124–130.

Fine, M. J., & Nissenbaum, M. S. (2000). The child with disabilities and the family: Implications for professionals. In M. J. Fine & R. L. Simpson (Eds.), *Collaboration with parents and families of children with exceptionalities,* 2nd ed. (pp. 3–26). Austin, TX: PRO-ED.

Fish, M. C. (2000). Children with special needs in nontraditional families. In M. J. Fine & R. L. Simpson (Eds.), *Collaboration with parents and families of children with exceptionalities,* 2nd ed. (pp. 49–68). Austin, TX: PRO-ED.

Flaherty, E., & Glidden, L. M. (2000). Positive adjustment in parents rearing children with Down syndrome. *Early Education and Development, 11*(4), 407–422.

Fox, L., & Dunlap, G. (2002). Family-centered practices in positive behavior support. *Beyond Behavior,* 24–26.

Fox, L., Vaughn, B. J., Wyatte, M. L., & Dunlap, G. (2002). "We can't expect other people to understand": Family perspectives on problem behavior. *Exceptional Children, 68,* 437–450.

Francis, G., Gross, J. M. S., Turnbull, R., & Parent-Johnson, W. (2013). Evaluating the effectiveness of the Family Employment Awareness Training in Kansas: A pilot study. *Research & Practice for Persons with Severe Disabilities, 38*(1), 44–57.

Frankland, H. C., Edmonson, H., & Turnbull, A. P. (2001). Positive behavioral support: Family, school, and community partnerships. *Beyond Behavior, 10*(4), 7–9.

Frankland, H. C., Turnbull, A. P., Wehmeyer, M. L., & Blackmountain, L. (2004). An exploration of the self-determination construct and disability as it relates to the Diné (Navajo) culture. *Education and Training in Developmental Disabilities, 39*(3), 191–205.

Freedman, B. H., Kalb, L. G., Zablotsky, B., & Stuart, E. A. (2012). Relationship status among parents of children with autism spectrum disorders: A population-based study. *Journal of Autism and Developmental Disorders, 42*(4), 539–548.

French, G. S. (2008). Coordinated planning for parents, grandparents, and children with disabilities. *Exceptional Parent, 38*(12), 54–55.

Friend, M., & Cook, L. (2003). *Interactions: Collaboration skills for school professionals.* Boston: Allyn & Bacon.

Frost, J. (2002). Sarah syndrome: A mother's view of having a child with no diagnosis. *Exceptional Parent, 32,* 70–71.

Gallagher, G., & Konjoian, P. (2010). *Shut up about your perfect kid: A survival guide for ordinary parents of special children.* New York: Three Rivers Press.

Gallagher, P. A., Rhodes, C. H., & Darling, S. M. (2004). Parents as professionals in early intervention. *Topics in Early Childhood Special Education, 24*(1), 5–13.

Geisthardt, C., Brotherson, M., & Cook, C. (2002). Friendships of children with disabilities in the home environment. *Education and Training in Mental Retardation and Developmental Disabilities, 37*(3), 235–52.

Glidden, L. M., & Schoolcraft, S. A. (2003). Depression: Its trajectory and correlates in mothers rearing children with intellectual disability. *Journal of Intellectual Disability Research, 47*(4/5), 250–263.

Gorman, J. C. (2004). *Working with challenging parents of students with special needs.* Thousand Oaks, CA: Corwin Press.

Gotto, G. S., Beauchamp, D., & Simpson, M. (2007). Early childhood family supports community of practice … Creating knowledge and wisdom through community conversations. *Exceptional Parent, 37*(8), 52–53.

Gray, D. E. (2002). Ten years on: A longitudinal study of families of children with autism. *Journal of Intellectual and Developmental Disability, 27*(3), 215–222.

Griffith, G. M., Hastings, R. P., Oliver, C., Howlin, P., Moss, J., Petty, J., & Tunnicliffe, P. (2011). Psychological well-being in parents of children with Angelman, Cornelia de Lange and Cri du Chat syndromes. *Journal of Intellectual Disability Research, 55*(4), 397–410.

Grissom, M. O., & Borkowski, J. G. (2002). Self-efficacy in adolescents who have siblings with or without disabilities. *American Journal on Mental Retardation, 107(2),* 79–90.

Harland, P., & Cuskelly, M. (2000). The responsibilities of adult siblings of adults with dual sensory impairments. *International Journal of Disability Development and Education, 47,* 293–307.

Harper, A., Dyches, T. T., Harper, J., Roper, S. O., & South, M. (2013). Respite care, marital quality, and stress in parents of children with autism spectrum disorders. *Journal of Autism and Developmental Disorders, 43*(11): 2604–2616.

Hastings, R. P. (2006). Longitudinal relationships between sibling behavioral adjustment and behavior problems of children with developmental disabilities. *Journal of Autism and Developmental Disorders, 37,* 1485–1492.

Hastings, R. P., Beck, A., & Hill, C. (2005). Positive contributions made by children with an intellectual disability in the family: Mothers' and fathers' perceptions. *Journal of Intellectual Disabilities, 9*(2), 155–165.

Hauser-Cram, P. (2006). Young children with developmental disabilities and their families: Needs, policies, and services. In K. M. Thies & J. F. Travers (Eds.), *Handbook of human development for health care professionals* (pp. 287–305). Boston: Jones and Bartlett Publishers.

Heiman, T., & Berger, O. (2008). Parents of children with Asperger syndrome or with learning disabilities: Family environment and social support. *Research in Developmental Disabilities, 29*(4), 289–300.

Hu, X., Wang, M., & Fei, X. (2012). Family quality of life of Chinese families of children with intellectual disabilities. *Journal of Intellectual Disability Research, 56*(1), 30–44.

Huang, Y., Kellett, U., & St. John, W. (2010). Cerebral palsy: Experiences of mothers after learning their child's diagnosis. *Journal of Advanced Nursing, 66*(6), 1213–1221.

Iezzoni, L. I., & Long-Bellil. L. M. (2012). Training physicians about caring for persons with disabilities: "Nothing about us without us!" *Disability and Health Journal, 5*(3), 136–139.

Johnson, C. (2000). What do families need? *Journal of Positive Behavior Interventions, 2*(2), 115–117.

Jones, T. L., & Prinz, R. J. (2005). Potential roles of parental self-efficacy in parent and child adjustment: A review. *Clinical Psychology Review, 25*(3), 341–363.

Kazak, A. E. (1987). Families with disabled children: Stress and social networks in three samples. *Journal of Abnormal Child Psychology, 15*(1), 137–46.

Keen, D. (2007). Parents, families, and partnerships: Issues and considerations. *International Journal of Disability, Development and Education, 54*(3), 339–349.

Knox, M., & Bigby, C. (2007). Moving towards midlife care as negotiated family business: Accounts of people with intellectual disabilities and their families "Just getting along with their lives together." *International Journal of Disability, Development, and Education, 54*(3), 287–304.

Kolb, S. M., & Hanley-Maxwell, C. (2003). Critical social skills for adolescents with high incidence disabilities: Parental perspectives. *Council for Exceptional Children, 69*(2), 163–179.

Kresak, K. E., Gallagher, P. A., & Kelley, S. J. (2014). Grandmothers raising grandchildren with disabilities: Sources of support and family quality of life. *Journal of Early Intervention, 36*(1), 3–17.

Kyzar, K., Turnbull, A., Summers, J., & Gómez, V. (2012). The relationship of family support to family outcomes: A *synthesis of key findings from research on severe disability. Research and Practice for Persons with Severe Disabilities, 37*(1), 31–44.

Lach, L. M., Kohen, D. E., Garner, R. E., Brehaut, J. C., Miller, A. R., Klassen, A. F., & Rosenbaum, P. L. (2009). The health and psychological functioning of caregivers of children with neurodevelopmental disorders. *Disability and Rehabilitation, 31*(8), 607–618.

Laman, E., & Shaughnessy, M. F. (2007). An interview with Don Meyer on siblings of individuals with disabilities. *Exceptional Parent, 37*(7), 42–46.

Lamb, M. E., & Meyer, D. J. (1991). Fathers of children with special needs. In M. Seligman (Ed.), *The family with a handicapped child,* 2nd ed. (pp. 151–180). Boston: Allyn & Bacon.

Larson, Elizabeth A. (2000). The orchestration of occupation: The dance of mothers. *American Journal of Occupational Therapy, 54*(3), 269–280.

Lee, A. L., Strauss, L., Wittman, P., Jackson, B., & Carstens, A. (2001). The effects of chronic illness on roles and emotions of caregivers. *Occupational Therapy in Health Care, 14*(1), 47–60.

Lee, M., & Gardner, J. M. (2010). Grandparents' involvement and support in families with children with disabilities. *Educational Gerontology, 36*(6), 467–499.

Lee, S., Poston, D., & Poston, A. J. (2007). Lessons learned through implementing a positive behavior support intervention at home: A case study on self-management with a student with autism and his mother. *Education and Training in Developmental Disabilities, 42*(4), 418–427.

Leung, P., Erich, S., & Kanenberg, H. (2005). A comparison of family functioning in gay/lesbian, heterosexual and special needs adoptions. *Children and Youth Services Review, 27*(9), 1031–1044.

Levinson, E. M., McKee, L., & DeMatteo, F. J. (2000). The exceptional child grows up: Transition from school to adult life. In M. J. Fine & R. L. Simpson (Eds.), *Collaboration with parents and families of children with exceptionalities,* 2nd ed. (pp. 409–436). Austin, TX: PRO-ED.

Lightfoot, E., Hill, K., & LaLiberte, T. (2011). Prevalence of children with disabilities in the child welfare system and out of home placement: An examination of administrative records. *Children and Youth Services Review, 33*(11), 2069–2075.

Lobato, D. J., Kao, B.T., & Plante, W. (2005). Latina sibling knowledge and adjustment to chronic disability. *Journal of Family Psychology, 19*(4), 625–632.

Luckner, J. L. & Velaski, A. (2004). Healthy families of children who are deaf. *American Annals of the Deaf, 149*(4), 324–335.

Lucyshyn, J. M., Dunlap, G., & Albin, R. W. (2002). *Families and positive behavior support: Addressing problem behavior in family contexts.* Baltimore: Paul H. Brooks Publishing Company.

MacDonald E. E. & Hastings R. P. (2010a). Fathers of children with developmental disabilities. In M. E. Lamb (Ed.), *The role of the father in child development*, 5th ed. (pp. 486–516). Hoboken, NJ: John Wiley & Sons.

MacDonald E. E. & Hastings R. P. (2010b). Mindful parenting and care involvement of fathers of children with intellectual disabilities. *Journal of Child and Family Studies, 19*(2), 236–40.

MacInnes, M. D. (2008). One's enough for now: Children, disability, and the subsequent childbearing of mothers. *Journal of Marriage and Family, 70*(3), 758–771.

Mara, M. (2010). Guilt, denial, and videotape. In K. Anderson & V. Foreman (Eds.), *Gravity pulls you in: Perspectives on parenting children with autism spectrum* (pp. 11–21). Bethesda, MD: Woodbine House.

Marks, S. U., Matson, A., & Barraza, L. (2005). The impact of siblings with disabilities on their brothers and sisters pursuing a career in special education. *Research and Practice for Persons with Severe Disabilities, 30*(4), 205–218.

Martin, J. E., Van Dycke, J. L., Greene, B. A., Gardner, J. E., Christensen, W. R., Woods, L. L., & Lovett, D. L. (2006). Direct observation of teacher-directed IEP meetings: Establishing the need for student IEP meeting instruction. *Exceptional Children, 72*(2), 187–200.

Matuszny, R. M., Banda, D. R., & Coleman, T. J. (2007). A progressive plan for building collaborative relationships with parents from diverse backgrounds. *Teaching Exceptional Children, 39*(4), 24–31.

McCarthy, A., Cuskelly, M., van Kraayenoord, C. E., & Cohen, J. (2006). Predictors of stress in mothers and fathers of children with fragile X syndrome. *Research in Developmental Disabilties, 27*(6), 688–704.

McHatton, P. A. (2007). Listening and learning from Mexican and Puerto Rican single mothers of children with disabilities. *Teacher Education and Special Education, 30*(4), 237–248.

McHatton, P. A., & Correa, V. (2005). Stigma and discrimination: Perspectives from Mexican and Puerto Rican mothers of children with special needs. *Topics in Early Childhood Education, 25*(3), 131–142.

McHugh, M. (2003). *Special siblings: Growing up with someone with a disability.* Baltimore: Paul H. Brookes Publishing Company.

McKie, F. (2006). Heather at the neurologist's. *Equity and Excellence in Education, 39*(2), 115–123.

McStay, R., Dissanayake, C., Scheeren, A., Koot, H. M., & Begeer, S. (2014). Parenting stress and autism: The role of age, autism severity and problem behavior with high-functioning autism, *Autism, 18*(5), 502–510.

Meyer, D. (Ed.). (2005). *The sibling slam book: What it's really like to have a brother or sister with special needs.* Bethesda, MD: Woodbine House.

Migerode, F., Maes, B., Buysse, A., & Brondeel, R. (2012). Quality of life in adolescents with a disability and their parents: The mediating role of social support and resilience. *Journal of Developmental and Physical Disabilities, 24*(5), 487–503.

Moyson, T., & Roeyers, H. (2011). The quality of life of siblings of children with autism spectrum disorder. *Exceptional Children, 78*(1), 41–55.

Muscott, H. S. (2002). Exceptional partnerships: Listening to the voices of families. *Preventing School Failure, 46*(2), 66–69.

Neece, C. L., Blacher, J., & Baker, B. L. (2010). Impact on siblings of children with intellectual disability: The role of child behavior problems. *American Journal on Intellectual and Developmental Disabilities, 115*(4), 291–306.

Newacheck, P. W., Inkelas, M., & Kim, S. E. (2004). Health services use and health care expenditures for children with disabilities. *Pediatrics, 114*(1), 79–85.

Nielson, K. M., Mandleco, B. L., Roper, S. O., Cox, A., Dyches, T. T., & Marshall, E. S. (2012). Parental perceptions of sibling relationships in families rearing a child with a chronic condition. *Journal of Pediatric Nursing, 27*(1), 34–43.

Olson, D. (2011). Faces IV and the circumplex model: Validation study. *Journal of Marital and Family Therapy, 37*(1), 64–80.

Ong-Dean, C. (2009). *Distinguishing disability.* Chicago: University of Chicago.

Orsmond, G. I., & Seltzer, M. M. (2009). Adolescent siblings of individuals with an autism spectrum disorder: Testing a diathesis-stress model of sibling well-being. *Journal of Autism and Developmental Disorders, 39*(7), 1053–1065.

Orsmond, G.I., Lin, L., & Seltzer, M. M. (2007). Mothers of adolescents and adults with autism: Parenting multiple children with disabilities. *Intellectual and Developmental Disabilities, 45*(4), 257–270.

Ortiz, S. O. (2006). Multicultural issues in working with children and families: Responsive intervention in the educational setting. In R. B. Mennuti, A. Freeman, & R. W. Christner (Eds.), *Cognitive-behavioral interventions in educational settings* (pp. 21–36). New York: Routledge.

Parentlink (2011). *Children with a disability.* Retrieved August 18, 2011, from http://www.parentlink.act.gov.au/parenting-resources/parenting-guides/all-ages/children-with-a-disability.

Parette, H. P., Meadan, H., & Doubet, S. (2010). Fathers of young children with disabilities in the United States: Current status and implications. *Childhood Education, 86*(6), 382–388.

Parish, S. L., Rose, R. A., Grinstein-Weiss, M., Richman, E. L., & Andrews, M. E. (2008). Material hardship in U.S. families raising children with disabilities. *Exceptional Children, 75*(1), 71–92.

Pinkham, B. E. (2010). Is there anything else we should know? In

K. Anderson & V. Forman (Eds.), *Gravity pulls us in: Perspectives on parenting children with autism spectrum* (pp. 181–188). Bethesda, MD: Woodbine House, Inc.

Pipp-Siegel, S., Sedey, A. L., & Yoshinaga-Itano, C. (2002). Predictors of parental stress in mothers of young children with hearing loss. *Journal of Deaf Studies and Deaf Education, 7*(1), 1–17.

Platt, C., Roper, S., Mandleco, B., Freeborn, D. & Dyches, T. (2014). Sibling cooperative and externalizing behaviors in families raising children with disabilities. *Nursing Research, 63*(4), 235–242.

Pleck, J. H. (2010). Fatherhood and masculinity. In M. E. Lamb (Ed.), *The role of the father in child development* (pp. 27–57). Hoboken, NJ: John Wiley & Sons.

Poston, D., Turnbull, A., Park, J., Mannan, H., Marquis, J., & Wang, M. (2003). Family quality of life: A qualitative inquiry. *American Association on Mental Health, 41*(5), 313–328.

Poston, D. J., & Turnbull, A. P. (2004). Role of spirituality and religion in family quality of life for families of children with disabilities. *Education and Training in Developmental Disabilities, 39*(2), 95–108.

Raver, S. A. (2005). Using family-based practices for young children with special needs in preschool programs. *Childhood Education, 82*(1), 9–13.

Ravindran, N., & Meyers, B. (2012). Cultural influences on perceptions of health, illness, and disability: A review and focus on autism. *Journal of Family Studies, 21*(2), 311–319.

Rieger, A., & Scotti, J. (2004). Make it just as normal as possible with humor. *Mental Retardation, 42*(6), 427–444.

Risdal, D., & Singer, G. H. S. (2004). Marital adjustment in parents of children with disabilities: A historical review and meta-analysis. *Research & Practice for Persons with Severe Disabilities, 29*(2), 95–103.

Rivers, K. O. (2000). Working with caregivers of infants and toddlers with special needs from culturally and linguistically diverse backgrounds. *Infant Toddler Intervention: The Transdisciplinary Journal, 10*(2), 61–72.

Robey, K. L., Minihan, P. M., Long-Bellil, L. M., Hahn, J. E., Reiss, J. G., & Eddey, G. E. (2013). Teaching health care students about disability within a cultural competency context. *Disability and Health Journal, 6*(4), 271–279.

Romer, L., & Walker, P. (2013). Offering person-centered supports on a daily basis: An initial appreciative inquiry into the relationship between personal assistants and those seeking support. *Research & Practice for Persons with Severe Disabilities, 38*(3), 186–195.

Roper, S. O., Allred, D., Mandleco, B., Freeborn, D., & Dyches, T. (2014). Caregiver burden and positive sibling relationships in families raising children with disabilities and typically developing children. *Families, Systems, and Health, 32*(2), 241–246.

Rummel-Hudson, R. (2008). *Schuyler's monster: A father's journey with his wordless daughter*. New York: St. Martin's Press.

Rupiper, M., & Marvin, C. (2004). Preparing teachers for family centered services: A survey of preservice curriculum content. *Teacher Education and Special Education, 27*(4), 384–395.

Russell, L. M., & Grant, A. E. (2005). *Planning for the future: Providing a meaningful life for a child with a disability after your death*. Palatine, IL: Planning for the Future, Inc.

Saloviita, T., Itälinna, M. & Leinonen, E. (2003). Explaining the parental stress of fathers and mothers caring for a child with intellectual disability: A double ABCX model. *Journal of Intellectual Disability Research, 47*(4-5), 300–312.

Sandler, A. G., Warren, S. H., & Raver, S. A. (1995, August). Grandparents as a source of support for parents of children with disabilities. A brief report. *Mental Retardation, 33*, 248–250.

Santelli, B., Ginsberg, C., Sullivan, S., & Niederhauser, C. (2002). A collaborative study of parent to parent program: Implications for positive behavior support. In J. M. Lucyshyn & G. Dunlap (Eds.), *Families and positive behavior support: Addressing problem behavior in family contexts* (pp. 439–456). Baltimore: Paul H.

Brookes Publishing Company.

Segal, S. (2010). Sometimes, never. In K. Anderson & V. Forman (Eds.), *Gravity pulls you in: Perspectives on parenting children on the autism spectrum* (pp. 49–57). Bethesda, MD: Woodbine House.

Seligman, M., & Darling, R. B. (1989). *Ordinary families, special children*. New York: Guilford Press.

Shelden, M. L., & Rush, D. D. (2001). The ten myths about providing early intervention services in natural environments. *Infants and Young Children, 14*(1), 1–13.

Shogren, K. (2012). Hispanic mothers' perceptions of self-determination. *Research & Practice for Persons with Severe Disabilities, 37*(3), 170–184.

Shogren, K., Forber-Pratt, A., Nittrouer, C., & Aragon, S. (2013). The emergence of a human services cooperative to support families and young adults with disabilities: Implications for disability services and supports. *Research & Practice for Persons with Severe Disabilities, 38*(4), 259–273.

Siklos, S., & Kerns, K. A. (2007). Assessing the diagnostic experiences of a small number of children with autism spectrum disorders. *Research in Developmental Disabilities, 28*(1), 9–22.

Simmerman, S., Blacher, J., & Baker, B. L. (2001). Fathers' and mothers' perceptions of father involvement in families with young children with a disability. *Journal of Intellectual and Developmental Disability, 26*(4), 325–338.

Skotko, B., & Levine, S. P. (2009). *Fasten your seatbelt: A crash course on Down syndrome for brothers and sisters*. Bethesda, MD: Woodbine House.

Skotko, B.G., Levine, S.P., & Goldstein, R. (2011). Having a son or daughter with Down syndrome: Perspectives from mothers and fathers. *American Journal of Medical Genetics Part A, 155*(10), 2335–2347.

Smith, P. M. (2015). You are not alone: For parents when they learn their child has a disability. Retrieved February 23, 2015, from www .parentcenterhub.org /repository/notalone/.

Smith, L. E., Greenberg, J. S., & Seltzer, M. M. (2011). Social support and well-being at midlife among mothers of adolescents and adults with autism spectrum disorder. *Journal of Autism and Developmental Disorders, 42*(9), 1818–1826.

Smith, L. E., Hong, J., Seltzer, M. M., Greenberg, J. S., Almeida, D. M., & Bishop, S. L. (2010). Daily experiences among mothers of adolescents and adults with autism spectrum disorder. *Journal of Autism and Developmental Disorders, 40*(2), 167–178.

Steeves, P. (2006). Sliding doors—Opening our world. *Equity and Excellence in Education, 39*(2), 105–114.

Stone, J. H. (Ed.). (2005). *Culture and disability: Providing culturally competent services*. In *Multicultural Aspects of Counseling Series 21*. London: Sage Publications.

Stoneman Z. (2007). Examining the Down syndrome advantage: Mothers and fathers of young children with disabilities. *Journal of Intellectual Disability Research, 51*(12), 1006–1017.

Stoneman, Z. (2005). Siblings of children with disabilities: Research themes. *Mental Retardation, 43*(5), 339–350.

Stoneman, Z., & Gavidia-Payne, S. (2006). Marital adjustment in families of young children with disabilities: Associations with daily hassles and problem-focused coping. *American Journal of Mental Retardation, 111*(1), 1–14.

Strohm, K. (2005). *Being the other one: Growing up with a brother or sister who has special needs*. Boston: Shambhala Publications, Inc.

Taanila, A., Kokkonen, J. & Jaervelin, M. R. (1996). The long-term effects of children's early onset disability on marital relationships. *Developmental Medicine and Child Neurology, 38*(7), 567–577.

Taunt, H. M. & Hastings, R. P. (2002). Impact of children with developmental disabilities on their families: A preliminary study. *Education and Training in Mental Retardation and Developmental Disabilities, 37*(4), 410–420.

Tellegen, C. L., & Sanders, M. R. (2013). Stepping Stones Triple P-Positive Parenting Program for children with disability: A systematic review and meta-analysis. *Research in Developmental Disabilities, 34*(5), 1556–1571.

Theule, J., Wiener, J., Tannock, R., & Jenkins, J. M. (2012). Parenting stress in families of children with ADHD: A meta-analysis. *Journal of Emotional and Behavioral Disorders, 21*(1), 3–17.

Turbiville, V. P., & Marquis, J. G. (2001). Father participation in early education programs. *Topics in Early Childhood Special Education, 21*(4), 223–231.

Turbiville, Vicki. (1997). *Literature review: Fathers, their children, and disability*. Lawrence, KS: The Beach Center on Families and Disability, The University of Kansas.

Turnbull, A. P., & Turnbull, H. R. (2002). From the old to the new paradigm of disabilities and families: Research to enhance family quality and life outcomes. In J. L. Paul, C. D. Lavely, A. Cranston-Gingras, & E. L. Taylor (Eds.), *Rethinking professional issues in special education*. Westport, CT: Ablex Publishing.

Turner, M. H. (2000). The developmental nature of parent-child relationships: The impact of disabilities. In M. J. Fine & R. L. Simpson (Eds.), *Collaboration with parents and families of children with exceptionalities*, 2nd ed. (pp. 103–130). Austin, TX: PRO-ED.

Tynan, W. D., & Wornian, K. (2002). Parent management training: Efficacy, effectiveness, and barriers to implementation. *Report on Emotional and Behavioral Disorders in Youth, 2*, 57–58, 71–72.

Ulrich, M. E. (2003). Levels of awareness: A closer look at communication between parents and professionals. *TEACHING Exceptional Children, 35*(6), 20–23.

Vacca, J., & Feinberg, E. (2000). Why can't families be more like us?: Henry Higgins confronts Eliza Doolittle in the world of early intervention. *Infants and Young Children, 13*, 40–48.

Verté, S., Hebbrecht, L., & Roeyers, H. (2006). Psychological adjustment of siblings of children who are deaf or hard of hearing. *The Volta Review, 106*(1), 89–110.

Vohra, R., Madhavan, S., Sambamoorthi, U., & St. Peter, C. (2014). Access to services, quality of care, and family impact for children with autism, other developmental disabilities, and other mental health conditions. *Autism, 18*(7), 815–826.

Wang, M., Turnbull, A. P., Summers, J. A., Little, T. D., Poston, D. J., Mannan, H., & Turnbull, R. (2004). Severity of disability and income as predictors of parents' satisfaction with their family quality of life during early childhood years. *Research and Practice for Persons with Severe Disabilities, 29*(2), 82–94.

Ward, M. J., Cronin, K. B., Renfro, P. D., Lowman, D. K., & Cooper, P. D. (2000). Oral motor feeding in the neonatal intensive care unit: Exploring perceptions of parents and occupational therapists. *Occupational Therapy in Health Care, 12*(2-3), 19–37.

Warren, M. P., & Kirkendall, D. (1973). *Bottom to the high crowd*. New York, NY: Walker.

Werner, S., Edwards, M, Baum, N., Brown, I., Brown, R. I., & Isaacs, B. J. (2009). Family quality of life among families with a member who has an intellectual disability: An exploratory examination of key domains and dimensions of the revised FQOL Survey. *Journal of Intellectual Disability Research, 53*(6), 501–511.

Whitbread, K. M., Bruder, M. B., Fleming, G., & Park, H. J. (2007). Collaboration in special education: Parent-professional training. *Teaching Exceptional Children, 39*(4), 6–14.

Williams, P.D., Piamjariyakul, U., Graff, J. C. & Stanton, A. (2010). Developmental disabilities: Effects on well siblings. *Issues in Comprehensive Pediatric Nursing, 33*(1), 39–55.

Woodman, C. & Hauser-Cram, P. (2013). The role of coping strategies in predicting change in parenting efficacy and depressive symptoms among mothers of adolescents with developmental disabilities. *Journal of Intellectual Disability Research, 57*(6), 513–530.

Worthington, J., Hernandez, M., Friedman B., & Uzzell, D. (2001). *Systems of care: Promising practices in children's mental health, 2001 Series, Volume 11.* Washington D.C.: Center for Effective Collaboration and Practice, American Institutes for Research.

Young, D. M., & Roopnarine, J. L. (1994). Fathers' childcare involvement with children with and without disabilities. *Topic in Early Childhood Special Education, 14* (Winter), 488–502.

Young, E. L., Calderella, P., Richardson, M. J., and Young K. R. (2011). *Positive behavior support in secondary schools: A practical guide.* New York: Guilford Press.

Zhang, C., & Bennett, T. (2001). Multicultural views of disability: Implications for early intervention professionals. *Infant Toddler Intervention: The Transdisciplinary Journal, 11,* 143–154.

## Chapter 7

Abbott, L., McConkey, R., & Dobbins, M. (2011). Key players in inclusion: Are we meeting the professional needs of learning support assistants for pupils with complex needs? *European Journal of Special Needs Education, 26*(2), 215–231.

Alesi, M., Rappo, G., & Pepi, A. M. (2012). Self-esteem at school and self-handicapping in childhood: Comparison of groups with learning disabilities. *Psychological Reports, 111*(3), 952–962.

Alexander, C. P. (1994). Brain bane: Researchers may have found a cause for dyslexia. *Time, 144*(9), 61.

Algozzine, B., Wang, C., & Violette, A. S. (2011). Re-examining the relationship between academic achievement and social behavior. *Journal of Positive Behavior Interventions, 13*(1), 3–16.

American Psychiatric Association. (2013). Diagnostic and statistical manual of mental disorders, 5th ed. Arlington, VA: American Psychiatric Association.

American Speech-Language-Hearing Association. (2005). (Central) auditory processing disorders— The role of the audiologist [Position statement]. Retrieved from www.asha.org/policy.

Anderko, L., Braun, J., & Auinger, P. (2010). Contribution of tobacco smoke exposure to learning disabilities. *Journal of Obstetric, Gynecologic, And Neonatal Nursing: JOGNN / NAACO, 39*(1), 111–117.

Archer, A. L., & Hughes, C. A. (2011). *Explicit instruction: Effective and efficient teaching.* New York: Guilford.

Armbruster, B. B., Lehr, F., & Osborn, J. (2006). *Put reading first: The research building blocks for teaching children to read. Kindergarten through grade 3,* 3rd ed. Jessup, MD: National Institute for Literacy.

Ashkenazi, S., Black, J. M., Abrams, D. A., Hoeft, F., & Menon, V. (2013). Neurobiological underpinnings of math and reading learning disabilities. *Journal of Learning Disabilities, 46*(6), 549–569.

Baird, G., Dworzynski, K., Slonims, V., & Simonoff, E. (2010). Memory impairment in children with language impairment. *Developmental Medicine & Child Neurology, 52*(6), 535–540.

Barron, D. A., & Hassiotis, A. (2008). Good practice in transition services for young people with learning disabilities: A review. *Advances in Mental Health and Intellectual Disabilities, 2*(3), 18–24.

Beach, K. D., & O'Connor, R. E. (2015). Early response-to-intervention measures and criteria as predictors of reading disability in the beginning of third grade. *Journal of Learning Disabilities, 48*(2), 196–223.

Becker, A., McLaughlin, T. M., Weber, K. P., & Gower, J. (2009). The effects of copy, cover and compare with and without additional error drill on multiplication fact fluency and accuracy. *Electronic Journal of Research in Educational Psychology, 7*(2), 747–760.

Beirne-Smith, M., & Riley, T. F. (2009). Spelling assessment of students with disabilities: Formal and informal procedures. *Assessment for Effective Intervention, 34*(3), 170–177.

Bender, W. N. (2008a). *Learning disabilities: Characteristics, identification, and teaching strategies,* 6th ed. Boston: Allyn & Bacon.

Bender, W. N. (2008b). *Differentiating instruction for students with learning disabilities,* 2nd ed. Thousand Oaks, CA: Sage Publications.

Bender, W. N., & Waller, L. (2011). *The teaching revolution: RtI, technology, and differentiation transform teaching for the 21st century.* Thousand Oaks, CA: Corwin.

Berkeley, S., Mastropieri, M. A., & Scruggs, T. E. (2011). Reading comprehension strategy instruction and attribution retraining for secondary students with learning and other mild disabilities. *Journal of Learning Disabilities, 44*(1), 18–32.

Berninger, V. W., & May, M. O. (2011). Evidence-based diagnosis and treatment for specific learning disabilities involving impairments in written and/or oral language. *Journal of Learning Disabilities, 44*(2), 167–183.

Blue, E., & Tirotta, R. (2011). The benefits & drawbacks of integrating cloud computing and interactive whiteboards in teacher preparation. *TechTrends: Linking Research and Practice to Improve Learning, 55*(3), 31–39.

Bock, S. J, Michalak, N., & Brownlee, S. (2011). Collaboration and consultation: The first steps. In C. G. Simpson & J. P. Bakken (Eds.), *Collaboration: A multidisciplinary approach to educating students with disabilities* (pp. 3–15). Waco, TX: Prufrock Press.

Boudah, D. J. (2014). The main idea strategy: A strategy to improve reading comprehension through inferential thinking. *Intervention in School and Clinic, 49*(3), 148–155.

Bowman-Perrott, L., Burke, M. D., de Marin, S., Zhang, N., & Davis, H. (2015). A meta-analysis of single-case research on behavior contracts: Effects on behavioral and academic outcomes among children and youth. *Behavior Modification, 39*(2), 247–269.

Branum-Martin, L., Fletcher, J. M., & Stuebing, K. K. (2013). Classification and identification of reading and math disabilities: The special case of comorbidity. *Journal of Learning Disabilities, 46*(6), 490–499.

Bullock, C. E., & Hackenberg, T. D. (2015). The several roles of stimuli in token reinforcement. *Journal of the Experimental Analysis of Behavior.* Advance online publication.

Buttner, G., & Hasselhorn, M. (2011). Learning disabilities: Debates on definitions, causes, subtypes, and responses. *International Journal of Disability, Development and Education, 58*(1), 75–87.

Cahan, S., Forno, D., & Nirel, R. (2012). The regression-based discrepancy definition of learning disability: A critical appraisal. *Journal of Learning Disabilities, 45*(2), 170–178.

Cahill, S. M. (2009). Where does handwriting fit in? Strategies to support academic achievement. *Intervention in School and Clinic, 44*(4), 223–228.

Callinan, S., Cunningham, E., & Theiler, S. (2013). Revisiting discrepancy theory in learning disabilities: What went wrong and why we should go back. *Australian Journal of Guidance and Counseling, 23*(1), 1–17.

Carter, E. W., Trainor, A. A., & Ditchman, N. (2011). Community-based summer work experiences of adolescents with high-incidence disabilities. *Journal of Special Education, 45*(2), 89–103.

Castek, J., & Beach, R. (2013). Using apps to support disciplinary literacy and science learning. *Journal of Adolescent & Adult Literacy, 56*(7), 554–564.

Cerdan, R., Gilabert, R., & Vidal-Abarca, E. (2011). Selecting information to answer questions: Strategic individual differences when searching texts. *Learning and Individual Differences, 21*(2), 201–205.

Ciullo, S., Falcomata, T. S., Pfannenstiel, K., & Billingsley, G. (2015). Improving learning with science and social studies text using computer-based concept maps for students with disabilities. *Behavior Modification, 39*(1), 117–135.

Cleary, M. J., & Scott, A. J. (2011). Developments in clinical neuropsychology: Implications for school psychological services. *Journal of School Health, 81*(1), 1–7.

Clemow, D. B., & Walker, D. J. (2014). The potential for misuse and abuse of medications in ADHD: A review. *Postgraduate Medicine, 126*(5), 64–81.

Connor, C. M., Alberto, P. A., Compton, D. L., & O'Connor, R. E. (2014). *Improving reading outcomes for students with or at risk for reading disabilities: A synthesis of the contributions from the Institute of Education Sciences research centers. NCSER 2014-3000.* Retrieved from http://files.eric.ed.gov/fulltext/ED544759.pdf.

Cooper, L. L., & Tomayko, M. C. (2011). Understanding place value. *Teaching Children Mathematics, 17*(9), 558–567.

Cowden, P. A. (2010a). Social anxiety in children with disabilities. *Journal of Instructional Psychology, 37*(4), 301–305.

Cowden, P. A. (2010b). Preparing college students with moderate learning disabilities with the tools for higher level success. *College Student Journal, 44*(2), 230–233.

Crick. (2011). *WriteOnline.* Westport, CT: Crick. Retrieved from www.cricksoft.com/us/products/tools/writeonline/default.aspx.

Dalsgaard, S., Nielsen, H. S., & Simonsen, M. (2014). Consequences of ADHD medication use for children's outcomes. *Journal of Health Economics, 37*, 137–151.

Darsaklis, V., Snider, L. M., Majnemer, A., & Mazer, B. (2013). Assessments used to diagnose developmental coordination disorder: Do their underlying constructs match the diagnostic criteria? *Physical & Occupational Therapy in Pediatrics, 33*(2), 186–198.

Datchuk, S. M., & Kubina, R. M. (2013). A review of teaching sentence-level writing skills to students with writing difficulties and learning disabilities. *Remedial and Special Education, 34*(3), 180–192.

Davis, J. M., & Broitman, J. (2011). *Nonverbal learning disabilities in children: Bridging the gap between science and practice.* New York: Springer Science + Business Media.

Davis, O. S., & Plomin, R. (2010). Visualizing genetic similarity at the symptom level: The example of learning disabilities. *The Behavioral and Brain Sciences, 33*(2–3), 155–157.

Daviso, A. W., Denney, S. C., & Baer, R. M. (2011). Postschool goals and transition services for students with learning disabilities. *American Secondary Education, 39*(2), 77–93.

Deacon, S. H., Leblanc, D., & Sabourin, C. (2011). When cues collide: Children's sensitivity to letter- and meaning-patterns in spelling words in English. *Journal of Child Language, 38*(4), 809–827.

Decker, S. (2012). Dimensional integration of assessment outcomes with intervention services for children with specific learning disabilities. *Journal of Applied School Psychology, 28*(2), 175–199.

Devine, M., Taggart, L., & McLornian, P. (2010). Screening for mental health problems in adults with learning disabilities using the Mini PAS-ADD Interview. *British Journal of Learning Disabilities, 38*(4), 252–258.

Dexter, D. D., & Hughes, C. A. (2011). Graphic organizers and students with learning disabilities: A meta-analysis. *Learning Disability Quarterly, 34*(1), 51–72.

Doabler, C. T., & Fien, H. (2013). Explicit mathematics instruction: What teachers can do for teaching students with mathematics difficulties. *Intervention in School and Clinic, 48*(5), 276–285.

Dombrowski, S. C., & Gischlar, K. L. (2014). Ethical and empirical considerations in the identification of learning disabilities. *Journal of*

*Applied School Psychology, 30*(1), 68–82.

Dufault, R., Schnoll, R., Lukiw, W. J., Leblanc, B., Cornett, C., Patrick, L., Wallinga, D., Gilbert, S. G., & Crider, R. (2009). Mercury exposure, nutritional deficiencies and metabolic disruptions may affect learning in children. *Behavioral and Brain Functions: BBF 5*, 44.

Dunn, C., Rabren, K. S., Taylor, S. L., & Dotson, C. K. (2012). Assisting students with high-incidence disabilities to pursue careers in science, technology, engineering, and mathematics. *Intervention in School and Clinic, 48*(1), 47–54.

Dunn, M. W. (2010). Defining learning disability: does IQ have anything significant to say? *Learning Disabilities: A Multidisciplinary Journal, 16*(1), 31–40.

DuPaul, G. J., Gormley, M. J., & Laracy, S. D. (2013). Comorbidity of LD and ADHD: Implications of *DSM*-5 for assessment and treatment. *Journal of Learning Disabilities, 46*(1), 43–51.

Egeland, J., Ueland, T., & Johansen, S. (2012). Central processing energetic factors mediate impaired motor control in ADHD combined subtype, but not in ADHD inattentive subtype. *Journal of Learning Disabilities, 45*(4), 361–370.

Elias, M. J., & Leverett, L. (2011). Consultation to urban schools for improvements in academics and behavior: No alibis. No excuses. No exceptions. *Journal of Educational &*

*Psychological Consultation, 21*(1), 28–45.

Evans, M. K., Clinkinbeard, S. S., & Simi, P. (2015). Learning disabilities and delinquent behaviors among adolescents: A comparison of those with and without comorbidity. *Deviant Behavior, 36*(3), 200–220.

Farmer, T. W., Hall, C. M., & Weiss, M. P. (2011). The school adjustment of rural adolescents with and without disabilities: Variable and person-centered approaches. *Journal of Child and Family Studies, 20*(1), 78–88.

Fasmer, O. B., Riise, T., Eagan, T. M., Lund, A., Dilsaver, S. C., Hundal, Ø., & Oedegaard, K. J. (2011). Comorbidity of asthma with ADHD. *Journal of Attention Disorders, 15*(7), 564–571.

Ferguson, M., Jarrett, D., & Terras, M. (2011). Inclusion and healthcare choices: The experiences of adults with learning disabilities. *British Journal of Learning Disabilities, 39*(1), 73–83.

Fletcher, J. M., Stuebing, K. K., Morris, R. D., & Lyon. G. R. (2013). Classification and definition of learning disabilities: A hybrid model. In H. L. Swanson, K. R. Harris, & S. Graham (Eds.), *Handbook of learning disabilities,* 2nd ed. New York: Guilford.

Friend, A., & Olson, R. K. (2008). Phonological spelling and reading deficits in children with spelling disabilities. *Scientific Studies of Reading, 12*(1), 90–105.

Fuchs, L. S., & Fuchs, D. (2011). *Using CBM for progress monitoring in*

*reading.* National Center on Student Progress Monitoring. Retrieved from www.studentprogress.org.

Fuchs, L. S., Fuchs, D., & Compton, D. L. (2013). Intervention effects for students with comorbid forms of learning disabilities: Understanding the needs of nonresponders. *Journal of Learning Disabilities, 46*(6), 534–548.

Gall, M. D., Gall, J. P., & Borg, W. R. (2007). *Educational research: An introduction,* 8th ed. Boston: Allyn & Bacon.

Galway, T. M., & Metsala, J. L. (2011). Social cognition and its relation to psychosocial adjustment in children with nonverbal learning disabilities. *Journal of Learning Disabilities, 44*(1), 33–49.

Gardner, T. J. (2011). Disabilities in written expression. *Teaching Children Mathematics, 18*(1), 46–54.

Geary, D. C. (2011). Consequences, characteristics, and causes of mathematical learning disabilities and persistent low achievement in mathematics. *Journal of Developmental Behavior and Pediatrics, 32*(3), 250–263.

Geary, D. C., Hoard, M. K., Nugent, L., & Bailey, D. H. (2011). Mathematical cognition deficits in children with learning disabilities and persistent low achievement: A five-year prospective study. *Journal of Educational Psychology*, Online First Publication, September 12, 2011.

Gelfand, D. M., & Drew, C. J. (2003). *Understanding child behavior disorders,*

4th ed. (p. 238). Belmont, CA: Wadsworth. Used with permission.

Gerber, P. J. (2012). The impact of learning disabilities on adulthood: A review of evidence-based literature for research and practice in adult education. *Journal of Learning Disabilities, 45*(1), 31–46.

Gettinger, M., Schienebeck, C., Seigel, S., & Vollmer, L. (2011). Assessment of classroom environments. In M. A. Bray & T. J. Kehle (Eds.), *The Oxford handbook of school psychology* (pp. 260–283). New York: Oxford University Press.

Gilbert, J. K., Compton, D. L., Fuchs, D., & Fuchs, L. S. (2012). Early screening for risk of reading disabilities: Recommendations for a four-step screening system. *Assessment for Effective Intervention, 38*(1), 6–14.

Gilley, C., & Ringdahl, J. E. (2014). The effects of item preference and token reinforcement on sharing behavior exhibited by children with autism spectrum disorder. *Research in Autism Spectrum Disorders, 8*(11), 1425–1433.

Glascoe, F. P., & Trimm, F. (2014). Brief approaches to developmental-behavioral promotion in primary care: Updates on methods and technology. *Pediatrics, 133*(5), 884–897.

Goldstein, S. (2011). Learning disabilities in childhood. In S. Goldstein, J. A. Naglieri, & M. DeVries (Eds.), *Learning and attention disorders in adolescence and adulthood: Assessment and treatment,* 2nd ed. (pp. 31–58). Hoboken, NJ: John Wiley & Sons.

Graff, W. D., Miller, G., & Nagel, S. K. (2014). Addressing the problem of ADHD medications and neuroenhancements. *Expert Review of Neurotherapeutics, 14*(5), 569–581.

Greenbank, A., & Sharon, A. (2013). Recognizing non-verbal social cues promotes social performance in LD adolescents. *Alberta Journal of Educational Research, 59*(2), 266–284.

Grigal, M., Hart, D., & Migliore, A. (2011). Comparing the transition planning, postsecondary education, and employment outcomes of students with intellectual and other disabilities. *Career Development for Exceptional Individuals, 34*(1), 4–17.

Gronlund, N. E., & Waugh, C. K. (2009). *Assessment of student achievement,* 9th ed. Boston: Allyn & Bacon.

Haworth, C. M., Kovas, Y., Harlaar, N., Hayiou-Thomas, M. E., Petrill, S. A., Dale, P. S, & Plomin, R. (2009). Generalist genes and learning disabilities: A multivariate genetic analysis of low performance in reading, mathematics, language, and general cognitive ability in a sample of 8000 12-year-old twins. *Journal of Child Psychology and Psychiatry, and Allied Disciplines, 50*(10), 1318–1325.

Handal, B., Campbell, C., Cavanaugh, M., Petocz, P., & Kelly, N. (2013). Technological pedagogical content knowledge of secondary mathematics teachers. *Contemporary Issues in Technology and Teacher Education, 13*(1), 22–40.

Harris, M. L., Schumaker, J. B., & Deshler, D. D. (2011). The effects of strategic morphological analysis instruction on the vocabulary performance of secondary students with and without disabilities. *Learning Disability Quarterly, 34*(1), 17–33.

Harrison, A. G., Lovett, B. J., & Gordon, M. (2013). Documenting disabilities in postsecondary settings: Diagnostians' understanding of legal regulations and diagnostic standards. *Canadian Journal of School Psychology, 28*(4), 303–322.

Harrison, J. R., Vannest, K. J., & Reynolds, C. R. (2011). Behaviors that discriminate ADHD in children and adolescents: Primary symptoms, symptoms of comorbid conditions, or indicators of functional impairment? *Journal of Attention Disorders, 15*(2), 147–160.

Heath, N., Roberts, E., & Toste, J. R. (2013). Perceptions of academic performance: Positive illusions in adolescents with and without learning disabilities. *Journal of Learning Disabilities, 46*(5), 402–412.

Hills, J. (2011). Meeting the challenges of inclusion. *Primary Science, 117,* 9–11.

Hoekstra, P. J. (2011). Is there potential for the treatment of children with ADHD beyond psychostimulants? *European Child & Adolescent Psychiatry, 20*(9), 431–432.

Hollenbeck, A. F. (2011). Instructional makeover: Supporting the reading comprehension of students with learning disabilities in a discussion-based format. *Intervention in School and Clinic, 46*(4), 211–220.

Holmes, J., Gathercole, S. E., Place, M., Dunning, D. L., Hilton, K. A. & Elliott, J. G. (2010). Working memory deficits can be overcome: Impacts of training and medication on working memory in children with ADHD. *Applied Cognitive Psychology, 24*(6), 827–836.

Hoover, J. J. (2010). Special education eligibility decision making in response to intervention models. *Theory into Practice, 49,* 289–296.

Hord, C., & Xin, Y. P. (2013). Intervention research for helping elementary school students with math learning disabilities understand and solve word problems: 1996–2010. *Learning Disabilities: A Multidisciplinary Journal, 19*(1), 3–17.

Houston, S. M., Lebel, C., Katzir, T., Manis, F. R., Kan, E., Rodriguez, G. G., & Sowell, E. R. (2014). Reading skill and structural brain development. *Neuroreport, 25*(5), 347–352.

Hughes, L. A., Banks, P., & Terras, M. M. (2013). Secondary school transition for children with special educational needs: A literature review. *Support for Learning, 28*(1), 24–34.

Iseman, J. S., & Naglieri, J. A. (2011). A cognitive strategy instruction to improve math calculation for children with ADHD and LD: A randomized controlled study. *Journal of Learning Disabilities, 44*(2), 184–195.

Jackson, C. (2011). Your students love social media…and so can you. *Teaching Tolerance, 39.* Retrieved from www .tolerance.org/magazine /number-39-spring-2011 /your-students-love -social-media-and-so -can-you.

Janse, E., de Bree, E., & Brouwer, S. (2010). Decreased sensitivity to phonemic mismatch in spoken word processing in adult developmental dyslexia. *Journal of Psycholinguistic Research, 39*(6), 523–539.

Jenkins, J., & Terjeson, K. J. (2011). Monitoring reading growth: Goal setting, measurement frequency, and methods of evaluation. *Learning Disabilities Research & Practice, 26*(1), 28–35.

Jitendra, A. K., & Star, J. R. (2011). Meeting the needs of students with learning disabilities in inclusive mathematics classrooms: The role of schema-based instruction on mathematical problem-solving. *Theory Into Practice, 50*(1), 12–19.

Jitendra, A. K., Burgess, C., & Gajria, M. (2011). Cognitive strategy instruction for improving expository text comprehension of students with learning disabilities: The quality of evidence. *Exceptional Children, 77*(2), 135–159.

Job, J. M., & Klassen, R. M. (2012). Predicting performance on academic and non-academic tasks:

A comparison of adolescents with and without learning disabilities. *Contemporary Educational Psychology, 37*(2), 162–169.

Johnson, E. S., Semmelroth, C., Mellard, D. F., & Hopper, G. (2012). Using RtI within a comprehensive SLD evaluation: A review of a state's first year efforts. *Learning Disabilities: A Contemporary Journal, 10*(2), 1–15.

Johnson, T., Serrano, J. A, & Veit, D. (2013). Connecting schoolwork to life work: Students practice setting their own educational goals. *Odyssey: New Directions in Deaf Education, 14*, 22–25.

Joseph, L. M., & Eveleigh, E. L. (2011). A review of the effects of self-monitoring on reading performance of students with disabilities. *The Journal of Special Education, 45*(1), 43–53.

Judge, S., & Bell, S. M. (2011). Reading achievement trajectories for students with learning disabilities during the elementary school years. *Reading & Writing Quarterly: Overcoming Learning Difficulties, 27*(1–2), 153–178.

Kalikow, K. T. (2011). *Kids on meds: Up-to-date information about the most commonly prescribed psychiatric medications.* New York: W. W. Norton.

Kalloo, V. & Mohan, P. (2012). Correlation questionnaire data with actual usage data in a mobile learning study for high school mathematics. *Electronic Journal of e-Learning, 10*(1), 76–89.

Kamhia, A. G. (2011). What speech-language

pathologists need to know about auditory processing disorder. *Language, Speech, and Hearing Services in Schools, 42*(3), 265–272.

Kaufman, A. S. (2008). Neuropsychology and specific learning disabilities: Lessons from the past as a guide to present controversies and future clinical practice. In E. Fletcher-Janzen & C. R. Reynolds (Eds.), *Neuropsychological perspectives on learning disabilities in the era of RTI: Recommendations for diagnosis and intervention* (pp. 1–13). Hoboken, NJ: John Wiley & Sons.

Kavale, K. A., Spaulding, L. S., & Beam, A. P. (2009). A time to define: Making the specific learning disability definition prescribe specific learning disability. *Learning Disability Quarterly, 32*(1), 39–48.

Kebir, O., Grizenko, N., Sengupta, S., & Joober, R. (2009). Verbal but not performance IQ is highly correlated to externalizing behavior in boys with ADHD carrying both DRD4 and DAT1 risk genotypes. *Progress in Neuro-Psychopharmacology & Biological Psychiatry, 33*(6), 939–944.

Keeley, P. (2011). Formative assessment probes: With a purpose. *Science and Children, 48*(9), 22–25.

Kendall, S., Nino, M., & Stewart, S. (2010). Using the iPhone and iPod Touch@work. *Computers in Libraries, 30*(2), 14–19.

Kiger, D., Herro, D., & Prunty, D. (2012). Examining the influence of a mobile learning

intervention on third grade math achievement. *Journal of Research on Technology in Education, 45*(1), 61–82.

Kim, T., & Axelrod, S. (2005). Direct instruction: An educators' guide and a plea for action. *The Behavior Analyst Today, 6*(2), 111–120.

King-Sears, M. E., Swanson, C., & Mainzer, L. (2011). TECHnology and literacy for adolescents with disabilities. *Journal of Adolescent & Adult Literacy, 54*(8), 569–578.

Knowles, T. (2010).The kids behind the label: understanding ADHD [Condensed with permission from *Middle Matters,* 17 (June 2009), 1–3]. *The Education Digest, 76*(3), 59–61.

Koenig, D. (2011). Social media in the schoolhouse. *Teaching Tolerance, 39.* Retrieved from www .tolerance.org/magazine /number-39-spring-2011 /social-media-schoolhouse.

Kohnen, S., Nickels, L., & Coltheart, M. (2010). Training rule-of-(E): Further investigation of a previously successful intervention for a spelling rule in developmental mixed dysgraphia. *Journal of Research in Reading, 33*(4), 392–413.

Krawec, J. L. (2014). Problem representation and mathematical problem solving of students of varying math ability. *Journal of Learning Disabilities, 47*(2), 103–115.

Kushki, A., Schwellnus, H., & Ilyas, F. (2011). Changes in kinetics and kinematics of handwriting during a prolonged writing task in children with and without dysgraphia. *Research in Developmental Disabilities: A Multidisciplinary Journal, 32*(3), 1058–1064.

Lane, K. L., Menzies, H. M., & Bruhn, A. L. (2010). *Managing challenging behaviors in schools: Research-based strategies that work.* New York: Guilford Press.

Langberg, J. M., Vaughn, A. J., Brinkman, W. B., Froehlich, T., & Epstein, J. N. (2010). Clinical utility of the Vanderbilt ADHD rating scale for ruling out comorbid learning disorders. *Pediatrics, 126*(5), 990–991.

Langkamp, D. L., McManus, M. D., & Blakemore, S. D. (2015). Telemedicine for children with developmental disabilities: A more effective clinical process than office-based care. *Telemedicine Journal and E-Health, 21*(2), 110–114.

Lembke, E. S., Hampton, D., & Beyers, S. J. (2012). Response to intervention in mathematics: Critical elements. *Psychology in the Schools, 49*(3), 257–272.

Lenhart, A., Purcell, K., Smith, A., & Zickuhr, K. (2010). *Social media and mobile Internet use among teens and young adults.* Pew Research Center, Pew Internet & American Life Project. Retrieved from www.pewinternet.org/~/media//Files/Reports/2010/PIP_Social_Media_and_Young_Adults_Report_Final_with_toplines.pdf.

Lewandowski, L., Cohen, J., & Lovett, B. J. (2013). Effects of extended time allotments on reading comprehension performance of college students with and without learning disabilities. *Journal of Psychoeducational Assessment, 31*(3), 326–336.

Lieberman-Betz, R. G., Vail, C. O, & Chai, Z. (2013). Examining response to intervention using a framework of best practice from early childhood special education. *Exceptionality, 21*(1), 51–67.

Lindstrom, J. H., & Sayeski, K. (2013). Identifying best practice in a shifting landscape: Making sense of RtI in the context of SLD identification. *Exceptionality, 21*(1), 5–18.

Lobo, M. A., & Galloway, J. C. (2013). Assessment and stability of early learning abilities in preterm and full-term infants across the first two years of life. *Research in Developmental Disabilities, 34*(5), 1721–1730.

Loomis, J. W. (2006). Learning disabilities. In R. T. Ammerman (Ed.), *Comprehensive handbook of personality and psychopathology,* vol. 3 (pp. 272–284). Hoboken, NJ: John Wiley & Sons, Inc.

Lopez Fernandez, J. M., & Velazquez Estrella, A. (2011). Contexts for column addition and subtraction. *Teaching Children Mathematics, 17*(9), 540–548.

Luckner, J. L., & Bowen, S. K. (2010). Teachers' use and perceptions of progress monitoring. *American Annals of the Deaf, 155*(4), 397–406.

Lund, E. M., Miller, K. B., & Ganz, J. B. (2014). Access to assessment? Legal and practical issues regarding psychoeducational assessment in children with sensory disabilities. *Journal of Disability Policy Studies, 25*(3), 135–145.

Macaruso, P., & Rodman, A. (2011). Efficacy of computer-assisted instruction for the development of early literacy skills in young children. *Reading Psychology, 32*(2), 172–196.

Machek, G. R., & Nelson, J. M. (2010). School psychologists' perceptions regarding the practice of identifying reading disabilities: Cognitive assessment and response to intervention considerations. *Psychology in the Schools, 47*(3), 230–245.

Maehler, C., & Schuchardt, K. (2009). Working memory functioning in children with learning disabilities: Does intelligence make a difference? *Journal of Intellectual Disability Research, 53*(1), 3–10.

Maehler, C., & Schuchardt, K. (2011). Working memory in children with learning disabilities: Rethinking the criterion of discrepancy. *International Journal of Disability, Development and Education, 58*(1), 5–17.

Mammarella, I. C., Lucangeli, D., & Cornoldi, C. (2010). Spatial working memory and arithmetic deficits in children with nonverbal learning difficulties. *Journal of Learning Disabilities, 43*(5), 455–468.

Manci, D. B., Miller, S. P., & Kennedy, M. (2012). Using the concrete-representational-abstract sequence with integrated strategy instruction to teach subtraction with regrouping to students with learning disabilities. *Learning Disabilities Research and Practice, 27*(4), 152–166.

Mangina, C. A., & Beuzeron-Mangina, H. (2009). Similarities and differences between learning abilities, "pure" learning disabilities, "pure" ADHD and comorbid ADHD with learning disabilities. *International Journal of Psychophysiology, 73*(2), 170–177.

Martin, R. B., Cirino, P. T., Barnes, M. A., Ewing-Cobbs, L., Fuchs, L. S., Stuebing, K. K., Fletcher, J. M. (2013). Prediction and stability of mathematics skill and difficulty. *Journal of Learning Disabilities, 46*(5), 428–443.

Mason, L. H. (2013). Teaching students who struggle with learning to think before, while, and after reading: Effects of self-regulated strategy development instruction. *Reading and Writing Quarterly: Overcoming Learning Difficulties, 29*(2), 124–144.

Mason, L. H., Harris, K. R., & Graham, S. (2011). Self-regulated strategy development for students with writing difficulties. *Theory Into Practice, 51*(1), 20–27.

Maxam, S., & Henderson, J. E. (2013). Inclusivity in the classroom: Understanding and embracing students with "invisible disabilities." *Journal of Cases in Educational Leadership, 16*(2), 71–81.

McDonald, K. E., Keys, C. B., & Balcazar, F. E. (2009). Living with a learning disability and other marginalized statuses: A multilevel analysis. In C. A. Marshall, E. Kendall, M. E. Banks, & R. M. S. Gover (Eds.), *Disabilities: Insights from across fields around the world, Vol 1: The experience: definitions, causes, and consequences.* Santa Barbara, CA: Praeger/ABC-CLIO.

McGillivray, J. A., & Baker, K. L. (2009). Effects of comorbid ADHD with learning disabilities on anxiety, depression, and aggression in adults. *Journal of Attention Disorders, 12*(6), 525–531.

McLeskey, J., & Waldron, N. L. (2011). Educational programs for elementary students with learning disabilities: Can they be both effective and inclusive? *Learning Disabilities Research & Practice, 26*(1), 48–57.

McMaster, K. L., Du, X., & Yeo, S. (2011). Curriculum-based measures of beginning writing: Technical features of the slope. *Exceptional Children, 77*(2), 185–206.

McNamara, J. K., & Willoughby, T. (2010). A longitudinal study of risk-taking behavior in adolescents with learning disabilities. *Learning Disabilities Research & Practice, 25*(1), 11–24.

Mellard, D., McKnight, M., & Jordan, J. (2010). RIT tier structures and instructional intensity. *Learning Disabilities Research and Practice, 25*(4), 217–225.

Merit. (2011). *Starter paragraph punch.* New York: Merit Software. Retrieved from www.meritsoftware.com/index.php.

Miller, B., & McCardle, P. (2011). Moving closer to a public health model of

language and learning disabilities: The role of genetics and the search for etiologies. *Behavior Genetics, 41*(1), 1–5.

Miller, L. (2009). Informal and qualitative assessment of writing skills in students with disabilities. *Assessment for Effective Intervention, 34*(3), 178–191.

Moats, L. C. (2009). Teaching spelling to students with language and learning disabilities. In G. A. Troia (Ed.), *Instruction and assessment for struggling writers: Evidence-based practices* (pp. 269–289). New York: Guilford Press.

Moeller, K., Pixner, S., & Zuber, J. (2011). Early place-value understanding as a precursor for later arithmetic performance—a longitudinal study on numerical development. *Research in Developmental Disabilities: A Multidisciplinary Journal, 32*(5), 1,837–1,851.

Montague, M., Enders, C., & Dietz, S. (2011). Effects of cognitive strategy instruction on math problem solving of middle school students with learning disabilities. *Learning Disability Quarterly, 34*(4), 262–272.

Moore, D. R. (2011). The diagnosis and management of auditory processing disorder. *Language, Speech, and Hearing Services in Schools, 42*(3), 303–308.

Moorman, A., Boon, R. T., & Keller-Bell, Y. (2010). Effects of text-to-speech software on the reading rate and comprehension skills of high school students with specific learning disabilities.

*Learning Disabilities: A Multidisciplinary Journal, 16*(1), 41–49.

Morris, D., & Gaffney, M. (2011). Building reading fluency in a learning-disabled middle school reader. *Journal of Adolescent & Adult Literacy, 54*(5), 331–341.

Morris, M. A., Schraufnagel, C. D., Chudnow, R. S., & Weinberg, W. A. (2009). Learning disabilities do not go away: 20- to 25-year study of cognition, academic achievement, and affective illness. *Journal of Child Neurology, 24*(3), 323–332.

Murray, B. A., & Steinen, N. (2011). Word / map / ping: How understanding spellings improves spelling power. *Intervention in School and Clinic, 46*(5), 299–304.

Narkon, D. E., & Wells, J. C. (2013). Improving reading comprehension for elementary students with learning disabilities: UDL enhanced story mapping. *Preventing School Failure, 57*(4), 231–239.

National Center for Learning Disabilities. (2014). *The state of learning disabilities,* 3rd ed. New York: Author.

National Center on Response to Intervention. (2010). *Essential components of RTI—A closer look at response to intervention.* Washington, D.C.: Author.

National Coalition of Auditory Processing Disorders. (2015). *What is APD?* Retrieved from www.ncapd.org/What_is_APD_.html.

National Joint Committee on Learning Disabilities. (2011a). Learning

disabilities: Implications for policy regarding research and practice: A report by the National Joint Committee on Learning Disabilities. *Learning Disability Quarterly, 34*(4), 237–241.

National Joint Committee on Learning Disabilities. (2011b). Comprehensive assessment and evaluation of students with learning disabilities: A paper prepared by the National Joint Committee on Learning Disabilities. *Learning Disability Quarterly, 34*(1), 3–16.

National Reading Panel. (2000). *Teaching children to read: An evidence-based assessment of the scientific research literature on reading and its implications for reading instruction.* Rockville, MD: Author.

Nelson, J. M., & Harwood, H. R. (2011a). Learning disabilities and anxiety: A meta-analysis. *Journal of Learning Disabilities, 44*(1), 3–17.

Nelson, J. M., & Harwood, H. R. (2011b). A meta-analysis of parent and teacher reports of depression among students with learning disabilities: Evidence for the importance of multi-informant assessment. *Psychology in the Schools, 48*(4), 371–384.

Nelson-Walker, N. J., Fien, H., Kosty, D. B., Smolkowski, K., Smith, J. L. M., & Baker, S. J. (2013). Evaluation the effects of a systemic intervention on first-grade teachers: Explicit reading instruction. *Learning Disability Quarterly, 36*(4), 215–230.

Nguyen, H. T. (2012). General education and special education teachers collaborate to support English language learners with learning disabilities. *Issues in Teacher Education, 21*(1), 127–152.

Northwest Kinematics. (2011). *StoryBuilder.* Salem, OR: Mobile Education. Retrieved from http://mobile-educationstore.com.

Norton, E. S., Beach, S. D., Gabrieli, J. (2015). Neurobiology of dyslexia. *Current Opinion in Neurobiology, 30,* 73–78.

Nowicki, E. A., & Brown, J. D. (2013). "A Kid Way": Strategies for including classmates with learning or intellectual disabilities. *Intellectual and Developmental Disabilities, 51*(4), 253–262.

O'Brien, B. A., Wolf, M., & Lovett, M. W. (2012). A taxometric investigation of developmental dyslexia subtypes. *Dyslexia, 18*(1), 16–39.

Obrzut, J. E., & Mahoney, E. B. (2011). Use of the dichotic listening technique with learning disabilities. *Brain and Cognition, 76*(2), 323–331.

O'Donnell, P. S., & Miller, D. N. (2011). Identifying students with specific learning disabilities: School psychologists' acceptability of the discrepancy model versus response to intervention. *Journal of Disability Policy Studies, 22*(2), 83–94.

Olsen, A., LeMire, S., & Baker, M. (2011). The impact of self-efficacy and peer support on student participation with interactive white boards in the middle school mathematics class. *Journal of Computers in Mathematics and Science Teaching, 30*(2), 163–178.

Orosco, M. J. (2014). Word problem strategy for Latino English language learners at risk for math disabilities. *Learning Disability Quarterly, 37*(1), 45–53.

Orosco, M. J., & O'Connor, R. (2014). Culturally responsive instruction for English language learners with learning disabilities. *Journal of Learning Disabilities, 47*(6), 515–531.

Overvelde, A., & Hulstijn, W. (2011). Handwriting development in grade 2 and grade 3 primary school children with normal, at risk, or dysgraphic characteristics. *Research in Developmental Disabilities: A Multidisciplinary Journal, 32*(2), 540–548.

Passolunghi, M. C. (2011). Cognitive and emotional factors in children with mathematical learning disabilities. *International Journal of Disability, Development and Education, 58*(1), 61–73.

Paton, K., Hammond, P., Barry, E., Fitzgerald, M., McNicholas, F., Kirley, A., Robertson, I. H., Bellgrove, M. A., Gill, M., & Johnson, K. A. (2014). Methylphenidate improves some but not all measures of attention, as measured by the TEA-CH in medication-naïve children with ADHD. *Child Neuropsychology, 20*(3), 303–318.

Pierangelo, R., & Giuliani, G. A. (2006). *Learning disabilities: A practical approach to foundations, assessment, diagnosis, and teaching.* Boston: Allyn & Bacon.

Pieters, S., Desoete, A., Roeyers, H., Vanderswalmen, R., & Van Waelvelde, H. (2012). Behind mathematical learning disabilities: What about visual perception and motor skills? *Learning and Individual Differences, 22*(4), 498–504.

Ponce, H. R., Lopez, M. J., & Mayer, R. E. (2012). Instructional effectiveness of a computer-supported program for teaching reading comprehension strategies. *Computers and Education, 59*(4), 1170–1183.

Porter, J. (2005). Awareness of number in children with severe and profound learning difficulties: Three exploratory case studies. *British Journal of Learning Disabilities, 33,* 97–101.

Powell, S. G., Thomsen, P. H., & Frydenberg, M. (2011). Long-term treatment of ADHD with stimulants: A large observational study of real-life patients. *Journal of Attention Disorders, 15*(6), 439–451.

Powell, S. R. (2011). Solving word problems using schemas: A review of the literature. *Learning Disabilities Research & Practice, 26*(2), 94–108.

Prater, M. A., Redmond, A. S., Anderson, D., & Gibb, G. S. (2014). Teaching adolescent students with learning disabilities to self-advocate for accommodations. *Intervention in School and Clinic, 49*(5), 298–305.

PT Software. (2010). *My writing spot.* Retrieved from www.ptss.net.

Pugach, M. C., Blanton, L. P., & Correa, V. I. (2011). A historical perspective on the role of collaboration in teacher education reform: Making good on the promise of teaching all students. *Teacher Education and Special Education, 34*(3), 183–200.

Quinlan, M. M., Bates, B. R., & Angell, M. E. (2012). "What can I do to help?": Postsecondary students with learning disabilities' perceptions of instructors' classroom accommodations. *Journal of Research in Special Education Needs, 12*(4), 224–233.

Reed, M. J., Kennett, D. J., & Lewis, T. (2011). The relative benefits found for students with and without learning disabilities taking a first-year university preparation course. *Active Learning in Higher Education, 12*(2), 133–142.

Ritchey, K. D. (2011). The first "R": evidence-based reading instruction for students with learning disabilities. *Theory into Practice, 50*(1), 28–34.

Roberts, G. J., Solis, M., Ciullo, S., McKenna, J. W., & Vaughn, S. (2015). Reading interventions with behavioral and social skill outcomes: A synthesis of research. *Behavior Modification, 39*(1), 8–42.

Roivainen, E. (2014). Changes in word usage frequency may hamper intergenerational comparisons of vocabulary skills: An ngram analysis of Wordsum, WAIS, and WISC test items.

*Journal of Psychoeducational Assessment, 32*(1), 83–87.

Rojewski, J. W., Lee, I. H., & Gregg, N. (2014). Intermediate work outcomes for adolescents with high-incidence disabilities. *Career Development and Transition for Exceptional Individuals, 37*(2), 106–118.

Rojewski, J. W., Lee, I. H., Gregg, N., & Gemici, S. (2012). Developmental patterns of occupational aspirations in adolescents with high-incidence disabilities. *Exceptional Children, 78*(2), 157–179.

Rosenblum, Y., Larochette, A., Harrison, A. G., & Armstrong, I. (2010). The relation between comprehensive assessment procedures and diagnostic stability in school-aged children identified with learning disabilities. *Canadian Journal of School Psychology, 25*(2), 170–188.

Rosenzweig, C., Krawec, J., & Montague, M. (2011). Metacognitive strategy use of eighth-grade students with and without learning disabilities during mathematical problem solving: A think-aloud analysis. *Journal of Learning Disabilities, 44*(6), 508–520.

Rubenstein, K. B., Raskind, W. H., Berninger, V. W., Matsushita, M. M., & Wijsman, E. M. (2014). Genome scan for cognitive trait loci of dyslexia: Rapid naming and rapid switching of letters, numbers, and colors. *American Journal of Medical Genetics. Part B, Neuropsychiatric Genetics, 165B*(4), 345–356.

Sampango-Sprouse, C. A., Stapleton, E. J., Mitchell, F. L., Sadeghin, T., Donahue, T. P., & Gropman, A. L. (4014). Expanding the phenotype profile of boys with 47, XXY: The impact of familial learning disabilities. *American Journal of Medical Genetics. Part A, 164A*(6), 1464–1469.

Sayeski, K. L. (2011). Effective spelling instruction for students with learning disabilities. *Intervention in School and Clinic, 47*(2), 75–81.

Scanlon, D. (2013). Specific learning disability and its newest definition: Which is comprehensive? And which is sufficient? *Journal of Learning Disabilities, 46*(1), 26–33.

Scerri, T. S., & Schulte-Körne, G. (2010). Genetics of developmental dyslexia. *European Child & Adolescent Psychiatry, 19*(3), 179–197.

Scheeler, M. C., Macluckie, M., & Albright, K. (2010). Effects of immediate feedback delivered by peer tutors on the oral presentation skills of adolescents with learning disabilities. *Remedial and Special Education, 31*(2), 77–86.

Schieve, L. A., Gonzalez, V., Boulet, S. L., Visser, S. N., Rice, C. E., Van Naarden, B. K., & Boyle, C. A. (2012). Concurrent medical conditions and health care needs among children with learning and behavioral developmental disabilities, National Health Interview Survey, 2006–2010. *Research in Developmental Disabilities, 33*(2), 467–476.

Seethaler, P. M., & Fuchs, L. S. (2011). Using curriculum-based measurement to monitor kindergarteners' mathematics development. *Assessment for Effective Intervention, 36*(4), 219–229.

Semrud-Clikeman, M., Walkowiak, J., Wilkinson, A., & Minne, E. P. (2010). Direct and indirect measures of social perception, behavior, and emotional functioning in children with Asperger's disorder, nonverbal learning disability, or ADHD. *Journal of Abnormal Child Psychology: An official publication of the International Society for Research in Child and Adolescent Psychopathology, 38*(4), 509–519.

Shandra, C. L. (2012). The first sexual experience among adolescent girls with and without disabilities. *Journal of Youth and Adolescence, 41*(4), 515–532.

Shapiro, E. S., Hilt-Panahon, A., Gischlar, K. L, Semeniak, K., Leichman, E., & Bowles, S. (2012). An analysis of consistency between team decisions and reading assessment data within an RtI model. *Remedial and Special Education, 33*(6), 335–347.

Shaul, S., Arzouan, Y., & Goldstein, A. (2012). Brain activity while reading words and pseudo-words: A comparison between dyslexic and fluent readers. *International Journal of Psychophysiology, 84*(3), 270–276.

Sheehy, K. (2009). Teaching word recognition to children with severe learning difficulties: An exploratory comparison of teaching methods.

*Educational Research, 51*(3), 379–391.

Shifter, D., Callahan, R. M., & Muller. C. (2013). Equity or marginalization? The high school course-taking of students labeled with a learning disability. *American Educational Research Journal, 50*(4), 656–682.

Shiran, A., & Breznitz, Z. (2011). The effect of cognitive training on recall range and speed of information processing in the working memory of dyslexic and skilled readers. *Journal of Neurolinguistics, 24*(5), 524–537.

Shogren, K. A. (2011). Culture and self-determination: A synthesis of the literature and directions for future research and practice. *Career Development for Exceptional Individuals, 34*(2), 115–127.

Stetter, M. E., & Hughes, M. T. (2010). Using story grammar to assist students with learning disabilities and reading difficulties improve their comprehension. *Education & Treatment of Children (West Virginia University Press)*, 115–151.

Stock, P., Desoete, A., & Roeyers, H. (2010). Detecting children with arithmetic disabilities from kindergarten: Evidence from a 3-year longitudinal study on the role of preparatory arithmetic abilities. *Journal of Learning Disabilities, 43*(3), 250–268.

Stockard, J. (2010). Promoting reading achievement and countering the "fourth-grade slump": The impact of direct instruction on reading achievement in fifth grade. *Journal of*

Education for Students Placed at Risk (JESPAR), 15(3), 218–240.

Stothers, M. E., & Cardy, J. O. (2012). Oral language impairments in developmental disorders characterized by language strengths: A comparison of Asperger syndrome and nonverbal learning disabilities. *Research in Autism Spectrum Disorders, 6*(1), 519–534.

Stothers, M., & Klein, P. D. (2010). Perceptual organization, phonological awareness, and reading comprehension in adults with and without learning disabilities. *Annals of Dyslexia, 60*(2), 209–237.

Sundeen, T. H. (2012). Explicit prewriting instruction: Effect on writing quality of adolescents with learning disabilities. *Learning Disabilities: A Multidisciplinary Journal, 18*(1), 23–33.

Swanson, H. L. (2011). *Learning disabilities: Assessment, identification, and treatment.* New York: Oxford University Press.

Swanson, H. L., Moran, A. S., Bocian, K., Lussier, C., & Zheng, X. (2013). Generative strategies, working memory, and word problem solving accuracy in children at risk for math disabilities. *Learning Disability Quarterly, 36*(4), 203–214.

Taub, M. B. (2011). Review of the literature: Dyslexia. *Journal of Behavioral Optometry, 22*(2), 48–49.

Taylor, H. G., Espy, K. A., & Anderson, P. J. (2009). Mathematics deficiencies in children with very low birth weight or very preterm birth.

Developmental Disabilities Research Reviews, 15(1), 52–59.

Toland, J., & Boyle, C. (2008). Applying cognitive behavioural methods to retrain children's attributions for success and failure in learning. *School Psychology International, 29*(3), 286–302.

Torgesen, J. K., Wagner, R. K., & Rashotte, C. A. (2010). Computer-assisted instruction to prevent early reading difficulties in students at risk for dyslexia: Outcomes from two instructional approaches. *Annals of Dyslexia, 60*(1), 40–56.

Troia, G. A. (2011). How might pragmatic language skills affect the written expression of students with language learning disabilities? *Topics in Language Disorders, 3*(1), 40–53.

Unruh, S., & McKellar, N. A. (2013). Evolution, not revolution: School psychologists' changing practices in determining specific learning disabilities. *Psychology in the Schools, 50*(4), 353–365.

U.S. Department of Education. (2011). *The 30th annual report to Congress on the implementation of the Individuals with Disabilities Education Act, 2008.* Washington, D.C.: U.S. Government Printing Office.

U.S. Department of Education. (2013a). *Number and percentage distribution of 14-through 21-year old students served under Individuals with Disabilities Education Act (IDEA), Part B, who exited school, by exit reason, age, and type of disability:*

2009-10 and 2010-11. Washington, D.C.: U.S. Department of Education, National Center for Educational Statistics. Retrieved from http://nces.ed.gov/programs/digest/d13/tables/dt13_219.90.asp?current=yes.

U.S. Department of Education. (2013b). *Percentage distribution of students 6 to 21 years old served under Individuals with Disabilities Education Act, Part B, by educational environment and type of disability: Selected years, fall 1989 through fall 2011.* Washington, D.C.: U.S. Department of Education, Office of Special Education Programs, Individuals with Disabilities Education Act (IDEA) database. Retrieved from http://nces.ed.gov/programs/digest/d13/tables/dt13_204.60.asp?current=yes.

U.S. Department of Education. (2014a). *Percentage distribution of children ages 3–21 served under the Individuals with Disabilities Education Act (IDEA), Part B, by disability type: School year 2011–12.* Washington, D.C.: U.S. Department of Education, National Center for Education Statistics. Retrieved from http://nces.ed.gov/programs/coe/indicator_cgg.asp.

U.S. Department of Education. (2014b). *Digest of education statistics, Children 3–12 years old served under Individuals with Disabilities Education Act (IDEA), Part B, by type of disability: Selected years, 1976–2012–13. (Table 204.30).* Retrieved from https://

nces.ed.gov/programs/digest/d14/tables/dt14_204.30.asp?current=yes.

U.S. Department of Education. (2014c). *The 36th Annual Report to Congress on the Implementation of the Individuals with Disabilities Education Act.* Washington, D.C.: U.S. Government Printing Office.

Viel-Ruma, K., Houchins, D., & Fredrick, L. (2007). Error self-correction and spelling: Improving the spelling accuracy of secondary students with disabilities in written expression. *Journal of Behavioral Education, 16*(3), 291–301.

Viel-Ruma, K., Houchins, D. E., Jolivette, K., Fredrick, L. D., & Gama, R. (2010). Direct instruction in written expression: The effects on English speakers and English language learners with disabilities. *Learning Disabilities Research & Practice, 25*(2), 97–108.

Waesche, J. S. B, Schatschneider, C., Maner, J. K., Ahmed, Y., & Wagner, R. K. (2011). Examining agreement and longitudinal stability among traditional and RtI-based definitions of reading disability using the affected-status agreement statistic. *Journal of Learning Disabilities, 44*(3), 296–307.

Walker, S. O., & Plomin, R. (2005). The nature-nurture question: Teachers' perceptions of how genes and the environment influence educationally relevant behaviour. *Educational Psychology, 25*, 509–516.

Watson, S. M. R., & Gable, R. A. (2013). Cognitive

development of adolescents at risk or with learning and/or emotional problems: Implications for teachers. *Intervention in School and Clinic, 49*(2), 108–112.

Watson, S. M. R., Gable, R. A., Gear, S. B., & Hughes, K. C. (2012). Evidence-based strategies for improving the reading comprehension of secondary students: Implications for students with learning disabilities. *Learning Disabilities Research & Practice, 27*(2), 79–89.

Wei, X., Lenz, K. B., Blackorby, J. (2013). Math growth trajectories of students with disabilities: Disability category, gender, racial, and socioeconomic status differences from ages 7 to 17. *Remedial and Special Education, 34*(3), 154–165.

Weiser, B., & Mathes, P. (2011). Using encoding instruction to improve the reading and spelling performances of elementary students at risk for literacy difficulties: A best-evidence synthesis. *Review of Educational Research, 81*(2), 170–200.

Wilcutt, E. G., Petrill, S. A., Wu, S., Boada, R., DeFries, J. C., Olson, R. K., & Pennington, B. F. (2013). Comorbidity between reading disability and math disability: Concurrent psychopathology, functional impairment, and neuropsychological functioning. *Journal of Learning Disabilities, 46*(6), 500–516.

Wilkinson-Smith, A., & Semrud-Clikeman, M. (2014). Are fine-motor impairments a defining feature of nonverbal

learning disabilities in children? *Applied Neuropsychology Child, 3*(1), 52–59.

Wilson, J. K. (2012). Brisk and effective fluency instruction for small groups. *Intervention in School and Clinic, 47*(3), 152–157.

Woods, L. L., Sylvester, L., & Martin, J. E. (2010). Student-directed transition planning: Increasing student knowledge and self-efficacy in the transition planning process. *Career Development for Exceptional Individuals, 33*(2), 106–114.

Yew, S. G. K., & O'Kearny, R. (2013). Emotional and behavioural outcomes later in childhood and adolescence for children with specific language impairments: Meta-analyses of controlled prospective studies. *Journal of Child Psychology and Psychiatry, 54*(5), 516–524.

Zipke, M. (2014). Building an e-book library: Resources for finding the best apps. *Reading Teacher, 67*(5), 375–383.

## Chapter 8

Adelman, H. S., & Taylor, L. (2006). *The implementation guide to student learning supports in the classroom and schoolwide.* Thousand Oaks, CA: Corwin Press.

Algozzine, R., Serna, L., & Patton, J. R. (2001). *Childhood behavior disorders: Applied research and educational practices,* 2nd ed. Austin, TX: PRO-ED.

Allen-DeBoer, R. A., Malmgren, K. W., & Glass, M. (2006). Reading instruction for youth

with emotional and behavioral disorders in a juvenile correctional facility. *Behavioral Disorders: Journal of the Council for Children with Behavioral Disorders, 32*(1), 18.

American Psychiatric Association. (2013). *Diagnostic and statistical manual of mental disorders,* 5th ed. Arlington, VA: American Psychiatric Association.

Arter, P. S. (2007). The positive alternative learning supports program: Collaborating to improve student success. *Council for Exceptional Children, 40*(2), 38.

Artiles, A. J., Bal, A., Trent, S. C., & Thorius, K. K. (2012). Placement of culturally and linguistically diverse students in programs for students with emotional and behavioral disorders: Contemporary trends and research needs. In J. P. Bakken, F. E. Obiakor, & A. F. Rotatori (Ed.) *Behavioral disorders: Identification, assessment, and instruction of students with EBD (Advances in Special Education, Volume 22, Ch. 5).* Bingley, UK: Emerald.

Barber, B. K., Stolz, H. E., & Olsen, J. A. (2005). Parental control, psychological control, and behavioral control: Assessing relevance across time, culture, and method. *Monographs of the Society for Research in Child Development, 70*(4), 1–137.

Barker, E. D., Oliver, B. R., Viding, E., Salekin, R. T., & Maughan, B. (2011). The impact of prenatal risk, fearless

temperament and early parenting on adolescent callous-unemotional traits: A 12-year longitudinal investigation. *Journal of Child Psychology and Psychiatry, 52*(8), 878–888.

Beard, K. Y., & Sugai, G. (2004). First step to success: An early intervention for elementary children at risk for antisocial behavior. *Behavioral Disorders, 29*(4), 396–409.

Benitez, D. T., Lattimore, J., & Wehmeyer, M. L. (2005). Promoting the involvement of students with emotional and behavioral disorders in career and vocational planning and decision-making: The self-determined career development model. *Behavioral Disorders, 30*(4), 431–447.

Benner, G. J., Nelson, J. R., & Epstein, M. H. (2002). Language skills of children with EBD: A literature review. *Journal of Emotional and Behavioral Disorders, 10*, 43–59.

Birchmeier, Z. (2009). Stand by me: The effects of peer and teacher support in mitigating the impact of bullying on quality of life. *Psychology in the Schools, 47*, 636–649.

Bower, E. M. (1959). The emotionally handicapped child and the school. *Exceptional Children, 26*, 6–11.

Brotman, L. M., Calzada, E., Huang, K. Y., Kingston, S., Dawson-McClure, S., Kamboukos, D., Resenfelt, A., Schwab, A., & Petkova, E. (2011). Promoting effective parenting practices and preventing child behavior problems in school among ethnically diverse families from underserved, urban communities. *Child Development, 82*(1), 258–276.

Burke, M. D., Davis, J. L, Hagan-Burke, S., Lee, Y. H., & Fogarty, M. S. (2012). Using SWPBS expectations as a screening tool to predict behavior risk in middle school. *Journal of Positive Behavior Interventions, 16*(1), 5–17.

Burt, S. A. (2009). Rethinking environmental contributions to child and adolescent psychopathology: A meta-analysis of shared environmental influences. *Psychological Bulletin, 135*(4), 608–637.

Burt, S. A., & Neiderhiser, J. M. (2009). Aggressive versus nonaggressive antisocial behavior: distinctive etiological moderation by age, *Developmental Psychology, 45*(4), 1164–1176.

Capaldi, D. M., & Eddy, J. M. (2005). Oppositional defiant disorder and conduct disorder. In T. P. Gulotta & G. R. Adams (Eds.), *Handbook of adolescent behavioral problems: Evidence-based approaches to prevention and treatment*, 283–308. New York, NY: Springer Science + Business Media.

Carter, E. W., Wehby, J. H., Hughes, C., Johnson, S. M., Plank, D. R., Barton-Arwood, S. M., & Lunsford, L. B. (2005). Preparing adolescents with high-incidence disabilities for high-stakes testing with strategy instruction. *Preventing School Failure, 49*(2), 55–62.

Chang, H., Olson, S. L., Sameroff, A. J., Sexton, H. R. (2011). Child effortful control as a mediator of parenting practices on externalizing behavior: Evidence for a sex-differentiated pathway across the transition from preschool to school. *Journal of Abnormal Child Psychology, 39*, 71–81.

Child and Adolescent Bipolar Foundation. (2009). *About pediatric and bipolar disorder.* Retrieved March 25, 2009, from www.bpkids.org/site /PageServer?pagename =lrn_about.

Coleman, M. C., & Webber, J. (2002). *Emotional & behavioral disorders: Theory and practice.* Boston: Allyn & Bacon.

Conroy, M. A., & Brown, W. H. (2004). Early identification, prevention, and early intervention with young children at risk for emotional or behavioral disorders: Issues, trends, and a call for action. *Behavioral Disorders, 29*(3), 224–236.

Conroy, M. A., Hendrickson, J. M., & Hester, P. P. (2004). Early identification and prevention of emotional and behavioral disorders. In R. B. Rutherford, M. M. Quinn, & S. R. Mathur (Eds.), *Handbook of research in emotional and behavioral disorders* (pp. 199–215). New York: Guilford Press.

Crews, S. D., Bender, H., Cook, C. R., Gresham, F. M., Kern, L., & Vanderwood, M. (2007). Risk and protective factors of emotional and/or behavioral disorders in children and adolescents: A mega-analytic synthesis. *Behavioral Disorders:*

*Journal of the Council for Children with Behavioral Disorders, 32*(2), 64–77.

Crone, D. A., Hawken, L. S., & Horner, R. H. (2015). *Building positive behavior support systems in schools. Functional behavioral assessment,* 2nd ed. New York: Guilford.

Crundwell, R. M., & Killu, K. (2007). Understanding and accommodating students with depression in the classroom. *Council for Exceptional Children, 40*(1), 48–54.

Cullinan, D. (2004). Classification and definition of emotional and behavioral disorders. In R. B. Rutherford, M. M. Quinn, & R. Sarup (Eds.), *Handbook of research in emotional and behavioral disorders*, pp. 32–53. New York: Guilford.

Cummings, J. G, Pepler, D. J., Mishna, F., & Craig, W. M. (2006). Bullying and victimization among students with exceptionalities. *Exceptionality Education Canada, 16*, 193–222.

Cunningham, E. M., & O'Neill, R. E. (2007). Agreement of functional behavioral assessment and analysis methods with students with EBD. *Behavioral Disorders: Journal of the Council for Children with Behavioral Disorders, 32*(3), 211–221.

Davis, S. D., Young, E. L., Hardman, S., & Winters, R. (2011). Screening for emotional and behavioral disorders, *Principle Leadership, 11*(9), 12–17.

Dikel, W., & Stewart, D. (2011). Emotional/behavioral disorders and special education: Recommendations for

system redesign of a failed category. *34 Hamline Law Review, 589*, 589–610.

Doerfler, L. A., Conner, D. F., & Toscano, P. F. (2011). The CBCL bipolar profile and attention, mood, and behavior dysregulation. *Journal of Child and Family Studies, 20*(5), 545–553.

Donovan, S. A., & Nickerson, A. B. (2007). Strength-based versus traditional social-emotional reports: Impact on multidisciplinary team members' perceptions. *Behavioral Disorders: Journal of the Council for Children with Behavioral Disorders, 32*(4), 228–237.

Dunlap, G., Strain, P. S., Fox, L., Carta, J. J., Conroy, M., Smith, B. J., et al. (2006). Prevention and intervention with young children's challenging behavior: Perspectives regarding current knowledge. *Behavioral Disorders: Journal of the Council for Children with Behavioral Disorders, 32*(1), 29.

Eber, L., Breen, K., Rose, J., Unizycki, R. M., & London, T. H. (2008). Wraparound: A tertiary level intervention for students with emotional/ behavioral needs. *Teaching Exceptional Children, 40*(6), 18–10.

Eber, L., Hyde, K., & Suter, J. C. (2011). Integrating wraparound into a schoolwide system of positive behavior supports. *Journal of Child and Family Studies, 20*(6), 782–790.

Eber, L. & Keenan, S. (2004). Collaboration with other agencies: Wraparound and systems of care for children and youths with emotional and behavioral disorders. In R. B. Rutherford, M. M. Quinn, & S. R. Mathur (Eds.), *Handbook or research in emotional and behavioral disorders,* 502–516. New York: Guilford.

Eber, L., Sugai, G., Smith, C., & Scott, T. (2002). Wraparound and positive behavioral interventions and supports in the schools. *Journal of Emotional and Behavioral Disorders, 10,* 171–180.

Eivers, A. R., Brendgen, M., & Borge, A. I. H. (2010). Stability and change in prosocial and antisocial behavior across the transition to school: Teacher and peer perspectives. *Early Education & Development, 21*(6), 843–864.

Ensor, R., Marks, A., Jacobs, L., & Hughes, C. (2010). Trajectories of antisocial behaviour towards siblings predict antisocial behaviour towards peers. *Journal of Child Psychology and Psychiatry, 51*(11), 1208–1216.

Epstein, M. H. (1998). Using strength-based assessment in program with children with emotional and behavior disorders. *Beyond Behavior, 9*(2), 25–27.

Epstein, M. H., & Sharma, J. M. (1997). *Behavior and emotional rating scale.* Austin, TX: PRO-ED.

Espelage, D. L., & Swearer, S. M. (Eds.). (2011). *Bullying in North American Schools: A socioecological perspective on prevention and intervention*, 2nd ed. New York: Routledge.

Essa, E. (2003). *A practical guide to solving preschool behavior problems,* 5th ed. Australia: Thompson/Delmar Learning.

Etscheidt, S. (2006). Behavioral intervention plans: Pedagogical and legal analysis of issues. *Behavioral Disorders: Journal of the Council for Children with Behavioral Disorders, 31*(2), 223–243.

Forness, S. R., & Kavale, K. A. (2000). Emotional or behavioral disorders: Background and current status of the E/BD terminology and definition. *Behavioral Disorders, 25*(3), 264–269.

Forness, S. R., Kim, J., & Walker, H. M. (2012). Prevalence of students with EBD: Impact on general education. *Beyond Behavior, 21*(2), 3–10.

Forsman, M., Lichtenstein, P., Andershed, H., & Larsson, H. (2010). A longitudinal twin study of the direction of effects between psychopathic personality and antisocial behaviour. *Journal of Child Psychology and Psychiatry, 51*(1), 39–47.

Gable. R. A. (2004). Hard times and an uncertain future: Issues that confront the field of emotional/behavioral disorders. *Education and Treatment of Children, 27*(4), 341–352.

Gallagher, G., & Konjoian, P. (2010). *Shut up about your perfect kid: A survival guide for ordinary parents of special children.* New York: Three Rivers Press.

Graczyk, P. A., Connolly, S. D., & Corapci, F. (2005). Anxiety disorders in children and adolescents: Theory, treatment, and prevention. In T. P. Gullotta & G. R. Adams (Eds.), *Handbook of adolescent behavioral problems* (pp. 131–157). New York: Springer Science + Business Media, Inc.

Gresham, F. M., Van, M. B., & Cook, C. R. (2006). Social skills training for teaching replacement behaviors: Remediating acquisition deficits in at-risk students. *Behavioral Disorders: Journal of the Council for Children with Behavioral Disorders, 31*(4), 363.

Griffith, A. K., Trout, A. L., Hagaman, J. L. & Harper, J. (2009). Interventions to improve the literacy functioning of adolescents with emotional and/or behavior disorders: A review of literature between 1965 and 2005. *Behavior Disorders, 33*(3), 124–140.

Guerra, N. G., Boxer, P., & Kim, T. E. (2005). A cognitive-ecological approach to serving students with emotional and behavioral disorders: Application to aggressive behavior. *Behavioral Disorders, 30*(3), 277–288.

Haltigan, J. D., Roisman, G. I., Susman, E. J., Barnett-Walker, K., Monahan, K. C., & The National Institute of Child Health and Human Development Early Child Care Research Network. (2011). Elevated trajectories of externalizing problems are associated with lower awakening cortisol levels in midadolescence. *Developmental Psychology, 47*(2), 472–478.

Hansen, S. D., & Lignugaris-Kraft, B. (2005). Effects of a dependent group contingency on the verbal interactions of middle school students with emotional disturbances. *Behavioral Disorders, 30*(2), 170–184.

Harry, B., Hart, J. E., Klinger, J., & Cramer, E. (2009). Response to Kauffman, Mock, & Simpson (2007): Problems related to underservice of students with emotional or behavioral disorders. *Behavioral Disorders, 34*(3), 164–171.

Heilbrun, A. B. (2004). *Disordered and deviant behavior: Learning gone awry.* Lanham, MD: University Press of America, Inc.

Hollo, A., & Wehby, J. H. (2014). Unidentified language deficits in children with emotional and behavioral disorders: A meta-analysis. *Exceptional Children, 80*(2), 169–186.

Hughes, C. A., & Dexter, D. D. (2011). Response to intervention: A research-based summary. *Theory into Practice, 50*(1), 4–11.

Insel, T. (2012). *Director's blog: Spotlight on eating disorders.* National Institute of Mental Health. Retrieved from www.nimh.nih.gov/about/director/2012/spotlight-on-eating-disorders.shtml

Jeter, L. V. (2010). Conduct disorders: Are boot camps effective? *Reclaiming Children and Youth: The Journal of Emotional and Behavioral Problems, 19*(2), 32–36.

Johnson, C., Eva, A. L., Johnson, L., & Walker, B. (2011). Don't turn away: Empowering teachers to support students' mental health. *The Clearing*

House: A Journal of Educational Strategies, Issues and Ideas, 84(1), 9–14.

Johnson, W., McGue, M., & Iacono, W. G. (2009). School performance and genetic and environmental variance in antisocial behavior at the transition from adolescence to adulthood. *Developmental Psychology, 45*(4), 973–987.

Kauffman, J. M. (2005). *Characteristics of emotional and behavioral disorders of children and youth*. Upper Saddle River, NJ: Prentice-Hall.

Kauffman, J. M., & Landrum, T. J. (2009). *Characteristics of emotional and behavioral disorders of children and youth,* 9th ed. Upper Saddle River, NJ: Prentice-Hall.

Kauffman, J. M., Bantz, J., & McCullough, J. (2002). Separate and better: A special public school class for students with emotional and behavioral disorders. *Exceptionality, 10,* 149–170.

Kauffman, J. M., Simpson, R. L., & Mock, D. R. (2009). Problems related to underservice: A rejoinder. *Behavioral Disorders, 34*(3), 172–180.

Kendziora, K. T. (2004). Early intervention for emotional and behavioral disorders. In R. B. Rutherford, M. M. Quinn, & S. R. Mathur (Eds.), *Handbook of research in emotional and behavioral disorders* (pp. 327–351). New York: Guilford Press.

Kendziora, K., Bruns, E., Osher, D., Pacchiano, D. & Meija, B. (2001). Wraparound: Stories from the field. *Systems of Care: Promising practices in children's mental health, 2001 series*. Washington, D. C.: American Institutes for Research, Center for Effective Collaboration and Practice.

Knitzer, J., Steinberg, Z., & Fleisch, B. (1990). *At the schoolhouse door: An examination of programs and policies for children with behavioral and emotional problems*. New York: Bank Street College of Education.

Konopasek, D. E., & Forness, S. R. (2004). Psychopharmacology in the treatment of emotional and behavioral disorders. In R. B. Rutherford, M. M. Quinn, & S. R. Mathur (Eds.), *Handbook of research in emotional and behavioral disorders* (pp. 352–368). New York: Guilford Press.

Kostewicz, D. E., & Kubina, R. M. (2008). The national reading panel guidepost: A review of reading outcome measures for students with emotional and behavioral disorders. *Behavioral Disorders, 33*(2), 62–74.

Kowalski, R. M., & Fedina, C. (2011). Cyber bullying in ADHD and Asperger syndrome populations. *Research in Autism Spectrum Disorders, 5,* 1201–1208.

Lane, K. L. (2004). Academic instruction and tutoring interventions for students with emotional and behavioral disorders: 1990 to the present. In R. B. Rutherford, M. M. Quinn, & S. R. Mathur (Eds.), *Handbook of research in emotional and behavioral disorders* (pp. 462–486). New York: Guilford Press.

Lane, K. L. (2007). Identifying and supporting students at risk for emotional and behavioral disorders within multilevel models: Data driven approaches to conducting secondary interventions with an academic emphasis. *Education and Treatment of Children, 30,* 135–164.

Lane, K. L., Barton-Arwood, S. M., Nelson, J. R., & Wehby, J. (2008). Academic performance of students with emotional and behavioral disorders served in a self-contained setting. *Journal of Behavioral Education, 17*(1), 43–62.

Lane, K. L., Kalberg, J. R., & Menzies, H. M. (2009). *Developing schoolwide programs to prevent and manage problem behaviors: A step-by-step approach*. New York: Guilford.

Lane, K. L., Weisenbach, J. L., Phillips, A., & Wehby, J. H. (2007). Designing, implementing, and evaluating function-based interventions using a systematic, feasible approach. *Behavioral Disorders: Journal of the Council for Children with Behavioral Disorders, 32*(2), 122–139.

Levitt, J. L., Sansone, R. A., & Cohn, L. (Eds.). (2004). *Self-harm behavior and eating disorders: Dynamics, assessment, and treatment*. New York: Brunner-Routledge.

Lewis, T. J., Jones, S. E. L., Horner, R. H., & Sugai, G. (2010). School-wide positive behavior support and students with emotional/behavioral disorders: Implications for prevention, identification and intervention. *Exceptionality: A Special Education Journal, 18*(2), 82–93.

Lewis, T. J., Lewis-Palmer, T., Newcomer, L., & Stichter, J. (2004). Applied behavior analysis and the education and treatment of students with emotional and behavioral disorders. In R. B. Rutherford, M. M. Quinn, & S. R. Mathur (Eds.), *Handbook of research in emotional and behavioral disorders* (pp. 523–545). New York: Guilford Press.

Lopes, J. (2005). Intervention with students with learning, emotional, and behavioral disorders: Why do we take so long to do it? *Education and Treatment of Children, 28*(4), 345–360.

Lopez-Romero, L., Romero, E., & Luengo, M. A. (2012). Disentangling the role of psychopathic traits and externalizing behavior in predicting conduct problems from childhood to adolescence. *Journal of Youth and Adolescence, 41*(11), 1397–1408.

Maag, J. W. (2006). Social skills training for students with emotional and behavioral disorders: A review of reviews. *Behavioral Disorders, 32*(1), 4–17.

Maag, J. W., & Katsiyannis, A. (2010). Early intervention programs for children with behavior problems and at risk for developing antisocial behaviors: Evidence- and research-based practices, *Remedial and Special Education, 31*(6), 464–475.

Maag, J. W., & Katsiyannis, A. (2012). Bullying and students with disabilities:

Legal and practical considerations. *Behavioral Disorders, 37*(2), 78–86.

Mackie, L., & Law, J. (2010). Pragmatic language and the child with emotional/behavioural difficulties (EBD): A pilot study exploring the interaction between behaviour and communication disability. *International Journal of Language and Communication Disorders, 45*(4), 397–410.

Mattison, R. E., Hooper, S. R., & Carlson, G. A. (2006). Neuropsychological characteristics of special education students with serious emotional/behavioral disorders. *Behavioral Disorders, 31*(2), 176–188.

Mayer, M., Lochman, J., & Van Acker, R. (2005). Introduction to the special issue: Cognitive-behavioral interventions with students with EBD. *Behavioral Disorders, 30*(3), 197–212.

Menzies, H. M., & Lane, K. L. (2011). Using self-regulation strategies and functional assessment-based interventions to provide academic and behavioral support to students at risk within three-tiered models of prevention. *Preventing School Failure: Alternative Education for Children and Youth, 55*(4), 181–191.

Merrell, K. W., & Walker, H. M. (2004). Deconstructing a definition: Social maladjustment versus emotional disturbance and moving the EBD field forward. *Psychology in the Schools, 41*(8), 899–910.

Miller, M. J., Lane, K. L., & Wehby, J. (2005). Social skills instruction for students with high-incidence disabilities: A school-based intervention to address acquisition deficits. *Preventing School Failure, 49*(2), 27–39.

Moreno, G., Wong-Lo, M., & Bullock, L. M. (2014). Assisting students from diverse backgrounds with challenging behaviors: Incorporating a culturally attuned functional behavioral assessment in prereferral services. *Preventing School Failure: Alternative Education for Children and Youth, 58*(1), 58–68.

Mueller, T. G., Bassett, D. S., Brewer, R. D. (2012). Planning for the future: A model for using the principles of transition to guide the development of behavior intervention plans. *Intervention in School and Clinic, 48*(1), 38–46.

Murray, J., Irving, B., Farrington, D. P., Colman, I., & Bloxsom, C. A. J. (2010). Very early predictors of conduct problems and crime: Results from a national cohort study. *Journal of Child Psychology and Psychiatry, 51*(11), 1198–1207.

National Center for Education Statistics. (2013). *Table 48. Children 3 to 21 years old served under Individuals with Disabilities Education Act, Part B, by type of disability: Selected years, 1976–77 through 2010–11.* Retrieved December 12, 2014, from http://nces.ed.gov/programs/digest/d12/tables/dt12_048.asp.

National Institute of Mental Health. (2008). *Bipolar disorder in children and teens.* Retrieved March 25, 2009, from www.nimh.nih.gov/health/publications/bipolar-disorder-in-children-and-teens-easy-to-read/index.shtml.

National Mental Health Information Center. (2006). *National systems of care a promising solution for children with serious emotional disturbances and their families.* Washington, D.C.: Author. Retrieved July 19, 2006, from www.mentalhealth.samhsa.gov/publications/allpubs/Ca-0030/default.asp.

Nelson, J. R., Stage, S., Duppong-Hurley, K., Synhorst, L., & Epstein, M. H. (2007). Risk factors predictive of the problem behavior of children at risk for emotional and behavioral disorders. *Council for Exceptional Children, 73*(3), 367.

Nochajski, S. M., & Schweitzer, J. A. (2014). Promoting school to work transition for students with emotional/behavioral disorders. *Work: Journal of Prevention, Assessment, & Rehabilitation, 48*(3), 413–422

Nungesser, N. R., & Watkins, R. V. (2005). Preschool teachers' perceptions and reactions to challenging classroom behavior: Implications for speech-language pathologists. *Language, Speech, and Hearing Services in Schools, 36*, 139–151.

Pedersen, W., & Mastekaasa, A. (2011). Conduct disorder symptoms and subsequent pregnancy, child-birth and abortion: A population-based longitudinal study of adolescents. *Journal of Adolescence, 34*(5), 1025–1033.

Polsgrove, L., & Smith, S. (2004). Informed practice in teaching students self-control. In R. Rutherford, M. M. Quinn, & S. Mathur (Eds.), *Research in emotional and behavioral disorders.* New York: The Guilford Press.

Powell, N. P., Boxmeyer, C. L., Baden, R., Stromeyer, S., Minney, J. A., Mushtaq, A., & Lochman, J. E. (2011). Assessing and treating aggression and conduct problems in schools: Implications from the Coping Power Program. *Psychology in the Schools, 48*(3), 233–242.

Quinn, M. M., & Poirier, J. M. (2004). Linking prevention research with policy: Examining the costs and outcomes of the failure to prevent emotional and behavioral disorders. In R. B. Rutherford, M. M. Quinn, & S. R. Mathur (Eds.), *Handbook of research in emotional and behavioral disorders* (pp. 78–97). New York: Guilford Press.

Reinke, W. M., Herman, K. C., & Tucker, C. M. (2006). Building and sustaining communities that prevent mental disorders: Lessons from the field of special education. *Psychology in the Schools, 43*(3), 313–329.

Roberts, C., & Bishop, B. (2005). Depression. In T. P. Gullotta & G. R. Adams (Eds.), *Handbook of adolescent behavioral problems* (pp. 205–230). New York: Springer Science + Business Media, Inc.

Robinson, T. R. (2007). Cognitive behavioral interventions: Strategies to help students make wise behavioral choices. *Beyond Behavior, 17*(1), 7–13.

Rorie, M., Gottfredson, D. C., Cross, A., Wilson, D., & Connell, N, M. (2011). Structure and deviancy training in after-school programs. *Journal of Adolescence, 34*(1), 105–117.

Rose, C. A., & Espelage, D. L. (2012). Risk and protective factors associated with the bullying involvement of students with emotional and behavioral disorders. *Behavioral Disorders, 37*(3), 133–148.

Rosenberg, M. S., Wilson, R., Maheady, L., & Sindelar, P. T. (2004). *Educating students with behavior disorders,* 3rd ed. Boston: Allyn & Bacon.

Rutter, M. (2006). *Genes and behavior: Nature-nurture interplay explained*. Malden, MA: Blackwell Publishing.

Ryan, J. B., Pierce, C. D., & Mooney, P. (2008). Evidence-based teaching strategies for students with EBD. *Beyond Behavior, 17*(3), 22–29.

Ryan, J. B., Reid, R., & Epstein, M. H. (2004). Peer-mediated intervention studies on academic achievement for students with EBD: A review. *Remedial and Special Education, 25*(6), 330–341.

Sampers, J., Anderson, K. G., Hartung, C. M., & Scambler, D. J. (2001). Parent training programs for young children with behavior problems. *Infant Toddler Intervention: The Transdisciplinary Journal, 11*, 91–110.

Scibarras, E., Ohan, J. & Anderson, V. (2012). Bully and peer victimization in adolescent girls with attention-deficit/hyperactivity disorder. *Child Psychiatry & Human Development, 43*, 254–270.

Shoenfeld, N. A., & Konopasek, D., (2007). Medicine in the classroom: A review of psychiatric medications for students with emotional or behavioral disorders. *Beyond Behavior, 17*(1), 14–20.

Shores, R. E., & Wehby, J. H. (1999). Analyzing the classroom social behavior of students with EBD. *Journal of Emotional and Behavioral Disorders, 7*(4), 194–199.

Shriner, J. G., & Wehby, J. H. (2004). Accountability and assessment for students with emotional and behavioral disorders. In R. B. Rutherford, M. M. Quinn, & S. R. Mathur (Eds.), *Handbook of research in emotional and behavioral disorders* (pp. 216–231). New York: Guilford Press.

Sitlington, P. L., & Neubert, D. A. (2004). Preparing youths with emotional or behavioral disorders for transition to adult life: Can it be done within the standards-based reform movement? *Behavioral Disorders, 29*(3), 279–288.

SymTrend. (2012). *SymTrend ADL*. Belmont, MA: SymTrend.

U.S. Department of Education. (2006). *Federal Register*, August 14, 2006, Part II, 34 CFR Parts 300 and 301. Assistance to states for the education of children with disabilities and preschool grants for children; Final rule. Washington, D.C.: Author.

U.S. Department of Education. (2013a). *Thirty-fifth annual (2013) report to congress on the implementation of the individuals with disabilities act (vol. 1)*. Washington, D.C.: Author.

U.S. Department of Education. (2013b). Labor force participation, employment, and unemployment of persons 16–24 years old who are not enrolled in school, by age group, sex, race/ethnicity, and educational attainment: 2010, 2011, 2012 (Table 501.20). *Digest of Educational Statistics, 2013*. Retrieved from http://nces.ed.gov/programs/digest/d13/tables/dt13_501.20.asp

U.S. Department of Education. (2014). *Thirty-sixth annual report to Congress on the implementation of the Individuals with Disabilities Education Act, 2014*. Washington, D.C.: Author.

Vazsonyi, A.T. & Huang, L. (2010). Where self-control comes from: On the development of self-control and its relationship to deviance over time. *Developmental Psychology, 46*(1), 245–257.

Vieno, A., Nation, M. Pastore, M., & Santinello, M. (2009). Parenting and antisocial behavior: A model of the relationship between adolescent self-disclosure, parental closeness, parental control, and adolescent antisocial behavior. *Developmental Psychology, 45*(6), 1509–1519.

Vincent, C. G., & Tobin, T.J. (2011). The relationship between implementation of school-wide positive behavior support (sw-pbs) and disciplinary exclusion of students from various ethnic backgrounds with and without disabilities, *Journal of Emotional and Behavioral Disorders, 19*(4), 782–790.

Wagner, M., Kutash, K., Duchnowski, A.J., Epstein, M. H., & Sumi, W. C. (2005). The children and youth we serve: A national picture of the characteristics of students with emotional disturbances receiving special education. *Journal of Emotional and Behavioral Disorders Summer, 13*(2), 79–96.

Walker, H. M., Severson, H. H., & Feil, E. G. (2014). *Systematic screening for behavior disorders,* 2nd ed. Eugene, OR: Pacific Northwest Publishing.

Whitted. K.S. (2011). Understanding how social and emotional skill deficits contribute to school failure. *Preventing School Failure: Alternative Education for Children and Youth, 55*(1), 10–16.

Wicks-Nelson, R., & Israel, A. C. (2006). *Behavior disorders of childhood,* 6th ed. Upper Saddle River, NJ: Prentice Hall.

Wiley, A. L, Brigham, F. J., Kauffman, J. M., & Bogan, J. E. (2013). Disproportionate poverty, conservatism, and the disproportionate identification of minority students with emotional and behavioral disorders. *Education & Treatment of Children, 36*(4), 29–50.

Witt, J. C., Daly, E. M., & Noell, G. (2000). *Functional assessments: A step-by-step guide to solving academic and behavior problems*. Longmont, CO: Sopris West.

Witt, J. C., VanDerHeyden, A. M., & Gilbertson, D. (2004). Instruction and classroom management. In R. B. Rutherford, M. M. Quinn, & S. R. Mathur (Eds.), *Handbook of research in emotional and behavioral disorders* (pp. 426–445). New York: Guilford Press.

Woodruff, D. W., Osher, D., Hoffman, C. C., Gruner, A., King, M. A., Snow, S. T., & McIntire, J. C. (1999). The role of education in a system of care: Effectively serving children with emotional or behavioral disorders. Systems of Care: Promising Practices in Children's Mental Health, 1998 Series, Vol. III. Washington, D.C.: Center for Effective Collaboration and Practice, American Institutes for Research.

Woolsey, L., & Katz-Leavey, J. (2008). *Transitioning youth with mental health needs to meaningful employment and independent living*. Washington, D.C.: National Clearinghouse on Workforce and Disability for Youth, Institute for Educational Leadership.

Young, E. L., Calderella, P., Richardson, M. J., and Young K. R. (2011). *Positive behavior support in secondary schools: A practical guide*. New York: Guilford Press.

Young, E. L., Sabbah, H. Y., Young, B. J., Reiser, M. L., & Richardson (2010). Gender differences and similarities in a screening process for emotional and behavioral risks in secondary schools, *Journal of Emotional and Behavioral Disorders, 18*(4) 225–235.

## Chapter 9

AAIDD. (2013). *Definition of Intellectual Disability* Retrieved April 11, 2015, from http://aaidd.org/intellectual-disability/definition#.VSm_Cvm AHXo.

American Psychiatric Association. (2013). *Diagnostic and statistical manual of mental disorders* (5th ed.). Washington, DC: Author.

The ARC. (20011a). *Intellectual disability*. Washington, D.C.: The ARC. Retrieved April 11, 2015, from www.thearc.org/learn-about/intellectual-disability.

The ARC. (2015). *Life in the community*. Washington, D.C.: The ARC. Retrieved February 9, 2015, from www.thearc.org/who-we-are/position-statements/life-in-the-community.

Batshaw, M., Pellegrino, L., & Rozien, N. J. (2007). *Children with disabilities*, 6th ed. Baltimore: Paul H. Brookes.

Beirne-Smith, M., Patton, J. R., & Hill, S. (2010). *Introduction to intellectual disabilities*, 8th ed. Upper Saddle River, NJ: Merrill.

Berk, L. E. (2011). *Development through the lifespan*, 2nd ed. Upper Saddle River, NJ: Prentice-Hall.

Browder, D. M., Ahlgrim-Delzell, L. A., Courtade-Little, G., & Snell, M. E. (2011). General curriculum access. In M. E. Snell & F. Brown (Eds.), *Introduction to students with severe disabilities*, 7th ed. (pp. 489–525). Upper Saddle River, NJ: Prentice-Hall.

Browder, D. M., Jimenez, B. A., & Trela, K. (2012). Grade-aligned math instruction for secondary students with moderate intellectual disability. *Education and Training in Autism and Developmental Disabilities, 47*, 373–388.

Browder, D. M., & Spooner, F. (2011). *Teaching students with moderate and severe disabilities.* New York: Guilford Press.

Buxton, R. (2015). *Glee star has 1 request for fans: Stop using the "R-word."* Huffington Post. Retrieved February 7, 2015, www.huffingtonpost.com/2015/02/02/glee-actress-lauren-potter-r-word_n_6581562.html

Centers for Disease Control and Prevention. (2015). Measles. Retrieved February 8, 2015, from www.cdc.gov/measles/about/.

Children's Defense Fund. (2011). *The state of America's children*. Washington, D.C.: Author.

Crockett, M., & Hardman, M. L. (2009). Expected outcomes and emerging values. In J. McDonnell & M. L. Hardman, *Successful transition programs: Pathways for students with intellectual and developmental disabilities* (pp. 25–42). Los Angeles: Sage Publishing Company.

Drew, C. J., & Hardman, M. L. (2007). *Intellectual disabilities across the lifespan*, 9th ed. Columbus, OH: Merrill.

Falcomata, T., Wacker, D., Ringdahl, J., Vinquist, K., & Dutt, A. (2013). An evaluation of generalization of mands during functional communication training. *Journal of Applied Behavior Analysis, 46*(2), 444–454.

Flores, M., Hill, D., Faciane, L., Edwards, M., Tapley, S., & Dowling, S. (2014). The Apple iPad as assistive technology for story-based interventions. *Journal of Special Education Technology, 29*(2), 27–37.

Gargiulo, R. M. (2011). *Special education in a contemporary society: An Introduction to exceptionality*. London: Sage Publishing.

Hua, Y., Morgan, B., Kaldenberg, E., & Goo, M. (2012). Cognitive strategy instruction for functional mathematical skill: Effects for young adults with intellectual disability. *Education & Training in Autism & Developmental Disabilities, 47*(3), 345–358.

Kaiser, A. P. (2000). Teaching functional communication skills. In M. E. Snell & F. Brown (Eds.), *Instruction of persons with severe disabilities*, 5th ed. (pp. 453–492). Columbus, OH: Merrill.

Kagohara, D., van der Meer, L., Ramdoss, S., O'Reilly, M. F., Lancioni, G., Davis, T., & Sigafoos, J. (2013). Using iPods® and iPads® in teaching programs for individuals with developmental disabilities: A systematic review. *Research In Developmental Disabilities, 34*(1), 147–156.

Katims, D. S. (2000). Literacy instruction for people

with mental retardation: Historical highlights and contemporary analysis. *Education and Training in Mental Retardation and Developmental Disabilities, 35*(1), 3–15.

Kittler, P., Krinsky-McHale, S. J., & Devenny, D. A. (2004). Semantic and phonological loop effects on visual working memory in middle-age adults with mental retardation. *American Journal on Mental Retardation, 109*(6), 467–480.

Lakin, C. (2005). Introduction. In K. C. Lakin & A. Turnbull (Eds.), *National goals for people with intellectual and developmental disabilities* (pp. 1–13). Washington, D.C.: The ARC of the U.S. and the American Association on Intellectual and Developmental Disabilities (formerly AAMR).

Maulik, P. K, Mascarenhas, M. N., Mathers, C. D., Dua, T., & Saxena S. (2011, March-April). Prevalence of intellectual disability: A meta-analysis of population-based study. *Research on Developmental Disabilities, 32*(2), 419–436.

McDonnell, A. P., Hawken, L. S., Johnston, S. S., Kidder, J. E., Lynes, M. J., & McDonnell, J. J. (2014). Emergent literacy practices and support for children with disabilities: A national survey. *Education & Treatment of Children, 37*(3), 495–529.

Moore, B. J., & Montgomery, J. K. (2008). *Making a difference for America's children: Speech–language pathologists in public schools.* Greenville, SC: Super Duper Publications.

National Down Syndrome Society. (2015). Down syndrome facts. Retrieved February 5, 2015, from www.ndss.org /Down-Syndrome/Down -Syndrome-Facts/.

National Organization on Fetal Alcohol Syndrome. (2015). *What is fetal alcohol syndrome?* Retrieved April 11, 2015, from www.nofas.org /faqs/what-is-fetal -alcohol-syndrome-fas/.

President's Committee for People with Intellectual Disabilities. (2014). *Fact sheet: The role of the PCPID.* Retrieved February 8, 2015, from www.acl.gov/programs /aidd/Programs/PCPID/.

Siperstein, G. N., Heyman, M., & Stokes, J. E. (2014). Pathways to employment: A national survey of adults with intellectual disabilities. *Journal of Vocational Rehabilitation, 41*(3), 165–178.

Sternberg, R. J. (2008). *Cognitive psychology,* 5th ed. Florence, KY: Wadsworth.

Thurlow, M., Dillon, D., Abedi, J., & Brauen, M. (2012). PARA Accessible Reading Assessment Reports: Developing and Researching an Accessible Reading Assessment for Students with Disabilities. Partnership for Accessible Reading Assessment (PARA), Institute on Community Integration.

U.S. Department of Education. (2014). *The 36th Annual Report to Congress on the Implementation of the Individuals with Disabilities Education Act.* Washington, D.C.: U.S. Government Printing Office.

Wehman, P. (2011). *Essentials of transition planning.* Baltimore: Paul H. Brookes.

Werner, S., & Stawski, M. (2012). Mental health: Knowledge, attitudes and training of professionals on dual diagnosis of intellectual disability and psychiatric disorder. *Journal of Intellectual Disability Research, 56*(3), 291–304.

Westling, D., & Fox, L. (2009). *Teaching students with severe disabilities,* 4th ed. Upper Saddle River, NJ: Merrill/Prentice Hall.

## Chapter 10

Aarts, R., Demir, S., & Vallen, T. (2011). Characteristics of academic language register occurring in caretaker-child interaction: Development and validation of a coding scheme. *Language Learning, 61*(4), 1173–1221.

Adams, C. (2008). Intervention for children with pragmatic language impairments. In C. F. Norbury, J. B. Tomblin, & D. V. M. Bishop (Eds.), *Understanding developmental language disorders: From theory to practice* (pp. 189–204). New York: Psychology Press.

Adams, C., Lockton, E., Freed, J., Gaile, J., Earl, G., McBean, K., ... Law, J. (2012). The Social Communication Intervention Project: A randomized controlled trial of the effectiveness of speech and language therapy for school-age children who have pragmatic and social communication problems with or without autism spectrum disorder. *International Journal of Language & Communication Disorders, 47*(3), 233–244.

Allen, M. M. (2013). Intervention efficacy and intensity for children with speech sound disorder. *Journal of Speech, Language, and Hearing Research, 56*(3), 865–877.

American Psychiatric Association. (2013). *Diagnostic and statistical manual of mental disorders,* 5th ed. Washington, D.C.: Author.

American Speech-Language -Hearing Association. (2004). *Evidence-based practice in communication disorders: An introduction* [Technical Report]. Retrieved from www.asha.org/policy /TR2004-00001.htm.

American Speech-Language-Hearing Association (2015a). *The big nine.* Retrieved from www.asha.org/Events /SLP-Summit-Glossary/.

American Speech-Language-Hearing Association. (2015b). *Speech sound disorders— Articulation and phonology.* Retrieved April 13, 2015, from www.asha .org/PRPSpecificTopic.as px?folderid=8589935321 &section=Assessment.

American Speech-Language-Hearing Association. (2015c). *Stuttering.* Retrieved April 13, 2015, from www .asha.org/public/speech /disorders/stuttering/.

American Speech-Language-Hearing Association. (2015d). *Social communication disorders in school-age children.* Retrieved April 13, 2015, from www .asha.org/Practice-Portal /Clinical-Topics/Social -Communication-Disorders -in-School-Age-Children/.

Bastiaanse, R., & Thompson, C. K. (2012). *Perspectives on agrammatism*. Hove, East Sussex, UK: Psychology Press.

Battle, D. E. (2009). Language and communication disorders in culturally and linguistically diverse children. In D. K. Bernstein & E. Tiegerman-Farber (Eds.), *Language and communication disorders in children*, 6th ed. (pp. 536–575). Boston: Allyn & Bacon.

Bayley, N. (2005). *Bayley scales of infant and toddler development* (3rd ed.). Boston: Pearson.

Bernstein, D. K., & Levy, S. (2009). Language development: A review. In D. K. Bernstein & E. Tiegerman-Farber (Eds.), *Language and communication disorders in children,* 6th ed. (pp. 28–100). Boston: Allyn & Bacon.

Beukelman, D. R., & Mirenda, P. (2012). *Augmentative and alternative communication: Supporting children and adults with complex communication needs*, 4th ed. Baltimore: Paul H. Brookes.

Boone, D. R., McFarlane, S. C., Von Berg, S. L., & Zraick, R. I. (2010). *Voice and voice therapy*, 8th ed. (International Edition). Boston: Pearson.

Boyle, J., McCartney, E., O'Hare, A., & Law, J. (2010). Intervention for mixed receptive-expressive language impairment: A review. *Developmental Medicine & Child Neurology, 52*(11), 994–999.

Bretherton-Furness, J., & Ward, D. (2012). Lexical access, story re-telling and sequencing skills in adults who clutter and those who do not. *Journal of Fluency Disorders, 37*(4), 214–224.

Brinton, B., Fujiki, M., & Baldridge, M. (2010). The trajectory of language impairment into adolescence: What four young women can teach us. *Seminars in Speech and Language, 31*(2), 122–133.

Carey, B., O'Brian, S., Onslow, M., Block, S., Jones, M., & Packman, A. (2010). Randomized controlled non-inferiority trial of a telehealth treatment for chronic stuttering: The Camperdown Program. *The International Journal of Language & Communication Disorders, 45*(1), 108–120.

Chabon, S. S., & Cohn, E. R. (2011). *Communication disorders casebook: Learning by example.* Boston: Pearson.

Chang, S., & Zhu, D. C. (2013). Neural network connectivity differences in children who stutter. *Brain: A Journal of Neurology, 136*(12), 3709–3726.

Chavira, D. A., Garland, A. F., Daley, S., & Hough, R. (2008). The impact of medical comorbidity on mental health and functional health outcomes among children with anxiety disorders. *Journal of Developmental & Behavioral Pediatrics, 29*(5), 394–402.

Daymut, J. A. (2009). *Types of articulation errors: A simple guide.* Retrieved April 6, 2015, from www.superduperinc.com/handouts/pdf/201_TypesofArticulationErrors.pdf.

Drew, C. J., & Hardman, M. L. (2007). *Intellectual disabilities across the lifespan*, 9th ed. Columbus, OH: Merrill.

Dyches, T. T., Carter, N. J., & Prater, M. A. (2012). *A teacher's guide to communicating with parents: Practical strategies for developing successful relationships.* Upper Saddle River, NJ: Pearson.

Fama, M. E., & Turkeltaub, P. E. (2014). Treatment of poststroke aphasia: Current practice and new directions. *Seminars in Neurology, 34*(5), 504–513.

Ferrand, C. T. (2012). *Voice disorders: Scope of theory and practice.* Boston: Allyn & Bacon.

Flynn, T. W., & St. Louis, K. O. (2011). Changing adolescent attitudes toward stuttering. *Journal of Fluency Disorders, 36*(2), 110–121.

Fogle, P. T. (2013). *Essentials of communication sciences and disorders.* Florence, KY: Cengage Learning.

Freed, D. R. (2012). *Motor speech disorders & treatment,* 2nd ed. Florence, KY: Cengage Learning, Inc.

Froemling, K. K., Grice, G. L., & Skinner, J. F. (2011). *Communication: The handbook.* Boston: Pearson.

Gray, C. A. (1995). Teaching children with autism to "read" social situations. In K. A. Quill (Ed.), *Teaching children with autism: Strategies to enhance communication and socialization.* Albany, NY: Delmar.

Hartmann, E. (2008). Phonological awareness in preschoolers with spoken language impairment: Toward a better understanding casual relationships and effective intervention. A constructive comment on Rvachew and Grawburg's (2006) study. *Journal of Speech, Language, and Hearing Research, 51*(5), 1215–1218.

Johnston, S. S., Reichle, J., Feeley, K. M., & Jones, E. A. (2012). *AAC strategies for individuals with moderate to severe disabilities.* Baltimore: Paul H. Brookes Publishing Company.

Kaderavek, J. N. (2011). *Language disorders in children: Fundamental concepts of assessment and intervention.* Boston: Allyn & Bacon.

Klinto, K., Salameh, E., Svensson, H. & Lohmander, A. (2011). The impact of speech material on speech judgement in children with and without cleft palate. *International Journal of Language & Communication Disorders, 46*, 348–360.

Kosowski, T. R., Weathers, W. M., Wolfswinkel, E. M., & Ridgway, E. B. (2012). Cleft palate. *Seminars in Plastic Surgery, 26*(4), 164–169.

Kummer, A. W. (2006). Resonance disorders and nasal emissions: Evaluation and treatment using "low tech" and "no tech" procedures. *The ASHA Leader.* Retrieved from www.asha.org/Publications/leader/2006/060207/060207c.htm.

Manasco, M. H. (2014). *Introduction to neurogenic communication disorders*, 8th ed. St. Louis, MO: Mosby.

Martin, N. (2009). The roles of semantic and phonologic processing in short-term memory and learning: Evidence from aphasia. In A. S. C. Thorn & M. P. A. Page (Eds.), *Interactions between short-term and long-term memory in the verbal domain* (pp. 220–243). New York: Psychology Press.

Mayor, J. & Plunkett, K. (2014). Shared understanding and idiosyncratic expression in early vocabularies. *Developmental Science, 17*(3), 412–423.

McKinnon, D. H., McLeod, S., & Reilly, S. (2007). The prevalence of stuttering, voice, and speech-sound disorders in primary school students in Australia. *Language, Speech, and Hearing in the Schools, 38*(1), 5–15.

McLaughlin, M. (2011). Speech and language delay in children. *American Family Physician, 83*(10), 1183–1188.

Meinzen-Derr, J., Wiley, S. Grether, S., & Choo, D. I. (2011). Children with cochlear implants and developmental disabilities: A language skills study with developmentally matched hearing peers. *Research in Developmental Disabilities, 32*(2), 757–767.

Miller, C. A., & Wagstaff, D. A. (2011). Behavioral profiles associated with auditory processing disorder and specific language impairment. *Journal of Communication Disorders, 44*(6), 745–763.

Moore, B., & Montgomery, J. (2008). *Making a difference for America's children: Speech-language pathologists in public schools*, 2nd ed. Austin, TX: Pro-Ed.

National Institute on Deafness and Other Communication Disorders (2014). *Stuttering*. Retrieved from www.nidcd.nih.gov/health/voice/pages/stutter.aspx.

Norbury, C. F. (2014). Practitioner review: Social (pragmatic) communication disorder conceptualization, evidence and clinical implications. *Journal of Child Psychology and Psychiatry, 55*(3), 204–216.

Nyberg, J., Peterson, P., & Lohmander, A. (2014). Speech outcomes at age 5 and 10 years in unilateral cleft lip and palate after one-stage palatal repair with minimal incision technique: A longitudinal perspective. *International Journal of Pediatric Otorhinolaryngology, 78*(10), 1662–1670.

Owens, R. E., Jr. (2008). *Language development: An introduction*, 7th ed. (International ed.). Boston: Pearson.

Owens, R. E., Jr. (2010). *Language disorders: A functional approach to assessment and intervention*, 5th ed. Boston: Pearson.

Owens, R. E., Jr. (2011). Development of communication, language, and speech. In N. B. Anderson & G. H. Shames (Eds.), *Human communication disorders: An introduction*, 8th ed. (pp. 22–58). Boston: Allyn & Bacon.

Owens, R. E., Metz, D. E., & Farinella, K. A. (2011). *Introduction to communication disorders: A lifespan approach*, 4th ed. Boston: Allyn & Bacon.

Paul, D., & Roth, F. (2011). Guiding principles and clinical applications for speech–language pathology practice in early intervention. *Language, Speech, and Hearing Services in Schools, 42*(3), 320–330.

Pfeiffer, W. S., & Adkins, K. E. (2012). *Technical communication fundamentals.* Boston: Longman.

Phillips, D. A., & Lowenstein, A. E. (2010). Early care, education, and child development. *Annual Review of Psychology, 62*, 483–500.

Plante, E. M., & Beeson, P. M. (2013). *Communication and communication disorders: A clinical introduction*, 4th ed. Boston: Allyn & Bacon.

Plutarch (75). *Demosthenes.* Translated by John Dryden. Retrieved from http://classics.mit.edu/Plutarch/demosthe.html.

Portone, C., Johns, M. M., & Hapner, E. R. (2008). A review of patient adherence to the recommendation for voice therapy. *Journal of Voice, 22*(2), 192–196.

Przepiorka, A. M., Blachnio, A., St. Louis, K. O., & Wozniak, T. (2013). Public attitudes toward stuttering in Poland. *International Journal of Communication Disorders, 48*(6), 703–714.

Radziewicz, C., & Antonellis, S. (2009). Children with hearing loss: Considerations and implications. In D. K. Bernstein & E. Tiegerman-Farber (Eds.), *Language and communication disorders in children*, 6th ed. (pp. 370–401). Boston: Allyn & Bacon.

Ramig, P. R., & Dodge, D. M. (2010). *The child and adolescent stuttering treatment & activity resource guide,* 2nd ed. Florence, KY: Cengage Learning.

Rapin, I., & Allen, D. A. (1983). Developmental language disorders: Nosologic considerations. In U. Kirk (Ed.), *Neuropsychology of language, reading, and spelling* (pp. 155–184). New York: Academic Press.

Raposa, K. A. & Perlman, S. P. (2012). *Treating the dental patient with developmental disorders.* New York: Wiley.

Reed, V. A. (2012). *Introduction to children with language disorders*, 4th ed. Boston: Pearson.

Richardson, L. P., Russo, J. E., Lozano, P., McCauley, E., & Katon, W. (2008). The effect of comorbid anxiety and depressive disorders on health care utilization and costs among adolescents with asthma. *General Hospital Psychiatry, 30*(5), 398–406.

Robinson, N. B., & Robb, M. P. (2009). Early communication assessment and intervention: A dynamic process. In D. K. Bernstein & E. Tiegerman-Farber (Eds.), *Language and communication disorders in children*, 6th ed. (pp. 102–167). Boston: Allyn & Bacon.

Sampson, M., & Faroqi-Shah, Y. (2011). Investigation of self-monitoring in fluent aphasia with jargon. *Aphasiology, 25*(4), 506–528.

Schwartz, H. D. (2012). *A primer on communication and communicative disorders.* Boston: Pearson.

Snowling, M., & Hulme, C. (2012). Interventions

for children's language and literacy difficulties. *International Journal of Language & Communication Disorders, 47*(1), 27–34.

Starmer, H. M., Liu, Z., Akst, L. M., & Gourin, C. (2014). Attendance in voice therapy: Can an interdisciplinary care model have an impact? *Annals of Otology, Rhinology, and Laryngology, 123*(2), 117–123.

Steinfatt, T. M. (2009). Definitions of communication. In S. W. Littlejohn & K. A. Foss (Eds.), *Encyclopedia of communication theory*. Los Angeles: Sage.

Syrja, R. C. (2011). *How to reach and teach English language learners: Practical strategies to ensure success*. New York: Wiley.

Tager-Flusberg, H., Rogers, S., Cooper, J. Landa, R., Lord, C., Paul, R., … Yoder, P. (2009). Defining spoken language benchmarks and selecting measures of expressive language development for young children with autism spectrum disorders. *Journal of Speech, Language, and Hearing Research, 52*(3), 643–652.

Tiegerman-Farber, E. (2009). The role of the SLP. In D. K. Bernstein & E. Tiegerman-Farber (Eds.), *Language and communication disorders in children*, 6th ed. (pp. 404–435). Boston: Allyn & Bacon.

Tierney, C. D., Kurtz, M., Panchik, A., & Pitterle, K. (2014). "Look at me when I am talking to you": Evidence and assessment of social pragmatics interventions for children with autism and social communication disorders. *Current Opinion in Pediatrics, 26*, 259–264.

Torras-Mañá, M., Guillamón-Valenzuela, M., Ramírez-Mallafré, A., Brun-Gasca, C., & Fornieles-Deu, A. (2014). Usefulness of the Bayley Scales of Infant and Toddler Development, Third Edition, in the early diagnosis of language disorder. *Psicothema, 26*(3), 349–356.

U.S. Department of Education, Office of Special Education Programs. (2014). *The 36th annual report to Congress on the Implementation of the Individuals with Disabilities Education Act*. Washington, D.C.: U.S. Government Printing Office.

Vinson, B. P. (2012). *Language disorders across the lifespan*, 3rd ed. Florence, KY: Cengage Learning.

Vukovic, M., Vuksanovic, J., & Vukovic, I. (2008). Comparison of the recovery patterns of language and cognitive functions in patients with post-traumatic language processing deficits and in patients with aphasia following a stroke. *Journal of Communication Disorders, 41*(6), 531–552.

Weber-Fox, C., & Hampton, A. (2008). Stuttering and natural speech processing semantic and syntactic constraints on verbs. *Journal of Speech, Language, and Hearing Research, 51*(5), 1058–1071.

Weiss, A. L. (2009). Planning language intervention for young children. In D. K. Bernstein & E. Tiegerman-Farber (Eds.), *Language and communication disorders in children*, 6th ed. (pp. 436–495). Boston: Allyn & Bacon.

Williams, D. F. (2011). *Communication sciences and disorders: An introduction to the professions*. New York: Psychology Press.

Yairi, E., & Seery, C. H. (2011). *Stuttering: Foundations and clinical applications*. Boston: Pearson.

## Chapter 11

Abrahams, B. E., & Geschwind, D. H. (2008). Advances in autism genetics: On the threshold of a new neurobiology. *Nature Review Genetics, 9*(5), 341–356.

Alexander, J. L., Ayres, K. M., & Smith, K. A. (2015). Training teachers in evidence-based practice for individuals with autism spectrum disorder: A review of the literature. *Teacher Education and Special Education, 38*(1), 13–27.

American Psychiatric Association. (2000). *Diagnostic and statistical manual of mental disorders (DSM-IV-TR)*, 4th ed. (text rev.). Washington, D.C.: Author.

American Psychiatric Association. (2013). *Diagnostic and statistical manual of mental disorders (DSM-5)*, 5th ed. Washington, D.C.: Author.

Anckarsater, H. (2006). Central nervous changes in social dysfunction: Autism, aggression, and psychopathology. *Brain Research Bulletin, 69*(3), 259–265.

Ashbaker, B. Y., Dyches, T. T., Prater, M. A., & Sileo, N. M. (2012). Historical and legal foundations of family involvement in special education. In N. Sileo & M. A. Prater (Eds.), *Working with families of children with special needs: Family and professional partnerships and roles* (pp. 1–22). Boston: Pearson.

Asperger, H. (1944). Die 'Autistischen psychopathen' im kindesalter. *Arch Psychiatry, 117*, 76–136.

Autism Speaks (2011). *Autism: Should my child take medicine for challenging behavior?: A decision aid for parents of children with autism spectrum disorder*. Autism Speaks (Official Blog), September 14.

Autism Speaks (2014). *State Initiatives*. Retrieved from www.autismspeaks.org/state-initiatives.

Bauminger, N., Solomon, M., Aviezer, A., Heung, K., Brown, J., & Rogers, S. J., (2008). Friendship in high-functioning children with autism spectrum disorder: Mixed and non-mixed dyads. *Journal of Autism and Developmental Disorders, 38*(7), 1211–1229.

Becerra, T. A., von Ehrenstein, O. S., Heck, J. E., et al. (2014). Autism spectrum disorders and race, ethnicity, and nativity: A population-based study. *Pediatrics, 134*(1), e63–e71.

Bellini, S., & Akullian, J. (2007). A meta-analysis of video modeling and video self-modeling interventions for children and adolescents with autism spectrum disorders. *Exceptional Children, 73*(3), 264–287.

Bettelheim, B. (1967). *The empty fortress: Infantile autism and the birth of the self.* New York: Free Press.

Billstedt, E., Gillberg, I. C., & Gillberg, C. (2011). Aspects of quality of life in adults diagnosed with autism in childhood: A population-based study. *Autism, 15*(1), 7–20.

Bitterman, A., Daley, T. C., Misra, S., Carlson, E., & Markowitz, J. (2008). A national sample of preschoolers with autism spectrum disorders: Special education services and parent satisfaction. *Journal of Autism and Developmental Disorders, 38*(8), 1509–1517.

Blacher, J., & McIntyre, L. L. (2006). Syndrome specificity and behavioral disorders in young adults with intellectual disability: Cultural differences in family impact. *Journal of Intellectual Disability Research, 50*(3) 184–198.

Bolton, P. F., Golding, J., Emond, A., & Steer, C. D. (2012). Autism spectrum disorder and autistic traits in the Avon Longitudinal Study of Parents and Children: Precursors and early signs. *Journal of the American Academy of Child and Adolescent Child Psychology, 51*(3), 249–260.

Bondy, A., & Frost, L. (2008). *Autism 24/7: A family guide to learning at home and in the community.* Bethesda, MD: Woodbine House.

Bruns, D. A., & Thompson, S. D. (2012). *Feeding challenges in young children: Strategies and specialized interventions for success.* Baltimore: Brookes.

Burton, C. E., Anderson, D. H., Prater, M. A., & Dyches, T. T. (2013). Video self-modeling on an iPad to teach functional math skills to adolescents with autism and intellectual disability. *Focus on Autism and Other Developmental Disabilities, 28*(2), 67–77.

Butrimaviciute, R., & Grieve, A. (2014). Carers' experiences of being exposed to challenging behavior in services for autism spectrum disorders. *Autism, 18*(8), 882–890.

Cannon, L., Kenworthy, L., Alexander, K. C., Werner, M. A., & Anthony, L. (2011). *Unstuck and on target! An executive function curriculum to improve flexibility for children with autism spectrum disorders, Research edition.* Baltimore: Brookes.

Cappadocia, M., Weiss, J. A., & Pepler, D. (2012). Bullying experiences among children and youth with autism spectrum disorders. *Journal of Autism and Developmental Disorders, 42*(2), 266–277.

Carr, E. G., Dunlap, G., Horner, R. H., Koegel, R.L., et al. (2002). Positive behavior support: Evolution of an applied science. *Journal of Positive Behavior Intervention, 4*(1), 4–16.

Centers for Disease Control and Prevention (CDC). (2014). Prevalence of autism spectrum disorders among children aged 8 years: Autism and Developmental Disabilities Monitoring Network, 11 sites, United States, 2010. *MMWR Surveillance Summaries 63*(2), 1–22.

Dale, E., Jahoda, A., & Knott, F. (2006). Mothers' attributions following their child's diagnosis of autistic spectrum disorder: Exploring links with maternal levels of stress, depression and expectations about their child's future. *Autism, 10*(5), 463–479.

Daniels, A. M., & Mandell, D. S. (2014). Explaining differences in age at autism spectrum disorder diagnosis: A critical review. *Autism, 18,* 583–597.

DeRubeis, S., Poultney, C. S., Kou, Y., Fu, S., Brownfeld, J. M., Cai, J….Chiocchetti, A. G. (2014). *Nature, 515*(7526), 209–215.

Donovan, J. & Zucker, C. (2010, October). Autism's first child. *The Atlantic.* Retrieved January 16, 2015, from www .theatlantic.com /magazine/archive/2010 /10/autism-8217-s-first -child/8227/.

Draaisma, D. (2009). Stereotypes of autism. *Philosophical Transactions of the Royal Society B: Biological Sciences, 364*(1522), 1475–1480.

Dunlap, G., Carr, E. G., Horner, R. H., Zarcone, J. R., & Schwartz, I. (2008). Positive behavior support and applied behavior analysis: A familial alliance. *Behavior Modification, 8,* 682–697.

Dyches, T. T., Carter, N., & Prater, M. A. (2011). *A teacher's guide to communicating with parents: Practical strategies for developing successful relationships.* Needham Heights, MA: Pearson/ Allyn & Bacon.

Dyches, T. T., Prater, M. A., & Leininger, M. (2009). Juvenile literature and the portrayal of developmental disabilities. *Education and Training in Developmental Disabilities, 44,* 304–317.

Eaves, L. C., & Ho, H. H. (2008). Young adult outcome of autism spectrum disorders. *Journal of Autism and Developmental Disorders, 38*(4), 739–747.

Gabrielsen, T. P., Farley, M., Speer, L., Villalobos, M., Baker, C. N., & Miller, J. (2015). Identifying autism in a brief observation. *Pediatrics, 135*(2), e330–e338.

Gagnon, E. (2001). *The power card strategy: Using special interests to motivate children and youth with Asperger syndrome.* Shawnee Mission, KS: Autism Asperger Publishing Company.

Ganz, J. B., Davis, J. L., Lund, E. M., Goodwyn, F. D., & Simpson, R. L. (2012). Meta-analysis of PECS with individuals with ASD: Investigation of targeted versus non-targeted outcomes, participant characteristics, and implementation phase. *Research in Developmental Disabilities, 33*(2), 406–418.

Gaugler, T., Klei, L., Sanders, S. J., Bodea, C. A., Goldberg, A. P., Lee, A. B., …Buxbaum, J. D. (2014). Most genetic risk for autism resides with common variation. *Nature Genetics, 46*(8), 881–885.

Gibb, G. S., & Dyches, T. T. (2015). *IEPs: Guide to writing quality individualized education programs,* 3rd ed. Needham Heights, MA: Allyn & Bacon.

Grynszpan, O., Weiss, P. L. T., Perez-Diaz, F., & Gal, E. (2014). Innovative technology-based interventions for autism spectrum disorders: A meta-analysis. *Autism, 18*(4), 346–361.

Hall, L., & Kelley, E. (2014). The contribution of epigenetics to understanding genetic factors in autism. *Autism, 18*(8), 872–881.

Hansen, S. N., Schendel, D. E., & Parner, E. T. (2015). Explaining the increase in the prevalence of autism spectrum disorders: The proportion attributable to changes in reporting practices. *JAMA Pediatrics, 169*(1), 56–62.

Harrington, J. W., Patrick, P. A., & Edwards, K. S. (2006). Parental beliefs about autism: Implications for the treating physician. *Autism, 10*(5), 452–462.

Henault, I. (2006). *Asperger's syndrome and sexuality: From adolescence through adulthood.* London: Jessica Kingsley Publishers.

Hundert, J., Rowe, S., & Harrison, E. (2014). The combined effects of social script training and peer buddies on generalized peer interaction of children with ASD in inclusive classrooms. *Focus on Autism and Other Developmental Disabilities, 29*(4), 206–215.

Kamps, D., Mason, R., Thiemann-Bourque, K., Feldmiller, S., Turcotte, A., & Miller, T. (2014). The use of peer networks to increase communicative acts of students with autism spectrum disorders. *Focus on Autism and Other Developmental Disabilities, 29*(4), 230–245.

Kane, M., Connell, J. E., & Pellecchia, M. (2010). A quantitative analysis of language interventions for children with autism. *Behavior Analyst Today, 11*(2), 128–144.

Kanne, S., M., & Mazurek, M. O. (2011). Aggression in children and adolescents with ASD: Prevalence and risk factors. *Journal of Autism and Developmental Disorders, 41*(7), 926–937.

Kanner, L. (1943). Autistic disturbances of affective contact. *Nervous Child, 2*, 217–250.

Kellems, R. O., & Morningstar, M. E. (2012). Using video modeling delivered through iPods to teach vocational tasks to young adults with autism spectrum disorders. *Career Development and Transition for Exceptional Individuals, 35*(3), 155–167.

Koegel, R. L., & Koegel, L. K. (2012). *The PRT pocket guide: Pivotal response treatment for autism spectrum disorders.* Baltimore: Brookes.

Koegel, R. L., & Koegel, L. K. (2006). *Pivotal response treatments for autism: Communication, social, & academic development.* Baltimore: Brookes.

Kogan, M. D., Strickland, B. B., Blumberg, S. J., Singh, G. K., Perrin, J. M., & van Dyck, P. C. (2008). A national profile of the health care experiences and family impact of autism spectrum disorder among children in the United States, 2005–2006. *Pediatrics, 122*(6), e1149–e1158.

Johnson, R. A., Danis, M., & Hafner-Eaton, C. (2014). US state variation in autism insurance mandates: Balancing access and fairness. *Autism, 18*(7), 803–814.

Jones, C. R. G., Happé, F., Pickles, A., Marsden, A. J. S., Tregay, J., Baird, G., Simonoff, E., & Charman, T. (2011). "Everyday memory" impairments in autism spectrum disorders. *Journal of Autism and Developmental Disorders, 41*(4), 455–464.

Lai, M-C., Lombardo, M. V., Pasco, G., Ruigrok, A. N. V., Wheelwright, S. J., Sadek, ... Baron-Cohen, S. (2011). A behavioral comparison of male and female adults with high functioning autism spectrum conditions. *PLoS ONE 6*(6), e20835.

Lanou, A., Hough, L., & Powell, E. (2012). Case studies on using strengths and interests to address the needs of students with autism spectrum disorders. *Intervention in School and Clinic, 47*(3), 175–182.

LeBlanc, L. A. (2010). Using video-based interventions with individuals with autism spectrum disorders: Introduction to the special issue. *Education and Treatment of Children, 33*(3), 333–337.

Legoff, D. B., & Sherman, M. (2006). Long-term outcome of social skills intervention based on interactive LEGO play. *Autism, 10*(4), 317–329.

Lee, L. C., Harrington, R. B., Louie, B. B., & Newschaffer, C. J. (2008). Children with autism: Quality of life and parental concerns. *Journal of Autism and Development Disorders, 38*(6), 1147–1160.

Leininger, M., Dyches, T. T., Prater, M.A., & Heath, M. A. (2010). Teaching students with obsessive-compulsive disorder. *Intervention in School and Clinic, 45*(4), 221–231.

Levy, S. E., Giarelli, E., Lee, L., Schieve, L. A., Kirby, R. S., Cunniff, ... Rice, C. E. (2010). Autism spectrum disorder and co-occurring developmental, psychiatric, and medical conditions among children in multiple populations of the United States. *Journal of Developmental and Behavioral Pediatrics, 31*(4), 267–275.

MacFarlane, J. R., & Kanaya, T. (2009). What does it mean to be autistic? Inter-state variation in special education criteria for autism services. *Journal of Child and Family Studies, 18*(6), 662–669.

Magaña, S., Lopez, K., Aguinaga, A., & Morton, H. (2013). Access to diagnosis and treatment services among Latino children with autism spectrum disorders. *Intellectual and Developmental Disabilities, 51*(3), 141–153.

Maglione, M., Gans, D., Das, L., Timbie, J., & Kasari, C. (2012). Nonmedical interventions for children with ASD: Recommended guidelines and further research needs. *Pediatrics, 130*(Supplement 2), S169-S178.

Mandell, D., & Lecavalier, L. (2014). Should we believe the Centers for Disease Control and Prevention's autism spectrum disorder prevalence estimates? *Autism, 18*(5), 482–483.

Mandy, W., Charman, T., Puura, K., & Skuse, D. (2014). Investigating the cross-cultural validity of DSM-5 autism spectrum disorder: Evidence from Finnish and UK samples. *Autism, 18*, 45–54.

McConachie, H., McLaughlin, E., Grahame, V., Taylor, H., Honey, E., Tavernor, L., ...Le Couteur, A. (2014). Group therapy for anxiety in children with autism spectrum disorder. *Autism, 18*(6), 723–732.

Mohiuddin, S., & Ghaziuddin, M. (2013). Psychopharmacology of autism spectrum disorders: A selective review. *Autism, 17*(6), 645–654.

National Autism Center. (2009). *National Standards Report*. Randolph, MA: National Autism Center.

National Research Council. (2001). *Educating Children with Autism*. Committee on Educational Interventions for Children with Autism. C. Lord and J. P. McGee, Eds. Division of Behavioral and Social Sciences and Education. Washington, DC: National Academy Press.

Nicholas, J. S., Charles, J. M., Carpenter, L. A., King, L. B., Jenner, W., & Spratt, E. G. (2008). Prevalence and characteristics of children with autism spectrum disorders. *Annals of Epidemiology, 18*(2), 130–136.

Northey, W. F., Jr. (2009). Effectiveness research: A view from the USA. *Journal of Family Therapy, 31*, 75–84.

Nowell, K. P., Brewton, C. M., & Goin-Kochel, R. P. (2014). A multi-rater study on being teased among children/adolescents with autism spectrum disorder (ASD) and their typically developing siblings: Associations with ASD symptoms. *Focus on Autism and Other Developmental Disabilities, 29*(1), 195–205.

Paul, R., Orlovski, S., Marcinko, H., & Volkmar, F. (2009). Conversational behaviors in youth with high-functioning ASD and Asperger syndrome. *Journal of Autism and Developmental Disorders, 39*(1), 115–125.

Peters-Scheffer, N., Didden, R., Korzilius, H., & Sturmey, P. (2011). A meta-analytic study on the effectiveness of comprehensive ABA-based early intervention programs for children with autism spectrum disorders. *Research in Autism Spectrum Disorders, 5*(1), 60–69.

Perkins, M. R., Dobbinson, S., Boucher, J., Bol, S., & Bloom, P. (2006). Lexical knowledge and lexical use in autism. *Journal of Autism and Developmental Disorders, 36*(6), 795–805.

Radley, K. C., Ford, W. B., Battaglia, A. A., & McHugh, M. B. (2014). The effects of a social skills training package on social engagement of children with autism spectrum disorders in a generalized recess setting. *Focus on Autism and Other Developmental Disabilities, 29*, 216–229.

Rogers, S. J., & Ozonoff, S. (2006). Behavioral, educational, and developmental treatments for autism. In S. O. Moldin & J. L. R. Rubenstein (Eds.), *Understanding autism: From basic neuroscience to treatment* (pp. 443–473). Boca Raton, FL: CRC Press.

Roth, M. E., Gillis, J. M., DiGennaro Reed, F. D. (2014). A meta-analysis of behavioral interventions for adolescents and adults with autism spectrum disorders. *Journal of Behavioral Education, 23*, 258–286.

Saracino, J., Noseworthy, J., Steiman, M., Reisinger, L., & Fombonne, E. (2010). Diagnostic and assessment issues in autism surveillance and prevalence. *Journal of Developmental and Physical Disabilities, 22*(4), 317–330.

Schlosser, R. W., & Wendt, O. (2008). Effects of augmentative and alternative communication intervention on speech production in children with autism: A systematic review. *American Journal of Speech-Language Pathology, 17*(3), 212–230.

Sharma, S., Woolfson, L. M., & Hunter, S. C. (2011). Confusion and inconsistency in diagnosis of Asperger syndrome: A review of studies from 1981 to 2010. *Autism, 16*(5), 465–486.

Smith, L. M. (2007). Autism through my eyes. Parental first-person account to senior author. *Archives of Pediatrics and Adolescent Medicine, 161*, 324–325.

Spek, A., Schatorje, T., Scholte, E., & van Berckerlaer-Onnes, I. (2009). Verbal fluency in adults with high functioning autism or Asperger syndrome. *Neuropsychologia, 47*(3), 652–656.

Stacy, M. E., Zablotsky, B., Yarger, H. A., Zimmerman, A., Makia, B., & Lee, L. (2014). *Autism, 18*(8), 965–974.

Stahmer, A. C., Schriebman, L., & Cunningham, A. B. (2011). Towards a technology of treatment individualization for young children with autism spectrum disorders. *Brain Research, 1380*, 229–239.

Strang, J. F., Kenworthy, L., Daniolos, P., Case, L., Wills, M. C., Martin, A., & Wallace, G. L. (2012). Depression and anxiety symptoms in children and adolescents with autism spectrum disorders without intellectual disability. *Research in Autism Spectrum Disorders, 6*(1), 406–412.

Stewart, M., McAdam, C., Ota, M., Peppé, S. & Cleland, J. (2013). Emotional recognition in autism spectrum conditions from voices and faces. *Autism. 17*(1), 6–14.

Sung, M., Ooi, Y. P., Goh, T. J., Pathy, P., Fung, D. S., Ang, R. P., ...Lam, C. M. (2011). Effects of cognitive-behavioral therapy on anxiety in children with autism spectrum disorders: A randomized controlled trial. *Child Psychiatry and Human Development, 42*(2), 634–649.

Szidon, K., Ruppar, A., & Smith, L. (2015). Five steps for developing effective transition plans for high school students with autism spectrum disorders. *Teaching Exceptional Children, 47*(3), 147–152.

Tavassoli, T., Miller, L. J., Schoen, S. A., Nielsen,

D. M., & Baron-Cohen, S. (2014). Sensory over-responsivity in adults with autism spectrum conditions. *Autism, 18*(4), 428–432.

Taylor, L. E., Swerdfeger, A. L., & Eslick, G. D. (2014). Vaccines are not associated with autism: An evidence-based meta-analysis of case-control and cohort studies. *Vaccine, 32*(29), 3623–3629.

Tiegerman-Farber, E. (2009). Autism spectrum disorders: Learning to communicate. In D. K. Bernstein & E. Tiegerman-Farber (Eds.), *Language and communication disorders in children,* 6th ed. (pp. 314–369). Boston: Allyn & Bacon.

Toth, K., & King, B. H. (2008). Asperger's syndrome: Diagnosis and treatment. *American Journal of Psychiatry, 165*(8), 958–963.

Treffert, D. (2009). The savant syndrome: An extraordinary condition. A synopsis: past, present, and future. *Philosophical Transactions of The Royal Society, 364*(1522), 1351–1357.

Treffert, D. A. (2014). Savant syndrome: Realities, myths and misconceptions. *Journal of Autism and Developmental Disorders, 44*(3), 564–571.

U.S. Department of Education, Office of Special Education Programs. (2011). *The 30th Annual Report to Congress on the Implementation of the Individuals with Disabilities Education Act.* Washington, D.C.: U.S. Government Printing Office.

Viscidi, E. W., Johnson, A. L., Spence, S. J., Buka, S. L., Morrow, E. M., & Triche, E. W. (2014). The association between epilepsy and autism symptoms and maladaptive behaviors in children with autism spectrum disorder. *Autism, 18*(8), 996–1006.

Volkmar, F. R., & Wiesner, L. A. (2009). *A practical guide to autism: What every parent, family member, and teacher needs to know.* Hoboken, NJ: John Wiley & Sons.

Wass, S. V., & Porayska-Pomsta, K. (2014). The uses of cognitive training technologies in the treatment of autism spectrum disorders. *Autism, 18*(8), 851–871.

Weismer, S. E., Lord, C., & Esler, A. (2010). Early language patterns of toddlers on the autism spectrum compared to toddlers with developmental delay. *Journal of Autism and Developmental Disorders, 40*(10), 1259–1273.

Weitlauf, A. S., McPheeters, M. L., Peters, B., Sathe, N., Travis, R., Aiello, R. … Warren, Z. (2014). *Therapies for Children with Autism Spectrum Disorder: Behavioral Interventions Update.* Comparative Effectiveness Review No. 137. Rockville, MD: Agency for Healthcare Research and Quality. Retrieved from www.effectivehealthcare.ahrq.gov/reports/final.cfm.

White, S. W., Scahill, L., Klin, A., Koenig, K., & Volkmar, F. (2007). Educational placements and service use patterns of individuals with autism spectrum disorders.

*Journal of Autism and Developmental Disorders, 37*(8), 1403–1412.

Willis, C. (2009). *Creating inclusive learning environments for young children: What to do on Monday morning.* Thousand Oaks, CA: Corwin Press.

Wodka, E. L., Mathy, P. & Kalb, L. (2013). Predictors of phrase and fluent speech in children with autism and severe language delay. *Pediatrics, 131*(4), e1128–e1134.

Wong, C., Odom, S. L., Hume, K. A., Cox, A. W., Fettig, A., Kucharczyk, S. …Schultz, T. R. (2015). Evidence-based practices for children, youth, and young adults with autism spectrum disorder: A comprehensive review. *Journal of Autism and Developmental Disorders.* Advance online publication. doi:10.1007/s10803-014-2351-z

Zablotsky, B., Bradshaw, C. P., Anderson, C. M., & Law, P. (2014). Risk factors for bullying among children with autism spectrum disorders. *Autism, 18*(4), 419–427.

Zandt, F. (2007). Repetitive behaviour in children with high functioning autism and obsessive compulsive disorder. *Journal of Autism and Developmental Disorders, 37*(2), 251–259.

## Chapter 12

Abt Associates. (1974). *Assessments of selected resources for severely handicapped children and youth. Vol I: A state-of-the-art paper.* Cambridge, MA: Author (ERIC Document Reproduction Service No. ED 134 614).

The ARC. (2012). Causes and prevention of intellectual disabilities. Retrieved February 28, 2012, from www.thearc.org/page.aspx?pid=2453.

The ARC. (2014). *Position statement on education.* Retrieved February 14, 2014, from www.thearc.org/page.aspx?pid=2368.

Bagnato, S., Goins, D., Pretti-Frontczak, K., & Neisworth, J. (2014). Authentic assessment as "best practice" for early childhood intervention: National Consumer Social Validity Research. *Topics In Early Childhood Special Education, 34*(2), 116–127.

Batshaw, M., Pellegrino, L. & Rozien, N. J. (2008). *Children with disabilities,* 6th ed. Baltimore: Paul H. Brookes.

Beirne-Smith, M., Patton, J. R., & Hill, S. (2011). *Introduction to intellectual disabilities,* 8th ed. Upper Saddle River, NJ: Prentice-Hall.

Berk, L. E. (2005). *Development through the lifespan.* Boston: Allyn & Bacon.

Bishop, V. E. (2005). *Teaching visually impaired children,* 3rd ed. Springfield, IL: Charles C. Thomas.

Brown, F., & Snell, M. (2011). Measuring student behavior and learning. In M. E. Snell & F. Brown (Eds.), *Instruction for students with severe disabilities,* 7th ed. (pp. 186–223). Boston: Pearson.

Crockett, M., & Hardman, M. L. (2009). Expected outcomes and emerging values. In J. McDonnell & M. L. Hardman,

*Successful transition programs*, 2nd ed. (pp. 25–42). Los Angeles: Sage Publishing.

Drew, C. J., & Hardman, M. L. (2007). *Intellectual disabilities across the lifespan*, 9th ed. Columbus, OH: Merrill.

Entertainment Software Association. (2014). *Essential Facts about the Computer and Video Game Industry.* www.theesa.com/wp-content/uploads/2014/10/ESA_EF_2014.pdf.

Farber, M. (2014). Design challenge: DIY assistive game controllers. *Edutopia.* Retrieved March 1, 2015, from www.edutopia.org/blog/design-diy-assistive-game-controllers-matthew-farber.

Ford, A., Davern, L., & Schnorr, R. (2001, July/August). Learners with significant disabilities: Curricular relevance in an era of standards-based reform. *Remedial and Special Education, 22*(4), 214–222.

Gaumer Erickson, A., Noonan, P., Zheng, C., & Brussow, J. (2015). The relationship between self-determination and academic achievement for adolescents with intellectual disabilities. *Research In Developmental Disabilities, 36*, 45–54.

Giangreco, M. (2011). Educating students with severe disabilities: Foundational concepts and practices. In M. E. Snell & F. Brown (Eds.), *Instruction of students with severe disabilities*, 7th ed. (pp. 1–30). Boston: Pearson Group.

Gollnick, D., & Chinn, P. C. (2012). *Multicultural education in a diverse society,* 9th ed. Boston: Allyn & Bacon.

Hewitt, A., & O'Nell, S. (2009). *I am who I am: A little help from my friends.* Washington, D.C.: President's Committee on Intellectual Disabilities.

Horner, R. H., Albin, R. W., Todd, A.W., & Sprague, J. R. (2006). Positive behavior support for individuals with severe disabilities. In M. E. Snell & F. Brown (Eds.), *Instruction of students with severe disabilities*, 6th ed. (pp. 206–250). Upper Saddle River, NJ: Merrill Prentice Hall.

Johnston, S. (2003). Assistive technology. In J. McDonnell, M. Hardman, & A. McDonnell, *Introduction to persons with severe disabilities* (pp. 138–159). Boston: Allyn & Bacon.

Justen, J. (1976). Who are the severely handicapped? A problem in definition. *AAESPH Review, 1*(5), 1–12.

McDonnell, J., Hardman, M., & McDonnell, A. P. (2003). *Introduction to persons with moderate and severe disabilities*, 2nd ed. Boston: Allyn & Bacon.

Meyer, L. H., Peck, C. A., & Brown, L. (1991). Definitions and diagnosis. In L. H. Meyer, C. A. Peck, & L. Brown (Eds.), *Critical issues in the lives of people with disabilities* (p. 17). Baltimore: Paul H. Brookes.

Moore, B. J., & Montgomery, J. K. (2008). *Making a difference for America's children: Speech–language pathologists in public schools.* Greenville, SC: Super Duper Publications.

Oliver, C., Petty, J., Ruddick, L., & Bacarese-Hamilton, M. (2012). The association between repetitive, self-injurious and aggressive behavior in children with severe intellectual disability. *Journal of Autism & Developmental Disorders, 42*(6), 910–919.

Piche, L., Krage, P., & Wiczek, C. (1991). Joining the community. *IMPACT, 4*(1), 3–18.

Quenemoen, R., & Thurlow, M. (2012). *NCEO policy directions: Planning alignment studies for alternate assessments based on alternate achievement standards.* Retrieved February 28, 2012, from www.cehd.umn.edu/NCEO/OnlinePubs/Policy20/PolicyDirections20.pdf.

Rues, J. P., Graff, J. C., Ault, M. M., & Holvoet, J. F. (2006). Special health care procedures. In M. E. Snell & F. Brown (Eds.), *Introduction to students with severe disabilities*, 6th ed. (pp. 251–290). Upper Saddle River, NJ: Merrill.

Ryndak, D. L., Hughes, C., Alper, S., & McDonnell, J. (2012). Documenting impact of educational contexts on long-term outcomes for students with significant disabilities. *Education & Training In Autism & Developmental Disabilities, 47*(2), 127–138.

Sailor, W., & Haring, N. (1977). Some current directions in the education of the severely/multiply handicapped. *AAESPH Review, 2*, 67–86.

Snell, M. E. (1991). Schools are for all kids: The importance of integration for students with severe disabilities and their peers. In J. Lloyd, N. N. Singh, & A. C. Repp (Eds.), *The regular education initiative: Alternative perspectives on concepts, issues, and models* (pp. 133–148). Sycamore, IL: Sycamore.

Snell, M. E., & Brown, F. (2011). Selecting teaching strategies and understanding educational environments. In M. E. Snell & F. Brown (Eds.), *Introduction to students with severe disabilities*, 7th ed. (pp. 122–185). Boston: Pearson Group.

TASH. (2014a). *About us.* Retrieved February 28, 2014, from http://tash.org/about/.

TASH. (2014b). *TASH resolution on life in the community.* Retrieved February 24, 2014, from http://tash.org/about/resolutions/tash-resolution-life-community/.

U.S. Department of Education. (2013). National Center for Education statistics. *Digest of Education Statistics, 2012.* Retrieved February 5, 2014, from http://nces.ed.gov/pubsearch/pubsinfo.asp?pubid=2014015

Voss, K. S. (2005). *Teaching by design.* Bethesda, MD: Woodbine House.

Wehmeyer, M. L., Gragoudas, S., & Shogren, K. A. (2006). Self-determination, student involvement, and leadership development. In P. Wehman, *Life beyond the classroom: Transition strategies for young people with disabilities*, 4th ed. (pp. 41–69). Baltimore: Paul H. Brookes.

Wehmeyer, M. L., Abery, B. H., Zhang, D., Ward, K., Willis, D., Hossain, W. A., & …Goode, T. (2011). Personal self-determination and moderating variables that impact efforts to promote self-determination. *Exceptionality, 19*(1), 19–30.

Westling, D., & Fox, L. (2009). *Teaching students with severe disabilities,* 4th ed. Upper Saddle River, NJ: Merrill/Prentice Hall.

Ysseldyke, J. E., & Olsen, K. (2012). *Putting alternate assessments into practice: What to measure and possible sources of data.* NCEO Synthesis Report 28. Minneapolis: The National Center on Educational Outcomes, University of Minnesota. Retrieved February 1, 2012, from www.cehd.umn.edu/NCEO/OnlinePubs/archive/Synthesis/Synthesis28.htm.

Ysseldyke, J. E., Olsen, K., & Thurlow, M. (2012). *Issues and considerations in alternate assessments. NCEO Synthesis Report 27.* Minneapolis: The National Center on Educational Outcomes, University of Minnesota. Retrieved January 14, 2012, from www.cehd.umn.edu/NCEO/OnlinePubs/archive/Synthesis/Synthesis27.htm.

## Chapter 13

Alexander Graham Bell Academy. (2012). *Auditory Verbal Principles.* Retrieved April 29, 2015, from http://www.listeningandspokenlanguage.org/academydocument.aspx?id=563.

American Foundation for the Blind. (2015). *Educating students with visual impairments for inclusion in society: A paper on the inclusion of students with visual impairments.* Retrieved March 20, 2015, from www.afb.org/info/programs-and-services/professional-development/teachers/inclusive-education/1235.

American Printing House for the Blind, Inc. (2014). *Annual Report 2014.* Retrieved March 19, 2015, from www.aph.org/federal-quota/dist14.html.

American Speech-Language-Hearing Association (ASHA). (2012). *Cochlear implants quick facts.* Retrieved March 15, 2012, from www.asha.org/about/news/tipsheets/cochlear_quickfacts.htm.

Anghel, D. (2012). The development of theory of mind in children with congenital visual impairments. *Scientific Journal of Humanistic Studies, 4*(7), 229–235.

Barraga, N. C., & Erin, J. N. (2002). *Visual impairments and learning,* 4th ed. Austin, TX: Pro-Ed.

Batshaw, M., Roizen, N., & Lotrecchiano, G. (2012). *Children with disabilities.* Baltimore: Paul H. Brookes.

Berg, A. L., Ip, S. C., Hurst, M., & Herb, A. (2007). Cochlear implants in young children: Informed consent as a process and current practices. *American Journal of Audiology, 16*(1), 13–28.

Bouchard, D., & Tetreault, S. (2000). The motor development of sighted children and children with moderate low vision aged 8–13. *Journal of Visual Impairments and Blindness, 94,* 564–573.

Centers for Disease Control. (2015a). *Hearing loss in children.* Retrieved March 19, 2015, from www.cdc.gov/ncbddd/hearingloss/facts.html.

Centers for Disease Control. (2015b). *Table 39.* Retrieved March 20, 2015, from www.cdc.gov/nchs/data/hus/hus13.pdf#039.

Ching, T. T., & Dillon, H. (2013). A brief overview of factors affecting speech intelligibility of people with hearing loss: Implications for amplification. *American Journal of Audiology, 22*(2), 306–309.

Cook, B. (2013) *The Everygirl Career Profile: Tamika Catchings of the WNBA.* Retrieved March 21, 2015, from http://theeverygirl.com/feature/tamika-catchings-of-the-wnba.

Correa-Torres, S. M. (2008). The nature of the social experiences of students with deaf-blindness who are educated in inclusive settings. *Journal of Visual Impairment & Blindness, 102*(5), 272–283.

Cox, P. R., & Dykes, M. K. (2001). Effective classroom adaptations for students with visual impairments. *Teaching Exceptional Children, 33*(6), 68–74.

Cupples, L. Ching, T. Crowe, K. Day, J. & Seeto, M. (2014). Predictors of early reading skill in 5-year-old children with hearing loss who use spoken language. *Reading Research Quarterly, 49*(1), 85–104.

Dorr, R. E. (2006). Something old is new again: Revisiting language experience. *The Reading Teacher, 60*(2), 138–146.

Gilbertson, D., & Ferre, S. (2008). Considerations in the identification, assessment, and intervention process for deaf and hard-of-hearing students with reading difficulties. *Psychology in the Schools, 45*(2), 104–120.

Hallemans, A., Ortibus, E., Truijen, S., & Meire, F. (2011). Development of independent locomotion in children with a severe visual impairment. *Research In Developmental Disabilities, 32*(6), 2069–2074.

Heine, C., & Slone, M. (2008). The impact of mild central auditory processing disorder on school performance during adolescence. *Journal of School Health, 78*(7), 405–407.

Hintermair, M. (2008). Self-esteem and satisfaction with life and hard-of-hearing people—A resource-oriented approach to identity work. *Journal of Deaf Studies and Deaf Education, 13*(2), 278–300.

Jackson, C., & Schatschneider, C. (2014). Rate of language growth in children with hearing loss in an auditory-verbal early intervention program. *American Annals of the Deaf, 158*(5), 539–554.

Kaland, M., & Salvatore, K. (2012). *Psychology of hearing loss.* Retrieved March 9, 2012, from www.asha.org/Publications/leader/2002/020319/020319d/.

KidSource. (2012). *Undetected vision disorders are blinding children: Earlier testing needed to preserve good eyesight.* Retrieved January 26, 2012, from www.kidsource.com

/kidsource/content/news/vision.html.

Koenig, A. J., & Holbrook, M. C. (2005). Literacy skills. In A. J. Koenig & M. C. Holbrook (Eds.), *Foundations of education*: *Volume II Instructional strategies for teaching children and youths with visual impairments,* 2nd ed. (pp. 264–312). New York: AFB Press.

Kurzweil Technologies. (2012). *A brief career summary of Ray Kurzweil.* Burlington, MA: Lernout & Hauspie. Retrieved March 17, 2012, from www.kurzweiltech.com/aboutray.html.

Lederberg, A., Miller, E., Easterbrooks, S., & McDonald, C. (2014). Foundations for literacy: An early literacy intervention for deaf and hard-of-hearing children. *Journal of Deaf Studies & Deaf Education, 19*(4), 438–455.

Leigh, S. A., & Barclay, L. A. (2000). High school braille readers: Achieving academic success. *RE: View, 32,* 123–131.

Letcher, K. (2015). *Adapted physical education for the blind and visually impaired.* Overbrook School for the Blind. Retrieved March 21, 2015, from www.s118134197.onlinehome.us/page.php?ITEM=39.

Lewallen, S., Massae, P., Tharany, M., Somba, M., Geneau, R., MacArthur, C., & Courtwright, P. (2008). Evaluating a school-based trachoma curriculum in Tanzania. *Health Education Research, 23*(6), 1068–1073.

Library of Congress. (2012). *That all may read.* National Library Service for the Blind and Physically Handicapped (NLS). Retrieved March 2, 2012, from www.loc.gov/nls/.

Lund, S. K., & Troha, J. M. (2008). Teaching young people who are blind and have autism to make requests using a variation on the picture exchange communication system with tactile symbols: A preliminary investigation. *Journal of Autism and Developmental Disabilities, 38*(4), 719–730.

Marschark, M., & Spencer, P. E. (2011). *Oxford handbook of deaf studies, language, and education, Volume 2.* New York: Oxford University Press.

Marschark, M., Shaver, D. M., Nagle, K. M., & Newman, L. A. (2015). Predicting the academic achievement of deaf and hard-of-hearing students from individual, household, communication, and educational factors. *Exceptional Children, 81*(3), 350–369.

McAnally, P. L., Rose, S., & Quigley, S. P. (2005). *Language learning practices with deaf children,* 3rd ed. Austin, TX: Pro Ed.

McGowan, R. S., Nittrouer, S., & Chenausky, K. (2008). Speech production in 12-month-old children with and without hearing loss. *Journal of Speech, Language, and Hearing Research, 51*(4), 879–888.

McKeen, S. (2012). A new language for baby. *The Ottawa Citizen.* Retrieved February 25, 2012, from http://littlesigners.com/article3.html.

McLinden, M., & McCall, S. (2006). *Learning through touch: Supporting children with visual impairments and additional difficulties.* Milton Park Abingdon, UK: David Fulton Publishers.

Mikita, C. (2014). *Despite disabilities, U. student spreads message of hope.* Retrieved November 20, 2014, from www.ksl.com/?nid=148&sid=32239160#Asmv0R7VX9OZwthx.03.

Moore, D. R. (2007). Auditory processing disorders: Acquisition and treatment. *Journal of Communication Disorders, 40*(4), 295–304.

Moores, D. F. (2008). *Educating the deaf: Psychology, principles and practices plus guide to inclusion,* 5th ed. Boston: Houghton-Mifflin.

Narr, R. F. (2008). Phonological awareness and decoding in deaf/hard-of-hearing students who use visual phonics. *Journal of Deaf Studies and Deaf Education, 13*(3), 405–416.

National Institute on Deafness and Other Communication Disorders. (2015a). *Quick Statistics.* Retrieved March 19, 2015, from www.nidcd.nih.gov/health/statistics/Pages/quick.aspx.

National Institute on Deafness and Other Communication Disorders. (2015b). *Otitis media. Health information: Hearing and balance.* Retrieved March 9, 2015, from www.nidcd.nih.gov/health/hearing/pages/earinfections.aspx.

National Institute on Deafness and Other Communication Disorders. (2015c). *Cochlear implants. Health information: Hearing and balance.* Retrieved March 19, 2015, from www.nidcd.nih.gov/health/hearing/coch.asp.

National Institute on Deafness and Other Communication Disorders. (2015d). *American Sign Language. Health information: Hearing and balance.* Retrieved March 21, 2015, from www.nidcd.nih.gov/health/hearing/asl.asp.

National Technical Institute for the Deaf. (2006). *Welcome to C-Print.* Rochester, NY: Author.

New York State Department of Health. (2015). Report of recommendations: Vision impairment. Retrieved March 20, 2015, from www.health.ny.gov/community/infants_children/early_intervention/docs/2008-02_vision_impairment_recommendations.pdf.

Owen, D. T. (2007). Noise-induced hearing loss. *The Instrumentalist, 62*(3), 23–24, 26, 28.

Papadopoulos, K., Argyropoulos, V. S., & Kouroupetroglou, G. (2008). Discrimination and comprehension of synthetic speech by students with visual impairments: The case of similar acoustic patterns. *Journal of Visual Impairment & Blindness, 102*(7), 420–429.

Pester, P. (2012). *Braille bits.* Louisville, KY: American Printing House for the Blind. Retrieved March 16, 2012, from www.aph.org/edresearch/bits898.htm.

Phillips, J., Wiley, S., Barnard, H., & Meinzen-Derr, J. J. (2014). Comparison of two nonverbal intelligence tests among children who are deaf or hard-of-hearing. *Research in Developmental Disabilities, 35*(2), 463–471.

Poobrasert, O., & Cercone, N. (2009). Evaluation of educational multimedia support system for students with deafness. *Journal of Educational Multimedia and Hypermedia, 18*(1), 71–90.

Poon, T., & Ovadia, R. (2008). Using tactile learning aids for students with visual impairments in a first-semester organic chemistry course. *Journal of Chemical Education, 85*(2), 240–242.

Rathmann, C., Mann, W., & Morgan, G. (2007). Narrative structure and narrative development in deaf children. *Deafness and Education International, 9*(4), 187–196.

Riddering, A. T. (2008). Keeping older adults with vision loss safe: Chronic conditions and comorbidities that influence functional mobility. *Journal of Visual Impairment & Blindness, 102*(10), 616–620.

Sacks, S. Z., & Silberman, R. K. (2000). Social skills. In A. J. Koenig & M. C. Holbrook (Eds.), *Foundations of education, Volume II: Instructional strategies for teaching children and youths with visual impairments,* 2nd ed. (pp. 616–652). New York: AFB Press.

Scheetz, N. A. (2004). *Psychosocial aspects of deafness.* Boston: Pearson Education.

Social Security Administration. (2015). *Disability planner: Special rules for people who are blind.*

Washington, D.C.: Author. Retrieved March 19, 2015, from www.ssa.gov /ssi/text-eligibility-ussi .htm#blind.

Stanzione, C., & Schick, B. B. (2014). Environmental language factors in theory of mind development. *Topics in Language Disorders, 34*(4), 296–312.

Steinweg, S. B., Griffin, H. C., Griffin, L. W., & Gingras, H. (2005). Retinopathy of prematurity. *RE: view: Rehabilitation for blindness and visual impairment, 37*(1), 32.

Supalo, C. A., Malouk, T. E., & Rankel, L. (2008). Low-cost laboratory adaptations for precollege students who are blind or visually impaired. *Journal of Chemical Education, 85*(2), 243–247.

Tollefsen, M., Dale, Ø, Berg, M, & Nordby, R. (2011). *Connected!: Disabled and use of social media.* Retrieved March 12, 2012, from http://medialt.no /news/en-US/connected -disabled-and-use-of -social-media/737.aspx.

United Nations World Food Programme. (2012). *Hunger.* Retrieved February 1, 2012, from www.wfp.org /hunger.

U.S. Department of Education. (2014). *Thirty sixth annual report to Congress on the implementation of the Individuals with Disabilities Education Act, 2014.* Washington, D.C.: U.S. Government Printing Office.

## Chapter 14

AIDS.gov. (2012). *Legal disclosure.* Retrieved February 1, 2012, from http://aids.gov/hiv-aids -basics/diagnosed

-with-hiv-aids/your -legal-rights/legal -disclosure/.

Alba, A., & Chan, L. (2007). Pulmonary rehabilitation. In R. L. Braddom (Ed.), *Physical medicine & rehabilitation* (pp. 739–751). Philadelphia, PA: Saunders.

American Academy for Cerebral Palsy and Developmental Medicine. (2011). *What is cerebral palsy?* Retrieved January 11, 2012, from www.aacpdm.org.

American Academy of Pediatrics. (2011). *Contagious health problems in schools: AIDS/HIV infection.* Retrieved February 4, 2012, from www.healthychildren .org/English/ages-stages /gradeschool/school /Pages/Contagious -Health-Problems-in -Schools.aspx.

American Diabetes Association. (2014). *Statistics about diabetes.* Retrieved January 20, 2015, from www .diabetes.org/diabetes -basics/statistics/?loc =db-slabnav.

American Federation of Teachers. (2009). *The medically fragile child: Caring for children with special healthcare needs in the school setting.* Retrieved January 18, 2011, from http://www.aft.org /sites/default/files /medicallyfragilechild _2009.pdf.

Anwar, M., Boyd, B., & Romesburg, A. M. (2007). I have cerebral palsy … it doesn't have me! *Exceptional Parent, 37*(6), 100.

Asthma and Allergy Foundation of American. (2012a). *Prevention.*

Retrieved February 12, 2012, from www .aafa.org/display .cfm?id=8&cont=9.

Asthma and Allergy Foundation of America. (2012b). *Treatment.* Retrieved February 12, 2012, from www.aafa .org/display.cfm?id=8 &cont=8.

Asthma and Allergy Foundation of America. (2012c). *What causes asthma?* Retrieved February 12, 2012, from www.aafa.org/display .cfm?id=8&cont=6.

Asthma and Allergy Foundation of America. (2012d). *What is asthma?* Retrieved February 12, 2012, from http://www .aafa.org /display.cfm?id=8& cont=5.

Ball, J. W., & Bindler, R. C. (2008). Alterations in immune function. In J. W. Ball & R. C. Bindler (Eds.), *Pediatric nursing* (pp. 546–583). Upper Saddle River, NJ: Pearson Education.

Barbaresi, W. J. (2014). Update on long-term stimulant medication treatment of attention-deficit hyperactivity disorder. *Journal of Developmental & Behavioral Pediatrics, 35*(7), 46–47.

Barkley, R. A. (2006a). ADHD in adults: Development course and outcome of children with ADHD and ADHD in clinic-referred adults. In R. A. Barkley, *Attention-deficit hyperactivity disorder*, 3rd ed. (pp. 248–296). New York: Guilford Press.

Barkley, R. A. (2006b). Etiologies. In R. A. Barkley, *Attention-deficit hyperactivity disorder*, 3rd ed.

(pp. 219–247). New York: Guilford Press.

Barkley, R. A. (2006c). Psychological counseling of adults with ADHD. In R. A. Barkley, *Attention-deficit hyperactivity disorder,* 3rd ed. (pp. 692–703). New York: Guilford Press.

Batstra, L., Nieweg, E. H., Pijl, S., Van Tol, D. G., & Dadders-Algra, M. (2014). Childhood ADHD: A stepped diagnosis approach. *Journal of Pediatric Practice, 20*(3), 169–177.

Beljan, P., Bree, K. D., Reuter, A. E. F., Reuter, S. D., & Wingers, L. (2014). Private pediatric neuropsychology practice multimodal treatment of ADHD: An applied approach. *Applied Neuropsychology: Child, 3*(3), 188–196.

Best, S. J., Heller, K. W., & Bigge, J. L. (2004). Teaching Individuals with Physical or Multiple Disabilities, 5th ed. Upper Saddle River, NJ: Prentice Hall.

Blosser, C. G., & Reider-Demer, M. (2009). Neurologic disorders. In C. E. Burns, A. M. Dunn, M. A. Brady, N. B. Starr, & C. G. Blosser (Eds.), *Pediatric care,* 4th ed. (pp. 634–672). St. Louis, MO: Sanders.

Brady, M. A. (2009). Respiratory diseases. In C. E. Burns, A. M. Dunn, M. A. Brady, N. B. Starr, & C. G. Blosser (Eds.), *Pediatric care,* 4th ed. (pp. 767–794). St. Louis, MO: Sanders.

Browder, D. M. & Spooner, F. (2011). *Teaching students with moderate and severe disabilities.* New York: Guilford.

Bullough, R. V. (2011). *Adam's fall: Traumatic brain injury, the first 365 days.* Santa Fe, NM: The Sunstone Press.

Bussing, R., Mason, D. M., & Bell, L. (2010). Adolescent outcomes of childhood attention-deficit/hyperactivity disorder in a diverse community sample. *Journal of the American Academy of Child & Adolescent Psychiatry, 49*(6), 595–605.

Bussing, R, Porter, P., Zima, B. T., Mason, D., Garvan, C., Reid, R. (2012). Academic outcome trajectories of students with ADHD: Does exceptional education status matter? *Journal of Emotional and Behavioral Disorders, 20*(3), 131–143.

Cahill, B. S., Coolidge, F. L., Segal, D. L., Klebe, K. J., Marle, P. D., & Overmann, K. A. (2012). Prevalence of ADHD and its subtypes in male and female adult prison inmates. *Behavioral Sciences & the Law, 30*(2), 154–166.

Centers for Disease Control and Prevention. (2012a). *Adolescent and school health: Childhood obesity facts.* Retrieved February 4, 2012, from www.cdc.gov/healthyyouth/obesity/facts.htm.

Centers for Disease Control and Prevention. (2012b). *Facts about ADHD.* Retrieved February 6, 2012, from www.cdc.gov/ncbddd/adhd/facts.html.

Centers for Disease Control and Prevention. (2013). *Epilepsy fast facts.* Retrieved from www.cdc.gov/epilepsy/basics/fast_facts.htm.

Centers for Disease Control and Prevention. (2014a).

*Spina bifida data and statistics.* Retrieved from www.cdc.gov/ncbddd/spinabifida/data.html.

Centers for Disease Control and Prevention. (2014b). *HIV in the United States: At a glance.* Retrieved from www.cdc.gov/hiv/statistics/basics/ataglance.html.

Centers for Disease Control and Prevention. (2014c). *Attention-Deficit/Hyperactivity Disorder (ADHD) data & statistics.* Retrieved from www.cdc.gov/ncbddd/adhd/data.html.

Centers for Disease Control and Prevention. (2015a). *HIV surveillance in adolescents and young adults.* Retrieved from www.cdc.gov/hiv/pdf/statistics_surveillance_Adolescents.pdf.

Centers for Disease Control and Prevention. (2015b). *Asthma fast stats.* Retrieved from www.cdc.gov/nchs/fastats/asthma.htm.

Centers for Disease Control and Prevention. (2015c). *Traumatic brain injury in the United States: Fact sheet.* Retrieved from www.cdc.gov/traumaticbraininjury/get_the_facts.html.

Centers for Disease Control and Prevention. (2015d). *Sickle cell disease: Data & statistics.* Retrieved from www.cdc.gov/ncbddd/sicklecell/data.html.

Cerebral Palsy Alliance. (2015). *What causes cerebral palsy?* Retrieved May 6, 2015, from www.cerebralpalsy.org.au/what-is-cerebral-palsy/causes/.

Child Care Law Center. (2005). *Caring for children with HIV or AIDS in child care.* San Francisco: Child Care Law Center.

Cifu, D. X., Kreutzer, J. S., Slater, D. N., & Taylor, L. (2007). Rehabilitation after traumatic brain injury. In R. L. Braddom (Ed.), *Physical medicine & rehabilitation* (pp. 1133–1174). Philadelphia: Saunders.

Clark, C. D. (2003). *In sickness and in play: Children coping with chronic illness.* Piscataway, NJ: Rutgers University Press.

Compassionate Friends. (2012). *You need not walk alone.* Retrieved January 18, 2011, from www.compassionatefriends.org/Brochures/you_need_not_walk_alone.aspx.

Comstock, E. J. (2011). The end of drugging children: Toward the genealogy of the ADHD subject. *Journal of The History of The Behavioral Sciences, 47*(1), 44–69.

Cystic Fibrosis Foundation. (2012a). *About cystic fibrosis.* Retrieved February 6, 2012, from www.cff.org/AboutCF/.

Cystic Fibrosis Foundation. (2012b). *Frequently asked questions: Who gets cystic fibrosis?* Retrieved February 6, 2012, from www.cff.org/AboutCF/Faqs/.

Daley, D., & Birchwood, J. (2010). ADHD and academic performance: Why does ADHD impact on academic performance and what can be done to support ADHD children in the classroom? *Child: Care, Health and Development, 36*(4), 455–464.

Defense and Veterans Brain Injury Center. (2014).

*TBI and the military.* Retrieved May 6, 2015, from dvbic.dcoe.mil /about/tbi-military.

Dooley, J., Gordon, K. E., Dodds, L., & MacSween, J. (2010). Duchenne muscular dystrophy: A 30-year population-based incidence study, *Clinical Pediatrics, 49*(2), 177–179.

Doyle, E. A., & Grey, M. (2010). Diabetes mellitus (Types 1 and 2). In P. J. Allen, J. A. Vessey, & N. A. Shapiro (Eds.), *Child with a chronic condition,* 5th ed. (pp. 427–446). St. Louis, MO: Mosby.

DuPaul, G. J., & Kern, L. (2011a). Assessment and identification of attention-deficit/hyperactivity disorder. In *Young children with ADHD: Early identification and intervention* (pp. 23–46). Washington, D.C.: American Psychological Association.

DuPaul, G. J., & Kern, L. (2011b). Psychotropic medication treatment. In *Young children with ADHD: Early identification and intervention* (pp. 149–165). Washington, D.C.: American Psychological Association.

DuPaul, G. J., Weyandt, L. L., & Janusis, G. M. (2011). ADHD in the classroom: Effective intervention strategies. *Theory Into Practice, 50*(1), 35–42.

Efron, D. & Sciberras, E. (2010). The diagnostic outcomes of children with suspected attention deficit hyperactivity disorder following multidisciplinary assessment. *Journal of Paediatrics and Child Health, 46,* 392–397.

Elkins, I. J., Malone, S., Keyes, M., Iacono, W. G., & McGue, M. (2011). The impact of attention-deficit/hyperactivity disorder on preadolescent adjustment may be greater for girls than for boys. *Journal of Clinical Child & Adolescent Psychology, 40*(4), 532–545.

Epilepsy Foundation. (2009a). *Understanding epilepsy.* Retrieved April 6, 2009, from www .epilepsyfoundation.org /about/types/causes /index.cfm.

Epilepsy Foundation. (2009b). *What is epilepsy?* Retrieved April 6, 2009, from www.epilepsyfoundation .org/about/index.cfm.

Epilepsy Foundation. (2014). *About epilepsy: The basics.* Retrieved January 20, 2015, from www .epilepsy.com/start-here /about-epilepsy-basics.

Fahrner, R., & Romano, S. (2010). HIV infection and AIDS. In P. J. Allen, J. A. Vessey, & N. A. Shapiro (Eds.), *Child with a chronic condition,* 5th ed. (pp. 527–545). St. Louis, MO: Mosby.

Fowler, M. (2010). Increasing on-task performance for students with ADHD. *Education Digest: Essential Readings Condensed for Quick Review, 76*(2), 44–50.

Frodl, T. (2010). Comorbidity of ADHD and substance use disorder (SUD): A neuroimaging perspective. *Journal of Attention Disorders, 14*(2), 109–120.

Froehlich, T. E., Lanphear, B. P., Epstein, J. N., Barbaresi, W. J., Katusic, S. K., Kahn, R. S. (2007). Prevalence, recognition, and treatment of attention-deficit/hyperactivity disorder in a national sample of us children. *Archives of Pediatrics & Adolescent Medicine, 161*(9), 857–864.

Gebel, E. (2012). *Pushing for diabetes cure.* Retrieved February 4, 2012, from http://forecast.diabetes .org/magazine/features /pushing-a-diabetes-cure.

Geng, G. (2011). Investigation of teachers' verbal and nonverbal strategies for managing attention deficit hyperactivity disorder (ADHD) students' behaviours within a classroom environment. *Australian Journal of Teacher Education, 36*(7), 17–30.

Glass, K., Flory, K., Martin, A., & Hankin, B. L. (2011). ADHD and comorbid conduct problems among adolescents: Associations with self-esteem and substance use. *Attention Deficit and Hyperactivity Disorders, 3*(1), 29–39.

Goldstein, S. (2011). Attention-deficit/hyperactivity disorder. In S. Goldstein & C. R. Reynolds, Eds., *Handbook of neurodevelopmental and genetic disorders in children,* 2nd ed. (pp. 131–150). New York: Guilford Press.

Gorodzinsky, A. Y., Hainsworth, K. R., & Weisman, S. J. (2011). School functioning and chronic pain: A review of methods. *Journal of Pediatric Psychology, 36*(9), 991–1002.

Graf, R. (2009). Stem cells for dummies: A few questions answered. New University. Retrieved April 17, 2009, from www.newuniversity .org/2007/10/features /stem_cells_for _dummies42/.

Graziano, P. A., Geffken, G. R., & Lall, A. S. (2011). Heterogeneity in the pharmacological treatment of children with ADHD: Cognitive, behavioral, and social functioning differences. *Journal of Attention Disorders, 15*(5), 382–391.

Hale, J. B., Reddy, L. A., Semrud-Clikeman, M., Hain, L. A., Whitaker, J., Morley, J., Lawrence, K., Smith, A., & Jones, N. (2011). Executive impairment determines ADHD medication response: Implications for academic achievement. *Journal of Learning Disabilities, 44*(2), 196–212.

Harty, S. C., Miller, C. J., Newcorn, J. H., & Halperin, J. M., (2009). Adolescents with childhood ADHD and comorbid disruptive behavior disorders: Aggression, anger, and hostility. *Child Psychiatry and Human Development, 40*(1), 85–97.

Hazle, L. A. (2010). *Cystic fibrosis.* In P. J. Allen, J. A. Vessey, & N. A. Shapiro (Eds.), *Child with a chronic condition,* 5th ed. (pp. 405–426). St. Louis, MO: Mosby.

Hedin, L. R., Mason, L. H., & Gaffney, J. S. (2011). Comprehension strategy instruction for two students with attention-related disabilities. *Preventing School Failure, 55*(3), 148–157.

Higgens, E. S. (2009, July). Do ADHD drugs take a toll on the brain? *Scientific American.* Retrieved from www.scientificamerican

.com/article.cfm?id=do -adhd-drugs-take-a-toll.

Jahns, V. (2008). Educating your child with spina bifida: One size does not fit all. In M. Lutkenhoff (Ed.), *Children with spina bifida: A parents' guide* (pp. 239–262). Bethesda, MD: Woodbine House.

Kahn, A. B. (2009). *Assistive technology for children who have cerebral palsy: Augmentation communication devices.* Retrieved March 10, 2009, from www.newhorizons.org /spneeds/inclusion /teaching/kahn.htm.

Kalikow, K. T. (2011). *Kids on meds.* New York: W. W. Norton and Company, Inc.

Kent, K. M., Pelham, W. E., Jr., Molina, B. S. G., Sibley, M. H., Waschbusch , D. A., Yu, J., Gnagy, E. M., Biswas, A., Babinski, D. E., & Karch, K. M. (2011). The academic experience of male high school students with ADHD. *Journal of Abnormal Child Psychology, 39,* 451–462.

Kraft, D. P. (2010). Nonmedication treatments for adult ADHD: Evaluating impact on daily functioning and well-being. *Journal of American College Health, 59*(1), 57–59.

Laverdure, P. A., & Rose, D. S. (2012). Providing educationally relevant occupational and physical therapy services. *Physical & Occupational Therapy in Pediatrics, 32*(4), 347–354.

Lazzaretti, C. C., & Pearson, C. (2010). Myelodysplasia. In P. J. Allen, J. A. Vessey, & N. A. Shapiro (Eds.), *Child with a chronic condition,* 5th ed.

(pp. 671–685). St. Louis, MO: Mosby.

Lee, S. S., Humphreys, K. L., Flory, K., Liu, R., & Glass, K. (2011). Prospective association of childhood attention-deficit/hyperactivity disorder (ADHD) and substance use and abuse/ dependence: A meta-analytic review. *Clinical Psychology Review, 31*(3), 328–341.

Levine, E. S., & Anshel, D. J. (2011). "Nothing works!" A case study using cognitive-behavioral interventions to engage parents, educators, and children in the management of attention-deficit/ hyperactivity disorder. *Psychology in the Schools, 48*(3), 297–306.

Light, J., & McNaughton, D. (2012). Supporting the communication, language, and literacy development of children with complex communication needs: State of the science and future research priorities. *Assistive Technology, 24*(1), 34–44.

Liverman, C. T., Altevogt, B. M., Joy, J. E., & Johnson, R. T. (Eds.). (2005). *Spinal cord injury: Progress, promise, and priorities.* Washington, D.C.: National Academies Press.

Mao, A. R., Babcock, T., & Brams, M. (2011). ADHD in adults: Current treatment trends with consideration of abuse potential of medications. *Journal of Psychiatric Practice, 17*(4), 241–250.

Mayo Clinic. (2012a). *Absence seizure (petit mal seizure): Definition.* Retrieved February 4, 2012, from www.mayoclinic .com/health/petit -mal-seizure/DS00216.

Mayo Clinic. (2012b). Diabetes causes. Retrieved February 25, 2012, from www.mayoclinic.com /health/diabetes/DS01121 /DSECTION=causes.

McConaughy, S. H., Volpe, R. J., & Antshel, K. M. (2011). Academic and social impairments of elementary school children with attention deficit hyperactivity disorder. *School Psychology Review, 40*(2), 200–225.

McNaughton, D., & Light, J. (2013). The iPad and mobile technology revolution: Benefits and challenges for individuals who require augmentative and alternative communication. *Augmentative and Alternative Communication, 29*(2), 107–116.

Mitchell, J. T., Robertson, C. D., Kimbrel, N. A., & Nelson-Gray, R. O. (2011). An evaluation of behavioral approach in adults with ADHD. *Journal of Psychopathology and Behavioral Assessment, 33*(4), 430–437.

Muscular Dystrophy Association. (2011). *Facts about Duchenne & Becker muscular dystrophies.* Tucson, AZ: Muscular Dystrophy Association.

Muscular Dystrophy Association. (2012). Diseases: Duchenne muscular dystrophy (DMD). Retrieved January 18, 2012, from www.mdausa.org /disease/dmd.html.

National Center for HIV/ AIDS, Viral Hepatitis, STD, and TB Prevention. (2012). *What are HIV and AIDS?* Retrieved from http://www.cdc.gov /hiv/basics/whatIshiv .html.

National Institute of Mental Health. (2008). *Attention deficit hyperactivity disorder.* Bethesda, MD: Author.

National Institute of Mental Health. (2012a). *Attention deficit hyperactivity disorder (ADHD): What is attention deficit hyperactivity disorder?* Bethesda, MD: National Institute of Mental Health.

National Institute of Mental Health. (2012b). *Attention deficit hyperactivity disorder in children and adolescents fact sheet.* Bethesda, MD: National Institute of Mental Health.

National Institute of Neurological Disorders and Stroke. (2012a). *NINDS epilepsy information page.* Retrieved February 4, 2012, from www .ninds.nih.gov/disorders /epilepsy/epilepsy.htm.

National Institute of Neurological Disorders and Stroke. (2012b). NINDS muscular dystrophy information page: Muscular dystrophy. Retrieved January 18, 2012, from www.ninds.nih .gov/disorders/md/md .htm.

National Institute of Neurological Disorders and Stroke. (2012c). *Seizures and epilepsy: Hope through research.* Retrieved February 4, 2012, from www.ninds.nih .gov/disorders/epilepsy /detail_epilepsy.htm #192293109.

National Institute of Neurological Disorders and Stroke. (2012d). *Seizures and epilepsy: hope through research.* Retrieved February 13, 2012, from www.ninds

.nih.gov/disorders /epilepsy/detail_epilepsy .htm#192443109.

National Institute of Neu-rological Disorders and Stroke. (2012e). *NINDS traumatic brain injury information page: What is traumatic brain injury?* Retrieved February 6, 2012, from www.ninds .nih.gov/disorders/tbi /tbi.htm.

National Resource Center on ADHD. (2012). *So-cial skills in adults with ADHD.* Retrieved February 14, 2012, from www.addforums.com /forums/showthread .php?t=16804.

National Spinal Cord Injury Statistical Center. (2014). *Facts and figures at a glance.* Birmingham, AL: University of Alabama at Birmingham. Retrieved from https://www.nscisc .uab.edu/PublicDocu ments/fact_figures_docs /Facts%202014.pdf.

Nehring, W. M. (2010). Cerebral palsy. In P. J. Allen, J. A. Vessey, & N. A. Shapiro (Eds.), *Child with a chronic condition,* 5th ed. (pp. 326–346). St. Louis, MO: Mosby.

Nikolas, M. A., & Burt, S. A. (2010). Genetic and en-vironmental influences on ADHD symptom dimensions of inatten-tion and hyperactivity: A meta-analysis. *Journal of Abnormal Psychology, 119*(1), 1–17.

Owens, J. S., & Fabiano, G. A. (2011). School mental health programming for youth with ADHD: Ad-dressing needs across the academic career. *School Mental Health, 3*(3), 111–116.

Palisano, R. J., Begnoche, D. M., Chiarello, L. A.,

Bartlett, D. J., McCoy, S. W., & Chang, H. J. (2012). Amount and focus of physical therapy and occupational therapy for young children with cerebral palsy. *Physical & Occupational Therapy in Pediatrics, 32*(4), 368–382.

Parent Project Muscular Dystrophy. (2012). *Steroids/nutritional supplements/antibiotics.* Retrieved January 18, 2012, from www .parentprojectmd.org/site /PageServer?pagename =Care_physical_supple ments_options.

Parkes, J., & Hill, N. (2010). The needs of children and young people with cerebral palsy. *Paediatric Nursing, 22*(4), 14–19.

Posey, W. M., Bassin, S. A., & Lewis, A. (2009). Preschool ADHD and medication … More study needed?! *Journal of Early Childhood and Infant Psychology, 5,* 57–77.

Powell, S. G., Thomsen, P. H., & Frydenberg, M. (2011). Long-term treat-ment of ADHD with stimulants: A large observational study of real-life patients. *Journal of Attention Disorders, 15*(6), 439–451.

Pugach, M. C., & Winn, J. A. (2011). Research on co-teaching and teaming: An untapped resource for induction. *Journal of Special Education Lead-ership, 24*(1), 36–46.

Rabiner, D. L., Anastopou-los, A. D., & Costello, E. J. (2010). Predictors of non-medical ADHD medication use by college students. *Journal of Attention Dis-orders, 13*(6), 640–648.

Ramachandran, Priya. (2010). *From science

fiction to reality: Exo-skeletons.* The National Spinal Cord Injury Asso-ciation. Retrieved from www.spinalcord.org /from-science-fiction-to -reality-exoskeletons/.

Ratcliffe, M. M., & Kieckhefer, G. M. (2010). Asthma. In P. J. Allen, J. A. Vessey, & N. A. Shapiro (Eds.), *Child with a chronic condition,* 5th ed. (pp. 168–196). St. Louis, MO: Mosby.

Reid, R., & Johnson, J. (2011). *Teacher's Guide to ADHD.* What works for special-needs learn-ers series. New York: Guilford Publications.

Ricci, S. S., & Kyle, T. (2009a). Nursing care of the child with a neu-rologic disorder. In S. S. Ricci & T. Kyle, *Ma-ternity and pediatric nursing* (pp. 1138–1186). Philadelphia: Lippincott, Williams, & Wilkins.

Ricci, S. S., & Kyle, T. (2009b). Sexually trans-mitted infections. In S. S. Ricci & T. Kyle, *Ma-ternity and pediatric nursing* (pp. 141–170). Philadelphia: Lippincott, Williams, & Wilkins.

Riley, J. L., McKevitt, B. C., Shriver, M. D., & Allen, K. D. (2011). Increas-ing on-task behavior using teacher attention delivered on a fixed-time schedule. *Journal of Behavioral Education, 20*(3), 149–162.

Ryan, J. B., Katsiyannis, A., & Hughes, E. M. ( 2011). Medication treatment for attention deficit hyper-activity disorder. *Theory Into Practice, 50*(1), 52–60.

Schachar, R. (2014). Genetics of attention deficit hyper-activity disorder (ADHD):

Recent updates and fu-ture prospects. *Current Developmental Disorders Reports, 1,* 41–49.

Science Codex. (2009). *Studies investigate child-hood obesity, diabetes and related conditions.* Retrieved April 11, 2009, from http://sciencecodex .com/studies_investigate _childhood_obesity _diabetes_and_related _conditions.

Selekman, J. (2010). Attention-deficit hyper-activity disorder. In P. J. Allen, J. A. Vessey, & N. A. Shapiro (Eds.), *Child with a chronic condition,* 5th ed. (pp. 197–217). St. Louis, MO: Mosby.

Shute, N. (2009). ADHD medication: Can your child go without? *U.S. News & World Report.* Retrieved from http:// health.usnews.com /health-news/family -health/brain-and -behavior/articles/2009 /01/14/adhd-medication -can-your-child-go -without_print.html.

Spinal Cord Injury Resource Center. (2012). *Spinal cord 101.* Retrieved January 18, 2012, from www .spinalinjury.net/html /_spinal_cord_101.html.

Sprich, S. E., Knouse, L. E., & Cooper-Vince, C. (2010). Description and demonstration of CBT for ADHD in adults. *Cog-nitive and Behavioral Practice, 17*(1), 9–15.

Springer, C., & Reddy, L. A. (2010). Measuring parental treatment ad-herence in a multimodal treatment program for children with ADHD: A preliminary investiga-tion. *Child & Family Behavior Therapy, 32*(4), 272–290.

Stark, C., Hoyer-Kuhn, H. K., Semler, O., Hoebing, L., Duran, I., Cremer, R., Schoenau, E. (2014). Neuromuscular training based on whole body vibration in children with spina bifida: A retrospective analysis of a new physiotherapy program. *Child's Nervous System: CHNS*. Advance online publication: Internet *ISSN:* 1433–0350 (Electronic).

Stiens, S. A., Fawber, H. L., & Yuhas, S. A. (2013). The person with spinal cord injury: An evolving prototype for life care planning. *Physical Medicine and Rehabilitation Clinics of North America, 24*(3), 419–444.

Storm, B. C., & White, H. A. (2010). ADHD and retrieval-induced forgetting: Evidence for a deficit in the inhibitory control of memory. *Memory, 18* (3), 265–271.

Stroh, J., Frankenberger, W., Cornell-Swanson, L., Wood, C., & Pahl, S. (2008). The use of stimulant medication and behavioral interventions for the treatment of attention deficit hyperactivity disorder: A survey of parents' knowledge, attitudes, and experiences. *Journal of Child & Family Studies, 17*(3), 385–401.

Taylor, A., Deb, S., & Unwin, G. (2011). Scales for the identification of adults with attention deficit hyperactivity disorder (ADHD): A systematic review. *Research in Developmental Disabilities, 32*(3), 924–938.

Thorell, L. B., & Rydell, A-M. (2008). Behaviour problems and social competence deficits associated with symptoms of attention-deficit/hyperactivity disorder: effects of age and gender. *Child: Care, Health & Development, 34*(5), 584–595.

United Cerebral Palsy. (2012). *Cerebral palsy information*. Retrieved January 11, 2012, from www.ucp.org.

U.S. Department of Education. (2006). *Assistance to states for the education of children with disabilities and preschool grants for children with disabilities; Final rule, 34 CFR Parts 300, 301, and Part C§636*. Retrieved from www.ed.gov/policy/speced/guid/idea/idea2004.html#law.

VGo. (2012). VGo Communications, Inc. Retrieved February 22, 2012, from www.vgocom.com/remote-student.

van de Loo-Neus, G. H. H., Rommelse, N., & Buitelaar, J. K. (2011). To stop or not to stop? How long should medication treatment of attention-deficit hyperactivity disorder be extended? *European Neuropsychopharmacology, 21*(8), 584–599.

van Kraayenoord, C. E., Miller, R., & Moni, K. B. (2009). Teaching writing to students with learning difficulties in inclusive English classrooms: Lessons from an exemplary teacher. *English Teaching: Practice and Critique, 8*(1), 23–51.

Vaughan, B. S., Roberts, H. J., & Needelman, H. (2009). Current medications for the treatment of attention-deficit/hyperactivity disorder. *Psychology in the Schools, 46*(9), 846–856.

Velde, S. V., Biervliet, S. V., Bruyne, R. D., & Winckel, M. V. (2013). A systematic review on bowel management and the success rate of various treatment modalities in spina bifida patients. *Spinal Cord, 51*(12), 873–881.

Wilens, T. E., Martelon, M., Joshi, G., Bateman, C., Fried, R., Petty, C., & Biederman, J. (2011). Does ADHD predict substance-use disorders? A 10-year follow-up study of young adults with ADHD. *Journal of the American Academy of Child and Adolescent Psychiatry, 50*(6), 543–553.

Williamson, P., & McLeskey, J. (2011). An investigation into the nature of inclusion problem-solving teams. *Teacher Educator, 46*(4), 316–334.

Willcutt, E. G. (2012). The prevalence of DSM-IV attention-deficit/hyperactivity disorder: A meta-analytic review. *Neurotherapeutics, 9,* 490–499.

Yamamoto, M. S. (2007). Cerebral palsy. In B. J. Atchinson & D. K. Dirette (Eds.), *Conditions in occupational therapy: Effect on occupational performance* (pp. 9–22). Baltimore: Lippincott, Williams, and Wilkins.

Youngstrom, E. A., Arnold, L. E., & Frazier, T. W. (2010). Bipolar and ADHD comorbidity: Both artifact and outgrowth of shared mechanisms. *Clinical Psychology: Science and Practice, 17*(4), 350–359.

## Chapter 15

Adams, C. M. (2006). Articulating gifted education program goals. In J. H. Purcell & R. D. Eckert (Eds.), *Designing services and programs for high-ability learners: A guidebook for gifted education* (pp. 62–72). Thousand Oaks, CA: Corwin Press.

Baum, S. (Ed.). (2004). Introduction to twice-exceptional and special populations of gifted students [Introduction]. In *Twice-exceptional and special populations of gifted students* (pp. xxiii–xxxiii). Thousand Oaks, CA: Corwin Press.

Baum, S. M., Schader, R. M., & Hebert, T. P. (2014). Through a different lens: Reflecting on a strength-based, talent-focused approach for twice-exceptional learners. *Gifted Child Quarterly, 58*(4), 311–327.

Benjamin, A. (2013). *Differentiated instruction: A guide for middle and high school teachers*. New York: Routledge.

Berlin, J. E. (2009). It's a matter of perspective: Student perceptions of the impact of being labeled gifted and talented. *Roeper Review, 31*(4), 217–223.

Binet, A., & Simon, T. (1905). Methodes nouvelles pour le diagnostique du niveau intellectuel desanomaux. *L'Anee Psychologique, 11,* 196–198.

Binet, A., & Simon, T. (1908). Le development de intelligence chez les enfants. *L'Anee Psychologique, 14,* 1–94.

Bireda, M. R. (2011). *Schooling for minority children*. Lanham, MD:

Rowman & Littlefield Education.

Borland, J. H. (2003). Evaluating gifted programs: A broader perspective. In N. Colagnelo & G. A. Davis (Eds.), *Handbook of gifted education* (pp. 293–307). Boston: Pearson Education.

Burns, D. E., Purcell, J. H., & Hertberg, H. L. (2006). Curriculum for gifted education students. In J. H. Purcell & R. D. Eckert (Eds.), *Designing services and programs for high-ability learners: A guidebook for gifted education* (pp. 87–111). Thousand Oaks, CA: Corwin Press.

Callahan, C. M. (2008). Assessing and improving services provided to gifted students: A plan for program evaluation. In F. A. Karnes & K. R. Stephens (Eds.), *Achieving excellence in gifted and talented* (pp. 230–245). Upper Saddle River, NJ: Pearson.

Callard-Szulgit, R. (2003). *Parenting and teaching the gifted.* Lanham, MD: Scarecrow Press.

Caraisco, J. (2007). Overcoming lethargy in gifted and talented education with contract activity packages: "I'm choosing to learn!" *Journal of Educational Strategies, Issues and Ideas, 80*(6), 255–260.

Cattell, R. B. (1971). *Abilities: Their structure, growth, and action.* Boston: Houghton Mifflin.

Center for Comprehensive School Reform and Improvement. (2008). *Issue brief: Gifted and talented students at risk for underachievement.* Austin, TX: Learning Point Associates.

Clark, B. (2008). *Growing up gifted,* 7th ed. Columbus, OH: Merrill.

Clark, B. (2013). *Growing up gifted,* 8th ed. Upper Saddle River, NJ: Pearson.

Claxton, G., & Meadows, S. (2009). Brightening up: How children learn to be gifted. In T. Balchin, B. Hymer, & D. J. Matthews (Eds.), *The Routledge international companion to gifted education* (pp. 3–9). New York: Routledge.

Cohen, S. (2005, March 19). *Child prodigy's apparent suicide: "He knew he had to leave," mother says.* New York: Associated Press.

Colangelo, N., & Assouline, S. (2009). Acceleration: Meeting the academic and social needs of students. In T. Balchin, B. Hymer, & D. J. Matthews (Eds.), *The Routledge international companion to gifted education* (pp. 194–202). New York: Routledge.

Colangelo, N., Assouline, S. G., & Gross, M. U. M. (2004a). *A nation deceived: How schools hold back America's brightest students,* Vol. I. Iowa City: University of Iowa.

Colangelo, N., Assouline, S. G., & Gross, M. U. M. (2004b). *A nation deceived: How schools hold back America's brightest students,* Vol. II. Iowa City: University of Iowa.

Colangelo, N., Assouline, S. G., & Lupkowski-Shoplik, A. E. (2004). Whole-grade acceleration. In N. Colangelo, S. G. Assouline, & M. U. M. Gross (Eds.), *A nation deceived: How schools hold back America's brightest students,* Vol. II (pp. 77–76). Iowa City: University of Iowa.

Coleman, L. J. (2005). *Nurturing talent in high school: Life in the fast lane.* In *Education and psychology of the gifted series.* New York: Teachers College Press.

Colombo, J., Shaddy, D. J., Blaga, O. M., Anderson, C. J., & Kannass, K. N. (2009). High cognitive ability in infancy and early childhood. In F. E. Horowitz, R. F. Subotnik, & J. J. Matthews (Eds.), *The development of giftedness and talent across the lifespan* (pp. 23–42). Washington, D.C.: American Psychological Association.

Colvin, G. (2008). *Talent is overrated: What really separates world-class performers from everyone else?* New York: Penguin.

Conant, J. B. (1959). *The American high school today.* New York: McGraw-Hill.

Cooper, C. R. (2006). Creating a comprehensive and defensible budget for gifted programs and services. In J. H. Purcell & R. D. Eckert (Eds.), *Designing services and programs for high-ability learners: A guidebook for gifted education* (pp. 125–136). Thousand Oaks, CA: Corwin Press.

Cross, T. L., & Coleman, L. J. (2014). School-based conception of giftedness. *Journal of Education of the Gifted, 37*(1), 94–103.

Davis, G. A., & Rimm, S. B. (2004). *Education of the gifted and talented,* 5th ed. San Francisco: Allyn & Bacon.

Davis, G. A., Rimm, S. B., & Siegle, D. (2011). *Education of the gifted and talented,* 6th ed. Boston: Pearson.

DeHann, R., & Havighurst, R. J. (1957). *Educating gifted children.* Chicago: University of Chicago Press.

Eckert, R. D. (2006). Developing a mission statement on the educational needs of gifted and talented students. In J. H. Purcell & R. D. Eckert (Eds.), *Designing services and programs for high-ability learners: A guidebook for gifted education* (pp. 15–22). Thousand Oaks, CA: Corwin Press.

Eckstein, M. (2009). Enrichment 2.0: Gifted and talented education for the 21st century. *Gifted Child Today, 32*(1), 59–63.

Esping, A., & Plucker, J. A. (2008). Theories of intelligence. In F. A. Karnes & K. R. Stephens (Eds.), *Achieving excellence in gifted and talented* (pp. 36–48). Upper Saddle River, NJ: Pearson.

Firmender, J. M., Reis, S. M, & Sweeny, S. M. (2013). Reading comprehension and fluency levels ranges across diverse classrooms: The need for differentiated reading instruction and content. *Gifted Child Quarterly, 57*(1), 3–14.

Ford, D. Y. (2003). Equity and excellence: Culturally diverse students in gifted education. In N. Colagnelo & G. A. Davis (Eds.), *Handbook of gifted education,* 3rd ed. (pp. 506–520). Boston: Pearson Education.

Ford, D. Y., Coleman, M. R., & Davis, J. L. (2014).

Racially, ethnically, and linguistically different gifted and talented students. *Gifted Child Today, 37*(3), 133–134.

Gagné, F. (1999). My convictions about the nature of abilities, gifts, and talents. *Journal for the Education of the Gifted, 22*(2), 109–136.

Gallagher, J. J. (Ed.). (2004). Public policy in gifted education. In *Essential readings in gifted education*. Thousand Oaks, CA: Corwin Press.

Gardner, H. (1983). *Frames of mind: The theory of multiple intelligences*. New York: Basic Books.

Gibbons, M. M., Pelchar, T. K., & Cochran, J. L. (2012). Gifted students from low-education backgrounds. *Roeper Review, 34*, 114–122.

Gottfried, A. W., Gottfried, A. E., & Guerin, D. W. (2009). Issues in early prediction and identification of intellectual giftedness. In F. E. Horowitz, R. F. Subotnik, & J. J. Matthews (Eds.), *The development of giftedness and talent across the lifespan* (pp. 43–56). Washington, D.C.: American Psychological Association.

Graham, G. (2009). Giftedness in adolescence: African American gifted youth and their challenges from a motivation perspective. In F. E. Horowitz, R. F. Subotnik, & J. J. Matthews (Eds.), *The development of giftedness and talent across the lifespan* (pp. 109–129). Washington, D.C.: American Psychological Association.

Gross, M. U. M. (2004). Radical acceleration. In N. Colangelo, S. G. Assouline, & M. U. M. Gross (Eds.), *A nation deceived: How schools hold back America's brightest students*, Vol. II (pp. 87–96). Iowa City: University of Iowa.

Gubbins, E. J. (2006). Constructing identification procedures. In J. H. Purcell & R. D. Eckert (Eds.), *Designing services and programs for high-ability learners: A guidebook for gifted education* (pp. 49–61). Thousand Oaks, CA: Corwin Press.

Guilford, J. P. (1950). Creativity. *American Psychologist, 5*, 444–454.

Guilford, J. P. (1959). Three faces of intellect. *American Psychologist, 14*, 469–479.

Harris, B., Plucker, J. A., Rapp, K. E., & Marinez, R. S. (2009). Identifying gifted and talented English language learners: A case study. *Journal for the Education of the Gifted, 32*(3), 368–393.

Hoogeveen, L., van Hell, J. G., & Verhoeven, L. (2014). Socio-emotional characteristics of gifted accelerated and non-accelerated students in the Netherlands. *British Journal of Educational Psychology, 82*, 585–605.

Horowitz, F. D. (2009). Introduction: A development understanding of giftedness and talent. In F. D. Horowitz, R. F. Subotnik, & D. J. Matthews, (Eds.). *The development of giftedness and talent across the life span* (pp. 3–19). Washington, D.C.: American Psychological Association.

Hughes, J. (2009). Teaching the able child … or teaching the child to be able. In T. Balchin, B. Hymer & D. J. Matthews (Eds.), *The Routledge international companion to gifted education* (pp. 161–168). New York: Routledge.

Isaacson, W. (2011). *Steve Jobs*. New York: Simon and Shuster.

Johnsen, S. K. (2008). Identifying gifted and talented learners. In F. A. Karnes & K. R. Stephens (Eds.), *Achieving excellence in gifted and talented* (pp. 135–153). Upper Saddle River, NJ: Pearson.

Johnsen, S. K. (2013). Resources for addressing assessment and accountability challenges in providing services to gifted students. *Gifted Child Today, 36*(1), 81–82.

Johnsen, S. K., VanTassel-Baska, J., & Robinson, A. (2008). *Using the national gifted education standards for university preparation programs*. Thousand Oaks, CA: Corwin Press.

King, K. A., Kozleski, E. B., & Lansdowne, K. (2009, May–June). Where are all the students of color in gifted education? *Principal Magazine*, pp. 17–20.

Knight, S. (2009). *Is high IQ a burden as much as a blessing?* Retrieved May 15, 2009, from www.ft.com/intl/cms/s/0/4add9230-23d5-11de-996a-00144feabdc0.html.

Kulik, J. (2004). Meta-analytic studies of acceleration: Dimensions and issues. In N. Colangelo, S. G. Assouline, & M. U. M. Gross (Eds.), *A nation deceived: How schools hold back America's brightest students*, Vol. II (pp. 13–22). Iowa City: University of Iowa.

Leppien, J. H., & Westberg, K. L. (2006). Roles, responsibilities, and professional qualifications of key personnel for gifted education services. In J. H. Purcell & R. D. Eckert (Eds.), *Designing services and programs for high-ability learners: A guidebook for gifted education* (pp. 161–182). Thousand Oaks, CA: Corwin Press.

Liu, W. M., Shepherd, S. J., & Nicpon, M. F. (2008). "Boy are tough, not smart": Counseling gifted and talented young and adolescent boys. In M. S. Kiselica, M. Englar-Carlson, & A. M. Horne (Eds.), *Counseling troubled boys: A guidebook for professionals* (pp. 273–292). New York: Routledge.

Lubbard, T., Georgsdottir, A., & Besançon, M. (2009). The nature of creative giftedness and talent. In T. Balchin, B. Hymer, & D. J. Matthews (Eds.), *The Routledge international companion to gifted education* (pp. 42–49). New York: Routledge.

MacKinnon, D. W. (1962). The nature and nurture of creative talent. *American Psychologist, 17*(7), 484–495.

Manning, S., & Bestnoy, K. D. (2008). Special populations. In F. A. Karnes & K. R. Stephens (Eds.), *Achieving excellence in gifted and talented* (pp. 116–134). Upper Saddle River, NJ: Pearson.

Matthews, M. S., & Shaunessy, E. (2008).

Culturally, linguistically, and economically diverse gifted students. In F. A. Karnes & K. R. Stephens (Eds.), *Achieving excellence in gifted and talented* (pp. 99–115). Upper Saddle River, NJ: Pearson.

McHugh, M. W. (2006). Governor's schools. Fostering the social and emotional well-being of gifted and talented students. *Journal of Secondary Gifted Education, 17*(3), 50–58.

Mersino, Deborah. (2012). How grade skipping changed everything. *Ingenious: Strategic communication, gifted perspective* (blog), Copyright © Deborah Mersino. Reprinted with permission from www.ingeniosus.net/archives/category/acceleration.

Montgomery, D. (2009). Special educational needs and dual exceptionality. In T. Balchin, B. Hymer, & D. J. Matthews (Eds.), *The Routledge international companion to gifted education* (pp. 218–225). New York: Routledge.

Mooij, T. (2013). Designing instruction and learning for cognitively gifted pupils in preschool and primary school. *International Journal of Inclusive Education, 17*(6), 597–613.

Moon, S. M. (2006). Developing a definition of giftedness. In J. H. Purcell & R. D. Eckert (Eds.), *Designing services and programs for high-ability learners: A guidebook for gifted education* (pp. 23–31). Thousand Oaks, CA: Corwin Press.

Moran, S. (2010). Creativity in school. In K. Littleton, C. Wood, & J. K. Staarman (Eds.), *International handbook of psychology in education* (pp. 319–359). Bingley, UK: Emerald.

Morawska, A., & Sanders, M. R. (2009). Parenting gifted and talented children: Conceptual and empirical foundations. *Gifted Child Quarterly, 53*(3), 163–173.

National Association for Gifted Children. (2012). Frequently asked questions: Is there a definition of "gifted"? Retrieved March 10, 2012, from www.nagc.org/index2.aspx?id=548.

National Association for Gifted Children. (2014). *2012–2013 state of the states in gifted education, Table C: State mandates and funding levels*. Retrieved from www.nagc.org/sites/default/files/Gifted-by-State/Table%20C%20(mandates%20%20funding).pdf

North, J. (2007). Practical gifted kidkeeping. In L. B. Golden & P. Henderson, (Eds.), *Case studies in school counseling* (pp. 223–233). Upper Saddle River, NJ: Pearson.

Olszewski-Kubilius, P., & Lee, S. Y. (2004). The role of participation in in-school and outside-of-school activities in the talent development of gifted students. *The Journal of Secondary Gifted Education, XV*(3), 107–123.

Olszewski-Kubilius, P., & Lee, S. (2008). Specialized programs serving the gifted. In F. A. Karnes & K. R. Stephens (Eds.), *Achieving excellence: Educating the gifted and talented* (pp. 192–208). Upper Saddle River, NJ: Pearson.

Olszewski-Kubilius, P., & Lee, S. Y. (2011). Gender and other group differences in performance on off-level tests: Changes in the 21st century. *Gifted Child Quarterly, 55*(1), 54–73.

Passow, A. H. (2004). The nature of giftedness and talent. In R. J. Sternberg (Ed.), *Definitions and conceptions of giftedness* (pp. 1–11). Thousand Oaks, CA: Corwin Press.

Phillipson, S. N., & McCann, M. (2007). *Conceptions of giftedness: Sociocultural perspectives*. Mahwah, NJ: Lawrence Erlbaum Associates, Inc., Publishers.

Piffer, D. (2012). Can creativity be measured?: An attempt to clarify the notion of creativity and general directions for future research. *Thinking Skills and Creativity, 7,* 258–264.

Piirto, J. (1999). *Talented children and adults: Their development and education*. Upper Saddle River, NJ: Prentice-Hall.

Plomin, R., & Price, T. S. (2003). The relationship between genetics and intelligence. In N. Colangelo & G. A. Davis (Eds.), *Handbook of gifted education,* 3rd ed. (pp. 113–123). Boston: Pearson Education.

Purcell, J. H., & Eckert, R. D. (2006). *Designing services and programs for high-ability learners: A guidebook for gifted education.* Thousand Oaks, CA: Corwin Press.

Ramos-Ford, V., & Gardner, H. (1991). Giftedness from a multiple intelligences perspective. In N. Colangelo & G. A. Davis (Eds.), *Handbook of gifted education* (pp. 55–64). Boston: Allyn & Bacon.

Ramos-Ford, V., & Gardner, H. (1997). Giftedness from a multiple intelligences perspective. In N. Colangelo & G. A. Davis (Eds.), *Handbook of gifted education,* 2nd ed. (pp. 54–66). Boston: Allyn & Bacon.

Reis, S. & Renzulli, J. S. (2004). Current research on the social and emotional development of gifted and talented students: Good news and future possibilities. *Psychology in the Schools, 41*(1), 119–130.

Renzulli Learning. (2012). Differentiation engine. Retrieved March 17, 2012, from www.renzullilearning.com/ToolsAndServices/differentiationengine.aspx.

Renzulli, J. S. (Ed.). (2004). *Identification of students for gifted and talented programs*. In *Essential readings in gifted education*. Thousand Oaks, CA: Corwin Press.

Renzulli, J. S., & Reis, S. M. (2003). The schoolwide enrichment model: Developing creative and productive giftedness. In N. Colangelo & G. A. Davis (Eds.), *Handbook of gifted education*, 3rd ed. (pp. 184–203). Boston: Pearson Education.

Richert, E. S. (2003). Excellence with justice in identification and programming. In N. Colangelo & G. A. Davis (Eds.), *Handbook of gifted education,* 3rd ed.

(pp. 146–161). Boston: Pearson Education.

Rimm, S. (2008). Parenting gifted children. In F. A. Karnes & K. R. Stephens (Eds.), *Achieving excellence in gifted and talented* (pp. 262–277). Upper Saddle River, NJ: Pearson.

Rimm, S. B. (1982). *PRIDE: Preschool and primary interest descriptor.* Watertown, WI: Educational Assessment Service.

Rimm, S. B., & Davis, G. A. (1983, September/October). Identifying creativity, Part II. *G/C/T,* 19–23.

Davis, G. A., & Rimm, S. B. (2004). *Education of the gifted and talented, 5th ed.* (p. 33). San Francisco: Allyn & Bacon.

Roberts, J. L. (2008). Teachers of the gifted and talented. In F. A. Karnes & K. R. Stephens (Eds.), *Achieving excellence in gifted and talented* (pp. 246–261). Upper Saddle River, NJ: Pearson.

Robinson, A., Shore, B. M., & Enerson, D. L. (2007). *Best practices in gifted education: an evidenced-based guide.* Waco, TX: Prufrock Press, Inc.

Rogers, K. B. (2004). The academic effects of acceleration. In N. Colangelo, S. G. Assouline, & M. U. M. Gross (Eds.), *A nation deceived: How schools hold back America's brightest students,* Vol. II (pp. 47–58). Iowa City: University of Iowa.

Rogers, K. B. (2006). Connecting program design and district policies. In J. H. Purcell & R. D. Eckert (Eds.), *Designing services and programs for high-ability learners: A guidebook for gifted*

education (pp. 207–223). Thousand Oaks, CA: Corwin Press.

Savant, M. (2012). *About Marilyn.* Retrieved April 10, 2012, from http://marilynvossavant.com/about-marilyn/.

Scott, M. T. (2014). Using the Blooms-Banks matrix to develop multicultural differentiated lessons for gifted students. *Gifted Child Today, 37*(3), 163–168.

Silverman, L. K. (1986). What happens to the gifted girl? In C. J. Maker (Ed.), *Critical issues in gifted education: Defensible programs for the gifted,* Vol. 1 (pp. 43–89). Austin, TX: PRO-ED.

Sosniak, L. A., & Gabelko, N. H. (2008). *Every child's right: Academic talent development by choice, not chance.* New York: Teacher College Press.

Stephens, K. R., & Karnes, F. A. (2000). State definitions for the gifted and talented revisited. *Exceptional Children, 66*(2), 219–238.

Sternberg, R. F., Jarvin, L., & Grigorenko, E. L. (2011). *Explorations in giftedness.* New York: Cambridge University Press.

Sternberg, R. J. (1997). A triarchic view of giftedness: Theory and practice. In N. Colangelo & G. A Davis (Eds.), *Handbook of gifted education,* 2nd ed. (pp. 43–53). Boston: Allyn & Bacon.

Sternberg, R. J. (2006). Creativity is a habit. *Education Week, 25*(24), p. 64.

Sternberg, R. J. (2009). Wisdom, intelligence, creativity, synthesized: A model of giftedness. In T.

Balchin, B. Hymer, & D. J. Matthews (Eds.), *The Routledge international companion to gifted education* (pp. 255–264). New York: Routledge.

Subotnik, R. F., & Calderon, J. (2008). Developing giftedness and talent. In F. A. Karnes & K. R. Stephens (Eds.), *Achieving excellence in gifted and talented* (pp. 49–61). Upper Saddle River, NJ: Pearson.

Subotnik, R. F., Olszewski-Kubilius, P., & Worrell, F. C. (2011). Rethinking giftedness and gifted education: A proposed direction forward based on psychological science. *Association for Psychological Science, 12,* 3–54.

Tannenbaum, A. J. (2003). Nature and nurture of giftedness. In N. Colangelo & G. A Davis (Eds.), *Handbook of gifted education,* 3rd ed. (pp. 45–59). Boston: Allyn & Bacon.

Terman, L. M. (1925). *Genetic studies of genius: Vol. 1. Mental and physical traits of a thousand gifted children.* Stanford, CA: Stanford University Press.

Ternus-Bellamy, A. (2013, March 7). The story of a gifted child. *The Davis Enterprise,* p. A1. Retrieved from www.davisenterprise.com/local-news/the-story-of-a-gifted-child/.

Thomsen, D., & Olszewski-Kubilius, P. (2014). The increasingly important role of off-level testing in the context of the talent development perspective. *Gifted Child Today, 37*(1), 33–40.

Tomlinson, C. A., & Hockett, J. A. (2008). Instructional

strategies and programming options for gifted learners. In F. A. Karnes & K. R. Stephens (Eds.), *Achieving excellence: Educating the gifted and talented,* pp. 154–169, Upper Saddle River, NJ: Prentice Hall.

Tomlinson, C. A., & Jarvis, J. M. (2014). Case studies of success: Supporting academic success for students with high potential from ethnic minority and economically disadvantaged backgrounds. *Journal for the Education of the Gifted, 37*(3), 191–219.

Tomlinson, C. A., Doubet, K. J., & Capper, M. R. (2006). Aligning gifted education services with general education. In J. H. Purcell & R. D. Eckert (Eds.), *Designing services and programs for high-ability learners: A guidebook for gifted education* (pp. 224–238). Thousand Oaks, CA: Corwin Press.

Torrance, E. P. (1961). Problems of highly creative children. *Gifted Child Quarterly, 5,* 31–34.

Torrance, E. P. (1965). *Gifted children in the classroom.* New York: Macmillan.

Torrance, E. P. (1966). *Torrance tests of creative thinking.* Bensenville, IL: Scholastic Testing Service.

Torrance, E. P. (1968). Finding hidden talent among disadvantaged children. *Gifted and Talented Quarterly, 12,* 131–137.

Treffinger, D. J. (2004). Creativity and giftedness. In S. M. Reis, *Essential readings in gifted education.* Thousand Oaks, CA: Corwin Press.

Treffinger, D., Nassab, C. A., & Selby, E. C. (2009). Programming for talent development: Expanding horizons for gifted education. In T. Balchin, B. Hymer, & D. J. Matthews (Eds.), *The Routledge international companion to gifted education* (pp. 210–217). New York: Routledge.

VanTassel-Baska, J. (1989). *Counseling the gifted.* Denver, CO: Love.

VanTassel-Baska, J. (2009). The role of gifted education in promoting cultural diversity. In T. Balchin, B. Hymer, & D. J. Matthews (Eds.), *The Routledge international companion to gifted education* (pp. 273–280). New York: Routledge.

VanTassel-Baska, J. (2012). Analyzing differentiation in the classroom: Using the COS-R. *Gifted Child Today, 35*(1), 42–48.

VanTassel-Baska, J. (2013). Curriculum, instruction, and assessment for the gifted: A problem-based scenario. *Gifted Child Today, 36*(1), 71–75.

Warwick, I., & Matthews, D. J. (2009). Fostering giftedness in urban and diverse communities: Context-sensitive solutions. In T. Balchin, B. Hymer, & D. J. Matthews (Eds.), *The Routledge international companion to gifted education* (pp. 265–272). New York: Routledge.

Williams, F. E. (1980). *Creativity assessment packet*. East Aurora, NY: DOK.

Worrell, F. C. (2009). What does gifted mean? Personal and social identity perspectives on giftedness in adolescents. In F. E. Horowitz, R. F. Subotnik, & J. J. Matthews (Eds.), *The development of giftedness and talent across the lifespan* (pp. 131–152). Washington, D.C.: American Psychological Association.

Worrell, F. C., & Erwin, J. O., (2011). Best practices in identifying students for gifted and talented programs. *Journal of Applied School Psychology, 27*(4), 319–340.

# Author Index

Bodea, C. A, 275
Bogan, J. E., 186
Bol, S., 269
Bolt, S. E., 72
Bolton, P. F., 271, 272, 275
Bondy, A., 281
Boon, R. T., 167
Boone, D. R., 256
Borg, W. R., 152
Borge, A. I. H., 188
Borkowski, J. G., 136
Borland, J. H., 403
Bos, C. S., 55, 68, 69, 70
Boscardin, M. L., 144
Boström, P. K., 131, 134, 135
Bouchard, D., 327
Boucher, J., 269
Boudah, D. J., 166
Boulet, S. L., 173
Bowen, S. K., 162
Bower, E. M., 179
Bowles, S., 165
Bowman-Perrott, L., 168
Boxer, P., 193
Boxmeyer, C. L., 194, 195
Boyce, W. T., 101
Boyd, B., 355
Boyle, C., 168
Boyle, C. A., 173
Boyle, J., 237
Boyraz, G., 125, 131, 132, 142, 143
Braddock, D., 10
Bradshaw, C. P., 284
Brady, M. A., 377
Brams, M., 392
Brandes, J., 32
Branscombe, N. R., 5
Branum-Martin, L., 159
Bratter, J. L., 101
Brauen, M., 211
Brault, Matthew W., 20
Braun, J., 161
Braziel, P. M., 72
Bree, K. D., 129, 392
Breen, K., 193, 198, 199, 200
Brehaut, J. C., 126, 131, 135, 139
Bremer, C. D., 87
Brendgen, M., 188
Bretherton-Furness, J., 248
Brewer, R. D., 190
Brewton, C. M., 284
Breznitz, Z., 159
Briggs, C. J., 409
Brigham, F. J., 186
Brigham Young University, 116
Brinkman, W. B., 168
Brinton, B., 112, 243
Brisk, M. E., 116
Broberg, M., 131, 134, 135
Broitman, J., 154
Brondeel, R., 139
Brooke, V., 143
Brookman-Frazee, L., 126
Brotherson, M., 141
Brotherson, M. J., 139
Brotman, L. M., 195
Brouwer, S., 156
Browder, D., 55, 87
Browder, D. M., 211, 219, 392
Brown, F., 297, 299, 304
Brown, G., 135, 136, 137
Brown, I., 126
Brown, J., 281
Brown, J. D., 172
Brown, L., 294
Brown, M. W., 128
Brown, R. I., 126
Brown, W. H., 187, 190

Brown-Chidsey, R., 144
Brownfeld, J. M., 275
Brownlee, S., 172
*Brown v. Board of Education of Topeka, Kansas*, 28
Bruder, M. B., 143, 139
Bruhn, A. L., 168
Brun-Gasca, C., 239
Bruno, A., 102, 105
Bruns, D. A., 269
Bruns, E., 201
Brussow, J., 302
Bruyne, R. D., 362
Bryant, B. R., 72
Bui, Y. N., 144
Buitelaar, J. K., 392
Buka, S. L., 272
Bullock, C. E., 168
Bullock, L. M., 192
Bullough, R. V., 380
Burbidge, J., 125, 133, 135
Burgess, C., 152
Burke, M. D., 168, 183
Burkett, Ellen, 123
Burns, D. E., 416
Bursuck, W. D., 32, 51, 52, 69, 88
Burt, S. A., 187, 391
Burton, C. E., 281
Buschbacher, P., 143
Bussing, R., 392
Butrimaviciute, R., 269
Buttner, G., 150, 152, 154, 160
Buxbaum, J. D., 275
Buxton, R., 206
Buysse, A., 139
Byrne, D., 5
Byrnes, M. A., 32

Cabrera, N. J., 64
Cahan, S., 158
Cahill, B. S., 392
Cahill, S. M., 160
Cai, J., 275
Calderella, P., 142, 189
Calderon, J., 409, 411
Callahan, C. M., 413
Callahan, R. M., 170
Callard-Szulgit, R., 407
Callinan, S., 153
Calzada, E., 195
Cameto, R., 32
Campbell, C., 165
Cannon, L., 269, 275
Capaldi, D. M., 186
Capitani, J., 130
Cappadocia, M., 284
Capper, M. R., 416
Caputi, P., 124, 125
Caraisco, J., 412
Cardy, J. O., 160
Carey, B., 251
Carlo, M., 102
Carlson, C. D., 102, 104
Carlson, E., 277
Carlson, G. A., 184
Carlson, N. R., 18
Carpenter, B., 138
Carpenter, L. A., 274
Carpenter, S., 97
Carr, E. G., 280, 281
Carstens, A., 128, 129
Carta, J. J., 194, 195
Carter, E. W., 87, 143, 144, 169, 186
Carter, N., 286
Carter, N. J., 131, 143, 231, 232
Case, L., 272
Case-Smith, J., 59

Cassidy, D., 50
Cassidy, R. C., 99
Cassidy, V. M., 27
Castek, J., 167
Cattell, R. B., 399, 401
Cavaiuolo, D., 81, 82
Cavanaugh, M., 165
Cavin, M., 87
Center for Applied Special Technology, 74
Center for Comprehensive School Reform and Improvement, 423, 424
Center on Human Policy at Syracuse University, 21
Center on Teaching and Learning, 104
Centers for Disease Control and Prevention, 215, 216, 272, 273, 274, 275, 317, 325, 328, 361, 367, 369, 372, 374, 377, 379, 380, 389, 391
Cercone, N., 324
Cerdan, R., 156
Cerebral Palsy Alliance, 357
Cervantes, H. T., 115
Chabon, S. S., 240, 246
Chai, Z., 164
Chambers, C. R., 137, 143, 144
Chan, J. B., 133
Chan, L., 376
Chang, H., 195
Chang, H. J., 358
Chang, S., 248, 249
Chapadjiev, S., 129, 145
Charles, J. M., 274
Charman, T., 272, 274
Chavira, D. A., 257
Chenausky, K., 335
Cheney, D. A., 106
Chesnut, P., 32
Cheung, W. S., 52
Chiarelle, L. A., 358
Child and Adolescent Bipolar Foundation, 184
Child Care Law Center, 368
Children's Defense Fund, 216
Ching, T. T., 323, 324
Chinn, P. C., 51, 98, 101, 107, 115, 301
Chiocchetti, A. G., 275
Choo, D. I., 240
Christensen, W. R., 141
Chudnow, R. S., 158, 169
Ciancio, J., 89
Cifu, D. X., 380
Cirino, P. T., 104, 165
Ciullo, S., 164, 168, 172
Clare, M. M., 105
Clark, B., 401, 403, 404
Clark, C. D., 374
Clarke, S., 143
Claxton, G., 401
Cleary, M. J., 161
Cleland, J., 268
Clemow, D. B., 173
Clinkinbeard, S. S., 168, 169
Cloutier, H., 82
Cochran, J. L., 423
Cohen, J., 126, 131, 134, 171
Cohen, S., 421
Cohn, E. R., 240, 246
Cohn, L., 181
Colangelo, N., 416
Colby, S. L., 99
Coleman, L. J., 412, 418
Coleman, M. C., 183
Coleman, M. R., 423
Coleman, T. J., 145
Coll-Black, S., 104

Collier, C., 107, 117
Collier, P., 81
Collier, V. P., 97, 108, 113, 114
Collins, B. C, 89
Colman, I., 187
Colombo, J., 411
Coltheart, M., 157–158
Colvin, G., 397, 408
Combs, M. C., 97, 108, 113, 114
Compassionate Friends, 366
Compton, D. L., 163, 164, 165, 166, 171
Compton, D. R., 131
Comstock, E. J., 391
Conant, J. B., 403
Conley, D. T., 87
Connell, J. E., 279
Connell, N. M., 198
Conner, D. F., 184
Connolly, S. D., 184
Connor, C. M., 164, 165, 166
Connor, R. T., 55, 64
Connors, C., 125
Conroy, M. A., 114, 187, 188, 190, 194, 195
Cook, B., 314
Cook, C., 141
Cook, C. R., 187, 188, 189, 199
Cook, L., 52, 112, 114, 130
Coolidge, F. L., 392
Cooper, C. R., 416
Cooper, J., 235, 239
Cooper, J. L., 99
Cooper, L., 165
Cooper, P. D., 143
Cooper-Vince, C., 392
Copeland, S., 88
Corapci, F., 184
Cornell-Swanson, L., 391
Cornett, C., 161
Cornoldi, C., 158
Correa, V. I., 142, 144, 145, 171
Correa-Torres, S. M., 317
Costello, E. J., 391
Courtade-Little, G., 211, 219
Courtwright, P., 330
Cowden, P. A., 160, 163, 168, 170
Cox, A. W., 137, 278, 279
Cox, C., 138
Cox, P. R., 341
Craig, W. M., 185
Cramer, E., 186
Crane, J. L., 58
Crawford-Brooke, E., 102
Cremer, R., 362
Crews, S. D., 187, 188
Crick, 167
Crider, R., 161
Cridland, E. K., 124, 125
Cristol, D., 114
Crockett, M., 81, 90, 209, 226, 305
Crockett, M. A., 57
Crone, D. A., 190
Cronin, K. B., 143
Cross, A., 198
Cross, T. L., 412
Crowe, K., 324
Crowe, Taylor, 278, 284, 285
Crundwell, R. M., 179
Cullinan, D., 179
Cummings, J. G., 185
Cummins, R. A., 128
Cunningham, A. B., 276
Cunningham, E., 153
Cunningham, E. M., 190
Cupples, L., 324
Cuskelly, M., 126, 131, 134, 137

Huang, Y., 126
Huber, J. J., 127, 128
Hudson, R. F., 142
Huefner, D. S., 38, 43, 44, 67
Huff, R. M., 104
Hughes, C., 143, 144, 186, 187, 306
Hughes, C. A., 165, 166, 189
Hughes, E. M., 391
Hughes, J., 407
Hughes, K. C., 165
Hughes, L. A, 169
Hughes, M. T., 167
Hulme, C., 245, 246, 247
Hulstijn, W., 157, 160
Hume, K. A., 278, 279
Humphrey, N., 52
Humphreys, K. L., 391
Hundal, Ø., 154
Hundert, J., 283
Hunt, J. M., 56
Hunt, P. H., 57
Hunter, S. C., 266
Hurst, M., 332
Hyde, K., 198

Iacono, W. G., 186, 187, 392
Iarusso, K., 52
Iezzoni, L. I., 144
Ilyas, F., 157
Imbeau, M., 73
Inkelas, M., 126
Insel, T., 181
Ip, S. C., 332
Irving, B., 187
Isaacs, B. J., 126
Isaacson, W., 408
Iseman, J. S., 159
Israel, A. C., 184, 187, 188, 199
Itälinna, M., 134

Jackson, B., 128, 129
Jackson, C., 166, 323
Jackson, R., 72
Jacobs, L., 187
Jaervelin, M. R., 126
Jahns, V., 362
Jahoda, A., 284
James, William, 17
Janse, E., 156
Janusis, G. M., 392
Jarrett, D., 169
Jarvin, L., 398, 400, 402, 403, 408, 422
Jarvis, J. M., 409
Javitz, H., 32
Jenkins, J., 162, 167
Jenkins, J. M., 126
Jenner, W., 274
Jeter, L. V., 198
Jimenez, A. M., 101
Jimenez, B., 55
Jimenez, B. A., 211
Jitendra, A. K., 152, 158
Job, J. M., 169
Johansen, S., 154
Johns, M. M., 257
Johnsen, S. K., 409, 413
Johnson, A. L., 272
Johnson, C., 135, 177, 179, 180, 186
Johnson, D., 80
Johnson, E. S., 153, 173
Johnson, G. O., 27
Johnson, J., 391
Johnson, J. H., Jr., 99
Johnson, K. A., 173
Johnson, L., 177, 179, 180, 186
Johnson, R. A., 276

Johnson, R. T., 363
Johnson, S. M., 186
Johnson, T., 169, 170
Johnson, W., 186, 187
Johnston, S., 304
Johnston, S. S., 218, 241
Jolivette, K., 169
Jones, C. R. G., 272
Jones, E. A., 241
Jones, M., 251
Jones, N., 391
Jones, S. C., 124, 125
Jones, S. E. L., 189
Jones, T. L., 143
Joober, R., 158
Jordan, A. M., 27
Jordan, J., 164
Joseph, L. M., 89, 166, 167
Joshi, G., 389
Joy, J. E., 363
Judge, S., 156
Justen, J., 294
Justice, L. M., 63

Kachgal, M., 87
Kaderavek, J. N., 63, 235
Kagohara, D., 220
Kahn, A. B., 358
Kahn, R. S., 389
Kaiser, A. P., 211
Kaland, M., 323, 324
Kalb, L., 268
Kalb, L. G., 126
Kalberg, J. R., 189, 192, 198
Kaldenberg, E., 210
Kalikow, K. T., 173, 391
Kalloo, V., 165
Kamboukos, D., 195
Kamhia, A. G., 160
Kamps, D., 283
Kan, E., 161
Kanaya, T., 267, 268
Kandel, W. A., 102, 105
Kane, M., 279
Kanenberg, H., 131
Kanga, A., 113
Kannass, K. N., 411
Kanne, S. M., 269
Kanner, L., 264, 273, 275
Kao, B. T., 142
Karch, K. M., 392
Karen, T. J., 73
Karnes, F. A., 403
Kasarda, J. D., 99
Kasari, C., 277
Katims, D. S., 211
Katon, W., 257
Katsiyannis, A., 179, 184, 194, 391
Katusic, S. K., 389
Katzir, T., 161
Katz-Leavey, J., 201
Kauchak, D., 55
Kauffman, J. M., 114, 183, 186, 198
Kaufman, A. S., 160
Kavale, K. A., 151, 152, 179
Kazak, A. E., 126
Kebir, O., 158
Keeley, P., 162
Keen, D., 139, 141, 142
Keenan, S., 193, 198
Kellems, R. O., 281
Keller-Bell, Y., 167
Kellett, U., 126
Kelley, E., 275
Kelley, S. J., 124, 138
Kelly, N., 165
Keltner, B., 108, 110, 111

Kendall, S., 167
Kendziora, K. T., 195, 201
Kennedy, M., 165
Kennedy, W., 87
Kennett, D. J., 171
Kent, K. M., 392
Kenworthy, L., 269, 272, 275
Kern, L., 187, 188, 391, 392
Kerns, K. A., 127
Kessler Foundation and the National Organization on Disability, 13, 14, 80
Ketterlin-Geller, L. R., 72
Keyes, M, 392
Keys, C. B., 169
Kidder, J. E., 218
KidSource, 328
Kieckhefer, G. M., 369
Kientz, M., 81
Kiger, D., 165
Killu, K., 179
Kim, J., 186
Kim, P., 101, 104
Kim, S. E., 126
Kim, T. E., 166, 193
Kimbrel, N. A., 392
King, B. H., 283
King, K. A., 423
King, L. B., 274
King, M. A., 201
King-Sears, M. E., 167
Kingston, S., 195
Kirby, R. S., 271, 272
Kirkendall, D., 123
Kirkendall, Don, 123
Kirley, A., 173
Kishiyama, M. M., 101
Kittler, P., 210
Kiuhara, S., 81
Klassen, A. F., 126, 131, 135, 139
Klassen, R. M., 169
Klebe, K. J., 392
Klei, L., 275
Klein, E., 55
Klein, P. D., 157
Kleinert, H., 89
Klin, A., 276, 277
Kline, M. V., 104
Klinger, J., 186
Klinger, J. K., 72, 73
Klingner, J., 105, 113
Klinto, K., 244
Knight, R. T., 101
Knight, S., 399
Knitzer, J., 198
Knokey, A., 80, 81, 89
Knoster, T. P., 142
Knott, F., 284
Knouse, L. E., 392
Knowles, T., 160
Knox, M., 138
Koegel, L. K., 270, 272, 284
Koegel, R. L., 270, 272, 280, 284
Koenig, A. J., 342, 343
Koenig, D., 166
Koenig, K., 276, 277
Kogan, M. D., 276
Kohen, D. E., 126, 131, 135, 139
Kohnen, S., 157–158
Kolb, S. M., 141
Konjoian, P., 140, 143, 177
Konopasek, D., 200
Konopasek, D. E., 200
Konrad, M., 89
Koot, H. M., 126
Korzilius, H., 277
Kosowski, T. R., 257

Kostewicz, D. E., 186
Kosty, D. B., 166
Kotering, L., 72
Kou, Y., 275
Kouroupetroglou, G., 326
Kovas, Y., 161
Kowalski, R. M., 184
Kozleski, E. B., 52, 98, 105, 106, 112, 113, 115, 423
Kraft, D. P., 392
Krashen, S. D., 114
Krauss, M. W., 126
Krawec, J. L., 156, 158
Kresak, K. E., 124, 138
Kreutzer, J. S., 380
Krinsky-McHale, S. J., 210
Kroger, X., 87
Kubina, R. M., 157, 186
Kucharczyk, S., 278, 279
Kulik, J., 416
Kummer, A. W., 255, 256, 257
Kurtz, A., 82
Kurtz, M., 252, 254, 255
Kurzweil Technologies, 345, 348
Kushki, A., 157
Kutash, K., 186
Kyle, T., 368, 372
Kyzar, K., 139

Lach, L. M., 126, 131, 135, 139
Ladew, P., 89
Lai, M-C., 274
Lakin, C., 227
LaLiberte, T., 126
Lall, A. S., 391
Lam, C. M., 281
Laman, E., 131, 135, 136, 137, 144
Lamb, M. E., 134
Lamonte, M., 50
Lancioni, G., 220
Landa, R., 235, 239
Landrum, T. J., 186
Lane, K. L., 87, 168, 178, 186, 189, 190, 192, 198
Langberg, J. M., 168
Langkamp, D. L., 172
Lanou, A., 272, 277, 284
Lanphear, B. P., 389
Lansdowne, K., 423
Laracy, S. D., 154, 173
Larochette, A., 161
*Larry P. v. Riles*, 112
Larson, Elizabeth A., 133
Larsson, D., 101, 104
Larsson, H., 187
Lattimore, J., 201
*Lau v. Nichols*, 112
Laverdure, P. A., 359
Law, J., 184, 237, 253, 254
Law, P., 284
Lawrence, K., 391
Layton, C. A., 88
Lazzaretti, C. C., 360
Leader-Janssen, E., 53
Leafstedt, J. M., 50
Lebel, C., 161
Leblanc, B., 161
Leblanc, D., 156
LeBlanc, L. A., 281
Lecavalier, L., 274
Le Couteur, A., 281
Lederberg, A., 335
Lee, A. B., 275
Lee, A. L., 128, 129
Lee, I. H., 168, 169
Lee, L., 271, 272
Lee, L. C., 284

# Subject Index

National Center for Culturally Responsive Educational Systems (NCCRES), 97, 110
National Institute of Child Health and Human Development (NICHD), 212
*National Longitudinal Transition Study-2* (NLTS-2), 80–81
National Mental Health and Special Education Coalition, 179
National Organization on Disability (NOD), 14
National Society for Autistic Children, 10
National Technical Institute for the Deaf, 339
*A Nation Deceived*, 416
Native Hawaiian/Pacific Islander, 99f, 100f
Natural supports, 51, 81, 209
Nature vs. nurture, 16, 217, 406–407
Nazi Germany, 9
NCCRES (National Center for Culturally Responsive Educational Systems), 97, 110
NCLB (No Child Left Behind Act), 43, 51
Needed support, classification based on, 209
Neural tube defects (NTD). *See* Spina bifida
Neurological factors, in learning disabilities, 161
Neuromotor problems, 381
Neurotic disorders, 18
*New York Times*, 346
NICHD (National Institute of Child Health and Human Development), 212
NIDDM (Noninsulin-dependent diabetes mellitus), 373. *See also* Diabetes
NLTS-2 (*National Longitudinal Transition Study-2*), 80–81
*Nobody Nowhere* (Williams), 270
No Child Left Behind Act (NCLB), 43, 51
NOD (National Organization on Disability), 14
Nondiscriminatory assessment, 112
Nondiscriminatory collaboration, 111–112
Noninsulin-dependent diabetes mellitus (NIDDM), 373. *See also* Diabetes
Nonverbal communication, 252, 268
Nook, 345
Normalcy, 5, 15
Normal eyeballs, 322f
Normative sample, 207
Norm-referenced assessment, 162
Norm-referenced standardized assessment, 217
Note Teller, 345
Nurture vs. nature, 16, 217, 406–407
Nystagmus, 322

Observational learning techniques, 255
Occlusion, 244, 244f

Occupational therapist, 17, 358
Oelwein, Patricia, 305
Office of Special Education and Rehabilitative Services, 28
Off-level, 410
*Olmstead v. L.C. & E.W*, 19–20
Olson Circumplex Model, 124–125
Opportunistic infection, 368
Oppositional defiant disorder, 181
Optacon scanner, 345
Optic atrophy, 322, 330
Optic nerve, 318, 319f
Oral approach to teaching communication, 336–337
Oral expression, 342–343
Orientation, and vision loss, 327, 341
Orthopedic impairment, 356
Orthopedic impairments, 31
Other health impaired, 356
Otitis media, 329
Otologist, 331
Otosclerosis, 328
Overprotectiveness, 133–134

Pain syndromes, 364
Paralytic conditions, 357t
Paraplegia, 357t
PARC (Pennsylvania Association for Retarded Citizens), 11–12
*PARC v. Commonwealth of Pennsylvania*, 12
Parental negativism, 236
Parental reactions, 126–130
Parental safeguards and involvement, 31–32
"Parentese," 245
Parent organizations, 10–11
Parents
  involvement of in culturally and linguistically diverse populations, 110–111
  as part of multidisciplinary school-wide assistance teams, 54
  severe and multiple disabilities, 302
  as valued partners, 52–53
Parent-to-parent programs, 142, 143
Parent training, 143, 195, 301
Parkin, Terence, 325
Partial hearing, 317
Partial inclusion, 50
Partially sighted, 321
Partial sight, 321
Partner-notification laws, 368
Partner relationships, 131–133
Pathology, 15
Patient's disease, 16
PBIS (Positive behavior intervention and support), 280–281
PBS (Positive behavioral supports)
  emotional/behavioral disorders, 188, 189, 192, 193, 198
  and family support, 141–142
  and response to intervention, 70
PCI Education, 56
PDAs (Personal digital assistants), 345, 346
PDD (Pervasive developmental disorders), 265

PECS (Picture Exchange Communication System), 280, 304, 306
Peer-mediated instruction, 55
Peer support, 55
Peer tutoring, 55
Pennsylvania Association for Retarded Citizens (PARC), 11–12
*Pennsylvania Association for Retarded Citizens v. Commonwealth of Pennsylvania*, 28t
People First, 12
Perception problems, 159
Perceptual-motor development, 327
Perceptual-motor theories, 151
Perfectionism, 420
Perseveration, 270
Personal digital assistants (PDAs), 345, 346
Personal exoskeletons, 365
Personal independence, 223, 225, 297
Person-centered transition planning, 83–86, 85f
Person-first language, 8, 30
Pervasive developmental disorders (PDD), 265
Pervasive support, 209
Phantom pain, 364
Phenylketonuria (PKU), 215, 298
Phonics, 166
Phonology, 233
Photophobia, 330
Physical and healthcare needs, and severe and multiple disabilities, 298
Physical development, and intellectual and developmental disabilities, 212–213
Physical disabilities
  acquired immunodeficiency syndrome (AIDS), 367–369
  adult years, 389
  asthma, 369–371
  attention deficit/hyperactivity disorder, 389–393
  cerebral palsy, 356–359
  community support, 387–389
  cystic fibrosis, 376–377
  definition of, 356
  diabetes, 373–376
  early childhood years, 387
  elementary school years, 387–388
  human immunodeficiency virus (HIV), 367–369
  introduction to, 355–356
  muscular dystrophy, 365–367
  secondary and transition years, 388–389
  seizure disorders (epilepsy), 371–373
  sickle-cell disease, 377–379
  spina bifida, 360–363
  spinal cord injury, 363–365
  traumatic brain injury, 379–386
Physical therapists, 17, 358, 362
Pica, 181
Picture books, 264t
Picture Exchange Communication System (PECS), 280, 304, 306
Pinel, Phillippe, 16

Pitch, 316, 317
Pitch disorders, 256
PKU (Phenylketonuria), 215, 298
Placement, for special education, 39
Place value, 158
Point card, 199f
Portable picture schedule, 283f
Position-sensitive device (PSD), 342
Positive behavioral supports (PBS)
  emotional/behavioral disorders, 188, 189, 192, 193, 198
  and family support, 141–142
  and response to intervention, 70
Positive behavior intervention and support (PBIS), 280–281
Positive impacts of children with disabilities on their families, 125–126
Positive replacement behaviors, 195
Postlingual loss, 317
Postnatal disease, and hearing loss, 329
Postschool outcomes, 80–81
Potter, Lauren, 205
Poverty
  cultural and linguistic diversity, 100–101, 100f
  emotional/behavioral disorders, 186, 187
  intellectual and developmental disabilities, 216–217
  and schools, 104–105
Practical adaptive skills, 207f
Practical intelligence, 402
Pragmatics, 234, 254
Prednisone, 366
Predominantly hyperactive-impulsive type of ADHD, 389
Predominantly inattentive type of ADHD, 389
Pregnancy, problems during, 215–216
Prelingual loss, 317
Prematurity, 215, 322–323
Prenatal care, 334
Prenatal disease, and hearing loss, 328–329
Preschool-age children. *See also* Early childhood years/education
  age-appropriate placement, 61–62
  developmentally appropriate practice, 61
  early intervention services, 58–59f
  evidence-based instructional approaches, 58–65
  functional life skills, 62
  inclusion, 62–64
  individualized, intensive, and comprehensive services, 60
  overview of, 58–59
  referral, assessment, and IEP development, 60–61
  service delivery, 59–60
  severe and multiple disabilities, 301
  transition to elementary school, 64–65

5.5 Beginning special education professionals develop and implement a variety of education and transition plans for individuals with exceptionalities across a wide range of settings and different learning experiences in collaboration with individuals, families, and teams.

5.6 Beginning special education professionals teach to mastery and promote generalization of learning.

5.7 Beginning special education professionals teach cross-disciplinary knowledge and skills such as critical thinking and problem solving to individuals with exceptionalities.

## STANDARD 6:
## PROFESSIONAL LEARNING AND ETHICAL PRACTICE

Beginning special education professionals use foundational knowledge of the field and the their professional ethical principles and practice standards to inform special education practice, to engage in lifelong learning, and to advance the profession.

6.1 Beginning special education professionals use professional ethical principles and professional practice standards to guide their practice.

6.2 Beginning special education professionals understand how foundational knowledge and current issues influence professional practice.

6.3 Beginning special education professionals understand that diversity is a part of families, cultures, and schools, and that complex human issues can interact with the delivery of special education services.

6.4 Beginning special education professionals understand the significance of lifelong learning and participate in professional activities and learning communities.

6.5 Beginning special education professionals advance the profession by engaging in activities such as advocacy and mentoring.

6.6 Beginning special education professionals provide guidance and direction to paraeducators, tutors, and volunteers.

## STANDARD 7:
## COLLABORATION

Beginning special education professionals collaborate with families, other educators, related service providers, individuals with exceptionalities, and personnel from community agencies in culturally responsive ways to address the needs of individuals with exceptionalities across a range of learning experiences.

7.1 Beginning special education professionals use the theory and elements of effective collaboration.

7.2 Beginning special education professionals serve as a collaborative resource to colleagues.

7.3 Beginning special education professionals use collaboration to promote the well-being of individuals with exceptionalities across a wide range of settings and collaborators.

SOURCE: National Council for the Accreditation of Teacher Education. (2012). Washington, DC: Author. Retrieved from www.cec.sped.org/Standards /Special-Educator-Professional-Preparation/CEC -Initial-and-Advanced-Preparation-Standards.

# Council for Exceptional Children Standards Correlation Chart

As in the previous edition, the contents of *Human Exceptionality: School Community and Family*, 12th edition, correspond with the Council for Exceptional Children (CEC) standards. Icons in the margins highlight the relevant CEC standards. This handy correlation chart provides a chapter-by-chapter summary of where specific CEC standards are covered in each chapter

| Part/Chapter | Council for Exceptional Children (CEC) Standards |
| --- | --- |
| **Part I Through the Lifespan** | |
| Chapter 1<br>Understanding Exceptionalities in the 21st Century | 1 Learner Development and Individual Learning Differences, p. 12<br>2 Learning Environments, p. 20<br>6 Professional Learning and Ethical Practice, pp. 5, 14<br>7 Collaboration, p. 17 |
| Chapter 2<br>Education for All | 1 Learner Development and Individual Learning Differences, pp. 30, 32, 35, 38, 39<br>4 Assessment, pp. 31, 38<br>5 Instructional Planning and Strategies, pp. 31, 32<br>6 Professional Learning and Ethical Practice, pp. 27, 28, 30, 31, 43 |
| Chapter 3<br>Inclusion and Multidisciplinary Collaboration in the Early Childhood and Elementary School Years | 1 Learner Development and Individual Learning Differences, pp. 49, 51, 68<br>2 Learning Environments, pp. 49, 59, 64<br>5 Instructional Planning and Strategies, pp. 55, 60, 64, 72<br>6 Professional Learning and Ethical Practice, pp. 51, 57<br>7 Collaboration, pp. 52, 66 |
| Chapter 4<br>Secondary Education and Transition Planning | 1 Learner Development and Individual Learning Differences, pp. 87, 88<br>2 Learning Environments, p. 80<br>5 Instructional Planning and Strategies, pp. 81, 83, 87, 88, 90<br>6 Professional Learning and Ethical Practice, pp. 80, 82, 83 |
| **Part II Perspectives on Diversity and the Family** | |
| Chapter 5<br>Cultural and Linguistic Diversity | 1 Learner Development and Individual Learning Differences, pp. 99, 102<br>2 Learning Environments, pp. 96, 97, 102<br>4 Assessment, p. 112<br>5 Instructional Planning and Strategies, pp. 106, 115<br>6 Professional Learning and Ethical Practice, pp. 107, 114<br>7 Collaboration, pp. 110, 111 |
| Chapter 6<br>Exceptionalities and Families | 1 Learner Development and Individual Learning Differences, p. 133<br>2 Learning Environments, p. 142<br>4 Assessment, p. 127<br>6 Professional Learning and Ethical Practice, pp. 138, 141, 143, 144, 145<br>7 Collaboration, pp. 135, 137, 138, 140, 141, 142 |
| **Section III People Who Are Exceptional** | |
| Chapter 7<br>Learning Disabilities | 1 Learner Development and Individual Learning Differences, pp. 150, 154<br>2 Learning Environments, pp. 164, 169<br>4 Assessment, p. 161<br>5 Instructional Planning and Strategies, pp. 164, 169<br>7 Collaboration, p. 171 |
| Chapter 8<br>Emotional/Behavioral Disorders | 1 Learner Development and Individual Learner Differences, pp. 178, 183, 186, 188, 193<br>2 Learning Environments, pp. 191, 193, 195, 198, 201<br>4 Assessment, pp. 188, 190, 194, 195, 198, 201<br>5 Instructional Planning and Strategies, pp. 191, 193, 194, 195, 198, 201<br>7 Collaboration, pp. 184, 189, 191, 193, 194, 195, 198, 201 |
| Chapter 9<br>Intellectual and Developmental Disabilities | 1 Learner Development and Individual Learning Differences, pp. 207, 210, 217, 218<br>2 Learning Environments, pp. 219, 227<br>4 Assessment, pp. 217, 218<br>5 Instructional Planning and Strategies, p. 218<br>6 Professional Learning and Ethical Practice, pp. 206, 225 |